ISBN 978-1-5284-5915-0
PIBN 10933109

1 MONTH OF
FREE
READING

at

www.ForgottenBooks.com

By purchasing this book you are eligible for one month membership to ForgottenBooks.com, giving you unlimited access to our entire collection of over 1,000,000 titles via our web site and mobile apps.

To claim your free month visit:
www.forgottenbooks.com/free933109

English
Français
Deutsche
Italiano
Español
Português

www.forgottenbooks.com

Mythology Photography **Fiction**
Fishing Christianity **Art** Cooking
Essays Buddhism Freemasonry
Medicine **Biology** Music **Ancient**
Egypt Evolution Carpentry Physics
Dance Geology **Mathematics** Fitness
Shakespeare **Folklore** Yoga Marketing
Confidence Immortality Biographies
Poetry **Psychology** Witchcraft
Electronics Chemistry History **Law**
Accounting **Philosophy** Anthropology
Alchemy Drama Quantum Mechanics
Atheism Sexual Health **Ancient History**
Entrepreneurship Languages Sport
Paleontology Needlework Islam
Metaphysics Investment Archaeology
Parenting Statistics Criminology
Motivational

THE

REVISED REPORTS

BEING

A REPUBLICATION OF SUCH CASES

IN THE

ENGLISH COURTS OF COMMON LAW AND EQUITY,

FROM THE YEAR 1785,

AS ARE STILL OF PRACTICAL UTILITY.

EDITED BY

SIR FREDERICK POLLOCK, BART., D.C.L., LL.D.,
LATE CORPUS PROFESSOR OF JURISPRUDENCE IN THE UNIVERSITY OF OXFORD.

ASSISTED BY

O. A. SAUNDERS AND ARTHUR B. CANE,
BOTH OF THE INNER TEMPLE,
BARRISTERS-AT-LAW.

VOL. LXII.

1842–1844.

2 HARE; 4 QUEEN'S BENCH; 3 GALE & DAVISON; 10 MEESON & WELSBY; 9 CARRINGTON & PAYNE; 2 MOODY & ROBINSON; 5 JURIST.

LONDON:
SWEET AND MAXWELL, LIMITED, 3, CHANCERY LANE.

BOSTON:
LITTLE, BROWN & CO.
1903.

BRADBURY, AGNEW, & CO. LD., PRINTERS,
LONDON AND TONBRIDGE.

PREFACE TO VOLUME LXII.

WE know on the authority of Sir G. Jessel that Equity does not even pretend to be ancient ; it may now perhaps be said that the pretence is no less abandoned in matters of pure common law. The language of Wigram, V.-C. at p. 103 of this volume shows that sixty years ago authority was still needed to define the duty of reasonable vigilance on which constructive notice depends. Want of diligence in informing oneself, or drawing inferences from the information at hand, need not, for this purpose, be such gross negligence as the Court considers equivalent to fraud. *Foss* v. *Harbottle*, p. 185, is still important on the limits of the right of an individual corporation to object to alleged invalid acts of the governing body in the corporation. *Morley* v. *Rennoldson*, p. 236, is among the monuments of the perplexed doctrine about conditions in restraint of marriage, a doctrine which shows how dangerous is a little borrowing from a foreign system.

In the common-law portion we have several much cited and discussed cases. *Smout* v. *Ilbery*, p. 510, has been much and not favourably observed upon by text-writers, and it is quite possible that the Court of Appeal may some day reduce it to insignificance, if not overrule it, and establish a consistent and rational body of rules as to the determination of an agent's authority.

Winterbottom v. *Wright*, p. 534, looks a hard case at first sight. But all it really decides is that the implied warranties of a man who sells or lets out a chattel do not run with that chattel in favour of all persons who use it. The question how far one may be liable for sending out a chattel into the world of possible users with known defects is not touched. Here the defect is latent. *Davies* v. *Mann,* p. 698—the well-known "donkey case"—is a decision on very peculiar facts; it has been criticized, especially in America, but is believed to be quite sound.

It will be observed that there are several Nisi Prius rulings on evidence, most of them now rather elementary. Perhaps the profession might well have dispensed with some of them; but, being reported, they could not safely be omitted.

This preface is written at Toronto, within a quarter of an hour's walk of Osgoode Hall; the writer can bear witness that the Common Law is as keenly studied and as diligently taught in the Province of Ontario as in any English-speaking jurisdiction. In one respect, indeed, the law school of Osgoode Hall is unique by reason of its intimate connexion with the practical side of the profession. It is not only a recommended but a necessary road to being called to the Bar of the Province. Our Canadian brethren do not believe that sound knowledge comes by examinations alone.

F. P.

HIGH COURT OF CHANCERY.

1842—1844.

(5 & 6 VICT.—7 & 8 VICT.)

LORD LYNDHURST, 1841—1846 . . . *Lord Chancellor.*

LORD LANGDALE, 1836—1851 . . . *Master of the Rolls.*

SIR LANCELOT SHADWELL, 1827—1850 .⎫

SIR J. L. KNIGHT BRUCE, 1841—1851 . .⎬ *Vice-Chancellors.*

SIR JAMES WIGRAM, 1841—1850 . .⎭

COURT OF QUEEN'S BENCH.

LORD DENMAN, 1832—1850 . . . . . *Chief Justice.*

SIR JOHN PATTESON, 1830—1852 . .⎫

SIR JOHN WILLIAMS, 1834—1846 . . .⎬

SIR JOHN T. COLERIDGE, 1835—1858 . .⎬ *Judges.*

SIR WILLIAM WIGHTMAN, 1841—1863 . .⎭

COURT OF COMMON PLEAS.

Sir N. C. Tindal, 1829—1846 . . . . *Chief Justice.*

Sir John B. Bosanquet, 1830—1842 .

Sir Thomas Coltman, 1837—1849 . .

(1) Thomas Erskine, 1839—1844 . .

Sir William H. Maule, 1839—1855 . . } *Judges.*

Sir C. Cresswell, 1842—1858 . .

Sir William Erle, 1844—1846 . . .

COURT OF EXCHEQUER.

Lord Abinger, 1834—1844 . . . } *Chief Barons.*

Sir Frederick Pollock, 1844—1866 . }

Sir John Gurney, 1832—1845 . . .

Sir E. H. Alderson, 1834—1857 . . } *Barons.*

Sir James Parke, 1834—1856 . . .

Sir Robert M. Rolfe, 1839—1850 . . }

Sir Frederick Pollock, 1841—1844 . } *Attorneys-General.*

Sir W. W. Follett, 1844—1845 . . }

Sir W. W. Follett, 1841—1844 . . } *Solicitors-General.*

Sir Frederick Thesiger, 1844—1845 }

Sir Edward Burtenshaw Sugden . . { *Lord Chancellor of Ireland.*

(1) The description of Mr. Justice Erskine as a knight in the earlier volumes of Manning and Granger's Reports was erroneous. As a peer's son he would not have been knighted in the ordinary course; and the lists of the Judicial Committee in Moore's Privy Council Reports, and of the Benchers of Lincoln's Inn in the Law List down to 1863 (confirmed by the description of the Right Hon. Thomas Erskine in a deed of which a copy is before me), show that in fact he was not.—F. P.

TABLE OF CASES

REPRINTED FROM

2 HARE; 4 QUEEN'S BENCH; 3 GALE & DAVISON; 10 MEESON & WELSBY; 9 CARRINGTON & PAYNE; 2 MOODY & ROBINSON; 5 JURIST.

Note.—Where the reference is to a mere note of a case reproduced elsewhere in the Revised Reports, or omitted for special reasons, the names of the parties are printed in italics.

TABLE OF CASES.

NOTE.

———

The first and last pages of the original report, according to the paging by which the original reports are usually cited, are noted at the head of each case, and references to the same paging are continued in the margin of the text.

The Revised Reports.

VOL. LXII.

CHANCERY.

LEEMING *v.* SHERRATT.

(2 Hare, 14—25; S. C. 11 L. J. Ch. 423; 6 Jur. 663.)

1842.
March 23.
April 18.
———
WIGRAM,
V.-C.
[14]

A testator gave certain pecuniary legacies to his daughters respectively, one-half to be invested and secured from the control of any husband, the interest to be paid to them in the meantime, and the principal disposed of as they should direct, to their issue; but in case they should die without issue, he gave the principal among the survivors of his children in equal shares: Held, that the first bequest was limited to issue living at the death of the children, and that the gift over on failure of issue referred to the same objects.

Gift of a residue of real and personal estate to trustees to sell, get in, and pay and divide the money arising therefrom, unto and equally among the testator's children, so soon as the youngest should attain twenty-one,—the daughter's shares to be invested and secured, and the interest paid to such daughter, and the principal to be disposed of amongst her children as she might direct; if no child, the share to be divided amongst the survivors of the testator's children equally, and, in case of the death of any of his children leaving lawful issue, the testator gave to such issue the share the parent would have been entitled to have: Held,

(1) That the residuary share of a child, who attained twenty-one, and died before the time of division, passed to his representatives.

(2) That the word "survivors" in the residuary clause, must be construed in its natural sense, and not as importing "others," and that this construction of the word in one part of the will must govern the construction of the same word in the other parts.

(3) That the gift of the part or share of a parent dying leaving issue, to such issue, applied both to the original and accruing shares of the residue, but not to the particular legacies.

THOMAS LEEMING, by his will, after bequeathing certain legacies, gave to each of his children, Sarah, *James, Maria, Joseph, Frances, and Henry, 1,000*l.* each, to be paid respectively on their attaining

[*15]

the ages of twenty-one, excepting to such of them as were girls, in which cases he ordered that one-half part should be placed out at interest to be secured from the control of any husband with whom they might intermarry, the interest in the meantime to be paid to them, and the principal disposed of, in such manner as they might direct, to their issue; but, in case they should die without issue, he gave the principal among the survivors of his children in equal proportions. The testator then gave, devised, and bequeathed to his son, Thomas Leeming, John Sherratt, and Thomas Belshaw, whom he appointed his executors, all his freehold property, and also all the residue of his personal estate; and he declared the trusts thereof as follows: "To sell and dispose of my freehold property, and to collect and get in all my personal property, and to pay and divide the money arising therefrom, so soon as my youngest child shall attain the age of twenty-one, unto and equally amongst my children, share and share alike; but I direct one-half of the shares of such of them as are daughters shall be placed out at interest, and be secured from the control of any husband with whom they may intermarry, the interest in the meantime to be paid to such daughter, and the principal to be disposed of, in such manner as she may direct, amongst her children, if any; but, if there be no children, then such share to be divided equally amongst the survivors of my children; and, in case of the death of any of my children, leaving lawful issue, I direct and give to such issue the part or share the parent so dying would have been entitled to have."

The testator died in 1807. Nine of his children survived him, and attained twenty-one years of age, namely, John (who died
[*16] without issue before Henry, *the youngest, attained twenty-one), Sarah (who died without issue after Henry attained twenty-one), Thomas, Elizabeth, and Frances, (who died leaving issue after Henry attained twenty-one), and James, Joseph, Maria, and Henry, living at the institution of the suit.

The suit was instituted for the administration of the testator's estate, and to obtain the declaration of the Court upon the interests of the surviving legatees, and the representatives of those who were dead. On further directions,

Mr. Temple, Mr. Sharpe, Mr. Walker, Mr. Bacon, Mr. Bagshawe, Mr. Mylne, Mr. Elderton, and *Mr. Taylor,* appeared for the several parties.

THE VICE-CHANCELLOR:

Four questions have been raised in this case. First, on the meaning to be attached to the expression, "in case they die without issue." The second, whether the residuary share of John Leeming, who died in the year 1811, without leaving lawful issue before the youngest child of the testator attained twenty-one years of age, having himself attained twenty-one, was transmissible to his representative, or is undisposed of by the will. The third question, on the meaning of the word "survivors;" and the fourth question, what parts of the testator's property are affected by that clause of the will in which, "in case of the death of any of his children leaving lawful issue," he gives "to such issue the part or share the parent so dying would have been entitled to have."

Upon the first question my opinion is, that the words *"in case they die without issue," must be construed with reference to the issue before spoken of; as if the words were "in case they die without such issue:" *Ellicombe* v. *Gompertz* (1). I am further of opinion that the issue before spoken of does not mean issue indefinitely: *Target* v. *Gaunt* (2),—a construction which is fortified by the subsequent parts of the will, in which it is manifest from the words themselves, that an indefinite failure of issue was not the event the testator contemplated.

Upon the second point I think that the share of the residue of John Leeming was transmissible to his representatives.

The argument against this construction may be thus stated: It was said that the gift of the residue is future,—that there is no gift of such residue, except in the direction to pay, and that it is a settled rule, in the construction of wills relating to personal estate, that, where a legacy is given at a future time, and there is no gift of the legacy, except in the direction to pay, the legatee can claim nothing unless he is living at the time when the legacy becomes payable. That the Court has, in many cases, expressed itself very nearly in this manner, I do not deny; but I am satisfied that I should be misapplying the rule intended to be expressed by the Court in such cases, if I were to hold that John's share of the residue was not transmissible to his representatives, only because he died before the testator's youngest child attained twenty-one. The rule of construction referred to (as I understand it) is simply this: Courts of equity, in the construction of wills relating to

(1) 45 R. R. 234 (3 My. & Cr. 127),　　(2) 1 P. Wms. 432.
and see the cases there cited.

personal estate, follow the rules of the civil law. By that law, when a legacy is given absolutely, *and the payment is postponed to a future definite'period, the Court considers the time as annexed to the payment and not to the gift of the legacy, and treats the legacy as *debitum in præsenti solvendum in futuro*. This rule being established, a question was made, whether, in the simple case of a direction to pay a legacy at a future period, without any gift of the legacy independently of that direction, the legacy would be transmissible to the representatives of the legatee dying before the time of payment; and the Court, in that simple case, has sometimes considered the time of payment as annexed to the legacy itself, and not merely to the payment of it. But the Court, in so deciding, has not, I conceive, intended to decide that the gift of a legacy, under the form of a direction to pay at a future time, or upon a given event, was less favourable to vesting than a simple and direct bequest of a legacy at a like future time, or upon a like event; but, in fact, has intended only to assimilate those cases to each other, and to distinguish both from the class of cases to which I first referred, in which there has been a gift of the legacy, and also a direction to pay at a future definite time distinct from that gift.

I have examined most of the reported cases upon the subject, and am confirmed in the opinion I entertained during the argument, that the question is one of substance and not of form. The question in all the cases has been, whether the testator intended it as a condition precedent that the legatees should survive the time appointed by him for the payment of their legacies; and the answer to this question has been sought for out of the whole will, and not in particular expressions only like those relied upon in this case. [On this point, which no longer needs authority, his Honour referred to *Barnes* v. *Allen* (1), *Saunders* v. *Vautier* (2), *Hanson* v. *Graham* (3), *Thicknesse* v. *Liege* (4), and other authorities.]

[21]   The question, therefore, I am now bound to consider is, whether (excluding the cases in which there has been a gift of the legacy distinct from the direction for payment) the testator has made the shares in the residue of such of his children as should die without leaving issue contingent upon their surviving the time when the youngest should attain twenty-one. In considering this question, I may be bound to advert to the circumstances, that the gift of the

(1) 1 Br. C. C. 181.   (3) 5 R. R. 277 (6 Ves. 246, 247).
(2) 54 R. R. 286 (1 Cr. & Ph. 240).   (4) 3 Br. P. C. 365, 373, Tom. ed.

residue is future, and that there is no gift of such residue, except in the direction for payment; but they are only circumstances, and certainly not conclusive.   The persons to whom the residue is given are all the testator's children as tenants in common; and the clause, which afterwards substitutes the issue of a deceased child for the parent dying leaving lawful issue, shows, or strongly *tends to show, that the persons to whom, in the first instance, the residue was given meant all the testator's children who should survive him, and not all those only who should be living when the youngest should attain twenty-one.   Then the residue is given to trustees. For whom are they trustees? Obviously for all the children of the testator who should survive him, except so far as he should otherwise direct. Of what are they trustees?   The income of the property between the death of the testator and the time of dividing the residue would accumulate for the benefit of those to whom the residue in terms is eventually given.   The trustees, therefore, are trustees of the residue, and of the interim profits thereof, for all the testator's children (except so far as he has afterwards substituted others for those children) upon the happening of an event which in fact has happened, namely, the youngest child attaining twenty-one.   Again, the testator directs, that, in case any of his children dies leaving lawful issue, that issue shall take "the part or share the parent so dying would have been entitled to have." The words "would have been entitled to have" were relied upon in argument, as showing that the testator himself supposed the parent spoken of to have lost his share in the residue in the event he provides for. But I do not think those words are so full of meaning as that argument supposes. I think the clause is nothing more than the common clause of substitution of one legatee for another in the event spoken of. The substitution is not general. It is confined to the case of a child of the testator dying leaving lawful issue, and does not extend to the case which has happened of the child of the testator dying not leaving lawful issue. If the will had not contained the clause of substitution, and one or more of the testator's children had died leaving lawful issue before the youngest attained twenty-one, the argument in favour of the *legacy being transmissible would have been irresistible; and if the bequest of the residue would, in the absence of the clause of substitution, have given to John an interest transmissible to his representatives, I do not understand why the clause of substitution can alter the construction of the will in a case to which that clause will not apply.

[*22]

[*23]

The circumstances which, in cases of residuary gifts, the Court has relied upon for preventing an intestacy, as in *Booth* v. *Booth* (1), and in *Love* v. *L'Estrange* (2), were certainly not stronger than occur in this case. *Lore* v. *L'Estrange*, I may observe, is approved of by Sir WILLIAM GRANT in *Hanson* v. *Graham*, and by Lord COTTENHAM in *Saunders* v. *Vautier*. There is nothing of improbability in the supposition that the testator intended his children to take absolute interests in the residue, except in the event of their dying leaving issue before the period of division. If there is any case which decides, as an abstract proposition, that a gift of a residue to a testator's children, upon an event which afterwards happens, does not confer upon those children an interest transmissible to their representatives merely because they die before the event happens, I am satisfied that case must be at variance with other authorities.

In the observations I have made upon this case, I have noticed the fact that John Leeming had attained twenty-one, for this reason : The testator having postponed the division of the residue until his youngest child attained that age, I think no child, who did not attain that age, could have been intended to take a share therein. But this is consistent with the proposition, that all who lived to that age should participate in the residue as soon as the youngest child, who should *attain that age, had reached it, which is the intention I ascribe to the testator. I think, in fact, the case more analogous, in principle, to such cases as *Barnes* v. *Allen* than to such as *Thicknesse* v. *Liege*, in which the Court has discovered a manifest intention that the gift of the residue should be for all purposes contingent upon the legatee's surviving the period of division.

[*21]

Upon the third point, I think the word "survivors" must be understood in its natural sense, and not in the sense of "others" in which it has sometimes been construed. In *Davidson* v. *Dallas* (3), Lord ELDON's language obviously imports that the word "survivors" is to be construed in its natural sense, unless the will itself shows that it was used by the testator in a different sense, and *Crowder* v. *Stone* (4) is to the same effect. In *Barlow* v. *Salter* (5), the *dictum* of the Court tends rather to treat the word as

(1) 4 R. R. 235 (4 Ves. 399).
(2) 5 Br. P. C. 59, Tom. ed.
(3) 9 R. R. 350 (14 Ves. 576).
(4) 27 R. R. 68 (3 Russ. 217).

(5) 17 Ves. 479; but this view has not been accepted by later authorities.
--O. A. S.

having a technical meaning (that of "others") impressed upon it in practice. According to *Davidson* v. *Dallas*, one reason for construing "survivors" to mean "others" has been to take in all persons who should be born before the period of distribution. In other cases, the object suggested has been to prevent a family losing the provision intended for it by the death of a parent leaving children. The reason of the former of these cases could not occur here, in the case of the residue, because the testator's own children are the legatees of that residue. And, according to the construction that I feel myself at liberty to put upon that clause in the will which, in certain cases, substitutes the issue for the parents, I think the testator has guarded against the second inconvenience ; and, so far at least as the residue is concerned, I think, *that, in the residuary clause, the word "survivors" must be construed in its natural sense, and that this construction of the word, in one part of the will, must, in this will, determine its construction in the other part also. With respect to the cases of *Cripps* v. *Walcott* (1), *Hoghton* v. *Whitgreave* (2), and other cases of the same class which were cited during the argument, they appear to me to raise a question distinct from that in the case before me.

[*25]

I see nothing in the words of the will to prevent me from applying the clause of substitution both to an original share of the residue, and to a share in the residue of the daughter, who died without issue, which is the question involved in the fourth point; and the intention of the testator will best be satisfied by my so applying that clause. But I cannot extend that substitutionary clause to the particular legacies.

BOURNE *v.* BOURNE.

(2 Hare, 35—39; S. C. 11 L. J. Ch. 416 ; 6 Jur. 775.)

The old form of mortgage by way of trust for sale did not work a conversion unless and until the property was sold.

1842.
June 6, 28.

WIGRAM,
V.-C.

[35]

WILLIAM BOURNE being seised in fee-simple in possession of certain hereditaments and premises at Shrawley, in the county of Worcester, subject to a mortgage to William Dunn, executed certain indentures of lease and release, dated the 13th and 14th of

(1) 20 R. R. 268 (4 Madd. 11).   (2) 20 R. R. 259 (1 Jac. & W. 146).

BOURNE
v.
BOURNE.

June, 1822, the latter being made between W. Bourne, of the first, W. Dunn, of the second, S. Good, of the third, J. Southall, of the fourth, and the trustee of a term for the fifth, part, whereby, in consideration of 1,000*l.*, then advanced and paid to W. Bourne by S. Good, out of which the mortgage to W. Dunn was discharged, W. Bourne and W. Dunn conveyed and released the said hereditaments unto and to the use of J. Southall, his heirs and assigns, upon trust, in case W. Bourne, his heirs, executors, administrators, or assigns, should pay S. Good the sum of 1,000*l.* and interest at 5 per cent. on the 14th of June then next, to permit W. Bourne to retain possession of the said hereditaments, and receive the rents thereof, until the said 1,000*l.* and interest should become payable, and, in case the same should be then discharged, to re-convey the said hereditaments to W. Bourne, his heirs and assigns; but, in case default should be made for the space of three calendar months in payment of the said 1,000*l.* and interest, or any part thereof at the time aforesaid, then upon trust that J. Southall, his heirs or assigns, should thereupon enter into possession of the said hereditaments, and should, at any time thereafter, at his or their discretion, sell and dispose of the said hereditaments and premises as therein mentioned, and, out of the proceeds of such sale, in the

[*36] *first place, pay and retain all costs and expenses attending the sale or otherwise to be incurred in execution of the trusts thereby declared, and, in the second place, to pay and satisfy to the said S. Good, his executors, administrators, or assigns, the said sum of 1,000*l.*, and the interest and arrears of interest thereof, or such parts of the said principal and interest monies as should be then due and unpaid, together with all costs and expenses (if any) attending any non-payment thereof, and, after all the aforesaid principal and interest monies, costs and expenses, should be wholly paid and satisfied, then in trust to pay over the residue or surplus of the said trust monies to arise by the means aforesaid unto the said W. Bourne, his heirs, executors, administrators, or assigns, for his or their own benefit. In November, 1826, W. Bourne made a deed of further charge on the hereditaments, to the amount of 150*l.*, to S. Good. In June, 1831, W. Bourne died, having, by his will, duly executed to pass freehold estate, devised an estate at Ombersley for the payment of his debts, expressly including the monies due on the mortgage of his said hereditaments at Shrawley, and having devised the said hereditaments unto W. Holdsworth and the defendant, R. B. Bourne, for a term of ninety-nine years,

in trust to permit the testator's wife, Mary Bourne, one of the plaintiffs, to receive the rents and profits for her life, and, from and after her decease, to the use of his son, the defendant, Robert Bourne, and his assigns for his life, with remainder to his issue in tail,—remainder to the testator's daughter, the plaintiff, Jane Bourne, and her assigns for her life,—remainder to her issue in tail,—remainder to the defendant, R. B. Bourne, his heirs and assigns.

BOURNE
v.
BOURNE.

The defendant, R. B. Bourne, disclaimed the estate thereby devised to him. In June, 1834, S. Good assigned *his mortgage debt of 1,150*l.* to Samuel Higgins, and the hereditaments comprised in the mortgage were conveyed to the defendant, Robert Higgins, upon and subject to the powers and provisoes of the release of the 14th of June, 1822. Robert Higgins, in July, 1837, under the said trusts for sale, sold the mortgaged hereditaments, the proceeds of which, after paying thereout the debt and costs, left a surplus of upwards of 1,000l. in his hands. The plaintiffs, the widow and daughter of the testator, filed their bill, praying a declaration that the said balance of the purchase-money which arose from the sale of the said hereditaments was subject to the devises and limitations in the will, and that the same might be secured, and the interest paid accordingly. The bill stated, that there was no personal representative of the testator in existence.

[*37]

The defendant, R. Higgins, by his answer, submitted to pay the balance as the Court should direct.

Mr. Sharpe and *Mr. Parry*, for the plaintiffs.

Mr. Cameron, for the defendants R. B. and R. Bourne.

Mr. Girdlestone and *Mr. Piggott*, for the defendant Higgins:

The estate in this case has been converted into personalty, and the defendant is accountable to the personal representative of the testator, who is not before the Court. * * *

Mr. Sharpe, in reply:

[38]

The surplus of the estate retains the character which the estate had at the death of the testator: if it had been sold in his lifetime, it would have been personal estate; not having been so, it is real.

BOURNE
v.
BOURNE.

THE VICE-CHANCELLOR:

The question is upon the effect of the release of June, 1822. Bourne being seised in fee of the Shrawley estate, subject to a mortgage to Dunn, another person, named Samuel Good, advanced money to pay off that charge, and the estate was conveyed to Southall, a trustee, in the first place, to secure the sum due to Good.

(His Honour stated the terms of the instrument.)

This is merely a charge by way of mortgage : there is no indication of any intention to convert the property from real into personal. If a person charges his real property with the payment of his debts, unless there is a clear indication that it shall be converted out and out, it retains its character of realty, so far as the charge does not extend, until it is actually converted. If the trustee had taken the property with absolute directions to sell and convert it, the circumstance, that the directions had not been carried into effect at the death of the testator, might have been immaterial, and it might have been treated as personalty. But, in this case, there was no absolute or compulsory direction for the sale or conversion of the estate ; it is merely an authority, in a certain event, to enter into possession of this estate, and at the discretion of the trustee [*39] *to sell it, for the purpose of recovering payment of the debt for the mortgagee. The direction to re-convey the estate, in case of payment of the mortgage-money, is inconsistent with the notion that there was any intention that the property should be absolutely converted by the effect of the conveyance.

The event, upon the happening of which the trustee might, at his discretion, have sold the estate, namely, the default in payment of the mortgage-money, took place in the lifetime of the testator ; but the discretion to sell had not been exercised at the time of his death. The consequence is, that the estate passed to his devisees as realty, subject to the mortgage, and the trustee must, therefore, account to the devisees for the surplus proceeds of the sale.

The cases on this subject are all collected and commented upon in the exceedingly able work of Mr. Dalzell, on the Law of Conversion (1).

(1) Page 89. His Honour mentioned *Wright* v. *Rose*, 25 R. R. 209 (2 Sim. & St. 323); *Shudforth* v. *Temple*, 51 R. R. 230 (10 Sim. 184); [and other cases where an imperative trust was held to be necessary to work a conversion.—O. A. S.]

BLACKLOW v. LAWS(1).

(2 Hare, 40—54.)

1842.
June 23.
July 5.
Dec. 22, 23.

WIGRAM,
V.-C.

[40]

Where an estate was directed by the testator to be sold after the death of a certain person, and the sale was made during the life of that person, under a decree. some of the persons interested in the proceeds being infants or not *sui juris*, the Court would not compel the purchaser to accept the title.

The conditions of sale provided that all objections to the title disclosed by the abstract, not taken within a certain time after delivery of the abstract to the purchaser, should be deemed to be waived: Held, that the time for objecting was not to be computed from the time of the delivery of an imperfect abstract; and that the purchaser was not precluded from taking an objection which arose out of evidence called for before the expiration of the time fixed.

The sale took place under a decree. The abstract stated that the person, at whose death the sale was to be made, proved the will of the testator, but it did not state the pleadings in the cause. or whether that person was living or dead: Held, that this was not a sufficiently distinct intimation to the purchaser that the time of sale had, without any sufficient ground, been anticipated.

.The testator directed an annuity to be paid by the trustees, appointed by his will, into the proper hands of his daughter A., the wife of L., for her own proper use and benefit: Held, that it was not a trust for the separate use of the daughter (2).

SAMUEL CHRISTIE, by his will, dated in September, 1830, devised and bequeathed all his freehold and leasehold, and all his personal estate, not specifically bequeathed, to J. Laws and two other trustees, as to his estate at Preston, in trust for sale as therein mentioned; and upon further trust to receive and take the rents and profits of his freehold estate, situate in Queen Street and Charles Street, until sale thereof as thereafter directed; and out of such rents and profits and the produce arising from the sale of his said estate at Preston, and of his other effects, pay unto the proper hands of his daughter-in-law Agnes the sum of 130*l.*, to and for her own sole use and benefit, which he desired might be paid to her, her executors, or administrators, free of legacy duty; then to pay one annuity of 150*l.* into the proper hands of his said wife Alice during her natural life, for her own proper use and benefit; and he declared his will to be that such annuity should be paid into the proper hands of the said Alice, from time to time as the same should become due, and that the same should not be received by anticipation, and that she should not be at liberty either to raise any money on security thereof, or in any manner to dispose of the

(1) *Want* v. *Stallibrass* (1873) L. R. 8 Ex. 175, 42 L. J. Ex. 108, 29 L. T. 293. [As to this case see Law Quarterly Review, xix., 161.]

(2) *Surman* v. *Wharton* [1891] 1 Q. B. 491, 60 L. J. Q. B. 233.

[*41]

same, and if she should so do, such annuity should immediately
thereafter cease and be no longer payable. And upon further trust,
by and out of the monies to arise from the sale of his said estate
at Preston, and other effects which should come to the hands of his
said *trustees (as follows), " to pay one annuity or clear yearly sum
of 50l., during the natural life of my said wife Alice, into the proper
hands of my youngest daughter Anne (now the wife of James Laws),
for her own proper use and benefit." And the testator directed
that so soon after the decease of his wife Alice as conveniently
might be, his said trustees should, either by public auction or
private contract, as they should deem most expedient, sell and
dispose of his freehold estates situate in Queen Street and Charles
Street aforesaid, for the best prices that could be reasonably obtained
for the same, and out of the proceeds arising from such sale, pay
into the proper hands of his said daughter Anne the sum of 500l.,
to and for her own sole use and benefit absolutely ; and he directed
that the residue of his property should be held by his trustees, upon
trust to be divided into six equal parts, one part thereof for his
daughter Jane wife of J. Davies, one other part thereof in trust for
Sarah Davies widow, one other part thereof in trust for Harriet the
wife of J. Simpson, one other part thereof in trust for Eliza, the
wife of W. Pugh,—which last-mentioned sixth share he directed
should be invested by his trustees, and the dividends and interest
paid into the proper hands of his said daughter Eliza, whose
receipt alone notwithstanding her coverture should be a sufficient
discharge for the same ; provided that if his said trustees should
see occasion they should be at liberty, at any time during the lifetime of his said daughter Eliza, to transfer any portion of the
bequest made in her favour, not exceeding one-half part thereof,
for her immediate use, and in that case her receipt alone should be
a sufficient discharge to them for the same, notwithstanding her
coverture, and that such remaining moiety should remain vested in
his trustees, in trust for her, and be subject to such disposition as
she should by her last will and testament direct and appoint not-

[*42]

withstanding her present or any future *coverture, and in default
of appointment the same to be equally divided as therein mentioned,
and one other part thereof in trust, for his said daughter Anne.
And he declared that the respective receipts of such of them as
should be married should be a sufficient discharge, although under
coverture. And the testator appointed Alice his wife, and the said
three trustees, his executrix and executors. The testator died soon

after the date of his will, leaving his wife Alice surviving him ; and his will was proved by Alice the widow, and James Laws.

The bill was filed in January, 1839, by some of the persons beneficially interested in the residuary estate of the testator, against the executrix and executor, and the other residuary legatees, and prayed the usual accounts of the real and personal estate, and that the trusts of the will might be executed under the direction of the Court.

By the decree, made the 14th of December, 1841, it was declared, that the trusts of the will ought to be performed and carried into execution. An inquiry was directed of what lands and hereditaments, and what estate therein the testator had at the date of his will, and of his death ; and it was ordered that the real estate, of which the testator was seised at the date of his will, and at the time of his death, or such parts thereof as then remained unsold, should be sold with the approbation of the Master.

Under this decree, the estates in Queen Street and Charles Street were put up to sale in January, 1842, upon printed conditions ; and W. Hains became the purchaser. By the 8th condition of sale, the purchaser was within twenty-one days next after the delivery of the abstract, to deliver to the vendor's solicitors a statement in writing of such objections to the title *disclosed by the abstract as he should be advised to take, and every objection not so taken, and communicated within such period, should be deemed waived.

[*43]

The report of the purchase was made and confirmed. The abstract was delivered to the purchaser's solicitors on the 1st of March. This abstract did not contain any statement of the pleadings in the cause, but stated, amongst other instruments, the will of the testator, and contained in a short line at the foot of the will, as part of the abstract relating to that instrument, these words :

"Will proved in the Prerogative Court of Canterbury, the 24th of June, 1831, by said Alice Christie, James Simpson, and James Laws; said Thomas Bayley having renounced probate."

The purchaser's counsel in advising on the title said, " It should be ascertained by a brief of the pleadings, that all proper parties are before the Court." The objections to the title, not including any objection on the ground of the sale having been made during the life of the widow, were delivered on the 22nd of March : and in answer to the observation referred to, the vendors' solicitors, on the 5th of April, wrote, " A brief of the pleadings can at any time be seen at our office." About the 21st of April, the purchaser's counsel gave this further opinion, " Upon procuring a brief of the pleadings, I do not find that any cause is shown for decreeing a sale before the time fixed by the testator's will,—his widow's death. Probably it would appear by the decree, the Court having power to decree a sale for payment of all debts. It also appears that two of the trustees of the will have disclaimed, and that one of those two is dead, though the facts are not noticed in the abstract." The

[*44] purchaser ultimately insisting upon the objection *that the decree for sale was premature, the question was submitted to the Court by motion, on behalf of the vendors, that the purchaser should pay his purchase-money into Court, and on behalf of the purchaser, that he might be discharged from his purchase.

Mr. Sharpe, for the vendors, argued first, that the purchaser was precluded by the 8th condition, when more than twenty-one days had elapsed after the delivery of the abstract, from taking the objection as to the time of sale. The abstract had contained all the facts upon which the state of the title might have been known. It appeared that the widow had proved the will ; and no mention was made of her death. It was not the practice to state in the abstract that parties interested in the estate were still alive : their existence was assumed, unless the contrary was stated. Secondly, the decree for sale was made in a suit in which the widow was a party, with her consent. The Court must be presumed to have been satisfied that it was for the benefit of the infants that the estate should be sold : the circumstance that there was no inquiry whether it was for their benefit, does not impair the presumption, for the Court may be satisfied of the fact without inquiry, which is only one mode of deriving information. The property consisted of houses, and may be deteriorated, but is not likely to be improved. An erroneous conclusion in fact, if it were so, may be occasion for appeal, but is not error in the decree.

Mr. Dunn, for the purchaser :

The 8th condition did not apply, for the abstract was not complete even at the time when the objection was taken, which was discovered not from the abstract, but from a different document,

[*45] *the brief in the cause: *Tanner* v. *Smith* (1) ; *Hobson* v. *Bell* (2) ; *Dalby* v. *Pullen* (3). Any infant, interested in the estate, might, on

(1) 51 R. R. 277 (10 Sim. 410).   (3) 30 R. R. 123 (3 Sim. 29, 1
(2) 50 R. R. 90 (2 Beav. 17).   Russ. & My. 296).

attaining twenty-one, procure the cause to be reheard, and displace the decree.

THE VICE-CHANCELLOR:

The vendors in this case contend, first, that the objection taken by the purchaser to the title is not tenable, for they say the Court may anticipate the time of sale directed by a will, where it is for the benefit of the parties interested (although they may be infants), that an earlier sale should take place than the testator has prescribed; and therefore, that a sale in the lifetime of the widow is not error in the decree. Secondly, that the facts upon which the present objection is founded appear sufficiently upon the abstract, and that the purchaser is now precluded by the 8th condition of sale from taking the objection.

The purchaser, on the other hand, alleges, first, that the objection is fatal to the title, or at all events, that the title is one which a court of equity will not compel a purchaser to take; secondly, that the facts raising the objection were not sufficiently disclosed upon the abstract; and, thirdly, that the twenty-one days mentioned in the 8th condition are to be computed from the day when a perfect abstract was delivered: *Hobson* v. *Bell;* and he insists that the abstract first delivered was imperfect; that his objection was taken within the twenty-one days; and, in fact, that the abstract is not yet perfect.

Upon the principal question, I am of opinion, that the *sale in the lifetime of the widow creates such a defect in the title, that a court of equity ought not to compel a purchaser to accept it. In order to justify that opinion, I need not deny the power of the Court in any possible case to anticipate the time prescribed in a will for selling an infant's estate. All that I need say is, that a decree anticipating the sale of the estate is a departure from the trusts of the will; and that a case should be made for the exercise of such an extraordinary power. That case must be made either upon the pleadings, or upon a reference to the Master, or some other proceeding informing the Court of the case, which is relied upon as calling for so unusual an act. It has not been suggested at the Bar that the decree can be supported upon the ground that the debts of the testator require the sale. The trustees therefore could not have made a good title to the estate; and in the absence of special circumstances, the Court, as a general proposition, does nothing more than the trustees might have done in the due execution

[*46]

of the express trusts of the will. This bill asks the execution of
the trusts of the will as they are set out in the pleadings; no case
for departure from those trusts is made; and it is impossible to
read the decree without seeing that the Court intended to do
nothing more than execute the trusts of the will. It directs the
trusts of the will to bè performed, and the Master to sell such, if
any, of the testator's estates as then remained unsold. If any of
the infant defendants were now to rehear the cause, I cannot doubt
but that the Court would alter the decree, unless a case were made
as the result of future inquiry or evidence to justify the Court
in renewing the existing decree for sale.

Then has the purchaser accepted this defective title according to
the construction of the 8th condition, so as to preclude himself from

[*47]
taking the objection to it, *by the expiration of the twenty-one days
there mentioned ?

Now the first observation is : The abstract does not contain the
pleadings in the cause : the pleadings were called for by the purchaser's counsel on the 12th of March, before the expiration of the
twenty-one days; and on the 5th of April, after the expiration of
that time, the vendors' solicitors tender the brief for inspection at
their office. If it has in truth been out of the inspection of these
pleadings that the objection has arisen, it would be impossible for
the vendors successfully to contend that it was not competent to
the purchaser, after the twenty-one days, to insist upon an objection to the title arising out of the inspection of a document which
had been called for within that time. But this is the state of the
case between the parties, unless the contents of the abstract are
such as to deprive the purchaser of any argument founded upon
the difference of the information disclosed by the pleadings and
that disclosed by the abstract. In considering this, I must have
regard to the principles of the Court as explained by the MASTER OF
THE ROLLS in *Burroughs* v. *Oakley* (1). The Court must anxiously
protect the purchaser. The question must be whether as a conclusion of fact the Court is satisfied the purchaser intended to
waive, and has waived his right to object to this defect in the title.
And in a question between the purchaser and vendors only, I
cannot hold that he has done so unless the contents of the abstract
are such as clearly to raise the present objection. If the purchase
had been completed, it would undoubtedly have been difficult for
the purchaser in a contest with a stranger, to have contended with

(1) 19 R. R. 188 (3 Swanst. 159).

effect, that the statement in the abstract, of the will having been
proved by Alice Christie and *Laws, did not affect him with notice
that Alice the tenant for life survived the testator, and with all the
consequences resulting from such notice. But the statement is not
inconsistent with the supposition, that a good title might be made
notwithstanding the widow was living. The suggestion on the
remarks upon the abstract, and the argument of the vendors at the
Bar show this. If the fact that the widow survived the testator
and is still living, was absolutely inconsistent with the decree being
right, the argument in favour of a waiver would be far stronger
than it is. It was by the pleadings, and only by the pleadings,
that the defect in the title really appeared. But in truth the
abstract does not state that the widow survived the testator, except
incidentally in stating another fact,—the probate of the will; and
the decree as abstracted purports duly to carry into effect, not to
vary, the trusts of the will as expressed therein. In these circumstances, and looking at the evidence before me, I think myself
bound to hold, in a question between the vendors and purchaser
before conveyance, that the abstract does not so point to the facts
out of which the present objection arises, that I can consider the
purchaser as having waived it. The abstract itself did not raise
the objection, and if it did, the objection is established by the
evidence which the purchaser called for before the twenty-one days
expired.

The cause came on for further directions. The only material
question was, whether the gift of the annuity to the testator's
daughter Anne, created a trust for her separate use.

Mr. *Sharpe* and Mr. *Rolt*, for the plaintiffs, relied on *Tyler* v.
Lake (1), as an authority that the annuity did not vest in the
daughter to her separate use.

Mr. *Simpkinson*, for Anne, the daughter, contended that a
series of decisions, anterior to *Tyler* v. *Lake*, had established that
words of equivalent import to the words of this bequest were
sufficient to create a separate use; and that *Tyler* v. *Lake* was
distinguishable, because the use of similar words of gift to a son
showed that the testatrix had not any special intention to exclude
the husband of the daughter.

(1) 34 R. R. 53 (2 Russ. & My. 183).

THE VICE-CHANCELLOR :

The case of *Tyler* v. *Lake* was an appeal from the VICE-CHANCELLOR, who held that words very nearly similar to the words of this gift had not the effect of creating a separate interest in the wife. Lord BROUGHAM said that, "If a sufficient strength of negative words is not to be found in the gift or limitation, you are not allowed to fish about for indications of intention from other parts of the instrument," and his Lordship refers to a case of *Stanton* v. *Hall* (1), where he says the same principle was acted upon. And Lord COTTENHAM, in the subsequent case of *Massey* v. *Parker* (2), which, though afterwards reversed by himself on one point, remains untouched on this, says : "The cases require very distinct and unequivocal expressions to create a separate interest in the wife. In *Tyler* v. *Lake*, the LORD CHANCELLOR says, that the husband is not to be excluded except by words which leave no doubt of the intention, and of the principle the case of *Tyler* v. *Lake*, which is also reported before the Vice-Chancellor (3), and

[*50] the *case of *Stanton* v. *Hall*, afford strong illustration. In neither of these cases did the claim of the wife prevail; although in *Stanton* v. *Hall*, the whole machinery of the instrument proved that such must have been the intention, but the required words of exclusion were wanting ; and in *Tyler* v. *Lake*, the trustees were directed to pay the shares of the trust fund, into the proper hands of the married women, to and for their own use and benefit, and if they should be dead to pay the same to their husbands." Now, without presuming to question these *dicta*, I confess I do not understand how far either Lord BROUGHAM or Lord COTTENHAM meant to say the rule in these cases goes. I take the rule to be universal, that nobody can entitle himself to an interest under a written instrument, unless he can make out that he is entitled to the interest he claims by the words of that instrument; and where the Court, by what is called implication, as distinguished from express gift, gives property to a claimant, it does not by so doing contravene the rule that an unequivocal intention to give must be found in the instrument itself (4). Now if the cases of *Tyler* v. *Lake*, *Stanton* v. *Hall*, and *Massey* v. *Parker*, are to be understood as laying down the rule, that in these particular cases of the marital right there must be negative words in the words of limitation,—

(1) 34 R. R. 49 (2 Russ. & My. 125).   (4) See *Ancaster* v. *Mayer*, 1 Br.
(2) 2 My. & K. 174.   C. C. 460—462.
(3) 4 Sim. 144.

certainly the marital right is protected by stricter rules than are applicable, at the present day, to any other right of property; for, with the exception of a few technical words, (the words "heir" or "exchange," for example, in a deed), courts of justice invariably affirm the proposition, that an intended gift shall take effect, provided the Court can find in the instrument a declared intention to give, although the simple words of limitation, unaided by implication arising out *of other parts of the instrument, might [*51] leave the intention uncertain. I do not know whether the learned Judges meant to go the length of saying, that the words of limitation themselves must, in this particular case, be absolutely unequivocal; but the authorities referred to place me in this situation,—that I must construe the will in this case with the utmost strictness. If strictness of construction is to be relaxed, in a case of this class, it must be by a higher authority than mine.

With regard to the case of *Tyler* v. *Lake*, I presume to say it might well be supported without furnishing a necessary rule for the present case. The trust was to pay the proceeds of real estate into the proper hands of a married woman for her own use and benefit. And in certain events similar expressions were used, declaring trusts in favour of male persons. The direction to pay into the proper hands of the lady left untouched the marital right to the money when in her hands, and it was previously settled that the word "own" will not create a separate interest in the wife: coupling this with the gift in the very same words to a male, the VICE-CHANCELLOR held that a separate use was not created. Lord BROUGHAM, however, did not form his judgment upon the same reasoning. He took a broader ground—after enforcing the necessity of finding direct words of exclusion, he said, that the word "proper" is the Latin form of the word "own," and therefore payment into her proper hands signifies the same thing, as into her "own" hands, and her "own" has no exclusive meaning, and upon that ground alone he determined that the gift in that case was not a gift for the wife's separate use. Now the present case is, in one respect, distinguishable from *Tyler* v. *Lake*, for the word "proper" is repeated in describing in what manner the wife is to hold and enjoy the property; and reported cases of great *authority certainly [*52] take a distinction, where there is a simple direction that a woman should receive, and where to that direction is superadded a direction, as to the manner in which she is to hold and enjoy the

BLACKLOW
v.
LAWS.

property. In *Tyrrell* v. *Hope* (1), there was an agreement that the wife should enjoy and receive the issues and profits : that is the mere legal consequence of the receipt of the money by her ; yet in that case the direction that she should enjoy was held to create a separate use. In *Prichard* v. *Ames* (2), a like decree was made upon a similar ground ; and in *Atcherley* v. *Vernon* (3), to the words "to be by her laid out in what she shall think fit," the same construction was applied. The gift in *Margetts* v. *Barringer* (4) was " for her own use and benefit, independently of any other person," which was held to exclude the husband. *Wardle* v. *Claxton* (5) seems to be the case of a gift to the separate use of the wife within those cases ; but the VICE-CHANCELLOR said that the direction to apply the fund for the maintenance of her children as well as herself, prevented the case from being brought within the language of the authorities (6). It was these cases, and the very strong expressions in the case before me, showing that this was meant to be a gift to the separate use of the females, that led me to look into the authorities.

Admitting, then, that a direction to pay into the proper hands of a woman would not be a gift to her separate use, and that I am only to try whether the superadded words are to have any effect ; the first thing which, independently of authority, I should have to

[*53]

consider is, the meaning of the word "proper," according *to the ordinary use of the English language. Now the word "proper" is defined as meaning "peculiar," — "not belonging to other persons,"—"not common to other persons." And the ordinary rule of construction is to give, where it is possible, some effect to all the words. Now, if, in *Margetts* v. *Barringer*, a declaration, that the property was to be held by the lady "independently of any other person," created a separate use, it is difficult to see why the same effect should not be given to a direction (superadded to the direction to pay into her hands) that she shall hold it,—for her " peculiar use,"—so as not to belong to any other, —or so as not to be enjoyed by others "in common" with her. If the words are to have any operation, they must make it a gift to her separate use, as in *Margetts* v. *Barringer*, and other cases. Lord BROUGHAM, however, rejecting or not relying upon the VICE-CHANCELLOR's reasoning, goes (I might almost say) out of his way

(1) 2 Atk. 561.
(2) 24 R. R. 31 (T. & Russ. 222).
(3) 10 Mod. 518.
(4) 7 Sim. 482.

(5) 9 Sim. 524.
(6) See *Kirk* v. *Paulin*, 7 Vin. Abr. 96, pl. 43.

to decide that the word " proper " is mere repetition or surplusage, and means nothing more than " own," overruling a decision in which Lord ALVANLEY (1) held, that the use of the word " proper " would create a separate use. And I cannot, in the face of a decision of Lord BROUGHAM, so recently given, and the remarks of Lord COTTENHAM on the same point, act on any impression of my own as to the word " proper," when applied as in this case.

Some observations were made on the language in other parts of this will; and it is remarkable that, though the testator creates separate interests in several instances, he adopts, in almost every case, a different set of words for doing so. And it may also be observed, that, in giving legacies to persons who are widows, he gives them to the sole use of the widows. The *case is open to the observation which Lord BROUGHAM makes in *Tyler* v. *Lake*, that one cannot help seeing that the testator did not know the meaning of the words he was using. Although with a strong opinion that I decide this case against the real intention of the testator, my decision must be governed by that in *Tyler* v. *Lake*.

BLACKLOW
v.
LAWS.

[*54]

WARRINGTON *v.* WARRINGTON (2).

(2 Hare, 54—57; S. C. 6 Jur. 872.)

A testatrix gave the residue of her real and personal estate equally between her brother, her sister, and her "nephew W., and E. his wife," (E. being the niece of the testatrix): Held, that the husband and wife took one share each, and not merely one share between them.

1842.
July 11, 14.

WIGRAM,
V.-C.
[54]

THE question was, whether, under the will of Elizabeth Warrington, made in 1840, the defendants, William Henry, and Emma his wife, the nephew and niece of the testatrix, took one share, or two shares, of the residuary estate. The only material passage in the will was as follows :

" My share of the estate called Cynon, in the county of Montgomery, and all other my real and personal estate, with the exception of Carlton Lodge, and that I leave to my dear niece and nephew, Emma and William Henry Warrington, having but one half of that house and garden ; and all other my real and personal estate and property in the joint-stock bank called Gloucestershire

(1) *Hartley* v. *Hurle*, 5 R. R. 113 (5 Ves. 545).
(2) *In re March* (1884) 27 Ch. D. 166, 54 L. J. Ch. 143, 51 L. T. 380,
C. A. ; *In re Jupp* (1888) 39 Ch. D. 148, 57 L. J. Ch. 774, 59 L. T. 129; *In re Dixon* (1889) 42 Ch. D. 306, 61 L. T. 718.

and Cheltenham Bank, with all the rest, residue, and remainder of my trust estate and property whatever and wherever not herein disposed of, I leave equally between my brother Thornhill Warrington, my sister Anne Van Corlandt, widow, my nephew, William Henry Warrington, and Emma his wife, their heirs and assigns, nevertheless subject to any bequest and legacy herein mentioned."

[55]

Mr. Sharpe and *Mr. Berrey*, for the plaintiff:

The rule in joint-tenancy is thus stated by Littleton: "If a joynt-estate be made of land to a husband and wife, and to a third person, in this case the husband and wife have in law, in their right, but the moiety. And the cause is, for that the husband and wife are but one person in law; and are in like case as if an estate be made to two joyntenants, where the one hath, by force of the joynture, the one moiety, and the other, the other moiety. In the same manner it is, where an estate is made to the husband and wife and to two other men; in this case the husband and wife have but the third part, and the other two men, the other two parts " (1). *Bricker* v. *Whalley* (2); *Anon.*, Skin. (3); *Green d. Crew* v. *King* (4); *Back* v. *Andrews* (5); *Doe d. Freestone* v. *Parratt* (6). There is no reason in the nature of a tenancy in common, for applying a different rule in this respect from that which is applied in joint-tenancy.

Mr. Lewin, for the defendant Anne Van Corlandt.

Mr. Purvis and *Mr. Toller*, for the defendants William Henry Warrington, and Emma his wife:

The case of *Bricker* v. *Whalley* turned on the peculiarity of expression by which the husband and wife were separated in the gift by the conjunction "and" from the other persons—"to B., C., and D., and the *wife of D." In the simple case of a devise to a husband and wife, and a third person equally, POPHAM, Ch. J., is reported to have laid it down that they were tenants in common, inasmuch (*quia*) as they took every one of them a third part: *Lewin* v. *Cox* (7). In *The Attorney-General* v. *Bacchus* (8), a residuary

[*56]

(1) Sect. 291.
(2) 1 Vern. 233; *S. C.* 4 Vin. Abr. p. 154, tit. Baron and Feme, (M. a). pl. 9.
(3) Skin. 182; *S. C.* 4 Vin. Abr. p. 154, pl. 10.

(4) 2 W. Bl. 211.
(5) 2 Vern. 120; *S. C.* Prec. Cha. 1.
(6) 5 T. R. 652.
(7) Serjt. Moore, 558, pl. 759.
(8) 9 Pri. 30; *S. C.* 11 Pri. 547. See 35 R. R. 746, *n*.

bequest to a husband and wife was treated as a gift to two persons, and the legacy duty distinguished accordingly.

THE VICE-CHANCELLOR :

I cannot concur in the argument that the quantity of the interest to be taken by the husband and wife in this residuary gift depends upon the question whether the gift creates a joint-tenancy or a tenancy in common.   The quantity of land which the husband and wife take, under a devise like that before me, is a different question from that of the manner in which they take it.   They may take their shares by entireties, and not by moieties as between themselves; but this legal result, as between the husband and wife, cannot affect the amount of the gift, as between them and third persons. The number of shares into which the residue is divided must be determined by counting the legatees, among whom it is equally given.   It may be observed, that Littleton, in stating the rule which has been referred to, always illustrates it by placing the husband and wife as the first parties to whom the estate is made; and in *Bricker* v. *Whalley*, the occurrence of the word " and " before the names of the husband and wife is adverted to by the LORD KEEPER.   The circumstances relied on in that case exist here : the husband and wife are equally of kin to the testatrix : and there *is nothing in the disposition of the names which can import any intention to treat either of them differently from the other legatees. I cannot do otherwise than hold the gift to be a gift in severalty to several persons ; and the residue must therefore be divided into four shares, and the husband and wife declared to be entitled each to one of such shares.

[*57]

EDWARDS *v.* MEYRICK (1).

(2 Hare, 60—79; S. C. 12 L. J. Ch. 49; 6 Jur. 924.)

On a question of the propriety of a purchase by a solicitor from his client, the solicitor, in order to sustain the transaction, must, if he was solicitor *in hâc re*, show that he gave his client all that reasonable advice against himself, which his office of solicitor would have made it his duty to have given him against a third person ; but the nature of the proof varies according to the subject of the purchase, the relative situation of the parties, and the equality of the footing upon which they stand, in reference to the subject of the contract; and,.although the relationship of attorney

----

(1) *Luddy's Trustee* v. *Pearl* (1886) 33 Ch. D. 500, 55 L. J. Ch. 884, 55 L. T. 137; *In re Haslam* and *Hier-Erans* [1902] 1 Ch. 765, 71 L. J. Ch. 374, 86 L. T. 663, C. A.; *Wright* v. *Carter* [1903] 1 Ch. 27, 72 L. J. Ch. 138, C. A.

and client may exist, yet if it has no existence *in hâc re*, the rule with regard to the *onus* of proof may no longer be applicable.   Nor does the rule require the solicitor to point out the speculative possibility that a railway which is known to be in contemplation may improve the value of the property which he is buying from his client.

On proof of some specific errors and overcharges in an account and bill of costs, inquiries were directed with respect to an account made up—and the balance of which was secured by a mortgage made thirteen years before the bill was filed.

IN the year 1815, the defendant W. Meyrick, a solicitor at Merthyr Tydvil, became acquainted with the fact of the existence of a settlement under which the plaintiff, Lewis Edwards, a farmer in that neighbourhood, was entitled to property of considerable value.   The defendant having informed the plaintiff of that fact, the latter, in 1817, instructed him to take proceedings for the recovery of the settled property, and a bill was accordingly filed in the Court of Great Session in Wales.   In this suit various proceedings were had, —an issue was directed,—a suit to impeach the settlement was commenced in this Court, and several ejectments were brought.   In 1827 terms of compromise were adopted, and the same were finally carried into effect in 1829.

The plaintiff was also the owner of two farms known as Tyr Twppa and Yscwddgwyn, which were not connected with the property in dispute ; these farms were subject to a mortgage for 600*l.*   Being indebted to the defendant for money advanced and costs incurred in the proceedings adverted to, the plaintiff executed indentures dated 1st and 2nd of January, 1823, whereby he conveyed [*61] the farms Tyr Twppa and Yscwddgwyn to *the defendant in fee, by way of mortgage, to. secure the sum of 1,109*l.* 1*s.* 3*d.*, the alleged amount due to him at that time, of which the charge in respect of costs appeared to be about 816*l.*   In 1825 the plaintiff offered the two farms for sale to different persons, and the defendant ultimately proposed to become himself the purchaser, at the price of 2,100*l.*   The plaintiff accepted the offer, and by indentures of the 1st and 2nd of February, 1825, which were prepared by the defendant, and the execution of which by the plaintiff was attested by another solicitor, the farms Tyr Twppa and Yscwddgwyn were conveyed to the defendant absolutely, in consideration of 697*l.*, due for principal and interest to the prior mortgagee, 1,224*l.* 10*s.* 11*d.* stated to be due to the defendant on his mortgage, and a sum of 178*l.* 9*s.* 1*d.* in cash, making up the 2,100*l.*   It was alleged that 100*l.* only was paid to the plaintiff, and the remaining 78*l.* 9*s.* 1*d.* retained by the defendant on account of his then current bill of costs against the

plaintiff. The defendant, it was admitted, did not act as the
solicitor of the plaintiff after the year 1832, and according to the
statement of the defendant their relation of solicitor and client
ceased in 1829.

In October, 1835, the plaintiff applied to redeem the two farms,
upon payment to the defendant of what should be due to him,—
treating the property as a security for that sum. In June, 1836,
the plaintiff filed his bill, charging that the mortgage in 1823 was
obtained from him without any settlement of accounts, the plaintiff
being involved in suits and actions in respect of the litigated property, and the defendant being his sole solicitor and attorney : that
the plaintiff reluctantly consented to the subsequent sale, upon being
pressed thereto by the defendant, who knew that the plaintiff had
no other means of discharging the heavy demands for costs ; that
no solicitor was employed on his behalf; and that he had *never   [*62]
received more than the 100*l.* of the purchase-money. The bill
charged that the farms were, at the time of sale, even for the
surface rent, worth considerably more than the consideration
expressed to be given, and that there were valuable beds of coal
and other minerals underneath, making the whole value 5,000*l.* at
the least ; that the bills of costs of the defendant contained numerous
errors and overcharges, many of which to the amount of upwards
of 100*l.*, the bill specifically stated ; and it also alleged that credit
had not been given for several sums which the defendant had
received.

The bill alleged that the plaintiff was a Welch yeoman of very
little education, and incompetent to examine bills of costs, if any
had been delivered by the defendant ; and it charged that the mortgage, sale, and conveyance of the said farms to the defendant ought
to be declared fraudulent, or to stand only as a security for what
was, at the time of the execution thereof, justly due to the defendant,
and that, upon payment thereof, the said farms ought to be re-
conveyed: that the pretended settlement of accounts, and alleged
mortgage security on the foot thereof, were not, under the circumstances, valid or conclusive in equity, and that the plaintiff was
entitled to have the accounts unravelled.

The bill prayed that the mortgage, sale, and conveyance might
be declared to be fraudulent, and be set aside ; or if the Court should
be of opinion that the defendant was entitled to hold the same as a
security for his costs, then that the same might be declared to stand
only as a security for what was justly due to the defendant at the

[*63]

time of the execution thereof ; and that an account thereof might be taken, as also an account of the rents and profits of the said farms come to the hands of the defendant, and of the incumbrances paid off by him ; and that the farms might be re-conveyed to the *plaintiff, on payment of what should be due from him.   The bill also prayed, in the alternative, that if the Court should be of opinion that the purchase and conveyance ought to be established, then that an account might be taken of what was due to the plaintiff in respect of the purchase-money, and that the alleged settled account and mortgage security might be opened, and the accounts taken without reference thereto ; or if the Court were of opinion that the plaintiff was not entitled to have the mortgage set aside, and the bill of costs opened for general taxation, that the plaintiff might be at liberty to surcharge and falsify the same, and question the propriety of the work, and the reasonableness of the charges.

The defendant, by his answer, denied all pressure or improper influence, and insisted that the plaintiff was perfectly competent to act for himself in the matters in which he had been engaged, and which were now the subject of enquiry.   He said it was only upon the solicitation of the plaintiff that he had consented to become the purchaser of the two farms ; that the consideration was adequate,— the amount retained for his advances and costs justly due,—and the plaintiff, in fact, still indebted to him : that the taxation of costs in the Courts of Great Session in Wales was not governed by the same rules as in the Courts of Westminster : that the errors of computation or casting which appeared in the accounts were, he believed, owing to omissions and clerical errors, but which, in consequence of the death of Watkins, one of his clerks, by whom the accounts had been kept and made up, he was not fully able to explain.

The effect of the evidence on several of the material facts will sufficiently appear in the foregoing statement (1), and in the judgment.   The witnesses produced *on behalf of the defendant stated that the value of the farms had greatly improved since the purchase, by the making of the Rhymney Railway, in 1826 and 1827, through the parish of Gellygare, in which the farms were situated : they also proved that Watkins, the clerk of the defendant, who had attended to the account and bills of costs in question, died in 1828, and that many documents and papers had been lost by accident from the office.

[*64]

(1) *Supra,* p. 24.

Mr. Sharpe and *Mr. W. M. James*, for the plaintiff :

This was a conveyance obtained by a solicitor from his client ; and, therefore, unless in peculiar circumstances, and with the clearest proof of fairness on his part, cannot be sustained. [On this point they cited *Gibson* v. *Jeyes* (1) ; *Hatch* v. *Hatch* (2) ; *Wood* v. *Downes* (3) ; *Hunter* v. *Atkins* (4) ; *Jones* v. *Thomas* (5), and other cases.] The instruments were prepared by the defendant himself—no attorney was interposed on behalf of the plaintiff. It cannot be supposed, that, as a local solicitor, the defendant was ignorant of the projected railway. No proof was adduced that the plaintiff was informed of that circumstance. Secondly, the security given for the costs did not amount to a settlement of the bill, so as to preclude taxation. [On this point they cited *Waters* v. *Taylor* (6), *Horlock* v. *Smith* (7), and earlier cases.]

The *Solicitor-General, Mr. Girdlestone*, and *Mr. Romilly*, for   [65]
the defendant :

There is no rule which, as against a solicitor, invalidates a con-tract merely because it is made between him and his client. [On this point they cited *Montesquieu* v. *Sandys* (8), *Champion* v. *Rigby* (9), and other cases.] The intended railway, if of any   [66] importance as a matter of consideration at the time of the sale, must be taken to be as well known to the owner of the property as to the solicitor. This proceeding is instituted thirteen years after the mortgage, eleven years after the purchase ; and when any relation of solicitor and client between the parties had ceased to exist for seven years : after that lapse of time the Court will not open these accounts : *Waters* v. *Taylor ; Horlock* v. *Smith*. The inaccuracies, if they are ultimately shown to have existed, are but of small amount compared with the purchase-money ; and are not of sufficient importance to affect the settled account, in the circumstances. * * *

THE VICE-CHANCELLOR :   [67]

The plaintiff in this case, who is described by one of the witnesses

(1) 5 R. R. 295 (6 Ves. 266).   (6) 45 R. R. 129 (2 My. & Cr. 526).
(2) 7 R. R. 195 (9 Ves. 292).   (7) 45 R. R. 125 (2 My. & Cr. 495).
(3) 11 R. R. 160 (18 Ves. 120).   (8) 11 R. R. 197 (18 Ves. 302).
(4) 41 R. R. 30 (3 My. & K. 135).   (9) 31 R. R. 107 (1 Russ. & My.
(5) 47 R. R. 449 (2 Y. & C. Ex. Eq.   539).
498).

as a hill farmer, is the owner of some property in Wales; and, according to the evidence to which I shall refer, a person perfectly competent to understand his own interests. The defendant is a solicitor practising in the same neighbourhood. It appears, that, in 1815, the defendant discovered the title of the plaintiff to some estates, of which he was not then in possession; and having communicated the fact to the plaintiff, he was retained by him as his solicitor in the proceedings necessary to recover these estates. Those proceedings were commenced in the Court of Great Session, and were prosecuted there, and in other Courts, during several years. In the year 1823, before these proceedings were brought to a close, the defendant claimed from the plaintiff a sum of about 1,100*l.*; which, to the extent of 800*l.* or more, appears to have been made up of costs incurred, or said to have been incurred, in the conduct of the business I have adverted to. The defendant appears to have asked either for payment or security : and the result was, that the plaintiff gave him a mortgage for 1,100*l.*, and upwards, on two farms belonging to him, of which he was then in possession, not being part of the estates which were the subject of the then existing suits. In those suits, the defendant still continued to act as the solicitor of the plaintiff; and in the year 1825, having then a further claim on the plaintiff, he became the purchaser of the two farms of which he was mortgagee. The purchase-money agreed to be paid for the two farms was 2,100*l.* The defendant was to pay off a prior mortgage, and after retaining the defendant's mortgage-debt, and certain costs, in respect of which some other credit was to be taken, the balance of the account, amounting to

[*68]

178*l.*, was to be paid to *the plaintiff. In point of fact, the sum of 100*l.* only was paid to the plaintiff, and the remaining 78*l.* were retained on account. It is clear, that the whole of the purchase-money was not paid. The litigation which first brought the plaintiff and defendant into communication with each other, does not appear to have terminated until 1829; down to which time, the defendant acted as solicitor for the plaintiff. I am not satisfied that there is any evidence of his so acting later than 1829. The present bill was filed in June, 1836.

(His Honour stated the substance of the prayer.)

It was not insisted in argument that a solicitor is under an actual incapacity to purchase from his client. There is not, in that case, the positive incapacity which exists between a trustee and his cestui que trust; but the rule the Court imposes is, that

inasmuch as the parties stand in a relation which gives, or may give,
the solicitor an advantage over the client, the *onus* lies on the
solicitor to prove that the transaction was fair : *Montesquieu* v.
Sandys (1) ; *Cane* v. *Lord Allen* (2). The rule is expressed by Lord
ELDON (3) to be, that if the attorney " will mix with the character
of attorney that of vendor, he shall, if the propriety of the transaction comes in question, manifest that he has given his client all
that reasonable advice against himself that he would have given
him against a third person." It was argued that the rule I have
referred to has no application, unless the defendant was the
plaintiff's solicitor *in hâc re*, and this argument is no doubt well
founded : *Jones* v. *Thomas* (4) ; *Gibson* v. *Jeyes* (5). It appears to
me, however, that the question *whether Meyrick was the solicitor   [*69]
in hâc re, is one rather of words than of substance. The rule of
equity which subjects transactions between solicitor and client to
other and stricter tests than those which apply to ordinary transactions, is not an isolated rule, but is a branch of a rule applicable
to all transactions between man and man, in which the relation
between the contracting parties is such as to destroy the equal
footing on which such parties should stand. In some cases, as
between trustee and cestui que trust, the rule goes to the extent of
creating a positive incapacity ; the duties of the office of trustee
requiring on general principles, that that particular case should
be so guarded. The case of solicitor and client is, however,
different. In the case of *Gibson* v. *Jeyes*, there was evidence that
the client was of advanced age, and of much infirmity, both in
mind and body, that the consideration was inadequate,—and of
various other circumstances. Lord ELDON there shows how each
of those circumstances gave rise to its appropriate duty on the part
of the attorney. In other cases, where an attorney has been
employed to manage an estate, he has been considered as bound
to prove that he gave his employer the benefit of all the knowledge
which he had acquired in his character of manager or professional
agent, in order to sustain a bargain made for his own advantage :
Cane v. *Lord Allen* (6). But as the communication of such knowledge by the attorney will place the parties upon an equality,—
when it is proved that the communication was made, the difficulty
of supporting the transaction is *quoad hoc* removed. If, on the

(1) 11 R. R. 197 (18 Ves. 302).   498).
(2) 2 Dow, 289.   (5) 5 R. R. 295 (6 Ves. 266).
(3) 5 R. R. at p. 306 (6 Ves. 278).   (6) 2 Dow, p. 294.
(4) 47 R. R. 449 (2 Y. & C. Ex. Eq.

EDWARDS
v.
MEYRICK.

[*70]

other hand, the attorney has not had any concern with the estate respecting which the question arises, the particular duties to which any given situation of confidence might give rise cannot of course attach upon him, whatever may be the other duties which the mere office of attorney *may impose. If the attorney, being employed to sell, becomes himself the purchaser, his duties and his interests are directly opposed to each other, and it would be difficult,—and without the clearest evidence that no advantage was taken by the attorney of his position, and that the vendor had all the knowledge which could be given him in order to form a judgment, it would be impossible—to support the transaction. In other cases the relation between the parties may simply produce a degree of influence and ascendancy, placing the client in circumstances of disadvantage ; as where he is indebted to the attorney, and is unable to discharge the debt. The relative position of the parties, in such a case, must at least impose upon the attorney the duty of giving the full value for the estate, and the *onus* of proving that he did so. If he proves the full value to have been given, the ground for any unfavourable inference is removed. The cases may be traced through every possible variation until we reach the simple case where, though the relation of solicitor and client exists in one transaction, and, therefore, personal influence or ascendancy may operate in another, yet the relation not existing *in hâc re*, the rule of equity to which I am now adverting may no longer apply.

The nature of the proof, therefore, which the Court requires must depend upon the circumstances of each case, according as they may have placed the attorney in a position in which his duties and his pecuniary interests were conflicting, or may have given him a knowledge which his client did not possess, or some influence or ascendancy or other advantage over his client; or, notwithstanding the existence of the relation of attorney and client, may have left the parties substantially at arm's length and on an equal footing : this seems deducible from the cases.

[His Honour here referred to the cases cited for the plaintiff, *ante*, p. 27.]

[71]

I have, therefore, to consider the position in which these parties actually stood to each other. And I certainly am not treating the case of the plaintiff too strictly when I exclude all considerations which the bill does not state as having existed ; and, according to the statements in the bill, it does not appear that the defendant had any peculiar or exclusive knowledge of these particular farms or the value of them, or that he had undertaken any particular duties respecting them which were opposed to his becoming a purchaser. No equity appears to me to arise, except that which might arise from the mere possibility of the relation of attorney and client, giving the attorney some influence or ascendancy over the client, and the circumstance that the plaintiff was pressed by him to pay his bill of costs. On the evidence in the cause I am satisfied that the only ground upon which I can proceed, is this bare relation between the parties. Taking the obligations of the defendant to stand as high as the relative position of the parties enable me to place them,—admitting the defendant to be the attorney *in hác re,* —I cannot consider that he is bound to do more than prove that he gave the full value for the estate.

On the question of whether the full value was given for the estate, it has been proved that this was property situated in a coal country, although coal had never been worked under it. It does not appear that any coal works had approached so near to property in this *neighbourhood that the value of the coal had ever been taken into account in sales of such property. The evidence shows that coal was known to be under it; but it clearly proves that in sales before this transaction the price was determined or the property valued with a view to alienation, according to the surface value founded upon the rental, at a certain number of years' purchase. In considering the evidence as to value I shall, therefore, confine myself to the surface value of the estate.

[*72]

(His Honour examined the evidence with regard to value, adduced by both parties, and which varied from 70*l.* to 85*l.* a year net, and from twenty to thirty years' purchase. It appeared that the plaintiff had let the property at a rent of 70*l.* for the year preceding the sale, and it did not appear that he had at any time received a higher rent for the property. After the purchase by the defendant it was let at 90*l.* per annum, with an allowance of 10*l.* for repairs. It was stated by the steward of Lord Bute that he (the steward) felt himself justified in offering 2,100*l.* for the estate, Lord Bute having particular reasons for possessing the property.)

In *Montesquieu* v. *Sandys,* Lord ELDON by no means intimates that, where the transaction is fair in every other respect, no advantage having been taken of the relation of attorney and client, the fact that the amount given for the property, even if a third less than the value, would affect the transaction. He does not express any opinion upon that point. In this case, according to the highest estimate in the evidence referred to, so far as it is founded upon any calculation, (for I disregard general statements, the grounds of which are not given), the amount paid would be one-eighth less than the value. I do not think it too much to presume that the plaintiff *himself knew the value of the estate : I do not find any evidence given by him to show that he had let the estate at an under value, or to explain why it was so let. There is no evidence that the defendant had any peculiar knowledge with respect to the estate : there is every possible reason to suppose that the plaintiff knew the value of it better than the attorney, and it has not been thought by him to be worth more than 70*l.* a year. On that footing the purchase was made. If the case had stopped there, no question could have been made that the full and fair value of the estate had been given, even supposing Meyrick to be considered the purchaser as well as, *in hâc re*, the attorney.

[*73]

The material fact upon which any question of value is raised, is this,—that it is proved, and indeed, admitted, that the estate is worth more than 2,100*l.* at the present time ; and I think I may add, that it became worth much more very soon after the purchase was made. But to what do the parties attribute this? The whole of the evidence shows, that, up to the time of the purchase, the formation of a railroad had never been taken into account in the valuation of estates in that district ; and that sales and purchases were made with reference only to the surface value. The purchase was made in February, 1825. In May, 1825, a bill for making a railroad through that part of the country received the Royal assent; and in consequence of the railroad being made, there arose a probability of coal being worked at a period less remote than there was previously reason to anticipate ; and, therefore, coal speculators would give a higher price for the property than they otherwise would have done.

The question then comes to this,—whether I could, as against the defendant, hold, that the relation in *which he stood as the plaintiff's attorney, in the suits I have referred to, imposed on him the obligation to prove that he gave the plaintiff notice that a railroad might be made, and that by possibility there might be an opportunity for working the coal under the land with advantage, and that, if it was worked, the land would be of greater value : the whole of these considerations being purely of a speculative character ? Now, certainly, looking at the relation in which these

[*74]

parties stood, I have no ground for supposing that this would be
more likely to be present in the mind of Meyrick, than of any other
person. He had nothing to do with these farms. The advantage
to be derived from the proposed undertaking was a point as much
open to one party as to the other, and was a merely speculative
result, the communication of which I think I ought not now to
require the defendant to prove, unless, in fact, the land had at that
time become of an improved value, owing to that circumstance.
This, however, would be in the knowledge of the plaintiff; and he
has not suggested any such case. The fact relating to the railroad
is not to be found in the pleadings: it comes out casually in the
evidence that a railroad bill was at that time in contemplation;
and then an argument is raised upon the assumption that Meyrick
knew it, and took advantage of that knowledge. It is true, that
the *onus* lies on the defendant to show that the treaty was fairly
conducted; but I do not think that in this case I can reasonably
hold the possibility of a speculative and consequential advantage
of this kind to fall within those communications which an attorney
is bound to prove he disclosed to his client. I cannot, on this part
of the case, from anything which is before me, form any conclusion
whether this possible improvement ought or not to have been in
the mind of any person dealing with the property. Considering,
as I do, that the Court is bound to watch strictly transactions
between attorney *and client, I do not think that the Court is
bound to allow a contingent advantage, which may or may not
have been in the contemplation of the parties at the time, to
afford ground for imputing fraud or improper concealment to the
attorney, because he does not prove that he communicated it to
his client.

I think that I should be carrying the doctrine of the Court
farther than it has ever yet been carried, if I were to hold that a
vendor, who has obtained from his solicitor thirty years' purchase
for the estate, at the highest rent ever given for it up to the time
of sale, so far as the evidence goes,—the solicitor being in no way
connected with that estate,—can rescind the transaction after a
lapse of eleven years from the time of the sale; the only new
circumstance occurring during that time being the formation of a
railway which has added to the value of the property. The acquiescence for so many years, coupled with the fact, that the foundation
of the argument on the effect of the railroad was not brought forward
in the pleadings, satisfies me that the plaintiff felt that his case

EDWARDS
v.
MEYRICK.

[*75]

could derive no strength on that ground, and that it is, in fact, an after-thought.

I must make the same order as Lord ELDON made in *Montesquieu* v. *Sandys*, and dismiss so much of this bill as seeks to rescind the contract, without costs.

It being determined that the contract is to stand, it follows that the plaintiff is entitled to the purchase-money; and then the question is, whether 1,109*l.* is to be taken conclusively as the sum which was due at the date of the mortgage. Of the other part of the purchase-money there must be an account taken.

[*76]   The first and most convenient way of looking at this *part of the case would be, to suppose that I had before me the bill of costs actually made out by Meyrick, and which constituted the particulars of the charge of the 1,109*l.* secured by the mortgage. The bill charges minute and specific errors in that bill of costs, an error in the casting up of upwards of 40*l.*, and improper professional charges; the result of which, if proved, would be, that something more than 100*l.* would be taken off the whole bill of costs. I do not mean that this is the result of the evidence; for if that were so, there would be no doubt of the right of the plaintiff to have the bill taxed. If the transaction also were recent, the allowance of the amount in the mortgage would not preclude the taxation of the bill. But, with regard to the effect of the acquiescence, I do not understand that the answer sets up time as a bar to the taxation. Then the case stands thus,—specific errors are alleged to exist in a bill to an amount which it would be most improper to disregard in taking the account of what is due in respect of the purchase-money; and which the plaintiff should have an opportunity of proving. In *Waters* v. *Taylor*, the VICE-CHANCELLOR OF ENGLAND held, that more than twenty years was not a bar to the taxation of a bill, even without proving specific errors, where a mortgage had been given pending the relation of solicitor and client. Lord COTTENHAM did not confirm that judgment; but decided, that after a settlement of accounts, and long acquiescence, the transaction ought to stand, unless specific errors were proved. I did not understand that judgment as importing, that if the bill were proved to be erroneous, the Court would not open it so far as was necessary to do justice between the parties.

I have hitherto assumed that the bill itself has been produced. I think the defendant has proved that the bill was
[*77]   made out by Watkins, and other clerks; that a *copy of that

bill was given to the plaintiff; and that the plaintiff, on one occasion, called with the copy of the bill, and had it explained to him
by Watkins; and it is plain that he was so far satisfied with it
as to execute a mortgage for securing the payment of it.   These
circumstances would materially affect the extent to which the
decree of the Court should go; especially adverting to the fact,
that Watkins, the clerk to whom the business was entrusted,
is dead.

The parties have placed the Court as well as themselves in
considerable difficulty in dealing with the question as to the bill
of costs.   The defendant sets out in his schedule what he describes
as a copy of the bill made out by Watkins for the plaintiff, which
would make up the sum secured by the mortgage; and he gives
explanations of several parts of the bill.   The plaintiff being unwilling
to take his account of the bill from the answer, with the explanations which the answer gives, avoided reading that part of the
answer which related to it.   The question then arises whether there
is evidence of any errors whatever in the identical bill, the amount
of which was the consideration for the mortgage.   The plaintiff
produces a bill of costs or supposed bill of costs, and has examined
witnesses to prove particular errors in it, and he proves the existence
of errors in a bill which, for anything that appears in evidence,
might not be a bill in any way connected with these transactions.
In strictness I have no evidence to connect them, and I certainly
cannot think the fact that the bill agrees in amount with that which
I find in the answer would justify me in taking it to be identified
by the plaintiff's evidence; but the defendant produces a bill, not
proved to be the bill delivered by himself, and he gives general
evidence of its fairness.   Each party produces a paper containing
a number of items, there is nothing to identify either of these
papers *with the bill, the propriety and correctness of which is   [*78]
impeached in this suit, but witnesses are examined on both sides
to show the fairness or unfairness of a bill about which I know
nothing, and can assume nothing.   The plaintiff then goes one step
further, he identifies two items contained in that supposititious bill
which he has produced as charges which have been actually made.
I am called upon to infer, that the bill of costs as to which the
witnesses have been examined must be the bill delivered by the
defendant.   I can have no doubt of the fact.   In the answer I find
a bill of costs on which both parties have examined witnesses,
corresponding with the bill of costs which the defendant says he

EDWARDS
c.
MEYRICK.

has made out. It would be trifling with justice if I did not send it for inquiry.

Another point then arises. It was said by Lord ELDON that, where a bill has been acquiesced in and paid, or security has been given for it, if, after many years have elapsed, there appear to be errors in it so gross as to amount to fraud, the Court will open it altogether, but the Court will not open it after it has been paid merely because there are charges in it which would not be allowed on taxation. One important difficulty in the present case is, that the bill relates to matters with regard to which we are very little conversant. It was for business done in the Court of Great Session in Wales, and we have very imperfect means of knowing whether the charges were or were not regularly made. If in taxing the bill, one sixth is taken off, will the Court hold that reduction to be so far evidence that the bill of costs was fraudulent in its character ; or will the Court hold the fact of the abatement in amount to be such evidence of misconduct as to disallow the defendant his costs of the taxation ? At present there is no evidence of fraud ; I cannot

[*79]

assume that the items in this bill, which was *settled in 1823, to some extent confirmed by the sale in 1825, and so long afterwards acquiesced in, are fraudulent.

This Court doth dismiss so much of the plaintiff's bill as seeks to set aside the sale in the pleadings mentioned, but without costs ; and it is ordered, that it be referred to the Master to whom, &c., to take an account of what (if anything) is due in respect of the purchase-money on such sale, and, in taking such account, the Master is to inquire and state what was the bill of costs and account which made up the sum of 1,109*l*. 1*s*. 3*d*. for which the mortgage of the 2nd day of July, 1823, in the pleadings mentioned, was taken ; and whether any and which of the items of such bill and account were improper, and ought not to be allowed on taxation ; and it is ordered, that each of the parties be at liberty to show that they have not had credit for sums or business done for which credit ought to have been given ; and it is ordered, that the said Master do tax the subsequent bill of the defendant as solicitor for the plaintiff, and take an account of subsequent money transactions between the plaintiff and the defendant, and for the better taking, &c., the parties are to produce, &c., and are to be examined upon interrogatories as the said Master shall direct, who, in taking the said accounts, is to make unto the parties all just allowances ; and the Master is to be at liberty to state any circumstances specially

as he shall think fit ; and this Court doth reserve the consideration
of all further directions and of the costs of this suit not hereinbefore
disposed of, until after the said Master shall have made his report.
Liberty to apply.

EARL OF GLENGALL *v.* FRAZER (1).

(2 Hare, 99—105; S. C. 12 L. J. Ch. 128; 6 Jur. 1081.)

In answer to a bill seeking to impeach a security and requiring the
defendant to set forth what communications passed between his solicitor
and agents in the transaction and the plaintiff; and what letters were
written and received, and entries made on the subject by such solicitors, it
is not sufficient for the defendant to say, that the solicitors had ceased for
several years since the transaction to be his solicitors or agents, and that he
does not know what communications or entries they had or made : the
defendant, if he has not personal knowledge of the facts, must at least
show that he has endeavoured to acquire the imformation from his agents
in the transaction in question.

IN the year 1825, the plaintiff, in consideration of the loan of
2,999*l.* by the defendants, granted them an annuity of 298*l.* 11*s.*
for the term of 100 years, if the plaintiff should so long live ;
which annuity was charged on the estates of the plaintiff in
Ireland. The sum so borrowed was also further secured by a
bond for 6,000*l.*, and by warrant of attorney to confess judgment
both in England and Ireland, for the same sum.

In June, 1842, the bill was filed, alleging that the memorial of
the annuity enrolled in pursuance of the statute, under the title
" consideration and how paid," stated, " 2,999*l.* of lawful money of
the United Kingdom of Great Britain and Ireland, of English value
and currency paid to the said Richard, Earl of Glengall, at the
time of the execution of the said indenture, in notes of the Governor
and Company of the Bank of England, payable to bearer on
demand ; " whereas, the same was, in fact, paid partly in notes
and partly in sovereigns. The bill charged that the securities were
therefore void, and prayed that they might be set aside, and
defendants restrained from taking proceedings founded upon the
judgments either at law or in equity, in England or Ireland.
The bill contained charges, upon which interrogatories to the
following effect were founded : Whether the plaintiff, about the
time of granting the annuity, did not have some, and what, interviews with the defendants, and with Messrs. Dawson, Capron,

[*100]

---

(1) *Bolckow, Vaughan & Co.* v.   *Incandescent Gas Lighting Co.* v. *New*
Fisher (1882) 10 Q. B. Div. 161, 52   *Sunlight Incandescent Co.* [1900] 2
L. J. Q. B. 12, 47 L. T. 724 ; *Welsbach*   Ch. 1, 69 L. J. Ch. 546, 83 L. T. 58, C. A.

Rowley, and Weld ; and whether the plaintiff did not also write and send some and what letters to the defendants, and to Messrs. Dawson & Co., with reference to the money to be advanced by the defendants to the plaintiff, or to the annuity which he was in consideration thereof to grant to them, or to the mode in which such annuity was to be secured. or for some other purpose ; and whether Messrs. Dawson & Co., at that or some time, were not or did not act, and whether they are not now, or do not act as, the solicitors of the defendants ; or how long had they ceased to act as such solicitors ; and whether the defendants, and Messrs. Dawson & Co., had not made some and what entries in books ; and whether they had not respectively written, sent, or received, to or from each other, or to and from other and what persons, some and what letters or letter relating to or mentioning the consideration-money agreed to be paid to the plaintiff for the said annuity ; and whether thereby the truth of the matters alleged would not appear ; and whether such books and letters were not in the possession or power of the defendants, or Messrs. Dawson & Co.

The defendants, in their answer, said they believed that the plaintiff had some interviews with Messrs. Dawson & Co., who acted as the plaintiff's solicitors, with reference to the money to be advanced by the defendants to the plaintiff, and to the said annuity, and *the mode in which such annuity was to be secured ; but save, as aforesaid, the defendants severally said they did not know, and they could not answer, as to their information, belief, or otherwise, whether the plaintiff, at such time, or at any time, did or not have any or what interviews or interview with Messrs. Dawson & Co., or any of them, or whether the plaintiff did or not also write and send letters to Messrs. Dawson & Co. with reference to the said matters (following the words in the bill).   And the defendants said that Messrs. Dawson & Co. had respectively ceased to act, and they had not, nor had any of them, acted as the solicitors &c. of the defendants, or either of them, for the space of seven years and upwards.   The defendants said that one of the defendants had occasionally had interviews with Messrs. Dawson & Co. to obtain information with respect to the payment of the annuity by the plaintiff, but not as the attornies or solicitors of the defendants, or either of them ; and that the last of such interviews took place in August, 1842.   The defendants said they did not know, and could not answer, as to their information, belief, or otherwise, whether Messrs. Dawson & Co. had &c. (following the

[*101]

interrogatory as to entries, letters, &c.), or whether thereby the truth of the alleged matters would appear; and save as aforesaid, the defendants denied that any such books or letters were then in the possession or power of the defendants, or either of them; and they did not know, and could not answer, as to their information, belief, or otherwise, whether such books or letters were then in the possession or power of Messrs. Dawson & Co.

Exceptions for insufficiency of the answer were taken, and allowed by the Master.

> *Mr. James Parker,* for the defendants, in support of exceptions to the Master's report: [102]

* * The information sought by these interrogatories is within the reach of the plaintiff, by *subpœna duces tecum*. Messrs. Dawson & Co. are mere witnesses. The connection of solicitor and client between them and the defendants has long ceased. This fact distinguishes the present case from *Taylor* v. *Rundell* (1). [They cited *Christian* v. *Taylor* (2), *Freeman* v. *Fairlie* (3), and other cases.]

> *Mr. Temple* and *Mr. Tripp,* for the plaintiff: [103]

The defendants are bound to show, at least, that they have made some attempt to acquire a knowledge of the facts in question; for it is admitted that Messrs. Dawson & Co. were their solicitors at the time of the transaction. It is not necessary, in this case, to say what the rule may be where the information is in the possession of one wholly a stranger.

THE VICE-CHANCELLOR:

The only question in this case is, whether the answer going only to the personal knowledge, information, and belief of the defendants, is sufficient; or whether the defendants ought not to have ascertained, or made, at least, an attempt to ascertain, by inquiry of their late solicitors, what are the facts which are made the subject of charge and interrogatory. I think it must be taken as admitted, that Messrs. Dawson & Co. were the solicitors of the defendants, and as between the plaintiff and the defendants, the question of privilege which was suggested in argument, does not necessarily arise (4). I should also guard myself against being understood to

---

(1) 54 R. R. 227 (Cr. & Ph. 104).   (4) See 36 R. R. 261 (1 My. & K.
(2) 54 R. R. 411 (11 Sim. 401).   101).
(3) 17 R. R. 7 (3 Mer. 44).

express any opinion that a defendant is bound, in all cases, to seek
information which is equally accessible to both parties, and which
is not either in his own possession or knowledge, or that of his
agents, or of persons within his control, or for whose acts, with
reference to the matter in question, he is answerable. Take for
[*104] example the case put in argument: I do *not think that the
plaintiff, calling on the defendant to state whether a person did
or not die on a certain day, as a general rule, has any right, in
order to procure that information, to require him to examine the
parish register. But how does the case stand, regard being had to
the simple fact, that Messrs. Dawson & Co. were the defendants'
agents?   Suppose the extreme case of the vendor of an estate
selling it through his agent,—the whole matter being transacted
between the purchaser and the vendor's agent,—and suppose the
agent, by gross misrepresentations, to induce the purchaser to give
for the estate a price ten times the value. If the purchaser, in
such a case, filed a bill to have the transaction set aside on the
ground of fraud, it could not be sufficient for the vendor, by his
answer, to say, that he did not know whether his agent made
such false representations or not. The sufficiency of the answer
would be at once tried, by inquiring whether, if the defendant had
put in an answer, saying that he had been informed by his agents,
and believed it to be true, that such misrepresentations were made,
that would or would not be material. In the case of a mere witness,
the statement might not bind the defendant; but that which an agent
said, in the case I have supposed, would bind his principal; and
for that reason, the admission, that the plaintiff was informed, and
believed the agent did make the misrepresentation, would be material.
It is impossible the Court can, in this case, say that the letters or
communications which passed between the plaintiff and the agents
of the defendants may not, if admitted, be sufficient to entitle the
plaintiff to a decree.

The defendants are bound to give some information by their
answer, or to say that they have made the attempt to procure it,
but have failed. It is not sufficient for one party, acting by his
[*105] agent simply, to tell the *other party that he does not know what
his agent did. I proceed on the ground, that the acts of the agent
would bind the principal; and the answer as to those acts may,
therefore, be material evidence for the plaintiff. I think the point
is not new, although I am not aware of any reported case upon the
subject.

It was said, that the plaintiff might himself make the inquiries of the solicitors, and might call them as witnesses.   The answer to that argument is, that the plaintiff is, in this Court, entitled to an answer from the defendant, not only in respect of facts which he cannot otherwise prove; but also as to facts, the admission of which, will relieve him from the necessity of adducing proof from other sources.

Exceptions to the Master's report overruled.

MORLEY v. COOK.

(2 Hare, 106—115; S. C. 12 L. J. Ch. 136.)

1842.
Dec. 17, 19,
23.

WIGRAM,
V.-C.

[106]

A condition of sale provided that in case the purchaser should raise objections to the title which the vendor should not be able or willing to remove, the vendor might rescind the contract, on notice and repayment of the deposit to the purchaser; and objections not delivered within fourteen days after delivery of the abstract to be treated as waived, in which respect time was to be essential.   The purchaser returned the abstract with queries within the fourteen days, and the vendor answered the queries; the purchaser on the same day objected to the answers: the correspondence on the subject of the title continued for several weeks, and then the vendor gave notice that he rescinded the contract: Held,

That the continuance of the treaty for the completion of the title, after the first objection of the purchaser, was a waiver of the condition as to the rescinding of the contract.

That such a condition of sale ought to be discouraged; and ought not to receive a construction oppressive on the purchaser.

That the vendor's right to rescind the contract under the condition must be co-extensive with the purchaser's right to object to the title under the same condition.

That the vendor was only bound *bonâ fide* to deliver an abstract of such title as he had at the time of delivering it; and so long as the condition remained in force, was not bound to deliver any supplemental abstract of title afterwards acquired.

THE sale of certain property, and amongst the rest of a leasehold estate, was announced to take place by auction, on the 14th of January, 1841, according to stated conditions, the sixth of which was as follows: That the vendor of the freehold will deliver to the purchaser an abstract of his own conveyance; but all other abstracts, or the inspection of any other deeds or documents, or other evidence of title whatever, that may be required, are to be prepared and obtained at the purchaser's expense.   That each vendor of the leaseholds will deliver to the purchasers an abstract of the lease under which such vendor holds the premises, and such purchasers shall not require the production of

MORLEY
v.
COOK.

the lessor's title, nor the production of any deeds or documents in any of such leases, or intermediate assignments recited or referred to, nor require any indemnity against any rents or covenants to which the premises may, with others, be subject or liable to; and the production of the last receipt for rent shall be conclusive evidence that the covenants contained in the leases have been fulfilled.

[*107] All attested, official, or other copies or extracts *from deeds, wills, or other documents, and all deeds of covenant for the production of title-deeds or documents as respects all the lots, are to be prepared at the purchaser's expense. In any case where the title-deeds relate to other property, the vendor will retain the same, and, if required, covenant for their production. And in case any of the purchasers shall raise objections not herein provided for, and which the vendors shall not be able or willing to remove, the vendors shall be at liberty to rescind the contracts, by writing under their hands, on repaying to such purchaser or purchasers his or her deposit, without interest, costs, or further compensation, and all objections not made in writing and delivered to the vendors' solicitors within fourteen days after the delivery of the abstract shall be treated as waived; in this respect time shall be deemed the essence of the contract.

On the 25th of January, the vendor delivered an abstract, which was returned with queries on the 6th of February. The abstract was re-delivered, with answers to the questions on or before the 17th of February, and on the 17th of February the purchaser objected to the answers as insufficient. A correspondence on the subject then took place between the parties, and continued until the 25th of March, when the vendor giving some further explanation respecting the title, in a letter to the solicitor of the purchaser, added—"If your client is unwilling to complete the purchase with the above answers, I must avail myself of the power contained in the 6th condition of the above particulars of sale, to rescind the contract, and I do hereby rescind the contract."

[*108] On the 21st of May, 1841, the purchaser filed his bill *against the vendor for a specific performance of the contract of sale (1). On the hearing,

(1) The bill charged the vendor with fraud in not stating, in his abstract, deeds which he had and which would have removed objections. It was not argued, that this frame of the record precluded relief on the simple ground of contract (as in *Whitworth* v. *Gougain*, 54 R. R. 315 (1 Cr. & Ph. 333)). The vendor said he had made out the best title in his power. This was immaterial to the principal point of construction on which the case is reported.

Mr. Teed, and *Mr. Bilton*, for the plaintiff, argued that the vendor having continued the treaty beyond the time specified, and thereby led the purchasers into further expense, in anticipation that the contract would be fulfilled, could not afterwards avail himself of the sixth condition, and retire from the contract: *Tanner* v. *Smith* (1); *Page* v. *Adam* (2); *Cutts* v. *Thody* (3); *Hobson* v. *Bell* (4).

Mr. Sharpe, and *Mr. Glasse*, for the defendant, insisted upon the plain and distinct terms of the sixth condition, enabling the vendor to rescind the contract: *Williams* v. *Edwards* (5); *Bennett* v. *Fowler* (6); *Sainsbury* v. *Jones* (7). The point did not call for decision in *Tanner* v. *Smith*.

THE VICE-CHANCELLOR:

The plaintiff has in this case insisted, that according to the judgment of the VICE-CHANCELLOR OF ENGLAND, in *Tanner* v. *Smith*, upon a condition very similar to the present, the vendor must at once elect between one of two courses, when objections to the title are taken: *first, waive his right to insist upon the condition enabling him to rescind the contract; or, secondly, put an end to the contract, and thereby relieve the purchaser, as well as himself, from the pendency of it. On behalf of the vendor it was argued, that the question of the effect of the condition did not, in fact, judicially arise in the case of *Tanner* v. *Smith*; the bill in that case having been brought by the vendor, who could not have insisted, by his own bill, upon exercising his right to rescind under the condition. My own impression (having been counsel in the appeal motion) is, that the question did distinctly arise, and that it was decided by the VICE-CHANCELLOR in the way which the plaintiff has contended. The argument for the purchaser in that case was, that, under the condition in question, the vendor had a right to· rescind the contract at any time before the decree, and that it would be unjust that a vendor retaining such a right should keep the deposit. The VICE-CHANCELLOR held, that the vendor was not in a position to rescind the contract. He said the condition was waived by the vendor, and he granted the injunction to restrain the action for the recovery of the deposit, thereby deciding against

[*109]

(1) 51 R. R. 277 (10 Sim. 410).   (5) 29 R. R. 61 (2 Sim. 83).
(2) 55 R. R. 70 (4 Beav. 269).   (6) 50 R. R. 184 (2 Beav. 302).
(3) 1 Coll. 212.   (7) 48 R. R. 217 (5 My. & Cr. 1).
(4) 50 R. R. 90 (2 Beav. 17).

MORLEY
v.
COOK.

[*110]

that construction of the condition for which the vendor now contends (1). It was with reference to that argument that Lord COTTENHAM *said, "This case shows the inconvenience of hearing the merits of a cause upon motion;" and he said, that whether the vendor did or did not retain the right to rescind the contract, (not having rescinded it upon the first objection), he had reserved to himself the right to contend that he was in a position to rescind the contract to the latest moment; and that it would be unjust to allow a vendor in such circumstances to keep the purchaser's money in his pocket. Lord COTTENHAM's judgment, however, neither overruled nor disapproved of the VICE-CHANCELLOR's opinion of the construction and effect of the condition.

The case of *Page* v. *Adam* (2) at the Rolls, which was cited for the plaintiff, may, perhaps, raise a question whether Lord LANGDALE agrees with the VICE-CHANCELLOR in the construction of the condition as expressed in *Tanner* v. *Smith*. The VICE-CHANCELLOR held, that a treaty and correspondence between the vendor and purchaser, after the first objection taken, with a view to complete the title, was a waiver of the condition. It was not meant in *Page* v. *Adam*, to decide that the vendor could take the benefit of the condition after he had waived it; and the case rather points to the conclusion, that Lord LANGDALE did not consider the treaty and correspondence as necessarily a waiver; and his observations about

[*111]

the good faith of the proceeding on the part of the vendor, *point

---

(1) During the argument of *Tanner* v. *Smith*, 15th January, 1840, the VICE-CHANCELLOR OF ENGLAND having expressed an opinion to the effect which is reported (10 Sim. 411), that when objections are delivered, the vendor, under the 7th condition, had then the opportunity of deciding whether he was able and willing to remove them, the following observations passed:

Mr. Jacob:

The vendor may deliver a supplemental abstract, which may fail still to make out his title.

THE VICE-CHANCELLOR:

It seems to me a condition which is capable of being exercised at one time only. When objections are delivered and the vendor says—" I am able and

willing to remove them," he cannot afterwards rescind the contract.

Mr. Jacob:

If he at that time thinks himself able, and proves not to be able, may he not afterwards exercise the option?

THE VICE-CHANCELLOR:

My opinion is, that the 7th condition applies to the mode in which the vendor chooses to deal with the objections. If he says that he is able and willing to remove them, he is excluded at any time afterwards, whether upon the same objections or future objections, from availing himself of that condition to rescind the contract on the ground that he is not able or willing. Repr. MS.

(2) 55 R. R. 70 (4 Beav. 269).

the same way. In that case, an abstract was delivered and returned in due time with observations and queries. Answers to the queries were returned. Upon these answers, observations were made; and it was with reference to these last observations that the vendor's solicitors claimed a right to rescind the contract : that case would rather impeach than confirm the authority of *Tanner* v. *Smith*.

If, however, I am to follow *Tanner* v. *Smith*, I can only do so by rejecting the second part of the plaintiff's argument in which (for some purpose of this suit) he imputed fraud to the vendor in the suppression of part of his abstract. It was said that the vendor was bound to furnish the purchaser with a perfect abstract of his title; and that the vendor was not bound to deliver his objections until such perfect abstract was delivered, *Hobson* v. *Bell* (1) ; that in this case a perfect abstract had not been delivered ; and, therefore, that the time for delivering objections had not yet expired.

If by the expression "perfect abstract," is meant the most perfect abstract in the vendor's possession (actual or constructive) at the time of his delivering it, I should probably accede to the plaintiff's argument; for, undoubtedly, a court of equity would not permit a vendor, who had a good title, and the means of showing such title on his abstract, fraudulently to deliver an imperfect abstract to which objections would necessarily be taken; and, upon these objections being taken, avail himself of his own fraud to avoid his contract, under the condition. In any other sense of the words "perfect abstract," I should have difficulty in following the argument. A perfect abstract in the strict sense of the term would *show a good title; but the conditions clearly mean to provide for the case of an abstract not showing a good title.

[*112]

It is clear, however, that it was not in any qualified sense of the term that the expression "perfect abstract" was used in the argument. The argument was, that the vendor had been guilty of a fraud (depriving him of the benefit of the condition in question), because he had withheld from the purchaser a policy of assurance and a conveyance of the equity of redemption of the purchased premises, both of which were, *ex concessis*, obtained by him in the month of March, 1841. Now, it appears to me impossible to hold that the vendor was under an obligation to deliver these documents, if the argument derived from *Tanner* v. *Smith* be right. The vendor cannot be bound to do more than, *bonâ fide*, deliver such abstract of title as he has at the time of delivering it, if (as the

(1) 50 R. R. 90 (2 Beav. 17).

purchaser contended) the effect of doing more towards the completion of the title, in answer to the purchaser's requisition, is to have
the effect of a waiver of any condition of sale.

It was attempted to reconcile the argument I have adverted to,
with *Tanner* v. *Smith*, by saying, that the days within which the
purchaser was bound to take his objection, must be computed from
the time when a perfect abstract was delivered; and that, if the
vendor made any addition to the abstract first delivered, a new
period of fourteen days would run in the purchaser's favour, from
the time of delivering such addition. That the purchaser must be
at liberty, after addition to the abstract, to take new objections to
the title, (at least to the extent of objections arising upon or out of
the additional matter), cannot be disputed. But if I am to understand the purchaser as admitting that every answer, *(not being
merely argumentative) which the vendor gives to the purchaser's
requisition, and to that length the argument went, is to be considered as an addition to the original abstract, giving the purchaser
under the condition of sale a new period of fourteen days, within
which to take objections to the abstract originally delivered, I
cannot but think that *Tanner* v. *Smith* is given up altogether by
the argument; for, if the conditions are held to apply to that new
state of circumstances, so as to give or rather limit the purchaser
to the fourteen days, prescribed by the conditions for taking objections to the title, it appears to me irresistibly to follow, that the
vendor must have a new right to rescind the contract, upon the
new objections being taken. So long as the purchaser's right to
object to the title upon the footing only of the conditions of sale is
claimed,—so long the right of the vendor to rescind the contract
under the same conditions in answer to the objections must remain.
Those who rely upon *Tanner* v. *Smith*, must, for the purposes of
their argument, contend, that the vendor in this case had delivered
his abstract ; or, at least, that whatever the rights of the purchaser
might be, the vendor was estopped from saying he had not delivered
an abstract,—that by treating for the completion of the title, after
objections taken, he had waived his right to rescind under the
condition, and that all parties were consequently remitted to the
ordinary rules of a court of equity, in reference to questions of
title, unfettered by the particular conditions of sale.

I shall, therefore, pass by the imputed fraud, and return to the
consideration of the actual position of the parties in this case.

Upon many of the possible cases alluded to, I need not express a

[*113]

decided opinion. I agree that a vendor, *in a case like the present,
is bound to deliver the best abstract that he can; and a court of
equity would not do a very violent act in holding, that a vendor
who, under conditions of this kind, having a perfect abstract,
fraudulently delivered one which was imperfect, had, by such
fraudulent breach of the conditions on his part, forfeited the benefit
of the conditions in his favour.

No question however can arise upon that point, because it is
not suggested that the vendor, at the time he delivered his abstract,
was in the possession of any better or other abstract than that
which he delivered. Nor is it necessary I should say in what
manner the Court would deal with a case in which a vendor acting
bonâ fide should deliver a second abstract (properly so-called) after
objections taken to a first abstract. For the purposes of the present
case, I assume that the abstract delivered by the vendor was his
abstract of title, or, at least, that he is not in a condition to say
that it was not. The case is then reduced to the same point which
arose in *Tanner* v. *Smith;* namely, an abstract delivered,—objections taken to it by the purchaser,—answers (not merely argumentative) to the purchaser's requisitions, furnished by the vendor,—
and a correspondence and treaty between the vendor and purchaser
continued down to the 25th March, upon the footing of the vendor
proceeding to complete his title. The question is, whether such
correspondence and treaty, after the first objections were delivered,
is or is not a waiver of the 6th condition, which involves the preliminary question, whether the 6th condition is not confined to the
objections first taken after the abstract is delivered. I cannot say
that the language of the 6th condition imperatively decides the
question. Nor can it, on the other hand, be denied that the language
of the 6th condition *is consistent with the construction put upon
it in *Tanner* v. *Smith*, or that such construction reaches the reasonable and probable intention of the parties. Nor am I prepared to
say, that the interests of a purchaser might not in many cases be
best consulted by a different interpretation of the condition; nor
that a skilful practitioner may not in all cases by the addition of
a few words in his answer to objections to title, such, for, instance,
as "without prejudice," obviate the effect of the rule laid down in
Tanner v. *Smith*. But I am bound to come to that conclusion
which, with reference to the majority of cases, appears most
consonant to justice. Proceeding upon that principle, I have no
hesitation in saying that I think conditions of sale like those before

MORLEY
v.
COOK.

me (the meaning of which no purchaser knows until *ex post facto* decisions of a court of justice informs him of it) ought to be discouraged, and that I am but offering such discouragement by putting a strict construction upon them in favour of a purchaser, and by holding that they are not to have a construction which might subject purchasers to a great expense and inconvenience at the mere will of a vendor; that the 6th condition in this case ought to have that construction which the VICE-CHANCELLOR put upon a similar condition in *Tanner* v. *Smith;* that a treaty between the vendor and purchaser for the completion of the title by the former, after the purchaser's objections have been taken to the abstract, ought to be deemed a waiver of that condition; and that in equity, as at law, the condition once waived is gone for ever.

I have reason to know that the VICE-CHANCELLOR remains of the opinion correctly attributed to him in *Tanner* v. *Smith,* and that he intended to re-assert the same opinion in the late case of *Cutts* v. *Thody.*

1842.
Nov. 8, 9, 10.
Dec. 3, 10, 19.

WIGRAM,
V.-C.
[120]

PINKETT *v.* WRIGHT.

(2 Hare, 120—140.)

[AFFIRMED on appeal to the House of Lords under the title of *Murray* v. *Pinkett,* as reported in 12 Cl. & Fin. 764, for which see a later volume of the Revised Reports.]

1842.
Dec. 16, 17.

WIGRAM,
V.-C.
[144]

CALDECOTT *v.* BROWN(1).

(2 Hare, 144—146; S. C. 7 Jur. 693.)

A tenant for life cannot lay out monies in building or improvements on the estate, and charge them on the inheritance; and, therefore, the Court will not direct an inquiry what sums were expended by the tenant for life, in substantial improvements, beneficial to the inheritance.

B. BROGDEN devised and bequeathed his real and personal estate upon trust to permit his wife Sarah to receive and take the clear rents, issues, and profits of all and singular his said real and personal estate for her life, for her own sole use and benefit; and after the decease of his wife, the testator directed the said real and personal estate to be sold, and the proceeds of such sale to be divided amongst his children.

The testator died in 1799. Sarah, the widow, who was one of

(1) See the note to *Hibbert* v. *Cooke,* 24 R. R. 225.—O. A. S.

the devisees, and an executrix, proved the will, and entered into CALDECOTT
v.
BROWN. possession of her life estate. The widow died in 1840. The bill was filed in 1841, for the administration of the estate of the testator, by the parties entitled in remainder, against the representatives of the widow, his executrix.

The representatives of the widow, by their answer, alleged that the personal estate had been exhausted by the charges upon it, and that the widow had expended out of her own monies, during the continuance of her life estate, the sum of 2,000l., and upwards, in substantial and lasting improvements of the said hereditaments and premises and the inheritance thereof, and they claimed to be allowed the same in taking the account of the estate of the testator, as monies expended by the tenant for life and executrix. The defendants, by evidence in the cause, proved that 2,000l. and upwards had been expended by the executrix in building on the property. At the hearing of the cause—

Mr. Blunt, for the defendants, asked for a reference *to inquire [*145] whether any and what sums had been laid out by the tenant for life in permanent improvements of the premises, beneficial to the inheritance, or such other inquiry to that effect, as would bring before the Court the advantage which the plaintiffs, the parties entitled in remainder, derived from the expenditure made by the tenant for life: *Hibbert* v. *Cooke* (1) ; *Graves* v. *Graves*.(2).

Mr. Follett, for the plaintiffs, opposed the application for the reference.

THE VICE-CHANCELLOR:

I am of opinion that I ought not to make the order for the reference which the defendants seek in this case. I was referred to the case of *Hibbert* v. *Cooke* as an authority for the inquiry; but in that case Sir JOHN LEACH refused to direct an inquiry of the expenses incurred by the tenant for life in repairs to the mansion-house, which had been rendered necessary owing to the dry rot, although the inquiry was not opposed. If the mansion-house was affected by the dry rot, it would certainly be a substantial improvement to remove it; but the Court in *Hibbert* v. *Cooke* said, that it was an expense to which a tenant for life, choosing to occupy the

(1) 24 R. R. 225 (1 Sim. & St. 552).   (2) M. R., March, 1822, cited 24
                                                R. R. 226 (1 Sim. & St. 553).

CALDECOTT
v.
BROWN.

property, must submit. I do not know how to consider that case otherwise than as overruling *Graves* v. *Graves*.

I do not mean to lay it down as an imperative rule, that no case could arise in which the Court would sanction the expenditure of monies by a tenant for life for the benefit of the inheritance, by making such expenditure *a charge upon the inheritance. The case may be suggested, of a devise of lands in strict settlement, and a direction to lay out personal estate to the same uses: it might be more beneficial to the remainder-men that a part of the trust fund should be applied to prevent buildings on the settled estate from going to destruction, than that the whole should be laid out in the purchase of other lands. Other like cases might perhaps be supposed.

[*146]

In *Bostock* v. *Blakeney* (1), Mr. Justice BULLER, sitting for the Lord Chancellor, directed, at the hearing of the cause, an inquiry what substantial and lasting improvements had been made by the tenant for life of the estate; but the decree was reheard by the LORD CHANCELLOR, and reversed on this point; and in the case of *Nairn* v. *Marjoribanks* (2), the Court was asked to direct a reference whether it would be for the benefit of the parties interested in the property, that a new roof to the mansion-house should be constructed at the expense of the testator's estate; but Lord ELDON refused to make any order upon the petition, observing, that he would not confirm the report, even if the Master should find that it would be beneficial to all the parties.

I do not think that the alleged fact of the insufficiency of the personal estate of the testator in this case affects the question.

1843.
Jan. 11.

WIGRAM,
V.-C.

[147]

SHUTTLEWORTH v. SHUTTLEWORTH.

(2 Hare, 147.)

Testamentary guardian of an infant trustee, who was residing out of the jurisdiction, appointed guardian *ad litem*, without either the appearance of the infant in Court, or a commission.

MR. ROMILLY moved, that the testamentary guardian of an infant defendant, who was the heir of the last survivor of several trustees, and had no beneficial interest in the subject of the suit,

(1) 2 Br. C. C. 656.   (2) 3 Russ. 582.

might be appointed his guardian, *ad litem*, without the appearance of the infant in Court, and without a commission.

The VICE-CHANCELLOR, upon affidavits of the facts above stated, made the order.

COLMAN v. NORTHCOTE.

(2 Hare, 147—148; S. C. 12 L. J. Ch. 255; 7 Jur. 528.)

The answer of a married woman, who is an infant, cannot be taken either separately or jointly with her husband, until she has had a guardian assigned.

1843.
Jan. 31.
March 2.
___
WIGRAM,
V.-C.
[147]

THE clerk of records and writs refused to file the joint answer of Augustus Northcote, and Emma his wife, the wife being an infant, and yet having no guardian.

Mr. Randell moved that the answer might be taken without a guardian.

[148]

The VICE-CHANCELLOR said that the practice had been, to require the appointment of a guardian to an infant defendant, notwithstanding she was a married woman: the VICE-CHANCELLOR OF ENGLAND had followed that practice in cases before him.

Motion refused.

NEESOM v. CLARKSON.

(2 Hare, 163—176; S. C. 12 L. J. Ch. 99; 6 Jur. 1055; rehearing, 4 Hare, 97—106; S. C. 9 Jur. 82.)

A. contracted to purchase real estate, and died, having made his widow his universal devisee and legatee. The widow married B., who, in 1793, took a conveyance of the premises contracted to be purchased by A., to himself and a trustee, reciting the contract by A., his will and death, and the marriage of his widow with B.; and that "thereupon B. became entitled to the beneficial interest in the purchase." B., in 1817, sold the premises to C., and C. took a conveyance from B. and his trustee, reciting, that, by certain good and sufficient assurances in the law, the premises stood limited to B. and the trustee, but not reciting the deed of 1793. The widow died, leaving her heir-at-law an infant, who came of age in 1825, in the lifetime of B. The bill was brought by the heir-at-law in 1836, after the death of B., for a conveyance of the estate.

Held, that the recital in the deed must be understood as stating that the widow was devisee of the purchased premises, and that the title of B. accrued by the marriage; that the Court would not presume, in favour of a purchaser, that B. had any other title than was so represented; that C. must be presumed to have been cognizant of, and to have taken the title of B. his vendor; that the equitable title of the heir-at-law of the widow was

1842.
Nov. 12, 14.
Dec. 10.
___
WIGRAM,
V.-C.
On rehearing.
1844.
Nov. 15, 18,
20.
Dec. 19.
1845.
Jan. 18.
___
WIGRAM,
V.-C.
[163]

not affected by the lapse of time; and that the heir-at-law was entitled to the decree for a conveyance of the estate, and to an account of the rents and profits as against C. on the footing of wilful default (1).

That the Court would not direct the account to be taken with annual rests where no special case for that form of decree had been made on the pleadings.

JOHN COWLING, in 1792, purchased, at a sale by auction, certain freehold premises at Leeds, known as the "Angel Inn," for the sum of 1,500*l.*, but before any conveyance of the estate was executed, or the purchase-money paid, Cowling died, having by his will, made in January, 1793, devised all his real estate to Ann, his widow, and made her his residuary legatee and executrix. Ann the widow proved the will. In July, 1793, Ann the widow married William Sykes.

By indentures of lease and release, dated the 24th and 25th of September, 1793, the latter made between Wade Brown (the vendor of the premises), devisee in trust thereof, appointed by the will of Alice Bywater, deceased, of the first part; the said William Sykes and Ann his wife (who was the widow and relict of the said John Cowling, deceased), of the second part; and L. Nicholson, of the third part; reciting the will of Alice Bywater, and reciting that the said Wade Brown, in pursuance of the trust in him reposed by the said will, caused the tenements and hereditaments thereinafter mentioned, (being all the residue of the real estate of the said Alice Bywater), to be advertised in the public newspapers for [*164] *sale by auction on the 3rd day of October, 1792, on which day a meeting was held; and the said John Cowling, being the highest bidder at such sale, became the purchaser of the said tenements and hereditaments, at or for the price or sum of 1,500*l.*, being the best price that could be had or gotten for the same; and reciting, that the said John Cowling had since departed this life, having first made and duly executed his last will and testament, and thereof appointed the said Ann Sykes, his then wife, universal devisee and legatee, and sole executrix; and reciting, that the said William Sykes had, since the death of the said John Cowling, intermarried with the said Ann his widow, and thereupon become entitled to the beneficial interest in the said purchase, and had agreed to complete the same, but not being provided with the whole of the purchase-money, the said Wade Brown had agreed to let the

(1) In *Parkinson* v. *Hanbury* (1867) L. R. 2 H. L. 18, Lord WESTBURY describes this case "as a very strong stretch of the authority of the Court." The exact form of the decree in this case was very fully considered on a re-hearing by the Vice-Chancellor, as reported in 4 Hare, p. 97; see *post*, p. 61.—O. A. S.

sum of 1,100l. part thereof remain in the hands of the said William
Sykes, upon security of the said tenements and hereditaments,
in manner hereinafter mentioned and expressed, — the said
premises called the "Angel Inn" were conveyed and assured to
L. Nicholson, and his heirs, as to a term of 1,000 years, to the
use of the said Wade Brown, for securing payment of the said
1,100l. and interest thereon; and as to the remainder, to the
use of the said William Sykes and L. Nicholson, and their
heirs, in trust, nevertheless, as to the estate of the said L.
Nicholson, and his heirs, for the said William Sykes, his heirs
and assigns.

By an indenture of demise and mortgage of the 5th of September,
1800, made between the said William Sykes of the first part;
Nicholson of the second part; and Wade Brown of the third
part, William Sykes and Nicholson demised the premises to Wade
Brown, his executors, &c., for the term of 1,000 years, subject to a
*proviso for redemption of the said premises on payment of 500l.,   [*165]
with interest as therein mentioned.

In pursuance of a contract for the sale of the premises by William
Sykes to Benjamin Clarkson, an indenture, dated the 30th of
September, 1817, was made between the said William Sykes of the
first part; L. Nicholson of the second part; Wade Brown of the
third part; Benjamin Clarkson of the fourth part, and T. Hampshire
(a trustee for Clarkson) of the fifth part; reciting that, under and
by virtue of certain good and sufficient conveyances and assurances
in the law, the said premises then stood limited and assured to the
use of the said William Sykes and L. Nicholson, and their heirs,
nevertheless as to the estate and interest of the said L. Nicholson
and his heirs therein, in trust for the said William Sykes, his heirs
and assigns for ever, subject only to the mortgage next thereinafter
mentioned; and reciting the said demise by way of mortgage of the
5th September, 1800, that the estate of the said Wade Brown thereunder had become absolute at law, and that the sum of 150l. only
remained due on the said mortgage; and reciting that Benjamin
Clarkson had, sometime previously, contracted and agreed with
William Sykes for the absolute purchase of an estate of inheritance
in fee simple, in possession, free from all incumbrances of and in
the said premises, at or for the price or sum of 2,700l., out of which
it had been agreed that the said sum of 150l., so due and owing to
the said Wade Brown, should in the first place be paid; and reciting
that the said William Sykes had applied to, and prevailed upon,

NEESOM
r.
CLARKSON.

[*166]

the said L. Nicholson and Wade Brown to join in conveying and assuring the said hereditaments to the said Benjamin Clarkson and his heirs, to the uses and in manner thereinafter mentioned ; and the said premises and the said term therein, were thereby conveyed and assigned to Benjamin Clarkson and his heirs in fee. Clarkson *afterwards died, having devised the premises to the defendants.

Ann Sykes (formerly the widow of Cowling) died on the 9th of September, 1821, leaving the plaintiff, her daughter by a former husband, her heiress-at-law, then an infant. The plaintiff attained twenty-one years of age in August, 1825, and intermarried with Neesom, the other plaintiff, in January, 1826. William Sykes died in August, 1835.

In August, 1836, the bill was filed against the devisees of Clarkson, praying that they might be decreed to convey the premises to the plaintiff, and to account for the rents and profits, the plaintiff offering to pay what might be due to the defendants in respect of the purchase-money.

The answer stated, that Cowling, as the defendants believed, never entered into any written or binding contract for the purchase of the premises ; that at his death his property was sworn to be under the value of 40l., and that he was in fact insolvent; that Sykes entered into an independent contract for the purchase, and to complete the same borrowed 1,100l. from Wade Brown, and paid the residue out of his own monies. The answer stated the indentures of the 24th and 25th of November, 1793, and that the premises were thereby conveyed and assured in the manner above stated.

[*167]

The *answer of the defendants said they did not believe that any interest in the premises passed by the will of Cowling to Ann Sykes, or that Ann Sykes had ever any interest in them ; and they insisted that they were purchasers for valuable consideration, without notice of any such interest, and as such had been in undisturbed possession since 1817.

     Mr. Wakefield, Mr. C. P. Cooper, Mr. Kenyon Parker, and *Mr. Hodgson,* for the plaintiff :

The contract made by Cowling, for the purchase of the premises in question, being made at a sale by auction, must, at this distance of time, be presumed, without evidence of any written contract, to have been made in a manner which was binding within the Statute of Frauds. The auctioneer, for that purpose, is the agent of both parties. *Emmerson* v. *Heelis* (1) ; *White* v. *Proctor* (2) ; 1 Sugd. Vend. & Pur. p. 188, 10th ed. The effect of the contract was, therefore, to vest in Cowling the equitable interest in the premises. His widow took the same interest as his devisee. Supposing that the widow had then died intestate,—the plaintiff would have taken the premises as heiress-at-law, either subject to the payment of the purchase-money in the nature of a mortgage, or with the right of having the purchase-money raised and paid out of the personal estate. The equitable interest, however, remained vested in the widow at the time of her marriage with Sykes. Nothing has since taken *place to divest the widow and her heirs of that interest: it could not pass without fine, the widow having died in the lifetime of Sykes. The defendants are bound by the recitals in the deed of 1793, and they do not in fact, by their answer, suggest that they derive their title in any other manner : Gilbert on Evidence, p. 86 ; *Fort* v. *Clarke* (3). There was no reason for making Nicholson a party to the deed of 1817, except in respect of his interest as a trustee for Sykes, and that interest he acquired only by means of the previous conveyance to Sykes ; the circumstance shows that Clarkson derived his title under the conveyance of 1793, and from the erroneous conclusion of law upon which that conveyance was founded ; and it also affects him with notice of that failure in the title.

> *Mr. Sharpe, Mr. Koe, Mr. Coote*, and *Mr. Elmsley*, for the defendants :

The presumption will be in favour of *bonâ fide* purchasers, whose title had been undisturbed for twenty years ; and, therefore, in the absence of evidence that Clarkson had actually any knowledge of the deed of 1793, before the completion of his purchase, or that he claimed or derived title under that deed, the Court would not presume, against him, that he must necessarily have done so. If the defendants are to be bound by the recital, it must be by the whole of that recital. The plaintiffs are not at liberty to take one part and reject the other ; and if the whole recital is taken, then the title of the defendants appears : *Earl of Mountague* v. *Lord Preston* (4). The purchasers from Sykes cannot, after his death, explain the recital ; but several interpretations *may be suggested,

NEESOM
v.
CLARKSON

[*168]

[*169]

(1) 11 R. R. 520 (2 Taunt. 38).   (4) 18 Vin. Ab. p. 163, tit. Recital,
(2) 13 R. R. 580 (4 Taunt. 209).   pl. 9 ; *S. C.* Vent. 140.
(3) 1 Russ. 601.

NEESOM
v.
CLARKSON.

not inimical to the validity of the title of Sykes. Brown, the
vendor, might have cancelled the first contract (the estate of Cowling
being insolvent), and might have made a new contract with Sykes;
1 Sugden, Ven. & Pur. 306, ed. 10th; *Whittaker* v. *Whittaker* (1);
or the widow might have assigned the benefit of the contract to
Sykes by a letter to Brown, or any other form of memorandum;
or it might have been conditionally assigned, in the event of the
marriage taking place; or, at the utmost, the recital that "thereupon" (*i.e.* the marriage) Sykes became entitled, is only a mistake
in fact: it is not to be read as "thereby." At least, when the
recital may be consistent with the truth, the contrary will not be
assumed: *Tenny* v. *Jones* (2); *Lewis* v. *Davison* (3). The length of
time during which the plaintiff, with a knowledge of her alleged
rights, has acquiesced in the possession of the defendants, deprives
her of any right to the assistance of a court of equity: *Stockley* v.
Stockley (4); stat. 3 & 4 Will. IV. c. 27, s. 27.

THE VICE-CHANCELLOR:

The argument which has been addressed to me in this case,
requires that I should observe on three points. First, excluding
the time that has elapsed, I am to consider how the case would
stand if the bill had been filed against Sykes in his lifetime?
Secondly,—still excluding the question of time, what is the position
of the defendants, supposing them to claim under Sykes? Thirdly,
how far the time that has elapsed ought to affect the question?

[170]   Now, if this were the case of a bill filed against Sykes in his lifetime, I should have, as against Sykes, to determine simply the
construction of the recitals contained in the purchase-deed of 1793.
I put this point without going into any question of the right of the
plaintiff to relief, if the general case of the defendant is sustained.
It has not been argued before me, that if the property did in point
of fact belong to the wife, and the conveyance was taken during the
coverture, that Sykes could, in that case, as against his wife, claim
to be entitled to the property. The argument has been wholly
directed to show, that I ought not, in the circumstances of this case,
to presume such was the state of the title; at least, that I ought
not to presume it against the parties who are the defendants upon
this record.

(1) 4 Br. C. C. 30.   (3) 4 M. & W. 654.
(2) 10 Bing. 75; *S. C.* 3 Moo. & S.   (4) 12 R. R. 184 (1 V. & B. 23).
472.

(His Honour stated the purchase-deed of 1793 (1).)

Now, unless I am to disregard the plain and obvious meaning of language, it would be impossible, in a case in which Sykes was living, and the defendant in the cause, that I could put any other interpretation upon these recitals than this: that the property was advertised for sale; that on a day fixed for the sale, Cowling attended and became the highest bidder at such sale (which clearly imports a sale by auction, if that were material, which I think it is not); and that Cowling, who is so stated to have become the purchaser, made his will, and devised the property to Ann, his widow, afterwards Ann Sykes. It is obvious that the meaning of this is, that Ann Sykes, as devisee of Cowling, had become the owner of the property; and when the deed states, that, upon the marriage of Sykes with the devisee of Cowling, Sykes *became entitled to the property, it appears to me, that I should be spelling out a meaning against the plain and obvious sense of the language, if I did not understand the deed to state, that in consequence, and by the effect of, the marriage, Sykes became entitled to the property. In point of fact, the only substantial question that can be asked with respect to this recital is, whether Sykes does not intend to represent that he was about to take a conveyance from Wade Brown in execution of the contract for the sale of the property to Cowling? I am clear, upon reading these recitals, that it is impossible to put any other construction upon the contract as against Sykes; and that is the construction which I must put upon the deed, unless I can find any reason in the altered situation of the parties, or otherwise, to regard it differently. If, therefore, I were trying the question against Sykes, I should construe the deed as stating, that by the effect of the marriage of Sykes with the devisee of Cowling, he had become entitled to call for a conveyance to himself of the property which Cowling had contracted to purchase.

[*171]

The property having been conveyed to Sykes, I have next to advert to the question as against the Clarksons. In 1817, Sykes conveyed the property to Clarkson.

(His Honour stated the deed of the 30th of September, 1817 (2).)

The material recital here is, that, " by certain conveyances in the law, the property had been granted and conveyed to the use of William Sykes, and Lucas Nicholson, and their heirs; nevertheless, as to the estate and interest of Lucas Nicholson and his heirs, in

---

(1) *Ante*, p. 52.   (2) *Ante*, p. 53.

NEBSOM
v.
CLARKSON.

[*172]

trust for William Sykes, his heirs and assigns for ever." It appears, therefore, that this property, the identity of which *with the property comprised in the deed of 1793 is not in dispute, was, in 1817, conveyed by Sykes to Clarkson as the purchaser.

Another deed, the deed of 1793, having come out of the possession of the defendants who claim under Cowling, is then put in evidence. This deed conveys the identical property to Sykes. The property which the defendants had purchased, is the property comprised in the deed of 1793; which, by that deed, was conveyed to Sykes. Sykes, in the deed of 1793, recites the title I have mentioned; and as these parties claim under Sykes, it is impossible, unless Sykes had a different title to the property from that acquired by the deed of 1793, that the recitals of the deed of 1793 should not be evidence (I will not say conclusive) against Clarkson the purchaser. On the plainest principles of law, the recitals contained in that purchase deed of 1793 must be evidence against all parties to whom Sykes may have conveyed the property he has thus purchased; and he does, in 1817, convey the property to Clarkson. I do not say that that conveyance is necessarily conclusive. I am very far from saying it is so; and if this case were one in which the plaintiffs had stated the general case against the defendants, and upon coming into Court for the first time, had surprised them by the production of this deed, the bare possibility, that there might have been some intermediate or collateral title, might have entitled the parties to an inquiry, with the view of showing what the title of Sykes really was. All I am stating now against the defendants is this, that *primâ facie* I must presume the title that Sykes conveyed in 1817, was the same title which he took in 1793; I must presume it, unless some reason can be given to me for showing why I ought not to act on that presumption. But the

[*173]

defendants have had the opportunity of bringing forward, *if they were able, a case to show that such presumption is not well founded, and knowing what their own title is they have not done so. I do not look into the answer for the purpose of giving the plaintiff the benefit of any evidence to support and make out his case; I take the plaintiff's case to be made out by the presumption I have already adverted to, and I refer to the answer for the purpose of seeing whether a case is there suggested which I ought to inquire into further, before I give the plaintiff the benefit of that presumption which I think is raised in his favour by the production of the deed.

The plaintiff, however, in strictness is entitled to have his case
put higher.   The deed of 1817, although it recites generally a title in Sykes, expressly refers to the conveyance under which Sykes became entitled; and that is stated to be a conveyance by which the property was conveyed to the use of Sykes and Nicholson,—to Nicholson as a trustee for Sykes : and the mention of Nicholson in the deed of 1817 is material, because it identifies the deed thus referred to with the deed under which Sykes took the conveyance in 1793. And the rule of law I take to be perfectly clear, that wherever you find one deed referred to by another, the person who claims under the deed referred to is bound, at his peril, to ascertain the contents of that deed.   I believe the rule of this Court to be in accordance with what Sir JOHN LEACH said in the case of *Jackson* v. *Rowe* (1), that every purchaser is presumed to have investigated and known his vendor's title ; and if nothing more were proved in this case than the mere fact that the purchaser took a conveyance in 1817, and upon inspecting the title which was assumed to be conveyed to him, it appeared that it was one which in truth gave no title to the vendor, the Court would consider the *onus* thrown on the purchaser *to show why [*174] he had not inquired into that title with a view to his protection. It appears to me indispensably necessary that such should be the law of this Court, for otherwise a purchaser might take a title, shutting his eyes to a defect in it, and then, on the ground of the absence of actual knowledge, require this Court to pronounce a judgment in his favour against the right of the party justly entitled to the estate, when nothing but wilful blindness or culpable negligence could have prevented him from knowing the real state of the title.

In this case, however hard it may be on the parties who may have innocently paid their money for the estate, it is impossible, looking at the case upon the answer, which does not suggest any other title in Sykes than that which appears upon the deed coming out of the possession of the defendants,—it is impossible, if I am to affect them with notice of what their professional adviser knew, or must be presumed to have known, that I can suppose the real state of the title to have been unknown to them.

I must therefore, as against Sykes, have construed the deed in the way I have mentioned ; and I must presume the defendants to have had notice of the actual state of Sykes' title, and to have

(1) 25 R. R. 250 (2 Sim. & St. 475).

NEESOM
r.
CLARKSON.

purchased under that title. I must deal with the case, as against them, as I should have dealt with it against Sykes, unless the length of time is to make any difference.

With regard to the lapse of time; there was a continuing coverture from the time of the purchase in 1793, until the death of Mrs. Sykes. The title then descended on the female plaintiff; this happened during her infancy, and it was not until August, in the year 1825, that she attained her age of twenty-one years. This is the earliest moment from which I can reckon the time.

[*175] *There was then a period of five months before her marriage, during which there was no disability. Taking, however, the whole period of ten years and a half before the bill was filed, which is the utmost time that, in fact, elapsed, it is clear that it constitutes no bar to the claim; and being no bar, it clearly is not a case in which this Court can raise a presumption to destroy the title of the plaintiff. The question therefore comes to this, whether there has been such delay in asserting the title, that the Court should presume in favour of the defendants, that which it would not presume in favour of Sykes. The great difficulty in the defendants' way is this; that I could not in any possible view of the case raise a presumption in their favour, which would not, according to the way that I have read the deed, be contradicted by the words of the deed. If the words were equivocal, or ambiguous, or doubtful, and if a case were suggested in the answer as to the existence of any other title, I might possibly, in the circumstance of great delay, have raised a presumption in favour of the defendants; but I cannot raise a presumption in the defendants' favour against what I think is the plain and obvious meaning of the language of the recitals.

If these parties bought the estate on the supposition that they were purchasing an estate free from defect of title, they have great reason to complain of those who advised them; but I am satisfied I cannot, consistently with the rules on which courts of justice proceed, do otherwise than make a decree in the plaintiff's favour: and I must make the decree with costs, for when the claim was once asserted, the parties were bound, at their peril, to see if they had any ground for resisting it: having in their possession this deed of 1793, and having no ground for suggesting any intermediate or other title in Sykes, under which the defendants could derive a title different from that contained in the deed of 1793, it
*176] appears *to me they must have contested this only for the chance

of anything that might arise in their favour, and not because they have been advised, they could resist it successfully, if the truth of the case were disclosed.

:The decree directed an account against the defendants of the rents and profits as from the death of Ann Sykes on the 9th September, 1821, on the footing of wilful default and an unlimited account of all expenditure by William Sykes, Benjamin Clarkson, and the defendants respectively for necessary repairs and lasting improvements, with interest at 4 per cent.   On a subsequent rehearing, reported in 4 Hare, 97, both accounts were directed to commence as from the completion of the purchase by William Sykes in 1793.]

NEESOM
v.
CLARKSON.

The case came on again, upon a petition of the plaintiff's for a rehearing, as to that part of the decree which directed an account to be taken of the rents and profits received by Sykes, and those claiming under him, from the death of his wife in September, 1821, but did not confine the account of necessary repairs and lasting improvements (1), to the period subsequent to that date.

1844.
[4 Hare, 97]

Mr. Cooper, Mr. Kenyon Parker, and *Mr. Shee,* for the plaintiffs, argued, that the husband, being seised in right of his wife, during her life, was not entitled to charge the estate with monies laid out by him during that period; and, therefore, that the account, as to lasting improvements, ought to commence at the wife's death : *Bostock* v. *Blakeney* (2), *Hibbert* v. *Cooke* (3), *Caldecott* v. *Brown* (4).

[98]

Mr. Koe and *Mr. Elmsley,* for the defendants, argued, that Sykes, and those who represented him, were entitled to the protection of the Court, from the consequences of the mistake as to their rights under which they had acted ; that the Court would require the plaintiff, who came for equity, to make an equitable compensation to the defendants for the money which had been laid out, owing to the misconception as to the right,—and that would be effected by charging the estate with the monies expended in lasting

---

(1) The right of the defendants to an account of the monies expended on lasting improvements was conceded at the original hearing, without argument; and the only question raised upon the petition of rehearing was at what time that account should begin ?

(2) 2 Br. C. C. 653.
(3) 24 R. R. 225 (1 Sim. & St. 552).
(4) *Ante,* p. 48.

NEESOM
v.
CLARKSON

improvements, that there was no distinction as to this right between monies expended in the lifetime of the wife, and monies expended since her decease; the error extended throughout the whole time which elapsed from the completion of the purchase by Sykes, until the claim of the plaintiff was first set up; that the right to recover the monies so laid out by mistake was wholly independent of the account of interest on the purchase-money on the one side, and rents and profits on the other. The account of rents and profits ought to begin at the death of the wife, for, during her life, the husband was absolutely entitled to them in her right, and ought not to be treated as accountable.

[99]　　THE VICE-CHANCELLOR:

The account of lasting improvements contained in the decree in this cause was submitted to without argument, and the present petition of rehearing raises a question only as to the time at which that account is to commence. The propriety of the account itself is not questioned. Applying my present observations to this state of the proceedings,—the question is, not whether the husband was entitled to receive the rents and profits of the estate, and apply them as he pleased, during the lifetime of his wife, but whether, claiming that right, he could at the same time insist upon charging his expenditure on the estate in the shape of lasting improvements. The consequences would be extravagant. It could be neither right nor just that the husband should charge the wife's estate with expenditure on lasting improvements, when he may have every year received in surplus rents, after paying the interest on the purchase-money, a sum, perhaps, greatly exceeding what he had expended in lasting improvements. It is necessary to remember what the state of things was upon which the decree in this case was founded. The husband had always thought and acted on the supposition that he had acquired an absolute interest in the wife's estate. When the husband was receiving the rents and expending them, and laying out money in improvements, he supposed himself seised in fee of the estate; he sold, and the Clarksons purchased, the estate on that assumption, and the recital was that he was seised in fee; that was the hypothesis on which all the transactions proceeded. It is true, therefore, that no means were taken to protect the husband in respect of the sums he had paid for the benefit of the wife's inheritance; and that no declaration was made by him for the purpose of showing he intended his wife not to have the benefit of *his expenditure; but the absence of any declaration of that nature, cannot, under these circumstances, be referred to an intention on his part that the wife's estate should have that benefit, for the husband clearly acted on the belief that the estate was his own. It turned out that the wife's estate had never been displaced. The question then arose, whether the husband, having paid off the vendor's lien, under a mistaken supposition as to the interest he acquired by doing so, the purchase-money so paid was or was not to be deemed a charge upon the estate? and whether, that being the way in which the case would stand if Sykes, or the parties representing his estate, had been the defendants, the case was different as against the Clarksons?

The Clarksons have purchased the estate of Sykes,—what have the Clarksons paid? They have paid Sykes for all the improvements which he made on the estate, both in the lifetime of his wife and after her death; and the Clarksons say, they have themselves also expended money under the same mistake respecting the property, of which improvements the plaintiff has the benefit. I decided, rightly or wrongly is not now the question, that, where all this had taken place under a mistake, the husband might be considered in the same situation as if the purchase-money had been paid by a stranger, who had thereby acquired a lien on the estate. This appeared to me to be in accordance with what I found decided in *Pitt* v. *Pitt*(1). The ground that I went upon certainly was, that the mistake was one against the consequences of which the Court ought to relieve the husband, and those who claimed under him, to the extent to which a stranger paying off the vendor's lien would have been entitled to charge the *estate. I thought they were entitled to this relief in a suit in which the heir of the wife was the plaintiff, on the ground, that the plaintiff who would have equity must do equity. That, as I have often had occasion to say, is a rule of unquestionable justice, but which decides nothing in itself; for you must first inquire what are the equities which the defendant must do, and what the plaintiff ought to have. It may be, that the doctrine of retainer cannot strictly be applied, except in cases where the party claiming the right of retainer is a defendant, or is in some form the party charged in the suit; but, unless that state of things in any respect qualifies the rule, I think it may be generally said, that, unless the equity which the defendant claims from the plaintiff is one which the defendant

(1) 24 R. R. 15 (T. & Russ. 435, 180).

might enforce by bill, it is not a term which the Court has a right to impose on the plaintiff. The Court is bound to look into the position of the parties, and see what their relative rights are, and, having ascertained them, it tells the plaintiff that it will not give him what he seeks unless he submits to give to the defendant what the defendant might in equity have asked, but has not asked, at least by any distinct suit, from the plaintiff. In his character of defendant, the only relief he can have is the dismissal of the bill; but the Court obviates that difficulty of form, by giving the plaintiff what he is entitled to, only on the condition that he submits to give the defendant what the defendant might equitably require. That is my view of the rule, and is what I acted upon in this case.

[*102]   I had then to consider what were the equities between *the parties. Supposing Sykes never to have sold the estate, and himself, or his heir or devisee, to have been in possession, I was of opinion, as I have said, that he would be entitled to be reimbursed his expenditure owing to the mistake; and, being of that opinion, it appeared to me, that this relief would be properly worked out by treating Sykes as having been in the situation of a mortgagee in respect of the vendor's lien, and making the same decree as would be made either for or against a mortgagee in possession.

Having come to that conclusion, I think I suggested, at the hearing of the cause, that the better course would be, to begin the account from the death of the wife. The decree, however, has been so drawn up, that, according to its literal form, the account of the rents and profits on the one side, and the interest on the other, is given from the death of the wife; but the account to be taken of lasting improvements is general, and not confined to that date. The question then is, how the case is to be now dealt with—the only point in dispute being when the account is to commence.

If the husband, or those who here represent him, should contend, that during the wife's life he was in possession, not as mortgagee, but as seised in fee of the wife's estate, one of the consequences of that position is, that he cannot charge on the estate his expenditure in lasting improvements. If, on the other hand, the husband succeeds in establishing that, during his wife's life, he is to be considered as mortgagee in possession, that will give him a right, as the record and proceedings stand, to charge the wife's estate with the expenditure on such improvements; but then he necessarily

abandons his claim of a seisin in fee, in right *of his wife : he
claims a possession by a title paramount to his wife,—that of a
mortgagee ; and then, if he is entitled as mortgagee, while on the
one hand he may charge his lasting improvements, on the other he
would be charged with the rents and profits. If, therefore, the
account is carried back to the time of the purchase for one purpose,
it must be carried back to the same time for the other ; or if it
begins from the death of the wife, in respect of the rents and
profits and interest, it must begin at the same time as to lasting
improvements.   The decree is erroneous if its construction be, that
it directs the account of the rents and profits to begin at one time,
and the account of the lasting improvements at another, unless
there is some special reason for doing so, which in this case there
is not.   I am certain that was not intended.   But, although I
ought to make the decree uniform and consistent, it would be
proper to give the other party the opportunity of insisting that the
decree should be amended, not by bringing down the account of
lasting improvements, but by carrying back the account of rents
and profits to the time of the purchase.   I certainly cannot follow
the argument which has been addressed to me on the part of the
plaintiff.   Why may I not carry back the account during the life
of the wife, as well as take it up after her death?   Every argument
that the party has no lien, and no right of retainer, would apply to
one form of decree as much as to the other.   If, therefore, the
decree is right in carrying the account back to the death of the
wife,—if the situation in which the parties are placed, owing to this
mistake, entitles the defendants to be repaid an expenditure, the
benefit of which the plaintiff gets, it must be equally right to carry
the account back during the life of the wife, if that be the proper
mode of taking such an account.   The decree, as I have before
observed, was taken, as to this part, *without any judgment having
been pronounced upon it, and the present proceeding does not
impeach it.

NEESOM
v.
CLARKSON.
[*103]

[*104]

The VICE-CHANCELLOR said, the petitioners were entitled to have
the decree altered ; there was a manifest inconsistency as it stood.
Upon a petition of rehearing by the plaintiffs, the whole case was
open to the defendants,—not, perhaps, that they could ask for any
variation of the decree, without a petition for that purpose, but that
they were at liberty to go into the whole case, for the purpose of
showing that the relief sought by the petitioners was not proper to

Nov. 20.

be granted. The alteration proposed by the petitioners would, however, make the decree more, rather than less, erroneous. It appeared to him, that in strictness, upon the principle the decree went upon, the right way was to carry back the account to the time of the purchase, and, therefore, that he could not grant the petition of rehearing. The petitioners might, however, amend their petition of rehearing, praying in the alternative, either that both accounts might be restricted to the later, or both carried back to the earlier period.

Dec. 19.

The petition was amended, and the decree ordered the whole account to be taken from the time Sykes completed the purchase and entered into possession. The case was then mentioned, at the motion of the plaintiff, upon the question of annual rests. * * *

1845.
Jan. 18.

[*105]

The VICE-CHANCELLOR said, that, if the account was to be taken against the defendants as mortgagees in *possession, that account must be taken in the common form, unless a special case was made. The case of *Donovan* v. *Fricker* (1) was very different from the present case. There the Court assumed, that the parties had made a case of the rents and profits exceeding the amount of the interest and other charges,—a circumstance which was wholly wanting in this case. There was no suggestion to that effect ; and, unless it was to be said, that wherever a mortgagor filed a bill for redemption, he was entitled to rests as of course, without giving the Court any special case, or any fact to found its judgment upon, he could not but direct the account to be taken in the usual way. There was no case for making a special decree as to rests, nor was there any case for keeping the question open, in order that the parties might thereafter have the opportunity of bringing that case forward. There was no more ground laid for one than for the other. The only facts were, that an account of rents and profits on the one side, and interest on the other, was to be taken, and allowances were to be made for lasting improvements. All he could do was to make the usual decree, as in a mortgagee's suit. If, as the counsel for the plaintiff had contended, the practice of the Court enabled a party to come, upon petition, although no further directions were reserved, to obtain a special order on the subject of rests, when the state of the account was known,—if that were the practice of the Court, and the result of the account warranted it, the plaintiff would have that opportunity.

(1) Jac. 165.

The accounts of the purchase-money and interest thereon, and of necessary repairs and lasting improvements, and of interest thereon, and of rents and profits and occupation rents in the said decree mentioned, to be taken from the 25th of September, 1793, instead of the 9th of September, 1821 ; and, in addition to the accounts directed by the said decree let the Master take an account of the rents and profits of the said estate received by W. Sykes, deceased, or by any *person or persons by his order, or for his use, or which, without his or their wilful default, might have been so received. And, in case it shall appear that the said William Sykes has been in possession of the said estate, or any part thereof, during any time or times since the 25th of September, 1793, let the Master fix an occupation rent or rents on such part or parts, during the time of such occupation, and take an account thereof, and include the same in the said account of rents and profits.

NEESOM
v.
CLARKSON.

[106]

CHRISTIAN *v.* FIELD (1).

(2 Hare, 177—185 ; S. C. 11 L. J. Ch. 97 ; 5 Jur. 1130.)

1842.
Nov. 24, 25.
Dec. 3.

WIGRAM,
V.-C.

[2 Hare, 177]

The solicitor of the executrix and devisee, paying a sum of money in exoneration of an adverse claim on part of the testator's estate, does not, as against creditors of the testator, necessarily and by force of the transaction alone, acquire a lien upon the estate, or on the title-deeds, for the sum which he so paid.

The solicitor of the executrix having paid a sum which was due to a third party, who had a lien on title-deeds belonging to the testator's estate for the amount, gave a receipt for the deeds in the name of the executrix, and, as her solicitor, carried into the Master's office her examination, in which the sum he had so paid was stated to have been paid by the executrix, and was allowed accordingly : Held, that the solicitor must, in the circumstances, be presumed to have made the payment on the behalf and on the personal security of his client; and that he could not claim a lien upon the deeds for the amount.

THE plaintiff instituted a creditors' suit—*Christian* v. *Chambers* —against the executrix and devisees of the debtor, and a decree was made for the sale of the real estate of the testator for the payment of his debts. The defendant Field had been the solicitor of the testator, and was the solicitor of the executrix in the cause ; and he claimed a lien on the title-deeds of the real estate of the testator, which were in his possession : these deeds or muniments were of three classes, and liable, as was alleged, to three several

(1) *In re Hawkes* [1898] 2 Ch. 1, 15, 67 L. J. Ch. 284, 78 L. T. 336, C. A.

CHRISTIAN
v.
FIELD.

claims. First, copies of Court rolls, deposited with the defendant,
by the testator, as a security for costs, of which no bill had then
been delivered, but in respect of which the defendant alleged, by
his answer, that 74l. was at that time due. Secondly, certain deeds
which were, at the death of the testator, in the hands of a certifi-
cated conveyancer, whose claim, amounting to 8l. 8s., the defendant
Field had paid, and to whom a receipt for the deeds had been given
in the name of the executrix, Field affixing his name as a witness.
And, thirdly, certain other deeds relating to property, an adverse
claim to which had been set up, after the testator's death, by
strangers,—and had been compromised for a small sum of money,
5l. of which was paid by the defendant Field, who prepared the
release executed on that occasion.

[*178]

The present bill was filed (as supplemental to the *suit of
Christian v. *Chambers*) against Field and the defendants in the
original suit ; alleging that the sale directed by the Court could not
proceed, owing to the detention of the title-deeds by the defendant,
and praying that Field might be decreed to deliver up the deeds,
or, if it should appear that he had any lien thereon, to deliver
them up upon payment of what might be found due to him in
respect of such lien.

The defendant, by his answer, claimed a lien on the several
grounds above stated upon the different classes of instruments.

It appeared that the solicitors of the plaintiff had repeatedly
applied for an account of the defendant's demand, but had been
unable to obtain a statement from him either of the deeds which he
held or the amount of his claim : that an attempt had been made
to examine him upon interrogatories before the Master, but that
the defendant had objected to such examination, and his objection
had been allowed. The defendant, however, had offered to prepare
and deliver an abstract of the property comprised in the deeds in
his possession at the plaintiff's expense. It also appeared that the
executrix, in her discharge sworn in taking the account before the
Master, and carried in by the defendant Field, as her solicitor in
the suit (*Christian* v. *Chambers*), had taken credit for the sums
in respect of which the two latter claims of lien were made, as
having been actually paid by her, as executrix, on account
of the estate; and such payments were allowed to her in that
account.

Mr. Sharpe and *Mr. Francis Bayley,* for the plaintiff. * * *

Mr. Walker and *Mr. E. Montagu*, for the defendant:

   * * The suit of *Christian* v. *Chambers* is *res inter alios acta:* the defendant in this cause is neither bound by any thing which was done in that suit, nor is it evidence against him. * * *

If this form of suit can be sustained, the defendant must be protected by being allowed the same benefit of lien as he would have had if the executrix herself was plaintiff; all the right which she could confer, the defendant has acquired. * * As to the second class of documents, the defendant discharged an unquestionable lien, and he is entitled to stand in the place of the party thus paid off: *Glaholm* v. *Rowntree* (1). The defendant, as a mortgagee, was not bound to disclose his securities before payment: *Browne* v. *Lockhart* (2). The application for the particulars of claim were not accompanied by any offer to pay what was due to the defendants; and there *i⁸ no ground, if any decree is made, for dealing with the case as to costs otherwise than as a common bill for redemption.

Mr. Kenyon Parker and *Mr. Stinton*, for the other defendants.

Mr. Sharpe, in reply. * * *

THE VICE-CHANCELLOR:

The plaintiff, having instituted a suit on behalf of himself and all the other creditors of the testator, in which he obtained a decree for the sale of the real estate, has filed this bill, in order to carry out the sale so directed, by recovering the title-deeds in the possession of the present defendant, treating it as supplemental to the former suit. The first objection which has been urged on behalf of the defendant is, that it neither appears upon the bill, nor is admitted or proved in this cause,—called the supplemental cause,—that the plaintiff is either a creditor or otherwise interested in the estate of the testator; and it is said that the defendant Field not being a party to the other suit, in which the debt of the plaintiff is established, that suit, as regards Field, is *res inter alios acta*, and the decree inoperative against the defendant. The rule of law, that *res inter alios acta non nocet*, no doubt applies to protect *the rights of a party from being prejudiced by a decision in another cause, in which he has had no opportunity of defending them; but it has no application to a case of this kind, where the proceeding, the effect of which is objected to, was properly constituted to determine the

(1) 45 R. R. 599 (6 Ad. & El. 710,   (2) 51 R. R. 284 (10 Sim. 421).
716).

[*181]

[*182]

question then in contest, and where that question was determined
between the only parties competent to contest it, namely, the
creditors and the executrix. The result of that suit, by establishing
claims upon the estate, may, if the estate is insufficient, affect the
interest of the other creditors; but this effect must always attend a
judgment recovered against a debtor, whose property is insufficient
for the payment of his debts. And it would be not more unreasonable for the other creditors of a person in such circumstances to
object to the operation of a judgment against their debtor, as being
res inter alios acta, than it is for the defendant to make the same
objection in this case. The first suit has not, however, even the
consequential effect I have adverted to upon the interests of the
defendant in this suit; for the question now is, what are the rights
of the defendant as mortgagee of property belonging to the estate
of the testator, and it is unimportant to him whether he has to
litigate that question with the executrix, as executrix, or with any
established creditor or claimant on the estate. The defendant may
justly contend, that he is not liable, in respect of the documents in
question, to the suit of any person who is not interested in the
estate of the testator; but, if a party has established his interest in
the documents against those who represent that estate, it cannot be
denied that he is entitled to enforce or give effect to the title or
interest he has so established against any party in possession of the
documents. Take, for example, the case of one who has obtained
[*183]   a decree for the specific performance of a contract for *the purchase
of an estate, and afterwards finds the title-deeds of the estate in the
possession of a third party claiming a lien upon them: in such
a case the interest which the purchaser has acquired under the
decree would be a sufficient foundation upon which to demand, and,
if necessary, to sue for the recovery of the deeds, although the suit
for specific performance, as against the holder of the deeds, might
be *res inter alios acta*: his lien or claim might not be affected; but
the purchaser would be entitled, as against him, to enforce all such
rights as the vendor could give, and had in fact given him.

The plaintiff, in this case, has obtained a decree, in a suit against
all proper parties, for the sale of the estate; and that decree is not
impeached. He has thereby acquired a sufficient interest enabling
him to sustain a suit, for the purpose of giving effect to and
obtaining the benefit of the decree, and that is all which he now
·contends for. The question, then, is, what is the extent of the lien
to which the defendant Field is entitled?

The deposit of the copies of the Court rolls has been proved by CHRISTIAN
the defendant to have been made to secure the payment of his costs, FIELD.
and he is, therefore, entitled to hold them as a security for the
costs due at the time of the deposit.

(His Honour stated the circumstances under which the claims of
lien were made by the defendant Field on the second and third
classes of deeds (1).)

It has been insisted, with regard to the second of these claims,
that, inasmuch as the conveyancer, in *whose possession the deeds [*184]
were, had a lien upon them as against the estate of the testator, the
same lien was, on the payment by Field, transferred to him. This
is by no means a necessary consequence of that payment; and
there are several reasons which prevent it having that effect in this
case. In the first place, the deeds are delivered up to the executrix,
and not to Field; and then the executrix, in her examination on
oath, in which Field acts as her solicitor, states the payment to
have been made by her, and the amount is allowed in her accounts
accordingly. It would be impossible to treat the defendant Field
as a creditor of the estate for the same sum, without taking some
steps to relieve the estate from the former payment. But the
presumption rather is, that the first charge by the executrix is
accurately made : nothing is more common than for a solicitor to
advance money on the personal security of his client in cases of this
nature. I am of opinion, that I ought to treat it as the payment
of the executrix by the hand of Field, her solicitor; and that the
solicitor has, therefore, no lien on the estate of the testator for
that sum.

The third claim of the sum paid by Field in respect of the compromise of an adverse claim to part of the property of the testator,
is even more clearly untenable than that which was last adverted
to. The adverse claimants had no lien on the property, nor could
Field acquire any such lien by the payment of the whole or any
part of the price for which their claims were extinguished.

The only question which remains is that of the costs of this suit.
The plaintiff, by his bill, wholly denies the claim of the defendant
to a lien upon any document for any purpose whatever, and this
justified the defendant in carrying the suit to a hearing; for, to
some extent, he *had a lien. I think, therefore, the plaintiffs are [*185]
not entitled to costs against Field. On the other hand, the claim
of the defendant goes much beyond what he was entitled to. Nor

(1) *Supra*, p. 68.

can I overlook the fact, that part of his claim is in direct contradiction to a case which, under his conduct as solicitor, Mrs. Chambers made and verified by her oath. I also repeat,—what I have before stated and acted upon,—that, in deciding upon questions of costs, not depending exclusively upon regularity of practice in the strict sense of the word, I shall always consider myself bound to see whether the parties, by reasonable care, might not have avoided the necessity for litigation.

(His Honour, adverting to the evidence of applications by the solicitors of the plaintiff for the amount of the lien claimed before the institution of the suit, said that no satisfactory reason had been given by the defendant for disregarding these applications. No costs of the suit should be given to Field. The decree to be, that Field should deliver up the deeds on payment of the other costs (exclusive of the sums disallowed), without prejudice to any right of the plaintiff and the other defendants to retain their costs of the suit out of the estate, or receive them in the other suit.)

———

GOLDSMID v. GOLDSMID.

(2 Hare, 187—199 ; S. C. 12 L. J. Ch. 113; 7 Jur. 11.)

Property subject to a special power of appointment may, with the concurrence of one of the objects of the power, be appointed and settled upon trusts for the benefit of persons some of whom are not objects of the special power.

THE Act 1 Geo. IV. c. 42, intituled, "An Act to authorize a composition for the debt remaining due to his Majesty from the late Abraham Goldsmid, merchant, and his surviving partners," recited that, at the death of Abraham Goldsmid, a sum of 466,700l. was due to his Majesty from the co-partnership, and recited also a deed of inspectorship confirmed by a former Act (52 Geo. III. c. 75), whereby Thomas Bainbridge, Alexander Baring, William Joseph Denison, and George Ward, nominated by the Lords of the Treasury to superintend, direct, and controul the administration of the property of the several concerns therein mentioned, were appointed inspectors accordingly ; and it confirmed an arrangement to discharge the estates of the parties on payment of a dividend of 17s. 6d. in the pound. The Act then proceeded as follows: "And be it further enacted, that so much of the property of the said Aaron Goldsmid and Thomas Moxon, and of the estate and effects of the said Abraham Goldsmid which shall be so acquitted and discharged as aforesaid, as, in case such acquittance and discharge had not been made, would have been applicable to the payment in full of the said debt of 466,700*l.* and the said other debts, under the arrangement so acceded to on the part of the Crown, as hereinbefore is mentioned, shall immediately after such certificate as aforesaid shall have been signed by the said Commissioners of the Treasury, or any three of them, be paid, disbursed, divided, or settled to, amongst, upon, or in trust for, or for the *benefit of the said Aaron Goldsmid and Thomas Moxon, or their respective descendants, and the widow and descendants of the said Abraham Goldsmid, or any one or more of the aforesaid several persons, exclusively of the other or others of the said Aaron Goldsmid, and Thomas Moxon, or their respective descendants, and the widow and descendants of the said Abraham Goldsmid, and the same shall be an interest or interests vested in and paid and payable to them or any of them, on or at such age, day or time, or respective ages, days or times, and be divided between and among them in such shares, and charged and chargeable with the payment of such annual or other sum or sums of money to them or any of them, and shall be upon such conditions, under such restrictions, and subject to such powers, declarations and agreements, and generally in such manner for the benefit of the persons hereinbefore mentioned or any of them, as they the said T. Bainbridge, A. Baring, W. J. Denison, and G. Ward, or the survivors or survivor of them, or the executors or administrators of such survivor, shall think reasonable, and shall by any deed or deeds, or instrument or instruments in writing, with or without power of revocation or new appointment, direct or appoint; and for that purpose be and be considered, deemed and taken as one fund, without any regard to the separate or conflicting interests, if any such conflicting interests there be, of the parties interested in the same, inasmuch as the concessions made by the said creditors, and hereby authorized to be made by the Crown, are to prevent any of them the said Thomas Moxon, Aaron Goldsmid, and Nathan Solomons, and the representatives of the said Abraham Goldsmid, or the legatees under the same, or any other person or persons claiming or deriving any right, title, or interest under the same (so far as respects the trust fund, subject to the provision of the said indenture of the 27th of November, 1810), *from having any claim or demand on the others or other of them, for any excess which they respectively may have paid beyond their due proportion of the debts of the said

[*188]

[*189]

co-partnerships, or either of them, or the greater proportion of their respective property brought into the fund, subject to the provisions of the said indenture of the 27th of November, 1810, or the greater amount of the debts or demands to which they respectively were subject or liable."

A deed-poll dated the 24th of April, 1821, was executed by T. Bainbridge, A. Baring, W. J. Denison, and G. Ward, whereby, reciting their said powers, they disposed of seven-twentieths and three-twentieths of the fund which, under the arrangement and the Act, had been released from the claims of the creditors, and they then directed, appointed, and declared, as follows : " And the other or remaining ten equal twentieth shares or moiety thereof shall belong and be paid, transferred, and assigned unto the said Ann Goldsmid, Daniel Eliason, and Isaac Lyon Goldsmid, their executors, administrators, and assigns, upon and for the trusts, intents, and purposes, and with, under, and subject to the powers, provisoes, agreements, and declarations intended to be declared and contained concerning the same, for the benefit of the said Ann Goldsmid, the widow, and Moses Goldsmid, Esther Goldsmid, Mary Levein, and Elias Goldsmid, children of the said Abraham Gold-smid, and their issue, by and in an indenture already prepared and engrossed, and intended to bear date the day next after the date of these presents, and to be made between the said T. Bainbridge, A. Baring, W. J. Denison, and G. Ward, of the first part, Thomas Moxon of the second part, the said Ann Goldsmid of the third part, and the said Ann Goldsmid, Daniel Eliason, and Isaac Lyon Goldsmid of the fourth part, and moreover that the said indenture,
[*190] so *already prepared and engrossed, shall be forthwith executed by the several parties thereto accordingly."

By an indenture of the 25th of April, 1821, being the deed referred to, and executed by all the parties, as expressed in the preceding deed-poll, reciting an agreement that the property should be dis-posed of as thereinafter mentioned, it was expressed that, in pursuance of, and in obedience to the said deed-poll, and in con-sideration of the premises,—it was thereby agreed and declared between and by the parties thereto, that they the said Ann Gold-smid, Daniel Eliason, and Isaac Lyon Goldsmid, and their executors, administrators, and assigns, should, subject to the power of revocation reserved by the said deed-poll, stand and be possessed of, and interested in, all and singular the ten equal twentieth shares or moiety by the said deed-poll appointed unto

them, of and in the remaining funds or property thereby distributed, upon trust from time to time to lay out and invest the
said trust monies, and, during the life of the said Ann Goldsmid,
pay the interest, dividends, and annual produce of the same unto
or permit the same to be received by the said Ann Goldsmid and
her assigns, for her and their own benefit; and that from and
immediately after the decease of the said Ann Goldsmid, the said
trust monies and the interest, dividends, and annual produce
thereof should be divided into four equal shares, and one of such
shares allotted to each of them the said Moses Goldsmid, Esther
Goldsmid, Mary Levein, and Elias Goldsmid, and the shares so
respectively allotted to each such son or daughter of the said
Abraham Goldsmid, to respectively remain and be upon and for
such trusts, intents, and purposes, and with, under, and subject to
such powers, provisoes, and declarations in favour or for the benefit
of the son or daughter to whom such share should be allotted, and
his respective wife and child or children, *or her respective child   [*191]
or children (as the case may be), with such provisions for his or
her or their respective maintenance and education, and at such
time or respective times and in such shares and manner, and with
such limitations over in favour of all or any other of such sons or
daughters to whom such shares are so respectively allotted, and
their, his, or her respective issue, as the said Ann Goldsmid by
her last will and testament in writing, or any codicil or codicils
executed as therein mentioned, should direct or appoint; and in
default of such direction or appointment, and so far as such direction or appointment, if incomplete, should not extend, then the said
share so respectively allotted to each such son or daughter as aforesaid should respectively remain and be in trust for him or her
respectively, and his or her respective executors, administrators,
and assigns, for his or her absolute benefit.

Ann Goldsmid by her will dated in December, 1825, expressed to
be in exercise of her power under the said deed-poll and indenture,
appointed the fund amongst the four sons and daughters of Abraham
Goldsmid, who were to be the objects of it; and with regard to one
share she directed that the trustees or trustee thereof should from
time to time apply and dispose of all or any part or parts of the
same unto or for the benefit of Moses Goldsmid in such manner as
they or he the said trustees or trustee should in their or his uncontrolled discretion think fit; and subject thereto should, during the
life of the said Moses Goldsmid, pay the annual produce of the

GOLDSMID
v.
GOLDSMID.

same, or of so much thereof as should remain unapplied and undisposed of under the trusts aforesaid, unto the said Moses Goldsmid for his own benefit, until he should assign, charge, or otherwise dispose of the same or any part thereof by way of anticipation, or agree so to do, or should do some act whereby the same or any part thereof, *if payable to himself, would become vested in some other person or persons, but in case the said Moses Goldsmid should assign, charge, or otherwise dispose of the same or any part thereof by way of anticipation, or agree so to do, or should do some act whereby the same or any part thereof would, if payable to himself, become vested in some other person or persons, then should thenceforth during the life of the said Moses Goldsmid apply the same annual produce in such manner as the said trustees or trustee should, in their or his uncontrolled discretion, think fit, for the benefit of all or any more exclusively of the other or others of them the said Moses Goldsmid and the person or persons who, under the trusts and provisions thereinafter declared and contained, would, for the time being, be entitled to the same annual produce in case the said Moses Goldsmid were then actually dead, and should, after the decease of the said Moses Goldsmid, pay the said annual produce unto the widow (if any) of the said Moses Goldsmid, during her life if she should so long continue a widow; and after the decease of such widow in trust for the children or child of the said Moses Goldsmid in manner therein mentioned.

[*192]

Ann Goldsmid afterwards died. The bill was filed by Moses Goldsmid against the other objects of the power, and the trustees of the fund, charging that the power of the trustees under the Act had not been well executed, and praying a declaration that he was absolutely entitled to one fourth share of the fund.

Mr. Tinney, and *Mr. Calvert*, on the argument that the effect of the instruments was an unlawful delegation of a trust, cited [*Combe's* case (1) ; *Alexander* v. *Alexander* (2) ; *Ingram* v. *Ingram* (3) ; *Phipson* v. *Turner* (4) ; *Bray* v. *Bree* (5), and other authorities] .

[193]

Mr. Sharpe, and *Mr. Goldsmid*, for the defendants Esther and Elias. contended that the power of the trustees was absolute : they might have appointed the whole fund to Ann, or given her a general

(1) 9 Co. Rep. 75.
(2) 2 Ves. Sen. 640.
(3) 2 Atk. 88.
(4) 47 R. R. 229 (9 Sim. 227).
(5) 37 R. R. 172 (2 Cl. & Fin. 453).

power of appointment over it; they had, in fact, appointed it to her, and by the same instrument she concurred in limiting her own power, and took it in a restricted form. None of the authorities were opposed to the validity of such an exercise of a power. [They cited *Routledge* v. *Dorril* (1) ; *Wade* v. *Paget* (2) ; *West* v. *Berney* (3) ; *Crompe* v. *Barrow* (4), and other authorities.]

THE VICE-CHANCELLOR :

With a view to the opinion I am about to express, it *will be [*194] sufficient to observe that, by the Act 1 Geo. IV., a trust or confidence is reposed in the four gentlemen who are there named for the payment, division, or settlement of a fund derived from the estate of Mr. Abraham Goldsmid and his partners, and that the person for whose benefit they are to exercise that trust or confidence are to be Aaron Goldsmid, Thomas Moxon, or their descendants, and the widow and descendants of Abraham Goldsmid, or one or more of them, exclusive of the others. That is a power to be exercised for the benefit of certain objects, not including, in terms, the wives of any of the persons who are named as the objects of the power : the wives are not the objects of this power, unless they are so under the direction to settle for the benefit of the individuals named.

The fund having been ascertained, the gentlemen in whom this power is vested, on the 24th of April, 1821, executed a deed-poll. (His Honour stated the material parts of the deed-poll (5).)

The question in this cause arises with respect to the ten-twentieths, the trusts of which were to be declared by a deed dated the day after the date of the deed I have just mentioned. On the 25th of April, 1821, the indenture referred to was executed by all the parties, including Ann Goldsmid, and thereby, after reciting the agreement that the property should be settled and disposed of in the way therein mentioned, the indenture witnessed—(His Honour stated the substance of the indenture, and of Ann Goldsmid's will (6).)

It is upon this exercise of the power expressed to be given to [*195] Mrs. Goldsmid, whereby she appoints a share *of the fund in favour of the plaintiff Moses Goldsmid, in the qualified way which the bill specifies, and gives also an interest therein to his widow, that the question in this cause turns. Moses Goldsmid by his bill

(1) 2 R. R. 250 (2 Ves. Jr. 357).
(2) 1 Br. C. C. 364.
(3) 32 R. R. 237 (1 Russ. & My. 431). *
(4) 4 R. R. 318 (4 Ves. 681).
(5) *Ante*, p. 74.
(6) *Ante*, pp. 74, 75.

insists that the declaration of trust and the will of Ann Goldsmid have made a disposition of the fund which the Act does not authorize ; and he founds his claim in this suit on the ground that the declaration of trust and the will are inoperative on the subject with which they profess to deal.   The argument for the plaintiff was—that the trustees had, in effect, assumed a power to delegate to others the execution of the trust reposed in themselves,—that a person in whom a trust or confidence was reposed could not so delegate it to others,—and that the declaration was therefore void.   It was objected further that the deed authorized the creation of estates for the benefit of the wives or widows of the descendants of Abraham Goldsmid, which were not warranted by the power ; and that the will itself carried out that illegal intention by giving an interest to the widow of Moses Goldsmid, who it was said was not an object of the power.   On behalf of the defendant it was said that a settlement upon the widow of one of the objects of the bounty would ·be a benefit to the party himself, and, therefore, that a direction to settle property for the benefit of a certain individual would, in fact, be properly executed by giving a part to his widow.   The case of *The Duke of Devonshire* v. *Lord George Cavendish* (1) was referred to on this point, and that of *Alexander* v. *Alexander* (2) might also be added.   In answer to the argument on the main question in the cause, whether there was an unlawful attempt to delegate the trust, it was said that the declaration of trust of the 25th of April, 1821,

[*196]

had a two-fold *operation,—that it operated, first, as an appointment to Ann absolutely, and, secondly, as a settlement by Ann as such appointee ; and if that proposition can be made out, then I am of opinion that the deed of trust of the 25th of April, 1821, and the execution of the power given to Ann by that deed, would constitute a perfectly valid appointment.

There is no doubt that cases of the description which the latter argument supposes have been decided, but before I expressed any opinion upon it I desired to see under what restrictions such a mode of executing a power was placed by those cases.   It is clear that where a person has a power of selection out of a number of given objects, he must have very great influence over each of those objects. Now if the donees of the power thought it right, in the exercise of the discretion confided in them, to give the whole to one object absolutely, they might have given it to Ann, and Ann, by a separate

(1) 4 T. R. 741, *n.*   See 6 R. R.   (2) 2 Ves. Sen. 640,
455, *n.*

deed, might have disposed of the property as she thought fit; but
it appeared to me impossible to deny the force of the observation
that, where the donee of the power makes the appointment in the
way which is done by this deed, to which the appointee is a party,
the case might be open to the suspicion of the exercise of undue
influence to induce the appointee to dispose of the property in
favour of persons who were, in truth, not the objects of the bounty
of the appointee, but of the donee of the power.   •

I have examined the cases on the subject, and I find that they
lay down the rule with great clearness, *and bear out the proposition that, in equity, a valid appointment may be made to persons
who are not objects of the power, with the approbation of the
persons who are the objects of the power; and the case is explained
in the manner in which it was put in argument, namely, that the
deed operates in two ways, first, as an appointment by the donee
of the power, and, secondly, as a settlement by the appointee of the
property in question; and I do not find that the suspicion which
possibly might attach to the disposition, has induced the Court to
place cases of that description under any sort of control. In the
simple case where there has been nothing more than the concurrence of the donee of the power and one of the objects of the power,
to whom an exclusive appointment might be made, or to whom an
appointment might be made co-extensive with the amount of the
property disposed of, the Court has treated the appointment as valid
and effectual. That point being expressly decided, the only question
is, whether this case is governed by the same rule.

[*197]

I think the cases to which I have adverted are quite decisive to
this extent, that if the estates created by the will of Ann had been
inserted in the deed of appointment itself, instead of being left to
be carried out by the will of Ann, those estates would have been
perfectly good, although the estates were not given to persons who
are named as objects of the power in the Act of Parliament. The
cases expressly decide it on the principle I have before mentioned;
that is, an appointment to Ann, and then a settlement by Ann of
the property she so acquired. If then the estates would have been
good, had they been actually set out and created in the deed of the
25th of April, 1821, the question is, whether any difficulty arises
from the circumstance that they are left to Ann afterwards to
appoint. Now, if the *power given by the appointment had been
a general power to Ann, there would have been that which the
Court considers as equivalent to a gift of the property; and then

[*198]

GOLDSMID
v.
GOLDSMID.

the case of *Bray* v. *Bree* (though not wanted as an authority) would have borne out the proposition that the power was well executed. But it was argued on behalf of the plaintiff, that the limitation imposed, in this case, took away that character from the appointment, and gave it the character of an unlawful delegation of power. If, however, the general gift would have had the effect attributed to it, I confess it appears to me at least open to argument whether, in the case of a limited gift of property, the trustees being expressly authorized to limit the property, it would not have been sufficient; but I think it is much safer to put this question upon the broad ground which the cases I have referred to establish, namely, that where the appointee, an object of the power, joins in the deed of appointment, and the deed shows that that which is done has been so done by agreement with that party, the Court considers that party as making a settlement of the property. If Ann, therefore, to whom unquestionably an exclusive appointment might have been made, agrees that the property shall be settled as in this case it has been, what possible difference can it make whether the property is given to Ann in the form of an interest, or whether a control over the property is given to Ann in the form of a power. The act complained of is not, according to the construction of the cases, the act of the donee of the power, but it is the separate act of Ann, which she acquired the power of exercising by means of the appointment first made by the donees of the power.

The only shadow of distinction which I can discover is, that
[*199] Ann, to whom the powers are given, is not named *as a separate party to the deed, she is named as one amongst several trustees. If Ann had been named as a separate party in the deed it appears to me the case would not have admitted of a doubt, for then it would have been simply that Ann, to whom, according to the construction I have mentioned, the estate is appointed, agreed that the property should be so settled ; and when I find Ann is one of the parties—one who assents and agrees to the arrangement, and that the appointment is actually made to Ann herself, it appears to me it would be a departure from the principles already established by the cases I have mentioned, to draw any distinction between those cases and the present. I have no doubt, therefore, that I am bound to declare that these instruments constitute a valid execution of the power.

WOODGATE *v.* FIELD.

1842.
July 4, 7.
Nov. 10, 21,
23.

WIGRAM,
V.-C.

[211]

(2 Hare, 211—217; S. C. 11 L. J. Ch. 321; 6 Jur. 871.)

In a suit by a creditor on behalf of himself and all other creditors, if the debt of the plaintiff be admitted or proved, and the executor or administrator admits assets, the plaintiff is entitled at the hearing to an immediate decree for payment, and not to a mere decree for an account.

A mistake of the law or practice of the Court is not, *per se*, a ground for allowing a party to go into further evidence, on facts at issue at the hearing of the cause, *semble.*

THE plaintiff, claiming to be a creditor of the intestate, on a promissory note, filed his bill on behalf of himself and all other creditors, against the administrator, for payment. The defendant, by his answer, admitted assets, but denied the debt, and suggested that the pretended promissory note was a forgery.

The plaintiff went into evidence, and proved the note. At the hearing,

Mr. Teed, and *Mr. Bagshawe,* for the plaintiff, asked for the immediate decree of the Court against the defendant, for payment of the debt: *Wall* v. *Bushby* (1).

Mr. Girdlestone, and *Mr. Allfrey,* for the defendant:

The decree must be for an account in the usual way. The admission of the executors does not entitle the plaintiff to a personal decree, without giving the other creditors an opportunity of contesting the claim: *Owens* v. *Dickenson* (2). [Other creditors have an interest in requiring that the suit shall be prosecuted in such a manner as will give them the benefit of it: *Sterndale* v. *Hankinson* (3).]

Mr. Teed, in reply. * * *   [212]

THE VICE-CHANCELLOR:

The suit is instituted by a simple contract creditor on behalf of himself and all other creditors, seeking the payment of a debt alleged to be secured by the promissory note of the intestate. The defendant, by his answer, says he believes the note to be a forgery, and that no debt was due to the plaintiff, but admits assets sufficient to pay the amount, and all other debts of the intestate. He suggests no ground for his belief as to *the debt [*213] and note. Evidence has been gone into on the part of the plaintiff

(1) 1 Br. C. C. 488, per Lord   (2) 54 R. R. 195 (Cr. & Ph. 48).
THURLOW.   (3) 27 R. R. 210 (1 Sim. 398).

WOODGATE
v.
FIELD.

to prove the debt, and he asks an immediate decree for payment. The defendant says it ought to be referred to the Master to take the account, not only of the estate, but of what other debts are owing from the testator.   This inquiry is said to have two objects : one, that the plaintiff's debt may be proved in the Master's office ; the other, that the rest of the creditors may have an opportunity of getting their debts paid in the suit.   In a creditors' suit, where there is no admission of assets, that is no doubt the usual form of the decree, and though the plaintiff may have proved his debt at the hearing, it may still be displaced by evidence in the Master's office ; but the question is, whether that form of decree is applicable when assets are admitted ?

The reason for, and the principle of, the usual form of decree, are stated in *Owens* v. *Dickenson* (1), but that reasoning has no application where assets are admitted, for the executor thereby makes himself liable to the payment of the debt.   In such a case, the other creditors cannot be prejudiced by a decree for payment of the plaintiff's debt ; and the object of the special form of the decree in a creditor's suit fails.

I entertained no doubt upon this point, nor can I, upon inquiry, find that it was ever doubted in the other branches of the Court. In effect, the rule is proved by the fact that the creditor and the defendant, the executor, may settle the matter pending the suit, by the latter paying the debt and costs of the suit.   And it has twice been decided at the Rolls, that the Court will order the same thing

[*214]

to be done, even when *the suit had proceeded to a considerable extent.   If then the Court would compel a creditor to accept payment of his debt when the executor offers to pay it, with the costs of suit, where is the line to be drawn, beyond which the plaintiff cannot be allowed to have the exclusive benefit of his own suit.   I am satisfied that in this case there ought to be a decree for immediate payment.

It was objected, however, that in *Sterndale* v. *Hankinson*, Sir A. HART said that, on the filing of a creditor's bill, every creditor has an inchoate right in the suit ; the meaning of that expression is, that a right then commences which may indeed fail, but may also be perfected by decree ; and it is not inaccurately called an inchoate right.   After the decree, every creditor has an interest in the suit ; but the question is, whether the plaintiff, until decree, is not *dominus litis*, so that he may deal with the suit as he pleases.

(1) 54 R. R. 195 (Cr. & Ph. 48).

There is nothing to prevent other creditors from filing bills for a like purpose; and there is nothing more common than for several suits to exist together, and the Court permits them to go on together until a decree in one of them is obtained, because it is possible, before the decree, that the litigating creditor may stop his suit.

The only question then is, whether the plaintiff has sufficiently proved his debt. The defendant admits that he saw the note before putting in his answer: he therefore knew what was upon the face of it. It purports to be signed by the intestate, and it has two attesting witnesses. They depose that it was produced to them, written as it now appears, except that the interlineation of the name of the payee was omitted: that the interlineation was inserted in their presence, and that it was then signed in their presence by the intestate: I see no ground for saying that the evidence was not sufficient. *It is quite clear that it would be sufficient at law. The defendant might have cross-examined the attesting witnesses; or, if necessary, he might have filed a cross-bill for discovery. There is no evidence that the note was a forgery, and no statement of the ground for that suggestion.   [*215]

The only point suggested at the Bar as a reason why the decree should not now be made, was, that the practice was supposed to be different, and that therefore the defendant should have an opportunity of contesting the debt by a trial at law. If, upon a special application, the defendant can show that there was in fact a slip, which will operate as a surprise upon him, and will undertake in any event to pay the costs of the trial,—rendered necessary by his own neglect,—unless the Court shall otherwise order, I will consider whether I am at liberty, at the hearing of the cause, after the case is fully proved, to entertain such an application. Such an application is not to be acceded to, except under special circumstances.

1842.
Dec. 9, 10, 12,
13, 19.
1843.
Jan. 18, 19,
24.
———
Wigram,
V.-C.
[218]

FISHER v. TAYLER.

(2 Hare, 218—238.)

A partner has no implied authority to pledge the credit of the firm for money expressly borrowed for the purpose of permanent employment as an addition to the capital already employed by the firm, unless the money is in fact required or applied for the ordinary purposes of the business as already carried on by the firm.

Two partners in a firm announced their intention of adding 16,000*l*. to their capital, by admitting one or more additional partners. W. entered into a negotiation with one of the partners, then acting on behalf of both, on the subject of the announcement, but afterwards declining to enter into the firm, advanced a sum of 4,000*l*. to that partner by way of loan, on the security of the bills of the firm, and also of the partner's separate estate : Held, that W. had, so far as this evidence went, notice that the loan of 4,000*l*. was an advance, not within the implied authority of the partner obtaining it, the other partner having authorized the capital to be raised in a different mode; but, inasmuch as the original partnership was then existing, and the advance might have been within the scope of the partnership authority, without reference to the proposed increase of capital, liberty was given to W., for the purpose of trying that question, to bring an action on the bills against the executors of the other partner.

Under the decree in a creditors' suit for an account of the estate and debts of the testator, D. F. Tayler, a claim was carried in by Simon Wilkin, of the sum of 4,000*l*. upon promissory notes in the name of a firm in which the testator was a partner. The debt arose in the following manner :

In January, 1832, a partnership was formed between Henry Shuttleworth, Joseph Wartnaby, and the testator, under the firm of D. F. Tayler & Co., for the manufacture of patent solid-headed pins, and it was agreed that Shuttleworth and Wartnaby should advance in moieties 8,000*l*., or such other sum as should be required for the patent and machinery, which was then to become the property of the partnership, in equal shares. Shuttleworth and Wartnaby were also to bring in 1,500*l*. in money, to be considered as a debt, and bear five per cent. interest. If, at any future time, it should be thought necessary to increase the capital, such addition to be advanced in equal shares; and any partner advancing, with the consent of the other, more than by the articles he was bound to do, the same to be entered in the partnership books as a debt, and carry the like interest. Wartnaby, who, according to the representation of the defendants, brought in his required share

[*219] of the capital, only by the assistance of Shuttleworth, died *in November, 1834; and, upon that representation, if the firm was then indebted to the estate of Wartnaby, the estate of Wartnaby was indebted to Shuttleworth.

In November, 1838, the surviving partners, Shuttleworth and the testator, caused the following advertisement to be inserted in the newspapers : " Partnership. In a most highly respectable and well-established wholesale mercantile concern, the very first house in its line in the kingdom, an additional capital of about 16,000l. is wanted to extend the business and pay off a deceased partner's advances. It is therefore proposed to admit one or more gentlemen, whose shares will be proportioned to the amount of their capital. Principals or their solicitors addressing to V. R., post-paid, Law Club, Chancery Lane, may have the most candid explanation, and full particulars." Wilkin answered the advertisement, and shortly afterwards received the following letter :

" 25th January, 1838.

" SIR,—Owing to the illness of the acting partner, your letter addressed to V. R. respecting the advertisement for a partnership was not opened till this morning. It is hoped that his health will be sufficiently restored by the middle of next week to enable him to give you a meeting, with a view to enter into the necessary explanation. We are instructed, therefore, to request you will attend at our office on Wednesday next, the 31st inst., at 11 o'clock, for that purpose, &c.

" We remain, &c.,

" S. WILKIN, Esq."   " BATTYE, FISHER, and SUDLOW."

Wilkin accordingly attended at the place appointed and met Shuttleworth and Mr. Sudlow, but no agreement was then made.

Mr. Sudlow stated that, to the best of his recollection, *the amount of capital Wilkin offered to advance was too small, and that the negotiation for a partnership went off, and was entirely abandoned.   [*220]

Wilkin's state of facts thus represented the circumstances : Mr. Sudlow (the solicitor of the testator, and occasionally of the firm) introduced Wilkin to Shuttleworth as one of the partners in the firm of D. F. Tayler & Co., and a conversation then took place on the subject of the advertisement, in which Shuttleworth told Wilkin that the partners in the business were the testator and himself; that the testator, who was the active and managing partner, was prevented by illness from being present at that meeting; and that a large portion of the capital required was to replace that of a deceased partner. Wilkin then informed Shuttleworth and Mr. Sudlow of the amount of capital which he would be able to bring in ; and after some further conversation, the treaty was adjourned. Wilkin afterwards employed Mr. Wood as his attorney, and being advised not to enter into a partnership, it was ultimately arranged that he should act as the accountant and superintendent of the firm, at a salary, and that his duty should be the management of their accounts, and cash account. The negotiation was continued by Shuttleworth, as such partner, on behalf of the firm, and by Mr. Wood, as the attorney of Wilkin, Shuttleworth stating, that the object for which the money was intended to be raised was to pay off the advances of a deceased partner, and for other partnership purposes. Mr. Wood advised Wilkin not to make the proposed advance to the firm, without the separate security of Shuttleworth as well as that of the firm, and Shuttleworth having acquiesced in that requisition, a memorandum, as heads of the agreement, was drawn up and signed, as follows:

[221]　　　" Bond from Henry Shuttleworth, of Market Harborough, in the county of Leicester, to Simon Wilkin, of Cossey, Norfolk, for 4,000*l.* at 5 per cent. interest, 3,000*l.* to be paid down immediately, and the remaining 1,000*l.* as soon as obtained by Mr. Wilkin, and in the meantime Mr. W. is to give Mr. S. a declaration, that, although the bond for 4,000*l.* is given, 3,000*l.* part thereof only is paid."

" Agreement between the said H. S. and S. W., that the said 4,000*l.* is lent to H. S., as the partner of D. F. Tayler and as part of the capital of the firm of D. F. Tayler & Co., of Light Pool Mills, Gloucestershire, and Nos. 9 and 10, King Street, Cheapside, patent solid-headed pin and brass wire manufacturers, and that the said S. W. is to be employed by the said firm, as assistant and superintendent, and general agent, at a salary of 200*l.* per annum, payable quarterly, together with the use and occupation of the house and furniture at No. 10 in King Street ; and if Mr. W. relinquishes the use and occupation of the house in King Street, then he is to be allowed 80*l.* per annum, towards paying the rent, &c. of another house. Mr. W. is to attend regularly to the business of the firm. Proviso that agreement and bond to be void on payment of the 4,000*l.* and interest, and after six calendar months' notice by either party. Agreement to commence on the 25th of March next.—HENRY SHUTTLEWORTH.—SIMON WILKIN."

On the 27th of February, 1838, Wilkin paid to Shuttleworth 1,600*l.*, on the 1st of March, 1838, 1,400*l.*, on the 16th of April, 1838, 500*l.*, and on the 28th of April, 1838, 500*l.*, making together

4,000*l.*, for which several sums Shuttleworth gave to Wilkin the promissory notes, in the name of the firm of D. F. Tayler & Co. Shuttleworth executed also his separate bond for 8,000*l.*, conditioned for the payment of 4,000*l.*, to Wilkin, at six *months' notice, and deposited with Wilkin, as a further security, the title-deeds of certain real estate, the property of Shuttleworth.

Of the sum lent by Wilkin, a part (about 400*l.*) was proved to have been immediately applied in the payment of a partnership debt.

Wilkin entered upon his duty under the agreement, in May, 1838. The testator, having received a complaint from Flick, a clerk, whose office Wilkin was to fill, remonstrated with Shuttleworth, by a letter of the 28th of April, on the impropriety, on his sole authority, of superseding Flick; the testator afterwards, on the occasion of visiting the counting-house in King Street, appeared to have recognised Wilkin as a person whom he expected to find there. On the 31st of July, the testator caused a notice to be served upon Wilkin, distinctly apprising him, that he (the testator) had never seen, and knew nothing of any agreement between Wilkin and Shuttleworth; that Wilkin was not to consider himself employed by the firm, and that the firm would not be answerable for any wages, or other remuneration for his services; that Shuttleworth had not authority to appoint him, and that he must look to the latter alone for his remuneration. And on the 30th of July the testator caused a notice in the name of the firm to be delivered to Flick, directing him not to make any payment to Wilkin, as he was not employed by the firm.

On the 1st of January, 1839, the partnership between the testator and Shuttleworth was dissolved, and an agreement was made by which Shuttleworth was to become the purchaser of the partnership property. Wilkin subsequently acted as the clerk of Shuttleworth. Shuttleworth became bankrupt in December, 1839. It *did not appear that Wilkin had ever demanded payment of the loan from the testator, until the 11th of January, 1840, when the testator was served with a writ at the suit of Wilkin, against both Tayler and Shuttleworth, in an action of assumpsit for 4,000*l.* and interest from the 19th of November, 1839. The testator died on the 2nd of February, 1840. Shuttleworth died in April of the same year.

The Master rejected the claim, and Wilkin excepted to the report.

Mr. Sharpe, and *Mr. Romilly,* for Wilkin, commented on the various circumstances in evidence, and submitted, as the necessary

FISHER
v.
TAYLER.

[*222]

[*223]

conclusion, that the 4,000*l.* was borrowed by Shuttleworth, on behalf
of the firm, for partnership purposes, and was actually employed in
such purposes with the knowledge of Tayler, and that the loan had
been made upon the credit of the partnership, and not upon the
credit of Shuttleworth alone. * * *

Mr. Teed, Mr. Lee, and *Mr. Heathfield,* for the executors,
[*224] *contended, that the circumstances under which the negotiation
originated, the position of the partners at that time, the material
departure from the purpose intimated in the advertisement, which
the agreement with Wilkin involved, the separate security taken
from Shuttleworth, the repudiation by the testator of any contract
with Wilkin, and the acquiescence of the latter after that repudiation,—all contributed to prove that the loan of 4,000*l.* was not
made to the partnership, but was an advance to Shuttleworth
alone. * * *

Mr. Kenyon Parker, for the plaintiffs.

Mr. Sharpe, in reply. * * *

[232] THE VICE-CHANCELLOR:

Tayler and Shuttleworth carried on trade together with an agreed
amount of capital ; part of which had been withdrawn after the
death of Wartnaby, and the survivors agreed to replace the capital
so withdrawn, and also to raise the aggregate capital to the sum of
16,000*l.* For this purpose additional monies were to be brought in
so as to form a permanent increase of the capital ; but it was to be
raised in such a manner as not to charge Tayler personally. In
point of fact from the beginning Tayler was exempted from bringing
in capital, he was to pay no part of the 8,000*l.*, nor of the 1,500*l.* ;
he was only to bring in a share of the monied capital in case an
addition should be found necessary, exceeding the 1,500*l.* to be
brought in by the other partners. The advertisement, which is the
act of both the partners, is therefore evidence of an agreement
having been come to between Tayler and Shuttleworth, whereby the
former agreed that the concern should no longer be carried on with
the limited amount of capital, but that the same, as between the
partners, should be increased, not by borrowing any money on the
credit of Tayler, or by rendering him in any way chargeable for the
increase, but by finding some person willing to advance the capital,
in consideration of a share in the concern. This was the undoubted

contract between the partners, and upon *that contract the question is, whether Shuttleworth had any authority to go into the market and raise money on the credit of Tayler's name as well as his own : that he possibly might have succeeded in charging Tayler by borrowing money of a person who was ignorant of this special contract,—I do not say to the amount of 16,000*l*.,—but that he might have charged him for ordinary partnership purposes, may be admitted ; but if, having that advertisement in his hand, he goes to a person willing to lend money, and says " this is my authority to raise capital," can that person lend the money on the credit of Tayler's name and hold Tayler bound by the amount of that advance ? I will suppose the contract between Tayler and Shuttleworth to have been that Shuttleworth should find the whole money, and Tayler should find no part of it,—if that appeared on the face of the contract, it is impossible that any person lending the money to Shuttleworth, for that very purpose, could say that Tayler was bound by it, for on the face of the written authority he would in fact have notice that Shuttleworth was exceeding his authority when he made use of Tayler's name as a security for repaying the money. It appears to me that such a case would not be more conclusive than the case which has actually happened. How does Mr. Wilkin represent the case in his own state of facts ? he says that he received an answer to his letter from the solicitor of the firm; that the meeting which took place between him, that solicitor, and Shuttleworth, was adjourned, without anything having been done; that an adjourned meeting was had, and that it was ultimately arranged that he should make the intended advance as a loan to the firm, and that he should act as accountant, at a salary ; that the negotiation was continued and carried on by Shuttleworth as such partner on behalf of the firm of D. F. Tayler & Co., and the object for which the money was intended to be raised was stated by *Shuttleworth to be the payment of the estate of a deceased partner and for other partnership purposes. In point of fact having met to negotiate for becoming a partner and advancing capital, whereby Tayler could not have been subjected to any charge in respect of the capital so advanced,—instead of doing that—he declines to become a partner, and then, as he himself says, makes the intended advance as a loan to the firm ; and not only receives notes by which the firm was to be bound, but at the same time enters into a very special agreement connected with the security. (His Honour stated the agreement(1).)

FISHER
v.
TAYLER.
[*233]

[*234]

(1) *Supra*, p. 86.

It appears therefore plainly, that this is not the case of money borrowed merely for the general and current purposes of a firm, in which case no question could have been anticipated, but that it is a large sum of money advanced as part of the permanent capital of the firm, and advanced to a partner who, on meeting Wilkin, gave him notice that he had authority to borrow, but in a totally different way, and one which would be attended with very different consequences. It is not merely a common bill or note given in the ordinary course of business, but it is an advance accompanied by an agreement for the employment of this gentleman by the firm with a view to the protection of his own interest,—for giving six months' notice of payment, and embracing other special terms. I have not the slightest doubt that, in a case of this description, where two partners have agreed to make a permanent addition to their capital, and to make it in a particular mode, that no party can, with knowledge of that special agreement, bind the absent partner in any way other than that which the special agreement would authorize. Suppose the case of two partners carrying on business with a capital of 2,000*l.*, each contributing 1,000*l.* The operations *of that firm are necessarily carried on to an amount proportionate to the employed means, and each partner is safe so long as the affairs of the concern are well conducted; but if that capital is to be permanently increased, doubled, or trebled, or if the operations of the concern are to be so, monies advanced for that object cannot be treated as monies advanced for the ordinary purposes of the trade; it is in fact wholly altering the character of the business. If, then, one of the partners agrees with the other that the capital shall be doubled or trebled, provided the other party will find the whole, it comes in principle within the reasoning of the learned Judges in *Greenslade* v. *Dower*, that if a bill could be accepted for this purpose the effect would be that, whereas one partner was to find all the capital or a portion of it, yet he would have the power to bind his co-partner to find the whole.

[*235]

There would, as I have observed, be difficulty in the case of an established concern, if the money was borrowed from a party who had no notice. But here Wilkin had notice that the large sum of 16,000*l.*, being nearly double the capital previously employed, was to be raised in a given mode. Confining myself solely to this view of the case, if it stood alone, I could not but agree with the Master. Upon the attendant circumstances only, I should infer that the 4,000*l.* were advanced as part of the 16,000*l.*, and if the whole

16,000*l*. had been advanced I am satisfied there could not have been
room for any question. But the case does not depend on inference
alone ; it stands on direct evidence. It is so laid in Wilkin's state
of facts, which is his bill for the purpose of this proceeding. And
it was not (so far as my recollection goes) until after I had called
for a second argument on the point, that any attempt was made to
treat the loan in question, as unconnected with the sum *mentioned in the advertisement. But, however that may be, it is
unquestionable that Wilkin met Shuttleworth as a person authorized
to raise money in a particular manner and for a special purpose,
not falling within the scope of the dealings of the concern, and with
full knowledge that such was the case he lent money upon a security
which charged Tayler, a consequence which the manner of raising
the money pointed out by Tayler would have excluded.

FISHER
v.
TAYLER.

[*236]

Then is there anything in the evidence before me to alter this
view of the case ? The evidence of Wood tends to confirm it ; and,
as the professional adviser of Wilkin, I cannot assume that he has
not disclosed everything within his knowledge, material to his
client's case. There certainly is evidence that Shuttleworth said
he had communicated the matter to Tayler ; but there is no direct
evidence that Tayler knew anything of the transaction, unless it
may be inferred from the evidence of Flick and Crawley, of what
took place in London. This evidence is certainly of the most
meagre kind. Wilkin was on the premises acting, or going to act,
as clerk. Tayler came there when Wilkin was present, and he
acknowledged Wilkin in a way which showed he had heard of him
before. No doubt he had heard of him from Shuttleworth, as
a person treating to become a partner. Perhaps Shuttleworth
deceived Tayler, by telling him he would become, or expected to
become, a partner, and wished to look into the concern beforehand ;
but it is perfectly consistent with the transaction to suppose that
Tayler had heard of Wilkin, and supposed Wilkin was there with
a view to some transaction to be carried out, without knowing the
fact that bills or notes had been given, by which Tayler himself
might be bound. Any inference to be drawn from this evidence
is far outweighed by the conduct of Wilkin, after the receipt of
*the letter of the 31st of July. Instead of replying to that letter,
by saying, " I advanced money to the firm, and Shuttleworth
told me you were informed of it," he acquiesces from that time
until Shuttleworth having become unable to pay, and Tayler's
estate being apparently solvent, he sets up this demand. On

[*237]

the case before the Master, I have no doubt his conclusion was right.

There is another view, however, which may be taken of the case. It is true that there was 16,000l. to be raised by way of increase of capital, and in order to enlarge the transactions of the firm, but there is no suggestion that the old firm was not to go on in the mean time. On the contrary the very circumstance that the transactions were proposed to be enlarged, shows that the old firm was intended to be carried on until the increase of the capital should be raised; and it is not disputed that such was the intention of the parties. Now, if the old concern was to go on, undoubtedly all the partnership rights of Shuttleworth, and all the partnership liabilities of Tayler would remain with respect to that partnership. If it were necessary to borrow money with a view to preserve or carry on the old concern, there was nothing in the circumstance that they proposed to enlarge their partnership transactions, that would necessarily make it illegal in Shuttleworth to borrow money for their general purposes; and I understood *Mr. Romilly's* argument to be, that, inasmuch as it appears, the firm was much pressed at this time, and Wartnaby's estate was demanding payment of money, the 4,000l. was a sum which reasonably might be necessary to carry on and preserve the old firm. There are thus, so to express it, two antagonistic principles which might apply. I have the strongest impression that Shuttleworth was not justified in binding the firm in respect of any advance of the 16,000l.; at the same time, I have
[*238] nothing to lead me *with certainty to the conclusion that he might not be justified in borrowing, or Wilkin in lending, money to some extent, with a view to carry on the old concern. Wilkin may not have known that such borrowing was unlawful as between the partners. Although the parties are bound to bring forward their case in the first instance, and the Court, in general, holds them bound by that case; yet, considering the great injury to Wilkin on the one hand, if I confirm the report, and the comparatively small injury to the other party of the short delay which will be occasioned by my allowing Wilkin to bring an action,—and being satisfied there is a question to be tried more fit for the decision of a jury than of this Court,—while I think the Master was right upon the case before him, I think I am best consulting the ends of justice by giving Wilkin (if he is willing to incur the risk) to bring an action on the promissory notes, before I finally determine the case against him.

The exceptions to stand over, and, in the mean time, Wilkin to be at liberty to bring an action on the notes against the executors of Tayler, it being admitted for the purposes of the action that Tayler survived Shuttleworth.

KING *v.* SMITH.

(2 Hare, 239—245; S. C. 7 Jur. 694.)

The Court will not, on the application of a mortgagee out of possession, restrain the mortgagor from proceeding to fell timber growing upon the mortgaged estate, unless the security is insufficient.

W. SMITH conveyed and surrendered certain freehold and copyhold estates to the use of J. Reid and his heirs, by way of mortgage, to secure 2,700*l.* and interest.   W. Smith, by his will, gave all his real and personal estate to the defendant S. Smith (who was also his heir-at-law, customary heir, and sole executor), "in hopes that he might be able to pay his (the testator's) just debts, and find a surplus for his trouble."   J. Reid devised his legal interest in the mortgaged premises to the plaintiffs, and appointed them his executors.   The plaintiffs, by their bill, charged, that the mortgaged premises were a " scanty security " for the principal and interest due, and that the plaintiffs were entitled and claimed to be specialty creditors upon the general estate of the mortgagor for the deficiency; and that, to ascertain the same, the mortgaged premises ought to be sold.   The bill prayed an account of the mortgage debt,—a sale accordingly,—and payment out of the proceeds; and, if the same were insufficient, that the plaintiffs might be declared to be specialty creditors upon the estate for the deficiency: that, if necessary, the suit might be taken as being on behalf of the plaintiffs, and all other the unsatisfied creditors of W. Smith, and the personal and real estate duly administered and applied.

After appearance, and before answer, the plaintiffs filed their supplemental bill, stating that, since the original bill was filed, the defendant had felled, and was proceeding to fell and carry away large numbers of timber and timber-like trees, which were growing on the mortgaged premises,—that many of such trees were *lying upon the lands, and had been advertised for sale: and praying an account of the trees felled, and of the monies produced by the sale, and an injunction to restrain the felling and sale of trees from the mortgaged premises.

[*240]

The plaintiffs moved for the injunction, according to the prayer.

Mr. W. T. S. Daniel, for the motion.   *   *   *

Mr. James, for the defendant.   *   *   *

[241]   *Mr. W. T. S. Daniel,* in reply.   *   *   *

[242]   THE VICE-CHANCELLOR:

It is now an established rule, that, if the security of the mortgagee is insufficient, and the Court is satisfied of that fact, the
mortgagor will not be allowed to do that which would directly
impair the security,—cut timber upon the mortgaged premises.   It
has been argued, that, if the bill be for a foreclosure, when the
mortgagee seeks to take the whole estate, the Court will not prevent
him, pending that suit, from cutting timber or receiving rents, or
doing any other act incident to the ownership; but that, if the
plaintiff sued as a general creditor, the Court would give him the
relief by injunction.   That, however, is not the distinction.   The
rule would be rather the other way.   The plaintiff, in a foreclosure
[*243]   suit, asks nothing more *than the estate, whilst the plaintiff, in a
creditors' suit, seeks the application, not only of the mortgaged
estate, but, if necessary, of the general estate also, in payment of
his debt.   It is very difficult to suppose that a mere creditor can
have any such right as the argument assumes.   On what principle
is the executor and trustee of real estate to be restrained at the suit
of a general creditor from acting according to his judgment in the
management of the property.

I think the allegation in the bill, that the mortgaged premises
are a scanty security for the debt, is a sufficient foundation for
admitting evidence of the value of the estate.

Jan. 13.   THE VICE-CHANCELLOR:

The cases decide that a mortgagee out of possession is not of
course entitled to an injunction to restrain the mortgagor from
cutting timber on the mortgaged property.   If the security is sufficient, the Court will not grant an injunction merely because the
mortgagor cuts, or threatens to cut, timber.   There must be a
special case made out before this Court will interpose.   The difficulty I feel is in discovering what is meant by a "sufficient
security."   Suppose the mortgage debt, with all the expenses, to be
1,000*l.*, and the property to be worth 1,000*l.*, that is, in one sense,
a sufficient security; but no mortgagee, who is well advised, would
lend his money, unless the mortgaged property was worth one-third

more than the amount lent at the time of the mortgage. If the
property consisted of houses, which are subject to many casualties
to which land is not liable, the mortgagee would, probably, require
more. It is rather a question of prudence than of actual value.
*I think the question which must be tried is, whether the property
the mortgagee takes as a security, is sufficient in this sense,—that
the security is worth so much more than the money advanced,—
that the act of cutting timber is not to be considered as substantially impairing the value, which was the basis of the contract
between the parties at the time it was entered into. I have read
the affidavit, and I cannot find that either the rental or income of
the property appears; but it seems that the substantial part of it
consists of houses, which might make it a more serious question,
whether the Court should permit the mortgagor to cut the timber.
The supplemental bill, which states the circumstances with respect
to the timber, and prays the injunction, contains no case with
reference to the insufficiency of value, nor does the plaintiff, by his
affidavit, make any such case. The bill and affidavit appear to
proceed on the supposition that the mortgagor has no right to cut
the timber under any circumstances. In the valuation which is
attempted to be shown, I am not told the quantity of the land, or
the rental; nor can I discover of what class the houses are, or
whether they are tenanted or not, or what is the nature of the
property generally.

It is stated, on the defendant's affidavits, that he did not cut any
of the trees with the intention of injuring the estate, but, on the
contrary, he did it in the due and proper course of husbandry and
management. What is meant by felling twenty-one large elm trees
in due course of husbandry, I cannot comprehend. It is obvious,
that the defendant is using language, of which he does not know
the effect. There being, however, no abstract right on the part of
a mortgagee to say that the mortgagor shall not cut timber, I am
satisfied that there must be clearer evidence of the value before me,
or I cannot grant the injunction.

Let the motion stand over, with liberty to apply. If the defendant proceeds to cut more .timber, the plaintiff can then renew his
application, and bring before me a case upon which I can adjudicate,
and then the costs of this motion will be disposed of. I should be
very reluctant to decide it without knowing what is the actual value
of the security which has been accepted by the mortgagee, or
whether he is really secured or not.

1843.
Jan. 14, 30.

WIGRAM,
V.-C.

[246]

SAMUEL *v.* JONES (1).

(2 Hare, 246—248; S. C. 12 L. J. Ch. 496; 7 Jur. 845.)

In an administration or creditors' suit against an executor becoming bankrupt or insolvent, and who is, at the same time, indebted to the estate of his testator, the costs of the executor incurred before his bankruptcy or insolvency will be set off against his debt; and the costs of the same executor incurred in the proper performance of the duties of his trust, after his bankruptcy or insolvency, will be allowed out of the estate.

AN administration suit. The bill was filed in January, 1833: and, on the 7th of February, the defendant Lloyd, one of the executors, became bankrupt. On the 14th of May he obtained his certificate; and, in June he put in his answer in this cause. The defendant Jones, the other executor, became bankrupt in February, 1834; and afterwards obtained his certificate. The decree in 1836 directed the costs of all parties to be taxed as between solicitor and client, and reserved the payment of the defendants' costs, and the further directions and subsequent costs. The executors, Jones and Lloyd, were found debtors to the estate in the amount of upwards of 1,000*l.* each. On further directions,

Mr. Wray, for the executors, submitted, that, notwithstanding they had been defaulters to the estate, they were entitled to receive their costs as executors, incurred subsequently to their bankruptcy. The executors' costs before the bankruptcy must, there was no doubt, be set off against the balance owing by the executors to the estate; but that balance, as a debt, was extinguished by the bankruptcy; and afterwards there was nothing against which their costs could be set off, and no ground for requiring them to act as trustees at their own expense. He referred to the case of *Gibbons* v. *Hawley* (2).

(1) *In re Basham* (1882) 23 Ch. D. 195, 52 L. J. Ch. 408, 48 L. T. 476.

(2) A creditor's suit against the administratrix, who had carried on the business of the intestate, her husband, after his death, and had become indebted to his estate. After the institution of the suit, the administratrix took the benefit of the Insolvent Act. The decree, on further directions, on the 10th of May, 1832, ordered that her costs should be deducted from the sum of 773*l.* 8*s.* 9*d.*, found to be due from her to the testator's estate; and, if the said costs should exceed the amount of the said debt, that the receiver should pay the excess thereof out of the monies which might come to his hands; and, if such costs should fall short of the amount of such debt,—- it appearing that the said administratrix had taken the benefit of the Act for the Relief of Insolvent Debtors,— that the Master should inquire, and state to the Court, whether it was for the benefit of the said creditors, that any and what steps should be taken for obtaining of the excess of the said debt over the said costs, or of any dividend on such excess. The cause

Mr. Koe, for the plaintiffs, said, that the consent of the plaintiff in *Gibbons* v. *Hawley*, rendered that case wholly inapplicable as an authority for the present, in which the plaintiff did not consent : *Harmer* v. *Harris* (1) [and other cases].

SAMUEL
v.
JONES.
[247]

THE VICE-CHANCELLOR :

I think that an executor, although a defaulter to the estate at the time of his bankruptcy, yet properly conducting *himself in his character of executor after the bankruptcy, is entitled to his subsequent costs, like any other executor. A different rule would be very harsh. Suppose the case of an executor, who has had the misfortune to be made a bankrupt, and who is a debtor to the estate of his testator in a small sum, whilst the chief part of the estate has been got in and secured by his diligence : is a party in such a situation not to have his costs as executor until after the whole of his debt at the time of his bankruptcy shall have been repaid ? The bankruptcy is the statutory mode by which, in such a case, the debt is discharged. In other respects, the bankruptcy does not affect the trust character. I shall, therefore, direct the costs of the executors from the time of their bankruptcy to be taxed. No case of misconduct or of unnecessary litigation has been shown, but if, on taxing the costs, it should appear that any unnecessary expenses have been incurred, the parties will not be precluded from bringing forward their objections to such charges.

[*248]

came on again for further directions on the 13th of June, 1839, and the decree then made contains the following direction : " And, inasmuch as the defendant became a debtor to the estate of the testator, and was discharged by virtue of the Acts in force for relief of insolvent debtors in respect of the amount of her default, and inasmuch as the said defendant has since, by her solicitor, Mr. T. Smith, greatly facilitated the realizing of the assets of the said testator, her husband, and rendered her aid and assistance to the said plaintiff in prosecuting this suit, and the various proceedings thereunder ; and the said defendant having applied to have costs allowed to her subsequent to the order made on further directions on the 10th of May, 1832, and to her said default, and the said plaintiff not objecting thereto : it is ordered, that the costs of the plaintiff and defendant, subsequent to the order on further directions, be taxed by the said Master between solicitor and client, and paid as hereafter mentioned " : *Gibbons* v. *Hawley*, Rolls, 10th May, 1832 ; 13th June, 1839.

(1) 25 R. R. 20 (1 Russ. 155).

1843.
Jan. 16, 17.
Feb. 11.

WIGRAM,
V.-C.

[249]

WEST *v.* REID.

(2 Hare, 249—263; S. C. 12 L. J. Ch. 245; 7 Jur. 147.)

In 1816, D. assigned a policy of insurance on his life to a trustee to secure a sum of money owing to W.; and soon afterwards, the solicitor of W. caused a memorandum to be entered in the office of the Insurance Company, directing that all letters were to be sent to him, and the premiums were thenceforth paid by W., through the hands of his solicitor; but the Insurance Company were not informed on whose behalf the solicitor acted. In 1826, D. became bankrupt, and his assignees declined to interfere respecting the policy. The premiums continued to be paid by W., through his solicitor, during his life, and by the executors of W., through their bankers, after his death. D. died in 1839.

Held, that the policy was in the order and disposition of the bankrupt, and that there was not any notice given to the insurance office of the assignment of the policy to take it out of such order and disposition.

That the conduct of the assignees did not amount to an abandonment of any right which they had to the benefit of the policy.

That the executors of W. had a lien on the policy for the amount of the premiums which had been paid by W., and his estate, and the interest thereon; and that they were entitled to payment of the amount thereof out of the monies payable under the policy (1).

Negligence, as applied to cases of constructive notice, supposes the disregard of a fact known to the purchaser, which indicated the existence of the fact, the knowledge of which the Court imputes to him; and such negligence may, without a fraudulent motive, be so gross as to justify the charge of constructive notice.

A purchaser may be presumed to have investigated every instrument, which directly or inferentially forms a link in the title to the property, but not instruments which are neither directly nor presumptively connected with it, and may only by possibility affect it.

By a policy of insurance, bearing date the 16th of August, 1813, the defendant Reid, and two other Directors of the Rock Life Assurance Company, in consideration of the annual premium of 95*l.* 18*s.* 2*d.*, covenanted to pay to the executors, administrators, or assigns of James Daniell, three months after his decease, the sum of 2,500*l.*, and any bonuses which might be allotted thereto. On the 23rd of February, 1816, James Daniell assigned his interest in several funds and securities, including the policy of assurance, to Mr. Wimburn (of the firm of Collett and Wimburn, solicitors), in trust to secure 5,000*l.* and interest lent to Daniell by one Woodroffe; and by the same assignment, the policy was at the same time delivered to Mr. Wimburn, and thenceforward remained in his possession. On the 17th of May, 1816, the interest of Woodroffe in the securities comprised in the indenture of the 23rd of February preceding, including his interest in the policy, was assigned *to James West, for whom Mr. Wimburn afterwards remained the trustee.

[*250]

(1) *Falcke* v. *Scottish Imperial Insurance Co.* (1886) 34 Ch. Div. 234, 56 L. J. Ch. 707, 56 L. T. 220.

It appeared that, in the year, 1816, Mr. Collett (the partner of Mr. Wimburn) made some communication to the Rock Life Assurance Company, the only information given respecting the particulars or contents of which was contained in a memorandum entered by an officer of the Company, dated the 23rd of July, 1816, in the margin of the declaration made by James Daniell at the time of making the insurance,—in the following words: "Letters to Collett and Wimburn, Chancery Lane, by Mr. Collett's order." From the time that James West became interested under the assignment of the 17th of May, 1816, until his death, the annual premiums were paid by him through the hands of his solicitors, Messrs. Collett and Wimburn.

On the 3rd of January, 1826, James Daniell became bankrupt, and Barnes and Palmer were appointed his assignees. Daniell informed his assignees of the interest of West in the policy, and a correspondence on the subject took place soon afterwards between the solicitors of West and the solicitors of the assignees, in which it was proposed, and appeared to be agreed between them, that the better course was to sell the policy and apply the proceeds towards the discharge of the debt due to West. The policy was at this time valued by the Rock Life Assurance Company at the sum of 875*l.* At the time of the bankruptcy the sum due to West was 910*l.* 12*s.* 7*d.* for principal and interest on the original debt,—575*l.* 9*s.* for premiums paid on the policy, and 82*l.* 19*s.* 3*d.* for interest thereon. On the 4th of August, 1827, the solicitors of West wrote to the solicitors of the assignees, recommending that the sale should be carried into effect, and also stating that the annual premium was on the *point of becoming due, and offering to pay it, in order to keep the policy on foot, if authorized to do so by the assignees. Barnes and Palmer were afterwards removed from being assignees of the estate of Daniell, and the defendant Solarte and others substituted in their place, by whom new solicitors were appointed, who refused to interfere with respect to the sale, or payment of the premiums. James West died in November, 1829. From the death of West the annual premiums on the policy were paid by the plaintiffs, his executors, through their bankers. On the 25th of December, 1839, James Daniell died. The sum at this time due to the executors of James West in respect of the original debt, premiums, and interest, amounted to 4,049*l.* 12*s.* 9*d.* The sum payable on the policy was 3,667*l.* 10*s.*

The bill was filed by the executors of West, and Mr. Wimburn,

[*251]

their trustee, against J. Reid, the Director of the Rock Life Assurance Company,—the surviving assignees,—and the executor of
Daniell, praying a declaration that the plaintiffs were entitled to
the policy of insurance, and the benefit thereof, and to the monies
to be received thereby; and that the Rock Life Assurance Company might be decreed to pay to the plaintiffs, the executors, the
said sum of 3,667l. 10s., or such other sum as was then due and
owing from the Company on account of the policy; or if, under the
circumstances, the assignees of the estate and effects of James
Daniell had a right to redeem the policy, then that the plaintiffs,
the executors, might be declared to have a lien thereon for what
was due to the estate of West, as well for principal and interest on
the bonds therein mentioned, as for the amount of premiums paid
by West or his executors, together with interest on such premiums,
according to the indentures of the 23rd of February and the 17th

[*252]   May, 1816; and in the latter *case praying an account of what
was due to the plaintiffs for principal and interest upon the
security of the said policy of insurance, and that the said
assignees might be decreed to pay to the plaintiffs what should
appear to be due to them on the said account, together with the
costs of the suit; or in default thereof, that they might be foreclosed
of the equity of redemption of the said policy.

The Rock Life Assurance Company paid into Court the sum of
3,667l. 10s., due upon the policy, which was the only property comprised in the indenture of the 23rd of February and 17th of May,
1816, which became available for the payment of the plaintiffs'
debt.

The assignees of James Daniell under his bankruptcy claimed
the monies arising from the policy, on the ground that the policy
was in the order and disposition of the bankrupt; but it was
admitted at the Bar, on the part of the assignees, that the plaintiffs
were entitled to a lien on the policy for the amount of the premiums
paid on account of West and of his estate, and the interest
thereupon.

Mr. Boteler and *Mr. Walpole*, for the plaintiffs, argued that
the policy was not in the order or disposition of Daniell at the time
of his bankruptcy, within the meaning of the statute (1); [and that

(1) 6 Geo. IV. c. 16, s. 72. The   so that the cases cited upon that point
corresponding section in the Bank-   have no longer any application.—
ruptcy Act, 1883, see sect. 44 (iii.) is O. A. S.
not applicable to policies of assurance,

the notice given to the office, and the payment of the premiums by
West and the plaintiffs, had taken it out of such order and
disposition].

    Mr. Kenyon Parker and *Mr. Sidebottom*, for the assignees of   [253]
Daniell's estate under his bankruptcy. * * *

    Mr. Hardy, for the executors of Daniell.   [254]

[The arguments and cases cited sufficiently appear in the
judgment.]

THE VICE-CHANCELLOR:

    It being now admitted on the part of the assignees of Daniell
that they cannot resist the claim of the plaintiffs to a lien on the
policy in respect of the premiums which have been paid by West
and his executors, the question is, whether I can, upon any of the
other grounds relied upon by the plaintiffs, give them a better
decree than that which the assignees are willing that they should take.

    Upon the first point, whether the policy of assurance was or not
within the clause of the Bankrupt Act, which, in case of bankruptcy, gives to reputed ownership the effect of actual ownership,
I shall (as I intimated during the argument) follow the example set
me by the Chief Judge of the Court of Review, in the late case
Ex parte Pott, *Re Daintry* and *Ryle* (1). If the cases which have
decided that a policy of assurance is a chattel, within the meaning
of the clause of the Bankrupt Act, relating to order and disposition,
are to be disturbed, the decision which is to have that effect should
come from the LORD CHANCELLOR. I shall trust myself with this
observation only, that the reasoning upon which the cases have
proceeded appears to me to be logically correct, and that I must not
be understood *from anything which fell from me during the   [*255]
argument, to have intimated an opinion that the existing decisions
will be or ought to be disturbed.

    The second question is, whether enough was done by West or his
executors to take the policy in this case out of the order and
disposition of the bankrupt.

    The question of reputed ownership is always a question of fact:
Edwards v. *Scott* (2). In the particular case of the assignment of a
debt or policy of assurance, notice to the debtor in the one case, and
to the insurers in the other, has generally been considered the

    (1) 12 L. J. Bank. 33, 7 Jur. 159.   (2) 1 Man. & Gr. 962.

test by which the question of change of reputed ownership of the debt, or money secured by the policy, is to be determined; because it is by such notice that the debtor, or Insurance Company, would be prevented from paying the money to any other than the party claiming, as in this case, by assignment. In the absence of some modern authorities, which are entitled to the greatest respect, I might, perhaps, have had difficulty in coming to the conclusion that the want of express notice was in all cases material, and that the possession (by an assignee of a chose in action) of the instrument securing or evidencing the debt, and the practice of each particular assurance office, might not be sufficient in deciding the question of reputed ownership of a debt in a court of equity.

[His Honour here cited a number of cases which established that notice of assignment to the insurance office was necessary under the old bankruptcy law to take a policy out of the order and disposition clauses, and continued as follows:]

[256]   I cannot, therefore, consider myself at liberty, in this particular case, to do more than inquire, whether in fact the office had such a notice of the assignment as would have subjected them to the liability to pay the amount of the policy a second time, if they had paid it to Mr. Daniell's assignees in bankruptcy. Now the fact that the premiums were paid by Messrs. Wimburn and Collett out of the funds of West during his life, and that they were paid by the bankers of West's executors, after his death, cannot *per se* make any difference. The office had a right to the premiums, and until the person paying them, or some other, gave notice that the original position of the parties was altered, the office would be justified in

[*257]   considering the premiums as paid under and *in conformity with the original contract. It is not suggested that there was anything in the mere mode of paying the premiums from which the office had notice of any change in the position of the parties; and in answer to a question I put upon this point, it was admitted that there was no alteration; that the premiums were paid, and the receipts given as from Daniell.

The only remaining fact upon which notice to the office could be inferred was the memorandum entered in the margin of Mr. Daniell's declaration (1).

Upon this part of the plaintiffs' case I was referred to *Hiern* v. *Mill* (2), *Tibbits* v. *George* (3), and to my own judgment in *Jones* v.

(1) *Supra*, p. 99.   (3) 5 Ad. & El. 107.
(2) 9 R. R. 149 (13 Ves. 114).

Smith (1). In applying (as I think I am bound to apply) to the case
now before me the principle upon which I acted in *Jones* v. *Smith*,
I shall take the opportunity of repudiating a conclusion which I
have been told has been drawn from the language I used in that
case, but which I think the language does not warrant, unless in a
single expression, corrected in that respect as well by the immediate
context as by the other parts of the judgment. I have been told
that, according to the language I made use of in that case, the
grossest negligence would in no case justify the Court in charging
a party with constructive notice, unless the negligence proceeded
from a fraudulent motive existing in the mind of the party at the
time. Nothing, certainly, would have been further from my intention, than to say any thing which should lead to the conclusion that
there may not be a degree of negligence so gross (*crassa negligentia*)
that a court of justice may treat it as evidence of fraud—impute a
fraudulent *motive to it—and visit it with the consequences of
fraud, although (morally speaking) the party charged may be
perfectly innocent,—a meaning which, I should have thought, had
been sufficiently conveyed by my expression, that negligence might
be evidence of fraud, but that it was not the same thing. In *Jones*
v. *Smith*, the mortgagee knew that the mortgagor was married, and,
therefore, knew that he might have made a settlement, and might
have included in such settlement the property proposed to be
included in the mortgage. But there was nothing in the fact of
marriage which raised a legal presumption or inference that it was
settled, and, therefore, nothing upon which to found a charge of
negligence as distinguished from mere want of extreme caution in
the mortgagee. The mortgagee was credibly informed both by
Jones (the mortgagor) and his wife,—one of whom (the wife) at all
events, according to her evidence in the cause, believed she was
speaking the truth,—that the property about which he was treating
was not comprised in their marriage settlement. He was informed,
that the wife's property was settled, and that the husband made no
settlement; and a reasonable excuse was made for not producing
that deed. Believing what was told him, he became mortgagee of
the property, and got in the legal estate. There was no pretence,
in that case, for imputing actual fraud to the purchaser, nor was
there a single fact or circumstance in the case raising, or tending
to raise, an inference, or create a suspicion that the husband's
property was in settlement.

(1) 58 R. R. 22 (1 Hare, 43).

Having satisfied myself that Smith had acted *bonâ fide*, and that he had not notice of any fact raising a presumption, or creating a suspicion, that the husband's property was in settlement, I could not possibly hold that he had notice of that fact. A decision to that effect would have been merely arbitrary, and inconsistent *with the facts of the case. Extreme caution, no doubt, might have led Smith to inquire after a mere possibility, the existence of which he had no ground to surmise. But the omission to exercise such caution is not negligence in the legal sense of the term, nor, indeed, in any sense. Negligence, as I understand the term, supposes a disregard of some fact known to a purchaser, which at least indicated the existence of that fact, notice of which the Court imputes to the purchaser.

[*259]

I do not deny that difficulty may sometimes arise in drawing the line between the degree of negligence, which shall be sufficient to charge a purchaser, and that mere want of extreme caution which, in the absence of fraud, will excuse him. But the distinction is founded in principle,—and the difficulty is one with which (upon the very question of gross negligence) courts of justice are in the daily habit of grappling ; and the difficulty in principle is not distinguishable from that which occurs in every other case in which antagonist principles come into immediate conflict with each other.

The distinction, which is taken in terms by Sir Edward Sugden (1), is fully borne out,—by the cases which decide that a person purchasing without obtaining the title-deeds, is not affected by notice of an equitable mortgage : *Plumb* v. *Fluit* (2) ; *Evans* v. *Bicknell* (3),—by Lord THURLOW's judgment in *Cothay* v. *Sydenham* (4),—by a judgment of Lord HARDWICKE, and other cases referred to in the judgment in *Jones* v. *Smith*. If that distinction be not admitted in a case like *Jones* v. *Smith*, the unavoidable consequence must *be, that a man, who mortgages a fraction of his estate, will thereby throw a cloud upon the title to the rest of his estate ; and a devise of a single acre of land by a will, which does nothing more, will throw a cloud upon the title of an heir-at-law to his descended estates ; for, it is clear, that neither the mortgagor in the one case, nor the heir in the other, can command the production of the mortgage-deed or will ; and it is equally clear, that nothing but the production of the original itself would be sufficient, if a representation such as Smith relied upon be not sufficient.

[*260]

(1) Vend. & Pur.   (3) 5 R. R. 245 (6 Ves. 174).
(2) 3 R. R. 605 (2 Anst. 432).   (4) 2 Br. C. C. 391.

Similar observations would apply to a codicil partially revoking a will; and to every deed executed after the date of a will.

In short, let the doctrine of constructive notice be extended to all cases (it is in fact more confined : *Plumb* v. *Fluit*, *Evans* v. *Bicknell*, *Cothay* v. *Sydenham*, and other cases,—but) let it be extended to all cases in which the purchaser has notice that the property is affected, or has notice of facts raising a presumption that it is so, and the doctrine is reasonable, though it may sometimes operate with severity. But once transgress the limits which that statement of the rule imposes—once admit that a purchaser is to be affected with constructive notice of the contents of instruments not necessary to, nor presumptively connected with, the title, only because, by possibility, they may affect it (for that may be predicated of almost any instrument) ; and it is impossible, in sound reasoning, to stop short of the conclusion, that every purchaser is affected with constructive notice of the contents of every instrument of the mere existence of which he has notice.   A purchaser must be presumed to investigate the title of the property he purchases, and may, therefore, be presumed to have examined every instrument forming a link, directly or by inference, in that title ; and that presumption I take to be the foundation of the whole *doctrine. But it is impossible to presume that a purchaser examines instruments not directly nor presumptively connected with the title, only because they may by possibility affect it.

[*261]

The same principle must govern my judgment in the case now before me. Had the office, before the bankruptcy, notice of any fact which created a change of Daniell's interest in the policy ? If Collett and Wimburn required the letters to be addressed to them as Mr. Daniell's solicitors, they would naturally have given it in the simple form in which the office received it.   If they gave it not as Mr. Daniell's solicitors, but as the solicitors of a party claiming a new interest, the office had a right to expect that the notice they received should have been more explanatory.   The circumstance that one member of a firm of solicitors requests that all letters respecting the policy effected by Daniell may be sent to the firm of which that solicitor is a member, does not raise any inference that Daniell's interest in the policy had undergone any change. I do not deny that extreme caution might have led the office to inquire whose solicitors Wimburn and Collett were ; but in the absence of actual fraud, I could not hold that this was a case of that gross negligence to which courts of justice impute fraud,

WEST
v.
REID.

and visit with the consequences of fraud. I am not considering a case which has happened, but I am speculatively to determine whether the insurance office, having no notice of West's interest except that, if any, which is to be inferred from the note in the margin of the declaration, would have been liable to the plaintiffs for the amount of the policy, if they had paid it to the assignees of

[*262]

Daniell *under his bankruptcy. I feel bound to decide that they would not have been so liable. Upon that evidence alone I should say, as between these parties only, that the negligence was in those who omitted to give the office actual notice of West's claim, and not in the office, who, receiving from one of a firm of solicitors a communication which was perfectly consistent with the original position of the parties, did not infer that any change had taken place. Whatever I might have thought, if the question were untouched by decision, yet finding it decided that parting with the policy will not alone take the debt out of the order and disposition of the bankrupt, I cannot hold that the case is altered by a communication of the character I have referred to,—a communication in every respect consistent with the original right.

Upon the third point,—the suggested abandonment by the assignees, —I am also of opinion against the plaintiffs.

It does not follow, that, because the assignees may now have a right to demand from the office the money due upon the policy, they could have recovered the policy in trover during Daniell's life : and inasmuch as the right of the creditors was fixed by the bankruptcy itself, the correspondence can have no effect except as evidence of a subsequent contract, or intentional abandonment of right. No such contract is suggested, nor can it be said that there was any intentional abandonment, adverting to the knowledge of their interests which the parties had. There is no consideration between West and his estate on the one hand, and the assignees under the bankruptcy on the other, entitling the former to claim the policy adversely.

[*263]

I must therefore declare that West's estate is entitled *to be repaid out of the fund the amount of the premiums paid by West. or by his executors, together with interest on such payments from the times at which they were respectively made. The plaintiffs are entitled to the costs of so much of the suit as was directed to that part of the case on which they have been successful. The right to the premiums was given up at the Bar, yet it was not given up on the pleadings, nor indeed was it at first given up at the Bar.

There was therefore an absolute necessity for coming into Court to establish that claim.   As to the rest of the costs of the suit, I at firs thought that I ought to make the plaintiffs pay them; but adverting to the recent decisions by Sir JOHN CROSS, I think any party was justified in taking the opinion of the Court upon the question, whether the former decisions in *Williams* v. *Thorp* (1), and *Ex parte Colville* (2), and other cases, are to be taken as the rule of the Court or not.   On that part of the case, therefore, I think there should be no costs.   The balance of the money in Court will be paid to the assignees; and the costs of Dawson, the executor of Daniell, who appears to have been unnecessarily made a party, must be paid by the plaintiffs.

GRAY *v.* GARMAN (3).

(2 Hare, 268—274 ; S. C. 12 L. J. Ch. 259 ; 7 Jur. 275.)

Gift by a testator of his real and personal estate to his wife for her life, and the residue to be equally divided between her brothers and sisters, and, in case any of them should be dead at the time of her decease, leaving issue, such issue to stand in their parents' place : Held, first, that no brother or sister, who died before the date of the will, was capable of taking under the bequest, and, therefore, the issue of any brother or sister, who was dead before the date of the will, could not take by substitution; secondly, that it was not an original and substantive gift to the issue of those brothers and sisters who were dead at the death of the wife; and, thirdly, that the brothers and sisters, who survived the testator, and afterwards died without issue in the lifetime of the wife, were entitled to shares in the residue.

THE testator, by his will, dated in 1812, gave his real and personal estate to his wife for her life, and directing a sale of the real estate, and bequeathing some pecuniary legacies to be paid after her death, he disposed of the residue as follows : " All the rest, residue, and remainder of my estate and effects I desire may be equally divided between the brothers and sisters of my said wife, Elizabeth Rockwell ; and, in case any or either of them shall be dead at the time of the decease of my said wife, Elizabeth Rockwell, leaving issue, then such issue to stand in the place of their respective parents or parent."

The testator died in 1813, and the said Elizabeth, his widow, died in August, 1839.   There had been fifteen brothers and sisters of Elizabeth the wife, of whom seven died in the lifetime of the testator without leaving issue, and one, named John, died before the date of the will, leaving six children.   Of the seven who

(1) 29 R. R. 96 (2 Sim. 257).   (3) *In re Wood* [1894] 3 Ch. 381, 63
(2) 2 Sim. 570, *n.*   L. J. Ch. 790, 71 L. T. 413, C. A.

survived *the testator, two died in the lifetime of the widow without
issue, and five survived the widow.

The six children of John survived the testator, and three of
them died in the lifetime of the widow,—two leaving issue, and
one without issue and intestate,—one left England in 1828, and
was not afterwards heard of,—and two survived the widow, and
appeared in the cause.

*Mr. Temple, Mr. Teed, Mr. Roupell, Mr. Anderdon, Mr.
Chandless, Mr. Bagshawe, Mr. Cooke,* and *Mr. Glasse,* appeared
for the various parties interested. * * *

THE VICE-CHANCELLOR:

Two questions have been discussed in this case: first, whether
the issue of John—John having died before the date of the will—
are entitled to a share in the residue of the testator's estate? and,
secondly, whether, of the seven brothers and sisters of the wife
who survived the testator, the two who died without issue, in the
lifetime of the widow, were entitled to participate in the same
residue?

The answer to the first of these questions must be found in the
words of the will.   And, as there clearly is not in this will (as the
Court thought there was in *Giles* v. *Giles* (1), *Jarvis* v. *Pond* (2), and
other like cases) any thing in the context of the will by which the
language of the clause I have cited can be modified or controlled,
the simple consideration is, what does that clause express?   This
depends upon the meaning of the word "them" in the second
branch of that clause, in which the issue of brothers and sisters
are substituted for the parents.   If the word "them" refers to the
brothers and sisters to whom the legacy is primarily given, and to
no other brothers and sisters, it is impossible that the issue of
John can have any interest in the question before me.   If, on the
other hand, the word "them" is to be understood as referring to
brothers and sisters generally, and is not confined to the brothers
and sisters before spoken of,—the issue of John may possibly bring
themselves within the description of the issue contemplated.

That the first branch of this proposition is correct, must, I conceive, be clear, both upon the language of the clause itself, and
upon authority.   Under that clause, no brother or sister had ever a
capacity to take who was not living at the date of the will.   And

(1) 42 R. R. 205 (8 Sim. 360).   (2) 47 R. R. 309 (9 Sim. 549).

as, by the supposition, the issue spoken of was issue of brothers
and sisters, whom the testator supposed capable of taking under
his will,—the issue of a brother or sister not living at the date of
the will cannot bring themselves within the description : *Christopherson* v. *Naylor* (1) ; *Butter* v. *Ommaney* (2) ; *Waugh* v. *Waugh* (3) ;
Peel v. *Catlow* (4).

It has, indeed, been made a question, whether the capacity of
the primary legatee (at the date of the will) to take the legacy
was alone sufficient,—whether such legatee must not survive the
testator, and become a legatee *in esse*, and not have been a legatee
in posse only, to entitle his issue to claim in substitution : *Thornhill*
v. *Thornhill* (5). But later cases appear to sanction a more liberal,
though still a literal, construction of language like that I am considering. And it has been held, that the issue of a person primarily
pointed out as the object of a testator's bounty, and living at the
date of the will, may take by substitution for that party dying in
the lifetime of the testator,—*Smith* v. *Smith* (6) ; *Collins* v. *Johnson* (7) ; *Le Jeune* v. *Le Jeune* (8),—a construction which is certainly
fortified by very important analogies. No such question arises here ;
but it was necessary that I should notice the point, because it explains
and gets rid of many of the cases which were cited at the Bar.

On the other hand, if the word " them " is not to be taken as
referable exclusively to brothers and sisters before spoken of ; if
the entire clause is to be read as containing an original and substantive gift to two classes of legatees, namely, first to brothers
and sisters living at the death of the wife, and, secondly, to the
issue of brothers and sisters who may be dead at the time of the
death of the wife,—there is nothing in the description of the second
class to prevent the issue of John (though he were dead when the
will was made) from bringing themselves within the very words of
the will : *Tytherleigh* v. *Harbin* (9) ; *Rust* v. *Baker* (10) ; *Bebb* v.
Beckwith (11). The description (upon this hypothesis) requires only
that the brother or sister be dead at the time of the wife's decease,
and there is nothing in that description which makes the time of
their death material.

I have, therefore, simply to decide which of the above construc-

---

(1) 15 R. R. 120 (1 Mer. 320).

(2) 28 R. R. 6 (4 Russ. 70).

(3) 39 R. R. 129 (2 My. & K. 41).

(4) 47 R. R. 263 (9 Sim. 372).

(5) 20 R. R. 315 (4 Madd. 377).

(6) 42 R. R. 203 (8 Sim. 353).

(7) 41 R. R. 211 (8 Sim. 356, *n.*).

(8) 44 R. R. 327 (2 Keen, 701).

(9) 38 R. R. 121 (6 Sim. 329).

(10) 8 Sim. 443.

(11) 50 R. R. 188 (2 Beav. 308).

GRAY
v.
GARMAN.

tions the word "them" is to receive. Now, in the absence of authority, I cannot say there is a serious question to be argued. If there be no authority giving to plain words a technical meaning, beyond or differing from their natural meaning, the word "them" in this clause must refer, and exclusively refer, to the immediate antecedent. But it was argued for the issue of John, that authority requires me to put a more extensive meaning upon the word, in order to take in the issue of every brother and sister who was dead at the date of the will. Such is not my conclusion from the authorities. In *Christopherson* v. *Naylor*, the question was,—as in this case,—whether the children of a brother or sister, who died before the date of the will, could take? Sir WILLIAM GRANT said, the question was, whether there was a substitution? and, therefore, it came to this,—not what description of issue could take under the second clause, supposing it an original substantive limitation,—but what description of parents might have taken under the first,— and he ultimately held, that the issue of children not living at the date of the will could not take. He did not hold that the plain meaning of the words could be controlled upon any abstract notion that the testator must be supposed to have intended any thing more than his words expressed. In *Butter* v. *Ommaney*, the gift was,

[*273]

after the death of *the testator's wife and his brother Joseph, to be equally divided between the children of Joseph and his late sister Betty, and late brother Jacob (except Bernard), who should be then living, in equal shares and proportions; and as to such of them as should be then dead, leaving a child or children, such child or children were to be or stand in the place or places of his, her, or their parent or parents. It appears that the children, who died in the testator's lifetime, were all dead at the date of his will (1); and it was held, as in *Christopherson* v. *Naylor*, that those who died in the testator's lifetime were not entitled to any share. Upon the decision in *Waugh* v. *Waugh*, some doubt may perhaps be felt, so far as it depends upon the mere language of the will : *Tytherleigh* v. *Harbin*. But the case directly follows, and supports the two cases I have already cited,—and the only question upon it is, whether the peculiar language of the will did not take it out of the reach of the principle applied to it by Sir J. LEACH ?

The case of *Peel* v. *Catlow* is to the same effect. A case of substitution, and not of original substantive gift to issue, and the decision was in conformity to the principle I have adverted to.

(1) See note, 28 R. R. 8 (4 Russ. 73).

In *Giles* v. *Giles*, and in *Jarvis* v. *Pond*, the wording of the clauses
giving the legacies apparently imported substitution as in the cases
I have mentioned; but the Court, upon a critical examination of the
will, found it impossible to satisfy all parts of the will, without
treating the gift to the issue as original and substantive, and not as
substitutionary. It was upon the express ground that the special
language of the will required that construction, that the Court distinguished the case from those *to which I have referred. The other   [*274]
cases cited apply to questions differing from that before me.

The division of the reported cases into two classes, first,—where
the question has been, whether the issue of parties dying after the
date of the will in the lifetime of the testator would take by substitution ; and, secondly, those in which there has been an original
and substantive gift,—appears to me to remove all doubt with
reference to their operation and effect.

On the second question, I have no hesitation in saying that the
representatives of the brothers and sisters of the wife, who died
after the testator, but in the lifetime of the widow, leaving no
issue, are entitled to shares in the residue. The gift to the
brothers or sisters who survived the testator, was determinable
only on one event, their death, leaving issue : that event did not
happen, and their interest in the gift was, therefore, not taken away.

Declare, that the issue of John took no interest ; and direct the
residue to be divided in seven equal shares, &c.

DOVER v. ALEXANDER.

(2 Hare, 275—285; S. C. 12 L. J. Ch. 175; 7 Jur. 124.)

A married woman, having several legitimate children, and one illegitimate child, and being separated from her husband, and *enceinte* with a
second illegitimate child, appointed a fund to her illegitimate child then
born, reserving a power of revocation, as to a moiety, in favour of any
after-born children she might have born of her body. After the birth of
the second illegitimate child, she revoked the appointment of the moiety,
and appointed the entire fund equally between the two illegitimate
children : Held, that the after-born children, for whose benefit the revocation might be made, must be taken, in the primary and legal sense, as
applying to legitimate children only ; that, therefore, the second illegitimate child was not an object of the reserved power, and could not take
under the latter appointment.

BY indenture, dated the 24th of November, 1804, made between
Henry Whatton and Elizabeth, his wife, and their trustees, and

other parties, a sum of 3,083*l.* was directed to be paid to trustees, upon trust to purchase the sum of 4,200*l.*, Three per cent. Consols, to the intent that the dividends thereof might produce an annuity of 126*l.*, secured to Elizabeth Whatton for her separate use as therein mentioned, during the joint lives of herself and her said husband, and, after the decease of such one of them—Henry Whatton and Elizabeth his wife—as should first die, to transfer the same stock and dividends thereof, and stand and be possessed thereof respectively, and of all and every part thereof, in trust for such person or persons, and for such ends, intents, and purposes, and in such manner and form, parts, shares, and proportions, as the said Elizabeth Whatton, as well when covert as sole, and notwithstanding her coverture by her then present or any future husband, and either absolutely and with or without revocation and new appointment, by any deed or deeds, instrument or instruments, in writing, to be executed in manner therein mentioned, or by her last will and testament, or any codicil or codicils thereto, to be executed in manner therein mentioned, should direct or appoint; and, in default thereof, in trust for Elizabeth Whatton, for her sole and separate use.

[276]   By an indenture, dated the 28th of November, 1804, made between Elizabeth Whatton, of the one part; and Charles Watkinson, otherwise Charles Watkinson Arkinstall, of the other part,—Elizabeth Whatton, in consideration of natural love and affection, and in order to make a provision for Charles Watkinson Arkinstall, in the event of her decease, by virtue of the powers vested in her by the indenture of the 24th of November preceding, limited and appointed the said sum of 3,083*l.*, and the funds and securities in or upon which the same was or might be invested, saving her life interest therein, to hold the same unto Charles Watkinson Arkinstall, his executors, administrators, and assigns, absolutely, subject to a power of revocation therein contained as to one moiety of the said reversionary monies, funds, and securities, in favour of any after-born child or children the said Elizabeth Whatton might have born of her body, but not otherwise (1).

(1) This deed was recited in the following deed of April, 1813 (which was proved on behalf of the plaintiffs), and it was only stated in the bill as being so recited, without any other evidence of its existence: it was ultimately argued that Elizabeth Whatton should be taken as still having her general power of appointment, under the deed of the 24th of November, 1804, at the time she executed the deed of April, 1813. The Court held, that it was not open to the plaintiffs on the pleadings thus to put their case.

The 4,200l. stock was purchased in the names of the trustees,
upon the trusts of the indenture of the 24th of November. At the
date of the indenture of the 28th of November, Elizabeth Whatton
was living separate from her husband, and had four legitimate
children, namely, Henry, John, William, and George. Elizabeth
Whatton had also one illegitimate child, the said Charles Watkinson Arkinstall, and she was at the same time *enceinte* of another
illegitimate child, Margaret Brookshaw, *otherwise Mary Brook-   [*277]
shaw Arkinstall, who afterwards intermarried with Dover, and was
with him, the plaintiff in the cause. Henry Whatton died in the
lifetime of Elizabeth, his wife.

By indenture, dated the 2nd April, 1818, made between Elizabeth
Whatton, of the one part; and Charles Watkinson Arkinstall, and
the plaintiff, Margaret Brookshaw Arkinstall, of the other part,
reciting the indenture of the 24th of November, 1804,—the purchase of the stock,—that the children of Elizabeth Whatton living
were the said Henry, John, William, and George, and the said
Charles, known by the name of Charles Watkinson Arkinstall, and
the said Margaret, known as Margaret Brookshaw Arkinstall,—
that Margaret had been born since the appointment of the 24th of
November, 1804,—that both Charles and Margaret were infants,—
and that Elizabeth Whatton, being very anxious and desirous that
they should be provided for in equal proportions, as far as the same
was possible, in the event of her death, the said Elizabeth Whatton,
in pursuance of her said powers, and in performance of her agreement to that effect thereinbefore recited, and in consideration of
her natural love and affection for her said infant children, Charles
and Margaret, and for their advancement in the world, revoked and
made void so much of the indenture of the 28th of November, 1804,
as related to one moiety of the 4,200l. stock, and appointed and
assigned all her (the said Elizabeth Whatton's) reversionary right
and interest in the said 4,200l. stock (subject to her life estate
therein) unto the said Charles Watkinson Arkinstall, and Margaret
Brookshaw Arkinstall, their executors, administrators, and assigns,
equally between them, share and share alike, as tenants in common,
and not as joint-tenants; and, in case either of them should die
during his or her minority without leaving lawful issue, *then   [*278]
the share of him or her so dying to go to the survivor of them, his
or her executors, &c., absolutely.

Charles Watkinson Arkinstall died in 1819, an infant, and
unmarried. The plaintiff, Margaret Brookshaw Arkinstall, inter-

married with the plaintiff Dover, in 1826. Elizabeth Whatton, their mother, died in April, 1839.

The bill was filed in October, 1839, by the said Margaret Brookshaw and her husband, and their trustees,—their interest in the fund having been settled on marriage,—praying a declaration that the plaintiffs were entitled, under the indenture of the 2nd April, 1818, to the 4,200*l.* stock, and the dividends since the death of Elizabeth Whatton.

At the hearing,

Mr. Temple and *Mr. Lloyd,* for the plaintiffs, submitted, first, that, under the original deed, giving Elizabeth Whatton the power of appointment, it was competent to her to appoint the fund to any person whomsoever, and that the power of revocation, which she reserved on executing that power, ought, as to the moiety to which it extended, to be construed as reserving all her previous powers, or, if the latter construction was excluded, and the power confined to a revocation in favour of after-born children, the meaning of the word " children " should be ascertained by reference to the deed containing the reservation, in which the appointment was made in favour of one who was her illegitimate child. [They cited *Earle* v. *Wilson* (1), *Wilkinson* v. *Adam* (2), *Gordon* v. *Gordon* (3), *Mortimer* v. *West* (4), and other cases.]

[280]   *Mr. Roupell, Mr. Anderdon, Mr. Lovat, Mr. Wood, Mr. Bagshawe,* and *Mr. Blunt,* appeared for several parties claiming the funds, either under other alleged appointments, or in default of appointment.

Mr. Spence, for the representative of the surviving trustee of the fund.

THE VICE-CHANCELLOR :

The bill, in effect, alleges, and it is admitted that the plaintiff Margaret, in whose favour the appointment was attempted to be made, and Charles, who is since dead, were both illegitimate. No issue is tendered as to that fact. And, indeed, whatever the law may formerly have been, the cases in which the question of adulterine

(1) 11 R. R. 130 (17 Ves. 532).   (3) 15 R. R. 88 (1 Mer. 151).
(2) 12 R. R. 255 (1 V. & B. 446).   (4) 27 R. R. 98 (3 Russ. 375).

bastardy has arisen show, that, where the husband and wife are in   DOVER
v.
ALEXANDER.
such circumstances that all presumption of access is rebutted, the
children will be regarded as illegitimate.

It has been insisted, in argument, that the after-born illegitimate
of a woman are capable of taking from their *mother an interest,   [*281]
in the character of children, in cases where such children of a man
could not take any interest in that character. What the decision
ought to be in a case where that argument applies, I am not called
upon to give any opinion ; but if I wanted authorities to show that,
with reference to the children of females as well as those.of males,
the word " child," uncontrolled by the facts, and unexplained by
the context of the deed or will, must have its primary and legal
meaning, I should have no difficulty in finding them. The cases
of *Wilkinson* v. *Adam* and *Mortimer* v. *West* leave no doubt that the
opinions of the learned Judge before whom those cases were argued
was against the proposition, that even an after-born illegitimate
child of a female can take under the simple description of a child
of that person.

The original power of appointment, vested in Elizabeth Whatton,
would have enabled her to appoint to any children, whether
illegitimate or not, if it was exercised in a form that the law could
support. By the deed of the 28th of November, 1804, the whole
fund was appointed to Charles, reserving a power of revocation as
to one moiety "in favour of any after-born child or children the
said Elizabeth Whatton might have born of her body, but not
otherwise." Elizabeth Whatton does not in this deed speak of
Charles as being her son, either legitimate or illegitimate, but
simply describes him by his reputed name. There is nothing
whatever, so far as I can discover, from which any light can be
thrown upon the sense in which she intended to use the word
" child." If she had there described Charles as her child, perhaps
an argument might have arisen, whether the word " child,"
employed afterwards, was not used in the same sense. I do not
say that it would have affected the case. The word " child " *has   [*282]
often been construed in two different senses in the same instrument.
If a gift were made to the children of A. now living,—if A. had
none but illegitimate children, and they had acquired by reputation
the character of his children,—they would, no doubt, take under
the gift ; and a bequest by the same will to the after-born children
of A. would be satisfied by construing the word " child " in its
proper sense, and in the latter bequest illegitimate children would

take no interest. *Fraser* v. *Pigott* (1) is not the only decision on that point.

In the argument of this case, I have called on the counsel for the plaintiffs to show me that I have any right to suppose that other than legitimate after-born children were intended. It does not appear to me that the words " born of her body, but not otherwise," add any thing to the effect of the word " child." They leave the legal interpretation uncontrolled. The cases of *Cartwright* v. *Vawdry* (2), *Godfrey* v. *Davis* (3), *Fraser* v. *Pigott*, *Wilkinson* v. *Adam* (4), *Swaine* v. *Kennerley* (5), *Harris* v. *Lloyd* (6), *Mortimer* v. *West* (7), and *Bagley* v. *Mollard* (8), all decide that the word "child," taken *simpliciter*, means a legitimate child only, unless there are any words by which that sense may be controlled, or any thing in the context showing that the word is intended to be used in a secondary sense, or some extrinsic facts and circumstances, which show that the word "child" could not have been used in its only proper sense. In this case, it does not appear to me that there is anything on the face of the instrument to divert the expression from its proper meaning.

[283]   On the controlling effect of extrinsic circumstances upon the construction of words used in an instrument, I may refer to the case of *Gill* v. *Shelley* (9), where a testatrix directed that the residue of her estate would be divided amongst certain classes of persons mentioned in her will, and added, "amongst whom I include the children of the late Mary Gladman." Mary Gladman was then dead, having left two children only,—one legitimate, and the other illegitimate,—so that the plural term "children" could not be satisfied by giving the property to the single legitimate child; and Sir JOHN LEACH held, that both of the children were entitled. The express ground was, that the words were not capable of being satisfied without a departure from their primary sense. In *Pocock* v. *Bishop of Lincoln* (10), a father seised in fee of a perpetual advowson devised it to his son, who, at that time, was the incumbent of the living: there it was urged that, inasmuch as the devisee had a life interest at the time in the subject of the devise, unless the words "perpetual advowson" were construed to carry more than a life interest, he took nothing by the devise. There could

(1) 34 R. R. 290 (1 Younge, 354).
(2) 5 R. R. 108 (5 Ves. 530).
(3) 5 R. R. 204 (6 Ves. 43).
(4) 12 R. R. 255 (1 V. & B. 465).
(5) 12 R. R. 269 (1 V. & B. 469).
(6) 24 R. R. 68 (1 T. & R. 310).
(7) 27 R. R. 98 (3 Russ. 370).
(8) 32 R. R. 281 (1 Russ. & My. 586).
(9) 34 R. R. 106 (2 Russ. & My. 336).
(10) 3 Brod. & B. 27.

scarcely be a stronger case for implication. The Court, however,
refused to enlarge the meaning of the words, upon this ground,—
that, if the incumbent resigned the living, or accepted preferment,
or in certain other possible events, the devise would give the right
of presentation to the living, and, therefore, in such possible event,
the words might have some operation, without departing from their
proper sense. In *Doe* d. *Oxenden* v. *Chichester* (1), a testator devised
his estate of " Ashton " to Oxenden. It was *proved that the   [*284]
testator had an estate, which he used to call his " Ashton estate,"
the accounts relating to which were kept under that name, though
a small portion only of the estate was locally situated at Ashton ;
and the Court said, that the words, strictly interpreted, meant the
small portion of the estate which was locally situated at Ashton ;
and though, from the evidence tendered, there was no more doubt
of his intention to devise the whole estate than if he had used the
most unequivocal words to that effect, yet they said the rule was
inflexible, that, if the words, strictly interpreted, had a sensible
operation, their meaning ought not to be departed from.   So, in
Doe d. *Westlake* v. *Westlake* (2), a devise of an estate to " Matthew
Westlake, my brother, and unto Simon Westlake, my brother's
son,"—the testator had three brothers, each of whom had a
son, named Simon,—and evidence was tendered to prove that
the testator meant Simon, the son of his brother Richard ;
and the Court received the evidence.   Upon a motion for a
new trial, it was held, that, in strict construction, the Simon
who was meant must be the son of Matthew, the brother,
who was previously mentioned,—the last antecedent in the will ;
and the evidence which the Court below had received was
rejected.

The strongest cases upon this point are those which relate to
powers.   Before the late Statute of Wills came into operation,
it had repeatedly been decided, that, under a devise of " my real
estate," property of the testator subject to a power would pass, if
he had no real estate which would satisfy the devise ; and that
if there were any real estate belonging to the testator upon which   [*285]
the will could operate, it was otherwise.   *But a bequest of " all
my personal estate " was never held to pass property over which
the testator had only a power of appointment, because, as the will
would pass after-acquired personal estate, the words might possibly
have a sensible construction, without departing from their strict

(1) 16 R. R. 32 (4 Dow, 65).   (2) 22 R. R. 621 (4 B. & Ald. 57).

and primary meaning. The rule undoubtedly is, to ascertain, in the first place, whether the words can, with reference to the facts, have a sensible operation in their primary sense; and they must be construed in the primary sense, if the facts do not exclude it.

Suppose that, in the case before the Court, Elizabeth Whatton had afterwards married again, and had had a family of legitimate children,—it is possible to say that an illegitimate child would have been within the power? There is, in fact, nothing to show that the parties did not look to that event. The bill must, therefore, be dismissed.

BARKLEY v. LORD REAY.

1842.
June 11.
___
1843.
Jan. 27.
___
WIGRAM,
V.-C.
[306]

(2 Hare, 306—310.)

In a suit against the trustees of real estate, having the legal fee, and full powers of sale—the object being to raise a legacy charged on such estate—the legatee is not entitled to the appointment of a receiver where no default is attributable to the trustees.

ROBERT HOME GORDON, by his will, dated in 1812, devised his real and personal estate in Jamaica to the defendant Lord Reay and others, upon trust by sale or mortgage of all or any part thereof, to levy, raise and pay so much of his debts (except mortgage debts) and his funeral and testamentary expenses, and the legacies thereinafter bequeathed, as his other real and personal estate therein mentioned should not be sufficient to pay, and also upon trust to pay certain annuities; and, subject to such trusts, the testator directed that his trustees should permit Susan Harriet Hope to receive the rents, profits and produce of the said real and personal estate for her life, and after her decease levy, raise and pay certain other annuities therein mentioned; and upon further trust, within six months after the death of Susan Harriet Hope, to levy, raise and pay the sum of 5,000l. unto his cousin George Home Murray; and, subject to such trusts, the testator directed that his trustees should, after the decease of the said Susan Harriet Hope, convey and assure all such part or parts of the said real and personal estate in Jamaica as should not have been sold for any of the said purposes, to the use of Sir Orford Gordon and his assigns during his life, without impeachment of waste, with remainder to trustees to preserve contingent remainders, and remainder to the use of his first and other son and sons successively

in tail male, according to their priority of birth, with divers BARKLEY
v.
LORD REAY.
remainders over: and the testator declared, that the receipts of
the trustees, or the survivor of them, should be good and sufficient
discharges to the purchasers or mortgagees of any parts of the
said real *and personal estate in Jamaica; and he afterwards   [*307]
bequeathed several other legacies. The testator died in 1826: the
will was proved by Lord Reay. George Home Murray died in
1833, and bequeathed his legacy of 5,000*l.* to the plaintiffs, whom
he appointed his executrixes. Susan Harriet Hope died in July,
1839. The bill was filed against Lord Reay, the surviving trustee,
in whom the whole legal fee of the Jamaica estate had become vested,
Sir Orford Gordon, the equitable tenant for life, and his eldest son,
William Home Gordon, the equitable tenant in tail of the same
estate, and Margaret Mackenzie, an annuitant under the will,
praying that the legacy of 5,000*l.*, together with the other legacies
and annuities charged on the Jamaica estate, might be paid out
of the assets of the testator received by Lord Reay, or that it might
be raised and paid by sale or mortgage thereof, and that the
necessary accounts might be taken and a receiver appointed.
The bill also prayed, under the Order XXIII., of August, 1841,
that William Home Gordon and Margaret Mackenzie might, upon
being served with copies of the bill, be bound by all proceedings
in the cause.

The answer of Lord Reay stated that he did not know whether
the plaintiffs were or not the representatives of George Home
Murray, the legatee, but admitted that no part of the 5,000*l.* or
interest thereon had been raised or paid to the plaintiffs, and
stated the course which had been adopted in the management of
the estate, and that, in the year ending in May, 1840, there was
a balance of 184*l.* of the produce of the estate after payment of
the expenses: in the year ending May, 1841, the balance of the
expenses beyond the produce amounted to 2,920*l.*, and that he
believed the produce of the year 1842 would be greatly insufficient
to pay the charges and outgoings, and that at the end of the year
*there would be a large balance against the estate. The defendant   [*308]
said that he believed the 5,000*l.* could not, in the depreciated condition of property in Jamaica, be raised by mortgage thereon, and
he did not consider it prudent to sell the estate for the purpose
of raising it.

The plaintiffs moved for a receiver.   1842.
June 11.
——

BARKLEY
v.
LORD REAY.

Mr. *Roupell* and Mr. *Finelly*, for the motion, and Mr. *Sharpe* and Mr. *James Parker, contrà*.

The VICE-CHANCELLOR refused the motion, observing that there was no evidence of any improper management of the estate, and nothing to show that the appointment of a receiver or other consignee would probably be attended with any benefit to the estate. The bill in fact did not ascribe any mismanagement to Lord Reay, and the Court would not, at the instance of one of several parties interested in an estate, displace a competent trustee, or take the possession from him, unless he wilfully or ignorantly permitted the property to be placed in a state of insecurity, which due care or conduct would have prevented.

[The report further states that at the hearing upon the defendant objecting that William Home Gordon was a necessary party, the Vice-Chancellor said :]

1843.
Jan. 27.
—
[310]

THE VICE-CHANCELLOR :

The substantial purpose of the suit is to sell the settled estate, and that is direct relief against the tenant in tail, although the prayer may not express it in terms. The 23rd Order was not intended to apply to such a case. The object of the Order was to relieve suitors from the necessity of having numerous parties in the same interest, against whom no relief is prayed, uselessly appearing in the cause.

Liberty to amend by adding parties.

————

1841.
Dec. 14.
1843.
Jan. 18, 27, 31.

WIGRAM,
V.-C.
[310]

WHITAKER *v.* WRIGHT (1).

(2 Hare, 310—325 ; S. C. 12 L. J. Ch. 241 ; 7 Jur. 320.)

In the proof of a bond debt, before the Master, it is not the practice to require an affidavit of the consideration, unless a case of suspicion against the bond is raised.

Under a decree in a suit by a bond creditor on behalf of himself and the other creditors on the estate, the executor may, in the Master's office, impeach the validity of the bond upon grounds which were not in issue in the cause at the hearing.

THIS was a creditor's suit, instituted, in 1838, by William Whitaker (and afterwards revived by his executors) against the personal representatives of Strethill Wright, the younger, seeking payment of a debt alleged to be due on a bond, dated the 10th of

(1) *Cardell* v. *Hawke* (1868) L. R. 6 Eq. 464, 19 L. T. 47.

February, 1817, whereby P. W. Dumville, therein described as the   WHITAKER
principal debtor, and S. Wright, and the said Strethill Wright, the   *v.*
younger, became jointly and severally bound to the said William   WRIGHT.
Whitaker in the sum of 1,800*l.*, with a condition making void the
same on payment to him of 900*l.*, and lawful interest, on the 10th
of November then next. The bill stated, that, after deducting
certain dividends on the debt received under the bankruptcies *of   [*311]
Wright, the elder, and Dumville, the sum of 835*l.* still remained
due on the bond.

The defendants, by their answer, not admitting the debt, the
plaintiffs examined J. Roscoe, the attesting witness, and proved the
bond. The defendants exhibited cross-interrogatories, and examined
J. Roscoe as to the consideration for the bond.

At the hearing, the defendants insisted that the effect of the   1841.
evidence was to show that the transaction had been usurious, and   *Dec.* 14.
that a part of the alleged consideration had been returned to   ———
Whitaker by way of bonus. The plaintiffs contended that, no issue
on this point having been raised on the pleadings, the evidence
directed to it could not be taken into consideration, and that any
payment to Whitaker was at the utmost nothing more than an item
in the account of the debt which was to be taken: *Walker* v.
Woodward (1). The evidence was entered as read, and the common
decree in the suit of a specialty creditor was made.

The Master by his report stated the charge carried in by the
plaintiffs of the sum alleged to be due for principal and interest on
the bond, and also the contents of the bond, and that a state of facts
and counter-charge had been laid before him by the defendants,
wherein it was alleged that no good or sufficient consideration
passed between the parties for giving such bond, but that such bond
was made and executed to cover an usurious transaction between
William Whitaker and P. W. Dumville, and that the plaintiffs ought
to prove the consideration, and that the bond is in fact *void under   [*312]
the provisions of the statutes respecting usury, and that in support
of such counter state of facts and charge the deposition of the said
J. Roscoe had been produced and read; and on consideration of
such charges, and of the evidences laid before him in support
thereof respectively, he was of opinion that there was sufficient
ground for calling on the plaintiffs to prove the consideration of
the bond, and he accordingly requested them so to do; and the

(1) 25 R. R. 9 (1 Russ. 107).

plaintiffs having declined so to do, he had not thought fit to allow
the charge so brought in by them as a debt against the estate of
Strethill Wright the younger, until the consideration of such bond
should have been so proved as aforesaid, and no other debt having
been claimed before him in consequence of the advertisement, he
had not thought it necessary to proceed to take the accounts
directed to be taken by the said decree.

The plaintiffs excepted to the report, on the ground that they
ought not to be required to prove the consideration.

Mr. Romilly and *Mr. Follett*, for the plaintiffs, cited *Rundell* v.
Lord Rivers (1) [and other cases].

Mr. Temple and *Mr. Elmsley*, for the representatives of the
obligor, mentioned *Owens* v. *Dickenson* (2), *Ferrall* v. *Shaen* (3).

1843.
Jan. 31.

[*313]

THE VICE-CHANCELLOR :

The bill is filed by a plaintiff claiming to be a bond-creditor, *on
behalf of all the creditors of the obligor.   No issue, impeaching the
bond on the ground of usury, or any other ground which has been
since the subject of contest, was tendered by the answer of the
representatives of the obligor ; but, in the cross-examination of the
attesting witness to the bond, some evidence was given by him,
which the Master has since thought raised a suspicion against its
validity.   The decree made was nothing more than that which is
usual in a creditor's suit ; and the evidence, therefore, having no
effect on the decree, the formal admission of it was not objected to
on the part of the plaintiff, and it was accordingly received.   The
cause, when in the Master's office, assumed a different aspect ; for
the defendants, representing the debtor doing that which it is not
disputed in this case they had a right to do, have endeavoured to
show that the bond was founded upon an usurious contract or
consideration ; and have, by their state of facts, raised a question
in the office, which was not raised on the pleadings before the
Court.   The defendants gave in evidence the cross-examination,
which had been previously read in the cause, but which could not
then be noticed, inasmuch as it did not apply to any question in
issue on the pleadings.   The Master has not reported either for or
against the bond ; he has only refused to allow the debt against the

(1) 59 R. R. 586 (11 L. J. Ch. 27).   (3) 1 Wms. Saund. 294.
(2) 54 R. R. 195 (Cr. & Ph. 48).

estate until the consideration should be proved; and, in this state, WHITAKER
v.
WRIGHT. the case comes before me.

Two points were suggested in argument before me,—one was, as to the effect of the decree,—the other, as to what was the duty of the Master in the investigation of the case, as distinct from the question of the form of the decree.

With respect to the form of a decree in a creditors' suit,—the Court does not treat the decree as conclusive *proof of the debt. It [*314] is clear, that it is not so treated for all purposes; for any other creditor may challenge the debt, *Owens* v. *Dickenson* (1); and it is equally clear, that, in practice, the executor himself is allowed to impeach it. If, in a case where the plaintiff sues on behalf of himself and all the other creditors, and the defendants, who represent the estate, do not admit assets, it is objected, at the hearing, that the debt is not well proved,—the Court tries the question only whether there is sufficient proof upon which to found a decree; and, however clearly the debt may be proved in the cause, the decree decides nothing more than that the debt is sufficiently proved to entitle the plaintiff to go in to the Master's office; and a new case may be made in the Master's office, and new evidence may be there tendered. The real question is, in what way the new case is to be tried, or what is the course to be pursued in the Master's office?

[His Lordship then dealt with this question and in so doing referred at great length to the proceedings in *Rundell* v. *Lord Rivers* (2), and then continued as follows:]

It is manifest, therefore, that [in *Rundell* v. *Lord Rivers*] the [319] LORD CHANCELLOR did not mean to decide more than this; that the Master, who had admitted the bond debts as *good, refusing the [*320] opposite party the opportunity of impugning them, had miscarried in his judgment. The LORD CHANCELLOR decided nothing on the nature or effect of the evidence to be given,—as to which party should be called on to give evidence,—or on the course of the investigation. He decided only that the Master should have entertained the question, exercising his discretion in calling on the creditor to give, where the creditor is in a condition to do so, such evidence of the consideration of his debt as may be necessary to repel any adverse implication arising out of the case, as well in respect of debts on bond as by simple contract. I do not understand the LORD CHANCELLOR as deciding abstractedly that the validity of a

(1) 54 R. R. 195 (1 Cr. & Ph. 48).   (2) 59 R. R. 586 (11 L. J. Ch. 27).

debt in equity is to be investigated upon principles different from
that which would govern the right at law, or in a different manner.

In the case before me, the Master, proceeding upon the language
of the judgment in *Rundell* v. *Lord Rivers*, required some proof to
be given of the consideration, the creditor not suggesting any
difficulty in giving it, but simply refusing to do so. The Master
having required him to do something more than he had done, the
plaintiffs have at once concluded, that, in consequence of the
evidence elicited by the cross-examination of the attesting witness,
the Master would throw upon the obligee the *onus* of proving a
negative, and of showing that the consideration of the bond was not
usurious. I have the Master's authority for saying that he had no
such intention, and that he had decided only, upon the authority
of *Rundell* v. *Lord Rivers*, that he was bound to ascertain the
validity of the bond, not deciding what the creditor should do.

Without attempting to define the limits of the discretion given to
the Master, and not admitting the conclusion that *Rundell* v. *Lord

[*321] Rivers* has reversed the *legal position of the parties, or that such
position is in fact altered, I am forced in this case to send the cause
back again to the Master ; for if I were to allow the exceptions, the
case must go again to the Master, in order that the defendants
might have an opportunity of making that defence to the bond
which they have not hitherto been called upon to make, in
consequence of the Master having required something more of the
plaintiffs. If I overrule the exceptions, I must also remit the case
back to the Master, for he has not decided that the bond may not
constitute a good charge against the estate.

Remit the case to the Master to review his report (not allowing
the exception), and reserve the costs.

1848.
Feb. 15, 16, 17,
18, 24.

WIGRAM,
V.-C.

[326]

DU VIGIER *v.* LEE.

(2 Hare, 326—341; S. C. 12 L. J. Ch. 345 ; 7 Jur. 299.)

The price of redeeming the mortgaged premises is the same in a suit by
the mortgagor to redeem as it would be in the like circumstances in a suit
by the mortgagee to foreclosure.

If the debt and interest are secured only by the mortgage, the mortgagee
is entitled to no more than six years' arrear of interest, *semble.*

[THIS case was partly overruled by *Hunter* v. *Nockolds* (1850)
1 Mac. & G. 640, and in further part by *Heath* v. *Pugh* (1881)
6 Q. B. D. 345, affirmed, 7 App. Cas. 235, and the principal point

decided in the case is now superseded by 37 & 38 Vict. c. 57, s. 8 : see
In re Frisby (1889) 43 Ch. Div. 106, 59 L. J. Ch. 94, 61 L. T. 632.
The only part of the judgment remaining untouched which appears
to be of possible utility is the following general observation, which
is independent of the facts of the case.—O. A. S.

THE VICE-CHANCELLOR, in the course of his judgment, said :]

I think, that in order to determine the price of redemption upon   [335]
a bill to redeem a mortgage, the Court ought to inquire what the
terms of redemption would be in a suit to recover the mortgage-
money out of or by means of the charge upon the land ; and if, on
the result of that inquiry, the Court should find that in a suit for
foreclosure, or other suit seeking to affect the land, no more than
six years' interest would be recoverable by the mortgagee, I think it
would be bound to fix the same limit in determining the price of the
redemption in a suit to redeem. So far I feel bound to reject, or
at least not to found my judgment upon, the arguments which
have been relied upon by the plaintiffs.

JONES *v.* HOWELLS.

(2 Hare, 342—354 ; S. C. 12 L. J. Ch. 365 ; affirmed, 15 L. J. Ch. 115.)

A party suing as executor or administrator cannot sustain proceedings to
recover a larger sum than that upon which the probate duty is calculated.

[UPON the point mentioned in the above head-note the VICE-
CHANCELLOR said :]

I should not now advert to it, if it had not been stated in argu-   [354]
ment that the practice of the VICE-CHANCELLOR OF ENGLAND was to
allow a cause to proceed where it appeared that the stamp was paid
in respect of a smaller sum than that which was in question in the
cause, but to compel the parties to procure the larger stamp before
payment of the fund which might be recovered. I find upon inquiry
that this is not the practice in that branch of the Court ; and that
the rule laid down by Lord BROUGHAM in *Killock* v. *Greg*, requiring
the party to show that he represents the estate to a sufficient
amount to cover his claim, is the rule of that branch of the
Court.

1843.
Jan. 18, 17,
25.

Wigram,
V.-C.

[355]

HILLERSDON *v.* LOWE.

(2 Hare, 355—372; S. C. 12 L. J. Ch. 321; 7 Jur. 482.)

Where the words introducing a testamentary gift in remainder are repugnant to the previous gifts and to the general scheme of the will, and introduce a capricious and irrational construction which may lead to an intestacy, the Court may modify or reject those words.

The testator, John Hillersdon, by his will, dated in 1806, after giving to J. Lowe and another all his real and personal estate and effects (not otherwise thereby disposed of), declared the trusts thereof as follows :

Upon trust, during the life of my nephew John Grove, to pay the rents and annual interest thereof unto John Grove; and after his death, in case he shall leave issue one or more son or sons, then to apply the rents and annual interest thereof in the maintenance of such son of John Grove, as for the time being shall be the eldest son or only son of John Grove, until such eldest son or only son shall attain the age of twenty-one years, and when such eldest son or only son of John Grove shall attain the age of twenty-one years, then to convey, assign, transfer, and pay my said real and personal estate unto such eldest son or only son; but in case John Grove shall leave no son who shall survive him and live to attain the age of twenty-one years, then, during the life of my second nephew Joseph Grove, to pay the rents and annual interest of my said real and personal estate unto Joseph Grove; and after the death of Joseph Grove, in case Joseph John Grove, the son of Joseph Grove, shall happen to survive Joseph Grove, his father, then to pay the rents and annual interest of my real and personal estate unto Joseph

[*356] John *Grove, the son, during his life; and after the decease of the survivor of them, Joseph Grove, the father, and Joseph John Grove, the son, in case Joseph John Grove, the son, shall leave one or more son or sons who shall survive the survivor of them, Joseph Grove and Joseph John Grove, the son, then to apply the rents and annual interest thereof in the maintenance of such son of Joseph John Grove, the son, as for the time being shall be the eldest son of, or only son of Joseph John Grove, the son, until such eldest son or only son shall attain the age of twenty-one years, and when such eldest son or only son shall attain the age of twenty-one years, to convey, assign, transfer, and pay my said real and personal estate unto such eldest son or only son of Joseph John Grove, the son; but in case Joseph John Grove, the son, shall die in the lifetime of Joseph Grove, the father, without leaving issue male, who shall

survive Joseph Grove, the father, and live to attain the age of HILLERSDON
twenty-one years, and Joseph Grove, the father, shall die, leaving   *v.*
other issue one or more son or sons, then to apply the rents and   LOWE.
annual interest of my real and personal estate in the maintenance
of such son of Joseph Grove, the father, as for the time being shall
be the eldest son or only son of Joseph Grove, the father, until such
eldest son or only son shall attain the age of twenty-one years, and
when such eldest son or only son shall attain the age of twenty-one
years, then to convey, assign, transfer, and pay my real and personal estate unto such eldest son or only son ; but in case none of
them John Grove, Joseph Grove, the father, and Joseph John Grove,
the son, shall happen to leave any son or sons who shall survive the
survivor of them John Grove, Joseph Grove, and Joseph John Grove,
and live to attain the age of twenty-one years, then, during the life
of my third nephew Henry Grove, to pay the rents and annual
interest of my real and personal estate *unto Henry Grove ; and   [*357]
after the death of Henry Grove, in case he shall leave issue one or
more son or sons, then to apply the rents and annual interest thereof
in the maintenance of such son of Henry Grove, as for the time being
shall be the eldest son or only son of Henry Grove, until such eldest
son or only son of Henry Grove shall attain the age of twenty-one
years, and when such eldest son or only son of Henry Grove shall
attain the age of twenty-one years, then to convey, assign, transfer,
and pay my real and personal estate until such eldest son or only
son ; but in case none of them John Grove, Joseph Grove, Joseph
John Grove, and Henry Grove, shall happen to leave any son or
sons who shall survive the survivor of them John Grove, Joseph
Grove, Joseph John Grove, and Henry Grove, and shall live to
attain the age of twenty-one years, and John Grove shall leave
issue one or more daughter or daughters, who shall survive the
survivor of them John Grove, Joseph Grove, Joseph John Grove,
and Henry Grove, then from and after the death of the survivor of
them John Grove, Joseph Grove, Joseph John Grove, and Henry
Grove, and of their issue male under the age of twenty-one years,
to pay all the rents and annual interest of my real and personal
estate for the maintenance of such daughter of John Grove, as for
the time being shall be the eldest daughter or only daughter of
John Grove, until such eldest daughter or only daughter shall
attain the age of twenty-one years ; and when such eldest daughter
or only daughter shall attain the age of twenty-one years, then to
convey, assign, transfer, and pay my real and personal estate unto

'[*358]

such eldest daughter or only daughter ; but in case there shall be
no such issue female of John Grove, then, from and after the
decease of the survivor of them John Grove, Joseph Grove, Joseph
John Grove, and Henry Grove, and of their issue *male under the
age of twenty-one years, to pay all the rents and annual interest of
my real and personal estate for the maintenance of such daughter
of Joseph Grove, as for the time being shall be the eldest daughter
or only daughter of Joseph Grove, until such eldest daughter or only
daughter shall attain the age of twenty-one years; and when such
eldest daughter shall attain the age of twenty-one years, then to
convey, assign, transfer, and pay my real and personal estate unto
such eldest daughter or only daughter of Joseph Grove; but in case
there shall be no issue female of Joseph Grove, then from and after
the decease of the survivor of them John Grove, Joseph Grove,
Joseph John Grove, and Henry Grove, and of their issue male
under the age of twenty-one years, to pay all the rents and annual
interest of my real and personal estate for the maintenance of such
daughter of Joseph John Grove, as for the time being shall be the
eldest daughter or only daughter of Joseph John Grove, until such
eldest daughter or only daughter shall attain the age of twenty-one
years ; and when such eldest daughter or only daughter shall attain
the age of twenty-one years, then to convey, assign, transfer, and
pay my real and personal estate unto such eldest or only daughter
of Joseph John Grove ; but in case there shall be no issue female of
Joseph John Grove, then from and after the decease of the survivor
of them John Grove, Joseph Grove, Joseph John Grove, and Henry
Grove, and of their issue male under the age of twenty-one years,
to pay all the rents and annual interest of my real and personal
estate for the maintenance of such daughter of Henry Grove, as
for the time being shall be the eldest daughter or only daughter of
Henry Grove, until such eldest or only daughter shall attain the
age of twenty-one years; and when such eldest or only daughter

[*359]

shall attain the age of twenty-one years, then *to convey, assign,
transfer, and pay my real and personal estate unto such eldest or
only daughter of Henry Grove.

The testator then proceeded to direct that John Grove, Joseph
Grove, Joseph John Grove and Henry Grove and their issue male
and the husbands of their issue female, entitled to the rents and
annual interest or to the conveyance and assignment of the real
and personal estate, should, within twelve months after so becoming
entitled, take the name and arms of Hillersdon, or in default thereof

that the person or persons who would be entitled in case the person or persons neglecting the same were then dead, should, upon complying with such directions, take and receive the said rents, interest, or conveyance and assignment in the same manner as if the person or persons neglecting to take and use the same was or were then dead without issue, and he gave and devised and bequeathed the same accordingly.

The testator then proceeded, "But in case none of them, John Grove, Joseph Grove, Joseph John Grove and Henry Grove shall happen to leave issue male or female who shall survive the survivor of John Grove, Joseph Grove, Joseph John Grove and Henry Grove, and live to attain the age of twenty-one years, or if they John Grove, Joseph Grove, Joseph John Grove, and Henry Grove or their issue, when and as they shall respectively become entitled to the rents and annual interest, or to a conveyance, assignment and transfer of my real and personal estate, or within twelve months afterwards, shall omit, neglect, or decline to take and use my name and arms in the manner hereinbefore directed, then upon trust, and I give, devise and bequeath my said real and personal estate and effects unto and amongst all and every of my nieces, the daughter and daughters of my sister Louisa Grove, and all and *every the child and children male and female of such my nieces [*360] who shall be living at the time of my death, and to his, her, and their heirs, executors and administrators for ever, equally share and share alike, to take as tenants in common, and not as joint tenants, and I direct my trustees, &c., to convey, assign, transfer and pay the same accordingly." And he appointed his said trustees, and John Grove, his executors.

The testator died in 1807, leaving the said John, Joseph, Joseph John and Henry, and also some daughters of Louisa, surviving. The residuary estate of the testator consisted of freehold, copyhold, and leasehold estates, and of stock in the public funds. John Grove took the name and arms of Hillersdon, and received the rents and interest until his death. He died in 1839, leaving the plaintiff, his only son (who had previously attained his age of twenty-one) surviving. The bill was filed by the plaintiff after the death of his father, praying that the trustees might be decreed absolutely to convey, surrender, and assign the said estates unto the use of the plaintiff, his heirs, executors, administrators, and assigns respectively, and to transfer the said stock to him, for his own use and benefit.

At the hearing the question arose whether the two nephews, Joseph Grove and Joseph John Grove, were necessary parties to the suit, and the case was argued, first, on the point of parties, and then, by direction of the Court, on the construction of the will.

Mr. Kenyon Parker and *Mr. Haldane*, for the plaintiff. * * *

[361]   *Mr. Koe, Mr. Roupell, Mr. Lovat, Mr. Campbell, Mr. Bacon, Mr. Wood, Mr. Renshaw, Mr. Grove,* and *Mr. Wilkinson,* appeared for the several defendants.

[The arguments of counsel sufficiently appear in the judgment. *Lord Stamford* v. *Hobart* (1), *Papillon* v. *Voice* (2), *Jenkins* v. *Herries* (3), and other cases were cited, but were not referred to in the judgment.]

THE VICE-CHANCELLOR :

The plaintiff, in this case, claims an absolute interest in the estates which are the subject of the gift, upon the ground that he has performed the two conditions which are annexed to such gift to him—one being that he should survive his father, John Grove, and the other that he should attain the age of twenty-one. The plaintiff relies upon the simple words which, he contends, direct that, in case he should attain twenty-one and survive his father, the trustees shall convey to him the real estate in fee. On the other hand, the special words used in the will to describe the event on which other parties are to take, are relied upon as excluding the absolute interest of the plaintiff. The defendants have argued that although the plaintiff, surviving his father and attaining twenty-one, has acquired some present interest in the property, yet, in the event of his not surviving the survivor of the three, or in the event of no son of some one of them surviving the survivor of the three, the estate is given over. The persons interested in this view of the question are Henry,—any son *Henry may have,—the daughters, if any, of John Grove, Joseph Grove, and Joseph John Grove, and, lastly, the daughters of Louisa, to whom the estate is given by the ultimate limitations in the will, provided others do not take.

[*362]

In order to explain the view which I take of this case, I shall first advert to that clause which, as I have said, describes the event on which Henry is to take ; and without saying what the construction

(1) 3 Br. P. C. 31.   (3) 20 R. R. 272 (4 Madd. 82).
(2) 2 P. Wms. 471.

of that clause taken with the whole will is, I think it can admit HILLERSDON
of no doubt (and, in fact, it was conceded in argument), that if the LOWE.
words which describe the events upon which the gift to Henry is to
take effect were omitted, the direction to the trustees to convey,
transfer, assign, and pay the real and personal estate of the testator
to the first son of John who should survive his father, and attain
twenty-one, is sufficient to give and would give to such son of John
an absolute interest in the real and personal estate. I think it is
equally clear, that, if the words which describe the event upon
which the gift to Henry is to take effect stood alone, these words
would entitle Henry to claim an interest in the testator's estate,
unless a son of any one of his three nephews, John, Joseph, and
Joseph John, should survive the survivor of such three nephews,
and attain the age of twenty-one. The plaintiff, however, says
that, taking the latter clause, not alone, but in connection with the
whole will, the intention is clearly expressed that the trustees are
to convey, assign, and pay the real and personal estate absolutely
to a son of John, surviving him, and attaining twenty-one, and that
such conveyance, assignment, and payment will supersede all the
subsequent directions in the will. He says that the gifts to Joseph
and Joseph John, and their sons, are made by way of substitution
of the estate given to him, the plaintiff, only in case John Grove
*should leave no son who should survive him, and live to attain   [*363]
twenty-one; and that, inasmuch as that event has happened, the
gift to Joseph, and the other parties, can never take effect, and that
the estate to himself has therefore become absolute. He contends,
in effect, that the scheme of the will is to retain the estate in the
hands of the trustees until such son of John should take, or, failing
such son, until some other person, described in the will, should be
entitled to call for a conveyance or assignment, and that the first
person who should so become entitled was intended to take the
estate absolutely.

I am clearly of opinion with the plaintiff, upon the gifts in the
will preceding that to Henry, unless the clause describing the
events upon which Henry is to take is sufficient to control the
antecedent words of the will. The plaintiff's construction is
according to the natural import and effect of the words of the will,
and is fortified by the consideration that the direction to the
trustees to convey and assign to different persons mentioned in the
will, necessarily supposes that no conveyance or assignment can
have been previously executed. The difficulty of the plaintiff is in

HILLERSDON reconciling his construction with the clause which, according to
v.   the defendants' argument, gives the estate over to Henry in the
LOWE.   event specified.

Upon the question what effect (if any) that clause should have
upon the gift to the plaintiff, different views have been presented
to me by different parties opposing the plaintiff's claim to an
absolute interest.   All agree in contending that the plaintiff's
construction of the will is erroneous; but they differ widely in their
views of what its effect should be.   On behalf of the sisters of the
[*364]   plaintiff, it has been contended that the *clause in question reduces
the plaintiff's interest to an estate for life, giving estates in
remainder for life, by implication, to Joseph and Joseph John, in
the event of the plaintiff's dying in the lifetime of Joseph and
Joseph John, and of the survivor of them, and requiring the Court
to respite the conveyance, assignment, and payment, which the
will directs, during the lives of Joseph and Joseph John, and the
survivor.

On the other hand, Henry, and the children of Louisa and other
parties opposing the plaintiff, have admitted that the plaintiff is
entitled to call for a conveyance and transfer of the entire interest,
but contend that the instrument of conveyance should contain a
proviso for determining the plaintiff's interest in the event of the
son of any of the three nephews surviving the survivor of them,
and attaining twenty-one; and that the Court must secure the
personal estate until the event shall be determined.   On this point,
with respect to which the defendants thus differ, I have no hesitation in saying I think the argument, which requires me to give the
plaintiff a life estate only, and to imply life estates to Joseph and
Joseph John, and to respite the conveyance, assignment, and payment, cannot be supported.   The direction to convey and transfer,
taken alone, is (as I have already intimated) a direction to pass the
absolute interest.   Construing that direction according to the legal
as well as natural import of the words, it must carry the entire
interest.   What is there to limit the plaintiff's estate to an estate
for life?   His death will not give the estate over.   It is given over,
not on his death, but only in case none of the nephews named
should have a son surviving such three nephews.   His estate, the
defendants admit, may continue after his own death, and ultimately
become absolute, by reason of one of the sons surviving the survivor
[*365]   of the nephews.   And if I should *give a life interest only to the
plaintiff, and he should die, leaving Joseph or Joseph John, upon

what principle can I give life estates in remainder to them by   HILLERSDON
implication? The testator has given them express estates, not by   *v.*
way of remainder, but in case John Grove shall leave no son who   LOWE.
shall survive him and attain twenty-one years of age. Nor, if I
were to give the plaintiff a life estate only, is there any thing in the
will to carry the estate to any other person during the lives of
Joseph and Joseph John and the survivor, if either of them should
outlive the plaintiff. Again, if I respite the conveyance, assignment, and payment during the lives of Joseph and Joseph John,
what interest can the plaintiff claim in the interval? There is no
gift to him except in the direction to convey, assign, transfer, and
pay. The effect of the argument I am now considering would,
therefore, be to create intestacies, against which the will itself
provides. And why should I do this? If the testator, according
to the true construction of his will, has given his estate to Henry,
and a son of Henry, in the event of the plaintiff, or some other son
of one of the three nephews not surviving them,—why should the
Court depart from the mode of giving effect to this intention, in the
manner pointed out by the will, namely, by executory devise, and
which, if the intention be made out, is effectual for the purpose,
and avoids the inconvenience which the contrary argument would
introduce. Admitting that, according to the construction I have
suggested, there may be some contingencies in some events not
fully provided for, there is nothing in that aspect of the case to
justify the Court in giving a preference to the defendants' argument.

The observations I have made have been applied only to the
clause descriptive of the event upon which Henry, and a son of
Henry, are to take; but they apply to each *successive clause in   [*366]
the will, in which the estate is given over in terms similar (*mutatis
mutandis*). I conclude, therefore, that the plaintiff is entitled to a
conveyance of the whole interest, and that he is entitled now to call
for such conveyance; and the only question is, whether it is to be
absolute or subject to an executory limitation over, in the event of
there being no son of any of the three nephews surviving them,—
the Court, in the latter case, securing the personal estate until the
event shall be determined.

Now, I do not mean to deny the right of a testator to be
capricious in the disposition of his property, but where a plain,
simple, and rational scheme for the disposition of property, is
made by a testator in one part of his will, and a clause (certainly
not of inflexible construction) afterwards occurs, which, according

to one construction of it, subverts that scheme, and disappoints the
primary objects of the testator's bounty; and that, without any
cause assigned by the testator, or discoverable by the ingenuity of
counsel, it is clearly the duty of the Court to examine it with care,
and to see whether, by any reasonable construction, of which its
words are fairly susceptible, it may not be reconcilable with that
scheme of the will, about which, when separately considered, no
question can arise.   In this case the intention ascribed to the
testator by the defendants' argument is most capricious and
irrational.   I will take a single example.   The objects of the
testator's bounty are,—1st, John; 2nd, sons of John; 3rd, Joseph;
4th, Joseph John; 5th, sons of Joseph John; 6th, Henry; and
7th, Henry and his male issue.   Now, any thing which, upon the
failure of an estate given to one of those, should give the estate
over to the other next in succession is intelligible; but a clause,
which arbitrarily determines the estate of any of them, without

[*367]   reference to the interest *of the others, must excite a doubt as to
the accuracy of the expression, unless that expression be very
clear and precise.   The plaintiff, next to John, was the first object
of the testator's bounty.   By the events of surviving his father
and attaining twenty-one, he becomes entitled to the estate: but of
necessity he excludes all the other nephews.   The plaintiff, I will
suppose, has a family; he calls for and obtains a conveyance of
the estate, which the trustees are directed to make,—he dies,
leaving a family and Joseph and Joseph John surviving him.
Now, what is the effect of the conveyance?   Does his death
determine his estate?   Certainly not.   Nothing can be more clear
than that, if an estate be given to a person, with a limitation over
on a certain event, the first estate is absolute, unless that event
happens.   Notwithstanding the plaintiff dies, the estate remains in
his family, and will go either to his heir-at-law, or to his devisee,
or in any way in which he may dispose of it, subject only to the
question, whether it will not go over according to the devise in the
events described by that which is stated, as being an executory
limitation.   The death of the plaintiff in the lifetime of Joseph, or
Joseph John, does not therefore, in this view, determine the
plaintiff's estate; but a certain event may happen which would
determine it, and that not in favour of any of the objects who
come next in the distribution of the testator's bounty.   The estate
would continue as part of the plaintiff's estate, until it was seen
whether a son of John, other than the plaintiff, or a son of Joseph,

or a son of Joseph John, should survive the survivor of the three HILLERSDON
nephews, and attain the age of twenty-one; in that case the estate LOWE.
will not go over to Henry, but will remain absolute in the plaintiff.
The proposition is not that the plaintiff must himself survive
Joseph and Joseph John, in order that the estate may become
absolute, but that some one of the excluded parties may *do so,   [*368]
and that will give him the estate absolutely.   The question
whether the plaintiff's estate is to become absolute is not made to
depend on whether he himself shall survive them, but whether one
of those persons who cannot, by any possibility, touch the estate at
all, shall survive them.   I think it is quite impossible that could
have been the intention of the testator.   He could not have
intended that the interest of the plaintiff in the estate should be
contingent on persons surviving the survivor of the three nephews,
where the persons so surviving were not only to take nothing in
the estate on the happening of that event, but whose chance of
succession to the estate was for ever excluded by the events which
had happened.

The only question is, whether the testator has left light enough
in this case to guide the Court in endeavouring to preserve his real
intention.   In order to get at his meaning, I have gone back to the
clause in which the form of expression, on which the question
arises, occurs for the first time.   It is in the devise to the eldest son
of Joseph John (1),—" after the decease of the survivor of them,
Joseph Grove, the father, and Joseph John Grove, the son, in case
Joseph John Grove, the son, shall leave one or more son or sons
who shall survive the survivor of them, Joseph Grove, the father,
and Joseph John Grove, the son."   The expression is there very
accurate, Joseph and Joseph John take only life estates : and the
testator did not by the form of expression interfere with any estate
previously given.   He then proceeds in like manner, substituting
one estate for another to the sons of Joseph, and the sons of Joseph
John, contingently upon their surviving individuals named, and
attaining the age of twenty-one, provided those individuals *do not   [*369]
themselves become entitled to the estates, but not otherwise ; and
in no case does the estate given contingently to any of these parties
interfere with any estate previously given, until he arrives at the
clause describing the event in which the estate is given to Henry.
And I may observe that throughout the will the same care is taken
not to interfere with one estate by the substitution of another for

(1) *Supra*, p. 126.

it, except where the testator uses the expression, "survive the survivor," which occurs in the clause I am now considering. Adverting to this, and to the use first made of that form of expression, I cannot but think that the testator, in the clause describing the events in which Henry was to take, has intended only to describe the failure of the previous contingent gifts in the will.

The testator had so disposed of his property that there could be no intestacy, unless none of the three sons should leave a son who should survive him, and attain the age of twenty-one. If any one of the three left a son surviving him, and who attained the age of twenty-one, the property was completely disposed of; and the testator had then only to dispose of the property in the event of none of the three having left a son who should survive his father, and attain the age of twenty-one. Now, at the time of making the will, John, Joseph, and Joseph John, were all living, and it was uncertain in what order they would die: but, according to the contingent dispositions, the survivor of them, whoever he might be, might have a son, who, by surviving him, and attaining twenty-one, would become entitled to the estate. The testator then addressing himself by anticipation to this case of intestacy,— to a state of things not existing at the time of the will, that is, assuming some two of his nephews to have died without having left a son who should attain twenty-one, and that the survivor, whoever *he might be, had also died without leaving a son who should survive him, and attain twenty-one,—makes use of the language on which the question arises,—language which would be accurate if the events had actually happened, which the testator supposes, but is certainly not accurate without that explanation. The testator's meaning is, if all his three nephews should die without leaving a son who should survive his parent, and attain twenty-one, then the estate should go to Henry.

[*370]

I think I am justified in giving this construction to the will, on several grounds: The opposite construction is capricious and irrational; and it subverts that scheme of the will, which is expressed in clear and unambiguous language in all other parts of it; it would also render the direction to the trustees to convey, transfer, and pay, except in a single instance, incapable of execution; whereas it is capable of complete execution upon the principle that the estates are given by way of substitution. There is also the theory which I have founded on the antecedent language,—that the

testator himself supposes events to have happened which have not
taken place, and has, therefore, contemplated a state of things
which does not exist.   I may mention another ground, which
though of little weight alone, yet fortifies this view of the case,—
when the testator comes to the limitations to daughters he refers to
his former disposition, and describes the events which would leave
the estates undisposed of, as occurring " after the decease of the
survivor of them, the said John, Joseph John, and Henry, and of
their issue male under the age of twenty-one." After a gift to issue
coming within a special description, a reference to such issue, by
the general term of issue male, would, on the general rule of
construction, be regarded merely as an *inaccurate reference to   [*371]
what had gone before, and meaning the same thing; but I am
satisfied that the testator here meant to describe the estates, which
he supposed he had previously given in certain events ; and that he
intended to point out that the taking effect of the estates he was
then giving depended on the failure of issue male of the three
nephews attaining twenty-one.

In giving to this will the construction that I feel bound to give,
and according to which the plaintiff takes an absolute interest,
the testator's unequivocal directions,—that the trustees shall
convey, assign, transfer, and pay over the real and personal
estate,—have their full effect, which, if the opposite construction
were admitted, they could not have. I give those estates to the
persons,—in the order,—upon the contingencies,—and for the
estates and interests mentioned in the will, according to the
literal and proper import of the words. I do this with reference
to those parts of the will which contain the primary intentions
of the testator, in which the directions are simple, and the purpose
is clear; and in which, therefore, the chance of his having failed
correctly to express his meaning is the least. In giving effect to
this part of the will, I avoid the intestacies and incongruities which
I have pointed out as the consequences of the construction urged
by the defendants, and I modify the testator's words in that part
of his will in which his directions are the most complex, and the
chance of inaccuracy of expression is therefore greatest. Language,
which I cannot give effect to in its literal import, without imputing
to the testator the most capricious, if not inconsistent, intentions,
I modify—so as to avoid those consequences—but without any
direct violence to the clause in which that language is found.
Admitting that, between two inconsistent clauses in a will, the

last should prevail, it is a sound rule of construction, that *an intention plainly declared shall not be avoided by subsequent words of doubtful import, which are not necessarily irreconcilable with the intention first expressed.

The difficulty arises, in this case, from a cause which is fertile in producing litigation. If a testator, having made a disposition of his property on a certain event, would be content with simply saying that, "failing that gift," he gave it over to some ulterior object of bounty, or if he would repeat in terms what he had said before, he would seldom fail in effecting his intention. The difficulties commonly occur when, after making a disposition of a complicated nature, the testator, intending to make another disposition if the first should fail, but neither simply stating that intention, nor taking the pains to repeat the exact words, endeavours to give an abstract of the former gift. The want of correspondence between the words describing the limitations over, and those which define the previous estates, is a source of numerous suits, although morally the intention is clear,—being, in point of fact, only to give the estate over in the event of the previous limitation not taking effect; and the whole tendency of the modern decisions is so to construe them. In the case of *Ellicombe* v. *Gompertz* (1), the gift was to particular grandchildren, and failing all grandchildren, then over; but Lord COTTENHAM construed the latter gift as a mere inaccurate mode of referring to the former.

I am of opinion that the plaintiff is entitled to take the estates absolutely, and the decree must be to that effect.

1843.
Feb. 20, 27,
28.

WIGRAM,
V.-C.

[373]

BURGE v. BRUTTON.

(2 Hare, 373—380; S. C. 12 L. J. Ch. 368; 7 Jur. 988.)

An executor who acts as solicitor in a cause, in which he is a party in his representative character, though he is only allowed personally, as against the estate, such costs as he actually pays, held entitled to be allowed, as against the estate, that proportion of the whole costs which his town agent in the cause was entitled to receive.

The representative of a deceased executor, in accounting for the executor's receipts of the trust estate,—held not to be entitled, by way of discharge, to the amount of a debt owing to the executor and his partner jointly from his testator, without evidence of retainer of the debt by the executor

(1) 45 R. R. 234 (3 My. & Cr. 127).

in his lifetime: the amount can only be claimed as a debt against the   BURGE
estate (1).   *v.*
An executor is not entitled to be allowed the costs of a suit in respect of   BRUTTON.
the estate, prosecuted by a solicitor whom he did not employ : the solicitor
himself is the party to apply for costs, as a lien on the fund which he has
recovered.

ELEANOR CORNETT, by her will, made in 1814, appointed John
Brutton and another, her executors. Brutton was in partnership
with Mr. H. M. Ford, as solicitor, at Exeter, and they were the
solicitors of the testatrix.   The testatrix died in 1816, and her will
was proved by Brutton alone, the other executor having renounced.
At the time of the death of the testatrix, a suit for redemption
(*Chaplin* v. *Cornett*) was pending against her ; and after her death,
Brutton, as her personal representative, was made a party to the
suit by revivor.   Brutton and Ford continued to act as solicitors in
the defence of the suit, and in the other business of the testatrix's
estate, until 1818, when Brutton became, from illness, incapable
of transacting business.   In 1820, the family of Brutton entered
into an arrangement with Ford, by which the latter became the
purchaser of Brutton's share in the partnership business.   Ford
thenceforward acted as solicitor for the defendant in the suit.
Brutton died in 1827, and administration, with his will annexed,
was granted to the defendant Margaret Brutton, his daughter.
Margaret Brutton then entered into possession of the property
of the testatrix, including that which was the subject of the
redemption suit, and she was made a party to that suit by
supplement.

The present bill was filed in 1832, by one of the residuary
legatees, who was also administrator *de bonis non* of the testatrix,
for an account of her estate received by Brutton, and by the
defendant.   The accounts were decreed *to be taken.   The defen-   [*374]
dant claimed, by way of discharge, the amount of two bills of
costs : 1st. The bill of defendant Margaret Brutton's solicitor,
against the representatives of the testatrix, from 1808 to 1832,
72*l.* 1*s.* 6*d.*   2nd. The bill of defendant's solicitor, in the suits
Chaplin v. *Cornett; Same* v. *Brutton; Same* v. *M. Brutton,*
341*l.* 6*s.* 11*d.*   The Master disallowed both of these bills of costs.
The defendant excepted to the report.

The exceptions depended on the following questions: 1st.
Whether the Master ought not to have allowed so much of the

(1) *Talbot* v. *Frere* (1878) 9 Ch. D.,   Q. B. 347, 68 L. J. Q. B. 804, 80 L. T.
see p. 575; *In re Rhoades* [1899] 2   742, C. A.

BURGK
c.
BRUTTON.

bills of costs as was due from the testatrix to Brutton and Ford, her solicitors, at the time of her death, which amounted to about 30*l.* 2nd. Admitting that Brutton, being the executor, could not charge the testatrix's estate with costs to himself: *Moore* v. *Frowd* (1), or to himself and his partner Ford: *Collins* v. *Carey* (2) ; yet, inasmuch as, being solicitors practising in the country, they were obliged to employ a town agent,—whether the Master ought not,—from the death of the testatrix until January, 1821, when the agreement, dissolving the partnership between Brutton and Ford, took effect,—to have allowed, besides other sums actually paid out of pocket, a moiety of the costs in the suits, being the proportion which it is the custom for the town agent to receive. 3rd. Whether the Master ought not, after the dissolution of partnership between

[*375]   Brutton and Ford, to have *allowed so much of the defendant's claim as consisted of the bills of costs of Mr. Ford alone.

Mr. Simpkinson and *Mr. Prior* supported the exceptions.

Mr. Temple, Mr. Lovat, and *Mr. Walpole,* in support of the Master's report.

On the first point, the costs incurred in the testatrix's lifetime, the plaintiff contended that, if the defendant had any claim on this ground, it ought to have been made in her capacity as executrix of Brutton, or by Ford, as a debt due from the testatrix's estate, and not by way of discharge: that it could not be claimed in discharge, unless it had been retained by Brutton in his lifetime, of which retainer there was no evidence.   The defendant contended that such retainer ought to be presumed.   [*Layfield* v. *Layfield* (3), *Padget* v. *Priest* (4), *Curtis* v. *Vernon* (c), *Loomes* v. *Stothard* (6), *Player* v. *Foxhall* (7), and other cases, were also cited.]

THE VICE-CHANCELLOR:

A claim was made by the defendant Margaret Brutton to have an allowance made to her in respect of certain costs which she insists had either been paid by, or by the estate of, her intestate, Brutton, or which that estate was liable to pay.   It does not

[*376]   distinctly appear *whether there had been any payment, or whether it was merely a question of liability.   These costs extended over

(1) 45 R. R. 205 (3 My. & Cr. 45).   (5) 1 R. R. 774 (3 T. R. 587).
(2) 50 R. R. 124 (2 Beav. 128).   (6) 24 R. R. 209 (1 Sim. & St. 458).
(3) 40 R. R. 91 (7 Sim. 172).   (7) 25 R. R. 133 (1 Russ. 538).
(4) 1 R. R. 440 (2 T. R. 97).

many years, and have been considered with reference to the circumstances existing during three distinct periods. The first period
was in the lifetime of the testatrix. Brutton was a partner with
Ford; and they, in the lifetime of the testatrix, acted as her
solicitors, and a sum of 30*l.*, or thereabouts, became due from her
to the two. The Master disallowed this claim. The argument on
behalf of Margaret Brutton was, that, inasmuch as Brutton was the
executor of the testatrix, he had a right to retain this debt, and
therefore, in the way of retainer, it ought to have been allowed in
discharge of his estate. Now it appeared,—in fact it was the case
of Margaret Brutton to say,—that from January, 1821, the partnership between Brutton and Ford was dissolved, in consequence
of Brutton, owing to a paralytic attack, having become totally
incapable of business. The affidavits on that point are very
strong. The business was afterwards carried on by Ford alone.
It does not appear that Brutton had ever exercised his right of
retainer. I do not mean to question the proposition that one of
two partners to whom a debt is due, being made an executor, might
retain that debt. The same reason seems to apply in that case as
to a case of his being a sole creditor. In point of fact, however,
there was no retainer, nor anything done that showed an intention
to retain. In 1821, this arrangement took place; in 1827, Mr.
Brutton died, and before any right of retainer had been thought of,
the legal interest in the debt had wholly devolved on Ford alone,
and, therefore, the reason which would give the right of retainer
had ceased to exist. It appears to me that that alone is sufficient
to dispose of the case; but I desired to look at the affidavits, to see
whether the equitable interest had not also passed, for, if it had,
that would be an additional *consideration for holding that the   [*377]
right of retainer was extinguished. It appeared to me impossible
to read the affidavits without understanding from them that Mr.
Ford claimed to be absolutely entitled to all the profits of the
business, up to the time of the arrangement of the business in
1821, including the debt in question.

(His Honour read the affidavits, with reference to the illness and
incapacity of Brutton, and the arrangement with his family and
friends, by which Ford purchased all his interest in the partnership,
as well in respect of the business which had been done, as of the
good-will.)

I think, therefore, that, in equity as well as at law, Brutton
had ceased to have any interest in the debt; and, there having

been no retainer in fact, nor any evidence of intention to retain,
that the Master's conclusion was right with respect to the costs
comprised in the first period.

The second period includes the time between the death of the
testatrix and the dissolution of the partnership of Brutton and
Ford; and, during that period, it appears that the Master has
allowed all payments actually made by Brutton, with this exception,—Mr. Brutton, a solicitor in the country, had employed a
London agent, and payments had been made to that London agent.
The question before the Master was, whether he was to treat such
payments as payments actually made, and which ought to be
allowed, or whether he was to consider them as only a part of those
profits which the Court does not allow an executor or trustee to
make, and which he, therefore, could not claim. The reason why
a trustee is not permitted to make a profit of the business which
arises out of the office he holds, is, that he is bound to exercise a
[*378] control *over the solicitor he employs, to watch the proceedings,
and see that they are proper ; and the Court guards the performance of that duty, by excluding him from any pecuniary interest
in the steps that are taken. If the application of that reasoning
were carried to its extreme length, it appears to me it would go to
exclude the executor from receiving the sums which have been
allowed as payments, for it may be said that he had a pecuniary
interest in conniving at improper steps being taken ; but the Court
does not go that extreme length. In this case, the Master has
allowed the sums paid by Brutton, in the course of the proceedings
during the period to which I am referring, and, I think, correctly
allowed them. The Court invariably does so, unless there is some
attempt to impeach the propriety of what has been done. Then
the Court, having so far said that the steps shall be recognised, the
question is whether the Master ought not to have allowed the
expenses paid to the agent, which stand upon the same footing as
the sums actually paid ; in point of fact, whether by pursuing that
course he would not have done all which the Court affects to do,
which is to deprive a solicitor and trustee of all profit from the
business. The considerations on this point are so nicely balanced,
that I have hesitated very much in disturbing the conclusion to
which the Master has come ; but, upon the whole, I think that he
has drawn the line with more than necessary strictness, in stopping
at the precise point at which he has made the allowance to cease.
I think I may declare that the Master ought to have allowed the

expenses actually paid to the agent; and refer it back to him to
review his report, regard being had to that declaration.   That will
confine the alteration to that point; everything else will stand.

I have had great difficulty in knowing how to deal *with the claim
for costs, incurred between the time of the alleged dissolution of
partnership of Brutton and Ford and the death of Brutton.   The
Master, I understand, was of opinion, that, inasmuch as Mr. Brutton
was incapable of acting, no one had power to dissolve the partnership for him : that he must be considered as having been a partner
throughout, and, therefore, that the case will be governed by the
same considerations which previously applied.   It is not very
material which way the case is taken.   If he is to be considered as
a partner, the Master was clearly right except as to the agency, if
there were any such, expenses.   I confess, however, that, as the
defendant's case is, that the partnership was dissolved,—the representative of Brutton, in fact, adopting and confirming the transaction, and as the family, who sold his share and took the benefit of
such sale, do not affect to impeach the transaction, I think I am
pursuing the strict course of justice in holding that the partnership
was dissolved.   But what difference does it make?   I must now
consider Mr. Ford as standing in one of two characters,—he was
either a solicitor retained by somebody, or he was acting officiously.
Then by whom was he retained?   The original retainer was given
by John Brutton to the firm of Ford and Brutton.   When that
partnership was dissolved, a new retainer would have been
necessary, in order that Ford should be properly retained as the
solicitor in the cause.   Who could give him this retainer?   I
cannot upon these proceedings hold that Mr. Brutton gave it, for
the whole case raised by Margaret Brutton is that, at the time of
the dissolution in 1821, and thenceforward until his death, he was
in a state of complete incapacity either to give a retainer or do any
other act.   The most favourable way in which I can therefore treat
Mr. Ford, is as a solicitor who has acted officiously, and carried the
*cause to a successful result.   The consequence is, that which
Mr. Baron ALDERSON held, and in which I agreed with him in *Hall* v.
Laxer(1), that those who claim the benefit of the suit,—not complaining
of the mode of conducting it,—shall pay the costs of carrying it on,
although they may not have employed the solicitor by whom it
was prosecuted.   This principle does not, however, help the defendant Margaret Brutton's case, for the person to make application

(1) 58 R. R. 198 (1 Hare, 571, 575).

BURGE
v.
BRUTTON.

[*379]

[*380]

BURGE
v.
BRUTTON.

for the costs is not Margaret Brutton, but the solicitor who has so acquired a title to receive them. Mr. Ford might on that ground think fit to petition that the funds now in Court shall not go out until the proper costs are provided for, but this is not that proceeding. It is the claim of Margaret Brutton, who never retained him, and who is a mere stranger to the transaction ; and I do not think I can possibly do otherwise than confirm the Master's report; although the disallowance of this sum may merely produce a circuity, and ultimately throw the same costs on the fund in another shape.

1843.
Feb. 13, 16.

WIGRAM,
V.-C.
[383]

TIPPING *v.* CLARKE (1).

(2 Hare, 383—393.)

Answers to interrogatories should be explicit, for otherwise, unless they contain a clear and sufficient statement which meets the whole case, they will be treated as evasive.

Construction of an answer, containing a general denial of the facts charged, in the terms of the charge, with a saving so far as the other statements in the answer admits or explains them.

A clerk is under an implied contract not to divulge information coming to his knowledge in the course of his employment, and persons threatening to avail themselves of information thus obtained may be restrained by injunction from using it.

THE plaintiff, a factor, had dealings with the defendant, a merchant, and disputes arising between them, the defendant, in a letter to the plaintiff, stated in effect, that he had, with much time and trouble, acquired a knowledge of the contents of the plaintiff's books, not only relating to his (the defendant's) account, but also to the accounts of all the plaintiff's other Irish friends, and that he (the defendant) intended to call a meeting of the latter, his object being to make a public exhibition of the plaintiff's books. The plaintiff thereupon filed his bill, charging that the defendant had by surreptitious and fraudulent means obtained access to the plaintiff's accounts, books, and other documents, relating to the plaintiff's business, and had by the like means made or obtained copies thereof, not only in reference to his own transactions with the plaintiff, but *also in reference to the plaintiff's dealings with other persons, and in particular with various connexions and friends of the plaintiff in Ireland and elsewhere, in which the defendant had no concern. The bill charged that the defendant ought to set forth a list and description of all copies

[*384]

(1) *Merryweather* v. *Moore* [1892] 2 Ch. 518, 61 L. J. Ch. 505, 66 L. T. 719.

of, and extracts or entries from, and of all other particulars
respecting the said accounts, books, and documents, relating to
such transactions, at any time or in any manner obtained by him,
or which were in any way then in his possession or power, or under
his control, or to which he had any means of access, and ought also
to set forth how and when, and from whom, he obtained the same,
and what means of access he then had thereto, and when he parted
with the custody of any of the said several particulars which were
not then, but formerly were, in his possession or power, or under
his control, and where the same then were, and what had become
thereof.

The bill inquired, 1st, whether it was not true that the defendant
had by surreptitious and fraudulent means, or by some and what
means obtained access to the plaintiff's accounts, books, and other
documents relating to his business, or to some and which of them.
2ndly, whether he had not in some and what manner made or
obtained copies, or a copy, or extracts, or an extract, therefrom, or
of some and what part or parts thereof. 3rdly, whether he had
not made or obtained such copies or extracts, not only in reference
to his own transactions with the plaintiff, but also in reference to
the plaintiff's dealings with other persons, and in particular with
various, or some and what friends of the plaintiff in Ireland and
elsewhere, with which he had no concern. 4thly, the bill called
upon the defendant to set forth a list and short description of all
copies of, and extracts or entries from, and of all other the particulars
aforesaid in *his possession or power. 5thly, how and when, and   [*385]
from whom, he obtained the same, and what means of access he
then had thereto: and 6thly, when he parted with the custody of
any of the said several particulars which were not then, but formerly
were, in his possession or power, and where the same then were,
and what had become thereof.

The bill prayed that the defendant might be restrained by injunction
from printing or otherwise copying, and from publicly exhibiting or
making known, and from distributing or parting with any copies, or
otherwise in any way publishing the said accounts, books, and
documents, and any copies of, or extracts from, the same, and
might be decreed to deliver up to the plaintiff, or to destroy, all
such copies and extracts; and might also be decreed to pay the
costs of the suit.

The defendant, by his answer, said that, suspecting the plaintiff
had rendered him false statements of the sales of the goods

consigned to him by the defendant, and appropriated to his own use part of the proceeds which he ought to have accounted for to the defendant, he (the defendant) made inquiries, and exerted himself to obtain information respecting the matters aforesaid, and to ascertain the true state of the case with respect thereto, and by the means aforesaid he obtained information respecting it, relating to the defendant's own affairs and property, and the dealings of the plaintiff, as his factor, in respect thereof, and the accounts relating to the same, and the defendant had some private memorandums relating to the same matters, and of the information so obtained, which memorandums were written on several separate papers, and were in the defendant's possession; and the defendant had a few other memorandums of a similar nature, which he was then unable [*386] to find, although *he had searched for the same, and, in consequence, believed that the same had been lost or destroyed, and was unable to set forth any other description or account thereof, or when the defendant parted with the same, or where the same then were, and what had become thereof.   And the defendant insisted that he was entitled to retain all such memorandums, and that he ought not to be compelled to produce or make any discovery respecting the same or any of them, for they related exclusively to the defendant's property and goods, and the sales thereof, with the exception only, that two of the memorandums contained notes made by the defendant of information obtained by him, of differences between the accounts of the proceeds realized and received by the plaintiff, from merchandize of the defendant, and also of some other persons therein mentioned, being also connections in trade of the plaintiff, he having, as the defendant believed, improperly, unfairly, and fraudulently retained and appropriated to his own use the sums constituting such differences; but the defendant denied that he had, by surreptitious and fraudulent means, or by any means except as aforesaid, and by an order in a suit in which he was plaintiff, obtained access to the plaintiff's accounts and books, or other documents, or any of them, or save as therein mentioned had, in any manner, made or obtained copies or a copy thereof, or extracts or an extract therefrom, or of any part thereof: and the defendant said that he had in his possession or power the memorandums or papers thereinbefore mentioned and described, which he insisted he was not bound to produce or discover in any manner to the plaintiff, and that the plaintiff had not by his bill shown any ground, or made any case, entitling him

to the production or discovery thereof, and, except as aforesaid, the TIPPING
v.
CLARKE.
defendant denied the possession of any documents,—following the
terms of the interrogatory.

The plaintiff took six exceptions for insufficiency, in respect of [387]
the interrogatories which are above distinguished. The Master
overruled the exceptions. Upon exceptions to his report,

Mr. Roupell and *Mr. Rolt* submitted that the answer was evasive,
and that, even supposing the bill were demurrable, the 38th Order
of August, 1841, was not intended to alter the rules of pleading,
to the extent of giving to an answer the effect of a demurrer to the
relief. It was intended only to give to an answer the effect of a
demurrer to the discovery. On the title to relief they cited *Gee* v.
Pritchard (1).

Mr. Bazalgette, for the defendant, argued that the interrogatories
were in terms answered, and that the specific answers, referred to in
the general denial, applied to all the facts which were material to
any relief that could be given ; for the plaintiff was not entitled to
any part of the relief prayed with respect to the accounts of his
dealings with the defendant himself, whatever might be his title to
relief with respect to the accounts of the plaintiff's dealings with
third persons. Under the 38th Order of August, 1841, the Master
had, therefore, correctly overruled the exceptions, as to inquiries
leading to that part of the relief which might have been demurred
to ; and the inquiries not covered by that principle were properly
held to be immaterial, under the power given to the Master by the
74th Order of April, 1828.

THE VICE-CHANCELLOR, after stating the subject of the bill, and of
the exceptions :

I have, in this case, to consider three points : first, *whether the [*388]
defendant has sufficiently answered the matter of the exceptions,
admitting that he has verbally answered the interrogatories: secondly,
whether (if he has not sufficiently answered) it is material to the relief
prayed, that he should answer the matters in question, with reference
to the 74th Order of April, 1828 : and thirdly, whether the defendant
is relieved from the necessity of answering by the effect of the 38th
Order of August, 1841. With regard to the first point, whether the
defendant has answered or not, I make the observation, which is

(1) 19 R. R. 87 (2 Swanst. 402).

very commonly and usefully made by all Judges who have to
consider this question,—which is, that, if the defendant will simply
answer in the terms of the bill, he avoids all difficulty on the
subject ; but if, instead of doing so, he gives an answer which is
not precise with reference to all the matters on which he is interro-
gated, and then endeavours to shelter himself under a general denial,
coupled with the words " except as aforesaid," or similar expressions,
he makes it often difficult to decide whether the answer is sufficient
or not.   The rule, since I have known the practice of the Court, has
been, that wherever the defendant denies the bill to be true, " except
as aforesaid," or "except as appears by the other parts of the
answer," if there be not found on the answer a clear and sufficient
statement, which, to a reasonable extent, meets the whole case, the
answer is deemed to be evasive.   Then, does the previous part of the
answer to the subject of the three first exceptions meet the questions
put by the bill, and explain the matters, so far as it relates to the
allegation that the defendant has had access to, and has taken copies
or extracts from, the plaintiff's books, and that such copies and
extracts relate to accounts between the plaintiff and third persons,
as well as between him and defendant ? I am clear that the defendant
[*389]   has not given any such sufficient or explanatory statement.   *(His
Honour read that part of the answer.)   The statement the defendant
makes is perfectly consistent with the supposition that the defendant
may have had access to, and taken copies and extracts from, the
books, relating as well to his own affairs as to the affairs of other
persons.   It is a general denial, "except as aforesaid ; " but there
is not any previous allegation which excludes the suggestions to
which this qualified denial applies.   It is a mere general denial,
in answer to a specific charge, with which the Court never requires
a plaintiff to be satisfied.   The first, second, and third exceptions
must, therefore, be allowed.

The fourth exception stands on a different footing, for the
substance of the answer is, that the defendant has in his possession
no documents relating to the dealings between the plaintiff and
other persons, except two,—that those two have upon them certain
memoranda to the effect mentioned in the bill, as to the transactions
between the plaintiff and other persons therein named.   The answer
would enable the Court, on motion, to order the production of those
two documents.   If the documents produced under that order should
not correspond with the representation in the answer, or the names
of the persons with whom the dealings took place should not appear

on them, or if the memoranda upon them do not agree with the   TIPPING
description in the answer, the plaintiff may move for an order that   *v.*
the defendant should make a further discovery on oath ; and enable   CLARKE.
the plaintiff to obtain the production of the identical documents.
If the documents correspond with the description in the answer,
that *primâ facie* will be sufficient to identify them, and show that
the order of the Court has been complied with.   It may be answered
that it would be possible for the defendant to substitute other documents for those so described ; but the same may be said of almost
every document.   If they were distinguished by several marks *and   [*390]
successive numbers, the Court cannot guard against the possibility
of fraud by substitution of other documents bearing similar marks
or numbers.   With respect to those two documents I think the
answer is sufficient.   The other documents, however, the defendant
does not even affect to number; and, supposing he is bound to
produce or give them up, the answer is not sufficient.

The subject of the fifth exception, when and from whom the
defendant obtained the documents, falls within the observation I
have already made.   Until the defendant has given a specific
answer to the question, whether he has the documents in his
possession, I cannot be satisfied with a general answer from him.

The answer to the sixth exception is insufficient for a different
reason; and I have very little doubt that the answer was meant to
be sufficient, and that the plaintiff will not be benefited by my
allowing the exception ; but the answer is made evasive in saying
that the defendant cannot set forth when he parted with the papers
or memoranda, and what had become thereof.   When a defendant
answers conjunctively by saying he is unable to answer half-a-dozen
things, and does not add " or any of them," it is obvious that the
answer may be evasive.

The next point is with regard to the materiality of the exceptions.
The 74th Order directs the Master to consider the relevancy or
materiality of the question or statement.   The Master undoubtedly
has always to read the bill, and to see what the scope of it is, on
the question of materiality ; but the Order is not imperative that
the Master shall weigh that question with a nicety which is necessary on questions of a right to property ; but—having regard to it,
—if the statement is clearly immaterial, he is to take that circumstance into account *in determining on the sufficiency of the answer.   [*391]
If the plaintiff is entitled to relief at the hearing of the cause, or
if the effect of the bill being demurrable (supposing it to be so) is

TIPPING
v.
CLARKE.

not to protect the defendant,—the plaintiff may have occasion to prove that the defendant has copies of his books, which he has threatened to publish; and that the plaintiff has a right to restrain him from publishing them. It is impossible to say the discovery in this case may not be material. The fact of having access to the books may be very material. It may be an important link in the chain of evidence to prove that the defendant in truth had taken the copies or extracts. It is material also with a view to the injunction, for, if I had to decide that question on motion, I might probably say that it involved so much difficulty, that I could not try the cause before the hearing; but then the mischief of publication being one which the Court could not repair, and which could scarcely be adequately repaired in damages, I might possibly grant the interim injunction until the right was decided. Again, at the hearing, the plaintiff may be entitled to have the documents, or some of them, delivered up to be cancelled, or to have them impounded; and, if any relief of that kind is to be given, the plaintiff would be bound to prove in some way what the documents are; and whatever he is bound to prove at the hearing, he is at liberty to prove, if he can, by the oath or admission of the defendant. The documents must, therefore, be so far described that the Court may be in a condition to make a decree at the hearing, if the plaintiff should be entitled to a decree. The answer may be material also with regard to the costs of the suit. I give no opinion on the right of the plaintiff to the production of the documents: that is not the present question.

[*392]   The only other point arises on the suggestion that *the bill is demurrable, and that, in such case, the 38th Order of August, 1841, gives the defendant the benefit of a demurrer in this form.

Those who are familiar with the old cases on the subject before Lord Thurlow, Lord Rosslyn, and Lord Eldon, know the contest which for a long time existed on the point, whether the defendant answering could refuse to answer fully, unless the question itself was immaterial, or a breach of professional confidence, or calculated to subject him to pains and penalties, or any question of that nature, which the Court never obliges a defendant to answer, even where the right to relief is admitted. In the consideration of those cases, a distinction was constantly taken in argument between a bill which was demurrable, and on which the Court might, therefore, see that the discovery would be useless, and the case of a plea

or answer where the question of right to discovery depended on a
fact, the truth of which the Court could not ascertain before the
hearing of the cause. But this distinction was not allowed by
the Court, Lord ELDON saying the Master could not try whether
the bill was demurrable.   Now the 38th Order was certainly
intended to alter this practice where the bill was clearly demurrable ; and I conceive that, as the case goes first before the Master,
the Court, by the order in question, placed the Master in the same
situation as the Court in that respect ; and although the general
rule is, that a bill must be so stated as to show that the plaintiff
would be certainly entitled to relief, and it is not sufficient to say
he may be entitled to it, yet the Court very commonly exercises a
discretion in saying, that a question is of too much difficulty to
decide upon demurrer. The right to discovery in cases like the
present may be put on three grounds. First, on the ground of
property in the books, which depends on the statute of Anne ;
secondly, on a *breach of contract between the parties ; and the
third ground, which is common to all cases, is, that the Court
interposes to prevent a positive wrong, the consequences of which
cannot be adequately measured or repaired in damages. I do not
mean to give any opinion in this stage of the case, how far these
principles may ultimately apply to it, or whether or not a party has
a property in the contents of his books of account.   To draw a line
between different classes of books, on the question of property,
requires much consideration. I cannot, without argument, decide
that there may not be a property in these books in the plaintiff, as
the bill charges there is.   Looking at the case with reference to
contract, I cannot say that the defendant shall not make known to
the world his own dealings with another party ; but it is clear, that
every clerk employed in a merchant's counting-house is under an
implied contract that he will not make public that which he learns
in the execution of his duty as clerk : if the defendant has obtained
copies of books, it would very probably be by means of some clerk
or agent of the plaintiff, and if he availed himself surreptitiously of
the information, which he could not have had except from a person
guilty of a breach of contract in communicating it, I think he could
not be permitted to avail himself of that breach of contract. I
cannot say that a serious injury may not arise by the publication
of accounts under such circumstances ; nor am I in a condition to
say, with any satisfaction to myself, that this is not a case in which
the Court will give relief of the nature which is sought.   The

TIPPING
v.
CLARKE.

[*393]

TIPPING
v.
CLARKE.

question arising only incidentally, on exceptions to the answer, and the answer being evasive, I think the Master should have allowed the exceptions.

Exceptions to the report allowed.

1843.
Feb. 22, 23,
24.
March 3.

WIGRAM,
V.-C.

[394]

FULLER *v.* BENETT.

(2 Hare, 394—407 ; S. C. 12 L. J. Ch. 355 ; 7 Jur. 1056.)

The solicitors for a purchaser pending completion of the purchase received written notice of a prior incumbrance. The purchase was not completed until five years later, and the same solicitors subsequently acted both for the purchaser and for mortgagees to whom he subsequently mortgaged the property. Held that the mortgagees had constructive notice of the prior incumbrance (1).

IN February, 1831, Sir J. J. Dillon, who was the owner of an undivided moiety of an estate called the Hatch estate, in Wiltshire, subject to a mortgage to Mollan, commenced a treaty with the defendant Benett, the elder, for the sale to him of the said moiety. The draft of an agreement was drawn up in writing by J. Benett, the elder, and altered and signed by Sir J. J. Dillon ; the alterations did not appear to have been adopted by Benett, but the abstract was delivered, and a correspondence commenced between Sir J. J. Dillon, and Messrs. Farrer & Co., the solicitors of Benett, with respect to the title, with a view to the purchase. In the draft of agreement as made by Benett and signed by Sir J. J. Dillon, the stipulated purchase-money was 13,000*l.*

On the 18th of November, 1831, Sir J. J. Dillon being indebted to P. M. Chitty, a solicitor, in respect of costs and disbursements, signed a memorandum in writing, whereby he agreed to execute a mortgage to Chitty of the Hatch estate for securing such sum of money as was due from him to Chitty, on the balance of account not exceeding the sum of 2,000*l.*, as soon as such mortgage could be prepared. The draft of a mortgage-deed was afterwards prepared and sent to Mr. Stephens, the solicitor of Sir J. J. Dillon, but the proposed deed was not executed.

[*395]

Chitty, by way of security for a debt which he owed to the plaintiffs G. and R. Fuller, who were bankers, in *March, 1832, assigned to the plaintiff Smith, as trustee for them, the debt owing to him (Chitty) from Sir J. J. Dillon, and all securities for the same. On the 29th of March, 1832, Messrs. Smith and Allistons,

---

(1) See now the Conveyancing Act, 31 Ch. D. 671, 55 L. J. Ch. 662, 54
1882, s. 3, and see *In re Cousins* (1886)   L. T. 376.—O. A. S.

the solicitors of the plaintiffs, gave Messrs. Farrer & Co., the solicitors of J. Benett the elder and J. Benett the younger, notice of the assignment by Chitty to the plaintiffs, of the debt for which he held the undertaking to execute a mortgage of the estate contracted to be sold to Benett, and requested to be informed of the time when the purchase was to be completed, that they might attend and receive the amount due to Chitty. In November, 1832, Chitty became bankrupt.

In August, 1832, Sir Hyde Parker filed his bill against Sir J. J. Dillon, the defendant J. Benett the elder, and others, and thereby claimed to be equitably entitled to the said moiety of the Hatch estate. The defendant Benett, the elder, by his answer in that suit claimed the benefit of the contract of sale; but did not acknowledge that he was bound by it. The cause (*Parker* v. *Dillon* and others) was heard in November, 1835, and the bill was dismissed with costs. After the termination of Parker's suit, Sir J. J. Dillon, being desirous of enforcing the performance of what he considered to be the contract he had made with the defendant J. Benett the elder, for the sale of the Hatch estate, with which Benett declined to proceed, caused a bill to be prepared for that purpose; but, in February, 1837, before further steps were taken, Sir J. J. Dillon died, having by his will devised all his estates, including the said moiety of the Hatch estate, to his sister Henrietta Dillon, who was also his heiress-at-law, and having also appointed her his residuary legatee and sole executrix.

Soon after the death of Sir J. J. Dillon, an agreement was entered into between Henrietta Dillon and the defendant J. Benett the elder, by which the latter, on *behalf of himself and J. Benett [*396] the younger, agreed to purchase the said moiety of the Hatch estate, and to accept the title as it then stood, at the reduced sum of 11,500*l*. The plaintiffs alleged that this was merely a completion of the former contract with an abatement of price: the defendants alleged that it was an entirely new agreement; the former agreement having been abandoned. By indentures, dated the 2nd and 3rd of October, 1837, Henrietta Dillon in consideration of 11,500*l*., paid by the defendants J. Benett the elder and J. Benett the younger, to her and to her order, conveyed the said moiety of the Hatch estate to the use of J. Benett the elder and J. Benett the younger, as therein mentioned. The purchase-money was applied in paying off the mortgage to Mollan and other incumbrances (not including the claim of the plaintiffs under the agreement of

November, 1831), and the balance, amounting to 3,820*l.*, was paid
to Henrietta Dillon.

By indentures dated the 23rd and 24th of June, 1839, J. Benett
the elder and J. Benett the younger conveyed the Hatch estate,
together with other estates, to the defendant Edward Marjoribanks,
and his heirs, by way of mortgage for securing 129,000*l.* and
interest. Messrs. Farrer & Co. were the solicitors of both the
defendants, Benett and Marjoribanks, in the business of this
mortgage.

The bill was filed in April, 1840, against J. Benett the elder,
J. Benett the younger, E. Marjoribanks, Henrietta Dillon, and the
assignees of Chitty, stating that the plaintiffs had then lately
discovered that the purchase was completed, and the Hatch estate
conveyed to the several defendants by the deeds of October, 1837,
and June, 1839; and praying that an account might be taken of
the debt due to the plaintiffs from Chitty, secured by the agreement
of March, 1832, and to Chitty from Sir J. J. Dillon, secured by the
[*397]   *agreement of November, 1831, and that the defendants Henrietta
Dillon, J. Benett the elder, and J. Benett the younger, and
E. Marjoribanks, might be decreed to pay to the plaintiffs the
amount, not exceeding 2,000*l.*, which should be found due from
Dillon to Chitty at the date of the agreement of November, 1831,
with interest, in part satisfaction of the debt secured to the plaintiffs
by the agreement of March, 1832, with the costs of the suit; and
in default of such payment that the said defendants and the
assignees of Chitty might be foreclosed of the equity of redemption
of the said moiety of the Hatch estate, and that the said defendants
might be decreed to convey the said moiety to the plaintiffs, and
deliver up to them the deeds relating thereto, and the possession
thereof.

The defendants J. Benett the elder, J. Benett the younger, and
E. Marjoribanks claimed to be purchasers of the Hatch estate,
without notice of the agreement of November, 1831. The defendant
J. Benett, the elder, said that there was, before that agreement, a
contract binding in law upon Dillon for the sale of the estate,
although it was not in law binding upon him (the defendant); that
such agreement was abandoned after the institution of the suit of
Parker v. *Dillon;* and that the subsequent contract with the
defendant Henrietta Dillon was an entirely new transaction, having
no reference to the former; that no mention was made in the conveyance of any former treaty or contract; and that the purchase-

money was paid to Henrietta Dillon as the vendor, and not as the
personal representative of Sir J. J. Dillon. Henrietta Dillon was
out of the jurisdiction, and did not appear in the cause.

Evidence was entered into on both sides, but the material facts
of the case were scarcely in dispute. The questions were with
regard to the inferences or conclusions *which were to be drawn   [*398]
from the particular facts. It did not appear whether the notice
which they had received of the agreement of November, 1831, was
or not in the actual recollection of Messrs. Farrer & Co. at the time
of the completion of the purchase by their clients, the defendants
Benett, and the payment of the balance of the purchase-money to
Henrietta Dillon. Mr. Parkinson, the partner in the firm of
Farrer & Co., who acted in this business, was examined as a
witness, and the following passage in his depositions was noticed in
the judgment:

"I have some recollection that the produced notices (of the
agreement and assignment) were, on some occasion previously to
the death of the said Sir J. J. Dillon, referred to, or noticed by me,
in some conversation or conversations which I then had with the
said J. Benett the elder; but at what precise time between the date
of the said last-mentioned documents I had these communications,
I cannot state as to my recollection or belief; nor can I recollect to
what extent I apprised the said J. Benett, the elder, of the contents
of the said last-mentioned documents, and even if I could, I should
decline to state the same, as I consider the communications between
myself and my client, the said J. Benett, the elder, as confidential
and privileged. I am confident that, after the death of the said Sir
J. J. Dillon, neither I nor any of my partners had any conversation
with the said J. Benett, the elder, on the subject of the said produced
paper writings, or made known to him the contents thereof, as at
that time the treaty for the purchase of the said estates had been
put an end to; and both my partners and myself considered that
there was no binding contract subsisting between the parties."

And the following passage in the depositions of the same witness
was also read in the judgment:

"I believe that neither I nor any of my partners ever communi-   [399]
cated to the said plaintiffs or their solicitors the result of the said last-
mentioned suit, or the completion of the purchase of the moiety of
the said estate by the said John Benett the elder, and John Benett
the younger, inasmuch as I and my partners considered that there
was no binding contract between the said Sir John Dillon and the

FULLER
v.
BENETT.

said John Benett the elder. These matters were not purposely kept
secret from the said plaintiffs or their solicitors, by myself, or my
partners, or our client; we certainly did not consider ourselves
under any obligation to give the said plaintiffs or their solicitors,
spontaneously, any notice of the termination of the said suit, or of
the completion of the said purchase by the said defendants, John
Benett the elder, and John Benett the younger; but we should not
have refused to give the said plaintiffs or their solicitor any information thereof, if they had made any inquiry respecting the same;
such inquiry or information, however, was never, as far as I recollect
or believe, made or sought after. I cannot state, as to my knowledge
or belief, whether the said plaintiffs and their solicitors were wholly
or in any way ignorant of the termination of the suit, instituted as
aforesaid, by the said Sir Hyde Parker, or of the completion of the
said purchase by the said Messrs. Benett, until a short time previous
to the institution of this suit." At the hearing,

Mr. Temple and *Mr. Heathfield*, for the plaintiffs.

Mr. Purvis and *Mr. Sidebottom*, for the defendants, J. Benett
the elder, and J. Benett the younger, argued that the vendor, after
he had bound himself by a contract for sale, could not charge the
estate by the agreement to mortgage it; that there had been *laches*,
or at least negligence on the part of the plaintiffs, in suspending
their claim from 1832 until after the purchase-money was *paid;
that the contract with Henrietta Dillon was an entirely new and
distinct transaction; and that it was neither reasonable in fact, nor
consistent with law, to deem that the solicitor, after such a lapse of
time, had the circumstances of the former transaction present in
his mind, so as to affect his client with constructive notice. They
contended also, that the bill was not correctly framed, supposing
the plaintiffs were entitled to relief; for it should have prayed that
a proper mortgage-deed might be executed, and not a foreclosure.

[*400]

Mr. Romilly and *Mr. Giffard*, for E. Marjoribanks.

Mr. Hislop Clarke, for the assignees of Chitty.

[*Dawson* v. *Ellis* (1), *Mountford* v. *Scott* (2), *Winter* v. *Lord
Anson* (3), *Hargreaves* v. *Rothwell* (4), and earlier cases, were cited.

(1) 21 R. R. 227 (1 Jac. & W. 524).   *S. C.* 3 Russ. 488).
(2) 24 R. R. 55 (T. & R. 274).   (4) 44 R. R. 48 (1 Keen, 154).
(3) 27 R. R. 171 (1 Sim. & St. 434;

The VICE-CHANCELLOR, at the conclusion of the argument, stated his opinion to be, that there was no complete contract between Dillon and Benett before the agreement of November, 1831, but that the matter was then in treaty only; that there was no ground for imputing *laches* to the plaintiffs; and that the record was not improperly framed, so as to preclude the plaintiffs from obtaining relief, if upon the merits they were entitled to it.

THE VICE-CHANCELLOR :

Referring to what I said on a former day, the only question which I have to try is that of notice or no notice to Benett and Marjoribanks of the contract between Chitty and Sir J. J. Dillon.

In order to understand the point of law upon which the answer to the question depends (for the material facts are not substantially in dispute), it is necessary only to state, that Mr. Parkinson, of the firm of Farrer & Co., on behalf of that firm, was the solicitor and legal adviser of Mr. Benett in and throughout his original treaty with Sir J. J. Dillon, in February, 1831, and thenceforward until the institution of the suit of *Parker* v. *Dillon*, in November, 1832 ; that the same firm (acting by Mr. Bannister) were the solicitors for Mr. Benett in the cause of *Parker* v. *Dillon*, in which Mr. Benett insists, by his answer, that he held Sir J. J. Dillon bound by a contract for sale of the Hatch estate ; that Messrs. Farrer & Co. by Mr. Parkinson continued to act for Mr. Benett, in the transaction respecting the alleged sale of the Hatch estate, from the month of November, 1835, (the date of the dismissal of Sir Hyde Parker's suit), until the death of Sir J. J. Dillon, in 1837 ; that he afterwards, in the same character, acted for Mr. Benett in the treaty between that gentleman and Miss Dillon, which terminated in the agreement for sale and purchase in October, 1837 ; and that he or Messrs. Farrer & Co. were the solicitors for Mr. Marjoribanks, as well as of Mr. Benett, in the transaction which terminated in the mortgage of June, 1839. Mr. Parkinson has been examined by the defendants, or some of them, as a witness in the cause, and cross-examined by the plaintiffs. He does not controvert the fact of notice given to his house by Smith and Allistons in 1832, nor his recollection *of that notice in 1835, 1837, or 1839. His evidence upon this point tends the other way, if that were material. (His Honour read that part of Mr. Parkinson's deposition which has been already stated (1).) I should here observe, that the notices I have

(1) *Supra*, pp. 155, 156.

Right margin:

FULLER
v.
BENETT.

March 3.

[401]

[*402]

FULLER
v.
BENETT.

referred to as having been sent by Smith and Allistons to Messrs. Farrer & Co. in March, 1832, came out of the possession of the defendants Benett in this cause; and that there is some evidence that the notices formed the subject of a conversation between Mr. Parkinson and Mr. Benett in the lifetime of Sir J. J. Dillon. It is not, however, upon these facts that my opinion on this case has been formed.

The plaintiffs have argued, that the treaty for the purchase of the estate, which commenced in February, 1831, was suspended only by Sir H. Parker's suit in 1832, and is to be considered as one continuous transaction until its completion in 1837; and that the notice, which, in March, 1832, was given to Farrer & Co., on behalf of the plaintiffs, will affect both Benett and Marjoribanks. The defendants insist, that the treaty and contract for purchase with Miss Dillon, after Sir J. J. Dillon's death, was altogether a new transaction, unconnected with the treaty in the lifetime of Sir J. J. Dillon, and that notice to a solicitor in one transaction is not notice to his client in a new transaction.

The general propositions, first, that notice to the solicitor is notice to the client; secondly, that, where a purchaser employs the same solicitor as the vendor, he is affected with notice of whatever that solicitor had notice in his capacity of solicitor for either vendor or purchaser in the transaction in which he is so employed; and, [*403] thirdly, that the notice to the solicitor, *which alone will bind the client, must be notice in that transaction in which the client employs him,—have not, as general propositions, been disputed at the Bar; but with respect to the last proposition, it was argued, for the plaintiffs, that, where one out of two matters transacted by the same solicitor follows so close upon the other, that the earlier transaction cannot have been out of the mind of the solicitor when engaged in the latter, there is no ground for restricting the notice to the client to the second transaction only, and that he will be affected with notice of both; and for this reference was made to *Winter* v. *Lord Anson* (1), *Mountford* v. *Scott* (2), and *Hargreaves* v. *Rothwell* (3), to which I may add the case of *Brotherton* v. *Hatt* (4).

According to the plaintiffs' argument upon this part of the case, carried to its full extent, the question is one of memory only on the part of the solicitor, irrespective of the circumstance which has entered into all the cases cited for the plaintiffs, that the same

(1) 27 R. R. 171 (3 Russ. 488).   (3) 44 R. R. 48 (1 Keen. 154).
(2) 24 R. R. 55 (T. & Russ. 274).   (4) 2 Vern. 574.

solicitor was employed by both parties, the vendor and the purchaser. According to the defendants' argument, the knowledge which the solicitor has must be acquired after and during the retainer, or it will not affect the client. I am certainly not prepared to accede to either proposition to the full extent. Cases may easily be suggested in which it would be impossible that a solicitor should have forgotten a fact recently under his view, with notice of which, however, it would be impossible to affect his client, unless the circumstance of his being solicitor for two parties be introduced into the case. And it is equally clear, where that circumstance forms part of the case, that a purchaser may be affected with notice of *what the solicitor knew as solicitor for the vendor, although, as solicitor for the vendor, he may have acquired his knowledge before he was retained by the purchaser. Whatever the solicitor, during the time of his retainer, knows as solicitor for either party, may possibly in some cases affect both, without reference to the time when his knowledge was first acquired. If, therefore, in order to decide the cause now before me, it were strictly necessary that I should decide, as an abstract question, that a purchaser, who for the first time employs a solicitor (not being also the solicitor of the vendor), can be affected with constructive notice of anything known to the solicitor, save that of which the solicitor acquires notice after his retainer, and during his employment by the purchaser,—I should certainly feel great difficulty in coming to the conclusion. The rule, that notice to the solicitor will not bind the client, unless it be in the same transaction, or at least during the time of the solicitor's employment in that transaction, I have always understood to be a rule *positivi juris*, adopted by courts of justice in favour of innocent purchasers ; and the reason and policy of the rule appear to me to show that such is the case. "It is settled," says Lord HARDWICKE, "that notice to the agent or counsel, who was employed in the thing by another person, or in another business, and at another time, is no notice to his client who employs him afterwards. It would be very mischievous if it was so ; for the man of most practice and greatest eminence would then be the most dangerous to employ "(1). The expression commonly used in explaining the rule, namely, that the agent may have forgotten the former transaction, points at the same conclusion; and I cannot think that Lord ELDON, in the language he used extrajudicially in *Mountford* v. *Scott*, intended to shake the *general

FULLER
v.
BENNETT.

[*404]

[*405]

(1) 3 Atk. 392 ; 2 *Id.* 242.

FULLER
v.
BENETT.

doctrine which himself, as well as Lord HARDWICKE and other Judges, had so often insisted upon : *Warrick* v. *Warrick* (1), *Steed* v. *Whitaker* (2), *Hiern* v. *Mill* (3), *Mountford* v. *Scott* (4), *Kennedy* v. *Green* (5). It is not necessary so to understand Lord ELDON's language when construed with reference to the circumstances of the case before him. The rule limited as above, is, I presume to say, best adapted to, and fully sufficient for, the purposes of justice.

It appears to me, however, that it may not be necessary that I should give an opinion upon the abstract question. The cases of *Brotherton* v. *Hatt, Winton* v. *Lord Anson, Mountford* v. *Scott,* and *Hargreaves* v. *Rothwell,* do not appear to me necessarily to impeach the rule. The circumstances of those cases were, for the present purpose, in substance the same. The mortgagors had at different times employed the same solicitor in effecting different incumbrances upon the same estate; and the incumbrancers, with whom the contest arose, had employed the mortgagor's solicitor in the several transactions in which they were respectively concerned. The Court held the puisne incumbrancer affected with constructive notice of the prior incumbrances ; for having, in that case, employed the mortgagor's solicitor, he would necessarily be affected with notice of the prior transaction, unless it should be held that the common solicitor (in his character of solicitor to the mortgagor) was not to be considered as recollecting the old transactions when engaged in the new. If that were admitted—if the notice which the solicitor of the mortgagor *had in the old transaction were not continued in the new transaction,—I do not know what should prevent the solicitor of the mortgagor from himself becoming an incumbrancer upon the estate, and insisting upon his incumbrance against the mortgagees, whose mortgages he had himself on former occasions prepared : this was in fact unsuccessfully attempted in the late case of *Perkins* v. *Bradley* (6). In the absence of special circumstances to affect the conclusion, and in the absence certainly of any rule of law affecting the case, it might be right to hold that the solicitor for the mortgagor had (like the mortgagor himself) notice of the prior transaction, in that very transaction in which he was employed by the mortgagee. It was one continuous dealing with the same title. If, as solicitor for the mortgagor, he had such notice in the new transaction, he had it in that new transaction as solicitor for

[*406]

(1) 3 Atk. 294.
(2) Barnard. Chan. Rep. 220.
(3) 9 R. R. 149 (13 Ves. 120).

(4) 18 R. R. 189 (3 Madd. 34).
(5) 41 R. R. 176 (3 My. & K. 699).
(6) 1 Hare, 219.

both. The reasoning is technical ; and, in a case like that I am
supposing, the technicality as well as the common sense of the case
appears to me to be in favour of the decisions I am now considering.
But, however that may be, the decisions must govern the present
case, whether my attempt to reconcile them with the positive rule
I have referred to be right or not.

In the case now before me, I consider it to be immaterial whether
the treaty between Sir J. J. Dillon and Mr. Benett, and that
between Mr. Benett and Miss Dillon, after Sir J. J. Dillon's death,
were the same or not,—whether the latter was a continuance of the
first or a new treaty,—Messrs. Farrer & Co. were the solicitors of
the defendant Benett from the commencement of the treaty in 1831
to its close. The notices of the plaintiffs' interest were given to
them in March, 1832, as the solicitors of Benett. Those notices
were retained and preserved by them ; and in this suit they come
out of their *possession from the answer of their clients. Upon
the intermediate circumstances, and Mr. Parkinson's evidence, I
have already observed, I cannot discover any ground upon which
Mr. Benett can escape from the consequences of the notice.

If Mr. Benett is bound by the notice, Mr. Marjoribanks must be
bound by it also, not because abstractedly he is to be bound by
facts which came to the knowledge of his solicitor in other transactions, but because the solicitor he employed in the business of
the mortgage had notice of the plaintiffs' interest, as the solicitor
of the mortgagor, in the very transaction in which he (the
mortgagee) so employed him.

FULLER
v.
BENETT.

[*407]

BOWER v. COOPER.

(2 Hare, 408—411 ; S. C. 11 L. J. Ch. 287 ; 6 Jur. 681.)

An agreement to sell land, not expressing what interest in it, is
construed to mean the whole of the interest of the vendor in the
land.

An agreement to purchase land for an annuity for the life of the vendor,
to be a charge on the land, and to be paid quarterly, entitles the vendor,
not only to the security of the charge, but to the covenant of the purchaser
for the payment of the annuity.

Separation of the costs occasioned by a defence, founded on a statement
of fact, disproved by the evidence.

THE bill was brought for the specific performance of the following
agreement : " Memorandum of an agreement made this 22nd day

1842.
April 22, 26,
27.
May 3.
1843.
Jan. 27.

WIGRAM,
V.-C.

[408]

of January, 1841, between Reuben Cooper, of Hinton, of the one part, and Charles Bower, of High Cliff, both in the parish of Christchurch, in the county of Southampton, of the other part. The said R. Cooper hereby agrees to sell to the said Charles Bower the following : A certain cottage and land recently purchased by the said R. Cooper of J. Lane; two cottages and land purchased of W. Lane; both in the parish of Christchurch,—the cottage and garden purchased by the said R. Cooper and T. Burt, in the parish of Milton, in the said county, which premises were lately in the respective occupations of J. Davy, the said R. Cooper, T. Cratchley, and W. Church, and one of the said cottages purchased of W. Lane, being now or lately void,—together with the crop in the ground thereof, for an annuity of 30l., payable during the life of the said R. Cooper; and the said C. Bower hereby agrees to purchase the said premises for the said annuity: and it is hereby agreed that the said annuity shall be charged on the said premises by an instrument giving the said R. Cooper power, upon non-payment of the same, to sell such premises for the purpose of raising the arrears thereof; and it is further agreed that the said annuity shall be payable quarterly from the 5th day of January, and that the first payment thereof shall be made in advance, and that the said C. Bower shall be entitled to the possession and rents and profits of the same premises from the said *5th day of January, and that all expenses incurred in or about the said sale shall be borne by the said C. Bower, and that the deeds of the said premises shall be deposited with Mr. Druitt, of Christchurch, solicitor, on behalf of both parties. (Signed) REUBEN COOPER, CHARLES BOWER." The first quarterly payment of the annuity was made in advance on the execution of the agreement.

[*409]

The performance was resisted on four grounds : first, on the allegation, that the defendant was in a state of intoxication at the time of making and executing the agreement, and that the plaintiff took advantage of his incapacity : *Coles* v. *Trecothick* (1), *Lightfoot* v. *Heron* (2). Secondly, that the agreement was uncertain, inasmuch as it did not express what interest in the premises it was intended should pass to the plaintiff: *Western* v. *Russell* (3). Thirdly, that, by the agreement, no provision was made for any covenant or security to be given for the payment of the annuity to

(1) 7 R. R. 167 (9 Ves. 234).   (3) 13 R. R. 178 (3 V. & B.
(2) 51 R. R. 406 (3 Y. & C. Ex.   187).
Eq. 586).

the defendant beyond the security of the premises. [And lastly that the consideration was uncertain and inadequate (1).]

BOWER
v.
COOPER.

Mr. Sharpe and *Mr. Lewin*, for the plaintiff; and *Mr. Anderdon* and *Mr. James*, for the defendant.

May 3.
———
[410]

The VICE-CHANCELLOR held, that the agreement must be construed as referring to and importing the whole of the defendant's interest in the premises; that, under the agreement, the defendant was entitled, not only that the annuity should stand as a charge upon the premises, but also to the personal covenant of the plaintiff for its payment; and that the defendant had failed in proving any incapacity on his part to enter into the contract: none of the first three grounds relied upon by the defendant, therefore, constituted any defence; and the plaintiff must be declared to be entitled to the costs occasioned by the defence, founded on the alleged incapacity, which had failed: *Wright* v. *Howard* (2), *Deggs* v. *Colebrooke* (3), *Watts* v. *Manning* (4), *Mounsey* v. *Burnham* (5); although the separation of the costs was not to be adopted in practice upon light grounds, nor unless the respective costs applied to distinct cases, and were considerable, with reference to the whole evidence given in the cause.

[On the question of inadequacy his Honour directed a reference as to the respective values of the property and of the annuity.]

The Master found that the value to sell of the premises and crop, at the date of the contract, was 302*l.* 10*s.*; and that the value at the same time of an annuity of 90*l.* per annum, on the life of a party of the age of the defendant, was 278*l.* 18*s.* 2*d.*

[411]

Decree for specific performance, with costs.

1843.
Jan. 27.
———

(1) The defence of inadequacy is covered by modern authority, which settles that inadequacy is no defence unless it amounts to evidence of fraud, and so much of the report as deals with that defence is accordingly omitted.—O. A. S.

(2) 24 R. R. 169 (1 Sim. & St. 205).
(3) 1 Atk. 396.
(4) 1 Sim. & St. 421.
(5) 58 R. R. 11 (1 Hare, 22).

1843.
Feb. 24, 25,
28.

WIGRAM,
V.-C.

[413]

GAUNT *v.* TAYLOR (1).

(2 Hare, 413—423.)

Administration of an estate, where a creditor had obtained judgment upon a plea of *plenè administravit* by two of the executors, and a confession of assets to a certain amount by another executor,—such assets consisting of money in the hands of bankers not reached by the execution,—which the two executors prevented from being paid upon the cheque of the third executor to the judgment creditor, and which was afterwards paid into Court.

An executor, who, in an action at law by a creditor of the testator, has pleaded according to the truth of the case, is, when the assets are taken from him, and administered in equity, entitled to the protection of the Court against any personal liability in respect of such plea.

Notwithstanding an order on further directions in a creditor's suit, that the costs of all parties should be taxed as between solicitor and client, and paid out of a fund in Court,—the fund proving insufficient to pay all the costs,—the Court ordered the costs of the executors to be paid in the first place.

Interest on debts by judgment recovered against the executor.

J. TAYLOR, the testator, married Hannah, the widow of R. Stringer, and borrowed of Waterhouse, Holt, and Cooper, the executors of Stringer, the sum of 1,200*l.* Taylor, who was not a trader, died in January, 1830, indebted in that sum, and also indebted to other persons; and entitled to some real estate, subjected by his will to the payment of his debts, and to other real estate which did not pass by his will. He appointed Hannah, his widow, Tottie and Shaw, his executrix and executors. In June, 1830, Waterhouse, Holt, and Cooper, brought their action in the Common Pleas against the executrix and executors of Taylor, for recovery of the 1,200*l.* and interest; to which the executrix and executors of Taylor pleaded *plenè administravit.* In the same month of June, the plaintiff in this suit, a creditor of the testator Taylor, filed his bill on behalf of himself and the other unsatisfied creditors, for the administration of the estate. Hannah Taylor, the executrix, withdrew her plea of *plenè administravit* to the action by the executors of Stringer (2), and instead thereof pleaded *plenè administravit præter* the sum of 388*l.* 6*s.* 7*d.* (part of the testator's assets, which the executrix and executors had received and deposited in their joint names in the

[*414] Bank of Messrs. Brown & Co. at Leeds), and *goods and chattels of the value of 481*l.* 13*s.* 6*d.* (being the furniture and effects in the testator's house), making together 865*l.* 0*s.* 1*d.* Waterhouse, Holt,

(1) *Staniar* v. *Evans,* 34 Ch. D. 470, 56 L. J. Ch. 581, 56 L. T. 87.

(2) The executrix also severed in her defence in this suit, having a different interest from her co-executors; and it was held to be a case in which two sets of costs should be allowed. See *Gaunt* v. *Taylor,* 50 R. R. 197 (2 Beav. 346).

and Cooper then entered a *nolle prosequi* on the plea of the executors   GAUNT
Tottie and Shaw, with payment of assets *in futuro* as against them ;   *v.*
and an interlocutory judgment was signed against Hannah Taylor,   TAYLOR.
the executrix, for the assets confessed, with an award of a writ of
inquiry to assess the damages. The writ of inquiry was executed
on the 2nd of November, 1830, and the damages (the debt and
interest) were assessed at 1,249*l.* with 31*l.* 13*s.* costs, and final
judgment was signed on the 11th of November, upon which execution issued to levy 865*l.* 0*s.* 1*d.*, part of the said damages and costs,
of the goods and chattels of the testator, acknowledged by Hannah
Taylor to be in her hands. Under this execution the sheriff seized
and sold the furniture and effects, and paid the sum produced by
the sale, amounting after deducting the expenses to 400*l.* 9*s.* 5*d.*, to
Waterhouse, Holt, and Cooper, in part satisfaction of the judgment.
Waterhouse, Holt, and Cooper applied to Hannah Taylor for payment of the 383*l.* 6*s.* 7*d.*, and she gave them a cheque on Messrs.
Brown & Co., dated the 15th of November, 1830, for 380*l.* The
bankers, however, refused payment, alleging that they had received
notice from Shaw, one of the executors, not to part with the money.
Under an order of the 8th of February, the 383*l.* 6*s.* 7*d.* was paid
into Court, in the cause. The decree was made in June, 1831, and
the usual accounts were directed. The Master, in taking the
account of the debt due to the executors of Stringer, allowed interest
on the principal sum of 1,200*l.* from the time of assessment of
damages until the time of the levy under the execution, and on the
balance of such principal sum, after deducting the sum levied, from
the time of the levy to the date of his report. Exceptions to the
report in respect of such allowance *of interest were taken and   [*415]
allowed (1) ; and the amount reported to be due was reduced to
880*l.* 3*s.* 7*d.*

   In December, 1840, by an order made on further directions, and
on the petition of Waterhouse and Cooper (Holt being dead), it was
ordered that,—there being a deficient fund for the payment of the
creditors of the testator in full,—the Master should tax the costs
of the plaintiff as between solicitor and client, and any costs,
charges, and expenses he had incurred, not being costs in the
cause,—and tax the costs of the defendant James Taylor the
heir-at-law,—and tax the costs of the defendant Hannah Taylor, as
between solicitor and client, and her costs, charges, and expenses,
not being costs in the cause,—and tax the costs of the defendants

_____

(1) *Gaunt* v. *Taylor*, 3 My. & K. 302.

Tottie and Shaw, as between solicitor and client, and their costs.
charges, and expenses, not being costs in the cause. And, without
prejudice to any question as to the ultimate appropriation thereof,
an inquiry was directed of how much of 2,732*l.* 6*s.* 11*d.* Consols,
standing to the credit of the cause, was purchased with the
383*l.* 6*s.* 7*d.* paid into Court by the executrix and executors, and
what interest had arisen therefrom ; and so much of the fund as
was so purchased and accumulated was ordered to be carried over
to a " special account ; " and an inquiry was also directed of how
much of the 2,732*l.* 6*s.* 11*d.* Consols arose from legal assets of the
testator, and so much as should be found to have so arisen was
ordered to be carried over to the same " special account." And the
residue of the Consols was ordered to be applied in payment of the
[*416]   costs, and costs, charges, and expenses before ordered *to be taxed.
And it was ordered that a case should be sent to the Common
Pleas, for the opinion of the Judges of that Court, on the following
questions : first, whether it was necessary to docket the judgment
recovered by E. Holt, W. Waterhouse, and W. Cooper, against the
defendants Hannah Taylor, T. W. Tottie, and J. H. Shaw, as
executors of J. Taylor deceased, in order to give preference against
the executors in the administration of the testator's estate, in pursuance of the 4 & 5 W. & M. c. 20 ; and if the Judges of the
said Court should be of opinion that it was necessary to docket
such judgment, then, secondly, whether such judgment was duly
docketed.

In Michaelmas Term, 1841, the Judges of the Common Pleas
certified that it was not necessary the judgment should have been
docketed to give priority to the judgment creditor.

The Master, by his separate report, in April, 1842, found that a
part of the fund, consisting of 497*l.* 12*s.* 8*d.* Consols, and 156*l.* 14*s.* 3*d.*
interest thereon, was produced by the 383*l.* 6*s.* 7*d.* ; and that
1,312*l.* 15*s.* 2*d.* Consols, arose from legal assets of the testator.
And by his general report, in July following, he certified that he
had taxed the costs, charges, and expenses of the plaintiff at the
sum of 1,367*l.* 11*s.* 6*d.*, of J. Taylor, the heir-at-law, at 127*l.* 6*s.* 9*d.*,
of the executrix Hannah Taylor, (deducting sums due from her), at
971*l.* 13*s.* 6*d.*, of the executors Tottie and Shaw, at 552*l.* 13*s.* 9*d.* :
making in the whole 2,997*l.* 16*s.* 8*d.*

Feb. 24.   At the time the cause came on for further directions, 1,597*l.* 2*s.* 2*d.*
[417]   Consols, and 45*l.* 12*s.* 10*d.* cash, were standing to the "special
account," and 1,497*l.* 13*s.* 3*d.* Consols, and 111*l.* 1*s.* 1*d.* cash, to

the credit of the cause generally.   Cooper, who had survived   GAUNT
Waterhouse and Holt, the other executors of Stringer, by his   v.
petition, prayed that the fund produced by the 383*l*. 6*s*. 7*d*. might   TAYLOR.
be paid to him, in satisfaction of the judgment recovered against
Hannah Taylor, upon her confession as to that sum.

Mr. Anderdon and *Mr. E. Montagu*, for the plaintiff, contended
that he was entitled to be paid his costs out of the entire fund before
specialty creditors, whether of the testator or of the executors. * * *

Mr. Spence and *Mr. Parker*, for the executors, Tottie and   [*418]
Shaw, argued that the creditors, who recovered *judgment, and
obtained the cheque from the executrix, of which the executors had
prevented the payment, did not thereby acquire any right to the
money in the hands of the bankers as against the two executors and
the general creditors ; and that the costs of the executors must first
be paid.

Mr. Roupell and *Mr. Elderton*, for Hannah Taylor, the
executrix, contended that she was justified in pleading as she had
done, and in endeavouring to pay the judgment creditor ; and that
the costs of the executrix and executors were now the first charge.

Mr. Kenyon Parker and *Mr. Shee*, for the petitioner Cooper,
contended, that the effect of the judgment, as now determined by
the certificate from the Common Pleas, was to give the creditor a
prior right to the monies which the executrix had confessed ; and
that they were thereby taken out of the reach of the Court for the
purposes of administration.

Mr. Shebbeare, for the heir-at-law.

THE VICE-CHANCELLOR, after stating the facts, and disposing of
the costs of the motion in the cause, which had been a
subject of discussion :

With regard to the claim of the judgment creditor to the sum of
383*l*. 6*s*. 7*d*. in the banker's hands, it is now settled that money in
the hands of a banker is not in the nature of a chattel deposited
with a third party, but is merely a simple contract debt; it is a
mere debt owing to the executors : the judgment creditor had no
means of reaching it at law, unless he acquired the power of doing
so by means of the cheque, which he obtained from the executrix.
The cheque was subject *to be countermanded before payment, and   [*419]

it was in fact countermanded by the other two executors ; and the money was paid into Court. The payment into Court does not affect the right of any party : it is only secured for the party who shall be found entitled to it when all the facts are brought before the Court. Now, the case of *Lepard* v. *Vernon* (1), and other cases, show that, although this Court does not deprive the creditor of any legal advantage which he has acquired, yet, if, without its assistance, he cannot obtain payment even out of legal assets, in priority to other creditors, the Court does not give him assistance to enable him to obtain that advantage.

In this case, I have to consider the effect of any order which I might make for the distribution of the produce of this particular fund, either in payment of costs or otherwise, with reference to the position in which Hannah Taylor may be placed, in consequence of the proceedings at law. Hannah Taylor, by her plea at law, acknowledged the possession of this sum of 383*l*. 6*s*. 7*d*. ; and, upon that confession, the judgment against her proceeded : the execution did not give the judgment creditor possession of the money, and the Court has since taken it out of the hands of the executors. What the personal liability of an executor may be, where he has pleaded a false plea at law,—or what degree of protection he may be in that case entitled to in this Court,—I am not now called upon to decide. That is not the present case. The plea of the executrix was in accordance with the truth of the case ; and it is impossible I can say, as an abstract proposition, that the executrix, who frames her plea at law according *to the truth, has done wrong,—or that she is not entitled, in this Court, where the estate ultimately comes to be administered, to all the protection which the Court can give her against any consequences resulting from the interference of this Court and the nature of the plea at law. If the effect of the judgment was to charge the executrix to the extent of her acknowledgment, and immediately to give the creditor a right at law to recover these funds, the executrix is entitled to be indemnified by means of such an application of the fund as will give the creditor the benefit of his legal right, and so protect her from any personal liability under which she might be placed by the judgment against her. I think the proper course in this case will be to retain this portion of the fund until the creditor shall have had an opportunity of taking such proceedings at law as he may think proper, in order to establish his title to it.

[*420]

(1) 13 R. R. 13 (2 V. & B. 51).

I have felt much difficulty in disposing of the question of costs in this case. The order made on further directions, in December, 1840, directed the costs, charges, and expenses, ordered to be taxed, to be paid out of the residue of the fund in Court, after carrying over part to the special account. In the case of *Swale* v. *Milner* (1), the Court considered itself to be bound by a similar order to apply the fund in payment of the costs rateably, where it proved to be insufficient to pay the whole of the costs in full, although the ordinary rule of the Court gave to some of the parties a priority over the others in respect of costs. The order of payment which I directed in the case of *Tipping* v. *Power* (2), was merely following the old rule of the Court. And, if that is the order in which the parties are entitled *to the payment of their costs, and yet the Court is to be bound to apply the fund rateably, in consequence of the language of the prior direction, it follows that an effect is given to that direction which I cannot consider the Court to have intended,—for it involves a disposition of the fund (being deficient to pay all) which is not in accordance with the rights of the parties. Does the order which has been made force upon me the conclusion come to in *Swale* v. *Milner* ? I cannot say that I think the language of the order so stringent as that case supposes. If a fund were ordered to be paid to creditors, and some were creditors by specialty, and others by simple contract, and the fund proved to be insufficient to pay them all, I cannot think the Court would be bound to interpret an order, the language of which is plainly flexible, so as to contravene a well-established and undisputed rule of practice. I proceed upon the ground that the order merely amounts to a charge upon the fund in favour of the parties entitled, according to their admitted rights.

I think the proper course in this case is to carry the order of December, 1840, into effect, with those specific directions which the circumstances now appearing render necessary; and that the direction to apply the fund in payment of the costs must be executed by making that payment in the order in which the respective parties are entitled to their costs, according to the general rule of the Court. I do not in this respect vary the order on further directions, I only give to it a specific interpretation consistent with the language in which it is expressed.

*   *   *   *   *

(1) 6 Sim. 572.   (2) 58 R. R. 113 (1 Hare, 412).

1843.
Feb. 21, 22,
25.
March 11, 14.
────
WIGRAM,
V.-C.

On Appeal.
1843.
March 17, 18,
29.
────
Lord
LYNDHURST,
L.C.

[424]

SUISSE v. LORD LOWTHER.

(2 Hare, 424—439; affirmed, 12 L. J. Ch. 315—320; 7 Jur. 407.)

Several bequests to a servant of the testator, made in eight different instruments, held to be all cumulative, notwithstanding the gift to the party by the last codicil was much larger than any of the preceding gifts to him; and the whole amount given by that codicil was expressed as being given to provide for the servants of the testator.

Where a testator makes several gifts to a stranger by different instruments, the presumption is, that such gifts are cumulative, and the circumstance of differences in their character or amount, or of a further motive or reason assigned upon the instrument, tends to strengthen the presumption.

Circumstances in which one testamentary instrument is held to be in substitution for, or a mere repetition of, another.

THE plaintiff entered the service of the late Marquis of Hertford (then Lord Yarmouth) in 1822, and continued in such service until the death of the Marquis, in 1842. The bill sought a decree against the executors for payment of various legacies, amounting in the whole to 19,500l., under the will, and numerous codicils made by the Marquis, dated respectively in 1823, 1827, 1829, 1833, 1835, 1837, and 1839. The executors admitted assets. The question was, whether some of these legacies expressed to be given to the plaintiff were not merely in substitution for others which had been made in the previous instruments, or whether they were all cumulative.

The several parts of the will and codicils material to the question are successively stated in the judgment.

*   *   *

[426]   Mr. Roupell, Mr. Goodeve, and Mr. De Gex, were then heard. for the plaintiff, on the questions of construction,—and Sir C. Wetherell and Mr. Follett, for the defendant.

[In addition to the cases mentioned in the judgment, many other cases were cited, including Mackenzie v. Mackenzie (1), Bartlett v. Gillard (2), Fraser v. Byng (3), Watson v. Reed (4), Mackinnon v. Peach (5), Spire v. Smith (6), Robley v. Robley (7).]

THE VICE-CHANCELLOR:

The plaintiff claims to be entitled to several legacies under the will and seven of the codicils made by Lord Hertford. Under six

(1) 26 R. R. 64 (2 Russ. 262).   (5) 44 R. R. 283 (2 Keen, 555).
(2) 27 R. R. 45 (3 Russ. 149).   (6) 49 R. R. 396 (1 Beav. 419).
(3) 32 R. R. 154 (1 Russ. & My. 90).   (7) 50 R. R. 112 (2 Beav. 95).
(4) 35 R. R. 178 (5 Sim. 431).

of these instruments, he claims as a legatee named; and, under the other two, as being one of a class to whom legacies are given. The *question to which the argument was directed was, whether the legacy of 8,000*l.*, given by the Marquis to his executors by the last codicil, was to be in addition to, or in substitution for, the legacies given by the previous instruments; and, to determine this question, I must first consider the construction of the previous instruments to which the last is supposed to refer.

The first claim is under a gift to servants, in these words: " I give and bequeath to every servant, who shall be living in my service at the time of my death (except such of them as were living in my service as Lord Yarmouth), clear of legacy-duty, one whole year's wages; and to every servant that shall be living in my service at the time of my death, and was also living in my service as Lord Yarmouth, clear of legacy-duty, three whole years' wages " (1). The testator divides his servants into two classes, and apportions his bounty according to the time of their service. There is no question that Suisse will take under this gift, according to his description or character, whatever that may be.

The next gift is, " I give all my servants three years' wages who have lived with me three years,—to others, one year's." This is a gift to servants whose qualifications to take will differ materially from those under the first gift. And, further on, in the same codicil, the testator removes all necessity for resorting to any presumption; for, he adds, " All bequests made by this codicil to be in addition to any bequests I may have previously made to these legatees; and I confirm all codicils to my will (the only one I have made since my father's death) wheresoever and whatsoever " (2). By express words therefore, as well as by the presumption *of law to which I shall advert, Suisse would be entitled to take both these legacies.

The next gift is this: " I give to my valet, Nicholas Suisse, if he be living with me at the time of my death, 1,000*l.*, over and above any other bequest" (3). Here is a legacy differing in substance from those which went before. They were to be measured by the wages and the time of service,—here it is a gift of a certain sum upon a condition, with an express declaration that it shall be additional. Upon that there can be no question.

(1) Will, dated in February, 1823.   (3) Eighth codicil, dated October,
(2) Third codicil, dated February,   1829.
1827.

The next instrument is in these words : "This is a codicil to the will of me, Francis Charles, Marquis of Hertford, one copy of which is at Coutts's, the other at Hopkinson's : I give to C. L. Strachan, my ward, over and above any and every other bequest, 15,000*l.* : I give to Nicholas Suisse similarly 2,000*l.*: both legacies to be paid within three months of my death " (1).   Even if there were nothing in these words importing that the legacy to the plaintiff was to be additional, there is nothing to exclude the presumption, that, being of a different amount from the former legacies, and given by a different instrument, he would take both.   But there is nothing to which the word "similarly" can be referred, except the words "over and above," annexed to the previous legacy given to C. L. Strachan.   In this case, also, we find an express direction that the legacy shall be taken in addition to previous legacies.

There then comes the legacy of 3,000*l.*, upon which it is contended that a question of substitution first arises.   It is in these words : "This is a codicil ; I give these legacies in addition to what I have
in most *instances given to the same persons by other codicils and bequests, all of which I confirm, as well as the repealing codicils in some instances ; but this the dates will regulate ; to the Right Hon. J. W. Croker, 7,000*l.* additional ; to (name struck through), for medical attendance on me, when I die, 3,000*l.* ; to Nicholas Suisse, my valet, 3,000*l.*"   The codicil also contains legacies to several other persons (2).   Now, it was argued, on the part of the estate, that the 3,000*l.* given by this codicil, following the other two codicils giving 1,000*l.* and 2,000*l.*, was, in point of fact, a mere repetition of the other two ; and the argument was important for this reason,—that the last codicil giving 8,000*l.* is thereby made sufficient, in point of amount, to satisfy the preceding gifts.   And if the 3,000*l.* is to be taken as a mere repetition of the 2,000*l.* and 1,000*l.*, then, it was said, the 8,000*l.* given to Suisse by the last codicil would exceed the amount of the legacies given to him by the prior instruments.   If, on the other hand, the 3,000*l.* was to be taken as cumulative, then the 8,000*l.* given by the last codicil would not in amount be a satisfaction of the legacies previously given.

The argument against the cumulative character of the legacy given by the codicil I am now considering was founded, first, on the coincidence in amount between the two former legacies and

(1) Fourteenth codicil, dated July,   (2) Twenty-fourth codicil, dated
1833.   September, 1835.

the latter; and, secondly, on the fact, that the other legacies, given to Mr. Croker and others in the same codicil, have the word "additional" appended to them, while in the legacy to Suisse that word is not used. Leaving out the introductory part of the codicil, the question would certainly arise, whether the effect of the word "additional" annexed to some of the gifts, and omitted in that to the *plaintiff, would be to leave his legacy as a substitution for [*430] prior gifts. The cases, however, have expressly decided the point,— that, where there is nothing but the circumstance of omitting such words, the Court does not consider it sufficient to control that which, *primâ facie*, is the meaning of the bequest. Where the mere bounty of the testator is the only apparent motive for the bequest, and no other is expressed, the rule is, that the legatee shall take in addition. But I confess I do not understand how to give to the introductory words their plain meaning, unless I take the legacy to be expressly additional. I have no right to strike out the words, "I give these legacies in addition to what I have in most instances given to the same persons by other codicils," in their application to the plaintiff's legacy. It can only be by first assuming that this legacy was not meant to be cumulative, that I can come to the conclusion, that those words were not meant to apply to it. I am of opinion, that the plaintiff takes the 3,000*l.* as a distinct legacy, and that he was, therefore, at the date of this codicil, a legatee to the extent of 6,000*l.*,—a fact which materially alters the amount to which he was entitled before and at the time when the last codicil was made.

On the next codicil no question arises. It is in these words: "I give, above all other legacies, to Charlotte L. Strachan, 11,000*l.*; to the Right Hon. John W. Croker, 9,000*l.*; to T. Tomkinson, equally in addition, 1,000*l.*; and to Nicholas Suisse, equally in addition, 2,600*l.*" (1). The codicil which contains the next gift to the plaintiff is equally unambiguous: "Independent of, and in addition to, all other legacies I have given to Nicholas Suisse, I leave him 2,000*l.* for continued good services" (2). If the express words had not avoided the *necessity of all argument, the mere [*431] fact, that this gift is contained in a separate instrument, would of itself probably be sufficient; but the additional fact, that, at this date, the testator speaks of Suisse's "continued good services," would be a reason, within the authority of decided cases, for holding that that also was an additional legacy. Down to this time,

(1) Twenty-seventh codicil, dated   (2) Twenty-ninth codicil, dated
Milan, January, 1837.   September, 1837.

therefore, the plaintiff is a legatee to an amount considerably above 10,000*l.* Then follows the codicil to which I before referred, and upon which the argument has been founded. It is in these words : " This is a further codicil to the last will of me, Francis Charles, Marquis of Hertford, K.G. : I give and bequeath 16,000*l.* to my executors, that they may provide for my servants as follows—first, half of the same to Nicholas Suisse, my head valet, an excellent man : then I desire that the remaining eight may be split into three parts, one to Charlemagne, my cook, one to Fiorini, my courier, another to Robert (really Thomas) Foote : there will then remain a quarter and an eighth, which I desire may be divided at my executors' pleasure, attending first to James, my coachman's, claims, and next to those who have slept under my roof, and been abroad with me " (1).

Now, passing over the gift for the benefit of Suisse in the first part of this codicil, it is quite impossible that, as regards the legacies to the other servants, substitution can have been the object of the testator ; for the servants, who took under the former legacies, were selected in a manner totally different : they took absolutely, provided they fell under a certain description. Here the legacies remained at the pleasure of the executors, and the persons indicated are those servants who have slept under the roof and been abroad with the testator. *Many of the servants, entitled under the will and former codicils, might not fall within that description ; and it is impossible I could deprive them, by the effect of this codicil, of the bounty previously given.

[*432]

On questions of repetition or accumulation, most of the Judges have referred, as Lord ELDON did in the case of *Hemming* v. *Gurrey* (2), to the judgment in *Hooley* v. *Hatton* (3), as containing a sound exposition of the law upon the subject,—and, in the case of *Hurst* v. *Beach* (4), Sir JOHN LEACH drew his conclusion from the cases with great precision, and, as it appears to me, with great accuracy : he stated the rule to be, that, where legacies are given by different instruments, the presumption is, *primâ facie,* that two legacies are intended. But, inasmuch as if a testator were by one instrument to give a particular ring, or horse, or specific chattel, and were, by another instrument, to give precisely the same thing, it would follow that the second must be a repetition,—so, if the

(1) Thirty-fourth codicil, dated   1 Bligh, N. S. 479).
November, 1839.   (3) 1 Br. C. C. 390, *n.*
  (2) 30 R. R. 56 (2 Sim. & St. 311 ;   (4) 21 R. R. 304 (5 Madd. 358).

bounty given by one instrument be, in terms, a repetition of that
which has gone before, the Court has presumed that the second
was intended to be repetition, and not accumulation.   It is clearly
decided, however, that the mere fact that the amount is the same,
is not such an identification of the second with the first as would
prevent both from taking effect as cumulative; but if, in addition
to the amounts being the same, the testator connects a motive with
both, and the express motive is also the same, the double coincidence induces the Court to believe that repetition, and not accumulation, was intended.   Except in such cases, and the class of cases
to which I am about to advert, the Court does not infer that
repetition was the *object, unless it be so declared, or it is to be
collected from the words of the will itself.

   The presumption, in the case of several gifts by different instruments, being in favour of accumulation, it is clear that the claim of
the plaintiff in this case must be strengthened by any circumstances
of difference between the two gifts,—whether it be found in the
amount,—in the character in which it is given,—in the mode of
enjoyment,—in the extent of the interest,—or in the motive for the
bounty.   All these considerations tend, in the judgment of the
Court, to support the argument in favour of accumulation.   Now,
in the legacy to Suisse by the last codicil, there is a particular
description of Suisse, which imports a motive of a later date than
the former legacies : he is described as " an excellent man,"—and
the amount being different, and less beneficial to Suisse than the
amount of the previous gifts to him, this adds to the presumption
already in his favour, that a distinct gift was intended; and the
only question, therefore, is, whether there is any thing in the word
" provide," as used in the last codicil, which should lead the Court
to the construction that the legacy is not cumulative.

   Much argument has been founded in this case upon the use of
the word " provide."   The technical sense of the word, it was said,
should be taken by analogy from those cases in which, in gifts from
a parent to a child, or from a person standing *in loco parentis*
towards the legatee, the Court had laid great stress on it.   The
language of the Court in those cases is, that it "leans against
double portions,"—a rule which, though sometimes called technical,
Lord COTTENHAM, in *Pym* v. *Lockyer* (1), said, was founded on good
sense, and could not be *disregarded without disappointing the
intentions of donors.   But, although the presumption is, that

   (1) 48 R. R. 219 (5 My. & Cr. 34, 46).

SUISSE
v.
LORD
LOWTHER.

[*433]

[*434]

The next instrument is in these words: "This is a codicil to the will of me, Francis Charles, Marquis of Hertford, one copy of which is at Coutts's, the other at Hopkinson's: I give to C. L. Strachan, my ward, over and above any and every other bequest, 15,000*l*.: I give to Nicholas Suisse similarly 2,000*l*.: both legacies to be paid within three months of my death" (1). Even if there were nothing in these words importing that the legacy to the plaintiff was to be additional, there is nothing to exclude the presumption, that, being of a different amount from the former legacies, and given by a different instrument, he would take both. But there is nothing to which the word "similarly" can be referred, except the words "over and above," annexed to the previous legacy given to C. L. Strachan. In this case, also, we find an express direction that the legacy shall be taken in addition to previous legacies.

There then comes the legacy of 3,000*l*., upon which it is contended that a question of substitution first arises. It is in these words: "This is a codicil; I give these legacies in addition to what I have

[*429] in most *instances given to the same persons by other codicils and bequests, all of which I confirm, as well as the repealing codicils in some instances; but this the dates will regulate; to the Right Hon. J. W. Croker, 7,000*l*. additional; to (name struck through), for medical attendance on me, when I die, 3,000*l*.; to Nicholas Suisse, my valet, 3,000*l*." The codicil also contains legacies to several other persons (2). Now, it was argued, on the part of the estate, that the 3,000*l*. given by this codicil, following the other two codicils giving 1,000*l*. and 2,000*l*., was, in point of fact, a mere repetition of the other two; and the argument was important for this reason,—that the last codicil giving 8,000*l*. is thereby made sufficient, in point of amount, to satisfy the preceding gifts. And if the 3,000*l*. is to be taken as a mere repetition of the 2,000*l*. and 1,000*l*., then, it was said, the 8,000*l*. given to Suisse by the last codicil would exceed the amount of the legacies given to him by the prior instruments. If, on the other hand, the 3,000*l*. was to be taken as cumulative, then the 8,000*l*. given by the last codicil would not in amount be a satisfaction of the legacies previously given.

The argument against the cumulative character of the legacy given by the codicil I am now considering was founded, first, on the coincidence in amount between the two former legacies and

(1) Fourteenth codicil, dated July, 1833.

(2) Twenty-fourth codicil, dated September, 1835.

the latter; and, secondly, on the fact, that the other legacies, SUISSE
r.
LORD
LOWTHER.
given to Mr. Croker and others in the same codicil, have the word
"additional" appended to them, while in the legacy to Suisse that
word is not used. Leaving out the introductory part of the codicil,
the question would certainly arise, whether the effect of the word
"additional" annexed to some of the gifts, and omitted in that to
the *plaintiff, would be to leave his legacy as a substitution for [*430]
prior gifts. The cases, however, have expressly decided the point,—
that, where there is nothing but the circumstance of omitting such
words, the Court does not consider it sufficient to control that which,
primâ facie, is the meaning of the bequest. Where the mere bounty
of the testator is the only apparent motive for the bequest, and no
other is expressed, the rule is, that the legatee shall take in addition.
But I confess I do not understand how to give to the introductory
words their plain meaning, unless I take the legacy to be expressly
additional. I have no right to strike out the words, "I give these
legacies in addition to what I have in most instances given to the
same persons by other codicils," in their application to the plaintiff's
legacy. It can only be by first assuming that this legacy was not
meant to be cumulative, that I can come to the conclusion, that
those words were not meant to apply to it. I am of opinion, that
the plaintiff takes the 8,000*l.* as a distinct legacy, and that he was,
therefore, at the date of this codicil, a legatee to the extent of
6,000*l.*,—a fact which materially alters the amount to which he was
entitled before and at the time when the last codicil was made.

On the next codicil no question arises. It is in these words: "I
give, above all other legacies, to Charlotte L. Strachan, 11,000*l.*;
to the Right Hon. John W. Croker, 9,000*l.*; to T. Tomkinson,
equally in addition, 1,000*l.*; and to Nicholas Suisse, equally in
addition, 2,600*l.*" (1). The codicil which contains the next gift to
the plaintiff is equally unambiguous: "Independent of, and in
addition to, all other legacies I have given to Nicholas Suisse, I
leave him 2,000*l.* for continued good services" (2). If the express
words had not avoided the *necessity of all argument, the mere [*431]
fact, that this gift is contained in a separate instrument, would of
itself probably be sufficient; but the additional fact, that, at this
date, the testator speaks of Suisse's "continued good services,"
would be a reason, within the authority of decided cases, for holding
that that also was an additional legacy. Down to this time,

(1) Twenty-seventh codicil, dated   (2) Twenty-ninth codicil, dated
Milan, January, 1837.   September, 1837.

given? the rule of law being, for the reasons I have stated, in favour of the last legacy being cumulative. I am clear I have no right to speculate on any *views the Marquis may have had, or to hold that the last codicil was merely intended to provide for the payment of the former gifts.

Looking at the case as it stands upon these testamentary papers, without reference to any of the considerations to which I have adverted, taking it as clear that there is no presumption against any of the legacies, independently of the form of the instruments in which they are found, and that, *primâ facie*, they are cumulative, the question may still be, whether the instruments are in substitution one for another,—so that if one is to take effect, another is to be regarded as cancelled? The cases of *The Duke of St. Albans* v. *Beauclerk* (1), *Hemming* v. *Gurrey*, and *Russell* v. *Dickson* (2), illustrate that subject very clearly. In *The Duke of St. Albans* v. *Beauclerk*, the instruments were almost repetitions one of the other. In several instances, the testator had given the identical thing by the second which he had given by the first instrument,—such as particular jewels, and certain specific articles which were of necessity nothing but repeated gifts of the same thing. In the case of *Hemming* v. *Gurrey*, also, the testator was in the habit of copying his will; and although there were some differences, yet the two instruments were, to the eye and in substance, very nearly a repetition the one of the other. In *Russell* v. *Dickson*, the paper, which the testator called his last will, was construed as a final declaration of his will, excluding all that had gone before it. But it is impossible to apply that reasoning in this case; for the will and the several codicils dispose of property, to a very large amount,

among a number of persons who are obviously very *marked and favoured objects of the testator's bounty, but of whom there is no mention in the last codicil, which touches nobody but Suisse and some particular servants. It is impossible, therefore, to treat the last instrument, in any sense of the word, as being the will of the Marquis substituted by him for and superseding all his former testamentary dispositions.

I may observe another fact, which strongly tends to convince me of the obligation I am under to give effect to the last codicil, as containing additional gifts to the plaintiff: in pursuing the language of the testator through the various codicils, you find that, having begun by giving his property to persons who had naturally a claim

(1) 2 Atk. 636.   (2) 59 R. R. 674 (2 Dr. & War. 133).

upon him, he is afterwards continually cutting down the provisions he had made for those persons, and giving his property to strangers. Why he should not have intended to make this liberal provision for Suisse, as well as gifts, to an enormous amount, to other persons who had no natural claim upon him, I have no ground for saying. It is nothing but conjecture. I do not find any thing in this will to deprive Suisse of the whole amount which he claims.

SUISSE
v.
LORD
LOWTHER.

Decree for payment of the legacies, without costs.

[The executors appealed from this judgment, as reported in 12 L. J. Ch. 315.]

Sir C. *Wetherell* and *Mr. Follett* appeared for the appellants; and

[12 L. J. Ch. 316]

Mr. *Roupell*, Mr. *Goodere*, and Mr. *De Gex*, for the plaintiff. * * *

THE LORD CHANCELLOR:

March 29.

This is a question arising out of the will and codicils of the late Marquis of Hertford; and the question is, whether or not the legacies bequeathed to Nicholas Suisse in those codicils are to be considered as cumulative or substitutional. They are of three descriptions: first, those legacies which are given generally to the servants by the will and by one of the codicils; secondly, with respect to a legacy of 3,000*l.*, given by one of the codicils; and, lastly, with respect to a legacy of 8,000*l.*, which is given by another codicil.

First, then, with respect to the legacy given to the servants generally, under which Nicholas Suisse claims as one of the servants in the service of the late Marquis of Hertford. By the will, one year's wages are given to those servants who should be living with the Marquis at the time of his death, free of the legacy duty. Those legacies are to be paid within three months after the death of the Marquis. To those who were living with him when he was Earl of Yarmouth he gives three years' wages, free of the legacy duty, to be payable in like manner. By the codicil, to which reference is made, he gives to those servants who shall have lived with him for three years, three years' wages and board wages: nothing is said with respect to the legacy duty. To the rest of the servants he gives one year's wages and board wages: nothing is said with

SUISSE
v.
LORD
LOWTHER.

[*317]

respect to the time of payment. Now those legacies are given by different instruments, and they are legacies of different amounts ; and therefore they must be taken, in the first instance, as distinct and independent legacies: the one cannot be considered as a substitution for the other, unless there is something in the instrument clearly *manifesting that such was the intention of the testator. Now I look in the codicil for the purpose of ascertaining whether there is anything clearly manifesting such an intention, and I find nothing whatever to that effect. There are some circumstances, too, existing in this case, that have been relied upon by the Court in support of the principle of cumulation. First of all, the legacies are different in point of amount: those which are given by the will are free of the legacy duty ; those which are given by the codicil make no reference whatever to the legacy duty : those which are given by the will consist only of wages ; those which are given by the codicil consist of wages and board wages : those which are given by the will are payable within three months after the death of the testator ; there is no limitation as to the time when those given by the codicil are payable. I think, therefore, it is perfectly clear, according to the rules laid down for the construction of instruments in these cases, and which have been acted upon, that one cannot be considered as a substitution for the other, even upon the general terms of the will.

But there is a distinct clause, which has been relied upon in confirmation of that which I have stated. The clause is in these terms : " All bequests by this codicil to be in addition to any bequest I may have previously made to these legatees." " All bequests by this codicil : " these are bequests given by this codicil ; they are to be " in addition to any bequest I may have previously made to these legatees." What legatees ? The legatees taking under this codicil. It appears to me, therefore, upon the natural and obvious construction of this passage, that it imports, in confirmation of what I have stated, that these legacies to the servants, given by this codicil, were to be cumulative. It was said at the Bar, that the words " these legatees," in their natural construction, apply to the persons who were named immediately previously to this clause ; but I think to put such a construction upon those words would be inconsistent with the previous words, " all bequests by this codicil " comprehending all the bequests contained in the codicil. However, without deciding the question upon the construction of this clause, it appears to me to be sufficient to decide it upon the general terms of the codicil, and I am of opinion, as I have before stated, according to the rules that have been laid down in the decisions of the Courts with respect to instruments of this kind, that these bequests to the servants are to be considered as cumulative.

The next question for consideration relates to a legacy of 3,000*l.* given by one of the codicils. The testator had previously given a legacy of 1,000*l.*; he had also given another legacy of 2,000*l.*, and by this codicil he gives a legacy of 3,000*l.* That 3,000*l.* being equal in amount to the 2,000*l.* and the 1,000*l.*, therefore it is said that this 3,000*l.* must be considered as substituted for the two previous legacies of 2,000*l.* and 1,000*l.*, as they correspond in amount. But that is not sufficient; they are given by distinct instruments, and being given by distinct instruments, unless there is something, as I have before stated, to satisfy the Court, not merely as to conjecture, but to satisfy the Court that it was the intention of the testator that one should be substituted for the others, the Court must act according to the principles I have already laid down. But there are some circumstances here also similar to those which have been relied on by the Court in cases of this kind, to which it is necessary I should advert. The first legacy of 1,000*l.* is not given absolutely, but given upon a condition, namely, that Nicholas Suisse should be living with the testator at the time of his death. The second legacy is payable three months after the death of the testator. Now, when you come to the legacy of 3,000*l.*, there is no such restriction, nor is there any such limitation as to the time of payment. These circumstances, therefore, are confirmatory of the general proposition that these legacies are to be considered as cumulative.

But there is also in this case, as in the former case, a general clause, importing, as I think clearly, the intention of the testator that the legacies should be considered as cumulative. The clause to which I refer is in these terms (this is the codicil) : " I give these legacies "—that is, the legacies in this codicil—" in addition to what I have in most instances given to the same persons by other codicils and bequests, all of which I confirm." " In addition to what I have in most instances *given to the same persons "—now [*318] if I look through this codicil, I find in most instances he had given to the persons therein named legacies, but there are persons also mentioned in this codicil who are not mentioned previously, either in his will, or in any of the antecedent codicils. The will, therefore, corresponds with this clause, which I have read, " I give these legacies in addition to what I have in most instances given to the same persons." Among the "most instances" is included Nicholas Suisse; therefore, by the very terms of the codicil, "I give these legacies in addition to what I have in most instances given to the same persons," it is quite clear, as it appears to me, that the testator intended that the legacy given to Nicholas Suisse should be in addition to the legacies he had before given. The legacy, therefore, is cumulative.

The principal point, however, turns upon the last legacy, the legacy of 8,000*l.* The codicil is in these terms: it is material and necessary to read them. "This is a further codicil to the last will of me, Francis Charles Marquis of Hertford. I give and bequeath the sum of 16,000*l.* to my executors, that they may provide for my servants as follows: first, one half of this sum to Nicholas Suisse, my head valet, an excellent man; then I desire that the remaining eight may be split into three parts, one to Charlemagne, my cook, one to Fiorini, my courier, another to Robert (really Thomas) Foote. There will then remain a quarter and an eighth, which I desire may be divided at my executors' pleasure, attending first to James my coachman's claims, and next to those who have slept under my roof, and been abroad with me." That is the codicil out of which the question arises. It is material, I think, with a view to this codicil, to advert to a previous codicil; it is the last codicil but two. One codicil intervenes between this and the last codicil. He says, "independent of, and in addition to all the legacies I have given to Nicholas Suisse, I leave him 2,000*l.* for continued good services: I give Fiorini, my courier, 1,500*l.* for the same reason, and Charlemagne, my cook, 1,000*l.*, because I know he has made money in my service, and not because he deserves less. To Robert Foote I make up former legacies to 1,500*l.*, and to all the other servants indiscriminately one year's wages and board wages." Now then, with respect to the last codicil. It is a sum of 8,000*l.*, given by a separate instrument. It is suggested that the 8,000*l.* was intended to be substituted for the former legacies. It is given by a separate instrument: it is different in amount; therefore it is to be taken, in the first instance, as a distinct and independent gift, unless there is something appearing, as I before stated, upon the instrument, to show manifestly it was the intention of the testator that it should be taken as substitutional. Now it is suggested that this was given to the executors according to the terms of the legacy, "to provide for my servants as follows;" that is, that it was a

final provision for the servants, to be dispensed and distributed by
the executors according to the terms of this codicil, and that that
was the construction that is to be put upon it.   It was said, that
that was the intention of the testator.   No such intention was
expressed, but such, it is said, by construction, was the intention
of the testator.   If that be so, it must have been the intention of
the testator to reduce his bounty and the gift which he had before
given to Nicholas Suisse, because he had before given to Nicholas
Suisse legacies amounting to the sum, altogether, I think, of 11,600*l.*,
so that he was reducing Nicholas Suisse, if this construction is to
prevail, by the amount of 3,600*l.*   No such intention, I think,
appears upon the instrument ; but, on the contrary, a directly
opposite inference, I think, is to be drawn from all the circumstances.   In the immediately previous codicil, where Suisse is
mentioned, he gives him 2,000*l.* for continued good services.   He
gives him 8,000*l.* by this codicil, and the motive appearing on the
face of the codicil is, that he is " an excellent man."   I am justified,
therefore, in inferring, from these circumstances, rather the opposite
conclusion,—that he had no intention to diminish or lessen his
bounty towards Nicholas Suisse.   No intention is expressed upon the
face of the instrument ; and if we are to judge from inference and
from probabilities, the inference, as I have before stated, appears
to me to be directly the other way.   But it is not confined to
Nicholas Suisse alone, because it would affect the other legatees who
are specially named here, *namely, the courier, the cook, and the   [*319]
footman.   In the previous codicil to which I have referred, he gives
them also 4,000*l.* between them for " continued good services."
No intention appears upon the face of this codicil to diminish that
bounty, and yet by the effect of it, if this is to be considered as the
final provision for the servants and a substitution for former
legacies, that which he had previously given in the antecedent
codicil for good services is reduced to the amount of one-half ; it is
reduced to the amount of 2,000*l.*   If we are to act, therefore, upon
conjecture and inference, I think the inference is strongly against
the supposition that these legacies were meant as substitutions for
the former bounty of the Marquis.   Then it is said that this is—
and it certainly appears to be—a very large sum of money to have
been given all at once to a person in the situation of Nicholas Suisse ;
but any person who will take the trouble to read through these
codicils, will see that he cannot construe them by the ordinary rules
of probability : and, after all, if we compare this codicil with the

SUISSE
v.
LORD
LOWTHER.

former acts of the testator with reference to this same individual, it does not appear to be at all improbable; it is a mere continuation of what he had previously done. He began by including him among the general servants. He then gives him 1,000*l.* by a codicil, depending upon what? Upon his being in his service at the time of his death. He had not acquired that confidence which he seems afterwards to have acquired. He then gives him 2,000*l.* by name, without that contingency. He then gives him another legacy of 8,000*l.* Then a legacy, after an interval of about a year or so, of 2,600*l.* Then a further legacy of 2,000*l.* for continued good services. And then, after an interval of two years, which it is material to advert to, in which he has given him nothing, he gives him this sum of 8,000*l.* Now between 1835 and 1837, though he had given it him at three intervals, he gives him about the same sum: he gives him, in 1835, 3,000*l.*, and, between 1835 and 1837, he gives him 2,600*l.* and 2,000*l.*, making altogether 7,600*l.* So that, in the previous two years, he had given him nearly the same sum; and the last of those grants was "for continued good services." Then he gives him, after two years, the same sum of 8,000*l.*, or about the same sum, describing him as "an excellent man." It appears to me that there is nothing improbable in this; on the contrary, it is perfectly consistent with the former exercise of his bounty in favour of the same individual.

But then it is said, why give this to the executors to be distributed among the servants, and to provide for them? Why create two funds? Why it is very difficult always to account for the caprices of men. It does not appear, when you look at this instrument, that he had any legal advice at the moment. It is obviously drawn up by himself; and I think, therefore, no inference can be drawn from the form of the instrument. But if we are to conjecture, I think I can give a reason why it is not improbable that he took this form. Upon all the other occasions, he had given precise sums to the individuals by name; in this particular case he gives a large sum to the executors—16,000*l.*—a very considerable proportion of which was to be distributed entirely at the discretion of the executors; the individuals were not named; the amounts were not named; the amounts were to be fixed and assigned by the executors themselves; they had perfect liberty to do, in that respect, as they thought proper. Giving, therefore, a sum over which the executors were to exercise a control in the distribution at their pleasure, it was not unnatural that he should give that sum directly to the executors.

I think that is a reasonable explanation of the different forms of these legacies. It is by no means necessary to assign any reason for the particular form which he took; no inference can be drawn from it beyond mere conjecture. It cannot influence the decision of the Court in a case of this kind.

Then there was another argument pressed strongly, and which is possessed of some weight, with respect to the care which the Marquis, in his will, seems generally to have taken, where he intended a legacy to be cumulative, to state that it was to be "in addition to former legacies." He does this in every instance where Suisse is concerned, and he does it generally throughout the codicils to his will. But he does not do it consistently. Several *instances have been pointed out to me, which I have examined, in which, where he obviously meant the legacy to be cumulative, he has not made use of this expression "in addition" in terms; and it only shows, therefore, that men who are generally accurate and precise, sometimes relax in their vigilance and their precision: and though the argument was entitled to some weight, that in the other instances where Suisse is made the object of the bounty of the testator (it is stated in *all* the instances, I think,) the legacies are to be "in addition to former legacies"; and though that is a consideration entitled to weight, and to be examined, it does not appear to me that the inference drawn from that circumstance is sufficient to outweigh the other circumstances to which I have referred. Therefore, upon the whole, I do not, upon the face of this codicil, see anything to lead me to a satisfactory conclusion that it was the intention of the testator that this legacy to Suisse should be in substitution of the former legacies which he had given him by the previous codicils, and, therefore, the judgment of the VICE-CHANCELLOR must be affirmed.

[*320]

FOSS v. HARBOTTLE (1).

(2 Hare, 461—506.)

1843.
March 4, 6, 7,
8, 25.

WIGRAM,
V.-C.

[2 Hare, 461]

A bill was filed by two of the proprietors of shares in a Company incorporated by Act of Parliament, on behalf of themselves and all other the proprietors of shares except the defendants, against the five directors, (three of whom had become bankrupt), and against a proprietor who was not a director, and the solicitor and architect of the Company, charging the

(1) Many references to later cases in which the principle here established has been applied will be found in the case of *Burland* v. *Earle* [1902] A. C.

83, 71 L. J. P. C. 1, 85 L. T. 553; and see *Punt* v. *Symons & Co. Lim.* [1903] 2 Ch. 505, 516.—O. A. S.

defendants with concerting and effecting various fraudulent and illegal transactions, whereby the property of the Company was misapplied, aliened, and wasted; that there had ceased to be a sufficient number of qualified directors to constitute a board; that the Company had no clerk or office; that in such circumstances the proprietors had no power to take the property out of the hands of the defendants, or satisfy the liabilities or wind up the affairs of the Company; praying that the defendants might be decreed to make good to the Company the losses and expenses occasioned by the acts complained of; and praying the appointment of a receiver to take and apply the property of the Company in discharge of its liabilities, and secure the surplus: the defendants demurred.

Held, that, upon the facts stated, the continued existence of a board of directors *de facto* must be intended; that the possibility of convening a general meeting of proprietors capable of controlling the acts of the existing board was not excluded by the allegations of the bill; that in such circumstances there was nothing to prevent the Company from obtaining redress in its corporate character in respect of the matters complained of; that therefore the plaintiffs could not sue in a form of pleading which assumed the practical dissolution of the corporation; and that the demurrers must be allowed.

THE bill was filed in October, 1842, by Richard Foss and Edward Starkie Turton, on behalf of themselves and all other the shareholders or proprietors of shares in the Company called "The Victoria Park Company," except such of the same shareholders or proprietors of shares as were defendants thereto, against Thomas Harbottle, Joseph Adshead, Henry Byrom, John Westhead, Richard Bealey, Joseph Denison, Thomas Bunting and Richard Lane; and also against H. Rotton, E. Lloyd, T. Peet, J. Biggs and S. Brooks, the several assignees of Byrom, Adshead and Westhead, who had become bankrupts.

The bill stated, in effect, that in September, 1835, certain persons conceived the design of associating for the purchase of about 180 acres of land, situated in the parish of Manchester, belonging to the defendant Joseph Denison and others, and of enclosing and planting the same in an ornamental and park-like manner, and erecting houses thereon with attached gardens and pleasure grounds, and selling, letting, or otherwise disposing thereof; and the defendants Harbottle, Adshead, Byrom, Westhead, Bealey, Denison, Bunting and Lane, agreed to form a joint-stock Company, to consist of themselves and others, for the said purpose: that in [*462] October, 1835, *plans of the land, and a design for laying it out, were prepared: that after the undertaking had been projected and agreed upon, Denison purchased a considerable portion of the said land of the other original owners, with the object of re-selling it at a profit, and Harbottle, Adshead, Byrom, Westhead, Bunting and Lane, and one P. Leicester, and several other persons, not members

of the association, purchased the said land in parcels of Denison
and the other owners, so that at the time of passing the Act of
incorporation Harbottle, Adshead, Byrom, Westhead, Bunting and
Lane owned more than half of the land in question, the remainder
being the property of persons who were not shareholders: that
Denison and the last-named five defendants made considerable
profits by re-selling parts of the said land at increased chief rents
before the Act was passed.

The bill stated, that between September, 1835, and the beginning
of 1836, various preliminary steps were taken for enabling the
projectors of the said Company to set it on foot: that in April,
1836, advertisements, describing the objects of the proposed Company, and the probabilities of its profitable result, were published,
in which it was proposed to form the association on the principle of
a tontine: that the first eight named defendants and several other
persons subscribed for shares in the proposed Company, and among
others the plaintiff Foss subscribed for two shares, and the plaintiff
Turton for twelve shares of 100*l.* each, and signed the contract, and
paid the deposit of 5*l.* per share: that at a public meeting of the
subscribers, called in May, 1836, it was resolved that the report of
the provisional committee should be received, and the various
suggestions therein contained be adopted, subject to the approval
of the directors, who were requested to complete such purchases of
land, and also such other acts as they might *consider necessary   [*463]
for carrying the objects of the undertaking into effect; and it also
resolved that Harbottle, Adshead, Byrom, Westhead and Bealey
should be appointed directors, with power to do such acts as they
might consider necessary or desirable for the interests of the
Company; and Westhead, W. Grant and J. Lees were appointed
auditors, Lane architect, and Bunting solicitor: that in order to
avoid the responsibilities of an ordinary partnership, the defendants
Harbottle and others suggested to the subscribers the propriety of
applying for an Act of incorporation, which was accordingly done:
that in compliance with such application, by an Act, intituled "An
Act for establishing a Company for the purpose of laying out and
maintaining an Ornamental Park within the Townships of Rusholme,
Charlton-upon-Medlock and Moss Side, in the County of Lancaster,"
which received the Royal assent on the 5th of May, 1837, (7 Will. IV.),
it was enacted that certain persons named in the Act, including
Harbottle, Adshead, Bealey, Westhead, Bunting and Denison and
others, and all and every such other persons or person, bodies or

FOSS
v.
HARBOTTLE.

body politic, corporate or collegiate, as had already subscribed or should thereafter from time to time become subscribers or a subscriber to the said undertaking, and be duly admitted proprietors or a proprietor as thereinafter mentioned, and their respective successors, executors, administrators and assigns, should be and they were thereby united into a Company for the purposes of the said Act, and should be and they were thereby declared to be one body politic and corporate by the name of "The Victoria Park Company," and by that name should have perpetual succession and a common seal, and by that name should and might sue and be sued, plead or be impleaded at law or in equity, and should and might prefer and prosecute any bill or bills of indictment or

[*464]

information against any person or *persons who should commit any felony, misdemeanor, or other offence indictable or punishable by the laws of this realm, and should also have full power and authority to purchase and hold lands, tenements, and hereditaments to them, and their successors and assigns, for the use of the said undertaking, in manner thereby directed. [The bill stated several other clauses of the Act, of which the principal provisions are set forth below (1).]

(1) Section 3 empowered the Company to purchase the lands mentioned in the schedule; 5, and other lands within a mile from the boundary of the said lands. * * 38 provided that the business affairs and concerns of the Company shall, from time to time, and at all times hereafter, be under the control of five shareholders, (to be appointed directors), who shall have the entire ordering, managing, and conducting of the Company, and of the capital, estates, revenue, effects, and affairs, and other the concerns thereof, and who shall also regulate and determine the mode and terms of carrying on and conducting the business and affairs of the Company, conformably to the provisions contained in this Act; and no proprietor, not being a director, shall, on any account

[*465, *n.*]

or pretence whatsoever, *in any way meddle or interfere in the managing, ordering, or conducting the Company, or the capital, estates, revenue, effects, or other the business, affairs, or concerns thereof, but shall fully and entirely commit, entrust, and leave

the same to be wholly ordered, managed, and conducted by the directors for the time being, and the persons whom they shall appoint, save as hereinafter mentioned. 39. That the said T. Harbottle, J. Adshead, H. Byrom, J. Westhead, and R. Bealy shall be the present and first directors of the Company. 40. Three directors to constitute a board, and the acts of three or more to be as effectual as if done by the five. * * 45. Books of account of all the transactions of the Company to be kept, and half-yearly reports and balance sheets to be made: the proprietors to have access to, and to be at liberty to inspect all books, accounts, documents, and writings belonging to the Company, at all reasonable times. 46. That a meeting of the proprietors of the Company shall be convened and held on the first Monday in the month of July, 1837, and on the same day in every succeeding year, at eleven o'clock in the forenoon, at their office, or such other convenient place in Manchester as the directors may think proper to

The bill also stated the schedule annexed to the Act, whereby the
different plots of the said land, numbered *from 1 to 37, were

appoint, of which meeting the clerk or secretary for the time being of the Company shall give fourteen days' previous notice, by an advertisement in one of the Manchester newspapers; and each meeting so to be convened and held shall be called "The Annual General Meeting," and the proprietors respectively qualified to act and vote therein, according to the provisions therein contained, and who personally, or by such proxy as hereinafter authorised, shall attend the same, shall have full power and authority to decide upon all such matters and questions as by virtue of this Act shall be brought before such annual general meeting. 47. Board of directors empowered to call extraordinary general meetings. 48. That ten or more proprietors of the Company for the time being, qualified to vote as hereinafter mentioned, or three full fourth parts in number and value of all the proprietors for the time being of the Company, may, at any time, by writing under their hands, require the board of directors for the time being to call an extraordinary general meeting of the proprietors, and every such requisition shall set *forth the object of such extraordinary meeting, and shall be left with the clerk or secretary for the time being at the principal office of the Company, at least one calendar month before the time named in the requisition for the meeting to be holden, otherwise the said board shall not be bound to take notice thereof; but in case the directors shall refuse or neglect for fourteen days, after such requisition shall be so left as aforesaid, to call such extraordinary meeting, then, the proprietors signing the requisition may, for the purposes mentioned in such requisition, call an extraordinary general meeting of the proprietors, by notice signed by them, and advertised in one or more of the Manchester newspapers, at least fourteen days before the time fixed for holding the meeting; and in every

such advertisement, the object of such extraordinary meeting, and the day and hour and place in the town of Manchester of holding the same, and the delivery of the requisition to the said board, and of its refusal to call such extraordinary meeting, shall be specified. 65. Two of the directors selected by lot amongst themselves to retire from office at the annual general meeting in July, 1841, and be replaced by two qualified proprietors, to be then elected by the majority of votes at such meeting, and two others, the longest in office, or so selected to retire, at every subsequent annual general meeting; but the retiring directors to be re-eligible. 67. No person shall be a director who shall not be a holder in his own right of the number of shares hereinafter mentioned in the capital of the Company, viz. who shall not be a holder of ten shares at least, so long as the total number of the shares shall exceed 500; and from and after the total number of shares of the Company shall be reduced to and shall not exceed 100, then, who shall not be a holder of five shares at least; and if any of the then or future directors shall cease to hold the respective number of shares aforesaid in his own right, his office as director shall thereupon and thenceforth become vacated. 68. Directors may vacate by resigning their offices. 70. Board of directors to appoint qualified persons to fill up the offices of directors dying, resigning, removed, or becoming disqualified before their time of retirement; such appointments to be subject to the approbation of the next general meeting. 73. Cheques, bills, notes, and other negotiable securities, to be signed, &c. by the treasurer or such other officer of the Company as the board should by minute appoint, and no others to be binding on the Company. 74. That all actions, suits, and other proceedings at law or in equity, to be commenced and prosecuted by or on

stated to have been purchased by the Victoria Park Company from the various persons whose *names were therein set forth, and including the following names: " Mr. P. Leicester and others; " " Mr. Lacy and another; " " Mr. Lane " and " Mr. Adshead: " that *the land so stated to be purchased of " P. Leicester and others," was at the time of passing of the Act vested partly in P. Leicester and partly in Westhead, Bunting, and Byròm, and the land so stated to be purchased of " Mr. Lacy and another," was at the time of the passing of the Act vested partly in Mr. Lacy and partly in Lane.

The bill stated, that the purchase and sale of the said land as aforesaid was the result of an arrangement fraudulently concerted and agreed upon between Harbottle, Adshead, Byrom, Westhead, Denison, Bunting, and Lane, at or after the formation of the Company was agreed upon, with the object of enabling themselves to derive a profit or personal benefit from the establishment of the said Company; and that the arrangement amongst the persons who were parties to the plan was, that a certain number from amongst themselves should be appointed directors, and should purchase for the Company the said plots of land from the persons in whom they were vested, at greatly increased and exorbitant prices: that it was with a view to carry the arrangement into effect that Harbottle, Adshead, Byrom, and Westhead procured themselves to be appointed directors, and Denison procured himself to be appointed auditor: that accordingly, after the said plots of land had become vested in the several persons named in the schedule, and before the passing of the Act, the said directors, on behalf of the Company, agreed to purchase the same from the persons named in the schedule, at rents or prices greatly exceeding those at which the said persons had purchased the same: that after the Act was

[*467, n.] behalf of the *Company, shall and lawfully may be commenced and instituted or prosecuted in the name of the treasurer, or any one of the directors of the Company for the time being, as the nominal plaintiff for and on behalf of the Company; and all actions, &c. against the Company shall be commenced and instituted and prosecuted against the treasurer, or any one of the directors of the Company for the time being, as the nominal defendant for and on behalf of the Company. * * 129. That in all cases wherein it may be requisite or necessary for any person or party to serve any notice, or any writ or other legal proceedings upon the said Company, the service thereof upon the clerk or secretary to the Company, or any agent or officer employed by the said director, or leaving the same at the office of such clerk or secretary, agent or officer, or at his last or usual place of abode, or upon any one of the said directors, or delivery thereof to some inmate at his last or usual place of abode, shall be deemed good and sufficient service of the same respectively on the Company or their directors.

passed, Harbottle, Adshead, Byrom, Westhead, and Bealey continued to act as directors of the incorporated Company in the same
manner as before : that Adshead continued to act as director until
the 18th of July, 1839, Byrom until the 2nd of December, 1839,
and *Westhead until the 2nd of January, 1840, at which dates
respectively *fiats* in bankruptcy were issued against them, and they
were respectively declared bankrupts, and ceased to be qualified to
act as directors, and their offices as directors became vacated.

The bill stated that upwards of 3,000 shares of 100*l.* in the
capital of the Company were subscribed for : that the principle of
tontine was abandoned : that before 1840, calls were made,
amounting, with the deposit, to 35*l.* per share, the whole of which
were not, however, paid by all the proprietors, but that a sum
exceeding 35,000*l.* in the whole was paid.

The bill stated, that, after the passing of the Act, Harbottle,
Adshead, Byrom, Westhead, Bunting, and Lane, with the concurrence of Denison and of Bealey, proceeded to carry into execution
the design which had been formed previously to the incorporation
of the Company, of fraudulently profiting and enabling the other
persons who had purchased and then held the said land, to profit
by the establishment of the Company and at its expense ; and that
the said directors accordingly, on behalf of the Company, purchased,
or agreed to purchase, from themselves, Harbottle, Adshead, Byrom,
and Westhead, and from Bunting and Lane, and the other persons
in whom the said land was vested, the same plots of land, for
estates corresponding with those purchased by and granted to the
said vendors, by the original owners thereof, charged with chief or
fee-farm rents, greatly exceeding the rents payable to the persons
from whom the said vendors had so purchased the same : that of
some of such plots the conveyances were taken to the Victoria Park
Company, by its corporate name ; of others, to Harbottle, Adshead,
Byrom, Westhead, and Bealey, as directors in trust for the Company ; *and others rested in agreement only, without conveyance :
that by these means the Company took the land, charged not only
with the chief rents reserved to the original landowners, but also
with additional rents, reserved and payable to Harbottle, Adshead,
Byrom, Westhead, Denison, Bunting, Lane, and others : that in
further pursuance of the same fraudulent design, the said directors,
after purchasing the said land for the Company, applied about
27,000*l.* of the monies in their hands, belonging to the Company,
in the purchase or redemption of the rents so reserved to themselves,

Harbottle, Adshead, Byrom, Westhead, Denison, Bunting, Lane, and others, leaving the land subject only to the chief rent reserved to the original landowners.

The bill stated, that the plans of the park were contrived and designed by Lane, in concert with Denison, the directors, and Bunting, so as to render the formation of the park the means of greatly increasing the value of certain parcels of land, partly belonging to Denison and partly to Lane, situated on the outside of the boundary line of the park, but between such boundary line and one of the lodges and entrance gates, called Oxford Lodge and Gate, erected on a small part of the same land purchased by the Company; and through which entrance, and the land so permitted to be retained by Denison and Lane, one of the principal approaches to the park was made: that the said land so retained by Denison and Lane was essentially necessary to the establishment of the park, according to the plans prepared by Lane, and the same was virtually incorporated in the park, and houses erected thereon would enjoy all the advantages of the park, and plots thereof were in consequence sold by Denison and Lane for building land at enhanced prices.

[471]   The bill stated, that, after the purchase of the land as aforesaid, the directors proceeded to carry into effect the design of converting the same into a park, and they accordingly erected lodges and gates, marked out with fences the different crescents, terraces, streets, and ways; formed drains and sewers, and made road-ways, and planted ornamental trees and shrubs: that they also caused to be erected in different parts of the park several houses and buildings, some of which only were completed; and that the directors alleged the monies expended in the roads, drains, and sewers amounted to 12,000l., and in the houses and buildings to 39,000l., or thereabouts: that the said directors sold and let several plots of land, and also sold and let several of the houses and buildings, and received the rents and purchase-money of the same.

The bill stated, that Harbottle, Denison, Bunting, and Lane did not pay up their calls, but some of them retained part, and others the whole thereof; Harbottle and Lane claiming to set off the amount of the calls against the chief rents of the lands which they sold to the Company, Bunting claiming to set off the same against the chief rents, and the costs and charges due to him from the Company; and Denison claiming to set off the amount of the calls against the rents payable to him out of the land which he sold to persons who re-sold the same to the Company.

The bill stated, that owing to the large sums retained out of the calls, the sums appropriated by the said directors to themselves, and paid to others in reduction of the increased chief rents, and pay-ment of such rents, and owing to their having otherwise wasted and misapplied a considerable part of the monies belonging to the Company, the funds of the Company which came *to their hands [*472] shortly after its establishment were exhausted: that the said directors, with the privity, knowledge, and concurrence of Denison, Bunting, and Lane, borrowed large sums of money from their bankers upon the credit of the Company: that, as a further means of raising money, the said directors, and Bunting and Lane, with the concurrence of Denison, drew, made, and negotiated various bills of exchange and promissory notes; and that the said directors also caused several bonds to be executed under the corporate seal of the Company for securing several sums of money to the obligees thereof: that by the middle or latter part of the year 1839, the directors, and Bunting and Lane, had come under very heavy liabilities; the chief rents payable by the Company were greatly in arrear, and the board of directors, with the concurrence of Denison, Bunting, and Lane, applied to the United Kingdom Life Assurance Company to advance the Victoria Park Company a large sum of money by way of mortgage of the lands and hereditaments comprised in the park; but the Assurance Company were advised that the Victoria Company were, by the 90th section of their Act, precluded from borrowing money on mortgage, until one half of their capital (namely, 500,000l.) had been paid up, and on that ground declined to make the required loan: that the directors finding it impossible to raise money by mortgage in a legitimate manner, resorted to several contrivances for the purpose of evading the provisions of the Act, and raising money on mortgage of the property of the Company, by which means several large sums of money had been charged by way of mortgage or lien upon the same: that to effect such mortgages or charges, the directors pro-cured the persons who had contracted to sell plots of land to the Company, but had not executed conveyances, to convey the same, by the direction of the board, to some *other person or persons in [*473] mortgage, and afterwards to convey the equity of redemption to the directors in trust for the Company: that the directors also conveyed some of the plots of land which had been conveyed to them in trust for the Company to some other persons, by way of mortgage, and stood possessed of the equity of redemption in trust for the Company: that, for the same purpose, the board of directors caused the common seal of the Company to be affixed to several conveyances of plots of land which had been conveyed to the Company by their corporate name, and to the directors in trust for the Company, whereby the said plots of land were expressed to be conveyed for a pretended valuable consideration to one or more of the said directors absolutely, and the said directors or director then conveyed the same to other persons on mortgage to secure sometimes monies advanced to the said directors, and by them paid over to the board, in satisfaction of the consideration-monies expressed to be paid for the said prior conveyances under the common seal, sometimes antecedent debts in respect of monies borrowed by the board, and sometimes monies which had been advanced by the mortgagees upon the security of the bills and notes which had been made or discounted as aforesaid: that, in other cases, the said directors and Bunting deposited the title-deeds of parcels of the land and buildings of the Company with the holders of such bills and notes, to secure the repayment of the monies due thereon, and in order to relieve the parties thereto: that, by the means aforesaid, the directors, with the concurrence of Denison, Bunting, and Lane, mortgaged, charged, or otherwise incumbered the greater part of the property of the Company: that many of such mortgagees and incumbrancers had notice that the said board of directors had not power under the Act to mortgage or charge the property of the Company, and that the *said mortgages, charges, and incumbrances were fraudulent and void as against the Company, but that the defendants allege, that some of the said incumbrances were so planned and contrived, that the persons in whose favour they were created had not such notice.

[*474]

That the said directors having exhausted every means which suggested themselves to them of raising money upon credit, or upon the security of the property and effects of the Company, and being unable by those means to provide for the whole of the monies due to the holders of the said bills and notes, and the other persons to whom the said directors in the said transactions had become indebted as individuals, and to satisfy the debts which were due to the persons in whose favour the said mortgages and incumbrances had been improperly created, and in order to release themselves from the responsibility which they had personally incurred by taking conveyances or demises of parts of the said land to the said directors as individuals in trust for the Company, containing covenants on their parts for payment of the reserved rents,—the said directors resolved to convey and dispose of the property of the Company, and they accordingly themselves executed, and caused to be executed under the common seal of the Company, divers conveyances, assignments, and other assurances, whereby divers parts of the said lands and effects of the Company were expressed to be conveyed or otherwise assured absolutely to the holders of some of the said bills and notes, and some of the said mortgagees and incumbrancers, in consideration of the monies thereby purported to be secured; and also executed, and caused to be executed under the common seal of the Company, divers conveyances and assurances of other parts of the said lands to the persons who sold the same to the Company, in consideration of their releasing them from *the payment of the rents reserved and payable out of the [*475] said lands: that many of such conveyances had been executed by Harbottle, Adshead, Westhead, and Bealey, and a few by Byrom, who had been induced to execute them by being threatened with suits for the reserved rents: that Harbottle, Adshead, Byrom, Westhead, and Bealey threatened and intended to convey and assure the remaining parcels of land belonging to the Company to the holders of others of the said bills and notes, and to others of the said mortgagees and incumbrancers and owners of the chief rents, in satisfaction and discharge of the said monies and rents due and to become due to them respectively.

The bill stated, that, upon the bankruptcy of Byrom, Adshead, and Westhead, their shares in the Company became vested in the defendants, their assignees, and that they (the bankrupts) had long ceased to be, and were not, shareholders in the Company: that the whole of the land re-sold by them was vested in some persons unknown to the plaintiffs, but whose names the defendants knew and refused to discover: that, upon the bankruptcy of Westhead, there ceased to be a sufficient number of directors of the Company to constitute a board for transacting the business of the Company, in manner provided by the Act, and Harbottle and Bealey became the only remaining directors whose office had not become vacated, and no person or persons had been appointed to supply the vacancies in the board of directors occasioned by such bankruptcies, and consequently there had never been a properly constituted board of directors of the Company since the bankruptcy of Westhead.

That Byrom, Adshead, and Westhead, nevertheless, and after their respective bankruptcies, executed the several *absolute [*476]

13—2

conveyances and other assurances of the lands and property of the
Company, which were so executed for the purposes and in manner
aforesaid, after the directors had exhausted their means of raising
money upon credit, or upon the security of the property of the
Company.

That about the end of the year 1839, or commencement of the
year 1840, the said directors discharged Brammell, the secretary of
the Company, and gave up the office taken by the Company in
Manchester, and transferred the whole or the greater part of the
title-deeds, books, and papers of the said Company into the hands
of Bunting; and from that time to the present the Company had
had no office of its own, but the affairs of the Company had been
principally conducted at the office of Bunting.

That the only parts of the land bought by the Company which
had not been conveyed away either absolutely or by way of mortgage, and the only part of the other property and effects of the
Company which had not been disposed of and made away with in
manner aforesaid, remained vested in, and in the order and disposition of, Harbottle, Adshead, Byrom, Westhead, Bealey, and
Bunting, in whose custody or power the greater part of the books,
deeds, and papers belonging to the Company which had not been
made away with remained : that by the fraudulent acts and proceedings in the premises to which Harbottle, Adshead, Byrom,
Westhead, Bealey, and Bunting were parties, the property and
effects of the said Company had been and then were involved in
almost inextricable difficulties, and if such property and effects
were any longer allowed to remain in their order and disposition,
the same would be in danger of being wholly dissipated and irre-
[*477]   trievably *lost : that the said Company were then largely indebted
to their bankers and other persons who had *boná fide* advanced
money to the Company, and to the builders and other persons who
had executed some of the works in the park, and provided materials
for the same; while, in consequence of the property of the Company having been wasted and improperly disposed of by the
directors, there were at present no available funds which could
be applied in satisfaction of the debts of the Company, and that
some of the creditors of the said Company had obtained judgments
in actions at law brought by them against the Company for the
amount of their debts, on which judgments interest was daily
accumulating.

The bill stated, that in the present circumstances of the Company,

and the board of directors thereof, the proprietors of shares had no Foss
v.
Harbottle.
power to take the property and effects of the Company out of the
hands of Harbottle, Adshead, Byrom, Westhead, Bealey, and
Bunting, and they had no power to appoint directors to supply
the vacancies in the board occasioned by the said bankruptcies, and
the proprietors of shares in the Company had no power to wind up,
liquidate, or settle the accounts, debts, or affairs of the Company,
or to dissolve the Company, nor had they any power to provide for
and satisfy the existing engagements and liabilities of the Company
with a view to its continuance, and the prosecution of the undertaking for which it was established, without the assistance of the
Court : that if a proper person were appointed by the Court to take
possession of and manage the property and effects of the Company,
and if the Company were to be repaid the amount of all losses and
expenses which it had sustained or incurred by reason of the fraudulent and improper acts and proceedings of the defendants in the
premises, and *which the defendants, or any of them, were liable to [*478]
make good to the said Company, as thereinafter prayed ; and if the
Company were decreed to take and have conveyed to them so much
of the said land which was retained by Denison and Lane as aforesaid, upon paying or accounting to them for the fair value thereof
at the time when the undertaking was first projected ; and Denison
and Lane were to pay or account to the said Company for the price
received by them, for so much of the same land as had been sold
by them, over and above what was the fair price for the same at the
time the undertaking was first projected ; and if the mortgages,
charges, incumbrances, and liens, and the said conveyances and
other assurances, by means of which the property and effects of the
Company had been improperly incumbered and disposed of, which
could be redeemed or avoided, as against the persons claiming
thereunder, were redeemed and set aside, and the property and
effects of the Company thereby affected were restored to it, and the
defendants, who had not become bankrupt, and who had not paid
up, but ought to have paid up, into the joint-stock capital of the
Company, the amounts of the several calls made by the directors on
their respective shares, were to pay up the same,—the lands, property, and effects of the Company would not only be sufficient to
satisfy the whole of its existing debts and liabilities, but leave a
surplus, which would enable the Company to proceed with, and
either wholly or in part accomplish, the undertaking for which it
was incorporated.

FOSS
v.
HARBOTTLE.

[*479]

[*480]

The bill stated, that the defendants concealed from the plaintiffs, and the other shareholders in the Company, who were not personally parties thereto, the several fraudulent and improper acts and proceedings of the said directors and the said other defendants, and *the plaintiffs and the other shareholders had only recently ascertained the particulars thereof, so far as they were therein stated, and they were unable to set forth the same more particularly, the defendants having refused to make any discovery thereof, or to allow the plaintiffs to inspect the books, accounts, or papers of the Company.

The bill charged that Harbottle and Bealey, and the estates of Adshead, Byrom, and Westhead, in respect of that which occurred before their said bankruptcies, and Adshead, Byrom, and Westhead, as to what occurred since their said bankruptcies, were liable to refund and make good to the Company the amount of the losses and expenses which it had sustained in respect of the fraudulent and improper dealings of the said directors of the Company with its lands and property : that Denison, Bunting, and Lane had counselled and advised the directors in their said proceedings, and had derived considerable personal benefit and advantage therefrom : that Denison, Bunting, and Lane were all parties to the said fraudulent scheme planned and executed as aforesaid, by which the several plots or parcels of land in the park were purchased and re-sold to the said Company at a profit and at a price considerably exceeding the real value of the same, and that Denison, Bunting, and Lane had derived considerable profit from the increased price or chief rents made payable out of the several plots or parcels of land which were purchased and re-sold by them in manner aforesaid, and from the monies which were paid to them as a consideration for the reduction of the same chief rents as before mentioned.

The bill charged that several general meetings, and extraordinary general meetings, and other meetings of *the shareholders of the Company, were duly convened and held at divers times, between the time when the Company was first established and the year 1841, and particularly on or about the several days or times thereinafter mentioned, (naming ten different dates, from July, 1837, to December, 1839), and that at such meetings false and delusive statements respecting the circumstances and prospects of the Company were made by the directors to the proprietors who attended such meetings, and the truth of the several fraudulent and improper acts and proceedings therein complained of was not disclosed.

The bill charged, that, under the circumstances, Denison,
Bunting, and Lane, having participated in and personally benefited by and concealed from the other shareholders the several
fraudulent and improper acts aforesaid, were all jointly and
severally liable together, with the said directors, to make good to
the Company the amount of the losses and expenses which had
been or might be incurred in consequence of such of the said
wrongful and fraudulent acts and proceedings as they were parties
or privies to: that Harbottle, Byrom, Adshead, Westhead, and
Bealey, respectively, had still some of the property and effects
belonging to the Company: that the said last-named defendants
had not paid up the calls due and payable on their respective
shares: that the plaintiffs had as yet paid only three of the calls
on their shares, not having paid the remainder in consequence of
learning, that, owing to some misconduct of the directors, the
affairs of the Company were in difficulties, the cause of which
difficulties the plaintiffs had but lately, and with considerable
difficulty, ascertained to have arisen from the proceedings aforesaid, but in all other respects the plaintiffs had conformed to the
provisions of the Act: that there were not any *shareholders in   [*481]
the Company who had not paid up the calls on their shares besides
the plaintiffs and the said defendants: that the names and places
of abode of the other persons who are not shareholders in the
Company, but are interested in or liable in respect of any of the
said matters, were unknown to the plaintiffs, and the defendants
ought to discover the same : that the number of shareholders in
the Company was so great, and their rights and liabilities were so
subject to change and fluctuation, by death and otherwise, that it
would be impossible to prosecute the suit with effect if they were all
made parties thereto.

The bill charged, that Bunting claimed a lien upon the documents
in his possession belonging to the Company for the costs of business
done by him as the attorney of the Company, but a great part of
such business consisted of the fraudulent acts aforesaid ; and that
he had received out of the funds of the Company divers large sums
of money exceeding the amount properly due to him : that Bunting
had deposited some of the deeds belonging to the Company with
certain bankers at Liverpool, and among the rest the contract
executed by the plaintiffs and the other shareholders before the
Act was passed, as a security for the payment of a bill of exchange
for 3,000*l.*, to which Bunting was individually a party, but for

Foss
v.
HARBOTTLE.

which he untruly pretended that the Company was responsible ; and that the holders of such deeds threatened to sue the plaintiffs for the said 8,000*l.*, as parties to the contract, on the ground that the capital was not paid up ; and also, that the said directors threatened to cause actions at law to be brought against the plain-tiffs, under the powers of the Act, in the name of Harbottle or Bealey, as the nominal plaintiff on behalf of the Company, for the amount of the unpaid calls on their shares.

[482]

The bill charged, that Harbottle and Bealey were two directors of the Company, but they respectively refused to use or allow either of their names to be used as the nominal plaintiffs in this suit on behalf of the Company ; but that Harbottle was a necessary party, not only in respect of his liability, but also as a nominal defendant on behalf of the Company.

After various charges, recapitulating in terms the alleged title of the plaintiffs to the relief and discovery sought by the prayer, the bill prayed that an account might be taken of all monies received by the defendants Harbottle, Adshead, Byrom, Westhead, Bealey, Denison, and Lane, or any of them, for the use of the Company, on which but for their wilful default might have been received, and of the application thereof ; also, an account of the losses and expenses incurred in consequence of the said fraudulent and improper dealings of the defendants with the monies, lands, and property of the Company, which they or any of them were liable to make good, and that they might be respectively decreed to make good the same, including in particular the profits made by Har-bottle, Denison, Bunting, and Lane, by buying and re-selling the said land, and the profits made by Denison and Lane out of the said land retained by them ; and that Denison and Lane might be decreed to convey the residue of the said land to the Company, upon payment of the fair value thereof at the time the undertaking was projected : that it might be declared that the said mortgages, charges, incumbrances, and liens upon the lands and property created as aforesaid, so far as regards the defendants who executed the same or were privy thereto, were created fraudu-lently and in violation of the provisions of the Act, and that Harbottle, Bealey, Denison, Bunting, and Lane, might be decreed

[*483]

to make good to the Company the principal *money and interest due and owing upon security of such of the mortgages, charges, and liens as were still subsisting, with all costs sustained by the Company in relation thereto ; and that it might be declared that

Harbottle, Adshead, Byrom, Westhead, and Bealey, by executing   Foss
v.
Harbottle.
the said conveyances and assurances of the lands and property of
the Company to the said mortgagees, holders of notes and bills,
and others, committed a fraudulent breach of trust, and that Harbottle, Adshead, Byrom, Westhead, Bealey, Denison, Bunting, and
Lane might be decreed to make good to the Company the purchase-
money and rents paid by the Company for such lands, and expended
in building and improving the same, with interest and expenses;
and that the monies so recovered from the defendants might be
applied in redeeming and re-purchasing the said lands, and restoring them to the Company. And that inquiries might be directed to
ascertain which of the mortgages and incumbrances, and of the
conveyances and assurances, of the lands and property of the
Company could be avoided and set aside as against the persons
claiming the benefit thereof, and that proceedings might be taken
for avoiding them accordingly. And that an account might be
taken of all the property and effects of the Company, and the
unpaid calls sued for and recovered, and that a sufficient part of
such property might be applied in liquidating the existing debts and
liabilities of the Company, and the residue secured for its benefit.
And that, for the purposes aforesaid, a receiver might be appointed
to take possession of, recover, and get in the lands, property, and
effects of the Company, and for that purpose to sue in the names of
Harbottle and Bealey, or otherwise, as occasion might require; and
that Harbottle, Adshead, Byrom, Westhead, Bealey, and Bunting
might be decreed to deliver up to *such receiver the property,   [*484]
effects, deeds, muniments, and documents belonging to the Company. And that the same defendants might be restrained by
injunction from holding, receiving, or intermeddling with the
property and effects of the Company, and from executing, or
causing to be executed, under the common seal of the Company,
any deed or instrument conveying, assigning, or disposing of the
same. And that Harbottle, Denison, Bunting, and Lane might be
restrained from entering or distraining upon any of the said lands
sold by them to or in trust for the Company as aforesaid. And the
plaintiffs thereby offered to pay into Court the amount of the unpaid
calls due from them to the Company.

The defendants Harbottle, Adshead, and Westhead demurred to
the bill, assigning for cause, want of equity, want of parties, and
multifariousness; and suggesting that all the proprietors of shares
in the Company, the assignees of P. Leicester, and the owners of

Foss
v.
Harbottle.

land named in the schedule to the Act, were necessary parties.
The defendant Bealey, the defendant Denison, and the defendants
Bunting and Lane, also put in three several demurrers, assigning
like causes.

Mr. *Lowndes* and Mr. *Rolt*, in support of the demurrers of
Harbottle, Adshead, and Westhead, and of Bunting and Lane.

Mr. *Walker* and Mr. *Glasse*, in support of the demurrers of
Bealey and Denison.

Mr. *James Russell*, Mr. *Roupell*, and Mr. *Bartrum*, for the
bill.

[485]   On the part of the defendants, it was contended, that the suit
complaining of injuries to the corporation was wholly informal, in
having only some of its individual members, and not the corporation itself, before the Court ; that this defect would not be cured
by adding the corporation as parties defendants, for the plaintiffs
were not entitled to represent the corporate body, even as distinguished from the defendants and for the purpose of impeaching the
transactions complained of ; and the plaintiffs' bill could not
therefore be sustained.

It was further argued, that the plaintiffs, if they had any ground
for impeaching the conduct of the defendants, might have used the
name of the corporation ; and, in that case, it would have been
open to the defendants, or to the body of directors or proprietors
assuming the government of the Company, to have applied to the
Court for the stay of proceedings, or to prevent the use of the
corporate name ; and, upon the application, the Court would have
inquired into the alleged usurpation or abuse of authority, and
determined whether the plaintiff should be permitted to proceed.
Or, the suit might have been in the shape of an information by the
Attorney-General, to correct the alleged abuse of powers granted for
public purposes. The statements of fact in the bill, it was also
contended, did not support the general charges of fraud upon which
the title to relief was founded. Several other points of equity, as
applicable to the cases made against the several defendants, and in
respect of the suggested defects of parties, were also made, but the
judgment did not turn on these points.

[*486]   On the part of the plaintiffs, so far as related to the *point on
which the decision proceeded, namely, their right to sustain the

bill on behalf of themselves and the other shareholders against the
it was argued, that the Company was not to be treated as an
ordinary corporation; that it was in fact a mere partnership, having
objects of private benefit, and that it must be governed by rules
analogous to those which regulated partnerships or joint-stock
Companies, consisting of numerous persons, but not incorporated.
The Act of incorporation was intended to be beneficial to the
Company, and to promote the undertaking, but not to extinguish
any of the rights of the proprietors *inter se.* The directors were
trustees for the plaintiffs to the extent of their shares in the Company;
and the fact that the Company had taken the form of a corporation,
would not be allowed to deprive the cestui que trusts of a remedy
against their trustees for the abuse of their powers. The Act of
incorporation, moreover, expressly exempted the proprietors of the
Company, or persons dealing with the Company, from the necessity
of adopting the form of proceeding applicable to a pure corporation;
for the 74th section (1) enabled them to sue and be sued in the
name of the treasurer, or any one of the directors for the time
being : the bill alleged, that the two remaining directors had refused
to institute the suit, and showed in fact that it would be against
their personal interest to do so, inasmuch as they were answerable
in respect of the transactions in question; if the plaintiffs could
not, therefore, institute the suit themselves, they would be
remediless. The directors were made defendants ; and, under the
74th clause of the Act, any one of the directors might be made the
*nominal representative of the Company; the corporation was   [*487]
therefore distinctly represented in the suit. The present proceeding
was in fact the only form in which the proprietors could now
impeach the conduct of the body to whom their affairs had been
intrusted. The 38th section expressly excluded any proprietor,
not being a director, from interfering in the management of the
business of the Company on any pretence whatever. The extinction
of the board of directors by the bankruptcy and consequent disqualification of three of them, (sect. 67), and the want of any clerk or
office, effectually prevented the fulfilment of the forms which the
46th, 47th, and 48th sections of the Act required, in order to the
due convening of a general meeting of proprietors competent to
secure the remaining property of the Company, and provide for its
due application.

(1) *Supra,* p. 189.

[The following (among other) cases were cited during the argument: *Adley* v. *The Whitstable Company* (1), *Hichens* v. *Congreve* (2), *Blain* v. *Agar* (3), *Richards* v. *Davies* (4), *Seddon* v. *Connell* (5), *Preston* v. *Grand Collier Dock Company* (6), *Attorney-General* v. *Wilson* (7), *Wallworth* v. *Holt* (8), *Bligh* v. *Brent* (9).]

March 25.

THE VICE-CHANCELLOR:

[488]   The relief which the bill in this case seeks, as against the defendants who have demurred, is founded on several alleged grounds of complaint; of these it is only necessary that I should mention two, for the consideration of those two grounds involves the principle upon which I think all the demurrers must be determined.   One ground is, that the directors of the Victoria Park Company, the defendants Harbottle, Adshead, Byrom, and Bealey, have, in their character of directors, purchased their own lands of themselves for the use of the Company, and have paid for them, or, rather, taken to themselves out of the monies of the Company a price exceeding the value of such lands: the other ground is, that the defendants have raised money in a manner not authorized by their powers under their Act of incorporation; and, especially, that they have mortgaged or incumbered the lands and property of the Company, and applied the monies thereby raised in effect, though circuitously, to pay the price of the land which they had so bought of themselves.

I do not now express any opinion upon the question, whether, leaving out of view the special form in which the plaintiffs have proceeded in the suit, the bill alleges a case in which a court of equity would say that the transactions in question are to be opened or dealt with in the manner which this bill seeks that they should be; but I certainly would not be understood by any thing I said during the argument to do otherwise than express my cordial concurrence in the doctrine laid down in the case of *Hichens* v. *Congreve* (2), and other cases of that class.   I take those cases to be in accordance with the principles of this Court, and to be founded

[*489]   on *justice and common sense.   Whether particular cases fall within the principle of *Hichens* v. *Congreve*, is another question.   In *Hichens* v. *Congreve*, property was sold to a Company by persons

(1) 11 R. R. 87 (17 Ves. 315 ; 1 Mer. 107).
(2) 32 R. R. 173 (4 Russ. 562).
(3) 27 R. R. 150 (2 Sim. 289).
(4) 34 R. R. 111 (2 Russ. & My. 347).

(5) 51 R. R. 209 (10 Sim. 58, 79).
(6) 54 R. R. 380 (11 Sim. 327).
(7) 54 R. R. 195 (Cr. & Ph. 1).
(8) 48 R. R. 187 (4 My. & Cr. 619).
(9) 47 R. R. 420 (2 Y. & C. 295).

in a fiduciary character, the conveyance reciting that 25,000*l.* had
been paid for the purchase; the fact being, that 10,000*l.* only had
been paid, 15,000*l.* going into the hands of the persons to whom
the purchase was entrusted. I should not be in the least degree
disposed to limit the operation of that doctrine in any case, in which
a person projecting the formation of a Company invited the public
to join him in the project, on a representation that he had acquired
property which was intended to be applied for the purposes of
the Company. I should strongly incline to hold that to be an invi-
tation to the public to participate in the benefit of the property
purchased, on the terms on which the projector had acquired it.
The fiduciary character of the projector would, in such a case,
commence from the time when he first began to deal with the
public, and would of course be controlled in equity by the representation he then made to the public. If persons, on the other
hand, intending to form a Company, should purchase land with a
view to the formation of it, and state at once that they were the
owners of such land, and propose to sell it at a price fixed, for the
purposes of the Company about to be formed, the transaction, so
far as the public are concerned, commencing with that statement,
might not fall within the principle of *Hichens* v. *Congreve.* A party
may have a clear right to say—"I begin the transaction at this
time; I have purchased land, no matter how or from whom, or at
what price; I am willing to sell it a certain price for a given
purpose." It is not necessary that I should determine the effect of
the transactions that are stated to have occurred in the present case.
I make these observations only, that I may not be supposed, from
any thing which fell from me during the argument, *to entertain   [*490]
the slightest hesitation with regard to the application, in a proper
case, of the principles I have referred to. For the present purpose,
I shall assume that a case is stated, entitling the Company, as
matters now stand, to complain of the transactions mentioned in
the bill.

The Victoria Park Company is an incorporated body, and the
conduct with which the defendants are charged in this suit is an
injury not to the plaintiffs exclusively; it is an injury to the whole
corporation by individuals whom the corporation entrusted with
powers to be exercised only for the good of the corporation. And
from the case of *The Attorney-General* v. *Wilson* (1), (without going
further), it may be stated as undoubted law, that a bill or information

(1) 54 R. R. 195 (Cr. & Ph. 1).

FOSS
v.
HARBOTTLE.

by a corporation will lie to be relieved in respect of injuries which the corporation has suffered at the hands of persons standing in the situation of the directors upon this record. This bill, however, differs from that in *The Attorney-General* v. *Wilson* in this, that instead of the corporation being formally represented as plaintiffs, the bill in this case is brought by two individual corporators, professedly on behalf of themselves and all the other members of the corporation, except those who committed the injuries complained of,—the plaintiffs assuming to themselves the right and power in that manner to sue on behalf of and represent the corporation itself.

It was not, nor could it successfully be argued, that it was a matter of course for any individual members of a corporation thus to assume to themselves the right of suing in the name of the corporation. In law, the corporation, and the aggregate members of the corporation, are not the same thing for purposes like this:

[*491]

and the *only question can be, whether the facts alleged in this case justify a departure from the rule which *primâ facie* would require that the corporation should sue in its own name and in its corporate character, or in the name of some one whom the law has appointed to be its representative.

The demurrers are,—first, of three of the directors of the Company, who are also alleged to have sold lands to the corporation under the circumstances charged; secondly, of Bealey, also a director, alleged to have made himself amenable to the jurisdiction of the Court to remedy the alleged injuries, though he was not a seller of land; thirdly, of Denison, a seller of land, in like manner alleged to be implicated in the frauds charged, though he was not a director; fourthly, of Mr. Bunting, the solicitor, and Mr. Lane, the architect of the Company. These gentlemen are neither directors nor sellers of land, but all the frauds are alleged to have been committed with their privity, and they also are in this manner sought to be implicated in them. The most convenient course will be, to consider the demurrer of the three against whom the strongest case is stated; and the consideration of that case will apply to the whole.

The first objection taken in the argument for the defendants was, that the individual members of the corporation cannot in any case sue in the form in which this bill is framed. During the argument I intimated an opinion, to which, upon further consideration, I fully adhere, that the rule was much too broadly stated on the part of the defendants. I think there are cases in which a suit might properly be so framed. Corporations like this, of a private nature, are in truth little more than private partnerships; and in cases which may easily be suggested, it would be too much to hold, that a society *of private persons associated together in undertakings, which, though certainly beneficial to the public, are nevertheless matters of private property, are to be deprived of their civil rights, *inter se*, because, in order to make their common objects more attainable, the Crown or the Legislature may have conferred upon them the benefit of a corporate character. If a case should arise of injury to a corporation by some of its members, for which no adequate remedy remained, except that of a suit by individual corporators in their private characters, and asking in such character the protection of those rights to which in their corporate character they were entitled, I cannot but think that the principle so forcibly laid down by Lord COTTENHAM in *Wallworth* v. *Holt* (1), and other cases, would apply, and the claims of justice would be found superior to any difficulties arising out of technical rules respecting the mode in which corporations are required to sue.

[*492]

But, on the other hand, it must not be without reasons of a very urgent character that established rules of law and practice are to departed from,—rules, which, though in a sense technical, are founded on general principles of justice and convenience; and the question is, whether a case is stated in this bill, entitling the plaintiffs to sue in their private characters. (His Honour stated the substance of the Act, sections 1, 38, 39, 43, 46, 47, 48, 49, 67, 70, 114, and 129 (2).) The result of these clauses is, that the directors are made the governing body, subject to the superior control of the proprietors assembled in general meetings; and, as I understand the Act, the proprietors so assembled have power, due notice being given of the purposes of the meeting, to originate proceedings for any purpose within *the scope of the Company's powers, as well as to control the directors in any acts which they may have originated. There may possibly be some exceptions to this proposition, but such is the general effect of the provisions of the statute.

[*493]

Now, that my opinion upon this case may be clearly understood, I will consider separately the two principal grounds of complaint to which I have adverted, with reference to a very marked distinction

(1) 48 R. R. 187 (4 My. & Cr. 635).

(2) *Supra*, p. 188, where most of these clauses are set forth.

between them. The first ground of complaint is one which, though it might *primâ facie* entitle the corporation to rescind the transactions complained of, does not absolutely and of necessity fall under the description of a void transaction. The corporation might elect to adopt those transactions, and hold the directors bound by them. In other words, the transactions admit of confirmation at the option of the corporation. The second ground of complaint may stand in a different position; I allude to the mortgaging in a manner not authorized by the powers of the Act. This, being beyond the powers of the corporation, may admit of no confirmation whilst any one dissenting voice is raised against it. This distinction is found in the case of *Preston* v. *The Grand Collier Dock Company* (1).

On the first point, it is only necessary to refer to the clauses of the Act to show, that, whilst the supreme governing body, the proprietors at a special general meeting assembled, retain the power of exercising the functions conferred upon them by the Act of incorporation, it cannot be competent to individual corporators to sue in the manner proposed by the plaintiffs on the present record. This in effect purports to be a suit by cestui que trusts, complaining
[*494] of a fraud committed or *alleged to have been committed by persons in a fiduciary character. The complaint is, that those trustees have sold lands to themselves, ostensibly for the benefit of the cestui que trusts. The proposition I have advanced is, that although the Act should prove to be voidable, the cestui que trusts may elect to confirm it. Now, who are the cestui que trusts in this case? The corporation, in a sense, is undoubtedly the cestui que trust; but the majority of the proprietors at a special general meeting assembled, independently of any general rules of law upon the subject, by the very terms of the incorporation in the present case, has power to bind the whole body, and every individual corporator must be taken to have come into the corporation upon the terms of being liable to be so bound. How then can this Court act in a suit constituted as this is, if it is to be assumed, for the purposes of the argument, that the powers of the body of the proprietors are still in existence, and may lawfully be exercised for a purpose like that I have suggested? Whilst the Court may be declaring the acts complained of to be void at the suit of the present plaintiffs, who in fact may be the only proprietors who disapprove of them, the governing body of proprietors may defeat

(1) 54 R. R. 380 (11 Sim. 327).

the decree by lawfully resolving upon the confirmation of the very
acts which are the subject of the suit. The very fact that the
governing body of proprietors assembled at the special general
meeting may so bind even a reluctant minority, is decisive to show
that the frame of this suit cannot be sustained whilst that body
retains its functions. In order then that this suit may be sustained,
it must be shown either that there is no such power as I have
supposed remaining in the proprietors, or, at least, that all means
have been resorted to and found ineffectual to set that body in
motion : this latter point is nowhere suggested in the bill : there
is no suggestion that an attempt has been made by any proprietor
to set the body of proprietors in *motion, or to procure a meeting   [*495]
to be convened for the purpose of revoking the acts complained of.
The question then is, whether this bill is so framed as of necessity
to exclude the supposition that the supreme body of proprietors is
now in a condition to confirm the transactions in question ; or, if
those transactions are to be impeached in a court of justice, whether
the proprietors have not power to set the corporation in motion for
the purpose of vindicating its own rights.

(His Honour recapitulated the history and present situation of
the Company, as it appeared upon the bill.)

I pause here to examine the difficulty which is supposed by the
bill to oppose itself to the body of proprietors assembling and acting
at an extraordinary general meeting. The 48th section of the Act
says, that a certain number of proprietors may call such a meeting
by means of a notice to be addressed to the board of directors, and
left with the clerk or secretary, at the principal office of the Company, one month before the time of meeting, or the board is not
bound to notice it. The bill says that there is no board of directors
properly constituted, no clerk, no principal office of the Company,
no power of electing more directors, and that the appointment of
the clerk being in the board of directors, no clerk can in fact now
be appointed. I am certainly not prepared to go the whole length
of the plaintiff's argument founded upon the 48th section. I admit
that the month required would probably be considered imperative ;
but is not the mode of service directory only?   Could the board of
directors de facto, for the time being, by neglecting to appoint a
clerk or have a principal office, deprive the superior body, the body
of proprietors, of the power which the Act gives that body over the
board of directors?   Would not a notice in substance,—a notice for
example such as the 129th section *provides for in other cases, be   [*496]

Foss
v.
Harbottle.

a sufficient notice? Is not the particular form of notice which is pointed out by the 48th section a form of notice given only for the convenience of the proprietors and directors? And if an impediment should exist, and, *à fortiori*, if that impediment should exist by the misconduct of the board of directors, it would be difficult to contend with success that the powers of the corporation are to be paralyzed, because there is no clerk on whom service can be made. I require more cogent arguments than I have yet heard to satisfy me that the mode of service prescribed by the 48th section, if that were the only point in the case, is more than directory. The like observations will apply to the place of service; but as to that, I think the case is relieved from difficulty by the fact that the business of the Company is stated to be principally conducted at the office of the solicitor, for I am not aware that there is anything in the statute which attaches any peculiar character to the spot designated as the principal office. In substance, the board of directors *de facto*, whether qualified or not, carry on the business of the Company at a given place, and under this Act of Parliament it is manifest that service at that place would be deemed good service on the Company.

If that difficulty were removed, and the plaintiff should say, that by the death or bankruptcy of directors, and the carelessness of proprietors, (for that term must be added), the governing body has lost its power to act, I should repeat the inquiries I have before suggested, and ask whether, in such a case also, the 48th section is not directory, so far as it appears to require the refusal or neglect of the board of directors to call a general meeting, before the proprietors can by advertisement call such a meeting for themselves. Adverting to the undoubted powers conferred upon the proprietors,

[*497]

to hold special general meetings without the consent and *against the will of the board of directors, and the permanent powers which the body of proprietors must of necessity have, I am yet to be persuaded that the existence of this corporation (for without a lawful governing body it cannot usefully or practically continue) can be dependent upon the accidents which at any given moment may reduce the number of directors below three. The board of directors, as I have already observed, have no power to put a veto upon the will of any ten proprietors who may desire to call a special general meeting; and if ten proprietors cannot be found, who are willing to call a special general meeting, the plaintiffs can scarcely contend that this suit can be sustained. At all events, what is there to prevent the corporators from suing in the name of the corporation? It cannot be contended that the body of proprietors have not sufficient interest in these questions to institute a suit in the name of the corporation. The latter observations, I am aware, are little more than another mode of putting the former questions which I have suggested. I am strongly inclined to think, if it were necessary to decide these points, it could not be successfully contended that the clauses of the Act of Parliament which are referred to are anything more than directory, if it be, indeed, impossible from accident to pursue the form directed by the Act. I attribute to the proprietors no power which the Act does not give them : they have the power, without the consent and against the will of the directors, of calling a meeting, and of controlling their acts ; and if by any inevitable accident the prescribed form of calling a meeting should become impracticable, there is still a mode of calling it, which, upon the general principles that govern the powers of corporations, I think would be held to be sufficient for the purpose.

It is not, however, upon such considerations that I *shall decide   [*498] this case. The view of the case which has appeared to me conclusive, is, that the existence of a board of directors *de facto* is sufficiently apparent upon the statements in the bill. The bankruptcy of Westhead, the last of the three directors who became bankrupt, took place on the 2nd of January, 1840 : the bill alleges that he thereupon ceased to be qualified to act as director, and his office became vacated ; but it does not say that he ceased to act as a director ; nor, although it is said that thenceforward there was no board " properly constituted," is it alleged that there was no board *de facto* exercising the functions of directors. These, and several other statements of the bill, are pregnant with the admission of the existence of a board *de facto*. By whom was the Company governed, and its affairs conducted, between the time of Westhead's bankruptcy, and that of the filing of the bill, in October, 1842 ? What directors or managers of the business of the Company have lent their sanction to the mortgagees, and other transactions complained of, as having taken place since January, 1840, and by which the corporation is said or supposed to be, at least to some extent, legally bound ? Whatever the bill may say of the illegal constitution of the board of directors, because the individual directors are not duly qualified, it does not anywhere suggest that there has not been during the whole period, and that there was not when the bill was filed, a board of directors *de facto*, acting in and

FOSS
v.
HARBOTTLE.

carrying on the affairs of the corporation, and whose acting must have been acquiesced in by the body of proprietors ; at least, ever since the illegal constitution of the board of directors became known, and the acts in question were discovered. But if there has been or is a board *de facto*, their acts may be valid, although the persons so acting may not have been duly qualified. The 114th section (1)

[*499]

of the Act provides *that "all acts, deeds, and things, done or executed at any meeting of the directors, by any person acting as a director of the said Company, shall, notwithstanding it may afterwards be discovered that there was some defect or error in the appointment of such director, or that such director was disqualified, or, being an interim director, was disapproved of by an annual general meeting of proprietors, be as valid and effectual as if such person had been duly appointed and was qualified to be a director." The foundation upon which I consider the plaintiffs can alone have a right to sue in the form of this bill must wholly fail, if there has been a governing body of directors *de facto*. There is no longer the impediment to convening a meeting of proprietors, who by their vote might direct proceedings like the present to be taken in the name of the corporation, or of a treasurer of the corporation, (if that were necessary) ; or who, by rejecting such a proposal, would, in effect, decide that the corporation was not aggrieved by the transactions in question. Now, since the 2nd of January, 1840, there must have been three annual general meetings of the Company held in July in every year, according to the provisions of the Act. These annual general meetings can only be regularly called by the board of directors. The bill does not suggest that the requisitions of the Act have not been complied with in this respect, either by omitting to call the meeting, or by calling it informally ; but the bill, on the contrary, avers that several general meetings, and extraordinary general meetings, and other meetings of the shareholders of the Company, were duly convened and held at divers times between the time when the Company was established and the year 1841 ; including, therefore, in this period of formality of proceeding, as well as of capacity in constitution, an entire year after Westhead's bankruptcy.

[500]

Another statement of the bill leading to the same inference, the existence of an acting board, is that which avers, that since the year 1839, down, in fact, to the time of filing the bill, that is, during these three years, the Company has had no office of its own.

(1) Not stated in the bill.

but the affairs of the Company have been principally conducted at
the office of Mr. Bunting. Now this, as I must read it, is a direct
admission that the affairs of the Company have been carried on by
some persons. By whom then have they been carried on ? The
statute makes the board of directors the body by whom alone those
affairs are to be ordered and conducted. There is no other person or
set of persons empowered by the Act to conduct the affairs of the Company ; and there is no allegation in the bill that any persons, other
than the board of directors originally appointed, have taken upon
themselves that business. In the absence of any special allegation
to the contrary, I am bound to assume that the affairs of the Company have been carried on by the body in whom alone the powers for
that purpose were vested by the Act, namely, a board of directors.

Again, the bill alleges, that, since the bankruptcy of Westhead,
the bankrupts have joined in executing the conveyances of the
property of the Company to mortgagees. It could only have been
in the character of directors that they could confer any title by
the conveyance ; in that character the mortgagees would have
required them to be parties, and it is in that character that I must
assume they executed the deeds.

If the case rested here, I must of necessity assume the existence
of a board of directors, and in the absence of any allegation that
the board *de facto*, in whose acting the Company must, upon this
bill, be taken to have acquiesced, have been applied to and have
refused to appoint *a clerk and treasurer, (if that be necessary),   [*501]
or take such other steps as may be necessary for calling a special
general meeting, or had refused to call such special general meeting,
the bill does not exclude every case which the pleader was bound
to exclude in order to justify a suit on behalf of a corporation, in a
form which assumes its practical dissolution. But the bill goes on
to show that special general meetings have been holden since
January, 1840. The bill, as I have before observed, states that
several general meetings, and extraordinary general meetings, have
been holden between the establishment of the Company and the
year 1841, not excluding the year 1840, which was during Westhead's disqualification, "and that at such meetings false and
delusive statements, respecting the circumstances and prospects of
the Company, were made by the said directors of the Company
to the proprietors who attended such meetings, and the truth of the
several fraudulent and improper acts and proceedings therein complained of was not disclosed ; " and the bill specifies some meetings

in particular. Against the pleader, I must intend, that some such meetings may have been holden at a time when there was no board properly constituted, and no clerk or treasurer or principal office of the Company, save such as appear by the bill to have existed ; and if that were so, the whole of the case of the plaintiffs, founded on the impracticability of calling a special general meeting, fails. Assuming then, as I am bound to do, the existence, for some time at least, of a state of things in which the Company was governed by a board of directors *de facto*, some of the members of which were individually disqualified, and in which, notwithstanding the want of a clerk, treasurer, or office, the powers of the proprietors were called into exercise at general meetings, the question is, when did that state of things cease to exist, so as to justify the extraordinary proceeding of the plaintiffs *by this suit? The plaintiffs have not stated by their bill any facts to show that such was not the actual state of things at the time their bill was filed, and, in the absence of any statement to the contrary, I must intend that it was so.

[*502]

The case of *Preston* v. *The Grand Collier Dock Company* was referred to as an example of a suit in the present form ; but there the circumstances were in no respect parallel with the present : the object of that suit was to decide the rights or liabilities of one class of the members of the corporation against another, in respect of a matter in which the corporation itself had no power to vary the situation of either.

I have applied strictly the rule of making every intendment against the pleader in this case, that is, of intending every thing to have been lawful and consistent.with the constitution of the Company, which is not expressly shown on the bill to have been unlawful or inconsistent with that constitution. And I am bound to make this intendment, not only on the general rule, but also on the rules of pleading which require a plaintiff to frame his case so distinctly and unambiguously, that the defendant may not be embarrassed in determining on the form which his defence should assume : *Attorney-General* v. *Corporation of Norwich* (1). The bill, I cannot but observe, is framed with great care, and with more than ordinary professional skill and knowledge ; but the averments do not exclude that which, *prima facie*, must be taken to have been the case, that during the years 1840, 1841, and 1842, there was a governing body, that by such body the business of the Company was carried on, that there was no insurmountable impediment to

(1) 44 R. R. 143 (2 My. & Cr. 406).

the *exercise of the powers of the proprietors assembled in general meetings to control the affairs of the Company, and that such general meetings were actually held. The continued existence of [*503] a board *de facto* is not merely not excluded by the averments, but the statements in the bill of the acts which have been done suppose, and even require, the existence of such a board. Now if the plaintiffs had alleged that there had been no board of directors *de facto*, and had on that ground impeached the transactions complained of, the defendants might have met the case by plea, and thereby have defended themselves from answering the bill. If it should be said that the defendants might now have pleaded, that there was a board of directors *de facto,* the answer is, that they might then have been told that the fact sufficiently appeared upon the bill, and therefore they ought to have demurred. Uncertainty is a defect in pleading, of which advantage may be taken by demurrer. If I were to overrule these demurrers, I might be depriving the defendants of the power of so protecting themselves ; and that because the plaintiffs have not chosen, with due precision, to put forward that fact, which, if alleged, might have been met by plea, but which, not being so alleged, leaves the bill open to demurrer.

I must further observe, that although the bill does, with great caution, attempt to meet every case which, it was supposed, might have been fatal to it upon demurrer, yet it is by allegations of the most general kind, and many of which cannot by possibility be true. It alleges the recent discovery of the acts complained of, but it gives no allegation whatsoever for the purpose of telling when or how such discovery was made, or what led to it. I am bound to give the plaintiff, on a general demurrer, the benefit of the allegation that the matters complained of have been recently discovered, whatever the term "recently *discovered" may mean; but when I [*504] look into the schedule to the Act I find that many of those matters must have been known at a very early period in the history of the Company. I find also provisions of the Act requiring that books shall be kept in which all transactions shall be fully and fairly stated ; and I do not find in the bill anything like a precise allegation that the production of those books would not have given the information, or that there have not been means of seeing those books at least at some time since 1835, or since the transactions in question took place, so that, in point of fact, many of the transactions might and may have been sooner known. These are observations upon which I do not found my judgment, but which I use as

explaining why it is I have felt bound in favour of the defendants
to construe this bill with strictness.

The second point which relates to the charges and incumbrances
alleged to have been illegally made on the property of the Company is open to the reasoning which I have applied to the first
point, upon the question whether, in the present case, individual
members are at liberty to complain in the form adopted by this
bill; for why should this anomalous form of suit be resorted to, if
the powers of the corporation may be called into exercise? But
this part of the case is of greater difficulty upon the merits. I
follow, with entire assent, the opinion expressed by the VICE-
CHANCELLOR in *Preston* v. *The Grand Collier Dock Company*, that,
if a transaction be void, and not merely voidable, the corporation
cannot confirm it, so as to bind a dissenting minority of its members. But that will not dispose of this question. The case made
with regard to these mortgages or incumbrances is, that they were
executed in violation of the provisions of the Act. The mortgagees
are not defendants to the bill, nor does the bill seek to avoid the
*security itself, if it could be avoided, on which I give no opinion.
The bill prays inquiries with a view to proceedings being taken
aliunde to set aside these transactions against the mortgagees. The
object of this bill against the defendants is to make them individually and personally responsible to the extent of the injury alleged
to have been received by the corporation, from the making of the
mortgages. Whatever the case might be, if the object of the suit
was to rescind these transactions, and the allegations in the bill
showed that justice could not be done to the shareholders without
allowing two to sue on behalf of themselves and others, very
different considerations arise in a case like the present, in which
the consequences only of the alleged illegal acts are sought to be
visited personally upon the directors. The money forming the
consideration for the mortgages was received, and was expended in,
or partly in, the transactions which are the subject of the first
ground of complaint. Upon this, one question appears to me to be,
whether the Company could confirm the former transactions, take
the benefit of the money that has been raised, and yet, as against
the directors personally, complain of the acts which they have done,
by means whereof the Company obtains that benefit which I suppose to have been admitted and adopted by such confirmation. I
think it would not be open to the Company to do this; and my
opinion already expressed on the first point is, that the transactions

which constitute the first ground of complaint may possibly be beneficial to the Company, and may be so regarded by the proprietors, and admit of confirmation. I am of opinion that this question,—the question of confirmation or avoidance,—cannot properly be litigated upon this record, regard being had to the existing state and powers of the corporation, and that therefore that part of the bill which seeks to visit the directors personally with the consequences of the impeached mortgages and charges, the benefit of which *the Company enjoys, is in the same predicament as that [*506] which relates to the other subjects of complaint. Both questions stand on the same ground, and, for the reasons which I stated in considering the former point, these demurrers must be allowed.

HOLLOWAY *v.* CLARKSON (1).

(2 Hare, 521—527; S. C. 6 Jur. 923.)

1842.
July 11, 12, 14.

1843.
Feb. 18, 25.
March 4, 11, 13.

Wigram, V.-C.

[521]

Bequests to females, some of whom were married and some single, for their separate use for their respective lives, and after their decease to such persons as they should respectively appoint; and in default of appointment, to their respective executors, administrators, and assigns:

Held, that the legatees, whether married or unmarried women, were entitled upon petition, without executing any formal appointment, to an immediate transfer or payment to themselves of the *corpus* of their respective shares of the fund.

John Holloway, by his will, made in 1808, devised his real estate to trustees, and directed them out of the rents and profits to pay certain annuities to persons therein mentioned for their lives, and to accumulate the remainder; and after the decease of persons therein named, he directed his trustees to sell such real estate, and stand and be possessed of the monies to arise thereby, and the said accumulations, for the benefit of the following sixteen persons (naming them; seven being males, and nine females:) or the child or children of such of them as should be then dead, and to divide the same into so many equal parts, and appropriate and set apart so many of the said parts as should be equal in number to such of the sixteen persons so living as should be males, and stand possessed of the same respectively, in trust for such male persons respectively, and his or their respective executors, administrators, and assigns, and appropriate and set apart for the portion of each of the said sixteen persons then living as should be females one of the remaining parts, and stand possessed of the same respectively,

(1) *In re Davenport, Turner* v. *King* [1895] 1 Ch. 361, 64 L. J. Ch. 252.

HOLLOWAY
r.
CLARKSON.

upon trust to pay the interest thereof to the sole and separate use of such female during her life, independently of any husband whom she had married or might marry, and without being in anywise subject to his debts, control, or engagements, and the receipts of her, or of such person or persons as she should from time to time appoint to receive the said interest and dividends, to be sufficient

[*522]

discharges for the same; and after the decease of such *female, upon and for such trusts, intents, and purposes as she should by deed or will appoint; and in default of appointment, in trust for her executors, administrators, and assigns, as part of her personal estate: and there followed a clause, substituting in their parents' place the child or children of any of the sixteen legatees who should be dead at the said time of distribution.   The testator died in 1821.

Of the nine female legatees, some were married and some single women at the date of the will; some others had married, and some became widows before the death of the testator, and the death of the tenants for life; and some were still married; and some were single women and widows at the time of the death of the last tenant for life.   A suit was then instituted to carry the trusts of the will into execution: the accounts were taken and the necessary inquiries made.

*   w   ⌋   *

[526]

Several of the married and single women presented their petitions, praying transfers of their respective shares of the fund.   In one case the petitioner had executed a formal appointment: in all the

[*527]

other cases the *petitioners prayed that the fund might be transferred or sold and the proceeds paid to them, but did not otherwise execute any appointment.

Mr. Kenyon Parker, Mr. Anderdon, and *Mr. Glasse,* for the several petitioners, submitted that they took an absolute interest in their shares, and that the demand made by the petition was a sufficient assumption of the fund in the character of property; as, in *Irwin* v. *Farrer* (1), the bill was an indication of the intention of the donee to take the legacy for her own benefit.

The VICE-CHANCELLOR said, that it being clear the executors of the several female legatees could only take the fund as part of the estates of such legatees, that the legatees were authorized to make

(1) 19 Ves. 86. See *Reith* v. *Seymour,* 28 R. R. 77 (4 Russ. 263).

an immediate disposition of their legacies, either by a revocable or
an irrevocable act; and that their executors could not dispute, or
claim in opposition to, the act of such legatees, he was of opinion
that the petition was in such a case equivalent to an appointment,
and that therefore the orders ought to be made as sought by the
petitions.

HOLLOWAY
v.
CLARKSON.

In the cases of the married women, the stock was ordered to be
sold, and the money to arise by the sale, and the dividends accrued,
to be paid to each petitioner on her sole receipt.

HYDE v. DALLAWAY.

(2 Hare, 528—530.)

A mortgagee in possession for six years, without making any
acknowledgment of the mortgagor's title, then purchased the interest of
the tenant for life of the equity of redemption, and continued in possession
for twenty years longer:

Held, that such possession was not adverse during the existence of the
life estate so purchased, and that the Real Property Limitation Act, 1833
(3 & 4 Will. IV. c. 27), s. 28 (1), was not therefore a bar to any suit for
redemption by the remainderman or reversioner.

1843.
March 1, 3, 4.

WIGRAM,
V.-C.
[528]

BILL for specific performance by vendors against a purchaser.
Reference of title. The Master reported that the plaintiffs had not
shown a good title. The plaintiffs excepted to the report.

Saville Hyde, being the mortgagee of the premises comprised in
the contract, under a mortgage thereof created by the tenant for
life and the remainderman, upon which the principal sum of 4,000l.
and a considerable arrear of interest was due, entered into possession
of the premises in the year 1817, in his character of mortgagee.
He afterwards, in the year 1823, purchased the interest of the
tenant for life of the equity of redemption. Saville Hyde continued
in possession of the premises until his death, in 1830. Saville
Hyde devised the premises to the plaintiffs, their heirs, executors,
administrators, and assigns ; and the plaintiffs continued in
possession or in receipt of the rents and profits until the same
were put up for sale by auction in June, 1839, when the defendant,
being the highest bidder, signed the contract in question for the
purchase of the premises, at the price of 2,700l. No acknowledgment of the title of any mortgagor or mortgagors to, or of any right
or equity of redemption of, the premises, was made or given by or

(1) Repealed. See now Real Property Limitation Act, 1874, s. 7.

to any person whomsoever, from the time that Saville Hyde entered into possession thereof as mortgagee, in 1817 (1).

The defendant insisted, that from the time that Saville Hyde, the plaintiffs' testator, purchased, in 1823, the interest of the tenant for life of the equity of redemption, *he could not be regarded as a mortgagee in possession ; and that interest not appearing to have determined, there was no adverse possession, or, at all events, no adverse possession for twenty years to constitute a bar to the owner of the equity of redemption, and consequently that the vendors could not convey an absolute, but only a mortgage title : *Corbett* v. *Barker* (2), *Ravald* v. *Russell* (3), *Raffety* v. *King* (4). The plaintiffs contended, that the Statute of Limitation having begun to run against the mortgagors, on the entry of the mortgagee into possession in 1817 (5), was not interrupted by the fact that he had endeavoured to strengthen his title by getting in the life interest in 1823. [They cited *Beckford* v. *Wade* (6) and other cases.]

[*529]

Mr. *Temple* and Mr. *Dunn*, for the plaintiffs, and Mr. *Roupell* and Mr. *Wood*, for the defendant.

THE VICE-CHANCELLOR, after disposing of other points in the cause :

[530]   I cannot compel the purchaser to take a title depending on the operation of the Statute of Limitations under the circumstances of this case. The possession of the mortgagee appears to me, in point of fact, not to have been adverse. The 28th section supposes the existence of a person to whom the acknowledgment is to be made, as well as that of the party to make it : there must be not only a party to redeem, but one to be redeemed. The parties in this case were not, I think, in the situation which the statute contemplates. as creating a bar. The mortgagee became, in effect, the tenant for life of the equity of redemption : the remainderman or reversioner may therefore properly look upon him as holding in that character. He would not necessarily refer his possession to any other title. It would be a surprise upon the parties interested in the property, after the expiration of the life interest, if they were told that the

(1) See stat. 3 & 4 Will. IV. c. 27, s. 28.

(2) 4 R. R. 856 (1 Anst. 138 ; *S. C.* 3 *Id.* 755).

(3) 34 R. R. 257 (1 Younge, 9).

(4) 44 R. R. 126 (1 Keen, 601).

(5) See 3 & 4 Will. IV. c. 27, ss. 2, 28, amended by 7 Will. IV. & 1 Vict. c. 28. [See note (1), last page.]

(6) 11 R. R. 20 (17 Ves. 99).

tenant for life had another and an adverse title, by means of which they are to be barred, and the tenant for life to acquire an absolute interest.

Exception overruled.

CHAMBERS *v.* BICKNELL (1).

(2 Hare, 536—540; S. C. 7 Jur. 167.)

A party to whom letters of administration have been granted, as the attorney of the person entitled to the grant, and for the use and benefit of such person, is liable to be sued in respect of the estate by the parties beneficially interested in it, in the same way as if he had obtained letters of administration in his own right.

W. CHAMBERS, by his will, dated in July, 1838, bequeathed the residue of his property, to be equally divided between Ann, his wife, and his two children. The testator died in India, leaving his wife and two children surviving. The widow resided in India, and by a power of attorney appointed the defendant Bicknell her agent in England. Under this power Bicknell *obtained letters of administration, as such attorney (2), of the estate of the testator in

---

(1) *Eames* v. *Hacon* (1880) 16 Ch. D. 407; affirmed, 18 Ch. Div. 347, 50 L. J. Ch. 740, 45 L. T. 196; *In re Rendell* [1901] 1 Ch. 230, 70 L. J. Ch. 265, 83 L. T. 625.

(2) The letters of administration were in the following form:

"William, by Divine Providence, Archbishop of Canterbury, Primate of all England and Metropolitan, to our well-beloved in Christ J. S. Bicknell, the lawful attorney of Ann Chambers, widow, the relict and one of the universal legatees named in the will of W. Chambers, late of &c., in the East Indies, deceased, greeting: whereas the said W. Chambers, having, while living, and at the time of his death, goods, chattels, or credits in divers dioceses or jurisdictions, did, as is alleged, in his lifetime, rightly and duly make his last will and testament hereunto annexed, and did not therein name any executor, and we, being desirous that the said goods, chattels, and credits may be well and faithfully administered, applied, and disposed of according to law, do therefore, by these presents, grant full power and

authority to you, in whose fidelity we confide, to administer and faithfully dispose of the said goods, chattels, and credits according to the tenor and effect of the said will; and first to pay the debts of the said deceased which he did owe at the time of his death; and, afterwards, the legacies contained and specified in the said will, so far as such goods, chattels, and credits will thereto extend: and the law requires you, having already been sworn, well and faithfully to administer the same, and to make a true and perfect inventory of all and singular the said goods, chattels, and credits, and to exhibit the same into the registry of our Prerogative Court of Canterbury on or before the last day of August, next ensuing; and also, to render a just and true account thereof: and we do, by these presents, ordain, depute, and constitute you administrator of all and singular the goods, chattels, and credits of the said deceased, with the said will annexed, for the use and benefit of the said Ann Chambers, now residing at Surat, in the Presidency of Bombay, in the East Indies, and unti

CHAMBERS
v.
BICKNELL.

this country. One of the children of the testator, in 1840, filed his bill against Ann (his widow), her second husband, and the other child, (all of whom were alleged to be out of the jurisdiction), and against Bicknell, for the administration of the testator's estate. Bicknell alone appeared.

[*538]

At the hearing,

Mr. Prior, for the defendant Bicknell, submitted that he was the agent of, and if not exclusively, at least primarily, accountable to, his principal, Ann the widow: that supposing there was any privity between him and the plaintiff, yet it was a material question whether he would be discharged by any thing done in a suit to which the widow was not a party. Bicknell, by the effect of the recital in the letters of administration, was made answerable to her : *De la Viesca* v. *Lubbock* (1). He was, however, willing to act as the Court should direct.

Mr. Kenyon Parker, for the plaintiff, [cited *Attorney-General* v. *Dimond* (2), and other cases].

THE VICE-CHANCELLOR:

It appears that administration of the estate of the testator has been granted to the defendant, as the attorney of the widow, and for her use and benefit; and a doubt has been suggested whether the grant in this form places Bicknell in such a position that the Court can act against him at the suit of the other parties beneficially interested in the estate, or at least can so act in the absence of the widow. It was said that he held the money as her agent, and was accountable to her, and to her alone. The case of *De la Viesca* v. *Lubbock* was referred to, upon which case I am not called upon, nor do I presume, to make any observation. The VICE-CHANCELLOR seems to have held that where administration has been granted to the attorney of a person, *for the use and benefit of that person, the latter may sue the administrator in this country without making the parties beneficially interested parties to the suit, and without taking out letters of administration in this country. That case certainly affirms the proposition that Bicknell is to be considered

[*539]

she shall duly apply for and obtain letters of administration (with the said will annexed) of the goods of the said deceased to be granted to her. Given, at London, the 3rd day of February,

in the year of our Lord 1840, and in the 12th year of our translation."

(1) 51 R. R. 326 (10 Sim. 629).
(2) 35 R. R. 732 (1 Cr. & J. 356).

as the agent of the widow, and accountable to her. I do not think   CHAMBERS
that it bears further upon the point now before me. The question   BICKNELL.
then arises whether the plaintiff is entitled to sue Bicknell or not.
The case of *Anstruther* v. *Chalmer* (1) is a very important case on
this subject. Catherine Anstruther, having made her will, died,
and Elizabeth Campbell her sister, and only next of kin, by her
power of attorney, authorized Chalmer and Fraser to obtain the
administration of the testatrix's estate from the Ecclesiastical Court
as her attornies, and they accordingly obtained such administration
as attornies of Elizabeth Campbell, and, as in the present case,
" for the use and benefit " of that person. The question was thereupon raised, whether, the letters of administration being expressed
to be granted to Fraser and Chalmer for the use and benefit of
Elizabeth Campbell, that circumstance did not exclude the parties
beneficially interested in the estate from any claim against the
attornies; that is, whether they were not merely agents. Sir
ANTHONY HART directed the case to stand over, that it might be
ascertained whether the question had not been decided by the
Ecclesiastical Court, in the form in which the letters of administration had been granted. A certificate from the deputy register of
the Prerogative Court was afterwards produced, which stated in
substance that the words used in the grant of letters of administration were invariably used when it was made under a power of
attorney from the parties entitled to representation, *and that these   [*540]
words did not exclude the claim of others to share in the estate.
It could not exclude those beneficially interested ; and it was decided
in that case that the plaintiff might sue. I am of opinion that the
plaintiff may, in this case also, sustain a suit against the administrator, notwithstanding the character in which he has taken upon
him that office. The suit, however, must be properly framed, and
for that purpose the plaintiff may have liberty to exhibit interrogatories to prove that the other defendants are out of the
jurisdiction.

The defendant Bicknell not opposing, an account of the testator's
estate received by him was directed, without prejudice to the rights
of the absent parties: the money in the hands of Bicknell was
ordered to be paid into Court, and liberty given to the plaintiffs to
exhibit interrogatories to prove that the other defendants were out
of the jurisdiction.

(1) 29 R. R. 48 (2 Sim. 1).

1843.
March 16.

WIGRAM,
V.-C.

[540]

[*541]

BROWN *v.* PERKINS (1).

(2 Hare, 540—542 ; S. C. 6 Jur. 727.)

In a suit for taking a partnership account between solicitors, the plaintiff is entitled to the discovery and production, in the usual way, of papers material to the account, although the papers relate to professional business transacted for their clients : *Semble.*

BROWN and Perkins were solicitors in partnership at Merthyr Tydvil (2). Brown died, and his representatives filed a bill against the surviving partner for an account; and an answer being put in, the plaintiffs moved for the production of the papers admitted in the answer of the defendant to be in his possession and material to the account. The defendant stated that *many of the papers referred to, related to the business of the clients of himself and his late partner, and concerned matters in which they had been entrusted in their professional character in secrecy and confidence; and that the disclosure of such matters to the solicitor of the plaintiffs, who practised in the same town and neighbourhood, might be prejudicial to such clients; and would be a breach of duty towards them; and that in several of such matters the solicitor of the plaintiffs was employed adversely, in his professional capacity, for other persons.

Mr. Roupell, for the motion, relied on the general rule entitling the plaintiff to the production of material documents.

Mr. W. M. James, contrà :

The Court will not compel a disclosure which will be a breach of confidence as against those by whom the parties have been entrusted. If any inconvenience should result from withholding the production, it is better that it should be suffered by the solicitor than the client.

THE VICE-CHANCELLOR :

The partners themselves, if they had been both living, and the question of account had arisen between them, would both have been entitled to see the papers which are part of the materials for taking the account; and it must, I think, follow that either of the partners might have employed a competent agent for the purpose of examining the papers on his behalf. If this be not so, no solicitor

(1) *Beran* v. *Webb* [1901] 2 Ch. 59, 70 L. J. Ch. 536, 84 L. T. 609, C. A.

(2) The case is reported on the argument of a plea to the bill : 5 R. R. 194 (1 Hare, 564.)

can employ another person to assist in the *settlement of his partnership accounts, without submitting to have such accounts taken
in an insufficient manner.

In this case, I should think it would be a reasonable course for
the papers to be inspected by some disinterested person,—such as
a town solicitor, or one not practising in the neighbourhood of
these parties: but such an arrangement, if made, must be by
consent.

The order for production was arranged between the parties, in
conformity with his Honour's suggestion.

BROWN
v.
PERKINS.
[*542]

PHILLIPS *v.* PRENTICE (1).

(2 Hare, 542.)

An affidavit which does not express that the deponent "made oath," is
not admissible.

AN affidavit, commencing in this form,—" A. B., of &c., saith
that," &c., not adding " maketh oath," or any words of like signification — was held, on the authority of *Oliver* v. *Price* (2), to be
inadmissible, notwithstanding the jurat expressed that it was
" sworn by the said A. B., at " &c.

Mr. Biggs and *Mr. Younge,* of counsel.

1843,
June 12.

WIGRAM,
V.-C.
[542]

COLBURN *v.* SIMMS.

(2 Hare, 543—565; S. C. 12 L. J. Ch. 388; 7 Jur. 1104.)

Where a defendant, having rendered himself liable to be sued, and being
sued, offers to submit to all the relief to which the plaintiff is entitled, the
Court will not give the plaintiff his costs of the subsequent prosecution of
the suit (3).

A plaintiff who is entitled to have an account taken of profits unlawfully
made by the defendant, is not bound to accept the statement of the
account on affidavit instead of by answer, but may call for an answer from
the defendant, without therefore disentitling himself to the costs in respect
of the answer, although he afterwards waives the account.

BY an agreement in writing, dated in July, 1839, between
Dr. Granville, of the one part, and Henry Colburn, of the other

1843.
March 24.
April 25, 26.

WIGRAM,
V.-C.
[543]

(1) *Allen* v. *Taylor* (1870) L. R. 10
Eq. 52, 39 L. J. Ch. 627, 22 L. T.
512 ; *Ex parte Torkington* (1874) L. R.
9 Ch. 298.

(2) 3 Dowl. Prc. 261.

(3) *Jenkins* v. *Hope* [1896] 1 Ch.
278, 65 L. J. Ch. 249.

part, for the considerations therein mentioned, Dr. Granville agreed to visit the principal spas and watering-places in England, and write an account of them, including advice to invalids, &c., on the plan of his work on the "Spas of Germany;" the work to be published by H. Colburn for his own use and benefit: and Dr. Granville thereby agreed to assign the copyright of the work to H. Colburn for the sum of 300*l.*, payable in manner therein mentioned: and Dr. Granville thereby further agreed not to be concerned in any other work of a similar description, but to give the entire results of his visits to the English spas in the said work, and also not to do anything that might at all interfere with the value of the copyright. Dr. Granville accordingly visited the English spas, and furnished the plaintiff with the manuscript of the work at different times. The volume containing the Northern Spas was first published in February, 1841; and another volume, containing the Southern Spas, was published in July, 1841. Before

[*544] the publication of the latter book, the plaintiff *observed an advertisement of an intended publication by Simms & Son of Bath, described as in the press, and intituled "The Invalid's and Visitor's Hand Book to the Hot Springs of Bath, by Dr. Granville, Author of the Spas of Germany, Spas of England, &c." The solicitor of the plaintiff, thereupon, by his direction, on the 29th of June, wrote to Henry Simms of Bath, acquainting him that Dr. Granville was under an engagement not to be concerned in any other work of a similar description to the "Spas of England," the copyright of which he had sold to the plaintiff; and as the plaintiff conceived the work announced was of a similar description to the book mentioned, so far as related to the mineral waters of Bath, he could not consent to the publication of the work; and that the plaintiff hoped to hear from Mr. Simms, that he would not insist on a right to introduce it to the public after that notice, or he would be compelled to commence proceedings for the protection of his property. In reply to this letter, Henry Simms, on the 1st of July, wrote to the plaintiff's solicitor, and informed him, that he (Henry Simms) and Mr. Green were the lessees of the baths and pump-room at Bath: that they had called on Dr. Granville very many months before the date of the letter, and arranged with him for a short book on the Bath waters, which they had since received from him. and for which they had paid him the sum he required: that the work was therefore justly their property, and they referred the plaintiff to Dr. Granville, as they were only publishing what was

strictly their own. He added, that their object in publishing the
little work was with no view to profit on the book, but simply as an
advertisement to their establishment.

The "Invalid's and Visitor's Hand Book" was published on the
30th of September, 1841, by the defendants, *S. Simms and S. W.
Simms, (who were in business as booksellers and publishers in
Bath, under the firm of Simms & Son), and by C. Tilt and D.
Bogue, publishers in London.

In October, 1841, the plaintiff filed his bill against Simms & Son,
Tilt and Bogue, and Dr. Granville, stating his agreement with
Dr. Granville, and the correspondence which had taken place; and
stating also, that he had since endeavoured unsuccessfully to communicate thereon with Dr. Granville, who had been abroad. The
plaintiff alleged that the "Hand Book" was, with very trifling
alterations, a copy of the chapters on Bath in the larger volume,
relating to the Southern English Spas: that the "Hand Book"
had not been published by the said Henry Simms or the said Mr.
Green, but by the defendants Simms & Son. The bill prayed that
an account might be taken of all and singular the copies of the
said "Invalid's and Visitor's Hand Book" which had been sold by
the defendants, and each or any of them, and of the profits which
would have been made by the plaintiff if he had sold the same
number of copies of the work called "The Spas of England,"
published by him, the copyright whereof had been infringed by the
publication and sale of the said "Hand Book;" and that the
defendants might be decreed to pay to the plaintiff the amount of
such profits; and that an account might be taken of all monies
paid and agreed to be paid to and received by Dr. Granville for or
in respect of the said "Hand Book;" and that the plaintiff might
be declared entitled to all such monies, and that the same might be
paid to the plaintiff accordingly; and that the defendants might
be restrained by injunction from printing, publishing, selling, or
otherwise disposing of the said "Hand Book," or any copy thereof,
or any part of the said "Spas of England" so published by *the
plaintiff, or any work written or composed by Dr. Granville of a
similar nature or description to the work so published by the
plaintiff, or to any part thereof: and that Dr. Granville might be
decreed specifically to perform the said agreement of July, 1839,
so far as the same remained to be performed on his part, and to do
and execute all such acts and instruments, if any, as might be
requisite for perfecting and confirming to the plaintiff the legal

title to the copyright in the said " Spas of England " so published
by him, and every part of the said work; and that Dr. Granville
might be restrained by injunction from assigning or otherwise
disposing of to the defendants, or any of them, or any other person,
the copyright of the same work, or of any part thereof, or of the
said " Hand Book," or any other work similar to or of the same
description as the work so published by the plaintiff, or any part
thereof, and from being concerned in any work of a similar description to, or which might interfere with the value of the copyright of,
the work so published by the plaintiff; and that the defendants
might be decreed to deliver up to be cancelled all copies of the said
" Hand Book " in their or any of their possession or power.

On the 30th of October the plaintiff obtained an injunction,
restraining Simms & Son, and Tilt and Bogue, from printing,
publishing, selling, or otherwise disposing of the " Hand Book ; "
and on the 6th of November he obtained a second injunction,
restraining Dr. Granville from printing or publishing that, or any
similar work.   No application was made to dissolve either of these
injunctions.

The answer of the defendants Simms & Son stated, that they
had caused the " Hand Book " to be printed, on account and at the
[*547] expense of the said Henry Simms *and W. Green ; that they (the
defendants) had no interest in the work, but only received the usual
allowance for its sale ; and that they were ignorant of the agreement between the plaintiff and Dr. Granville, or that the publication
involved any infringement of the plaintiff's rights.   They said that
they believed Dr. Granville wrote and composed the manuscript of
the " Hand Book " before he wrote and composed the chapter on
Bath in the plaintiff's book on the Southern Spas, and that the
" Hand Book " was printed from such manuscript.   They admitted
the publication of 508 copies of the " Hand Book ; " of which they
had sold 241, sent 100 to the defendants Tilt and Bogue, 10 to
Green and Simms, left one with the printer, and retained 373,
which, since the injunction, they had not offered for sale, and did
not intend to sell.   They stated that Green and Simms had paid
113*l.* 10*s.* in respect of the publication, and that 5*l.* 6*s.* 6*d.* had
been received for the copies sold.   They submitted, that as to part
of the relief, with which they had no concern, the bill ought to be
dismissed with costs as against them.

The defendants Tilt and Bogue by their answer stated that they
had no concern with the publication of the " Hand Book," save

that of having permitted their names to be used as the London COLBURN
v.
SIMMS.
publishers, and being employed to sell the work on commission,
for which purpose they had received 100 copies, 9 of which they
had sold before the injunction was issued, and the remaining 91
they had since returned to the solicitor of the defendants Messrs.
Simms.

Dr. Granville admitted the material facts, and said that he had
one copy of the " Hand Book," which was not for sale.

All the defendants submitted that the plaintiff was not entitled [548]
to the costs, inasmuch as he had called for the answers, and
unnecessarily proceeded with the suit; and in proof thereof, they
stated that their solicitor, on the 30th of January, 1842, in order
to terminate the suit, wrote to the solicitor of the plaintiff a letter
as follows:

" I am instructed by all the defendants to inform you that they
submit to the injunctions obtained against them respectively, and
that they are ready at once to pay the plaintiff his taxed costs of
the suit.   I herewith forward you a statement of the number of
the copies of the ' Hand Book ' published by the defendants, the
publishers thereof, and of those which had been sold, and of the
sums of money paid and received in respect of such work.   By this
statement you will perceive, that so far from the defendants' having
made any profit by the sale of the work in question, a very heavy
loss has been incurred.   My clients are ready to verify the account
contained in this statement by affidavit, if you require them to do
so.   With reference to Dr. Granville in particular, the plaintiff's
bill requires that the agreement should be specifically performed,
so far as the same remains to be performed on his part, and that
he may do and execute all such acts and instruments, if any, as
may be requisite for perfecting and confirming to the plaintiff the
legal title in the copyright of the ' Spas of England.'   Now, I am
instructed by that gentleman to say, that misapprehension of the
nature of his rights and obligations under his agreement with Mr.
Colburn alone could have caused him to have been a party to any
act which could be deemed an invasion of Mr. Colburn's rights
thereunder, and that he, Dr. Granville, has no intention of acting
contrary to the terms thereof, and is quite willing at once to execute
any instrument *you may deem proper to tender him for perfecting [*549]
your client's legal title to the copyright which he has purchased,
if indeed the Doctor has not already executed, as he believes he
has, such an instrument; for he says, that at the interview which

COLBURN
v.
SIMMS.

he had with Mr. Colburn, about the latter end of June last, he signed some document, which he then understood to be an assignment. If he is mistaken you will probably be good enough to undeceive him, and forward me a copy of the document which he did then sign. As to the relief asked by the plaintiff's bill with respect to the sum of money paid to Dr. Granville for the work in question, seeing that he will have to reimburse his co-defendants, the publishers, all their expenses incurred about the work, I am advised that the plaintiff is not entitled to what he seeks in respect thereof; neither is the plaintiff, as I am advised, entitled to insist upon having the books delivered up to be cancelled. With the concession here made, I submit, Mr. Colburn ought to be satisfied. I cannot help believing, that upon reflection you will deem it right to recommend Mr. Colburn to consent to discontinue the further prosecution of this suit upon payment of his costs, and which would be done immediately after the amount was ascertained: the injunction to continue perpetual. In the mean time, until I hear from you, my counsel will delay preparing the answer." And that on the 14th of February, 1842, the solicitor of the plaintiff wrote to their solicitor as follows:

"I have seen Mr. Colburn, and he altogether declined your proposal; and it seems to me he is right. Upon what principle it is to be contended that, because the act of your client has been unproductive to him, or his vendors, the plaintiff cannot therefore have sustained injury, I am at a loss to discover. After you have

[*550]

expended more than the sum in question between *us in additional costs, I hope you will discover that that is not the correct mode by which Dr. Granville will be allowed to decrease the payment to be made to Mr. Colburn for the offence of which he has been guilty."

At the hearing of the cause the plaintiff waived his right to the account, the defendants submitted to the perpetual injunction, and Dr. Granville to execute the assignment of the copyright.

Mr. Bazalgette and *Mr. Romilly*, for the plaintiff, on the only remaining relief prayed, namely, the right to delivery up of the copies, relied on the statutes 8 Ann. c. 19; 41 Geo. III. c. 107. s. 1, and 54 Geo. III. c. 156, s. 4 (1). * * The right to the

(1) These statutes were repealed by 5 & 6 Vict. c. 45, s. 1. Copies of pirated books are now legally vested in the registered proprietor of the copyright by 5 & 6 Vict. c. 45, s. 23; see *Muddock* v. *Blackwood* [1898] 1 Ch. 58, 67 L. J. Ch 6.—O. A. S.

decree for the delivery of the copies carried with it the right to the COLBURN
costs of suit.   But, with regard to costs, the plaintiff was not bound *v.*
to be satisfied with *the affidavits of the defendants as to the profits SIMMS.
they had made.   He was entitled to an answer, and having properly [*551]
called for an answer, he was not then under any obligation to
dismiss his bill.

Mr. Bearan, for the defendants S. Simms and S. W. Simms :

* * According to *Millington* v. *Fox* (1), the plaintiff is not
entitled to the costs, although the injunction is made perpetual—
the whole relief to which he was entitled having been offered to
him before answer. * * The Court will not order the delivery [552]
up of the copies in the absence of the owners.   The order for this
purpose can in fact be made against none other than the principals,
and through them the agents would be compelled to obey it.   The
delivery of the copies is to be ordered upon motion or petition, and
the hearing of the cause was unnecessary for that purpose : the
claim is not therefore a justification for incurring costs, after the
offer of the settlement, and the defendants ought to be indemnified
against the subsequent costs.

Mr. Headlam, for the defendants Tilt and Bogue, and *Mr.
Temple* and *Mr. Tripp,* for Dr. Granville, in support of the like
argument. * * *

THE VICE-CHANCELLOR :   *April* 24.

The defendants having in this case at the hearing submitted to [553]
a perpetual injunction, and Dr. Granville being ready to execute the
assignment, while, on the other hand, the plaintiff is satisfied with
the statement of account given by the answer, and has waived a
decree for an account, I have only to consider the question of the
delivery up of the copies of the " Hand Book " by the defendants
to the plaintiff, and the question of costs.

[The repeal of the statutes upon which the first question
depended makes it unnecessary to retain here that part of the
judgment which dealt with that point.   Upon the question of costs,
the VICE-CHANCELLOR said :]

The remaining question is as to the costs.   The plaintiff has suc- [560]
ceeded in the most material part of his case by making the injunction

(1) 45 R. R. 271 (3 My. & Cr. 338).

perpetual. The supposition, that at the hearing of the cause this Court could give the plaintiff something beyond the account, was, however, erroneous. It is true that the Court does not, by an account, accurately measure the damage sustained by the proprietor of an expensive work from the invasion of his copyright by the publication of a cheaper book. It is impossible to know how many copies of the dearer book are excluded from sale by the interposition of the cheaper one. The Court, by the account, as the nearest approximation which it can make to justice, takes from the wrong-doer all the profits he has made by his piracy, and gives them to the party who has been wronged. In doing this the Court may often give the injured party more, in fact, than he is entitled to, for *non constat* that a single additional copy of the more expensive book would have been sold, if the injury by the sale of the cheaper book had not been committed. The court of equity, however, does not give anything beyond the account, and I therefore think the defendants offered all that the plaintiff was entitled to. With regard to the costs incurred subsequently to the defendants' offer, the observations of Lord COTTENHAM in *Millington* v. *Fox* are important. The parties there were perfectly unconscious that they had committed a wrong by the use of another man's mark ; and Lord COTTENHAM, after saying that the plaintiffs were entitled to their decree, adds, that this abstract right of the plaintiff was not

[*561]

the only right he *had to guard : there was another object which the Court must keep in view—that of repressing unnecessary litigation, and of keeping litigation within the bounds which are essential to the establishment and vindication of the rights of the parties (1). If a plaintiff, immediately after the suit is commenced, is offered and may obtain all he seeks, and still thinks proper to go on with his suit, the Court may give him his decree, but will not give him the costs of the suit so unnecessarily prosecuted. I think that is the whole principle of the judgment in *Millington* v. *Fox*. Lord COTTENHAM had not his attention called to the fact, that the expense of filing the bill had been incurred before the plaintiffs received the letter offering compensation, and he certainly fortifies his judgment by saying that the defendants in that case were innocent parties, having committed the wrong ignorantly, which cannot be said of Dr. Granville in this case ; but I think I am justified by that authority in saying, that where a defendant offers to give all that

(1) 45 R. R. at p. 275 (3 My. & Cr. 353).

a plaintiff is entitled to, and the plaintiff refuses the offer, and   COLBURN
says, "Because you have committed a fraud I will exercise my   v.
power of harassing you with a Chancery suit," this Court will   SIMMS.
refuse the plaintiff his subsequent costs.

In *Kelly* v. *Hooper* (1), the only question was, up to what point
the plaintiff was justified in prosecuting his suit. It appears to
me that in this case the plaintiff was not bound to receive the
affidavits tendered by the defendants; and with respect to the
account prayed, I think he had a right to call for an answer ; I
cannot, therefore, *say that I think the plaintiff was wrong up to   [*562]
the time of getting in the answer. I think the plaintiff is entitled,
as against some of the defendants, to all the costs up to and including the answer, but that he is not entitled to his costs subsequent
to that time.   There is a difficulty as between the co-defendants :
Dr. Granville, by misleading the other parties, has occasioned the
suit, and he therefore must pay the costs of the defendants, who
have been misled by him.   Simms & Son had some notice of the
plaintiff's claim, but the time of that notice does not appear.   The
other defendants deny notice altogether, and there is nothing to
lead to the suspicion that they had notice. I shall, unless an
inquiry is asked, direct the plaintiff to pay all the defendants
(except Dr. Granville) their costs, and add them to his own
costs, to be paid by Dr. Granville ; but if Dr. Granville desires
it, I will direct an inquiry whether the other defendants had notice
of the plaintiff's right, and when they had such notice.

ATTORNEY-GENERAL *v.* LUCAS.

(2 Hare, 566—570 ; S. C. 12 L. J. Ch. 506 ; 7 Jur. 1080.)

A husband charged with procuring his marriage with a minor, by
falsely swearing that the consent of her parent had been given, cannot be
compelled to discover the facts relating to the charge, upon an information under the Marriage Act, 1823 (4 Geo. IV. c. 76, s. 23), seeking the
forfeiture of his interest in the wife's property, and a settlement of the
same upon her and her issue.

1843.
March 27, 28.

WIGRAM,
V.-C.

[566]

THIS information was filed under the Marriage Act, (4 Geo. IV.
c. 76 (2)), at the relation of R. Jago. The information stated, that
Elizabeth, the wife of the defendant Philip Lucas, was the only
child of the relator, and was an infant of the age of nineteen

(1) 1 Y. & C. C. C. 197.   (2) Sect. 23.

A.-G.
v.
LUCAS.

years: that on the 24th of August preceding, the defendant Philip
Lucas applied for and obtained a license for the solemnization of a
marriage between himself and the said Elizabeth, and that on the
31st of August the marriage was solemnized by virtue of such
license: that the license was procured by means of the defendant
Philip Lucas swearing, among other things, that the consent of the
relator to such marriage had been obtained, whereas the defendant
well knew that such consent had never been given, but on the contrary, that the said marriage had been solemnized without the
consent of the relator or his wife, (the mother of the said Elizabeth); and that the relator and his said wife had always objected
thereto, alleging divers circumstances in evidence thereof, and in
particular that the defendant induced the said Elizabeth to leave
the relator's house clandestinely, previous to and for the purpose of
the said marriage: that the defendant had in his possession various
letters and papers, from which the truth of the said allegations
would appear. The information alleged, that the said Elizabeth
was entitled to certain real and personal property, expectant on the
decease of the relator and his wife; and it prayed a declaration
that the defendant Philip Lucas had forfeited all interest in such
property, and that an account might be taken of all the property to
[*567]   which the said Elizabeth was entitled at the time of *her marriage,
and that the same might be settled under the direction of the Court
for the benefit of the said Elizabeth and her issue. The defendant
Philip Lucas, by his answer admitting the marriage, insisted that
he was not bound to answer whether the said Elizabeth was not a
minor, whether he did not obtain the license by swearing that he
had the consent of the relator, or whether the marriage took place
by virtue of such license, or whether the relator had always withheld his consent, or as to the circumstances stated as evidence
thereof; for the defendant said that it appeared on the face of the
information that the same was filed for the purpose of having it
declared that he had forfeited his interest in the real and personal
estate of the said Elizabeth, and of enforcing such forfeiture; and
further, that he was thereby charged with matters which would, if
true, render him liable to an indictment and to punishment for
misdemeanor.

Exceptions for insufficiency were taken with respect to the facts
which the defendant had so declined to answer. The Master
reported the answer sufficient, and exceptions were taken to the
Master's report.

Mr. Roupell and *Mr. Bilton*, for the informant:

  * * The rule, that a defendant shall not be compelled to answer
with respect to circumstances which might occasion a loss or forfeiture of property, applies only where that forfeiture is to be enforced
at law; if the relief is to be given in equity, the defendant must
answer, however prejudicial to his interests the answer might be:
this is proved by the common practice of the Court, and the cases
are consistent with it. The defence, on the alleged ground of the
liability to punishment as for a misdemeanor, is answered by the
fact that such liability does not exist: *Rex* v. *Thomas Foster* (1),
Woodman's case (2). There are some of the facts to which the
objections to answer certainly do not apply.

Mr. Tinney and *Mr. Heathfield*, for the defendant:

  * * As to the separation of the discovery, *which might be
harmless, from that which clearly led to forfeiture or penalty, they
referred to *Paxton* v. *Douglas* (3). The Order XXVIII., of August,
1841, enabled the defendant, by answer, to decline answering.

THE VICE-CHANCELLOR:

  The object of the suit is to deprive the husband of property
which he acquires in his marital right. A court of equity compels
a defendant to give discovery generally in aid of the plaintiff's
case; but whatever the merits of the case may be, there are
certain questions which the defendant is not bound to answer.
Among these are questions the answers to which would involve
the disclosure of privileged communications, and such matters as
may subject the defendant to pains, penalties, and forfeitures.
With respect to these questions it is perfectly immaterial whether
the objection be taken by demurrer or answer: the defendant is
equally protected. The thirty-eighth Order of August, 1841, therefore, has no application. That Order was not necessary in such a
case: it was intended to provide for cases in which the defendant
could not previously protect himself by answer. I think this case
is not of that class in which the fact, the subject of inquiry, has
been attended with a mere determination of interest by force of an
original limitation, but that the present case is within the rule
applicable to penalties and forfeitures, and that the defendant
cannot therefore be compelled to answer any of the interrogatories
which are the subject of these exceptions.

  (1) Russ. & Ry. Cr. Ca. 459.   (3) 12 R. R. 175 (16 Ves. 239; 19
  (2) 1 Leach, Cr. Ca. 64, *n.*   *Id.* 225).

A.-G.
v.
LUCAS.
[568]

[*569]

It has been argued, however, that a different principle applies where the bill is for relief as well as discovery, *and the effect of the discovery is to be worked out in equity. This distinction is not to be found in any of the cases, and it appears to me to be unfounded in principle. I think I should be introducing an unmeaning refinement, if I decided that the same principle did not govern the case, whether the relief was at law or in equity.

Exceptions overruled.

1843.
April 4, 19,
20.
May 6.

WIGRAM,
V.-C.
[570]

MORLEY *v.* RENNOLDSON (1).

(2 Hare, 570—587; S. C. 12 L. J. Ch. 372; 7 Jur. 938.)

A testator bequeathed the residue of his personal estate to his daughter upon trust for her maintenance and support, until she attained twenty-one, or married with the consent of his trustees under that age, and upon her attaining such age or her marriage, for her separate use, with remainder to her children; and in case of her death without issue, he bequeathed the same to certain legatees in remainder. The testator afterwards declared by a codicil, that, in consequence of a nervous debility, his daughter was unfit for the control of herself, and his will was that she should not marry, and in case of her marriage or death, he gave the property he had bequeathed to her over to the same legatees in remainder.

Held, that the limitation over by the codicil, being in general restraint of marriage, was void as to the life interest of the daughter (2).

That the Court would not inquire into the fact of whether the testator was mistaken or not, with reference to his daughter's health or capacity.

W. RENNOLDSON, by his will, dated the 4th of November, 1834, gave and bequeathed all his household goods and furniture, plate, glass, linen, china, books, prints, and pictures, unto and to be equally divided between his wife Emma and his daughter Margaret; and he also gave to his said wife and daughter Margaret, the sum of 150*l.* each for mourning, to be paid to them within two calendar months next after his decease; the said legacy to his daughter to be paid and applied to her use by his executors, if she had not then attained twenty-one. And he gave his leasehold house in Turner Street unto his wife, and directed that she should

[*571]

provide a *suitable apartment therein for the residence of his said daughter Margaret, so long as she should remain single and unmarried, and desired to live with his wife, to whose care he strongly recommended her. And he gave and bequeathed the residue of his personal estate to trustees therein named, upon trust to pay and

(1) The daughter subsequently married and died leaving children, and it was held that the daughter's children were entitled to the fund, see *Morley* v.   *Rennoldson* [1895] 1 Ch. 449, 64 L. J. Ch. 485, 72 L. T. 308, C. A.—O. A. S.
(2) *Bellairs* v. *Bellairs* (1874) L. R. 18 Eq. 510, 43 L. J. Ch. 669.

apply certain sums for the benefit of his said wife, and his daughter
Emma, and the issue of his daughter Emma, and upon further
trust to pay and apply all, or a competent part (in the discretion of
his trustees) of, the residue of the annual proceeds of the trust
monies, in the maintenance and support of his daughter Margaret,
until she should attain twenty-one, or be married under that age
with the consent of the said trustees, or the greater number of
them, in such manner as the trustees should think fit; and the
remainder of such annual proceeds, from time to time, to be added
to the principal; and immediately after his daughter Margaret
should attain the age of twenty-one, or be married under that
age with such consent as aforesaid, then upon trust to pay the
interest and dividends of the said residue of the trust monies unto
his daughter Margaret, for her sole use and benefit, without power
of anticipation; and after her decease, he directed that the residue
of the said trust monies should be in trust for all and every her
child and children, as therein mentioned. And in case his said
daughter should die without leaving any such child or children, he
directed that his said trustees should stand possessed of the said
trust monies, or so much thereof as remained undisposed of, upon
trust to pay and transfer three fourth parts thereof unto his
daughter Emma, and his nephews William Rennoldson and John
Dalton, equally, and the other fourth part thereof unto his niece
Mary Harvey, for her separate use.

By a codicil, dated the 15th of February, 1836, the *testator   [*572]
revoked the last-mentioned ultimate bequest of the residue of his
personal estate in fourths, in case of the death of his daughter
Margaret without issue, and bequeathed one moiety of the same to
his daughter Emma, and the other moiety to his said nephews and
niece: and he appointed the defendant R. Linkson executor and
trustee, instead of one of the first-named executors, who was dead.

The testator made a second codicil, dated the 30th of October,
1836, upon which the question in the cause arose: this codicil was
as follows: "In consequence of the continued nervous debility
under which my daughter Margaret is labouring, (originally occasioned by a fright at the age of five years), and considering that
it totally unfits her for the control of herself, I deem it advisable,
for her better protection and of the several legacies and bequests
to her by my said will, to direct that my trustees and executors
shall apply all monies bequeathed to my said daughter for her use
and benefit, in such manner as they shall think fit, and the most

for her comfort and welfare, and my will and mind is that for the reason aforesaid my said daughter Margaret shall not at any time contract matrimony; and in case of the marriage or death of my said daughter Margaret, then I direct that the trustees and executors for the time being shall stand possessed of all the residuary stocks, funds, and securities, which I have bequeathed to her, as mentioned in my said will, and pay and transfer one half part thereof unto my daughter Emma, and the other half part thereof unto and equally between my nephews William Rennoldson and John Dalton, and my niece Mary Harvey."

[*573]
The testator died in February, 1837, leaving all the said legatees surviving. The executors, Morley, Sadgrove, *Graham, and Linkson, proved the will. After providing for the legacies, there was a residue of about 5,000l. Three per cent. Stock.

On the 9th of January, 1842, the testator's daughter Margaret intermarried with R. Linkson, one of the executors. The bill was filed by the other three executors to obtain the declaration of the Court on the rights of the parties, as they might be affected by the marriage of Margaret, and that the trusts might be performed under the direction of the Court. The defendants were the testator's widow, his daughter Emma, an infant, R. Linkson and Margaret, his wife, William Rennoldson, John Dalton, and Mary Harvey and her husband.

The defendant William Rennoldson submitted, that the testator's residuary estate, on the marriage of his daughter, became payable to the other persons named in the second codicil: or, if Margaret had not attained twenty-one when she married, and had married without the said consent, then that only a part of the interest of the residue ought to be applied for her benefit during her life or her minority, or at all events that he was entitled to one-third of a moiety of the residue, in the event of the death of Margaret without children. The testator's widow, and his daughter Emma, an infant, submitted their rights to the Court. John Dalton and Mary Harvey and her husband were out of the jurisdiction, and did not appear in the cause.

The defendants R. Linkson and Margaret, his wife, submitted that the second codicil did not operate as an alteration of the benefits given to Margaret and her children by the will; and that the codicil was made when the testator was at a very advanced age, and suffering from acute disease, and under a mistaken notion of
[*574]
*the state of his daughter's health; and that neither then nor

previously was she under any nervous debility unfitting her for the control of herself.   They admitted that her health had been for a short time impaired by a fright when about five years old, but said that she very soon recovered from the effects of it.

Jane Linkson, a child of R. Linkson and Margaret, his wife, born after the commencement of the suit, was made a party by supplemental bill.

At the hearing—

Mr. Teed and *Mr. Rogers*, for the plaintiffs.

Mr. Romilly, for the defendants Linkson and wife, and their child :

The testator has by the codicil attempted to impose an absolute restriction on the liberty of marriage, and to fortify it by a penalty. This the law does not permit : *Low* v. *Peers* (1), *Hartley* v. *Rice* (2). It is not necessary to contend that a party may not in some cases create a valid limitation of property until marriage, or that he may not alter his bounty upon that event; but in all cases it is always a question of intention, whether the testator truly intends, on such an event, the benefit of the object in whose favour the legacy is limited over, or *bonâ fide* intends the simple performance of the condition, or whether his real object be to compel the celibacy of the legatee.   In the former case the limitation may be good, in the latter it is invalid.   Thus, "when on any condition, however restrictive of marriage, the legacy is given over to pious *uses, the intention of the party shall be deemed to regard those uses, and not to have aimed at the objectional purpose of restraining marriage " (3).   So, again, the testator may make the consent of another person to the marriage a lawful condition; but if he requires the consent of a person whose interest it is to refuse, or who would unreasonably refuse, the condition is void (4).   The validity of every limitation until marriage depends upon the intention ; and, if found to be in general restraint of marriage, there is no case in which the limitation in that respect has been upheld, except where the legatee was the testator's own widow: *Rishton* v. *Cobb* (5), *Keily* v. *Monck* (6), *Long* v. *Dennis* (7).   *   *   *

[*575]

(1) 4 Burr. 2225.
(2) 10 R. R. 228 (10 East, 22).
(3) Per Lord THURLOW, *Scott* v. *Tyler*, 2 Dick. 722.

(4) *Scott* v. *Tyler*, 2 Br. C. C. 488.
(5) 48 R. R. 256 (5 My. & Cr. 145).
(6) 3 Ridg. P. C. 205.
(7) 4 Burr. 2052.

Mr. Anderdon and *Mr. Cripps*, for the defendants Emma Rennoldson and Emma Rennoldson, the younger :

* * The utmost that Margaret can claim, supposing the condition to be construed as unlawful with respect to the restraint upon her, is the life-interest. There is no authority for the proposition that a party may not make the marriage of A. an event upon which property shall pass from B. to C.: that is no restraint on

[*577] the *marriage of A. The gift in remainder to the children of Margaret is therefore well revoked, and passes by the codicil to the legatees over in the case of her marriage.

Mr. Toller, for the defendant William Rennoldson, in support of the like argument, cited, also, *Clarke* v. *Parker* (1) and *Malcolm* v. *O'Callaghan* (2) :

The limitation over takes effect upon breach of the condition. There is no principle upon which the Court can say that the parties claiming under the last limitation are to be excluded, merely for the benefit of those taking under the first,—one party being as much an object of the testator's bounty as the other.

Mr. Romilly, in reply, as to the alleged revocation of the gift to the children of Margaret, said that the expression in the codicil, importing the testator's intention that the legatee should forfeit her legacy on marriage, would not be construed to imply more than her own interest in it: the reason of the provision obviously went no further; and the same provision, in case of her death, would be made intelligible and consistent with the will by reading it as death without issue. The testator would therefore be deemed to say, that, if his daughter married, she should lose her life-interest; if she died without issue, the capital should go over. The will and codicil must be taken together, and regard had to the principle, that a revocation, to be operative, must be as distinctly shown as the original gift : *Hearle* v. *Hicks* (3).

[Other cases mentioned in the argument are referred to in the following judgment :]

May 6.　THE VICE-CHANCELLOR :

[578] The bill is filed by some of the executors, who are trustees, against the other trustee, who has married the testator's daughter Margaret, and against the other parties beneficially interested, or

(1) 12 R. R. 124 (19 Ves. 13, 23).　　(3) 36 R. R. 1 (8 Bing. 475).
(2) 38 R. R. 28 (2 Madd. 349).

claiming to be interested, in the estate. The plaintiffs suggest, that, in consequence of Margaret's marriage, a question has arisen, whether she is entitled to the income of the fund for her life, or whether her life-interest has not become forfeited, and vested in the ultimate legatees. The defendants, Mr. Linkson and his wife, state by their answer, that, although the latter had suffered some time from nervous debility, yet that her health was perfectly restored, and they insist that the codicil is to be considered as merely *in terrorem* and of no effect. The whole question in the case arises between co-defendants, and no other facts appearing, I simply have to determine upon the face of the will as it stands, what decree I ought to make.

The rule of the civil law was referred to in the argument, as it has usually been on questions of this *nature, but that law—founded, as Lord LOUGHBOROUGH observes (1), on social maxims and public polity, so essentially different from our own, as to render it difficult to conceive how it could have been adopted by our Courts on this subject—has not been followed with regard to conditions operating in restraint of marriage. The extent to which the civil law has been gradually departed from is to be collected from Lord THURLOW's judgment in *Scott* v. *Tyler* (2). In the English law a distinction has been taken between the cases in which the restraint operates as a condition precedent, and those in which it is expressed to take effect as a condition subsequent. A distinction has also been made as to whether it is a particular restraint, (a partial and reasonable restraint), or whether it is a general restraint; and the decision is generally made to depend upon the question, whether there is a gift over, or no gift over. In *Stackpole* v. *Beaumont* (3), Lord LOUGHBOROUGH appears to have said, that, such was the state of the authorities, a Judge could not be considered to act too boldly whichever side of the proposition he should adopt (4). There are some points, however, which seem clearly settled, according to the law as administered in courts of justice in this country; one is, that, if the restraint is a general restraint, and the condition is subsequent, then the condition is altogether void, and the party retains the interest given to him, discharged of the condition; that is, supposing a gift of a certain duration, and an attempt to abridge it by a condition in restraint of marriage, generally the condition is, *primâ facie*, void, and the original gift remains. But, until I heard the argument of this case, I had certainly understood, that,

[*579]

(1) 8 R. R. 59 (3 Ves. 96).   (3) 3 R. R. 52 (3 Ves. 88).
(2) 2 Dick. 712.   (4) 3 R. R. 61 (3 Ves. 98).

without doubt, where property was limited to a person until *she
married, and when she married then over, the limitation was
good. It is difficult to understand how this could be otherwise, for
in such a case there is nothing to give an interest beyond the
marriage. If you suppose the case of a gift of a certain interest,
and that interest sought to be abridged by a condition, you may
strike out the condition, and leave the original gift in operation ;
but if the gift is until marriage, and no longer, there is nothing to
carry the gift beyond the marriage. With reference to that point,
and also in order that the grounds of my decision might clearly
appear to those parties against whom it might be, I wished to look
into the authorities ; and I am satisfied, from an examination of
the authorities, that there is no reason to alter my opinion, that a
gift until marriage, and when the party marries then over, is a
valid limitation. In the case of a widow there is no question of the
validity of such a limitation. It was decided in *Jordan* v. *Holkham* (1),
that, where an estate was given during widowhood, the estate was
determinable by the second marriage ; and an annuity given
during widowhood is also good : *Barton* v. *Barton* (2). In *Scott* v.
Tyler (3), Lord THURLOW, speaking of the change which the civil
law had undergone in its descent, observes that, in the novels,
widowhood was excepted, and an injunction to keep that state was
a lawful condition (4). *Scott* v. *Tyler* was certainly a peculiar case ;
but, referring to the canon law, Lord THURLOW, citing Godolphin,
says, that the use of a thing may be given " during celibacy, for
the purpose of intermediate maintenance, and will not be interpreted maliciously to a charge of restraining marriage " (5) ;

[*581]
affirming, therefore, the *general doctrine, that a gift until
marriage would be good. In the case of *Low* v. *Peers* (6), Chief
Justice WILMOT goes through the cases upon the subject, and shows
that, according to his apprehension of the law, a gift until marriage
is perfectly good. He notices the case of college fellowships, of
customs of manors, of limitations of estates during celibacy, and
the express distinction between limitations and conditions ; and he
remarks that that distinction is recognised and established, and
that the common law allows it. I may refer to the cases, and
amongst them to the later ones of *Bird* v. *Hunsdon* (7), and *Marples*

(1) Amb. 209.
(2) 2 Vern. 308.
(3) 2 Dick. 712.
(4) *Id.* 721.

(5) 2 Dick. 722.
(6) Ch. J. Wilmot's Cases, 369.
(7) 19 R. R. 82 (2 Swanst. 342).

v. *Bainbridge* (1), as affirming the same proposition. In those cases all the reasons the Court referred to were superfluous, if a limitation during celibacy is not good. The Court might have taken the short course, and have said that it was in the nature of a restraint, and therefore could not be supported. I wish to exclude the supposition, that I proceed, in any respect, upon the ground taken in argument upon this point.

The question to be considered is that upon which, in fact, I reserved my judgment, whether, according to the true intent of the second codicil, it must be considered as confirming the gifts made by the will, and then seeking to determine them on the event of marriage, or whether it was not a complete substitution of new bequests, amounting, in substance, to a limitation during celibacy. Without saying the case is clear, the conclusion to which I have come is, that this codicil does, in point of fact, recognise and confirm the prior bequests by the will. The testator does not intend to say, "I substitute a new bequest,"—but he says, "It is advisable for her better protection, *as to the several legacies and bequests to which by my will she is entitled, to direct that my trustees shall apply the money in a certain way." He then proceeds to say his will is, that she shall not, for the reasons he has mentioned, contract matrimony ; and that, in case of her marriage or death, the residuary stocks, funds, and securities which he has bequeathed to his daughter, as mentioned in his will, shall go over to other parties. That is the next clause. In the case of *Malcolm* v. *O'Callaghan*, which was cited, marriage with consent was a condition precedent, by the will, and the codicil giving the legacy to the survivor of the daughters who should die before the age of twenty-five, or marriage with consent, was held to keep alive the condition. The testator in this case has so expressed himself, as to import an intention to create a general restraint upon the marriage of the legatee, and the limitation over, with that object, is therefore, *primâ facie*, void. I need not repeat the cases on this point, the last of which (*Rishton* v. *Cobb* (2)) is a very important one, although there were some words in that case which might be open to observation.

The only other point upon the face of this case is, whether circumstances may not exist, justifying the testator in prohibiting his daughter altogether from contracting marriage, notwithstanding the general rule I have mentioned. Although, upon this will and

[*582]

(1) 16 R. R. 271 (1 Madd. 590).   (2) 48 R. R. 256 (9 Sim. 615;
                                    affirmed, 5 My. & Cr. 145).

codicil taken together, the testator says that the state of mind of
his daughter totally unfits her for the control of herself, it is
impossible to read the will, made in 1834, and the codicil, made in
1836, in the latter of which the testator does not speak of any new
fact having occurred, but of continuous debility, produced by an
[*583]   antecedent *cause, without seeing that on the face of the will he
admits a capacity in his daughter to contract marriage.   He supposes it in 1834,—he supposes the same state to continue at the
time of making the codicil ; and on that supposition it is that he
thinks it necessary to interpose, and provide by his will that she
shall not contract marriage.   Upon the face of these instruments
there is a recognition, therefore, by the testator, of a capacity on
the part of his daughter to contract marriage ; and, therefore,
taking the case as unencumbered with any other facts, it seems to
me, that I cannot do otherwise than hold that this is a conditional
gift in general restraint of marriage, by which the testator seeks to
cut down an interest which he had given by the will, and therefore
that I must hold this to be a void condition.   Attending, however,
to the qualification which I must annex to the decree in respect of
the interests of the absent parties,—to the fact, that this is a case
between co-defendants,—and to the suggestion, that, if the truth of
the case was before the Court, it might receive a different consideration, all I at present decide is, that, simply reading the will, in a
case in which there has been no opportunity for contest between
the co-defendants with respect to extraneous circumstances, I am
of opinion that the condition is invalid.

There were other parts of the case argued, which I do not think
it necessary to decide, and which I notice only to exclude them, as I
would most emphatically do, from being considered to form any part
of the grounds of my judgment.   It was said that this was a case of
mistake on the part of the testator.   I cannot advise the parties—on
the contrary, I think it would be idle for them to attempt to found
any case upon such a supposition as that of there being a mistake
[*584]   in the testator's *mind with respect to the competency or incom-
petency of his daughter for marriage.   I could not hold the codicil
void on the ground of such mistake, supposing it to be proved.
Although I admit that mistake may be a ground for equitable
relief, this is a case, in which a party, having the object of his
bounty before his eyes, thinks proper to form his own opinion on
her fitness for a certain state of life, and, forming that opinion, he
declares that she ought not to marry ; and if she does, he directs

that the bounty which he intended for her should go to others. If
he could by law impose such a restraint, I cannot inquire into the
soundness of the judgment which led him to do so.

I was asked to decide also the case as to the children. In the
decree I intend to make, the case of the children will incidentally
be noticed. I give the income to Margaret, with liberty to all
parties to apply. The case of the children of Margaret may stand
upon a different footing from that of Margaret herself. Suppose
the testator had said, " I have given my daughter a life-interest,
and I have given A. B., a stranger, the remainder; but now I do
not choose that my daughter shall marry, and if she do marry, I
revoke the bequest to A. B." Is it quite clear that the revocation
would not be effectual as to A. B., although, as to the daughter, the
attempt to revoke the legacy, on her marriage generally, would be
void? Here the testator says his daughter ought not to marry, and
she shall not marry; and he has given the property, after her
marriage or death, to other parties. I will not decide, in this stage
of the case, in what way, if at all, the interests of the children of
Margaret may be affected by the condition, which is inoperative as
regards the interests of Margaret herself (1).

As to the form of the decree,—this bill being filed by trustees,
I must treat the co-defendants as making claims adverse to each
other, and avoid anything which might endanger the interests of
the absent parties. Emma Rennoldson, who would take half of
the residue given over by the codicil, and William Rennoldson, who
would take one-sixth, are before the Court; and therefore the decree
which I propose to make will properly bind the four sixth parts of
the residue that would pass to them. The parties who would be
entitled to the other two-sixths, namely, John Dalton and Mary
Harvey, are out of the jurisdiction. The decree must be guarded
with reference to this portion of the residue. The case of *Steven-
son* v. *Anderson* (2), before Lord Eldon, may seem to throw a doubt
upon the necessity for this caution : that was a case of interpleader;
and only one of the suggested claimants of the property was before
the Court, the others being out of the jurisdiction : the Court
granted an injunction, (which I should have no difficulty in doing
in this case, if any injunction were needed) (3); and Lord ELDON
said, that, the Court having proof that the plaintiff in interpleader
had done all he could to bring the parties before the Court, and

[585]

(1) See note, *ante,* p. 236.
(2) 13 R. R. 126 (2 V. & B. 407).

(3) See *Chambers* v. *Bicknell, ante,*
p. 223.

MORLEY
v.
RENNOLD-
SON.

[*586]

had not succeeded, the consequence would be, that the only person within the jurisdiction must have that which was represented as the subject of competition, and the Court would ·indemnify the interpleading party against those who were out of the jurisdiction. Many reasons apply to that case which do not apply here. Where the remedy of the claimant is against the bailee personally, the Court places that claimant in no worse situation by making its declaration upon the case which the bailee presents to the Court. *The case is different where the Court is disposing of a fund under its control. In such a case I cannot allow the money to be received by the parties before the Court, saving the rights of those who are absent ; for the decree to that effect would prejudice their rights if it were erroneous. It would deprive them of the security of the fund itself. The utmost which I think I can do, is, to secure the fund in which the absent parties are interested. There are several provisions in this will which may yet remain in operation, upon which I am not now called to give any opinion. The funds will be brought into Court, and the dividends, to which Margaret is declared to be entitled, will be directed to be paid to her.

Declare, that, as against Emma Rennoldson, the younger, and William Rennoldson, such interest as the defendant Margaret Linkson, late Rennoldson, took under the will of William Rennoldson, the testator, in the pleadings, &c., did not determine by force of her marriage with the defendant Robert Linkson, in the pleadings mentioned ; but this declaration is to be wholly without prejudice to the rights (if any) of the defendants John Dalton and Mary Harvey, who are out of the jurisdiction of this Court, and without prejudice to any right of the defendants Emma Rennoldson, the younger, and William Rennoldson, to file a bill to establish their rights (if any) in the residue not inconsistent with the above declaration, and refer it to the Master of this Court, in rotation, to inquire and state to the Court what children there have been of the marriage of the said defendants Robert Linkson and Margaret, his wife, and whether any of them are since dead ; and if the said Master shall find that all the surviving children of the said marriage are before the Court, parties to these suits, then let it be referred to the said Master to take an account of the personal estate not specifically bequeathed of the testator, &c. Plaintiff, and defendant R. Linkson, to transfer and pay (the several parts of the trust funds) into Court, in trust in these causes. (Directions with respect to the payments to be made to the defendants Emma Rennoldson and Emma Rennoldson, the younger.) And let four-sixths of the dividends that have accrued due on the said (describing the residuary trust funds) previously to the transfer thereof as aforesaid, and which may be paid into Court *pursuant to this order, and of the dividends hereafter to accrue due thereon, when so transferred, be paid to the defendant Margaret Linkson, for her separate use, and on her sole receipt, until the further order of this Court, but without prejudice to the payment of the costs of this suit.   Liberty generally to apply.

GRIFFITHS *v.* GRIFFITHS.

(2 Hare, 587—596; S. C. 12 L. J. Ch. 387; 7 Jur. 573.)

Where a party has employed, as his solicitors in a cause, a firm of two solicitors in partnership, the retirement from the business of one partner, under an arrangement with the other, operates as a discharge of the client by the solicitors, and the client is thereupon entitled to require that the papers in the cause necessary for its prosecution shall be delivered up to his new solicitor, upon the usual undertaking for saving the lien of the discharged solicitors.

THE petition of the plaintiff, Elizabeth Jane Griffiths, an infant, by W. Fallowfield, her next friend, stated, among other things, that, it having, in 1840, been determined by George Gordon and Susan, his wife, two of the defendants in the cause, (Susan being the mother and testamentary guardian of the petitioner), that the petitioner should be made a ward of Court, and a suit instituted on her behalf, the said George Gordon applied to W. Fallowfield, and requested him to act as such next friend, which he consented to do, and accordingly signed a written authority, prepared by Messrs. Gregory and Cook, the solicitors of the said George Gordon, authorizing them (Messrs. Gregory and Cook) to use his (W. Fallowfield's) name as the next friend of the petitioner in the cause: that this suit was thereupon commenced, and various proceedings had, as thereby stated.   That Messrs. Gregory and Cook had recently dissolved partnership, and on the occasion of such dissolution some arrangement had been made between them, whereby this suit, and the further prosecution thereof on behalf of the petitioner, had been attempted to be assigned or given over to Mr. Cook alone, and that Mr. Gregory had since ceased to conduct the same or interfere therewith.   That, on the 15th of March, 1843, W. Fallowfield moved this Court that he might be at liberty to change his solicitor in this cause, by appointing Mr. George Hume as such *solicitor, in the place and stead of Messrs. Gregory and Cook, and which was ordered accordingly: that under and by virtue of such order, which had been duly served in pursuance of the general order of this Court in that behalf, Mr. George Hume had been duly substituted for the said Messrs. Gregory and Cook as the solicitor of W. Fallowfield, the next friend of the petitioner in this cause, and proper notice required in that behalf had been given to the clerk of the records and writs of this Court. That Mr. George Hume, by the authority of W. Fallowfield, had applied to Messrs. Gregory and Cook, and requested them to deliver up the papers in this cause held by them as theretofore such solicitors as aforesaid, but Messrs. Gregory and Cook had refused to' deliver up the same unless their bill of costs was first paid.

The petitioner therefore prayed that Messrs. Gregory and Cook might respectively be ordered, within a week from the date of the order to be made on the petition, to deliver up on oath to Mr. Hume, the present solicitor of the said W. Fallowfield, as the next friend of the petitioner, all briefs, office copies of answers, cases for the opinion of counsel, opinions of counsel, and all other papers and writings whatsoever in or connected with this cause, in the possession or custody of Messrs. Gregory and Cook or either of them as the solicitors or solicitor, or acting as the solicitors or solicitor, of the petitioner, or of W. Fallowfield, as her next friend in this cause, which upon inspection Mr. Hume might deem necessary on behalf of the petitioner on the hearing of this cause, the said Mr. Hume undertaking to receive and hold all such papers and writings without prejudice to any right of lien thereon to which Messrs. Gregory

[*589]   *and Cook, or either of them, were, or was, or might be entitled, and to return the same undefaced to Messrs. Gregory and Cook within fourteen days after the hearing of this cause.

Mr. Roupell and *Mr. Lloyd*, for the petition :

The retainer was given to the partners jointly: by the dissolution of their partnership, under which one party ceases to act in the cause, the solicitors, in effect, discharge themselves; and the client is entitled to treat them in the same manner as solicitors who have been discharged by their own voluntary act, and not by the act of their client: *Earl of Cholmondeley* v. *Lord Clinton* (1), *Cook* v. *Rhodes* (2), *Colegrave* v. *Manley* (3), *Heslop* v. *Metcalfe* (4), *In re Smith* (5).

(1) 13 R. R. 183 (19 Ves. 261).   (4) 45 R. R. 248 (3 My. & Cr. 183).
(2) 13 R. R. 190, n. (19 Ves. 273, n.).   (5) 55 R. R. 88 (4 Beav. 309).
(3) 24 R. R. 83 (1 T. & Russ. 400).

Mr. Temple and *Mr. Toller, contrà.* * * *

THE VICE-CHANCELLOR:

I take the law of the Court in the abstract to be *free from [*590]
doubt. If a client discharges his solicitor, the Court does not take
the papers from the latter, unless upon payment of his bill. If, on
the other hand, the solicitor discharges himself, then, according to
the decision in *Heslop* v. *Metcalfe* (1), the Court will compel him to
give over the papers to the new solicitor, saving his lien upon them.
There was a doubt before that case, whether the rule was to allow a
new solicitor, on behalf of his client, to inspect papers in the hands of
the old solicitor, and take copies of them, or whether the papers
were to be delivered over. Lord COTTENHAM, in that case, made an
observation, the force of which every one must feel, that the only
effect of obliging the new solicitor to take copies is to put the client
to expense, without any benefit to the old solicitor; for, when the
copies are taken, nothing more is wanted. The case of papers in a
cause is different from that of deeds, which have an intrinsic value,
that cannot be imparted to copies.

The question I have here to try, is, whether the dissolution of the
partnership operates as a discharge of themselves by the solicitors,
or a discharge of the solicitors by their client. I do not see any
other question. With regard to the dissolution of partnership, it
seems to me, that I am simply to apply to this case, as between
solicitor and client, what Lord ELDON manifestly, in *Cholmondeley*
v. *Clinton* (2), applies to every species of contract between man and
man. Where a person employs two solicitors, who are partners,
Lord ELDON says, in that case the client stipulates for the activity
and services of both: that is his contract. Apply that to a contract
of any other kind. A man contracts with two persons to do a
certain thing; suppose one of those persons subsequently to refuse
or incapacitate himself *from acting in the business against the [*591]
will of the other; that I will suppose might raise a question as to
the position of the other; but if the withdrawal of one partner from
his contract has taken place by arrangement between the two, for
purposes of their own, can any obligation to one alone remain upon
the party with whom the two made the contract? Is he to rely on
the responsibility of one alone? The argument for Mr. Cook has
been, that the two partners were retained, that Mr. Gregory has
retired, and that his retirement only has led to this application for

(1) 45 R. R. 248 (3 My. & Cr. 183).   (2) 13 R. R. 183 (19 Ves. 261).

GRIFFITHS   the papers. When one party retires, I ask, as Lord ELDON did, in
v.
GRIFFITHS. *Cholmondeley* v. *Clinton*, what is the client to do? He cannot have
the services of both: he must have the services of one, or of none;
but he never consented to trust his affairs to one alone. If the
continuing partner, for his private purposes, has consented to the
retirement of the other, as is admitted to have been the case here,
the question, whether he was the party principally employed or
not, makes no difference. If the proposition be put, as I incline to
think it must be, that the solicitors have discharged themselves,
how can one of them say he has nevertheless a right to continue
the solicitor for the party? He has voluntarily, for purposes with
which the client had nothing to do, and of which he knew nothing,
thought fit to come to an arrangement with his co-partner, by
which the client has been deprived of the benefit of part of his contract, the services of that co-partner. If the continuing partner
can say that he has a right to insist upon being the solicitor of the
client of the two, the consequence would be that the client must,
whether he confides in the continuing partner or not, continue to
employ him, or relieve himself from such an obligation by paying
his bill of costs, and this where it is not by his own act, but by the
act of the solicitor, that his situation has been so materially
altered. What I have to consider is, whether the solicitors, not-

[*592] withstanding *their own acts have changed the relative situation of
their client and themselves, have yet a right to say at any given
moment, "You must pay our bill of costs, or you shall not have
the papers." That they may not be bound to go on and incur
further costs, is another proposition; but that they may not retain
the papers from the client where they have discharged themselves,
if such be the case here, is the very point decided in *Heslop* v.
Metcalfe. My present impression is, that, where there are two
solicitors, and they choose to dissolve their partnership, one, and
perhaps he that was principally trusted by a client, retiring from the
firm, the remaining partner can have no right to say, "I will lock
up the papers and not let the client use them, unless he will employ
me alone as his solicitor." The consequence seems to me to be,
that to some extent these papers must be made available to the
petitioner.

April 20. THE VICE-CHANCELLOR:

The law of the Court, as I stated at the conclusion of the argument, is perfectly settled; that, if a party discharges his solicitor

by his own arbitrary act, he cannot obtain from that solicitor even
an inspection of papers in his hands, much less a delivery of them
up for the purposes of the cause, without paying the solicitor's bill.
If, on the other hand, the client is discharged by the solicitor, the
rule is the other way. It is unquestionably clear in that case, that
the client has a right to have an inspection of the papers to an
extent necessary to enable him to carry on the cause in a convenient
manner,—" with as much ease and celerity," to use Lord ELDON's
expression in *Colegrave* v. *Manley* (1), as if the solicitor had not discharged him. According to the earlier cases, it appears to have
been held, that all *which the client was entitled to was the inspec-   [*593]
tion of the papers in the hands of the solicitors. In the case of
Colegrave v. *Manley*, an order was made, which in terms gave the
client who was discharged by his solicitor the possession of the
documents, undertaking to return them to the first solicitor. Notwithstanding that case, it was not until *Heslop* v. *Metcalfe* (2), that
the point was considered to be settled, that the client would have a
right to the possession of the documents upon an undertaking to
return them. In the latter case, Lord COTTENHAM, referring to
Colegrave v. *Manley*, said, that the principle was, that the client must
be able to carry on his case with the same ease and celerity, and as
little expense, after his solicitor had discharged himself, as before ;
and he made an order in the terms asked by this petition. I do
not understand Lord COTTENHAM to have laid down an absolute rule
with regard to the form of the order, but only to have held, that
the mere circumstance of the change of the solicitor is not to be
made the occasion of depriving the client of those facilities for the
conduct of the suit, which he had before the connexion between
him and his solicitor was dissolved ; and upon this principle the
Court will make such an order as *primâ facie* appears to be the
most beneficial to the client, not disregarding the protection of the
solicitor, and the order would commonly be as in *Heslop* v. *Metcalfe*,
unless it be shown by the solicitor that the delivering up of the
papers is practically unnecessary.

The question is brought to this, whether I am to consider Messrs.
Gregory and Cook not as discharged by their client, but as discharging
themselves, in which case the order will be in the terms of the
prayer of the petition. Now, if I am to look at the case upon
principle, *it seems impossible to entertain a doubt upon it. The   [*594]
retainer in this case was given to the two partners. The affidavits

(1) 24 R. R. 83 (1 T. & R. 402).   (2) 45 R. R. 248 (3 My. & Cr. 183).

on the part of the solicitors in terms state that fact. It appears
that the two did to some extent act in the business of the cause, but
unquestionably Mr. Gregory was the acting solicitor. Of that there
is no doubt. In a letter in which he recommended Mr. Cook as a
man of talent, and one who could be safely trusted to carry on the
cause, he took credit to himself for having, as he says, " with great
labour and much anxiety, got the whole of it up." I do not, however, think this material to the application, for, if the retainer was
given to the two, and one thinks proper to retire, I think the
principle of law is the same, whether the retiring or the continuing
partner happened to be more or less conversant with the particular
business. I notice it only to show how important it is that the
principle should be observed. It often happens that a partner
retiring assigns his business to a clerk in whom he has great
confidence, but in whom his clients may have no confidence whatever ; or a party may have continued his business with a firm of
more than one partner, solely from the confidence he had in an elder
partner, or member of the firm, whom he has always trusted. If
that partner might retire, and insist that the person whom he had
taken into the business, or the partners who were left in the
business, but whom the client had not trusted, should alone have
the conduct of that client's affairs, it would enable him materially
to alter the relation of the parties, without the consent of the party
most interested. It seems to me, the agreement between the two
solicitors, that the partnership shall be dissolved, being made for
their own benefit without any communication with their client, the
moment one of them retires he has discharged himself, and the
relation of attorney and client is dissolved between .them. Now

[*595] *in this case Mr. Gregory discharged himself, and thereupon the
retainer which was given to the two is gone altogether, and the
client is left at liberty either thenceforward to employ the continuing
partner, or to take a new solicitor. In either case it is, in substance,
a new retainer. Upon principle, as I have said, I have no doubt
upon the subject. If, instead of considering it on principle, I refer
to what Lord ELDON said, in *Cholmondeley* v. *Clinton* (1), it is
impossible not to see that it was his opinion also. He is represented
as saying, in effect, that the better course for the client was to
continue to employ the partner who remains ; yet the whole of his
reasoning shows, that in such a case he considered the solicitors to
have discharged themselves, and not to have been discharged by

(1) 13 R. R. 190—191 (19 Ves. 273).

GRIFFITHS
v.
GRIFFITHS.

their client, and that the client has, in truth, to give a new retainer. In *Re Smith* (1), Lord LANGDALE held that Smith had so acted as make it impossible that his client in the country could trust him any longer; and, as it was by the act of Smith that the other parties were obliged to discharge him, that he must be considered, for the purposes of the application, to have discharged himself, and his lien be dealt with accordingly. *Redfearn* v. *Sowerby* (2) is an important case: there the solicitor died, and the question was, whether the client must pay the bill of costs before he obtained possession of the papers. And Lord ELDON takes this distinction: he says, the proceedings are stayed by the act of God, and not by any default of the party, and he could not say that the client could take the papers out of the hands of the solicitor's representatives without first discharging the lien,—indirectly affirming the proposition, which indeed common sense would dictate, that where the connexion is broken off by the voluntary act of the solicitor, the Court will *hold that the solicitor discharges himself; which is, in truth, the obvious effect of his act.

[*596]

Being therefore of opinion, upon principle, that the retirement of Mr. Gregory, in this case, had the effect of discharging himself and Mr. Cook as solicitors in this cause, and thinking that this opinion is also supported by the authorities, so far as they go, although I can find do case which is precisely similar, I must hold that Mr. Fallowfield is entitled to the benefit of the rule applicable where the relation of solicitor and client is terminated by the act of the solicitor, and that, therefore, he is entitled to have the papers delivered up to the new solicitor, upon the terms mentioned in the prayer of the petition.

THORP v. OWEN (3).

(2 Hare, 607—617; S. C. 12 L. J. Ch. 417; 7 Jur. 894.)

A testator, by his will, desired that every thing, during the life of his wife, should remain as it was, for her use and benefit; and after her decease he gave his real estate to his male heir, and his personal estate to his children; adding, that he gave the above devise to his wife, that she might support herself and her children according to her discretion, and for that purpose.

Held, that the widow took an absolute interest for her life in the real and personal estate.

1843.
April 26.
May 2, 3, 6, 25.
June 12.
—
WIGRAM,
V.-C.
[607]

THE suit was brought to determine the construction of a will, which was in the following words: "This is the last will and

(1) 55 R. R. 88 (4 Beav. 315).   (3) *In re Booth* [1894] 2 Ch. 282;
(2) 18 R. R. 31 (1 Swanst. 84).   63 L. J. Ch. 560.

testament of me, Henry Owen, of &c. I desire every thing to
remain in its present position during the lifetime of my wife, for
her use and benefit; and after her decease I devise my real estate
to my then male heir and his heirs in strict tail male, and I wish
my personal estate to be then equally divided among all my children;
and I appoint my friends James Bridger and his brother George
Bridger, both of &c., my executors, hereby revoking all former and
other wills, and declaring this only to be my last will and testament,
dated the 26th day of June, 1841. I give the above devise to my
wife that she may support herself and her children according to her
discretion, and for that purpose."

The testator died on the same day, leaving his widow and eleven
children—five males and six females—surviving. The eldest son
was at that time upwards of thirty, and the youngest child about
ten years of age: several of the children were married in the lifetime
of the testator.

The executors named in the will renounced probate, and letters
of administration with the will annexed were granted to the widow.

[608]   The bill was filed by the greater part of the children, and the
husbands of the married daughters, against the widow, the heir-at-
law, and the other children of the testator, and prayed the execution
of the trusts of the will, and a declaration of the rights of the parties.
At the hearing of the cause, the common inquiries with respect to
the family and the accounts of the estate were directed. The cause
now came on for further directions.

Mr. *Roupell* and Mr. *Lindsell*, for the plaintiffs, contended that
the widow was a trustee of the income of the real and personal
estate during her life, for the benefit of herself and all the children,
either in equal shares or in such proportions as the Court might
determine, having regard to their relative necessities, and that the
widow had a discretion only in respect of the application of the
shares of the children during their infancy.

Mr. *Walker*, Mr. *Koe*, and Mr. *Trotter*, for the defendants
having substantially the same interests as the plaintiff.

Mr. *Tinney* and Mr. *Stinton* for the widow:

If it be admitted that the widow takes the property during her life
charged with the maintenance of the children, that obligation must
be confined within some definite limits; it must be confined to the

maintenance of the children during their infancy, or, at the utmost,
during the time they continue to form part of the household of their
mother.   The mode in which the children are entitled to participate
in the estate must be such as to admit of the exercise of the mother's
discretion in the *application of it for their use. If the income
should be divided amongst all the children, whether married and
settled in life, or what is termed "foris familiated," or not, it ceases
to be a fund for the support of the widow and children, according
to her discretion.   The meaning as well as the intention of the
bequest evidently is, that the mother shall take the income for the
maintenance of her household, the testator relying upon her to
afford, by that means, a home and support for her children forming
part of that household.

[The principal cases cited are referred to in the judgment.]

THE VICE-CHANCELLOR, after stating the will :

Several of the children of the testator and of the defendant, his
wife, were minors at the time of his death; all the minors have
since been maintained by the widow, and the only question argued
before me was, whether the adult children, male or female, either
living at home or foris familiated, were entitled to participate in the
income which was given to the wife for life.

Two points were conceded in the argument on the part of the
widow: first, that, according to the true construction *of the will,
a trust is declared in favour of the children of the testator, whether
during infancy or not is another question, but that a trust is
declared, excluding the widow from an absolute interest in the
property for life: secondly, that, notwithstanding the indefinite
character of the trust with respect to the amount to which the
children are to participate in the life interest of the widow, the
Court might execute such a trust in favour of adults as well as
of infants. It was, however, argued, that the support of the
children during their minorities, and nothing more, was contemplated by the will.   Supposing a trust to be declared, the latter of
the two concessions, was, I think, unavoidable upon the authorities.
Whatever difficulties might originally have been supposed to exist
in the way of a court of equity enforcing a trust, the extent of which
was unascertained, the cases appear clearly to decide that a court of
equity can measure the extent of interest which an adult as well
as an infant takes under a trust for his support, maintenance,

THORP
v.
OWEN.

advancement, provision, or other like indefinite expression, applicable
to a fund larger, confessedly, than the party entitled to the support,
maintenance, or advancement can claim, and some interest in which
is given to another person.   If that is to be altered, it should not
be by any but the highest branch of the Court.   I may mention on
this point, *Broad* v. *Bevan* (1), *Wetherell* v. *Wilson* (2), *Woods* v.
Woods (3), *Pride* v. *Fooks* (4), *Jubber* v. *Jubber* (5), *Kilvington* v.
Gray (6), *Soames* v. *Martin* (7), *Gilbert* v. *Bennett* (8).   *   *   *

[611]   Now, with respect to the first concession, that a trust was
declared, and that the widow could not claim the absolute interest
during her life, I was not satisfied at the time of the argument that
the counsel for the widow had not paid a greater degree of deference
to the language of some modern cases than the learned Judges by
whom those cases were decided would claim in favour of their own
decisions.   The case is one of a class respecting which it is perhaps
to be expected that an apparent discrepancy would exist in the
decisions, a discrepancy, however, which might be attributed not
to any difference of opinion as to the principle which should govern
the cases, but only on the manner of applying admitted principles.
I doubt whether the concession ought to have been made.

The cases should be considered under two heads: first, those in
which the Court has read the will as giving an absolute interest to
the legatees, and as expressing also the testator's motive for the
gift; and, secondly, those cases in which the Court has read the
will as declaring a trust upon the fund, or part of the fund, in the
hands of the legatee.   A legacy to A. the better to enable him to
pay his debts expresses the motive for the testator's bounty, but
certainly creates no trust which the creditors of A. could enforce in
this Court; and, again, a legacy to A. the better to enable him to
maintain, or educate and provide for, his family must, in the
abstract, be subject to a like construction: it is a legacy to the
individual, with the motive only pointed out.   This is very clearly,
and in my opinion very correctly, laid down by the VICE-CHANCELLOR
in the late case of *Benson* v. *Whittam* (9); and the cases of *Andrews* v.
[*612]   *Partington* (10), *Brown* v. *Casamajor* (11) and *Hammond* v. *Neame* (12)
illustrate the same principle.   At the same time, a legacy to a

(1) 25 R. R. 123 (1 Russ. 511, n.).   (7) 50 R. R. 249 (10 Sim. 287).
(2) 44 R. R. 27 (2 Keen, 80).   (8) 50 R. R. 268 (10 Sim. 371).
(3) 43 R. R. 214 (1 My. & Cr. 401).   (9) 35 R. R. 113 (5 Sim. 22).
(4) 50 R. R. 227 (2 Beav. 430).   (10) 2 Cox, 223.
(5) 47 R. R. 291 (9 Sim. 503).   (11) 4 Ves. 498. See 35 R. R. p. 116.
(6) 50 R. R. 250 (10 Sim. 298).   (12) 18 R. R. 15 (1 Swanst. 35).

parent upon trust to be by him applied, or in trust, for the main-
tenance and education of his children, will certainly give the
children a right in a court of equity to enforce their natural
claims against the parent in respect of the fund on which the
trust is declared. And a similar rule, as I have already observed,
has prevailed in favour of adult cestui que trusts, notwithstanding
the difficulty of measuring the amount of interest in those cases.

It is, I am aware, difficult to reconcile all the decisions on cases
of this nature, but although those decisions may not appear recon-
cileable with each other, I am satisfied that the learned Judges by
whom they have been pronounced did not mean to disregard the
distinction I have noticed, or in any way to break in upon it. The
difference has arisen in the different modes of applying admitted
principles. In *Raikes* v. *Ward* (1), and *Crockett* v. *Crockett* (2), I
thought, and still think, a trust was declared as well as a motive
expressed; and I am satisfied that neither Lord COTTENHAM in
Woods v. *Woods*, nor Lord LANGDALE in *Wetherell* v. *Wilson*, intended
to negative the distinction to which I have adverted.

I do not at present give any opinion upon the question, whether
the direction in this will is confined to minority or not. *Mr. Tinney*
argued, with force which appeared to me almost irresistible, that the
obvious intention was, that the widow should have the spending of
*her life income in one establishment. Supposing a child were willing
to reside with the mother, and no reasonable objection could be
urged against it, the testator having directed that every thing should
remain as it was, whether the Court would in that case allow the
widow arbitrarily to refuse support to such child merely because he
or she had attained the age of twenty-one, is one question; but
it does appear to me to be another and a serious question, whether,
if a son or daughter chooses to marry, and become foris familiated,
leaving the house of the widow, and perhaps having a family, in
that case, the intention of the testator, expressed in this will,
requires that the widow should apportion a certain part of her
income for the benefit of such son or daughter; whether, in such
circumstances, she should no longer spend her income in one estab-
lishment, but divide it into as many different incomes as there are
children, possibly not giving enough for their support to any, and
not leaving enough for her own support. The question is, whether
the testator did not mean to leave it entirely to the natural
affection of the mother to provide for the children during

THORP
r.
OWEN.

[*613]

(1) 58 R. R. 131 (1 Hare, 445).   (2) 58 R. R. 135 (1 Hare, 451).

THORP
v.
OWEN.

her life, afterwards giving the property to them, as in fact he has done.

Having considered the authorities on the subject, it is impossible but that I should have formed an opinion on this case. It appears to me, that if I decide the case on the question of the adult or infant maintenance alone, it might be open to an appeal, the expense of which may perhaps be saved to the parties, by giving all the reasons that occur to me, as the grounds of my decision. If the counsel for the widow should think the authorities on the question, whether the gift creates an absolute interest or a trust, do not govern the present case, I should prefer to hear them, and also the counsel for the plaintiffs, upon that point alone. My [*614] *object is, that my decision may be satisfactory to the parties, and that, so far as possible, they may be relieved from the necessity and expense of discussing this question elsewhere.

June 12.

The case was again argued by *Mr. Roupell* and *Mr. Lindsell*, for the plaintiffs, and *Mr. Tinney* and *Mr. Stinton*, for the widow. [In addition to the cases mentioned in the judgment, they cited *Meredith* v. *Heneage* (1), *Cape* v. *Cape* (2), *Stubbs* v. *Sargon* (3), *Ford* v. *Fowler* (4), *Knight* v. *Knight* (5), and other cases.]

THE VICE-CHANCELLOR:

I am satisfied that, however long this case may be under consideration, there would be still some doubt upon it with reference to the authorities. I cannot, however, doubt the principle laid down by the VICE-CHANCELLOR in *Benson* v. *Whittam;* it is plain to common sense that the law must be as it is there explained. If you give property to persons to accomplish an object, increasing their funds so that they might be the better able to do it, that is, in point of fact, a gift to them, and there is no trust which others can enforce. And I think those cases of *Bushnell* v. *Parsons* (6), *Hammond* v. *Neame, Burrell* v. *Burrell* (7), *Andrews* v. *Partington*, [*615] *and others, are all cases in support of the same proposition, and recognising the principle with great clearness. A great number of these cases might be cited, but I will not go through them; the principle cannot be at all doubted, although Judges may differ as to the mode of applying it. I think it equally clear, if property be

(1) 27 R. R. 243 (1 Sim. 566).
(2) 47 R. R. 458 (2 Y. & C. Ex. Eq. 543).
(3) 44 R. R. 250 (3 My. & Cr. 508, 513).
(4) 52 R. R. 72 (3 Beav. 146).
(5) 52 R. R. 74 (3 Beav. 148).
(6) Prec. Chan. 218.
(7) Amb. 660.

given to a parent upon trust to maintain herself and her children,
that, although she takes a beneficial interest, and though to some
extent there is an uncertainty as to the *quantum* she is bound to
apply, it is impossible for me to hold that the cases do not decide
that the Court will find the means of measuring the extent of the
children's interest. The only question here is, under which of the
two principles I am to say that this case falls; at the same time I
agree with the argument, that if the expression, that the gift is
to support the children, extends to the support of the children
throughout the whole of their lives, in the various situations that
may arise, the impossibility, I may almost say, of measuring the
gift to each child by any rule to be laid down by a court of justice,
is—in a case where there is no trust excluding the mother from
taking whatever she is not obliged to part with—a strong argument
against holding that the expressions which refer to the children
were meant to create a trust binding on her. Lord ELDON's language,
in the cases of *Morice* v. *The Bishop of Durham* (1), *Wright* v.
Atkyns (2), and the other cases referred to, goes to show that where
words of trust are not used so imperatively as to exclude the
legatee from taking any thing beneficially, there the difficulty of
ascertaining how much that legatee was bound to give away is a
strong argument against construing the gift to be a trust. If it be
a clear case of trust, then it appears to me, on the *authorities,   [*616]
that the Court has held that the trust shall not in the case of
children be void, but that it will find the means of ascertaining how
much the parties to be benefited are to take. It was on that ground
I went in the cases of *Raikes* v. *Ward* and *Crockett* v. *Crockett.* In
those cases the gift was made in terms which obliged the legatee to
give something to the children. If it is not in such terms, of course
there is no trust to exclude the legatee.

I considered this case very much in private, before I called for
the second argument, and the conclusion to which I have come is,
that the words of this will import a gift to the mother for life, and
that afterwards the personal estate is to go to the testator's
children, and the real estate to his heir-at-law. The testator adds
to the gift an explanation which appears to me merely to express
what actuated his mind in the gift. He trusts to the affection of
the mother towards her children, and says, "I have given to her
this large provision, in order that she may be able to support her
children during her life." The gift is to her, and the support is to

(1) 7 R. R. 232 (10 Ves. 534).   (2) 24 R. R. 3 (T. & Russ. 157).

THORP
v.
OWEN.

be administered according to her discretion. I do not deny that the will may be construed another way, you may construe it thus: "I give it to my wife for the purpose of being applied by her in the support and maintenance of the children;" but the words are equally consistent as importing, "I give it to her that she may be able to support her children." I cannot see anything in the mere words used in that particular part of the will, which leads one way rather than the other; but I am satisfied, from the language of the whole will, that the gift is to her, to be applied according to her discretion. The absence of any expression excluding the wife from taking, and the moral impossibility that any court of justice

[*617]

can measure *the suggested bounty of the testator, in favour of all the children, in every possible state of circumstances, are grounds on which it appears to me I ought to decide that, in this case, the widow is not controlled by any equitable interest in the children.

I confess I have the less regret in coming to this conclusion, because, so far as respects the maintenance of the children during their minority, there appears to be no practical reason for deciding the case one way rather than another,—all such children having, in fact, been maintained, and being still maintained, by the widow. With regard to the other children the difficulty of applying the fund in many cases which may arise, or be suggested, is such that I can hardly see any way of effecting it. The best legal conclusion I think is this: The testator has given the property to his wife absolutely, during her life, and in order that the children may not suppose that they have been overlooked during that time, the testator tells them his reason for giving the property to the mother. I think, therefore, that the construction of the will is, that the widow takes the property absolutely for her life (1).

1843.
May 8, 11, 29.

WIGRAM,
V.-C.

[624]

WEATHERBY v. ST. GIORGIO.

(2 Hare, 624—630; S. C. 12 L. J. Ch. 412; 7 Jur. 717.)

A testator directed his debts to be paid, and appointed executors in England, and other executors in Italy, directing the English executors to transmit the residue to the Italian executors, and bequeathing such residue amongst classes of persons alleged to reside in Italy: Held, that the sum to be paid over, being the residue, after payment of debts, the Italian executors must be regarded as simply trustees of that fund, and not as executors holding it charged with debts; and that therefore inquiries

---

(1) See *Longmore* v. *Elcum*, 60 R. R. 192 (2 Y. & C. C. C. 363).

must be directed to ascertain the persons beneficially entitled to the fund WEATHERBY
under the bequest.   *v.*
    Held also, that where a trust fund is to be administered under the direc- ST. GIORGIO.
tion of the Court, the general rule requiring the cestuis que trust to be
parties, is applicable to foreign trustees and cestuis que trust, residing out
of the jurisdiction, unless a special case of difficulty or inconvenience
in the application of the rule be shown.

JOHN ST. GIORGIO, a native of Italy, by his will, dated in March,
1833, after directing all his debts and funeral and testamentary
expenses to be paid as soon as conveniently might be, appointed
Weatherby, the plaintiff, and W. S. Lewis, executors of his will, so
far as related to his property in England and Ireland, and elsewhere, (except in Italy), and Doctor Francesco Ciceri and Signior
Advocato Giuseppe Montanara, of Milan, executors of his will, so
far as related to his property in Italy, and not elsewhere, and after
giving certain legacies, the testator gave and bequeathed unto
Lewis and the plaintiff the residue of his estate and effects in
England and Ireland, or elsewhere, (except in Italy as aforesaid),
upon trust, as to certain parts thereof, for his son John Nathaniel
St. Giorgio, and the children of his said son as therein mentioned.
And (after payment of the legacies bequeathed by any codicil he
might make) the testator directed his said executors in England to
transmit the residue, and every part thereof, to his said executors
in Italy, to be by them jointly disposed of, together with all
property and effects that he should possess in Italy, or be entitled
to at the time of his decease, amongst all and every his *nephews   [*625]
and nieces, the children of his late sisters Annunziata De Micheli
and Teresa Corbetta, who should be living at his decease, or the
husbands or wife of such of them respectively as should be then
dead, without leaving issue then living or born in due time afterwards, to be equally divided between them in equal proportions as
tenants in common, and if but one such child, husband, or wife, to
pay the whole to such only child, husband, or wife, subject to the
proviso, that if there should at his decease be living any child or
children of his said nephews or nieces who should have died in his
lifetime, then, that the share of such deceased parent in such
residue should be paid to his or her child or children in equal
portions.
    The testator made a codicil to his will, of the same date, by
which he gave certain legacies. He made a second codicil, dated
the 16th of March, 1833, whereby he bequeathed certain debts
and securities to his said son, in trust for his grandchildren.

Subsequently, in the same year, the testator left England, where he had resided, and returned to Monza, in Lombardy. He there made several other codicils to his will, in the Italian language, bequeathing various legacies. The translation of one of these, dated the 5th of February, 1835, was as follows :

"When my testament in London, and also in succession my codicil at Milan, shall be completely fulfilled, I will, that all the surplus residue be given to the descendants of my sisters *per stirpes*, and not *per capita*. My executor shall be the advocate, Giuseppe Montanara, whom I join with Doctor F. Ciceri, of Milan." By a later codicil, dated in March, 1838, the testator gave a legacy to a charitable institution in Monza.

[*626]   The testator died at Monza, in August, 1840, leaving *W. S. Lewis, the plaintiff Weatherby, and the defendant Giuseppe Montanara, surviving. Ciceri died in the lifetime of the testator. Montanara duly published and proved the will and codicils, and filed the same of record in the Imperial Royal Municipal Court of Monza, and sent official copies to the plaintiff, who proved translations thereof in the Ecclesiastical Courts in England and Ireland. Lewis renounced probate.

The plaintiff filed the bill against the son and grandchildren of the testator, and Giuseppe Montanara, praying that the estate might be administered, and the trusts of the will and codicils performed under the direction of the Court. Montanara, though out of the jurisdiction, appeared, and put in his answer. The cause was heard on the 24th of June, 1842, and by the decree then made it was referred to the Master, to inquire whether Montanara was the duly constituted executor or representative of the testator, so far as related to his property in Italy, according to the laws in force there ; inquiries were also directed in the ordinary form with regard to the children of the testator's sisters, and whether they or their representatives were out of the jurisdiction, and if so,—the plaintiff submitting to account, the usual accounts were directed. The inquiries were prosecuted before the Master only on the first point, on which the draft-report was prepared, finding that Montanara was the duly constituted executor or personal representative, as to the property in Italy. In order to avoid the expense of making in this country the inquiries as to the families of the Italian legatees, Montanara, before taking the report, presented his petition of rehearing, thereby suggesting, that, as such executor and legal personal representative in Italy, he was, under and

according to the terms and fair construction of the will and codicils, WEATHERBY
entitled to *receive and apply in Italy, according to such will and ST. GIORGIO.
codicils, the testator's estate thereby given and directed to be paid   [*627]
to him for the purposes therein mentioned.

Mr. Roupell and *Mr. G. L. Russell*, for the plaintiff, submitted
that the decree was right, but that an inquiry as to the domicile of
the testator might be properly added.

Mr. Koe for the son and grandchildren of the testator.

Mr. Tinney and *Mr. Rogers* for the defendant Montanara :

The testator has appointed a person to administer his estate in
Italy, and he has directed the surplus in this country to be transmitted to that person. What prevents this from being done? An
artificial rule of this Court, by which it assumes the power of
executing all trusts brought within its direction. But is not this
rule confined to cases in which it can adequately and conveniently
perform the office of trustee,—namely, to cases where the objects
of the trust are subjects of this kingdom, and within the operation
of its laws? The principle upon which the Court acts in assuming
the administration of trusts, is founded on justice and convenience;
but the difficulty and expense of undertaking a trust, where all the
facts upon which the Court is to proceed, and the law by which it
is to be guided, must be collected by inquiries in a foreign country,
take the case altogether out of the operation of that principle. If
the objects of the testator's bounty were simply indicated, and no
hand interposed *as the medium of distribution, the Court might   [*628]
have no alternative but that of administering the estate amongst
such objects; but where that course is not absolutely necessary,
and where, as in this case, there is a foreign executor, the Court
will not undertake that office. The distinction between the cases
of English and foreign trusts is seen in the cases of legacies to
foreign charities, which the Court does not undertake to administer,
but merely ascertains the hand to receive the legacy.

[The following (among other) cases were cited : *Attorney-General*
v. *Levine* (1), *Preston* v. *Lord Melville* (2), *Emery* v. *Hill* (3), *Hall* v.
Dewes (4), and *Thorp* v. *Owen* (5).]

(1) 19 R. R. 55 (2 Swanst. 181).   (4) 23 R. R. 27 (Jac. 189).
(2) 54 R. R. 1 (8 Cl. & Fin. 1).   (5) *Ante*, p. 253.
(3) 25 R. R. 11 (1 Russ. 112).

THE VICE-CHANCELLOR:

The testator first directs all his debts to be paid, and then that his executors in England shall transmit the residue to his executors in Italy, to be by them disposed of, together with all his property in Italy, among certain legatees. It is clear, therefore, that the fund which he had in his contemplation was the residue after the debts were paid, and it appears to me impossible to escape the conclusion that the executors in Italy must be taken to be legatees

[*629] in trust. I am now called upon *to decide a perfectly abstract proposition. The rule in England is, that if property is given to a trustee for certain cestui que trusts, the Court will pay it to the cestui que trusts, and not to the trustee. If I were not to follow that rule in this case, I should, in effect, decide, that in every case where there is a direction to pay money to a foreign trustee, to be by him paid to another person, that such other person is not a necessary party to the suit; or, in other words, that the rule, which is applicable in England, ceases to apply where the trustee and objects of the trust are the subjects of a foreign country, and out of the jurisdiction of the Court. There is nothing at present before me to show that there is any difficulty in this case to justify a departure from the ordinary rule: at the same time, the case must be open to the same observations as all other cases are with respect to parties,—that wherever a great practical inconvenience arises in applying the general rule, there the Court has power to relax it, in order to prevent that which was laid down for the purposes of justice from working the contrary; and that would no doubt be the case, if, where a small property had to be divided among a great number of foreigners, all the cestuis que trust were compelled to prove their right in the Master's office in England. I must continue the direction for inquiry with respect to the parties abroad. I cannot introduce a rule different from that which prevails in all ordinary cases, without seeing that there is in truth some particular difficulty in following it.

I endeavoured at first to adopt the argument that Montanara and Ciceri should be considered as strictly executors; for I then should have had less difficulty in directing the money to be paid over to them, as they would in that case have been bound to pay any debts

[*630] *which might have existed, and would have been accountable for the residue: but it is admitted that the debts must be paid in this country, and the executors here are directed to pay over the surplus to the executors in Italy. It is therefore a payment by a trustee to a trustee.

I mean to decide nothing beyond what I am forced to decide. I WEATHERBY
only abstain from deciding, that where the legatees are foreigners, *v.*
St. GIORGIO.
the rule requiring the cestui que trusts, to whom personally the
money is to be paid, to be made parties, does not *primâ facie* apply.
The case is different from that of a charity where there is no
direction to pay personally.

It appears to me that much difficulty might be avoided by
Montanara having the carriage of so much of the order as directs
the inquiries, for he will probably be in a condition to show to the
Master better than any other party the state of the families, and
what difficulties there are in following out the order.

(The inquiries proper to be made were afterwards considered in   *May* 29.
detail.)

IN THE QUEEN'S BENCH.

1842.
Nov. 19.
1843.
Jan. 18.

[2]

REG. *v.* SIR MARTIN ARCHER SHEE AND OTHERS (1).

(4 Q. B. 2—17; S. C. 3 G. & D. 80; 12 L. J. M. C. 53; 7 Jur. 810.)

The President, Council and Members of the Royal Academy of Arts were rated to the poor for the " Exhibition Rooms, Royal Academy."

The Royal Academy was established by an instrument under the sign manual of George III., for the improvement of painting, sculpture and architecture. The Society has no charter, and is not incorporated. The King nominated the original Academicians; and the appointment of subsequent ones, though made by the Society, is subject to the King's approbation : so also is the election of officers, who hold during his pleasure. No change in the fundamental rules or establishment can be made without the Royal assent. At first the King furnished such funds as were wanted out of the Privy Purse; but latterly the Society's whole outlay has been supplied by the proceeds of the annual exhibition of paintings, to which the public is admitted for money. Out of these receipts are paid the expenses of exhibition ; of schools for students, who are instructed gratis ; allowances to travelling students; salaries to officers and lecturers; pensions to members of the Society who may be in want, or their widows, and some other allowances and expenses. There is a surplus, which is laid out in stock, in trust for the general purposes of the Society. The treasurer, who receives the dividends and profits, and pays the expenses, is appointed by the Crown from among the Academicians, and his accounts finally submitted to the Keeper of the Privy Purse. An officer called the Keeper of the Academy has private apartments in the building, communicating internally with the Society's rooms, and which he occupies for the more convenient performance of his duties and for his own domestic purposes. The Council, consisting of the President and eight Academicians, meet from time to time, and are paid for their attendance. Visitors, also paid, attend the schools. The exhibition rooms, also used as lecture and school rooms, are the property of the Crown, and are distinct from the rest of the building. All works approved by the Academy are admitted for exhibition ; the Academicians have the privilege of exhibiting more works than other persons. Pictures intended for sale are entered in a register, which is open for the inspection of purchasers. The members of the Society neither derive personal advantage or emolument from the premises, nor occupy them, otherwise than as above stated.

When the Academy was founded, the King permitted the Society to have the use of certain apartments in his Palace of Somerset House : when that Palace was appropriated to public offices, the King ordered part of it to be prepared for the use of the Academy ; and they were put in possession of that part. And, when the new building called the National Gallery was erected, King William IV. ordered that they should be removed thither, and should have the rooms now in question on the same terms and tenure, and for the same purposes, as they had had the use of the apartments formerly assigned to them. They have no lease or written contract, and pay no rent.

Held, that they were not rateable for the rooms.

ON appeal against a rate for the relief of the poor of the parish of St. Martin in the Fields in the county of Middlesex, whereby

(1) Comm. *Reg.* v. *Temple* (1853) 3 El. & Bl. 160, 173, 22 L. J. M. C. 129.—A. C.

Sir Martin Archer Shee, Sir Robert Smirke, and others, the Presi-   REG.
dent, Council and Members of the Royal Academy of Arts, were   *v.*
assessed as the occupiers of " Exhibition Rooms, Royal Academy,"   SHEE.
the Sessions confirmed the rate, subject to the opinion of this Court
upon the following case.

A part of the building called the National Gallery, situate in   [3]
Trafalgar Square, in the parish of St. Martin in the Fields, in the
county of Middlesex, consisting of six rooms or picture galleries,
hall, staircase and other apartments, is used by the members of the
Royal Academy, for the purposes and under the circumstances
hereinafter stated.   The rate and assessment in question was duly
made, allowed and published, pursuant to a local Act of Parliament,
10 Geo. III. c. 75 (1), whereby the churchwardens, overseers of the
poor, vestrymen, constables and other ancient inhabitants, in vestry
assembled, are empowered and authorised to make rates or assessments for and towards the relief of the poor, and for the several
purposes of the Act, "upon all and every person or persons who do
or shall inhabit, hold, occupy, possess, or enjoy any land, house,
shop, wharf, warehouse, or any other building, tenement, or
hereditament, or any other person or persons who by law is
or are chargeable and assessable for and towards the relief of
the poor."

The appellants are the President, Treasurer and Members of the
Royal Academy of Arts.   The said Royal Academy is a Society
established and instituted by King George III. in 1768, for the
express purpose of cultivating and improving the art of painting,
sculpture and architecture.   The instrument of institution is under
the Royal sign manual, and is signed by every member upon his
appointment : but the Society is not incorporated ; nor has it any
charter or letters patent.   The King named the original Academicians, in number *forty ; and each new Academician still receives   [*4]
his appointment from the Sovereign, although such appointment is
made in favour of those who have been elected by the general body
of Academicians.   All the officers of the Society are either actually
selected and appointed by the Sovereign, or are elected by the
Society subject to the approbation of the Sovereign, and hold
their offices during his pleasure.   No new laws or changes in the

(1) " For building a workhouse in   See it more fully set out, *Regina* v. *St.*
the parish of St. Martin in the Fields,   *Martin's in the Fields*, 61 R. R. 196
within the liberty of Westminster, in   (3 Q. B. p. 205, note (a)).
the county of Middlesex."   Sect. 13.

fundamental rules or establishment can be made without the vote
of a General Assembly and the assent of the Sovereign.

At the commencement of the Society, the King supplied the
deficiency of their funds out of his Privy Purse, and was also in the
habit of affording such relief, in the way of gratuities and charitable
donations, as is now given by the Royal Academy out of their own
funds.   But the Academy, by their prosperity and by the
economical management of their surplus profits, have, for many
years, had no occasion to resort to the Royal bounty.

The Society consists of forty members, who are called the
Academicians of the Royal Academy.   The government of the
Society is vested in a President and Council, and the General
Assembly of the Members.   The Council consists of eight Academicians and the President, who have the entire direction and
management of the business of the Society, subject to the approbation of the Sovereign.   There is a Treasurer, who is appointed by
her Majesty from among the Academicians, whose business is to
receive the dividends and profits of the Academy, and to pay its
expenses.   His accounts are examined by members appointed to
audit them, and finally submitted to the Keeper of her Majesty's
Privy *Purse.   Since the establishment of the Society, another
order of members, called Associates, has been instituted, who are
selected by the Academicians from exhibitors in the annual exhibition.   Vacancies in the body of Academicians are always filled up
from the Associates; but, until so elected, they have no voice or
control in the management of the Royal Academy.

[*5]

An annual exhibition of paintings, sculptures and designs, in
which all artists of merit are permitted to exhibit such of their
works as are approved by the Academy, takes place upon the
premises in respect whereof the appellants are assessed, and
continues open to the public for six weeks or more if deemed
expedient.   Persons admitted to view this exhibition are charged
by the Society 1s. each for their admission; which payments produce an annual gross income amounting on the average to 5,000l.,
including the sale of catalogues of the said works of art, which
catalogues are sold on the said premises by the servants of the
Society.   The Academicians enjoy the privilege of exhibiting a
larger number of works of art than other persons : and they are
each under an obligation to exhibit annually some original work of
art.   An officer of the said Academy registers the prices of such of
the works as are intended for sale; which register is open to the

inspection of persons desirous of purchasing them. Three days or
more, according to the conveniency of the management and the
discretion of the committee, are allowed to all the members of the
Royal Academy, for the purpose of varnishing or painting on their
pictures in the places which have been allotted to them previously
to the day appointed for the annual dinner hereinafter mentioned
in the exhibition rooms. There is a library, formed by *the   [*6]
Society, to which all members and students have access under
certain regulations. The library is distinct from the exhibition
rooms. An annual dinner of the members of the Society takes
place in the great room of the Academy previous to the opening of
the exhibition ; invitations to which are issued by the said President
and Council to persons in elevated situations, of high rank,
distinguished talents, or known patrons of the arts, who attend as
guests on those occasions.

The funds of the Royal Academy arise from the proceeds of the
said annual exhibition, and from the dividends of money vested in
the public funds, being the surplus from time to time of such
proceeds. Out of these funds the following annual expenses are
paid. The expenses of the exhibition, amounting to from 1,400*l.*
to 1,500*l.*, and of the annual dinner ; the pensions and donations
hereinafter mentioned ; the expense of the schools for students ; of
the purchase of books, drawings, prints and works of art for the
use of such students ; of one or more travelling students ; and of
servants and occasional attendance. The secretary, keeper,
treasurer and librarian, being all members of the Royal Academy,
are paid salaries, in respect of the duties performed by them, out
of the funds of the said Academy. The professors of painting,
sculpture, architecture and perspective, being also members, are
paid 60*l.* each for six lectures out of such funds. There are also
other professors who are not members. The keeper resides in
private apartments within the same building, which communicate
internally with the other rooms of the Society, and which he
occupies, as well for his own private and domestic purposes as for
the more convenient performance of his duties as keeper. The
*Council at each meeting receive 4*l.* 10*s.*, equally divided among the   [*7]
members attending. Absent members of the Council are subject to
a fine.

The principal object of the establishment, and one of the
heaviest charges upon its funds, is the maintenance of schools for
the instruction of students : these are numerous. Any person who

presents himself with testimonials of moral character, and whose capacity has been shown to the satisfaction of the Council, is accepted as a student, and becomes entitled to study daily in the Academy, and for that purpose to have access to models, painting, sculpture, books, &c., to receive the instruction and advice of the visitors appointed for each school, to attend the lectures of the professors, and to enjoy all other privileges of students, for ten years. For these advantages no payment whatever is made by any student, or by any one in his behalf; but the same are wholly gratuitous. An annual distribution of prizes among the students is made by and at the expense of the Academy: and one of those who have obtained the highest prizes is enabled, at the same expense, to pursue his studies on the Continent for three years. The visitors of the said schools, who are also members, attend in rotation, and receive one guinea for each time of attending.

A certain portion of the funded property is set apart for pensions. The amount of this, and of the several pensions that may be paid out of it, is fixed; and no variation can be made in either without the assent of the General Assembly of Academicians and the sanction of the Crown. These pensions vary from 45l. to 105l., and are grantable to Academicians and Associates or their widows, provided they be in absolute want and without any other source

[*8] of adequate subsistence or income. *Besides these pensions, pecuniary donations, not exceeding 50l., are occasionally made in cases of particular distress. These pensions and donations have in most instances been given to widows of Academicians and of Associates; and neither now nor at the time of making the rate is or was any Royal Academician in the receipt of any pension or other relief from that fund.

After payment of the various expenses above mentioned out of the receipts of the Society, there has been usually in late years a surplus of variable amount, sometimes considerable, at other times small, which is applied towards the increase of the stock belonging to the Society. This stock is invested in the names of four trustees, in trust for the general purposes of the institution as above set forth, and for no other purpose, use or trust whatsoever.

The rooms in respect of which the Society is rated are the property of the Crown: they are distinct from the other portions of the building, and have separate entrances from the street. When not in use for the annual exhibition, they are used for the lectures of the professors, and schools of the students. The members of the Society derive no other personal advantage or emolument from the use of them : nor have they any other occupation of them, nor any personal participation in the profits or dividends belonging to the Society, excepting the advantage, emolument, occupation and participation hereinbefore stated and specified.

When the Society was first founded (1768), they received the permission of the King to have the use of certain apartments in his Palace of Somerset House.   When the Palace was replaced by the official buildings now called Somerset House, the King directed *that a certain part of it should be prepared for the use [*9] of the Royal Academy.   They were accordingly put into possession of the part so designed for them, and continued to use it for the purposes of their institution above set forth, and for no other purposes, for about sixty years.   His late Majesty King William IV. intimated his pleasure that the Royal Academy should be removed to the new building called the National Gallery, and that they should have the use of the portion appropriated to them exactly on the same terms and tenure, and for the same purposes, as they had always theretofore had the use of the apartments which he and his predecessors had from time to time been pleased to assign to them.   There is no lease, contract or other written instrument under which they hold or occupy the above premises: nor is any rent reserved, demanded or paid in respect of them.

The question for the opinion of the Court was : whether, under the above circumstances, the Society is liable to be assessed in respect of the premises above specified.   If the Court should be of opinion that the Society is liable to be assessed in respect of the whole of the above premises, the order of Sessions was to stand confirmed.   If the Court should be of opinion that the Society is not liable to be so assessed, the order to be quashed.   If the Court should be of opinion that the Society is liable to be rated for a portion only of the premises, the rate to be adjusted accordingly.

The case was argued in last Michaelmas Term (1).

Erle and *Bodkin* in support of the order of Sessions :

The premises in this case were properly rated.   They are *occupied (though the case does not use the word) by the Society, [*10] and yield a profit, which, to the forty Academicians, is a private

(1) November 19th, 1842.   Before Lord Denman, Ch. J., Williams, Coleridge and Wightman, JJ.

and personal one. The pictures, which they paint for profit, are
exhibited in the rooms. The funds raised by means of the building produce also salaries to the professors and allowances to the
Council, and a residue which is applied to the purpose of education.
The premises, therefore, are rateable according to the decisions on
stat. 43 Eliz. c. 2 ; and the local Act, 10 Geo. III. c. 75, (if it
were necessary to resort to that) is more comprehensively worded.

[They referred to *Reg.* v. *Sterry* (1), *Lord Amherst* v. *Lord
Sommers* (2), *Rex* v. *Green* (3), *Rex* v. *Terrott* (4), *Rex* v. *The
Chelsea Waterworks Co.* (5), and *Reg.* v. *Ponsonby* (6).]

[11]   *Sir F. Pollock*, Attorney-General, *Sir W. W. Follett*, Solicitor-
General, and *Smirke, contrà :*

There is no person distinct from the Crown who can be rated for
this property. The Academy was originally formed in a Royal
Palace, and afterwards in the public buildings established on its
site. King William IV. assigned to it the apartments now in
question in the National Gallery, on the same terms and tenure
and for the same purposes. The Crown still superintends the
proceedings of the Society, appoints the officers, or sanctions their
appointment, audits the accounts, and controls the application of
the profits, and might, as it would seem, cause the prices of
entrance to the exhibition rooms to be raised or lowered. If no
entrance money were demanded, the expenses now defrayed out of
this fund would probably have to be paid, if at all, from the Royal
purse. If the receipts fell short of the expenses, the difference
would be so paid. The establishment was formed by the Crown ;
and, if the Crown is now indemnified wholly or in part by money
paid for admission, that cannot affect the principle of rateability.
The Academicians receive the money, and dispose of it, and use the
premises, as servants of the Crown, to carry out the purposes of
[*12]   the Crown in keeping *up the institution. The sums taken at the
times of exhibition are like those received from the public for
admission to some parts of the Tower. The rate, if grounded on
the receipt of this revenue, is an assessment on the Crown. *Reg.* v.
Sterry (1) was a very different case : the decision there was, in effect,
that private property, which, if occupied in the usual manner,
would have been clearly rateable, was not the less so because

(1) 54 R. R. 546 (12 Ad. & El. 84).   (4) 7 R. R. 502 (3 East, 506).
(2) 1 R. R. 497 (2 T. R. 372).   (5) 39 R. R. 438 (5 B. & Ad. 156).
(3) 32 R. R. 639 (9 B. & C. 203).   (6) 61 R. R. 128 (3 Q. B. 14).

applied to charitable purposes. * * The Academicians are not
a voluntary or independent Society, but exist at the will of the
Crown.   They have no exclusive occupation of the rated premises ;
the Crown might at any time use part of them for other purposes :
the case differs in this respect from *Rex* v. *The Chelsea Water
Works Company* (1) and *Reg.* v. *Ponsonby* (2).   *   *   *

Cur. adv. vult.

LORD DENMAN, Ch. J., in this Term (January 18th), delivered the
     judgment of the COURT.   After stating the subject of the
     appeal, his Lordship proceeded as follows :

     The question arises upon the peculiar nature and character of
the property, and the purposes for which it is used ; no doubt
existing but that, if there be nothing specially to exempt them,
the premises (" a part of the building " &c.) are presumably the
subject of lawful assessment, and that, too, independent of the
local Act of the 10 Geo. III. c. 75.   Because, although that Act
does contain some more general description of property (" tenement " for instance) than is to be found in the statute of Elizabeth,
no reliance was placed in the argument upon that circumstance,
because the case was considered (and properly we think) as coming
within the earlier statute, or neither.

     The principles upon which the rateability of any person or
persons occupying any portion of the property of the Crown or
the public depends are, we think, defined with sufficient distinctness and well understood; the difficulty (whatever that may be)
depending upon the application of those principles to the facts
*and circumstances of each particular case.   The case of *Rex* v.
Terrott (3), in conformity with preceding ones, seems to have
settled this branch of the law.   There a lieutenant-colonel of
artillery was rated in respect of property, stated to be " the
property of the Crown, and part of a barrack : " and this Court
was of opinion that he was properly so rated, on account of the
private benefit which he derived from the apartments occupied by
him, beyond what was necessary for the discharge of his public
duty.   Lord ELLENBOROUGH, however, in delivering the judgment
of the Court, stated the general rule thus.   " The principle to be
collected from all the cases on the subject is, that if the party

---

(1) 39 R. R. 438 (5 B. & Ad. 156).   below (10 M. & W. 117).
(2) 61 R. R. 128 (3 Q. B. 14). *At-*   (3) 7 R. R. 502 (3 East, 506).
torney-General v. *Donaldson*, see p. 540

rated have the use of the building or other subject of the rate as a
mere servant of the Crown, or of any public body, or in any other
respect for the mere exercise of public duty therein, and have no
beneficial occupation of or emolument resulting from it in any
personal and private respect, then he is not rateable." It by no
means follows therefore that, if the residence had been merely
what was requisite for purposes of discipline or command, there
would have been the same decision. Such an inference, indeed,
is expressly guarded against in very precise terms. "Whether"
(it is said) "the commanding officer could withdraw himself from
the rate, by contracting his occupation in some proportionable
degree within the same narrow limits of merely necessary enjoyment with the soldier in his barracks, will be a question to be
decided when it shall occur."

This point lately came before us in the case of certain occupiers
of separate apartments in the Palace of Hampton Court (1), and
was determined in strict conformity *with this decision. The
enjoyment of those apartments ·by the occupants severally was
complete, and for the private benefit of each person, wholly
independent of any object or purpose of maintaining, as servants
or otherwise, the Palace for the use of her Majesty. The residence
of the parties was, in truth, in no respect distinguishable from that
of the occupier of a set of chambers in an Inn of Court, or of a house
in any street or square ; and therefore the parties were adjudged to
be rateable. In the present instance, there is no beneficial occupation in the shape of actual residence upon the premises rated, or
any part of them, by the appellants, to assimilate this to the case
of *Rex* v. *Terrott* (2), and the class to which it belongs. If, therefore, this be the property of the Crown or the public (for we are
not aware that the terms are otherwise than synonymous), and is
used expressly for public purposes, we think that this case must
come within the general principle of exemption laid down with so
much distinctness in the language above quoted (3).

Now this Society (which is not a corporation) was, as it appears,
instituted by his Majesty King George III., in the year 1768, "for
the express purpose of cultivating and improving the art of painting,
sculpture and architecture ; " a public purpose, surely, if such an
one can be stated. The place where the meetings of the Society

(1) 61 R. R. 128 (*Reg.* v. *Ponsonby*, 3
Q. B. 14).

(2) 7 R. R. 502 (3 East, 506).

(3) But see *Mersey Docks* v. *Cameron*
(1865) 11 H. L. Cas. 443, 463, 507,
511, 35 L. J. M. C. 1.—A. C.

were to be held, and where, until a very late period, they were in fact held, was a part of the Royal Palace of Somerset House. The apartments appropriated by his late Majesty William IV. for the use of the Society (those now assessed) are *stated to be "the property of the Crown." "All the officers of the Society are either actually selected and appointed by the Sovereign, or are elected by the Society subject to the approbation of the Sovereign, and hold their offices during his pleasure." The treasurer, who receives the profits and pays the expenses of the Society, is appointed by her Majesty; and his accounts are finally submitted to the Keeper of the Privy Purse. At the commencement of the Society, the King supplied the deficiency in their funds out of his Privy Purse: and even now, if the profits from the annual exhibition should fail, and the sums which the providence of the Society has invested in the funds be expended, the Society must probably fall, unless sustained by the bounty of the Crown. Lastly, the Society has no lease or certain term of holding; but the Crown, so far as appears, might at any time resume possession.

Seeing, therefore, that in this case, there is (as has been before observed) no beneficial occupation in the shape of actual residence upon the premises assessed, and no beneficial occupation at all, apart from the purposes of the institution, and that the appellants may well be considered as the ministers or agents of the Crown for furthering the objects for which property of the Crown is employed, those objects being merely national and public, we are of opinion that the assessment cannot be sustained, and that the order of Sessions must be quashed.

Order quashed.

REG. <i>v.</i> The GRAND JUNCTION RAILWAY COMPANY.

(4 Q. B. 18—46; S. C. Dav. & M. 237; 13 L. J. M. C. 94; 8 Jur. 508; 4 Ry. Cas. 1.)

Where a Railway Company, incorporated by Act of Parliament in the usual form of such Acts, made their profit partly by fare as carriers, and partly by tolls received from other carriers: Held that, in assessing them to a poor rate, the proper measure of rateable value was, not the amount of the tolls actually received, or which would have been received if all the carrying business had been performed by others, but the rent (after the deductions required by the Parochial Assessment Act, 6 & 7 Will. IV. c. 96) at which the railway might be reasonably expected to let to a yearly tenant, having the same powers and advantages as the Company.

The Sessions ascertained the rent by taking the gross receipts of the Company in respect of their own railway, and making the following deductions from them : viz. 1. Interest on the capital invested in the moveable stock of the Company. 2. A per-centage on the same capital for tenant's profits and profits of trade. 3. A per-centage on the same sum for annual depreciation of stock beyond ordinary annual repairs. 4. The actual annual expenses of conducting the business of carriers, maintenance of way, repairs of buildings, insurance, direction, rates, taxes and other disbursements as railway owners and carriers. 5. The fair annual value of stations and buildings rated separately from the railway. 6. An annual sum per mile for the renewal and reproduction of the rails, sleepers, &c.

Held, that these deductions (the amount of which was for the Sessions to determine) included all that was properly referable to trade, and that the Sessions might fairly infer that a yearly tenant of the railway, under the circumstances above stated, would give the balance as rent.

ON appeal against a rate made for the relief of the poor of the parish of Seighford, in the county of Stafford, whereby the above Company were rated, in respect of so much of the railway and land adjoining as lay within the parish, in the sum of 1,050*l.*, the Sessions confirmed the rate, subject to the following case.

The appellants were incorporated, and the Grand Junction Railway formed, by and under an Act, 3 & 4 Will. IV. c. xxxiv. (local and personal, public), altered and extended by other Acts of Parliament, namely, 4 & 5 Will. IV. c. lv. ; 5 & 6 Will. IV. c. viii. ; 5 & 6 Will. IV. c. ix. ; 1 & 2 Vict. c. lix. ; 3 & 4 Vict. c. xlix. (all local and personal, public) ; which were to be taken to be part of the case.   Under these Acts, not only has the line of railway,

[*19]   *as originally contemplated from Warrington to Birmingham, been constructed, but other railways, made by other parties from Warrington to Newton and from Crewe to Chester, have become the property of the appellants, and now form part of the Grand Junction Railway ; and the whole is managed, as to accounts and otherwise, as one entire business.   Over all these railways, and also over the Liverpool and Manchester Railway, between Newton and Liverpool in the one direction and Newton and Manchester in the other, the appellants exercise the right of being carriers, on their own account, of passengers and goods, providing for themselves stations or stopping places, locomotive power, carriages, coke and watering places, and all other things necessary and convenient for conveyance of passengers and goods, and charging for such conveyance reasonable fares and freights, in addition, as regards the said Grand Junction Railway, to the tolls or tonnages which they are authorised by the said Acts to take : and by this carrying trade, as well as by the toll, the appellants make profits.   Other parties also exercise the right of being carriers over various parts of the Grand Junction Railway ; and, amongst others, over that part which is in the respondent

parish; providing for themselves, without the consent or concurrence of the appellants, and independently of them (subject, however, to the control of the appellants under the provisions of the said Acts, and of the several Acts for the regulation of railways), locomotive power, carriages, coke and watering places, and all other things necessary and convenient for the conveyance of passengers and goods, and separate stations with needful branches into or communications with the same: and they, like the appellants, make profits of *their trade so carried on over the railway, and pay to the appellants the tolls or tonnages duly fixed by the appellants pursuant to the said Acts, being the same tolls as formed the basis of the calculations hereinafter mentioned as contended for by the appellants. A third class of carriers over the Grand Junction Railway hire from the Company locomotive engines and the use of stations &c., but find their own carriages; and these likewise make profits over the railway. They also pay to the appellants tolls or tonnages, besides a compensation for the use of the power, stations and other accommodations provided for them.

[*20]

The total length of so much of the railway as lies between Birmingham and Newton is eighty-four miles, and from Crewe to Chester twenty-one miles; making together one hundred and five miles. The distance along the Liverpool and Manchester Railway from Newton to Liverpool is fifteen miles, and from Newton to Manchester sixteen miles. The length of railway within the respondent parish is one mile: and there is no station, stopping place or property of the appellants there, other than the railway itself. The appellants have duly caused toll boards or lists to be made and published as required by sects. 165 and 166 of the first Act above mentioned, and have duly kept accounts of tolls as required by sects. 19 and 20 of stat. 1 & 2 Vict. c. lix. and sect. 27 of stat. 3 & 4 Vict. c. xlix., and have afforded free access to them as required by those Acts. The fares and charges for the conveyance of passengers and goods by the appellants, as carriers, are regulated by the number of miles through which they are carried, as well as by weight, bulk, value, &c., and various *other circumstances, in the same manner as the fares and charges of other carriers.

[*21]

The gross sum received by the appellants as tolls, including what they receive from other Companies or persons using the railway as carriers, and also tolls, of which an account is kept, calculated upon all the passengers, goods, &c., carried by them for their own profit, amount together to the sum of 1,500*l.* in respect of so much of the railway as lies in the respondent parish, and for the current year of rating ; and this is the gross produce of the land which the appellants, if not carriers, or which a lessee of the tolls, as such, would in fact have received, howsoever or by whomsoever the carrying business of the railway was conducted. And the appellants contended that this sum of 1,500l. ought to form the basis of any rate upon them in respect of their property in the respondent parish.

The gross yearly receipts of the Company, including as well the tolls actually received by them as the tolls, fares, freights and profits of every kind derived by them as carriers upon, and owners of, the Grand Junction Railway and its appurtenances in all the parishes between Birmingham and Newton and Crewe and Chester, and including also the profits of their stock in trade, and personal property as carriers in connection with and upon the entire Grand Junction Railway, and also the rents, profits and value of all their stations and other conveniences at and between Birmingham and Newton and Chester and Crewe, but excluding their receipts over the Liverpool and Manchester and other Railways which do not belong to them, but for passing over which, as carriers, they pay toll in the same way as the independent carriers over the Grand Junction Railway *are agreed for the purposes of this case to amount to the sum of 440,366l. for the current year of rating. Adopting the principle of a mileage division thereof, that is to say, dividing the same by 105, the total length of the railway, the amount is 4,190l. (and a fraction) in respect of so much thereof as lies in the respondent parish. And it is, for the purpose of the present case, admitted that the mileage principle of division is fair and equal as respects the respondent parish.

[*22]

It was admitted and agreed (subject to the opinion of the Court as to the propriety and principle of each item of deduction) that, if the amount of tolls, namely 1,500l., is to be adopted as the basis of calculation, then the full net annual value of the appellants' rateable property within the respondent parish will be 712l. 10s., being 1,500l., *minus* the following deductions, which the Court of Quarter Sessions find to be reasonable in fact : (that is to say)

(1.) 20l. per cent. thereof for the tenant's subsistence (1) and profits ; regard being had, in this case, to the extensive amount of responsibility, risk, &c.

(2.) 2l. 10s. per cent. for the collection of the tolls.

(1) This was explained in the course of argument to mean subsistence out of the profits.

(3.) 350*l.* per mile for the maintenance of the railway with the works and fences, and gate keepers ; and also for engineers and police, as to so much of the two latter items as are fairly chargeable on the proprietors of the railway as such.

(4.) 70*l.* per mile for poor rates, highway rates, church rates, and tithe commutation rent charge.

(5.) 80*l.* per mile for renewing or reproducing those portions of the subject of the rate which are of a perishable nature, such as the rails, chairs and sleepers &c., when rendered necessary by accident or decay.

[23]

The parish officers adopted, and the Court of Quarter Sessions sanctioned by their judgment, a different mode of arriving at the net annual rateable value of the property of the appellants in the parish. They ascertained the gross yearly receipts of the Company throughout the railway as stated above, viz. the sum of 440,366*l.*, and then made therefrom the following deductions ; the propriety, principle and completeness of such deductions, as well as the propriety and principle of this mode of arriving at the net annual rateable value of the rateable property of the appellants in the parish, being referred to the opinion of this Court, and the Court of Quarter Sessions finding such deductions to be reasonable in fact ; (that is to say)

(1.) 5*l.* per cent. for interest on 255,000*l.* ; being the capital necessary for and actually invested by the appellants in the purchase of engines, carriages and all the other moveable stock necessary for the business of carriers as conducted by them in manner aforesaid.

(2.) 20*l.* per cent. on the same sum for the tenant's profits, and the fair profits of such a trade carried on by means of so large a capital and with such large risks.

(3.) 12*l.* 10*s.* per cent. on the same sum as the fair annual amount of the depreciation of such stock considered to be in the hands of a tenant from year to year, beyond all needful and usual annual repairs and expenses.

(4.) 198,962*l.* per annum ; being the appellants' reasonable annual costs of conducting their business during *the same year in which their earnings as aforesaid amounted to 4,190*l.* per mile in Seighford parish ; namely (in the coaching department) wages of guards, conductors, porters, station keepers, clerks and policemen, repairs of carriages, trucks and horse boxes, horsing parcel carts, oil, grease, &c., for carriages, and duty on passengers ; and (in the merchandize department) salaries and wages of agents, clerks,

[*24]

porters, &c., repairs of waggons, and carriages of live stock expenses; and (in both departments, and generally) locomotive power, engine-men's and firemen's wages, engineering, repairing and cost of materials, including coke, maintenance of way, repairs of stations and buildings, office and general expenses including insurance and advertising, charge for direction, compensation account, rates and taxes, law expenses, and, generally, petty disbursements attendant on the several businesses of railway owners and railway carriers.

(5.) As the stations, offices, stores and buildings, and repairing works and premises throughout the railway have been and are sepa-rately rated in the several parishes in which they are situated, though necessarily used and occupied for the purposes of, and in connection with, it, and with the conduct of the traffic upon it, the respondents further deducted the fair annual value thereof, viz. 9,150*l.*

(6.) 30*l.* per mile for renewing or reproducing rails, chairs, sleepers, &c. as before (1).

[25]   The balance, amounting to the net sum of 135,589*l.*, was taken to be the net annual value of the whole railway, independently of the stations and other buildings rated separately ; and the Sessions found, as an inference from the above facts, that the railway and other corporeal hereditaments of the Company in connection with the railway might reasonably be expected to let to a tenant from year to year at the last mentioned sum of 135,589*l.*, exclusive of the rent of the stations and other buildings rated separately, such tenant being assumed to have the power of using the railway and all its appurtenances now the property of the Company under the same circumstances as the Company, and with no other privileges and advantages than the Company now possess.   The principle of mileage being agreed upon by both parties as fair for the purposes of this rate, both as applied to the expenses and deductions as well as receipts, the net annual rateable value of so much of the railway as lies in the respondent parish is to be taken at 1,050*l.* at least supposing the principle of rating adopted by the parish officers be just and correct.

Of the total receipts of the Company only about 30,000*l.* per annum are received in the shape of tolls from all other parties using the railway on their own account.

(1) It was suggested in argument that this deduction and that of No. 3, *supra*, for depreciation of the moveable stock and of the fixtures of the way, ought not to be allowed over and above the annual expense of repairs, &c. specified in No. 4. The decision of the Court was that enough had been deducted, not that all the deductions were proper.

All the other rateable property in the respondent parish is rated upon an estimate of the net annual value thereof within the meaning of the Parochial Assessment Act (6 & 7 Will. IV. c. 96), and without directly taking into account any receipts, expenses or allowances having reference to the amount of actual profits made thereon.

The appellants have not any stations or buildings in *the respondent parish. In various parishes along the line of railway the parties who (as before mentioned) use the railway as carriers, and have stations with buildings, and branches into the railway, and other conveniences connected with the railway, are not rated in the particular parishes or elsewhere upon or in respect of, or with any reference to, the Grand Junction Railway ; but solely for their own stations. The appellants derive no pecuniary profit whatever from their land in the respondent parish, except from the tonnage and tolls and from their fares and other receipts hereinbefore mentioned, and their trade as carriers in common with all other carriers over the same, if, indeed, these latter profits are to be considered as profits arising from the land, which the appellants contend that they are not.

The appellants contend that, even supposing the rate to be founded on a just principle and proper basis, the deductions allowed by the respondents do not include all the items necessary to bring out the net annual value ; that is to say, the rent at which what the respondents contend is the appellants' rateable property might reasonably be expected to let from year to year ; amongst which omitted deductions the appellants instance, by way of example, an annual allowance for goodwill.

The Court of Quarter Sessions adopted the principle of rating and the deductions contended for by the respondents as furnishing the net annual value of the rateable property pursuant to the Parochial Assessment Act, and confirmed the rate accordingly ; but, on the application of the appellants, granted a case for the opinion of this Court on the several questions hereinbefore *raised and stated ; the Court to have the power of amending, quashing or otherwise dealing with the rate, as they may deem right.

The case was argued, November 15, 1843 (1), by *Kelly* and *Smirke* in support of the order of Sessions, and *Sir W. W. Follett*, Solicitor-General, and *M. D. Hill*, *contrà*. A second argument as upon a *concilium* was then directed by the Court: and in Hilary Term,

(1) Before Lord Denman, Ch. J., Williams, Coleridge and Wightman, JJ.

REG.
v.
THE GRAND
JUNCTION
RAILWAY
COMPANY.

[*26]

[*27]

17th January, 1844 (1), the case was re-argued by *Kelly* on one side and by *M. D. Hill* on the other.

Arguments in support of the order of Sessions:

There is no essential difference between this case and *Reg.* v. *The London and South-Western Railway Company* (2). The differences in fact are, that there is here a real active competition of carriers on the railway, which did not exist, and was supposed to be practically impossible, in that case. The right of the Board of Trade (3) to interfere, in order to prevent any bye-laws or regulations of the Company from excluding strangers from the safe, profitable or convenient use of the railway, has probably given rise to a real competition. Another difference is that a part, though comparatively inconsiderable, of the profits of the Company really arises out of tolls paid by other carriers and Companies who use the railway. It is observable, also, that sect. 156 of stat. 3 & 4 Will. IV. c. xxxiv. (4) limits the amount of fares payable by passengers ; so [*28] that there is a maximum for fares as well *as for tolls. But these facts cannot affect the principle of rating. They merely tend to diminish the profits of the Company, and consequently the rateable value. To assume the tolls, which would have been taken if the Company had not been carriers, as the basis of the rate is to found it on a state of things almost wholly fictitious. Toll is only a part of the profits, even supposing it to be the criterion where toll is paid ; for the whole profit of the small parcel department (sect. 159), and of the mail contracts under stat. 1 & 2 Vict. c. 98 (5), is in addition to, and independent of, toll ; so that, if the Company made no use of the way but to carry small parcels and mails, or carried no tollable articles, they would not be rateable at all according to the argument. But the real test of rateable value is what a tenant will give for the railway itself for the purpose of trading, or taking toll, or any other available profit. The question is, not what profit a lessee of the tolls would take, but what a lessee of the railway would be able to earn. If the case were before a jury, witnesses would be called to prove what a lessee would give for the railway. Tolls are not the natural profits or real produce of the land, any more than fares. Both are equally the remuneration for the work,

---

(1) Before Lord Denman, Ch. J.,   5 & 6 Vict. c. 55.
Patteson, Coleridge and Wightman, JJ.   (4) See note (3), p. 285, *post.*
(2) 55 R. R. 351 (1 Q. B. 558).   (5) " An Act to provide for the con-
(3) Stats. 3 & 4 Vict. c. 97, and   veyance of the mails by railways."

labour and outlay of the Company in constructing, maintaining and working the railway, and for their permitting others to use it. It makes no difference that the remuneration is partly fixed by Parliament. If the prices of admission to a theatre, licensed for dramatic entertainments, were regulated by the Lord Chamberlain, yet, if the owner could calculate upon a further *annual profit derived from balls, concerts, dinners and public meetings, the overseers would doubtless be entitled to consider that source of profit when they make their rates. If competition were to interfere with the Company's profits so much as to drive them from the trade of carriers and to reduce their profits to that of toll alone, then toll would become the real test of value, and the railway would resemble a canal which usually yields to the proprietors no profit except toll: *Rex* v. *The Trustees of the Duke of Bridgewater* (1). So little is toll a necessary representative of value, that it is easy to imagine a case in which the whole profits of the Company's trade might not exceed the maximum amount of tolls; as if there were a rival and preferable railway between the same *termini*. There would then be no competition on the same railway; consequently no tolls would be taken, and no profit would be made of it except by carrying at prices which might not exceed the maximum tolls. Would the Company then consider themselves fairly rated on the amount of imaginary tolls, which they did not and could not get any one to pay, and which included all their profits as carriers? To the argument that tolls may be arbitrarily reduced to a nominal amount, an answer was attempted in *Reg.* v. *The London and South-Western Railway Company* (2) by saying that they must be fixed at a "reasonable" amount. But, where a tax is imposed, the lower it is, the more reasonable it may be justly called. In such a case "reasonable" means as small as possible. A Company free from competition of carriers may safely reduce their tolls indefinitely, and thus exempt themselves from local taxation by reason *of the very circumstance that increases their profits and their ability to pay. The question of value depends on the rent which a tenant may be expected to pay. Here the Sessions have expressly found that; and, if they had simply stated such finding, it would have been conclusive; but, to obtain the direction of this Court, they have disclosed the means by which they reached the result, and submit their inference to the judgment of this Court in case they

REG.
r.
THE GRAND
JUNCTION
RAILWAY
COMPANY.

[*29]

[*30]

(1) 32 R. R. 574 (9 B. & C. 68).   (2) 55 R. R. 351, 362 (1 Q. B. 558, 573).

shall think proper to exercise it on that which seems to be rather a question of fact than of law : for, although this Court has often pronounced on the deductions to be made from the ascertained rent or gross annual value of the land, it has not hitherto been called upon to determine the proper method of finding out such rent or gross value itself, or to verify the calculations upon which the estimate has been founded.

Supposing the inquiry now open, the rateable value has been thus attained. The Sessions have taken the gross receipts. These are clearly not the immediate subject of a rate; but they must necessarily include the rateable subject. They must include the profits of the railway as such, unless there are no such profits at all. The problem therefore is to cut down this gross sum to the net rent. For this purpose all trade expenses and trade profits must be excluded: all that can be referred to these is to be found in the first four items of deduction; and the residue must be the sum earned by the Company as railway owners. Again, clear this residue of the expense of maintaining the railway and all the fixtures and buildings connected with it, and all the rates and taxes upon them, and the balance is the net profit of the railway which a tenant will make independently of his trade of carrier. From this there must be a further *deduction of tenant's profits, in order to bring out the net rent at which it may be expected to let to him. All these deductions have been made: and it may be doubted whether more has not been allowed than the Company can fairly claim (1). The appellants do not point out any other or more satisfactory way of bringing out the net value. This species of property has acquired, as yet, no such known average market value as to enable surveyors to speak of it from their common experience, as in the case of houses and farms. These have a current value, according to their class and situation, which supersedes the necessity of any other mode of calculating it. To estimate the value from the profits of trade has been said to be as unwarrantable as to rate Coutts's banking house according to the profits of the business: but there the profits have no connection with the house, and are not dependent on it. An incoming tenant would not regard them.

[*31]

(COLERIDGE, J.: He might give more for it as a banking shop.)

(1) As all the deductions claimed were insufficient to reduce the value below the rate, the parish allowed them all. Some doubtful items are referred to in note (1), p. 280, *ante.*

It might perhaps add to the value. Indeed houses often derive a value from a trade independent of them; thus Dr. A. Smith mentions that the rent of houses near the sea in the Shetland Islands is in proportion to the profit the tenant can make by fishing, as well as by the land (1). The present case, however, rather resembles that of lands or buildings applicable exclusively to some particular purpose: as a chapel, a factory, a billiard or news room, or a brewer's plant; and the tenement rated is not the mere habitation of a trader, but is parcel of *his fixed stock, and the instrument whereby his profits are made.

REG.
v.
THE GRAND
JUNCTION
RAILWAY
COMPANY.

[*32]

Arguments for the appellants:

The Court in *Reg.* v. *The London and South-Western Railway Company* (2) cautiously guarded against the inference that their judgment applied to other railways regulated under different Acts of Parliament, and worked under different circumstances. Various clauses of their Act show that the Legislature contemplated the use of the railway by other carriers in common with the appellants (3); and the only question now is, whether the Company are to be subject to a burden from which other companies or parties carrying on the railway will be exempt. It is plain that the Company were in that case considered to be in the exclusive use of the railway; here other carriers use it adversely to the Company, and the Company enjoys no advantage whatever over other carriers. If there be any advantage arising from the position of the stations, that increases the value of the stations, and not of the railway as distinguished from them. It is an error to suppose that a lessee of the railway will get any profit out of the land but toll. He will take by the demise not a right of carrying on it, for that he has already by force of the statute, but a right to receive the tolls. As soon as he has entered on the subject of the demise, the *Company may still continue to carry as before and to use their stations for that purpose, paying toll to their own tenant. The fallacy consists in supposing the Company to be obliged to withdraw from competition, which they would not be; and, if they were, the consideration

[*33]

---

(1) Wealth of Nations, B. 1, Ch. XI.
(2) 55 R. R. 351 (1 Q. B. 558).
(3) The clauses of stat. 3 & 4 Will. IV. c. xxxiv., to which counsel referred, do not differ materially from those which are contained in the Act for the London and South-Western Railway, and of which there is an abstract at the end of the report of that case. Stat. 3 & 4 Vict. c. xlix., ss. 19, 20, obliges the Company to keep an account of tolls actually received by them.

paid for this would not be rent, but a payment in respect of good-will. If, therefore, the rent, found by the Sessions to be reasonable in amount, supposes the tenant to be in the place of the Company, this item ought to be deducted. Whatever an incoming tenant pays to the outgoing one for the advantage of succeeding to his business is, in substance, for goodwill, by whatever name it may be called. Any calculation of value based on the gross receipts of trade must be wrong, because those profits are not rateable either in whole or in part: and any deductions which leave a residue exceeding the amount of tolls must be insufficient, for toll is the only profit which the Company can by law receive from the mere use of the land; fare being the remuneration, not for the use of the land, but for carriage of the passenger or goods.

Nor is there any difficulty here arising from an arbitrary amount of toll; for as there is an active competition there is evidently no interest to fix any rate except the maximum ; and the case is, there-fore, exactly parallel to that of a canal, where the tolls are the measure of value even were the canal owner is a carrier, and takes fares and not tolls: *Rex* v. *The Trustees of the Duke of Bridge-water* (1). All the cases relied upon as instances in which value is supposed to be independent of the land are in truth instances of

[*34] land increased in *value by something incidental to it. [He referred to *Rex* v. *The Proprietors of the Liverpool Exchange* (2) and *Rex* v. *Bradford* (3).] There is no case in which the personal profits of the tenant can be fairly brought into the account in estimating the value or rent of his house. If it were otherwise, a banker who establishes a bank next door to Messrs. Coutts, in a house of equal dimensions but in which he carries on a less extensive business, would, on that account, be assessed at a less rate. The principle of this rate would justify taking into account the profits made by the appellants in running their carriages on the other railroads ; whereas the respondents disclaim any right to do this. All the anomaly and hardship of such a mode of calcula-tion is removed by making the tolls, fixed at a fair amount, and earned by all carriages, to be the sole criterion of rateable value. By assuming the fictitious case of a tenant at will in the enjoyment

[*35] of all the privileges and trade profits of the *Company, the Com-pany, who at their own cost and risk constructed the railway, are put in a position to contend with rival carriers at a great

(1) 32 R. R. 574 (9 B. & C. 68).   (3) 4 M. & S. 317.
(2) 1 Ad. & El. 465.

disadvantage; which could not have been intended by the
Legislature.

Cur. adv. vult.

LORD DENMAN, Ch. J. now delivered judgment:

This case of appeal against a poor rate was argued in Michaelmas
Term last, and again on a *concilium* in Hilary Term, and has been
heard by all the members of the Court.

Independently of certain questions of detail which we will consider hereafter, the main argument of the appellants was directed
to show that this case was distinguishable from that of *The London
and South-Western Railway Company* (1) in points which went to the
principle of the judgment in that case; while the respondents contended that the two cases were in principle the same, and that that
judgment must govern the Court in this. It is necessary, therefore,
in the first place to compare the two cases. If they shall be found
to be different in material circumstances, the principle of that decision may lead to a contrary one in this; at all events that decision
will not bind in the present case. If they shall be found to be
substantially the same, it may be necessary to consider whether our
own reflection, or any thing urged in these arguments, should
induce the Court to depart from the former decision.

In that case the facts found (and it must never be forgotten that
the propriety of a poor rate can only be determined with reference
to the facts found to be actually existing when it was made) were
that the Company *was in the sole and exclusive occupation of the
railway, warehouses, stations, and landing places; and, being so,
were solely and exclusively carrying on a large business as carriers
thereon; that, although the Legislature had, under certain limitations, made the railway a highway, and given to all the liege
subjects, under these, a right to use it, as such, either as
carriers or for individual travelling, and in such case provided
for the payment of tolls to the Company, yet, in fact, no one having
availed himself of the right, nor, as then appear to us, having the
power of doing so conveniently or effectually, no tolls were in fact
earned. To this state of facts we applied the established principles
of rating—that the rate is to be on the occupier in respect of the
beneficial nature of his occupation, in estimating which as to
amount, or, to put it in other words, in ascertaining how much
net rent such or such an occupation may be expected to command,

[*36]

(1) 55 R. R. 351 (1 Q. B. 558).

parish officers are to consider, not drily and only what would legally pass by a demise of it, but all the existing circumstances, whether permanent or temporary, wherever situated, however arising or secured, which would reasonably influence the parties to a negociation for a tenancy as to the amount of rent to be asked or given. We therefore thought it impossible in that case to separate the three or four miles of railway within the respondent parish from the whole line running through many other parishes, or that whole line from the warehouses, stations, and landing places, or these again from the peculiar conveniencies which a tenant would have for carrying on as occupier a lucrative business, if not the effective monopoly, which the provisions of the Act appeared to give to the occupier for carrying it on. What *under the Act was possible by law, what in point of fact might be in future, however near, we thought immaterial as to the principle, though very fit to be taken into account when making the calculation as to the *quantum ;* but in principle the parish officers were to look to the actual state and value of the occupation.

[*37]

In the case now under consideration there are some facts entirely different from those we have just mentioned. The case finds that other parties, as well as the appellants, exercise the right of being carriers over various parts of the railway, including therein that part of it which is within the respondent parish; providing for themselves, independently of the Company (subject however to its controul under the Acts of Parliament), carriages, fuel and all other things necessary and convenient for conveyance of passengers and goods, and separate stations, and the needful branches into or communications with the railway. These make profits of their carrying trade, as do the appellants, and pay them the tolls which they have fixed under the powers given them by their Acts. Besides these, another class of carriers hire from the appellants engines and the use of stations, landing places, &c., but find their own carriages ; these also make profits of their carrying trade on the railway, and pay to the appellants both tolls and a compensation for the use of the engines, stations and other accommodations provided for them.

As the appellants receive tolls from these two classes of carriers in respect of the goods and passengers conveyed by them on the railway, so they keep an account, as directed by their Act, of the tolls which would have been produced by their own conveyance of such goods and passengers, if not upon their own account. These,

[*38]

*with the compensation above mentioned, form the total produce of

the land, which the Company, if not carriers, or a lessee of the
railway carrying on no traffic upon it, would receive; and upon the
aggregate of these alone, after due deductions made, the Company
contend that the rate ought to be imposed. We understand them,
though it is not precisely so stated, to admit the principle of considering the whole line as entire, and to arrive at the exact sum, at
which they contend the rate in the respondent parish should be
fixed, by a mileage division of the whole length; a principle very
convenient in itself, and rightly adopted by consent.

It is unnecessary after this statement to point out the difference
in fact between the two cases. But we cannot perceive how this
difference bears upon the principle on which the present rate is to
be examined, or which governed the Court in the former decision.
For that proceeded, not upon speculations as to what might be in
future, but expressly on the then existing state of facts. Each of
the two Companies must be rated in respect of the occupation of
the land: one of them derives no benefit from that occupation
except by carrying on upon the land the business of conveying
goods and passengers; the division of that profit into tolls and
fares we think merely nominal: the other, in addition to this mode
of profitably occupying, also derives a profit from allowing others to
carry goods and passengers on the land also; and this latter profit
is properly called tolls. Still in both the enquiry must be the
same: what is the value of the occupation, from whatever source
derived? In neither can the profits of trade, as such, be brought
into the rate; but, if the ability to carry on a gainful trade upon
the land adds to the value of the land, that value *cannot be
excluded merely because it is referable to the trade. Suppose a
house occupied by a private family to-day, which, having great
advantages of situation for the purposes of trade, is turned into a
shop to-morrow, and in consequence lets for double or treble the
former rent; would not the rate be properly increased in proportion? Could it be objected that to do so was to rate the profits of
trade? Again, supposing that the occupier was to let out different
rooms to other persons carrying on the same trade as himself, and
this mode of occupying was still to increase the value of the house
to let; would this at all vary the principle on which he was rated,
though it might increase the *quantum*? Or, lastly, supposing that,
instead of this species of underletting being at the option of the
occupier, all persons using the same trade had a right by some
statute, under certain restrictions, to carry it on in the different

REG.
v.
THE GRAND
JUNCTION
RAILWAY
COMPANY.

[*39]

rooms of the house, paying a large compensation to the occupier, would not the principle of the rate be still the same ?   Would it be material to enquire how the occupation became more valuable, except it might be for making greater or less deductions, which the nature of the occupation might make just ?   We may all remember when the large premises in Soho Square, now used as a bazaar, were occupied as private residences.   The present mode of occupation probably increases the rent; but whether one man, being the tenant, alone carried on the various trades now exercised there, or sold goods himself at part of the stands and let out the others, and so derived his profit in part directly from trade, in part from the rent paid him by traders, or let out all the stands and so earned no profit but from the rents paid him by traders, the result would be

[*40]   in either case exactly *the same ; the overseers could only enquire what was the fair rateable value of buildings so occupied.   Nor, as we have said before, could the enquiry be at all affected, if the occupier of the bazaar held it under some statutable licence, which compelled him to allot his stands to all persons paying certain rents and submitting to certain regulations.

But it is said that in the cases supposed all is referable to the occupation under the supposed lease: that conveys the exclusive dominion ; and thence flow entirely the means of making the profits. We have in truth already given the answer to this ; but it will be plainer, if it be observed that there is a fallacy in confounding that which the lease conveys a legal title to, and that which it gives the lessee the means of doing or enjoying.   No two things can be more distinguishable: and it is the latter which regulates the rent a tenant will give, and not the former.   Suppose two estates of equal size and in all respects of equal fertility ; but one is surrounded by excellent roads, or has a canal near to it, or is near to a large market, and the other is without these advantages ; of course the rent and the rateable value of the one will be larger than the other ; yet the tenant would take no more by the lease of the one than of the other ; the lease would give him no legal title, which he had not before, to use the roads, the canal or the market.   Or suppose a more peculiar case : A., the owner and occupier of Blackacre, and having the command of a stream of water which he can turn over Whiteacre, on that account desires to rent it ; to him it will be more valuable than to any other occupier, because he can fertilize it at little expense ; he will therefore give a larger rent than any

[*41]   other person ; yet by *the lease he would take no more than any

other person, though he ought undoubtedly to pay a higher rate. Apply the principle of these cases to the railway of the appellants. It is quite true that, if they were to let it to a tenant, the lease would convey the land and railway only, and give a title to the tolls only ; but the lessee would undoubtedly consider the facilities and advantages which the occupation as tenant would afford him for carrying on a lucrative trade as carrier ; and, in whatever proportion that consideration would increase his rent, in the same, after due allowances, would his rate be raised also.

Two propositions are equally true, that the rate is not to be imposed in respect of the profits of trade, and that it is to be imposed in respect of the value of the occupation ; and two propositions that are true, and applicable to the same subject-matter, cannot be inconsistent ; and we think the respondents in the present case, by the scheme they propose, have shown that they are not so. The gross yearly receipts of the Company as occupiers of, and carriers on, the railway must at least include the proper subject-matter of the rate. They have, therefore, taken a sum agreed to represent them as the first point to start from. They then assume an amount of capital employed in the trade, and deduct from the former sum two per-centages on the latter for the interest of this capital and the profits which ought to be made on it, and a third for the depreciation of stock beyond usual repairs and expenses ; fourthly, they deduct from the gross receipts the annual costs of conducting the trade; fifthly, they deduct the annual value of all the land occupied by stations, &c., and elsewhere rated ; and, sixthly, a sum per mile for the reproduction *of rails, chairs, sleepers, &c. These deductions, taken together, seem to us to include whatever is properly referable to the trade, and distinguishable from the increased value which that trade gives to the land. We do not now speak of the amounts allowed under each item ; and we decline to give any opinion on this point, which is properly for the Sessions : but, if these are the proper heads of deduction, then the residue must represent the value of the occupation ; and, if so, this alone is brought into the rate, and the profits of trade are excluded. Accordingly the Sessions have found, as an inference from the facts, that the residue is the sum which a tenant from year to year might reasonably be expected to give for the railway and corporeal hereditaments now occupied by the Company in connection with the railway, exclusive of the stations and other buildings rated separately, such tenant being assumed to have the same and no

[*42]

other power of using the railway, the same and no other advantages and privileges, as the Company now possess.   If the deductions exhaust that portion of receipts referable to trade, the inference of the Sessions is fair.   If the advantages and privileges which the Company possess are attributable to their occupation and would pass with it, their assumption is well founded.   We agree with them in both.

The appellants, however, contend that, even if the principle of the rate be fair, some reasonable deductions are omitted.   We have used the sufficiency of the deductions made as a mode of trying the principle ; but the objection of the appellants now to be considered is one of detail.   The only instance which they specify and rely on is that an allowance ought to be, and is not, made for goodwill.

[*43] We presume by this is meant that a person, *bargaining with the Company to become their yearly tenant of the railway in the expectation of succeeding to their trade as a probable consequence of succeeding to their occupation, would properly be called on to pay them something for the goodwill of that trade ; and that this would be in the nature of an outgoing, a deduction from profits. This objection appears capable of two answers ; the first and a decisive one is, that the purchase of goodwill implies that a trade is sold ; that the Company are to be bound to surrender their trade to the lessee, and no longer to be carriers on the line ; but the calculation of the Sessions proceeds on no such supposition ; all those special advantages, indeed, for carrying it on, which the occupation gives them, whatever they may be, they must necessarily surrender : but, the moment they had leased the railway, they would become a part of the public and have the right to carry on their trade, retaining all the goodwill, with all those advantages which the statutes have carefully reserved for the public.   Secondly, though the supposition of a tenancy is to be made, yet what the incidents of the tenancy must be as to actual terms and allowances must be determined, for the purpose of fixing the amount of the rate, by the actual state of things ; for this supposition of a tenancy is only a mode of ascertaining the existing value of the occupation to the existing occupier.   Now here there is no tenancy in fact ; no goodwill is in fact paid for, and, therefore, no deduction ought in fact to be made on account of its price.

Again, it is contended that the existing facts of this case show the unreasonableness of the rate.   The carrying trade of the Com-
[*44] pany goes beyond their own line *upon the railways of other sets of proprietors ; but the receipts arising from this have been excluded

from the rate ; this, it is said, is inconsistent.   How can the profits which the same engine earns by drawing goods over one mile be of a different character from those which it earns in the same employ over the next mile?   So far from there being any inconsistency in this, it is necessarily involved in the principle on which the rate rests : that the distinction can be made, and has been made, is no slight proof of the soundness of that principle.   The moment that the engine leaves the railway of the Company, what it earns ceases to have any connection with their occupation of the railway ; it may and of course does increase the value of the occupation of that other line on which it then works, and will of course in the shape of toll proportionably increase the rate which the occupier will pay ; but, if it were allowed to swell the charge on the Company, it could only do so in respect of the profits of trade ; and these our principle excludes.

But it is said, lastly, that this principle works injustice between the Company and those other corporations or individuals who carry on their line.   Their engines and their trade, it is said, pay nothing to the poor rate directly, and indirectly only in respect of their toll, which may be supposed to be calculated so as to bear its own rate ; whereas the Company pay both on their tolls and their fares. Colour is given to this objection from the fact, which might seem to explain it, that the Company fill two characters ; the other parties one only.   But the proper answer is a denial of the fact ; the Company do not pay directly or indirectly on their fares ; *they pay only on the increased value of their occupation of land occasioned by whatever circumstances.   If a trader should underlet to a lodger a room in his house in which he drove the most profitable trade imaginable, such lodger would pay no poor rate at all ; but, as the trader would proportion the rate at which he let the lodgings to the advantage which such lodger derived from them, the total rent which the trader would pay, and the rate which would be imposed on him, would be proportionately increased : but could he complain of any injustice, or say that he carried on his own trade in the residue of the house to a disadvantage, because in his rate the value, which his trade so carried on in the residue gave to his occupation, was also taken into the account in fixing the *quantum* of the rate?   Yet those parties who carry on a trade upon the Company's line are, in effect, but in the nature of lodgers or parties enjoying a profitable easement on the line, and, by the consideration they pay, increasing its general value.

[*45]

In the examination which this case has compelled us to make, we have necessarily been led into a reconsideration of the principles on which the decision in the case of the South-Western Railway proceeded.   That decision was not directly impugned in the argument; but the distinction of fact relied on has appeared to us, on examination, so unsubstantial, that it was necessary, in order to a decision against this rate, to examine the principle on which that was upheld : and, in a matter of such vast importance and such apparent novelty, where, too, the decision of this Court cannot be reviewed in a court of error, we were not unwilling again to examine the question.

[46]   Upon the whole we are satisfied with the decision of the Sessions. It appears to us founded on a just application of established principles, in accordance with several decided cases and conflicting with none.   Our judgment, therefore, will be for the respondents.

Order of Sessions confirmed.

1843.
Jan. 25.

[132]

REG. *v.* THE INHABITANTS OF WORTH.

(4 Q. B. 132—140; S. C. 3 G. & D. 376 ; 12 L. J. M. C. 47 ; 7 Jur. 172.)

On the trial of an appeal, respondents, to defeat an alleged settlement by hiring and service in 1824, 1825, produced a book in which the master, then dead, had kept minutes of his contracts with servants, and which contained the following entries in his writing.

"April 4th, 1824.   W. W." (the pauper) "came; and to have for the half year 40s.

"September 29th.   Paid this 2l.

"October 27th.   Ditto came again, and to have 1s. per week : to March 25th, 1825, is 21 weeks 2 days : 1l. 1s. 6d.

"25th.   Paid this."

Held, that these entries were not admissible, either as made against the writer's interest, or as written in the course of a business or employment, or as embodying a contract.

The Sessions, in stating a case for the opinion of this Court, ought not to direct that, in any particular event, the case shall be sent back to the Sessions for final determination.

ON appeal against an order of justices removing William Worsell and his wife and children from the parish of Worth, in Sussex, to the parish of Horne, in Surrey, the Sessions quashed the order, subject to the opinion of this Court upon the following case.

The respondents had removed the pauper and his family upon a settlement obtained in the appellant parish by hiring and service for a year with one Thomas Booker in 1821.   The appellants admitted the settlement upon the hearing of the appeal, and

relied upon a subsequent settlement, alleged in the grounds of appeal to have been gained in the respondent parish by hiring and service for a year with one Thomas Stone in or about 1824. · For the purpose of establishing this settlement the appellants called the pauper and his father, who both deposed to the contract of service having been for a year, though neither could recollect at what wages. The pauper further stated in evidence that he worked for Mr. Stone under the contract for six months at Gibsaven Farm, in the parish of Worth; that he then went away at his master's request for about three weeks, during which time he worked for his father and received remuneration from him, his boxes and clothes remaining all the time at Mr. Stone's; that he afterwards returned and completed his year's service with Mr. Stone; and that he received his whole year's wages in one sum from *Mr. Stone at the end of the year. For the purpose of   [*133]
rebutting this evidence, and showing that no such contract of hiring and service for a year in fact took place, the respondents called Mrs. Amelia Creasy, daughter of Mr. Stone, who proved that her father died in 1827; that he carried on the business of a farmer at the farm in question for upwards of twenty years; that in the course of his business he was in the habit of hiring farm servants; and that his practice was, when he did so, to make an entry of the time and terms of such hiring in a memorandum book kept by him for that purpose, which memorandum book was returned with the present case. This book, which had been in the custody of Mrs. A. Creasy from the time of her father's decease, was then produced and tendered in evidence by the respondents, but objected to on the part of the appellants. It contained, amongst numerous minutes of the time and terms of hiring of farm servants, many such being for the year, and of payments made to them in respect of their services, the following entries with reference to the hiring and service of the pauper, proved to be in the handwriting of Mr. Stone; but the witness was not present when the entries were made.

"April 4th, 1824. W. Worsell came; and to have for the half-year 40s.

"September 29th. Paid this 2l.

"October 27th. Ditto came again; and to have 1s. per week: to March 25th, 1825, is 21 weeks two days: 1l. 1s. 6d.

"25th. Paid this."

The Sessions rejected this evidence, and quashed the order of removal, subject to the opinion of the Court upon the question, whether the memorandum book containing *the above entries was admissible for the respondents or not.   If the Court should be of opinion that it was, the appeal was to be sent back to the Quarter Sessions to be reheard (1) ; if the Court should be of opinion that it was not, the order of justices was to be quashed.

Cobbett and *Creasy*, in support of the order of Sessions (2) :

This memorandum was not admissible as the entry of a deceased person.   It was not against the writer's interest : on the contrary, he had an interest in representing his farm servant as hired for only half a year, to avoid burdening his parish.   The case in this respect is like *Rex* v. *Debenham* (3).

(COLERIDGE, J. : It was against his interest to charge himself with a debt of 2*l*.   Conflicting interests cannot be balanced.)

He discharges himself at the same time.

(COLERIDGE, J. : Not at the same time.   And accounts are evidence though the writer, upon the whole result, discharges himself.)

The benefit by relieving the parish from a settlement would be greater than the injury by acknowledging a contract for payment of 2*l*. ; and, if the entry might, upon the whole, be in favour of the maker's interest, the evidence is inadmissible, 1 Phill. on Ev. 306, c. 7, s. 7 (4), citing *Outram* v. *Morewood* (5).

(COLERIDGE, J. : His liability to the poor rate might not amount to 2*l*.)

The entry here is not a direct acknowledgment of a debt, *but only a statement of a contract, and that in a private document, which would not bind the party writing it.   The certificate in *Chambers* v.

---

(1) Lord DENMAN, Ch. J. observed, on this part of the statement : "The question is improperly put. According to this practice, we might have a case reserved a second and a third time. The Sessions should find one way or the other.   But we will go on with the case." See *Reg.* v. *The Justices of*

Kesteven, 61 R. R. 406, note (1) (3 Q. B. 810, 815, note (*d*)).

(2) The case was in part heard on January 21st.

(3) 20 R. R. 401 (2 B. & Ald. 185).

(4) 9th ed.

(5) 12 R. R. 542 (5 T. R. 121).

Bernasconi (1) was as much against the interest of the party making it as the memorandum here ; yet it was held not admissible; and clearly the rules of evidence do not let in every writing which may, under some imaginable circumstances, operate to the writer's prejudice. The principal decisions on this subject are collected in *Higham* v. *Ridgway* (2), and the comment upon it in 2 Smith's Leading Cases, 193—197 (3) ; also in *Barker* v. *Ray* (4).   This is not a case where the entry has been made in the course of any duty or employment, as in *Doe* d. *Patteshall* v. *Turford* (5) ; and, if it were, the requisites to make such an entry admissible are wanting : as, proof that the entry was contemporaneous with the act ; corroborative circumstances ; and the absence of any motive to misstate. The cases in which entries of this kind have been received have several times been remarked upon as going so far that their doctrine ought not to be extended : *Marks* v. *Lahee* (6), *Chambers* v. *Bernasconi* (7), and *Doe* d. *Gallop* v. *Vowles* (8), cited in 1 Phill. on Ev. 333, note (1) ; Part 1, c. 16, s. 2 (9).

Platt and *Roupell, contrà :*

The question is not as to the weight of the evidence, but whether it can be received at all ; and it was admissible on the principle *acted upon in *Higham* v. *Ridgway* (2), that the writer, by making   [*136] the entry, furnished evidence against himself.

(Lord Denman, Ch. J. : The entry here stated only what he had agreed to pay.)

It was his interest not to be bound at all. As to the poor rate, it is not probable that he had that in contemplation when he wrote this memorandum.   The interest on that account, therefore, was not such a present interest as makes evidence inadmissible.

(Patteson, J. : Your argument would apply equally if he had made the most advantageous bargain ; as if he had agreed to deliver goods at a very high price.)

(1) 40 R. R. 604 (1 Cr. M. & R. 347 ; *S. C.* 4 Tyr. 531). See *Chambers* v. *Bernasconi*, 1 Cr. & J. 451. *S. C.* 1 Tyr. 335.
(2) 10 R. R. 235 (10 East, 109).
(3) 11th ed. vol. 2, p. 327.
(4) 2 Russ. 63, 66, 67, n.
(5) 37 R. R. 581 (3 B. & Ad. 890).
(6) 3 Bing. N. C. 408, 418.
(7) 40 R. R. 604 (1 Cr. & J. 451, 459 ; *S. C.* 1 Tyr. 335, 344).
(8) 1 Moo. & Rob. 261.
(9) 8th ed. The note is omitted in ed. 9 : vol. i. p. 318, c. 7, s. 8.

The party shows himself bound to make a payment: that acknowledgment may be presumed adverse to himself. It is true that the entry limits the amount which he is to pay: but that might be said if he had mentioned the most extravagant sum. At all events, it is evidence which might be used against him by a party seeking to enforce the contract.

(COLERIDGE, J.: If Mrs. Creasy had stated that she heard her father say that he only hired the pauper for six months, do you say that that would have been evidence in a suit between third parties? This entry is only a declaration in writing, made after the time of contracting.)

That does not appear by the statement. If the entry was made at the time, it is as if the master had written a separate paper containing the terms of the agreement, and delivered it to the servant. In *Outram* v. *Morewood* (1), the entry was in favour of the right of the party making it. In *Rex* v. *Debenham* (2) the entry was of a fact which it was the interest of the writers to establish. In *Spiers* v. *Morris* (3) entries by an executor charging

[*137]

himself *with the receipt of rent (for which he had afterwards been obliged to account) were held to be evidence of the perception of rents by him as executor.

(PATTESON, J.: Here the party charges himself with an agreement only.

COLERIDGE, J.: You must contend that an admission of any contract takes effect as a declaration against interest, in an action between third parties.)

The case is like that of a steward charging and discharging himself by one set of entries.

(COLERIDGE, J.: There the writer does, by one part of the entries, completely charge himself.)

This evidence is also maintainable on the second ground (if it be necessary to call that in aid), that the entries were made in the ordinary course of employment in the party's profession, as in *Doe* d. *Patteshall* v. *Turford* (4). The question ultimately comes to this,

(1) 12 R. R. 542 (5 T. R. 121).   (3) 9 Bing. 687.
(2) 20 R. R. 401 (2 B. & Ald. 185).   (4) 37 R. R. 581 (3 B. & Ad. 890).

whether there is a reasonable probability that the entry was a true one: and here the contents of the book and the general circumstances of the case support that probability.   (Some observations on these are omitted.)

LORD DENMAN, Ch. J. :

I have always a great disposition to admit any evidence that can reasonably be tendered : but there must be some limits.   In a case of this kind the entry must be against the interest of the party who writes it, or made in the discharge of some duty for which he is responsible.   The book here does not show any entry operating against the interest of the party.   The memorandum could only fix upon him a liability on proof that the services referred to had been performed : and whether, on dispute, a jury would have *found him liable for the sum entered, or more or less, we cannot say. Nor was this an entry made in the course of duty, as in *Doe* d. *Patteshall* v. *Turford* (1).   The act there was performed by a principal in the firm, and not by a clerk ; but it was done by a person acting under the same responsibility ; therefore no distinction favourable to the respondents arises from that part of the case.

[*138]

PATTESON, J. :

This was not an entry against the interest of the maker.   It showed only an agreement, which we must suppose to have been made on fair and equitable terms : and, on that supposition, it was as much for the party's interest to have the service as against his interest to pay for it.   At the time of making the entry nothing more than an agreement subsisted, though after performance the party hiring would be a debtor.   As to the argument that this entry was made in the course of the party's employment, the writer in this case was a principal : in *Doe* d. *Patteshall* v. *Turford* (1) the person who acted, though a partner in the attorneys' firm, gave the notice as an agent.   That was properly a matter of employment within the rule.

It was suggested in argument that this writing might be considered as the contract itself between Stone and the pauper.   But it is not signed by the parties : it is only a memorandum made by the master for his own purposes : and, in a case referred to in 1 Phill. on Ev. 419, Part 1, c. 8 (2), it is said that " where an agent for the plaintiff made a verbal agreement with the defendant, and

(1) 37 R. R. 581 (3 B. & Ad. 890).   (2) 9th ed.

afterwards put it down in *writing, (which was not signed by the parties,) as a memorandum to assist his recollection, such writing is not the best evidence, nor indeed any evidence of the agreement, though it may be used by the agent for the purpose of refreshing his memory " (1). It is true that, in this case, if the pauper had not been paid according to the agreement, this entry, if he could have got at it, would have been evidence against Stone, the employer ; but still it was not the contract, and would not have been evidence for Stone, or against a third person.

COLERIDGE, J. :

This was not an entry against the party's interest, unless the mere making of a contract be so : and, if that were the case, the existence of a contract would be against the interest of both parties to it. It was argued that we might enquire whether a reasonable probability appeared that the entries were true, and that for this purpose we might go into the contents of the book beyond the particular entry. But the question is, not what may be inferred from other entries, but whether the particular entry, at the time when it was made, imported something contrary to the maker's interest. As to the other point : it cannot be contended that Stone made these entries in the course of any duty. In *Doe* d. *Patteshall* v. *Turford* (2) the person who did the act relied upon was a partner in the firm of attorneys : but both attorneys were equally the agents of the client ; and it was the duty of each to serve the notices by himself or by his clerk. It was usually done by a clerk ; but on [*140] the particular occasion the *attorney himself did it ; and, while so doing, he was actually in the discharge of a duty to another person. This is an entirely different case.

WIGHTMAN, J. :

The admitting entries of this kind is an exception to the general rules of evidence. The cases in which they have been admitted are where the person has entered a receipt of money for which he would be accountable, or the payment of a debt due to himself. There the entry would be *primâ facie* against the writer's interest, as making him liable or discharging some one else. But this is merely a memorandum of a contract to be performed in future. When the entry is, in effect, "I owe so much," the result is an

(1) See *Rex* v. *St. Martin's, Leicester*,   *Tomlin*, 44 R. R. 612 (5 Ad. & El. 856).
2 Ad. & El. 210.   Also *Lord Bolton* v.   (2) 37 R. R. 581 (3 B. & Ad. 890).

immediate liability to pay, and nothing else : but here the party would not be liable unless the service were performed. The argument by which this objection was met would show that every thing which proves a contract is against the interest of the contracting party. As to the suggestion that this writing contains the contract, the entry, though it might prove a contract as against the master, would be no evidence to bind the pauper, he denying that such a contract had been made.

Order of Sessions confirmed.

REG. *v.* WHIPP.

(4 Q. B. 141—146; S. C. 3 G. & D. 372; 12 L. J. M. C. 64.)

Under stat. 5 & 6 Will. IV. c. 76, s. 88 (1), the town council of a borough took on themselves the powers given to inspectors under stat. 3 & 4 Will. IV. c. 90, as to lighting a township in the borough, and made an order on overseers to collect and pay a sum named.

Within the township was a parochial church or chapel, being the only place where poor rates had ever been published ; but there were also within the township two other churches of the Established Church, recently built, and some dissenting places of worship.

The rate made by the overseers, in compliance with the order, was published in the first named church or chapel only.

Held, an insufficient publication, under stat. 7 Will. IV. & 1 Vict. c. 45, s. 2 : and that the rate ought to be quashed on appeal.

ON the appeal of James Whipp against a rate made by the church-wardens and overseers of the township of Clitheroe, the Sessions confirmed the rate, subject to the opinion of this Court upon a case which, so far as regards the point decided, was substantially as follows (2).

The appeal was against a rate made by the respondents, dated 6th April, 1842, to raise 250*l.* for lighting the township of Clitheroe, in the borough of Clitheroe, and for carrying into effect the provisions of the Parochial Lighting and Watching Act, 3 & 4 Will. IV. c. 90.

On the trial of the appeal, the respondents proved the rate, and that it was made by virtue of an order (3) or warrant, under the common seal of the borough of Clitheroe, by which the aldermen and councillors, being the council of such borough, having taken upon them the powers given to the inspectors named in a certain Act &c. (3 & 4 Will. IV. c. 90), so far as the same related to the

(1) Rep. Municipal Corporations Act, 1882, s. 5.

(2) The case, as stated, raised some points not here reported, upon which

no decision was given.

(3) See stat. 5 & 6 Will. IV. c. 76, s. 88. [Municipal Corporations Act, 1882 (45 & 46 Vict. c. 50), s. 197.]

REG.
v.
WHIPP.

[*142]

lighting of the township, required the overseers of the poor of the said township to collect and levy, pursuant to such Act, 250*l.*, being the amount of money fixed and determined to be called for in the year from 17th February, 1842, to 17th February, 1848, for the *purpose of lighting the said township, and for carrying into effect the provisions of the said Act in that behalf, and to pay the same to the treasurer within three calendar months &c. The order was addressed to the overseers.

The rate was proved to have been duly declared, signed and allowed by two magistrates, according to the laws in force respecting the signature and allowance of rates for the relief of the poor. And it was, on the Sunday next after the allowance, namely on the 10th April, 1842, published by a written notice affixed to the door of the church or parochial chapel of St. Michael's, in the said township of Clitheroe, which is usually called the old church, that being the only place where the rates for the relief of the poor had theretofore been published. The chapelry of Clitheroe is a perpetual curacy within the parish of Whalley ; and the said church was, until about four years ago, the only church or chapel in connection with the Established Church in the chapelry or township : but, at the time of the publication of the rate in question, there were two other churches of the Established Church in the township of Clitheroe, namely the church of St. James, which had been used for Divine worship for about three years, and another church, which had been opened for Divine worship a short time previous to the publication of the rate in question, but was not then completely finished. There were also various chapels for the religious worship of persons dissenting from the United Church of England and Ireland, in the township. There was no other publication of the rate in question than as above mentioned.

[*143]

The township of Clitheroe is situate within the municipal *borough of Clitheroe : and the said township, at the time of the passing of the Municipal Corporation Act, was not within the provisions of any local Act : nor was there any power of levying rates for lighting the same. The rate is assessed upon all the occupiers in the township, numbers of whom live at a considerable distance from the part of the township which is lighted, namely the part which is properly called the town of Clitheroe.

It was objected, on the part of the appellant, that the rate was not published as by law required. The Court overruled the objection, and confirmed the rate, subject to the case.

Sir W. W. Follett, Solicitor-General, and *Tomlinson* now showed
cause :

It was not necessary to make the publication in any church
besides that in which the poor rates had been ordinarily published.
By sect. 5 of stat. 3 & 4 Will. IV. c. 90, the time and place of
meetings to be held for determining whether the provisions of that
Act shall be adopted by a parish must be notified by "affixing a
notice on the principal outer door of every parish church or chapel
situate within such parish, or on the usual place of affixing notices
relating to the parochial affairs of any such parish, and also by
publication of the same in the parish church or chapel," on the
Sunday before the meeting, "during or immediately after Divine
service." By sect. 10, notice of a poll is to be fixed on the outer
door of every parish church or chapel, or the usual place for parish
notices, as before. Sect. 15 makes the same provision for notice of
the adoption of the Act. Any one of these clauses is satisfied by
publication on the door of the place where parochial rates have
been *published. By stat. 7 Will. IV. & 1 Vict. c. 45, s. 2, "all   [*144]
proclamations or notices, which under or by virtue of any law or
statute, or by custom or otherwise, have been heretofore made or
given in churches or chapels during or after Divine service, shall
be reduced into writing, and copies thereof either in writing or in
print, or partly in writing and partly in print, shall previously to
the commencement of Divine service on the several days on which
such proclamations or notices have heretofore been made or given
in the church or chapel of any parish or place, or at the door of
any church or chapel, be affixed on or near to the doors of all the
churches or chapels within such parish or place; and such notices
when so affixed shall be in lieu of and as a substitution for the
several proclamations and notices so heretofore given as aforesaid,
and shall be good, valid, and effectual to all intents and purposes
whatsoever." That proviso is reasonably satisfied ; the notice has
been given in the customary place under the Act last mentioned :
it is sufficient to publish the poor rate, made upon a district of a
parish maintaining its own poor, on the door of the church belonging
to that separate district, though there are other chapelries in the
same parish having each its own chapel (1). The principle is, that
all parties interested in the rate have practically notice of the rate.
Under stat. 3 & 4 Will. IV. c. 90, s. 73, a part of a parish may

(1) See *Reg.* v. *Marriott*, 54 R. R. 698 (12 Ad. & El. 779).

REG.
v.
WHIPP.

adopt the Act: but the rule to be contended for on the other side would, in such a case, make it necessary to publish the rate in districts of the parish which could not be interested in the rate.

(COLERIDGE, J.: Does stat. 3 & 4 Will. IV. c. 90, contain no express provision as to the publication of the rate?)

[*145]   Sect. 9, under which the *amount is fixed, makes no such provision.

(COLERIDGE, J.: Do you say that no notice is requisite?)

It must be discretionary, or conformable to the ordinary publication of rates: in either case the publication here will be good. Sect. 33 gives the overseers, for the purpose of collecting, raising and levying the rate, the same powers, remedies and privileges as for "levying" money for the relief of the poor.

(COLERIDGE, J.: The foundation of all seems to be stat. 17 Geo. II. c. 3, s. 1, which enacts that no poor rate "shall be esteemed or reputed valid and sufficient so as to collect and raise the same," unless public notice of the rate have been given in the church on the next Sunday after its allowance. "Levying" and "raising" seem to mean the same thing.)

There is much obscurity in the provisions of stat. 3 & 4 Will. IV. c. 90: and, as nothing is specifically enacted as to the notice of the rate, it seems enough to take care that the notice shall be reasonable.

Clarkson and *Whigham*, *contrà*, were stopped by the COURT.

LORD DENMAN, Ch. J.:

Stat. 7 Will. IV. & 1 Vict. c. 45, after stating, in sect. 1, the expediency of altering the mode of giving the notices required by divers Acts relative to highway and poor rates and land tax, and other matters, enacts, by sect. 2, that the notices shall be affixed to the doors of "all the churches and chapels within such parish or place." Then, under stat. 3 & 4 Will. IV. c. 90, a rate for the township is made which, instead of being published in all the churches and chapels of the township, is published in one only.

[*146]   Nothing *can be clearer than that this is insufficient. The appeal must prevail.

PATTESON, J. concurred.

COLERIDGE, J. :

I think this rate is as much within the meaning of stat. 7 Will. IV. & 1 Vict. c. 45, as a poor rate.

WIGHTMAN, J. concurred.

REG.
v.
WHIPP.

Order of Sessions quashed.

REG. *v.* MORTON (1).

(4 Q. B. 146—150; S. C. 3 G. & D. 400; 12 L. J. Q. B. 123.)

1843.
Jan. 27.

[146]

A rule *nisi* having been obtained for an information in the nature of a *quo warranto* against M. for exercising the office of councillor of a borough, M. resigned the office : on his afterwards showing cause, it appeared that the presiding officer had declared him duly elected, and that the town clerk had served notice upon him to accept the office, with a warning that, in default of his doing so, he would be liable to a fine.

M. appearing in this Court but not defending his title, the Court made the rule absolute, M. paying the costs of the application, but ordered that, if it should be necessary to file the information, it should be done at the prosecutor's expense, and that, M. now undertaking to disclaim if required, he should do so at the prosecutor's expense.

SIR *W. W. FOLLETT*, Solicitor-General, obtained a rule in last Term, calling on George Morton to show cause why an information in the nature of a *quo warranto* should not be exhibited against him, to show by what authority he claimed to be a councillor of the borough of Leeds.

By the affidavits in support of the rule it appeared that, on 1st November, 1842, an election was held for the West Ward of Leeds, to elect three councillors for the ward, two vacancies having been created by councillors going out in rotation, and another by a councillor having resigned. Robert Craven, Richard Bramley, George Morton, John Patrick, and Joshua Hobson were candidates. The votes, as taken to fill the two vacancies created by rotation, were, for Craven 585, *for Bramley 547, for Morton 543, for Patrick 540, for Hobson 53. On 3rd November, the names of the persons elected not having been published, the presiding alderman and one of the assessors rejected the names of five voters who had voted for Bramley and Patrick. Another vote for Bramley and two votes for Morton were also rejected. This made the votes for Bramley and Morton equal, namely 541: and the alderman and the one assessor, on 3rd November, published the names of Craven and Morton as the two councillors elected to supply the vacancy created by rotation. The five votes first mentioned were rejected on the ground that

[*147]

(1) Cited in *Reg.* v. *Tugwell* (1868) L. R. 3 Q. B. 704, 713, 37 L. J. Q. B. 275. —A. C.

there had been no fresh burgess roll made out for the then current year, and the election had been made from the old burgess roll, and that the five voters in question had been enrolled in such roll as voters in other wards besides the West Ward, and had, on previous elections, voted in such other wards (1). Morton had made and subscribed the declaration required by stat. 5 & 6 Will. IV. c. 76, s. 50 (2), and had acted as councillor.

The affidavits in answer stated the following facts. On 3rd November, 1842, Morton received notice from the town clerk that he was elected councillor; that, in default of his accepting the office and making and subscribing the declaration, within five days after notice, he would be liable to a fine of 50*l*. (3) ; and that attendance would be given at the Court House, on 4th November, by persons duly authorised to administer the declaration. Morton attended accordingly, and accepted office by making and subscribing the declaration; and *he deposed that, at the time of so doing, he believed that he was legally elected. After being served with a copy of the rule *nisi*, he resigned his office, by deed poll, (which was set out on affidavit), to the Mayor, aldermen and burgesses : and the deed was deposited with the town clerk. The mayor, at the request of Morton, had called a meeting for the 18th January, 1843, and Morton, by affidavit dated 11th January, 1843, deposed that he intended to be present at such meeting and there resign his office (4) ; and that he had given notice to the relator of his having resigned as aforesaid, and of such his intention. On 1st November, 1842, the town clerk published by placard a notice that the *Attorney-General* had given his opinion that a party could not vote for a ward after having selected another ward to vote in on a former election, until there was a fresh registration, and that the alderman and assessors ought to reject such vote if tendered : and such opinion had been read at a meeting of the aldermen and assessors on 31st October, 1842, notice thereof having been given to each by a circular.

[*148]

Jervis and *T. F. Ellis* now showed cause :

Morton does not propose to defend his office : and, upon the

(1) See stat. 5 & 6 Will. IV. c. 76, s. 44. See now Municipal Corporations Act, 1882 (45 & 46 Vict. c. 50), ss. 45 (6) and 51. The ground of the objection to the other votes became immaterial. The affidavit also impeached another vote given for Morton.

(2) See now Municipal Corporations Act, 1882 (45 & 46 Vict. c. 50), s. 35. —A. C.

(3) Stat. 5 & 6 Will. IV. c. 76, s. 51. (Municipal Corporations Act, 1882, s. 34.)

(4) See *Rex* v. *The Mayor of Rippon*, 1 Ld. Ray. 563.

facts, it appears that he is free from blame. The resignation does
not of itself discharge the rule, according to *Rex* v. *Warlow* (1):
nor can Morton disclaim *in vacuo*, there being as yet no information : *Rex* v. *Marshall* (2). But the precedent in *Rex* v. *Holt* (3)
may be followed, where a party, appearing to be free from *blame,
was allowed to disclaim without costs.

REG.
v.
MORTON.

[*149]

(LORD DENMAN, Ch. J.: There seems to be some mistake in the
report of that case: unless there was an information, how could
there be any record so as to enable the party to disclaim ?)

The meaning probably was that the information might be filed,
and a disclaimer entered, without costs. That may be done here.
Or, since the object of the relator is already obtained, and the
resignation gets rid of the plenarty, so that Bramley may be
admitted or a *mandamus* may go for his admission, and the
information thus becomes unnecessary, this rule may be discharged without costs. The granting of the information is a
matter in the discretion of the Court. Had notice of this motion
been given to Morton, he would have resigned immediately, and
have rendered all legal proceedings unnecessary.

Sir W. W. Follett, Solicitor-General (with whom was *R. Hall*),
contrà :

The relator has been under the necessity of proceeding, and must
have his costs. The resignation is nugatory if Morton never was a
councillor at all. The information must be exhibited ; and then
the defendant may disclaim : but there is nothing in the case to
prevent the ordinary rule as to costs from being applied.

LORD DENMAN, Ch. J.:

I think the relator must have his costs up to this time ; but, if
an information be necessary, the defendant should be allowed to
disclaim without additional expense. He may undertake so to
do now.

PATTESON and WIGHTMAN, JJ. concurred (4).

[150]

The following rule was afterwards drawn up :

" Ordered, that an information in the nature of a *quo warranto*

(1) 14 R. R. 592 (2 M. & S. 75).   (4) Coleridge, J., was absent, in
(2) 2 Chitt. 370.   consequence of a domestic affliction.
(3) 2 Chitt. 366.

20—2

be exhibited against the said George Morton, to show " &c. (as in
the rule *nisi*), "upon the several grounds mentioned in the rule of
this Court made in this prosecution on the 25th day of November
last; the prosecutor hereby undertaking not to file such information unless legally necessary; and the said defendant hereby
undertaking to pay to the said prosecutor, or his attorney, the
costs of this application within three weeks next ensuing; the
said prosecutor hereby further undertaking, if an information
should be necessary, to file the same at his own expense, and
the said defendant also hereby further undertaking, if required,
to disclaim thereto, at the prosecutor's expense. And it is further
ordered that the costs above mentioned, if necessary, be taxed by
the coroner and attorney of this Court."

IN THE MATTER OF THE CAMBERWELL RENT-CHARGE ALLOTMENT, No. 606.

(4 Q. B. 151—157; S. C. 3 G. & D. 365; 12 L. J. Q. B. 155.)

If the half-yearly payments of a rent-charge on land under the Tithe
Commutation Act, 6 & 7 Will. IV. c. 71, be in arrear and no sufficient distress found, the owner of the rent-charge may recover such arrear for a
period not exceeding two years, by assessment and writ of *habere facias
possessionem* under sect. 82. Although he may not have attempted to levy
the arrear by distress, under sect. 81, at the end of each, or any but the
last, of the half-years; and although at the end of one or more of the
previous half-years there may have been a sufficient distress for the amount
then due.

A RULE was obtained in last Easter Term, calling upon Charles
James Jones, the lessee of the Camberwell rent-charge allotment
606, to show cause why the writ for the assessment of arrears of the
said rent-charge allotment 606, and all proceedings thereon, should
not be set aside for irregularity.

The writ, dated March 23, 1842, and addressed to the sheriff of
Surrey, was issued under sect. 82 of the Tithe Commutation Act,
[*152] 6 & 7 Will. IV. c. 71 (1). It recited an *agreement for commutation

------

(1) Stat. 6 & 7 Will. IV. c. 71, s. 67,
enacts : "That from the first day of
January next following the confirmation of every such apportionment"
(sects. 33, 55, 63, &c.) " the lands of
the said parish shall be absolutely discharged from the payment of all tithes,
except so far as relates to the liability
of any tenant at rack rent dissenting

as hereinafter provided, and instead
thereof there shall be payable thenceforth to the person in that behalf mentioned in the said apportionment a sum
of money equal in value, according to
the prices ascertained by the then
next preceding advertisement, to the
quantity of wheat, barley, and oats
respectively mentioned therein to be

of the vicarial tithes of St. Giles, Camberwell, for a rent-charge, in
pursuance of the Act, and an apportionment by which 1*l*. 15*s*. 9*d*.

payable instead of the said tithes, in the nature of a rent-charge issuing out of the lands charged therewith ; and such yearly sum shall be payable by two equal half-yearly payments on the 1st day of July and the 1st day of January in every year, [the first payment, except in the case of barren reclaimed lands, as hereinafter provided, being on the 1st day of July next after the lands shall have been discharged from tithes as aforesaid,†] and such rent-charge may be recovered at the suit of the person entitled thereto, his executors or administrators, by distress and entry as hereinafter mentioned." " Provided always, that *nothing herein contained shall be taken to render any person whomsoever personally liable to the payment of any such rent-charge."

Sect. 80 enacts that " every tenant or occupier who shall occupy any lands by any lease or agreement made subsequently to such commutation, and who shall pay any such rent-charge, shall be entitled to deduct the amount thereof from the rent payable by him to his landlord, and shall be allowed the same in account with the said landlord."

Sect. 81 enacts : "That in case the said rent-charge shall at any time be in arrear and unpaid for the space of twenty-one days next after any half-yearly day of payment, it shall be lawful for the person entitled to the same, after having given or left ten days' notice in writing at the usual or last known residence of the tenant in possession, to distrain upon the lands liable to the payment thereof, or on any part thereof, for all arrears of the said rent-charge, and to dispose of the distress when taken, and otherwise to act and demean himself in relation thereto as any landlord may for arrears of rent reserved on a common lease for years; provided that not more than

two years' arrears shall at any time be recoverable by distress."

Sect. 82 enacts : "That in case the said rent-charge shall be in arrear and unpaid for the space of forty days next after any half-yearly day of payment, and there shall be no sufficient distress on the premises liable to the payment thereof, it shall be lawful for any Judge of his Majesty's Courts of record at Westminster, upon affidavit of the facts, to order a writ to be issued, directed to the sheriff of the county in which the lands chargeable with the rent-charge are situated, requiring the said sheriff to summon a jury to assess the arrears of rent-charge remaining unpaid, and to return the inquisition thereupon taken to some one of his Majesty's Courts of law at Westminster, on a day therein to be named, either in Term time or vacation ; a copy of which writ, and notice of the time and place of executing the same, shall be given to the owner of the land, or left at his last known place of abode, or with his known agent, ten days previous to the execution thereof; and the sheriff is hereby required to execute such writ according to the exigency thereof; and the costs of such inquisition shall be taxed by the proper officer of the Court; and thereupon the owner of the rent-charge may sue out a writ of *habere facias possessionem*, directed to the sheriff, commanding him to cause the owner of the rent-charge to have possession of the lands chargeable therewith until the arrears of rent-charge found to be due, and the said costs, and also the costs of such writ and of executing the same, and of cultivating and keeping possession of the lands, shall be fully satisfied : provided always, that not more than two years' arrears over and above the time of such possession shall be at any time recoverable."

[*152, *n*.]

---

† Rep. by Statute Law Revision Act, 1890.

per *annum was apportioned as rent-charge payable to the vicar on certain land numbered 606 in the plan annexed to the said apportionment; a demise of the rent-charge by the vicar to Charles James Jones; and that, since the demise and during its continuance, four half-yearly payments of the rent-charge so apportioned on the said land had become due and were in arrear and unpaid to the lessee; "and the same have been in arrear and unpaid for the space of forty days next after the days of payment when the same became due respectively, amounting together to the sum of 3l. 12s. 1d., and there is no sufficient distress for the said half-yearly payments or either of them on the said premises, liable to the payment thereof, as it is said: Therefore we command you that, pursuant to the statute in that case made and provided, and by the oath of twelve good and lawful men of your county " &c., "to be summoned by you for that purpose, you diligently assess the arrears of the amount of the said rent-charge apportioned on the said land and premises numbered " &c., " remaining unpaid, . according to the prices of corn as directed by the said Acts; and that you return the inquisition " &c.

By the affidavits in support of this rule, it appeared that the lessee, on the 4th or 5th of October, 1841, demanded of the tenant, on whose behalf the present rule was obtained, arrears of rent-charge for the last three half-years, when the tenant stated that he had only held the land from the preceding January, and did not think it right to pay the debt of his predecessor; but he offered to pay the rent-charge for the half-year ending in July, 1841. This was refused. The affidavits also contained statements showing that there had been, at all *times from January, 1841, sufficient distress on the premises to answer the whole amount stated in the writ to be due.

The affidavits in opposition denied the offer to pay the half-year's rent-charge; and stated that, on 5th October, 1841, the lessee went to the land for the purpose of distraining for the three half-years' rent-charge, there being then sufficient distress, but forbore to distrain, on the tenant's promise to pay: and that he again went to the land in March, 1842, and then found that the hay and stock had been removed and nothing left for a distress but a roller, the value of which, for sale, was stated to be below 20s. The affidavits on the other side raised the value to 5l.

The irregularity complained of was that the writ used the words " there is no sufficient distress for the said half-yearly payments or either of them," whereas the affidavit on which the writ was granted, after mentioning the arrears of three half-years, stated only that there was no sufficient distress "for the said arrears of rent-charge;" and it was therefore contended that the writ had not issued "upon affidavit of the facts" according to sect. 82. But, the rule not having been obtained on reading this affidavit, the Court thought that the objection (assuming it to be valid in itself) could not be noticed; and it was ultimately given up, the applicant relying only on the want of authority under the statute to issue a writ for arrears of more than a single half-year.

Sir F. *Pollock*, Attorney-General, *Buller* and *Attree*, now showed cause:

This proceeding is warranted by the plain words of sect. 82, which enacts that, "in case the said *rent-charge shall be in arrear and unpaid for the space of forty days next after any half-yearly day of payment, and there shall be no sufficient distress on the premises liable to the payment thereof," the writ of assessment may issue. The limitation imposed by sect. 81 is, "that not more than two years' arrears shall at any time be recoverable by distress." To support the present objection, "two years" must be read as "half a year." It cannot have been meant that the owner of a rent-charge should be obliged to distrain at the end of a single half-year, however small the sum in arrear might be.   [*155]

Sir W. W. *Follett*, Solicitor-General, *contrà*:

The same rule must prevail for small and for great sums. This question now is, not as to the power of distraining, but as to the circumstances under which the owner of a rent-charge may seize the land. That power is given if there be not a sufficient distress. It is consistent with the writ that there may have been a sufficient distress at the end of each successive half-year. Can the owner of a rent-charge voluntarily allow the arrears to accumulate and at last seize because there is not enough on the land to answer the arrear of a year and a half? The language of the writ itself, "no sufficient distress for the said half-yearly payments or either of them," seems to admit that, if there were enough to satisfy one such payment, the proceeding would be unwarranted; and it may fairly be concluded from the affidavits that there would have been sufficient distress for one half-year.

LORD DENMAN, Ch. J. :

This is an important question. The statute, in my opinion,
would be a nuisance if *enforced in the manner contended for in
support of this application ; and I think it is not to be construed
according to the rule suggested. Its meaning is, that the owner of
a rent-charge, if he does not delay his remedy so as to extend it
over more than two years, may recover all the arrears by the process described in sect. 82 : and this though at the end of each
half-year there may have been sufficient distress for the arrear
then payable. This is too clear for doubt ; and the reasonableness
of the construction is obvious. The rule must be discharged.

PATTESON, J. :

The remedy given by this Act for the recovery of rent-charge is
by distress under sect. 81, provided that not more than two years'
arrears shall be so recoverable, and, in default of such distress, by
seizure and possession of the land under sect. 82, provided that
"not more than two years' arrears over and above the time of such
possession shall be at any time recoverable." Why should one
section be construed differently from the other ? There is no
reason to suppose that, although a party might distrain for an
arrear of two years, the Legislature intended that he should
not enforce the remedy under sect. 82 unless he attempted to
distrain at the end of a single half-year, and no distress were
found. The construction of both clauses must be the same. In
the case of proceedings on a vacant possession (1), it never was
contended that, if the landlord omitted to enforce his remedy at
the end of a first year, he could not avail himself of it afterwards.

[157]   WIGHTMAN, J. (2) :

Sects. 81 and 82 must receive the same construction ; and
cases of hardship are provided for by the clauses limiting the
recovery to two years' arrears.

Rule discharged.

(1) Stat. 11 Geo. II. c, 19, s. 16.   (2) Coleridge, J. was absent in consequence of a domestic affliction.

REG. *v.* ABRAHAMS AND OTHERS.

(4 Q. B. 157—161; S. C. 3 G. & D. 382; 12 L. J. Q. B. 118; 7 Jur. 129.)

1843.
Jan. 30.

[157]

An individual conveyed lands to private persons in trust to distribute the rents periodically among the poor of a certain parish. The deed provided that a receiver should be appointed, and should account to the parishioners from time to time; and that a coffer, of which there should be three locks and three keys, should remain in the parish church, for keeping all writings and accounts, and trust monies unexpended; one key to be kept by the receiver, another by the incumbent or curate, and the third by one of the churchwardens. An information was afterwards exhibited in Chancery, praying that a scheme might be approved of for the future management of the charity and application of the funds; and a scheme was accordingly prepared and decreed, regulating the matters referred to in the above prayer, but making no mention of the coffer or keys. On motion for a *mandamus* to the trustees to deliver one key to the churchwardens:

Held, that the claim of the churchwardens was not merely equitable, but that they had a legal right which might be enforced by *mandamus*. Also,

Held, no objection to the rule that the charity was a private institution.

HENRY BEAUMONT, by his will, dated March 17th, 1590, directed that 800*l.* should be employed in the purchase of land, of which land he gave to the poor of Ottery St. Mary, Devon, 5*l.* a year for ever, and made his wife Elizabeth executrix. The said Elizabeth, "in performance of the said will, and for the special trust and confidence which she reposed in the twelve persons therein named, then inhabitants of the town and parish of O. St. M., that they and their heirs and assigns would be faithful in disposing of the rents for the relief and succour of the aged and impotent poor people which then were and thereafter should be inhabiting in the said town and parish, by her deed indented, bearing date 1st June, 36 Eliz., granted and enfeoffed *unto* " twelve trustees and their heirs certain lands and tenements, " upon trust to apply the rents thereof, first in defending all titles and claims that should be made to the same by any person whomsoever, and to distribute the residue of the said rents yearly, quarterly, monthly or weekly for ever, as need should require, amongst the most aged, impotent and poor people inhabiting within the said parish of O. St. M., in such manner as the said trustees should think most convenient." There was a provision for appointing new trustees when it should be necessary, and a receiver of the rents, to be elected for the year, who was to render his account to the parishioners at a stated time. " And it was provided that a coffer, of which there should be three locks and three keys, should remain in the parish church of Ottery for keeping all writings and accounts, and the trust moneys remaining unexpended; one of such keys to be kept by the receiver during

[*158]

REG.
v.
ABRAHAMS.

his year, the second by the parson, vicar, or curate there, and the third by one of the churchwardens."

A rule *nisi* was obtained in last Michaelmas Term, calling upon the then feoffees to show cause why they should not deliver up one of the said keys to the churchwardens. The affidavit on which the rule was moved for alleged the making of the above will and deed, and set forth the material parts ; and stated further that the churchwardens had demanded the key of the feoffees, who refused it, saying that they did not feel justified in giving one to any person not a member of the trust.

The affidavits in answer stated that an information had been filed in Chancery against the feoffees, praying that it might be referred to one of the Masters to approve of a scheme for the future

[*159]

regulation and management *of the said charity, and application of the charity moneys; and that such further and other orders and directions might be given for the conduct and management of the said charity, and in respect of the other matters and things in the information before stated, as the nature of the case might require. It was further deposed that the Master, in 1829, reported to the Court his approval of a scheme; and the Court, in 1830, decreed that the charities in question in the cause ought to be established and regulated, and the accruing and other rents distributed, according to that scheme ; which had since been done. The scheme was annexed to the affidavits : it contained various directions for the management of the affairs and distribution of the revenues by the trustees and the receiver to be elected by them, who was to give security &c., and account to the trustees yearly. The scheme made no mention of the coffer or keys, or of the churchwardens, and contained nothing that had any direct reference to the subject of the present application.

Bompas, Serjt. and *Kelly* now showed cause :

This is an application to compel the execution of a private trust, a matter peculiarly for the Court of Chancery, and which that Court has regulated by a scheme, taking no notice of the point now insisted upon. The effect of the proposed *mandamus* would be to overthrow that arrangement. It is not shown that at present any key or chest exists ; the substantial object of this rule is that a chest may be kept in which money and documents shall be deposited, and that the churchwardens may have access to these. The Court will not interfere for such a purpose.

(LORD DENMAN, Ch. J. : Only two years ago we ordered a   REG.
mandamus to the master of *the Earl of Leicester's Hospital in   *v.*
Warwick to seal an instrument of presentation (1).   That was the   ABRAHAMS.
case of a private charity.)   [*160]

The right there was a right at law.

(LORD DENMAN, Ch. J. : A *mandamus* lies to restore the minister of
an endowed dissenting chapel ; yet the foundation there is private.)

That right is of a legal character. In *Rex* v. *The Marquis of
Stafford* (2), where the application was for a *mandamus* to allow
and present a person to the Ordinary to be stipendiary priest or
curate of an endowed chapel, in order that he might obtain the
Ordinary's license, he having been elected by the inhabitants of a
town in whom that power was vested, Lord KENYON said : " It
seems as if the inhabitants have only an equitable right. If so,
this Court cannot interfere at all ; or if the inhabitants have a legal
right, such right may be asserted in a *quare impedit*." BULLER, J.
added : "It appears to me on these affidavits that this is a trust,
and therefore that the remedy is in a court of equity. A party
applying for a *mandamus* must make out a legal right." Lord
ELLENBOROUGH lays down the same rule in *Rex* v. *The Archbishop
of Canterbury* (3). Here keeping the chest and keys is one of the
trusts of the deed, and not to be enforced in this manner. It is
not sworn that any chest or key has ever been provided. If a key
exists, detinue may be brought for it.

   Rogers, contrà :

   This is so far a private institution, that the funds are provided
by an individual. But duties connected with the administration
of such charities have been enforced by *mandamus* in many
instances ; *as in those, already cited, of dissenting ministers,   [*161]
and in the cases of lecturers, and persons holding offices in colleges.
As to the claim being equitable, the only real cestui que trusts here
are the poor. In the proceedings in Chancery the churchwardens
were not before the Court ; nor had they any equitable rights to
enforce. The suit was on behalf of the inhabitants, and regarded
the entire management and application of the funds. If the
present motion was as general in its objects, the argument against
it might be well founded.

(1) 55 R. R. 275 (*Reg.* v. *Kendall*, 1   (2) 3 T. R. 646.
Q. B. 366).   (3) 8 East, 213.

LORD DENMAN, Ch. J. :

I think the claim of the churchwarden to have a key, as being one of the parties named in the deed for that purpose, is a legal right. It is independent of the general administration of the funds. The Court does not interfere in the case of dissenting ministers, and in other instances where the establishments are private. It is true that, in *Ex parte the Trustees of the Rugby Charity* (1), a *mandamus* to pay certain persons an increased allowance was refused ; but that would clearly have been an interference with the administration of the funds. We need not hear you farther on this point. But we wish to be satisfied whether or not the late churchwardens had a key.

After some further discussion on the affidavits,

The COURT (2) granted a

Rule absolute.

WILLIAM YATES *v.* WILLIAM ASTON.

(4 Q. B. 182—196; S. C. 3 G. & D. 351 ; 12 L. J. Q. B. 160.)

Defendant borrowed money of B., and conveyed land in trust for him, with a power of sale, in trust to pay him principal and interest, and pay over the residue to defendant ; defendant afterwards borrowed other money of B., and charged that also on the land, but without any power of sale. Afterwards, plaintiff paying both sums to B. and advancing an additional sum to defendant, by deed between plaintiff, defendant, B., and B.'s trustee, the former securities were assigned to plaintiff (B. giving plaintiff a power of attorney to sue in his name as to the first sum borrowed), and the lands were conveyed to plaintiff, to hold them to the same trusts, but for his own benefit, as were mentioned in the other deeds with respect to B. None of the deeds contained a covenant to pay.

Plaintiff sued defendant in debt, payable on demand, for money paid, money lent, interest, and on an account stated. Held, that he was entitled to recover the whole sum, on proof that he had paid it as above : and that he was not bound to declare on the deed.

ON the trial of this cause, before Wightman, J., at the Middlesex sittings after Michaelmas Term, 1841, a verdict was found for the plaintiff for 1,952*l.* and costs, subject to the opinion of this Court upon the following case.

The declaration contained the ordinary *indebitatus* counts in debt, payable on request, for money paid, money lent, interest,

(1) 9 Dowl. & Ry. 214.
(2) Lord DENMAN, Ch. J., and WIGHTMAN, J. PATTESON and COLE-

RIDGE, JJ. took no part in the decision, being interested in the result.

and on an account stated. The only plea material to the present statement was Never indebted. The action was brought to recover the sum of 1,500*l.*, and interest thereon, hereinafter mentioned to have been advanced by the plaintiff.

By deeds of lease and release, dated 11th and 12th September, 1829, certain premises were conveyed by the defendant and his brother Thomas Aston, since deceased, to one John Blagg, by way of mortgage to secure a sum of 1,000*l.*, lent by Blagg. That sum was subsequently increased to 1,200*l.*: and, by a deed of assignment dated 3rd October, 1829, the property was further charged to that amount. In January, 1833, the defendant and Thomas Aston were called upon by Blagg to pay off the principal and interest then due: but they, being unable to do so, and being desirous of obtaining a further loan, *applied to Yates, the plaintiff, to advance [*183] and pay the same to Blagg, and to lend them a further sum of 300*l.* Yates accordingly agreed to advance 1,500*l.*, upon the security of, and comprised in, the deed hereinafter mentioned: and his then solicitor received directions from the defendant in what manner that sum was to be applied. In conformity therewith, the solicitor, on a subsequent day, being the day after that upon which the deed last mentioned was executed, paid over 1,394*l.* to Blagg, as and for principal and interest then due, and for certain costs due to Blagg's solicitor: 43*l.* was retained as his own costs in and about effecting the loan; and the residue was paid over to the solicitor of the defendant, on defendant's account. This took place on 15th January, 1833.

A copy of the deed last mentioned was annexed to the case; and, so far as material to the point here decided, was as follows:

The indenture was made, 14th January, 1833, between John Blagg of the first part, Robert Fisher (a trustee nominated by John Blagg) of the second part, William Aston and Mary his wife of the third part, Thomas Aston of the fourth part, and William Yates of the fifth part. It recited indentures of lease and release, of 11th and 12th September, 1829, between William Aston and Mary his wife, of the first part, Thomas Aston of the second part, John Blagg of the third part, Robert Fisher of the fourth part, and James Griffiths of the fifth part, whereby (after recital of certain interests of William and Thomas Aston in the premises after described), in consideration of 1,000*l.* advanced by Blagg to W. Aston and T. Aston, and 10*s.* paid by Fisher, W. Aston and Mary his wife, and T. Aston, at the request *and by the direction of Blagg, did, [*184]

according to their respective estates and interests, convey the
messuages, lands, &c., therein particularly described unto and to
the use of Robert Fisher, his heirs and assigns (but, as to parts of
the property, during the lives respectively of W. Aston and T. Aston),
on the trusts thereinafter mentioned. · The trusts of the recited deed
were, that W. and T. Aston should possess and enjoy the premises
till 12th March, 1888, according to their respective interests, and
then that Fisher might sell, and, out of the purchase money, pay
Blagg the principal and interest of the 1,000l., and pay the residue
of the purchase money to W. Aston and T. Aston, according to their
respective interests. The indenture of 14th January, 1833, further
recited that no sale had taken place, and that the 1,000l., and 200l.
more for money lent by Blagg to W. Aston and T. Aston and
secured with interest by the indenture after mentioned, was due to
Blagg, and that W. Aston and T. Aston had "requested and
prevailed upon" Yates (plaintiff) "to advance and pay the same,
which he hath agreed to do, and also to lend them the further sum
of 300l. upon the security of the aforesaid hereditaments and
premises." The indenture then witnessed that, in pursuance of the
agreement, and in consideration of 1,200l., of lawful &c., "to the
said John Blagg in hand well and truly paid at or before the sealing
and delivery of these presents by the said William Yates, at the
request and by the direction of the said William Aston and Thomas
Aston, testified by their being parties hereto (the receipt of which
said sum of 1,200l., and that the same is in full discharge and
satisfaction of the said principal sum of 1,000l. and all arrears of
interest thereof, and the said principal sum of 200l. and interest,
[*185] and *all other monies owing to him on the said recited securities,
the said John Blagg doth hereby acknowledge, and of and from the
same doth acquit, release, exonerate and for ever discharge the said
William Yates, his executors, administrators and assigns, and also
the said messuages, lands and hereditaments, by these presents and
by the receipt or acknowledgment for the same sum, hereupon
endorsed), he the said John Blagg, at the request, nomination and
appointment of the said William Aston and Thomas Aston, testified
as aforesaid, hath bargained, sold, assigned, transferred and set
over, and by these presents doth bargain, sell, assign, transfer and
set over, and the said William Aston and Thomas Aston have
assigned, ratified and confirmed, and by these presents do assign,
ratify and confirm, unto the said William Yates, his executors,
administrators and assigns, all that the said mortgage debt or

principal sum of 1,000*l.*, so due and owing upon the said hereinbefore in part recited security, and all interest and arrears of interest, and all and every other sum and sums of money which now is, or are, or hereafter shall or may grow or become, due and owing for or in respect of the same; and also the said hereinbefore in part recited indenture of release, and the bargain and sale for a year accompanying the same, and all other deeds, securities, writings and evidences of title whatsoever, of or belonging to or in the custody or power of him the said John Blagg relative thereto, or to the said hereditaments, or any part of the same, respectively; and all benefit and advantage to arise or be had, received and taken by or from the same respectively; and all the estate, right, title, interest, use, trust, property, benefit, claim and demand whatsoever, both at law and *in equity, of him the said John Blagg, of, in, to or concerning the said mortgage debt, or principal sum and interest, and securities and premises hereby assigned, or mentioned, or intended so to be, and every of them respectively : to have, hold, receive, take and enjoy the said mortgage debt or principal sum of 1,000*l.* and interest, and all and singular other the moneys, securities and premises hereinbefore assigned, or otherwise assured or intended so to be, unto him the said William Yates, his executors, administrators and assigns, from henceforth for ever, as and for his and their own proper moneys and effects, and to and for his and their own use and benefit." There was then a power of attorney from Blagg to Yates, his executors, &c., empowering him and them to demand, recover, &c., from W. Aston and T. Aston, their heirs, executors, &c., and all persons to whom it might belong to pay the same, the 1,000*l.*, and all interest now or hereafter due, to give receipts and discharges, and to prosecute actions and suits in the name of Blagg, his executors, &c.   And Fisher, by the direction of Blagg, did grant, bargain, sell and release, " and also, in consideration of the further sum of 300*l.* of such lawful money as hereinbefore mentioned in hand well and truly paid to the said William Aston and Thomas Aston by the said William Yates, at or before the execution of these presents (the receipt whereof, and the payment by him the said William Yates of the said sum of 1,200*l.* to the said John Blagg, making together the sum of 1,500*l.*, the said William Aston and Thomas Aston do, and each of them doth, hereby acknowledge, and of and from the same, and every part thereof, do, and each of them doth, acquit, release and discharge the said William *Yates, his executors, administrators and assigns, and also

[*186]

[*187]

YATES
v.
ASTON.

and T. Aston, "hath bargained, sold, assigned, transferred and set over, and by these presents doth bargain," &c., "unto the said William Yates, his executors, administrators and assigns, all and singular the said hereinbefore and in the said hereinbefore in part recited indenture of assignment mentioned rents and profits, to arise by and from all and singular the hereinbefore mentioned and described messuages," &c., "and from henceforth to become due and payable; and also all the said surplus money which shall or may arise and remain by and from the sale of the aforesaid hereditaments and premises so vested in the said Robert Fisher, his executors, administrators and assigns in trust to sell as hereinbefore recited and expressed, after payment of all costs attending the execution of such trusts as aforesaid, and of the said sum of 1,000l. and the interest thereof, as by the said trust is provided, and all the estate, right, title and interest of the said John Blagg and Robert Fisher therein and thereto: To have and to hold the said rents and profits, and all the said surplus money hereinbefore mentioned, and hereby, or intended to be hereby, assigned, unto the said William Yates, his executors, administrators and assigns, from henceforth, upon the same trusts, and to and for the like ends, intents and purposes, but to and for the sole use and benefit of the said William Yates, his executors, administrators and assigns, as in the said recited indenture of assignment is mentioned in respect of the said John Blagg." Then followed a covenant on the part of Blagg and Fisher, their heirs, executors and administrators, with Yates, his heirs, executors, administrators and assigns, against incumbrances by Blagg *or Fisher on the rents or profits, or surplus monies, to arise from the premises so vested in Fisher.

[*191]

On the indenture were receipts, by Blagg of the 1,200l. and by W. Aston and T. Aston of the 300l., from Yates, "being the consideration money within mentioned to be paid by him" to the parties respectively signing the two receipts.

The question for the opinion of the Court was stated to be:

Whether, under the circumstances, an action of debt in the present form (1) is maintainable between these parties for any part of the said demand for which the action is brought. If the Court should be of opinion that the plaintiff is entitled to maintain this action in its present form for the whole or any part of his demand,

---

(1) It will be observed that the question was really one of substance: owing to the form of the deed the plaintiff could not have declared in covenant.—A. C.

the verdict is to stand, or be entered, accordingly. If the Court shall be of opinion that the plaintiff is not entitled to maintain the action at all, or in part, the verdict is to be entered for the defendant for the whole, or in part, as the case may be.

The case was argued in last Michaelmas Term (1).

Whitmore, for the plaintiffs :

The defendant denies that he is indebted to the plaintiff at all, or that it is a debt of the kind described in the declaration. Now, first, there plainly was a debt; or there had been a direct loan from plaintiff to defendant, besides the payment made by plaintiff for defendant. There is no covenant to pay the debt, in this deed : but a mortgage, though without covenant or bond to pay, implies a loan ; *and every loan implies a debt : *King* v. *King* (2), which is conformable to the earlier case of *Howel* v. *Price* (3), and to *Cope* v. *Cope* (4). It is true that the parties may, by a special agreement, limit or waive the ordinary remedy for debt, as was done in *The South Sea Company* v. *Duncomb* (5) ; but that case shows that such waiver must be express and distinct; and nothing of the sort appears here. The fact of the advances is found by the case ; and the recitals in the deed treat the transaction as a payment by the plaintiff for the defendant, and a loan by the one to the other. Then, secondly, the remedy is not merged in the specialty. *Atty* v. *Parish* (6) will be cited on the other side. But there the action was for the carriage of goods, and the whole contract was created by the charter-party, which was a deed : the deed was therefore the foundation of the action ; and it was properly held that the plaintiff could not declare in debt generally and give the deed in evidence. The principle upon which a simple contract is merged in a higher security is that a higher remedy is created ; but that principle does not apply where, as the case is here, the specialty gives no remedy at all. The rule is expressed differently in different authorities, but will be found reducible to the principle now stated. The rule laid down by BAYLEY, J. in *Twopenny* v. *Young* (7) is that, "in general, where a simple contract security for a debt is given, it is extinguished by a specialty security, if the remedy given by the latter is co-extensive with that which the creditor had upon the

[*192]

(1) November 15th, 1842. Before Lord Denman, Ch. J., Williams, Coleridge and Wightman, JJ.
(2) 3 P. Wms. 358.
(3) 1 P. Wms. 291.
(4) 2 Salk. 449.
(5) 2 Str. 919.
(6) 1 Bos. & P. N. R. 104.
(7) 3 B. & C. 208.

former." In *Allenby* v. *Dalton* (1), a case which occurred *in 1827, it was considered that assumpsit was maintainable for money lent, though a mortgage had been given for it.

S. Martin, contrà :

The contract is the deed : whenever parties embody the transaction between them in a deed, that deed is not collateral to the contract, but is the contract itself. The action must then be on the deed. The cases on this point are collected in 2 Stark. Ev. 104, note (*n*) (2). But, on this deed, no action at all arises : there is no covenant to pay ; and the parties themselves clearly contemplate only actions to be brought by Yates in the name of Blagg.

(WIGHTMAN, J. : That seems to be so only as to the 1,000*l*.)

The real remedy reserved is the power of sale.   In *Howel* v. *Price* (3) the question was merely between the heir and personal representatives ; and it is said that the "LORD CHANCELLOR seemed to be strongly of opinion, that the personal estate should be applied in ease and exoneration of the real estate."   At an earlier stage of the same case, *Howel* v. *Price* (4), Lord Chancellor HARCOURT decided against the heir.   *King* v. *King* (5) was a case of the same kind : it is not there suggested that there was a remedy by an action at law on the simple contract.   An equitable remedy was allowed by Lord Chancellor HARCOURT, in *Thomas* v. *Terry* (6), to a mortgagee against the mortgagor's executors where there was no covenant upon which the mortgagee could sue : but that affords a presumption against the existence of any legal remedy.   In a similar case, *Hodges* v.

[*194]   *The Croydon Canal Company* (7), *Lord LANGDALE, M. R. evidently assumes the absence of any legal remedy.   *Cope* v. *Cope* (8) was also a case in equity.   In *The South Sea Company* v. *Duncomb* (9) the jury expressly affirmed the existence of an agreement to discharge the person of the defendant; here that is the question for the Court.   If, however, there be any right of action, it must be one on the special contract.   The defendant was entitled to *profert* and *oyer*.   *Atty* v. *Parish* (10) cannot be distinguished from this case:

(1) 5 L. J. (O. S.), K. B. 312.
(2) Ed. 3.   And see vol. iii. Appendix, pp. 133, 139.
(3) 1 P. Wms. 291.
(4) 2 Vern. 701.
(5) 3 P. Wms. 358.

(6) Gilb. Rep. Eq. 110.
(7) 52 R. R. 44 (3 Beav. 86).
(8) 2 Salk. 449.
(9) 2 Str. 919.
(10) 1 Bos. & P. N. R. 104.

there the deed proved that there was a debt between the parties, as much as the deed does here.   *   *   *

Whitmore, in reply :

195

The defendant must show that the deed dispossesses the plaintiff of his remedy ; which it can do only by giving another co-extensive. In all the cases cited on the other side there was such a remedy given.   The earlier decision of *Howel* v. *Price* (1) cannot prevail against the later (2).   *Atty* v. *Parish* (3) is inapplicable for the reason already stated : but, if it were necessary to impugn that case, it might be argued that it must be at least received with much qualification since *Tilson* v. *The Warwick Gas Light Company* (4).

(COLERIDGE, J. : May there not be a distinction between the 1,200*l.* and the 300*l.* ?   As to the 300*l.*, there is a direct loan, a mortgage with power of sale, and no covenant for payment. Cannot we infer from this that the security was meant to be only collateral, and that there was a distinct contract to pay ?)

That is the necessary inference, where the accompanying security gives no remedy by action for the money : and the present security gives no such remedy for any part of the advance, in which respect, the transaction resembles that in *Bristoe* v. *Knipe* (5).

Cur. adv. vult.

LORD DENMAN, Ch. J., in this Term (January 17th), delivered the judgment of the COURT :

We are of opinion that the plaintiff is entitled to judgment, and that the verdict ought to stand.

196

The case states that the plaintiff, at the request of the defendant and another, agreed to pay the sum of 1,200*l.* to Blagg, and to lend them the further sum of 300*l.*   The plaintiff accordingly advanced 1,500*l.* upon the security of a mortgage, which contained no covenant for payment of the money advanced by the plaintiff, but merely gave the plaintiff the security of the mortgaged premises. And it was contended, on the part of the defendant, that, because the plaintiff had taken as a security a conveyance of premises by a mortgage deed, an action of debt or assumpsit on an *indebitatus* for

(1) 2 Vern. 701.

(2) *Howel* v. *Price*, 1 P. Wms. 291.

(3) 1 Bos. & P. N. R. 104.

(4) 28 R. R. 529 (4 B. & C. 962, 968).

(5) Yelv. 206.   *S. C.*, as *Briscoe* v. *King*, Cro. Jac. 281.

YATES
v.
ASTON.

money lent or paid could not be supported, the only contract being, as it was said, by the deed.

We think that the advance, being made at the request of the defendant, raised a contract by parol for the repayment, which was not merged in a security of a higher nature. The mortgage does not appear to have been taken in satisfaction, but as a security collateral to the contract raised by the request and the advance in consequence. There was no covenant in the mortgage deed, either express or implied, upon which an action for the money advanced could be maintained : and the case appears to fall within the principle of the decision in *Burnett* v. *Lynch* (1), and the distinction taken in *Baber* v. *Harris* (2) between cases where an action may be supported on the deed for the same cause and where it may not.

Judgment for the plaintiff.

1842.
Nov. 15.
1843.
Jan. 20.

[197]

EDMUND THOMAS FOLEY *v.* ADDENBROOKE
AND OTHERS, EXECUTORS OF ADDENBROOKE.
(4 Q. B. 197—208; S. C. 3 G. & D. 64; 12 L. J. Q. B. 163.)

Declaration, in covenant at the suit of E., stated that F. and W. demised lands and iron mines of one undivided moiety of which F. was seised in fee, to defendant for a term of years, defendant covenanting with F. and W., and their heirs, executors, &c., to erect and work furnaces, to repair the premises, and work the mines; and that F. died, and plaintiff was F.'s heir : and breaches of the covenants were assigned, committed since F.'s death. Plea, that W. survived F.

Held, on demurrer, that the action, brought by E. without W., could not be maintained.

COVENANT. The plaintiff "complains of Edward Addenbrooke Addenbrooke, John Addenbrooke Addenbrooke and Henry Addenbrooke, executors of the last will and testament of John Addenbrooke Addenbrooke deceased, and the defendants in this suit, who have been summoned " &c. The declaration stated that, before and at the time of making the indenture after mentioned, one Edward Foley and Eliza Maria Foley, his wife, were seised in their demesne as of fee, in right of the said E. M. Foley, of and in one undivided moiety, the whole into two equal moieties to be divided, of and in the lands, tenements, mines and veins of ironstone and hereditaments, with the appurtenances, after mentioned to have

(1) 29 R. R. 343 (5 B. & C. 589).
(2) 9 Ad. & El. 532. [The only question in this case was as to whether

the form of action was covenant or assumpsit.—A. C.]

been demised : and, being so seised, heretofore, in the respective
lifetimes of the said E. Foley and E. M. Foley, and J. A. Addenbrooke, deceased, to wit on 8th January, 1799, by indenture then
made between Edward Foley and E. M. Foley, and one Mary
Whitby, of the one part, and the said J. A. Addenbrooke, deceased,
of the other part, (*profert*, the date being the day and year aforesaid), it was witnessed that E. Foley and E. M. Foley and
M. Whitby did demise, lease, set, and to farm let, direct and
appoint, unto J. A. Addenbrooke, deceased, his executors, administrators and assigns, certain closes therein mentioned, together with
certain powers, licences, &c., therein also mentioned, and, amongst
others, licence to J. A. Addenbrooke, deceased, his executors, &c.,
during *the continuance of the demise, to have the use of certain   [*198]
land for coking coals, burning stone, making sawpits for timber,
laying spoil, rubbish or cinders, or otherwise for the use and
accommodation of the intended iron works to be erected in
pursuance of the indenture, making reasonable satisfaction, &c.,
to E. Foley, E. M. Foley and M. Whitby, and the heirs and
assigns of E. M. Foley and M. Whitby, respectively, for such
damage as should be occasioned to certain pieces of land in the
indenture mentioned, and not thereby hindering E. Foley, E. M.
Foley and M. Whitby, and the heirs and assigns of E. M. Foley and
M. Whitby, respectively, from erecting any engine or machine on
the pieces of land last mentioned, or sinking any pits therein for
raising coals and fire clay, or making roads, &c., or doing any
act necessary for getting and raising coal and fire clay out of
the same lands : *habendum* to J. A. Addenbrooke, deceased, his
executors, administrators and assigns, for forty-two years from 25th
December then next.   And the said J. A. Addenbrooke, deceased,
did, by the said indenture, for himself, his heirs, executors and
administrators, covenant, promise and agree to and with E. Foley
and E. M. Foley and M. Whitby, and the heirs and assigns of
E. M. Foley and M. Whitby respectively, that he, J. A. Addenbrooke, deceased, his executors, &c., would in one year erect on one
of the pieces of land demised a furnace or iron work and fire engine
for making and smelting iron, with other buildings requisite for
carrying on the iron trade, and such dwelling houses as should be
necessary for workmen; and that, if it should appear that a
sufficient quantity of ironstone could be got and raised by J. A.
Addenbrooke, deceased, his executors, &c., out of the lands to
supply a second *furnace during the continuance of the demise,   [*199]

then J. A. Addenbrooke, deceased, his executors, &c., within ten years should erect and build a second furnace, &c., for making and smelting iron ; and would, during the term, carry on and effectually work the said furnace and iron works and second furnace, as the case might be, without intermission, &c., save and except only for such times as there should be a necessity for stopping for repairs, accident or want of necessary materials, or in case the ironstone to be got was insufficient to supply the furnaces or iron works, or would not make good pig iron: and also that J. A. Addenbrooke, deceased, his executors, &c., would, during the demise, repair, &c., scour, &c., and keep in good, sufficient and tenantable order and repair all the gates, rails, stiles, hedges, ditches, mounds and fences, of and belonging to the said thereby demised lands and premises, and the furnace and furnaces, fire engine, ironworks, dwelling houses, and other erections and buildings to be erected and built by the said J. A. Addenbrooke, deceased, his executors, administrators or assigns, on the said demised lands (being allowed clay for bricks, &c.), and, at the expiration of the lease, leave, yield up, &c., the furnace, &c., and all other erections (except iron work castings and moveable implements), so repaired, &c., into the hands and quiet possession of E. Foley, E. M. Foley, and M. Whitby, and the heirs and assigns of E. M. Foley and M. Whitby, respectively. And it was by the indenture further witnessed that E. Foley, E. M. Foley, and M. Whitby did demise, lease, &c., to J. A. Addenbrooke, deceased, his executors, &c., all the mines and veins of ironstone in the indenture described, with certain liberties in the indenture specified, and, among *others, the liberty for J. A. Addenbrooke, deceased, his executors, &c., during the demise, to raise, get and work the mines of ironstone ; *habendum* to J. A. Addenbrooke, deceased, his executors, &c., for forty-two years, to commence from 25th December then next: and J. A. Addenbrooke, deceased, did, for himself, his heirs, executors and administrators, further covenant, promise and agree to and with E. Foley, E. M. Foley and M. Whitby, and the heirs and assigns of E. M. Foley and M. Whitby, respectively, that he, his executors, &c., would at all times during the demise work the said mines of ironstone under the lands in a proper and workmanlike manner (as to which details were set forth).

[*200]

The declaration then stated that J. A. Addenbrooke, deceased, to wit on 25th December, 1799, entered upon the demised premises, and became possessed, and continued so until his death, to wit till 19th November, 1835, when defendants, as executors, entered and became possessed, and continued so until the demise expired, to wit till 25th December, 1841: that, during the term, to wit on 1st January, 1805, E. Foley and E. M. Foley died seised of the reversion of their said one undivided moiety, whereby the said reversion of the said undivided moiety descended to plaintiff, then being son and heir of E. Foley. And that J. A. Addenbrooke, deceased, erected two furnaces. The breaches assigned were: 1. That, after the deaths of E. Foley and E. M. Foley, to wit on 1st January, 1834, and on divers days between that day and the expiration of the lease, the furnaces were not carried on and effectually worked (negativing the exceptions). 2. That J. A. Addenbrooke, deceased, his executors, &c., (though they had been allowed clay &c.) *did not at all times after the death of E. Foley and E. M. Foley well and sufficiently repair &c., nor leave and yield up in repair &c., but on the contrary thereof &c. (giving details of waste). 3. That, after the deaths of E. Foley and E. M. Foley, to wit on 1st January, 1834, J. A. Addenbrooke, deceased, in his life time, did not, nor after his death did the defendants, executors as aforesaid, work the mines of ironstone in a proper and workmanlike manner.

Plea 6. That the several causes of action in the declaration mentioned did not accrue to plaintiff after the premises came to defendants, in manner and form &c.: conclusion to the country. Special demurrer. Joinder in demurrer.

Plea 7. That heretofore, to wit 22nd June, 1803, E. Foley died, leaving E. M. Foley, his wife, and M. Whitby, him surviving; after whose death, to wit on 9th July, 1805, E. M. Foley died, leaving M. Whitby surviving: verification. Special demurrer, assigning for cause that the plea is uncertain, inasmuch as it does not appear whether the defendants rely on the action having survived to the said M. Whitby alone, or that the said M. Whitby or her representative ought to be joined as co-plaintiff in the action; also that it does not appear on the pleadings that any right of action in the declaration mentioned was vested in the said M. Whitby, or could have survived to her. Joinder in demurrer.

There were also demurrers to the 8th, 9th, 10th, and 11th pleas; on which severally the plaintiff joined in demurrer (1).

The case was argued in last Michaelmas Term (2).

---

(1) The decision of the Court having proceeded exclusively on the seventh plea, no report of the argument on the other pleas is given.

(2) November 15th, 1842. Before Lord Denman, Ch. J., Williams, Coleridge and Wightman, JJ.

R. V. Richards, for the plaintiff :

The seventh plea raises the question, whether Mary Whitby, having joined with the ancestor of the plaintiff in this demise, and being a joint covenantee, should necessarily have been joined in this action. M. Whitby can be only tenant in common with the plaintiff ; the interests of tenants in common are several ; and they may sue severally upon a covenant made with all. If the cause of action be joint, no doubt all the covenantees must join, even if the covenant be joint and several in its terms : *Eccleston* v. *Clipsham* (1). Now tenants in common have no privity in title ; they have only privity in possession. Hence they may avow separately, though they should join in a personal action for rent : Littleton, ss. 316, 317 ; Lord KENYON in *Harrison* v. *Barnby* (2). On a similar principle, where the duty is no longer to two jointly, there can be no joint action : thus, where two make a man their factor, and one of the two dies, the survivor must sue the factor alone, and cannot join the executor of the deceased, "for the remedy survives, but not the duty : " *Martin* v. *Crompe* (3). In *Wilkinson* v. *Hall* (4) TINDAL, Ch. J. said : " parties cannot join in an action for damages, unless the damages when recovered would accrue to them jointly." In *Kitchen* v. *Buckly* (5) it was certainly held that tenants in common may join in *an action for breach of a covenant to repair ; but it does not follow that they are bound to do so.

[*203]

Ogle, contrà :

What the interest of Mary Whitby is or was does not appear on the record : she may possibly have been joined only as a trustee. But, even if she had no beneficial interest, she ought to have been made a plaintiff. Either of two joint covenantees has a legal interest, though the covenant be exclusively for the benefit of the other covenantee : *Anderson* v. *Martindale* (6). There a covenant was made with two, for the benefit of one ; and it was held that, on the death of the party beneficially interested, his executor had no right of action, but the remedy survived entirely to the surviving covenantee. The same principle is illustrated by the cases of *Rolls* v. *Yate* (7) and *Southcote* v. *Hoare* (8). It is true

---

(1) 1 Saund. 153.

(2) 2 R. R. 584 (5 T. R. 246, 249).

(3) 2 Salk. 444. *S. C.*, more fully, 1 Ld. Ray. 340.

(4) 43 R. R. 728 (1 Bing. N. C. 713, 718).

(5) 1 Lev. 109. *S. C.* Sir T. Raym. 80 ; *S. C.* as *Kitchin* v. *Compton*, Sid. 157.

(6) 6 R. R. 334 (1 East, 497).

(7) Yelv. 177.

(8) 12 R. R. 600 (3 Taunt. 87).

that, where the interest is several, the covenant, though joint in its
terms, may be taken as several : *James* v. *Emery* (1).   But here the
interest is joint, because the covenant is for the performance of
works on a property the possession of which is joint.   The duty is
entire.   The case is not like that of an avowry for rent.   To what
amount could each party, suing separately, recover damages for
the breaches of the duty ?   The rule is thus stated in Walford's
Treatise on the Law respecting Parties to Actions, vol. i., p. 423.
" Tenants in common, then, where they conclude any contract
relative to their tenements, are entitled to sue thereon jointly or
severally, according as the contract contemplates the performance
of one entire duty to all, or of several duties to each of the
covenantees. Thus, *if tenants in common make a joint lease,
reserving an entire rent, they shall join in an action brought to
recover the same ; but if there be a separate reservation to each,
or the demises are altogether separate, there must be several
actions of debt for the rent.   This same rule applies equally to
any other contract concluded with tenants in common, relative
to the subject-matter of the tenancy."   *Powis* v. *Smith* (2) and
Wilkinson v. *Hall* (3) are cited as instances of the rule.

(COLERIDGE, J. : Then you maintain that Mary Whitby should
have sued alone, in this case, as survivor.)

That would have been the proper course.

(COLERIDGE, J. : Ought she to have recovered in respect of more
than her own interest ?)

She ought to have recovered the whole ; but, as to so much as
exceeded her own interest, she would have been a trustee for the
representatives of the deceased covenantees, as in *Anderson* v.
Martindale (4). In *Wallace* v. *M'Laren* (5) a lease was made by
tenants in common, reserving rent to them according to their
several and respective rights and interests : and it was held that
the survivors might sue for the whole rent. In *Petrie* v. *Bury* (6) a
party covenanted with three persons to pay them an annuity for
the use of another ; two of the covenantees did not execute ; yet it
was held that the three might, and therefore must, join in an
action on the covenant. Here all that appears as to Mary Whitby

FOLEY
v.
ADDEN-
BROOKE.

[*204]

is that she joins in the demise, and that the covenant is made to
her jointly with the others. But, even if it appeared that she
had an undivided moiety, her interest in the covenant would be
joint.

[205]   *R. V. Richards*, in reply.   *   *   *

                                        Cur. adv. vult.

1843.   LORD DENMAN, Ch. J., in this Term (January 20th), delivered the
            judgment of the COURT:

This was an action of covenant upon an indenture of demise
between Edward Foley and Eliza Maria Foley, his wife, and Mary
Whitby, of the one part, and J. A. Addenbrooke, of the other part:
by which it was witnessed that the said Edward Foley and Eliza
Maria his wife, and the said Mary Whitby, did demise to the said
J. A. Addenbrooke, deceased, his executors, administrators and
assigns, certain lands and premises for a term of forty-two years,
with covenants on the part of the lessee for himself, his heirs,
executors and administrators, with the said Edward Foley and
Eliza Maria his wife and Mary Whitby, and the heirs and assigns
of the wife and Mary Whitby, respectively, for building and
working furnaces and iron works, and for repairing the premises,
[*206]   &c.   The declaration contained an inducement *that Edward
Foley and Eliza Maria his wife, at the time of the demise, were
seised in fee, in right of the wife, of one undivided moiety of the
demised premises.   The declaration averred the death of the lessee,
and that the defendants, as executors, entered upon the demised
premises, and continued possessed till the lease expired; and that,
during the term, Edward Foley and Eliza Maria his wife died;
and that the reversion of her undivided moiety descended to the
plaintiff, as her son and heir.   Breaches of the covenants were
then assigned, as well during the lifetime of the lessee as after his
death.

The defendants pleaded several pleas; to the sixth, seventh,
eighth, ninth, tenth, and last of which there were demurrers: and
the defendants, upon the argument, abandoned all but the sixth and
seventh.

Upon these pleas two questions were raised: first, whether the
defendants, who were named executors in the declaration, but were
not charged in terms as such, nor as assignees, were liable for
breaches of covenant as well in their own time as in that of their

testator; and, secondly, whether the action is maintainable by the plaintiff only without joining the other lessor Mary Whitby, who is still living.

As upon the latter point our opinion is in favour of the defendants, it is unnecessary to consider the other question raised, the defendants being entitled to judgment on the demurrer by reason of the nonjoinder of Mary Whitby, one of the lessors and covenantees.

The indenture shows a joint demise by Edward Foley and his wife, and Mary Whitby; and the covenants are with Edward Foley and his wife, and Mary Whitby, and the heirs and assigns of the wife and Mary Whitby, respectively. *Referring to the indenture only as set out in the declaration, it must be taken that Edward Foley and his wife and Mary Whitby had such an interest as would enable them jointly to demise the whole of the premises. It appears, however, by the inducement, that Edward Foley and his wife had only an undivided moiety: and therefore it is to be inferred, though her interest is not shown by averment, that Mary Whitby had the other moiety, making up the whole interest in the premises demised. It is clear that upon the face of the declaration Mary Whitby cannot be taken to be a person having no interest in the premises: and, whether she were a coparcener or a tenant in common with Eliza Maria Foley, she would be a tenant in common with the plaintiff.

[*207]

We are of opinion that, the demise being joint, and the covenants upon which the action is brought entire, and made with both the lessors, the cause of action is joint, and that both the covenantees ought to sue; though, as between themselves, their interests may be separate.

Several cases were cited upon the argument: *Anderson* v. *Martindale* (1), *James* v. *Emery* (2), *Kitchen* v. *Buckly* (3), *Harrison* v. *Barnby* (4), *Eccleston* v. *Clipsham* (5), and others which it is not necessary more particularly to refer to. But the result of the cases appears to be this, that, where the legal interest and cause of action of the covenantees are several, they should sue separately, though the covenant be joint in terms; but the several interest and the several ground of action *must distinctly appear, as in the case of covenants to pay separate rents to tenants in common upon

[*208]

(1) 6 R. R. 334 (1 East, 497).
(2) 19 R. R. 503 (8 Taunt. 245).
(3) 1 Lev. 109.
(4) 2 R. R. 584 (5 T. R. 246).
(5) 1 Saund. 153.

demises by them; or as, in the instance cited from *Slingsby's*
case (1) in note (1) to the case of *Eccleston,* v. *Clipsham* (2), where a
man by indenture demised Blackacre to A., Whiteacre to B., and
Greenacre to C., and covenanted with them, and each of them,
that he had good title, each might maintain an action for his
particular damage by a breach of that covenant.   On the other
hand, it appears from several cases that, if the cause of action be
joint, the action should be joint though the interest be several:
Coryton v. *Lithebye* (3), *Martin* v. *Crompe* (4), *Wilkinson* v. *Hall* (5).
In the present case the covenants for breach of which the action is
brought are such as to give the covenantees a joint interest in the
performance of them: and the terms of the indenture are such
that it seems clear that the covenantees might have maintained a
joint action for breach of any of them.   Upon this point the case
of *Kitchen* v. *Buckly* (6) is a clear authority: and the case of *Petrie*
v. *Bury* (7) shows that, if the covenantees could sue jointly, they are
bound to do so.

Our judgment therefore is for the defendants.

Judgment for defendants.

———————

GEORGE HARPER AND RICHARD PARRY JONES *v.* DAVID WILLIAMS (8).

(4 Q. B. 219—235; S. C. 12 L. J. Q. B. 227.)

Attorneys, assignees of a mortgage of lands, brought an action in the
name of the mortgagee against W., the mortgagor, for principal and
interest; and W. pleaded.   The attorneys had obtained from E., their
client, a loan to W. on further mortgage of the same lands, and had
brought an action, for E., against W. for principal and interest due on that
mortgage; and W. had pleaded.   They had also obtained a verdict against
W., and certificate for execution, in an action of debt at their own suit.   D.,
an attorney, but not employed as such by the mortgagor (who was the
brother of D.'s professional agent), wrote to the plaintiffs, promising that, if
they would not issue execution for two months, the pleas should be withdrawn and judgment suffered by default in the first two actions; and
further undertaking as follows.   "I shall pay all the principal, interest
and costs through a friend of mine in London, to whom a transfer of all the
securities you have will have to be made."   "The cash will be ready, if the
securities will, on the 16th instant."   The plaintiffs agreed, and forbore

(1) 5 Rep. 18 b.   (6) 1 Lev. 109.
(2) 1 Wms. Saund. 155.   (7) 27 R. R. 383 (3 B. & C. 353).
(3) 2 Saund. 115.   (8) Dist. *Duncombe* v. *Brighton Club*
(4) 1 Ld. Ray. 340.   *Co.* (1875) L. R. 10 Q. B. 371, 375, 44
(5) 43 R. R. 728 (1 Bing. N. C. 713).   L. J. Q. B. 216.—A. C.

issuing execution ; but the party referred to by D. did not advance the   HARPER
money.   *v.*
    Held : 1. That D. was personally liable in assumpsit on the above under-   WILLIAMS.
taking, for the amount claimed by the plaintiffs in the first two actions.

    2. That they were sufficiently interested in the recovery of the sum due
to E., their client, to sue on D.'s agreement in respect of it, in their own
names.

    3. That they might recover interest on the sums due, as damages in the
action against D., though not under stat. 3 & 4 Will. IV. c. 42, ss. 28, 29.

ASSUMPSIT.   The declaration contained two special counts ; to each
of which several pleas were pleaded, and issues joined thereon :
also counts for work and materials, for money paid, and on an
account stated : to which, and the special counts, a payment into
Court was pleaded : replication, damages *ultrà :* issue thereon.
On the trial, before Cresswell, J., at the Spring Assizes for Shrop-
shire, 1842, a verdict was found for the plaintiffs on all the issues
raised upon the first count, and for the defendant on the remaining
issues, subject to the opinion of this Court on a special case as to
the right of the plaintiffs to recover on the agreement set forth in
the first count.

    The first count was abstracted in the case as follows :

    It sets forth, by way of inducement, that, before the making of
the defendant's promise, William Williams and John Kyffin Williams
borrowed from John Lowe 2,000*l.*, secured by a mortgage of certain
estates and a joint and *several covenant of W. Williams and J. K.   [*220]
Williams to pay principal and interest. That J. Lowe afterwards
assigned the said mortgage debt by indenture to the plaintiffs for
an advance of 2,000*l.*   That afterwards J. K. Williams applied to
the plaintiffs to procure him a further loan of 325*l.* ; and that
Elizabeth Humphreys, at the request of the plaintiffs, advanced
him the sum of 325*l.* on the security of a further mortgage of the
estate before mortgaged as aforesaid, and subject thereto, and of
the joint and several covenant of the said J. K. Williams and
W. Williams for the payment of principal and interest. That
W. Williams was further indebted to the plaintiffs in the sum of
164*l.* 7*s.* 11*d.*   That, the covenant of the said W. Williams with the
said J. Lowe having been broken, the plaintiffs, as the attorneys of
the said J. Lowe, but for their own behoof, sued out a writ against
the said W. Williams for damages for non-payment of the said sum
of 2,000*l.* and interest, and declared in that action, and the said
W. Williams pleaded thereto. That, the covenant of the said
W. Williams with the said E. Humphreys having been also broken,
the plaintiffs, as her attorneys, sued out another writ against the

said W. Williams for damages for the non-payment of the said sum
of 325*l.* and interest, and declared in the said action, and the said
W. Williams pleaded thereto.   That the plaintiffs also commenced
an action of debt against the said W. Williams to recover the said
sum of 164*l.* 17*s.* 11*d.* due to themselves, and recovered a verdict
therein for the said debt, for 1*s.* damages and 40*s.* costs, and a
certificate of execution for the 17th day of August then next.   That
afterwards, on 1st August, 1841, in order to put an end to the
several suits and litigations, it was agreed between the plain-

[*221]   tiffs *and defendant that the plaintiffs should stay execution
in the said last mentioned suit for two months from the
said 1st August, 1841, and should furnish defendant with an
abstract of the deed of assignment from the said J. Lowe to the
plaintiffs; that the pleas of the said W. Williams in the said
actions first and secondly mentioned should be withdrawn, and
judgment suffered therein by the said W. Williams by default;
that judgment should be entered up in the said action at the suit
of the plaintiffs, but that no writ of execution should be levied or
put in force in the said actions or any of them for the space of two
months from the said 1st August; that the defendant should
prepare drafts of transfer and assignment of the said several
securities before mentioned to a certain person to be procured by
the defendant, to wit Robert Dixon, Esq., and should send them to
the plaintiffs; and, if the plaintiffs should approve of the same, the
defendant should get them engrossed and return them to the
plaintiffs, who should procure them to be executed by the parties
by whom such assignments and transfers were to be made; and
that thereupon, and as soon as the same should have been so
executed as aforesaid, he, the defendant, would pay to the plaintiffs
all the principal monies and interest then due by the said
W. Williams to the said several parties respectively on the said
securities, together with the costs of the two first mentioned actions
respectively, and would also pay to the plaintiffs the said debt and
damages recovered in the said action at the suit of the plaintiffs,
together with the full costs of suit in the said action.   The declaration proceeds, after the usual statement of mutual promises, to
aver that the plaintiffs did stay execution in their own action; that

[*222]   the pleas in *the other actions were withdrawn, and judgment
entered up; that the plaintiffs did not levy or enforce, or cause or
permit to be levied or enforced, any writ of execution in either or
any of the said actions, nor was any execution levied in the said

actions or either of them ; that they furnished an abstract of the HARPER
deed of assignment from the said John Lowe to the plaintiffs ; that, WILLIAMS.
the said transfer and assignments of securities having been prepared
and approved, the plaintiffs caused them to be duly executed by the
several parties, and were ready and willing to deliver them so
executed : of all which premises the defendant had notice : and
assigns for a breach the non-payment of the several principal
monies and interest and the costs of the two first mentioned actions,
and of the debt and costs in the action at the suit of the plaintiffs.

The case then proceeded as follows :

The defendant, by his pleas to the first count, denied, first, the
agreement ; secondly, the alleged assignment and transfer by Lowe
to the plaintiffs ; thirdly, that the plaintiffs stayed execution
according to the terms of the agreement ; fourthly, that the
plaintiffs were ready and willing to deliver the transfers and
assignments duly executed by the necessary parties ; on all which
traverses issues were joined.

To prove the agreement as set forth in the first count, the
plaintiffs put in the following letters, all of which were admitted
by the counsel for the defendant.

"GRAY'S INN COFFEE HOUSE, LONDON,
"31st July, 1841.

" MY DEAR SIR,—Upon coming up here three days back I found
that there was some squabbling work *going on between my agent   [*223]
and yourself, and that you had instituted proceedings against his
brother for different sums due to you and your clients. Having
been consulted on the subject, and not exactly understanding how
matters stand, will you do me the favour to inform me how things
are, and be good enough to say whether you will have any objection to wait a couple of months, by taking judgments with a stay
of execution for that period : and I have no doubt arrangements
can be made by then to settle every thing. I shall be obliged by
your early reply, addressed to me here.

"Yours very truly,
"GEO. HARPER, Esq.   "DAVID WILLIAMS."

"*Selves* v. —— *Williams, Esq.*
"*Humphreys* v. *Same.*
"*Lowe* v. *Same.*

" MY DEAR SIR,—Mr. Williams has nothing to do but suffer
judgment in each of the above : let us complete them by taxing

our costs; and rely upon this as our undertaking that, although we shall issue execution, we shall not put it in force for two months from this date.   We shall have no objection to give you personally any explanation, or your friend Mr. Williams," &c.: (the letter then proceeded to blame the conduct of the latter).

"We are" &c.

"HARPER and PARRY JONES.

"Whitchurch, 1st August, 1841."

"GRAY'S INN COFFEE HOUSE, LONDON,
"3rd August, 1841.

"MY DEAR SIR,—I beg to acknowledge the receipt of your letter and to thank you for your courtesy. I regret that you have [*224] grounds to complain" &c. "Will *you be kind enough to send me an abstract of the deed from Lowe to Jones, and also of the one affecting the policy for 600*l.* which you effected. I shall pay all the principal, interest and costs through a friend of mine in London, to whom a transfer of all the securities your clients have will have to be made. The concurrence of Mr. Williams and his son as directing parties to the transfer will not be required on behalf of the gentleman to whom the transfer will be made; and I take it for granted that you will not consider it necessary on the part of the mortgagees. The pleas shall be withdrawn as you request; but I hope you will not require executions to be issued, as the money will be ready immediately to pay the whole, including your bill of costs for which you obtained a verdict at Shrewsbury, and which should be settled without being taxed. As soon as you send up the abstracts mentioned above, a draft transfer will be sent down for your perusal; and, if you approve of it, you can get it engrossed and executed so as to send the engrossment complete to your agents or bankers in London to be exchanged for the money. The cash will be ready, if the securities will, on the 16th instant. Hoping that you will be so good as to allow the transaction to be completed with as little expense as circumstances will permit, believe me" &c.

"GEO. HARPER, Esq.   "DAVID WILLIAMS."

"DEAR SIR,—We beg to send you, as requested, an abstract of the assignments from Mr. Lowe to ourselves, and also an abstract of a deed of arrangement between Mr. Williams and his son on the loan from Miss Humphreys, which we presume is what you want. [*225] We never effected any policy for Mr. Williams except one for *100*l.*, on which we have not now any charges: the policy and a satisfied assignment of it have been given up to Mr. Williams. We shall not require the concurrence of the mortgagees to the proposed transfers. In July, 1837, we entered into a covenant with Mr. Peachey of Salisbury Square for the production of Mr. Williams's title deeds to some property at Islington: this covenant is defeasible on our giving up the deeds and procuring a similar covenant from the party to whom the deeds are handed over: the mortgagees also covenanted with us to indemnify in respect of such deed of covenant. Shall you require abstracts of these?" &c.

> " We are " &c.
>
>> " HARPER and PARRY JONES.

" Whitchurch, 4th August, 1841.

" DAVID WILLIAMS, Esq."

The case then set out several other letters written by the parties respectively while endeavouring to carry into effect the above arrangement, which terminated (as appeared by the correspondence) in the defendant's failure to obtain the expected advance. The case then proceeded as follows.

It was admitted that, pending the arrangement, viz. on the 25th [226] September, 1841, the defendant married a daughter of the said W. Williams. Upon these letters *and facts it was agreed between [*227] the counsel for the several parties that a verdict should be entered for the plaintiffs on all the issues upon the first count, subject to the opinion of the Court on this case: and a verdict was accordingly taken for 2,725l. damages, to which interest was to be added from the 1st of October, if this Court should be of opinion that such interest was recoverable.

The questions for the opinion of the COURT were: 1. *Whether [*228] the agreement set forth in the first count was made out by the evidence: and, if the Court should be of that opinion, then 2. Whether the damages should be reduced by striking out the sum of 325l. advanced by the said Elizabeth Humphreys to the said W. Williams, and the interest thereon. 3. Whether the plaintiffs are entitled to interest on the whole or any part of the said damages from 1st October, 1841.

The points for argument on behalf of the plaintiffs were stated in their paper books as follows.

1. That the letters taken together, coupled with the circumstances

of the case, constitute an agreement binding on the defendant to
the effect set forth in the first count of the declaration.

2. That there is no ground for reducing the damages by striking
out the said sum of 325*l.*, inasmuch as the promise by the defendant
is one and entire, and the plaintiffs have a sufficient interest in the
sum to be recovered for the benefit of the said E. Humphreys to
entitle them to sue the defendant for the breach of his promise in
not paying that sum.

3. That, as the debts were all such as bore interest, the plaintiffs
are entitled to recover interest by way of damages.

The case was argued in the last Term (1) by *Talfourd*, Serjt. for
the plaintiffs, and *Sir W. W. Follett*, Solicitor-General, for the
defendant. The material points of the argument will appear
sufficiently from the judgment of the COURT. *Burrell* v. *Jones* (2)
and *Appleton* v. *Binks* (3) were cited.

Cur. adv. vult.

[229]   LORD DENMAN, Ch. J., in this vacation (February 11th), delivered
the judgment of the COURT:

The plaintiffs in this case are solicitors, and assignees of a
mortgage granted by William and John Kyffin Williams to secure
an advance of 2,000*l.* made to them by one Lowe; they had also
procured for J. K. Williams, from a client, one Elizabeth Humphreys,
a further advance of 325*l.* on the same security, and with a covenant
by the two Williamses for its repayment. W. Williams was also
indebted to them in the sum of 164*l.* 17*s.* 11*d.* They had instituted
proceedings on all these causes of action, and recovered a verdict
in the last. Under these circumstances it is alleged on their part
that the defendant intervened and entered into an agreement by
which, in consideration of a stay of execution for two months in the
last mentioned action, and furnishing defendant with an abstract
of the assignment of the mortgage, the pleas were to be withdrawn,
and judgment suffered by default in the first and second, on which
no execution was to issue for two months from a day named; and
further the defendant was to prepare a transfer of the mortgage to
a certain person to be procured by him, for the execution of which
by the proper parties the plaintiffs undertook; and thereupon the
defendant was to pay to the plaintiffs all principal monies and

(1) January 17th. Before Lord   (2) 22 R. R. 296 (3 B. & Ald. 47)
Denman, Ch. J., Patteson, Coleridge   (3) 7 R. R. 672 (5 East, 148).
and Wightman, JJ.

interest due to the respective parties, with the costs in the two
first actions, and the debt and costs in the last. The plaintiffs
have in all respects performed their part of the agreement: and, so
far as regards the withdrawal of pleas and suffering judgment, the
defendant has performed his; but the gentleman whom he expected
to take the transfer and pay the money has declined to do so; and
the same remains unpaid. The declaration has been framed on
this agreement: and, *the defendant having pleaded *Non assumpsit*,   [*230]
two principal questions are made: the first, whether any such
agreement has been entered into; the second, if it has, whether
the defendant has entered into it as principal: and the answer to
these is to be extracted from a long correspondence stated in a
special case for our consideration.

We have no difficulty in answering the first of these questions
in the affirmative. One of the letters, the third in the series (1),
furnishes abundant evidence of an agreement such as that stated,
to which the plaintiffs and the defendant are at least the ostensible
parties. The second requires more consideration. The principle
on which it is to be answered is not a technical one. Several cases
similar in kind have occurred, such as *Burrell* v. *Jones* (2); *Iveson*
v. *Conington* (3); *Scrace* v. *Whittington* (4); and *Jones* v. *Downman*,
in this Court, not reported (5). It will be found, however, that the
judgment in each has been arrived at only by an examination of
the particular circumstances in each: one decision will scarcely
serve as an authority for any other, except in so far as we may
ascertain from it the weight to be allowed to any particular fact
which may be found in any one of these cases and the present also.
Further, in a case where we are to extract our evidence from
letters, it is essential to avoid laying too much stress on single
expressions, the object being to ascertain fairly, from the whole of
the correspondence, what was the real intention and understanding
of the parties. It is obvious also that the earlier letters, where
the parties are less attentive to personal consequences and in
apprehension *of no difficulties, where consequently they write more   [*231]
naturally, are the most important.

We have examined these letters on these principles, and have
come to the conclusion that they make the defendant personally
liable. We do not rely on the fact, which has been thought of

---

(1) 3rd August, 1841. P. 338, *ante.*   (4) Stated 31 R. R. 556 (2 B. & C. 11).
(2) 22 R. R. 296 (3 B. & Ald. 47).   (5) P. 344, note (1), *post.*
(3) 25 R. R. 344 (1 B. & C. 161).

importance in some cases, that he was a solicitor ; because it seems
clear, not only that he was not employed by the Williamses as
such, but that he did not voluntarily intervene as their solicitor :
they had at the time their own solicitor, employed in the conduct
of their defences ; and the different steps in the suits taken on
their behalf in consequence of the negotiation were taken by him.
The defendant's interference is not therefore the mere undertaking
of an attorney in a cause. Still less do we rely on a fact, which
we mention only because it was somewhat relied on in the argument, that the plaintiff was paying his addresses to the daughter
of W. Williams, and married her in the course of the negotiation.
This circumstance may have been the motive for his interference,
but it would act as such equally whether he was conducting a
treaty only on behalf of W. Williams or entering into one on his own
responsibility. The stipulations on the part of the defendant were
twofold : first, that certain things should be done by the Williamses
as to the first and second suits ; secondly, that the money to be
recovered in all the suits should be paid. It does not appear that
he professed, or was understood by the plaintiffs to profess, to
have any original power as to the former, or to intend to pay the
latter out of his own proper monies : but his language imports
him to undertake absolutely and as a principal, in both cases, that,
[*232]   if the plaintiff would grant the Williamses *certain indulgence in
the suits, and do certain other acts, the pleas should be withdrawn,
the judgments suffered, and the monies paid : and there is nothing
improbable in his having so undertaken, however seriously the
responsibility may press on him. In the result he might feel quite
certain that the Williamses would do all that he promised should
be done in the suits. The plaintiffs evidently had them so entirely
in their power that there could be no doubt that they would do as
they did in fact, for the sake of the time gained and expense saved :
and it is equally clear, from many expressions in the early part of
the correspondence, that the defendant had not the least doubt of a
Mr. Dixon taking the transfer of the mortgage and paying off the
incumbrances. We cannot but infer that the Williamses had so
represented the value of the mortgaged property to him as to make
him believe there would be no difficulty on that head. It is a familiar
principle in the law of agency, " that, wherever a party undertakes to do any act, as the agent of another, if he does not possess
any authority from the principal, or if he exceeds the authority
delegated to him, he will be personally responsible therefor to the

person with whom he is dealing for or on account of his principal." These are Mr. Justice Story's words, in his Commentaries on the Law of Agency, c. x. s. 264 (1) accompanied by a qualification, that the want of authority is not known to the other party. This test has been often applied in our Courts, when the question has turned on the liability of an admitted agent: it is, in effect, scarcely a different question whether one has acted as principal or agent, and the same test has been and may properly be applied. If such person has not *made any other person liable as principal, a strong presumption arises that he himself is liable as such, because it cannot be taken that he intended to procure from the other party some benefit even for third persons, or to subject that party to loss or inconvenience, upon the faith of some promised consideration, and yet give him no recourse to any one for its recovery. Now, in the present case, the defendant holds out to the plaintiffs a promise that they shall receive their principal and interest, and their costs, if they will give the Williamses certain indulgence : they give it in consequence, forbear to press them with executions, and run the risk of losing all effectual remedy against them : but it is clear that neither against them nor against Mr. Dixon, the intended assignee who was to advance the money and take the transfer, have the plaintiffs any recourse. No other principal is suggested ; no one therefore is liable, unless the defendant be : and, as we ought to presume against his holding this dishonest intention, we must hold him to have intended to make himself liable. Though many parts of his letters show that he relied on being borne harmless, there is no expression in them, prior to Mr. Dixon's refusal, which is not consistent with this conclusion.

We are of opinion, therefore, that the count is well proved. A second question proposed to us is, whether the damages should be reduced by striking out the sum of 325*l.* advanced by Elizabeth Humphreys to Williams, and the interest thereon. It was not argued that any promise was made to her, or that she could have sued the defendant : the doubt was, whether the plaintiffs had sufficient interest in the subject-matter of the promise to sue for its non-performance. As to this, they, the solicitors of E. Humphreys, had induced her to advance her money, *they had sued for it in her name, and then stayed their proceedings on the promise of the defendant to pay them the money. First, then, it is far from clear that the plaintiffs might not be liable to her if the money were lost

HARPER
v.
WILLIAMS.

[*232]

[*234]

(1) P. 226. (London, 1839.)

HARPER
v.
WILLIAMS.

by this unauthorized delay on their parts. Secondly, it is clear that she cannot recover it except in their name; for he has entered into no agreement with her. On these two grounds, of interest in the plaintiffs, and that they alone can recover what it must be taken that the defendant intended some one should be able to recover from him, we think that this sum should not be deducted from the damages. The plaintiffs of course will be trustees as to the amount for her.

The remaining question is, whether the plaintiffs are entitled to recover interest on all or any part of the damages from the 1st October, 1841. We do not think this case is brought within either section, the 28th or 29th, of stat. 3 & 4 Will. IV. c. 42. Assuming that the sums recovered were sums certain, because they might be made so by calculation, yet they were not payable " at a certain time " " by virtue of some written instrument ; " nor, being payable otherwise than at a certain time, has any demand in writing been made according to the provisions of the 28th section. And, as to the 29th section, this is not one of the actions there enumerated. The only question is, whether a jury should have been recommended to add the interest to the damages independently of the statute. Looking to the nature of the two principal items of which the damages are composed, the 2,000*l.* and the 325*l.*, for which no doubt interest has been computed to the 1st October, 1841, and forms part of the 2,725*l.* for which the verdict has been taken, and assuming that no interest has been paid on those sums since that

[*235] date, we *think that it should be added to the verdict, and computed from that date to the day of final judgment. Beyond this the case furnishes no materials upon which we can decide that the plaintiffs should recover any interest.

         *Verdict to be entered for plaintiffs for damages and
         interest as above* (1).

---

(1) See *William Jones* v. *Downman,* 4 Q. B. 235, *n.* [This case will be reported with the case of *Downman* v. *Williams* in the Exchequer Chamber (7 Q. B. 103; 14 L. J. Q. B. 226), where the judgment herein was reversed for reasons arising out of the form of the special verdict.]

REG. *v.* The INHABITANTS of MIDVILLE.

(4 Q. B. 240—259; S. C. 3 G. & D. 522.)

Previously to the passing of the local and personal public Acts after mentioned, a district was extra-parochial and uninhabited.

Stat. 41 Geo. III. (U. K.) c. cxlii. empowered Commissioners to divide the district into allotments, and set out roads, which, upon the confirmation, within a certain time, of a certificate from the surveyors, but not before, were to be repaired by the inhabitants of the respective parishes, townships and places having right of common in the district. The Commissioners set out a road, which was used by the public; but no certificate was ever made; and the time for confirmation expired.

Stat. 50 Geo. III. c. cxxix. provided for the erection and endowment of chapels in the district by a deduction from certain allotments to be made therein.

Stat. 52 Geo. III. c. cxliv. recited that it would be of public utility if the lands, roads, &c., of the district were made to constitute distinct townships, and if the public laws in force concerning constables and for the relief of the poor were put in force in such townships; and enacted that a certain part of the district, comprehending the road in question, should be the township of M.; that all public laws in force or to be made relating to constables or the relief of the poor should be put in force in the townships in like manner as in any parish; and that the inhabitants and occupiers in any township should not be liable to contribute to the relief of the poor, or to any other parochial rates, in any other parish, &c., and *vice versâ*.

Stat. 58 Geo. III. c. xlvi. empowered trustees to erect additional chapels, and houses of residence for the ministers, and assign stipends from the rents of the land allotted; and enacted that chapelwardens should be appointed for the chapels; and a chapel was accordingly built in M. Overseers, chapelwardens, surveyors of the highways, and constables were also regularly appointed in M. Highway rates were laid; and some repairs performed by the township upon the road.

Held, that the inhabitants of M. were not bound to repair the road, either by force of the above statutes, or on any general principle of law.

INDICTMENT for non-repair of a road.

The first count charged "that there was and yet is a certain common and ancient Queen's highway, at the township of Midville in the county of Lincoln, used for all the liege subjects of our said lady the Queen, with their horses, carts and carriages, to go, return, pass, ride and labour, at their free will and pleasure; and that a certain part of the said common Queen's highway, in the said township of Midville in the county aforesaid, beginning at " &c. (describing the part by *termini*), " containing in length" &c., on 20th July, 4 Vict., "at the township aforesaid, in the county aforesaid, was and yet is ruinous," &c., "for want of due reparation and amendment of the same, so that the liege subjects of " &c. "in, along," &c., "could not, nor yet can, safely go " &c., "to the great damage and common nuisance " &c. "And that the inhabitants of the township of Midville the said common Queen's highway, so in

[*241]

*decay as aforesaid, have been used and accustomed, and still of right ought, to repair and amend, when and so often as need shall require."

Second count.   " That, before and at the time of the passing of the Act of Parliament next hereinafter mentioned, certain lands and grounds situate and being in a certain place called the East Fen, and in the said Act mentioned and described, were extra-parochial: and thereupon, at a certain Session of Parliament holden, to wit " &c. (52 Geo. III.), " a certain Act of Parliament was passed, intituled, ' An Act for forming into townships certain extra-parochial lands in Wildmore Fen, and in the West and East Fens, in the county of Lincoln : ' and thereby, and by the said Act, it was enacted and provided that certain of the said lands and grounds in the said Act specified and mentioned should, from and after the passing of the said Act, be a distinct township of itself, and be called by the name of Midville within the soke of Bolingbroke and parts of Lindsey in the county of Lincoln ; as by the said Act more fully and at large appears, reference being had thereto." " That, after the passing of the said Act, the said lands and grounds became, and the same thence hitherto have been, and still are, the township of Midville, as by the said Act provided.   And that there since the passing of the said Act hath been, and still is, a certain common Queen's highway, at the said township of Midville, in the said county of Lincoln, used for all the liege subjects of our said lady the Queen, with their horses," &c. (as in the first count).   " And that a certain part of the said common Queen's highway, in the said township of Midville, in the county aforesaid, beginning " &c. (describing the part by *termini*), " containing in length " &c., " after

[*242]

*the passing of the said Act, to wit " 21st July, 4 Vict., " at the township aforesaid, in the county aforesaid, was and yet is ruinous," &c. (as in the first count).   " And that the inhabitants of the said township of Midville the said common Queen's highway, so in decay as aforesaid, have been used and accustomed, and still of right ought, to repair and amend, when and so often as need shall require."

The third and fourth counts omitted the description of the part of the road out of repair, and in other respects corresponded respectively with the first and second counts.

On the trial, before Parke, B., at the Lincolnshire Summer Assizes, 1841, a verdict was found for the Crown, subject to the opinion of this Court on a case substantially as follows : the indictment to form part of the case, and the defendants to be at liberty to move in arrest of judgment.

The road mentioned in the indictment has been constantly used as a public highway since the passing of the Inclosure Act, 41 Geo. III. (U. K.) c. cxlii., hereinafter mentioned; and the part indicted is ruinous and out of repair, and lies wholly within the township of Midville in the county of Lincoln. Midville is a separate and distinct township, maintaining its own poor since it was created a township by Act of Parliament as hereinafter mentioned. And, in 1823, the township appointed surveyors, and have since made highway rates and repaired the road in question so far as hacking in the ruts. Before the passing of the Acts of Parliament hereinafter mentioned, the land over which the road so indicted passes was part of a certain extra-parochial fen, called the East Fen, which was then uninhabited.

By stat. 41 Geo. III. (U. K.) c. cxlii. (local and personal, *public), entitled " An Act for dividing and allotting certain fens, called the East and West Fens, in the county of Lincoln," it is (amongst other things) enacted (sect. 1) " that the said East and West Fens shall be divided and allotted by such Commissioners, and in such manner, and under such powers and authorities, and subject to such rules, orders, and directions, as are hereinafter mentioned, appointed, and declared." Sect. 30 of the said Act enacts " that the said Commissioners shall, as soon as conveniently may be, and before they proceed to set out the allotments hereinafter mentioned, make, set out, and appoint such public and private roads and ways as they shall judge necessary, and also such drains, watercourses, mounds, fences, banks, cloughs, engines, bridges, tunnels, shuttles, gates, stiles, and other works, in, over, through, or upon the said fens hereby directed to be divided and allotted, as they shall judge necessary and proper, so as all such public carriage roads shall be and remain forty feet " &c. (directions as to the dimensions of public and private roads, and other regulations respecting the same); " and after the said public roads shall have been set out as aforesaid, the said Commissioners shall, and they are hereby empowered and required, by writing under their hands, to appoint some proper person or persons to be surveyor or surveyors of the said roads, and such surveyor or surveyors shall cause the same to be properly formed and completed, and put into good and sufficient repair, and shall be allowed such salary or reward " &c.; " which salary or reward, and also the expenses of forming the said roads, and of putting the same in good and sufficient repair, shall be raised and paid in like manner as the charges and expenses of

obtaining and passing this Act, and *carrying the same into
execution, are hereinafter authorized and directed to be raised and
paid ; and that the inhabitants of the said respective parishes,
townships, or places having right of common on the said fens,
shall not be charged or chargeable towards the forming or repairing
of the said public roads, until the same shall be made fit for the
passage of travellers and carriages, and shall have been certified
so to be by the said surveyor or surveyors, by writing under his or
their hand or hands, to be delivered to the clerks of the peace at
some Quarter Sessions of the peace to be holden for the parts of
Lindsey or division of Holland aforesaid, within which such roads
respectively shall lie, and until such certificate shall have been
allowed and confirmed by the justices at such Sessions ; which said
certificate shall be so delivered to the clerk of the peace at the
Quarter Sessions for the said parts or division next after the said
roads shall be formed, completed, and put into good and sufficient
repair as aforesaid, and within the space of two years next after
the execution of the award or instrument hereinafter directed to be
made, unless sufficient reason be given to the satisfaction of the
said justices, that a further time is necessary for that purpose, in
which case the said justices may, and they are hereby empowered
to allow such further time for delivering in the said certificate as
they should think proper, not exceeding twelve calendar months ;
and in case the said surveyor or surveyors shall neglect or refuse to
deliver in such certificate within the time before limited, he or they
shall forfeit and pay any sum, not exceeding " &c. ; " and after such
certificate shall have been delivered to the said clerk of the peace by
the said surveyor or surveyors as aforesaid, and shall have been

[*245]   allowed and *confirmed at such Sessions, the said roads shall be
from time to time amended and kept in repair by the inhabitants
of the respective parishes, townships, and places having right of
common on the said fens, in the same manner as the other public
roads within the said respective parishes, townships, and places are
by law to be amended and kept in repair ; and that the said private
roads or ways, so as to be made, set out, and appointed, shall at all
times thereafter be kept in repair at the expense of such person or
persons, and in such shares and proportions as the said Commissioners shall order, direct, and appoint ; and that after such public
and private roads and ways shall be set out and made, it shall not
be lawful for any person or persons to use any roads or ways, either
public or private, in, over, through or upon the said fens hereby

directed to be divided and allotted, either on foot or with cattle, horses, or carriages, other than such as shall be set out and appointed by the said Commissioners by virtue of this Act; and that all former roads and ways which shall not be set out and appointed as the roads and ways through the said intended division, shall be deemed part of the lands and grounds to be divided and allotted by virtue of this Act, and shall be divided and allotted accordingly, as part thereof; and all such ditches, mounds, fences, banks, drains, watercourses, cloughs, engines, bridges, tunnels, shuttles, gates, stiles, and other works so to be made, set out, and appointed by the said Commissioners as aforesaid, shall at all times thereafter be repaired, cleansed, maintained, and kept in repair, either by parochial assessments, or by such person or persons, and in such manner, as the said Commissioners shall direct *or appoint in and   [*246] by their award or instrument in writing hereinafter directed to be made."

The said Commissioners, by their award in writing dated 30th June, 1820, set out and awarded as follows. "One other public carriage road of the width of fifty feet, beginning " &c. (the case then stated the description given in the award, which directed that the road should run along the west bank of the Hob Hole Drain)· The road indicted is part of the highway so set out.

The said highway was not put into good and sufficient repair by the surveyors appointed under the said Act; nor was it certified to be so by them, or any of them, in writing under their hands to the clerk of the peace for any Quarter Sessions.

By stat. 50 Geo. III. c. cxxix. (local and personal, public), "for amending and rendering more effectual an Act" (41 Geo. III. (U. K.) c. cxlii.); "and for dividing and inclosing the parochial allotments, lands and grounds belonging to and in certain parishes having right of common on the said fens, and for declaring to what parishes such allotments shall belong," it was enacted (sect. 14) that the Commissioners under the recited Act should, as soon as convenient after the allotment or allotments should be made out of the said East and West Fens in lieu of manerial rights in, over and upon the East and West Fens, deduct from the manerial allotment or allotments such part or parts as should, in their judgment, be equal in value to one ninth part of such allotment or allotments; and such deductions, when made, should be in lieu of, and in full compensation and satisfaction for, all tithes, great and small, arising and renewing upon or from the allotment or *allotments so   [*247] made in lieu of manerial rights.   And (sect. 15) that such one ninth part should be appropriated to the erection and endowment of chapels in the fens.

Parts of the fens were accordingly allotted to trustees for those purposes.

By stat. 52 Geo. III. c. cxliv. (local and personal, public), entitled &c. (see p. 346, *ante*), reciting (sect. 1) the passing of six Acts, all local and personal, public: namely, 41 Geo. III. (U. K.) c. cxxxv., entitled "An Act for the better and more effectually draining certain tracts of land called Wildmore Fen, and the West and East Fens, in the county of Lincoln, and also the low lands and grounds in the several parishes, townships, and places, having right of common on the said fens, and other low lands and grounds lying contiguous or adjoining thereto;" 41 Geo. III. (U. K.) c. cxli., entitled "An Act for dividing and allotting a certain fen, called Wildmore Fen, in the county of Lincoln;" 41 Geo. III. (U. K.) c. cxlii., before mentioned; 42 Geo. III. c. cviii., entitled "An Act for altering, amending, and rendering more effectual, an Act" &c. (41 Geo. III. (U. K.) c. cxli.); "and for dividing, allotting in severalty, and inclosing, the parochial or general allotments set out, or to be set out, in pursuance of the said Act, for compensating for the tithes of such allotments, and for declaring and determining to what parish or parishes the several allotments of the said fen shall belong;" 43 Geo. III. c. cxviii., entitled "An Act for amending an Act" &c. (41 Geo. III. (U. K.) c. cxxxv.); and 50 Geo. III. c. cxxix. (before mentioned): and reciting that "certain persons in the several above recited Acts named, were thereby severally appointed *Commissioners for putting the said Acts in execution;" and "were severally empowered and required to sell and dispose of such parts or parcels of the said fens, as they should judge most proper and expedient: and whereas large portions of the said fens hereinafter particularly set forth and described, containing" &c., "have been sold to divers persons in pursuance of the said Acts; and about fourteen acres of the said fens have been set out, and are intended to be sold for the purposes of the said Act" &c.: "and whereas certain parts of the said fens hereinafter also particularly set forth and described, have been allotted to lords of manors in lieu of their manerial rights, and to trustees for the erection and endowment of chapels for Divine worship in the said fens; and that none of the said lands so sold or intended to be sold or allotted as before mentioned, are by any of the said Acts directed to be annexed to,

[*248]

or form part of any parish or parishes adjoining or near to the said
fens, and such lands, and the drains, banks, roads, and silt pits,
within the bounds and limits hereinafter described, or adjoining to
some part thereof, are now considered to be extra-parochial: and
whereas the population in the said fens is rapidly increasing, and it
would be of public utility and convenience if such lands, drains,
banks, roads and silt pits were divided into, and made to constitute
seven distinct townships, as hereinafter mentioned; and if all the
general public laws now in force concerning constables, and for the
relief and employment of poor people in England, were put in force
within such townships as hereinafter directed : " it was enacted :

Sect. 2: "That all that precinct of land included within the
bounds and limits next hereinafter described; *(that is to say)"
&c. (here followed the description of the district), "shall, from and
after the passing of this Act, be a distinct township of itself, and be
called by the name of Midville, within the soke of Bolingbroke and
parts of Lindsey, in the county of Lincoln, and such last mentioned
township shall be considered to be within the deanery of Bolingbroke,
and in the diocese and jurisdiction of the Bishop of Lincoln."
Sect. 9 : " That all the general public laws and statutes now in
force, or hereafter to be made concerning or relating to constables,
and for the relief and employment of poor people in England,
subject to the proviso hereinafter contained, shall be executed and
put in force within each and every of the said several townships of
Eastville, Midville," &c. (naming the others), "in like manner as
such laws and statutes are or may be executed and put in force in
any parish in England; and all inhabitants of, and occupiers of
lands within the said townships of Eastville, Midville," &c., "are
hereby declared to be subject and amenable to all such laws and
statutes, subject to the proviso hereinafter contained, in like manner
as inhabitants and occupiers of lands, within any parish in England,
are or may be subject and amenable to such laws and statutes."
Sect. 10: "That the inhabitants and occupiers of lands in all the
said townships shall be liable to maintain and support the poor
people in their respective townships, and shall be liable and chargeable to all payments, charges, expenses and orders in respect of
poor people, in the township where he, she, or they may inhabit or
occupy lands, in like manner and form as inhabitants and occupiers
of lands within any parish in England, are now, by any general
law or *statute, liable and chargeable for or towards the maintenance
and support of poor people in any parish in England, subject to the

REG.
r.
THE INHABI-
TANTS OF
MIDVILLE.

[*249]

[*250]

proviso hereinafter contained." Sect. 11 : "Provided always" &c.,
"that the said inhabitants or occupiers of lands within such
respective townships shall not be subject or liable, or be required in
any manner to pay or contribute towards the relief of poor people
in any other parish, township or place, or to bear or pay a proportional part of any other parochial rates whatsoever in any other
parish, township or place ; neither shall the inhabitants or occupiers
of lands or tenements in any other parish, township or place, be
liable or be required to pay or contribute towards the relief of poor
persons in any township by this Act formed or created, or to bear
or pay a proportional part of any other parochial rate or rates
whatsoever to be levied or raised in such townships or any of them ;
any law, statute, custom or usage to the contrary in any wise
notwithstanding."

By stat. 58 Geo. III. c. xlvi. (local and personal, public), entitled
"An Act for amending two Acts of his present Majesty, so far as
the same relate to the establishment of chapels in the East, West
and Wildmore Fens in the county of Lincoln," after (sect. 1) reciting
stats. 42 Geo. III. c. cviii. and 50 Geo. III. c. cxxix., certain trustees
were appointed for carrying that Act into execution, and (sect. 2)
were empowered to erect additional chapels, and houses of residence
for the ministers : and (sect. 14) such chapels, when built, and the
chapels already erected, were to be consecrated and dedicated to the
service of the Almighty ; and the houses of the ministers for the
time being were to be appropriated for their residence: and

[*251]   (sect. 15) the *trustees and their successors for the time being were
directed from time to time to nominate ministers to officiate at the
chapels so erected or to be erected, and, out of the rents of the
allotted land, to assign them such a stipend as they should think
fit: and (sect. 21) such ministers and inhabitants were to appoint
chapelwardens.

Shortly after passing the last mentioned Act, the trustees therein
named erected and endowed a chapel in Midville : and thenceforth
hitherto an officiating minister and chapelwardens have been duly
and regularly appointed. And overseers of the poor, surveyors of
the highways, and a constable, have been regularly and duly
appointed within and for the said township.

All the statutes above referred to were to be taken as part of
the case.

In 1837, the Commissioners of drainage and enclosures cleaned
out the drains, and covered the roads in question, to two or three

feet in depth, with the mud &c., and left the materials on it, and
levelled the same.

The township was not in existence till stat. 52 Geo. III. c. cxliv.;
before which time the road was extra-parochial.

There was duly set out and certified by the Commissioners, and
put into proper repair, a public highway on the opposite side of
the Hob Hole Drain, the whole way, with the road indicted, and
only separated from it by the drain.

If the Court should be of opinion that the inhabitants of the
township of Midville were bound to repair the highway indicted,
the verdict for the Crown was to stand : if of a contrary opinion,
to be entered for the defendants.

The case was argued in last Michaelmas Term (1).

Waddington, for the Crown :

Before stat. 41 Geo. III. (U. K.) c. cxlii., there was no liability in
any one to repair the roads : the place was extra-parochial ; and
had neither inhabitants nor roads.   Sect. 30 of that statute provides
for defraying the expenses of repair by the inhabitants of the
parishes, &c., having right of common, when the road shall have
been constructed, and certified so to be within two years after the
execution of the award, or, if the justices allow, within twelve
calendar months after that time has elapsed.   This conditional
liability has never attached, no certificate having been made ; nor
can it now ever attach, as the utmost time allowed has expired.
The liability contemplated in section 30 was a liability contrary
to common law, and therefore would not attach unless the statutory
condition precedent was strictly complied with.   This was decided
in *Rex* v. *Hatfield* (2) under sect. 9 of stat. 41 Geo. III. (U. K.) c. 109
(the General Inclosure Act).   Then stat. 52 Geo. III. c. cxliv.
recites that the lands are extra-parochial, and that it would be of
public utility that the lands, roads, &c., should be divided into
townships ; and the district is accordingly divided into townships.
Does the indictment, then, lay a legal liability, under these circumstances ?   There can of course be no charge in respect of custom
or prescription, the roads and the townships themselves being
recent.   But, except in name, each of the new districts constitutes a parish : it has the legal attributes of a *parish, such as
overseers, chapelwardens, surveyors, reputed highways, highway

RE G.
v.
THE INHABI-
TANTS OF
MIDVILLE.

[252]

[*253]

(1) November 9th, 1842.   Before   ridge and Wightman, JJ.
Lord Denman, Ch. J., Williams, Cole-   (2) 43 R. R. 322 (4 Ad. & El. 156).

rates. It will be contended, on the other side, that the first count of the indictment cannot be sustained, because it does not appear that the township is not within a parish, in which case immemorial liability ought to be averred. That objection, at any rate, does not apply to the second count, which sets forth the facts specially: and this raises the question, whether the common law liability to repair roads does not, upon general principles, attach to the district in which the roads are, when such district is invested with the other attributes which the statute here creates. If the statute had expressly made this district a parish, it would hardly have been disputed that the district immediately became subject to all the liabilities which the common law imposes on ancient parishes. The principle of this rule must be, not that the district is called a parish, or that it constitutes an ecclesiastical division, but that it is separate and not subordinate to any other district recognised by the law as liable to the repair of roads. This question arose in *Rex* v. *Kingsmoor* (1), but was not decided; though BEST, J. certainly there expressed an opinion against the liability of extra-parochial districts. The authority of 27 Ass. fol. 138, pl. 44, enumerating the articles to be inquired of in K. B. by inquest of office (cited in the argument in *Rex* v. *Kingsmoor* (1)), is in favour of such liability; for article 21 seems to assume the general liability of "villes" to repair roads. *Rex* v. *Yarton* (2), cited in the same argument, is indeed an authority of little weight, as appears by [*254] comparing Siderfin's report with the report of the *same case under the title of *Rex* v. *Yarenton* (3) in Keble, alluded to in the note at the end of *Rex* v. *Kingsmoor* (4). In *Rex* v. *Ecclesfield* (5) it was contended that an indictment charging a particular district of a parish by immemorial custom for the district to repair the roads within it was bad for not showing consideration: but the indictment was held good; and Lord ELLENBOROUGH (6) considered this (like the liability of counties to repair bridges) an instance of the common law liability incumbent on the inhabitants of a territory

(1) 26 R. R. 307 (2 B. & C. 190).
(2) 1 Sid. 140.
(3) 1 Keb. 277, 498, 514. The *placitum* in p. 277 turns upon different pleadings from that in p. 498. Keble (p. 498) speaks of Yarenton as a parish; Siderfin as a hundred: for the purposes of the respective reports, either statement appears sufficient, as the plea, whether by a parish or by a hundred, would have been bad. Serjt. Williams, in note (10) to *Rex* v. *Stoughton* (2 Wms. Saund. 159 a), seems to adopt Siderfin's statement. See the notices of *Rex* v. *Yarenton* in 4 Vin. Ab. 509, tit. Chimin Common (E.), pl. 19, 20.
(4) 26 R. R. 307 (2 B. & C. 190).
(5) 19 R. R. 335 (1 B. & Ald. 348).
(6) 1 B. & Ald. 357.

to perform the repair of ways within that territory. Here immemorial liability is not charged : but it is averred that the inhabitants have been used and accustomed to repair the road ; that is,
as long as the district has been a township.   The moment the
township began to exist, the common law principle of liability
applied : at any rate that was so as soon as the township took
upon itself the liability, and performed the repairs and appointed
surveyors.   It will be argued that the recital in sect. 1 of stat. 52
Geo. III. c. cxliv. speaks only of the utility of applying the public
laws concerning constables and the relief of the poor ; and that the
enactment in sect. 9 goes no farther.   But the liability of parochial
districts to poor laws is created by statute, and would not attach
without express enactment : the same necessity for express enactment would not exist in the case of a common law liability : and
the recital in sect. 1 does state that it *would be of public utility if
the " roads," among other things, were divided into townships.

(COLERIDGE, J. : Is not the law concerning constables as much
common law as that concerning roads ?)

It seems very doubtful whether a new township, not having before
been in any parish or within the jurisdiction of any leet, would
have constables.   The exemption, in sect. 11 of stat. 52 Geo. III.
c. cxliv., from parochial rates in other parishes is not confined to
poor rates ; this is a recognition of the general liability of the
district.   The language of PARKE, J., in *Rex* v. *Leake* (1), explains
the principle of mutual benefit by which districts, instead of joining
to maintain all roads, maintain their own respectively : upon which
principle it was there decided that a parish must repair roads newly
dedicated to the public.   That principle applies to the case of a
district newly created.

N. R. Clarke, contrà, was stopped by the COURT.

LORD DENMAN, Ch. J. :

This case has been very ably argued for the Crown.   We will
consider whether it is necessary to call upon the other side.

Cur. adv. vult.

LORD DENMAN, Ch. J. now delivered the judgment of the COURT :

This is an indictment against the inhabitants of the township of

(1) 39 R. R. 521 (5 B. & Ad. 469, 482).

Midville, for non-repair of a public highway situate within the same: and the question before us is raised on the form of the indictment, and a case reserved for our opinion.

[*256] It thereby appears that a certain district called the East and West Fens has, under sundry Acts of Parliament *(the provisions of some of which, and of one particularly, will require notice hereafter), been recovered by drainage, the place over which the highway passes having been previously uninhabited and extra-parochial.

The first Act bearing upon the question is stat. 41 Geo. III. (U. K.) c. cxlii., whereby power was given to certain Commissioners to divide and allot the said East and West Fens, and to set out public and private roads therein. The indicted road was, with others, so set out as a public road, and has been used as such ever since. By a clause in the said Act, certain surveyors to be appointed by the said Commissioners were to certify to the clerk of the peace for the said county that the said roads were in good repair; and, upon such certificate being given, the said roads, so put into repair, were thereafter to be repaired by the inhabitants of the respective parishes, townships and places having right of common on the said fens. The case, however, states that this was never done, the road in question, though used as a public road (as above mentioned), never having been so certified; and therefore the liability to repair, above pointed out, never has attached.

The question mainly turns upon one of the subsequent Acts of Parliament, 52 Geo. III. c. cxliv., entitled "An Act for forming into townships certain extra-parochial lands in Wildmore Fen, and in the East and West Fens, in the county of Lincoln." Of seven such townships, so newly created, the township indicted was one. The manner in which this is done, and the language used for the purpose in the last-mentioned Act, it will be very material to attend to.

Before we do this, however, it may be proper to premise that the facts relied upon in support of the prosecution are, that the road
[*257] in question is a public road *situate within the township, and out of repair: that, since the year 1828, surveyors of highways have been appointed; and that, in the shape of repairs, the ruts have been hacked in; and the highway rates have been raised since that time. It further appears (with this, to a certain extent, material bearing on the case, as showing that the Legislature did not then contemplate the bringing the roads in this district within the general rule of the law as to repairs, but to provide for it in a special

manner) that, since the passing of stat. 58 Geo. III. c. xlvi., a chapel has been erected, and there has been an officiating minister; and, lastly, that there have been overseers and constables for the township.

From these facts, however, the origin of every thing (including the township and the road itself) being clearly ascertained, no inference can be raised as to the liability of the defendants to repair the road by usage or prescription. Nor was it attempted to question the principle upon which that liability of a township is founded. On the contrary, the learned counsel for the prosecution very properly abandoned, in his argument, the first count of the indictment, because that only stated the road to be situate within the township and out of repair, and that the township is bound to repair it, without more. Reliance was placed upon the second count, which is founded upon the said statute of 52 Geo. III. c. cxliv. It is plain, therefore, that the question depends upon the effect of that statute; because, if the district had been merely created a township, it is manifest from the concession with respect to the first count of the indictment that the conviction could not be supported.

The material clauses, to which we have before referred, are to the following substance and effect. The *first clause states, by way of recital, that it would be of public utility if certain lands (therein described) were made to constitute seven distinct townships, and if all the general public laws now in force concerning constables, and for the relief and employment of poor people in England, were put in force therein. The second clause (1) enacts that the said townships shall be subject to all the general public laws relating to constables and the relief of the poor in England, subject to a proviso thereinafter contained. The third clause (2) enacts that the inhabitants and occupiers of lands in all the said townships shall maintain the poor therein, in the same manner as is done within any parish in England, subject to the said proviso; dropping all mention of the laws concerning constables. Then follows the said proviso (3), whereby it is enacted that the inhabitants, &c., of the said townships shall not be liable to contribute to the relief of the poor in any other parish or place, or to pay a proportional part of any other parochial rates whatsoever in any other parish or place.

[*258]

(1) Sect. 9.
(2) Sect. 10.

(3) Sect. 11.

Neither in the recital, therefore, nor in either of the enacting clauses, is there any mention made of the repair of the roads within the said several townships, though it is obvious that the few words "and the repair of roads" in the first enacting clause would have removed all doubt and difficulty. And how can we account for such omission, if the general law relating thereto had been meant to be introduced? Or how can we supply such omission? Or, if the insertion of the words above suggested would have not been sufficient for the purpose, what could have been easier than to have simply *enacted that the said several townships should repair all the public roads within the same?

[*259]

It is true that, in the proviso exempting the said townships from any contribution towards the expenses of any other parish or place, "other" rates, in addition to those for the relief of the poor, are mentioned, and that thereby rates for the repair of the roads may be understood. But it seems to be a hazardous construction to supply, by inference, the place of enactment, and that, because "other" rates may mean highway rates, therefore the township is bound to repair its own roads; and that, too, when it may have been meant merely to declare that there should be a total exemption from all foreign contribution, without any other object.

The case, therefore, resolves itself into this: that a new independent district, forming no part of any parish, is created. As to this, certain liabilities as to relief of poor, &c., depending upon statute, are expressly created also. That this district, so made a township, is wholly distinguishable from a township generally forming a part of a parish is obvious. In the absence, however, of any case wherein the *primâ facie* liability by law belonging to a parish has been held to extend to any other district or division whatever, we do not feel ourselves authorized in deciding that such independence of the district as has been before alluded to *ipso facto* attracts liability; and the more so, as such liability might so easily (if intended) have been created by the Legislature in any of the acts respecting this township.

Judgment for defendants.

IN THE EXCHEQUER CHAMBER.

(ERROR FROM THE QUEEN'S BENCH.)

SANDERS, SNOW AND COCKINGS *v.* VANZELLER(1).

(4 Q. B. 260—297; S. C. 3 G. & D. 580; 12 L. J. Ex. 497.)

Indebitatus assumpsit for freight and primage for goods carried on board plaintiff's ship at defendant's request, for work and labour performed by plaintiff for defendant, and for the use of plaintiff's ship kept on demurrage at defendant's request. Plea, *Non assumpsit;* and issue thereon. Special verdict finding the following facts.

By charter-party (not stated to be under seal), between B. and plaintiff, being owner of a vessel, it was agreed that the vessel should proceed to I., and there load from B.'s agents a cargo, and proceed therewith to London, and deliver the same on being paid freight at a rate specified, half in cash and half by bills at three months, a certain rate being also specified for demurrage.

The vessel arrived at I., and shipped goods from B.'s agent. By the bills of lading, the goods were to be delivered to B. or his assigns, he or they paying freight, as per charter-party, and primage. Before the ship arrived in London, B. sold part of the goods to defendant, and indorsed to him the corresponding bills of lading. When the ship arrived in London, the goods sold were, by defendant's order, entered in his name at the Custom House and the docks, defendant paying the duties: and defendant obtained possession of the goods under the bill of lading and indorsement. The jury referred it to the Court, whether the defendant did or did not promise as alleged in the declaration.

Held, by the Court of Exchequer Chamber, affirming the judgment of the Court of Queen's Bench, that, whether or not the facts found were evidence of a contract by defendant with plaintiff to pay freight for the goods sold (as to which, *quære*), no such contract was implied in law from the facts; that the Court could not assume such a contract on this finding; and that the defendant was entitled to judgment.

Held, by the Court of Exchequer Chamber, that, assuming the facts to be evidence of such a contract, the contract would not support the declaration.

And, by the same Court, that, if the bills of lading had not referred to the charter-party, but had merely stated that the goods were to be delivered to the consignee or his assigns on their paying freight, the taking the goods under the indorsement would have been evidence from which a jury might have inferred a contract between defendant and plaintiff to pay freight ; but that, even in such a case, no such contract would arise by mere implication of law.

The Court of Queen's Bench, after giving judgment for the defendant, refused to order a new trial for the purpose of having the contract expressly found or negatived, or to order a case to be stated with liberty for that

---

(1) See the Bills of Lading Act, 1885 (18 & 19 Vict. c. 111), s. 1; *Sewell* v. *Burdick* (1884) 10 App. Ca. 74, 54 L. J. Q. B. 156; and notes to *Cock* v. *Taylor*, 12 R. R. 378, and *Moorsom* v. *Kymer*, 15 R. R. 261. —A. C.

1841.
Jan. 15, 19.
May 27.
1842.
Jan. 27.
Feb. 1.
Nov. 26, 28.
1843.
Feb. 2.

[260]

Court to draw its inference from the facts, or to allow an amendment of the special verdict; and the Court of Exchequer Chamber held that the plaintiff was not entitled to a *venire de novo* on the ground of ambiguity in the finding.

ASSUMPSIT.   The declaration charged that defendant, on &c., was indebted to plaintiffs in 1,000*l.* for freight and primage, payable by defendant to plaintiffs for the carriage and conveyance of certain goods in and on board of a ship or vessel of plaintiffs from and to

[*261] divers places at defendant's request; in 1,000*l.* for *work and labour performed by plaintiffs for defendant at his request; in 500*l.* for the use of a ship or vessel of plaintiffs retained and kept on demurrage for a long time then elapsed at defendant's request; in 1,000*l.* for money paid by plaintiffs to the use of defendant at his request; and in 1,000*l.* on an account stated: and that defendant afterwards, on &c., in consideration of the premises, promised plaintiffs to pay &c. on request.   Breach, nonpayment.

Plea. *Non assumpsit.*   Issue thereon.

On the trial, before Lord Denman, Ch. J., at the London sittings after Michaelmas Term, 1838, a special verdict was taken, which was substantially as follows.

The plaintiffs were, on 19th December, 1835, the owners of the brig *Oscar.* George Bell then carried on business in London, under the firm and style of George Bell & Co., having a correspondent and agent at Ibrail carrying on business under the firm of Bell and Anderson.   And (1) on that day entered into the following memorandum of charter with George Bell & Co.

"LONDON, 19th December, 1835.

"Memorandum for charter.

"It is this day mutually agreed between Samuel Cockings and the other owners of the good ship or vessel called the *Oscar*, of the measurement of " &c., "now at Torquay, and Messrs. George Bell & Co. of London, merchants, that the said ship, being tight," &c., "shall, after delivery of her outward cargo at Constantinople, with all convenient speed sail and proceed to Ibrail in

[*262] the river Danube, or so near thereunto *as she may safely get, and there load, from the factors of the said charterers, a full and complete cargo of such lawful goods and merchandise as may be sent alongside the vessel, not exceeding " &c.; "and, being so loaded, shall therewith proceed to London, Liverpool, or Bristol, calling at Cork or Falmouth for orders, or so near thereunto as she

(1) The words " the plaintiffs " appear to be here omitted.

may safely get, and deliver the same, on being paid freight, at the

> 60s. per ton for tallow, 11l. per ton
> for unpressed wool, 7l. per ton for
> pressed wool, 40l. per mille for pipe
> staves, 60s. per load for wainscot or
> square oak logs.
>
> Other goods, if any, in proportion.

} With five per cent. primage.

" Restraint of princes and rulers," &c., " always excepted. The
freight to be paid on unloading and right delivery of the cargo, half
in cash, and half by bills in London at three months' date. Fifty
running days are to be allowed to the said merchant (if the ship is
not sooner dispatched) for loading the said ship at Ibrail, and
unloading at her port of delivery, to commence from the time the
vessel is ready to take in, whether in quarantine or not, and ten
days on demurrage, over and above the said laying days, at 5l. per
day. Penalty for non-performance of this agreement 1,000l. The
quantity of staves not to exceed " &c. " And, if the vessel requires
to be lightened in passing the bar, the lighterage to be at the
charterers' expense.

" GEORGE BELL & Co."

The ship sailed on her voyage to Ibrail, where she safely arrived,
and received on board there the goods *mentioned in the following   [*263]
bills of lading, which were signed by the captain, and forwarded by
the said correspondents and agents of Bell & Co. from Ibrail to
the said George Bell & Co. at London. The bills of lading, bearing
date respectively the 3rd, 6th, 25th, and 26th August, 1836, were
in the following form :

" Shipped in good order, and well conditioned, by Bell and Anderson, in and upon the good ship called the *Oscar*, whereof is master
for this present voyage William Field, now riding at anchor in the
river Danube, and bound for London, to say,

$\overset{\text{G B}}{\underset{\text{A}}{}}$ 201 @ 230 bales of unwashed zigai wool.

$\overset{\text{G B}}{\underset{\text{B}}{}}$ 41 @ 55 fifteen bales of do.   do.

being marked and numbered as in the margin, and are to be
delivered in the like good order, and well conditioned, at the aforesaid port of London (the act of God," &c. " excepted), unto Messrs.
George Bell & Co. or to their assigns, he or they paying freight
for the said goods as per charter-party, with primage and average

accustomed. In witness whereof the master or purser of the said
ship hath affirmed to three bills of lading, all of this tenor and date;
the one of which three bills being accomplished, the other two to
stand void. Dated in the port of Ibrail, 3rd August, 1836."

Indorsed, "GEORGE BELL & Co."

On 16th July, 1836, the following contract was made and entered
into between George Bell & Co. and the defendant (W. G. Colchester
being the agent of Messrs. George Bell & Co. and the defendant).
Messrs. George Bell & Co. had previously purchased the wools
[*264]   *hereinafter mentioned, according to the recitals in the following
contract.

"LONDON, 16th July, 1836.

"Whereas, by a contract made on the 4th January last, between
Messrs. Bell and Anderson of Bucharest on the one part, and
Messrs. Jacob N. Gallanter and Schonfield, of Bucharest, and
Messrs. Leigh, Reiss & Co. of Jassy, on the other part, Messrs.
Bell and Anderson purchased a quantity of wool, to be delivered
at Ibrail or Galatz before the 1st of October next, a copy of which
contract is hereto annexed; and whereas the said wool was bought
for and on account of Messrs. George Bell & Co. of this city, and is
at their entire disposition: Now be it known that I have this day
sold, for Messrs. George Bell & Co., to Francis Ignatius Vanzeller,
Esq., the 200,000 okes of the washed zigai wool specified in the
annexed copy, for the sum of 22,000*l.* The wool is to be put on
board the ships by the sellers, or their agents, at the ports of Ibrail
or Galatz, or any other port on the Danube, as the same may be
delivered: and the buyer agrees to perform and fulfil all charter-
parties and agreements for freight for the said wool heretofore
made, or to be made, by the sellers, excepting any charges that may
be made for demurrage, for which the buyer is in no case to be
liable to pay. And the sellers are, immediately upon the receipt of
the bills of lading for the said wool, to hand the same over to the
buyer properly assigned; it being understood that the 200,000
okes of washed wool, delivered by the before mentioned parties to
Messrs. Bell and Anderson under the said contract, vests absolutely
from this day in the buyer. And, as, by a subsequent agreement,
[*265]   *Messrs. Bell and Anderson consented to take a portion of wool in
an unwashed state, according to a certain rate, in lieu of a part of
the wool agreed to be delivered washed under the before mentioned
contract, it is agreed between the said Messrs. George Bell & Co.

and Francis Ignatius Vanzeller, Esq. that the wool shall be delivered
and received by them upon the conditions of the said contract and
the subsequent agreement.   And whereas the buyer has already
paid to the sellers the sum of 9,000l. on account of this purchase,
the remainder of the purchase-money is to be paid in manner
following, viz. the sum of 3,500l. by the buyer's acceptance of the
sellers' draft at two months from this date, 3,500l. by the like
acceptance at three months, and 4,000l. by a like acceptance at four
months from this date, and 2,000l. to be paid in cash at such time
or times as the sellers may require the same, they giving to the
buyer ten days' previous notice in writing.
" W. G. COLCHESTER."

The defendant, under the said contract of 16th July, paid to
George Bell & Co. in London for the said wools, and made his
advances thereon before the arrival of the ship and cargo in this
country.   The bills of lading were indorsed and delivered by George
Bell & Co. to the defendant.

One hundred bales of wool were shipped by the said Messrs. Bell
and Anderson on board a vessel called the *Ann*, as and for part of
the said 200,000 okes of wool so contracted to be sold as aforesaid,
which said vessel arrived in the port of London on 27th October,
1836.   On the arrival of the *Ann*, the said one hundred bales were
found to be, and they in fact were, *wool of a quality other than   [*266]
and different from and very inferior to the quality of the said wool
so contracted to be sold to defendant.   And thereupon, and before
the arrival in the port of London of the *Oscar*, the defendant gave
notice to Messrs. Bell and Anderson that he would not accept the
said wool, so arrived by the *Ann*, or the further parcel thereof
about to arrive by the *Oscar*, as and for wool so contracted to be
sold to him as aforesaid, but that he defendant would receive the
same and sell and dispose thereof for and on account of Messrs.
G. Bell & Co., and pay himself out of the proceeds the advances
he had made on the goods.   Messrs. G. Bell & Co. thereupon, and
before the arrival of the *Oscar*, agreed with the defendant that he
should receive the said wool by the *Ann* and the *Oscar*, and sell
and dispose of the same for and on account of the said Messrs. G.
Bell & Co., and carry the proceeds to their credit against the sums
so paid and advances made by the defendant.   Messrs. G. Bell
& Co. afterwards paid the freight for the said one hundred bales of
wool which had, as before mentioned, arrived by the *Ann*.

The said several bills of lading of the said wool, so shipped on board the *Oscar*, arrived before the said vessel arrived, and were indorsed and handed over to the defendant, some on 29th August, and the residue on 14th September, 1836.

The defendant, before the arrival of the wools, sold part of them, on 8th November, 1836.

The *Oscar* arrived in St. Katherine's Docks on 21st November, 1836. The wools were entered in the defendant's name, by his order, at the Custom House in London, and the duties for the same *267] paid by the defendant. *They were also entered at the St. Katherine's Docks in the defendant's name. The wools were landed from the *Oscar* on to the St. Katherine's Docks wharf, and were of the same inferior quality as that which had been landed from the *Ann*.

On 22nd November, 1836, the following order, signed by the defendant, was delivered by the defendant or his agents to the St. Katherine's Docks Company.

" Please allow the bearer to draw two samples.
                              " For Cooper and Spratt,
                                        " S. BENTLEY.
     " LONDON, November 22nd, 1836.
     " To the superintendent of the St. Katherine's Docks.
     " Please deliver to Messrs. Cooper and Spratt the under mentioned wools, entered by us, *ex Oscar*, Field, at Ibrail."

The order set forth in the margin the marks and numbers, and added :

" Two hundred and ninety-nine bales of sheep's wool. They paying all charges.
                              " F. J. VANZELLER."

Indorsed, " Deliver the within to our carts,
     " Charges to deposit account.
                         " Your obedient servants,
                                   " COOPER AND SPRATT."

And the said wools were accordingly, under that order, then delivered to Cooper and Spratt, and removed thence by them to certain warehouses on the defendant's account. And, on 30th November, 1836, the defendant sold the residue of the wools by [*268] public auction, on the account of George Bell & Co., as had *been agreed upon between Mr. Bell and the defendant as aforesaid.

The defendant obtained possession of the wools under the bills of lading and the indorsement and delivery thereof to the defendant

Payment of the freight, according to the memorandum of charter,
and now sought to be recovered in this action, for the said wools
assigned to the defendant under the said four bills of lading, was
demanded by the plaintiffs of Messrs. George Bell & Co., after the
same had been removed, and not before.   And afterwards payment
of the same freight was demanded by the plaintiffs of the defendant,
and refused to be paid by him, before this action was brought.

There was other wool and other goods on board the *Oscar*,
shipped by Bell and Anderson, and consigned in a similar way to
George Bell & Co., or their order: the bills of lading whereof
(precisely similar in tenor and effect to those indorsed to the defendant) had been indorsed and delivered by them to Messrs. Holford
for securing advances made by them to Bell & Co.   There were
also other goods on board the *Oscar*, shipped by Bell and Anderson,
and consigned to Messrs. Holford or their order, the bills of lading
whereof were precisely similar in tenor and effect to those indorsed
to the defendant.   The last mentioned goods were consigned to
Messrs. Holford & Co., for securing advances made by them to
Messrs. George Bell & Co.

The plaintiffs by their broker, after the said wool had been so as
aforesaid delivered to the defendant, and removed to the warehouses
as before mentioned, viz. 6th December, 1836, gave notice to the
St. Katherine's Dock *Company to detain the cargo then in the   [*269]
docks for the whole of the freight payable under the charter-party.

The goods so delivered to Messrs. Holford were, at the time the
said notice were given, in the warehouses of the said Dock
Company, and were detained by the said Company, pursuant to the
said notice.   And, in order to obtain possession thereof, Messrs.
Holford paid the freight of their own goods and indemnified the
Company against the claims of the plaintiffs.   Messrs. Holford's
goods realised, after payment of their freight, 558*l.*

The demand of the plaintiffs in this action for freight of the
defendant's wool is 520*l.* 6*s.*

The sums received by the defendant on the sale of the said wools
are insufficient to cover his said advances on them : and there is
still a large balance due to the defendant on his said advances upon
the wools.

" The jury, on their oaths aforesaid, further say that the plaintiffs
are entitled to recover interest, if the plaintiffs are entitled to the

judgment of the Court. But whether or not, upon the whole matter aforesaid by the jurors aforesaid in form aforesaid found, the said Francis Ignatius Vanzeller did promise, the jurors aforesaid are altogether ignorant; and thereupon they pray the advice of the Court of the said lady the Queen, before the Queen herself. And, if, upon the whole matter aforesaid, it shall seem to the said Court that the said F. I. Vanzeller did promise, then the jurors aforesaid, upon their oath aforesaid, say that the said F. I. Vanzeller did promise in manner and form as the said Robert Roger Sanders," &c., "have within thereof complained against him; and in that case they assess the damages of the plaintiffs, by reason thereof, over and above their costs and charges," &c., to 520*l.* 6*s.*, with

[*270] interest at 5 per *cent. from 17th March, 1837, the day on which this action was brought, and for costs 40*s.* "But if, upon the whole matter aforesaid, it shall seem to the said Court that the said F. I. Vanzeller did not promise, then the jurors aforesaid, upon their oath aforesaid, say that the said F. I. Vanzeller did not promise in manner and form as the said R. R. Sanders," &c., "have within thereof complained against him."

The case was argued in the Court of Queen's Bench in Hilary Term, 1841 (1), by *Sir W. W. Follett* for the plaintiffs, and *R. V. Richards* for the defendant. The line of argument will sufficiently appear by the argument on error. Besides the authorities there cited, *Pinder* v. *Wilks* (2) and *Heisch* v. *Carrington* (3) were referred to in the Court of Queen's Bench.

Cur. adv. vult.

LORD DENMAN, Ch. J., in Trinity Term following (May 27th, 1841), delivered the judgment of the COURT :

Messrs. Bell of London chartered a vessel of the plaintiffs, by a memorandum agreeing that she should proceed to the Danube, and load from the factors of the charterers a cargo of lawful merchandize to be delivered in England, "on being paid freight" at certain specified rates for tallow, various kinds of wool, and other merchandize, "the freight to be paid on unloading and right delivery of the cargo, half in cash, and half by bills in London at three months'

[*271] date," with other stipulations not material *to our present inquiry. The ship sailed, received a large quantity of wool, with bills of

---

(1) January 15th and 19th. Before   (2) 5 Taunt. 612.
Lord Denman, Ch. J., Littledale,   (3) Note (*e*) to *Johnston* v. *Usborne*,
Patteson and Coleridge, JJ.   52 R. R. 445 (11 Ad. & El. 555).

lading addressed to Messrs. Bell, or their assigns, "he or they
paying freight for the said goods as per charter-party, with primage
and average accustomed."   The agent of Messrs. Bell sold his wool
to the defendant for 22,000*l.*, "the wool to be put on board the
ships by the sellers, or their agents" at Ibrail, or any other port
on the Danube, "as the same may be delivered: and the buyer
agrees to perform and fulfil all charter-parties and agreements for
freight for the said wool heretofore made, or to be made, by the
sellers, excepting any charges that may be made for demurrage, for
which the buyer is in no case to be liable to pay.   And the sellers
are, immediately upon the receipt of the bills of lading for the said
wool, to hand the same over to the buyer properly assigned."   The
defendant immediately paid Messrs. Bell for the said wool, which,
on its arrival, was found to be of inferior quality; and he gave them
notice that he would not accept it as the wool contracted for, but
would sell it on account of Messrs. Bell, and pay himself his
advances out of the proceeds.   To this Messrs. Bell acceded.   The
wools were entered by the defendant at the Custom House, and the
duties paid by him in his own name ; and he sold them, part by
private contract, part by auction.   The special verdict finds that
the defendant obtained possession of the wools under the bills of
lading, and that payment of the freight, demanded by plaintiffs,
first of Messrs. Bell, afterwards of the defendant, was refused.
Some other goods brought by the same vessel to other merchants
had paid freight to the plaintiffs ; but 520*l.* still remains due in
respect of the wool.   The proceeds of the sales made by the defendant
as aforesaid are insufficient to pay the advances made by *him ;   [*272]
and a large balance is still due to him from Messrs. Bell.

In this case we had written a detailed judgment, observing on
the cases cited on the argument, being, principally, *Moorsom* v.
Kymer (1) for the defendant, *Cock* v. *Taylor* (2), and *Wilson* v.
Kymer (3) for the plaintiffs.   That first named established that the
indorsee's acceptance of goods under a bill of lading does not of
itself constitute an agreement to pay freight, &c., according to the
bill of lading, where the ship has been engaged by a charter-party
under seal.   And to this extent we fully coincide with that decision.
Neither do we in any degree impugn the cases quoted on the other
side, which appear consistent with reason and have been often
recognised as authority.   They prove that such an acceptance may

(1) 15 R. R. 261 (2 M. & S. 303).   (3) 1 M. & S. 157 (see 52 R. R. 812,
(2) 12 R. R. 378 (13 East, 399).   813).

be evidence (stronger or weaker according to other circumstances) of a new contract to make the payments stipulated by the bill of lading, between the shipowner and the indorsee to whom the goods are delivered.

In the present case we find a charter-party under seal; and *Moorsom* v. *Kymer* (1) shows that this privity is not created by operation of law. But, though we find evidence of the new contract alluded to, we must not forget that we are dealing with a special verdict, which states and confines us to the facts found by the jury. We have no right to infer any thing, however probable in appearance. One of the facts, therefore, that are essential to entitle the plaintiffs is wanting; and our judgment must be for the defendant.

Judgment for defendant.

[273]   After the above judgment was given, *Sir W. W. Follett*, in the same Term, obtained a rule to show cause why a new trial should not be had, or why the facts found at the trial should not be stated in a special case for the opinion of the Court, with liberty to the Court to draw their inference from the facts, or why the special verdict should not be amended in such way as to raise the question of law for the opinion of the Court. * * *

[275]   In Hilary Term, 1842 (2),

Sir F. Pollock, Attorney-General, and *Richards* showed cause. * * *

Sir W. W. Follett, Solicitor-General, and *Hoggins, contrà*. * * *

Cur. adv. vult.

[276]   LORD DENMAN, Ch. J., in the following vacation (February 1st, 1842), delivered the judgment of the COURT:

In this case the parties came before me and settled the special verdict, upon which judgment has been given. Application is now made for a new trial, in order that an additional fact, that of a contract, may be introduced. Such an application, if founded on a suggestion of fraud or of misunderstanding at Nisi Prius or in
[*277]   banc, should *not have been so long deferred. But, independently of this, we held the facts, by which we considered ourselves to be bound, insufficient to warrant a judgment for the plaintiffs: and

(1) 15 R. R. 261 (2 M. & S. 303).   Denman, Ch. J., Patteson, Coleridge
(2) January 27th. Before Lord   and Wightman, JJ.

the answer to this application is that, if the facts are sufficient, error may be brought on our judgment; and, if they are not, such facts as would have been sufficient ought, if true, to have been inserted in the first instance. Probably no judgment ever was delivered as to which the losing party might not have made a complaint similar to that which is made here.

Rule discharged.

Error was brought in the Exchequer Chamber upon the judgment on the special verdict: and the case was argued in last Michaelmas vacation (1), before Tindal, Ch. J., Coltman and Erskine, JJ., and Parke, Alderson, Gurney and Rolfe, Barons.

Sir W. W. Follett, Solicitor-General, for the plaintiffs in error (the plaintiffs below):

The facts stated in the special verdict raise a contract and promise in law; and therefore the judgment ought to have been entered for the plaintiffs. But, if, as the Court of Queen's Bench has considered, this was a question to be determined expressly by the jury, the finding is imperfect, and there must be a *venire de novo*.

First, the defendant has received the cargo, as indorsee of a bill of lading, which specifies that freight is to be paid on the unloading and delivery of the cargo. In *Roberts* v. *Holt* (2) it was holden to be a good custom *of merchants that the consignee of a bill of lading should be liable for the freight. Then in *Cock* v. *Taylor* (3) it was held that, if the assignee of a bill of lading, by which the goods are to be delivered to the order of the consignee or to his assigns, he or they paying freight, demand and take the goods from the master, that is evidence of a contract by the assignee to pay the freight, upon which he may be sued in *indebitatus assumpsit* for freight. In conformity with these cases, the law is thus laid down in Abbott on Shipping, p. 285 (4). "If a consignee receive goods in pursuance of the usual bill of lading, by which it is expressed that he is to pay the freight, he by such receipt makes himself debtor for the freight, and may be sued for it." The author then, after mentioning cases in which it had been held that a purchaser from the consignee was not under such liability, goes on as follows. "But the point, having been since more maturely considered, it has been decided, that although there

[*278]

(1) November 26th and 28th, 1842.
(2) 2 Show. 443.
(3) 12 R. R. 378 (13 East, 399).

(4) Part III. c. 7, § 4, ed. 5. See ed. 7, p. 420, part IV. c. 9, § 4.

be no original privity of contract between the purchasers from consignees and the owner, yet the taking of goods by purchasers under a bill of lading is evidence of a new agreement by them, as the ultimate appointees of the shippers, to pay the freight for the carriage of the goods, the delivery being stipulated with the shippers to be made to the consignees named in the bill of lading or their assigns, he or they paying freight for the same. And this opinion seems most consonant to sound reason; for if a person accepts any thing, which he knows to be subject to a duty or charge, it is rational to conclude that he means to take the duty or charge upon himself; and the law may very well imply a promise

[*279]
to perform *what he so takes upon himself " (1). The principle, therefore, is that the taking, under these circumstances, is a virtual assent to the terms of the bill. The promise is implied by law, just as upon the sale and delivery of goods. In *Wilson* v. *Kymer* (2) it was held that an implied assumpsit did not arise where the assignees of a similar bill of lading took the cargo, not (as here) under the bill, but by a special order from the original consignees, after it was landed in the names of the consignees: but, nevertheless, that the implied assumpsit did arise, even there, upon proof that, under such circumstances, the assignees had been in the habit of paying the freight. It is, however, to be observed that in that case the whole ship was let by charter-party to the consignees, and the plaintiffs (the shipowners) had proved against them, on their bankruptcy, for freight, under that charter-party. [He also referred to *Jesson* v. *Solly* (3), Abbott on Shipping, p. 247, part III. c. 8, s. 11 (ed. 5) (4), *Moorsom* v. *Kymer* (5), *Schack* v. *Anthony* (6), *Harman* v. *Clarke* (7), *Harman* v. *Mant* (8), *Scaife* v. *Tobin* (9), *Tobin* v. *Crawford* (10), *Christy* v. *Row* (11), *Shepard* v. *De Bernales* (12), *Domett* v. *Beckford* (13), *Ward* v. *Felton* (14), *Anonymous* (15), *Paul* v. *Birch* (16) and *Small* v. *Moates* (17).]

(1) See *Renteria* v. *Ruding*, Moo. & Mal. 511, 513.

(2) 1 M. & S. 157 (see 52 R. R. 812, 813).

(3) 13 R. R. 557 (4 Taunt. 52).

(4) See ed. 7, p. 376, part IV. c. 5, s. 4.

(5) 15 R. R. 261 (2 M. & S. 303).

(6) 1 M. & S. 573.

(7) 16 R. R. 768 (4 Camp. 159).

(8) 16 R. R. 770 (4 Camp. 161).

(9) 37 R. R. 500 (3 B. & Ad. 523).

(10) 52 R. R. 695 (5 M. & W. 235). Affirmed on error in Exch. Ch., *Tobin* v. *Crawford*, 52 R. R. 701 (9 M. & W. 716).

(11) 9 R. R. 776 (1 Taunt. 300).

(12) 12 R. R. 442 (13 East, 565).

(13) 29 R. R. 145 (5 B. & Ad. 521).

(14) 1 East, 507.

(15) 1 Leon. 293, pl. 401.

(16) 2 Atk. 621, 622.

(17) 35 R. R. 613 (9 Bing. 574).

The Court of Queen's Bench, however, consider that the con- SANDERS
tract itself should have been found by the jury.   That would *v.*
VANZELLER.
make it almost impossible to frame *a special verdict in an action   [284]
of assumpsit.   The contract is, legally speaking, found by finding   [*285]
the facts which raise it. [He cited *Tobin* v. *Crawford* (1),
Monkhouse v. *Hay* (2), *Goodtitle* d. *Jones* v. *Jones* (3) and *Bird*
v. *Appleton* (4).]

Richards, contrà: [286]

The principal stress appears to be laid upon *Cock* v. *Taylor* (5).
There *Artaza* v. *Smallpiece* (6), and *The Theresa Bonita* (7) were
overruled : but it is not necessary, for the purpose of the present
*case, to contest the decision.   At one time an opinion seems to   [*287]
have prevailed that the contract was ambulatory, and that the
shipper ceased to be liable when the goods were delivered, his
liability being then transferred to the party taking them.   That
opinion is now admitted to be incorrect : but, upon such an
assumption, there might be no inconsistency in holding that the
party taking the goods became primarily liable.   When, however,
it is admitted that the shipper continues liable on his original
contract, it is difficult to understand how, upon the same contract,
two different parties can be simultaneously under the same
liability (8).   It is not like the case of a suretyship, or a joint liability :
but, according to the view taken on the other side, two distinct
parties are severally and primarily liable for the conveyance of
the same goods under a single contract.   No legal meaning can be
assigned to the words " adoption of a contract," as used in the
argument for the plaintiffs.   Can the goods have been carried for
the indorsee and also for the shipper ?   In *Domett* v. *Beckford* (9)
the goods belonged to the defendant, and were shipped originally
on his account, though, by the bill of lading, they were consigned
to other parties, they paying freight : and it was there held that
such a shipping creates a contract with the shipper without
any charter-party, which contract may be enforced even after a

(1) 52 R. R. 701 (9 M. & W. 716).
The decision in the Court of Exchequer
was on a case reserved, with leave to
turn the case into a special verdict
(see *Tobin* v. *Crawford*, 52 R. R. 695,
5 M. & W. 235), which was done ;
and the argument in the Exchequer
Chamber was on the special verdict.

(2) 8 Price, 256.

(3) 7 T. R. 43, 48.

(4) 5 R. R. 468 (1 East, 111, see
note (a)).

(5) 12 R. R. 378 (13 East, 399).

(6) 1 Esp. 23.

(7) 4 Chr. Rob. Adm. Rep. 236.

(8) See now Bills of Lading Act, 1855
(18 & 19 Vict. c. 111), s. 2.—A. C.

(9) 29 R. R. 145 (5 B. & Ad. 521).

[*288]

delivery to the consignees without payment. In *Drew* v. *Bird* (1) Lord TENTERDEN held that, where there was no charter-party, and the goods were, by the bill of lading, to be delivered to a party other than the shipper, or to the assigns of such other party, he or they paying freight, the shipper was not liable if the goods were delivered without payment of freight, unless there were *some additional circumstances to show a contract between him and the shipowner.

(PARKE, B. : That is not the law now.)

The shipper would be liable, certainly, if he shipped on his own account.

(PARKE, B. : According to a manuscript note which I have of *Mr. Taddy's* argument in *Moorsom* v. *Kymer* (2), he there stated that in *Cock* v. *Taylor* (3) the goods, when shipped, were the property of the defendant : if that was so, the doctrine, that a party may contract by taking goods under the bill of lading, would not have been necessary there, though it has been subsequently sanctioned.)

(*Sir W. W. Follett*: That must have been a mistake arising from the indorsement of the bill to Peters, the defendant's agent at Gibraltar.)

Suppose even that there had been no charter-party here: the shippers might have been sued on the contract shown by the bill of lading. But the bill in fact refers to the charter-party for the terms : the shippers therefore were liable to pay freight for the whole, half in bills and half in cash. How can the indorsees here be liable on that contract ? What is the breach to be ? Were the indorsees to give bills for half and cash for half of the parcel which they received ? Is such a special contract to be applied to every parcel of goods which is the subject of a separate bill of lading, if the bill be indorsed ? It is observable that, according to the report of *Cock* v. *Taylor* (3), Lord ELLENBOROUGH there considers that there was evidence of a new agreement between the shipowner and the indorsee, and LE BLANC, J. treats the abandonment of the lien as evidence of such a contract. That would not support the

(1) Moo. & Mal. 156.   (3) 12 R. R. 378 (13 East, 399).
(2) 15 R. R. 261 (2 M. & S. 303).

declaration there, which was *indebitatus assumpsit* for freight : but,
upon *the explanation of that case, just suggested by PARKE, B.,
the allegations in the declaration would of course be proved. In
Wilson v. *Kymer* (1) there was a count stating the facts specially,
and it was held that a new contract might be implied from the
usage of the parties. So in *Roberts* v. *Holt* (2) the contract was
implied from the custom of merchants, which is part of the law of
the land. *Moorsom* v. *Kymer* (3) is decisive against the plaintiffs.
It is unimportant that the charter-party there was under seal : the
effect of the decision is that the shipowner, if he gives up the goods
without payment, must resort to the original contract with the
shipper, whether such contract be under seal or not, or whether it
be evidenced by a charter-party or by the mere act of shipping. In
Dougal v. *Kemble* (4) an indorsee of a bill of lading, framed as the
bill is here, was held liable for freight, on the authority of *Cock* v.
Taylor (5) : but both BEST, Ch. J. and PARK, J. evidently consider
that, if there were a previous contract with any other party, that
party would be solely liable ; and *Moorsom* v. *Kymer* (3) is explained
in that way. *Bell* v. *Kymer* (6) was decided on the authority of
Cock v. *Taylor* (5). Afterwards, in *Domett* v. *Beckford* (7), the
liability of the original owner and shipper of the goods, independently of a charter-party, was established : and that decision
qualifies, in a great degree, the views upon which some of the
learned Judges decided the earlier cases. *Coleman* v. *Lambert* (8)
shows that the mere consignment of goods does not *make the
consignee liable for freight on receiving the goods, where there is
no bill of lading. It is true, as contended on the other side, that
an indorsee of a bill of lading which stipulates for demurrage is
liable for demurrage to the shipowner. The new contract which
arises may be proved by the terms of the bill ; the indorsee must
be understood as contracting in the character of owner of the goods
which he has purchased ; and, as owner of the goods, he must
answer for the delay which causes the demurrage. That does not
prove that he becomes primarily liable on the original contract for
freight between the shipper and the shipowner. The only recent
authority for the doctrine that the contract of shipment is adopted
by the indorsee of the bill of lading is some of the language in

(1) 52 R. R. 812, 813 (1 M. & S. 157).   (6) 5 Taunt. 477 ; *S. C.* at N. P., 3
(2) 2 Show. 443.   Camp. 545.
(3) 2 M. & S. 303.   (7) 39 R. R. 559 (5 B. & Ad. 521).
(4) 28 R. R. 648 (3 Bing. 383).   (8) 52 R. R. 811 (5 M. & W. 502).
(5) 12 R. R. 378 (13 East, 399).

SANDERS
v.
VANZELLER.

[291]

[293]

[*294]

Small v. *Moates* (1), which, perhaps, might properly be reconsidered. * * *

Then, as to the form of the verdict. The jury profess to leave to the Court whether the facts legally establish a contract; and, if such a contract be not constituted, then they find that the defendant did not promise. That is perfectly distinct and unambiguous, if the facts do not raise the promise at law: though possibly, if they do, the defendant might insist on a *venire de novo* for want of a positive finding.

Sir *W. W. Follett*, Solicitor-General, in reply. * * *

Cur. adv. vult.

TINDAL, Ch. J. now delivered the judgment of the COURT:

The questions in this case arise upon a special verdict in the Court of Queen's Bench, in an action of *indebitatus assumpsit*, stating the defendant to be indebted to the plaintiffs for freight and primage payable by the defendant to the plaintiffs for the carriage and conveyance of certain goods, on board a vessel of the plaintiffs, from and to divers places, at the defendant's request, and for work and labour, with the money counts and account stated. There was a plea of *Non assumpsit*; and issue thereon. And, on the trial, the facts were found by the jury.

The jury found that the plaintiffs, the owners of the brig *Oscar*, on the 19th December, 1835, by a memorandum per charter made between them and Messrs. George Bell & Co., agreed that the said vessel should proceed to Ibrail in the river Danube, and there load from the charterers' agents a full cargo of lawful merchandise, and therewith proceed to London, or some other port therein named, and deliver the same, on being paid freight, at the rate of 60s. per ton for tallow, 11l. per ton for unpressed wool, &c.: the freight to be paid on unloading and right delivery of the cargo, half in cash, and half by bills in London at three months' date. That the ship received on board a certain quantity of wool from the agents of Messrs. Bell & Co., under bills of lading dated 26th August, 1836, by which the goods were made deliverable to Messrs. George Bell & Co., or their assigns, he or they paying freight for the said goods as per charter-party. The special verdict then found a contract of sale between Messrs. Bell & Co. and the defendant, dated the 16th July, 1836, by which Bell & Co. sold to the

(1) 35 R. R. 613 (9 Bing. 574).

defendant the wools expected to arrive, and it was agreed that the
property should vest in the defendant from the time of the contract: that the bills of lading were indorsed and delivered by Messrs. Bell & Co. to the defendant on their arrival in England; and that the defendant afterwards obtained possession of the wools under the bills of lading.   There were other facts found in the special verdict, which do not appear material to the consideration of the points raised before us.

The Court of Queen's Bench gave judgment for the defendant. And, on the argument before us, it was insisted by the plaintiff in error that the judgment was erroneous: first, because, on the facts found by the jury, there was a promise implied by law from the defendant to the plaintiffs to pay the freight of the goods at the rate specified in the charter-party; and, secondly, if there was not, that there was evidence of such a contract to go to the jury, and that the special verdict was defective, and that therefore there should be a *venire de novo*.

We are of opinion that the judgment of the Court of Queen's Bench was right, and that the special verdict was not defective; and that the defendant is entitled to judgment in his favour.   Such facts as are found by the jury are found without any ambiguity; and there is no defect in the verdict in that respect; and the question referred by the jury to the Court is one of law: viz. whether the law would, upon these facts, imply a contract *by the [*295] defendant with the plaintiff to pay the freight at the rate specified. We are satisfied that it would not, even if this were the case of an indorsee of a bill of lading which specified that the goods were to be delivered by the shipowner to the consignee or his assigns, he or they paying a certain specified sum for freight, without any reference to a charter-party, and the indorsee had received the goods by virtue of that bill: there would have been no promise implied by law, though there would have been evidence to warrant the jury in finding that there was such a contract; and it has been so much the practice for the indorsee of such a bill of lading to pay the specified freight, if he accepts the goods under it, that there is little or no doubt that the jury would, on such a question, have found in favour of the shipowner if the indorsee received the goods without a disclaimer of his liability to the freight.   But there is no authority for saying that, under such circumstances, there is a contract raised by law to pay the freight which another, viz. the consignor, has contracted with the shipowner to pay.   Upon

SANDERS
v.
VANZELLER.

principle, it cannot be contended that the contract runs with the property in the goods and is transferred with it; and there is no decision to that effect. We do not dispute the propriety of the judgment in *Cock* v. *Taylor* (1), which may be treated as the origin of questions of this nature; but that decision was merely that the receipt of the goods under the bill of lading was evidence of a new agreement; and it is so spoken of by all the Judges. In the subsequent case of *Wilson* v. *Kymer* (2) the previous mode of carry-

[*296]

ing on business between the parties was held to be evidence of *the same nature; and it was left to the jury to consider whether they would imply a similar promise from the former habits of dealing by the evidence of the defendant having obtained the goods under orders from the consignee, but having paid the freight: and, though some of the Judges, particularly Mr. Justice LE BLANC in the subsequent case of *Moorsom* v. *Kymer* (3), speak as if the case of *Cock* v. *Taylor* (4) had decided that the law would imply a promise, it is evident that the expression is an inaccurate one and not justified by the case itself. The ground on which the latter case is distinguished from the former by all the Judges except Lord ELLEN-BOROUGH, viz. that there was a remedy for the same freight by the shipowner against the consignee, cannot certainly be supported.

We are therefore of opinion that the law would not imply any contract in this case, if the bill of lading had made no reference to the charter-party, but had specified a certain sum of money to be payable for freight; and, consequently, that our judgment should be for the defendant.

But it is said that the Court should draw reasonable inferences from the facts, even on a special verdict; and that, as a matter of fact, such a contract ought to be inferred.

We are not prepared to say that a jury would be warranted, on the facts in this case simply, to find that there was a contract by the defendant to pay any freight; because the reference in the bill of lading to the charter-party is, in the opinion of some of us, intro-

[*297]

duced for the purpose of keeping the charter-party *unvaried, and preserving the lien for the charter-party freight, and not for the purpose of creating a new contract, viz. to deliver the goods in each bill of lading on the payment of a freight for each according to the rate in the charter-party. But we all agree that the Court can draw no inference that a contract was made by the defendant

(1) 12 R. R. 378 (13 East, 399).   (3) 15 R. R. 261 (2 M. & S. 303).
(2) 52 R. R. 812, 813 (1 M. & S. 157).   (4) 12 R. R. 378 (13 East, 399).

with the plaintiff to pay any freight in consideration of the delivery to him of the goods comprised in such bill of lading.

We are also of opinion that, if the jury had found such contract, it would not support this declaration, which ought to have been a count in special assumpsit, or at least *indebitatus assumpsit* for the freight for goods delivered to the defendant at his request. If the law had been that there was an implied contract, on the ground that the obligation to pay freight was transferred with the goods to the indorsee, so that he would have been indebted for the freight, this declaration would have been proper; but that is not the law.

The judgment must therefore be affirmed.

Judgment affirmed.

MARTIN *v.* TEMPERLEY (1).

(4 Q. B. 298—313; S. C. 3 G. & D. 497; 12 L. J. Q. B. 129; 7 Jur. 150.)

By statute 7 & 8 Geo. IV. c. lxxv. (for regulating watermen and lighter-men on the Thames), and the by-laws ordained in pursuance thereof, no one besides freemen, or apprentices to freemen or to widows of freemen, of the Watermen and Lightermen's Company (with certain exceptions not material), may navigate craft on the river for hire within the limits of the Act, under a penalty; but any persons may keep and use craft for carrying their own goods by their servants, being such freemen or apprentices: and on board of every barge, &c., there must be at least one able and skilful man authorized by law to navigate. There are about 6,000 freemen and apprentices.

The owner of a barge hired two qualified persons to navigate it within the limits; and, by their negligent management of the barge, another vessel was injured.

Held, that the owner of the barge was liable to a civil action for the mischief.

And that it made no difference whether the navigators were hired for the job or by time.

THE declaration stated that, whereas plaintiff, on &c., before and at the time of the grievance hereinafter mentioned, was lawfully possessed of a certain boat of great value, to wit &c. then lawfully being in the river Thames; and defendant was also then possessed of two barges in the same river, and then had the care, direction and management of the same: yet defendant, not regarding his duty in that behalf, whilst the said boat of plaintiff so was in the river Thames aforesaid, to wit on &c., took so little and such bad care of, and so carelessly, negligently and improperly managed, governed and directed, his said barges, that one of them, by and through the carelessness, misdirection and mismanagement,

(1) *The Guy Mannering* (1882) 7 P. Div. 132.

MARTIN
v.
TEMPERLEY.

negligence and improper conduct, of defendant and his servants in that behalf, then with great force and violence ran foul of and struck against the said boat or vessel of plaintiff, and thereby then greatly broke, damaged and injured the same : and by means of the premises the said boat of plaintiff then became and was filled with water, and sunk in the said river : and thereby divers goods and chattels, to wit &c. (special damage from the loss of goods on board, expense of repairs and deprivation of the use of the vessel, and other expenses in respect of goods on board, and of the vessel).

[299]

Pleas. 1. Not guilty. 2. That defendant had not, at the time of the committing &c., the care, direction or management of the two vessels or barges, or either of them : conclusion to the country. Issue thereon.

On the trial, before Lord Denman, Ch. J., at the London sittings after Hilary Term, 1842, it appeared that the defendant had hired by the year the two barges mentioned in the declaration from one Covington, who was the owner of the barges and a freeman of the Company of Watermen and Lightermen, incorporated by stat. 7 & 8 Geo. IV. c. lxxv. (1), s. 4 : that it was usual to hire barges in this manner : and that the barges so hired were entirely under the control of the persons hiring them. The accident occurred within the limits named in the title of the Act, and was occasioned by the two barges, which at the time were lashed together, coming into collision with the plaintiff's boat. The barges were at that time under the management of two men named Wickings and Martin. Martin was a freeman of the Company of Watermen and Lightermen ; and Wickings was an apprentice to his own brother, Joseph Richard Wickings. J. R. Wickings was a freeman of the Company, and foreman to the defendant : he was paid by the defendant weekly ; and he had let out himself and his apprentice, by the week. He hired Martin for the particular job, and was also paid by the defendant for what Wickings the apprentice did, by the job. The defendant's counsel contended that the defendant was not liable for the damage, inasmuch as he was bound to employ only

[*300]

persons authorized to navigate, under stat. *7 & 8 Geo. IV. c. lxxv. s. 37. A copy of the by-laws, made under sect. 57 of the statute, was put in : by the 25th of which it was ordained that, during all the time that any barge, &c., should be navigating or passing

---

(1) Local and personal, public: "for the better regulation of the watermen and lightermen on the river Thames, between Yantlet Creek and Windsor." Printed in the statutes at large.

along the river within the limits, one able and skilful man,   MARTIN
authorised by law, should be constantly on board the same, for the   *v.*
TEMPKRLEY.
navigation and management thereof: and, if the owner or owners
of any such barge, &c., should permit or suffer the same to pass
along any part of the limits aforesaid without having at least one
such able or skilful man or other person, authorized as aforesaid,
to navigate the same, he or they, or any of them, should forfeit for
every such offence 40*s.*: and, if the person or persons on board
should quit or leave the barge, &c., at any time during the navigation or passage through the limits, he or they should forfeit and
pay for every such offence 40*s.*; and it should be lawful for any
harbour master and his assistants to remove the said barge, &c.;
and the charges and expenses thereof respectively should · be paid
by the owner or owners or master thereof.   It appeared that there
were about six thousand freemen and apprentices.   The jury being
of opinion that negligence was proved, the LORD CHIEF JUSTICE
directed a verdict for the plaintiff, giving leave to move for a nonsuit, or a verdict for the defendant on the second plea.   In Easter
Term, 1842, *Richards* obtained a rule *nisi* for a nonsuit or verdict
for defendant, or for a new trial.

   Thesiger and *Borill* now showed cause:

   The question is whether the persons navigating were the servants
of the defendant: if they were, the maxim *respondeat superior*
applies.   The defendant was the owner of the barges, under his
contract with Covington.   But it is *said that, as the defendant   [*301]
was obliged to employ the freemen or apprentices of the Company
of Watermen and Lightermen, under sect. 37 of stat. 7 & 8
Geo. IV. c. lxxv., the persons so employed were not his servants.
By that section, " if any person, not being a freeman of the said
Company, or an apprentice to a freeman or to the widow of a
freeman of the said Company, (except as hereinafter is mentioned (1),)
shall at any time act as a waterman or lighterman, or ply, or work
or navigate, or cause to be worked or navigated, any wherry,
lighter, or other craft, upon the said river, from or to any place or
places, or ship or vessel, within the limits of this Act, for hire or
gain (except as hereinafter is mentioned,) every such person shall
forfeit and pay for every such offence any sum not exceeding 10*l.*"
Sect. 102 enacts " that nothing in this Act contained shall prevent any person or persons from keeping, and using and rowing

   (1) The exception did not arise in the present case.

MARTIN
v.
TEMPERLEY.

by their servants, any lighter or lighters, or other large craft for carrying their own goods, provided such servants be freemen, or apprentices to freemen, or to the widows of freemen of the said Company." Sect. 103 enacts "that if such person or persons shall carry or cause to be carried in his or their lighter or lighters, or other large craft, any passenger or passengers for hire, or any goods, wares, or merchandises for hire, or otherwise than their own as aforesaid, or shall row in or navigate, or permit or suffer any person or persons to row in, navigate, or work any such vessel or vessels, who is not a freeman, or an apprentice to a freeman, or to a widow of a freeman of the said Company, he and they shall for

[*302]

any such offence forfeit and pay any sum *of money not exceeding 10l." It is clear, even from the language of sect. 102, that the persons employed are the servants of the employers, though they must be taken from a particular class. [They cited *Randleson* v. *Murray* (1), *Milligan* v. *Wedge* (2), *Quarman* v. *Burnett* (3), *Laugher* v. *Pointer* (4), *Rapson* v. *Cubitt* (5), *Bush* v. *Steinman* (6).]

[305]   *R. V. Richards* and *Peacock, contrà :*

The enactments of stat. 7 & 8 Geo. IV. c. lxxv. had in view the security of the navigation on the river Thames; and they take the discretion out of the hands of parties employing navigators duly qualified. Here, therefore, is no contract of master and servant, in the proper sense of the words. And, further, the hiring is for the

[*306]

particular job ; *and it places the persons hired in an employment as independent as that of a postilion hired to drive to a given place. The postilion, if required, would probably drive on a part of the road pointed out by the person hiring; but he would not be bound to do it. So, here, the navigators would not be bound to obey the defendant's particular directions as to the manner of navigating, though probably they would in general do so. [In addition to the cases cited by the plaintiff they referred to *The Maria* (7), *Lucey* v. *Ingram* (8) and *Carruthers* v. *Sydebotham* (9).]

[308]   LORD DENMAN, Ch. J. :

It is quite clear that the defendant is the party liable. In the

(1) 47 R. R. 513 (8 Ad. & El. 109).

(2) 54 R. R. 677 (12 Ad. & El. 737).

(3) 55 R. R. 717 (6 M. & W. 499). See *M'Laughlin* v. *Pryor*, 4 Man. & G. 48.

(4) 29 R. R. 319 (5 B. & C. 547).

(5) 60 R. R. 873 (9 M. & W. 710).

(6) 1 Bos. & P. 404.

(7) 1 W. Rob. Adm. R. 95, 106, 107.

(8) 55 R. R. 621 (6 M. & W. 302).

(9) 16 R. R. 392 (4 M. & S. 77).

first place, every man is liable for the misconduct of his servants:
and, in the second, the men here undoubtedly were the servants of
the defendant; and men so employed are even called servants in
stat. 7 & 8 Geo. IV. c. lxxv. s. 102. But a question is made,
whether the limitation of the defendant's power of choice deprived
the party injured of the remedy against him. I cannot think it
can be reasonably contended that it does: the inconvenience would
be enormous. *Mr. Bovill's* argument on the statute respecting
apprentices bears very strongly on the point. Before the repeal of
that statute, persons could not be employed in trades without
having been apprenticed: the selection therefore was limited just
as much as here. Sect. 89 of stat. 7 & 8 Geo. IV. c. lxxv. makes
an unskilful navigator liable, to the amount of 5*l.*, for the mischief
he may do; but he is not touched in this respect by any other
provision of the Act. The decision of Dr. LUSHINGTON in *The
Maria* (1) cannot be applied to this case. Dr. LUSHINGTON must be
understood as assuming that the master was there bound to take
the first licensed pilot who offered himself. He clearly considers
that, *under sect. 6 of the Newcastle Pilot Act, 41 Geo. III. (U. K.)   [*309]
c. lxxxvi., the master of the ship, being foreign, was bound to take
the pilot on board, without any power of selection; and indeed in
the case of a foreign vessel in a strange port there could seldom be
any ground for preferring one pilot to another, and therefore little
practical power of selection, even if two or three offered themselves
at the same time. The rule of *respondeat superior* is not impeached:
the only question is who is the superior. Under stat. 6 Geo. IV.
c. 125, the authority of the master is absolutely superseded by that
of the pilot. *Milligan* v. *Wedge* (2) has been fairly pressed upon
us: but the distinction between that case and the present is clear.
The drover there was pursuing a separate trade: to drive the
bullocks was no part of the butcher's business; he had only to
select the licensed drover, who was the person that set in motion
the servant whose negligent driving did the mischief; and the
owner of the bullock had no longer any control over it. In the
present case it was otherwise; and therefore our decision here is
not inconsistent with that in *Milligan* v. *Wedge* (2).

PATTESON, J.:

I am of the same opinion. The first question is, whether the
relation of master and servant existed between the defendant and

(1) 1 W. Rob. Adm. R. 95.   (2) 54 R. R. 677 (12 Ad. & El. 737).

MARTIN
v.
TEMPERLEY.

those managing his barges ; and next, if it did, whether there be any thing in stat. 7 & 8 Geo. IV. c. lxxv. that prevents the legal consequences following from such a relation. On the part of the defendant it is argued, without reference to the statute, that this

[*310]

is the case, not of master and servant, *but of an independent contract to perform the work, as in *Milligan* v. *Wedge* (1) and *Quarman* v. *Burnett* (2). But that is clearly erroneous. Independently of the Act, the men navigating the barges would clearly be the defendant's servants. If the defendant, being at liberty to employ whom he pleased, engaged persons to manage his barges on the Thames, I cannot see how it is possible to contend that they were not his servants as much as a man whom he might employ to drive his carriage. Where, indeed, a man hires another man's servant from him, though such servant be employed to drive where the person hiring pleases, it has been held in *Quarman* v. *Burnett* (2) that the servant so hired is not the servant of the person so hiring. That case certainly carried the exception a great way : but there the servant hired was ordinarily in the employment of the person from whom he was hired, and who let horses along with the driver. That case is not like the present. The second question, then, is as to the effect of stat. 7 & 8 Geo. IV. c. lxxv. That indeed confined the defendant to employing as his servants only individuals of a particular class. It narrowed the number of persons from whom he could select. But that is very different from the state of things created by the Pilot Act, where a party must take the first pilot who offers himself. Here the defendant had the power of selection, though from a limited number : and no case has gone so far as to decide that the person hired ceases to be the servant of the person hiring if he is necessarily selected from a number, though limited. I was much struck with the argument deduced from the old statute

[*311]

of apprenticeship. According to the doctrine *contended for on the part of the defendant, it would hardly have been possible, while that Act was in force, to employ a man as a servant. I do not put the case on the largeness of the number from which the selection may here be made : the principle seems to me the same whether the number be five hundred or five thousand. If there be a power of selection, and not, as in the Pilot Act, a provision preventing any choice, the person hired is the servant of the person hiring. At first I felt the difficulty raised by *Lucey* v. *Ingram* (3). That case

(1) 54 R. R. 677 (12 Ad. & El. 737).   (3) 55 R. R. 621 (6 M. & W. 302).
(2) 55 R. R. 717 (6 M. & W. 499).

however was decided on the words of the Pilot Act, 6 Geo. IV.
c. 125. It is true that the defendant there came within the
exemption of sect. 63 of the Act, and was not obliged to take a
pilot. But the pilot, under sect. 72, was compelled to act when
called upon : and the Court rested their decision on the precise
words of sect. 55, which " exempts the owner from responsibility in
respect of accidents happening by reason of the default of any pilot,
acting under or in pursuance of the provisions of the Act " (1) ; and
they held that the pilot was so acting, whether the owner was compelled to employ him or not. And they conclude as follows. " The
case before us is clearly within the words of the exempting clause ;
and we must therefore hold it to be within its spirit and meaning,
unless (which is not the case) some manifest inconvenience or
inconsistency should result from our so doing." The decision, so
explained, is inapplicable to the present question.

COLERIDGE, J. :

Though this case has been argued at some length and with much
ingenuity, the point is not *difficult. The question is, were the   [*312]
defendant and the persons employed by him master and servants ?
If they were, the general principle applies. And the tests leave no
doubt that they were. First, the men were selected by the defendant : secondly, they were paid by him : thirdly, they were doing
his work : fourthly, they were under his control ; that is, in doing
the work in the ordinary way. It is said that a difference arises
where the workman is paid so much for doing the whole job. But
the defendant might pay either for a given time or a given work ;
and the men here were as much under the defendant's control as a
gentleman's coachman is under that of his master. The master
cannot order the coachman to do an illegal act, as to drive furiously,
or on the wrong side. But, subject to that, the master has the
control over the coachman. So here the defendant had the control
over the persons navigating the barge, subject to the rules of the
river. They are, practically, selected by him. Suppose the owner
of a barge, seeing a number of watermen on the side of the river,
chose to hire one who was incompetent : would not he have made
the selection ? Then, if the men here were the defendant's
servants, on what grounds is the defence put? On two only. First,
that the defendant was bound to select from a particular class :
secondly, that he was not allowed to do the work for himself. But

(1) 55 R. R. 621 (6 M. & W. 316).

MARTIN
v.
TEMPERLEY.

[*313]

neither of these grounds is sufficient. As to the first, it is true that the defendant was bound to select from a class; and so we all practically are limited by the necessity of choosing persons of skill and fitness; but, if we can choose from a class, whether large or small, our contract places us in the situation of a party responsible for the acts of those whom he does choose. And, as to *the defendant not being able to do the work for himself, the law, for the public safety, imposes a qualification, and makes the apprenticeship a test of fitness. Though the defendant was obliged to employ one qualified person, he still made those whom he did employ his servants by the contract. Both grounds of defence therefore fail.

Rule discharged (1).

———•———

1843.
Feb. 4.
———
[361]

MARY LANE *v.* GOODWIN.

(4 Q. B. 361—366; S. C. 3 G. & D. 610; 12 L. J. Q. B. 154; 7 Jur. 372.)

A licence under which marriage has been solemnized, and in which one of the parties is described by a name wholly different from his own, is not void by the misdescription.

Semble (per PATTESON, J.), that it would be void if the name of one person had been inserted with a fraudulent intention that the licence should be used by another.

TROVER for cider, apples, casks, &c. Pleas: 1. Not guilty. 2. Plaintiff not possessed &c. 3. Leave and licence. Replication to pleas 1 and 2, *Similiter:* to plea 3, *De injuriâ.* Issue thereon. On the trial, before Patteson, J., at the Gloucestershire Spring Assizes, 1842, the material facts proved were as follows.

The goods were conveyed to the defendant by bill of sale (July 29th, 1841) from George Rudman, with whom the plaintiff was living as his wife. Afterwards the plaintiff preferred a charge of bigamy against Rudman, alleging that, when he married her, he was already married to one Mary Tibbells, then living. On the making of this charge the defendant took possession of the goods.

[*362]

The *plaintiff, as a *feme sole,* laid claim to them as her own; but defendant sold them and converted the proceeds. In 1814, Rudman was taken into custody at the instance of the parish officers of Stanford in the Vale, Berkshire, as the reputed father of a child of which Mary Tibbells was pregnant, and was married to her by licence. He gave his name as George Neate at the times of the apprehension and marriage, and was named so in the licence, but

———

(1) Wightman, J. was absent.

had never gone by that name before (1). It was objected, on the
trial, that the licence was invalid on this account, and the marriage
null; and *Rex* v. *Tibshelf* (2) was cited. PATTESON, J., on the
authority of *Cope* v. *Burt* (3), overruled the objection; and the
plaintiff had a verdict. In Easter Term, 1842, a rule *nisi* was
obtained for a new trial. The COURT now called upon

 Greaves, in support of the rule:

The authority of *Cope* v. *Burt* (3) need not be disputed; but it
differs from this case. The wife there had been known for several
years by the name under which she was married; and Sir W.
SCOTT, in the Consistory Court, gave that as a reason for his
judgment in favour of the marriage. That reason prevailed also
in *Rex* v. *Burton-upon-Trent* (4), a case of marriage by licence, and
would be recognised (as appears from *Rex* v. *Tibshelf* (2)) in the
case of a marriage by banns. But here it did not appear that
Rudman had ever passed by the name of Neate *before the
occasion on which the marriage took place. Banns would have
been void under the same circumstances; and there is no distinction, on this point, between banns and a licence. These are
the only legal modes by which an intended celebration of marriage
in facie ecclesiæ is to be made known; the latter mode (though
once questioned) having been established, at the time of the
Reformation, by stat. 25 Hen. VIII. c. 21, s. 8, 2 Burn's Ecc.
Law, 462 e (5), tit. Marriage, IV. 1 (6). Licences are the substitute
for banns, and should fulfil the same purpose; they ought, therefore, to have the same requisites as to description of parties. If
an untrue name be inserted in the licence, it may be impossible to
ascertain that the conditions of Canon 103 (7) have been fulfilled in
obtaining it. By the Constitutions of 1597, referred to by Gibson
in a note to that Canon (8), when a licence is obtained, the true
names of parents or guardians consenting must be given to the
Judge on oath, if they do not themselves appear: much more
ought the names of the principal parties to be truly stated in the
licence. By suppressing the true names, a licence might be obtained

[*363]

(1) The first wife said, on the trial:
"I never heard the name of Neate till
we married: I knew him only by the
name of George."

(2) 1 B. & Ad. 190.

(3) 1 Phill. Ecc. Rep. 224. *S. C.*, in
the Consistory Court, 1 Hag. Consist.
Ca. 434.

(4) 16 R. R. 350 (3 M. & S. 537).

(5) 9th ed. by R. Phillimore.

(6) *Greaves* also referred to 1 Gibs.
Cod. tit. xxii. c. 6, pp. 424, 425, and
425, note *x* (2nd ed.).

(7) 1 Gibs. Cod. 428.

(8) 1 Gibs. 428, note (*a*).

LANE
v.
GOODWIN.

[*364]

for persons under the age of twenty-one. The provisions which have
from time to time been made for the registration of marriages,
Canon 70 (1), stats. 26 Geo. II. c. 33, s. 15, 4 Geo. IV. c. 76, s. 28,
and other Acts, show the importance of enforcing, in the case of
marriage by licence, a correct insertion of names in the licence.
The party signing an untrue name in the register *must have
committed a felony : stat. 4 Geo. IV. c. 76, s. 29.   It is not necessary that a fraud should have been practised on one of the parties
to the marriage, if, in effect, a fraud on the law has been committed :
this has been held in the case of banns : *Wakefield* v. *Wakefield* (2),
Rex v. *Tibshelf* (3).   In *Rex* v. *Beck* (4) LEE, Ch. J. held that the
unauthorised insertion of the name of a parish, as one of those
in which the marriage might be solemnized, did not make the
licence void, because " the place is not of the essence of a licence : "
it may be inferred that, in his opinion, falsification of an essential
particular would have avoided it.   In *Rex* v. *Burton-upon-Trent* (5)
the marriage was held good, because the name in the licence was
that which the husband had acquired by reputation : and Lord
ELLENBOROUGH laid it down that, if the name had been assumed
in order to practise a fraud upon the woman, the Court would not
have given effect to such a purpose ; but he did not say that, in the
absence of such fraudulent purpose, the licence, though in a name
not acquired by reputation, would have been good.   When a party's
name is essential, the act done under it is valid only where the name
has been adopted in certain modes known to the law : Co. Litt. 3 a ;
Com. Dig. Abatement (E. 18), (E. 19), (F. 18) ; Fait (E. 3).

(LORD DENMAN, Ch. J. : Is *Cockburn* v. *Garnault* (6) materially
distinguishable from this case ?)

[*365]

There is no distinct report of that decision ; it seems to have proceeded on a peculiar state of facts, and is observed upon, in the
*argument of *Cope* v. *Burt* (7), as a case not of conclusive authority
on the general point now in question.

Erle and *W. J. Alexander*, in opposition to the rule, were not
heard.

(1) 3 Burn, Ecc. L. 460 : tit.
Register Book, I.
(2) 1 Hag. Consist. Ca. 394, 401.
(3) 1 B. & Ad. 190.
(4) 2 Stra. 1160.
(5) 16 R. R. 350 (3 M. & S. 537).

(6) Cited in *Cope* v. *Burt*, 1 Hag.
Consist. Ca. 436, 437, 438, and 1
Phill. Ecc. Rep. 228, 231.
(7) 1 Hag. Consist. Ca. 434 ; 1 Phill.
Ecc. Rep. 224.

LORD DENMAN, Ch. J. :

There is no authority for the general proposition that a marriage
licence is made absolutely void by a mistake in the name of one
party.   The reason for which banns are held invalid on this
account does not extend to licences.   There might perhaps be
reasons for making the rule as to banns extend to licences:
mischiefs may result from fraud, as *Mr. Greaves* has ingeniously
pointed out.   But the protection given by the one is of a different
kind from that afforded by the other.   No fraud is suggested here:
and although *Cope* v. *Burt* (1) does not entirely agree in circumstances with the present case, yet the language used by Lord
STOWELL in that case, in the Consistory Court, shows the prevailing opinion in the Ecclesiastical Courts as to the distinction
between banns and licence: and my brother PATTESON, on enquiry,
finds the existence of that opinion confirmed.

PATTESON, J. :

I acted on the authority of *Cope* v. *Burt* (1) at the trial, though
without having the case itself before me.   I have enquired as to
the opinion of the Ecclesiastical Courts on this subject, and find
that *Cope* v. *Burt* (1) and *Cockburn* v. *Garnault* (2) have always been
considered decisive authorities there.   The *distinction between
banns and licences is clear: and, although perhaps, if a licence
were obtained for one person with the intention that it should be
used for another, such a licence might not be valid, that is not the
case here: and the objection cannot prevail.

COLERIDGE, J. :

The rule on this subject does not rest merely on the decisions in
Cope v. *Burt* (1) and *Cockburn* v. *Garnault* (3), but on the opinion
entertained in the Ecclesiastical Courts since the latter decision,
which is thus expressed by Lord STOWELL: " I had considered this
point to be so much *res adjudicata*, under the authority of the case
which has been cited, that it was not without surprise that I received
this libel."   And he adds a reason for the decision: " The Judge took
the distinction between banns and licence, which has been noticed
in the argument,—that, in publication by banns, it is essentially
necessary that the publication should be in the true name, as it

LANE

v.

GOODWIN.

[*366]

(1) 1 Hag. Consist. Ca. 434; 1   438; 1 Phill. Ecc. Rep. 228.
Phill. Ecc. Rep. 224.   (3) 1 Hag. Consist. Ca. 436; 1 Phill.
    (2) 1 Hag. Consist. Ca. 436, 437,   Ecc. Rep. 228, 231.

would otherwise be defective in substance, and no one would be put on their guard by such publication ; whilst a licence is not of the same notoriety, but is granted by the Ordinary, on the evidence which he is content to receive,—the oath of the party, as required by the canons of the Church."

Rule discharged (1).

DOE D. GEORGE WYNDHAM, EARL OF EGREMONT *v.* GRAZEBROOK.

(4 Q. B. 406—416; S. C. 3 G. & D. 334; 12 L. J. Q. B. 221 ; 7 Jur. 530.)

Lessor of plaintiff in ejectment claimed as remainderman in tail. To establish the pedigree, he proved cohabitation and reputation of marriage between his alleged father and mother. He also produced a parish register signed by them, stating the performance of a marriage ceremony between them at a private house; and the Archbishop's *fiat* for a special licence, with the affidavit upon which the *fiat* was obtained. No search had been made for the licence ; and it appeared that there was no regular place of custody for such licences: Held, that the affidavit, *fiat* and register were admissible evidence, without production of the licence, to confirm the evidence of cohabitation and reputation, and as showing that parties bearing the names of the alleged father and mother had been engaged in taking measures for contracting a marriage.

Lessor of plaintiff, as part of his case, proved that defendant, and those through whom he claimed, for more than twenty years before the action brought (the action being brought within twenty years of the accruing of the title of lessor of plaintiff), held under a lease granted by a tenant for life (2) under the same settlement which created the estate tail. The settlement gave power to tenants for life to lease for, or for a term of years determinable upon, one, two or three lives, reserving the ancient and accustomed heriots " or more." By a pattern lease, which was for ninety-nine years, determinable upon the lives of J., E. and M., there were reserved the three best beasts, or 6*l.* 13*s.* 4*d.*, at the choice of the reversioner, on the deaths of each of J., E. and M., provided that, living J., E. and M., no heriot should be taken on E.'s death, nor, living J. or E., on M.'s death. The disputed lease, produced by lessor of plaintiff, was for ninety-nine years, determinable upon two lives, H. and A. ; and the reservation was of 6*l.* 13*s.* 4*d.* as a heriot on the death of each of H. and A. (without any alternative or proviso). The Judge told the jury that it was for the defendant to satisfy them that the latter reservation was more than that in the pattern lease : Held (on motion for a new trial after verdict by plaintiff) that the direction was right.

EJECTMENT for lands in Somersetshire.

On the trial, before Erskine, J., at the Somersetshire Spring Assizes, 1842, it appeared that the premises had been held in fee by Charles, Earl of Egremont, who died 21st August, 1763, leaving a will dated 31st July, 1761. By the will, certain lands in Somersetshire,

---

(1) Wightman, J. was absent.　　　　(2) See now Settled Land Acts, 1882 to 1890, tit. Leases.—A. C.

which included those claimed in the present action, were devised
to the testator's eldest son, George O'Brien, Lord Cockermouth,
for life, remainder (after intermediate limitations which did not take
effect) to the fourth, fifth, and all and every other son and sons of
the devisor, in tail male. The fourth son was William Frederick
Wyndham, who died 18th February, 1828, and whose eldest son
the lessor of the plaintiff claimed to be. The will contained a
power enabling any tenant for life, being in actual possession, to
lease for one, two or three lives, or for a term of years determinable upon one, two, or *three lives, any part of the premises
usually so leased, with certain restrictions, one of which was as
follows. "So that there be reserved, in every such lease, during
the continuance thereof, the ancient and accustomed rent and
heriots for the premises therein contained, or more." On the part
of the lessor of the plaintiff a counterpart of a lease was produced,
under which he showed that the tenant in possession held. The
lease was granted by George O'Brien, Earl of Egremont, formerly
Lord Cockermouth, the devisor's eldest son, who became tenant
for life on 21st August, 1763, and died 11th November, 1837. It
was dated 30th June, 1783, and was for ninety-nine years, determinable on the lives of Hannah Broughton and Elizabeth Ann
Broughton. The only reservation therein contained as to heriots
was as follows: "Yielding and paying, on the several deaths and
deceases of them the said Hannah Broughton and Elizabeth Ann
Broughton, the sum of 6l. 13s. 4d., they dying after the commencement of the term hereby granted, whether in succession or otherwise, of like lawful money of Great Britain, for and in the name of
an heriot." A lease of the same premises was then produced, on
the part of the lessor of the plaintiff, as a pattern lease, being of
the date 13th September, 1734, and the lease in existence at the
time of the making the will. It was granted by Sir William
Wyndham, the then owner of the property, and was for ninety-nine
years, determinable on the lives of John Baker, Elizabeth Baker
and Margaret Harris. The reservation of the heriots there was as
follows: "Yielding and paying, upon the death and deaths of each
and every of them the said John Baker, Elizabeth Baker and
Margaret Harris, three of his, her and their best beasts, or three of
the best beasts of the then tenant in possession of the *premises, or
that shall be then thereon depasturing or feeding, or the full sum
of 6l. 13s. 4d. of good and lawful money of Great Britain, at the
choice and election of the said Sir William Wyndham, his heirs

DOE d.
THE
EARL OF
EGREMONT
v.
GRAZE-
BROOK.

[*407]

[*408]

DOE d.
THE
EARL OF
EGREMONT
v.
GRAZE-
BROOK.

and assigns, for and in the name of an heriot or farlief (1) : provided
that, living the said John Baker, no such heriot or sum of money in
lieu thereof shall be paid or demanded on the death of his sister,
the said Elizabeth Baker, or, living the said John Baker or Elizabeth
Baker, on the death of their mother, the said Margaret Harris."
For the lessor of the plaintiff it was contended that the reservation of
the heriot in the lease of 1783 was not in pursuance of the power, and
that the lease was therefore invalid as against the remaindermen.

In the course of proving the descent, a question arose, which was
stated as follows by Lord DENMAN, Ch. J., in delivering the judgment
of the Court in banc.

"Two objections were made to the learned Judge's conduct on
the trial : first, that he admitted improper evidence ; secondly, that
he misdirected the jury.

"The evidence was offered to support the proof of marriage
between the father and mother of the lessor of the plaintiff in
1784. The marriage was said to have taken place in August in
that year, at a private house, under a special licence from the
Archbishop of Canterbury. There was some evidence of cohabitation and reception : but the plaintiff's counsel also offered in
evidence an affidavit made for the purpose of obtaining a special
licence to be married at a private house, and a *fiat*, signed by the
[*409]   Archbishop, directing a licence to be *made out, as prayed, for a
marriage-between the parties : both which documents were produced
from the proper Ecclesiastical Office (2). No search had been made
for the original licence : and there was proof that such licences
are not kept in any regular custody (3). The plaintiff also offered
in evidence a copy of the register of the parish of St. Pancras,
which stated the marriage to have been at a private house, by
special licence, and professed to be signed by the parties. The
objection was taken to the *fiat*, as being neither more nor less than
secondary proof of the contents of a document for which no search
had been made. And, though the learned counsel confessed that
the marriage might have been sufficiently proved by cohabitation
and reception alone, yet they contended that the plaintiff took
the chance of this evidence being held admissible, and must

---

(1) "In some manors westward,
they distinguish Farleu to be the best
good, as Heriot is the best beast, payable at the tenant's death." Cowel,
Interp. in voc. "Farley or Farleu."
[To same effect Blount's Law Dict.

And see Eng. Dial. Dict. *s.v.*—F. P.]
(2) The Office of Faculties.
(3) The evidence was that they were
generally handed over to the officiating
clergyman, and not taken back from
him.

submit to have his verdict set aside if the Court should hold it
inadmissible."

The learned Judge, after argument, admitted the whole of this
evidence.

The objection to the Judge's direction arose as follows. The
counsel for the defendant contended that, though the heriot reservation in the lease of 1783 was not the " ancient and accustomed "
heriot, as appeared by comparison with the lease of 1734, yet the
reservation in that respect was "more" than in the lease of 1734,
and therefore the lease followed the power. The learned Judge left
it to the jury to say whether this was so, telling them that it was
for the defendant to show *that the reservation in the lease of 1783   [*410]
was more than that in the lease of 1734.

The verdict was for the plaintiff. ERSKINE, J. reserved leave to
move for a nonsuit: and, in Easter Term, 1842, *Bompas*, Serjt.
obtained a rule *nisi* for a nonsuit or a new trial. In this vacation (1),

Sir W. W. Follett, Solicitor-General, *Erle*, *Crowder*, and *Montague Smith* showed cause :

First, as to the evidence of descent. The proof of cohabitation
and reputation was, on a question of pedigree, legally sufficient to
entitle the plaintiff to a verdict. In confirmation of this, it was
shown that the alleged parents had taken steps to procure a licence ;
and for this purpose there can be no doubt that the Archbishop's
fiat and the affidavit were good evidence. Confirmatory evidence
also was properly given, though such evidence was not necessary,
that the same parties went through a ceremony which, at any rate,
was professedly a marriage. This evidence was not offered as in
itself proving a marriage, but as confirming the previous evidence
of the relation which the parties appeared to bear to each other.
But, even if it were necessary to prove the fact of the marriage by
direct evidence, this was a legitimate and sufficient proof. The
ceremony is performed at a private house ; and, it is true that, by
stat. 26 Geo. II. c. 33, ss. 1, 4, 6(2), and stat. 25 Hen. VIII. c. 21,
ss. 3, 4, 8, a marriage in a private house is void without the *fiat* of
the Archbishop. But it is not necessary to prove the licence : if it
were, then in every case of marriage by licence in a church the
licence must be proved ; for there can be *no difference between a   [*411]

(1) February 7th and 8th. Before   (2) Repealed by 4 Geo. IV. c. 76,
Lord Denman, Ch. J., Patteson, and   s. 1. See *Ibid.*, s. 20.
Williams, JJ.

Doe d.
THE
EARL OF
EGREMONT
v.
GRAZE-
BROOK.

Doe d.
THE
EARL OF
EGREMONT
v.
GRAZE-
BROOK.

special and a common licence in this respect: and, indeed, even in the case of a marriage by banns, it would be necessary to prove the publication of the banns. But no proof is ever required of a common licence or of publication of banns. If, however, the licence required proof, it was proved here. The licence is properly the *fiat* of the Archbishop. What is commonly called the licence is merely the communication to the clergyman of the fact of the Archbishop's assent: properly speaking, the *fiat* is itself the licence. Thus, the act of the Court in granting administration proves the administration without the letters of administration: 2 Phil. Ev. 173 (1). The Court rolls of a manor give the title without the copy.

(PATTESON, J.: Are those cases similar? The *fiat* is not an order that the marriage shall be solemnised, but that the licence shall issue.)

If it be necessary to prove the licence, then the *fiat* and subsequent marriage constituted good secondary evidence of it: and search for the original was not possible; for it appeared that there was no proper place of custody.

Secondly, as to the heriots, it is not pretended that the reservation of heriots made in the lease which is questioned is the same with that in the pattern lease. But, for the defendant, it is said to be possibly "more;" and the argument is that according to the reservation in the disputed lease there will necessarily be taken a sum in lieu of a heriot on each death, whereas, under the pattern lease it might be that, by the proviso, one heriot only could be taken on the three deaths. But the words in the power, "or

[*412]

more," cannot be understood *as referring to such a balance of contingencies. They must mean that, things otherwise remaining the same, either more beasts may be reserved, or a larger sum of money; or else that the limiting proviso may be omitted. But, even if the most extensive meaning were given to the word "or more," it was for the defendant to show to the satisfaction of the jury, which he did not do, that "more" was reserved.

(PATTESON, J.: On moving for the rule it was argued that, as the plaintiff made it part of his title that there was a bad lease, the burthen of showing the badness lay on him: and it was said that the case was in this respect distinguishable from cases where the plaintiff sets up a *primâ facie* title, and the defendant undertakes to meet that by showing a good lease.)

(1) 9th ed. *Elden* v. *Keddell*, 9 R. R. 404 (8 East, 187), is cited.

That statement misrepresents the position of the parties. The lessor of the plaintiff proved his title as remainderman in tail : that, without more, entitled him to a verdict. It can make no difference that he chose to anticipate the expected defence by proving the lease and the holding under it. The case is analogous to that of a justification set up in right of a tenant for life ; there the party justifying must aver the continuance of the life : *Dayrell* v. *Hoare* (1).

Doe d.
THE
EARL OF
EGREMONT
v.
GRAZE-
BROOK.

Bompas, Serjt. and *Butt, contrà :*

First, as to the pedigree. If the plaintiff had ventured to go to the jury on the mere evidence of cohabitation and reputation, the verdict could not have been disputed. But, evidence in confirmation having been offered and received, the question is whether that was admissible. Now what was offered was clearly meant for direct evidence of *the marriage. The performance of a ceremony was proved. If this had taken place in a church, it would *primâ facie* have been a good marriage ; and the jury would properly have been told to presume that either a common licence had been obtained or banns published. But the ceremony was shown to have been performed in a private house. That is not, *primâ facie*, a good marriage. Therefore the plaintiff endeavoured to give evidence of what alone could make such a ceremony a good marriage, namely, of a special licence. In order to do this, he proved the affidavit upon which a *fiat* was obtained, and the *fiat*. The *fiat* is a direction, by the Archbishop, that a licence shall issue ; but it is not the licence. In this respect the case differs from those which have been suggested, of letters of administration and grants in Court of copyhold land. In those cases, if no letters of administration issue and no copies of Court roll are made out, the parties are nevertheless administrators (2) and copyholders. But, if nothing is done beyond the *fiat*, if no licence actually issues, the clergyman has no power to perform the ceremony, and if he does so it is invalid. Therefore the evidence received was in truth secondary evidence of the licence, which was inadmissible without proof of the best practicable search.

As to the heriots. The plaintiff chose to make it part of his case that the defendant held under a bad lease. As there had been so long a holding, there would have been an adverse possession

[*413]

(1) 54 R. R. 565 (12 Ad. & El. 356).   (2) See *Doe* d. *Bassett* v. *Mew*, 7 Ad. & El. 240.

Doe d.
THE
EARL OF
EGREMONT
r.
GRAZE-
BROOK.

[*414]

in the defendant, unless it had been shown that the possession was not adverse. To show this, the plaintiff was obliged to rest his case on the lease; and then, having insisted on *the defendant's title being that of a leaseholder, he could not get rid of the title without proving the invalidity of the lease. The learned Judge, therefore, ruled incorrectly in throwing the burthen of proof of validity on the defendant: and, in a case where the two reservations were of such doubtful relative value, this was very important. *Dayrell* v. *Hoare* (1) is inapplicable; there the right of the tenant for life was set up in the first instance by the defendant. And, even in such a case, if the life were shown to have been recently in existence, the proof of death would lie on the plaintiff: *Nepean* v. *Doe* d. *Knight* (2).

LORD DENMAN, Ch. J. now delivered the judgment of the COURT:

After stating the facts respecting the evidence received in proof of the marriage (as *ante*, p. 390), his Lordship proceeded as follows:

We think that the *fiat* was an act done in the course of official duty, showing that two persons bearing the names of the lessor of the plaintiff's parents were at that time engaged in taking measures for contracting a marriage; and that it may be properly taken into consideration by the jury as confirming the evidence of their union which arose from cohabitation and reception. The affidavit and register were proofs of the same general fact. The same objection was taken in a former trial between the lessor of the plaintiff and another lessee, but was abandoned when the new trial was argued in this Court (3).

The imputed misdirection respected the mode of proving a lease void, as made by a tenant for life, not *warranted by the leasing power in the will under which he held. The power required the old rent and heriot to be reserved, or more; the pattern lease gave to the landlord the option of receiving the three best beasts or the sum of 6*l*. 18*s*. 4*d*. on the death of the persons named, contingent on their surviving each other as specified. The actual lease reserved only the 6*l*. 18*s*. 4*d*., giving no option, but payable on the death of each life successively. On the trial, the defendant's counsel argued that the change was in effect a beneficial one, but complained that the learned Judge ruled that the burthen of proof was on the defendant, and that he was bound to show this reservation to be of

(1) 54 R. R. 565 (12 Ad. & El. 356).   (3) *Doe* d. *The Earl of Egremont* v.
(2) 46 R. R. 789 (2 M. & W. 894).   *Date*, 61 R. R. 326 (3 Q. B. 609).

Doe d.
THE
EARL OF
EGREMONT
v.
GRAZE-
BROOK.

equal or greater advantage to the landlord.   The defendant had no evidence to prove this; the jury did not agree to his argument, and found against the lease.

We are not prepared to say that this burthen of proof lies in all possible cases on a lessee under a power.   For, though a lease made by tenant for life can only bind the remainderman when it conforms to the power, general evidence of such conformity may be sufficient to launch the case.   But, when the lease avowedly varies from the pattern lease in so important a point as to deprive the landlord of an option between a sum of money and the three best beasts, the change in the reservation throws upon the lessee the burthen of making out that the new state of things is as beneficial as the old.

But it was further contended that the objection was not open to the lessor of the plaintiff in this case, because he had been obliged to produce the lease in the first instance, and the defendant had not given it in evidence in support of his own right, but the lessor of *the plaintiff produced it, meaning to show that defendant held   [*416] by that title, and then prove that title a bad one.   No authority was cited for this distinction; and there is no reason for it.

Rule discharged.

STEPHENS *v.* DE MEDINA.

(4 Q. B. 422—429; S. C. 3 G. & D. 110; 12 L. J. Q. B. 120; 3 Ry. Cas. 454.)

To enforce a contract for transfer of railway shares, if the transfer requires a deed, the purchaser must tender a conveyance to the vendor for execution; the same rule prevailing as on sales of real property.

So held where the Railway Act (6 & 7 Will. IV. c. lxxvii.) gave a very short and simple form of transfer under seal, and made shares personal property.

And a declaration by purchaser against vendor for not having completed the contract of sale, stating that defendant promised to make over and transfer the shares in a reasonable time, and that plaintiff was ready and willing to pay for and accept the shares, and requested defendant to make over and transfer them, but defendant did not nor would make over &c., but neglected and refused, was held bad on special demurrer for not averring that plaintiff tendered a conveyance.

ASSUMPSIT.   The declaration stated that heretofore, and after the passing of an Act &c. (6 & 7 Will. IV. c. lxxvii., local and personal, public, " for making a railway from Cheltenham and from Gloucester, to join the Great Western Railway near Swindon, to be called ' The Cheltenham and Great Western Union Railway,' with a branch to Cirencester "), to wit on &c., " the plaintiff at the request of the

STEPHENS
v.
DE MEDINA.

defendant bargained and agreed with the defendant to buy of the defendant, and the defendant then bargained and sold to the plaintiff, divers, to wit ten, shares in the Cheltenham and Great Western Union Railway Company, established and incorporated under and by virtue of the said statute, at and for the price or sum of 1*l.* 2*s.* 6*d.* for each and every of the said ten shares, and which ten shares in the said Company the defendant then professed and represented that he was possessed of, each and every of the said ten shares to be made over and transferred by the defendant to the plaintiff in a reasonable time then next following; and, in consideration thereof, and that the plaintiff, at the like request of the defendant, had then promised the defendant to accept and receive the said ten shares and to pay him for the same at the rate or price aforesaid, he the defendant then promised the plaintiff to make over and transfer the

[*423] said ten shares *to the plaintiff as aforesaid in a reasonable time then next following; and, although the plaintiff hath always been ready and willing to pay the defendant for the said ten shares at the rate or price of 1*l.* 2*s.* 6*d.* each as aforesaid, and although a reasonable time for the defendant to make over and transfer the said ten shares to the plaintiff hath long since, before the commencement of this suit, elapsed, and although the defendant was afterwards, to wit on " &c., " requested by the plaintiff to make over and transfer to him the said ten shares, and although the plaintiff hath always been ready and willing to accept and receive the same; and of all which premises the defendant then and always had notice : yet the defendant, not regarding his said promise, did not nor would, when so requested as aforesaid, or at any other time, make over or transfer the said ten shares, or any or either of them, to the plaintiff, and hath hitherto wholly neglected and refused, and still wholly neglects and refuses, so to do: whereby the plaintiff hath lost and been deprived of divers great gains " &c.

Demurrer, assigning for causes : That it does not appear by the declaration that the plaintiff did at any time tender to the defendant any deed of sale or transfer of the said shares or of any or either of them, whereas the tender of such deed of sale or transfer by the plaintiff was a condition to be done and performed by him precedent to the accruing to him of any right of action against the defendant for not transferring the said shares as in the said declaration mentioned : and also for that the declaration does not aver that the plaintiff ever tendered or offered to pay the defendant the said price for the said shares.

Joinder in demurrer.

The demurrer was argued last Michaelmas Term (1).

Martin, for the defendant:

The Railway Act requires that the conveyance of shares shall be
in writing, and gives a form (2). Then it lay upon the vendee to
tender the written instrument for signature. This question may
never have arisen on the purchase of railway shares; but the case
is analogous to that of a sale of lands. There the vendee must
tender a conveyance; and a declaration against the vendor for not
completing the sale must aver such tender, on the principle that,
in declaring on a *contract, performance of a condition precedent   [*425]
must be pleaded. [He cited 1 Sugd. Vend. & Purch. 373 (3), *Baxter*
v. *Lewis* (4), *Webb* v. *Bethel* (5), *Poole* v. *Hill* (6), and *Pickford* v. *The
Grand Junction Railway Company* (7).]

Barstow, contrà: [426]

First: it is not necessary to contend for any distinction as to
sales of this kind of property. Sir E. Sugden in the section just

___

(1) November 15th, 1842. Before
Lord Denman, Ch. J., Williams, Coleridge, and Wightman, JJ.

(2) Stat. 6 & 7 Will. IV. c. lxxvii.
(local and personal, public), s. 148,
enacts "that it shall be lawful for the
several proprietors of shares in the
said undertaking, and their respective
executors, administrators, and successors, to sell and dispose of any shares
to which they shall be entitled therein,
subject to the rules and conditions
herein mentioned; and the conveyance
of such shares shall be in writing, and
may be in the following words or to
the like effect, varying the names and
descriptions of the contracting parties
as the case may require; (that is to
say,)

"'I, A. B.   of   in consideration of the sum of   paid to
me by C. D. of   do hereby assign
and transfer to the said C. D.
share (*or* shares) numbered   of
and in the undertaking called the
Cheltenham and Great Western Union
Railway, to hold unto the said C. D.,

his executors, administrators, and
assigns (*or* successors and assigns),
subject to the several conditions on
which I held the same immediately
before the execution hereof; and I the
said C. D. do hereby agree to accept
and take the said share (*or* shares)
subject to the conditions aforesaid.
As witness our hands and seals the
    day of   .'

"And on every such sale the deed
or conveyance (being executed by the
seller and purchaser) shall be kept by
the said Company, or by the secretary,"
&c.: then follow directions for entering a memorial of such transfer and
sale, &c.

Sect. 147 enacts that the shares
"shall to all intents and purposes be
deemed personal estate," and not "of
the nature of real property."

(3) 10th ed. ch. iv. sect. iv. §§ 53—59.
(4) Forrest, 61.
(5) 1 Lev. 44.
(6) 55 R. R. 805 (6 M. & W. 835).
(7) 58 R. R. 742 (8 M. & W. 372).

cited (1), after referring to the *dicta* which lay down "that it is incumbent on the vendor to prepare and tender a conveyance," observes that this, "as a general rule, certainly seems to have prevailed when the simplicity of the common law prevailed, and possession was the best evidence of title ; but upon the introduction of modifications of estates, unknown to the common law, and which brought with them all the difficulties that surround modern titles, it became necessary to make an abstract of the numerous instruments relating to the title, for the purpose of submitting it to the purchaser's counsel : and it then became usual for him to prepare the conveyance." Here the statute gives a form perfectly simple and in very few words : the reason, therefore, which led to the preparation of conveyances by the vendee (2) does not apply ; and there is no ground for assuming that a tender of conveyance by the purchaser ought to have appeared in this declaration. But, secondly, supposing that the rule insisted on applies generally to conveyances under this statute, the contract stated in the declaration shows a direct engagement by the defendant to do the act of conveying, which binds him independently of any tender by the plaintiff. The words are, "in consideration thereof, and that the plaintiff, at the like request" &c., "had then promised the defendant to accept and receive the said ten shares and to pay him for the same at the rate &c.," "the defendant then promised the plaintiff to make over and transfer the said ten shares to the plaintiff as aforesaid in a reasonable time then next following." The *intention is clear, that the act of conveying should originate with the party who was to make the transfer. Besides, the argument for the defendant assumes that the vendor's contract could not be broken unless a conveyance were tendered and execution refused. But an issue might properly be taken on the refusal only : and the tender, if made, would be merely part of the evidence showing the refusal. An issue on the fact of refusal would put the tender in issue, if the case were one which required that fact : but the contract might be broken in other ways than by refusing to execute a conveyance actually tendered. An appointment might be made for completing the contract, and a conveyance prepared, and the vendor might decline to attend, saying that he had sold the property.

[*427]

  Martin, in reply. • • •

              Cur. adv. vult.

(1) 1 Sugd. Vend. & Purch. 374, ch, iv, sect. iv. § 56.

(2) See *Reg.* v. *Kendall*, 55 R. R. 275 (1 Q. B. 366, 385, note (c)).

LORD DENMAN, Ch. J., in this vacation (February 2nd), delivered
the judgment of the COURT :

This is an action for not transferring to the plaintiff ten shares
in the Cheltenham and Great Western Union Railway : and the
plaintiff alleges that he was always ready to pay the stipulated
price and accept the transfer, that he has requested the defendant
to make the transfer, and that a reasonable time has elapsed for the
making it ; but he does not aver that he tendered to the defendant
any conveyance for execution : and the question raised, upon special
demurrer, is whether such tender is a condition precedent to the
maintenance of the action.   Upon the argument it was not denied
that in the conveyance of real property, where no special provision
is made in the contract, the expense of the conveyance falls upon
the purchaser, nor that in such a case, in the absence of any
stipulation to the contrary, it becomes his duty to prepare and to
tender such conveyance : neither was it disputed that the same
practice prevailed with regard to terms for years : but it was urged
that in all these cases the rule had been established because generally
there was or might be more or less of complexity of title or in the
mode of conveyance ; and that, as the purchaser was to secure
himself in respect of the former, and to prescribe all the peculiarities
which he insisted on in the latter, it was proper that his legal
adviser should prepare the instrument : and it was insisted on that
the reason did not apply in a case like the present, where the form
of conveyance was simple and prescribed in terms by the Act of
Parliament.   It does not appear to us that this is the true reason
of the rule, which seems rather to be a consequence from the fact
that the purchaser is to pay for the conveyance, *the contract on
the part of the vendor being simply this : "In consideration of
such a sum I will execute any proper conveyance of the estate which
you tender me."

But, whatever be the true ground for the rule, whether this alone,
or partly for the security of the purchaser, it appears to us that we
ought not to introduce a different rule in the present case, even if
the same reasons do not exist in full force, unless there be some
inconvenience or injustice in adhering to it.   Conveyances of property
of this description and under similar circumstances are becoming
exceedingly frequent ; they have now been in use for some time ;
and we do not find that any practice has grown up varying from the
uniform rule as to sales of land or leases : there is, therefore, a clear
convenience in its being understood that one uniform rule will be

maintained. Some expense must be incurred in the necessary stamps if in no other way: and, if nothing is said in the contract, this must, on general principles, fall on the purchaser: the vendor is to receive the purchase money in full; and, if so, it is reasonable that the purchaser should do what he is to pay for: if he is to prepare the instrument, it is with him, and he must tender it to the vendor for execution before he can maintain any action for his non-execution.

We therefore think the demurrer sustained: and our judgment must be for the defendant.

Judgment for defendant.

CRAIG *v.* HASELL.

(4 Q. B. 481—492; S. C. 3 G. & D. 299; 12 L. J. Q. B. 181; 7 Jur. 368.)

Declaration in case charged that defendant, falsely and maliciously and without probable cause, made affidavit in the Court of Exchequer that plaintiff was indebted to the Queen in a sum named, and was in embarrassed circumstances, and that the debt was in danger; by means whereof defendant, maliciously and without probable cause, caused a commission to issue and an inquisition thereon to be taken, whereby it was found that plaintiff was indebted to the Queen in the sum named; and defendant afterwards, falsely, maliciously and without probable cause, procured a writ of extent to be issued and delivered to the sheriff, upon which plaintiff's goods were seized, which writ of extent was afterwards superseded in the Court of Exchequer, "and the said writ of extent was then and is ended:" whereas plaintiff was indebted only in a small portion of the sum named, and was not in embarrassed circumstances, and the debt was not in danger, as defendant knew: and special damage was alleged, from loss of credit, by a creditor selling plaintiff's property under a power of sale given as a security, and another creditor making an affidavit and giving notice to make plaintiff a bankrupt.

Held, on demurrer to the plea, that the declaration was good, without showing that the proceedings in the Exchequer were at an end otherwise than by the averment that the writ was at an end, the issuing of the writ being the grievance.

Plea, that the writ was superseded at request of plaintiff, and by the grace and favour of the Queen, on terms of plaintiff paying costs of the execution of the writ of extent, and was not otherwise superseded or ended.

On special demurrer, for that the plea did not avoid any allegation of the declaration, or was an argumentative denial of the *supersedeas* and termination of the suit: Held, that the plea was ill, being consistent with the facts in the declaration and not justifying the act complained of.

CASE. The declaration alleged that defendant, maliciously intending and devising to oppress and injure plaintiff, and to cause him to be unjustly arrested and imprisoned by our sovereign lady the Queen, and to cause and procure his goods and chattels,

lands and tenements, debts and credits, to be wrongfully appraised, CRAIG
extended, taken and seized into the hands of our said lady the HASELL.
Queen, and thereby wrongfully and injuriously to deprive plaintiff
of his personal liberty, and of the use, &c., of his lands, &c., and
to bring plaintiff into great disgrace, &c., and to put him to great
expense, &c., heretofore, to wit on 26th December, 1840, in order
to carry into effect his said malicious, &c., wrongfully, deceitfully,
falsely and maliciously, and without any reasonable or probable
cause whatever for issuing an extent to the amount hereafter
mentioned, did suggest and represent, and cause to be suggested
&c., and cause to be made and exhibited a *certain affidavit of   [*482]
defendant in her Majesty's Court of Exchequer at Westminster,
representing and stating, that plaintiff was then justly and truly
indebted to our sovereign lady the Queen, in the two several sums
of 301l. 0s. 7d. and 194l. 11s. 4d., making together 495l. 11s. 11d.,
being so much of her Majesty's money issued to plaintiff by
defendant for the service of the Westmoreland regiment of
yeomanry cavalry, and unaccounted for by plaintiff; and that the
said sums of &c. then remained wholly unpaid by plaintiff; and
that plaintiff then was in embarrassed and insolvent circumstances; and that, unless some method more speedy than the
ordinary course of proceeding at law should be forthwith had
against plaintiff for the recovery of the debt so falsely represented
by defendant, and stated in the said affidavit, to be due and owing
to her Majesty, the same was in danger of being lost: and, by
means of such unjust, false and deceitful representations and
affidavit, there did issue out of the said Court of Exchequer, and
the defendant, in order to carry into effect his said purposes &c.,
afterwards, to wit on the day and year aforesaid, wrongfully, &c.,
and without any reasonable &c. (as before), caused and procured
to be issued by and out of her Majesty's said Court of Exchequer,
a certain writ of our lady the Queen, directed to William Burchell
and Francis Allen the younger, gentlemen, whereby &c. The
declaration then stated the purport of the commission for an
inquisition in respect of the debt mentioned in the affidavit,
returnable 11th January then next. By virtue of which said writ,
and by the means and representations aforesaid, defendant afterwards caused a certain inquisition to be taken within the said
county of Middlesex, and there was taken an inquisition *within   [*483]
the said county, on 26th December, 1840, before the said W. B.
and F. A., on the oath of divers, to wit twelve, &c.; whereby it

was found that plaintiff, on the day of taking that inquisition, was justly and truly indebted to her Majesty in the several sums of &c. (as before), being so much of her Majesty's moneys issued &c.; as by the said writ and return thereof, and the inquisition thereto annexed, remaining in her Majesty's said Court of Exchequer at Westminster, appears: and, by reason of, and upon, the said false, unjust and deceitful suggestion and representation and affidavit so made as aforesaid, and for the malicious intents and purposes aforesaid, afterwards, to wit on 26th December, 1840, there did issue out of her said Majesty's Court of Exchequer, and the defendant did wrongfully, &c., and without any reasonable &c. (as before), cause and procure to be issued by and out of her Majesty's said Court of Exchequer, a certain other writ of our said lady the Queen, directed to the sheriff of the county of Cumberland, by which said writ, after reciting the said inquisition, the said sheriff was commanded &c. The declaration then stated the purport of the writ of extent in chief, against plaintiff's body, lands, tenements, goods, chattels, debts and specialties. And, by means of the said false representations and affidavit, the said last mentioned writ was delivered to the sheriff of the county of Cumberland, on 1st January, 1841. And defendant, in further prosecution of his said malicious &c., afterwards, and before the return of the last mentioned writ, to wit 1st January, 1841, wrongfully and maliciously procured to be delivered the last mentioned writ to Sir George Musgrave, Baronet, then being sheriff of the said county of Cumberland, to be executed in due form of law. By

[*484] *virtue whereof the said sheriff, afterwards, and before the return of the last mentioned writ, to wit on &c., within the bailiwick &c., seized and took into her Majesty's hands divers goods and chattels of plaintiff, and kept and detained the same in his custody by virtue of the said last mentioned writ of extent, until the said writ of extent was superseded, as hereinafter is mentioned. That afterwards, to wit on 1st June, in the year last aforesaid, the said writ of extent was superseded in respect of the plaintiff by virtue of her Majesty's writ of *supersedeas*, issued out of her Majesty's Court of Exchequer at Westminster for that purpose; and the said writ of extent was then, and is, ended. Whereas, in truth and in fact, plaintiff, at the time of such false and deceitful representation and suggestion, and at the time of the making and filing such affidavit, was not justly and truly indebted to our said lady the Queen in the said sum of 301*l*. 0*s*. 7*d*., or any part thereof, nor

was plaintiff indebted to our lady the Queen in the said sum of 194*l.* 11*s.* 4*d.*, but only in a small portion thereof, to wit in the sum of 70*l.* 11*s.* 8*d.*, and no more, for moneys of her Majesty issued to the plaintiff by defendant for the service &c., or in any other manner; and whereas, in truth and in fact, plaintiff was not in embarrassed and insolvent circumstances; and whereas, in truth and in fact, the said supposed debt was not in danger of being lost unless some method more speedy than the ordinary course of proceeding at law should be then forthwith had against plaintiff for the recovery of the supposed debt so represented by defendant to be due and owing to her Majesty. Which said matters and things defendant, at the times aforesaid, well knew. By means of which said false and deceitful representation *and suggestion and affidavit, and malicious suing out and prosecuting of the said writ of extent against plaintiff, and the proceedings thereon had before the same could be superseded, the plaintiff lost the use &c.: the declaration then alleged damage by the loss of the use of the goods and chattels, and his being prevented from cultivating his land and obtaining payment of divers debts, and disabled from discharging divers debts owing from him, and his being injured in his credit, so that divers creditors required immediate payment of debts, and in particular James Cookson, to whom money was owing which plaintiff by reason of the premises was unable to discharge, sold at a price below the value thereof certain buildings and hereditaments of plaintiff, vested in J. C. as a security for the money by way of mortgage with a power of sale: and one Charles Byres, being a creditor of plaintiff, made an affidavit and gave a notice, for the purpose of making plaintiff a bankrupt: and plaintiff, by means of the premises, has been compelled to pay to other creditors divers sums due, sooner than they would otherwise have been required, and to pay costs and expenses in defending himself from the said proceeding, and procuring the *supersedeas,* &c.

[*485]

Third plea. That, although true it is that the execution of the writ of extent was superseded, yet that, before the issuing of the *supersedeas,* to wit 1st June, 1841, it had been and was, at the request of the plaintiff, and by the grace and favour of our said lady the Queen, granted and allowed to the plaintiff by and on behalf of the Queen that the execution of the said writ of extent should be superseded upon certain terms being then therefore complied with by the plaintiff, to wit that the plaintiff should pay to the sheriff the costs and charges of the *sheriff, of and relating and incidental to the execution of the said writ of extent; which said terms being then assented to and complied with by the plaintiff, the execution of the said writ of extent was thereupon then accordingly superseded by virtue of her said Majesty's said writ of *supersedeas* as aforesaid; and that the said writ of extent was not, nor has been, nor is, superseded or ended otherwise or on any other account, or for any other cause, than as in this plea aforesaid.   Verification.

Demurrer, showing for cause that the plea does not deny or confess and avoid any allegation of the declaration : that, if it be a denial of the *supersedeas*, as stated in the declaration, there should·have been a traverse thereof, and the plea should have concluded to the country : and that it is only an argumentative denial of the *supersedeas* and the termination of the suit.

The demurrer was argued in last Term (1).

W. H. Watson, for the plaintiff:

The plea does not deny the termination of the proceeding; and it is immaterial, for the purposes of this action, whether the proceeding terminated by means of a compromise or in any other way.   All that is necessary is, that the proceeding should be at an end.   The plea merely sets up a collateral contract between the plaintiff and the Crown.   A declaration for a malicious prosecution must show that the prosecution is at an end, because otherwise the plaintiff might, after he had recorded a verdict against the defendant, be convicted.   But such a result cannot happen if the
[*487]
prosecution is at an end, however the termination *may have been brought about.   In an action for holding to bail in too large a sum, the plaintiff might recover, though he had paid the costs to get rid of the action.

Cowling, contrà:

The affidavit averred, first, that the plaintiff was indebted to the Crown; secondly, that the debt was in danger.   The declaration does not deny that he was indebted in a part of the sum named in the affidavit.   Further, the Court cannot assume that the inquisition of the jury is false.

(1) January 24th, 1843, before Lord   before Lord Denman, Ch. J., Patteson
Denman, Ch. J., Patteson, Coleridge   and Wightman, JJ.
and Wightman, JJ.; and January 27th,

(PATTESON, J.: The inquisition would hardly be more than   CRAIG
evidence upon an issue raising the question as to the fact of   *v.*
the debt.)   HASELL.

The plea negatives the want of reasonable cause. The case does
not resemble that of an action for holding to bail in too large
a sum. The complaint is that a false suggestion has been made
to the Crown, which has induced it to set the process in motion.
The plaintiff was bound to show the falsehood by informing the
Court how the proceeding had terminated. But all that the
declaration shows is, not the termination of the proceeding, but
that the writ of extent is ended. A *scire facias* may still issue on
the inquisition. The plaintiff may, for any thing that the declaration shows, have claimed his goods, and have failed on the claim.
A declaration for maliciously holding to bail would not be sufficient,
if it merely showed that the arrest was set aside, without showing
the termination of the suit. In the case of a civil action there
must be a judgment, though in that of a prosecution it is enough
to show a verdict of acquittal without averring a judgment:
Hunter v. *French* (1). In *Goddard* v. *Smith* (2) an action *was   [*488]
brought for a false and malicious indictment of barratry; and it
appeared only that there had been a *nolle prosequi* by the *Attorney-
General;* and this was held insufficient, because there ought to
have been an acquittal on the merits.

(COLERIDGE, J.: If the gravamen here be the procuring the writ
to issue, it is sufficient to show that the writ is at an end.

WIGHTMAN, J.: In an action for maliciously and falsely holding
to bail on the pretext that the party was leaving England, the
plaintiff might recover on proof of his discharge from arrest,
though the debt really existed.)

According to *Parker* v. *Langley* (3) it must be shown what has
become of the action itself. In an action for maliciously suing
out a commission of bankrupt, it must be shown that the commission is superseded: *Whitworth* v. *Hall* (4); because in that case
(though not in this) the *supersedeas* is what finally terminates
the whole proceeding complained of. Even where a decision of

(1) Willes, 517, 519.   K. B. 163.
(2) 1 Salk. 21; 2 Salk. 456; 3 Salk.   (4) 36 R. R. 715 (2 B. & Ad. 695).
245.   See *Atkinson* v. *Raleigh,* 3 Q. B. 79.
(3) 10 Mod. 145, 209; Gilb. Rep.

CRAIG
r.
HASELL.

sub-commissioners of excise on an information against the plaintiff was reversed on appeal, it was held that the judgment of the sub-commissioners, being averred in the declaration as well as the reversal, negatived malice in the informant and was an answer to an action against him for a malicious prosecution : *Reynolds* v. *Kennedy* (1) : and LEE, Ch. J. said that the plaintiff himself had shown that the prosecution was not malicious, because the sub-commissioners gave judgment for the defendant, and therefore the Court could not infer any malice in him.   The same principle applies to the inquisition here.   In *Vanderbergh* v. *Blake* (2) the

[*489]

action was brought against a party who *had procured the seizure and condemnation of goods in the Exchequer, as aliens' goods imported under pretence of being denizens' goods ; and judgment was given for the defendant ; HALE, C. B. saying that, " if such an action should be allowed, the judgment would be blowed off by a side-wind."   It is true that the goods there were seized and condemned : that, however, may have been so here.   But further, even if the declaration be good, the plea explains how the writ is at an end, and shows that there has been no decision on the merits. And this is an instance of the danger of not requiring the declaration to show the end of the whole proceeding.   The writ may be at an end merely from forbearance on the part of the Crown ; and the affidavit may be quite true.   If an action has terminated in a *stet processus* by consent of the parties, no suit can be maintained for a malicious arrest : *Wilkinson* v. *Howel* (3).   In *Bird* v. *Line* (4) it was held that an action does not lie for a malicious suit, *pendente lite*.

W. H. Watson, in reply :

The want of cause, malice and *scienter* are all alleged in the declaration.

(WIGHTMAN, J. : Where does the complaint begin ?

PATTESON, J. : May not the causing of the writ to issue be mere aggravation ?)

It is the gist of the complaint.   The affidavit is like the oath before the grand jury in the case of a malicious prosecution, or the

(1) 1 Wils. 232.
(2) Hardr. 194, 195.
(3) Moo. & Mal. 495.

(4) 1 Com. 190.   See *Norrish* v. *Richards*, 3 Ad. & El. 733.

affidavit to hold to bail in the case of a malicious arrest. In
8 Wentw. Pleading, p. 324, there is a precedent like this declaration,
drawn by Mr. Baron WOOD.

CRAIG⸱
r.
HASELL.

(WIGHTMAN, J.: He very possibly drew a declaration which he
knew to be bad for want *of better facts.)

[*490]

There was a verdict for the plaintiff.

(PATTESON, J.: There is some mistake there. It is a case of
extent in aid against the plaintiff, where the defendant represented
himself to be debtor to the Crown: yet it is said that the original
writ of extent against the plaintiff is to be recited: but that writ
would be against the defendant.   The precedent however is
inapplicable ; for in the case of an extent in aid the writ of extent
in aid is the whole grievance ; here the original proceeding is
a grievance.)

No stress can be laid on the fact that the finding on the inquisition
remains: that is an *ex parte* proceeding, no notice being given to
the alleged debtor : West on Extents, 22.   In the cases mentioned
on the other side both parties were or might have been heard, as
in *Vanderbergh* v. *Blake* (1), where the COURT pointed out that
there was a proclamation before the condemnation.   The inquisition amounts to no more than the affidavit, or a deposition at
Bow Street.   The writ here is finally set aside: no new one
can issue.

(PATTESON, J.: I am not aware of any authority for that
position.)

The question as to the existence of the debt arises upon disputing
the writ.   An action lies for arresting a party upon a cause of
action on which a suit is still pending between the parties, in
which suit the person arrested has been discharged only through
the other's delay in declaring : *Heywood* v. *Collinge* (2).   In an
action for abusing the process of the Court in order to compel the
plaintiff to surrender property, it is not necessary to show that
the first suit is at an end: *Grainger* v. *Hill* (3).   There is no
regular proceeding by which the affidavit here can be got rid of.

(1) Hardr. 194, 195.   (3) 4 Bing. N. C. 212.
(2) 9 Ad. & El. 268.

The plea is no *more, at the utmost, than an argumentative denial of the want of probable cause.

Cur. adv. vult.

LORD DENMAN, Ch. J., in this vacation (February 11th), delivered the judgment of the COURT.   After stating the pleadings, his Lordship proceeded as follows :

The plaintiff argued that his declaration did all required by law to found this action, having given a history of what was done with the writ averred to be so sued out.   The answer made at the Bar was that, the verdict of the jury and the inquisition remaining still in Court unreversed and in full force, the declaration itself negatived the necessary fact of the cause having reached its termination ; and, at all events, that that fact, appearing in the declaration, negatives the want of reasonable and probable cause, and forbids the Court to infer the malice which is also essential for the maintenance of this action.

Much learning was employed in the argument; and several expressions drawn from particular cases, which it would not be easy to make consistent in all respects with each other.   But we are of opinion that there is a fallacy in treating the inquisition as any part of the proceeding complained of.   The debt, though found by the jury on *ex parte* evidence, may perhaps have been a just and true debt ; and yet a party suing it out maliciously and with a view to annoy the plaintiff by ulterior proceedings, and afterwards, with that object, praying an extent for securing that debt as if it was in danger of being lost to the Crown when he knew it not to be in danger, may produce consequences injurious [*492] and even ruinous to the debtor, by this latter proceeding so *well calculated to affect his credit and bring demands upon him.   The writ of extent is the grievance: and all that the rule of law, in cases of malicious prosecution, requires is that the writ of extent should be traced to its close ; and that is done by showing it discharged by the Court, though upon an arrangement and by consent.   It is by no means improbable that the Crown may, in such a case, be induced to accord its grace from a persuasion that the proceeding originated in malice.   Such a termination of the case negatives no fact essential to maintaining the action : and, notwithstanding some language used in the case in Wilson (1), it is not necessary that either that or any fact in the declaration

(1) *Reynolds* v. *Kennedy*, 1 Wils. 232.

should lead the Court to infer malicious motives. This at least is solely in the province of the jury.

The declaration being sufficient, the plea is clearly bad. Consistently with all the facts stated in it, the writ of extent may have been sued out by the defendant without any reasonable or probable cause ; and yet, if it was, the facts stated do not justify the defendant in so doing. The judgment must be for the plaintiff.

Judgment for plaintiff.

REG. *v.* THE INHABITANTS OF BARNOLDSWICK (1).

(4 Q. B. 499—510; S. C. 3 G. & D. 545; 12 L. J. M. C. 44.)

To charge a township with liability by custom to repair all highways within it which would otherwise be repairable by the parish comprising such township, it is not necessary to prove that there are or have been ancient highways in the township. Without such proof, a jury may infer the custom from other evidence. As, that the parish consists of five townships, one of which is the township in question : that four have always repaired their own highways ; that no surveyor has ever been appointed for the parish ; and that the township in question has repaired a highway lately formed within it.

INDICTMENT against a parish for non-repair of a highway.

Plea : that the said parish of Barnoldswick now is, and at the time of the taking of the said inquisition was, and from time whereof &c. hath been, divided into divers, to wit five, districts and different townships, one whereof hath immemorially been and still is called Admergill ; and that within the said parish there now is, and at the time of the taking &c. was, and during all the time aforesaid hath been, a certain ancient and laudable custom there during all the time aforesaid used and approved of, that is to say, that each of the said several townships from time whereof &c. have repaired, maintained and amended, and have used and been accustomed to repair, &c., and during all the time aforesaid of right ought to have repaired, &c., and still of right ought to repair, &c., all and every the Queen's common highways lying and being within their own respective townships that would be otherwise repairable *by the said parish of Barnoldswick at large, when and as often as necessary : and that the inhabitants of the said parish at large have not during all or any part of the time aforesaid repaired, maintained or amended, and have not been used or accustomed to

[*500]

(1) Dist. in *Reg.* v. *Rollett* (1875) L. R. 10 Q. B. 469, 483, 44 L. J. M. C. 190.—A. C.

REG.
v.
THE INHABI-
TANTS OF
BARNOLDS-
WICK.

repair, &c., and of right ought not to repair, &c., the Queen's common highways within the said parish, or any of them or any part thereof : and that so much of the said common Queen's highway as in the said indictment is mentioned &c. to be ruinous and in decay is situate and lying within the said district and township called Admergill, and before and at the time of the said inquisition found was, and hitherto and continually from thenceforth hath been, and still is, a common Queen's highway in that district and township, and that but for the said custom would be repairable by the inhabitants of the said parish at large ; and that the same part of the said highway of right has always been repairable, and of right always ought to have been repaired, maintained and amended, and still of right ought to be repaired, &c., by virtue of the said custom, by the inhabitants of the said district and township called Admergill, when and as often as necessary, and not by the inhabitants of the said parish of Barnoldswick at large. Verification.

Replication, averring as before that the inhabitants of the said parish of Barnoldswick the said common Queen's highway so as aforesaid being in decay ought to repair and amend when and so often &c., and that within the said parish there is not, nor from time whereof &c. hath there been, &c. ; traversing the existence of the custom : conclusion to the country. Issue thereon.

On the trial, before Parke, B., at the York Spring Assizes, 1842, it appeared that the parish of Barnoldswick *consisted of the township or district of Admergill (1) and four other townships. Admergill was situated in a moorland country at an extremity of the parish, and contained only six or seven farms. The road in question ran through it, and was a turnpike road, made about 1804. It began to need repair about 1816 : and since that time repairs had been done upon it by most (but not all (2)) of the occupiers of land in Admergill. Each of the other townships had public roads within it, and had always repaired them : and no surveyor had ever been appointed for the whole parish. It did not appear that Admergill had ever had any surveyor or other parochial or township officer, or contributed in any way to the general parochial

[*501]

(1) It was urged on the argument that Admergill did not appear by the evidence to be a township of itself. PATTESON and WILLIAMS, JJ. observed that the fact was not denied on the pleadings.

(2) The occupier of one farm had not contributed. Some evidence was given (and left to the jury) to account for this consistently with the alleged obligation.

burdens. Others of the townships had surveyors. There were
traces of old roads in Admergill; but it was not proved that they
had ever been public; and the prosecutors contended that they were
only occupation roads.

The learned Judge, in summing up, said (1) : " The defendants,
the indicted parish, allege that there is a custom in the parish of
Barnoldswick, which is divided into more districts or townships
than one, that each and every one of the districts repair their own
roads. If the defendants fail in proving that to you, the verdict
will be for the Crown : if they satisfy you of it, your verdict will be
for the defendants." After stating that the custom was proved as
to each of the districts, *except Admergill, his Lordship said :   [*502]
" Are you satisfied that this custom, which prevails in four-fifths
of the parish, prevails in the other fifth?" " There is some
evidence for your consideration which tends to show it does."
" There is a good foundation for the custom on a presumed bargain,
made before the time of living memory by the inhabitants of each
of the townships, that each should take on itself the repair of its
own roads. In order to render the custom binding, it has been
said to be necessary that there should be at that time existing in
each township highways which some one was bound to repair. It
is not absolutely necessary. The counsel for the prosecution says
this custom must fail, unless you are satisfied that there was, at
some time or other beyond the time of living memory, some highway within the district of Admergill. I do not think it necessary
that should be so ; for there may be a perfectly valid custom in
point of law, that the inhabitants of either township should repair
any high roads which from time to time become public high roads.
A highway may exist by modern dedication." " I think there may
have been a perfect valid bargain beyond the time of legal memory,
that each district should repair such roads as might be created
within it." " No doubt it is extremely reasonable to suppose that, if
the custom applies to four districts out of five, it would be likely to
extend to the other. You will say if it did." He then observed
that, if the case depended on the question, whether or not there
were ancient public roads in the township of Admergill, the proof
that there were such roads did not appear satisfactory ; " but," he
added, " it is not absolutely necessary for the existence of such a
custom that in the particular township there should have been

(1) The observations of the learned Judge are taken from a shorthand
note used in showing cause.

REG.
v.
THE INHABI-
TANTS OF
BARNOLDS-
WICK.

[*503]

any. They may be *bound by ancient usage and custom to repair all such roads as from time to time may be created within the limits of the township. Now is there such a custom prevailing here ? " And he left it to the jury to say whether the repairs done upon the road made in 1804, if done by the township, were attributable to such alleged custom, or were done merely to avoid litigation, and because the inhabitants were uncertain who ought to repair. The jury found that Admergill was bound to repair its own roads ; and the verdict was entered for the defendants : but PARKE, B. gave leave to move this Court upon the question whether or not it was essential to the custom, as affecting Admergill, that ancient roads should be proved to have existed in the township : repeating, as his own clear opinion, that proof of that fact was not necessary, and that the custom might be well founded on a bargain applicable to future roads (1).

Baines, in the ensuing Term, moved for a rule to show cause why the verdict should not be entered for the Crown, relying upon the want of evidence that ancient highways had existed in Admergill, and contending that the custom was not made out. A rule *nisi* was granted.

Dundas and *Sir G. A. Lewin* now showed cause :

The proof bore out the plea. There was some evidence for the jury that old roads had existed in Admergill : and even without that fact the case was sufficient. A township may be liable by custom to repair such new roads as may be formed within it : *Rex*

[*504]

v. *Hatfield* (2), judgment *of HOLROYD, J. : and the custom here might reasonably originate in a bargain between Admergill and the other townships.

(COLERIDGE, J. : The other townships would have no consideration for such a bargain with Admergill, if it had no roads.)

It might be contemplated that roads would be made there, and that the repair of them would be an equivalent for what the other townships then undertook. *Rex* v. *Ecclesfield* (3) shows that a custom for the inhabitants of a district to repair roads within it

<hr>

(1) His Lordship consented to reserve the point, in order that the defendants might not be met by the objection usually made to motions for a new

trial, where the verdict, in a criminal case, has been found for the defendant.
(2) 22 R. R. 631 (4 B. & Ald. 75, 82).
(3) 19 R. R. 335 (1 B. & Ald. 348).

may be good, though the consideration do not appear ; and Lord
ELLENBOROUGH there cites 1 Bla. Com. 77, where it is said that
"Customs must be reasonable; or rather, taken negatively, they
must not be unreasonable." "A custom may be good, though the
particular reason of it cannot be assigned ; for it sufficeth, if no
good legal reason can be assigned against it." *Pigott* v. *Bayley* (1)
shows that, before Admergill had roads, a custom within the parish
for every township to repair its own roads might have been averred
and sustained. There a custom as to tithing was alleged to exist
within the parish of E., the bounds, limits and titheable places
thereof, and was held not to be negatived by proof of a *modus* in
one township, there being evidence of the custom in other parts of
the parish : and BAYLEY, J. said: "If that *modus* should hereafter
be proved to be a bad one, the evidence given in this case would, if
uncontradicted, be sufficient to establish the custom as to the township where that *modus* now exists." The facts here, that no
surveyor was ever appointed for the parish, and that the land-
holders in Admergill repaired the road in question in 1816, are
strongly in favour of the defendants.

(COLERIDGE, J. : If the custom might be found *to exist without   [*505]
proof that there were ancient roads in the township, no doubt there
was some evidence of the custom.)

Baines, R. Hall, and *F. Thompson, contrà :*

It is essential to a custom or prescription that there should have
been usage from time immemorial; or at least something upon
which the required usage might operate. If a period within
memory can be pointed out, from which the existence of the
subject-matter may satisfactorily be dated, the prescription or
custom fails: *Griffith* v. *Matthews* (2) ; *Rex* v. *Hatfield* (3). A prescription is entire, and must be proved as extensively as it is laid :
Morewood v. *Wood* (4) ; *Rogers* v. *Allen* (5). The allegation here is,
in effect, that the townships, including Admergill, "have repaired,"
and "been used and accustomed to repair," "and ought to have
repaired," such highways within them as would otherwise have been
repairable by the parish, from time immemorial. The evidence is
that that could not have been the case as to Admergill. In *Rex* v.

(1) 6 B. & C. 16.   (4) 2 R. R. 349 (4 T. R. 157).
(2) 2 R. R. 598 (5 T. R. 296).   (5) 10 R. R. 689 (1 Camp. 308, 314,
(3) 22 R. R. 631 (4 B. & Ald. 75).   315).

Great Broughton (1) ASHHURST, J. says that, when persons are charged against common right, " it is not enough to show that they immemorially ought to repair : it should be shown, that they have repaired." The same is stated in Com. Dig. Chimin, (A. 4). Other authorities on the point are cited in note (9) to *Rex* v. *Stoughton* (2), where it is shown that an indictment against a township alleging only that from time whereof &c. they ought to have repaired, and not that they have repaired, would be bad.

[*506] The law as laid down *by these authorities is supported by the judgment of Lord ELLENBOROUGH in *Rex* v. *Ecclesfield* (3) ; and he there observes (4), referring to a passage cited for the present defendants from 1 Bla. Com. 77, that " the matter of this rule applies " " to the inhabitants of a known district of country, and to a subject existing within that district." It is essential to a custom that it should have been actually used from time out of mind : Litt. sect. 170. Had the custom here been established, it would have been no objection that the road was newly introduced : *Rex* v. *Netherthong* (5) ; but the custom itself is not proved. The repair in 1816 is of no weight ; and, if the present question had arisen before that time, the custom clearly could not have been supported.

(WILLIAMS, J. : Do you say that the defendants were bound to prove the existence of roads at some former time ?)

The evidence here proved their non-existence down to a time within legal memory. The existence in one or more townships of a custom to repair their own roads does not conclusively show that other townships in the same parish have the same custom. It is common in the North of England for part of the roads in a parish to be repaired by a particular township, and part by the parish. Where such a general unity of customs and liabilities is shown to exist in several districts that they constitute an integer, proof of a custom in one may of itself be conclusive evidence that the same custom exists in another. The places from which tithe was claimed, in *Pigott* v. *Bayley* (6), formed such an integer. But no such community exists between Admergill and the other townships in Barnoldswick. If the inhabitants of Admergill had been

[*507] indicted, and the indictment *had shown the facts here relied upon by the parish as a defence, the indictment would have been

(1) 5 Burr. 2700, 2702.   (4) P. 357.
(2) 2 Wms. Saund. 158 e.   (5) 2 B. & Ald. 179.
(3) 19 R. R. 335 (1 B. & Ald. 348).   (6) 6 B. & C. 16.

bad, according to *Rex* v. *Kingsmoor* (1), for not showing that this township " neither forms part of, nor is connected with, any other larger district, the inhabitants of which are liable to repair the road in question." If the particular division, from whatever cause, has not been, or has ceased to be, liable, the burden falls of course upon the parish, by operation of law: *Rex* v. *Sheffield* (2). The learned Judge at Nisi Prius put the case on the supposition of an agreement among the townships ; but, if there were immemorial highways in the other townships, and not in Admergill, there could be no consideration for the agreement on the part of this township. That such an agreement, to discharge the parish from its common law liability, cannot be aided by any presumption, may be inferred from *Rex* v. *Scarisbrick* (3). If the parish was once liable to repair, " no agreement with any person whatever can take off this charge which the law lays upon them :" *Anonymous* (4) case in Ventris. The liability, having attached, could not afterwards be apportioned : *Reg.* v. *The Duchess of Buccleuch* (5). If, therefore, an agreement be relied upon as exonerating the parish, it ought to appear that such compact was made before the public had acquired a right to have the roads repaired by the parish : that is, if the parish was conterminous with a manor (as parishes seem originally to have been, 1 Bla. Com. 114), that the arrangement took place when the manor was granted.

(COLERIDGE, J. : Why may not the arrangement *here have been made before the parish was liable ?)   [*508]

There is no evidence of it.

(COLERIDGE, J. : The repair by four townships is some.)

No unity of customs among the five townships is shown.

(COLERIDGE, J. : That bears only upon the degree of probability. In *Reg.* v. *The Duchess of Buccleuch* (5) an original liability seems to have been traced to a particular person.)

Here it is in the parish, no evidence appearing to the contrary. It ought to have been shown that Admergill had ancient highways, and had actually repaired them. The fact that no surveyor was

(1) 26 R. R. 307 (2 B. & C. 190).
(2) 1 R. R. 442 (2 T. R. 106).
(3) 45 R. R. 554 (6 Ad. & El. 509).

(4) 1 Ventr. 90.
(5) 1 Salk. 358.

appointed for the parish at large is accounted for by the
evidence that the four townships repaired their own roads, and
Admergill had none.

LORD DENMAN, Ch. J. :

The point reserved is, whether it was necessary in this case to
prove the existence of ancient highways in Admergill. According
to the learned Judge's report he had no doubt that it was unnecessary. And I am of opinion that direct evidence on this point was
not essential. It was not proved that there had been none ; and
there was some evidence that they had existed. And I think that
the custom was maintainable without proof that there were ancient
highways in the township. It is sufficient for this purpose if we
find evidence of a practice long existing, consistent with the
custom, and no proof of the origin of that practice, except such
as the parties claiming exemption have brought before the jury.
We are not, in such a case, to look at the degree of probability ;
that is only matter for comment to be addressed to a jury. I think
the learned Judge was right in directing the jury that the custom
[*509]   might be found without proof that there had *been ancient roads.
Suppose the state of things proved here were shown to have existed
three hundred years ago ; could it be said that that was no evidence
of the custom? And we cannot draw a line between such proof
and that now before us.

PATTESON, J. :

The question here is narrowed to the point whether, in support of
the allegation that every township in this parish had immemorially
repaired its own highways, it was necessary to prove that ancient
highways in Admergill had been repaired by that district. I think
it was not necessary to prove that any particular highway had
actually been so repaired. The required inference might be
raised, although there had been no repair which any person
living remembered. There was complete evidence of repair by
the four townships ; and no surveyor had ever been appointed by
the parish. It is true that Admergill was an inconsiderable place,
and had had no surveyors within living memory ; and the existence
of ancient ways within it was not satisfactorily made out. But I
think it was not necessary that this fact should have been directly
proved ; and it was shown that repairs had been done by Admergill
upon the road in question after the trustees had ceased attending

to it, which was some admission of a liability by custom, though no other act of repair appeared to have been done within living memory.

WILLIAMS, J. :

The parish consists of five townships, four of which have been accustomed to repair their own highways; and no surveyor has ever been appointed for the whole parish. Then the question is, whether it be essential to sustain this plea, that some repair of ancient *highways should be proved to have taken place in Admergill. On the evidence here given I think it may very well be (and there is no sufficient proof to negative the supposition) that the alleged custom has existed, and that Admergill has done repairs under it.

COLERIDGE, J. :

I think we are only at liberty here to consider whether the learned Judge's opinion was right upon the point reserved, namely whether, to sustain the plea, direct proof was necessary that there had been ancient highways in Admergill. So limiting the inquiry, I think that it was not necessary. Whatever may have been the origin of customs like this, so many of them exist that it is too late now to question their legality; and here I think that, consistently with the evidence, every thing may have existed as in those places where customs like the present are undoubtedly good. There may, consistently with the facts before us, have been ancient roads in Admergill; to require that their existence should be actually proved is imposing a greater burden than, in my opinion, is necessary. Therefore, limiting the question as I have already done, I think that the present rule must be discharged.

Rule discharged.

BETTELEY v. REED.

(4 Q. B. 511—518; S. C. 3 G. & D. 561; 12 L. J. Q. B. 172; 7 Jur. 507.)

1843.
Feb. 2, 11.
_____

[511]

Defendant, a wharfinger, received malt from and for B.; and B., to cover an usurious transaction, made a colourable sale of the malt to plaintiff; defendant transferring the malt in his books to plaintiff. Afterwards B. became bankrupt; and his assignees sued plaintiff in trover for the malt. Pending the dispute, plaintiff, defendant and the assignees agreed that the malt should be sold, and the proceeds paid into a bank, except a part, which defendant was to retain on account of a lien which he had against B., but that this transaction should not prejudice the rights of any party. Defendant had no lien against plaintiff. Afterwards the assignees abandoned the action

BETTELEY
v.
REED.

against plaintiff, on his giving up a part of the proceeds. Plaintiff then
brought assumpsit against defendant for money had and received :

Held, that he might maintain such action, without joining the assignees
as plaintiffs ; and that defendant could not therein set up the usurious nature
of the transaction between B. and plaintiff, as invalidating the transfer.

ASSUMPSIT for money had and received. Plea (besides others not
here material) : *Non assumpsit.* Issue thereon.

The cause was tried before Lord Denman, Ch. J., at the London
sittings after Hilary Term, 1842, when the defendant had a
verdict, under circumstances which were detailed as follows by
Lord DENMAN, Ch. J., in the introductory part of the judgment
of the COURT afterwards delivered.

"This was an action for money had and received, to recover a
sum of about 528l., being part of the proceeds of a quantity of malt
deposited in the warehouse of the defendant, and the right to which
had been disputed between the plaintiff and the assignees of one
Bradley, who had become a bankrupt. The defendant pleaded
Non assumpsit.

"It appeared that the defendant, who is a wharfinger, had received
a quantity of malt on account of a person of the name of Bradley,
a corndealer, who was from time to time accommodated with money
by the plaintiff, upon the terms that Bradley should make a sale to
the plaintiff of a sufficient quantity of malt to cover the amount
required, with a condition annexed for repurchase by Bradley at an
advanced price. The malt, of which the money in question was
[*512] part of the proceeds, had been *sold by Bradley to the plaintiff
upon the terms above mentioned, and had been regularly transferred by the defendant in his books from Bradley to the plaintiff ;
and, had nothing further occurred, was held by the defendant at
the disposal of the plaintiff.

"Bradley, however, became bankrupt : and his assignees brought
an action of trover against the plaintiff to recover the malt held by
the defendant on his account, on the ground that the sale of the
malt to the plaintiff by Bradley was not a *bonâ fide* sale, but merely
colourable, to be a sort of security for an usurious contract between
the plaintiff and Bradley. To avoid expense of warehouse rent,
and to take advantage of a rising market, it was agreed that the
malt should be sold : and accordingly, by an order of Mr. Justice
LITTLEDALE, the malt was directed to be sold ; and, out of the
proceeds, the charges of the defendant were to be paid, and the
remainder was to be paid into the Bank in the joint names of the
present plaintiff and the official assignee of Bradley, with a proviso

that the order should not operate to the prejudice of any right of action which the present plaintiff might have against the defendant or the assignees of Bradley.

"In order to effect this arrangement, it was necessary to obtain the consent of the defendant, in whose custody the malt was: and he agreed that, upon payment to him of 528*l*. 11*s*. 2*d*. (for which he claimed to have a lien upon the malt out of the proceeds), it should be sold, and that the sale and the receipt by the defendant of that money should not prejudice any right of action which the plaintiff Betteley might have against Reed, the present defendant, in respect of the malt; nor was the acceptance of that sum to prejudice the rights of *any of the parties. Under this arrangement, the malt was sold, and the 528*l*. 11*s*. 2*d*. paid to the defendant, and the residue, amounting to above 4,000*l*., paid into the Bank as agreed. The 528*l*. 11*s*. 2*d*. was a sum which would not be chargeable against the plaintiff Betteley; nor would the defendant have had any lien as against him in respect of it upon the malt.

"When the action of trover came on to be tried, a compromise took place between the assignees of Bradley and Betteley; and, upon the former receiving a certain portion (about one-half) of the proceeds of the malt in the Bank, a juror was withdrawn, and the claim of the assignees abandoned.

"The plaintiff Betteley then brought his action against the defendant, to recover the 528*l*. 11*s*. 2*d*., as being part of the proceeds of the malt, which, as between him and the defendant, was undoubtedly his, unless Bradley or his assignees could establish a superior title. For the defendant it was contended that he had a right in this action to contest the validity of the sale as between Bradley and Betteley, and to show that, by reason of the transaction being usurious as between them, the transfer of the malt in the books of the defendant was wholly inoperative, and that he had a right to consider the property as still remaining in Bradley and his assignees upon his bankruptcy, against whom he could enforce his lien, though he could not against the plaintiff. At the trial of this cause he established a case of usury, to the satisfaction of the jury, in the sale of the malt by Bradley to the plaintiff, and obtained a verdict."

In Easter Term, 1842, *Erle* obtained a rule *nisi* for a new trial, on the grounds of misdirection, and that the *evidence of usury was not admissible. In this vacation (1),

(1) February 2nd. Before Lord Denman, Ch. J., Williams and Wightman, JJ.

BETTELEY
v.
REED.

[*513].

[*514]

27—2

BETTELEY
v.
REED.

Thesiger and *Ogle* showed cause :

The defendant was entitled to insist upon the nullity of the transfer by reason of usury. A sale made merely to colour an usurious transaction between the parties transfers no property : *Hargreaves* v. *Hutchinson* (1). It is contended, however, that this defence cannot be available to the defendant, whatever its validity might be as between the plaintiff and the assignees. In *Stonard* v. *Dunkin* (2) the defendants, having malt in their warehouse belonging to K., were ordered by K. to hold it for the plaintiff as purchaser from K., and gave plaintiff a written acknowledgment that it was held on his account ; and Lord ELLENBOROUGH decided that, in an action of trover, the defendant could not, as against the plaintiff, dispute that the property had passed by the purchase. The same principle was upheld in *Gosling* v. *Birnie* (3), where the acknowledgment by the defendant was verbal. These two cases are cited in Story's Commentaries on the Law of Agency, 179, ch. 7, s. 217 (4), where the rule is laid down as follows, " An agent is not, ordinarily, permitted to set up the adverse title of a third person, to defeat the rights of his principal, against his own manifest obligations to him ; or to dispute the title of his principal. If, therefore, he has received goods from his principal, and has agreed to hold them, subject to his order, or to sell them for him, and to account for the proceeds,

[*515] he will not be *allowed to set up the adverse title of a third person to the same goods, to defeat his obligations. An exception, however, is allowed, where the principal has obtained the goods fraudulently, or tortiously, from such third person." According to this qualification, the defendant might have set up the usury against the plaintiff, even if the assignees had not interfered. But they have themselves impugned the transaction, though the dispute between them and the plaintiff has since been compromised upon the plaintiff giving up a part of the proceeds. In *Hardman* v. *Willcock* (5) the agent defended himself successfully against his principal, on the ground that the latter had obtained the goods by fraud. If the assignees here had demanded the malt of the plaintiff, his refusal to deliver to them would have been proof of a conversion : *Wilson* v. *Anderton*(6). It is true that, if the agent is acquainted with all the facts at the time when he receives the

(1) 2 Ad. & El. 12.
(2) 11 R. R. 724 (2 Camp. 344).
(3) 33 R. R. 497 (7 Bing. 339).
(4) Ed. 1839. London. [9th Ed.

pp. 254, 255.]
   (5) Note to *White* v. *Bartlett*, 35 R. R. 566 (9 Bing. 382, note (a)).
   (6) 35 R. R. 348 (1 B. & Ad. 450).

goods, he is estopped from afterwards setting up against his BETTELEY principal a defence arising on such facts: but that is not the REED. case here. The defendant has never received the plaintiff's money: the malt was sold, and the money retained, with a reservation of the claim of the assignees. Further, this action should have been brought by the assignees and the plaintiff jointly: *Teed* v. *Elworthy* (1). The malt was sold on their joint account. And this objection is not merely technical; for the defendant has a lien against the assignees. "In cases of an advance of money, made under such circumstances as to constitute *money paid to the use of a third party, the [*516] nature of the compensation must clearly be determined by that of the fund out of which the advance is made:" 1 Walford's Treatise on the Law respecting Parties to Actions, p. 447, Book 3, c. 1, s. 1. Here therefore, before the compromise, the parties entitled to claim against the defendant would be the plaintiff and the assignees jointly: his liabilities and rights cannot be varied by a compromise to which he is no party. Nor, similarly, could he, by any thing which he chose to do in contravention of his original agency, relieve himself of, or qualify, his liability to the parties jointly interested: *Taylor* v. *Plumer* (2).

Erle, Hindmarch and *W. H. Watson, contrà :*

The defendant has consented that the sale shall not affect the rights of the parties. If, therefore, he could not have held the malt against the plaintiff, the money has been received by him to the plaintiff's use. The assignees could not have joined in an action to recover the malt; neither therefore could they join in an action for the money. The question is, not merely who made the agreement for the last sale, but who is really interested: *Skinner* v. *Stocks* (3). Now, first, there has been no usury. (The argument on this point is omitted.) The exception, by which it is attempted to modify the general rule that an agent cannot set up the *jus tertii* against his principal, would almost destroy the rule : the third party in fact almost always does intervene. There is no hardship in this case: an interpleader rule might have been obtained if justice had required it. *Hawes* v. *Watson* (4), *Gosling* v. *Birnie* (5), *Holl* v.   [*517]

(1) 14 East, 210.   See *Sims* v. *Bond*, 5 B. & Ad. 389.
(2) 16 R. R. 361 (3 M. & S. 562).   (4) 26 R. R. 448 (2 B. & C. 540).
(3) 23 R. R. 337 (4 B. & Ald. 437).   (5) 33 R. R. 497 (7 Bing. 339).

BETTFLEY
v.
REED.

Griffin (1), are conclusive authorities on the general rule. (They also argued that the defence did not arise upon *Non assumpsit :* the argument on this point is omitted.)

Cur. adv. vult.

LORD DENMAN, Ch. J., now delivered the judgment of the COURT. After detailing the facts (as *ante*, p. 418), his Lordship proceeded as follows :

The question is, whether he was entitled to set up that defence: And we are of opinion that he was not.

The defendant, who had dealt with the malt as being the malt of the plaintiff, and who had kept it in his warehouse for the plaintiff and in his name, proposes to answer the claim of the plaintiff by showing that the property in the malt is in the assignees of Bradley, and to set up their right against him, notwithstanding that the assignees had themselves abandoned it.

Upon the argument, a great many cases were cited to show that persons standing in similar situations to the defendant, as warehousemen, wharfingers and others, had been permitted to set up the *jus tertii*. But no instance could be adduced in which it was held that the *jus tertii* could be set up when the third person, being aware of the circumstances, had abandoned his claim. To allow a depositary of goods or money, who has acknowledged the title of one person, to set up the title of another who makes no claim or has abandoned all claim, would enable

[*518]

the depositary to keep for himself *that to which he does not pretend to have any title in himself whatsoever. After what passed, the defendant had no right to dispute the validity of the plaintiff's title, or to bring into question the validity of a contract to which he, the defendant, was no party, and which was no longer disputed by those between whom it was made, or their representatives.

With respect to the form of the action, we think that, as the plaintiff would have been entitled, under the circumstances of the case, to maintain an action of trover in case goods to the value of the sum now in dispute had been left in the hands of the defendant instead of money, he is entitled to maintain this action for money had and received.

The right of the official assignee and the plaintiff, jointly, applies

(1) 38 R. R. 817 (10 Bing. 246).

to the money paid into the Bank, and not to the money paid to the defendant.

Upon the whole, therefore, we are of opinion that the rule should be made absolute.

Rule absolute.

BETTELEY
r.
REED.

HEMP *v.* GARLAND, ADMINISTRATOR, &c. (1).

(4 Q. B. 519—524; S. C. 3 G. & D. 402; 12 L. J. Q. B. 134; 7 Jur. 302.)

> Defendant gave a warrant of attorney to secure a debt payable by instalments, the plaintiff to be at liberty, in case of any default, to have judgment and execution for the whole, as if all the periods for payment had expired: Held that, in an action of assumpsit on the implied promise to pay according to the terms of the defeazance, defendant might show, under a plea of the Statute of Limitations, that the first default was made more than six years before action; and that this was a complete defence, not only as to instalments due more than six years ago, but also as to those due within that period.

ASSUMPSIT against defendant as administrator of Charles Garland. The declaration stated that Charles Garland, in his lifetime, to wit on 25th April, 1832, was indebted to the plaintiff in 330*l.* for money found to be due on an account stated; and, being so indebted, and for securing payment, duly executed a warrant of attorney directed to certain persons &c. (the warrant was then set out), subject to a defeazance, indorsed thereon, to the tenor and effect following; that is to say: that the warrant of attorney was given by deceased to plaintiff, to secure payment of the said 330*l.*, the debt &c. due to the plaintiff, with interest at 5 per cent., and 7*l.* 7*s.* the costs of the warrant of attorney, in manner following; that is to say: 57*l.* 7*s.*, and interest on 50*l.*, on the 29th of September, 1832; 25*l.* and interest, on 25th of December, 1832; and 25*l.* and interest, on 25th of March, 24th of June, 29th of September, and 25th of December, in each and every succeeding year, until the whole of the said sums of 330*l.* and 7*l.* 7*s.* and interest as aforesaid should be fully satisfied; but, in case default should be made in payment of the said instalments, or any or either of them, or the interest thereon, or any part thereof, the plaintiff should be at liberty to enter up judgment on the said warrant of attorney, and thereupon to issue execution for levying, recovering and receiving all or so much of the *said sums of 330*l.* and 7*l.* 7*s.* and interest as should be unpaid at the time of such default, the same

1842.
Nov. 28.
1843.
Feb. 8.
——
[519]

[*520]

(1) Approved, *Reeves* v. *Butcher* [1891] 2 Q. B. 509, 60 L. J. Q. B. 619, C.A.
- A. C.

HEMP
v.
GARLAND.

as if all the periods for payment thereof had expired by effluxion of time, together with the costs of such judgment &c. That C. Garland then delivered the warrant of attorney to plaintiff, and plaintiff received it &c. That, thereupon, and in consideration that plaintiff, at the request of the said C. Garland, would forbear and give time to him for payment of the said debt and sum of 330*l.* so secured, until the times in the said defeazance specified, the said C. Garland promised plaintiff to pay him the said sum of 330*l.*, with interest from 24th of June, 1831, at the rate of 5 per cent. per annum, and 7*l.* 7*s.*, in the manner and at the times in the defeazance specified. The declaration then stated that plaintiff, relying &c., forbore and gave time to C. Garland, deceased, for such payment &c., until the several times in the defeazance specified, which time long since and in the lifetime of the deceased had elapsed ; and that, although the deceased, in part performance &c., had paid to plaintiff the first five of the said instalments and interest, yet the deceased disregarded his promise in not paying the 6th, 7th, 8th, 9th, 10th, 11th, 12th, or 13th of said instalments and interest, or any or either of them &c., nor would defendant, as administrator since the decease &c., pay the same or. any part thereof &c.

Plea (among others), that the causes did not accrue within six years before the commencement of the suit &c. Replication tendering issue thereon. Joinder.

On the trial, before Wightman, J., at the London sittings after Michaelmas Term, 1841, it appeared that the plaintiff, who relied upon the promise implied from the warrant and defeazance, had commenced *his action in March, 1841 : and it was admitted that all the unpaid instalments, except the last three payable in 1835, were barred by the Statute of Limitations : and the learned Judge was further of opinion that the last three, amounting, with interest, to 74*l.* 1*s.*, were also barred. A verdict was taken for the defendant, with liberty to move to enter a verdict for the plaintiff on the above point.

In Hilary Term, 1842, *Platt* obtained a rule *nisi* accordingly. In last Michaelmas Term,

[*521]

Deedes showed cause (1) :

The plaintiff's case is that, on 25th of December, 1833, the

(1) November 28th, 1842. Before Lord Denman, Ch. J., Coleridge and Wightman, JJ.

deceased made default.   The plaintiff then became entitled to levy
the whole debt: the plea is therefore a bar as to the whole:
Beckwith v. *Nott* (1), *Taylor* v. *Foster* (2), *Milles* v. *Milles* (3).   The
distinction is between assumpsit and debt.   Debt will not generally
lie till the last instalment has become due: *Rudder* v. *Price* (4) ;
but assumpsit will lie for each instalment; and here, by the terms
of the warrant and defeazance, not merely the instalment but the
whole debt was recoverable.

(COLERIDGE, J.: Was it obligatory on the plaintiff to sue for the
whole?   Might not he sue for each instalment without enforcing
payment of the whole?)

The statute runs from the time when the plaintiff might have
brought this action: Chitty on Contracts, 814 (3rd ed.).   *Rhodes* v.
Smethurst (5) illustrates the same doctrine.

Platt and *Whitehurst, contrà :*   [522]

The plaintiff could not have sued for the whole on the first
default.   He might have entered up judgment and levied the
whole; but the promise in the declaration is only to pay in the
manner specified in the warrant, that is, by instalments.   The
cases cited are therefore inapplicable.   But, supposing the plaintiff
entitled to sue for the whole on the first breach, he was not bound
to do so.   In *Rudder* v. *Price* (6) the doubt was, whether the
plaintiff was not bound to wait till every instalment was due.   At
all events, the plaintiff here might defer his action and sue for
each instalment when due: *Cooke* v. *Whorwood* (7) ; *Helps* v.
Winterbottom (8).

(LORD DENMAN, Ch. J.: In *Whitehead* v. *Walker* (9) the Court of
Exchequer held that the Statute of Limitations ran from the non-
acceptance of a bill of exchange, and could not be avoided by
deferring the action till nonpayment.)

The defendant in that case might clearly have been sued for the
whole upon non-acceptance.

Cur. adv. vult.

(1) Cro. Jac. 504.	(6) 1 H. Bl. 547.
(2) Cro. Eliz. 807.	(7) 2 Saund. 337.
(3) Cro. Car. 241.	(8) 36 R. R. 609 (2 B. & Ad. 431).
(4) 1 H. Bl. 547.	(9) 60 R. R. 811 (9 M. & W. 506).
(5) 51 R. R. 461 (4 M. & W. 42).	

LORD DENMAN, Ch. J., in this vacation (February 8th), delivered the judgment of the COURT:

This was an action of assumpsit: and the declaration stated in substance that, in 1832, the intestate was indebted to the plaintiff in a sum of 330*l.*, and that, for securing payment, the intestate executed a warrant of attorney with a defeazance stating that it was given to secure the payment of the debt with interest by certain instalments, the last of which would be payable on the 29th September, 1835; but that, in case default should *be made in the payment of any of the instalments, the plaintiff should be at liberty to enter up judgment and issue execution for so much of the principal debt of 330*l.* as should remain unpaid, as if all the periods for payment had expired.   The declaration then stated that, in consideration that the plaintiff would forbear until the times specified in the defeazance, the intestate promised to pay at those times: and then averred nonpayment of several instalments, three of which appeared to be due within six years before the action brought, and some were due more than six years.   The defendant pleaded several pleas, and, amongst others, the Statute of Limitations, upon which the present question arises; the plaintiff contending that he has a right to recover in respect of the instalments due within six years, and the defendant contending that, as all was to become payable upon the first default, the cause of action accrued at the time of such default, which was more than six years before the suit commenced.

We are of opinion that the defendant is right, and that the cause of action accrued upon the first default for all that then remained owing of the whole debt.   There was no other contract for forbearance or giving time than that which is expressed in or to be implied from the terms of the warrant of attorney.   The whole debt was due and payment might have been enforced at the time it was given: but the warrant of attorney and the power it gave was a good consideration for the forbearance contracted for; and as long as the terms were performed the plaintiff would be bound by it, and would have no cause of action against the intestate; but by the terms of that contract, which was the only valid consideration for the forbearance, the plaintiff was *not obliged to give further time in case of a default, but might, if he pleased, upon nonpayment of any instalment, proceed to recover all that remained due of the principal sum.

In this case there was a default more than six years ago; and

[*523]

[*524]

upon that the plaintiff might, if he pleased, have signed judgment
and issued execution for all that remained due, or he might have
maintained his action.   If he chose to wait till all the instalments
became due, no doubt he might do so; but that which was optional
on the part of the plaintiff would not affect the right of the defendant, who might well consider the action as accruing from the time
that the plaintiff had a right to maintain it.   The Statute of Limitations runs from the time the plaintiff might have brought his
action, unless he was subject to any of the disabilities specified in
the statute; and, as the plaintiff might have brought his action
upon the first default, if he did not choose to enter up judgment,
we think that the defendant is entitled to the verdict upon the plea
of the Statute of Limitations.

Rule discharged.

REG. *v.* The INHABITANTS of the Township
of HULME (1).

(4 Q. B. 538—542; S. C. 2 G. & D. 682; 12 L. J. M. C. 106; 7 Jur. 464.)

Pauper occupied a tenement of more than 10*l.* annual value for a year,
and paid the rent and poor rate for a year. In the rate, the landlord's
name was inserted under the head "name of owner;" but in the column
headed "name of occupier" no name was entered:
Held that pauper gained a settlement, as being sufficiently "assessed" to
satisfy 4 & 5 Will. IV. c. 76, the Poor Law Amendment Act, 1834 (s. 66.)

ON appeal against an order of two justices, whereby Joseph Gray
and Mary his wife were removed from the township of Hulme to
the township of Manchester, both in the borough of Manchester, the
Sessions quashed the order, subject to the following case:

It was admitted that the paupers had been entitled to a settlement in the township of Manchester: but it was contended, on the
part of that township, that Joseph Gray had subsequently acquired
a settlement in the township of Chorlton upon Medlock, by occupying
and renting a house therein, at the annual rent of 28*l.*, for one year
and upwards, during the years 1838, 1839, and 1840, in some or
one of them, and by being assessed to and having paid the poor
rate in respect of such tenement for one whole year. It was proved
that the pauper occupied and rented the house at the rent aforesaid, from June, 1838, to December, 1839, and paid the rent for
such period. It also appeared that, in the assessment for the poor
rate of Chorlton upon Medlock, which was made and allowed on

(1) *R.* v. *St. Anne, Westminster* (1860) 2 E. & E. 485; 29 L. J. M. C. 78, 83.

19th July, 1838, the house which the pauper so occupied was entered, but not the name of the tenant, the entry being as follows (1).

No. of Assess-ment.	Name of Occupier.	Name of Owner.	Description of property rated.	Gross estimated Rental.	Rateable Value.	Total amount to be collected	Date when paid.	Amount actually collected.
41	- -	Trustees of Otho Hulme.	House	- -	25l.	1l. 5s.	May 4	1l. 5s.

[539] It also appeared that 1l. 5s., the rate charged in that entry, was demanded from the pauper J. Gray, by and paid to the collector of the said poor rate by or on behalf of J. Gray on 4th May, 1839. The case then stated that in the next assessment J. Gray's name appeared, under the head " name of occupier ; " but that he did not pay the rate charged by this last assessment.

If the Court should be of opinion that the pauper might be deemed to have been assessed for the house during the first year of the tenancy, or that, by paying the rate for the first year and being assessed for the second year, the provisions of stat. 4 & 5 Will. IV. c. 76, s. 66, had been complied with, the order of Sessions was to be confirmed ; otherwise, to be set aside, and the order of removal confirmed.

Crompton in support of the order of Sessions :

A settlement was gained in Chorlton upon Medlock. Stat. 4 & 5 Will. IV. c. 76, s. 66, enacts that no settlement shall be acquired by occupying a tenement, " unless the person occupying the same shall have been assessed to the poor rate, and shall have paid the same, in respect of such tenement, for one year." Now, first, the assessment of July, 1838, satisfies this provision. It is not necessary that the rate should contain the name of the party paying. The requisites of the section do not materially differ from those of stat. 3 & 4 W. & M. c. 11, s. 6; only the word " assessed " is substituted for the word " charged " (the word in stat. 35 Geo. III. c. 101, s. 4, also), and assessment and payment for a whole year are now required. " Assessed " and " charged " cannot be differently construed. And it has been decided repeatedly that the word [*540] " charged," in stat. 3 & 4 W. & M. *c. 11, s. 6, is satisfied without the party being named, if the parish has notice of the party really

(1) Some headings not material to the point here decided are omitted.

rated : *Rex* v. *Walsall* (1) (though it was there admitted by the
COURT that *St. Mary le More* v. *Heavytree* (2) is misreported), *Rex* v.
Painswick (3), *Rex* v. *Brickhill* (4), *Rex* v. *Chew Magna* (5), *Rex* v.
Heckmondwicke (6). And these authorities are illustrated by cases
on the land tax : *Rex* v. *St. Lawrence, Winchester* (7), *Rex* v.
Mitcham (8) ; which show that, although both landlord's and tenant's
names appear on the rate, the occupier is the party really rated.
It is not, however, necessary here to contend that, if the name of
the landlord be expressly inserted, the tenant is assessed : and
where no name is inserted, and the tenant is not known by having
paid the rate or otherwise, he may not be legally the party rated,
as in *Rex* v. *Llangammarch* (9). But here is no doubt of notoriety
by payment. Secondly, the statute may be satisfied by the payment
in the first of the two years, and the assessment in the second. It
is not expressly required that the assessment and payment should
be for the same year ; and this clause, being restrictive, will be
construed narrowly. If it be argued that the omission of the name
in the rate makes the rate bad, the answer is, that a settlement may
be gained by payment under a bad rate.

> *Martin, contrà :*

The statute must be construed according to its plain words.
ABBOTT, Ch. J., in *Rex* v. *Turvey* (10), said, " I have often lamented,
that in so many instances, the Court has departed from the plain
and literal construction of the statutes relating to the settlement of
the poor." The construction adopted on the other side would make
assessment and payment the same thing ; but, if that were so, one
word only would have been used. The intention was, that settlements should not be gained by occupation, except where the occupation was notorious ; and for this purpose assessment by name, as
well as payment of rate, is required. Payment alone would give
no available notoriety: the parish officer would accept payment
from any one that offered it. The word " charged," in stat. 3 & 4
W. & M. c. 11, s. 6, must mean something different from the
word " assessed," in stat. 4 & 5 Will. IV. c. 76, s. 66 ; otherwise
the language would not have been changed. Under the earlier

REG.
v.
THE INHABI-
TANTS OF
HULME.

[*541]

(1) Cald. 35.
(2) 2 Salk. 478.
(3) Bur. S. C. 465.
(4) 8 Mod. 38.
(5) Cald. 365.
(6) Cald. 103.

(7) Cald. 379.
(8) Cald. 276.
(9) 2 T. R. 628.
(10) 2 B. & Ald. 520. See 2 Dwarris
on Statutes, 708.

REG.
v.
THE INHABI-
TANTS OF
HULME.

statute, the Courts avowedly acted on the principle of giving a lax interpretation to the words, as in *Rex* v. *Walsall* (1), *Rex* v. *Painswick* (2). Such a principle will not be applied to the late statute.

LORD DENMAN, Ch. J.:

It appears to me that there is no difference between the words "assessed" and "charged." *Mr. Martin* suggests that the Legislature must have had some reason for changing the expression; but at any rate they do not say so. It is not provided that the name of the party should be inserted, but only that he should be assessed, and pay the rate, for one year. That points only to the necessity of the assessment continuing for a year, and payment being made

[*542]

*by the same party; and this the individual in the present case has done.

PATTESON, J.:

The only question is, whether we can put a construction on the words of stat. 4 & 5 Will. IV. c. 76, s. 66, different from that which has been put on those of stat. 3 & 4 W. & M. c. 11, s. 6; and I think we cannot. And, whether it ought to be lamented or not, it is certain that the construction here adopted by the Sessions has been put on stat. 3 & 4 Will. IV. c. 11, s. 6, in scores of decisions.

WILLIAMS, J.:

I am of the same opinion. *Mr. Martin*, in his description of the requisites enforced by stat. 4 & 5 Will. IV. c. 76, s. 66, added the words "by name" to the word "assessed. Such an addition would make all the difference.

Order of Sessions affirmed.

1843.
April 27.
May 1.

[543]

BRUNE *v.* THOMPSON.

(4 Q. B. 543—553; S. C. Dav. & M. 221; 12 L. J. Q. B. 251; 7 Jur. 395.)

Where a party suing for port duties as owner of a port, gave no other evidence of title than the continual payment of a certain duty, which the jury found to be unreasonable in amount: Held, that he could not have a verdict for a less amount found by the jury to be reasonable.

Semble, that, where the duty is claimed under a grant from the Crown, which appears on the evidence to be enrolled of record, but is not produced

(1) Cald. 35.   (2) Bur. S. C. 465.

by the plaintiff, the jury ought not to be directed to presume such grant upon mere evidence of usage.

Quære, whether the Crown can grant, with the franchise of a port, the power to take tolls of undefined amount throughout the limits of the port and beyond the grantee's own land?

Quære also, whether ancient port duties can be made to apply to new articles of export or import?

Indebitatus assumpsit, with counts for port tolls, for manor tolls, and for tolls generally. Plea, payment of 10*l.* into Court as to all but the count on port tolls; and, as to the rest, *Non assumpsit*. Plaintiff accepted the 10*l.*, and joined issue on *Non assumpsit*. The contest on the trial was whether plaintiff was entitled to a port toll or to a manor toll only. The jury found plaintiff entitled to port tolls to the amount of 8*l.* Held, that plaintiff might take his verdict on the count for port tolls, and that defendant could not avail himself of the payment of money into Court, though plaintiff might have recovered the 8*l.* under the count for tolls generally (1).

INDEBITATUS ASSUMPSIT. The declaration contained counts for port tolls or dues; for tolls due to the plaintiff as owner of a manor; and for tolls and dues generally.

The defendant pleaded payment of 10*l.* into Court as to all the declaration, except the count for port tolls or dues; and, as to the residue, *Non assumpsit*. The plaintiff accepted the 10*l.* in satisfaction of so much as the first plea applied to.

Upon the trial, before Erskine, J., at the Cornwall Spring Assizes, 1842, it appeared that the plaintiff claimed, as owner of the port of Padstow, a toll or port duty on all articles imported and exported, and, among others, a duty of 3*d.* per ton on all ore exported in vessels from any part of the port; which port extended to both sides of the Padstow River for several miles between Wadebridge and a point at the mouth of it called Stipper Point. The plaintiff demanded, in his particular, a gross sum for port duties for iron ore exported from the port of Padstow during a certain period. The defendant contended that the plaintiff was entitled only in respect *of ore put on board and exported from certain quays [*544] within the port in the plaintiff's own manor of Padstow; and that the duty of 3*d.* per ton on the article exported by the defendant, viz. iron ore, was, at all events, unreasonable. Neither the declaration nor the particulars of demand specified the precise rate of toll claimed. It appeared that the plaintiff had, on a former trial of the same cause, given in evidence a grant from the Crown (to one Pope, who conveyed to plaintiff's ancestor) of the manor, with certain customs of anchorage, keelage, &c.; but the grant was not produced or proved by the plaintiff on this trial. One of the

(1) R. S. C. Ord. XXII., rr. 1, 2.

plaintiff's witnesses stated that it was enrolled among the public records, and accessible to any one.   The plaintiff's evidence proved an uniform payment for many years of 3*d.* per ton on tin, copper, lead and other ore ; but iron ore had only been recently exported, and that by the defendant, who had resisted the claim.   Ore was only one of a long list of articles of every kind on which the plaintiff claimed both an export and an import duty.   The learned Judge told the jury that they might from the evidence presume a grant by the Crown of a toll of 3*d.* per ton on all ore, or a grant of a reasonable toll in general terms, which reasonable toll might have been fixed by long usage at the amount claimed.   The jury found that the plaintiff was entitled to a duty upon ore exported from any part of the port, and not from the manor only ; that ¼*d.* per ton on iron ore would be a reasonable duty ; and that the plaintiff was therefore entitled only to the sum of 8*l.*   The Judge thereupon directed a verdict to be *entered for that amount on the count for the port duty, with liberty to move to enter a verdict for the defendant if the Court should be of opinion that the finding of the jury entitled him to it.   In the following Term,

[*545]

Erle obtained a rule *nisi* to enter a verdict for the defendant, or for a new trial, on the grounds that the evidence entitled the plaintiff to a verdict for 3*d.* per ton or nothing ; that, if 3*d.* was unreasonable, the verdict was for the defendant ; that a grant from the Crown could not, under the circumstances, be presumed, especially such a grant as was suggested by the Judge ; and that, at all events, the plaintiff was bound to take his verdict on the last count for tolls generally, on which count money had been paid into Court more than sufficient to cover the amount awarded by the jury. On this last point he cited *Early* v. *Bowman* (1), *Kennedy* v. *Withers* (2), and *Churchill* v. *Day* (3).

Sir W. W. Follett, Solicitor-General, *Crowder* and *Butt* now showed cause (4) :

The plaintiff claimed reasonable toll on all articles.   As to all ores but iron, the reasonableness of 3*d.* a ton was proved by long acquiescence and payment.   Iron ore was a recent export ; and the amount of toll was therefore subject to the opinion of the jury as to the reasonableness.   They would look to the nature of the article,

(1) 1 B. & Ad. 889.
(2) 3 B. & Ad. 767.
(3) 3 Man. & Ry. 71.

(4) The case was argued on April 27th and May 1st.

the duty upon similar articles, the extent of accommodation afforded   BRUNE
by the port, the date of the grant, and other circumstances.   The   v.
same mode of ascertaining the reasonableness of a duty on new   THOMPSON.
imports was adopted at Liverpool, and was *established by a verdict   [*546]
in a case tried (1) before Lord Denman, Ch. J., in which a bill of
exceptions was tendered, but eventually abandoned.

(LORD DENMAN, Ch. J.: This would be a difficult question for a
jury, and still more for a Judge.)

Not more so than to ascertain what shall be a reasonable market
toll; yet it was decided in *Corporation of Stamford* v. *Pawlett* (2),
affirmed on error, that a general grant of a market toll is legal, and
the Court clearly thought that the reasonableness of the amount
was for the determination of a jury.   A distinction was indeed
suggested in *Rex* v. *Corporation of Maidenhead* (3) between a market
toll and a toll against common right, as a toll thorough; but a port
toll is not against common right.   This is pointed out in *Warren* v.
Prideaux (4), and shows the distinction.   There is a consideration,
namely, the dedication of the port, and the appropriation of the
soil of it to the purpose of shelter and protection.   That no other
consideration is necessary is a doctrine now established: *Mayor &c.
of London* v. *Hunt* (5), *Crispe* v. *Belwood* (6), *Mayor of Yarmouth* v.
Eaton (7).   In *Jenkins* v. *Harvey* (8) all the authorities are collected.
A toll for passing along a highway, or navigating the sea, would be
a toll thorough: but that user is a very different thing from using
the port of a subject as a place of export, import or refuge.   Even
if the grant had specified the toll, its reasonableness *could not be   [*547]
withdrawn from a jury, as was observed by the Court in *Corporation
of Stamford* v. *Pawlett* (9): and this inconvenience would have
further resulted, that, if the jury had found it unreasonable, the
toll would have been wholly void, and the port or market free:

(1) *The Mayor, &c., of Liverpool*   ment in *Corporation of Stamford* v.
v. *Bolton* (tried at Westminster,   *Pawlett*, 35 R. R. 675 (1 Cr. & J. 74).
February 14th, 1843), of which there   The distinction is made by counsel in
is a note in Report of the Proceedings   argument.
of the associated Merchants of Liver-   (4) 1 Mod. 104.
pool, &c., 8vo, London, 1835.   (5) 3 Lev. 37.
(2) 35 R. R. 675 (1 Cr. & J. 57).   (6) 3 Lev. 424.
Affirmed on error, *Pawlett* v. *Corpora-*   (7) 3 Burr. 1402, 1406.
tion of Stamford, 35 R. R. 688(1 Cr. & J.   (8) 40 R. R. 769 (1 Cr. M. & R. 877;
400; *S. C.* 1 Tyr. 291). See *Wright* v.   2 Cr. M. & R. 393; *S. C.* 5 Tyr. 326,
Bruister,38 R. R. 232 (4 B. & Ad. 116).   871).
(3) Palm. 76, 84, cited in the judg-   (9) 35 R. R. 675 (1 Cr. & J. 81).

2 Inst. 220. A port duty is denied to be against common right by
ALDERSON, B. in *Jenkins* v. *Harvey* (1) ; and, on principle, it is in
the nature of a toll traverse, as appears by the description of such
petty customs and their presumed origin in Hale, De Portibus
Maris, p. 78. *Lord Falmouth* v. *George* (2) also illustrates the nature
of tolls traverse. As to the non-production of the grant supposed
to have been given in evidence on the former trial, the plaintiff
might rely upon user, and leave the jury to presume from it a
sufficient grant, or to find a title by prescription.

As to the payment of money into Court, *Early* v. *Bowman* (3),
Kennedy v. *Withers* (4) and *Churchill* v. *Day* (5) were decided before
the new rules of pleading, and are therefore not applicable. The
plaintiff and defendant both evidently went down to try whether
the plaintiff was entitled to a port toll or to a toll in respect of his
manor. The plea of payment into Court admitted a right to the
latter, but was made expressly inapplicable to the former ; the
second plea denied the right to port toll ; and the defendant
cannot now say that he always meant to admit a port toll to be
due. * * *

[548]   *Erle, Smirke* and *Montague Smith, contrà :*

The only toll demanded before trial or set up at the trial was one
of 3*d.* per ton on all ore. If that was unreasonable, and therefore
illegal, no title to any other was shown. The plaintiff's title
appeared to be derived under a grant from the Crown, which was
withheld from the jury. It was said that the defendant might as
easily have obtained access to the record of such a grant, and
produced it in evidence, as the plaintiff : but it was the plaintiff's
duty to produce it in order to make out his title ; and he could not
rely on mere user and prescription where the evidence showed that
another and different title was purposely concealed. Besides, the
plaintiff claimed under Pope ; and no conveyance subsequent to
that from the Crown was accessible to the defendant. The
defendant's objection was that Pope had no port duties to convey
to the plaintiff's ancestor. Of what avail, then, could it have been
for the defendant to prove a grant from the Crown to Pope which
did not contain such duties ? The plaintiff would, of course, deny
that to be the grant under which he claimed. Then the jury were

(1) 40 R. R. 769 (1 Cr. M. & R. 895 ;   (3) 1 B. & Ad. 889.
5 Tyr. 344).   (4) 3 B. & Ad. 767.
    (2) 30 R. R. 597 (5 Bing. 286).   (5) 3 Man. & Ry. 71.

told by the Judge that the original grant of the franchise may have
given a reasonable toll without specifying the precise amount, and
that user may have ascertained the amount at 3*d*.   But, first, the
jury have negatived the amount claimed by finding it to be
unreasonable ; therefore there has been no legal user to ascertain
the undefined amount; and the claim is unsupported by any
evidence.   Secondly, no such general grant of a port duty can be
presumed ; nor, if made, would it be legal.   The duty was one of
a great number of duties claimed on every kind of export and
import.   They were not confined to goods shipped from the plaintiff's
*land or soil, but charged on all goods passing in vessels up or
down a public navigable river within certain limits, independent of
his land, and included in the bounds of a public port.   This comes
within the description of a toll thorough.   It is a charge on the
subject for navigating an arm of the sea and using one of the *ostia
regni*, and is therefore classed among the tolls thorough in Com.
Dig. Toll, (C).   The distinction taken by counsel in *Rex* v.
Corporation of Maidenhead(1) is adopted by the Court of Exchequer
in *Corporation of Stamford* v. *Pawlett*(2), and is consistent with
reason.   *Mayor of Yarmouth* v. *Eaton* (3) and *Jenkins* v. *Harvey* (4)
are decisions which, though perhaps unexceptionable in themselves,
contain some extrajudicial opinions of very questionable authority.
In the first the declaration was held to contain a sufficient averment
of the plaintiff's title to a port duty without stating the consideration ;
but the doctrine there held by WILMOT, J., that a prescription for
a port duty is good without stating consideration or ownership of
the port or manor, merely because the Crown might first create
and then grant it, is an assumption capable of supporting any toll
thorough whatever.   So, as to *Jenkins* v. *Harvey* (4), it may well be
that a fee may be annexed by the Crown at this day to an office of
a public and useful nature ; but it is very doubtful whether the
Crown could lay duties on all manner of goods imported into a new
port, as seems to be there assumed ; and it is not a satisfactory
doctrine that juries are bound to presume an immemorial right
where there has been *" uninterrupted modern usage (5)."

BRUNE
v.
THOMPSON.

[*549]

[*550]

(LORD DENMAN, Ch. J. : I should like to know what length of
modern usage is to satisfy a jury.)

(1) Palm. 84.
(2) 35 R. R. 675 (1 Cr. & J. 74).
(3) 3 Burr. 1402.
(4) 40 R. R. 769 (1 Cr. M. & R. 877 ;

2 Cr. M. & R. 393 ; *S. C.* 5 Tyr. 326,
871).
  (5) 40 R. R. 769 (1 Cr. M. & R. 894 ;
5 Tyr. 342).

BRUNE
v.
THOMPSON.

The recital of stat. 12 Car. II. c. 4, s. 6, shows that consent of
Parliament is necessary to create port duties. There are indeed
precedents of grants by the Crown of small specified duties on
certain articles, for the maintenance or repair of ports, wharfs
and quays, of which Hale gives instances (1) ; but the " particular
sums " have been always expressed "in the patent ; " and no grant
or patent can be shown that professes to give the subject a right
to levy undefined duties on all exports and imports, subject to no
check but the accidental opinion of a jury impannelled in a cause,
whose notions of reasonableness will vary with times and circumstances. The reasonableness is considered by Lord Coke as a
question for the Judges, 2 Inst. 222 : and it seems the sum ought
to be so small that it cannot possibly operate as a check to commerce in any article liable to it, instead of being, as in the present
case, a very heavy burden (2). Wherever a toll has been claimed
on mere evidence of user, it has always been assumed that
uniformity of user was essential, as in *Lowden* v. *Hierons* (3) and
The Mayor of Truro v. *Reynalds* (4) ; which doctrine necessarily
excludes the notion of a power in the jury to reduce the amount
to a sum which was never in fact received. As to *The Mayor, &c.
of Liverpool* v. *Bolton* (5), the duties there had, in fact, been

[*551]

indirectly recognised by repeated statutes ; but the *case is, at
all events, of no value, for it ended in a reduction of the duties,
and the bill of exceptions was dropped (6). In some other instances,
as that of Bristol, where general *ad valorem* duties are taken by
prescription, it has been found necessary to confirm them by statute.

With respect to the point of pleading, it is certain that the
plaintiff might have recovered his whole demand on the last count
for tolls in general, on which money is paid into Court. * * *

[552]   LORD DENMAN, Ch. J. :

I feel no doubt on the last point ; and it is only by importing
technical reasons that any can be raised. Both parties went down
to try whether the defendant was liable to a port duty or to a
manor toll : and the plea of payment cannot be taken upon this
record to apply to a port duty (7).

With respect to the principal point, there ought to be a new

(1) De Portibus Maris, p. 78.
(2) See cases cited Com. Dig.
Market (F 1).
(3) 19 R. R. 542 (2 B. Moore, 102).
(4) 34 R. R. 713 (8 Bing. 275 .

(5) *Ante*, p. 433, note (1).
(6) This appears by the report cited,
ante, p. 433, note (1).
(7) See now R. S. C. Ord. XXII. rr.
1 and 2.—A. C.

trial. We think the jury could not properly be told that they might presume a grant where the plaintiff refused to produce it, especially a grant of a toll of unreasonable amount. This would be pressing the doctrine in *Jenkins* v. *Harvey* (1) too far. The doctrine held in that case is not indeed altogether satisfactory; and any person affected by it ought to have an opportunity of tendering a bill of exceptions. We also think it open to question whether the Crown can grant a right of taking toll indefinitely throughout a port beyond the limits of the grantee's land, and where the grantee may not even have it in his power to do repairs. The question, too, as to the legality of applying ancient port duties to new objects of commerce, raised in the *Liverpool* case but not decided, is proper to be considered.

PATTESON, J.:

As to the point on the plea of payment, it is really very clear. Since the late rules of pleading, the point in *Early* v. *Bowman* (2) cannot arise. It was an action by payee against acceptor, with a count on an *account stated. The plea to the first count would now be "*Non accepit;*" and, if a distinct issue were joined on it, the jury must find for the plaintiff if the acceptance were proved. The defendant could not insist on a nonsuit, or a verdict for himself on that count, merely because he had paid money into Court on the second count. Under the old practice, there was a plea of the general issue, on which the plaintiff would be nonsuited if the payment into Court covered the demand. Here the liability to a port duty, which was the only real question in the cause, was denied, and found by the jury; the plaintiff is therefore entitled to a verdict on the first count.

WILLIAMS, J. concurred.

Rule absolute for a new trial.

(1) 40 R. R. 769 (1 Cr. M. & R. 877 ; 2 Cr. M. & R. 393; *S. C.* 5 Tyr. 326, 871).
(2) 1 B. & Ad. 889.

REG. *v.* THE INHABITANTS OF ST. MARY,
NEWINGTON (1).

(4 Q. B. 581—584.)

By the Poor Law Amendment Act, 1834 (4 & 5 Will. IV. c. 76), s. 71,
the settlement of illegitimate children, born after the passing of the Act,
follows the mother's settlement acquired by marriage after their birth.

ON appeal against an order of two justices, whereby Eliza, lawful
child of Mary Ann Marks (late widow of William Marks), and
Henry and Ann, illegitimate children of M. A. Marks, were removed
from the parish of Cudham, Kent, to the parish of St. Mary,
Newington, Surrey, the Sessions confirmed the order as to Henry
and Ann, and quashed it so far as related to Eliza, subject to the
following case.

M. A. Marks (now Skeete) was, on or about 30th April, 1827,
married to William Marks, whose settlement at the time of his
death (in or about 1831) was in the appellant parish. On 15th
November, 1834, she was delivered of a male bastard child, the said
Henry, in the workhouse of the appellant parish. In 1838 she was
delivered of another bastard child, the said Ann, in the parish of
Hayes, in Kent. M. A. Marks gained no settlement in her own right
after the death of William Marks, up to and until 26th August, 1838,
when she was married to Samuel Henry Skeete, her present husband,
whose legal settlement is in the respondent parish.

The question for this Court was: whether the two children
(Henry and Ann) are to have the settlement to which their mother
was entitled immediately before her second marriage, or to take that
which she acquired by reason of such second marriage.

Erle and *Deedes* in support of the order of Sessions:

By stat. 4 & 5 Will. IV. c. 76, s. 71, the settlement of bastard
[*582]   *children is to follow that of the mother till they attain the age of
sixteen, &c., and they are to be part of her family; but that must
refer to a settlement gained by the mother in her own right, not to
a settlement in right of her husband, which, strictly speaking, is
not her settlement, since a *feme covert* can have no settlement of
her own. Sect. 57 requires the husband to maintain the children
which his wife has borne before marriage, whether legitimate or
illegitimate, up to the age of sixteen, during the life of the wife,

(1) See now The Divided Parishes   (1889) 14 App. Ca. 465, at pp. 483, 484,
Act, 1876 (39 & 40 Vict. c. 61), s. 35,   59 L. J. M. C. 29.—A. C.
and *Reigate Union* v. *Croydon Union*

and makes them part of his family: but it does not give them a settlement in the parish of such husband: *Rex* v. *Walthamstow* (1), *Reg.* v. *Wendron* (2); in the former of which cases the children were legitimate, and in the latter illegitimate. It follows that the liability to maintain, and the adoption into the family, do not create a settlement. And that seems to be assumed in *Lang* v. *Spicer* (3). There, and in *Reg.* v. *Wendron* (2), the children were born before the passing of stat. 4 & 5 Will. IV. c. 76; that, however, can make no difference as to the present question, which is, whether the marriage of the mother changed the previous settlement. Sect. 71 operates only so long as the mother is *sui juris*: when she marries, sect. 57 comes into operation. But sect. 57 operates without a change of settlement. Under the old law, also, the settlement of unemancipated children would follow that of the mother, but not after the mother's marriage, because she then lost the power of acquiring or imparting a settlement: *Wangford* v. *Brandon* (4); *Rex* v. *St. Giles in the Fields* (5); *Berkhampstead* *v. *St. Mary North Church* (6); POWELL, J. in *Cumner* v. *Milton* (7). By sect. 57, on the death of the mother the husband's liability ceases; it is scarcely consistent with this that the children should continue to be a charge on his parish. The words of sect. 71, " have and follow the settlement of the mother," do not seem to carry the enactment farther, in reality, than the word " have " would by itself; for that word would make the one settlement shift with the other: only, lest it should be supposed that the settlement of the child is to be finally that which the mother has at the time of its birth, the word "follow" is added. So that it cannot be assumed that the word "follow" is inserted with a view to the possibility of the mother's marriage: the word points to any change of her own settlement, properly so termed, not to a settlement, loosely so called, *jure mariti*. The ambiguity of sect. 71 is noticed in 3 Archbold's Justice of the Peace, &c., 300 (8).

Thesiger (with whom was *Bodkin*), *contrà*:

The Court will adhere to the language of the statute, even at the risk of partially counteracting some supposed intention of the

REG.
v.
THE INHABI-
TANTS OF
ST. MARY,
NEWINGTON.

[*583]

(1) 6 Ad. & El. 301.
(2) 7 Ad. & El. 819.
(3) 46 R. R. 290 (1 M. & W. 129;
S. C. Tyr. & Gr. 358).
(4) Carth. 449.

(5) Burr. S. C. 2.
(6) 2 Bott. 22, pl. 51 (6th ed.).
(7) 2 Salk. 528.
(8) 4th ed.

REG.
v.
THE INHABI-
TANTS OF
ST. MARY,[1]
NEWINGTON.

Legislature, according to the principle enforced in *Rex* v. *Barham* (1).
It is a fallacy to assume that the mother's settlement can be that
only which she acquires while she is a *feme sole.*

(PATTESON, J.: *Rex* v. *Walthamstow* (2) shows that legitimate
children do not gain the settlement which the mother acquires by
marrying after their birth.)

[*584]   But it is otherwise as to illegitimate children, by the express words
of sect. 71; if sect. 57 and sect. 71 appear inconsistent *in their
policy, the fault is in the enactment.

(PATTESON, J.: The children were illegitimate in *Reg.* v.
Wendron (3) ; but you will distinguish that case on the ground that
the children there were born before stat. 4 & 5 Will. IV. c. 76,
passed.)

Sect. 71 is expressly limited to the case of bastards born after the
passing of the Act.   The settlement which a woman acquires by
marriage is her own as much as any other settlement; she retains
it after the husband's death.   It cannot have been intended that
children under the age of sixteen, but above the age of nurture,
should be separated from their mother as soon as the husband
died.

(PATTESON, J.: But you admit that this will be so as to her
legitimate children by a former marriage; so that illegitimate
children will remain with the mother and legitimate children will
be taken from her.)

This is inconsistent : but the statute is so.   It is true that, under
the old law, the rule was that, if the mother " acquire a settlement by another marriage, it is not gained as the head of a family,
but as a subordinate part of some other, and therefore is not communicated to her former offspring : " 1 Nol. P. L. 308 (4th ed.).
Still the settlement so gained was her settlement : and therefore,
" wherever the husband " " has a settlement, that which the wife
had previous to marriage is absolutely superseded : " *Ib.* p. 291.
Consequently sect. 71 applies to such a settlement.   (He was then
stopped.)

(1) 8 B. & C. 99, 104.   (3) 7 Ad. & El. 819.
(2) 6 Ad. & El. 301.

Per Curiam (1) :

The words of sect. 71 cannot have the meaning for which the respondents contend.

Order of Sessions quashed as to the illegitimate children.

DOE d. EARL SPENCER and Others *v.* BECKETT.

(4 Q. B. 601—606 ; S. C. 12 L. J. Q. B. 236 ; 7 Jur. 532.)

1843.
May 6.

[601]

Lessor of plaintiff in ejectment proved a conveyance of the land to himself fifty years before the action brought: he had not occupied; but a person who had occupied proved payment of rent by himself to lessor of plaintiff, within thirty-three years of the action brought, at which time H. came into occupation. No lease to H. was shown. It was proved that, within twenty years before action brought, H., being in possession, declared that he was then paying rent to the lessor of the plaintiff; and that afterwards, and before action brought, defendant had said that he was tenant to H. H. died before the trial.

Held, that plaintiff was not barred by the Real Property Limitation Act, 1833 (3 & 4 Will. IV. c. 27), s. 2 (2), payment of rent being duly proved, by H.'s admission, so as to satisfy sect. 8, and defendant being bound by the evidence which was good as against H.

And that sect. 14, which requires acknowledgments of title to be in writing, was inapplicable to this case.

EJECTMENT for land in Wandsworth, Surrey. On the trial, before Alderson, B., at the Surrey Spring Assizes, 1842, the demise relied upon was that of Earl Spencer, which was laid on 1st February, 1841. It appeared, from documentary evidence, that in 1792 certain lands were conveyed by the Duke of Bedford to the late Earl Spencer, the father of the lessor of the plaintiff: and the present Earl was shown to be entitled, through and after the death of his father, to the lands described in the deeds produced. Evidence was given to identify the land in question as parcel of those included in the conveyance. It appeared, however, that neither the late nor the present Earl had been in actual possession from the time of the conveyance. William Matthews proved that, at that time and from thence to 1808, his father held as tenant to the Duke of Bedford and to the late Earl, and that he, the witness, had succeeded his father in that year, and held for ten years, during which he paid rent to the late Earl. In 1818 he was succeeded in the occupation by a person named Hampton ; and evidence was given that the defendant, in 1838, declared that he then held as tenant to Hampton. It was also proved that

(1) Lord Denman, Ch. J., Patteson and Williams, JJ.

(2) See now Real Property Limitation Act, 1874, s. 1.

Hampton, in 1835 or 1836, said to a surveyor employed by the lessor of the plaintiff, "You know as well as me what is Lord Spencer's property, *and what I hold. I have no property in Wandsworth but what I hold of Lord Spencer, and for which I pay 100*l.*" Hampton died before the trial. It was contended, for the defendant, that this evidence was not sufficient to take the case out of the operation of stat. 3 & 4 Will. IV. c. 27, ss. 2, 8. The learned Judge reserved leave to move for a nonsuit, and directed the jury to find for the plaintiff, if they were satisfied as to the identity of the land. Verdict for the plaintiff.

In Easter Term, 1842, *Shee*, Serjt. obtained a rule *nisi* for a nonsuit.

Platt and *Deedes* now showed cause:

The objection on the part of the defendant is that no payment of rent has been directly proved later than about 1818; that, as no lease is shown, the lessor of the plaintiff can insist only that Hampton and the defendant have been tenants from year to year; and therefore that the twenty years will run from 1818, under sect. 8 of stat. 3 & 4 Will. IV. c. 27. And it is said that the admissions of Hampton and the defendant do not meet this objection, since, by sect. 14, acknowledgments of title, in order to be equivalent to payment of rent, must be in writing. But there is a fallacy in assuming that the plaintiff uses the admissions as acknowledgments of title. Those of Hampton are insisted on as proofs of the payment of rent as late as 1835, under sect. 8; and the only question is whether payment of rent can be so shown. Now, as against either Hampton himself or the defendant, the payment of rent may be shown by the admission of Hampton,

made when he was in possession (1). Then *the defendant can have no better title than Hampton himself; for he has admitted that he holds as Hampton's tenant. This admission is not used as an acknowledgment of the title of the lessor of the plaintiff, but as proof of the connection between Hampton and the defendant, which may be shown by declarations of the defendant, as well as by any other evidence. If the payment by Hampton did not bind the defendant, a tenant from year to year might, by underletting, establish a title against his landlord, though he himself continued to pay the rent; for the undertenant never would pay rent to the

(1) See *Woolway* v. *Rowe*, 40 R. R.   v. *Coulthred*, 45 R. R. 714 (7 Ad. & El.
264 (1 Ad. & El. 114); *Doe* d. *Daniel*   235, 237).

owner of the fee. Mere non-payment of rent does not give an adverse title: in the case of a lease for a term, the twenty years will run from the determination of the term, though no rent has been paid: *Doe* d. *Davy* v. *Oxenham* (1) ; which was recognised in this Court in *Doe* d. *Newman* v. *Gopsall* (2). If it were *otherwise, a continued insolvency of the tenant would bar the landlord, unless he re-entered for nonpayment. Sect. 8 of stat. 3 & 4 Will. IV. c. 27, cannot apply to the payment of rent by the actual occupier, without reference to the nature of the holding. He might be let in by the immediate tenant to the landlord without any stipulation for rent, as a bailiff, or by mere favour. The owner of the fee is not bound to look beyond his own tenant. Sect. 14 applies to a matter not here in question, the effect of a formal acknowledgment of title between a claimant and the party of whom the claim is made.

(1) 56 R. R. 662 (7 M. & W. 131).

(2) Cited from 5 Jurist, 170, as *Doe* d. *Newman* v. *Godsill*.

The cause was tried before Lord Abinger at the Kent Summer Assizes, 1840. The premises had been conveyed to Newman, the lessor of the plaintiff, in 1809, by deed reciting that they were subject to a lease for sixty-one years at 4*l*. per annum. They were also subject to an annuity or rent-charge of 4*l*. payable to defendant. Newman had not received the rent, or had possession at any time during twenty years next before the bringing of this action; but the tenant had every year paid 4*l*. to the defendant. On the defendant's part it was suggested that this was a payment of rent to him, and showed that he held adversely to Newman. Lord ABINGER suggested to the jury that the payment might have been made in consequence of an arrangement among the parties that the tenant should pay defendant his annuity due from Newman instead of paying the same sum to Newman for rent: and he advised the jury, if they thought this probable, to find for the plaintiff. Verdict for plaintiff. *Thesiger*, in Michaelmas Term, 1840 (November 3rd, before Lord Denman, Ch. J., Littledale, Williams, and Coleridge, JJ.), moved for a new trial on the ground of misdirection, contending that the LORD

CHIEF BARON'S assumption was not borne out by any evidence, and that the payment was, on the face of the transaction, a payment of rent.

The Court took time to confer with Lord Abinger; and, in the same Term (November 24th),

LORD DENMAN, Ch. J. gave judgment.

After stating the material facts, his Lordship said:

The mere fact of non-payment of rent to the lessor of the plaintiff for twenty years would not be sufficient to bar his title, as was decided by the Court of Exchequer, this Term, in *Doe* d. *Davy* v. *Oxenham*, 56 R. R. 662 (7 M. & W. 131), in which decision we concur. But *Mr. Thesiger* said that the additional fact of a payment of 4*l*., the amount of the rent, to the defendant made a strong case in his favour. Lord ABINGER, however, thought it was for the jury to say, upon the evidence, whether the payments were made to the defendant on account of the annuity, or of rent due to him; and directed them, if they thought the former state of facts probable, to find for the plaintiff. The jury thought that the reasonable presumption, and found accordingly. We think the case was rightly submitted to them, and that there should be no rule.

Rule refused.

Shee, Serjt. and *Petersdorff, contrà :*

The argument on the other side appears rather to be directed against the policy of stat. 3 & 4 Will. IV. c. 27, than to show its inapplicability. The object of the Act was to put an end to disputes whether possessions were adverse or not, by laying down [*605] definite criterions for reckoning the *term of limitation. The attempt here is to evade the effect of sect. 14. The declarations of Hampton and the defendant were relied on substantially as acknowledgments of title: and they are unavailing for that purpose, because they were not in writing. *Doe* d. *Davy* v. *Oxenham* (1) is inapplicable: in that case there was a term of ninety-nine years created by a written lease, and the question arose on sect. 3. But here is no written lease ; and the utmost that can be implied is a tenancy from year to year, which comes under sect. 8. If the evidence of these declarations be sufficient, sect. 14 might be satisfied by the defendant having declared verbally that he had given a written acknowledgment of the title. It has been held that, under stat. 9 Geo. IV. c. 14, s. 1, a verbal acknowledgment of having paid money will not be an answer to the Statute of Limitations (2). The effect of the acknowledgment under stat. 3 & 4 Will. IV. c. 27, is for the Judge, not for the jury: *Doe* d. *Curzon* v. *Edmonds* (3) ; but, if the argument on the other side prevail, the jury will, in effect, have to interpret and apply written acknowledgments.

LORD DENMAN, Ch. J. :

I am of opinion that the learned Judge directed the jury quite properly. It was shown that Hampton paid rent for this land, while he held it, and within twenty years, to the lessor of the plaintiff : his declaration is good evidence of that fact. The defendant did not pay rent : but he was shown, by his own declara- [*606] tion, to hold under Hampton ; and an *undertenant cannot be permitted to dispute a title which is valid against the person of whom he holds.

WILLIAMS and WIGHTMAN, JJ. concurred.

Rule discharged.

(1) 56 R. R. 662 (7 M. & W. 131).
(2) See *Willis* v. *Newham*, 3 Y. & J. 518 ; *Bayley* v. *Ashton*, 12 Ad. & El. 493 ; and the cases mentioned in *Bevan* v. *Gething*, 3 Q. B. 740. Also *Doe* d. *Reed* v. *Harris*, 45 R. R. 469 (6 Ad. & El. 209).
(3) 55 R. R. 615 (6 M. & W. 295).

DOE D. SNELL AND SHORT v. TOM.

1843.
May 17.

(4 Q. B. 615—620; S. C. 3 G. & D. 637; 12 L. J. Q. B. 264; 7 Jur. 847.)

[615]

T. mortgaged land to B., and, by the mortgage deed, attorned to B. as tenant, at a quarterly rent, which was stated to be done for the purpose of securing the principal and interest, and in contemplation and part discharge thereof. The mortgage deed also gave B. a power of entry in default of payment. Held, that B., or his assignee, might bring ejectment against T., without giving him notice to quit.

T. mortgaged to B. for 150*l.*: afterwards, by a deed purporting to be between B., T. and S., in consideration of S. paying B. the 150*l.* and advancing 70*l.* to T., the mortgage was transferred to S.; but B. never executed. Held, that this was a transfer of a mortgage with an additional advance of 70*l.*, and therefore, under stat. 3 Geo. IV. c. 117, s. 2 (1), required only an *ad valorem* stamp as on a mortgage for 70*l.*

Afterwards B., by a new deed, transferred the mortgage to S., without any fresh advance. Held that, the deed required only a stamp as on a transfer of mortgage without additional advance, under stat. 3 Geo. IV. c. 117, s. 2 (2).

EJECTMENT for land in Cornwall. On the trial, before Atcherley, Serjt., at the last Cornwall Assizes, it appeared that, Thomas Tom, the defendant's father, being seised in fee of the land in question, by indentures of lease and release of 2nd and 3rd April, 1819, between the said Thomas Tom of the first part, Samuel Worden and Ralph Brown of the second, John Baker of the third, and Nicholas Penfound of the fourth part, the said Thomas Tom, in consideration of 150*l.* advanced to him by John Baker, granted, bargained, sold and released to Baker the premises in question, *habendum* to Baker in fee, with a proviso for. redemption on payment of 150*l.* on a certain day. The indenture also recited a previous mortgage, dated 16th April, 1802, by the said Thomas Tom, for 1,000 years, to one Cole, and an assignment by Cole to Worden and Brown in 1805, and that the mortgage debt secured by this term had been paid off, but the term had not been reassigned; and it was witnessed that Worden and Brown bargained, sold, assigned, transferred and set over to Penfound, his executors, &c., *habendum* to Penfound, his executors, &c., in trust to secure the payment of the 150*l.* and interest to Baker, and, after payment thereof, in trust for the said Thomas *Tom, his heirs, &c., to attend the inheritance. " And, lastly, for the better securing the said principal money and all interest and expenses, and in contemplation and part discharge thereof, the said Thomas Tom doth hereby attorn tenant to the said John Baker, his executors, administrators and assigns, for all the said premises, at the full and clear quarterly

[*616]

(1) See now Stamp Act, 1891 (54 & 55 Vict. c. 39), Sch. tit. Mortgage (4).
—A. C.

rent of 8l. for each quarter of a year, from the 25th day of March last, to be recoverable by distress and sale, action of debt, and otherwise however." A power of immediate entry and sale was also reserved to Baker upon default of payment.

By indentures of 28th and 29th of September, 1823, purporting to be between Baker of the first part, the said Thomas Tom of the second part, and Henry Short (one of the lessors of the plaintiff) of the third part, the mortgage of 1819 was transferred to Short, in consideration of his paying the 150l. to Baker, and advancing 70l. more to the said Thomas Tom, who covenanted to pay Short the 220l. and interest. This deed was executed by the said Thomas Tom and Short, but not by Baker. It had a 1l. 10s. stamp on the first skin, with progressive duty.

By indenture of release, dated 30th December, 1842, between William Baker, son and heir of the above-mentioned John Baker, deceased, of the first part, the said William Baker, Nathaniel Baker, and Thomas Baker, devisees and executors of John Baker deceased, of the second part, and John Orchard, administrator of Nicholas Penfound, above mentioned, deceased, of the third part, the said Henry Short of the fourth part, and John Henry Snell (one of the lessors of the plaintiff) of the fifth part, the mortgage of 1819 was transferred to Short and Snell, the latter as Short's trustee, without any further advance. This deed was executed by all the parties, and had a stamp of 1l. 15s., with progressive duty.

[617]   Thomas Tom, deceased, had continued in occupation till his death, when the present defendant succeeded him.

The stamps on the deeds of 1823 and 1842 were objected to as insufficient: and it was also objected that, since Thomas Tom, the father, was by the attornment in the deed of 1819 made tenant to Baker, the present defendant held as tenant from year to year, and that a notice to quit ought to be proved. The learned Serjeant directed a verdict for the plaintiff on the demise of Snell, reserving leave to move for a nonsuit.

In this Term, *Butt* obtained a rule accordingly.

Crowder now showed cause (1):

First, Baker and Tom did not contract the relation of landlord and tenant by the attornment in the deed of 1819. That attornment was merely to secure the payment of principal and interest, and in contemplation of part discharge thereof. It did not effect a

(1) Before Lord Denman, Ch. J., Patteson and Williams, JJ.

redemise from Baker to Tom. At any rate it could not preclude Baker from entering upon nonpayment. In this respect the case is like *Doe* d. *Garrod* v. *Olley* (1). And, further, Baker had not the legal estate ; that was in the trustees who held the term of 1,000 years. And, again, when Baker was paid off, there must have been a surrender : there is nothing to raise the presumption of a tenancy between Tom and the assignees of Baker's mortgage.

Next, the deed of 1823 was sufficiently stamped. That was a transfer of a mortgage, upon the further advance of 70*l.* Stat. 3 Geo. IV. c. 117, s. 2 (2), contemplates, first, the case where no further sum is advanced, and, secondly, the case where an addition is made to the sum already *secured. The latter case is that now before the Court ; and, in such case, " the *ad valorem* duty on mortgages " imposed by the former Acts is to " be charged only in respect of such further money." And, under stat. 55 Geo. III. c. 184, Schedule, Part I., title Mortgage, the *ad valorem* duty on a mortgage to secure 70*l.* is 1*l.* 10*s.* *Doe* d. *Bartley* v. *Gray* (3) is in point. And no deed stamp is necessary in addition : *Doe* d. *Barnes* v. *Rowe* (4). The case does not resemble *Lant* v. *Peace* (5), where an *ad valorem* stamp on the whole sum was held to be necessary because additional land was mortgaged upon the further advance.

[*618]

As to the deed of 1842, if it operated simply as a transfer, no additional sum being advanced, it required a stamp duty of 1*l.* 15*s.* with the progressive duty, under stat. 3 Geo. IV. c. 117, s. 2. That stamp has been affixed. Considered merely as a deed, it would require only the same stamp.

Butt, contrà :

First, it is true that the deed of 1819 could not be construed as effecting a redemise to Tom, if it merely stipulated for his remaining in possession : *Doe* d. *Parsley* v. *Day* (6). But here is a distinct agreement for a tenancy, and no clause, as there was in *Doe* d. *Garrod* v. *Olley* (7), that this shall not prejudice the right of entry.

Next, as to the deed of 1823, it is clear that, under stat. 55 Geo. IV. c. 184, Schedule, Part I., title Mortgage, a transfer of a

(1) 54 R. R. 607 (12 Ad. & El. 481).
(2) See now Stamp Act, 1891 (54 & 55 Vict. c. 39), Sch. tit. Mortgage (4).
—A. C.
(3) 3 Ad. & El. 89.
(4) 4 Bing. N. C. 737.
(5) 8 Ad. & El. 248.
(6) 57 R. R. 624 (2 Q. B. 147).
(7) 54 R. R. 607 (12 Ad. & El. 481).

Doe d.
SNELL
r.
TOM.

[*619]

mortgage, with an additional sum added, was liable to "the same duty or duties as an original mortgage." Now an original mortgage for 220*l.* would require an *ad valorem* stamp of 3*l.* So that, treating *the deed as a transfer, the only question is whether it be within the protection of stat. 3 Geo. IV. c. 117, s. 2. But it was not a transfer at all; for it was never executed by Baker nor by the trustees of the term. Therefore the cases of actual transfer, such as *Doe* d. *Bartley* v. *Gray* (1), and *Doe* d. *Barnes* v. *Rowe* (2), are inapplicable. The case much more nearly resembles *Lant* v. *Peace* (3), the effect being a new mortgage of the land. Or, even if it were taken simply as a covenant by Tom to pay interest on the 150*l.*, and as a mortgage for the 70*l.*, it would be a deed "not otherwise charged," and require a stamp of 1*l.* 15*s.*, under stat. 55 Geo. III. c. 184, Schedule, Part I., title Deed, in respect of the 150*l.*, and should also have a mortgage stamp of 1*l.* 10*s.* on the 70*l.*

Cur. adv. vult.

Lord Denman, Ch. J., in the following vacation (May 17th), delivered the judgment of the Court:

This was a motion for a nonsuit. Two objections to the plaintiff's case are stated.

First, that, although the action is by mortgagee against mortgagor, yet that the mortgage deed has a clause by which the mortgagor attorned tenant to the mortgagee at a rent of 32*l.* per annum, and that no notice to quit, or demand of possession, was proved. The answer is that there is also a clause for immediate entry in case of default in payment of the mortgage money; and therefore, whatever be the meaning of the clause of attornment, the case is brought within the authority of *Doe* d. *Garrod* v. *Olley* (4); and no notice or demand was necessary.

[620]

Secondly, that the stamps on the deeds are not sufficient. The lessor of the plaintiff claims as assignee of the original mortgagee: but the intended deed of assignment or transfer was not executed by the original mortgagee. A further sum was advanced at that time; and the deed is stamped with an *ad valorem* stamp on that sum. If the original mortgagee had executed it, the stamp would have been sufficient under stat. 3 Geo. IV. c. 117, s. 2, and according to the case of *Doe* d. *Bartley* v. *Gray* (5); but, as he did not execute,

(1) 3 Ad. & El. 89.
(2) 4 Bing. N. C. 737.
(3) 8 Ad. & El. 248.

(4) 54 R. R. 607 (12 Ad. & El. 481).
(5) 3 Ad. & El. 89.

it is contended that the deed operates as an original mortgage by the mortgagor, not only of the money newly advanced, but of the original sum also, and so ought to have had an *ad valorem* stamp applicable to the total amount. We do not think that it can be fairly said so to operate, and that it amounts to a further charge only, and comes under the same rule as if the mortgagee had executed it.

There was a subsequent deed in 1842, which was executed by the heir of the original mortgagee, who had died in the meantime, and thereby the transfer of the original mortgage was completed. That deed had a stamp applicable, under stat. 3 Geo. IV. c. 117, s. 2, to a transfer of a mortgage where no further sum is advanced: and no further sum was advanced at that time; therefore that deed also is properly stamped; and all is right.

The rule for a nonsuit must be discharged.

Rule discharged.

SEWELL, Executrix of Sewell, *v.* WILLIAM SEAL EVANS.

(4 Q. B. 626—634 ; S. C. 12 L. J. Q. B. 277, *n.*)

RODEN *v.* HENRY THOMAS RYDE.

(4 Q. B. 629—634 ; S. C. 3 G. & D. 604 ; 12 L. J. Q. B. 276 ; 7 Jur. 554.)

To prove the execution by defendant of an instrument on which he is sued, if it be shown that the instrument is executed by a person bearing defendant's name, it is not necessary to give evidence strictly identifying the person whose signature is proved with the party on whom process has been served, unless facts appear which raise a doubt of the identity.

In an action for goods sold, against William Seal Evans, it appeared that, about five years before action brought, William Seal Evans had been a customer, and had written a letter acknowledging receipt of the goods. The witness who proved these facts did not know whether defendant was the same W. S. Evans; nor was any further evidence given of the fact. Held a sufficient *primâ facie* case.

In an action against Henry Thomas Ryde as acceptor of a bill of exchange, it appeared that a Henry Thomas Ryde had kept cash at the Bank where the bill was made payable, and had drawn cheques which the cashier had paid. The cashier knew the party's handwriting by the cheques, and swore that the acceptance was in the same writing; but he had not paid any cheque for some time, did not know the party personally, and could not further identify him with defendant. Held a sufficient *primâ facie* case.

In *Sewell* v. *William Seal Evans* the action was debt on a bill of exchange drawn, by and in favour of the testator, upon and accepted by defendant; and for goods sold and delivered by testator to defendant, and on an account stated between testator and defendant.

Plea.   As to the bill of exchange, that defendant did not accept : as to the residue, Never indebted.

Issues thereon.

On the trial before Lord Denman, Ch. J., at the London sittings after Michaelmas Term, 1841, the plaintiff failed on the issues as to the bill of exchange and on the account stated.   As to the issue on the sale and delivery of goods, a witness swore that he introduced a person of the name of William Seal Evans to the testator as a customer, and that he saw the person so introduced write a letter ; which letter was produced in evidence, and (as was admitted) established the case against the defendant by acknowledgment, if the identity of the writer and the defendant was shown.   The facts occurred about five years before the action was brought.   The

[*627]

witness had not seen the person since, and did not *know whether that person was the defendant.   The defendant's counsel contended that there was no evidence to go to the jury : but the LORD CHIEF JUSTICE left the case to them ; and they found a verdict for the plaintiff on the issue as to goods sold and delivered.   In Hilary Term following (1),

Humfrey moved for a new trial :

There was nothing from which the jury could infer the identity of the defendant and the writer of the letter.

(LORD DENMAN, Ch. J. : How far do you go ?   Do you say that it was necessary to show the identity of that person with the person who was served with the writ ?)

In *Whitelocke* v. *Musgrove* (2) an action was brought upon a note which was signed with " the mark of Francis Musgrove."   The signature of an attesting witness was also proved : but the Court of Exchequer held that there was no case for a jury without evidence of the identity of the defendant.   And BAYLEY, B. (3) said : " It frequently happens that a subscribing witness says that he saw the bond executed, but that he did not know the person who executed to be the defendant.   What is the consequence ?   It is not presumed

(1) January 11th, 1842.   Before Lord Denman, Ch. J., Patteson, Coleridge and Wightman, JJ.
(2) 1 Cr. & M. 511; *S. C.* 3 Tyr.
541.
(3) 1 Cr. & M. 519 ; and see p. 521.

that he was the defendant, but the plaintiff is nonsuited." The case
there supposed is precisely the present case.

(LORD DENMAN, Ch. J.: Does the name go for nothing at all, in
any case? Suppose the name of the defendant had been William
Lemuel Gulliver Evans, and a sale had been proved to a party so
named.)

That point is noticed by BAYLEY, B. in *Whitelocke* v. *Musgrove* (1).
*He says: "We presume that the note was signed by a person of   [*628]
the name of Francis Musgrove; but how does that appear to be the
defendant?" *Middleton* v. *Sandford* (2) is to the same effect.

(COLERIDGE, J.: There proof was not given that the person signing
as Thomas Sandford was so named.)

No better proof, at any rate, was given here than in *Whitelocke* v.
Musgrove (3).

(PATTESON, J.: In *Nelson* v. *Whittall* (4) BAYLEY, J. said that there
was evidence to connect the defendant with the note.)

He clearly meant to intimate that some evidence, besides that of
identity of name, was always necessary: and it was shown, in
Whitelocke v. *Musgrove* (5), that the doctrine was not new.

(LORD DENMAN, Ch. J.: The opinion of BAYLEY, J., in *Nelson* v.
Whittall (4), was extrajudicial.)

In *Jones* v. *Jones* (6) it was held that, in an action on a note against
Hugh Jones, it was not evidence, to go to a jury, that a person
named Hugh Jones had signed it, the name appearing to be
common: and it is worth remarking that in that case there was a
plea of confession and avoidance. There PARKE, B. said that the
difficulty often occurred in ordinary cases of goods sold and delivered.
In *Bulkeley* v. *Butler* (7) the action was by indorsee against acceptor :
the payee and indorser was E. S.: and evidence of conduct, and
possession of the bill, by a person calling himself E. S., was
thought sufficient to enable a jury to infer the identity of this

(1) 1 Cr. & M. 515.	(4) 1 B. & Ald. 19, 21.
(2) 4 Camp. 34. See *Drew* v. *Prior*,	(5) 1 Cr. & M. 513; 3 Tyr. 546.
5 M. & G. 264.	(6) 9 M. & W. 75.
(3) 1 Cr. & M. 511 ; *S. C.* 3 Tyr. 541.	(7) 2 B. & C. 434.

SEWELL
v.
EVANS.
RODEN
v.
RYDE.
[*629]

person with the payee : but it was assumed that some evidence was requisite.

(PATTESON, J. : *In *Greenshields* v. *Crawford* (1), where Charles Banner Crawford was sued as acceptor of a bill, directed to Charles Banner Crawford, East India House, it was held enough to show that the acceptance was written by a person of that name, who had been a clerk in the India House, but had left it five years ago : according to your argument that was no evidence whatever.)

That case must have contained some other facts ; it is irreconcileable with *Whitelocke* v. *Musgrove* (2).

(PATTESON, J. referred to *Smith* v. *Henderson* (3).)

Cur. adv. vult.

In *Roden* v. *Henry Thomas Ryde* the declaration was in assumpsit by indorsee against acceptor of three bills of exchange, with a count on an account stated. Pleas : as to the bills, that defendant did not accept : as to the residue, *Non assumpsit.* Issues thereon.

On the trial, before Williams, J., at the sittings in Middlesex in last Hilary Term, it appeared that all the bills were accepted in the name of Henry Thomas Ryde, and made payable at the Regent Street Branch of the London and Westminster Bank. The plaintiff called a cashier of that Bank, who stated that he knew the handwriting of Henry Thomas Ryde, and that the acceptances were in his writing. Being cross-examined as to his means of knowledge, he stated that Henry Thomas Ryde had kept an account at the Regent Street Branch : that witness had never seen him write, and did not know him : that his only means of knowledge as to the handwriting consisted in his having, as cashier, paid cheques drawn in the name of the party alluded to by him ; and that he

[*630]

had paid none for some time. *For the defendant it was objected that there appeared no evidence to identify him with the Henry Thomas Ryde spoken of by the witness. The learned Judge thought that there was a *primâ facie* case of identity, and overruled the objection. Verdict for plaintiff. *Wordsworth*, in the same Term (January 13th), moved for a rule to show cause why a nonsuit should not be entered or a new trial had, contending that there had been no evidence of the identity. He cited no authorities, but

(1) 60 R. R. 740 (9 M. & W. 314).   541.
(2) 1 Cr. & M. 511 ; S. C. 3 Tyr.   (3) 60 R. R. 893 (9 M. & W. 798).

referred to the motion made by *Humfrey* in *Sewell* v. *Evans*, two days before, and the cases then mentioned.

Cur. adv. vult.

The COURT, in the same Term, January 25th, granted rules *nisi* in both cases, but directed that they should not be set down in the new trial paper.

In *Roden* v. *Ryde* (May 10th),

F. V. Lee was about to show cause; but the COURT called upon

Wordsworth in support of the rule:

(LORD DENMAN, Ch. J.: You admit that there was evidence of a person keeping an account at the Bank, whose handwriting was that produced; but you say he was not sufficiently identified with the defendant.)

That position is borne out by the judgment of the Court of Exchequer in *Whitelocke* v. *Musgrove* (1), where Lord LYNDHURST, C. B., though absent when cause was shown, concurred with the rest of the Court. And, on the motion of a rule *nisi*, his Lordship said: "It would be very extraordinary if some evidence of identity was not necessary" (2). "Were it *otherwise any person of the same name might be sued with effect. Why should the *onus* of proving a negative, viz. that he is not the person named in the note, be thrown on the defendant?" (3). In *Logan* v. *Allder* (4), which was an action of debt, on bond, against a party described as W. R. Allder, of H. House, in the county of Durham, a witness proved the execution of the bond at an inn in Sussex, but had not, either before or since, seen the person who executed, and did not know that the defendant was the person, or that he lived at H. House, Durham. The same question arose as in the present case; and the plaintiff was nonsuited. On a motion to set aside the nonsuit, BOLLAND, B. said: "The rule of law is the same in civil as in criminal proceedings. Now suppose a person to be tried for forging the signature of W. R. Allder of H. House to a bond, and that the subscribing witness said, 'I saw that bond signed at the inn I keep, but I never saw the party executing before or since,' could that prisoner's case be left to the jury?"

[*631]

(1) 1 Cr. & M. 511; *S. C.* 3 Tyr. 541.

(2) 3 Tyr. 542; see 1 Cr. & M. 523, note (*a*).

(3) 3 Tyr. 543.

(4) 3 Tyr. 557, note (*a*).

RODEN
v.
RYDE.

RODEN
v.
RYDE.

(PATTESON, J.: There must be some distinction in the modes of proof, according to circumstances. In a civil case the action may be against the executors of the party who signed. I do not understand the doctrine of BOLLAND, B. In a criminal case the prisoner would be in Court, and the witness would be asked whether that was or was not the man who signed the bond.)

In *Jones* v. *Jones* (1) the Court of Exchequer upheld the decision in *Whitelocke* v. *Musgrove* (2); and, the plaintiff failing to identify the party whose handwriting he proved with the defendant, a new trial was ordered. On a second trial, evidence of the identity was given, and the plaintiff *recovered (3). *Greenshields* v. *Crawford* (4) may be relied upon on the other side; but there some evidence of identity appeared.

[*632]

(LORD DENMAN, Ch. J.: How did the evidence there prove identity?

WILLIAMS, J.: The statement in the report does not show it.

PATTESON, J.: Nothing appears but that the person to whom the evidence related bore the same name with the party sued.)

No reason can be assigned for throwing the burden of disproof in such cases upon the defendant. In *Parkins* v. *Hawkshaw* (5), an action on a bond, HOLROYD, J. ruled that the plaintiff must identify the person sworn to have executed the bond with the person sued. Lord ELLENBOROUGH and BAYLEY, J., in *Nelson* v. *Whittall* (6), thought it doubtful whether mere evidence of the subscribing witness's handwriting was sufficient proof against a party sued as maker of a promissory note.

LORD DENMAN, Ch. J.:

The doubt raised here has arisen out of the case of *Whitelocke* v. *Musgrove* (2): but there the circumstances were different. The party to be fixed with liability was a marksman, and the facts of the case made some explanation necessary. But, where a person, in the course of the ordinary transactions of life, has signed his name to such an instrument as this, I do not think there is an

(1) 9 M. & W. 75.
(2) 1 Cr. & M. 511; S. C. 3 Tyr. 541.
(3) 9 M. & W. 78, note (a).
(4) 60 R. R. 740 (9 M. & W. 314).
(5) 19 R. R. 711 (2 Stark. N. P. C. 239).
(6) 1 B. & Ald. 19.

instance in which evidence of identity has been required, except *Jones* v. *Jones* (1).   There the name was proved to be very common in the country : and I do not say that evidence of this kind may not be rendered necessary by particular circumstances, as, for instance, length of time since the name was signed.   *But, in [*633] cases where no particular circumstance tends to raise a question as to the party being the same, even identity of name is something from which an inference may be drawn.   If the name were only John Smith, which is of very frequent occurrence, there might not be much ground for drawing the conclusion.   But Henry Thomas Rydes are not so numerous ; and from that and the circumstances generally there is every reason to believe that the acceptor and the defendant are identical.   The *dictum* of BOLLAND, B. (2) has been already answered.   Lord LYNDHURST, C. B. asks (3) why the *onus* of proving a negative in these cases should be thrown upon the defendant : the answer is, because the proof is so easy.   He might come into Court and have the witness asked whether he was the man. The supposition that the right man has been sued is reasonable, on account of the danger a party would incur if he served process on the wrong : for, if he did so wilfully, the Court would no doubt exercise their jurisdiction of punishing for a contempt.   But the fraud is one which, in the majority of cases, it would not occur to any one to commit.   The practice, as to proof, which has constantly prevailed in cases of this kind, shows how unlikely it is that such frauds should occur.   The doubt now suggested has never been raised before the late cases which have been referred to.   The observations of Lord ABINGER and ALDERSON, B. in *Greenshields* v. *Crawford* (4) apply to this case.   The transactions of the world could not go on if such an objection were to prevail.   It is unfortunate that the doubt should ever have been raised ; and it is best that we should sweep it away as soon as we can.

PATTESON, J. :   [634]

I concur in all that has been said by my Lord.   And the rule always laid down in books of evidence agrees with our present decision.   The execution of a deed has always been proved by mere evidence of the subscribing witness's handwriting, if he was dead. The party executing an instrument may have changed his residence. Must a plaintiff show where he lived at the time of the execution,

(1) 9 M. & W. 75.	(3) 3 Tyr. 543.
(2) 3 Tyr. 558.	(4) 60 R. R. 740 (9 M. & W. 314).

and then trace him through every change of habitation till he is
served with the writ?   No such necessity can be imposed.

WILLIAMS, J.:

I am of the same opinion.   It cannot be said here that there was
not some evidence of identity.   A man of the defendant's name
had kept money at the branch Bank; and this acceptance is proved
to be his writing.   Then is that man the defendant?   That it is a
person of the same name is some evidence till another party is
pointed out who might have been the acceptor.   In *Jones* v.
Jones (1) the same proof was relied upon; and Lord ABINGER said:
"The argument for the plaintiff might be correct, if the case had
not introduced the existence of many Hugh Jones's in the neighbourhood where the note was made."   It appeared that the name
Hugh Jones, in the particular part of Wales, was so common as
hardly to be a name: so that a doubt was raised on the evidence
by cross-examination.   That is not so here; and therefore the
conclusion must be different.

Rule discharged (2).

In *Sewell* v. *Evans*,

Fish, on May 11th, was about to show cause; but,

[635]   Per CURIAM:

This case must be considered as disposed of by the decision of
the Court yesterday in *Roden* v. *Ryde*.

Rule discharged.

---

[663]

DOE D. TIMMIS v. STEELE AND LIVERSAGE.

(4 Q. B. 663—668; S. C. 12 L. J. Q. B. 272; 3 G. & D. 622.)

A tenant in fee conveyed lands "to H., her heirs and assigns, to hold to
H. and her assigns during the life of G."   G. was H.'s heir-at-law:
Held that, after H.'s death, G. was entitled to hold for his life, as special
occupant, and that the land did not pass to H.'s executors (3) by the words
in the *habendum.*

EJECTMENT for lands in Cheshire.

On the trial before Coltman, J., at the Cheshire Spring Assizes,
1842, the plaintiff proved that, by indenture of 15th September,
1785, Sir Thomas Broughton, being seised in fee of the lands in

(1) M. & W. 75.
(2) See *Simpson* v. *Dismore*, 60 R. R.
663 (9 M. & W. 47).

(3) See now Land Transfer Act,
1897 (60 & 61 Vict. c. 65), ss. 1 and 2.
—A. C.

question, demised them to "Hannah Timmis, her heirs and assigns, to hold to the said Hannah Timmis and her assigns for and during the natural life of George Timmis." The George Timmis named in the indenture was the lessor of the plaintiff, and heir-at-law to Hannah Timmis, who was dead. The counsel for the defendants contended that the effect of the indenture was to give the land to the executors or administrators of Hannah Timmis. The learned Judge directed a verdict for the plaintiff, giving leave to move for a verdict for the defendants. In Easter Term, 1842, *Evans* obtained a rule *nisi* accordingly.

Jervis in this vacation (May 12th) showed cause:

The lessor of the plaintiff took as special occupant, by reason of the *word "heirs." The authorities are distinct on the effect of the word "heirs:" 3 Bac. Abr. 190, Estate for Life and Occupancy, (B), 3 (1). It is contended, on the other side, that the effect of this word is cut down by the *habendum*. The cases are collected in 4 Cruise's Digest, title XXXII. Deed, ch. 21 (2): and there, (sect. 67, p. 272) this rule is laid down. "With respect to the *habendum*, its office is only to limit the certainty of the estate granted; therefore no person can take an immediate estate by the *habendum* of a deed, where he is not named in the premises; for it is in the premises of a deed that the thing is really granted." And, at sect. 76, p. 273: "if lands are given in the premises of a deed to A. and his heirs, *habendum* to A. for life; the *habendum* is void; because it is utterly repugnant to, and irreconcileable with the premises:" and *Throckmerton* v. *Tracy* (3) is cited. In *Goodtitle d. Dodwell* v. *Gibbs* (4) land was conveyed to W. in fee, *habendum* to W. in fee after the death of H.; and it was held that W. took an immediate fee, and that the *habendum* could not so cut down the grant as to make the whole a conveyance of a freehold in future. There ABBOTT, Ch. J., in delivering the judgment of the Court, relied upon a distinction which he expressed as follows. "If no estate be mentioned in the premises, the grantee will take nothing under that part of the deed, except by implication and presumption of law, but if an *habendum* follow, the intention of the parties as to the estate to be conveyed will be found in the *habendum*, and, consequently, no implication or presumption of law can be made, and

DOE d.
TIMMIS
v.
STEELE.

[*664]

(1) 7th ed.
(2) 4th ed.
(3) Plowd. 145, 152, 153, in argument.
(4) 29 R. R. 366 (5 B. & C. 709).

if the intention so expressed be contrary to *the rules of law, the intention cannot take effect, and the deed will be void. On the other hand, if an estate and interest be mentioned in the premises, the intention of the parties is shown, and the deed may be effectual without any *habendum*, and if an *habendum* follow which is repugnant to the premises, or contrary to the rules of law, and incapable of a construction consistent with either, the *habendum* shall be rejected, and the deed stand good upon the premises."

Evans and *E. V. Williams, contrà :*

Where the *habendum* is repugnant to the premises it is void : but, where it merely qualifies, there it will take effect. " The office of the premises of the deed is twofold : first, rightly to name the feoffor and the feoffee ; and secondly, to comprehend the certainty of the lands or tenements to be conveyed by the feoffment, either by express words, or which may by reference be reduced to a certainty ; for *certum est quod certum reddi potest.* The *habendum* hath also two parts, viz. first, to name again the feoffee ; and secondly, to limit the certainty of the estate : " Co. Litt. 6 a.   In the position cited from Plowden by Cruise the *habendum* was contradictory to the premises, because no man can be heir to a living person. But here the word " heirs " is not a word of descent ; it merely describes a special occupant. In *Doe d. Blake* v. *Luxton* (1) Lord KENYON said that, if an estate *pur autre vie* " be given to A. and the heirs of his body, the heirs of the body will take as special occupants, if no disposition be made of it by the first taker : but it

[*666]

is absolutely in his power to make what disposition of it he *pleases.*" The estate here is for the life of George Timmis only ; the word " heir," in the conveyance of such an estate, has therefore no necessary repugnance to .the limitation in the *habendum*.

(PATTESON, J.: May not you reject as much of the *habendum* as is repugnant, and retain the rest ? The position cited from Plowden seems to go to that.)

In *Pilsworth* v. *Pyet* (2) land was conveyed to P. and his heirs, *habendum* to P. and his heirs for three lives ; and it was held that P. and his heirs took for the three lives only.

(PATTESON, J.: If a man give land to me and my heirs, *habendum* to me and the heirs of my body, there is no repugnancy, because

(1) 6 T. R. 289, 292.   (2) 2 (Thomas) Jones, 4.

the *habendum* explains the sense in which the word "heirs" is
used: but you want to strike the word out.)

That may be done where it is not a word of limitation. But it is
not generally true that words in the premises cannot be rejected.
In *Spyre* v. *Topham* (1) one Thickston, being seised in fee, leased
by bargain and sale for a year to Bass, and, the next day, by
release describing Bass as a person named in trust for Topham,
released to Topham in fee, describing the premises as in Topham's
possession by virtue of a bargain and sale of the day before, *habendum* to Bass in fee to the use of such person as Topham should
appoint; and it was held that Bass took in fee, by virtue of the
habendum in the release, and that the grant to Topham in the
premises might be rejected.

Cur. adv. vult.

LORD DENMAN, Ch. J. now delivered the judgment of the COURT:

The question in this case is, what effect ought to be *given to
the *habendum* in an indenture of lease. The words are: Sir Thomas
Broughton demises, &c., " to Hannah Timmis, her heirs and assigns,
to hold to the said Hannah Timmis and her assigns for and during
the natural life of George Timmis."

[*667]

It is clear that the *habendum* cannot be rejected altogether: for
the effect of that would be to give an estate in fee to Hannah Timmis,
whereas the estate intended to be given to her is for the life of
George Timmis; and, the proper office of the *habendum* being to
limit, explain or qualify the words in the premises, provided it be
not contradictory or repugnant to them, no doubt can be entertained but that the words " for and during the natural life of
George Timmis " must be allowed to limit the duration of the
estate and to explain and qualify the meaning of the word "heirs"
in the premises, so as to make the person designated by that word
take as special occupant, and not as heir by descent.

But the question arises upon the other words in the *habendum*,
namely, " to Hannah Timmis and her assigns."   Under these
words, there would be no special occupant, but the estate on the
death of Hannah Timmis would be personal assets by virtue of the
statutes 29 Car. II. c. 3, s. 12, and 14 Geo. II. c. 20, s. 9. Whereas,
under the words in the premises " to Hannah Timmis her heirs
and assigns," there is a special occupant, namely her heir. The

(1) 6 R. R. 559 (3 East, 115).

Doe d.
Timmis
v.
Steele.

[*668]

words of the *habendum* are therefore manifestly contradictory and repugnant to the words in the premises, and must, according to the general rule of construction in such cases, be disregarded.

The only case cited on the side of the defendants was *that of *Spyve* v. *Topham* (1), in which the words in the premises were, to "J. Topham" and "his heirs and assigns," and those in the *habendum*, to "G. Bass," "his heirs and assigns;" the deed was a release; and the lease for a year was to G. Bass. In the release, Bass was described as a trustee for Topham. The words "J. Topham" in the premises were obviously a clerical error. If effect had been given to them, nothing could have passed to any one by the release, and the whole object of the parties would have been defeated. The Court therefore read the release as if the words in the premises had been "G. Bass." The case was determined on the peculiar circumstances of it, and is no rule for any case not precisely like it.

We are clearly of opinion that the rule for a nonsuit must be discharged.

Rule discharged.

———————

1843.
May 2, 17.

[687]

WILLOUGHBY, Clerk v. Sir HENRY WILLOUGHBY, Baronet·(2).·

(4 Q. B. 687—706; S. C. 12 L. J. Q. B. 281.)

By an Act (6 & 7 Will. IV. c. 16, private), for dividing and allotting commons and wastes in a parish, the rector's tithes, and some detached portions of the glebe, were commuted for a rent-charge, on the principle of a corn rent: and an arbitrator was empowered to declare the amount by award. The rent-charge was to be charged on the lands of W., situate in the parish, in exoneration of the lands of all other proprietors therein: and the Act declared that it should be lawful for the arbitrator, by his award. to divide the rent-charge into so many portions as he should think fit, and to charge each portion on a separate part of W.'s lands, in order that each might be subject only to the portion charged thereon. Provision was made for revising the amount of rent-charge periodically at the end of seven years, at the instance of the rector or of W., his heirs or assigns, owners for the time being of the lands to be charged.

Held, that the arbitrator was not bound to particularize in his award the lands on which the rent-charge was imposed; but that an award charging it in one entire sum on "all and every the lands and grounds of "W., situate in the said parish, was sufficient.

The Act provided that, so often as the rent-charge should be three months in arrear, the rector, his executors, &c., should have "such and

(1) 3 East, 115.
(2) Distinguished in *Christie* v. *Barker* (1884) 53 L. J. Q. B. 537, 543. Cf. *Thomas* v. *Sylvester* (1873) L. R.

8 Q. B. 368, 42 L. J. Q. B. 237; and *Whitaker* v. *Forbes* (1875) L. R. 10 C. P. 583, 584, 44 L. J. C. P. 332 (affd. 1 C. P. Div. 51).—A. C.

the like powers and remedies for recovering the same, together with all expenses incident to the recovery thereof, as by the common law or statute are given to the landlords for the recovery of rent when in arrear." The Act gave compensation to W., by allotments of land, for the burden which his lands would suffer by the rent-charge.

Held, that the Act did not point out W. as the person by whom the rent-charge was to be paid.

Quære, whether the statute gave a remedy by action against any person. But held that, if any such action lay, it could be only against an occupier of the lands charged.

DEBT. The declaration stated that heretofore, and during all the time hereinafter mentioned, plaintiff was, and still is, rector of the rectory of the parish of Marsh Baldon, in the county of Oxford. That, before the making of the award after mentioned, by an Act of Parliament made &c. (6 & 7 Will. IV. c. 16, private (1)), *"for dividing, allotting, and laying in severalty lands in the parishes of Marsh Baldon and Toot Baldon in the county of Oxford," after reciting &c., it was enacted &c. The declaration then stated the following clauses (2):

Sect. 30. "And whereas a portion of the glebe lands of Marsh

[*688]

(1) The preamble (sect. 1) of the Act recites that there are, in the parishes of Marsh Baldon and Toot Baldon, divers open and common fields, and other commonable and waste lands and lot meadows; that Sir H. Willoughby, Bart., claims to be lord of the manor of Marsh Baldon, and as such to be entitled to the right of soil of the waste lands within the said parish of Marsh Baldon ; and that the Provost and Scholars of Queen's College, Oxford, claim the same right of soil in Toot Baldon, as lords of certain manors in that parish ; that Sir H. Willoughby is patron of the rectory of Marsh Baldon, and the Rev. Hugh Pollard Willoughby (the plaintiff) rector of the said rectory, and as such entitled to certain glebe lands, and to certain tithes of some of the lands in that parish ; and that Sir *H. W. is entitled to certain tithes of some of the said lands in the same parish, and also to the great and small tithes of all the said lands in the parish of Toot Baldon; and that Sir H. Willoughby, the Provost &c. of Queen's College, and others, are owners and proprietors of all other the lands, open and inclosed, within the

said parishes: it then refers to the general Inclosure Acts, 41 Geo. III. (U. K.) c. 109, and 1 & 2 Geo. IV. c. 23, and recites, further, that the lands in the said open and common fields lie intermixed &c. so as to render the cultivation inconvenient, and it would be advantageous to the proprietors if the parishes were separated, and the said open and common fields and other commonable and waste lands and lot meadows divided, allotted, &c., among the several proprietors according to their respective rights &c., and exchanges made &c., and if all the lands, as well open as inclosed, within the said parishes, were exonerated from tithes. The clause then appoints a Commissioner for dividing, allotting, &c., the said open and common fields and other commonable and waste lands and lot meadows, and for carrying this Act into execution.

[*688, *n.*]

(2) The enactments most material to the points reported are here stated in the words of the Act itself, which, by the subsequent pleadings, was put upon the record. Some sections mentioned in the declaration are omitted. as not important here.

WIL-
LOUGHBY
v.
WIL-
LOUGHBY.

Baldon is dispersed over the common fields of the parishes of Marsh Baldon and Toot Baldon, and some of the lands in the parish of Marsh Baldon yield great and small tithes to the rector of Marsh Baldon, and some of the lands in the same parish yield small tithes to the said rector: and whereas it is expedient to commute the said portion of the glebe lands, and also the said tithes, for a rent-charge on the principle of a corn rent, to be charged exclusively on the lands and grounds of the said Sir Henry Willoughby, in the parish of Marsh Baldon, in exoneration of the lands and grounds of all other proprietors in the said parish; be it therefore enacted, that Edmond

[*689]   Gibson Atherley, Esquire, of Gray's *Inn, barrister-at-law, be and he is hereby authorized and empowered to declare, by an award under his hand and seal, within six calendar months after the passing of this Act (and which award shall be final and conclusive on all parties), the annual amount of rent-charge on the principle of a corn rent, to be paid to the rector of Marsh Baldon and his successors, for ever, in lieu of all tithes, compositions, and moduses, issuing and payable from or in respect of all and every the lands and grounds in the parish of Marsh Baldon, and also in lieu of that portion of the glebe lands of the said rector of Marsh Baldon, which lies dispersed over the common fields of the parishes of Marsh Baldon and Toot Baldon, and also in lieu of all common rights belonging thereto, and to all other the glebe lands of the said rector of Marsh Baldon."

Sect. 31 enacts: "That the said rent-charge shall be, and the same is hereby charged on the lands and grounds of the said Sir Henry Willoughby, situate in the parish of Marsh Baldon, in exoneration of the lands and grounds of all other proprietors of lands and hereditaments in the said parish of Marsh Baldon."

Sect. 34 enacts: "That it shall be lawful for the said E. G. Atherley, by his said award, to divide and apportion the said rent-charge into so many parts or portions as he shall think fit, and to charge each such part or portion on a separate and distinct part of the lands and grounds of the said Sir H. W., in the said parish of Marsh Baldon, in order and to the intent that each such separate and distinct part of the said lands and grounds may be subject only to that part or portion of the said rent-charge which shall be so charged thereon, and to no further or greater part thereof."

. [690]   Sect. 35 enacts: "That the said rent-charge shall be paid and payable by even and equal half-yearly payments; that is to say, on the 6th day of April and the 11th day of October for ever, free and clear of and from all rates, dues, and assessments whatsoever, except land tax, the first payment thereof, or a proportionate part thereof, to commence on such of the said days as the said E. G. Atherley shall, by his said award, direct; and when and so often as the rector of the said parish of Marsh Baldon shall, by death or otherwise, cease to be the rector of the said parish, his executors or administrators, or he himself, if living, shall have or be entitled to a proportionate part of the said rent-charge in respect of such portion of the current half-year as shall have elapsed at the time he shall so cease to be the rector of the said parish of Marsh Baldon; and when and so often as the said rent-charge, or any part thereof, or such proportionate part as aforesaid, or any part thereof, shall be behind and unpaid by the space of three calendar months next after the same shall become due and payable, to the rector for the time being of the said parish of Marsh Baldon, his executors or administrators (1), shall have such and the like powers and remedies for recovering the same, together with all expenses incident to the recovery thereof, as by the common law or statute are given to landlords for the recovery of rent when in arrear; but nevertheless, no part of the lands or grounds to be charged with the said rent-charge shall be subject or liable to the payment of any further or greater part thereof than such part or portion thereof as by the said award shall be so fixed or charged thereon as aforesaid."

Sect. 39 provides for the substitution of another *referee, in case Mr. Atherley should die, or neglect or refuse to act, or become incapable of acting. .   [*691]

The declaration further alleged that "the said E. G. Atherley neglected to act in the matters so submitted to him as aforesaid, and did not declare by award under his hand and seal, within six calendar months next after the passing of the said Act, the annual amount of rent-charge to be paid to the rector of Marsh Baldon and his successors, according to the provisions of" the said Act, "but neglected so to do for the said space of six calendar months next after the passing of the said Act;" that another referee, John Maurice Herbert, Esquire, was substituted, and made and published his award, whereby, after certain recitals and findings (which it is not material to set out), he awarded to the plaintiff, rector as aforesaid, and his successors for ever, in lieu of all tithes, compositions, and moduses belonging and payable to him the said rector, and issuing and payable from or in respect of all and every the lands

(1) Sic.

and grounds which, at the time of the passing of the said Act, were
in the parish of Marsh Baldon, and in lieu of that portion of the
glebe which lay dispersed over the common fields of the two
parishes, and of all common rights belonging thereto and to all
other the glebe lands of the said rector, &c., " a clear yearly rent-
charge of 236*l*. 0*s*. 9*d*., the same to be paid and payable by even
and equal half-yearly payments of 118*l*. 0*s*. 4½*d*. each, on the 6th
day of April and the 11th day of October in each and every year for
ever, free and clear of and from all rates, dues," &c., except land
tax. The value of the rent-charge was then estimated according to
the prices of wheat and barley; and the referee further awarded
" that the said yearly rent-charge of 236*l*. 0*s*. 9*d*. should be, and
*the same was thereby, charged in one entire sum on all and every
the lands and grounds of the defendant situate in the said parish of
Marsh Baldon ; " the first half-yearly payment to commence on the
6th of April then next. The declaration then alleged " that the
said lands and grounds upon which the said rent-charge was so
charged as aforesaid were, at the time of the passing of the said
Act of Parliament, and from thence until and at the time of the
commencement of this suit, the lands and grounds of the
defendant ; " that two half-yearly payments of the rent-charge
became due ; and that defendant did not pay, &c.

The defendant set out the whole of the private Act, and prayed
that it might be enrolled in the records of the Court ; which was
done. The following clauses, not stated in the declaration, were
referred to in the argument.

The preamble is stated, p. 461, note, *ante.* Sect. 28 provides for
the setting out of allotments to the lords of the manors, equal to
one sixteenth part in value of the commons and wastes in each
manor respectively, in compensation, exclusively, for their respective
interests, in the soil of such commons and wastes.

Sect. 36 enacts : " That at the expiration of seven years from the
passing of this Act, and in like manner at the expiration of any
other period of seven years, but not at any intervening period, the
said rector of Marsh Baldon and his successors, or the said Sir H.
Willoughby, his heirs or assigns, owners and proprietors for the
time being of the lands and grounds to be charged with the said
rent-charge, may make application in writing for a reversion of the
amount of the said rent-charge at the first Quarter Sessions for the
county of Oxford after *the expiration of any such period of seven
years ; and the justices in Quarter Sessions assembled, or the major

[*692]

[*693]

part of them, may order and direct the amount of the said rent-charge to be increased or diminished on the several lands and grounds of the said Sir H. Willoughby, in the parish of Marsh Baldon, accordingly, as the average prices of wheat and barley in the market of the city of Oxford have increased or diminished during the preceding period of seven years, and according to the apportionment of the rent-charge on the several lands and grounds of the said Sir H. W. : " every rent-charge so settled to continue until a new revision shall have been made in manner aforesaid, &c.

Sect. 41 requires the Commissioner (appointed by sect. 1) to set out and allot to Sir H. Willoughby such part of the lands to be divided and allotted under the Act, situate in Marsh Baldon, as shall in his judgment be an equivalent for the glebe lands of the rectory lying dispersed in the common fields of Marsh and Toot Baldon, and for the rights of common, appertaining to the glebe, in the lands to be divided and allotted. Sect. 42 directs the Commissioner to allot to Sir H. Willoughby, in lieu of tithes issuing out of the lands to be divided and allotted, and out of the homesteads &c. and other ancient inclosures in Marsh Baldon and Toot Baldon, except the lands of Sir H. Willoughby, and the glebe lands of the rectory of Marsh Baldon, such parcels &c. of the lands &c. to be divided and allotted under the Act as will contain or be equal to &c. (stating the proportions); such allotments to be taken from and out of the shares of the lands to be divided and allotted, belonging to the parties whose lands shall be exonerated from tithe, or from or out of the lands to be allotted to *them respectively in lieu of their rights in the lands to be divided under the Act.

Sect. 53 enacts: " That when and so soon as the said Commissioner shall have ascertained the respective rights and interests of the said proprietors in the lands to be divided and allotted by virtue of this Act, and also the respective shares and proportions by him proposed to be allotted to such proprietors respectively in lieu thereof, the said Commissioner shall hold a sitting at some convenient time and place, when and where the proprietors may be informed of such allotments, and see the same set out and delineated upon a map or plan to be produced for their inspection;" and, if any proprietor, on inspection, shall be dissatisfied with the proposed allotments, the Commissioner shall receive complaints &c., and determine the same &c.

Sect. 69 enacts that the awards to be made by E. G. Atherley,

WIL-
LOUGHBY
v.
WIL-
LOUGHBY.

[*694]

or his successor, respectively, shall, "together with such maps and plans and references thereto as the said Commissioner shall think proper to annex to his award (which maps or plans and reference shall be deemed part thereof)," be delivered to the clerk of the peace, who is required to keep them among the records of the county, so that recourse may be had thereto by any person interested &c.: such awards (and such copies thereof as this clause specifies) to be evidence of the matters therein contained, &c.

Defendant pleaded, fourthly, as follows.

"That the said lands and grounds, upon which the said rent-charge was so charged as aforesaid, before and at the times when the said half-yearly payments and each of them became due, as in the declaration mentioned, and from thence, to wit hitherto, were and have been and are in the possession and occupation of divers [*695] *persons other than and different from the defendant; without this, that the defendant was possessed of the said lands and grounds, or any or either of them, or any part thereof, at the times when the said half-yearly payments, or any of them, became due, and from thence to the commencement of this suit, or any portion of such time or times, in manner and form" &c. Conclusion to the country.

Demurrer, assigning for causes: "That the issue tendered by that plea is immaterial: that the defendant has thereby traversed matter not alleged in or necessarily to be implied from the declaration; that the defendant admits by his plea that, at the times the payments became due, the lands and grounds upon which the rent-charge was charged were the lands and grounds of the defendant; and, if the traverse was intended to be a denial of that allegation, then that allegation should have been traversed in the words thereof. That the plea improperly concludes to the country, instead of with a verification."

Joinder in demurrer.

The plaintiff stated as his points for argument those assigned as causes of demurrer. The points for argument stated by the defendant were: "That the objections taken to the fourth plea are not valid; that it traverses what is impliedly stated in the declaration; and that, if possession is not so stated, the declaration is bad, and the action will not lie. Also that there is no remedy by action of debt on the award; and that the award is bad in consequence of not particularizing the lands and grounds on which the rent-charge is charged."

The demurrer was argued last Term (1).

Hugh Hill, for the plaintiff:

The real questions are: 1. Whether debt lies for the arrears of
this rent-charge; 2. If so, whether it lies against an owner, not
being occupier; 3. Whether the award is bad because it does not
particularize the lands on which the rent-charge is to be imposed,
but charges it in one entire sum on all the lands of the defendant
in Marsh Baldon. 1. Sect. 35 of the private Act gives " such and
the like powers and remedies for recovering" arrears "as by the
common law or statute are given to landlords for the recovery of
rent when in arrear." The action of debt is such a remedy. It
may be said that this charge is in the nature of a freehold rent, for
which, at common law, a personal action would not lie while the
estate of freehold continued. But this difficulty no longer exists
since stat. 8 Ann. c. 14, s. 4, which empowers "any person or
persons, having any rent in arrear or due upon any lease or demise
for life or lives, to bring an action or actions of debt for such
arrears of rent, in the same manner as they might have done, in
case such rent were due and reserved upon a lease for years." It
may be contended that the remedy by such action must be founded
on contract: but that is not universally so, as, for example, where
the right to the action of debt is founded on privity of estate, and
in other instances referred to in Com. Dig. Debt (A 1), (A 9). Under
the latter head it is stated that "debt lies upon any statute, which
gives advantage to another, for the recovery of it: as, upon the
stat. 32 Hen. VIII. c. 1, for money devised to be paid out of land:"
and an *Anonymous* (2) case in 6 Mod. is cited. HOLT, Ch. J., there
said that, "wherever a statute *enacts anything, or prohibits any-   [*697]
thing, for the advantage of any person, that person shall have
remedy to recover the advantage given him, or to have satisfaction for the injury done him contrary to law by the same
statute;" "and the action" (of debt, where money is devised out
of lands) "must be against the terre-tenant." The law there laid
down is recognized in *Webb* v. *Jiggs* (3), *Hopkins* v. *Mayor, &c. of
Swansea* (4), and *Mayor, &c. of Swansea* v. *Hopkins* (in error) (5).
Full effect ought to be given to the words of the private Act, " such

(1) May 2nd. Before Lord Denman,
Ch. J., Patteson and Williams, JJ.
(2) 6 Mod. 26; *S. C.* 2 Salk. 415, as
Ewer v. *Jones.*
(3) 16 R. R. 408 (4 M. & S. 113,

119).
(4) 51 R. R. 739 (4 M. & W. 621,
640).
(5) 58 R. R. 893 (8 M. & W. 901).

and the like powers and remedies." The Tithe Commutation Act, 6 & 7 Will. IV. c. 71, a statute *in pari materiâ*, passed in the same session of Parliament, gives powers (ss. 67' 81) for enforcing the rent-charge there imposed, but expressly provides, in s. 67, that nothing therein contained "shall be taken to render any person whomsoever personally liable to the payment of any such rent-charge;" a strong argument to show that, in the present Act, where no such proviso appears, the same restriction was not contemplated. 2. As to the person against whom this action lies, the only case which has been found at all resembling the present is *Newling* v. *Pearse* (1). The judgment of BAYLEY, J. (2) there is in favour of the present action. The situation of parties here is as if the rector had granted a lease of tithes to an owner of the lands held by Sir H. Willoughby. The word "terre-tenant" in the *dictum* of HOLT, Ch. J., before cited, does not mean a mere occupier. *Braithwaite* v. *Skinner* (3) illustrates this subject; and the judgments there delivered *tend to show the liability of an owner as such. "By tenants, *tenentes*, generally is meant the owners of the fee simple, and by occupiers, those who come in under them;" note (9) to *Jeffreson* v. *Morton* (4), citing Fitzh. N. B. 297 (127 B). Debt lies upon a contract in law as well as in deed, 1 Com. Dig. Debt (A 1); and here a statutable contract is created between the rector and the landowner. The provisions of the private Act point out Sir H. Willoughby as the person who was intended to be and ought to be liable. Sect. 31 names him as the party whose lands are to be charged; and sect. 42 gives him an equivalent. The declaration alleges that the lands charged were "the lands and grounds of the defendant:" and, if an owner is liable as such, the plea that he was not in possession tenders an immaterial issue. 3. The arbitrator was not obliged to particularize the lands and grounds subject to the rent-charge. Sect. 34 enacts only "that it shall be lawful" for him to apportion the rent-charge and lay it on distinct parcels. There are no compulsory expressions; and the words "it shall be lawful" are imperative only where public duty requires the thing to be done: *Rex* v. *Commissioners of the Flockwold Enclosure* (5), *Reg.* v. *St. Saviour's, Southwark* (6).

[*698]

---

(1) 1 B. & C. 437.
(2) He read the judgment, pp. 441, 442, from "I think this is" to "unoccupied."

(3) 5 M. & W. 313.
(4) 2 Wms. Saund. 9 e (6th ed.).
(5) 2 Chitt. Rep. 251.
(6) 7 Ad. & El. 925.

Cowling, contrà :

First, the award is bad, because the arbitrator has not specified the lands which are to be charged. If the owner wished to sell part of his estate, he could not say whether the rent-charge was issuing out of that or any other portion. The rector does not know where to distrain. The discretionary power of *the referee is, on this point, no answer. The statute is in the nature of an Inclosure Act: sects. 28, 41 and 42 show this. If the present award were good, the referee might as well have said merely that there should be à rent-charge.

[*699]

(PATTESON, J. : That would not have shown whether he meant the rent-charge to be distributed or not. You would say that, although he had power not to divide the rent-charge, still he must have set out the lands by metes and bounds.)

The Act renders it necessary. Sect. 30 shows the intention.

(PATTESON, J. : Could the referee conclude the other landowners by setting out metes and bounds ?)

There might be a difficulty with respect to them ; but that is no answer, the more especially if the Act imposes the duty. Sect. 36 also proves the intention. An individual claiming part of the lands through Sir H. Willoughby could not enforce that clause if the award did not show how his land was affected. In *Warner* v. *Potchett* (1), where part of a prebendal estate under lease had been sold to redeem land tax on the whole, under stat. 42 Geo. III. c. 116, s. 69, it was held that the prebendary could not distrain for the amount of such redeemed land tax as additional rent, under sect. 88, " until after the precise quantity of land, and the portion of the reserved rent to be sold, were ascertained," under sect. 83. In *Johnson* v. *Wilson* (2) an award for the dividing of common lands, keeping up of sea walls, and other purposes, was held altogether void, because imperfect in the clauses directing the partition. It is true that the present Act is *in pari materià* with stat. 6 & 7 Will. IV. c. 71, but sect. 55 of that Act, which (together with *sect. 61) corresponds with sect. 53 of the Act now in question, clearly shows an intention that the lands to be apportioned should be precisely ascertained and identified.

[*700]

(1) 3 B. & Ad. 921.   (2) Willes, 248.

WIL-
LOUGHBY
v.
WIL-
LOUGHBY.

(*Hill* referred to sect. 69 of the local Act (1).)

The maps there mentioned are only such as the Commissioner
"shall think proper" to annex to his award: and those would
probably be the general maps of the common lands, not plans of
the particular allotments in question. Secondly and thirdly, an
action of debt does not lie in this case against the landowner; at
least in that character. If he be subject to the action, it can only
be because the lands are in his possession. *Webb* v. *Jiggs* (2) shows
that, even since stat. 8 Ann. c. 14, debt is not the proper remedy
for a charge on freehold lands, while the estate of freehold subsists
in the defendant. The ordinary remedy for recovering arrears of
rent-charge is distress. The action of debt is not needed here.
In the cases under statutes, mentioned in Com. Dig. Debt (A. 1),
there would be no remedy if an action did not lie. The *dictum* of
HOLT, Ch. J. in the *Anonymous* (3) case has not been approved of
in all its generality. In *Braithwaite* v. *Skinner* (4) a qualified
construction was put upon it, which is consistent with the effect
given to it in *Hopkins* v. *Mayor, &c. of Swansea* (5), and *Mayor,*

[*701]

*&c. of *Swansea* v. Hopkins* (6). The analogy between stat. 6 & 7
Will. IV. c. 71, and the present statute is in the defendant's favour;
for the remedy given by sects. 67 and 81 is distress. If debt lie,
and the defendant be answerable as owner, he may be sued for
arrears which have accrued during several years and while tenants
were in possession. In *Warner* v. *Potchett* (7) the language of the
enactment pointing out the mode of recovering arrears of rent-
charge was like that used here; but the remedy taken was by
distress. The same observations apply to *Newling* v. *Pearse* (8).
The words in the present Act, sect. 35, are "the like powers and
remedies" "as by the common law or statute are given to the
landlords for the recovery of rent when in arrear." But that
must be taken with reference to the circumstances. The remedies
founded on express contract, of course, do not rest on the same

(1) *Hill* also mentioned sects. 12
and 14 of that Act, which it has not
been thought necessary to state particularly; the first enabling the Commissioner to settle disputes between
persons interested in the lands, but
not to determine the title to any
messuages, lands &c.; the latter
enabling parties dissatisfied with such
determination to try their rights at
law.

(2) 16 R. R. 408 (4 M. & S. 113).
(3) 6 Mod. 26; *S. C.* 2 Salk. 415, as
Ewer v. *Jones.*
(4) 5 M. & W. 313.
(5) 51 R. R. 739 (4 M. & W. 621).
(6) 58 R. R. 893 (8 M. & W. 901).
(7) 3 B. & Ad. 921.
(8) 1 B. & C. 437.

ground with those here given, and cannot apply. As to the
analogy which may be contemplated to the landlord's remedy on
an implied contract ; a landlord could not bring debt for use and
occupation against a person who had never actually occupied :
Edge v. *Strafford* (1). So here, if the preceding argument be
correct, the rector could not bring debt against a landowner who
had not possession at the time. And, if that be so, the plea puts a
material point in issue when it denies that the defendant was
possessed of the lands at the times when the half-yearly payments
or any of them became due, and from thence to the commencement
of this suit. The *dicta* of BAYLEY and HOLROYD, JJ., in *Newling* v.
Pearse (2), show how far, *in an analogous case, possession was
considered essential to liability. Sect. 42, which was relied upon
as giving Sir H. Willoughby an equivalent for the liability which
it is now sought to throw upon him, refers only to the loss which
he sustains in respect of his own rights to tithe.

WIL-
LOUGHBY
v.
WIL-
LOUGHBY.

[*702]

II. *Hill*, in reply :

The Court will not intend against this award that the lands are
not sufficiently marked out.

(LORD DENMAN, Ch. J. : We are all clearly of opinion that the
Act does not require the award to set out the particular lands.)

The words " such and the like powers and remedies " must be
construed in their usual and entire sense : one ordinary remedy of
the landlord is by distress ; but the words should not be narrowed
to that single meaning. The decision in *Braithwaite* v. *Skinner* (3)
does not impeach the *dictum* of HOLT, Ch. J., but shows only that
the parties there made defendants did not come within it. The
present Act does not, like the Tithe Commutation Act, preclude
any action against individuals ; nor does it direct that the occupier
shall pay the rent-charge. It creates a statutable privity between
the rector and Sir H. Willoughby, on which this action is well
grounded.

(PATTESON, J. : Sect. 35 gives " the like powers and remedies " as
" are given to landlords," but does not give them against any
specified person.

(1) 1 Cr. & J. 391; *S. C.* 1 Tyr.   (2) 1 B. & C. 437.
295.   (3) 5 M. & W. 313.

LORD DENMAN, Ch. J. : Would the vendee of any part of the lands be liable to an action for arrears of this rent-charge?)

[*703]

The inconvenience which may be supposed to arise from a division of the lands by sale is not very different whether the remedy *be distress or action. But limiting the remedy would make a material difference to the rector.

LORD DENMAN, Ch. J. :

On the question as to the award, my opinion is clear. *Johnson* v. *Wilson* (1) does not apply. The award there was held bad because it did not say by what deeds the partition should be completed; therefore the parties did not fully obtain the remedy they had contemplated. Here the lands to be charged are not specially marked out; but it is assumed that Sir Henry Willoughby's lands may be ascertained and fixed with the charge; and I think the award is sufficient.

PATTESON, J. :

I am of the same opinion. In *Warner* v. *Potchett* (2) the objection was, not that particular lands and fields had not been marked out, but that the quantity to be sold was not ascertained at all.

WILLIAMS, J. concurred.

On the other points,

Cur. adv. vult :

LORD DENMAN, Ch. J., now delivered judgment :

This was an action of debt against the defendant to recover a rent in lieu of tithes, due to the plaintiff, and charged upon the lands of the defendant by the award of a Commissioner, under an Act of Parliament passed in the 6 & 7 Will. IV., for dividing and allotting lands in the parishes of Marsh Baldon and Toot Baldon in the county of Oxford.

[704]

Two questions arise: first, whether an action of debt will lie at all; secondly, whether the Commissioner was bound by the provisions of the Act to specify in his award the lands on which the rent was to be charged.

On the second question we expressed our opinion in the course of

(1) Willes, 248.   (2) 3 B. & Ad. 921.

the argument. The Act provides that the rent shall be charged on
the lands of the defendant in exoneration of all other lands in the
parish, and gives the Commissioner power to apportion that rent on
the various lands of the defendant ; but it does not compel him to
do so : and, as he has not thought fit to exercise that power, it
was quite unnecessary for him to specify all the lands of the
defendant.

The first question depends upon the construction to be put on the
30th, 31st, and 35th sections of the Act, which are as follows. (His
Lordship then read them.) No person is mentioned by whom the
said rent-charge shall be paid and payable. No remedy is given
for the recovery of it until it shall be behind and unpaid by the
space of three calendar months ; and then the rector "shall have
such and the like powers and remedies for recovering the same,"
"as by the common law or statute are given to landlords for the
recovery of rent when in arrear." No demand is required to be
made by the rector or any person prior to his having recourse to
such powers and remedies.

The rent-charge in this case being perpetual, it is conceded that
no action of debt would lie for the recovery of it, according to the
case of *Webb* v. *Jiggs* (1), unless it be given by the 35th section of
the Act in question.

It cannot be denied that by law an action of debt for rent will lie
by a landlord against his tenant. If, therefore, this Act had stated
by whom the rent was to be paid, we should have had little
difficulty in saying that an action of debt would lie for it.

[705]

In the case of *Newling* v. *Pearse* (2), where a question arose
respecting a similar rent-charge, though not the same question
as the present, the Act of Parliament expressly provided that the
rent-charge should be paid by the occupier of the land charged.

The cases in the Court of Exchequer, which were cited, turned
on the Statute of Wills, and have no bearing upon the present
question.

It was argued that the statute respecting commutation of tithes,
6 & 7 Will. IV. c. 71, which was passed in the same session as the Act
in question, is *in pari materiâ*, and may assist in the construction
of this Act. That Act expressly excludes personal liability of any
one, but this Act does not ; and therefore it was argued that it
includes personal liability, and gives an action of debt. We do not
think this argument entitled to any weight whatever. The Act in

(1) 16 R. R. 408 (4 M. & S. 113).   (2) 1 B. & C. 437.

question is in effect a Parliamentary contract, and must speak for itself. Besides, the Tithe Commutation Act does not contain provisions as to the person who is to pay the rent-charge, and requires notice (1) to be left at the residence of the tenant in possession before any distress be made.

It was argued also that compensation is given to the defendant by the Act for the burthen thrown upon his lands in exoneration of those of other persons.   This is perfectly true, and arises out of an arrangement between *him and them; but it affords no argument whatever as to the mode in which it is intended that the rector should enforce his rent-charge.

[*706]

The powers and remedies given to the rector are " such and the like " as landlords have (again omitting to say against whom) for the recovery of rent when in arrear.   Now the remedy by action of debt which a landlord has is against the occupier; if, therefore, this Act of Parliament intended to give the rector an action of debt at all, we think it must be against the occupier; but we by no means lay it down that such is the meaning of the Act.   The declaration in this case does not state the defendant to be in possession of or the occupier of the lands charged; it states only that the lands charged are the lands of the defendant.

We think at all events that an action of debt will not lie against the defendant, for that reason.

We should also observe that, if the words just stated from the declaration involve the proposition that the defendant is in possession of the lands, there is a plea expressly denying that he is so possessed, to which the plaintiff has demurred ; therefore, if we are right in holding that the action of debt, if maintainable at all, must be brought against the person in possession, the defendant would be entitled to our judgment on that demurrer, as he is upon the declaration if no action of debt can be maintained against any one.

Judgment for defendant.

(1) Sect. 81.

GREGSON AND OTHERS *v.* RUCK AND OTHERS (1).

1843.
Feb. 1.
May 17.

[737]

(4 Q. B. 737—748.)

Declaration: detinue of goods, and an *indebitatus* count, in debt, for goods sold and delivered. Pleas, as to the detinue, *non detinent ;* plaintiffs not possessed; leave and licence : as to the debt, never indebted; payment after cause of action accrued; and receipt of a bill in satisfaction, after cause of action accrued. Issues thereon. It was proved that F., a broker, being authorised by plaintiffs to offer for sale goods of theirs in dock, reported to them an offer from defendants, which plaintiffs agreed to if for cash with the usual prompt, which meant (in the particular trade) cash on delivery at the end of two months, subject to a discount on earlier delivery. F., acting as broker for both parties, sold the goods to defendants without disclosing plaintiffs' names, and delivered to plaintiffs a sold note, stating the contract as "prompt two months;" whereupon plaintiffs indorsed and delivered to F. the delivery warrant. F. afterwards gave defendants a bought note, stating the contract, "prompt—bill @ two months," and handed to them the delivery warrants, under which they obtained the goods: he at the same time drew on them a two months' bill for the amount, which they accepted and paid when due. F. negotiated the bill, and appropriated the proceeds to his own use. Plaintiffs, on the expiration of the prompt, and after payment of the bill, being then ignorant both of the variance between the notes, and the payment by bill, applied to defendants for payment, which was refused. Plaintiffs made no specific demand of the goods. Verdict for defendants.

Held, on rule to enter verdict for plaintiffs, that, the variance between the bought and sold notes being material, there was no contract; that the delivery by plaintiffs, being on the supposition that there was a binding contract on the terms of the sold note, did not make out the plea of leave and licence ; and that plaintiffs were entitled to a verdict on all the issues on the count in detinue. Also, that defendants were entitled to a verdict on the plea of *nunquam indebitatus* to the count in debt, no contract having existed; but that they must fail on the other pleas to that count, as those pleas assumed the existence of the contract.

DETINUE for forty-five hogsheads of rum, stated to have come to defendants' possession by finding, *indebitatus* counts for goods sold and delivered, and on an account stated. Pleas : To the first count : 1. *Non detinent ;* 2. That the plaintiffs were not possessed as of their own property : To the second and last counts : 3. Never indebted ; 4. Payment after cause of action accrued; 5. As to 300*l.*, parcel &c., that, after the contracting of the debt as to that sum, and the accruing of the causes of action in respect thereof, and before the commencement &c., James Field and William Field, using the names and firm of James and William Field, as brokers and agents, for and by and with the authority of plaintiffs in that behalf, made

(1) Cf. *Thornton* v. *Charles* (1842) 60 R. R. 896 (9 M. & W. 802 ; 11 L. J. Ex. 302); *Sievewright* v. *Archibald* (1851) 17 Q. B. 103, 20 L. J. Q. B. 529 ; *Thompson* v. *Gardiner* (1876) 1 C. P. D. 777 ; Benjamin on Sales, 4th ed. 268—270, Blackburn on Sales, 2nd ed. 84, 114.—A. C.

[*738]

a certain bill of exchange, and directed the same to *defendants, and thereby required defendants, two months after the date thereof, to pay to the order of the said J. and W. Field 303*l.* 10*s.* 6*d.*, and they so drew the said bill, and defendants then accepted the same and delivered it to J. and W. Field, as brokers and agents, for and by and with the consent and authority of plaintiffs in that behalf ; and J. and W. Field, as such brokers and agents, and by and with the consent &c. of plaintiffs in that behalf, then took and accepted the said bill for and on account of said causes of action as to the said 300*l.*, parcel &c. ; and the said J. and W. Field indorsed and negotiated the said bill ; and defendants afterwards, and when the same became due and payable, paid the amount thereof, according to the tenor and effect thereof, to certain persons using the name and firm of Sir John Lubbock & Co., then being the holders thereof. Verification. 6. To the first count, leave and licence. Verification.

Replication, to the first three pleas, *similiter*. To the fourth plea, a traverse of the payment and acceptance in satisfaction. Issue thereon. To the fifth plea, that J. and W. Field made, drew, took and accepted the said bill of exchange as in that plea mentioned without the authority of the plaintiffs in that behalf, in manner and form &c. ; conclusion to the country. Issue thereon. To the sixth plea, that defendants of their own wrong, and without the leave and licence of plaintiffs &c., committed the several grievances &c. ; conclusion to the country. Issue thereon.

On the trial, before Lord Denman, Ch. J., at the London sittings after Michaelmas Term, 1841, it appeared by the evidence for the plaintiffs that they were colonial *merchants, and before the transaction in question had effected various sales of rum to the defendants, wholesale dealers in rum, through Messrs. Field, brokers, who, on each occasion, acted for both buyers and sellers. In the colonial trade a sale for prompt payment means payment in cash on delivery, the delivery taking place at the end of two months and three days' grace ; or deducting proportionable discount if the delivery be before the end of that period. In earlier transactions between the parties, the defendants had paid by accepting bills drawn by the plaintiffs : in the last previous transaction, the names of the plaintiffs were not mentioned, and the payment was by cash, deducting two months' interest. Early in November, 1840, the plaintiffs having instructed Messrs. Field to expose for sale East India rums, which were then a new article in the market, Messrs.

[*739]

Field reported an offer of a certain price by the defendants, which the plaintiffs agreed to accept, on the terms of their receiving cash with the usual prompt, saying that they would not draw any more bills: and, on 19th November, Messrs. Field delivered to plaintiffs a sold note bearing that date, not disclosing the purchaser's name, but stating the prompt in the following terms, "Prompt two months," and signed "J. and W. Field." The plaintiffs there-upon gave Messrs. Field the usual delivery warrant, authorising delivery "to Messrs. Field or their assigns:" under which the defendants ultimately received the goods. At the close of the plaintiffs' case the defendants applied for a nonsuit, on the ground that there was no evidence that the Fields were authorised by the defendants to make the contract. *His Lordship overruled the objection, reserving liberty to the defendants, if necessary, to move to enter a nonsuit.

[*740]

The defendants then produced evidence to the effect that the brokers, as between themselves and the plaintiffs, were to make up their account of sales and pay in three weeks; that, at the time of the sale, the brokers told the defendants that they, the brokers, should have to draw, as they would have to pay in three weeks; that, on the 20th November, the brokers delivered to the defendants a bought note, bearing that date, charging commission, and stating the prompt in the following terms, "Prompt bill @ two months," and signed by the brokers: that in the contract, as entered in the brokers' books (1), the prompt was originally as follows: "Bill at two months, Ruck Co.;" under which had been inserted, after an application by the plaintiffs' solicitors for copies, "prompt two months G. & Co.;" that the brokers had never held the bill of lading, nor was it indorsed to them; that the brokers had received payment, on delivery of the warrant, by the defendants accepting a bill at two months, drawn by the brokers, who became bankrupt before the expiration of the two months prompt, without having delivered to plaintiffs the bill, or any part of the proceeds; that the bill was paid at maturity; after which the plaintiffs being then ignorant of the variations in the contract, and of the payment, applied to defendants for the amount on the second day after the expiration of the three days' grace, the first being Sunday; and that in that trade it was customary, where the principal's name was not disclosed, for the broker to receive payment, whether it

_____

(1) It does not appear whether this entry was signed by the brokers; see   the authorities referred to on p. 475, n.—A. C.

was to be by bill *or in money.   The plaintiffs produced evidence
in reply, to the effect that there was no such custom in the trade.
The LORD CHIEF JUSTICE told the jury that, there being a material
discrepancy between the bought and sold notes, there was no
contract of sale, and the plaintiffs were entitled to recover on the
count in detinue; but that, assuming the bought note to constitute
the contract, the question was, whether the plaintiffs had authorised
the brokers to accept payment by bill at two months; in which
case the defendants were entitled to a verdict.   Verdict for the
defendants: liberty being reserved to move to enter a verdict for
the plaintiffs.

In Hilary Term, 1842 (1), *Cresswell* obtained a rule to show
cause why a verdict should not be entered for the plaintiffs, or a
new trial had: and, in the same Term (2), *Kelly* obtained a rule
nisi for a nonsuit, or a new trial.

Kelly, in last Hilary vacation (3), showed cause against the
plaintiffs' rule:

The bought note is the contract as regards the defendants, who
paid the bill when due, and did not hear of the plaintiffs having
any interest until two days after that payment: the defendants are
not to pay twice over merely because the plaintiffs' agent disobeyed
their secret instructions: a principal has his remedy against an
agent for such misconduct.   The defendants produced some evidence
to show that, according to the usage of this trade, the broker was

entitled to receive payment or to sell for *bills: they would have
produced more; but the jury expressed themselves satisfied on this
point: and the plaintiffs endeavoured to meet this intimation from
the jury by calling witnesses to prove the negative: but the jury
found that the broker himself was entitled to receive payment, and
that the buyer was not bound to enquire after the seller.

First, as to the issues on the pleading in detinue.   There is
certainly a material variance between the bought and sold notes;
and neither party was bound by the mere contract as long as nothing
had been done under it: but their rights had undergone a material
change before the action was brought.   A few days after the sale,
plaintiffs, knowing that the defendants were the purchasers,
delivered the goods to the broker to deliver to the purchasers, the

(1) 13th January.
(2) 14th January.
(3) February 1st.   Before Lord

Denman, Ch. J., and Patteson and
Coleridge, JJ.

plaintiffs thereby making him their agent for that purpose : and, even assuming that there was no binding contract, if, after a delivery by the broker to the defendants under that authority, the plaintiffs may still elect to disaffirm the sale, they cannot treat the defendants as wrongdoers without giving them notice of that election, and demanding the goods. * * The delivery also supports the plea of leave and licence, which had not been determined, there having been no demand of the goods.

The plaintiffs cannot maintain the count for goods sold and delivered, without affirming their agent's contract ; and, suing on it, they affirm it *in omnibus*.   Thus, where the agent for the sale of a horse is forbidden to give a warranty, but nevertheless sells with a warranty, if the principal sues on the contract he must abide by the warranty, for it entered into the price.   On that view the defendants make out their plea of payment : they purchased on terms without which they would not have contracted ; and they have paid accordingly.   Even assuming the contract not to have been binding originally, the plaintiffs have no right to disaffirm it now : for, on 19th November, they handed the goods to the broker for delivery to the defendants as under a sale ; he delivered them accordingly, and received payment in a bill ; and, though he might have no authority to sell for a bill, yet, *if the principal gives his agent the apparent absolute control, he is bound by the contract. No person would venture to buy in market overt, if a master could disaffirm his servant's sale there for less than the authorised price.

(PATTESON, J. : I am not prepared to say that the maxim *caveat emptor* would not apply.)

If the article had been stolen, the real owner would be bound by such a sale : as between innocent parties, it is the negligent that ought to suffer.

Bovill, contrà :

The general plea of payment, and the plea of payment by accepting the bill, both set up a defence in terms as arising after the cause of action accrued, which was not until the bill became due : *Goodchild* v. *Pledge* (1) : the evidence therefore does not support the pleas ; and, if it discloses a defence, it is one that ought to have been pleaded specially as a performance of the contract.

(1) 1 M. & W. 363.

GREGSON
v.
RUCK.

[743]

[*744]

(*Kelly*: If so, there never was a cause of action, and the plea of *nunquam indebitatus* is sufficient: if there ever was a cause of action, it accrued before the bill was paid.)

The defendants admit that on the count in debt the plaintiffs have a *primâ facie* case, to which there is no answer but the supposed payment: if there was a contract, it was the sold note, and the plaintiffs have not been paid: if there was not a contract, they are entitled to the goods.

The broker acted under special instructions to sell only for cash: and, the particular article being new in the market, there were no circumstances from which parties could infer that he had an implied authority to any greater extent. The broker acted as the agent of both *parties; the bought and sold notes constitute the contract: and the decisions from the time of Lord TENTERDEN to the present day show that, where these notes vary, the broker's book cannot be referred to, and there is no contract: *Grant* v. *Fletcher* (1), *Thornton* v. *Meux* (2), *Hawes* v. *Forster* (3). If the bought note was the contract, it was without authority: and, though the defendants knew nothing of the plaintiffs in the transaction, they knew they were dealing with brokers: that appeared on the face of the bought note, in which a charge is made for commission. The plaintiffs were not negligent in giving the delivery orders to the broker; for he was the proper person to hold them ready to be handed over: the delivery by the plaintiffs was on the terms of the sold note; and they applied to the defendants immediately the prompt expired, up to which time they were not aware of the variance. Therefore no property passed: the purchasers have their action against the brokers for deceit; and the seller has no such action. As to the necessity of a demand, if there was no contract the goods came wrongfully to the defendants' possession.

[*745]

(LORD DENMAN, Ch. J.: Do you conceive that a demand is necessary in detinue?)

No. The plea of Not possessed is inapplicable.

(PATTESON, J.: *Mr. Kelly* put it rather that the defendants had the possession by delivery of the plaintiffs, whose leave and licence has not been determined. '

(1) 29 R. R. 286 (5 B. & C. 436).   (3) 42 R. R. 803 (1 Moo. & Rob.
(2) 31 R. R. 711 (Moo. & Mal. 43).   368).

Lord Denman, Ch. J.: Even so I should say that the defendants'   GREGSON
possession of the goods is no more lawful than is the borrower's   *v.*
possession of money lent; yet debt for money lent lies without   RUCK.
previous demand.   It *may be different as to the plea of leave and   [*746]
licence.)

The authority to deliver was merely on the terms of the supposed
contract as disclosed in the sold note: if there was no contract,
there was no authority to deliver.   It is not necessary in detinue
to show a conversion.

   (*Kelly* referred to *Gledstane* v. *Hewitt* (1), as to pleading in
detinue.)

   Bovill then showed cause against the rule for entering a
   nonsuit :

The question is whether, at the close of the plaintiffs' case, there
was any evidence at all that the broker had authority from the
defendants to make the contract.   The plaintiffs say that the sold
note was signed by the broker as the defendants' agent: *Hawes* v.
Forster (2).   There certainly was some evidence of authority, the
slightness of which might have been commented upon, if the
defendants had rested their case there; and, if there was any
evidence of authority at that stage, it must now be taken as proved
upon the whole case as it stands.   The objection applies only to
the *indebitatus* count.

   Kelly and *Martin,* contrà :

At the trial no notice was taken of the count in detinue but by a
slight allusion at the close of the opening speech; and, but for the
importance of the case, the Lord Chief Justice would have
nonsuited the plaintiffs for want of evidence of authority.   The
evidence, as it stood at the close of the plaintiffs' case, was the sold
note, with proof of previous dealings, that the plaintiffs gave the
delivery order to the brokers indorsed generally, and that the
defendants ultimately *obtained possession of the goods.   Brokers   [*747]
are not the general agents of their principals, but special agents for
each particular transaction : no number of such previous contracts
would show a general authority.

(1) 1 Cr. & J. 565   (2) 42 R. R. 803 (1 Moo. & Rob.
                                          368).

GREGSON
v.
RUCK.

(PATTESON, J.: To fix a defendant, a contract must be shown, signed by him or his agent: this is signed by the plaintiffs' agent. All this arises from the practice of delivering a contract to the party who is bound by it. There ought to have been notice to the defendants to produce their part; and I do not see why that *per se* should be evidence of authority.

LORD DENMAN, Ch. J.: At the close of the plaintiffs' case there was no proof of there having been more than one note.)

In *Hawes* v. *Forster* (1) there was the proof of authority which is wanting here: and, as regards the count in detinue, the sold note, if not shown to have been delivered with the defendants' authority, was improperly admitted in evidence, and there ought to be a new trial.

Cur. adr. vult.

LORD DENMAN, Ch. J. now delivered judgment:

The first question in this case is whether the defendants ever were indebted to the plaintiffs for goods sold and delivered to be paid for on request.

The cases as to contracts made through the intervention of a broker acting for both buyer and seller are not clear: but they establish this point beyond all doubt, namely, that when the bought and sold notes differ in any material respect there is no contract. Here they differ essentially; and therefore there was no contract of sale at all: there was indeed a delivery; but it was under a [*748] mistaken notion as to the existence of a *contract which never did exist. No cause of action was therefore established for goods sold and delivered; and the defendants are entitled to succeed upon the plea of Never indebted. They must fail on the other pleas to the count in debt, because those pleas proceed on the supposed performance of a contract which never existed, and could not be performed.

The next question is as to the count in detinue. To this count three pleas are pleaded: *Non detinent;* that the plaintiffs were not possessed; and leave and licence. The evidence clearly established that the plaintiffs were possessed, and that the defendants did detain the goods. The other plea, of leave and licence, is said to be established by the defendants, because the plaintiffs delivered

(1) 42 R. R. 803 (1 Moo. & Rob. 368).

the goods to them; but the answer is that they were delivered under the mistaken notion that a contract had been made, such as the broker represented to the plaintiffs, whereas no such contract was made: the plaintiffs never authorised the broker to deliver the goods without payment; and the delivery, being unauthorised, cannot operate as a licence to the defendants to hold the goods.

GREGSON
v.
RUCK.

For these reasons we are of opinion that the rule must be made absolute to enter a verdict for the plaintiffs upon all the issues arising out of the count in detinue.

> *Verdict to be entered for plaintiffs, on the issues on the*
> *first count, for* 303*l., and on all the issues, but the*
> *first, on the counts in debt ; and for defendants on*
> *the issue upon Never indebted.*

On a subsequent day in this Term (May 30th) the defendants' rule was discharged.

———————

NASH AND ANOTHER *v.* ALLEN, ESQUIRE.

(4 Q. B. 784—791 ; S. C. Dav. & M. 16 ; 12 L. J. Q. B. 298.)

1843.
May 30.

[784]

Stat. 3 Geo. I. c. 15, s. 16, which, "for ascertaining the fees for executing of writs of *elegit*," so far as they affect real estate, enacts that the poundage to be taken by sheriffs "by reason or colour of their office," or "by reason or colour of their executing of any writ or writs of *habere facias possessionem aut seisinam*," shall not exceed a certain proportion of the yearly value of any lands "whereof possession or seisin shall be by them or any of them given," applies to the execution of writs of *elegit*, though not expressly named in the enacting part; and the sheriff taking more than the limited poundage for such execution is liable to the penalties imposed by stats. 8 Geo. I. c. 25, s. 5 (1), and 29 Eliz. c. 4, s. 1 (2).

CASE against the sheriff of Bucks for extortion in executing an *elegit*. Plea, Not guilty, by statute. Issue thereon. By consent of the parties, the following case was stated, under a Judge's order, for the opinion of this Court.

The plaintiffs in this action recovered a judgment for 1,000*l.* debt and 70*s.* costs, against one John Carter, and, for obtaining satisfaction thereof, issued, on the 18th day of August, 1841, a writ of *elegit* directed to the sheriff of Bucks, in the usual form,

———

(1) Repealed by Civil Procedure Acts Repeal Act, 1879 (42 & 43 Vict. c. 59), s. 2, and Sch.: see now Sheriffs Act, 1887 (50 & 51 Vict. c. 55), s. 29 (2). —A. C.

(2) Repealed by Sheriffs Act, 1887 (50 & 51 Vict. c. 55), s. 39, and Sch. III. ; see now *Ib.* ss. 20 and 39 (4), (5).—A. C.

NASH
v.
ALLEN.

against the lands of the said John Carter. That writ was indorsed by the plaintiffs to levy 1,008*l.* 10*s.* and interest from the 15th February, 1841, besides 50*s.* for that writ, and besides &c.; and, so indorsed, was delivered to the defendant, then sheriff of Bucks; and under this writ the defendant, the sheriff of Bucks, held an inquisition, and extended on that *elegit* lands of the said John Carter of the yearly value of 49*l.*; and the sheriff delivered to the

[*785]

plaintiffs *the said lands under the said writ. The sheriff claimed and received poundage for executing the said writ, the sum of 27*l.* 11*s.* 9*d.*, being the poundage on the sum indorsed on that writ.

The opinion of the Court is required, whether the sheriff is entitled to poundage on executing a writ of *elegit*, and, if so, whether poundage is payable on the whole debt, or only on the annual value of the land extended under the *elegit*. If the Court shall be of opinion that the poundage is payable on the whole debt, then the plaintiffs agree that a judgment of *nolle prosequi*, with costs, may be entered against them for the defendant, or otherwise, as the Court may think fit : but, if the Court shall be of a contrary opinion, then the defendant agrees that judgment shall be entered against him by confession for such sum of money and costs as the Court shall think they are entitled to, and that judgment shall be entered accordingly.

G. Atkinson for the plaintiffs :

Stat. 3 Geo. I. c. 15, s. 16 (1), "for ascertaining the fees for executing of writs of *elegit*, so far as the same relate to the extending of real estates, and for ascertaining the fees for executing of writs of *habere facias possessionem aut seisinam*," enacts that no sheriff, &c., " by reason or colour of their office or offices, or by reason or colour of their executing of any writ or writs of *habere facias possessionem aut seisinam*," shall demand or receive more than 12*d.* in the pound " of the yearly value of any manor, messuage, lands, tenements and hereditaments, whereof possession or seisin shall be by them or any of them given, where the whole exceedeth not the yearly value of 100*l.*, and the sum of 6*d.* only for every 20*s.* per

[*786]

*annum over and above the said yearly value of 100*l.* The defendant says that the execution of an *elegit*, being unnoticed in the enacting part of the clause, though mentioned in the recital, is *casus omissus*. The plaintiffs contend that the enactment includes

(1) Repealed by Sheriffs Act, 1887   Sch. III. : see now *Ib.* ss. 20 and 39
(50 & 51 Vict. c. 55), s. 39, and   (4), (5).—A. C.

the execution of an *elegit* as well as that of an *habere facias* NASH
possessionem, &c.   Two sets of words are used : " by reason or colour   *v.*
ALLEN.
of their office " &c., " or by reason or colour of their executing any
writ or writs of *habere facias* " &c. : and, "where the Legislature
in the same sentence uses different words, we must presume that
they were used in order to express different ideas : " per Lord
TENTERDEN, Ch. J. in *Rex* v. *Great Bolton* (1).   Here, if the former
words mean something different from the latter, they must mean
execution of an *elegit*.   If it be asked why a more definite expression
was not used, the answer may be, that it is difficult to point out
precisely when a *elegit* is in fact executed.   The poundage is
limited by the yearly value of the lands whereof " possession or
seisin " shall be given.   The term " possession " here applies
strictly to the execution of an *elegit*, under which a chattel interest
only passes : note (1) to *Underhill* v. *Devereux* (2).   Any doubt on
the meaning of stat. 3 Geo. I. c. 15, s. 16, is removed by stat.
8 Geo. I. c. 25, s. 5, which forbids the sheriff to take, on the executions there mentioned, " more than the same fees as are appointed
by an Act made " &c. (3 Geo. I. c. 15), " for executing a writ of
elegit and *habere facias possessionem or seisinam*."   No decision on
this clause has been found ; but a similar principle of interpretation has been sanctioned.   Under stat. 11 Geo. IV. *& 1 Will. IV.   [*787]
c. 60, s. 8, which enables the Court of Chancery, where lands have
been vested in a trustee, and, on his death, his heir cannot be found,
to appoint a person by whom the estate may be conveyed, it was
held in two cases, *In re Goddard* (3) and *In re Stanley* (4), that the
Court could not make such appointment on the death of a mortgagee, that case not being expressly provided for.   But in *Ex parte
Whitton* (5), decided after the passing of stat. 4 & 5 Will. IV. c. 23,
which, in sect. 2, assumes that the former Act, 11 Geo. IV. &
1 Will. IV. c. 60, s. 8, included mortgagees, Lord LANGDALE, M. R.
held " that mortgagees and the heirs of mortgagees were within
the eighth section, explained by the subsequent Act."

W. H. Watson, contrà :

The sheriff was entitled to poundage on the sum indorsed upon
the writ.   This point was touched upon, but not decided by the
Court, in *Price* v. *Hollis* (6).   Before stat. 3 Geo. I. c. 15, the sheriff

(1) 8 B. & C. 71, 74.   (4) 5 Sim. 320.
(2) 2 Wms. Saund. 68 f (ed. 6).   (5) 1 Keen, 278.
(3) 1 My. & K. 25.   (6) 1 M. & S. 105.

NASH
v.
ALLEN.

would have been entitled to poundage on the whole debt levied, at the rate of 1s. in the pound for the first 100l. and 6d. in the pound for the residue, by stat. 29 Eliz. c. 4, s. 1, which applied to executions on *elegit*: *Jayson* v. *Rash* (1), *Peacock* v. *Harris* (2), *Tyson* v. *Paske* (3), Com. Dig. Viscount (F. 1). The preamble of stat. 3 Geo. I. c. 15, s. 16, mentions writs of *elegit*; but the rest of the clause contains nothing which can be construed as including them: and the enacting part cannot be extended by the preamble, nor, unless ambiguous, restrained by it: 2 Dwarris on Statutes, 760,

[*788]

762; *Wilson* v. *Knubley* (4). The word " possession," *which has been relied upon, applies to the writ of *habere facias possessionem*. The form of a writ of *elegit* (5), " that " " you cause to be delivered to the said A. B. by a reasonable price and extent, all the goods " &c., " and also all such lands " &c., " to hold " &c. (6), does not imply an actual delivery of seisin or possession; the language of the old writ was similar; and in fact possession is not delivered.

(COLERIDGE, J.: It is said in 2 Tidd's Practice, 1036 (7), that " it was formerly usual for the sheriff to deliver actual possession of a moiety of the lands; but he now only delivers legal possession: " and *Rogers* v. *Pitcher* (8) is referred to (7).)

The practice not to deliver possession in fact has been uniform.

(COLERIDGE, J.: Your construction strikes out the words " by reason or colour of their office " in the enacting part of sect. 16. If the sheriff gave possession under an *elegit*, he would do so by reason of his office.)

There may have been good reason for omitting the writ of *elegit* in the enacting part. The debt may only be 20l., the annual value of the land 5,000l.: there a poundage on the annual value would be extravagant. The debt might be satisfied in half a year; yet the construction on the other side would give poundage on the value of the land for a year. The sheriff, at the time of executing the *elegit*,

(1) 1 Salk. 209.
(2) 1 Salk. 331.
(3) 1 Salk. 333.
(4) 7 East, 128.
(5) Under stat. 1 & 2 Vict. c. 110, s. 11.

(6) Tidd's Forms, 396, 397, ed. 1840.
(7) 9th ed.
(8) 25 R. R. 582, 586 (6 Taunt. 202, 207).

levies the entirety of the debt; and his poundage must be measured   NASH
by that: there is no subsequent levy.   Stat. 3 Geo. I. c. 15, s. 16,   *v.*
as construed on the other side, would repeal stat. 29 Eliz. c. 4, s. 1,   ALLEN.
as to poundage on executing an *elegit*, and leave the sheriff, in those   [*789]
cases, no authorized poundage except on the *annual value of lands.
In *Ex parte Whitton* (1) the supposition that the heirs of mortgagees
were included in the clause mentioning heirs of trustees did not
raise so much difficulty as attends the construction here argued for
by the plaintiffs.   Stat. 8 Geo. I. c. 25, s. 5, was not meant to extend
or explain stat. 3 Geo. I. c. 15, s. 16, but only to annex a penalty to
the violation of that clause.

   G. Atkinson, in reply :

   The effect of stat. 8 Geo. I. c. 25, s. 5, in law is, that writs of
elegit are included in sect. 16 of the former Act, unless the words
of sect. 16 are irreconcileable with such an assumption.   The words
" whereof possession or seisin shall be " given, in the latter
clause, apply sufficiently to the execution of an *elegit*, as described
by Tidd.

   (COLERIDGE, J.: The purport of the writ, as given by stat.
Westm. 2 (1 stat. 13 Edw. I. c. 18), is that the sheriff " shall
deliver " to the plaintiff all the chattels and half the land.)

As to the argument, that lands worth 5,000*l.* a year might be
taken for a debt of 20*l.*, it may as well be supposed on the other
hand that the debt might be 5,000*l.* and the yearly value of the
land 20*l.*   It appears, by an *Anonymous* (2) case in Siderfin, that
a sheriff was held indictable for taking 200*l.* as fees for executing
an *habere facias possessionem*, the Court saying that it was great
oppression in the sheriff, who had so much in the pound by statute
in case of execution against the personal estate, to take such fees
in a case against the real.   Therefore it appears that, where the
execution affected the real estate, no poundage at all could be taken
before *stat. 3 Geo. I. c. 15.   [*790]

   (*Watson :* The effect of that judgment is only that in a
case within stat. 29 Eliz. c. 4, where nothing was delivered but
the land, the sheriff could not have poundage because there was
nothing to measure it by.   Stat. 3 Geo. I. c. 15, s. 16, gives the
measure.)

   (1) 1 Keen, 278.   (2) 2 Sid. 155.

NASH
v.
ALLEN.

LORD DENMAN, Ch. J.:

I think the plaintiffs are entitled to judgment. Stat. 8 Geo. I. c. 25, s. 5 (1), assumes that stat. 3 Geo. I. c. 15, s. 16 (1), has prescribed a limit for the fees now in question. And this last mentioned clause, "for ascertaining the fees for executing writs of *elegit*, so far as the same relate to the extending of real estates," enacts that sheriffs shall not "by reason or colour of their office or offices" "demand, ask or receive any other or greater consideration, fee, &c.," than 12*d*. in the pound of the yearly value of any lands "whereof possession or seisin shall be by them or any of them given" &c. Passing over, as I have, the words as to executing writs of *habere facias possessionem aut seisinam,* and merely supposing that under an *elegit* the sheriff has given possession of lands by reason or colour of his office, I think the case comes within that limitation which the statutes, 8 Geo. I. c. 25, s. 5 (1), and 29 Eliz. c. 4, s. 1 (1), make it penal to transgress.

PATTESON, J.:

I am of the same opinion; and the construction we give to the clause in question of stat. 3 Geo. I. c. 15, cannot be called extending it by reference to the preamble. The enacting part does not speak of sheriffs receiving any greater consideration or fee &c., by reason of their office "in" executing any writ of *habere facias* &c., but by [*791] reason of their office or offices, "or" *by reason or colour of their executing &c. The words "by reason of their office" mean something else, I suppose, than executing the writs lastly named; and that meaning may be explained by the preamble.

WILLIAMS, J.:

Stat. 8 Geo. I. c. 25, s. 5, assumes that the sheriff takes fees under stat. 3 Geo. I. c. 15, s. 16, for executing an *elegit*: and therefore we may reasonably try to find something, in the clause referred to, whereby that may be done which the Legislature mentions as done. And I think enough appears for that purpose.

COLERIDGE, J.:

The taking of poundage for an *elegit*, so far as it affected goods and chattels, was already provided for by stat. 29 Eliz. c. 4, when

(1) Repealed: see notes (1), (2), p. 483, above.—A. C.

stat. 3 Geo. I. c. 15, passed. It remained only to provide for the
case, in which real estates were extended under the writ. Stat.
3 Geo. I. c. 25, s. 5, assumes that this has been done by stat.
3 Geo. I. c. 15, s. 16, and, if so, we should try to give a meaning
to that clause, consistent with the assumption. Now, by the old
writ of *elegit*, the sheriff was to "deliver" the moiety of lands to
the plaintiff. Then, construing the clause as my Lord has already
done, we may say that "by reason or colour of their office" applies
to the proceeding on a writ of *elegit*; and the words "whereof
possession or seisin shall be by them or any of them given" not
only refer to the writs specified immediately before, but are large
enough to include that which the sheriff is called upon to do under
an *elegit*.

NASH
v.
ALLEN.

Judgment for plaintiffs.

HENNIKER AND OTHERS *v.* LIONEL WIGG AND
OTHERS (1).

(4 Q. B. 792—795 ; S. C. Dav. & M. 160.)

1843.
May 30.
June 23.

[792]

Where a bond is given to secure payment by A. to B. of a specified sum,
it is not an invariable rule of law that all payments made by A. are to be
applied in immediate and final liquidation of the sum named, or of first
items in A.'s debit, or that, even if A., on a long course of transactions,
should, after the giving of the bond, be for a time in advance to B., the
bond is thereby satisfied.

It may, in default of express stipulation, be inferred from the language
and conduct of the parties after execution of the bond that they intended
the bond to stand as a continuing security ; and, that inference being
drawn, the above mentioned rule of application will not hold.

THIS was an action of debt, tried before Lord Denman, Ch. J.,
at the London sittings after Michaelmas Term, 1841, when a verdict
was found for the plaintiffs, subject to the opinion of the Court
upon a case.

The case was this day argued (2) by *Kelly* for the plaintiffs, and
Sir W. W. Follett, Solicitor-General, for the defendants. The
material points of the case and of the argument, so far as they
affect the general question, will be found sufficiently detailed in
the judgment.

(1) Followed, *City Discount Co. v.
McLean* (1874) L. R. 9 C. P. 692, 693,
43 L. J. C. P. 344; *Re Hallett, Knatch-
bull v. Hallett* (1880) 13 Ch. D. 696, 739,
49 L. J. Ch. 415; distinguished, *Re*

Boys, Eedes v. Boys (1870) L. R. 10 Eq.
467, 470, 39 L. J. Ch. 655.—A. C.

(2) Before Lord Denman, Ch. J.,
Patteson, Williams, and Coleridge, JJ.

HENNIKER
r.
WIGG.

Besides the authorities mentioned in the judgment, the following were referred to in argument:

Lysaght v. *Walker* (1) ; *Pease* v. *Hirst* (2) ; *Eyton* v. *Knight* (3) ; *Simson* v. *Ingham* (4) ; *Field* v. *Carr* (5).

Cur. adv. vult.

LORD DENMAN, Ch. J., in the vacation after this Term (June 23rd), delivered the judgment of the COURT:

[*793]

This was an action of debt on bond, brought by the plaintiffs, as trustees of the East of England Bank, *against the defendants, who severally executed the said bond. The condition (set out upon *oyer*) was simply for repayment of the amount (1,000*l.*) with interest, on or upon the 6th April, 1837, the bond itself bearing date the preceding 10th January. The plea was *Solvit post diem.* And upon that the question arises.

The facts materially bearing upon the question are as follows:

Lionel Wigg, the first-named defendant, having had dealings with the National Provincial Bank, and being indebted to them, applied to the plaintiffs' Bank for a credit of 1,000*l.*, to pay off the National Provincial Bank. That was declined : but they agreed to advance the defendant 1,000*l.* upon the other defendants joining him in a bond to that amount, which was accordingly executed by Lionel and Herbert Wigg on the 10th January, 1837, and by the other defendants on the 12th.

Before either of those days the first-named defendant had paid into the plaintiffs' Bank two several sums ; namely, 85*l.* on the 3rd of January, 196*l.* on the 7th, and, on the 12th, 102*l.* : he had also paid 35*l.* on the 11th. The defendant Lionel Wigg appears to have ceased dealing with the National Provincial Bank after paying to them the sum of 1,294*l.* 9*s.*, through the plaintiffs' Bank (which said sum of 1,294*l.* 6*s.* is the first item on the debit side of his account in the pass book of Lionel Wigg, viz. on the 12th January), but commenced a banking account with the plaintiffs, the first transactions being the payment by him into their Bank of the said sums, before the date of the bond, which formed the first items in his pass book on the credit side. It does not seem to be necessary to pursue minutely the details of the defendant Lionel Wigg's

[*794]

account with the plaintiffs, *because it does appear that, between

<hr/>

(1) 35 R. R. 1 (5 Bligh, N. S. 1 ; see p. 28).

(2) 34 R. R. 343 (10 B. & C. 122).

(3) 2 Jur. (1838), p. 8.

(4) 26 R. R. 273 (2 B. & C. 65).

(5) 5 Bing. 13.

the opening of his account and his failure at the close on the 10th September, 1840, when the balance was against him 1,505*l.*17*s.*11*d.*, the balance had been in his favour to a greater amount than was due upon the bond, both for principal and interest.

And the question is whether the payments by the defendant Lionel into the Bank beyond the amount of the bond, or, still more, the balances exceeding its amount, ought to have been applied in discharge of the bond.

It was contended that, as the bond was executed by some of the defendants on the 10th of January and by all on the 12th, the sum of 1,294*l.* 6*s.* above noticed must from the date have included the 1,000*l.* to secure which the bond was given; that the whole formed one account, and that an ordinary banking, in which, according to the language of Sir W. GRANT, M. R., all the sums paid in form one blended fund, the parts of which have no longer any separate exist- ence; and that " it is the first item on the debit side of the account, that is discharged, or reduced, by the first item on the credit side: *Clayton's* case (1); and *Bodenham* v. *Purchas* (2), in which case the doctrine of Sir W. GRANT was fully adopted. And it is presumed that, generally speaking, and with reference to a case like that which he was considering more especially, the doctrine of that eminent Judge admits of no doubt. But it is equally certain that a particular mode of dealing, and more especially any stipulation between the parties, may entirely vary the case: and that would be the effect, in the present *instance, if it should appear that this   [*795]
bond was given to secure the plaintiffs against advances which they might from time to time make to the defendant Lionel. That would show that the amount of it was not to be brought into account like any other item in the manner supposed by Sir W. GRANT. What was the precise nature of the agreement between the parties at the time of giving the bond does not very distinctly appear. But the conduct and language of the defendants, or some of them, which we find detailed in the case, have a strong bearing upon this point. In the month of September, 1840, Herbert, in the presence of Lionel Wigg, expressed a hope that the Bank would not stop his brother Lionel, as they had the security of the bond for 1,000*l.* In October following, the defendants Neriah and Edward expressly avowed their liability to pay 1,000*l.* on their bond. On the 7th of November following the defendant Neriah

(1) In *Devaynes* v. *Noble*, 15 R. R.   (2) 20 R. R. 342 (2 B. & Ald. 39).
151 (1 Mer. 530, 572 ; see p. 608).

HENNIKER
v.
WIGG.

wrote to the manager a letter in terms which admit his liability. And the same defendant shortly afterwards called at the Bank, and said he was aware he was liable for the principal, but was doubtful whether he was liable for interest. From this evidence, which is expressly submitted to our consideration, we know not at what conclusion we can possibly arrive except that this bond was given as a continuing security, and consequently has not been discharged.

Our judgment must therefore be for the plaintiffs.

Judgment for plaintiffs.

1843.
May 31.

[807]

REG. *v.* THE JUSTICES OF MIDDLESEX.

(4 Q. B. 807—810; S. C. Dav. & M. 289; 12 L. J. M. C. 134; 7 Jur. 669.)

Under stat. 8 & 9 Will. III. c. 30, s. 6, the appeal against an order of removal lies to Quarter Sessions only; not, therefore, to general Sessions, distinct from Quarter Sessions.

THE parish officers of St. John the Baptist, Stamford, Lincoln-shire, gave the parish officers of St. Pancras, Middlesex, notice of appeal, dated August 26th, 1841, against an order of two justices, removing Margaret, the wife of William Blake, and her children, from St. Pancras to St. John the Baptist. The notice stated that the appeal would ·be commenced and prosecuted "at the next general Sessions of the peace to be holden for the said county of Middlesex." By the practice of the Sessions, the notice ought to have been served on the 28th of August; but the agents for the appellant parish, not knowing the practice in this respect, did not serve the notice till September 2nd. The next general Sessions were holden on September 13th, when it was ordered by the Court that the officers of St. Pancras should have notice of the appeal, and attend on the 13th of October then next (1), to hear and abide by the judgment &c. of the Court. At the adjourned general Sessions holden October 13th, 1841, the appeal came on, and the service of notice of appeal on September 2nd was objected to, and the appeal consequently dismissed without hearing on the merits. The appellants' counsel asked the Court to enter continuances and respite the appeal: but they refused to do this, on the ground that they had no authority. *Clarkson*, in the ensuing Michaelmas

[*808]

Term, obtained a rule *nisi* for a *mandamus* to the Sessions to enter

(1) The appeal day of the general Sessions. according to the practice in Middlesex.

continuances and hear the appeal. Cause was shown in Hilary
Term, 1842, before WILLIAMS, J. in the Bail Court, on the part of
the respondents only: and the learned Judge, finding that the
question was one which materially affected the practice of the Court
of Quarter Sessions, enlarged the rule, in order that it might be
served on the justices, and that they, if they thought proper, might
show cause also.

   Sir F. Pollock, Attorney-General, now showed cause on behalf
      of the justices:

   The question is, whether or not the general Sessions have power
to exercise an original jurisdiction over an appeal, by entry and
respite.   The statute, 13 & 14 Car. II. c. 12, which first gives the
appeal against an order of removal, enacts (sect. 2) that the persons
aggrieved may appeal to the justices of the county " at their next
Quarter Sessions." Stat. 3 & 4 W. & M. c. 11, s. 9, gives an appeal
to " the next general Quarter Sessions of the peace, to be held for
the said county, riding, or division, city, or town corporate."   But,
by the clause now in question, stat. 8 & 9 Will. III. c. 30, s. 6,
" the appeal against any order for the removal of any poor person
from out of any parish, township, or place, shall be had, prosecuted,
and determined, at the general or Quarter Sessions of the peace for
the county, division, or riding, wherein the parish, township, or
place, from whence such poor person shall be removed, doth lie,
and not elsewhere."   The question is, whether the word " or "
gives an alternative, or merely connects two expressions which, for
the purpose of the clause, mean the same thing, and denotes that
the general Sessions are the Quarter Sessions.   The more ordinary
sense appears to be that which would give jurisdiction in this case;
but in *Rex* v. *The Justices of *London* (1), where this Court had   [*809]
under consideration a clause, 17 Geo. II. c. 38, s. 4, giving an
appeal to " the next general or Quarter Sessions," Lord ELLEN-
BOROUGH said: " This statute therefore limits the appeal (in terms)
to the next general or Quarter Sessions, and the question is whether
the word ' general ' is used with a view to those places which have
both general and Quarter Sessions, as London and Middlesex; or
whether it is not used as another word for Quarter Sessions, in
contradistinction to a special Sessions; every Quarter Sessions
being a general Sessions?   And we are of opinion that the latter
is the true construction."   The Court will now say, what rule of

   (1) 13 R. R. 540 (15 East, 632).

REG.
v.
THE
JUSTICES OF
MIDDLESEX.

practice the magistrates shall adopt for the future; but convenience is in favour of that which allows them to spread the business over eight Sessions, and not four only, in the year.

Bovill also showed cause for the respondents:

Stat. 8 & 9 Will. III. c. 30, s. 6, lays down a rule as to the county, division, or riding, in which an appeal shall be brought, but uses the expression "the" appeal against any order, &c., thus referring to a power of appeal given by previous statutes. And the subsequent words, "general or Quarter Sessions," have received a judicial construction in the case already cited. The observation of Lord ELLENBOROUGH there on the words "county, riding, or division," applies here; namely, that "there is no county but Middlesex, in which there are in fact general Sessions in addition to the Quarter Sessions; and they do not occur in any riding or division." Stat. 9 Geo. I. c. 7, s. 8, enacts that no appeal against an order of removal shall be proceeded upon "in any *Court or Quarter Sessions," unless notice of appeal shall have been given, the reasonableness of which shall be determined by the justices "at the Quarter Sessions, to which the appeal is made;" and, if it appear to them that reasonable notice was not given, "they shall adjourn the said appeal to the next Quarter Sessions." If an appeal lay to general Sessions by the prior Act, it is not to be supposed that in this clause they would have been so entirely overlooked.

[*810]

No counsel appeared for any other party.

LORD DENMAN, Ch. J.:

Assuming that the case is brought, as it seems to be, to this issue, whether the Quarter Sessions, and not the general Sessions, were the proper tribunal, I think there is no doubt that the Quarter Sessions were so. *Rex v. The Justices of London* (1) is an authority directly bearing on the point; and we must decide in accordance with it. The distinction between general and Quarter Sessions was held material in *Rex v. Turnock* (2) and *Rex v. Shaw* (3), and was recognized by the Court in *Taylor's* case (4). Lord KENYON, in *Rex v. The Guardians of the Poor of Chichester* (5), throws some doubt on *Rex v. Shaw* (3); but his judgment is not inconsistent with the

---

(1) 13 R. R. 540 (15 East, 632).   (3) 2 Salk. 482.
(2) 2 Salk. 474; *S. C.* (as *Rex v.*   (4) Palm. 44.
Turner) 5 Mod. 329.   (5) 3 T. R. 496.

decision in that case. I think that, by the terms of the Act now
before us, the appeal lay to the Quarter and not the general Sessions.

PATTESON, WILLIAMS, and COLERIDGE, JJ. concurred.

Rule discharged.

REG.
v.
THE
JUSTICES OF
MIDDLESEX.

THOMAS FLIGHT v. LEMAN (1).

(4 Q. B. 883—889; S. C. Dav. & M. 67; 12 L. J. Q. B. 353; 7 Jur. 557.)

1843.
June 9.
———
[883]

> A declaration in case alleged that defendant unlawfully and maliciously
> did advise, procure, instigate and stir up T. to commence and prosecute an
> action on the case against plaintiff, wherein certain issues were joined, as
> to which plaintiff was acquitted: Held, that no cause of action appeared,
> the declaration not showing maintenance (inasmuch as the action appeared
> not to have been commenced when defendant interfered), and not alleging
> want of reasonable and probable cause for the action.

CASE. The second count of the declaration alleged that the
defendant heretofore, to wit 1st January, 1838, and on divers &c.
between that day and 22nd November, 1838, contriving and maliciously intending to injure, harass and damnify plaintiff, and to
put him to great vexation, unlawfully and maliciously did advise,
procure, instigate and stir up John Thomas to commence and
prosecute an action of trespass on the case in the Court &c. (Queen's
Bench) against the now plaintiff together with certain other persons,
to wit one Edward Gill Flight and one John Knight; in which
*last mentioned action the now plaintiff and the said E. G. Flight
and J. Knight did appear, plead and defend the same, according to
the course and practice of the said Court: that, by and through
such advice, procurement, instigation and stirring up, John Thomas
did in fact afterwards, to wit 4th January, 1838, commence and
prosecute the last mentioned action, and did afterwards, to wit
13th February, 1838, according to the course and practice &c.,
declare in the last mentioned action against the now plaintiff and
the said other defendants therein; and John Thomas did, to wit
then, in and by the said declaration, complain against the now
plaintiff and the said other defendants in the said last mentioned
action, amongst other things, that, whereas &c. The present
declaration then set out three counts of a declaration in case at
the suit of John Thomas against the defendant, E. G. Flight and
J. Knight (2): and that such proceedings were thereupon had &c.:

[*884]

---

(1) Commented and distinguished,
Bradlaugh v. *Newdegate* (1883) 11
Q. B. D. 1, 8, 52 L. J. Q. B. 454.—A. C.

(2) *Thomas* v. *Flight* and others.
The declaration there, in fact, contained counts besides those set out in

averment of a trial at Nisi Prius at Dorchester, on 18th July, 1838, and that the defendants were then and there acquitted of the premises mentioned to be charged against them by John Thomas. And thereupon afterwards, to wit 22nd November, 1838, it was considered, in and by the said Court &c., amongst other things, that the said John Thomas be in mercy for his false claim against the now plaintiff and the said *E. G. Flight and J. Knight, defendants in the said last mentioned action as aforesaid, as to the premises aforesaid, whereof the now plaintiff and the said E. G. Flight and J. Knight, defendants as aforesaid, were acquitted in form aforesaid ; as by the record &c.   Whereby, and by reason of the said suit, action and false claim of the said John Thomas as to the said premises, and of such advice, procurement, instigation and stirring up as hereinbefore mentioned, the now plaintiff was not only put to great trouble and vexation in and about the defence of the said action, so far as the same related to the said false claim so made and prosecuted by the said John Thomas by the advice, procurement, &c. of the now defendant as aforesaid, and whereof the now plaintiff was so acquitted as aforesaid, but was also obliged to pay, and did in fact pay, a large &c., to wit 800l., in and about the defence of the said action, so far as the same related to the said false claim so then made by the said John Thomas as aforesaid, and the costs thereof and in relation thereto.

[*885]

The defendant pleaded, in effect, that the advice given by him was given in the character of an attorney.

Replication, *De injurià.*

Special demurrer. Joinder.

Sir W. W. Follett, Solicitor-General, for the defendant :

The declaration discloses no cause of action. It states that the defendant advised Thomas to commence an action against the defendant, and does not aver that such action was without reasonable or probable cause. In *Pechell* v. *Watson* (1) one count in case charged the *advising to commence an action without reasonable or probable cause ; and a second count charged the upholding and

[*886]

the present declaration. Several issues were joined ; on some of which the then plaintiff succeeded. The then defendants brought error in the Exchequer Chamber, on a bill of exceptions to the ruling of PARKE, B. at the trial at Dorchester; but the ruling was held good, and the judg-

ment of the Court affirmed : *Flight* v. *Thomas,* 52 R. R. 468 (11 Ad. & El. 688). The judgment of the Exchequer Chamber was affirmed in Dom. Proc., *Flight* v. *Thomas,* 54 R. R. 55 (8 Cl. & Fin. 231).

(1) 58 R. R. 843 (8 M. & W. 691).

maintaining of an action already commenced; and both were held good; but here the declaration differs from the first count in *Pechell* v. *Watson* (1) in not averring want of reasonable or probable cause, and from the second in showing that the action was not brought before the defendant gave his advice.   Maintenance consists, not in advising the commencement of an action, but in upholding an action already commenced.   In Co. Litt. 368 b, Lord Coke describes the offence as follows.   "Maintenance, *manutenentia*, is derived of the verb *manutenere*, and signifieth in law a taking in land, bearing up or upholding of quarrels and sides, to the disturbance or hindrance of common right."   He then goes on to explain two sorts of maintenance, one *in pais*, which is punishable only by indictment, the other in the Courts, which is that now in question.   Of this he says: "The other is called *curialis*, because it is done *pendente placito*, in the Courts of justice; and this was an offence at the common law, and is threefold."   The first and third kinds are not now in question: "the second is, when one maintaineth the one side, without having any part of the thing in plea, or suit; and this maintenance is twofold, general maintenance, and special maintenance."   In Hawk. Pl. Cr. B. 1, ch. 83 (2), this passage is referred to, and maintenance in the Courts is described as follows (sect. 3).   "Secondly, *curialis*, or in a court of justice, where one officiously intermeddles in a suit depending in any such Court *which no way belongs to him."   So, [*887] in Com. Dig. Maintenance (A 1), the act is explained to be sustaining a party in "a cause pending in suit;" for which 2 Inst. 208, 212, is cited.   To the same effect is 4 Blackst. Com. 134.   It is true that to procure the commencement of a suit without reasonable or probable cause, though it be not technically maintenance, is in some cases actionable: but one essential requisite to such an action is the want of reasonable or probable cause, which is not here averred.   The charge is analogous to that of a malicious prosecution. So it ought to be shown how the action terminated: it does not appear in this case that all the issues are set out, and what the general result was.   It is not even alleged that the defendant was not interested in the cause.   (He was then stopped by the COURT.)

Barstow, contrà :

The fallacy of the argument for the defendant consists in applying to all sorts of maintenance a definition of a particular kind of

(1) 58 R. R. 843 (8 M. & W. 691).   (2) Vol. II. p. 393, 7th ed.

FLIGHT
v.
LEMAN.

maintenance. One kind of maintenance consists in upholding suits already commenced; another in instigating the commencement of suits. The two are distinguished in 2 Inst. 213 (1). It is absurd to treat one as an offence, and not the other.

(COLERIDGE, J.: Suppose I know of a defect in your title to land, and, even from malice to you, inform the legal owner: is that actionable?)

[*888]

That might be actionable or not under the peculiar circumstances of the case. As to the objection that the defendant's interest is not negatived, it was held, in *Pechell* v. *Watson* (2), *that it lies on the defendant to aver his interest. Then, as to the result of the action, enough is shown; for it appears that on some issues, at all events, the parties were acquitted. The existence of reasonable or probable cause would be no justification in a case of maintenance. And, even if it were, the averment of such cause should come from the defendant, on the same principle which requires him to show his interest, if he has any.

LORD DENMAN, Ch. J.:

The case of *Pechell* v. *Watson* (2) proceeded on the principle that to maintain an action already commenced was unlawful. That is not here charged; and therefore the count ought to show the ingredients which make the instigation to a suit actionable. The plaintiff has not done this; for, beyond all doubt, the absence of reasonable or probable cause is one such ingredient, in the absence of which it does not appear that the plaintiff has been unlawfully disturbed.

PATTESON, J.:

I think this declaration is bad, for the reason already given. The case is analogous to that of a complaint of malicious prosecution or arrest; and here, as there, the want of reasonable or probable cause ought to be alleged.

WILLIAMS, J.:

The averments in this declaration might be sustained by proof that the defendant, not being an attorney, had held a conversation with Thomas, and had said, "if your story is correct, you might sue

---

(1) The distinction is the same as in
Co. Litt. 368 b, cited in the argument

for the defendant.
(2) 58 R. R. 843 (8 M. & W. 691).

Flight." No action could be maintained on that, unless *it further appeared that the now defendant knew that there was no right to sue the now plaintiff.

COLERIDGE, J. :

It is not asserted here that the suit maintained was without reasonable or probable cause: there are only general words, imputing an instigation and a stirring up. There should be added to these, in strict analogy with actions for malicious prosecution or arrest, as my brother PATTESON has pointed out, an averment of want of reasonable or probable cause: and without such averment this declaration shows no right of action.

Judgment for defendant.

REG. *v.* THE TOWN COUNCIL OF LICHFIELD.

(4 Q. B. 893—910; S. C. Dav. & M. 491; 12 L. J. Q. B. 308; 7 Jur. 670.)

Semble, that the council of a borough may prosecute at the expense of the corporation for an assault upon the mayor in the execution of his duty. But the opinion of the council must be taken before the prosecution is instituted; and, if this be not done, they cannot afterwards order payment of the costs out of the corporation funds (1).

The council of a borough, having borrowed money to pay debts incurred by the corporation since the passing of stat. 5 & 6 Will. IV. c. 76, (and not within stat. 7 Will. IV. & 1 Vict. c. 78, s. 28,) cannot order repayment of such loan out of the borough fund.

On a motion for a *certiorari* to bring up orders made for the above purposes, it is no answer that the alleged orders consist only of resolutions entered in the corporation minutes, and which would not of themselves be an authority for payment. Or that they are entered in a book which cannot be brought up without great inconvenience, and from which the resolutions could not be separated without injuring other entries.

A RULE was obtained, in last Easter Term, calling on the council of the city of Lichfield to show cause why a *certiorari* should not issue to remove into *this Court (2) "a certain order made by the said council," on 7th of April, 1843, for payment of 165*l.* 9*s.* 1*d.* to the late mayor, and "an order made by the said council," on the same day, for payment of 200*l.* and interest to Mrs. Mallett of the said city.

[*894]

The affidavits in support of the rule stated in substance the following facts. In and before 1838, the corporation of Lichfield was possessed of freehold property subject to the provisions of the

----

(1) See now Borough Funds Act, 1872 (35 & 36 Vict. c. 91), s. 2.
(2) Stat. 7 Will. IV. & 1 Vict.

c. 78, s. 44. [Municipal Corporations Act, 1882 (45 & 46 Vict. c. 50), s. 141 (2).]

Acts for regulating municipal corporations. In June, 1838, the corporation, with the approbation of the Lords of the Treasury (as directed by statute (1)) sold part of such property for 1,068*l.* The proceeds (except 100*l.*) were paid to the treasurer, and part of them, amounting to 700*l.*, invested in Exchequer bills in the treasurer's name. On November 9th, 1842, the council ordered that the Exchequer bills should be turned into money; which was done in January, 1843, and the proceeds, 735*l.*, received by the treasurer, and placed by him to the credit of the borough fund: and it remained in the treasurer's hands when this application was made.

After the passing of stat. 5 & 6 Will. IV. c. 76, Thomas Rowley, the then mayor, borrowed 200*l.* from Thomas Mallett, one of the then councillors, and gave his promissory note for the amount. No bond or obligation for the repayment was given in the name of the body corporate; nor was the money applied in discharging any debt incurred by them before the passing of the Act; but interest on the note was paid from time to time by the council out of the borough fund. Mallett died, and left the said Mrs. Mallett his executrix.

[895]

In October, 1842, a Court was held at the town hall for revising the burgess lists: a riot took place; and the mayor, Robert Sharp, was assaulted in the execution of his duty. He preferred a charge of riot and assault before the magistrates of the city against James Burton and three others, whom the magistrates bound over to appear at the next Quarter Sessions for the city, and there answer an indictment on the prosecution of Robert Sharp, for riot and assault. At those Sessions an indictment was preferred, by Sharp, for a riot, and for assaulting Sharp in the execution of his duty as mayor, and for an assault on him unconnected with his office. The indictment was removed by *certiorari*, and tried before a special jury at the Stafford Spring Assizes, March, 1843; and the defendants were acquitted. The Court made no order as to the prosecutor's costs.

At a council held on April 7th, 1843, the following " resolutions or orders " were agreed upon by the majority, and were signed by the mayor, but not by any of the councillors.

" Friday, April 7th, 1843. At a meeting and common hall of the council of this city this day held," &c. "It is agreed and ordered that the sum of 165*l.* 9*s.* 1*d.* be paid out of the borough fund to Mr. Alderman Sharp, late mayor of this city, in addition

(1) 5 & 6 Will. IV. c. 76, s. 94.   Local Government Act, 1882 (51 & 52
[See now Municipal Corporations Act,   Vict. c. 41), s. 72.—A. C.]
1882 (45 & 46 Vict. c. 50), s. 108, and

to any sums already paid to him on account of the mayor's salary; the above sum of 165*l.* 9*s.* 1*d.* being the amount of the bill of costs, now examined and allowed by the council, consisting of the charges, fees and disbursements of Messrs. Spurrier and Chaplin, solicitors, Birmingham, loss of time and travelling allowances of prosecutor and witnesses, justices' clerks' and Court fees, and expenses, in the prosecution of James Burton," &c., "for a riot and *assault on [*896] the said Robert Sharp on the 15th October last, when in the execution of his duty as mayor of this city on the revision of the burgess lists : the information and complaint of the said R. Sharp against the three first-named defendants for the said alleged offence having been heard and enquired into on the 20th and 24th of October last before ten of the justices of the peace for the said city, by whom the said R. Sharp was bound over to prosecute, and those defendants to appear and answer, at the ensuing Sessions for the city of Lichfield held on the 26th October last : the said R. Sharp having also preferred an indictment at such Sessions, which was found a true bill, and was moved by the defendants, after traversing, by *certiorari*, to Stafford ; and tried at the last Assizes, when the defendants were acquitted."

" It is agreed and ordered that the principal money, and interest thereon, due from this council to Mrs. Mallett of this city, widow, and secured by a promissory note to her late husband, be paid."

The councillors who dissented gave the treasurer notice not to make the payments, on the ground that they were illegal, and that an application would be made to this Court for the purpose of quashing them.

The affidavits further stated that the majority in council threatened to enforce the said orders for payment of the note, &c., and costs &c., " by and out of the said city or borough fund, and in particular by and out of the proceeds of the said Exchequer bills." That the balance standing to the credit of the borough fund when the orders were made consisted only of 20*l.*, which arose from the rents and other annual income of property belonging to the corporation, and of 735*l.*, the proceeds of the Exchequer bills. That, after payment of *the debts, expenses, and outgoings now properly incurred by the [*897] corporation, there would be no surplus applicable to the payment of the two sums mentioned in the resolutions, or for the benefit of the inhabitants, &c. And that the deponents believed that the proposed application of the proceeds of Exchequer bills had not been authorized by the Lords of the Treasury.

Reg.
v.
The
Council of
Lichfield.

It was further stated that an injunction had been obtained, restraining the mayor, aldermen and burgesses from ordering the treasurer to pay, and the treasurer from paying, the two sums in question out of any funds or property of the corporation till full answer, or till further order of the Court of Chancery.

The affidavits in opposition to the rule stated, among other things, as follows :

That the two resolutions or supposed orders of 7th April, 1843, "are not respectively orders in writing of the council of the borough of Lichfield, signed by three or more members of the said council, and countersigned by the town clerk of such borough, pursuant to the fifty-ninth section of the Act," &c. (5 & 6 Will. IV. c. 76) (1), " but that the same were and are resolutions of the council of the said borough entered in the minute book of the corporation of Lichfield, kept pursuant to the sixty-ninth section of the said Act, and signed only by the mayor, who presided at the meeting of the said council held on that day. That such original resolutions, so entered " &c., " and signed " &c., " are not orders upon which the treasurer of the said borough would pay the sums of money therein mentioned," " but that further orders, signed by three or more of the council of the said borough, and countersigned by the said town clerk, pursuant to the said fifty-ninth section," " would be

[*898]

necessary before the said treasurer would *pay the said sums of money ; " and that, upon payment of the money mentioned in such last-mentioned orders so made and countersigned as aforesaid, the said treasurer would keep such orders, together with any receipts which might be given by the person or persons receiving the said money, as his authority and vouchers for the payment of the said money." And that the resolutions so entered and signed " cannot be removed into this honourable Court by *certiorari* or otherwise without tearing the same out of the said minute book, and so destroying or injuring other entries contained in the said minute book relating to other matters, or without removing at the same time the said minute book itself, which could not be done without great inconvenience to the said corporation of Lichfield and the said council and officers thereof."

That the said majority of the council acted *bonâ fide*, and, before making the orders, ascertained that the 165*l.* 9*s.* 1*d.* was a necessary expense incurred on behalf of the council for the benefit of the

(1) See now Municipal Corporations Act, 1882 (45 & 46 Vict. c. 50), s. 141 (1).—A. C.

inhabitants in carrying into effect the above-mentioned statute by protecting the mayor while exercising the duties of his office, and prosecuting persons who had unlawfully and riotously obstructed him, &c.; and they had also ascertained "that the said sum of 200*l*. had been borrowed of the late Mr. Mallett on behalf of the council of the said borough with their assent, for the benefit of the inhabitants of the said borough, for the purpose of paying certain lawful debts and demands amounting to 199*l*. 15*s*. 9½*d*., to which the corporation were liable." A resolution of council (April 3rd, 1837), for borrowing the money, was set forth; and it was stated that the debt due from the corporation to the treasurer at that time exceeded 500*l*. The deponents also stated that repayment of the 200*l*. had been *secured by a note of the mayor, aldermen and burgesses, signed by Thomas Rowley as the mayor (1); and that the 199*l*. 15*s*. 9½*d*. had been expended (under proper orders) in paying such debts and demands as before mentioned, and the residue of the 200*l*. duly carried to account. The items in respect of which the payments were made consisted of pensions (granted by the former corporation, amounting to 10*l*.), salaries, fees of jury at Court leet, bill of clerk of the peace, payment to coroner, repairs &c., at the gaol, bread for prisoners, and expenses of a prosecution; all which payments had been agreed to and ordered by the council or the city Quarter Sessions. The resolutions made from time to time by the council for payment of interest on Mallett's note appeared, by extracts from their minutes, to have been concurred in by parties who were now promoting the application for a *certiorari*.

Statements were also made as to the riot and attack upon the mayor at the Revision Court: and it was deposed that the defendants removed the indictment into this Court, and that, on the trial, no application was made for costs of the prosecution, because it was considered that the Court had no power to award such costs on trial of an indictment removed by *certiorari*, and for no other reason.

(1) The note, stamped with the seal of the mayor, aldermen and burgesses, was as follows:
  "200*l*.
    "LICHFIELD, 11th April, 1837.
  "On demand, we, the mayor, aldermen and burgesses of the borough of the city and county of Lichfield, do promise to pay Mr. Thomas Mallett or order two hundred pounds with lawful interest for the same, at the rate of five pounds per centum per annum.
        "THOMAS ROWLEY,
                "Mayor.
  "Witness, CHARLES SIMPSON."

REG.
v.
THE
COUNCIL OF
LICHFIELD.
[*900]

It was also deposed that the purchase of Exchequer *bills referred to in the affidavits in support of the rule was not ordered by or made with the approval of the Lords of the Treasury ; that the investment of the produce of any sale of real property was not made one of the terms and conditions of such sale by the said Lords of the Treasury ; and, further, that the said purchase of Exchequer bills was not intended to be permanent, but only for a temporary purpose. That, when the resolutions of 7th April, 1843, were made, the borough fund in the treasurer's hands was more than sufficient to pay all the debts and legal liabilities of the corporation, including the sums mentioned in those resolutions. And that no borough rate had been at any time laid or levied in the said borough under stat. 5 & 6 Will. IV. c. 76.

Erle and *W. R. Cole* now showed cause:

[905]

The order for the costs of prosecution was rightly made (1). * * *
Then, as to the order for payment of the note. The fact is, merely, that, some small debts being due from the corporation, and its funds not immediately accessible, the council borrowed 200*l.* for the present purpose, refunding it, by the order in question, when they had money in hand. The payments, in each instance, were such as in honesty ought to have been made. *Holdsworth* v. *The Mayor &c. of Dartmouth* (2), in principle, bears out this order. Whether the liabilities which the money was borrowed to meet were incurred by the old or the new corporation is immaterial : with respect to such engagements the new corporation is merely the old continued : *The Attorney-General* v. *Kerr* (3) ; and it must have power to make the necessary provisions, by the general capacity resulting to it from stat. 5 & 6 Will. IV. c. 76, s. 6, as well as by the particular direction of sect. 92 (4).

[*906]

(COLERIDGE, J. : Your argument from sect. 92 requires that there should be a borough fund ; now it appears that there was none sufficient for the purposes of these orders, without taking into it money raised by sale of the real property. The *borough fund consists only of annual proceeds. You cannot make away with the capital stock.)

---

(1) See now Borough Funds Act, 1872 (35 & 36 Vict. c. 91), s. 2.—A. C.
(2) 52 R. R. 427 (11 Ad. & El. 490).
(3) 50 R. R. 221 (2 Beav. 420, 429,
430).
(4) See now Municipal Corporations Act, 1882 (45 & 46 Vict. c. 50), Sch. V. Pt. II. § 12.—A. C.

Where the Legislature has intended that capital arising from sales
should not be carried to the borough fund, express provision is
made to that effect, as in stat. 5 & 6 Will. IV. c. 76, s. 139(1); and
even that has been relaxed by stat. 6 & 7 Will. IV. c. 104, s. 3(2).

(COLERIDGE, J.: The treasurer does not hold the capital stock of
the borough, but only, under sect. 92, rents and annual proceeds.
By the practice contended for, all the real property of the borough
might be sold.)

If the borough fund is not now sufficient, that does not make the
orders illegal. A borough rate may be made, if necessary.

(COLERIDGE, J.: It would be retrospective. To avoid the un-
popularity of making a rate when it ought to have been made,
proceeds of the real property were taken into the borough fund.
Now, if a rate is made to pay the 200_l._, the inhabitants of the
borough will be rated for expenses incurred several years ago.)

Further, this writ is prayed for to remove certain orders. But
none have been made. Nothing exists but resolutions entered in
the minute book, and which could not be removed without the
inconvenience mentioned in the affidavits. Such minutes, made
under stat. 5 & 6 Will. IV. c. 76, s. 69(3), are different from orders
of the council; and the two are mentioned as distinct in stat. 7
Will. IV. & 1 Vict. c. 78, s. 22(4).

(LORD DENMAN, Ch. J.: If this be in itself an order, you cannot
say that writing it in a book which cannot be brought up makes
any difference.)

F. V. Lee, contrà, contended, as to the prosecution, that the
mayor ought, in the first instance, to have consulted *the council
on the expediency of undertaking it, and obtained from them an
order or resolution under the corporation seal. He referred to
Attorney-General v. *The Mayor of Norwich* (5). He also objected
that a municipal corporation could not bind itself by the note
here described; citing *Slark* v. *Highgate Archway Company* (6) and

[*907]

(1) See now Municipal Corporations
Act, 1882 (45 & 46 Vict. c. 50), s. 122.
—A. C.
   (2) *Ibid.* 122 (3).

(3) *Ibid.* Sch. II. § 12.
(4) *Ibid.* s. 233.
(5) 44 R. R. 143 (2 My. & Cr. 406).
(6) 5 Taunt. 792.

REG.
v.
THE
COUNCIL OF
LICHFIELD.

Broughton v. *The Manchester Water Works Company* (1).   (He was then stopped by the COURT.)

LORD DENMAN, Ch. J.:

Without saying that it is not quite proper that a corporation should incur expense to protect its officers in the performance of any necessary duty, I am of opinion that the objection to the first order in this case must prevail, namely, that the council of the borough did not previously authorize such expenditure (2).   It was their duty to consider in the first instance whether the prosecution was a proper one to be undertaken at the expense of the corporation. Such an enquiry is very easy and simple; and there is no injustice in exacting it.   Had they voted at first that the corporation would be at the expense of prosecuting, the present difficulty would not have arisen.   As to the 200*l.*, it appears to me no justification that the council borrowed this money to pay other debts.   They should have waited till funds came in, or raised them in the regular manner. Stat. 7 Will. IV. & 1 Vict. c. 78, s. 28 (3), expressly sanctions the borrowing of money to pay *debts contracted by the corporation before the passing of stat. 5 & 6 Will. IV. c. 76, and shows that the borrowing of money for other purposes is not sanctioned by the Legislature.

[*908]

PATTESON, J.:

Stat. 5 & 6 Will. IV. c. 76, s. 92 (4), authorizes payment of expenses " necessarily incurred : "   but the town council are to determine what are necessary ; and, if that question is not put to them before the expenses are incurred, they cannot afterwards decide upon repaying them.   As to the 200*l.*, if the borrowing of that sum was lawful, stat. 7 Will. IV. & 1 Vict. c. 78, s. 28 (5), must be deemed unnecessary.   That clause was introduced for the particular purpose of enabling new corporations to borrow money for the purpose of paying debts of the body corporate contracted before the Act of 5 & 6 Will. IV. passed.   Here the borrowing was not for such a purpose, and therefore is not within the statutes. Whether there be any remedy for the lender I do not now

(1) 22 R. R. 278 (3 B. & Ald. 1).   —A. C.

(2) See now Borough Funds Act, 1872 (35 & 36 Vict. c. 91), s. 2.—A. C.

(3) See now Municipal Corporations Act, 1882 (45 & 46 Vict. c. 50), s. 131.

(4) Municipal Corporations Act, 1882 (45 & 46 Vict. c. 50), Sch. V. Pt. 2, § 12.

(5) *Ibid.* s. 131.

enquire: there is none upon the note, because this is not a trading corporation.

WILLIAMS, J.:

As to the 200*l.*, the language of stat. 5 & 6 Will. IV. c. 76, expressly authorizing other modes of raising money, and not loans, is strongly against the order. If there existed a power of raising money to any extent for the purposes to which this sum was applied, it might be carried on to an entire dilapidation of the available property of the borough. I think this proceeding was not within the spirit or principle of the Act. As to the expenses of prosecution, the incurring of these was a matter concerning the whole corporation, and on which the council should have been consulted before *the step was taken; though, if the first magistrate is assaulted in the execution of his duty, it may be abundantly necessary that the corporation should prosecute.

[*909]

COLERIDGE, J.:

It may, no doubt, be very necessary that the corporation should prosecute, in a case of this kind, for the protection of its chief magistrate. But nothing could be more irregular than the proceeding adopted here. When this prosecution was undertaken, the borough fund was insolvent. An assault and riot are committed, and a charge made: the mayor does not consult the council as to the proceedings that shall be adopted: the magistrates direct a prosecution: parties are bound over to the Sessions: the case is removed by *certiorari* and tried by a special jury, and a verdict of Not guilty found. Then an order is made, to charge the expenses on the corporation. But, if application had been made to the council at first, they would perhaps have said: "In the present state of the borough fund we will consider whether or not a borough rate ought to be made:" and they might have been of opinion that it ought not. At all events they had no opportunity of deciding. In the mean time, real property of the borough having been sold, the proceeds, which ought not to have gone to the borough fund, have been taken into it; and then, from that miscalled borough fund, it is proposed to pay the costs of the prosecution. As to the 200*l.*, the practice contended for would lead to the grossest misapplications. There were, in this case, salaries, pensions and other demands to be paid out of the borough fund: but there was no borough fund to meet the payments.

Then, instead of making a rate, they borrow money to avoid that course, and *afterwards seek to pay the debt out of the capital stock of the corporation.

Rule absolute.

The orders were afterwards brought up (1), and quashed without opposition.

ARMYTAGE *v.* HALEY (2).

(4 Q. B. 917—918; S. C. Dav. & M. 139; 12 L. J. Q. B. 323; 7 Jur. 671.)

In an action for injury by negligence of defendant's servant, the jury found a verdict for plaintiff, with one farthing damages, though it appeared that plaintiff's thigh was broken, and that he had paid 10*l.* for surgical attendance.

This Court granted a new trial, on payment of costs by plaintiff within three weeks.

CASE for injury caused by negligence of defendant's servant in driving an omnibus belonging to defendant against plaintiff. Plea, Not guilty. Issue thereon.

On the trial, before Parke, B., at the Yorkshire Spring Assizes, 1843, the negligence was proved; and it appeared that plaintiff's thigh was broken, and considerable expense incurred in the consequent attendance of a surgeon, who also deposed that it was doubtful whether plaintiff would not be always lame. Verdict for plaintiff, damages one farthing.

In Easter Term, 1843, *Dundas,* for the plaintiff, obtained a rule to show cause why a new trial should not be had, unless defendant would consent to the damages being increased to 10*l.* 5*s.* 6*d.* (3).

W. H. Watson and *Pashley* now showed cause:

A new trial will sometimes be granted for smallness of damages in actions on contract, because there a definite measure of the injury may be assumed by the Court. But in actions for tort the

---

(1) The return (subscribed by the mayor and sealed with the common seal) was as follows: "On the 7th day of April" &c., "a meeting of the council of the city of Lichfield was duly held according to the Act" &c. 5 & 6 Will. IV. c. 76, "at which the following orders were made, and were then duly entered in the minute book of the proceedings of the said council pursuant to the said Act, that is to say"—The orders were then set out, and the return added, "Which are the orders mentioned in the writ hereunto annexed."

(2) Cf. *Kelly* v. *Sherlock* (1866) L. R. 1 Q. B. 686, 35 L. J. Q. B. 209; and *Phillips* v. *L. & S. W. Ry. Co.* (1879) 4 Q. B. D. 406, 5 Q. B. Div. 78, 49 L. J. Q. B. 233.—A. C.

(3) The alleged amount of the surgeon's bill.

general rule is, that a new trial will not be granted on that ground: ARMYTAGE
Rendall v. *Hayward* (1), *Mauricet* v. *Brecknock* (2), *Hayward* v.   *v.*
Newton (3), *Barker* v. *Dixie* (4), 21 Vin. Abr. 486, Trial, (Y. g),   HALEY.
Lord Gower v. *Heath* (5). So a new trial is seldom granted for
excessive damages: *Lord Townsend* *v. *Hughes* (6) is an instance   [*918]
of the unwillingness of the Court to interfere in such a case. The
jury here may have wished to deprive the plaintiff of costs, on
account of his conduct: but the Court will not take upon itself to
" unravel the grounds and motives which may have led to the
determination of a question once settled by the jurisdiction to
which the law has referred it: " *Reg.* v. *The Justices of the West
Riding* (7).

(LORD DENMAN, Ch. J.: A new trial on a mere difference of
opinion as to amount may not be grantable : but here are no
damages at all.)

The new trial, if granted, would be on payment of costs ; but can
the Court assume that the damages ought to have exceeded 20*l.* ?

Dundas and *Joseph Addison, contrà*, were stopped by the
COURT.

LORD DENMAN, Ch. J.:

The cases cited for the defendant were actions, not for injury to
the person, but, principally, for slander. There ought to be a new
trial here, on payment of costs.

PATTESON, WILLIAMS, and COLERIDGE, JJ., concurred (8).

> *Rule absolute, on payment of costs by plaintiff; if the
> rule absolute be not drawn up in three weeks, this
> rule to be discharged with costs* (9).

(1) 50 R. R. 730 (5 Bing. N. C. 424).
(2) 2 Doug. 509.
(3) 2 Str. 940.
(4) 2 Str. 1051.
(5) Barnes's Notes, 445.
(6) 2 Mod. 150.
(7) 55 R. R. 396 (1 Q. B. 624, 631).
(8) See *Cook* v. *Beal*, 1 Ld. Ray.

176; *S. C.* 3 Salk. 115; *Brown* v.
Seymour, 1 Wils. 5; *Austin* v. *Hilliers*,
Hard. 408.

(9) Tho rule absolute not being
drawn up in the time named, this rule
was discharged with costs, and an
entry made accordingly, July 7th,
1843.

IN THE COURT OF EXCHEQUER.

1842.
May 23.

Exch. of Pleas.

[1]

SMOUT *v.* MARY ANN ILBERY (1).

(10 Meeson & Welsby, 1—12; S. C. 12 L. J. Ex. 357.)

Where a man who had been in the habit of dealing with the plaintiff for meat supplied to his house, went abroad, leaving his wife and family resident in this country, and died abroad: Held, that the wife was not liable for goods supplied to her after his death, but before information of his death had been received; she having had originally full authority to contract, and done no wrong in representing her authority as continuing, nor omitted to state any fact within her knowledge relating to it; the revocation itself being by the act of God, and the continuance of the life of the principal being equally within the knowledge of both parties.

Debt for goods sold and delivered, and on an account stated.

Pleas, first, except as to 6*l.* 7*s.*, parcel, &c., *nunquam indebitatus :* secondly, except as to the said sum of 6*l.* 7*s.*, parcel, &c., payment; thirdly, as to the sum of 6*l.* 7*s.*, parcel, &c., payment into Court of that sum, and *nunquam indebitatus ultra.* The replication took issue on the first plea, denied the payment alleged in the second, and accepted the 6*l.* 7*s.*, in satisfaction as to so much of the debt demanded.

[2]   At the trial before Gurney, B., at the Middlesex sittings in Michaelmas Term, 1841, it appeared that the plaintiff was a butcher, and the defendant the widow of James Ilbery, who left England for China in May, 1839, and was lost in the outward voyage, on the 14th October, 1839. The news of his death arrived in England on the 18th of March, 1840. The plaintiff had supplied meat to the family before Mr. Ilbery sailed, and during his voyage, and the supply continued down to the time of the news of his death, and even afterwards. Upon the 14th October, 1839, the day of Mr. Ilbery's death, the amount of the debt was 52*l.* 13*s.* 11*d.* Between that day and the arrival of the news of the death, meat had been supplied to the amount of 19*l.* 9*s.*; and after that, the supply amounted to 6*l.* 7*s.*

(1) This decision has recently been applied in a case where a plaintiff sought to recover costs from the solicitor of the defendants, a Company which had become dissolved without the knowledge of the solicitor during the course of the action (*Salton* v. *New Beeston Cycle Co.* [1900] 1 Ch. 43, 69 L. J. Ch. 20). But it is not easy to reconcile the reasoning upon which the decision is based with the principle laid down in *Collen* v. *Wright* (1857) 8 E. & B. 647, 27 L. J. Q. B. 315, and the recent cases in which that principle has been applied (see *Firbank* v. *Humphreys* (1886) 18 Q. B. D. 54, 56 L. J. Q. B. 57; *Halbot* v. *Lens* [1901] 1 Ch. 344, 70 L. J. Ch. 125; *Oliver* v. *Bank of England* [1902] 1 Ch. 610, 71 L. J. Ch. 388, C. A.).—A. C.

This action was brought for these two sums (together) 25*l.* 16*s.* SMOUT
The defendant paid 6*l.* 7*s.* into Court, and relied on a payment of *v.*
20*l.*, as discharging her from the plaintiff's claim for meat supplied ILBERY.
after the date of her husband's death; and the counsel for the
defendant gave in evidence the following receipt signed by the
plaintiff, dated the 30th March, 1840: "Received of Mrs. Ilbery,
20*l.*" The plaintiff insisted that the 20*l.* had been paid generally
on account, and must be applied as a payment by the executors in
part satisfaction of the debt of the husband; and called Mr.
Dollman, the executor. From his evidence it appeared, that Mr.
Ilbery had left the management of his affairs in his hands, and
whenever Mrs. Ilbery wanted money, she had it from him.
Dollman and Mrs. Ilbery were, by Ilbery's will, appointed executor
and executrix; but he alone proved the will, on the 21st March,
1840, power being reserved in the usual way for her to prove also.
On the 28th March, Mr. Dollman gave Mrs. Ilbery five or six
cheques, and among others, one for 20*l.*, payable to the plaintiff.
This cheque she paid to the plaintiff, and took his receipt as above
mentioned.

At that time it was supposed that Ilbery's estate was solvent. It   [3]
turned out to be otherwise; and Dollman, who was engaged with
him in the adventure to China, had become bankrupt.

The question left to the jury was, whether the 20*l.* was paid on
the executorship account, or on the account of Mrs. Ilbery only,
and in discharge of that debt which (on both sides, as well as
in the learned Judge's opinion) was taken to have been due from her.

The jury found that it was paid on the executorship account, and
gave their verdict for the plaintiff for 19*l.* 9*s.*, the price of the meat
supplied between the day of Mr. Ilbery's death, and the arrival of
the intelligence of it. A rule having been obtained in Michaelmas
Term to show cause why that verdict should not be set aside, and
a new trial had, on the ground that the defendant was not liable
for the meat supplied after, but before she had any knowledge of,
her husband's death (1).

> *Hindmarch* (*Jervis* was with him) showed cause in the vacation
> after last Hilary Term:

There is no question here as to the appropriation of payments,
as the jury have found that the 20*l.* was paid on the executorship

(1) This point was not made at the trial, and therefore there could be no
motion for a nonsuit.

SMOUT
v.
ILBERY.

account. The only question is, whether the defendant (the widow) is liable for meat supplied to her from the time of her husband's death, until it became known in this country. It will be said on the other side, that the widow is not liable for meat supplied before the news of his death arrived, because she did not contract as his widow on her own account, but on her husband's credit. To support that proposition, it will be incumbent on the defendant to make out that the executor is liable, but that she cannot do, for the contrary was expressly held in *Blades* v. *Free* (1). * * If a man supplies goods to another, and he has them and uses them, the law will imply a promise by him to pay for them.

[5]

(ALDERSON, B. : The question is this, whether, where an agent contracts in the name of a principal, and it turns out afterwards that there is no principal, and there is no fraud in the case, the agent is liable as the principal. That is distinguishable from the case where he knows he has no principal, as in *Polhill* v. *Walter* (2). This question is a good deal discussed in Story on Agency, 226, 227, where the author seems to think that it may be taken that the party who makes the contract undertakes that he has a principal ; but that, he says, would be the subject of a special action.)

That point was not taken at the trial. In order to make the agent liable as principal, it is not necessary to import fraud into the case.

(ALDERSON, B. : Mr. Justice Story says (3), " There is no doubt of the personal liability of the agent in all cases where he falsely affirms that he has authority, as he does when he signs the instrument as agent of his principal, and knows that he has no authority. But another question has been made, whether he is liable when he supposes that he has authority, and he has none : as, for example, when he misconstrues the instrument conferring authority on him ; or where the instrument conferring the authority turns out to be a forgery, and he supposed it to be genuine. In *Polhill* v. *Walter*, Lord TENTERDEN, in delivering the opinion of the Court, seems to have thought that the right of action was founded solely upon there being an affirmation of authority, when the party knew it to be false ; and that therefore,

(1) 32 R. R. 620 (9 B. & C. 167 ; 4   (3) Pages 226, 227, note 3 (cf. 9th
Man. & Ry. 282).   ed. 312, 313).
(2) 37 R. R. 344 (3 B. & Ad. 114).

if the party acted under the authority of a forged instrument, supposing it to be genuine, he would not be responsible. But there is great reason to doubt this doctrine; for if a person represents himself as having authority *to do an act when he has not, and the other side is drawn into a contract with him, and the contract becomes void for want of such authority, the damage is the same to the party who confided in such representation, whether the party making it acted with a knowledge of its falsity, or not. In short, he undertakes for the truth of his representation." And then he adds, "In cases where a person executes an instrument in the name of another, without authority, there is some diversity of judicial opinion as to the form of action in which the agent is to be made liable for the breach of duty. In England it is held that the suit must be by a special action on the case: *Polhill* v. *Walter*.")

It is not necessary to import fraud into the case, to render the agent liable. If a party says, "I am agent of A. B.," he undertakes that he is so. The defendant must be taken to have held out to the plaintiff that she had authority to bind some person; and if that was untrue, she is herself bound. * * In *Thomson* v. *Davenport* (1), where at the time of making a contract of sale, the party buying the goods represented that he was buying them on account of persons resident in Scotland, but did not mention their names, and the seller did not inquire who they were, but afterwards debited the party who purchased the goods; it was held that the seller might afterwards sue the principals for the *price. There the vendor actually credited the agent, and yet the principal was held liable. The general principle is, that the law creates an implied contract from the receipt of the goods.

(ALDERSON, B.: Here each party thought the husband was responsible.)

That can make no difference, for it is clear that there could be no contract between the plaintiff and the dead man; and there was no contract by the executor with the plaintiff. * * *

Erle, in support of the rule:

The contract in this case was a continuing contract, which the parties, in *Blades* v. *Free*, failed to make out. This was a course of dealing which was continued in consequence of, and as part of,

(1) 32 R. R. 578 (9 B. & C. 78; 4 Man. & Ry. 110).

Marginal notes:

SMOUT
v.
ILBERY.

[*6]

[*7]

the former contract. An agent ought not to be held liable where he enters into a contract as agent, *bonâ fide* supposing himself to have authority, when it turns out that he had none, through an event which had happened, but of which he was not cognizant, and had no means of knowing. The evidence here was, that goods were supplied by the plaintiff to the husband during his residence here, and were afterwards continued to be supplied to his wife after he left this country; there is clearly no implied *contract arising from this state of things, that she would pay for them. Suppose the case of the husband and wife having both gone abroad, and having left a housekeeper in charge of the house and the children, and meat is supplied to the house, and the husband and wife are both drowned, is the housekeeper to be liable, because she ordered the meat for the use of the house?

[*8]

(ALDERSON, B. : In the same way it may be said, if a bachelor leaves a housekeeper in possession of his house, and goes abroad, and dies, is the housekeeper to be liable?)

In *Polhill* v. *Walter*, there was the making of a representation which the party making it knew to be untrue. If Ilbery had not died, he would have been clearly liable, and the account was in his name. As to the argument of there being an implied contract, that merely amounts to this, that a party to whom goods are delivered is liable for them; but that is where there is nothing to show that any other person was responsible. The case of *Blades* v. *Free* has nothing to do with the present.

Cur. adv. vult.

The judgment of the COURT was now delivered by—

ALDERSON, B. :

This case was argued at the sittings after last Hilary Term, before my brothers Gurney, Rolfe, and myself. The facts were shortly these. The defendant was the widow of a Mr. Ilbery, who died abroad; and the plaintiff, during the husband's lifetime, had supplied, and after his death had continued to supply, goods for the use of the family in England. The husband left England for China in March, 1839, and died on the 14th day of October, in that year. The news of his death first arrived in England on the 13th day of March, 1840; and the only question now remaining for the decision of the Court is, whether the defendant was liable for the goods supplied after her husband's death, and before it was possible that *the knowledge of that fact should be communicated to her.   There was no doubt that such knowledge was communicated to her as soon as it was possible ; and that the defendant had paid into Court sufficient to cover all the goods supplied to the family by the plaintiff subsequently to the 13th March, 1840.

We took time to consider this question, and to examine the authorities on this subject, which is one of some difficulty. The point, how far an agent is personally liable who, having in fact no authority, professes to bind his principal, has on various occasions been discussed.   There is no doubt that in the case of a fraudulent misrepresentation of his authority, with an intention to deceive, the agent would be personally responsible.   But independently of this, which is perfectly free from doubt, there seem to be still two other classes of cases, in which an agent who without actual authority makes a contract in the name of his principal, is personally liable, even where no proof of such fraudulent intention can be given. First, where he has no authority, and knows it, but nevertheless makes the contract as having such authority.   In that case, on the plainest principles of justice, he is liable.   For he induces the other party to enter into the contract on what amounts to a misrepresentation of a fact peculiarly within his own knowledge ; and it is but just, that he who does so should be considered as holding himself out as one having competent authority to contract, and as guaranteeing the consequences arising from any want of such authority.   But there is a third class, in which the Courts have held, that where a party making the contract as agent *bonâ fide* believes that such authority is vested in him, but has in fact no such authority, he is still personally liable.   In these cases, it is true, the agent is not actuated by any fraudulent motives; nor has he made any statement which he knows to be untrue.   But still his liability depends on the same principles as before.   It is a wrong, differing only *in degree, but not in its essence, from the former case, to state as true what the individual making such statement does not know to be true, even though he does not know it to be false, but believes, without sufficient grounds, that the statement will ultimately turn out to be correct.   And if that wrong produces injury to a third person, who is wholly ignorant of the grounds on which such belief of the supposed agent is founded, and who has relied on the correctness of his assertion, it is equally just that he who makes such assertion should be personally liable for its consequences.

On examination of the authorities, we are satisfied that all the

SMOUT
v.
ILBERY.

cases in which the agent has been held personally responsible, will be found to arrange themselves under one or other of these three classes. In all of them it will be found, that he has either been guilty of some fraud, has made some statement which he knew to be false, or has stated as true what he did not know to be true, omitting at the same time to give such information to the other contracting party, as would enable him equally with himself to judge as to the authority under which he proposed to act.

Of the first, it is not necessary to cite any instance. *Polhill* v. *Walter* (1) is an instance of the second; and the cases where the agent never had any authority to contract at all, but believed, that he had, as when he acted on a forged warrant of attorney, which he thought to be genuine, and the like, are instances of the third class. To these may be added those cited by Mr. Justice Story, in his book on Agency, p. 226, note 8. The present case seems to us to be distinguishable from all these authorities. Here the agent had in fact full authority originally to contract, and did contract in the name of the principal. There is no ground for saying, that in

[*11]

representing her authority *as continuing, she did any wrong whatever. There was no *mala fides* on her part—no want of due diligence in acquiring knowledge of the revocation—no omission to state any fact within her knowledge relating to it, and the revocation itself was by the act of God. The continuance of the life of the principal was, under these circumstances, a fact equally within the knowledge of both contracting parties. If, then, the true principle derivable from the cases is, that there must be some wrong or omission of right on the part of the agent, in order to make him personally liable on a contract made in the name of his principal, it will follow that the agent is not responsible in such a case as the present. And to this conclusion we have come. We were, in the course of the argument, pressed with the difficulty, that if the defendant be not personally liable, there is no one liable on this contract at all; for *Blades* v. *Free* (2) has decided, that in such a case the executors of the husband are not liable. This may be so: but we do not think that if it be so, it affords to us a sufficient ground for holding the defendant liable. In the ordinary case of a wife who makes a contract in her husband's lifetime, for which the husband is not liable, the same consequence follows. In that case, as here, no one is liable upon the contract so made.

(1) 37 R. R. 344 (3 B. & Ad. 114).

(2) 32 R. R. 620 (9 B. & C. 167; 4 Man. & Ry. 282).

Our judgment, on the present occasion, is founded on general principles applicable to all agents; but we think it right also to advert to the circumstance, that this is the case of a married woman, whose situation as a contracting party is of a peculiar nature. A person who contracts with an ordinary agent, contracts with one capable of contracting in his own name; but he who contracts with a married woman knows that she is in general incapable of making any contract by which she is personally bound (1). The contract, therefore, made with the husband by her *instrumentality, may be considered as equivalent to one made by the husband exclusively of the agent. Now, if a contract were made on the terms, that the agent, having a determinable authority, bound his principal, but expressly stipulated that he should not be personally liable himself, it seems quite reasonable that, in the absence of all *mala fides* on the part of the agent, no responsibility should rest upon him: and, as it appears to us, a married woman, situated as the defendant was in this case, may fairly be considered as an agent so stipulating for herself; and on this limited ground, therefore, we think she would not be liable under such circumstances as these.

For these reasons, we are of opinion that the rule for a new trial must be absolute; but as the point was not taken at Nisi Prius, we think the costs should abide the event of the new trial.

Rule absolute accordingly.

SMOUT
v.
ILBERY.

[*12]

STEPHENS *v.* HILL.

(10 Meeson & Welsby, 28—35; S. C. 11 L. J. Ex. 329; 1 Dowl. N. S. 669;
6 Jur. 585.)

Where an attorney has been guilty of misconduct in the course of a cause, the Court will grant a rule calling on him to show cause why his name should not be struck off the roll, even although the matter complained of may amount to an indictable offence; but the Court will not, under such circumstances, call upon him to answer the matters of an affidavit.

The affidavits to ground an application to strike an attorney off the roll for misconduct in a cause, may be intitled in the cause, though judgment has been obtained in it.

1842.
May 24.
——
Exch. of Pleas.
[28]

LUDLOW, Serjt., in Easter Term, obtained a rule calling upon the defendant's attorney in this cause to show cause why he should not be struck off the roll of attorneys, or be prohibited from

(1) But see now the Married Women's Property Act, 1882 (45 & 46 Vict. c. 75), s. 1 (2).—A. C.

STEPHENS
v.
HILL.

practising in this Court. It appeared from the affidavits in support of
the application, that the action was for the breach of a warranty of the
soundness of a horse, and the defendant, by his pleas, denied both
the warranty and the unsoundness. The evidence of the warranty
consisted of two letters, addressed by the defendant to the plaintiff,
which the defendant's attorney, on the usual notice and summons
being served on him, refused to admit. In order to prove that the
letters were in the defendant's handwriting, a person named Jackson,
an intimate friend of the defendant, was subpœnaed, and he
informed the defendant and his attorney of the circumstance, who
both endeavoured to persuade him, by threats and promises, not to
prove the handwriting. The defendant's attorney subpœnaed two
persons of the names of Cook and Cooper, who resided in the same
village with Jackson, in Yorkshire, and on the road from thence to
Gloucester, where the cause was to be tried, a conversation took
place between them and the defendant's attorney, as to the possibility of getting Jackson out of the way, the defendant's attorney
saying that Cook was the only person who had sufficient influence
over him for that purpose. Both Cook and Cooper, after their
arrival at Gloucester, urged Jackson to leave the place, and the
defendant's attorney offered him anything to do so, stating that his
evidence was the only thing he feared. On the evening previous to
the trial of the cause, Cooper went to the inn where the plaintiff's
witnesses were staying, and, under the pretence of taking a walk,
brought Jackson to the house where the defendant's attorney and

[*29]

Cook lodged. *The defendant's attorney and Cook then united in
urging Jackson to leave Gloucester on the following morning early,
and, after much persuasion, he at length consented. It was then
arranged that Cook should start with him to Birmingham, there to
await the arrival of the defendant's attorney, and, upon Cook's
representation that he would not be instrumental in procuring
Jackson's departure, unless the attorney indemnified the latter
from the consequences that might result from his absence, the
defendant's attorney gave Jackson the following guarantee:

"I hereby undertake to indemnify Mr. John Jackson for any
damage he may sustain or be put to, by reason of his going away
from Gloucester, as he is not a material witness in the case
Stephens v. *Hill.* Dated this 6th of August, 1841.

"JOHN WHITEHEAD,
"Solicitor for defendant.

"Witness, THOMAS COOK."

Cook and Jackson accordingly went to Birmingham early the
following morning.   The plaintiff's attorney having, before the
cause was called on, discovered that Jackson was gone, charged
the defendant's attorney with having sent him off, and threatened
to call him as a witness to prove the defendant's handwriting, and
at the same time served him with a *subpœna*.   The plaintiff's
counsel, in opening the case to the jury, commented in strong
language upon the conduct of the defendant's attorney, declaring
his intention to examine him as to the handwriting, whereupon
the defendant's counsel said he was instructed to admit that the
letters were written by the defendant's authority, but to deny they
were in his handwriting.   The plaintiff thereupon obtained a
verdict.

The affidavits on which this application was founded being intitled
in the cause *Stephens* v. *Hill,*

Wortley and *Keating,* on showing cause, took a preliminary
*objection that the affidavits were improperly intitled; that judg-   [*30]
ment having been long since given in the cause, the Court was
functus officio with respect to it, there being no such cause in the
Court; and that, the application not being a matter affecting the
cause, or the parties, but directed personally against the attorney,
they ought to have been intitled " in the matter of &c."

(ALDERSON, B.: It relates to the conduct of the cause.   Because
judgment has been given, it is not therefore out of Court.   The
affidavits are properly intitled.)

Then, as to the merits of the application, the Court will not
exercise its summary jurisdiction over an attorney, where the
misconduct charged amounts to an indictable offence.   The charge
here made, if true, amounts to a conspiracy, for which the attorney
may be indicted; and if he be indicted, the judgment of the
Court on this application might prejudice him on his trial.   The
complainant ought to resort in the first instance to his remedy by
indictment, and if the attorney were convicted, the Court might
then properly interfere.

(LORD ABINGER, C. B.: The Court will not grant a rule calling
upon the attorney to answer the matters of the affidavit in such a
case, but they will grant a rule to show cause why he should not
be struck off the roll.)

STEPHENS
v.
HILL.

STEPHENS
v.
HILL.

Although the Court will not call upon the attorney to answer the matters of the affidavit, yet if he does not do so the consequence would be that he would be struck off the roll. Such a distinction has never been recognised, and the position contended for was acted upon by the Court of Queen's Bench yesterday in the case of *Ex parte Cain, Harding* v. *Lee* (1). The Court there decided that, inasmuch as a portion of the charge would not affect the attorney in an indictable manner, they would enter into that; but said that had it been otherwise they would not have done so.

[*31]

   (ALDERSON, B.: *Then, according to the rule now contended for, the more serious the offence of the attorney, the longer he is to remain on the roll; he is to be left on the roll because he sets up that he has been guilty of an indictable offence ?)

No; but where the charge is indictable, it is incumbent on the Court not to prejudice the case upon affidavit.

   (ALDERSON, B.: Suppose nobody prosecutes ?)

If the Court punish the attorney summarily, the probability of there being no prosecution is increased, which is against public policy. The defendant's attorney is not an attorney of this Court.

   Ludlow, Serjt., in support of the rule, was stopped by the COURT.

LORD ABINGER, C. B.:

I never understood that an attorney might not be struck off the roll for misconduct in a cause in which he was the attorney, merely because the offence imputed to him was of such a nature that he might have been indicted for it. So long as I have known Westminster Hall, I never heard of such a rule as that; but in the case of applications calling upon an attorney to answer the matters of an affidavit, I have known Lord KENYON and also Lord ELLEN-BOROUGH frequently say, you cannot have a rule for that purpose, because the misconduct you impute to the man is indictable; but you may have one to strike him off the roll. Now an attorney who has been guilty of cheating his client, or the opposite party, in such a manner as to render himself indictable, is unfit to be allowed to

(1) 4 Jur. 220.

remain on the roll, or to practise in any Court; and I see no
objection, on principle, to the Court's removing him at once from
it. If, indeed, he were called on to answer the matters of an
affidavit, he would, by not complying, be guilty of a contempt for
which he might be punished by attachment, and if the offence
imputed to him were of an indictable nature, it would be most
unjust to *compel him to do so; for which reason a rule to answer [*32]
the matters of an affidavit is never granted in such a case, but only
a rule to strike him off the roll, which gives him a full opportunity
of clearing himself from the imputation, if he can, while, on the
other hand, it does not compel him to criminate himself. There
was a case in the Court of Queen's Bench (1), where a motion of
this nature was made by *Sir John Campbell*, and in which Lord
DENMAN states the distinction between applications to answer the
matters of an affidavit and to strike off the roll, in the same
manner I am now doing; although, unless that case is looked at
with attention, it might be taken to go further, and be considered
an authority against this rule: and the precise nature of the case
and ground of the motion are not given in the report. If, indeed,
a case should occur where an attorney has been guilty of some
professional misconduct for which the Court by its summary
jurisdiction might compel him to do justice, and at the same time
has been guilty of something indictable in itself, but not arising
out of the cause, the Court would not inquire into that with a view
of striking him off the roll, but would leave the party aggrieved to
his remedy by a criminal prosecution. I believe the first case to
be found of proceedings taken by the Court against an attorney for
something done by him in the way of his profession, is to be found
in a case in Strange's Reports (2), where an attorney having received
some deeds in his professional capacity, the Court of Queen's
Bench ordered him to re-deliver the deeds to the parties entitled to
them, saying that they would oblige all attornies to perform any
trust which might be reposed in them in virtue of the confidence
which the character of attorney produced in the mind of the client.
Ever since that time, applications of a similar nature have been
very *common in all cases where an attorney in his professional [*33]
capacity has received money, for which, although he might be
made accountable in a civil action, the Court will compel him to do
summary justice, without putting the client to the necessity of

(1) Referring to an *Anonymous* case, (2) *Strong* v. *Howe*, 1 Stra. 621.
5 B. & Ad. 1088.

bringing one. But in all cases where an attorney abuses the process of the Court of which he is an officer, and his proceedings are of such a nature as tend to defeat justice in the very cause in which he is engaged professionally, I never heard that, because by possibility he may thereby have exposed himself to be indicted as a cheat or for a conspiracy, he is to be permitted to remain on the roll; and if the cases in the Queen's Bench be carefully examined, it will be found that no such rule exists. Such a rule would be extremely injurious; for in no case could any remedy be had against the attorney, unless the client would first prosecute him to conviction, until which time he could not be struck off the roll or prevented from practising. Where, indeed, the attorney is indicted for some matter not connected with the practice of his profession of an attorney, that also is a ground for striking him off the roll, although in that case it cannot be done until after conviction by a jury. Now, with respect to the merits of the case before us, I cannot conceive how any attorney employed to prosecute or defend a suit in a court of justice can be justified in using any influence, directly or indirectly, for the purpose of preventing a witness who has been subpœnaed by his adversary from coming forward to give evidence. The present charge is therefore one of a very serious nature, as the proceeding complained of would, if unchecked, be an easy way for any attorney to win his causes; and is it to be said that no remedy can be had unless he is first indicted, and that the Court has no power at once to strike him off the roll? If an indictment is to be first preferred, the point at issue in it might, from its very nature, be one of which a jury would not be the best judges, and more proper to be determined by the Court, who are always

[*34]   the *fittest tribunal to decide on complaints of technical misconduct, and to determine not only the degree of severity which ought to be resorted to, but the proper cases for the exercise of that mercy which they are ever ready to extend where they see just grounds for it. Now, what is the present case? The attorney goes down to the Assizes where his client's cause has been put down in the list for trial on a certain day, on which he gives an indemnity to a witness relied upon by the opposite party to prove some matter in the cause, to save him harmless if he will disobey the writ of *subpœna* and absent himself. I do not go into the question of conspiracy which has been raised in this case; I treat it as if the indemnity were given to the witness by the attorney himself alone—an indemnity which he himself admits to be in his handwriting. As,

however, the man is not an attorney of this Court, all we can do is STEPHENS
to prohibit his practising here until the pleasure of the Court in *v.*
which he was admitted shall be known; and that branch of this HILL.
rule must therefore be made absolute.

ALDERSON, B.:

The question in this case is, whether the attorney has so misconducted himself in his character of an attorney, as to be an unfit
person to remain upon the roll.　I am by no means persuaded that
the letters were not in the handwriting of the defendant: but even
if they were not, and the testimony of Jackson was immaterial, the
defendant's attorney had no right to say who was or who was not a
material witness for the plaintiff.　If such a pretext were admitted,
it would be very easy for an attorney to frame an excuse for
sending away his opponent's witnesses, and afford a ready recipe
for obtaining a verdict.　To procure the absence of any witness is
gross misconduct in the course of a cause; and whether he may
be indicted or not, in my mind, makes no difference.　If persons
are to be accredited by the Court, it is our duty to watch over and
control their conduct; and where a man behaves in *such a way   [*35]
as this person has done, he ought to be no longer accredited.

GURNEY, B.:

There is a manifest distinction between a rule to answer the
matters of an affidavit, and to strike an attorney off the roll.　The
Court will not punish a man by imprisonment because he refuses
to criminate himself.　The rule here is in the proper form.

ROLFE, B.:

Unless there is some positive rule to prevent the Court from
interfering in such a case as this, it is our imperative duty to do
so.　The question therefore is, whether there is any authority to
show that we are precluded from entertaining this application,
because the offence is indictable.　Upon that point I at first
entertained some doubt.　It is observable, however, that the
simple act complained of is the sending of the witness away;
and this is rendered indictable, simply in consequence of its having
been done in concert with other persons.　We need not, therefore,
necessarily deal with that portion of the charge which is indictable;
but even were we compelled to do so, I agree in the distinction
which has been taken, and think we might entertain this motion.

The only authority I have been able to find is a case in Cowper (1), in which Lord MANSFIELD observes, "that having been convicted of felony, we think the defendant is not a fit person to be an attorney." There the defendant had been convicted of stealing a guinea, from which it is evident that it was not an act connected with his character of an attorney, but something perfectly collateral to it. If the Court will interfere in such a case, *à fortiori* they will do so in a case where the misconduct imputed is committed in the conduct of a cause.

Rule absolute, to prohibit the attorney from practising in this Court.

BARKER *v.* BIRT.

(10 Meeson & Welsby, 61—64; S. C. 11 L. J. Ex. 375; 6 Jur. 736.)

A Company having contracted a debt with the plaintiff, and the debt not being paid, he laid an attachment on money of theirs in the hands of bankers. While the attachment was in force, the defendant, representing himself to be a director of the Company, called on the plaintiff's attorney for the purpose of making an arrangement about the debt, when it was agreed that the following letter should be written by the defendant to the plaintiff, which was accordingly done: " As director of the B. W. Company, I have to request you will accept the sum of 50*l.* on account of your claim of 116*l.* 19*s.* 7*d.* against the Company ; and in consideration of your withdrawing the attachment against the funds of the Company, I agree on the part of myself and on behalf of the other directors, to pay you the balance of 66*l.* 19*s.* 7*d.* &c. on the 27th of August next:" Held, that this letter, coupled with the above facts, was evidence of an account stated ; and that it was no answer to show that the defendant was not a member of the Company when the original debt was contracted.

ASSUMPSIT for work and labour and materials, for money paid, for interest, and on an account stated. Plea, *non assumpsit.*

At the trial before Lord Abinger, C. B., at the London sittings after last Hilary Term, it appeared that the plaintiff was an advertising agent, to whom the British Waterproofing Company had incurred a debt of 116*l.* 17*s.* 6*d.* for advertisements, up to the month of July, 1839, when they ceased to employ him. The defendant did not become a member of the Company till the ensuing month of December, when he was also elected a director. In April, 1840, the plaintiff attached the funds of the Company in the hands of their bankers, whereupon the defendant called upon him, introducing himself as a director, and proposed that the

(1) *Ex parte Brounsall,* Cowp. 829.

attachment should be withdrawn upon the payment of 50*l.*, and the defendant's giving him the following undertaking, which was assented to:

"LONDON, 27th of April, 1840.

"SIR,—As a director of the British Waterproofing Company, I have to request you will accept the sum of 50*l.* on *account of your claim of 116*l.* 17*s.* 6*d.* against the directors of the Company, for advertisements; and I agree on my own part, and on behalf of the other directors of the Company, to pay you the balance of 66*l.* 17*s.* 6*d.*, with interest at 5*l.* per cent. per annum from this day, on the 27th day of August next.—I am, Sir, &c.

"To Mr. C. BARKER."   "W. BIRT."

[*62]

The 50*l.* was paid, and the attachment withdrawn, and this action was brought to recover a portion of the balance of 66*l.* 17*s.* 6*d.*, which had not been paid in accordance with the agreement. The above undertaking was put in and read at the trial, as evidence of an account stated. *Crowder*, for the defendant, proposed to show that the defendant was not a member of the Company at the time when the work was done, and contended that the above letter must be considered as a guarantee or special agreement to be answerable for the debt of another, and was not evidence of an account stated; and that, to render the defendant liable, a special count ought to have been inserted. The learned Judge, however, was of opinion that the promise contained in it, coupled with the fact of the attachment having been withdrawn, was evidence from which an account stated might be inferred, and directed the jury accordingly, who found for the plaintiff for the amount claimed.

Crowder having obtained a rule to show cause why there should not be a new trial on the ground of misdirection,

Martin now showed cause:

The letter, coupled with the other facts proved, was good evidence of an account stated. This document does not amount to a guarantee, but was merely evidence of the terms on which the defendant became a partner and took upon himself the debts of the Company, and was evidence to go to the jury of an account stated. It begins by requesting the plaintiff to accept the sum of 50*l.* *on account of his claim on the Company, and the writer agrees on his own part and on behalf of the other directors to pay the balance. There

[*63]

BARKER
v.
BIRT.

is nothing in the nature of a guarantee in that. It is a usual thing for persons coming into a Company to take upon them the debts of the Company. It is ample evidence on the account stated.

Crowder, in support of the rule:

The letter must be taken in conjunction with the evidence that the defendant became a director after the work was done and the debt incurred. The persons who were then members remained liable. This amounted to a special agreement between the parties, for a valid consideration, that if the plaintiff would withdraw the attachment, the defendant would pay the balance; and it ought therefore to have been declared on as such. When a man promises on good consideration to pay the amount of an account found to be due, unconditionally, it is agreed that that would be good evidence to support an account stated, because it is an acknowledgment that a debt is due at the time; but this is an agreement partly written and partly oral, whereby the defendant not only undertakes to pay the debt of other parties, but the promise is in its terms conditional. And the evidence is that the attachment was withdrawn the next day in pursuance of such agreement.

LORD ABINGER, C. B.:

If we take the words of this letter in their obvious meaning, they amount to an acknowledgment that the defendant and his brother directors were debtors to the plaintiff for the amount of the work done, and that he undertakes to pay the balance remaining due. The defendant contends that he is not liable, at least in this form of action, because he was not a member of the Company when the debt was contracted. I do not think he ought to be allowed to say so now, for he has admitted by this letter that he was a member of
[*64] it, and in *consequence of that admission got out of the hands of the bankers the money which the plaintiff would otherwise have had. In my opinion, if a party acknowledges the correctness of a stated account, and in consideration of an agreement to give him time, pays part of the debt, and undertakes to pay the balance, that is evidence of an account stated.

ALDERSON, B.:

Surely this letter is evidence of an account stated. It admits the correctness of the claim upon the Company of which the writer states himself to be a director, and promises, on his own account

and that of the other directors, to pay the balance. Then would
the fact proposed to be proved, that he was not a member at the
time the debt was contracted, be any answer ? I think not.

GURNEY, B. :

The letter contains an admission that a balance is due, and that
the defendant is a director of the Company. Is not that evidence
to show that he has taken this debt upon himself ?

ROLFE, B. concurred.

Rule discharged.

GIBBS v. POTTER.

(10 Meeson & Welsby, 70—75; S. C. 11 L. J. Ex. 376; 6 Jur. 586.)

On a shipment of a cargo from Valparaiso to England, the bill of lading
described the property as " 1,338 hard dollars," which was a coin current at
Valparaiso at the time : Held, that this was a sufficient compliance with the
provisions of the stat. 26 Geo. III. c. 86, s. 3 (1), it being the current coin
of the place where the shipment was made.

Quære, whether that statute is at all applicable to the case of shipments
made in places not subject to the British laws.

CASE. The declaration stated, that the plaintiffs shipped 1,338
hard dollars on board a certain ship belonging to the defendants,
to be by them carried in the said ship from Valparaiso in South
America to Liverpool or London, at the option of the consignees ;
and if at the former port, then to be further conveyed by the
defendants to London by land, saving all casualties arising from
the act of God or the Queen's enemies ; and averred a loss of the
said dollars by negligence on the part of the defendants.

Pleas, first, not guilty ; secondly, that at the time of the said
shipping and lading, the said dollars consisted of *a certain large
quantity of silver, and that the same were feloniously stolen out of
the said ship, without the privity of the defendants, and that neither
the owners nor the shippers thereof inserted in their bill of lading,
or otherwise made, any declaration in writing of the true nature,
quality, and value of the said goods, according to the form of the
statute, &c. Replication, *de injuriâ*.

At the trial before Alderson, B., at the last Spring Assizes for
Surrey, it appeared that the plaintiffs, who were English merchants

(1) Repealed by 17 & 18 Vict. c. 120,   1894 (57 & 58 Vict. c. 60), s. 502.—
s. 4 : see now Merchant Shipping Act,   A. C.

residing at Valparaiso, had there shipped these dollars on board a ship of which the defendants were registered owners, and delivered with them a bill of lading, which merely described them as "1,338 hard dollars." It appeared also from the evidence, that, at the time of the above shipment, hard dollars were current at Valparaiso but not in England; nor were they sold here as bullion, but by weight; and their value in the market was influenced by the rate of exchange between the two countries. The principal value of the dollar in England depended on what it might fetch on being sent abroad. On this state of the evidence, it was objected that the defendants were not liable, the provisions of the 26 Geo. III. c. 86, s. 3, not having been complied with. That statute enacts, that "no master or owner of any ship or vessel shall be subject or liable to answer for or make good to any one or more person or persons, any loss or damage which may happen to any gold, silver, diamonds, watches, jewels, or precious stones, which from and after the passing of this Act shall be shipped, taken in, or put on board any such ship or vessel, by reason or means of any robbery, embezzlement, making away with, or secreting thereof, unless the owner or shipper thereof shall, at the time of shipping the same, insert in his bill of lading, or otherwise declare in writing to the master, owner, or owners of such ship or vessel, the true nature, quality, and value of such gold, silver, diamonds, watches, jewels,

[*72]   or precious stones." *The learned Judge, however, overruled the objection, and directed a verdict for the plaintiffs for the value of the dollars, reserving leave to the defendants to move to enter a verdict on the second issue, on the point made at the trial.

Channell, Serjt., having obtained a rule to show cause accordingly,

Peacock (and *Thesiger* was with him) now showed cause:

First, the dollars were sufficiently described as dollars of the value they obtained according to the currency of the country where they were shipped. * * Secondly, the provision in the statute does not extend to contracts made abroad, and therefore the *lex loci contractus* would apply, and govern the engagement. The shipment was made at Valparaiso, and the contract was entered into there. There is no allegation in the plea that these parties were British subjects, or bound by the English law. There is no evidence of there being any law at Valparaiso which requires the nature, quality, and value of the goods to be described. The plea says, that neither the owners nor the shippers *thereof inserted in the bill of lading the true nature, quality, and value of the goods, according to the form of the statute.   That was an important allegation, which required to be proved, and the defendants ought to have shown that there was such a law at that place, and proved that law as all foreign laws are proved as matters of fact.   There is no allegation that this was a British ship, or that the parties were British subjects, and therefore the parties must be presumed to have contracted according to the law of the country where the contract was made.

GIBBS
v.
POTTER.
[*73]

Petersdorff, in support of the rule:

There is a condition precedent to the recovery of the price of articles of this nature, which have been stolen, that the value should be stated in the manner required by the laws of this country. * * *

LORD ABINGER, C. B.:

I am clearly of opinion that the verdict was right, and ought not to be disturbed.   Even supposing the Act does apply to the case of shipments made in foreign countries at all, it can only apply so far as to require the declaration of value to be made in the current coin of the country where the shipment is made ; for how absurd would it be for us in England to make a law to compel a Spaniard, who might have occasion to ship dollars *at Valparaiso, to declare on the back of his bill of lading the value of those dollars in English currency.   Such a law would manifestly be most absurd.   The object of the Act manifestly was to impose on the shipper the *onus* of giving notice to the shipowner of the nature of the goods entrusted to him to carry, and that is perfectly satisfied by the value being declared in hard dollars, or whatever else the current coin may be of the place where the shipment is made.   But I have great doubts as to the extent of the operation of this Act.   The present action is, it is true, brought on an English bill of lading, and so far may be distinguishable ; but suppose the case of a contract like this, transitory in its very nature, made in a foreign nature in a foreign port, between two parties who are foreigners, how absurd would it be for us to make laws regulating the mode in which they should transmit goods from one country to another !   At most, the statute could only apply where the shipment is made to England, and in which case a declaration of value according to the current coin

[*74]

of the country would be sufficient. This rule must therefore be discharged.

ALDERSON, B. :

I am still of the opinion I expressed at Nisi Prius in this case, that the second issue on this record ought to be found for the plaintiffs. There can be no doubt that the declaration of the value of the goods must be made at the place of shipment; and then comes the question, whether it is sufficient for the shipper to make that declaration according to the current coin of that place ; and I think that in holding the affirmative of that proposition, we shall give more effect to the provisions of this Act of Parliament, because the shipowner, who must know the value of the current coin at that place, is thereby enabled to form the most accurate judgment as to the degree of care to be bestowed on the goods entrusted to him. Suppose, instead of dollars, the articles shipped were jewels or
[*75]   *precious stones, would it not be by far the best plan to state how much they were worth in the coin of Valparaiso than in the coin of England, where their value would be in a great degree matter of speculation? The question, in short, is this ; does the Act require the value of the goods to be stated according to their actual value at the place of shipment, or according to a speculative value which they may possess on their arrival in another country ? The latter arrangement would be a very bad one.

GURNEY, B., concurred.

ROLFE, B. :

I am of the same opinion. At the time this rule was granted, I entertained some doubt on the point, owing to this consideration, that supposing a man at Valparaiso were to ship 10,000 sovereigns at that port for England, would it not be sufficient in his bill of lading to say that the shipment consisted of 10,000 sovereigns, without adding their value in dollars ? But I think that doubt arose from a misapprehension as to the words used in the Act, which does not say that you must state the money value of the goods shipped, but that you must state their "true nature, quality, and value," which means, not that you must state the actual true quality or value of the articles in money, which in many cases might be impossible, but that so far as the nature of the thing allows you to do so, you will give the value of the goods or precious stones as

nearly as you can. I do not, however, say that the description
might not be good either way, either describing them as being of
the value of so many pounds sterling, or as is the case here, 1,338
hard dollars only.

Rule discharged (1).

GIBBS
v.
POTTER.

BURTON *v.* HENSON AND KESBEY (2).

(10 Meeson & Welsby, 105—108; S. C. 11 L. J. Ex. 348.)

A parish clerk having been dismissed from his office by the rector, though
irregularly, and another appointed, the former entered the church before
Divine service had commenced, and took possession of the clerk's seat:
Held, that the churchwardens were justified in removing him from the
clerk's desk, and also out of the church, if they had reasonable grounds for
believing that he would offer interruption during the celebration of Divine
service.

1842.
June 2.

*Exch. of
Pleas.*
[105]

THIS was an action of assault, to which the defendants pleaded
not guilty by statute.

At the trial before Gurney, B., at the last Assizes at Chelmsford,
it appeared that the defendants were the churchwardens of the
parish of Northweald Bassett, in the county of Essex, and that the
plaintiff had been appointed clerk of the same parish in 1806. He
had continued to fill that office till the 1st July, 1841, when he was
dismissed by the vicar under the following circumstances: He had
originally been appointed at an annual salary of 5*l.* 5*s.*; but this
having been reduced, high words had ensued between the plaintiff,
the churchwardens, and the vicar; and although he officiated at
the clerk's desk during the sacrament, the plaintiff declined to
receive it, as he was on bad terms with these parties. An application
having subsequently been made to the Bishop of London by the
vicar, on the 15th June, 1841, the plaintiff was prevailed upon to
sign an apology for his absence and his disrespectful expressions,
with a promise of more becoming demeanour for the future. A few
days afterwards, in a conversation with the parish schoolmaster
respecting the terms of this document, and in answer to an observation made by the latter, that the vicar had said he had read it to
the plaintiff as loud as ever he read a lesson, the plaintiff said, that

(1) A cross rule had been obtained,
if necessary, on the part of the plaintiffs, for leave to enter judgment *non
obstante veredicto*, in the event of the
defendants' rule being made absolute,
on the ground that the Act did not at
all apply to the shipments made in

places not governed by British law:
but that point, in the result, it became
unnecessary to discuss.

(2) Comm. *Taylor* v. *Timson* (1888)
20 Q. B. D. 671, 678, 57 L. J. Q. B.
216.—A. C.

BURTON
c.
HENSON.

[*106]

if he said so he was a liar. The vicar, for this expression, dismissed him without summons, and one Holly was appointed in his place; and on Sunday, the 25th July, when the church doors were opened for Divine service, and the parishioners were assembling, the plaintiff came into the church, and proceeding to the clerk's seat, which was then occupied by Holly, attempted to enter it by the door, but was prevented from so doing by one of the rural police of the name of Pelby placing his back against the door. The defendants *thereupon desired him not to take this seat, but the plaintiff immediately entered an adjoining pew, and thence climbed over into the clerk's desk and took his seat there. The defendants then desired Pelby to remove him, which he did by force, and led him out of the church. Shortly after the service had commenced, however, he returned, and again attempted to enter the seat; but upon some communication being made to him by the defendants, he left the church. This forcible removal from the clerk's seat was the assault complained of. These facts having been proved at the trial, the learned Judge was of opinion that the dismissal was illegal, and therefore the plaintiff was entitled to a verdict, which the jury accordingly found for him, with one farthing damages. Leave was however reserved to the defendants to move to enter a verdict, if the Court should be of opinion, either that the removal was lawful, or that, under the circumstances, a dismissal *de facto* was sufficient to justify what the defendants had done.

Thesiger having, in Easter Term, obtained a rule accordingly,

Peacock (and *Shee*, Serjt., was with him) showed cause:

The learned Judge's direction was correct. The plaintiff having been appointed parish clerk, was in office for life, or as long as he behaved himself properly, and until he was legally dismissed. The churchwardens, therefore, had no right to turn him out as long as he continued *de facto* clerk.

(GURNEY, B.: The question is whether the clerk was justified in asserting his right in this indecent manner, and whether the church-wardens had not a right to remove him, under such circumstances.)

The clergyman had improperly dismissed him, and therefore he had a right to occupy the desk appropriated to the use of the clerk.

(ALDERSON, B.: There are authorities to show that the churchwardens have the power to regulate the seats ; here, in defiance of them, the plaintiff climbed over into the desk.)

The desk is the proper and peculiar place for the clerk ; it is especially set *apart for him, and differs from other seats.

107

(LORD ABINGER, C. B. : It is difficult to say that the churchwardens were not authorized to interfere. They could know nothing but that the minister had in fact dismissed him from the office. In the case of a dispute about a pew, the course is to try it by due course of law. Is a person to try such a right by insisting upon sitting there ? And if he finds another person there, and attempts to enter, cannot the churchwardens interfere ? The plaintiff would be in no way injured by being prevented from resorting to such an assertion of his title as this, for he may bring an action for money had and received.)

Although he might maintain such an action, it does not necessarily follow that he may not assert his right in this manner. He holds his seat *virtute officii*, which distinguishes it from the ordinary case of a pew. Besides, even supposing the defendants were justified in removing him from the pew, they had no right to remove him from the church. Perhaps, they might have been justified in taking him out of the church if the interruption had taken place during the performance of Divine service : but this took place before Divine service had commenced. Unless he was creating a disturbance during the service, they had no right to remove him.

Thesiger, in support of the rule, was stopped by the COURT, but in the course of the argument referred to *Reynolds* v. *Monkton* (1), where it was held by ROLFE, B., that churchwardens have a discretionary power to appropriate pews in the church amongst the parishioners, and might remove persons intruding on seats already appropriated.

LORD ABINGER, C. B. :

We think it makes no difference whether the service had actually begun, or was only about to begin, so long as the conduct of the plaintiff was such *as to lead the churchwardens reasonably to suppose that he would offer interruption to the service. The evidence shows that he was likely to create a disturbance. The question is

108

(1) 2 Moo. & Rob. 384.

whether the removal from the church was not at the time a fair exercise of judgment, that if they did not remove him he would create a disturbance. We think it was, and the jury seem to have been of the same opinion in awarding a farthing damages.

ALDERSON, B. :

In Hawkins's Pleas of the Crown, Book 1, c. 63, s. 29, it is laid down that " churchwardens, and, perhaps, private persons, may whip boys playing in church, or pull off the hats of those who obstinately refuse to take them off themselves, or gently lay hands on those who disturb the performance of any part of Divine service, and turn them out of the church." For these positions he quotes 1 Saund. 13, 1 Sid. 301, 3 Keble, 124, and 1 Mod. 168. *Hawe* v. *Planner* (1) is likewise an authority to show that churchwardens may interfere to preserve decorum in the church. Here the congregation were assembling for Divine service, and the defendants only did what was necessary to guard against interruption, and a most unseemly exhibition during its progress ; that they were fully entitled to do.

GURNEY, B., and ROLFE, B., concurred.

Rule absolute.

WINTERBOTTOM *v.* WRIGHT (2).

(10 Meeson & Welsby, 109—116 ; S. C. 11 L. J. Ex. 415.)

A. contracted with the Postmaster-General to provide a mail-coach to convey the mail-bags along a certain line of road ; and B. and others also contracted to horse the coach along the same line. B. and his co-contractors hired C. to drive the coach : Held, that C. could not maintain an action against A. for an injury sustained by him while driving the coach, by its breaking down from latent defects in its construction.

CASE. The declaration stated, that the defendant was a contractor for the supply of mail-coaches, and had in that character contracted for hire and reward with the Postmaster-General, to provide the mail-coach for the purpose of conveying the mail-bags from Hartford, in the county of Chester, to Holyhead : that the defendant, under and by virtue of the said contract, had agreed with the said Postmaster-General that the said mail-coach should, during the said contract, be kept in a fit, proper, safe, and secure state and

(1) 1 Saund. 13 ; 1 Sid. 301. See also Rogers on Ecclesiastical Law, 229.
(2) Foll. in *Collis* v. *Selden* (1868) L. R. 3 C. P. 495, 496, 37 L. J. C. P.
233 ; *Moule* v. *Garrett* (1870) L. R. 5 Ex. 132, 137 ; affd. 7 Ex. 101 : and dist. in *Heaven* v. *Pender* (1883) 11 Q. B. D. 503, 513, 52 L. J. Q. B. 702.—A. C.

condition for the said purpose, and took upon himself, to wit, under
and by virtue of the said contract, the sole and exclusive duty,
charge, care, and burden of the repairs, state, and condition of the
said mail-coach ; and it had become and was the sole and exclusive
duty of the defendant, to wit, under and by virtue of his said
contract, to keep and maintain the said mail-coach in a fit, proper,
safe, and secure state and condition for the purpose aforesaid : that
Nathaniel Atkinson and other persons, having notice of the said
contract, were under contract with the Postmaster-General to
convey the said mail-coach from Hartford to Holyhead, and to
supply horses and coachmen for that purpose, and also, not on any
pretence whatever, to use or employ any other coach or carriage
whatever than such as should be so provided, directed, and appointed
by the Postmaster-General : that the plaintiff, being a mail-coachman, and thereby obtaining his livelihood, and whilst the said
several contracts were in force, having notice thereof, and trusting
to and confiding in the contract made between the defendant and
the Postmaster-General, and believing that the said coach was in a
fit, safe, secure, and proper state and condition for the purpose
aforesaid, and not knowing and having no means of knowing to the
contrary thereof, hired himself to the said Nathaniel Atkinson and
*his co-contractors as mail-coachman, to drive and take the conduct   [*110]
of the said mail-coach, which but for the said contract of the
defendant he would not have done.   The declaration then averred,
that the defendant so improperly and negligently conducted himself,
and so utterly disregarded his aforesaid contract, and so wholly
neglected and failed to perform his duty in this behalf, that heretofore, to wit, on the 8th of August, 1840, whilst the plaintiff, as such
mail-coachman so hired, was driving the said mail-coach from
Hartford to Holyhead, the same coach, being a mail-coach found
and provided by the defendant under his said contract, and the
defendant then acting under his said contract, and having the
means of knowing and then well knowing all the aforesaid premises,
the said mail-coach being then in a frail, weak, infirm, and
dangerous state and condition, to wit, by and through certain latent
defects in the state and condition thereof, and unsafe and unfit for
the use and purpose aforesaid, and from no other cause, circumstance, matter or thing whatsoever, gave way and broke down,
whereby the plaintiff was thrown from his seat, and in consequence
of injuries then received, had become lamed for life.

   To this declaration the defendant pleaded several pleas, to two of

WINTER-
BOTTOM
v.
WRIGHT.

which there were demurrers; but as the Court gave no opinion as to their validity, it is not necessary to state them.

Peacock, who appeared in support of the demurrers, having argued against the sufficiency of the pleas,

Byles, for the defendant, objected that the declaration was bad in substance:

This is an action brought, not against Atkinson and his co-contractors, who were the employers of the plaintiff, but against the person employed by the Postmaster-General, and totally unconnected with them or with the plaintiff. Now it is a general rule, that [*111] *wherever a wrong arises merely out of the breach of a contract, which is the case on the face of this declaration, whether the form in which the action is conceived be *ex contractu* or *ex delicto*, the party who made the contract alone can sue: *Tollit* v. *Sherstone* (1). If the rule were otherwise, and privity of contract were not requisite, there would be no limit to such actions. [He also cited *Priestley* v. [112] *Fowler* (2), *Rapson* v. *Cubitt* (3), and *Witte* v. *Hague* (4).] *Levy* v. *Langridge* (5) will probably be referred to on the other side. But that case was expressly decided on the ground that the defendant, who sold the gun by which the plaintiff was injured, although he did not personally contract with the plaintiff, who was a minor, knew that it was bought to be used by him. Here there is no allegation that the defendant knew that the coach was to be driven by the plaintiff. There, moreover, fraud was alleged in the declaration, and found by the jury: and there, too, the cause of injury was a weapon of a dangerous nature, and the defendant was alleged to have had notice of the defect in its construction. Nothing of that sort appears upon this declaration.

Peacock, contrà:

This case is within the principle of the decision in *Levy* v. *Langridge.* Here the defendant entered into a contract with a public officer to supply an article which, if imperfectly constructed, was necessarily dangerous, and which, from its nature and the use for which it was destined, was necessarily to be driven by a coachman. That is sufficient to bring the case within the rule established by *Levy* v. *Langridge.* In that case the contract made by the

(1) 5 M. & W. 283.   (4) 2 Dowl. & Ry. 33.
(2) 49 R. R. 495 (3 M. & W. 1).   (5) 46 R. R. 689, 695 (4 M. & W.
(3) 60 R. R. 873 (9 M. & W. 710).   337).

father of the plaintiff with the defendant was made on behalf of
himself and his family generally, and there was nothing to show
that the defendant was aware even of the existence of the particular
son who was injured.   Suppose a party made a contract with
Government for a supply of muskets, one of which, from its mis-
construction, burst and injured a soldier : there it is clear that the
use of the weapon by a soldier would have been contemplated,
although not by the particular individual who received the injury,
and could it be said, since the decision in *Levy* v. *Langridge*, that
he could not maintain an action against the contractor ?   So, if a
coachmaker, *employed to put on the wheels of a carriage, did it so   [*113]
negligently that one of them flew off, and a child of the owner were
thereby injured, the damage being the natural and immediate consequence of his negligence, he would surely be responsible.   So, if a
party entered into a contract to repair a church, a workhouse, or other
public building, and did it so insufficiently that a person attending
the former, or a pauper in the latter, were injured by the falling of
a stone, he could not maintain an action against any other person
than the contractor ; but against him he must surely have a remedy.
It is like the case of a contractor who negligently leaves open a
sewer, whereby a person passing along the street is injured.   It is
clear that no action could be maintained against the Postmaster-
General : *Hall* v. *Smith* (1), *Humphreys* v. *Mears* (2), *Priestley* v.
Fowler.   But here the declaration alleges the accident to have
happened through the defendant's negligence and want of care.
The plaintiff had no opportunity of seeing that the carriage was
sound and secure.

(ALDERSON, B. : The decision in *Levy* v. *Langridge* proceeds upon
the ground of the knowledge and fraud of the defendant.)

Here also there was fraud : the defendant represented the coach to
be in a proper state for use, and whether he represented that which
was false within his knowledge, or a fact as true which he did not
know to be so, it was equally a fraud in point of law, for which he
is responsible.

LORD ABINGER, C. B. :

I am clearly of opinion that the defendant is entitled to our
judgment.   We ought not to permit a doubt to rest upon this
subject, for our doing so might be the means of letting in upon

(1) 2 Bing. 156.   (2) 1 Man. & Ry. 187.

WINTER-
BOTTOM
v.
WRIGHT.

[*114]

us an infinity of actions. This is an action of the first impression,
and it has been brought in spite of the precautions which were
taken, in the judgment of this Court in the case of *Levy* v.
Langridge, to obviate any notion that such an action *could be
maintained. We ought not to attempt to extend the principle of
that decision, which, although it has been cited in support of this
action, wholly fails as an authority in its favour; for there the gun
was bought for the use of the son, the plaintiff in that action, who
could not make the bargain himself, but was really and substantially
the party contracting. Here the action is brought simply because
the defendant was a contractor with a third person; and it is contended that thereupon he became liable to every body who might
use the carriage. If there had been any ground for such an action,
there certainly would have been some precedent of it; but with the
exception of actions against innkeepers, and some few other persons,
no case of a similar nature has occurred in practice. That is a strong
circumstance, and is of itself a great authority against its maintenance. It is, however, contended, that this contract being made on
the behalf of the public by the Postmaster-General, no action could
be maintained against him, and therefore the plaintiff must have a
remedy against the defendant. But that is by no means a necessary
consequence—he may be remediless altogether. There is no privity
of contract between these parties; and if the plaintiff can sue, every
passenger, or even any person passing along the road, who was
injured by the upsetting of the coach, might bring a similar action.
Unless we confine the operation of such contracts as this to the
parties who entered into them, the most absurd and outrageous
consequences, to which I can see no limit, would ensue. Where a
party becomes responsible to the public, by undertaking a public
duty, he is liable, though the injury may have arisen from the
negligence of his servant or agent. So, in cases of public nuisances,
whether the act was done by the party as a servant, or in any other
capacity, you are liable to an action at the suit of any person who
suffers. Those, however, are cases where the real ground of the
liability is the public duty, or the commission *of the public
nuisance. There is also a class of cases in which the law permits
a contract to be turned into a tort; but unless there has been some
public duty undertaken, or public nuisance committed, they are all
cases in which an action might have been maintained upon the
contract. Thus, a carrier may be sued either in assumpsit or case;
but there is no instance in which a party, who was not privy to the

[*115]

contract entered into with him, can maintain any such action. The plaintiff in this case could not have brought an action on the contract; if he could have done so, what would have been his situation, supposing the Postmaster-General had released the defendant? that would, at all events, have defeated his claim altogether. By permitting this action, we should be working this injustice, that after the defendant had done everything to the satisfaction of his employer, and after all matters between them had been adjusted, and all accounts settled on the footing of their contract, we should subject them to be ripped open by this action of tort being brought against him.

ALDERSON, B. :

I am of the same opinion. The contract in this case was made with the Postmaster-General alone; and the case is just the same as if he had come to the defendant and ordered a carriage, and handed it at once over to Atkinson. If we were to hold that the plaintiff could sue in such a case, there is no point at which such actions would stop. The only safe rule is to confine the right to recover to those who enter into the contract : if we go one step beyond that, there is no reason why we should not go fifty. The only real argument in favour of this action is, that this is a case of hardship; but that might have been obviated, if the plaintiff had made himself a party to the contract. Then it is urged that it falls within the principle of the case of *Levy* v. *Langridge*. But the principle of that case was simply this, that the father having bought the gun for *the very purpose of being used by the plain- [*116] tiff, the defendant made representations by which he was induced to use it. There a distinct fraud was committed on the plaintiff; the falsehood of the representation was also alleged to have been within the knowledge of the defendant who made it, and he was properly held liable for the consequences. How are the facts of that case applicable to those of the present ? Where is the allegation of misrepresentation or fraud in this declaration ? It shows nothing of the kind. Our judgment must therefore be for the defendant.

GURNEY, B., concurred.

ROLFE, B. :

The breach of the defendant's duty, stated in this declaration, is

WINTER-
BOTTOM
v.
WRIGHT.

his omission to keep the carriage in a safe condition; and when we examine the mode in which that duty is alleged to have arisen, we find a statement that the defendant took upon himself, to wit, under and by virtue of the said contract, the sole and exclusive duty, charge, care, and burden of the repairs, state, and condition of the said mail-coach, and during all the time aforesaid, it had become and was the sole and exclusive duty of the defendant, to wit, under and by virtue of his said contract, to keep and maintain the said mail-coach in a fit, proper, safe, and secure state and condition. The duty, therefore, is shown to have arisen solely from the contract; and the fallacy consists in the use of that word "duty." If a duty to the Postmaster-General be meant, that is true; but if a duty to the plaintiff be intended (and in that sense the word is evidently used), there was none. This is one of those unfortunate cases in which there certainly has been *damnum*, but it is *damnum absque injuriâ;* it is, no doubt, a hardship upon the plaintiff to be without a remedy, but by that consideration we ought not to be influenced. Hard cases, it has been frequently observed, are apt to introduce bad law.

Judgment for the defendant.

1842.
June 9.
———
Exch. of
Pleas.
[117]

THE ATTORNEY-GENERAL v. DONALDSON AND OTHERS (1).

(10 Meeson & Welsby, 117—125; S. C. 11 L. J. Ex. 338.)

An information of intrusion stated, that the defendants intruded and made entry on a certain messuage or dwelling-house, situate &c., and being parcel of the Royal Palace of Kensington, then in the occupation of our lady the Queen, and which was in the hands and possession of the Queen in right of her Crown. The defendants pleaded, in the form given by the stat. 23 Hen. VIII. c. 5, s. 11, that they committed the trespasses under the authority of a commission of sewers, for tax assessed by the said commission: Held, on demurrer, that this form of plea was not allowable in an information of intrusion at the suit of the Crown.

A distress cannot be levied for sewers' rates within the precincts of a Royal Palace, occupied as the residence of the Sovereign; and Kensington Palace is within this description.

But *semble,* that the averment in this information did not sufficiently show the Palace to be the residence of the Sovereign.

THIS was an information of intrusion. The information stated, that whereas heretofore, to wit, on &c., a certain messuage or

(1) Cited in *Att.-Gen.* v. *Dakin* (1870)   *Re Bonham* (1879) 10 Ch. D. 595, 601,
L. R. 4 H. L. 338, 354, 39 L. J. Ex.   48 L. J. Bk. 84.—A. C.
113; and *Ex parte Postmaster-General,*

dwelling-house, situate and being in the parish of St. Margaret, A.-G.
v.
DONALDSON. within the liberty of Westminster, in the county of Middlesex, and parcel of the Royal Palace at Kensington, long before then, and at that time in the occupation of our lady the Queen, was, and ought to have been, and of right is, or ought to be, in the hands and possession of our said lady Queen Victoria, as in right of her Crown of Great Britain and Ireland : yet the defendants heretofore, to wit, on &c., with force and arms, in and upon the possession of our said lady the Queen, of and in the premises aforesaid, entered, intruded, and made entry, and remained and continued thereon for a long time, to wit, &c.

Plea, that the trespasses in the information mentioned were committed by the defendants under the authority of a certain commission of sewers of our said sovereign lady the now Queen, before and at the said times when &c., being in full force, for tax assessed by the said commission, and according to the tenor and effect, true intent and meaning, of the several Statutes of Sewers made and then and now in force.   Verification.

Demurrer.   The following were the points of demurrer stated on the part of the *Attorney-General*.   First, that the Queen is not bound by the Statute of Sewers, so far as the same points out the mode of pleading.   Second, that the plea should have set out specially the whole of the grounds upon which the defendants' justification depends.   *Third, that the plea should have set forth [*118] more definitely the commission of sewers, and the assessment under it.

The case was argued in Easter Term (April 26), by

The *Attorney-General* for the Crown :

Two questions arise in this case : the first one of considerable importance, whether a Royal Palace, in the occupation of the Sovereign, is within the Statute of Sewers, and liable to be rated for the sewers' tax : the second, whether the defendants, in an information of intrusion at the suit of the Crown, are at liberty to plead the general form of plea given by the Statute of Sewers, 23 Hen. VIII. c. 5, s. 11.

With respect to the first point, it is impossible that a rate can be levied on a Palace in the occupation of the Sovereign. And in the case of *Winter* v. *Miles* (1), it was held that Kensington Palace, being kept in a constant state of preparation to receive the King, with his officers,

(1) 10 R. R. 391, 10 East, 578.

servants, and guards residing and doing duty there at all times, and some of the Royal family having apartments there (all which circumstances still exist with respect to it), was privileged as a Royal Palace against the intrusion of the sheriff for the purpose of executing process against the goods of a person having the use

[119] of apartments therein. *   *   *Netherton* v. *Ward* (1) will be cited for the defendants. There it was held that a tenement situate in the King's dock-yard, deriving a benefit from the public sewers, and occupied by an officer of Government, who paid no rent, was liable to be rated to the sewers' rate. But that case is altogether distinguishable from the present. It was decided upon the provisions of the stat. 23 Hen. VIII. c. 5, s. 9, which enacts in express terms, "that the same laws, ordinances and decrees to be made and ordained by the Commissioners, shall bind as well the lands, tenements, and hereditaments of the King our sovereign lord, as all other persons and their heirs, for such their interest as they shall fortune to have in any lands," &c. ; and the 3 & 4 Edw. VI. c. 8, which enacts, " that all scots, lots, and sums of money hereafter to be rated and taxed by virtue of such commission of sewers, upon any the lands, &c. of our sovereign lord the King, for any manner or thing concerning the articles of the said commission of sewers, shall be levied by distress." That was the case of Crown property applied by the Crown to public purposes, and held by a subject under the Crown, not of property in the occupation of the Sovereign himself. The Crown occupies in its public capacity, and no beneficial occupation can be supposed to be enjoyed by it.

Secondly, the defendants are not entitled to plead the general plea given by the statute. The 23 Hen. VIII. c. 5, s. 11, enacts, " that if any action of trespass, or other suit, shall happen to be

[*120] attempted against any person or persons *for taking any distress, or any other act doing, by authority of the said commission, &c., the defendant or defendants in any such action shall and may make avowry, cognizance, or justification, alleging in such avowry, &c. that the said distress, trespass, or other act was done by the authority of the commission of sewers, for lot or tax assessed by the said commission," &c. An information of intrusion cannot be considered an " action of trespass or other suit " within the meaning of this clause. It clearly refers to a suit between subject and subject. If the 11th section be held applicable, so also must the 12th, which enacts, that after such issue tried for the defendant, or

(1) 22 R. R. 284 (3 B. & Ald. 21).

nonsuit of the plaintiff, the defendant shall recover treble damages and costs; yet that obviously can have no reference to proceedings at the suit of the Crown.

Dundas, contrà:

The plea is good. The effect of the stat. 23 Hen. VIII. c. 5, as connected with and explained by the 3 & 4 Edw. VI. c. 8, is, that the Crown and the subject are placed in all respects, in reference to the commission of sewers, on the same footing. The 11th section of the former statute was framed with reference to all the subject-matters contained in the preceding clauses, and its words —"any action of trespass or other suit"—are very general. An information of intrusion is a civil suit: Savile, 48; *Attorney-General* v. *Allgood* (1); *Attorney-General* v. *Donaldson* (2). In the last case, the statute of Anne, allowing double pleading, was held not to apply, because all its provisions have reference to suits between subject and subject. But the Crown may be plaintiff in an action. This clause was introduced for the protection of the Commissioners in all cases where they act in the exercise of their public duty. At common law, the Crown might put a defendant in an information of intrusion on showing his title specially: *Com. Dig.*, Prerogative, (D.) 74, *Attorney-General* v. *Hudson* (3): but the object of this statute was to relieve the Commissioners from doing so. There would be vast inconvenience in being obliged to set out all their proceedings at length. Again, the Crown is bound by an Act of Parliament, although not named in it, where it is made for the advancement of religion, the maintenance of learning, or otherwise for the public good: *Willion* v. *Barkley* (4); *The Case of Ecclesiastical Persons* (5). This is a statute very much for the public good, having been made to protect the Commissioners, discharging a public and highly beneficial duty, from vexatious suits. No doubt the Crown cannot be nonsuited; but the Court may exercise its judgment distributively on the 11th and 12th sections, and apply them to the Crown where they can do so.

[*121]

Secondly, this rate was lawfully levied. It cannot be said, since the decision in *Netherton* v. *Ward*, that the Statutes of Sewers do not extend to the property of the Crown. (On this point he referred also to the statutes 23 Hen. VIII. c. 5, s. 8, and 13 Eliz.

(1) Parker, 10.
(2) 7 M. & W. 422.
(3) 2 Dyer, 238 b.

(4) Plowd. 236.
(5) 5 Co. Rep. 14 b.

A.-G.   c. 9, s. 1; *Whitley* v. *Fawsett* (1); *Holford* v. *Copeland* (2); 1 Nolan,
v.
DONALDSON.   P. L. 192, note; *Soady* v. *Wilson* (3); *Rex* v. *Matthew* (4).) The
case of *Winter* v. *Miles* has been referred to as showing that
Kensington Palace retains all the privileges of a Royal Palace: but
that was with reference to the case of process at common law. In
Rex v. *Stobbs* (5), however, it was held that process out of the
Palace Court was executable within the Palace of Westminster,
under the charter of Charles II. constituting that Court, and giving
it jurisdiction within the Palace. The Statute of Sewers has the
same operation, and so far limits the common-law prerogative of
[*122]   the Crown: *Jenkins's Century, 112, case 18; Dugdale on the
Statute of Sewers, 307 (6).

The *Attorney-General*, in reply.   *   *   *

Cur. adv. vult.

The judgment of the COURT was now delivered by

ALDERSON, B. :

There was a case of the *Attorney-General* v. *Donaldson* and others,
which was argued before this Court during the last Term. It was
an information against the defendant for intrusion into a certain
[*123]   messuage or *dwelling-house in the parish of St. Margaret, being
parcel of the Royal Palace of Kensington, long before then and at
that time in the occupation of our lady the Queen, and for committing certain trespasses therein. The defendants pleaded that the
several trespasses in the information mentioned were committed
by them under the authority and in pursuance of a commission of
sewers, at the time when &c., being in full force, for tax assessed
by the said Commissioners according to the tenor and effect of the
several Statutes of Sewers; and to this plea there was a general
demurrer. On the argument of this demurrer, two points were
made. First, that a Royal Palace, being the residence of the
Sovereign, was not within the authority of the Commissioners of
Sewers. Secondly, that the general form of pleading given by the
Statute of Sewers was not allowable on an information of intrusion
at the suit of the Crown. We are of opinion that the latter
objection must prevail, and consequently it is unnecessary to

(1) Styles, 12.   (5) 3 T. R. 735.
(2) 3 Bos. & P. 133.   (6) In his "History of Embanking,"
(3) 42 R. R. 379 (3 Ad. & El. 248).   1662.
(4) Cald. 1.

determine whether the averments in this information are sufficient
to show that Kensington Palace was a Royal residence at the time
of the alleged intrusion, assuming that a distress for non-payment
of a sewers' rate, which certainly may be levied on land in the
occupation of the servants of the Crown, by virtue of the 9th section of the 23 Hen. VIII. c. 5, and the 3 & 4 Edw. VI. c. 8, cannot
be levied, any more than the ordinary process of the law can be
executed, within the precinct of a Royal Palace occupied as the
residence of the Sovereign, by reason of the respect due to the
Royal person.   Upon this latter proposition we do not mean to
intimate any doubt, although we are not satisfied that sufficient
appears on the face of the record to give to Kensington Palace the
privilege that belongs to a Royal residence of the Sovereign.

The question whether a defendant at the suit of the Crown is
entitled to the privilege of the general plea, depends on the construction of the 11th section of 25 Hen. VIII. and the context of
that Act. It is a well-established rule, generally *speaking, in the
construction of Acts of Parliament, that the King is not included
unless there be words to that effect; for it is inferred *primâ facie*
that the law made by the Crown, with the assent of Lords and
Commons, is made for subjects and not for the Crown : *Willion* v.
Barkley. Now, in this case the 11th section gives the privilege
of a general plea in any action of trespass or other suit, and directs
that the plaintiff may reply generally ; and the 12th section gives
treble damages and costs to the defendant, by reason of his wrongful
vexation.   The language of both these sections is pointed at actions
between subjects merely, and not to suits in which the Crown is
concerned ; and, generally speaking, the Crown is not bound under
the terms "party to the suit:" *Reg.* v. *Tuchin* (1). Nor do the
terms "action or suit," where the privilege of double pleading is
given by the statute 4 & 5 Anne, c. 16, s. 5, apply to informations
of intrusion, as has been already decided by this Court in this very
suit, on the authority of *The Attorney-General* v. *Allgood ;* and we
cannot find any thing in the rest of the Act to control the ordinary
meaning of these terms, and to raise an implication that the Crown
was meant to be affected in its proceedings. The probability is,
that the Legislature never contemplated a case of distress being
necessary in respect of an assessment on Crown lands. Our
judgment on this demurrer must therefore be for the Crown.

Judgment for the Crown.

(1) 2 Ld. Ray. 1066.

A.-G.
v.
DONALDSON.

On a subsequent day (June 11),

Dundas applied to the Court for leave to plead *de novo*, or to amend the plea.

ALDERSON, B. :

[*125]

When this case was argued, the Court *entertained some doubt whether it sufficiently appeared on the face of the information that Kensington Palace was the residence of the Sovereign : but we cannot allow an amendment of the plea, because in point of fact there can be no doubt that it is so. Her Majesty has a right to go and live there, and there is no one who could resist her demand to take up her abode in the Palace.

The other Barons concurring,

Motion refused.

———————————

1842.
June 2.
———
Exch. of
Pleas.
[131]

FOX *v.* FRITH AND OTHERS.

(10 Meeson & Welsby, 131—137; S. C. 11 L. J. Ex. 336; Car. & M. 502.)

By a deed dated 7th May, 1839, a Company was formed called the West Mining Association, of which the defendants were Directors. The plaintiff, by an agreement dated 10th July, 1839, agreed to sell to this Company 1,000 shares in the Pennance Mills Mining Company, to be paid for by the sum of 1,385*l.*, and by the delivering to him of 200 scrip certificates of shares in the West Mining Association. The money was to be paid on the 1st of August, 1841. Immediately upon the execution of the agreement, 200 scrip certificates were obtained by the plaintiff's agent, and entered in the register book of the West Mining Association in the plaintiff's name. The defendants afterwards gave the plaintiff the following promissory note, dated August 17, 1839 : " We jointly promise to pay to J. F. (the plaintiff) 1,385*l.*, on the 1st of August, 1841, for value received in Pennance shares pursuant to annexed contract." This note was signed by all the defendants in their individual names. The deed of settlement of the West Mining Company provided that holders of scrip certificates should not be considered as qualified proprietors; and that a certain proportion of the net profits of the year should be divided amongst the shareholders and scrip certificate holders, in proportion to their several shares and interests. The plaintiff had not paid any instalments nor signed the deed of settlement, but continued to be the holder of the scrip certificates : Held, in an action brought upon the note, that a plea that the defendants made the note as Directors and on behalf of the mining co-partnership, and that the plaintiff was a partner with the defendants, was not supported by proof of the above facts.

ASSUMPSIT by the plaintiff as the payee, against the defendants as the makers, of a promissory note, dated the 17th of August, 1839, for 1,385*l.*, payable on the 1st of August, 1841.

Pleas, first, that the defendants did not make the note : secondly, that before the making of the agreement thereinafter mentioned, and of the said promissory note, the defendants and others were united in co-partnership under the name of the West Mining Association ; that on the 10th of July, 1839, a certain agreement in writing was-made between the plaintiff and the defendants, whereby the plaintiff agreed to sell, and the defendants, as such Directors, to purchase, 1,000 shares of the stock of the Pennance Mills Mining Company for 1,385*l.*, in part of such purchase, and also in consideration of the delivery to the plaintiff of 200 scrip or registered certificates of shares in the stock of the West Mining Association ; that upon the making of the said agreement, and before the making of the promissory note, the defendants delivered to the plaintiff, and the plaintiff accepted, the 200 scrip certificates, and the plaintiff then became the proprietor thereof, and entitled to share in the dividends and profits of the said co-partnership ; and that the defendants as such Directors, and for and on behalf of the *said co-partnership, made the promissory note to the plaintiff, for the purpose of securing payment of the sum of 1,385*l.* ; and that the plaintiff, before and at that time, was a partner with the defendants in the said co-partnership.

Replication, *de injurâ*.

At the trial before Erskine, J., at the last Spring Assizes for the county of Cornwall, the following facts were given in evidence. By a deed of settlement, dated the 7th of May, 1839, a Company was formed called the " West Mining Association," and the defendants were appointed Directors. By a clause in the deed, all bills and notes were to be drawn, indorsed, accepted, &c., by three Directors. On the 10th of July, 1839, another Company, called the " Pennance Mills Mining Company," was formed, of which all the shares were vested in the plaintiff. On the same day the plaintiff, by agreement, stipulated to sell 1,000 of these shares to the West Mining Association, to be paid for partly by the sum of 1,385*l.*, and partly by the delivery to the plaintiff of 200 scrip or registered certificates of shares in the West Mining Association, with the sum of 2*l.* certified to be paid on each of such shares. The sum of 1,385*l.* was not to be paid until the 1st of August, 1841. Immediately upon the execution of the above agreement, 200 scrip certificates were obtained by the plaintiff's agent, and were entered in the register-book of the West Mining Association in the plaintiff's name. A promissory note

Fox
v.
Frith.

was afterwards given by the defendants to the plaintiff, which was
as follows :

"1,385*l.*   " London, August 17th, 1839.
   " We jointly promise to pay to Joshua Fox the sum of 1,385*l.* on
the 1st day of August, 1841, for value received, in Pennance shares,
pursuant to annexed contract."

> (Signed by all the defendants, who were five of the
> Directors of the Company, but not stating them to
> be such.)

[133]   By the 25th clause of the deed of settlement it was provided, that
those proprietors only should be considered as qualified proprietors,
and entitled to vote, who should individually be proprietors of not
fewer than twenty-five registered shares. The 26th provided that
the holders of scrip certificates should not be considered as qualified
proprietors, and entitled to vote at general meetings in respect
thereof. The 86th clause provided that a certain proportion of the
net profits of the year, or so much as the Directors should determine, should be divided amongst the shareholders and scrip-
certificate holders, in proportion to their several shares and
interests accordingly. The plaintiff, it appeared, had not signed
the deed of settlement, nor paid the instalments due on the shares.
At the trial, a verdict was found for the plaintiff upon all the issues,
leave being reserved to the defendants to move to enter a verdict on
the second issue, if the Court should be of opinion that, under the
circumstances above stated, the second plea was proved.

Crowder having, in Easter Term last, obtained a rule accordingly,

   Erle and *Butt* now showed cause:

   The plaintiff was not a partner in the West Mining Association at
the time the agreement creating the debt was made, and therefore
the promissory note was binding upon the defendants, and the plea
was not supported. He could not become a partner until the
transfer to him of the 200 shares, which took place subsequently to
the making of the agreement. Besides, by the 26th clause of the
deed of settlement it is expressly provided, that the holders of scrip
certificates should not be considered as qualified proprietors ; and
the deed draws a marked distinction between shareholders and
scrip-certificate holders. The scrip certificates were transferable to
bearer ; there was no knowing who were the holders of them.
Secondly, this was a separate debt. The note not being signed by

the defendants as Directors, *or stated it to be made by them on behalf of the Company, the parties were bound individually, and the defendants have no right by parol to show that it was connected with the partnership transaction: *Emly* v. *Lye* (1); *Siffkin* v. *Walker* (2); *Woodbridge* v. *Spooner* (3). The plea states that the defendants as Directors made the note, but they did not do so. The distinction is, that where a partner draws on other partners by name, and they individually accept, he may recover against them, because by such an acceptance a separate right is acknowledged to exist; as was said by BEST, Ch. J., in *Neale* v. *Turton* (4), which is also shortly stated in Collyer on Partnership, 179. It makes no difference if it was in truth given on the partnership account, if it be given by the parties individually, and as a separate transaction. (They were then stopped by the COURT.)

Crowder, *Swann*, and *M. Smith*, in support of the rule:

The defendants are entitled to have the verdict entered for them. Although the note does not express that it is given by the defendants as Directors of the Company, the plaintiff and the defendants were jointly interested in the fund out of which the 1,385*l.* was to be paid, the plaintiff having become so interested as soon as he received and accepted the scrip certificates. If a dissolution of the partnership were to take place, the plaintiff would be entitled to his share of the funds of the Company. A court of equity is the proper place in which to sue the defendants, and the plaintiff has no right to sue the makers of the note in a court of law, for he is thereby suing himself. The plaintiff was still a scrip holder up to the commencement of the action, and therefore he had not parted with or forfeited his interest in the fund. The plea states that the defendants made the note as Directors, and they did so in fact, and it makes no difference that they signed it in their own *names. [They cited *Teague* v. *Hubbard* (5), *Goddard* v. *Hodges* (6), and *Mainwaring* v. *Newman* (7).]

LORD ABINGER, C. B.:

This is a plain case. The distinction is between an actual partnership and an inchoate right of partnership. It is true that

FOX
v.
FRITH.
[*134]

[*135]

[136]

(1) 13 R. R. 347 (15 East, 7).
(2) 11 R. R. 715 (2 Camp. 308).
(3) 22 R. R. 365 (3 B. & Ald. 233).
(4) 29 R. R. 531 (4 Bing. 151; 12 Moore, 365).
(5) 8 B. & C. 345.
(6) 1 Car. & M. 33.
(7) 5 R. R. 554 (2 Bos. & P. 120).

the plaintiff had a right to become a partner if he had chosen to
pay up his instalments ; but he did not determine to become a
partner, and he did not pay up his instalments, or sign the deed.
If then he did not become a partner, the plea is not proved, but the
debt is proved. Even if the plaintiff had signed the deed, I should
have had great doubts whether the defendants had not made themselves liable. It cannot be supposed that the plaintiff intended that
the contract should be such a one as should force him to seek his
remedy in equity. The defendants gave the plaintiff a promissory
note, in which they do not describe themselves as Directors; and
we must presume, that in the event of the note not being paid by
the partnership, they intended, as honest men, to make themselves
personally liable. Clearly, the plaintiff, in taking this promissory
note, had no intention of being driven to resort to a court of equity.
The rule, therefore, must be discharged.

Gurney, B., concurred.

Rolfe, B. :

[*137]   The defendants state in their plea, that they made the note as
Directors, and for and on behalf of the *co-partnership; but that
was not supported by the evidence. In one sense, indeed, they
may be said to have done so ; as in the event of their paying it,
they would have equitable rights as against the Company. It
certainly was not the intention of the plaintiff, that in the event
of the bill being unpaid, he should be driven to resort to a court
of equity.

                                        Rule discharged.

———————

Sir JOHN MORRIS, Bart., *v.* VIVIAN and Another.

(10 Meeson & Welsby, 137—141 ; S. C. 11 L. J. Ex. 367; 2 Dowl. N. S. 235.)

Where two of the jury, during the progress of a trial which lasted two
days, dined and slept at the house of the defendant on the evening of the
first day, and consequently before the summing up: Held, that this did
not avoid a verdict found for the defendant ;

Held, also, that it was discretionary with the Court whether they would
set aside the verdict and grant a new trial in such a case; and where the
party making the application declared that he did not entertain any belief
that the jurors, in giving their verdict, were influenced by their visit, and
there were no grounds for suspicion of unfairness, the Court refused to
set aside the verdict.

This was an action for damage to a mine, by permitting the
water to flow into it from an adjacent mine belonging to the

defendants, and was tried at the last Glamorganshire Assizes by a special jury, when a verdict was found for the defendants. In Easter Term, *E. V. Williams* obtained a rule for a new trial, upon affidavits which stated, that the trial lasted two days, and that on the evening of the first day, when the Judge had not commenced summing up, two of the jurors went to the defendant's house, and dined and slept there. Affidavits were filed in answer, which stated, that the defendant resided near Swansea, and that it was customary in Glamorganshire, at the Assizes, for gentlemen, coming from a distance to attend them, to be invited to the house of the neighbouring gentry; that there was but one inn, which afforded very indifferent accommodation, and that one of the two jurors, upon his arrival in the town, had met Sir John Morris, who expressed his regret that he was unable to entertain him, in consequence of the absence of Lady Morris; that Mr. Vivian was trustee of the mine, and had only a very slight interest in it, and that no allusion to the subject of the trial had been made *to or by either of the jurymen during their stay in the house. *E. V. Williams*, on moving for the rule, and also at the commencement of the argument, stated that neither he nor his client entertained a belief that the two jurors had been influenced in the slightest degree by their visit to Mr. Vivian in giving their verdict, and that he was instructed expressly to disclaim any imputation of that kind.

MORRIS
v.
VIVIAN.

[*138]

Chilton, J. *Evans*, and *Groves* showed cause:

In Co. Litt. 227 b, it is laid down, that " if the jury, after their evidence given unto them at the Bar, do at their own charges eat or drink, either before or after they be agreed on their verdict, it is finable, but it shall not avoid the verdict; but if, before they be agreed on their verdict, they eat or drink at the charge of the plaintiff, if the verdict be given for him, it shall avoid the verdict; but if it be given for the defendant, it shall not avoid it, *et sic e converso.*" The treating alluded to there is evidently such as the whole jury partake of, and that only after the summing-up is over. The cases of *Trewennarde* v. *Skewys* (1), *Rex* v. *Burdett* (2), and *The Duke of Richmond* v. *Wise* (3), are confined to treating under circumstances of that kind. No distinction is made between the period at which eating or drinking is finable, and that at which it shall avoid the verdict. Then, under the circumstances of this

(1) Dyer, 55 b.
(2) 2 Salk. 645.

(3) 1 Vent. 124.

MORRIS
v.
VIVIAN.

case, the Court will not exercise their discretionary power of granting a new trial, the plaintiff having expressly admitted that he has not been prejudiced by what occurred.

E. V. Williams, in support of the rule:

Although all the cases upon treating to be found in the books are where the jury had retired, yet the ground assigned for the rule which avoids a verdict is, that it induces favour and affection: Vin. Abr. "Trial," (G, g); Bro. Abr. tit. "Jurours;" *and that would be equally applicable to treating the jury at one time as another, either during the trial or after their being charged. In Buller's N. P., p. 308, it is said, "It is finable for the jury to eat at their own expense after they are departed from the Bar; but it will not avoid the verdict, as it will if they eat at the charge of him for whom the verdict was given, before they are agreed on their verdict." So in the same book, p. 326, it is said, "New trials are often granted for the misbehaviour of the jury, or if they cast lots for their verdict; so if they eat at his expense for whom they give the verdict." The law is so jealous upon this point, that the sheriff is not permitted to summon the jury, if he be in any way related to the parties, or interested in the cause. The policy of the law is to avoid the possibility of suspicion attaching to the jury; and the same suspicion of injustice will be created in the mind of the public, whether the treating occurs before or immediately after their retirement from the Bar to consider their verdict. But it is said that the treating must extend to the whole jury. The same reason, however, which forbids the treating of all, extends to the treating of any of them; the number can make no difference. If the contrary were the rule, a party might, without risk, treat eleven out of the twelve with impunity. It is a fixed and settled principle of law, quite independent of the circumstances of any particular case, that, where there has been treating of the jury, the verdict is void, and the setting of it aside is not a matter for the discretion of the Court.

[*139]

LORD ABINGER, C. B.:

It is our province to administer justice, and, in doing so, not to permit ourselves to be influenced by any apprehension of the opinion which the public may form. If the learned Judge who tried this cause had thought the verdict had been contrary to the weight of evidence,—a circumstance which would have induced us to look to some motive for it,—or if any *corrupt motive could at once be seen, we might have been inclined to set it aside: but here it is alleged to be the concurrent opinion of all parties, that there was neither corruption nor favour. If the public are to form an opinion, let them understand that this was a case in which all imputation of influence and favour was entirely disclaimed. Now, what are the facts of it? There was but one inn, which afforded very insufficient accommodation, and in consequence, two of the jury, one of whom would have been invited to his own house by Sir John Morris, but for an accidental circumstance, found their way to Mr. Vivian's. He had no substantial interest in the suit, and the matter was never there discussed. Under these circumstances, unless there is some positive peremptory rule, which compels us to set aside this verdict, we ought not to do so. Then do the cases establish this? On the contrary, they only show that, where all that remains for the jury is to deliberate upon and give their verdict, if they eat or drink at their own expense they may be fined, and if at the expense of the party for whom their verdict is given, it is void. Those cases seem to apply to the whole jury, and only to acts done by them after they are charged. It is quite clear that, in this case, they could not have been fined for eating or drinking at their own expense, and I do not see that they fall within the other branch of the rule. Then it is a case in which we are called upon to exercise our discretion; and I think we should not set aside this verdict, since by doing so we should be casting an unfounded imputation upon these gentlemen.

ALDERSON, B. :

I am of the same opinion. I disclaim laying down a rule for any case where suspicion of unfairness or bias can possibly attach; but here the parties, counsel, and every one else, concur in repudiating the notion that they intend to make any charge of the sort. There is no imperative rule which compels us to set *aside such a verdict as this, and the granting of a new trial is a matter for our discretion. Under these circumstances, I think we ought not to interfere.

GURNEY, B., and ROLFE, B. concurred.

Rule discharged.

MORRIS
v.
VIVIAN.
[*140]

[*141]

MOENS AND OTHERS *v.* HEYWORTH AND OTHERS (1).

(10 Meeson & Welsby, 147—160; S. C. 10 L. J. Ex. 177.)

A collateral statement, made at the time of entering into a contract, but not embodied in it, must, in order to invalidate the contract on the ground of its being a fraudulent statement, be shown not only to have been false, but to have been known to be so by the party making it, and that the other party was thereby induced to enter into the contract. (Per PARKE, B., and ALDERSON, B.; Lord ABINGER, C. B., *dissentiente*.)

A cargo of coffee was sold by a broker, for H., P., & Co., of Liverpool; and the words "invoiced to the sellers as of first shipping quality," were introduced into the bought and sold notes. At the same time the invoice was shown to the buyers, which stated the cargo to be shipped by H., Brothers, & Co., consigned to H., P., & Co., for sale on account and risk of whom it may concern—3,150 bags "first shipping quality." H., Brothers, & Co. were a branch house at Rio de Janeiro, composed of the same partners as the firm of H., P., & Co.: Held, in an action on the case against H., P., & Co. for deceit, that it was a proper question for the jury, whether the invoice imported that the coffee was invoiced to the defendants by distinct parties as the sellers thereof.

Quære, whether the action ought not to have been brought upon the contract, instead of in tort.

CASE. The first count of the declaration stated, that the plaintiffs, at the request of the defendants, bargained with them for the purchase by the plaintiffs of a cargo of coffee at a certain price, and upon certain terms (stating them); and that the defendants, by falsely and fraudulently warranting the said coffee to be of the first shipping quality, sold the said coffee to the plaintiffs at the price and upon the terms aforesaid, &c. &c. The second count alleged that the defendants were the consignees of the cargo of coffee, and that they, as a means to induce the plaintiffs to buy the said coffee, falsely, fraudulently, and deceitfully pretended, represented, and asserted to the plaintiffs, and by such fraud and false representation induced the said plaintiffs to believe and suppose, that the said last-mentioned coffee was of first shipping quality; and that the plaintiffs, confiding in the said representation and assertion of the defendants, then bought of them the said coffee, as coffee of the first shipping quality, at a certain price and upon certain terms (as in the first count). The third count stated, that the defendants, at the time of the committing of the grievance by them as thereinafter mentioned, exercised and carried on the trade and business of merchants at Liverpool, under the firm of Heyworth, Phipps, & Co., and also at Rio de Janeiro, in partnership together and with

(1) Cited in *Mackay* v. *Commercial Bank of New Brunswick* (1874) L. R. 5 P. C. 394, 410, 43 L. J. P. C. 31; *London Assurance* v. *Mansel* (1879) 11 Ch. D. 363, 368, 48 L. J. Ch. 331; and *Derry* v. *Peek* (1889) 14 App. Ca. 337, 366, 58 L. J. Ch. 864.—A. C.

Benjamin Butterworth and John Carlisle, under the firm and
description of Heyworth, Brothers, & Co. ; and so carrying on such
trade and business *in such co-partnership, had purchased, together
with the said Benjamin Butterworth and John Carlisle, a quantity
of coffee on the joint account and at the joint risk of the said firms,
which coffee was shipped at Rio de Janeiro and sent to England,
invoiced to the defendants, by the style and description of Heyworth,
Phipps, & Co. :. that, after the arrival of the coffee in England, the
defendants, in order to induce the plaintiffs to purchase the same,
wrongfully and injuriously contriving and intending to deceive,
defraud, and injure the plaintiffs, and to lead them to believe that
the said coffee was in good faith invoiced by distinct parties to the
defendants, as the purchasers or agents for the sale of the said
coffee, the plaintiffs being wholly ignorant, and the defendants well
knowing the plaintiffs to be wholly ignorant, of the premises above
mentioned, fraudulently and deceitfully represented and asserted
that the said coffee was invoiced to the sellers thereof as of the
first shipping quality, thereby causing and intending to cause the
plaintiffs to believe that the said coffee was so invoiced by some
distinct parties to the defendants, as the purchasers or agents for
the sale of the said coffee; and the defendants then exhibited a
certain invoice, purporting to be made out by the said firm of
Heyworth, Brothers, & Co. to the said firm of Heyworth, Phipps,
& Co., in proof of the said last-mentioned representation and
assertion; whereupon the plaintiffs, confiding in such representation, and believing that the said coffee was really and in good faith
so invoiced by distinct parties to the defendants, as the purchasers
or agents for the sale thereof, bargained with them for the purchase
thereof on certain terms (stating them); and that the defendants, by
means of such false representation and assertion, sold the said coffee
to the plaintiffs, who paid for the same.

The defendants pleaded not guilty to the whole declaration, and
nine other special pleas, traversing the material *allegations in each
count, upon all which issues were joined.

At the trial before Lord Abinger, C. B., at the London sittings
after Trinity Term, 1840, the following facts appeared : The defendants were merchants carrying on business at Liverpool, under the
firm of Ormerod Heyworth, Phipps, & Co., and at Rio de Janeiro
in America (where they had a branch establishment), under the firm
of Heyworth, Brothers, & Co. In the month of June, 1835, the
Liverpool house sent an order to the house at Rio for a cargo of

MOENS
v.
HEYWORTH.
[*148]

[*149]

MOENS
v.
HEYWORTH.

about 4,000 bags of coffee, of the first shipping quality. In execution of this order, the Rio house purchased, in December, 1835, that quantity of coffee, by sample, from respectable coffee dealers, on the joint account and risk of themselves and the Liverpool house, the price and duty being paid by the house at Rio as on coffee of the first shipping quality. The coffee was shipped on board the ship *Asia* for England, and a shipping invoice in the following form (which was proved to be that invariably adopted by merchants abroad shipping goods to Europe), was transmitted to the firm at Liverpool by the Rio house:

"Invoice of three thousand one hundred and fifty bags coffee, shipped by Heyworth, Brothers, & Co., of Rio de Janeiro, on board the British brig *Asia*, W. M. Bloomfield, master, for Cowes, and a market consigned to Messrs. Ormerod Heyworth, Phipps, & Co., of Liverpool, for sale on account and risk of whom it may concern—3,150 first shipping quality coffee."

In the spring of the year 1836, the defendants, in expectation of the arrival of the *Asia*, gave instructions to Messrs. Corrie & Co., their brokers in London, for the sale of the coffee on board of her. Corrie & Co., acting as brokers both for the buyers and sellers, entered into a negotiation for the sale of the coffee to the plaintiffs. The plaintiffs wished to have a warranty that it was of first shipping quality, but this Corrie & Co. declined, on the *ground that it was unusual to warrant a cargo which was afloat, but they showed the invoice to the plaintiffs, and consented to insert in the bought and sold notes the words " invoiced to sellers as first shipping quality." The contract was completed accordingly, and the plaintiffs paid for the coffee in cash, according to the terms of the contract, and on its arrival forwarded it to Amsterdam for sale. It was there discovered to be of an inferior quality, and the present action was brought to recover from the firm at Liverpool the amount of the loss sustained by the plaintiffs, by the consequent deficiency in the price obtained for it. The LORD CHIEF BARON was of opinion that there was no case to go to the jury on the first and second counts; and with respect to the third, he left it to the jury to say whether the plaintiffs were induced to accept the contract by any representation from the defendants that the coffee was invoiced to them by distinct parties. The jury found in the affirmative, and the verdict was thereupon entered for the defendants on the first and second counts, and for the plaintiffs on the third, leave being reserved to the defendants to move to enter a nonsuit.

[*150]

In the following Michaelmas Term, the *Attorney-General* (*Sir John Campbell*) obtained a rule accordingly, or for a new trial, citing *Haycraft* v. *Creasy* (1), and *Early* v. *Garrett* (2).   In Hilary Term, 1841 (Jan. 19),

Sir W. W. Follett, Kelly, and *Deedes* showed cause :

The third count of the declaration was proved by the evidence given on the part of the plaintiffs. It is clear that they purchased the coffee on the assumption induced by the terms of the contract, as agreed to by the brokers on behalf of the defendants, that it was invoiced to the defendants by distinct parties as consignors ; whereas in truth the houses at Rio and Liverpool were the same, and the coffee was purchased and shipped for England, and the invoice *made out, by the defendants themselves to themselves. If it be said that the third count does not disclose any cause of action, that would have been ground for a motion to arrest the judgment, not for a nonsuit. The only question now is, whether there was any evidence to go to the jury in support of the count. The complaint is not that the defendants specifically represented that the coffee was consigned to them by distinct parties ; the alleged misrepresentation is that which appears on the face of the contract, that it was "invoiced to sellers as of first shipping quality." The words "invoiced to sellers" would necessarily induce a belief that the two houses were distinct.

[*151]

(PARKE, B. : The question is, whether the words introduced into the contract import such a representation as is charged in the declaration.)

This was a mercantile instrument, and the interpretation of it was peculiarly a question for the jury. * * *

But there was also evidence to sustain the other counts of the declaration. The invoice not being in fact that of a *third party, but of the defendants themselves, when it was handed over to the plaintiffs, it became a representation by the defendants to the plaintiffs, that the coffee was of first shipping quality; which representation being false in fact, the allegations in the second count were thus proved.

[*152]

(ALDERSON, B. : Suppose Corrie had told the plaintiffs that the

(1) 6 R. R. 380 (2 East, 92).   (2) 33 R. R. 371 (9 B. & C. 928 ; 4 Man. & Ry. 687).

MOENS
v.
HEYWORTH.

houses were identical ; would it be a representation by the defendants to the plaintiffs, that the coffee was of first shipping quality?
It is merely a representation that it was invoiced by that invoice :
what the invoice imports is another question.)

The defendants allege that they did not represent the coffee as
being invoiced to them by third parties ; if that be so, then they
handed over the invoice as their own, and by doing so, they in
effect represented the coffee to be of the first shipping quality, and
the case becomes the same as if the coffee had been bought by the
plaintiffs under that invoice. It is, in effect, purchased from the
defendants under a written statement by them, which is false in
fact, that it was of first shipping quality : and although they
might have no knowledge of the inferiority of the coffee, yet,
being interested parties, they are responsible for their untrue
representation, which amounts to a fraud in law: *Hern* v.
Nicholls (1), *Schneider* v. *Heath* (2), *Pawson* v. *Watson* (3), *Cornfoot*
v. *Fowke* (4), *Humphreys* v. *Pratt* (5). It is not necessary they
should know the representation to be false ; it is sufficient that they
did not know it to be true.

Then as to the first count : as the representation in the invoice,
which is imported into the contract, was made by the defendants
themselves, it amounted to a warranty, for which the defendants
are liable. On this point they referred to *Shepherd* v. *Kain* (6),
Yates v. *Pym* (7), and *Bridge* v. *Wain* (8).

[153]   The *Attorney-General, Cresswell,* and *Cowling,* in support of
the rule :

It is not disputed that a representation which is false in fact,
although not proceeding from any immoral motive, amounts to a
fraud in law, and is the subject of an action of deceit : *Polhill* v.
Walter (9), *Foster* v. *Charles* (10) : but it is a wholly different question
how far it affects a party in relation to a contract. Whether a
particular statement in a contract be or be not false within the
knowledge of the party making it, is quite immaterial, for in any
case he is bound to perform it. On the other hand, it is equally

(1) 1 Salk. 289.
(2) 14 R. R. 825 (3 Camp. 506).
(3) Cowp. 785.
(4) 55 R. R. 655 (6 M. & W. 358).
(5) 35 R. R. 41 (5 Bligh, N. S. 154).
(6) 24 R. R. 344 (5 B. & Ald. 240).

(7) 16 R. R. 653 (6 Taunt. 446).
(8) 18 R. R. 815 (1 Stark. N. P. C.
504).
(9) 37 R. R. 344 (3 B. & Ad. 114).
(10) 31 R. R. 446 (6 Bing. 396; 7
Bing. 105; 4 Moo. & P. 61, 741).

clear, that a representation in a matter extraneous from and
collateral to the contract cannot affect him, even though it turn
out to be untrue, unless it were made fraudulently.   Here it is not
pretended that the whole transaction was not carried on with
perfect good faith.   But where is the falsehood in this case ?   The
coffee was invoiced to the sellers, *i.e.*, to Ormerod Heyworth, Phipps,
& Co., by the invoice which was produced, as of first shipping
quality.   The invoice was in terms precisely such as it was represented in the contract.   The word " sellers " merely means the firm
of Ormerod, Heyworth, Phipps, & Co.   Suppose the coffee had been
bought for them by their agents, and consigned and so invoiced to
them, could it have been said that this action was maintainable?
What difference, then, does it make, that it was bought by a house
abroad, of which the defendants, with two other persons, are
members ?

The first count clearly was not proved.   There is no warranty
whatever that the coffee was in fact of first shipping quality, but
merely a statement that it was invoiced as such.   It is said that
the invoice was handed over to the plaintiffs : but *quo animo ?*
Certainly not, according to the evidence, as a warranty, and it
cannot amount to more than a collateral representation, for which,
in the absence of fraud, the defendants are not liable.

(ALDERSON, B. : *It cannot be carried beyond this ; that, in   [*154]
some proceeding to which the defendants and others were parties,
it was represented as being coffee of first shipping quality : that is
a very different thing from an absolute warranty.

PARKE, B. : That part of the case is quite clear.)

The same answer applies with regard to the second count.

Then with respect to the third count.   It is not contended that
that count is bad in law ; if there had been evidence of fraud, it
might have been supported.   Thus, if it had been proved that the
Rio house had bought inferior coffee, and invoiced it to the defendants as of first shipping quality, and that the defendants, knowing
this, had instructed their brokers to hand over the invoice, the
plaintiffs might have been entitled to recover.   Or if the plaintiffs
had said to the broker, " Are these distinct houses ? " and the
latter had replied that they were, there would then have been a
suggestio falsi, which might have rendered the defendants liable.
But here, neither in writing nor by parol is there any representation

MOENS
v.
HEYWORTH.

that the two houses were distinct. It is therefore not material
what inference the purchaser might draw from the invoice, unless
the sellers meant him to draw it. Now the question left to the
jury was, what was the inference the plaintiffs drew from the terms
"invoiced to sellers as of first shipping quality?" There is
nothing, therefore, found by the jury to support any of the allegations in the count,—no finding either of moral fraud or even of
untrue statement.

(PARKE, B.: I do not see how this action can be supported without proving moral fraud; that is, that the defendants falsely
asserted that they were two distinct houses, when there was in fact
but one, and did so with a view of inducing the plaintiffs to enter
into the contract. It seems to me to be essential to support the
action, not merely that the plaintiffs surmised so and so, but that
the defendants exhibited the invoice, meaning that there was in
fact only one house, with the intention of inducing the plaintiffs to
[*155]   make the surmise that there were two distinct *houses, by one of
which the coffee was invoiced to the other as of a certain quality.)

It is said that this is a mercantile instrument, of the interpretation
of which the jury are the judges: but that is not so; the construction of a written instrument is in all cases for the Court, although
the meaning of particular mercantile terms may be a question for
the jury. The jury cannot alter the plain meaning of a written
contract. Neither was this a representation calculated to impose
upon a purchaser; it is merely collateral, and the plaintiffs might
have inquired into the fact had they desired the information. And
further, there is nothing to show that the purchase was in fact
induced by the representation, or that it would not have been made,
if the plaintiffs had possessed full knowledge that the houses at Rio
and at Liverpool were not distinct establishments.

LORD ABINGER, C. B.:

As this case has been so fully argued, I think it right to make
some remarks upon the arguments used by counsel. There has
been a misunderstanding in this case in regard to the meaning of
the word "fraud." The fraud which vitiates a contract, and gives
the party a right to recover, does not in all cases necessarily imply
moral turpitude. There may be a misrepresentation as to the facts
stated in the contract, all the circumstances in which the party may
believe to be true. In policies of insurance, for instance, if an

insurer makes a misrepresentation, it vitiates the contract: such contracts are, it is true, of a peculiar nature, and have relation as well to the rights of the parties as the event. In the case of a contract for the sale of a public-house, if the seller represent by mistake that the house realised more than in fact it did, he would be defrauding the purchaser, and deceiving him; but that might arise from his not having kept proper books, or from non-attention to his affairs; yet as soon as the other party discovers *it, an action [*156] may be maintained for the loss consequent upon such misrepresentation, inasmuch as he was thereby induced to give more than the house was worth. That action might be sustained upon an allegation that the representation was false, although the party making it did not know at the time he made it that it was so. It is not, however, necessary to go that length in this case. (His Lordship then stated the facts of the case, and continued:) It is plain, therefore, that the question is, whether the defendants have committed that species of fraud which renders them liable to an action.   That depends upon the correct interpretation of the invoice as a mercantile instrument, and upon that only. Now, it is for mercantile men, who are in the habit of seeing such documents frequently, to say whether or not the form of the invoice in this case is that generally adopted where the goods are to be shipped and sold on a joint account, or whether it imports a shipment of goods consigned by a distinct class of persons. Could any Judge, looking at this invoice, say that it means no such thing, or that the goods might not have been shipped by distinct parties to the house at Liverpool? I should think not; and if so, then it is for the jury to determine whether it imports, among mercantile men, a shipment by and to distinct parties. The defendants must be taken to know its import; and if it does import that which is untrue, viz. that the goods were invoiced by distinct parties to them, whereas the invoice was made by themselves to themselves, then, if they meant thereby to facilitate the sale, it is what may be termed a legal though not a moral fraud. It appeared to me, and I still think, that those facts ought to be decided by the jury. Whether the jury have drawn a right conclusion it is not for me to say. The Court are disposed to think that another jury might come to a different conclusion, and as the sum is large, I concur with the rest of the Court that there should be a new trial, on the single point as to the representation to *the plaintiffs that the goods were invoiced [*157] by distinct parties. That must be on payment of costs.

PARKE, B. :

With respect to the first and second counts, it is clear that no
warranty was meant to be given, and equally clear that the coffee
was not represented by the defendants to the plaintiffs as being of
first shipping quality ; on these counts, therefore, the defendants
are entitled to the verdict upon the plea of not guilty. It is on the
third count that the only question arises. To support that count,
it was essential to prove that the defendants knowingly, by words
or acts, made such a representation as is stated in the third count,
relative to the invoice of these goods, as they knew to be untrue,
and that the plaintiffs were thereby induced to purchase them,
which they otherwise would not have done. That question arises
on the peculiar allegations set forth in that count. (His Lordship
read the statement of the representation in the third count.) To
give a right of action for that representation, it was, I think,
essential to prove that, by words or acts of the defendants or their
agents, it was made falsely, and for the improper purpose of
inducing the plaintiffs to purchase the goods. I agree with the rest
of the Court, that there was some evidence to support that count ;
and therefore it seems to me that the defendants were not in a
condition to ask his Lordship to nonsuit the plaintiffs, nor to enter
the verdict for them. I think it essential that there should be
moral fraud, and indeed all the cases show that it is, though the
word *legal* fraud is used. That is a description of fraud not of so
grave and serious a character, that is to say, a representation made
without any private view of benefit to the party making it. The
case of a policy of insurance does not appear to me to be analogous
to the present ; those instruments are made upon an implied
contract between the parties, that everything material known to
[*158]   the assured should be disclosed by them. *That is the basis on
which the contract proceeds ; and it is material to see that it is not
obtained by means of untrue representation or concealment in any
respect. In this case the plaintiffs must prove a representation, by
words or acts, of that as being true which was known to the
defendants to be untrue ; as in the case of *Polhill* v. *Walter*, in
which a party had falsely represented that he was authorized to
accept a bill by procuration ; so also in *Foster* v. *Charles*, where
the allegation of the party was by a false representation of
character. In both these cases, there was not any deliberate
intention to deceive, yet it was called a fraud, though it was not of
so grave a character. Now the only inference of fraud in the

present case arises from the peculiar form of the instrument; that
is a part of the case which seems fit for a jury, the question being,
whether the invoice would necessarily be understood by mercantile
men as an invoice usually passing from one house to another. I
think my Lord could not have withdrawn that evidence from the
jury ; but if I were to give an opinion on the form of this invoice, I
should say that the mere similarity in the names would favour the
idea that it was a joint speculation, at all events sufficiently to
excite inquiry, if the plaintiffs meant to buy on the basis of this
being a representation that the goods were conveyed by a distinct
house. I think, therefore, that there should be a new trial on
payment of costs.

ALDERSON, B. :

I entirely concur in the propriety of a new trial. (His Lordship
then reviewed the evidence, and continued :) It has been urged by
counsel, that the representation was in terms true. I do not agree
to that, because I consider that if a person makes a representation,
or takes an oath, of that which is true, if he intend that the party
to whom the representation is made should not believe it to be
true, that is a false representation ; and so he who takes an oath in
one sense, knowing it to be administered to him *in another, takes   [*159]
it falsely.   This may be illustrated by an anecdote of a very
eminent Ambassador, Sir Henry Wotton, who, when he was asked
what advice he would give to a young diplomatist going to a foreign
Court, said—" I have found it best always to tell the truth, as they
will never believe any thing an Ambassador says, so you are sure
to take them in."   Now Sir Henry Wotton meant that he should
tell a lie.   This, no doubt, was only said as a witticism, but it
illustrates my meaning.   In the present case, the plaintiffs must
show that this invoice was sent to the broker, that he might
represent to the buyer, or that the buyer might think, that these
goods came to the defendants from an independent house, and that
the defendants were not interested in the shipment of them. I
think that was for the jury, and that there was some evidence for
them on that point, although very slight. We therefore cannot
make the rule absolute for entering a nonsuit, but we may grant a
new trial on payment of costs.

GURNEY, B. :

I have not heard the whole of the argument on either side, but

MOENS
v.
HEYWORTH.

in as far as I have been able to form a judgment, I concur in what my learned brothers have said.

Rule absolute for a new trial on the third count, on payment of costs.

The two first counts of the declaration having been struck out pursuant to the order of the Court, the cause was tried again before Lord Abinger, C. B., at the London sittings after last Trinity Term. It then appeared that the contract was signed and completed on the 4th of April, 1840, and it was not until the 8th of April that the shipping invoice was received by Corrie & Co. from Liverpool, and shown to the plaintiffs. Evidence was given by persons [*160] *connected with the coffee trade that such an invoice imported a sale by a house distinct from the consignee. It was insisted for the defendants, that there was no evidence to charge the defendants in an action of tort, and that the exhibiting of the invoice to the plaintiffs, after the completion of the contract, could not be taken into consideration, inasmuch as it was impossible that the plaintiffs could thereby have been induced to make the purchase. The LORD CHIEF BARON, in summing up, left it (in substance) to the jury to say whether the defendants knowingly represented to the plaintiffs that the coffee was invoiced to them by a distinct house, and the jury again found for the plaintiffs. In Michaelmas Term, *R. V. Richards* obtained a rule *nisi* for a new trial, on the ground that the action should have been brought upon the contract, and not in tort, the alleged representation being in truth, if anything, a material part of the contract itself: but the cause was compromised before the rule came on for argument.

1842.
May 31.

Exch. of Pleas.

[161]

WALKER AND OTHERS *v.* JACKSON AND OTHERS (1).

(10 Meeson & Welsby, 161—174; S. C. 11 L. J. Ex. 346; 12 L. J. Ex. 165.)

Declaration in case against the owners of a ferry stated, that the defendants were possessed of a ferry across the River Mersey, from Wood-side to Liverpool, and that the plaintiffs delivered to them certain goods, to wit, a phaeton, and certain jewellery and watches contained in it, to be by the defendants, for reward to them in that behalf, taken care of and carried in a certain steam-boat from Woodside to Liverpool, and there landed for the plaintiffs; that the defendants accepted and received the said carriage so containing the said jewellery and watches from the plaintiffs, and it became their duty to take proper care of them while they remained in their

(1) Followed in *Lebeau* v. *General Steam Navigation Co.* (1872) L. R. 8 C. P. 88, 97, 42 L. J. C. P. 1.—A. C.

custody, and in and about the carriage, conveyance, and landing of the
same as aforesaid.   Breach, that the defendants took such bad care of the
said carriage, jewellery, and watches, and so negligently conducted themselves in and about the carriage, conveyance, and landing of the same, that
they were injured.

Plea, that the plaintiffs did not deliver to the defendants, nor did they
accept and receive from the plaintiffs, the goods in the declaration mentioned, to be by them carried and conveyed in the said steam-boat from
Woodside to Liverpool, and there landed for the plaintiffs, for reward to
them in that behalf, *modo et formá.*

Held, that a contract to carry and land the carriage and jewellery, as
stated in the declaration, could not be implied from the mere character of
the defendants as owners of the ferry.   But that it was a question for the
jury, whether there was in fact a contract between the parties, either
express or implied from usage, to receive the carriage on board, and to land
it again at the end of the transit across the river.

It appeared that the plaintiff went on board the defendants' steam-boat,
with his horse and carriage, paying the defendants' charge for a "light
four-wheeled phaeton;" that jewellery and watches of great value, which
much increased its weight, were contained in a box under the seat; and
that he made no communication of that fact to the defendants.   The
carriage was taken safely across the river, and on the arrival of the boat
at the pier-head at Liverpool, two of the defendants' servants put the
carriage out upon the slip, and commenced drawing it up the slip towards
the quay, but in doing so were overpowered by its weight, and it ran down
into the river, whereby the jewellery and watches were injured: Held, that
the plaintiff's right of action for this injury was not affected by his not
having communicated the fact of the jewellery and watches being contained in the carriage: Held also, that it was a further question for the
jury (supposing a contract to land were established) whether the landing
was complete under the above circumstances.

Held, also, that to rebut evidence of a usage to take on board and land
the carriages of passengers, a notice stuck up at the door of entrance for
foot passengers to the slip at Woodside, but not visible to those who came
with carriages, nor shown to have been known to the plaintiff,—that the
defendants did not undertake to load or discharge horses or carriages, and
would not be responsible for loss or damage thereto,—was not admissible.

CASE against the defendants, three of the Directors of the Woodside Ferry Company.   The declaration stated, that the defendants,
before and at the time of the delivery of the goods and chattels to
them, and of the committing of the grievances thereinafter mentioned, to wit, on the 26th of August, 1840, were possessed of a
certain ferry across a certain arm of the sea called the River
Mersey, from Woodside, in the county of Chester, to Liverpool, in
the county of Lancaster; and thereupon afterwards, to wit, on &c.,
the plaintiffs, at the request of the defendants, then delivered to the
defendants certain goods and chattels of the plaintiffs of great
value, to wit, of the value of 10,000*l.*, to wit, a certain carriage, to
wit, a phaeton and *certain jewellery and watches, to wit, ten
boxes of jewellery and five bags of watches, contained and being in

WALKER
v.
JACKSON.

[*162]

the said carriage, to be by the defendants, for reward to them in
that behalf, taken care of and carried and conveyed in a certain
steam-boat, from Woodside aforesaid to Liverpool aforesaid, and
there, to wit, at Liverpool aforesaid, landed for the plaintiffs; and
the defendants, to wit, then took, accepted, and received the said
carriage so containing the said jewellery and watches as aforesaid,
of and from the plaintiffs, for the purposes aforesaid; and it then
became and was the duty of the defendants to take due and proper
care of the said carriage, jewellery, and watches, whilst they
remained in their custody for the purposes aforesaid, and to take
due and proper care in and about the carriage, conveyance, and
landing of the same as aforesaid. Yet the defendants, not regarding their duty in that behalf, but contriving &c., afterwards, to
wit, on &c., took so little and such bad and improper care of the
said carriage, jewellery, and watches, whilst they remained in their
custody for the purposes aforesaid, and took so little and such bad
and improper care, and so negligently conducted themselves in and
about the carriage, conveyance, and landing of the same as aforesaid, that the same then, by reason of the bad, imperfect, and
improper conduct of the defendants, their mariners and servants,
in that behalf, became and were very much broken, injured,
wetted, &c. &c.

Pleas, first, not guilty; secondly, that the plaintiffs did not
deliver to them the defendants, nor did they accept and receive
from the plaintiffs, the said goods and chattels in the declaration
mentioned, or any of them, or any part thereof, to be by the
defendants carried and conveyed in the said steam-boat from
Woodside aforesaid to Liverpool aforesaid, and there landed for the
plaintiffs, for reward to them the defendants in that behalf, in
manner and form &c. Thirdly, that the said goods and chattels in
the declaration mentioned were delivered by the plaintiffs to, and

[*163]   · *accepted and received by them the defendants, to be ferried across
the said ferry in the declaration mentioned, and there landed and
delivered to the plaintiffs, and the said reward in the declaration
mentioned to them in that behalf was for and in respect of such
ferryage, and landing and delivery, and for and in respect of
nothing else. And the defendants further say, that at the time of
the said delivery and acceptance and receipt of the said goods and
chattels, that is to say, on the said 26th day of August, 1840, it
was agreed by and between the plaintiffs and the defendants, as
part of the terms of the said acceptance and receipt, that they the

defendants were not to be in anywise answerable or accountable to WALKER
v.
JACKSON. the plaintiffs for any loss thereof or damage thereto which might occur in the course of the said ferryage and landing and delivery; and they the defendants then accepted and received the said goods and chattels to be so ferried and landed and delivered as aforesaid upon the terms of the said agreement, and upon no other terms whatsoever, whereof the plaintiffs then had knowledge and notice. And the defendants further say, that the said loss and damage of the said goods and chattels in the declaration mentioned happened and took place without any personal negligence or want of care whatsoever by the defendants themselves, and without any gross negligence or misfeasance of their mariners or servants, or otherwise howsoever. Verification.

The plaintiffs joined issue on the first and second pleas, and to the third replied *de injuriâ*, on which also issue was joined.

At the trial before Wightman, J., at the Liverpool Summer Assizes, 1841, it appeared that the plaintiffs were jewellers at Birmingham, and that on the 26th of August, 1840, one of the plaintiffs, travelling on behalf of the firm, put on board one of the defendants' steam-boats at Woodside, to be carried across to Liverpool, a horse and phaeton, the latter of which contained, in the box seat, jewellery and watches of *the value of several thousand pounds. [*164] The plaintiff paid 5*s.* for the ferryage of the phaeton and horse, which, according to the defendants' scale of charges, was the charge for " a light four-wheeled phaeton and one horse; " and he did not communicate the fact that the carriage contained any heavy or valuable property. The phaeton was carried safely over the river, and put out of the boat upon the slip at the Liverpool pierhead, and two of the defendants' servants endeavoured to draw it up the slip, but its weight overpowered them, and it ran back into the water, whereby the jewellery and watches were much injured. There was some conflict in the evidence as to the circumstances of the accident: according to the plaintiffs' witnesses, the men had drawn the phaeton some twenty yards up the slip before it ran back; and they stated also, that four men were necessary to bring it safely to the top of the slip: according to the evidence of the defendants' servants, they were overpowered by the weight of the carriage immediately on its being put out upon the slip, and on their endeavouring to turn it round for the purpose of being drawn up. The defendants' witnesses stated also, that the Company did not pay their men for putting carriages or horses on board the

WALKER
v.
JACKSON.

boats, or landing them; that the servants from the Woodside hotel generally brought down the carriages to the boats, but that if the defendants' servants put them on board or landed them, the owners of the carriages paid them for doing so.

The defendants' counsel contended, upon this state of facts, first, that there was no obligation on the defendants, by reason of their ownership of the ferry as alleged in the declaration, to land the carriage out of the steam-boat, but only to carry it safely across the river; and secondly, that the plaintiff was bound to have communicated to the defendants the fact, that the phaeton contained the jewellery and watches, the weight of which had occasioned the accident. The learned Judge reserved the first question; and

[*165]

*in summing up, left it to the jury to say whether there was any negligence or want of care on the part of the defendants: saying, that if the defendants undertook to land the carriage, they must do it safely; and he expressed his opinion that the plaintiff was not bound to give notice of the contents of the carriage. The jury found for the plaintiffs, damages 211*l.*

In Michaelmas Term, *Knowles* obtained a rule *nisi* for a new trial, on the ground of misdirection. He contended, first, that the learned Judge ought to have directed the jury that the defendants were entitled to a verdict on the second issue, it being no part of their duty as owners of the ferry to land the carriage; secondly, that even if the defendants were bound to land the carriage, they did in fact land it, by putting it out of the boat upon the slip; and thirdly, that the plaintiff was bound to give notice that there was an extra weight, the reward to the defendants being applicable to the phaeton alone.

Kelly and *Crompton* showed cause at the sittings after last Hilary Term (February 9):

The plaintiffs are entitled to retain their verdict. First, the declaration in this case is not founded on any duty in the defendants as owners of the ferry. They are liable upon their contract. If a ferryman, although not bound to do so, choose to receive goods to carry, he is liable like any other contractor. What took place in this case shows that the defendants were bound by their contract to land the carriage; if not, why did they set about doing it? they were not required to do so. Nor was there proof of any regular charge made against the owner of a carriage for putting on board or landing it. It was entirely a question of fact, what was the

contract between the parties, and not at all a question of law. It
is not as if the declaration had charged the defendants as common
carriers, or as proprietors of the ferry, and as a deduction of law
had alleged the duty; but this *is an action founded upon a contract. Who is to land carriages from the defendants' boats but the
servants of the defendants? the owners do not bring their servants
to do it. And whether the men do this as the employees of the
owner, or as the servants of the ferryman, is altogether a question
of fact for the jury, and which the defendants ought to have required
to be left to them.

In like manner, it is a mere question of fact what amounted to
a landing within the contract. It is obvious that if the defendants
were bound to land at all, they were bound to land safely; and
why did they attempt to take the phaeton up the slip, unless
because it was an ordinary part of their duty, under the contract,
to land it safely on the top. The question of negligence was entirely
for the jury; and whether the landing was over or not is part of
the question of negligence. Landing without negligence is landing
in a secure place.

Thirdly, the question as to the necessity of notice was also a
question of fact. But the defendants could not avail themselves
of this point without proof on their parts of some notice limiting
their liability; in the absence of that, the law will not raise any
such implied limitation. But again—if the injury arose from the
plaintiffs' having thrown the defendants off their guard, by sending
on board a carriage too heavily laden to be safely landed by the
ordinary means, that negatived negligence on the part of the
defendants; and the question of negligence was left to the jury.

Knowles and *Martin*, in support of the rule:

The only question left to the jury was, whether there was any
negligence or want of care on the part of the defendants, and the
question whether the landing was complete was never put to them.
First, the defendants did not contract to carry the concealed
jewellery, by which the weight of the carriage was doubled. There
was nothing to draw their *attention to its contents, and the plaintiff
paid only the charge for a "light phaeton." The defendants are
not common carriers, but mere bailees for hire, and liable only for
the want of reasonable care. The contract here was only to carry
a phaeton, which required no extraordinary care. If they had
known the additional weight, they might have exercised greater

WALKER
v.
JACKSON.

[*166]

[*167]

and adequate care in landing it. Before it can be said that a person in the situation of the defendants is guilty of negligence in carrying, it must appear that he knows what he is carrying, and therefore what degree of care is requisite to its security.

Secondly, the question whether the defendants contracted to land the carriage was not left to the jury; it was treated as a question of law. Now the only evidence of any contract at all was of a contract resulting from the defendants' situation and supposed duty as ferrymen. But the duty of a ferryman is only to supply a boat, to pass over passengers with their goods: Termes de la Ley; *Payne* v. *Partridge* (1). The ferryman never takes possession of the goods at all: they remain as much in the possession of the owner, as when a man drives over a bridge subject to a toll. It being, therefore, no part of his duty or contract as a ferryman to take the goods of the passengers into his possession, he is not chargeable in respect of their custody. They were then stopped by the COURT.

PARKE, B.:

Unfortunately we cannot collect exactly in what mode this question was left to the jury, but all the Court are clearly of opinion that it is a question for the jury, whether there was a contract between these parties, implied by usage or otherwise, to receive this carriage into the defendants' care, to put it on board, and to land it again at the expiration of the transit. The question is whether there was any such contract existing between these [*168]   *parties, and I think the simple circumstance of the defendants being ferrymen would not give rise to the contract laid in this declaration, nor import an obligation on the ferryman to take the trouble, either of putting a carriage on board or discharging it out the vessel on her arrival. It might be such a ferry as that by usage the ferryman takes that obligation upon himself; and the question will be, whether there is such a usage in this case, and whether the defendants contracted, not merely to carry across the river, but to take the carriage into their care, and to land it in safety: and then will arise the further question, whether it was properly taken care of by being placed at the bottom of the slip, and in a place of security. This carriage was left standing at the bottom of the slip, and the question is whether it ought not to have been carried up the slip immediately, so as never to have been in

(1) 1 Show. 257; 1 Salk. 12.

a state of insecurity; and whether such would not be the defendants' duty in landing it.   The questions, therefore, are, whether
there was a contract, by virtue of which the defendants were to
land the carriage at the expiration of the passage, and whether the
landing was complete by placing it at the bottom of the slip, or
whether they were not bound to take it up and put it on the quay.
These are questions of fact, which should have been determined
by the jury, and it does not appear to me that they have been
satisfactorily left, so as to enable the jury to determine them.

With regard to the other objections made on the part of the
defendants to this contract, we think they are not such as ought
to prevail.   There is no doubt that there was a delivery of the
carriage and its contents, and that included the jewellery; the
objection, therefore, urged by *Mr. Knowles*, that there was no
delivery of the jewellery, cannot prevail.   And I take it now to be
perfectly well understood, according to the majority of opinions
upon the subject, that if any thing is delivered to a person to be
carried, it is the duty of the person receiving it to ask such questions about it as may be necessary; if he ask no questions, and
there be no *fraud to give the case a false complexion, on the   [*169]
delivery of the parcel, he is bound to carry the parcel as it is.   It
is the duty of the person who receives it to ask questions; if they
are answered improperly, so as to deceive him, then there is no
contract between the parties; it is a fraud which vitiates the
contract altogether.   But in this case, if there was a delivery at
all of the carriage, with the jewellery in it, it was a delivery to be
carried for reward, namely, five shillings.   The objections made
on this ground, therefore, ought not to prevail: but we think there
ought to be a new trial, in order to establish these two points:
first, whether there was a delivery, as alleged in the declaration,
of the carriage to the defendants; and secondly, whether the
defendants entered into any contract, either express or implied, to
land the carriage upon its arrival on the shore, and in what way
such landing was to take place,—whether simply by leaving it at
the bottom of the slip, or whether it was their duty, according to
their contract, to carry it up the slip, and leave it on the pier-head.
If such was their duty, the only remaining question will be, whether
they were guilty of negligence in the performance of it.   All these
are questions to be disposed of by the jury, but it does not satisfactorily appear that they have at present decided upon them.   The
rule must therefore be made absolute.

WALKER
v.
JACKSON.

ALDERSON, B.:

If the question in this case depended simply upon this, whether there were negligence in the defendants, and whether the carriage ought to have been carried up the slip by four instead of two persons, considering the weight of it, and considering the circumstances connected with it, which the defendants might fairly be considered to be acquainted with, I think the verdict ought not only not to be disturbed, but that it would have been perfectly right. But a further question for the consideration of the jury, and which ought to have been submitted to them, is, whether there is any evidence of the phaeton, including the *jewellery, having been delivered to the defendants, to be carried by them on behalf of the plaintiffs. That is a question upon which the jury ought to have passed their judgment, and there is evidence by which they might have established that fact either one way or the other.

[*170]

Then the next question will be, what was the nature of the alleged contract? Was it to carry across, or to carry across and to land? And a further question is as to the landing itself; whether they were guilty of negligence in landing. What is a landing? That is for the jury to determine. Is it putting the carriage on shore in a secure place, where it would remain in safety unless it were removed out of that position? If that is a landing, then it will be for the jury to say whether that has been done in the present case. Even supposing, however, that the putting it at the bottom of the slip only is a landing, I apprehend that if the defendants themselves do not leave it there, but proceed to drag it up the slip, and in that conduct themselves negligently, by not applying a sufficient force, they would still be liable, notwithstanding they would have landed it under the circumstances; because it may be considered as one and the same act, and the criterion is not the length of time that it rests in that position, but whether the parties who so placed it at the bottom of the slip desisted, and left the rest to be done by other persons. All these are questions upon which the jury ought to exercise their judgment.

GURNEY, B., and ROLFE, B., concurred.

Rule absolute.

The case was again tried at the last Spring Assizes at Liverpool, before Rolfe, B., when it was proved to have been the invariable usage and custom for the defendants to land carriages put on

board their steam-boats, for the *purpose of being conveyed over
the ferry, on their arrival on the opposite side. The defendants,
for the purpose of rebutting the inference of a contract on their
part arising from this usage, tendered in evidence certain placards,
containing a list of the charges and ferryages by the Woodside
Ferry Company, subjoined to which was a notice that the proprietors did not undertake to load or discharge horses, carriages,
&c., and that they would not in anywise be responsible for any loss
thereof or damage thereto. These placards were proved to have
been hung up on each side of the covered gate by which foot
passengers entered the slip for the purpose of getting on board;
but it appeared that the plaintiff, and other persons with carriages,
went down to the boat by another entrance, at which there were
no notices, and persons going in carriages could not see the
notices at the foot passengers' gate. This evidence was objected to
by the plaintiffs' counsel, and the learned Judge refused to receive
it. The plaintiffs having again obtained a verdict, *Knowles*, in
Easter Term last, obtained a rule to show cause why there should
not be a new trial, on the ground that the above evidence ought to
have been received; against which

Baines and *Crompton* now showed cause:

The evidence was properly rejected. It was proved at the trial,
that it was the invariable usage of the defendants to land carriages
ferried over in their boats, and from that usage a contract was
properly inferred that they undertook safely to land the plaintiffs'
carriage; and that cannot be affected by a notice stuck up under
cover, in the entrance for foot passengers, which the plaintiff, going
with a carriage, had no means of seeing, and which it was not
shown had come in any way to his knowledge. The evidence was
therefore inadmissible; and if it had been admitted, must have
been utterly valueless. The only way in which it could possibly
be evidence, would have been for the purpose of explaining some
of the facts *which the plaintiffs had proved, as to the custom of
landing carriages; but it could not affect that question, because the
evidence showed that the notice was so placed, that it could not be
seen by persons going with carriages. If these placards were
admissible in evidence, they would be equally receivable if they had
been proved to have been stuck up in the most remote part of
Liverpool. The plaintiffs' evidence was confined to acts done by
the defendants, and did not include declarations to or by third

WALKER
v.
JACKSON.

[*171]

[*172]

persons; and this being a mere declaration by writing, it could not be used to explain the plaintiffs' case, and could not be any evidence against them, unless it were shown in some way to have come to their knowledge.

Knowles and *Martin*, in support of the rule:

This was not an action against the defendants as common carriers, but upon a contract safely to carry and land the plaintiffs' carriage; and the *onus* of proving that contract lay upon the plaintiffs. The defendants admit, if it had been otherwise, that this would not have been evidence, because in that case they could not have affected the plaintiffs without showing notice to them. But here, if there is any contract, it is one to be inferred from the general conduct of the defendants in their dealing with the public. Of that conduct the putting up of these placards formed an important part, and must be taken into consideration as restricting their liability. It is admitted that the defendants cannot in this way establish a new contract to cut down another; but the object of this evidence was not to cut down any contract established by the plaintiffs' evidence, but to explain the course of dealing from which a contract was sought to be inferred, and to show what that really was. The plaintiffs seek to establish a contract from the conduct of the defendants with respect to unknown persons, and from certain acts done by them: and this is not to be restricted to such facts only as make against *them. The exhibiting of this placard was an important part of their conduct, and was legitimate evidence to rebut the contract sought to be established.

[*173]

LORD ABINGER, C. B.:

This is a very clear case. It was established by an irresistible body of evidence, that it was the practice of the defendants to land carriages passing over the ferry, so as to support the contract set forth in the declaration; and in order to meet that evidence, the defendants proposed to read these notices. In general, in cases of this nature, it is usual to give some evidence of the probability that the parties were made acquainted with the contents of such notices. as by showing that the notice was inserted in a newspaper the plaintiff was in the habit of taking, or in a public office he was in the habit of frequenting; and I see no reason for an exception in this instance, for it appeared here that it was not at all likely that any parties who brought carriages could see these placards. As to the plaintiff himself, it is quite clear that there was no evidence to show that he did see them, or even that it was probable that he could have done so. The evidence, therefore, was properly rejected.

ALDERSON, B.:

I am of the same opinion. The acts proved by the plaintiffs, upon which they relied to substantiate the existence of a contract, were those done with respect to persons bringing carriages. These notices were stuck up in the way for foot passengers, and it appeared that the plaintiff did not go by that way; neither was it shown that any person with a carriage ever went by it. No reasonable probability, therefore, existed that the plaintiff, or any parties going with carriages, ever saw them.

GURNEY, B., concurred.

ROLFE, B.:

The defendants expressly admitted on the *trial, that they could not bring home to the plaintiff notice of these placards; but it now seems to be contended, that notice of them, even to third persons, would render them admissible. If it had been shown that these notices had been seen by a considerable number of the public bringing over carriages, there might have been some pretence for saying that they ought not to have been rejected; but this was not suggested, neither is there a particle of evidence of such a fact. On the contrary, all the evidence showed, that, with respect to such persons, it was just the same as if the notices had been kept in the desks of the Company.

[*174]

Rule discharged.

THE MARQUIS OF ANGLESEY *v.* LORD HATHERTON AND ANOTHER (1).

(10 Meeson & Welsby, 218—248; S. C. 12 L. J. Ex. 57.)

1842.
June 3, 4.

*Exch. of
Pleas.*

[218]

On a question as to the existence of a custom in a particular manor, evidence of a like custom in an adjoining manor, though within the same parish and leet, is not admissible.

Not even though there be evidence to show that the latter manor was a subinfeudation of the former; at least, unless it be clearly shown that they were separated after the time of legal memory, since otherwise they may have had different immemorial customs.

Evidence of payment of an annual sum of 4*s.* by the lord of the manor of

(1) Cited in *Duke of Portland* v. *Hill* (1866) L. R. 2 Eq. 765, 782, 35 L. J. Ch. 439; *Rajah Rup Singh* v. *Rani Baisni* (1884) L. R. 11 Ind. App. 163; *Johnstone* v. *Spencer* (1887) 30 Ch. D. 581, 595, 53 L. T. 502.—A. C.

W. to the lord of the manor of C. "for the manor of W.," was held not to be sufficient evidence that W. was such a subinfeudation of C.

A deed dated in 1605, made between the lord of the manor of C. of the one part, and a number of the copyholders of the manor of the other, reciting that the customs of the manor, of and concerning their copyhold premises, had immemorially been claimed to be as thereinafter expressed, proceeded to state in detail various alleged customs, among which no mention was made of any custom for the copyholders to take minerals. The deed then stated, that whereas, at the request of the said copyholders, and in consideration of 1,500*l.* paid by them to the lord, he had agreed that the said customs should be allowed, ratified, and confirmed, and that the copyholders were contented to submit to them : therefore the lord did thereby, for him and his heirs, allow all the said customs to be the true customs of the manor, for and touching all the said customary and copyhold lands before mentioned ; and the lord then covenanted with the said copyholders that he, his heirs and assigns, should be bound by the said customs for ever, and that the copyholders, their heirs and assigns, should enjoy them for ever without interruption ; and the copyholders covenanted with him that they would at all times thereafter submit themselves to and be bound by the said customs. It was then provided, that forasmuch as some matter or point of custom within the manor, not therein mentioned, might come in question, and doubts might be made of the true exposition of some matter or custom therein set forth, it was agreed between the parties that if any such matter, point, or custom, should come in question, it should be settled by a jury to be summoned as therein mentioned. And it was further agreed, that none of the ancient Court rolls of the manor should be showed or taken to prejudice or impugn any of the customs therein specified. This deed was confirmed in terms by a decree in Chancery, which contained a clause providing that it should not, nor should the said customs, extend but to the complainants and defendants (the copyholders who were parties to the deed, and the lord), and to the complainants' copyhold tenements, and should not be prejudicial to the lord concerning any other copyholds in the manor.

Held, that this deed was admissible in evidence, against a copyholder deriving title under one of the parties to it, to negative the existence of a custom of the manor for the copyholders to take the minerals under their respective copyholds.

Semble, that it would have been evidence for the same purpose, even against a copyholder not deriving title under any of the parties to it.

TROVER for coals, limestone, and ironstone. Pleas, first, as to the conversion and disposition of the said coals, parcel of the said goods and chattels in the declaration mentioned, that divers, to wit, 50 acres of land, with the appurtenances, situate in the parish of Cannock, in the county of Stafford, before and at the said time when &c. were, and from time immemorial have been, within and parcel of the manor of Cannock and Rugeley, in the said county of Stafford, and a customary tenement thereof, demised and demisable by the lord of the said manor, or his steward of the Courts of the said manor, for the time being, to any person or persons willing to take the same *in fee simple, at the will of the lord, according to the custom of the said manor, by and under the rents, customs, and

[*219]

services theretofore due and of right accustomed. And the defendants further say, that within the said manor there is and hath
been a certain ancient and laudable custom there used and approved
of, that is to say, that every customary tenant of each and every
customary tenement within and parcel of the said manor, for the
time being, from time whereof the memory of man is not to the
contrary, respectively hath and had used and been accustomed to
ˑhave, and of right ought to have had, and still of right ought to
have, for himself or herself respectively, all and every the mines,
veins, seams, and beds of coal lying or being or to be found under
the soil of each and every of the said customary tenements respectively, together with full and free liberty for each and every of the
said customary tenants respectively, and for his or her workmen or
servants, to open, search for, dig, get, and win the said mines,
veins, seams, and beds of coal, so lying and being or to be found
under the soil of each and every of the said customary tenements
respectively, and the coals thence arising to take, carry, convey, or
otherwise dispose of, at his or her free will. And the defendants
further say, that long before the said time when &c., to wit, on the
26th day of October, 1825, the plaintiff, then being lord of the said
manor, at his Court holden in and for the said manor, before
Thomas Hinckley, Esq., then steward of the said Court, granted to
the defendant Edward John Lord Hatherton (by his then name and
style of Edward John Littleton, Esq.), and to John Walhouse, Esq.,
since deceased (amongst other things), the said customary tenement
in this plea first mentioned, with the appurtenances, to hold the
same to the said Edward John Lord Hatherton and the said John
Walhouse, and the survivor of them, and their heirs for ever, at the
will of the lord of the said manor, according to the custom of the
said manor, by and *under the rents, customs, and services there-   [*220]
fore due and of right accustomed; by virtue of which said grant
the defendant Edward John Lord Hatherton, afterwards, and before
the said time when &c., to wit, on the day and year last aforesaid,
entered into the said last-mentioned customary tenement, with the
appurtenances, and became and was thence continually until and at
the said time when &c., seised thereof in manner aforesaid, and
entitled to the said mines, veins, seams, and beds of coal lying and
being or to be found under the soil of the said last-mentioned customary tenement; wherefore the said defendant Edward John Lord
Hatherton, whilst he was so seised and entitled as aforesaid, and
after the death of the said John Walhouse, and before the said time

MARQUIS OF
ANGLESEY
v.
LORD
HATHERTON.

when &c., to wit, on the 1st day of January, 1839, opened, searched for, and dug certain mines, veins, seams, and beds of coal then lying and being under the soil of the said last-mentioned customary tenement, and then took, got, won, and carried away therefrom divers, to wit, 1,000 tons of coals, which are the same coals as are in the said declaration and in the introductory part of this plea mentioned : and the defendants further say, that afterwards, and before the said time when &c., to wit, on the day and year last aforesaid, the said Edward John Lord Hatherton delivered the said coals to one Richard Roe, to be kept by the said Richard Roe to and for the use of him the said Edward John Lord Hatherton ; and the said Richard Roe afterwards, and just before the said time when &c., to wit, on the day and year last aforesaid, in violation of his said trust, delivered the said coals to the plaintiff, who thereby then became and was possessed thereof ; whereupon the said Edward John Lord Hatherton in his own right, and the said Henry Brierly as his servant and by his command, at the said time when &c., took the said coals from and out of the possession of the plaintiff, as they lawfully might for the cause aforesaid, which is the same conversion and disposition as *in the introductory part of this plea mentioned. Verification.

[*221]

The second and third pleas were precisely similar, except that they were pleaded as to the ironstone and limestone respectively. The fourth, fifth, and sixth pleas were similar to the first, second, and third respectively, except that they alleged the custom to be for every customary tenant of the particular customary tenement in question to take the coals, &c. under the soil of his own tenement.

The replication to each of the pleas traversed the custom as therein alleged ; on which issue was joined.

At the trial before Cresswell, J., at the last Worcester Assizes, no evidence was offered in support of the custom set up in the fourth and subsequent pleas ; but the question was as to the existence of a general custom in the manor of Cannock and Rugeley, for the customary tenants to get coals and other minerals under the soil of their respective customary tenement. In order to establish the custom, the defendant proved numerous instances of working for minerals by the customary tenants in different parts of the manor (without license or interruption, so far as appeared), and also gave evidence of appearances of old workings in various places within the manor. The defendant also tendered in evidence two leases, each for twenty-one years, by tenants of the manor, containing a clause

giving the lessees a right to take minerals, subject to a rent, and
dated respectively in 1800 and 1802. The Court rolls of the manor
were produced, which simply stated the inrolment of certain leases
corresponding with the above in the date and parties. The latter
of these two leases, which had no minute or description upon it to
identify it with the entry on the Court roll, was rejected; the former
had indorsed upon it a memorandum of the inrolment, and it was
received in evidence. The defendant also gave in evidence a
surrender *of a customary tenement within the manor, by way of
mortgage, by one Thomas Barton and Eliza his wife, and the
admittance thereon, dated in May, 1730. After the surrender of
the tenement followed these words: "Except always to the aforesaid
Thomas Barton and Eliza his wife, and their heirs and assigns,
from time to time, free liberty to make coal mines, sloughs, or
drains, and all other things necessary to search for coals within the
lands aforesaid, or any part or parcel thereof, and to convert the
coals so found to the sole use and behoof of the said Thomas Barton
and Eliza his wife, their heirs and assigns." Surrenders of other
tenements, in some cases expressly reserving the minerals to the
surrenderor, in others passing them by express words to the
surrenderee, were also proved. The defendant then gave in evidence
two accounts of the stewards of the adjoining manor of Wyrley, in
the reigns of Richard II. and Henry IV., taking credit for payments
made by them in respect of the manor, amongst which, under the
head of "rent absolute," was "four shillings to the Bishop of
Chester;" and annual payments were proved to have been made of
the like sum of four shillings by the Duke of Sutherland, the
present lord of the manor of Wyrley, to the plaintiff, by the hands
of the bailiff of the manor of Cannock, "for the manor of Wyrley,"
as it was expressed in the receipts. It was contended that this
payment, unexplained, led to a presumption that the manor of
Wyrley was a subinfeudation of the manor of Cannock, and therefore that evidence of the existence in the former manor of a similar
custom to that now claimed in respect of the latter, was admissible.
The learned Judge, however, refused to receive such evidence.

On the part of the plaintiff, a deed was tendered in evidence,
dated the 2nd November, 3 Jac. I. (1605), made between William,
Lord Paget, lord of the manor of (*inter alia*) Cannock and Rugeley,
of the one part, and Sir Walter Aston, and a great number of other
persons, copyholders of the several manors therein mentioned, of the
other part. *This deed recited, that whereas the said copyholders

[*222]

[*223]

87—2

MARQUIS OF
ANGLESEY
v.
LORD
HATHERTON.

did severally and respectively hold to them and their several heirs, the several copyholds mentioned in the several schedules thereunto annexed, of the said Lord Paget, as of his said several manors, by several and respective copies of Court rolls of the said manors, according to the several customs thereof, and by the several rents in the said schedules also mentioned; and whereas also the customs of the said several manors, of and concerning the said copyhold premises, all the time whereof the memory of man was not to the contrary, had been claimed to be in such manner and form as thereinafter expressed: the deed then proceeded to set forth the alleged customs, as to inheritance, descent, guardianship, dower, fines payable to the lord, powers of leasing and exchange, heriots, the right of felling timber without impeachment of waste, free common on the wastes of the manor, the right of getting heath, turf, clay, sand, earth, marl and gravel on the waste, escheat, suit and service at the lord's Courts, &c. &c.; but making no mention of any custom for the copyholders to take minerals. The deed then proceeded to state, that whereas, at the humble petition of the said copyholders, by them made to the said Lord Paget, and for consideration of the sum of 1,500*l.* by them paid to him, " when he, the said Lord Paget, is well pleased that the said customs shall be allowed, ratified, and confirmed, as also the said copyholders are contented to submit themselves to the same, to the end certainty may be left in that behalf to their posterity: " therefore the said Lord Paget, in accomplishment of so much as on his part was to be performed, did, by those presents, for him and his heirs, allow all and every the premises, and did thereby ratify and confirm the said customs and every of them, and was contented and well pleased that the customs before mentioned, and every of them, should for ever thereafter be the true customs of the said manors, for and touching all and every the said customary and copyhold lands and tenements

[*224] before mentioned. The Lord Paget then further *covenanted with the said copyholders and every of them, and every of their heirs, executors, and assigns, that he, his heirs and assigns, should and would be bound by the said customs for evermore; and that the said copyholders, and every of them, their heirs and assigns, should and might for ever thereafter enjoy and use the same customs and every of them, without any let, trouble, denial, or interruption of him the said Lord Paget, his heirs or assigns, or any of them. And the said copyholders severally covenanted with the Lord Paget, that they, their heirs and assigns, should and would, at all times

thereafter, submit themselves to the said customs, and be bound MARQUIS OF
thereby, and pay and perform every thing on their parts to be ANGLESEY
performed in those presents mentioned or expressed, &c.   Then *v.*
LORD
HATHERTON.
followed this clause : " And moreover, for that some matter or point
of custom within the said manors, or some of them, herein not
mentioned or expressed, may come in question, and for that also
some doubts may be made of the true exposition of some matter or
custom herein set forth, or of some circumstance thereof, therefore
it is fully concluded and agreed between all the said parties, and
every of them, that if any such matter, point, or custom shall, upon
just cause come in question, then an indifferent jury of fourteen or
sixteen copyholders of the same manor where such doubts shall
arise, at some Court for that purpose, shall be impanelled," &c. &c.,
to inquire and make presentment of the said matter, custom, or
question, and that their presentment should bind all the said parties
and their heirs for ever.   And it was also agreed, that none of the
ancient Court rolls of any of the said manors should be thenceforth
showed, nor should be esteemed or taken, to impugn, prejudice, or
hurt any of the customs in those presents specified or set down ;
and provision was made for the future keeping of the Court rolls in
a chest, with four locks and keys, in the church of Cannock, one
key to be kept by the steward of the manors, another by the lord's
bailiff, and the others by two indifferent copyholders.

Among the tenements specified in the schedule of the manor of [225]
Cannock, subjoined to this deed, were certain closes, stated to be
held by Thomas Sprott, jun., (one of the parties signing the deed),
which were shown to be part of a tenement of which the defendant
Lord Hatherton was now the owner (1).

The plaintiff also tendered in evidence a decree in Chancery,
dated 29th November, 4 Jac. I. (1606), in a suit wherein Sir Walter
Aston, knight, and others, were plaintiffs, and the Lord Paget,
defendant ; reciting, that they the said complainants, and their
several ancestors and those whose estate they severally have had,
claimed the customs of the said manors, of and concerning the
said copyhold premises, to be as thereinafter expressed, for and
touching which customs and claim divers suits, questions, and
controversies, had grown between the lords of the said manors and

(1) Much discussion took place, both
at Nisi Prius and before the Court, on
the question whether the identity of
this property was satisfactorily established in evidence : but it is assumed
for the purposes of this report that
it was.

the copyholders before named, and others before them, copyholders
of the said premises; for the final ending and determining of all
which questions, controversies, and debates, and for avoiding all
future doubts and controversies concerning the said customs, the
defendant Lord Paget, and they the complainants, of their mutual
consents and agreements, about six months then last past, did
conclude and agree that the customs of the said several manors, of
and concerning the said copyhold premises, thenceforth for ever
should be esteemed and taken to be in manner and form as thereinafter expressed, that is to say, (setting them forth precisely as in
the deed): and reciting, that the complainants further showed that
the said Lord Paget, in consideration of the sum of 1,500*l.* to him
by the said complainants paid, was well pleased that the said
customs should be allowed, ratified, and confirmed, and did

[*226] acknowledge and confess that he *was agreed that the customs
before mentioned, and every of them, thereafter for ever should be
the true customs of the said manors, for and touching all and
every the said customary and copyhold lands and tenements before
mentioned, and had promised that he the said Lord Paget, his heirs
and assigns, and every of them, should and would be bound by the
said customs for evermore, for and concerning the said copyhold
premises, &c. &c. (proceeding as in the deed, *ante*, p. 580): and
stating the answer of the Lord Paget, confessing the allegations of
the bill, and that he had promised and agreed to all the conclusions,
premises, and agreements therein specified, all which he alleged
that he was ready and willing to perform on his part, and was
contented that the same should appear and remain of record, and
be ordered and decreed by the Court to continue for ever, &c., so
as such order and decree, and the said customs, should extend only
to the said complainants, their heirs and assigns, and to their
copyhold lands, tenements, and hereditaments, and to none other,
and might not be hurtful nor prejudicial to the said Lord Paget,
his heirs nor assigns, of, for, or concerning any other copyhold
lands in any of the said manors, nor of, for, or concerning any
duty out of the same: it was therefore, by and with the assent and
consent of the said complainants and defendants, ordered and
decreed, that all and every the said customs, conclusions, and
agreements mentioned in the said bill, should have continuance
for ever, in manner and form as in the bill contained, and that the
said customs of the said several manors mentioned in the said bill,
and every of them, from thenceforth for ever should be, and be

esteemed and taken to be, the customs of the said manors, for and
touching all and every the said customary and copyhold lands and
tenements before mentioned, in manner and form as in the said
bill expressed, that is to say, (setting forth the customs in the same
terms as before).   The decree proceeded to confirm in all its parts
the agreement stated in the deed: and concluded with a clause
*stating that the said decree, nor anything therein contained, nor
any the customs aforesaid, should extend but only unto the said
complainants and defendants, their several heirs and assigns for
ever, and to the said complainants' copyhold lands, tenements, and
hereditaments, and to none other, and should not be hurtful nor
prejudicial to the said Lord Paget, his heirs nor assigns, of, for, or
concerning any other copyhold lands in any of the said manors,
nor of, for, or concerning any duty out of the same.

It was objected, on the part of the defendants, that the deed and
decree were not admissible in evidence, on the ground that they
constituted a mere agreement, for a pecuniary consideration,
between the lord and the particular copyholders who were parties
to the deed, in respect of the customs which were in future to
apply to their particular copyholds, but did not amount to any
admission of the non-existence of the particular custom alleged by
the defendant, so as to be evidence against him.   The learned
Judge, however, received the evidence, holding the deed to be a
declaration by Sprott, whose estate the defendant now had, what
were the then existing customs of the manor.

In summing up the case to the jury, his Lordship stated, with
reference to the surrender of May, 1730, produced on the part of
the plaintiff, and the exception of minerals contained therein, that
he was not prepared to say the steward could refuse to make the
entry of the surrender on the Court roll, or to make the admittance
thereon, whatever might be the terms of the exception which the
parties had introduced into the surrender, and whether they were,
in point of fact, entitled to the right excepted or not; but that it
was important as showing that the agent of the lord had distinct
notice that the parties were setting up a claim to the minerals, to
the prejudice of the lord, and it did not appear that any proceeding
was in consequence taken on his part to put a stop to the workings.
*He made a similar observation as to the other surrenders, and
the lease of 1800.   And after stating all the evidence, he left it to
the jury to say, whether they were of opinion that the copyholders
of the manor had been proved to have had, from time immemorial,

MARQUIS OF
ANGLESEY
v.
LORD
HATHERTON.

[*227]

[*228]

MARQUIS OF
ANGLESEY
v.
LORD
HATHERTON.

the customary right to take the mines and minerals. The jury found a verdict for the plaintiff.

In Easter Term, *Sir T. Wilde* obtained a rule *nisi* for a new trial, on the following grounds : first, that the evidence of the customs of the manor of Wyrley ought to have been received in evidence : on this point, the cases of *Champian* v. *Atkinson* (1), *Duke of Somerset* v. *France* (2), and *Rowe* v. *Brenton* (3), were cited : secondly, that the deed and decree of 1605-6 ought not to have been received : and thirdly, that the learned Judge had misdirected the jury, in stating it as his opinion that the steward was bound to receive and inrol surrenders which professed to pass, or to reserve, any right to which the surrenderor was not entitled by the custom of the manor, and therefore had given too little effect to the surrenders proved on the part of the defendant : and also that he had erroneously stated the deed of 1605 as evidence of what were the immemorial customs of the manor, whereas it amounted to no more than a creation of the customs agreed upon *in futuro.*

The *Solicitor-General, Talfourd,* Serjt., *R. V. Richards, Whateley,* and *Whitmore,* now showed cause against the rule :

I. The evidence of the custom of the manor of Wyrley was rightly rejected. It was suggested that that manor was a subinfeudation of the manor of Cannock ; but no ground was laid for such a conclusion. No connexion was shown between the Bishop of Chester, to whom the 4*s.* appeared to have been paid by the lord

[*229]

of the manor of Wyrley in *ancient times, and the lord of the manor of Cannock, or in any way with that manor. The whole basis, therefore, of the argument for the defendant on this point fails, no connexion whatever being made out between the two manors ; still less that that of Wyrley is a subinfeudation of the manor of Cannock. But even if it were, it does not follow that their customs should be identical. The subinfeudation must have been anterior to the Statute of *Quia Emptores,* but at what date there is no evidence whatever. Supposing the subinfeudation to have been created before the reign of Richard I., why may not the customs differ ? There is no foundation for the argument, unless

(1) 3 Keb. 90.
(2) 1 Stra. 654.

(3) 32 R. R. 524 (8 B. & C. 758 ; 3 Man. & Ry. 361).

it were shown when and how the manors were separated. The
decision in *Rowe* v. *Brenton* shows no more than this,—that where
the inquiry is as to the incidents of a particular estate existing in
a manor, and the same estate is found to prevail throughout a
district, its incidents throughout that district may be looked to, to
see what they are in the particular manor. The evidence was not
tendered in that case to prove a custom, but to prove the nature
of the general tenure in question. In the case of *The Duke of
Somerset* v. *France*, the question was whether a fine was payable
by the customary tenants of the manor to a tenant for life of the
manor under a marriage settlement, on the death of the last
admitting lord. Evidence was offered of instances of fines paid in
like cases to lords of other manors. Lord RAYMOND, Ch. J., says,—
" I have always looked upon it as a settled principle in the law,
that the custom of one manor shall not be given in evidence to
explain the custom of another manor; for if this kind of evidence
should be allowed, the consequence seems to be that it would let
in the custom of one manor into another, and in time bring the
customs of all manors to be the same." REYNOLDS, J., expressed
the same opinion; although, upon the supposed authority of
Champian v. *Atkinson*, and of a practice alleged at the Bar to
have existed on the northern circuit, the evidence was admitted.
*FORTESCUE, J., took the same distinction that was taken in *Rowe* v.
Brenton, between evidence as to the custom and as to the tenure
of a manor, and thought the evidence admissible as being referable
to the latter question. And it appears, from a note of the reporter,
that the Judges of the Common Pleas and Exchequer were all of
opinion that the evidence ought not to have been allowed. It
ought, therefore, in order to found this objection, to have been
shown that the manors were separated, with all their incidents,
since the time of legal memory.

(ALDERSON, B.: If a common origin were sufficient, which is the
utmost extent to which this case can be carried, all manors have a
common origin, namely, by grant from the Crown; therefore the
customs of all manors would be receivable. For aught that
appears, these manors might have had a common origin at periods
when the customs would be different.)

II. The deed and decree of 3 & 4 Jac. I. were rightly received in
evidence. It was shown that the present defendant derived title to

MARQUIS OF
ANGLESEY
v.
LORD
HATHERTON.

[*230]

MARQUIS OF ANGLESEY *v.* LORD HATHERTON.

a portion of his copyhold tenements from one of the parties to the deed. Now it is plain that that deed was executed in order to settle for all time to come the disputed customs of the manor as they then existed. The lord was thereby conceding the claims of the copyholders to their utmost limit, and receiving in return the large sum (at that day) of 1,500*l.*: and when they are stating the customs of the manor in their own favour, no mention whatever is made of any right to take the minerals. Is not the then declaration of the copyholders evidence what were the customs of the manor?

(ROLFE, B.: The argument on the other side is, that the deed is not evidence, on the ground that the Lord Paget had only agreed, in consideration of a sum of money, to admit such to be the customs in future.)

It is not merely an admission that they should be such in future, but that they had been so for all time. It is put as being a payment for forbearance to claim more extensive *rights; but it is much more: it is an admission by both parties of the existing customs, and is clearly evidence on a question touching the customs of the manor, arising at any time between the lord and the tenant of one of the same tenements therein mentioned.

[*231]

III. The learned Judge was guilty of no misdirection whatever. With respect to the leases, nothing was shown to have been done under them, and at best they were equivocal; because if the lord had given his customary tenant a license to work mines, the latter would for that purpose require such an agreement with his tenant. The supposed misdirection in this respect is, that the learned Judge told the jury the document was of no great weight, because the steward was bound to inrol the lease if brought to him, and it was not binding on the lord. But it is in no sense misdirection to give too much or too little weight to a fact, even if it appeared that it was done in this case. Then as to the supposed misdirection with respect to the deed of 1605, that objection, if it amounted to anything, would apply against the admissibility of the evidence. But in truth there was no misdirection in law, and the question in issue was clearly and fully left to the jury.

Sir T. Wilde, Ludlow, Serjt., and *W. J. Alexander, contrà:*

I. As to the admissibility of the deed and decree. This was a

contract by deed between the lord and certain tenants of the MARQUIS OF
ANGLESEY
manor, and the suit was by bill for a specific performance of that
contract, which was made in consideration of a sum of 1,500*l.*
Why should the lord exact such a sum of money for admitting
the ancient customs of the manor ? Reputation *post litem motam*
is not admissible evidence of a custom ; the deed, therefore, cannot
be receivable on that footing. This is an admission made on
payment of a sum of money by the one party to the other. As the
mere compromise of a dispute, it cannot be admissible against
other persons. It is said, however, that it is a *mutual admission   [*232]
as to their existing rights. Now it is part of the agreement that
the ancient Court rolls shall never be referred to, to disturb or
impugn it : that is altogether inconsistent with its being a definition
of the ancient rights of the parties. Besides, it is applicable only
to the particular copyhold tenements of which the complainants
were seised, and all the admissions have reference to them only,
not to the manor generally. A custom is a law governing the
district generally, and it is rather a prescription than a custom, if
it apply only to particular tenements. Here the consideration
and the admission are equally limited to the particular tenements.
There is no admission in terms, that for the future the customs
therein set forth shall be taken always to have prevailed. Then
the fact of the parties entering into mutual covenants shows that
the lord did not depend on the deed as being in itself a conclusive
admission of the existing customs. It is observable that the course
of descent provided for is not according to the custom of the
manor, but according to the course of descent at common law. So
as to the use of the coppice grounds ; it is not to be according
to the custom of the manor, but according to the laws as to the
realm ; and the same as to escheat. It is altogether a conventional
arrangement between the particular parties to whom the concessions
are made. Further, it clearly appears upon the face of the deed
itself that there were other customs not expressed therein ;
customs, doubtless, as to which there was no dispute, and which
therefore were not made the subject of the arrangement ; and
provision is made for settling them also if they should come in
question, not in regard to the manor generally, but as to the parties
to the deed, their heirs and assigns. And the decree expressly
provides, that the customs therein set forth shall not prejudice the
lord as to any other copyhold lands within the manor. It is, in
truth, a protest against their being taken to be customs of the

manor. This deed, therefore, was not *so made as to amount to a
declaration by the copyholders of the ancient customs of the manor,
so as to make it evidence as reputation, or as an admission by a
predecessor in estate. But even if it was admissible, the learned
Judge misdirected the jury, when he treated it as evidence of what
the immemorial customs of the manor were, and laid it down that
the omission, in the enumeration of the customs, of any mention of
the right to take the minerals, was evidence from which the jury
might infer that no such right existed immemorially.

II. The evidence of the custom in the manor of Wyrley ought to
have been received. The question is, if Wyrley was held of the
lord of the manor of Cannock at a chief rent of four shillings, what
must have been the nature of the connexion between the rent and
the manor? The payment of a chief rent imports the relation
of landlord and tenant; the circumstance of its being paid to
the bailiff of Cannock, (a manor in the same parish and leet),
afforded sufficient ground, in the absence of any explanation, for
the conclusion that the one manor was held of the other; and if the
manor of Wyrley had been separated from that of Cannock, *primâ
facie* their customs must be taken to have been the same. There
can be no inference of law that the customs have altered, although
in fact new customs may by possibility have grown up; but this
would constitute an objection to the value, not to the admissibility,
of the testimony. It follows as a legal consequence, at all events
until the presumption be rebutted by negative evidence, that, the
same customs having of course been applicable to all the copyholds
in the manor as it originally existed, upon the severance of a
portion of it by the subinfeudation, the part severed would retain
them. There having been a time when the customs were identical,
it is not to be presumed that on a sub-grant they have been altered.
The rule of law, that the customs of one manor are not admissible

in evidence on a question touching the *customs of another, is laid
down with this qualification in Phillipps on Evidence, Vol. I. p. 483
(8th edit.) : " Unless some connexion or relation is proved to have
existed between them, as by showing that they were all formerly
held under the same lord, or that the one manor was anciently
parcel of the other manor, such evidence is not admissible : " in
support of which position the case of *Moulin* v. *Dallison* (1) is
referred to. So BAYLEY, J., says in *Rowe* v. *Brenton* (2)—
" Generally speaking, a party cannot be allowed to prove the

(1) 1 Cro. Car. 484.   (2) 32 R. R. 524 (8 B. & C. 764).

custom of one manor by evidence of a custom in another, unless a
connexion between them be first established." The cases of *Champian* v. *Atkinson* (1), and *The Dean and Chapter of Ely* v. *Warren* (2),
are authorities to show that contiguity alone is sufficient to establish
this connexion, if the entire district be of the same nature, as was
the case here. So also, the case of *The Duke of Somerset* v. *France*
rests on the probability of connexion, and identity of customs,
which the same locality was reasonably presumed to afford. It
is obvious that the mode of showing such connexion must vary
according to the nature of the case, and cannot be universally
the same.

(The point as to the alleged misdirection with respect to the
leases and surrenders was abandoned.)

LORD ABINGER, C. B.:

This case has been fully argued, and I am of opinion that the
rule ought to be discharged.

Three points have been made for questioning the verdict.
The first relates to the non-admission of evidence of the working
of minerals in the manor of Wyrley; and it is contended that
evidence was given to connect the two manors, in such a way
as to authorize the reception of evidence of the customs of one
manor, in order to throw light upon the customs of the other.
The argument has been pushed by my brother *Ludlow* to such
a length in that respect, as to leave it a matter of doubt whether he
*does not contend that the general rule is, that the customs of one
manor, if the two lie contiguous, are evidence of the customs of the
other. But I have always understood, from the practice of the
Courts in ancient times, which has not been altered to the present
time, that there was no rule better established or more frequently
acted upon than this, that the customs of one manor could not be
given in evidence to prove the customs of another; because, as
each manor may have customs peculiar to itself, (and this, which
is contended for to-day, is admitted not to be a general or usual
custom), to admit the peculiar customs of another manor in order
to show the customs of the manor in question, would be a very
false guide for the purpose of leading to any such conclusion.
If no such custom exist, or can be found in the manor in
question, to show that such a thing existed in a neighbouring
manor, would be to put an end to all question as to the peculiar

(1) 3 Keb. 90.   (2) 2 Atk. 189.

MARQUIS OF
ANGLESEY
v.
LORD
HATHERTON.

[*235]

customs in particular manors, by throwing them open to the customs of all surrounding manors.

But there are, it is said, excepted cases; and one of the excepted cases that is contended for is, where one manor is held of another. Now that is a new proposition to me. I do not believe that can be satisfactorily established by any case. It was the custom of the Crown, in very ancient times, in granting a manor, to declare of what particular manor held by the Crown that manor should be held. Nobody ever contended that this gave an identity to the customs of the two manors. That which was the ancient custom, was followed out in almost all grants by the Crown since the dissolution of the monasteries; at least, in many cases which have come under my own knowledge, Crown manors were granted to be held of the manor of East Greenwich. It therefore is not at all a proposition based upon any established rule in Westminster Hall, that where one manor is held of another, their customs are identical. My brother *Ludlow* argues, that where one manor has been parcel

[*236]

of another, and has been separated by the lord and granted *out, such might be the case. In order to make that case out, if it be an exception to the general rule, it should be established clearly and beyond all controversy that the two manors originally formed one manor. That is not necessarily the case here. I do not see that the fact of one manor paying a chief rent, if you please, to the lord of another manor, is a necessary proof that the two manors were at one time one manor; and therefore the foundation of the argument fails in that respect. I think it also fails in the attempt to connect these manors together in point of fact. The evidence is, that this 4*s*. was paid to the Bishop of Chester in very early times, for this manor of Wyrley, as part of his fee. There is not a tittle of evidence to connect the Bishop of Chester with the manor of Cannock, or to show that the Marquis of Anglesey derives his title to the manor now in question from the Bishop of Chester. It may be so or it may not, but there is no evidence to show it; the only evidence is, that a receipt is given, which shows that 4*s*. was received for the use of the Earl of Uxbridge by the bailiff of the manor. But that does not prove how he came by it, or how he held the manor of Cannock, or that Wyrley was held of that manor. Then another argument is, that it is in the same parish. But is the contiguity of the two manors of the least importance? It is admitted it is not. Then it is within the same leet. But the lord, who has a leet granted to him, has it granted to extend over his own and other manors in the neighbourhood. There are well-known instances of that; for example, the Duke of Beaufort's leets. His Grace has a great many manors, and he holds one leet for several manors. In the North of England nothing is more common than to have many manors comprised in the same leet. There is nothing, therefore, in the fact of these manors being in the same leet or the same parish, which has the least efficiency to connect them with each other. I therefore think it was not shown, because the two manors were connected with the Earl of Uxbridge, that the one was *held of the other; and if it were, I think that would not alone be sufficient evidence to justify the proof of the customs of the one manor being received as evidence of the customs of the other. The excepted cases, when we come to look at them, really stand upon a very different footing. The case of the manors upon the border between England and Scotland is one. There prevails through those manors a particular species of tenure, called tenant-right. The tenure respecting those tenements is altogether different from the tenure respecting copyholds : they pass by lease and release, they descend from father to son, and there are peculiar customs belonging to that species of tenure. Now it being admitted that in these manors all the tenants hold under the same right, if it should happen that in one particular manor no example can be adduced of what is the custom in any particular case, it may be reasonable that in order to explain the nature of that tenure, which is not confined to one manor, but prevails in a great number, you may show what is the general usage with respect to that tenure ; and that is the whole extent to which those cases go.

But there is another connexion between manors, which might possibly admit this species of evidence; and that occurs in one of the cases which the learned Serjeant cited. It is well known that in the mining districts of Derbyshire and Cornwall, particular customs prevail. The custom in question in that case was not with respect to the minerals, but as to the rights of the miners. No question arose with respect to the right to the minerals as between the lord and the tenant; it was as to the rights of the miners as between each other : but if any question should arise with respect to the right to the minerals, in the mining districts, I do not pretend to say you might not give evidence of what has passed in one manor, for the purpose of showing what has been the custom as to the right to the minerals in another

manor. So again, the case of *Rowe* v. *Brenton*, which has been
cited, stands upon a ground perfectly distinct. That was not at all
a question of the customs *of the manor; it was a question of
what was the nature of the tenure of the assessional tenants;
whether they belonged to one manor or the other, they held under
the same title. It was not a manorial title. Since that case, by
modern Acts of Parliament, the nature of that title has, I believe,
been settled; but it certainly did not originate in their copyhold
interest; it apparently, and I believe really, originated in leases
granted for seven years, and renewable every seven years, and of
one year renewable every year, by the Assession Courts, embracing
the whole of what are called the assessional manors. That gave
an opportunity to say such was the custom, because at such a
Session such leases were granted in such a manor; and thus the
judgment of the Court of Queen's Bench in that case did not relate
to the tenure or the custom of the particular manor, but to the
nature of the assessional tenure in all the manors, as ascertained
from what was done in the one. Suppose there had been no manor
at all, but in truth the land had been held under such assessional
tenure, without being a manor; it would be evidence there in
exactly the same manner as if it had been a manor. This shows
that that decision has nothing to do with the question as to
admitting the customs of one manor to prove the customs of
another.

We then come to the second point, which is the more material
one in this case, viz., the admissibility of the deed of 1605. Now,
it will be observed, the issue the parties went down to try in this
case was not an issue upon the customs as to a particular copyhold,
or the claim of one single copyhold tenant, so that if the custom as
to all the rest were negatived, that tenant would be entitled to the
minerals; but the custom which the defendant undertakes to prove
is, that every customary tenant of a customary tenement within
the manor is entitled to the minerals. Would it not disprove that
issue, to prove that half the customary tenants of that manor had
positively disclaimed it? that not only they never did claim, but

that they declared *they were not entitled to it? Now a custom
lies in reputation; you prove a usage as far as you can prove the
fact from the time to which human memory goes; beyond that the
question in this case is open to evidence of reputation: and can it
be denied, that if you show that on a particular occasion half of
the tenants all stated what their customs were, and did not include

this custom of getting the minerals, that is evidence upon this issue, to show what in early times the tenants admitted as the customs? In that case of *Rowe* v. *Brenton*, there were several instances adduced of the tenants of the particular manors making a claim and a statement of their customs; and they were all received, on the ground that claims made fifty or a hundred years ago would be evidence of what the tenant alleged to be the customs. Therefore, if in this case there had been actually no proof of any identity of the tenement which Lord Hatherton holds with that which Sprott held, who signed the deed, I am not prepared to say (though I give no positive opinion upon the subject—it is not necessary) that a deed proved to be signed by a great many of the customary tenants a hundred and fifty years ago, alleging what the customs were, or what they conceived them to be, at that time, would not be receivable in evidence, to negative the claim that all the customary tenants were entitled to the minerals.   Suppose, instead of a deed, there had been a proceeding at the manor Court by the steward, and it was entered upon the Court rolls that the tenants were called upon to state what the customs were, that the steward might record it; and that the tenants had stated, and subscribed the statement, that they claimed the wood, but did not claim the minerals; can it be said this would not be evidence upon an issue of this kind—the issue not being with respect to a particular tenement, but whether a particular tenant had the right because the whole had the right? But I do not think it is necessary to go the length of deciding specifically that question, because it seems to me there is abundant evidence to show that Lord Hatherton holds one at least, if not more, *of the tenements   [*240] held by Sprott, who signed that deed. We have, therefore, the case of two parties to the same deed, because the defendant is made a party to it, claiming under a party who signed the deed— Lord Anglesey claiming under the then lord; and the question is, whether a deed signed by those under whom both parties claim, touching the customs, is not admissible in evidence. I think it is admissible, more especially when the case is of such a nature as to call for evidence of the reputation of early times. Then what is this deed? It is a claim by the different tenants who signed it, to what they conceive to be the immemorial customs of the manor generally; and it is an admission by the lord of those customs, so far as regards those tenements only. He is cautious, though admitting it generally, not to admit it for the rest of the manor;

but so far as regards their tenements, the claim they make to
certain immemorial customs is confirmed and ratified. It has been
argued that this was a creation of a new set of customs by con-
vention. I do not think the deed at all justifies that interpretation:
it is a claim of ancient customs by the tenants, and a ratification
and confirmation of the claim in the terms stated, by the lord. It
is true he takes care to prevent any prejudice arising to him from
any claim by a tenant who is not a party to the deed; but that
does not get rid of the effect derivable, not from the lord's
acquiescence, but from the claim of the tenants. As between him
and them, those are confessedly the customs of the manor for the
future, and are claimed and admitted to be the customs. Then
can any argument be more natural, or arise with more force from
the reading of that document, than the very argument used by the
learned Judge, and which is urged against him as a misdirection?
He says, when they are claiming their ancient usages and rights,
and when they, in order to purchase the lord's ratification of them,
have given him a sum of money, can it be doubted that they would
[*241]   not have omitted such a claim as this, to the *minerals, at the
very time that they claimed the trees, which could not belong to
them but by custom—when they claimed the marl and gravel to be
got from the lord's waste? I own it appears to me to be very
strong evidence, much stronger even than the learned Judge
represented it, that at that time it did not enter into their imagina-
tion that any custom existed in the manor that the customary
tenants should have the minerals; especially as it was proved that
minerals were worked at that period, and that they were of some
value. This is only an observation to show that they were less
likely to have omitted the notice of them, and that is the only use
the learned Judge made of it. Surely, if a custom existed at that
time to give them a right to the minerals, it was natural to expect
they would not have omitted it in an elaborate and minute statement of the customs, and they have not stated it. That is the
observation of the learned Judge, an observation so strong that I
do not wonder the jury should have felt the force of it, as I think I
should have felt upon the same issue, and should have determined
that the usage, of which evidence was given for a certain period,
was not referable to any right founded upon a custom. On the
other hand, the learned Judge makes an observation very favourable to the defendant's case; he says, usage cannot deceive you,
because that is matter of fact, and documents may be liable to

misapprehension and misinterpretation ; and therefore, although I
have made this observation upon the deed, it is for your judgment
and consideration : you are the persons to decide upon it. He
left the question to the jury as fairly, and I think as tenderly for
the defendant, as any Judge could possibly have done, and there is
no pretence for saying there was any misdirection. He stated the
effect of the deed as to this custom : what occasion was there to
go into the question of other customs ? There might be other
subordinate and immaterial customs—that would not answer the
argument. If among those customs existed one to claim the
minerals, was it not *natural that they should claim it at that
period ? How can one account for such an omission ? They had
a lord who would not even ratify the customs they did claim, unless
they gave him a sum of money. I do not think it is purchasing
his agreement to new customs, but his acquiescence in the ancient
customs. The question is what they claimed these to be, and it
cannot be denied they claimed them as immemorial customs ; and
surely among those customs they would have claimed the minerals.
I think, therefore, that the evidence was properly receivable ; that
the effect was actually stronger than the learned Judge was disposed
to give to it ; and consequently that there was no misdirection.
Upon these grounds, I think the rule should be discharged.

[*242]

ALDERSON, B. :

I am of the same opinion. It seems to me that the first point is
clearly in favour of the plaintiff : that no evidence of the customs
of the manor of Wyrley was properly receivable. Two things
must be made out, in order to entitle the party to give such
evidence : he must show that the customs of Wyrley are the same
as the customs of Cannock, and he must prove that Wyrley was
derived from Cannock. Now, neither of those things appears to
me to be established at all. There is no evidence which would at
all have satisfied me that Wyrley was held under Cannock. The
only circumstance is the payment to Lord Anglesey, through his
bailiff, upon several occasions, of 4s. It is clear that the same
payment was made in ancient times to the Bishop of Chester.
Some connexion between Lord Anglesey and the Bishop of Chester
is therefore shown, but it by no means appears that that connexion
arises out of the possession of the manor of Cannock. It may be
that it arises out of the possession of some other manor ; and if
that connexion were shown, it would prove that Wyrley was held

of another manor, and not of the manor of Cannock. The matter ought not to be left in ambiguity; it should be shown by the person *who proposes to tender the evidence of the customs of one manor as evidence of the customs of another, by some reasonable evidence, that the customs of the one are the same as the customs of the other. If, indeed, there be some general connecting link between them, as, for instance, if the customs in question be a particular incident of the general tenure which is common to the two manors, then you have a right to show what the custom of one manor is as to that tenure, for the purpose of showing what the custom of the other manor is as to that tenure: but you must begin by showing that there is a general tenure common to them both. That fact fails here; and therefore the case appears to me to fall within the general rule, that the customs of one manor cannot be given as evidence of the customs of another. The customs of manors are created by immemorial usage on the part of the lord and the copyholders. It is perfectly true, as was suggested in the argument by the *Solicitor-General*, that, inasmuch as this was a manor which must have been branched off, if ever it belonged to Cannock, before the Statute of *Quia Emptores*, and may have branched off long before the time of legal memory, there is nothing to show that the customs of the manor of Wyrley might not have originated after it parted from the manor of Cannock, and yet be beyond legal memory. It appears to me, therefore, that the learned Judge was quite right, upon the evidence before him, in rejecting the evidence of the customs of the manor of Wyrley.

Then was he right, which is the main question in the cause, in receiving the evidence of the deed and the decree? Now what is the issue here? It is an issue whereby the defendant undertakes to show that the customs of the manor authorize him to take these minerals. He is to establish the custom: he is to establish it, therefore, by evidence either of acts done by the lord and acts done by the copyholders, or declarations made by the lord, or acts which are entirely consistent with the existence of such a custom; and [*244] anything which negatives the conclusion to be drawn from *those acts must of necessity be evidence for the lord, in order to negative that custom. Now, if there be an agreement, or an acting by any of the copyholders of the manor, under circumstances, which, if it be true that they so acted and agreed, render it impossible to believe in the existence of the customs at the time when they so acted and agreed, that acting and that agreement must be evidence whereby the jury would conclude (if it be proved to have occurred after legal memory) that the custom did not then exist, that that is not a custom from time immemorial, and that the subsequent usage, on which the defendant relies, is referable to usurpation, and not to right. It is in that way that the learned Judge received and gave effect to the evidence of the decree and the deed. He did not give it effect as proving what were the customs of the manor, but as negativing this custom, which the defendant sets up as being a custom of the manor. He does not receive it as containing the customs of the manor, but as showing that the custom of the manor which the defendant sets up does not exist. That is the only use and only effect which ought to be given, and which the learned Judge, as it seems to me upon reading the whole of his summing up, did give, to the deed and to the decree.

Then, if that deed and decree were receivable in evidence, it was surely very reasonable for the Judge to say,—when those acts were done, would it not have been stated by the lord and his tenants, if the custom now set up had existed at that time ? He left that question fully to the jury, and I cannot say that I disagree with them in the conclusion to which they cáme. But further, it seems to me that the deed was receivable in evidence, because I think the connexion between Lord Hatherton and Sprott, who signed the deed for his copyhold lands, is fully made out as to the very land in question, upon which the coal and other minerals were got. Upon the whole, therefore, it seems to me that the evidence was properly receivable; and having read the whole of the summing up of the Judge from the shorthand *writer's notes, I must say, considering the length and complexity of the case, there is not only no misdirection, but that it is a marvellously correct summing up.

[*245]

GURNEY, B. :

I entirely agree with my Lord, that there is no ground whatever for the admission of the evidence with respect to the manor of Wyrley, inasmuch as the defendant wholly failed in showing that the chief rent, even supposing it to be the same which was paid to the Bishop of Chester, was paid to Lord Anglesey in respect of the manor of Cannock : and therefore there was no ground laid for the admission of the evidence. Then with respect to the deed, the identity of the lands which were held by Sprott appears to me to be clearly made out, and I think it is clear that the deed was

admissible. It is unnecessary to notice the observations made by
the learned counsel for the defendant, about the overwhelming
mass of evidence which was given of the usage. I only wish
to be understood as not assenting to its being an overwhelming
mass of evidence; I think the evidence of the usage is open to very
strong observations, and that it by no means deserves the character
he has given it.

ROLFE, B.:

I entirely concur with the rest of the Court upon both points.
With respect to the admission or non-admission of the evidence of
the customs of the manor of Wyrley, the ground upon which I
understood its admissibility to be rested by *Sir Thomas Wilde*,
was this: he does not contend generally that the customs of an
adjoining manor can be given in evidence to prove the customs of
the particular manor in question, but he says the manor of Wyrley
stands upon a distinct footing from a mere adjoining manor, for
this reason; I undertake to prove, he says, that it is a sub-infeudation of the manor in question; that it is a grant of the Crown, held
of the manor of Cannock. Having proved that, then he says it is
competent to him to show what are the customs of the sub-infeu-
[*246] dation, *because there can be no customs in that manor, which has
arisen from the sub-infeudation, that did not exist in the original
manor. Now I concur in thinking he has failed in showing, at
least with that distinctness with which in a question of this sort it
ought to be shown, that this is a sub-infeudation of the manor of
Cannock. The most that can be said is, that he has given evidence
which is perfectly consistent with it, and may render it not improbable that such may have been the fact. But he has wholly failed
in proving the other step of the proposition. It is impossible to
say there might not be a custom existing in the sub-infeudation,
different from those existing in the original manor, for the reasons
stated by my brother ALDERSON; because it must be shown that the
sub-infeudation took place after the time when the customs could
awfully have originated. There is an entire failure in that respect,
and therefore upon that ground it seems to me that the evidence
was properly rejected. I will just refer to one point upon this
subject, which was dwelt upon by my brother *Ludlow*—I allude to
the case which he relied upon, of *Champian* v. *Atkinson*; he says
it was decided there that in questions of this nature evidence of the
customs of other manors was receivable. I have looked at that case,

and it appears to me to be wholly different, and not to come at all within the same principle as this.   That was the case of a manor in Cumberland, and there being in that manor a custom to pay a fine on the death of a tenant, the question was, whether in such a case a grassum fine, as it is called, was payable when the lord succeeding was an infant; and upon that question, evidence was admitted to show what was the custom of other manors where the grassum fine prevailed.   That is not an analogous case to the present.   Prove in a particular manor that borough English prevails, and then you may see what the peculiarities of borough English are from other manors : prove that gavelkind prevails, and you may see what are the customs of gavelkind in other manors.   That appears to be *the principle on which the judgment in that case proceeds;   [*247] it is in very few words, but it points out the extent to which the Court meant to go : " Evidence for the defendant was, that other manors adjoining had the same custom, not to pay till age; which, per Curiam, is good, and was allowed of copyholds entailed in the manors of Thisleworth and Hammersmith, in Middlesex."   That I take to mean only this, that when it was proved there was a custom to entail, then the Court looked to another manor, where. the same custom of entail existed, to see what were the incidents of such tenure.   It appears to me, therefore, that that case in no respect established any such general proposition as has been attributed to it.

Then the other question is as to the admissibility of the deed.   I concur entirely in the other observations which have been made, but the clear ground upon which I think it is admissible is, that it is distinctly shown that Lord Hatherton claims in privity of estate under Sprott.   There is not the slightest doubt he claims an estate which he derives from Sprott, who was a party to the deed.   But then it is ingeniously suggested, that on spelling out this deed, it is not stated that the different copyholders who signed it, signed it in respect of all their copyhold tenements.   Now in the first place, I should say there is nothing to be picked out of the deed either way, but the probability of the case is that they did.   The improbability that the parties would not include the whole is so great, that I should have inferred that was the case; but I see circumstances in the deed which show me by necessary inference that the whole is included. See what the customs are.   One of them is, " If any copyholder die, the heir being within the age of fourteen years, then the next of kin to whom the inheritance may not descend, shall have the

MARQUIS OF
ANGLESEY
v.
LORD
HATHERTON.

[*248]

custody both of the body and lands of the same heir." Now the lands might be divisible, but if this custom does not extend to all the copyholders, what is to be the case as to the *body of the heir? the body must be one. It must be, therefore, that the party who signed this must have meant all his lands to be included, otherwise there would be one party to have the custody of the body, and by the custom some other person should have had the body in respect of the estate. There are other customs inconsistent with the notion of its not applying to all the lands. The single heriot on the death, —how is that to be apportioned, if there were a variety of estates to which this deed did not apply?

It seems to me therefore distinctly deducible from this deed, that Lord Hatherton's privy in estate was a party to the deed, and he states, as one of the parties to it, that from time whereof the memory of man is not to the contrary, such and such were the customs, and there is no mention amongst them of minerals. Upon such an occasion, is it not to the last degree improbable that such a custom, if it existed, should not be pointed out? It seems to me that it is, and that no more than the proper effect of the deed was given to it by the learned Judge; and that therefore there is no ground to complain, either of the admission of the evidence, or of the mode in which it was left to the jury.

Rule discharged.

————————

1842.
June 7.
————
*Exch. of
Pleas.*
[249]

WALKER *v.* HATTON (1).

(10 Meeson & Welsby, 249—259; S. C. 11 L. J. Ex. 361; 2 Dowl. N. S. 263.)

A messuage and premises were demised to the plaintiff by a lease bearing date the 10th of May, 1828, for the term of twenty-one years from the 25th of March then last; which lease contained covenants to paint the outside of the premises once in every three years, and the inside once in every seven years, and to repair and keep in repair the premises, and also to do any repairs which on a view of the premises by the lessor should be found wanting, of which notice should be given.

By a lease dated the 15th of June, 1830, the plaintiff demised the premises to the defendant for the residue of the term, wanting ten days, containing covenants, with the exception of a stipulation as to painting the outside wood-work, in precisely the same terms as those contained in the original lease. The original lessors having brought an action against the plaintiff for breaches of the covenant to repair, he applied to the defendant to perform the repairs, and for instructions as to the course he should pursue - with respect to the defence of the action. The defendant denied that any notice to repair had been given, and insisted that the premises did not

(1) Foll. in *Williams* v. *Williams* (1874) L. R. 9 C. P. 659, 666; 43 L. J. C. P. 382.—A. C.

require it; the plaintiff thereupon offered to suffer judgment by default,   WALKER
which the defendant refused to assent to. The plaintiff then gave the   *v.*
defendant notice, that as he had denied that any notice to repair had been   HATTON.
served, and insisted that the premises were not out of repair, he should
traverse the breaches of covenant assigned, and try the question, holding
the defendant responsible for the costs. This he accordingly did, and the
result was, that the original lessors recovered 68*l.* damages, and 58*l.* 12*s.*
for costs, and he himself incurred costs amounting to 53*l.* 14*s.* 4*d.*

Held, that the plaintiff was not entitled to recover from the defendant
the costs of defending the action, as they were not necessarily occasioned
by the defendant's breach of the covenant to repair.

Held, also, that although the covenants contained in the sub-lease were
(with the exception of that relating to painting) the same in words as those
contained in the original lease, they were, in effect, substantially different,
the periods at which the leases were granted being different.

Semble, that the plaintiff ought to have paid the amount of the dilapidations into Court, instead of defending the action.

COVENANT. The declaration stated, that, by an indenture dated
the 10th day of May, 1828, J. T. Coward, C. T. Coward, S. Henley,
and F. T. his wife, demised to the plaintiff a certain messuage and
premises, with the appurtenances, for the term of twenty-one years
from the 25th day of March then last, at a yearly rent; and that
the plaintiff thereby covenanted with the lessors, that he the
plaintiff, his executors, administrators, and assigns, should and
would, at his and their own costs and charges, once in every three
years of the term thereby granted, well and sufficiently paint all
the outside wood and iron work of the said messuage and premises
twice in good oil colour; and also once in every seven years of the
said term thereby granted well and sufficiently paint all the inside
of the said messuage and premises twice in good oil colour; and
also should and would, from time to time and at all times during
the said term thereby granted, well and sufficiently repair, uphold,
support, maintain, pave, cleanse, empty, amend, and keep the said
messuages and premises, with the appurtenances, *in, by, and with   [*250]
all and all manner of needful and necessary reparations, cleansings,
and amendments whatsoever (casualties by fire always excepted),
when, where, and as often as need or occasion should be or require;
and the said messuage and premises, being so well and sufficiently
repaired, supported, maintained, sustained, painted, paved, cleansed,
repaired, amended, and kept as aforesaid, should and would, at the
end and expiration of the term thereby granted, or other sooner
determination thereof, peaceably and quietly leave, surrender, and
yield up unto the said J. T. Coward, C. T. Coward, S. Henley, and
F. T. his wife, their heirs, executors, administrators, or assigns,
together with all erections and improvements made and added or

to be made and added thereon or therein, and all and singular
other the fixtures and things mentioned and comprised in the
schedule or inventory thereof thereunder written, in good plight
and condition (reasonable use and wear thereof, and casualties
happening by fire, to such fixtures in the meantime only excepted);
and further, that it should and might be lawful to and for the said
J. T. Coward, C. T. Coward, S. Henley, and F. T. his wife, their
heirs, executors, administrators, or assigns, either alone or with
workmen, at all reasonable times in the daytime, during the said
term, to enter upon any part of the said demised premises, to view,
search, and see the state and condition thereof, and upon any such
view that he the plaintiff, his executors, administrators, or assigns,
should and would, upon notice thereof being left at the said demised
premises, within three calendar months next after any such notice,
well and sufficiently repair, amend, and make good all and every
the wants of reparation, whereof any such notice should be given
or left as aforesaid (damage happening by fire excepted as aforesaid). After making *profert* of this indenture, the declaration

[*251]   proceeded to state, that by another indenture, made between *the
plaintiff and the defendant, on the 15th day of June, 1830, the
plaintiff demised the same premises to the defendant, for the term
of nineteen years, wanting ten days, from the 25th of March then
last, at a yearly rent, and the defendant thereby entered into
covenants with the plaintiff, which were set out, corresponding
precisely in terms with those contained in the original lease, save
that the outside painting was thereby stipulated to be done every
three, instead of every seven years, and leave was reserved to " the
original lessors," as well as to the plaintiff, to enter and view the
repairs, and give notice. The breaches assigned were, that the
defendant did not paint, that he did not repair, and that, although
the original lessors entered upon the premises to view the state of
repair, and, finding it defective, gave three months' notice of the
defects, the defendant omitted, within that period, to repair: by
reason of which said breaches of covenant, the plaintiff afterwards, and before the commencement of this suit, to wit, on the
4th December, 1842, was called upon, and forced and obliged to
pay, and did then pay to the original lessors, the sum of 68*l.* for
their damages, and 58*l.* 12*s.* for their costs, by them recovered in
an action of covenant, which they brought against the plaintiff on
account of certain breaches of the covenants entered into by the
plaintiff with the original lessors in the said indenture firstly

mentioned: and that the said covenants in the said indenture
firstly mentioned, and the said covenants in the said indenture
lastly mentioned, have a like force and effect, meaning and purport,
and are in fact the same, and that the breaches of covenant, for
and on account of which the original lessors recovered their
damages and costs, were the same and not other than the breaches
committed by the defendant; and the plaintiff was called upon,
and forced and obliged to pay, and did pay 53*l*. 14*s*. 4*d*. for his
costs, by him incurred in and about his defence to the said action.
The defendant *paid 1*s*. into Court, and pleaded that the plaintiff
had not sustained damage to any greater amount, upon which
issue was joined.

At the trial before Gurney, B., at the Middlesex sittings in last
Easter Term, it was proved that the original lessors, in April, 1841,
having surveyed the premises in question, left upon them a notice
to repair the dilapidations mentioned in it, more than three months
before they commenced an action against the plaintiff. The amount
of those dilapidations was estimated by the lessors at about 200*l*.;
and upon an action being commenced against the plaintiff, he had
the premises surveyed, and, finding them defective, applied to the
defendant to perform the repairs, and for instructions as to the
course he should pursue with respect to the defence of the action.
The defendant then denied that any notice to repair had been
served, and refused to make any arrangement, and even refused
permission to the plaintiff to enter and execute the repairs himself,
insisting that the premises did not require them. The plaintiff
thereupon offered to the defendant to suffer judgment by default,
but to this step he would not assent; and at last the plaintiff
served the defendant with a notice, that, as he denied that any
notice to repair had been served by the original lessors, and insisted
that the premises were not out of repair, he, the plaintiff, should ·
traverse the breaches of covenant assigned by the original lessors,
and try the question, holding the defendant responsible for the
costs he might incur by doing so. This course he ultimately
adopted, pleading a plea of *non est factum*. On the trial of that
action, the result was that the original lessors recovered 68*l*.
damages, and 58*l*. 12*s*. for costs, and the plaintiff incurred costs
to the amount of 53*l*. 14*s*. 4*d*. Upon the plaintiff claiming to be
allowed the amount of these costs as damages in the present
action, *the defendant objected that they were not the natural
consequences of his breaches of covenant, and therefore he was not

responsible for them. The learned Baron, however, overruled the objection, reserving leave to the defendant to move to reduce the damages to 68*l.*, and the plaintiff recovered a verdict for 180*l.* 6*s.* 4*d.*

Gunning having obtained a rule to reduce the damages accordingly,

Knowles and *Martin* showed cause:

The plaintiff is entitled to retain the verdict for the full amount. He must either have paid the sum demanded, or defended the action. He does the latter, by which he puts the parties to prove their case, and the lessors having recovered this amount of damages and costs from him, he is entitled to have them repaid him by the defendant. In *Neale* v. *Wyllie* (1), where the tenant, under a lease containing a covenant to repair, underlet the premises to one who entered into a similar covenant, and the original lessor brought an action on this covenant in the first lease, and recovered, it was held that the damages and costs recovered in that action, and also the costs of defending it, might be recovered as special damages in an action against the undertenant for the breach of his covenant to repair. That case is identical with the present. It was determined upon the ground that the plaintiff was entitled to recover the damages and costs which he had been compelled to pay in consequence of the defendant's breach of covenant. It may be said that the case of *Penley* v. *Watts* (2) has somewhat impaired that decision; but the Court expressly distinguished it from *Neale* v. *Wyllie*; and PARKE, B., there says, "If the circumstances had been exactly the same as they were in that case, we should have considered ourselves bound by it, although we cannot help thinking
[*254] that the Court on *that occasion had not exactly considered the relation of the parties, and the circumstance that the covenants were not in terms the same." In *Penley* v. *Watts* the covenants were substantially different; here the covenants are in effect the same: and therefore that case is no authority in the present. The cases on breaches of warranty are applicable to this case; because there the question is, what damages are the reasonable consequence of the breach of the contract of warranty. In *Lewis* v. *Peake* (3), the plaintiff recovered the costs of an action brought against him, in consequence of his having warranted a horse sold to him by the

(1) 27 R. R. 418 (3 B. & C. 533;   (3) 17 R. R. 475 (7 Taunt. 153;
5 Dowl. & Ry. 442).   2 Marsh. 481).
(2) 56 R. R. 810 (7 M. & W. 601).

defendant with a warranty. GIBBS, Ch. J., there says, "The
plaintiff was induced by the warranty of the defendant to warrant
the horse to a purchaser ; he gave notice to the defendant of the
action, and receiving no directions from the defendant to give
up the cause, he proceeded to defend, and was cast. Those costs
and damages are therefore a part of the damages which the
plaintiff has sustained by reason of the false warranty found
against the defendant."   That language exactly applies to
this case.

(PARKE, B. : If you look at the opinions expressed by the Court
in *Penley* v. *Watts*, you will find that that decision is very applicable
to this case.)

The covenants there were not alike, nor could the damages be so ;
here they are the same.   These are damages and costs which the
plaintiff was compelled to pay through the defendant's neglect to
repair.   In actions for breach of warranty, the plaintiff recovers
not only the difference between the value of the horse and the price
given, but also the incidental expenses, and the keep of the horse.
In *Borradaile* v. *Brunton* (1), which was an action for breach of
warranty of a chain cable, whereby the cable broke and an anchor
attached to it was lost, it was held that the plaintiffs might, in
addition to the value of the cable, recover the value of the lost
anchor *to which the insufficient cable was attached.   Therefore
it is clear that the damages may go beyond the strict line contended
for on the other side.

[*255]

(PARKE, B. : In *Lewis* v. *Peake*, the plaintiff was not aware at the
time he sold the horse that the warranty was not complied with,
and that was the ground on which the case was decided.   But in
Wrightup v. *Chamberlain* (2), where the plaintiff had purchased a
horse of the defendant with a warranty of soundness, and he sold
it with a like warranty to J. S., and the horse turning out to be
unsound, J. S. brought an action against him, which he defended,
and failed ; the jury having found that the plaintiff might, by a
reasonable examination of the horse, have discovered that it was
unsound at the time he sold it to J. S., it was held that he was not
entitled to recover as special damages the costs incurred by him in
defending the former action.)

(1) 20 R. R. 548 (8 Taunt. 535).   (2) 50 R. R. 855 (7 Scott, 598).

WALKER
v.
HATTON.

That was put entirely upon its being an improvident defence, and that the plaintiff could have found out the unsoundness by a reasonable examination. But here the plaintiff was misled by the defendant's false statement that he had not received notice, and also by his assertion that the premises did not require repairs, and he was not liable. The defence likewise was not improvident, as it was impossible for the plaintiff to ascertain what was the amount that ought fairly to be required, and it being a claim for unliquidated damages, he could make no tender, even if he had known the exact sum. The only method by which he could ascertain what he really ought to pay, was by bringing the matter before a jury to determine it.

Kelly and *Gunning*, in support of the rule:

The case of *Neale* v. *Wyllie* is distinguishable from the present in several respects. The covenants are not set out there, and it

[*256]

does not appear that the plaintiff knew he had no defence *to the action. In the present case, the plaintiff well knew that he had no defence, and it was his duty therefore to have suffered judgment by default. He had no right to go on, if he had no defence, when a third party was to be ultimately made chargeable; and here it is clear he was aware he had no valid defence. Even if there had been a covenant of indemnity, he would not have been justified in pleading a plea which he knew to be false, and incurring reckless and unnecessary expense. At the time when *Neale* v. *Wyllie* was decided, there were no means of paying money into Court, and a party was, therefore, obliged to suffer judgment by default, which the plaintiff in that case had accordingly done. * * Here, moreover, the covenants are substantially different, and the observations of PARKE, B., in *Penley* v. *Watts*, upon the points of difference, are applicable.

(PARKE, B.: The covenant to repair being general in both the original and the underlease, they would be different in effect; because the defendant, being a sub-lessee, is only bound to put the premises

[*257]

in *the same condition as he found them at the time of the lease to him. Suppose this were a lease of a new house for one hundred years, and there were a general covenant to repair, and at the end of fifty years a person were to take an underlease, with a covenant in the same words, the latter covenant must be construed with reference to the state of the premises at the time.)

That was so decided in *Stanley* v. *Towgood* (1), *Mantz* v. *Goring* (2),
and *Gutteridge* v. *Munyard* (3).   Here there was an interval of more
than two years between the two leases, and the covenants may
therefore apply to a very different state of things ; the one would
refer to the state of repair in 1828, and the other to that in 1830,
which might be widely different ; so that what would be a breach
of covenant in the one case, might be consistent with performance
in the other.   *   *   *

LORD ABINGER, C. B. :

I have come to the conclusion, with great reluctance, that this
rule must be made absolute.   I do not think that the covenant
entered into by the defendant extended to the payment of the whole
of these damages, but only of that portion of them which was
necessarily incurred by the plaintiff.   Now the real damage he
sustained was the sum of 68*l*., being the amount recovered by the
plaintiff in the former action.   The costs were certainly incurred
by the present plaintiff *in his own wrong, for he could have put   [*258]
an end to the controversy between him and his lessor by the payment of that sum in the first instance, or he might have subsequently
paid it into Court.   If we held that any more damages were recoverable, there would be no limit ; the only safe rule is, to confine the
verdict to those which were the necessary result of the act complained
of, viz. the want of repair ; and I cannot see how it can be
contended, that the costs of both the plaintiff and the defendant in
the former action were the natural or necessary consequence of that
act.   I think the case of *Neale* v. *Wyllie* is not law, and that it was
decided on a mistaken principle ; and I think it is better that I
should at once express that opinion, than attempt to make a
distinction between that case and the present, since making distinc-
tions which have no solid foundation only tends to keep up litigation.
I concur in the decision of this Court in *Penley* v. *Watts*, which
governs the present case.

PARKE, B. :

I entirely agree with my LORD CHIEF BARON.   This case is on
all fours with that of *Penley* v. *Watts*, which certainly makes it
extremely difficult to support the judgment in *Neale* v. *Wyllie*.

(1) 43 R. R. 569 (3 Bing. N. C. 4 ;   *Mantz*).
3 Scott, 313).   (3) 48 R. R. 773 (1 Moo. & Rob.
(2) 44 R. R. 759 (4 Bing. N. C. 451 ;   334 ; 7 C. & P. 129).
S. C. 6 Scott, 277, *nom. Young* v.

Although the covenants contained in the sub-lease are, with the exception of that relating to painting, the same in language with those contained in the original lease, yet they are different in substance; the periods at which the leases were granted being different. It is now perfectly well settled, that a general covenant to repair must be construed to have reference to the condition of the premises at the time when the covenant begins to operate; and as the one lease was granted in 1828, and the other in 1830, allowing an interval of two years, it is clear that the covenants would not have the same effect, but would vary substantially in their operation. With this explanation, there is no distinction

[*259]

between this case and *Penley* v. *Watts*. Then these costs *were unnecessarily incurred: if the plaintiff had paid the amount of the dilapidations into Court, they would have been spared.

GURNEY, B.:

I entirely concur with the rest of the Court. The plaintiff may have been extremely ill-used; but I think he has no remedy.

ROLFE, B.:

I think it would be very wrong for the Court to strain the meaning of covenants to that which may be thought reasonable, where the parties will not take the trouble to frame them in language by which their meaning can clearly be ascertained. We should be driven to great embarrassment, if we sought to supply what we considered as reasonably coming within the intention of the language used by them.

LORD ABINGER, C. B.:

I wish to add, that I am by no means clear that, even if this had been a covenant to indemnify, these costs would have been recoverable, as that would only extend to costs necessarily incurred.

Rule absolute.

WARWICK *v.* C. RICHARDSON (1).

(10 Meeson & Welsby, 284—296; S. C. 11 L. J. Ex. 351.)

A testator devised his real and personal estate to D. and R., upon trust to sell, and to invest the sum of 10,000*l.*, arising therefrom, in the public funds or real securities, for the benefit of certain persons mentioned in the will. The money was not so invested, but with D.'s consent was received by R., and used by him in his private trade; and R. gave to D. a bond,

(1) Cited in *Taylor* v. *Chichester, &c., Ry. Co.* (1867) L. R. 2 Ex. 390 (revd. L. R. 4 H. L. 628).—A. C.

conditioned to keep him harmless and indemnified against all actions, suits,   WARWICK
proceedings, claims, demands, loss, costs, charges, damages, and expenses,   v.
on account of the said sum of 10,000l., or by reason of R.'s being permitted   RICHARDSON.
to hold the same : Held, that this bond was valid in law.

The legatees having filed a bill in Chancery against the trustees and their
representatives, claiming payment of the 10,000l. and interest, obtained a
decree whereby it was declared that D. and R. were jointly and severally
liable to pay that sum: and the legatees carried in a claim against D.'s
estate for that amount, but no money was received therefrom : Held, that
the representatives of D. were entitled to recover from R., in an action on
the bond, the whole amount of 10,000l. and interest, and that their claim
was not limited to the amount of costs actually incurred and paid by them
in the Chancery suit.

THE following case was sent by the MASTER OF THE ROLLS for the
opinion of this Court:

John Pollard, by his will, dated the 10th of March, 1810, devised   [285]
his real and personal estate to the use of Ralph Day and John
Dingely Richardson, their heirs, executors, &c., upon trust to sell
the same, and from the monies arising therefrom, that they should
stand possessed of the sum of 10,000l., and invest the same in the
purchase of stock in the public funds, or in real securities, upon
trust to pay the annual proceeds thereof to Susan Cooper and
Joseph Yates Cooper, her husband, for their respective lives, and
after their deaths, to their children. By a codicil, J. Y. Cooper was
appointed an executor jointly with R. Day and J. D. Richardson.
The testator J. Pollard died in 1817, and in the same year J. D.
Richardson and R. Day alone proved the will, and acted under the
same. They did not invest the sum of 10,000l. in the purchase of
stock in the public funds, or in real securities, but the whole was,
with the consent of R. Day, received by J. D. Richardson, and used
by him in his private trade. In 1818 Cooper and Richardson gave
to Ralph Day a joint and several bond. In this bond it was recited,
that J. Y. Cooper and Susan his wife, and Richardson, had requested
Day to permit Richardson to employ the sum of 10,000l. in his
trade, according to an arrangement made between them; and that
Day had consented thereto, on being indemnified in respect of such
sum, and that such sum had been accordingly taken by and was
then in the hands of Richardson. The condition was, that if
Cooper and Richardson, or either of them, their heirs, executors, &c.,
" should at all times thereafter save, defend, keep harmless and
indemnified the said R. Day, his heirs, executors, &c., against all
manner of actions, suits, causes of action and suit, proceedings,
claims, demands, loss, costs, charges, damages and expenses whatsoever, which should be brought, commenced, prosecuted, or made

WARWICK
v.
RICHARDSON.

[*286]

against them, or which they should bear, pay, suffer, sustain, expend, or be put to, on account of the said sum of 10,000*l.*, or by reason of *Richardson being permitted to hold the same, then the obligation should be void, otherwise to remain in full force and virtue." Day died in 1818, having appointed T. Seddon his executor. Cooper died in 1833, leaving his wife and three children him surviving. Richardson died in 1833, and administration of his estate was granted to the present defendant. The sum of 10,000*l.* was never invested, and remained due and unaccounted for by Richardson at the time of his death. In 1833, two of the children of Cooper filed a bill in Chancery against Christopher Richardson and T. Seddon and others, claiming payment of the sum of 10,000*l.*, with interest, and a decree was obtained in 1836, whereby it was declared that J. R. Richardson and R. Day became jointly and severally liable to pay that sum. The plaintiffs in that suit have carried in, against the estate of Day, a claim to the sum of 10,000*l.* and interest. No payment has been made out of the estate of R. Day, on account of the sum of 10,000*l.*

It is admitted that Seddon has been put to costs in the suit of *Cooper* v. *Richardson*, and paid 10*l.* on account of such costs, out of the assets of Day. Seddon claims to be a creditor to the estate of Richardson, under the bond of 1818.

The question for the opinion of the Court is, whether Seddon, as the surviving executor of R. Day, is entitled to recover any and what sum of money under and by virtue of the said bond, from the personal representative of J. D. Richardson, to be paid out of his assets.

The point to be contended for by T. Seddon was, that he was entitled, as executor of Day, to recover under the bond, from the personal estate of J. D. Richardson, the sum of 10,000*l.*, with interest from the day of his death.

[*287]

The defendant's points were, first, that the bond was void in law, and that Seddon was not entitled to recover anything from the representative of Richardson. Secondly, *that Seddon, if entitled to recover anything, could only recover the sum of 10*l.*, paid by him out of the assets of Day for costs in the suit.

The case was argued on the 30th of May, by

W. H. Watson, for the plaintiff:

The plaintiff is entitled to recover the whole sum of 10,000*l.* upon this bond. This was a case where a sum of 10,000*l.* was appropriated to meet a specific legacy, but was lent to or retained

by the executor Richardson, and used by him in his trade, with the   WARWICK
assent of his co-executor, instead of being invested in real securities,   *v.*
pursuant to the trusts of the will.   There was no person to invest   RICHARDSON.
it in real securities, except Richardson or Cooper, and Day, the
obligors and obligee of this bond, which seems to have been given
for the express purpose of giving a right of action at law.   It is said
the bond is void, because this application of the money was a
breach of trust.   But the obligor cannot come into Court to say
that.   This is no question of public policy, but altogether a matter
of private interest.   There is nothing in the common or statute law
to render such a bond void.   Then, as to the amount to be recovered,
it is clear that at law the judgment would be for the whole penalty.
It will be said that the plaintiff can only recover the actual damages
sustained and paid ; even if that be so, yet the judgment must be
to recover 20,000*l.*, and to levy only 10*l.*: *Wilde* v. *Clarkson* (1),
Judd v. *Evans* (2).   But it is to be observed, that here the condition
is " to save, defend, keep harmless and indemnified the said R. Day,
his heirs, executors, &c., against all manner of actions, suits, causes
of action and suit, proceedings, claims, demands, loss, costs, charges,
damages, and expenses whatsoever, which should be brought, &c.,
or made against them, or which they should bear, &c., on account
of the said sum of 10,000*l.*, or by reason of Richardson *being per-   [*288]
mitted to hold the same."   It is not necessary, therefore, in order
to constitute a breach of the condition, that a suit should have
been commenced : the obligors are to interpose and save the parties
harmless against every claim and demand whatsoever.   The words
of the condition have a different and stronger meaning than merely
to indemnify against damages actually sustained.   The parties
clearly intended present payment, on demand, of the whole 10,000*l.*,
in order to its being invested pursuant to the will.   In Com. Dig.
Condition (I.), it is laid down that " a condition to indemnify
against A. is broken by his threatening to beat the obligee, by
reason of which he dares not go about his business."   There no
damage whatever is incurred, but merely an apprehension of injury.
So, " If a condition be to save harmless from an obligation in which
he is bound to A., the obligor ought to discharge it by release or
otherwise.   So, if it be to save harmless from all suits and demands
concerning that obligation."   " So, if the obligation be forfeited,
whereby he is liable to be sued : *à fortiori* if he be sued, although
the obligation be satisfied before execution."

        (1) 3 B. R. 178 (6 T. R. 303).   (2) 6 T. R. 399.
                                          39—2

WARWICK
v.
RICHARDSON.

(ALDERSON, B.: To restore a party to his former state, after suffering him to receive harm, is not to save him harmless.

ROLFE, B.: Does not the argument seem to go to this, that *eo instanti* that the bond was executed, the obligors were liable?)

No; but as soon as a demand was made for the investment of the money by the representatives of the obligee. *Abbots* v. *Johnson* (1), *Broughton's* case (2), *Barkly* v. *Kempstow* (3) are all authorities to show that the danger of being sued is a damnification, and a breach of the condition of such a bond as this, without actual suit or payment. It may be said, that Cooper, or the executors of Richardson, may pay the rest of the 10,000*l.* to the parties entitled under the will; but it was, by the terms of the bond, to be paid to *Day, that he and Richardson conjointly might invest it in real security. The statute 8 & 9 Will. III. c. 11, s. 8, will not affect this case; because, on the suit being instituted against Day's executor, there was an entire breach of the condition, and the whole damages were recoverable then or not at all. The statute applies only where there is a succession of breaches. [He cited *Lethbridge* v. *Mytton* (4), *Carr* v. *Roberts* (5), and *Lamb* v. *Vice* (6).]

[*289]

[290]

(ALDERSON, B., referred to *Penley* v. *Watts* (7).)

Day would be bound, in order to save himself from all harm, to invest the 10,000*l.* and pay the costs: then he who undertakes to save him from all harm must enable him to do that.

J. L. Adolphus, contrà :

First, this bond is void, the condition of it being against law, because in fraud of the trust under which the parties to it were acting. * * Even where trustees are empowered to lend money on personal security, one of them cannot be a borrower: —— v. *Walker* (8), *Brice* v. *Stokes* (9). This bond was given expressly that Day might not perform the duty imposed upon him by the will, and is therefore void.

(ALDERSON, B.: You are making a court of law the judge of a matter which is for the cognizance of a court of equity. How can

(1) 3 Bulstr. 233.
(2) 5 Rep. 24.
(3) Cro. Eliz. 123.
(4) 2 B. & Ad. 772.
(5) 39 R. R. 405 (5 B. & Ad. 78;

2 Nev. & M. 42).
(6) 55 R. R. 694 (6 M. & W. 467).
(7) 56 R. R. 810 (7 M. & W. 601).
(8) 5 Russ. 7.
(9) 8 R. R. 164 (11 Ves. 319).

we tell that a court of equity would hold it a breach of trust?

What violation is there of the common *or statute law?)

The Court will not refuse to take notice of plain points of equity. Courts of law take notice of trusts for some purposes. At all events, the Court will take cognizance of what these parties were bound to do as executors. In Shep. Touch. 371, it is said, "When the thing enjoined or restrained, to be or not to be done by the condition, is such a thing in its own nature as that the commission or omission thereof is *malum in se*, then not only the condition, but the whole obligation also, is void *ab initio*." And in another place, (*Id.* 132), "If the matter of the condition tend to provoke or further the doing of some unlawful act, or to restrain or forbid a man the doing of his duty, the condition for the most part is void." A similar rule is laid down by PARKER, Ch. J., in *Mitchel* v. *Reynolds* (1). The performance of this trust was a duty within the meaning of those authorities, and the bond was void for the violation of it. In the case of bonds to provide a settlement on the separation of husband and wife, no public policy intervenes, and yet they are void. So in the case of a security to one creditor for a greater proportion than his share of a composition, which is also void: *Cockshott* v. *Bennett* (2).

(ALDERSON, B.: There it is in the nature of a distinct fraud.)

So is this transaction, in the sense in which the word is there used. It is a collusion between two parties, to break their faith towards the persons for whose benefit they have undertaken the office of trustees. It is not a fraud in the sense of deceit, but a fraud in law, as being a private agreement tending to a breach of their fiduciary duty. That duty is, to take immediate steps to have the fund invested: *Jackman* v. *Mitchell* (3). In *Waldo* v. *Martin* (4), an agreement was held void merely as being wrongful against a third party. There are many authorities to show that a party cannot recover against another upon an indemnity against the *consequences of their jointly doing an unlawful act, although it do not amount to a criminal offence: *Shackell* v. *Rosier* (5), *Colburn* v. *Patmore* (6), *Merryweather* v. *Nixan* (7), *Prole* v. *Wiggins* (8). [*292]

(1) 1 P. Wms. 181.
(2) 1 R. R. 617 (2 T. R. 763).
(3) 9 R. R. 229 (13 Ves. 581).
(4) 28 R. R. 289 (4 B. & C. 319;
6 Dowl. & Ry. 364).
(5) 42 R. R. 666 (2 Bing. N. C. 634;
3 Scott, 59).
(6) 40 R. R. 493 (1 Cr. M. & R. 83).
(7) 16 R. R. 810 (8 T. R. 186).
(8) 43 R. R. 621 (3 Bing. N. C. 230;
3 Scott, 607).

WARWICK
v.
RICHARDSON.

The second question is, what sum the plaintiff is entitled to recover against the estate of Richardson, supposing the bond valid. That ought to be confined to the 10*l.*, the amount of the actual damage. * * The cases cited on the other side are distinguishable. *Broughton's* case was the case of a counter-bond, which was clearly forfeited. *Abbots* v. *Johnson* is a like case. The authorities cited from Com. Dig. are not disputed ; nor is it denied that here there has been a forfeiture of the bond to some extent. But it is not clear that Day's estate will pay, or be in danger of paying, anything beyond the 10*l.*; all may be paid from Richardson's estate. Day's executor is fully indemnified, if the 10,000*l.* be forthcoming, and his costs are paid. *Lethbridge* v. *Mytton* was the case of an absolute covenant to invest a certain sum of money in the year.

(ALDERSON, B. : Here the decree makes Seddon liable to invest the 10,000*l.*)

[*293]

It is merely declaratory on that point, for the instruction *of the Master.

(ALDERSON, B. : He is charged with a debt of 10,000*l.*; how do you save him harmless but by paying that debt ?)

The possibility that he may have to pay it is not a damage. It is for the plaintiff to show the amount of damage. In *Carr* v. *Roberts*, the party undertook not merely to indemnify, but to pay. The distinction between a contract to pay and indemnify, and to indemnify merely, is shown in *Penny* v. *Foy* (1), and *Collinge* v. *Heywood* (2). He cited also *Sparks* v. *Martindale* (3), and *Young* v. *Taylor* (4).

Watson was heard in reply.

                                        Cur. adv. vult.

The judgment of the Court was now delivered by

ALDERSON, B. :

In this case we shall certify our opinion to the MASTER OF THE ROLLS, that Thomas Seddon, as surviving executor of Ralph Day,

(1) 8 B. & C. 11.   (3) 8 East, 593.
(2) 48 R. R. 616 (9 Ad. & El. 633 ;   (4) 8 Taunt. 315.
1 P. & D. 502).

is entitled, under the bond executed by John Dingley Richardson, WARWICK
to prove for the full sum of 10,000*l.*, together with interest, and RICHARDSON.
the costs which he has incurred in the Chancery suit in which
the decree has been made.

We propose now to assign shortly our reasons for so doing.

The bond in question is dated the 28th of May, 1818, and by it
Joseph Yates Cooper and John Dingley Richardson, and their representatives, became bound in the penal sum of 20,000*l.* to Ralph
Day and his representatives. The condition of the bond, after
reciting the will of John Pollard, by which, among other bequests,
he left to Ralph Day and John Dingley Richardson 10,000*l.*,
in trust for his the testator's daughter, Mrs. Cooper, and her
children, *proceeded to state, that that sum had been accordingly   [*294]
raised, and was in the hands of John Dingley Richardson; that
Mr. and Mrs. Cooper had agreed with John Dingley Richardson
that he should hold and employ it in his business, and that Ralph
Day, the co-trustee, had consented thereto, on being indemnified.
And then it was provided, that if they, Mr. Cooper and John
Dingley Richardson, and their representatives, should from time to
time and at all times thereafter well and truly save, defend, keep
harmless and indemnified the said Ralph Day, his heirs, &c., from
all actions, suits, causes of action and suit, proceedings, claims,
demands, loss, costs, charges, and expenses whatsoever, which
might arise for or by reason of the said legacy of 10,000*l.*, or any
part thereof, or the interest thereof, or by reason of John Dingley
Richardson being permitted to hold the same, the obligation should
be void.

In consequence of this legacy having been thus dealt with by the
two trustees, the children of Mr. and Mrs. Cooper filed their bill
against the representatives of the trustees, (who are both dead), and
in the decree in that suit a declaration has been made that the
trustees are jointly and severally liable to make good the legacy,
with interest at the rate of 4 per cent. A charge has been since
carried in against the estate of Ralph Day, but no sum has as yet
been paid out of his funds. The case however states, that the
representative of Ralph Day has incurred costs in the course of that
suit.

The question now is, whether he has a claim against the estate
of Richardson under this bond; and if so, to what amount.

Two points were made in the argument—First, it was contended
that the bond was void, as being a bond of indemnity against a

WARWICK   breach of trust, and that the case therefore fell within the rule, that
*.   it is illegal to indemnify a party for doing a wrong.
RICHARDSON.
[295]   But we think that objection is not well founded. All that
appears on the face of this case is, that Richardson was to be
allowed to hold the money, upon giving this bond of indemnity.
It is true that, for certain reasons peculiar to a court of equity, the
estate of a trustee, who suffers trust-money so to remain, is held to
be liable to make good any eventual loss: but that is all. There
is nothing to show us, sitting in a court of law, that there is
anything necessarily illegal or wrong in the conduct of a trustee
who has been a party to such an arrangement. Indeed, many
cases might easily be put, which would exonerate him from blame
altogether. The whole circumstances of the case must be looked
at in a court of equity, before any opinion can properly be formed
on the subject; and we have no means of judging of them. This
objection therefore fails, and the question is reduced to the
consideration of the proper amount of damages.

Now, as to this point, the case may be shortly thus stated: A.
has agreed to save harmless his co-trustee, B., from any claim
which may arise out of B.'s permitting him to hold and use a
legacy of 10,000l., instead of investing it in a particular way, as they
were directed to do by the will under which they became trustees.
In consequence of this, a claim is afterwards made by the cestuis
que trust against him, the result of which is, that B. is ordered to
invest 10,000l., with interest at 4 per cent., and is forced to incur
costs in the discussion of that suit. Now, what ought A. to have
done, in order to save B. harmless from this claim? Manifestly
he ought to have invested 10,000l.; and not having done so, ought
now to pay that sum to B., and also to repay those costs and that
interest which B. is now obliged to pay. We think, therefore, that
this is the proper amount of the damages to which A. is liable
under the bond. For this will indemnify B. against the payments
[*296]   to which he has been rendered liable in consequence *of A. not
having saved him harmless, by investing the sum of 10,000l. as he
ought to have done.

The cases cited in argument are all distinguishable from the
present. The breach of the bond, in them, consisted in not
indemnifying against a payment, and none therefore took place till
a payment was made, and the amount depended upon and was
measured by the amount of such payment alone. Here, the breach
of the bond is not saving Ralph Day and his representative

harmless against the claim of the children of Mr. and Mrs.   WARWICK
Cooper, and the proper amount of damages is therefore that   RICHARDSON.
amount to which the making of the claim subjects him, which is
here the sum to be invested, and the actual loss which has been
subsequently added to that sum, in consequence of the claim
having been enforced by law upon the party to be indemnified.

These are the reasons upon which our certificate is founded.

A certificate was sent accordingly.

DALY *v.* THOMPSON, Secretary, &c., of the Anti-
Dry-Rot Company.

(10 Meeson & Welsby, 309—320.)

1842.
April 25.

*Exch. of
Pleas.*

[309]

Case against the Secretary of the Anti-Dry-Rot Company, for not making
out and delivering to the plaintiff a certificate in respect of each of 20 shares
purchased by him. The Act, 6 Will. IV. c. xxvi., provides that the capital
shall be 250,000*l.*, and that the number of shares shall be limited to 10,000;
and the 16th section enacts, that the Company shall keep a book, and cause
to be entered therein the name and designation of every person subscribing
for shares in the undertaking, and of every person entitled to any shares
therein, making a separate entry of each share in numerical order; and
that after the making of such entry a certificate shall be made out in
respect of every share, specifying the number of such share and the name
of the proprietor thereof, and such certificate shall be delivered to the proprietor upon demand. And the twentieth section provides that it shall be
lawful for the proprietor of every share to sell and transfer the same by
writing duly stamped, which transfer shall be exhibited to the Company, or
their secretary, to be filed and registered in the manner prescribed by the
Act. At the trial, the plaintiff produced in evidence twenty scrip certificates payable to bearer, signed by three of the directors, and countersigned
by one T., who had been secretary to the Company. It appeared that T.
had fraudulently re-issued a number of the shares, and this having become
known, the shares, at the time the plaintiff purchased, were at a low
discount. Notices had been given by the Company in the public papers of
the fraud which had been practised, and the broker who negotiated the sale
of the shares to the plaintiff knew of that fraud at the time. It appeared
that at the time the scrip certificates were brought by the plaintiff to be
registered, the whole number of 10,000 shares had been already entered in
the register, pursuant to the Act. It was thereupon objected that the
register being full, and the defendants having no power to add to the
number of shares, the action in this form would not lie; and the learned
Judge being of that opinion, nonsuited the plaintiff: Held, that the nonsuit
could not be supported; because the register might have been improperly
filled, in which case the Company would be taking advantage of their own
wrong.

Semble, that it was not sufficient for the plaintiff merely to produce scrip
certificates payable to bearer, which he had required to be registered, but
that he ought to have shown his title to have those shares registered, and to
have deduced a good title from the original subscriber and his assignees.

It was also objected at the trial, that the plaintiff was not the *bonâ fide*

DALY
v.
THOMPSON.

holder of these shares, inasmuch as he had purchased them after notice that many shares were fabricated by a person who was himself a director and secretary of the Company for a time, and that it might be that the plaintiff had acquired his title through some of those false certificates; and it was proved that the plaintiff had given a less price than the ordinary one; but *semble*, that that would not deprive him of the title he had by the transfer, unless it were shown that he was not the *bond fide* owner.

CASE. The declaration stated that theretofore, to wit, on the 27th December, 1838, the plaintiff became and was, and still is, entitled to divers, to wit, twenty shares in the undertaking mentioned in an Act of Parliament, passed in the sixth year of the reign of his late Majesty King William the Fourth, intituled "An Act to enable John Howard Kyan to assign to a Company certain Letters Patent," that is to say, twenty shares in the capital or joint-stock of the said Company : that the said Company had provided certain books for entering therein the names and designations

[*310]

of the *several persons or parties who had subscribed for any share or shares in the said undertaking, and of every person entitled to any share or shares therein, according to the provisions of the said Act; of all which premises the said Company theretofore, and before the commencement of the suit, and before the committing of the grievances thereinafter mentioned, to wit, on the day and year aforesaid, had notice. And the plaintiff avers, that before and at the times of committing the grievances thereinafter mentioned, being so as aforesaid entitled to the said shares in the said undertaking, he was entitled, under and by virtue of the said Act of Parliament, and according to the tenor and effect, true intent and meaning thereof, to have his name and designation, and each of the before-mentioned shares to which he was so entitled as aforesaid, entered by the said Company in the books of the said Company, and also to have made out by the said Company a certificate in respect of each of such shares, specifying therein the proper number of the said plaintiff as proprietor thereof, and to have such certificate delivered to him the said plaintiff on demand. That theretofore, and after he became entitled to the said shares as aforesaid, and before the commencement of this suit, to wit, on the 30th May, 1839, he the plaintiff did request the said Company to cause to be entered in the said books of the said Company the name and designation of the plaintiff as the person entitled to the said shares, making a separate entry of each of such shares, and that a certificate in respect of each of the said shares should be made out by the said Company, and did then demand of the said

Company that such certificate should be delivered to the plaintiff
as proprietor of the said shares, pursuant to the provisions of the
said Act of Parliament; and although a reasonable time for making
such entry in the said books, and for making out and delivering
such certificates, hath long since elapsed, yet the said Company,
well knowing the premises, and contriving and intending *to injure   [*311]
the plaintiff in this behalf, in utter disregard of the said Act of
Parliament and of their duty in that behalf, have hitherto wholly
neglected and refused, and still do neglect and refuse, to cause to
be entered in any of the said books of the said Company the name
and designation of the said plaintiff as the person entitled to the
said shares, or any or either of them; and although often requested
so to do, have hitherto wholly neglected and refused, and still do
neglect and refuse, to make out a certificate in respect of each of
the said shares, or any or either of them, and to deliver the same
to the plaintiff as proprietor thereof, whereby the plaintiff is
deprived of the evidence of his title as proprietor of the said
shares, and is prevented from receiving and enforcing payment
of the interest and dividends for and in respect of the said shares,
and thereby and otherwise the plaintiff is injured.

Pleas, first, not guilty; secondly, that the plaintiff did not
become, nor was he entitled to the said shares in the said undertaking in the declaration mentioned, or any or either of them, or
any part thereof, *modo et formâ*: on which issues were joined.

At the trial, before Lord Abinger, C. B., at the Middlesex sittings
after Trinity Term, 1841, it appeared that this was an action on
the case brought against the secretary of the Anti-Dry-Rot Company, for refusing to enter the plaintiff's name and designation in
the books of the Company in respect of twenty shares purchased
by him, and for not making out a certificate in respect of each of
such shares, and delivering the same to the plaintiff, pursuant to
the provisions of the Act of 6 Will. IV. c. xxvi., by which the
Company was established (1).   The number of shares were *by the   [*312]
16th section of the Act limited to the number of 10,000.   The

(1) The following clauses are appli-   shares in the said undertaking, and of
cable to this case: every person entitled to any shares or
  By section 19, it is enacted, that the   share therein, making a separate entry
Company or the directors thereof shall   of each share; and such share shall be
provide and keep a book or books, and   numbered, beginning with No. 1, and
cause to be entered therein the names   proceeding in arithmetical progression
and designation of the several persons   whereof the common excess shall
or parties who have subscribed or shall   always be one, and every such share
hereafter subscribe for any *share or   shall always be distinguished by the   [*312, n.]

DALY
v.
THOMPSON.

[*313]

plaintiff, at the trial, produced in evidence twenty scrip *certificates, dated January, 1836, payable to bearer, signed by three of the directors, and countersigned by one Terry, who had been secretary

number so to be applied to the same; and after the making such entries, a certificate shall be made out in respect to every share in the said undertaking, specifying therein the proper number of such share, and the name and designation of the proprietor or proprietors thereof, and every such certificate shall be delivered to the proprietor of such share or shares, his executors, &c. upon demand, and might be in the words, or to the effect, set forth in page 14 of the Act. And such certificate shall be admitted in all Courts whatsoever, as evidence of the title of such proprietor, his or her executors, administrators, and assigns, to the share therein specified, and to the profits and advantages accruing in respect of the same; but the want

[*313, *n.*]

of such certificate shall not deprive any proprietor or proprietors of any share or shares in the said undertaking of his, her, or their right or interest in or claim to a due proportion of the profits and advantages of the said undertaking, nor hinder or prevent the proprietor or proprietors of any such shares from selling or disposing of any such share or shares; and in case such certificate shall not be produced or forthcoming, then the said entry, or a true copy thereof certified by the secretary of the said Company, shall be deemed *primâ facie* evidence of the title thereto. [Cf. Companies Clauses Consolidation Act, 1845 (8 & 9 Vict. c. 16), s. 9.]

And it is further enacted by section 20, that it shall be lawful for the several and respective proprietors of any share or shares in the said undertaking, their executors, administrators, successors, and assigns, to sell and transfer, by writing duly stamped, any share or shares of which they shall respectively be possessed, and every such transfer may be in the form mentioned in such page. And every such transfer, executed by all the parties

thereto, should be exhibited to the said Company or their secretary, to be filed by the said secretary and kept for the use of the said Company, and every such transfer shall be registered in the books of the said Company, by an entry of the date of such registry and the date of such transfer, together with the names of the parties thereto, and number of the share or shares transferred; and a copy of such registry or entry signed by the secretary to the said Company, shall be sufficient evidence of every such sale and transfer, and shall be received as such in all disputes and in all trials before any judges, justices, and others; provided always, that until such transfer shall be so entered or registered in the books of the said Company, no purchaser or purchasers *of any share or shares, his, her, or their executors, administrators, successors, or assigns, shall have any part or share in the said undertaking and the profits and advantages thereof, nor shall receive any interest or dividends for or in respect of such share or shares so purchased, nor be entitled to vote at any meeting or meetings as proprietor or proprietors of or in the said undertaking: provided also, and it is further enacted, that, after any call for money shall have been made by virtue of the said Act, no person or persons shall sell or transfer any share or shares which he, she, or they shall possess in the said undertaking, after the day appointed for the payment of the said call, until the money called for in respect of his, her, or their share or shares intended to be sold shall be paid, together with the interest, if any, due thereon; and unless such money so called for, with interest as aforesaid, shall be paid, every such sale or transfer of any share or shares shall be void, and such share or shares shall be liable to forfeiture, as if no such sale or transfer had been made. [Cf. Companies Clauses Act, 1845, ss. 14—16.]

and managing director to the Company. It appeared, however,   DALY
that Terry had fraudulently re-issued a great number of the shares   *v.*
which had been brought into the office; and this having become   THOMPSON.
notorious, the shares, at the time the plaintiff purchased, were at
a very low discount, and the shares he now claimed to be registered
had been purchased at a low price. It appeared that the whole
10,000 shares had been disposed of, and entered in the register;
that notices had been given by the Company in several newspapers,
and placed upon the Stock Exchange, of the frauds practised with
the shares, and cautioning persons not to purchase them; and that
the broker who negotiated the sale of these shares to the plaintiff,
knew at the time of the frauds which had been practised by Terry
respecting the shares. It was objected for the defendants, that the
action would not lie, inasmuch as the register was full, and the
defendant had no right to add to the number of shares. On the
other hand, it was said that the plaintiff ought not to be a sufferer
by the frauds committed by the secretary of the Company; and the
scrip certificates being signed by three directors of the Company,
that the Company were responsible for them. The *learned Judge,   [*314]
being of opinion that the plaintiff was not entitled to succeed in
this form of action, nonsuited him, but gave him leave to move to
enter a verdict with 40*s.* damages, in case the Court should be of
a contrary opinion.

    Erle having, in Michaelmas Term last, obtained a rule
accordingly,

    Kelly and *Byles*, in the same Term (Nov. 12), showed cause:

    The 19th section of the Act prescribes the manner in which the
shares are to be registered. It enacts that the Company shall
provide and keep a book or books, and cause to be entered therein
the names and designation of the persons subscribing for any share
in the undertaking, and of every person entitled to any share
therein, making a separate entry of each share in numerical order;
and that after the making of such entries, a certificate shall be
made out in respect of every share in the undertaking, specifying
the number of such share, and the name &c. of the proprietor
thereof, and that every such certificate shall be delivered to the
proprietor of such share, his executors &c., upon demand. And it
then goes on to provide that such certificate shall be evidence of the
title to the share described therein; but that the want of such

DALY
v.
THOMPSON.

certificate shall not deprive the proprietor thereof of his right to a due proportion of the profits, or from selling or disposing of any such share; and in case the certificate shall not be forthcoming, a copy of the said entry, certified by the secretary of the Company, shall be deemed *primâ facie* evidence of the title thereto. Then the 20th section provides, that it shall be lawful for the proprietors of any share or shares to sell and transfer by writing, duly stamped, any share or shares of which they shall be possessed; and every such transfer shall be exhibited to the Company or their secretary, to be filed by the secretary and kept for the use of the Company; and every such transfer shall be registered in the books of the Company, by an entry of the date of such registry and the date of

[*315]

such transfer, together *with the names of the parties thereto and number of the shares transferred; and a copy of such registry or entry, signed by the secretary, shall be sufficient evidence of such sale. Now it is not pretended that the provisions of this latter section have been complied with in this sale.

(PARKE, B.: That section applies only to the sale of registered shares; it does not say that scrip certificates shall not be sold except in that way.)

It was impossible for the defendant to have entered these shares without a breach of duty, for the whole number of shares allowed had been already entered in the register pursuant to the Act.

(PARKE, B.: The question is, whether, if the Company permit these shares to be issued into the market, they are not bound to do that which the Act requires to be done respecting every share which shall be issued. The circumstance of the register being full is no answer to an action for refusing to register scrip issued by them.)

This is not an action for unlawfully issuing scrip certificates, but for refusing to register them. The right to have the certificates registered is confined to the 10,000. Perhaps the plaintiff might have maintained an action against the directors of the Company for improperly issuing shares beyond the number of 10,000 allowed by Act, whereby the plaintiff was unable to get his shares registered: but this is not such an action, but one founded on the right under the statute to have the shares registered. But the register being already full, the plaintiff could have no such right. Besides, in this

case advertisements had been published in the newspapers, and
notices placed upon the Stock Exchange, of the frauds practised
respecting the shares, cautioning persons not to purchase them :
and the plaintiff's broker, who was called as a witness, proved that
he had seen those notices before he purchased the shares in question.

DALY
v.
THOMPSON.

(PARKE, B. : Your argument assumes that the 10,000 shares were
rightly registered.)

Undoubtedly that must be assumed until it is shown that they
were not.

(PARKE, B. : The doubt is on *whom the burthen of proof should
lie.   Supposing that a person had bought shares in the market at
their ordinary price, and without any circumstances of fraud or
suspicion, would it be any answer to the person who brought the
shares to be registered that the register was already full ?)

[*316]

It is difficult to answer questions put in the abstract ; it is enough
to say, that these were not so purchased.   If the duty were imposed
upon the Company to show that the whole 10,000 shares were
properly registered, it would be next to impossible to do so.   The
plaintiff says he has a right to have the shares registered, and the
onus is on him to show that he has that right.   It is clear that the
plaintiff was bound to show his title to the shares.   He could only
be so entitled by being an original proprietor of the shares, or
having had them by assignment since.   Assuming the 10,000
shares to have been properly registered, the shares in question were
not shown to have been properly transferred.   The plaintiff ought
to have deduced a good title from the original subscriber and his
assignee, in order to have entitled himself to have his name entered
on the register.   But all that he did was to produce scrip certificates
payable to bearer, which was clearly not enough, as a person could
not acquire a right to shares by a transfer from hand to hand; and
the 19th section is not applicable to this case.

W. H. Watson, in support of the rule :

No point was made at the trial as to the transfer of the shares
having been properly made; if it had, the plaintiff might have
obviated it.   And if the learned Judge had decided against the
plaintiff, he might have tendered a bill of exceptions, and so raised
the point.

DALY
v.
THOMPSON.

[*317]

(LORD ABINGER, C. B.: As no point was made at the trial as to that, you need not trouble yourself upon it.)

Then the *onus* of showing that the register was properly filled lay upon the defendants. The Act distinguishes between a shareholder and a person entitled *to a share. The 16th section says, that the capital shall be considered as consisting of 10,000 shares. Then, the 19th section provides, that the Company shall keep a book, and cause to be entered therein the names of persons who have subscribed, or shall subscribe, for any share in the undertaking, and of every person entitled to any share; and after the making of such entry, a certificate shall be made out in respect to every share in the undertaking, and every such certificate shall be delivered to the proprietor of such share, his executors, &c., upon demand; and then it enacts, that the certificate shall be admitted as evidence of the title of such proprietor, his executors, &c. to the share therein specified. When once a party becomes registered under this Act, he becomes a proprietor of shares. This action is brought for not doing that for the plaintiff which the 19th section requires to be done. The plaintiff produces the scrip certificates in the handwriting of the directors, and requests them to register them pursuant to the 19th section. It is no answer to say that there are 10,000 names already entered in the book. The Company, who have issued these certificates, ought to show that they were not properly issued.

(PARKE, B.: The Company having proved notice that a number of shares had been improperly issued, and frauds committed, and the plaintiff having purchased these shares with a knowledge of that, the question is, whether he is not bound to show that they were genuine.)

It is no answer that the 10,000 shares were entered in the book, unless they were properly so entered, and they who entered them are bound to show that they were. If the Company wished to guard against frauds, they should have had it provided that the shares should pass only by indorsement in writing. If the defendant had made out that the plaintiff obtained these shares fraudulently, it might have been a different thing; but then the question is, whether that should not be raised by plea. No fraud has been imputed to the plaintiff, and he is therefore entitled to *have the shares registered; and it is no answer to say that the Company

have registered other shares, by which the register is full. The
defendants allege that their own servant has caused this: that is
their own negligence, and they ought to suffer for it, and not the
plaintiff. It was the act of the defendants in sending these shares
into the world, and they are answerable for it.

Cur. adv. vult.

The judgment of the COURT was now (April 25) delivered by

PARKE, B.:

There was a case of *Daly* v. *Thompson*, which was argued two or
three Terms ago, but stood over for the judgment of the Court. It
was an action on the case against the secretary of the Anti-Dry-Rot
Company, acting in the name and on the behalf of the Company, to
recover damages for not making out and delivering to the plaintiff
a certificate in respect of twenty shares alleged to have been purchased by him, and for refusing to register those twenty shares in
his name. There was a clause in the Act of Parliament, that the
capital should be 250,000*l.*, and the number of shares are to amount
to 10,000.

When this case came on to be tried before Lord Abinger at Westminster, it was objected, on behalf of the defendant, that this action
would not lie, because the register was full, and the defendants had
no power to add to the number of shares; and that appearing to be
the case, his Lordship was of opinion that the plaintiff ought to be
nonsuited; that although he might succeed in another form of
action, he could not here. When the matter, however, was brought
before the Court, it was thought that the objection taken before
Lord Abinger could not be sustained; because, if the register was
full, and had been improperly filled, the defendants must set up
their own misconduct as an answer to the action.

It was objected, on showing cause, that the plaintiff had not made   [319]
out a good title to these shares; all that he had done was to produce scrip certificates payable to bearer. It was contended that he
ought to have shown he was entitled to have those particular shares
registered, and moreover, that he ought to deduce a good title not
only from the original subscriber, but the assignee, in order to give
him a right to have his name entered on the register; and that the
clause in the Act of Parliament, by which it is provided that they
should be transferred, does not apply. The plaintiff must show
that he was entitled as assignee of an original subscriber; and

there is a serious question, whether he could show that merely by
the production of the scrip certificate payable to bearer, in which it
is stated that the share belongs to the bearer of the certificate. To
say the least of it, there is great doubt whether any person, not
authorized so to do, can make such evidence admissible by an act
of this description, as in the case of bills of exchange payable to
bearer, or promissory notes, or bills of lading, which are indorsed,
and the property of which passes to the *bonâ fide* bearer of that
indorsement: so also in the case of Exchequer bills and India
bonds. This objection, however, was not the ground upon which
my Lord ABINGER decided to nonsuit: and we think there ought to
be a new trial, to have that point considered; and if the plaintiff,
on that occasion, cannot trace his title to the original subscriber,
by showing who that subscriber was, and by proving an assignment
from that person, and so on from all the persons through whom the
plaintiff claims, it will be a question whether he will be entitled to
recover.

All the members of the Court are not quite agreed in their view
of the law upon this part of the case, and therefore I pronounce no
opinion upon it at present; but the plaintiff will have an opportunity afforded him of going down to a new trial, and giving such
[*320]   evidence as he may *be advised of his title; it will, however, be
only prudent on his part to take the course I have alluded to,
namely, that of deducing his title from the original subscriber.

One objection was taken, that the plaintiff was not the *bonâ fide*
holder of these shares, because he had purchased after notice in the
market that many shares were fabricated by a person who was
himself in the Company for a time; and that was the fact. All the
10,000 shares had been registered, and it may be that the plaintiff
has acquired his title through one of the false certificates. The
amount, however, of this was, that the shares were depreciated in
the market, and the plaintiff paid a less price than the ordinary
one; still that would not deprive him of the title he had by the
transfer of the certificates; it would, indeed, if the defendants were
to show that he was not the *bonâ fide* owner; but if that is not
proved, the circumstance of his giving a less price for the shares
themselves would not deprive him of the right the holder really
had. If it were otherwise, the consequence would be to deprive all
the shareholders, both good and bad, because they obtained a
transfer of the certificates at an under-price. The question will
come to this, whether the defendant really is entitled to any shares

in the company. As I have observed before, it will be for him to
tender any evidence he thinks right; but I cannot fail to observe,
that he will act wisely by deducing a title from the original subscriber; if he does that, he will probably succeed in the action;
if he does not, he probably will be defeated. That is matter,
however, for subsequent consideration. We think that if the
register was filled improperly, the nonsuit ought not to have taken
place on the ground that it was full, and that there must be a
new trial.

Rule absolute for a new trial.

ARDEN *v.* PULLEN (1).

(10 Meeson & Welsby, 321—328; 11 L. J. Ex. 359.)

Where the tenant of a house undertakes by his agreement to keep it in
as good repair as when he took it, fair wear and tear excepted, he is not
entitled to quit upon its becoming uninhabitable for want of other repairs
during the term; and the landlord is under no implied obligation to do
any repairs in such a case.

ASSUMPSIT. The declaration stated, that on the 25th of March,
1839, by an agreement made between the plaintiff and the defendant, the plaintiff agreed to let, and the defendant to take of the
plaintiff, for the term of three years, from the 25th of December,
1839, a house and premises at the yearly rent of 30*l.*, payable
quarterly; and the defendant, among other things, thereby agreed
with the plaintiff, that he the defendant would keep the said premises
in as good repair and condition as the same then were, and would
so leave the same on the termination of the said tenancy, fair wear
and tear excepted. Breach; that, although the defendant entered
and paid the rent up to the 29th of September, 1841, yet he did
not pay the two quarters' rent which became due on the 25th of
March, 1842.

Plea, that before the commencement of the period in respect of
which the rent was claimed, to wit, on the 29th of June, 1841, the
said house and premises, by means and in consequence of age and
natural decay, and the badness of the materials thereof, and the
bad and improper manner in which they were originally built, and
the rotten, foundrous, miry, and insecure state and condition of the
walls, timbers, and foundations thereof, and for want of good and
sufficient sewerage and drainage, and by and through the neglect
and default of the plaintiff, and not for want of any such repair as

(1) Cp. Gott v. Gandy (1853) 2 E. & B. 845.

40—2

ARDEN
v.
PULLEN.

the defendant was bound to do under or by virtue of the said agreement, or by or through any neglect or default of the defendant in
that behalf, became and were in a ruinous, bad, insecure, and
dangerous state and condition, and wholly unsafe and unfit for
habitation, whereof the plaintiff then had notice, and was then
requested by the defendant to put the said house and premises into
[*322]   a safe, habitable, and tenantable repair, and a *fit state and condition to enable the defendant to continue to inhabit and reside
therein in safety, which the plaintiff then wholly neglected and
refused to do.   That, after allowing the plaintiff a reasonable time
to put the premises into such a state, and before the commencement of the period in respect of which the rent was claimed, to wit,
on the 27th of July, 1841, the defendant quitted and left the said
house and premises, and relinquished and gave up the possession
thereof to the plaintiff, and had not at any time since used or
occupied the same, or any part thereof, or derived any benefit
therefrom.

Replication, that the said house and premises did not become,
nor were they or either of them in a ruinous, bad, insecure, and
dangerous state and condition, and wholly unsafe and unfit for
habitation, by means of the badness of the materials thereof, or by
or through the bad and improper manner in which the said house
and premises were originally built, and the rotten, foundrous, miry,
and insecure state and condition of the walls, and the timbers and
foundations thereof, and for want of good and sufficient sewerage
and drainage, and by and through the neglect and default of the
plaintiff; but that, on the contrary thereof, .the said house and
premises became and were in such condition and state as in the said
plea mentioned, for want of such repairs as the defendant was bound
to do under and by virtue of the said agreement, and by and through
the neglect and default of the defendant in that behalf; concluding
to the country : whereupon issue was joined.

At the trial before Lord Abinger, C. B., at the Middlesex sittings,
after last Easter Term, it was proved by the defendant that the
premises in question consisted of a dwelling-house, and that he had
taken it under the following agreement: " Memorandum of agreement made the 25th day of November, 1839, between T. Arden of
[*323]   the one part, and J. T. Pullen of the other part. The said T. *Arden
agrees to let, and the said J. T. Pullen agrees to take of the said
T. Arden, from the 25th of December, 1809, for the term of three
years, and, if he shall continue after that period, then as a yearly

tenant (subject to six months' legal notice from either party to the
other), a house and premises, situate No. 7, Holloway Terrace,
Middlesex, at the clear yearly rent of 30*l.* ; and the said J. T. Pullen
agrees to pay the said rent quarterly, and also all present and future
land-tax and sewer-rate, and all other rates and assessments whatsoever in respect of the premises, or any part thereof, on the landlord, tenant, or occupier thereof respectively, when due ; and in
default thereof, the said T. Arden is hereby authorized to pay the
same, or any part thereof, and then, without notice, to recover the
amount paid by distress upon the premises, as in case of distress
for rent in arrear, or by any other legal proceedings whatsoever,
with the expenses thereof respectively.   And the said J. T. Pullen
also agrees to keep the house and premises in as good repair and
condition as the same now are in, and to leave the same on the
termination of the tenancy or giving up possession, fair wear and
tear excepted, together with all the erections, fixtures, improvements, and other things whatsoever, that shall at any time be
erected, fixed, or put up therein.''

It appeared that very extensive settlements had taken place in
the building, and thus large gaps in the main walls had been occasioned, and the only mode by which the house could be supported
was by shoring it up : that in order to keep the basement free from
water, pumping for several hours a day was necessary, and it was
then so wet as to be utterly unfit for occupation : that the house
having become, from these causes, utterly uninhabitable, the defendant, after giving notice before Michaelmas, 1841, had quitted it by
the advice of a surveyor, who stated that had the defendant continued to reside in it, the house would certainly have fallen down.
It was also proved, that the only means by *which it could be
repaired was by shoring up and under-pinning the house, pulling
down the front wall and rebuilding it, laying an entirely new foundation, and making a sewer to carry off the water; and that the
mischief was not to be ascribed to the want of ordinary repairs, or
to any injury, but simply to the original badness of the foundation,
which consisted of soft brick, and to the marshy nature of the soil.
The jury thereupon found a verdict for the defendant, subject to a
motion to enter a verdict for the plaintiff, if the Court should be of
opinion that that portion of the defendant's plea which alleged the
dangerous state of the premises to have arisen from the neglect and
default of the plaintiff, was in issue, and in point of law was
not proved.

ARDEN
v.
PULLEN.

[*324]

Erle having obtained a rule for this purpose, and also for judgment *non obstante veredicto,*

Crowder (*Butt* was with him) now showed cause:

The issue joined on the replication is, whether the house became in the state described in the plea for want of such repairs as the defendant under his agreement was bound to make, and through his default. That is the only portion of the replication that traverses the defendant's plea; the rest is mere inducement. If it was the duty of the defendant at all events to make the house habitable, there ought to have been a verdict for the plaintiff: but the defendant was clearly not bound to do the repairs requisite for the purpose of preventing these dilapidations, which rendered the house quite uninhabitable: if he was, he must have reconstructed it altogether. The jury were therefore right in finding in favour of the defendant.

(ALDERSON, B.: What has the plaintiff omitted to do, which he ought by his bargain to have done?

LORD ABINGER, C. B.: The defendant says there is an implied contract that the premises are of such stability that they may last during the term, with proper repairs.)

[325]   Yes. The agreement is to be construed according to the ordinary understanding of mankind. It never could have been contemplated between the parties that the defendant should undertake to rebuild the house. An implied contract must be introduced, that the house is fairly habitable at the commencement of the term. It cannot be contended, that in the event of the house becoming uninhabitable, and utterly useless to the tenant, his liability to pay the rent should continue. [He referred to *Collins* v. *Barrow* (1), *Edwards* v. *Etherington* (2), *Baker* v. *Holtpzaffell* (3), and *Izon* v. *Gorton* (4).]

[326]   (LORD ABINGER, C. B.: The question is, is there, on letting a house on lease, an implied contract that the house shall endure for the term?)

It is submitted there clearly is.

(1) 1 M. & Rob. 112 (overruled, *Hart* v. *Windsor* (1843) 12 M. & W. 68; 13 L. J. Ex. 129).

(2) Ry. & M. 268; 7 Dowl. & Ry. 117 (overruled, *Hart* v. *Windsor* (1843)

12 M. & W. 68; 13 L. J. Ex. 129).

(3) 13 R. R. 556 (4 Taunt. 45).

(4) 50 R. R. 772 (5 Bing. N. C. 501; 7 Scott, 537).

Erle and *Ogle*, in support of the rule:

The material allegation in this plea is, that the house became uninhabitable "by and through the neglect and default of the *plaintiff," and not for want of any such repair as the defendant was bound to do under his agreement; that allegation is traversed by the replication, and this was the issue raised, which the defendant was bound to prove. But the plaintiff was under no obligation to the defendant to do these repairs, for there is no implied contract on the part of the landlord to that effect. If it were, it would necessarily extend to every defect which the tenant was not bound to remedy, and would entitle him to rescind the contract. The obligation to do such repairs as these would lie on the owner of the fee, and the plaintiff might be merely a lessee, and not bound himself to do them. The cases which have been cited only show that the tenant may put an end to the contract in cases where the landlord has been guilty of some default. (They were then stopped by the COURT.)

[*327]

LORD ABINGER, C. B.:

I am of opinion that, unless there has been some fraud or improper concealment on the part of the plaintiff, which is not suggested, the contract for letting this house was perfectly good. The defendant was, therefore, bound to perform it so long as the plaintiff performed her part of it; and the plea would have been bad if it had not contained the allegation, that the defects arose "by and through the default of the plaintiff." That allegation, being traversed by the replication, became the material part of the issue: and this raised the question whether, when a house turns out to be uninhabitable from such causes as existed in the present instance, the landlord is bound to repair it. I think, that without some express stipulation, he is under no such obligation; and the defendant, consequently, having failed to substantiate the only material part of the issue, the verdict must be entered for the plaintiff.

ALDERSON, B.:

I think the contract was perfectly good. *The rule laid down by TINDAL, Ch. J., in *Izon* v. *Gorton*, is the correct one, that, in order to enable a tenant to avoid his lease, there must be a default on the part of the landlord. He observes, that " the cases in which the tenant has been allowed to withdraw himself from the tenancy, and to refuse payment of rent, will be found to be cases where there

[*328]

has been either error or fraudulent misdescription of the premises which were the subject of the letting, or where the premises have been found to be uninhabitable by the wrongful act or default of the landlord himself." The case of *Collins* v. *Barrow* cannot be law, unless it is put upon that ground; and most probably that was the ground of the decision, and the statement of the facts in the report is imperfect; for it is to be observed, that some evidence is mentioned which would lead to the conclusion that the landlord must have engaged to make the sewer. Here the plaintiff has done no wrong; she has performed her duty, and therefore she is entitled to a verdict on the plea.

GURNEY, B., and ROLFE, B. concurred.

Rule absolute to enter a verdict for the plaintiff.

BROWN *v.* JOHNSON (1).

(10 Meeson & Welsby, 331—334; S. C. 11 L. J. Ex. 273; Car. & M. 440.)

By a charter-party made in London, upon a vessel for a voyage from London to Honduras and back to some port in the United Kingdom, 25 running days for every 100 tons of mahogany were to be allowed for loading the ship at Honduras, and 15 days for discharging at the destined port in the United Kingdom: Held, that in the absence of any custom, Sundays were to be computed in the calculation of the lay days at the port of discharge.

The ship arrived at Hull, the port of her destination, on the 1st of February, and was reported; on the 2nd, she entered the dock, and was given in charge of the dock-officer, but did not get to the place of unloading till the 4th, in consequence of the full state of the docks, the officer refusing to take her out of her turn; and the discharge was not completed till the 22nd: Held, that the lay days were to be calculated from the period of her arrival in dock, and not at the place of unloading.

DECLARATION by the plaintiff, as owner, against the defendant, as charterer, on a charter-party of the ship *Trinidad*, from London to Honduras, there to load at one of the usual places of loading, including the rivers Ulua and Dulce, a cargo of mahogany, and then proceed to some port in the United Kingdom; twenty-five running days for every hundred tons of mahogany to be allowed the defendant, if the ship were not sooner dispatched, for loading the said ship at Honduras, and fifteen days for discharging at her

---

(1) Followed, *Tapscott* v. *Balfour* (1872) L. R. 8 C. P. 46, 42 L. J. C. P. 16, 27 L. T. 710; distinguished, *Norden Steamship Co.* v. *Dempsey* (1876) 1 C. P. D. 654, 660, 45 L. J. C. P. 764; *Nelson* v. *Dahl* (1881) 6 App. Ca. 38, 43, 50 L. J. Ch. 411, 44 L. T. 381; approved, *Thiis* v. *Byers* (1876) 1 Q. B. D. 244, 249, 45 L. J. Q. B. 511, 34 L. T. 526; explained, *Neilsen* v. *Watt* (1885) 16 Q. B. Div. 67, 55 L. J. Q. B. 87, 54 L. T. 344.

destined port in the United Kingdom, and thirty days on
demurrage, over and above the said laying days, at 6l. per day.
Among other breaches, the declaration alleged, that the ship being
ordered to Hull upon her return, by the defendant, he would not
discharge the cargo at the said port of Hull within the said number
of fifteen days in the charter-party mentioned, but detained the
vessel after she was ready to discharge her cargo, and the
defendant had notice of it, for the space of six days over and
above the said fifteen laying days mentioned in the said charter-
party, whereby a demand for demurrage arose.

To this the defendant pleaded, amongst other pleas, that he did
not detain the vessel above the said fifteen laying days, in the said
charter-party in that behalf mentioned ; and also, that he was
prevented from unloading by the wrongful act, procurement,
neglect, and default of the plaintiff, and his servants and agents ;
whereupon issues were joined.

At the trial before Alderson, B., at the sittings in London *in
this Term, it appeared that, the charter-party having been entered
into in London, the ship proceeded on her voyage, and arrived with
her cargo at Hull, the port of destination, on the 1st of February,
1841, and was reported. On the 2nd she entered the dock, and
was given in charge of the dock officer, but did not get up to the
place of unloading till the 4th, in consequence of the full state of
the docks, the dock officer refusing to take the ship out of her
turn, and the discharge was not completed till the 22nd. The
defendant's counsel called several witnesses to prove that, by the
usage of the trade at Hull, the word " days " meant " working
days; " but this they failed to establish. There was evidence that
the plaintiff had been dilatory and negligent in the unloading; and
the learned Judge, in his summing up, directed the jury, that the
period from which the lay days was to commence was the day of
her coming into the dock, and not of her coming to her berth, and
that Sundays were to be included in the lay days. The jury
found a verdict for the plaintiff for 18l. for demurrage, declaring
that they had included Sundays in their computation of the time
allowed for unloading.

[*332]

    Jervis now moved for a new trial on the ground of mis-
       direction, on two points :

First, Sundays ought not to have been included in reckoning the
lay days. This was evidently the intention of the parties, from

DALY
v.
THOMPSON.

(LORD ABINGER, C. B.: As no point was made at the trial as to that, you need not trouble yourself upon it.)

Then the *onus* of showing that the register was properly filled lay upon the defendants. The Act distinguishes between a shareholder and a person entitled *to a share. The 16th section says, that the capital shall be considered as consisting of 10,000 shares. Then, the 19th section provides, that the Company shall keep a book, and cause to be entered therein the names of persons who have subscribed, or shall subscribe, for any share in the undertaking, and of every person entitled to any share; and after the making of such entry, a certificate shall be made out in respect to every share in the undertaking, and every such certificate shall be delivered to the proprietor of such share, his executors, &c., upon demand; and then it enacts, that the certificate shall be admitted as evidence of the title of such proprietor, his executors, &c. to the share therein specified. When once a party becomes registered under this Act, he becomes a proprietor of shares. This action is brought for not doing that for the plaintiff which the 19th section requires to be done. The plaintiff produces the scrip certificates in the handwriting of the directors, and requests them to register them pursuant to the 19th section. It is no answer to say that there are 10,000 names already entered in the book. The Company, who have issued these certificates, ought to show that they were not properly issued.

(PARKE, B.: The Company having proved notice that a number of shares had been improperly issued, and frauds committed, and the plaintiff having purchased these shares with a knowledge of that, the question is, whether he is not bound to show that they were genuine.)

It is no answer that the 10,000 shares were entered in the book, unless they were properly so entered, and they who entered them are bound to show that they were. If the Company wished to guard against frauds, they should have had it provided that the shares should pass only by indorsement in writing. If the defendant had made out that the plaintiff obtained these shares fraudulently, it might have been a different thing; but then the question is, whether that should not be raised by plea. No fraud has been imputed to the plaintiff, and he is therefore entitled to *have the shares registered; and it is no answer to say that the Company

[*317]

[*318]

have registered other shares, by which the register is full. The
defendants allege that their own servant has caused this: that is
their own negligence, and they ought to suffer for it, and not the
plaintiff. It was the act of the defendants in sending these shares
into the world, and they are answerable for it.

Cur. adv. vult.

The judgment of the COURT was now (April 25) delivered by

PARKE, B.:

There was a case of *Daly* v. *Thompson*, which was argued two or
three Terms ago, but stood over for the judgment of the Court. It
was an action on the case against the secretary of the Anti-Dry-Rot
Company, acting in the name and on the behalf of the Company, to
recover damages for not making out and delivering to the plaintiff
a certificate in respect of twenty shares alleged to have been purchased by him, and for refusing to register those twenty shares in
his name. There was a clause in the Act of Parliament, that the
capital should be 250,000*l.*, and the number of shares are to amount
to 10,000.

When this case came on to be tried before Lord Abinger at Westminster, it was objected, on behalf of the defendant, that this action
would not lie, because the register was full, and the defendants had
no power to add to the number of shares; and that appearing to be
the case, his Lordship was of opinion that the plaintiff ought to be
nonsuited; that although he might succeed in another form of
action, he could not here. When the matter, however, was brought
before the Court, it was thought that the objection taken before
Lord Abinger could not be sustained; because, if the register was
full, and had been improperly filled, the defendants must set up
their own misconduct as an answer to the action.

It was objected, on showing cause, that the plaintiff had not made   [319]
out a good title to these shares; all that he had done was to produce scrip certificates payable to bearer. It was contended that he
ought to have shown he was entitled to have those particular shares
registered, and moreover, that he ought to deduce a good title not
only from the original subscriber, but the assignee, in order to give
him a right to have his name entered on the register; and that the
clause in the Act of Parliament, by which it is provided that they
should be transferred, does not apply. The plaintiff must show
that he was entitled as assignee of an original subscriber; and

there is a serious question, whether he could show that merely by
the production of the scrip certificate payable to bearer, in which it
is stated that the share belongs to the bearer of the certificate. To
say the least of it, there is great doubt whether any person, not
authorized so to do, can make such evidence admissible by an act
of this description, as in the case of bills of exchange payable to
bearer, or promissory notes, or bills of lading, which are indorsed,
and the property of which passes to the *bonâ fide* bearer of that
indorsement: so also in the case of Exchequer bills and India
bonds.   This objection, however, was not the ground upon which
my Lord ABINGER decided to nonsuit : and we think there ought to
be a new trial, to have that point considered ; and if the plaintiff,
on that occasion, cannot trace his title to the original subscriber,
by showing who that subscriber was, and by proving an assignment
from that person, and so on from all the persons through whom the
plaintiff claims, it will be a question whether he will be entitled to
recover.

All the members of the Court are not quite agreed in their view
of the law upon this part of the case, and therefore I pronounce no
opinion upon it at present; but the plaintiff will have an opportunity afforded him of going down to a new trial, and giving such
[*320]   evidence as he may *be advised of his title; it will, however, be
only prudent on his part to take the course I have alluded to,
namely, that of deducing his title from the original subscriber.

One objection was taken, that the plaintiff was not the *bonâ fide*
holder of these shares, because he had purchased after notice in the
market that many shares were fabricated by a person who was
himself in the Company for a time ; and that was the fact. All the
10,000 shares had been registered, and it may be that the plaintiff
has acquired his title through one of the false certificates. The
amount, however, of this was, that the shares were depreciated in
the market, and the plaintiff paid a less price than the ordinary
one ; still that would not deprive him of the title he had by the
transfer of the certificates; it would, indeed, if the defendants were
to show that he was not the *bonâ fide* owner ; but if that is not
proved, the circumstance of his giving a less price for the shares
themselves would not deprive him of the right the holder really
had. If it were otherwise, the consequence would be to deprive all
the shareholders, both good and bad, because they obtained a
transfer of the certificates at an under-price. The question will
come to this, whether the defendant really is entitled to any shares

in the company. As I have observed before, it will be for him to tender any evidence he thinks right; but I cannot fail to observe, that he will act wisely by deducing a title from the original subscriber; if he does that, he will probably succeed in the action; if he does not, he probably will be defeated. That is matter, however, for subsequent consideration. We think that if the register was filled improperly, the nonsuit ought not to have taken place on the ground that it was full, and that there must be a new trial.

Rule absolute for a new trial.

ARDEN *v.* PULLEN (1).

(10 Meeson & Welsby, 321—328 ; 11 L. J. Ex. 359.)

Where the tenant of a house undertakes by his agreement to keep it in as good repair as when he took it, fair wear and tear excepted, he is not entitled to quit upon its becoming uninhabitable for want of other repairs during the term; and the landlord is under no implied obligation to do any repairs in such a case.

ASSUMPSIT. The declaration stated, that on the 25th of March, 1839, by an agreement made between the plaintiff and the defendant, the plaintiff agreed to let, and the defendant to take of the plaintiff, for the term of three years, from the 25th of December, 1839, a house and premises at the yearly rent of 30*l.*, payable quarterly; and the defendant, among other things, thereby agreed with the plaintiff, that he the defendant would keep the said premises in as good repair and condition as the same then were, and would so leave the same on the termination of the said tenancy, fair wear and tear excepted. Breach; that, although the defendant entered and paid the rent up to the 29th of September, 1841, yet he did not pay the two quarters' rent which became due on the 25th of March, 1842.

Plea, that before the commencement of the period in respect of which the rent was claimed, to wit, on the 29th of June, 1841, the said house and premises, by means and in consequence of age and natural decay, and the badness of the materials thereof, and the bad and improper manner in which they were originally built, and the rotten, foundrous, miry, and insecure state and condition of the walls, timbers, and foundations thereof, and for want of good and sufficient sewerage and drainage, and by and through the neglect and default of the plaintiff, and not for want of any such repair as

(1) Cp. *Gott* v. *Gandy* (1853) 2 E. & B. 845.

40—2

Martin, contrà :

The true construction of the deed is, that if the parties do work the mines, they shall do so in a proper and workmanlike manner; but if they choose not to work them, they are not bound to do so, paying the fixed rent. The very terms of the reservation of 20*l.* per annum, whether any coal should be worked or not, shows that it was to be optional with the defendant to work them or not. There is nothing in the covenant to compel him to work the mines. The clause reserving the 20*l.* contemplates that there may be no working of the coal, and there could be no breach without it.

Platt, in reply :

[*338]   If this in terms had been a grant of a *license merely to work the mines, as in *Muskett* v. *Hill* (1), it might perhaps have been different; but this is an actual demise of the mines themselves. The argument on the other side would go to the extent that nothing at all was demised. With respect to what has been said as to the 20*l.* being to be paid whether the mines were worked or not, there is nothing in that observation, for if the royalty amounts to more, the payment of that sum is to cease altogether.

Cur. adv. vult.

The judgment of the COURT was now delivered by

ALDERSON, B. :

This case was heard before my brothers Parke, Rolfe, and myself, in last Term, and the question arose on a demurrer to the second plea. The declaration states that the plaintiff, by deed dated the 13th October, 1889, demised to the defendant and two other persons, the mines which at the date of the demise had been, or during the term of twenty-one years thereby created should be, discovered or opened in or under certain lands called Dyffryn House, and the demesne lands thereto adjoining; and in the deed was a covenant by the lessees jointly and severally, that they would during the term work the demised premises in a workman-like manner, according to the custom. The declaration then avers a breach of that covenant, in not working the said demised premises in a workmanlike manner.

There are three counts in the declaration, founded on three separate demises of different mines, but they are all framed in

(1) 50 R. R. 832 (5 Bing. N. C. 694; 7 Scott, 855).

precisely the same language, so that the decision as to one governs the whole. The defendant pleads by his *second plea, that the mines in the first count of the declaration mentioned were not at any time before the demise worked, gotten, or cleared in any manner whatever, nor did the defendant and the other lessees, or any of them, work the same or get the mines in any manner whatever : and there are similar pleas as to the other counts. To these pleas the defendant demurred, and the question argued before us was, whether, it appearing by the pleas that the mines had not been worked at all, the defendant was liable on his covenant to work the demised premises, in a workmanlike manner.

It appears to us, on looking at the pleadings and the deeds in question, which are all set out on *oyer*, and are very long, that the defendant is clearly entitled to judgment; for the subject-matter of the demise in all the deeds is not the mines under the lands specified in the deed, but only such of the mines as had been or should be discovered or opened. It is therefore plain, that in order to show the defendant to have been guilty of any breach of covenant in not working, or not working in a workmanlike manner, the demised premises, it was absolutely necessary that the mines, the not working of which is the ground of the alleged breach of covenant, should have been discovered or opened. The contrary to this appears on the face of these pleadings, and we are therefore of opinion that the defendant is entitled to our judgment.

Judgment for the defendant.

RUSSELL AND OTHERS *v.* BELL AND ANOTHER (1).

(10 Meeson & Welsby, 340—354.)

Indebitatus assumpsit by the assignees of a bankrupt. The first four counts were for goods sold, money paid and had and received, and on an account stated, laying the promises to the bankrupt; the 5th, 6th, and 7th counts were for goods sold, money had and received, and on an account stated, laying the promises to the assignees. Pleas, first, except as to 320*l.* parcel, &c., and except as to 140*l.* parcel of the sums in the first, second, third and fourth counts mentioned, *non assumpsit*. Secondly, as to the said sum of 140*l.*, parcel of the monies in the first, second, third, and fourth counts mentioned, a plea of mutual credit, which had been demurred to, and on argument judgment given for the defendant. Thirdly, as to the 320*l.* payment of that sum into Court, which the plaintiffs took out and

(1) The point as to the particulars could hardly arise under the present practice. Upon the other points the case is still an authority.—A. C.

RUSSELL
v.
BELL.

joined issue, on the plea of *non assumpsit*. The following were the particulars of demand delivered prior to the pleas. "This action is brought to recover the sum of 140*l.*, the value of certain yarn; also the sum of 316*l.*, the proceeds of a bill of exchange, drawn by J. M. and indorsed by the bankrupt to the defendant; also 4*l.*, the proceeds of a cheque; and 80*l.* in cash; the said yarn, bill of exchange, cheque and cash having been received by the defendants from or by the authority of the bankrupt, about the months of September or October, 1839. The particular date is known to the defendants." At the trial, the cause proceeded for the recovery of the sum of 140*l.* only, and no evidence was adduced as to the 80*l.* cash. It was objected that the plaintiffs were not entitled to go into evidence as to the 140*l.*, as that sum was already satisfied by the judgment upon the demurrer, and that that sum must be struck out of the particulars of demand; but the learned Judge received the evidence, giving the defendant leave to move to enter a nonsuit. A rule having been accordingly granted on that ground: Held, that the plaintiff was entitled to give evidence of goods sold to the amount of 140*l.*, upon the other counts of the declaration, to which the plea was not pleaded, and might apply the particulars to those counts.

Where a debtor, upon applications made to him by creditors for payment of their debts, made appointments with them to meet him at specified times and places with reference to a settlement of their demands, but failed to keep such appointments: Held, that the failures to keep the appointments constituted acts of bankruptcy, although the places at which the appointments were made were not his usual places of business.

It appeared at the trial, that after the bankruptcy, 85 bundles of yarn, of the value of 114*l.*, had been delivered by the bankrupt to the defendants, as they alleged, to meet an accommodation bill which they were about to give the bankrupt. The goods were accompanied by an invoice, which stated them to be bought by the defendants of the bankrupt: Held, under these circumstances, that the assignees might waive the tort, and bring assumpsit for goods sold and delivered.

ASSUMPSIT. The first count of the declaration alleged, that the defendants, before the said J. Nicholl became bankrupt, were indebted to him in the sum of 500*l.* for goods sold and delivered; the second count was for money paid by the bankrupt for the defendants; the third for money had and received by the defendants for the use of the bankrupt; and the fourth was on an account stated between the defendants and the bankrupt; laying the promises to the bankrupt. The fifth count was for goods sold and delivered by the plaintiffs, as assignees, to the defendants; the sixth for money had and received to the use of the assignees; and the seventh was on an account stated between the defendants and the plaintiffs, as assignees; stating the promises to the plaintiffs as assignees.

[341]   The defendants pleaded, first, except as to the sum of 320*l.*, parcel of the sums of money in the declaration mentioned, and except as to the further sum of 140*l.*, parcel of the sums in the first, second, third, and fourth counts mentioned, *non assumpsit*.

Secondly, as to the said sum of 140*l.* parcel of the monies in the first, second, third, and fourth counts, and not being any part of the sum of 320*l.*, parcel &c. in the next plea mentioned, that before notice of any act of bankruptcy, and before the issuing of the *fiat*, and before action brought, they the defendants gave credit to the bankrupt to a large amount, by accepting certain bills of exchange for his accommodation; and at his request, without any consideration or value, which bills were, before notice of the bankruptcy, negotiated by the bankrupt for his own use and benefit; that the credits so given were likely to end in debts from the bankrupt to the defendants ; and that afterwards, and before action, the defendants paid the bills.   To this plea there was a special demurrer; but on argument, in Easter Term, 1841 (1), it was held to be sufficient, and judgment was accordingly entered, that the second plea was sufficient to bar the plaintiff from maintaining the action as to the said sum of 140*l.*, parcel &c.

The defendants, as to the sum of 320*l.*, pleaded payment of that sum into Court, which the plaintiffs took out, and joined issue on the plea of *non assumpsit.*

The following were the particulars of the plaintiffs' demand, delivered under a Judge's order the day prior to the delivery of the declaration :

" This action is brought to recover the sum of 140*l.*, the value of certain yarn ; also the sum of 316*l.*, the proceeds of a bill of exchange drawn on John Murgatroyd, and indorsed by Joseph Nicholl to the defendants ; also 4*l.*, the proceeds of a cheque (2) ; and the sum of 80*l.* *in cash ; the said yarn, bill of exchange, cheque, and cash, having been received by the defendants from or by the authority of the said Joseph Nicholl, about the months of September or October, 1839.   The particular date is known to the defendants."

[*342]

At the trial before Lord Denman, Ch. J., at the last Summer Assizes for the county of York, it appeared that the action was brought to recover the sum of 140*l.* for yarn sold and delivered to the defendants, and 80*l.* for money which it was alleged came to the defendant's hands after the bankruptcy ; as to the latter sum, however, no evidence was adduced.   It was objected, at the conclusion of the opening speech of the plaintiffs' counsel, that they were not entitled to go into evidence as to the 140*l.*, inasmuch as

(1) See 8 M. & W. 277.
(2) It will be perceived that these

sums of 316*l.* and 4*l.* together, made the sum of 320*l.* paid into Court.

judgment had been already given against them as to that sum on
the demurrer; that if it were otherwise, the plaintiffs would be
proceeding twice to recover the same sum; that if the judgment
had been the other way, and the plaintiffs were to obtain a verdict
now for that sum, they would recover the same sum twice over.
To this it was answered, that the second plea, on which judgment
had been given for the defendants, was confined to the first four
counts of the declaration. The learned Judge said he should
receive the evidence, giving the defendants leave to move to enter
a nonsuit.

The plaintiffs, in order to show acts of bankruptcy committed by
Nicholl (the bankrupt), proved repeated applications made to him
by several creditors for payment of debts owing to them from him;
that he had made appointments with them to meet him in the
months of July, August, and September, 1839, with reference to
an arrangement of their demands, at Bradford and Halifax markets,
and at certain public-houses; which appointments the bankrupt
failed to keep. There was no other evidence as to the bankrupt's
denying or absenting himself, but the case rested, in this respect,
on the neglect to keep the above appointments.

[343]   It was proved by a commission agent of the name of Froggatt,
that on the 15th of October, 1839, he had eighty-five bundles of
yarn of the bankrupt's in his possession, the value of which he
said was about 114l.; that the bankrupt urged him to buy it, which
he refused to do, but advised the bankrupt to sell it, which he said
he would try to do. He afterwards came and said he had sold it,
and sent a porter for it. Another witness proved that the defendant Bell had admitted to him that the bankrupt, Nicholl, had
pressed him to receive some goods which the bankrupt and a
porter brought to him, about the value of 100l., and that they the
defendants had received them. It was objected that there was no
evidence of a sale of the goods, or of money had and received by
the defendants to the use of the assignees; and the learned Judge
being of that opinion, was about to nonsuit the plaintiffs, when the
defendant Bell's examination was put in. On being asked when
the yarn was delivered, he stated that the goods were sent by the
bankrupt on account of an accommodation bill the defendants were
about to give him; that the amount was 114l. 15s., and that the
goods were received by them, he believed, on the 17th of September,
1839; that he could not swear to the precise day, but he had no
doubt of it; that the invoice which accompanied them bore that

date; that they received no yarns from Froggatt's warehouse but those on the 17th of September. The invoice was as follows :

"Messrs. Harrison & Bell.   Sept. 17, 1839.

" Bought of Joseph Nicholl.

" 170 gr. 40 weft at 13*s.* 6*d.*   .   .   .   .   £114 15   0."

It was still objected that there was no evidence of any sale of the goods by the assignees to the defendants, or of money had and received by the defendants to the use of the assignees. The learned Judge, however, thought the plaintiffs entitled to recover, and the jury, under his direction, found a verdict for 114*l.* on the fifth count of the declaration, with leave to the defendants to move to enter a nonsuit.

Wortley having, in Michaelmas Term last, obtained a rule to enter a nonsuit accordingly,   [344]

Cresswell and *W. H. Watson* now showed cause :

First, it is said that there having been a plea as to 140*l.*, parcel &c., on which judgment was given for the defendants, that sum of 140*l.* is to be struck out of the particulars delivered, and that no evidence can be given as to that sum : but that is treating the plea as pleaded to the particulars, and not to the declaration ; the particulars, however, are given merely to restrict the proof at the . trial. * * *

Then secondly, there was abundant evidence of acts of bank-   [345] ruptcy before the delivery of these goods. At the trial repeated appointments which the bankrupt had made with different creditors were proved, and that he had failed to keep those appointments, which was clearly sufficient. A trader's absenting himself from any place with intent to delay a creditor, is an act of bankruptcy : *Curteis* v. *Willes* (1).

Thirdly, there is abundant evidence of goods sold and delivered by the assignees. Here the goods were received by the defendants from the bankrupt after the bankruptcy, accompanied by an invoice stating the price of them, and the assignees are entitled to recover the exact sum invoiced, as they have done. Even supposing this to *be a conversion, the assignees have a right to   [*346] waive the tort and bring assumpsit. In *Smith* v. *Hodson* (2), the rule is laid down, that if a bankrupt on the eve of bankruptcy

(1) 1 Car. & P. 211 ; 6 Dowl. & Ry.   (2) 53 R. R. 93 (4 T. R. 211).
224 ; Ry. & M. 58.

fraudulently deliver goods to one of his creditors, the assignees may disaffirm the contract, and recover the value of the goods in trover; but if they bring assumpsit they affirm the contract, and then the creditor may set off his debt. Here the assignees have affirmed the contract. The defendants cannot say that they did not take the goods since the bankruptcy, and they are, therefore, clearly liable for them as goods sold by the assignees.

Wortley and *Crompton*, in support of the rule :

The object of the particulars is to apprise the defendants of what the plaintiffs seek to recover, and they must not be calculated to mislead them. Here the plaintiffs, amongst other things, set up a claim of 140*l.* for yarn sold and delivered. To the counts for goods sold and delivered, &c., by the bankrupt, the defendants have pleaded, as to the 140*l.*, a plea which, on demurrer, was held to be a good bar; and that plea states it to be a transaction between the bankrupt and the defendants.

(LORD ABINGER, C. B.: The particulars are sufficiently vague to admit of any parcel of yarn having been delivered to the defendants.

ALDERSON, B.: The plaintiffs' particulars restrict them to 140*l.* for yarn sold and delivered, but they may apply that to the other counts.)

It is submitted that the plaintiffs have been answered as to the 140*l.* * * *

[347] Then secondly, as to the act of bankruptcy. This person's merely failing to meet his creditors at Bradford and Halifax markets, or at certain public-houses which he had appointed, does not amount to an act of bankruptcy. In order to constitute it such, it must be a failure to meet his creditors, pursuant to an appointment, at his place of business.

(ALDERSON, B.: If he fails to meet a creditor to pay a debt, which he has appointed to do, it is an act of bankruptcy.)

Here there was no evidence that Nicholl stopped away in order to avoid his creditors.

(LORD ABINGER, C. B.: He is proved to have made six or seven different appointments, all of which he failed to keep, and unless a

reasonable excuse is given for it, that is an irresistible case to show   RUSSELL
v.
BELL.
that he avoided his creditors.)

Thirdly, there was no evidence of any sale or delivery of the goods
at all, but it is shown that the goods were delivered for a totally
different purpose.

(ALDERSON, B. : You receive goods with an invoice stating a sale
to you. It is true the defendant Bell states it to have been on the
17th of September, whereas it appears that it was not until the
15th of October.)

It is the ordinary custom, where goods are sent as a security, to
send *an invoice with them.   [*348]

(ALDERSON, B. : You received them under that invoice, stating
them to be bought of the bankrupt ; can you say that that was not
a sale in law ?)

The plaintiffs rely upon this, in one respect, as a fraudulent preference. It is true you may waive the tort ; but you must in that
case go on the very contract between the parties, which the law
under the circumstances will imply. Now, was there anything here
to show that these goods were to be paid for on request ? Certainly
not. An invoice is always sent in every transaction of this kind,
whether there is a sale or not. This was not a contract for the
.sale of goods to be paid for on request. *Strutt* v. *Smith* (1) shows
that, although you may waive the tort, still you are bound by the
very terms of the sale between the parties. *   * In *Bradbury* v.
Anderton (2), that principle is applied to a case like the present. It
appears, therefore, that where a party proceeds upon a contract
instead of insisting on what he might treat as a fraud, he must
abide by the terms of the contract. *   *   *

LORD ABINGER, C. B. :   [349]

It appears to me that the argument of the learned counsel for the
defendant is untenable on both points. First, as to the bill of
particulars. It is perfectly novel to say that a plea is to be construed by, or has any reference to, a bill of particulars ; what the
Courts have laid down as a settled rule is this—that where a bill of
particulars admits a sum of money to be paid, and the plaintiff goes

(1) 1 Cr. M. & R. 312.   (2) *Ibid.* 486.

for the balance only, the party shall not be bound to plead payment;
that is to say, on *non assumpsit* he shall be entitled to credit for
the amount stated in his bill of particulars without a plea of payment. The plea is to the declaration, and nothing but the declaration. To put the argument of the counsel for the defendant in the
light that appears to me to be the strongest, it is this; we have one
set of counts to which there is a plea of mutual credit, to which
there was a demurrer, which was determined in favour of the
defendants. They say, look at the consequence if you do not con-

[*350] sider that as disposing altogether of the plaintiff's *claim : if the
plaintiffs were to prove this claim, and attempt to show the very
debt which is the subject of the set-off in this case, will not this
judgment in favour of the defendants upon this plea be decisive
evidence between the same parties that they have satisfied the
debt by a set-off, and therefore the plaintiffs cannot prove it?
But to that argument there is an obvious answer. Suppose the
assignees had brought the action, and confined the declaration
altogether to counts in assumpsit which had been pleaded to, and
there had been judgment for the defendants; so far then the action
would have been decided in favour of the defendants : might not
the plaintiffs afterwards have brought an action of trover? Is it
not every day's practice, where a party is mistaken in his form of
action, and is therefore nonsuited, that he brings an action of
trover, and recovers the very same sum ? It is every day's practice;
and was it ever heard, where a defendant has recovered judgment
on demurrer, and the plaintiffs, not choosing to abide by that,
have brought a different action, and recovered the full amount, that
the defendant could set up the first judgment, and say the plaintiff
was satisfied, and could not prove the debt ? Here is a count that
is not applicable to the case, and the defendants have recovered
judgment by force of that; upon the count that is applicable the
plaintiffs have recovered a verdict. Can it be supposed that any
commissioner of bankrupt, upon the state of facts, would say the
plaintiffs cannot prove it under the commission? In truth, the two
separate sets of counts are just the same as two separate actions.
Suppose, for example, on the first class of counts the plaintiff had
recovered a verdict on the trial, the defendants having obtained a
verdict upon the other, would they not go before the commissioner
and say, the assignees cannot recover for anything due to the
bankrupt? The whole fallacy of this argument is, that this is a
plea to the bill of particulars, but that is not so. The plea is to

*the declaration, and to nothing else; and if a party delivers a bill of particulars, without saying he means to confine himself to the demand upon a particular count, he is quite entitled to take advantage of any count in the declaration to which the particulars apply; and if it turns out that the plea does not apply to one count, and does to the other, he may apply the bill of particulars to either. It is no objection, therefore, either in reason or law, to say that the parties are precluded by their particulars from going into evidence to support the second count.

Then as to the other points. *Mr. Wortley* insists that there is no sufficient evidence in this case of an act of bankruptcy, except that of a sale of the goods. I think I should not have hesitated in directing the jury that any one of these was an act of bankruptcy; but when they are all taken together, they leave no doubt as to the motives of the bankrupt in the evasions he made to his creditors, accompanied as they were by fraud, and this avoiding of creditors is precisely within the very letter of the Bankrupt Act (1). The case that has been quoted from the Nisi Prius Reports is only one of numerous examples of the same sort, in which the parties have made an appointment at a house, not the usual house of the bankrupt, and he failing to keep it, it has not been deemed an act of bankruptcy; but if, to avoid his creditors, a man says, I will meet you at a public-house, or I will meet you at such a place, at such a time, in such a way, and then pay you money, and he is not there at all, that has been held to be an act of bankruptcy. The cases are numerous, but they have not found their way into the reports, except that one case. I think it is clear there was an act of bankruptcy.

Then *Mr. Crompton* says, that if you treat this as a sale, you must treat it as a sale with all the circumstances belonging to it. That proposition is true, with this qualification—if the sale is made by an agent, and properly conducted for the supposed vendor, and the person buying is an honest *buyer, the vendor must stand to the sale, and is bound by the contract; but if a stranger takes my goods, and delivers them to another man, no doubt a contract may be implied, and I may bring an action either of trover for them, or of assumpsit. This is a declaration framed on a contract implied by law. Where a man gets hold of goods without any actual contract, the law allows the owner to bring assumpsit; that is the solution of it, and gets rid of the whole difficulty. Here the bankrupt took these goods, and delivered them to the defendants;

[*352]

(1) See now Bankruptcy Act, 1883 (46 & 47 Vict. c. 52), s. 4 (d).

on that an implied assumpsit arises that they are to pay the owners the value of the goods.   I think that is an answer to *Mr. Crompton's* argument, and a whole class of cases have decided this point, that you may convert a tort into an action of assumpsit, by bringing an action for the value of the goods so sold, waiving the tort.   Here the bankrupt is selling goods under false colours, in order to cover transactions he knew he could not otherwise cover ; and he has no right to set up his own fraudulent contract.   But the action being brought for goods sold and delivered by the assignees, and not by the bankrupt, the assignees have a right to waive the tort, and bring an action of assumpsit for goods sold and delivered.

ALDERSON, B. :

I am of the same opinion.   As to the first point, the effect of the bill of particulars, I apprehend, is entirely confined to the plaintiffs' evidence at the trial.   Where there is a declaration for goods sold and delivered, and the particulars specify the goods sold, with the amount, giving credit specifically for the sums paid ; there the particular is construed to mean, that the defendant is to understand that the plaintiff, at the trial, will be confined, on his general count for goods sold and delivered, to the unpaid-for goods ; it restrains his evidence to that.   You are not to expect, in such a case, that the plaintiff will give evidence of the whole of the goods [*353]   which he has delivered *to you, and that you are to get rid of it by showing you paid for them ; but by his particular he is restrained to a balance, and a balance alone.   That is the true construction of the particulars in this case ; they go in restraint of the plaintiff's evidence, and no more.   Here the plaintiffs have one claim which they state in two different forms in these counts : in the one case they treat it as a claim that arose to them as assignees, by reason of the sale the bankrupt made ; in another count they treat it as a sale made by themselves as assignees after the bankruptcy ; to which the defendant pleads in effect thus : " If you treat it as a sale by the bankrupt before the bankruptcy, the bankrupt owed me more money, and I have a good defence against you."   To that plea the plaintiffs demurred, and on the argument the Court were of opinion that the plaintiffs were wrong, and that if it was to be treated as a sale before the bankruptcy, the defendant had a good defence, it being clear that the defendant had counter claims amounting to more than 140*l.*   Then the plaintiffs say, that being so, they will go upon the count which treats it as a sale by the assignees after

the bankruptcy. It is true, at the trial they are restrained from
going for more than the 140*l.* on that count, but that is the only
restraint which the particulars impose upon them. That restraint
will not avail the defendants on the present occasion, because it
must be considered, that the plaintiffs have not given evidence of
any thing, excepting that one claim by the bankrupt; therefore it
seems to me that the particulars in this case do not restrain the
plaintiffs in the slightest degree; that their only effect at the trial
is to restrain the evidence they are to give, and has no reference
whatever to the pleadings.

Then the next point is, whether or not, that being the case, the
plaintiffs being at liberty to give evidence of goods sold and delivered
by the assignees to the defendant, for which they proceed to claim
payment, have they made out that? They show, long before the
15th day of October, *acts of bankruptcy committed by the bank- [*354]
rupt, Joseph Nicholl. There was abundant evidence to show not
only one but several acts of bankruptcy before the 15th of October;
appointments made with creditors, to meet them at particular places
in order to pay them money, and going away and making excuses
not founded in fact, and which indeed were no excuses at all, and
could leave no doubt in the minds of the jury that he absented
himself upon those occasions merely to delay his creditors. That
such an absenting is an act of bankruptcy is beyond all possibility
of doubt.

Then, if that be so, another question is, has there been a sale
subsequent to these acts of bankruptcy to the defendants? I am
supposing there are acts of bankruptcy proved prior to the 15th of
October. There is proof that Bell comes to the bankrupt and per-
suades him to sell the yarn to him; there is the examination of
Bell, in which he states that he has received the goods; and there
is the invoice, in which it is stated that Messrs. Harrison and Bell
(that is the defendants) bought of John Nicholl (that is the bankrupt) yarn to the amount of 114*l.* 15*s.* As against the defendants,
this is sufficient evidence that they received those goods under a
contract of sale for 114*l.* 15*s.* The defendant, when examined
before the commissioners, tells a story about the goods; are we
to take that story as it is, or are we not rather to take so much
only as may reasonably be taken against the defendant, rejecting
altogether the rest, and confine him to that on which he incurs
responsibility? He must be answerable for that which makes
against himself, where he is the offending party. If that be so, as

WILKS
v.
SMITH.
[358]

J. W. Smith, contrà:

The two questions resolve themselves into one; namely, whether the defendant's promise was in consideration of the plaintiff's promise, or of his performance. If the defendant promised in consideration of the performance of the contract by the plaintiff, performance must be averred; but if it was in consideration of the plaintiff's promise, the defendant has obtained that for which he contracted to pay the interest. In the present agreement no time is fixed for delivering possession of the land, but a time is fixed for the payment of the purchase-money. In *Mattock* v. *Kingslake*, LITTLEDALE, J. says, "A time being fixed for payment, and none

[*359]

for *doing that which was the consideration for the payment, an action lies for the purchase-money without averring performance of the consideration. An action for not executing a conveyance of the premises might have been maintained by the defendant before the day of payment; and in such action no allegation of payment would have been necessary. The covenants are independent, and each party has relied upon his remedy by action against the other." Here the defendant might at any time have brought an action against the plaintiff for non-performance of the agreement on his part. The promise is the consideration, and not the performance by the plaintiff. In *Campbell* v. *Jones* (1), the same principle is laid down; and that decision was recognised and approved by the Court in *Glazebrook* v. *Woodrow* (2). In *Pordage* v. *Cole* (3), the declaration was similar to the present, and there it was held that the covenant was an independent one, and that the vendor might bring an action for the money, before any conveyance by him of the land. * * *

Warren, in reply. * * *

[360]   PARKE, B.:

I am of opinion that the declaration is good, and that it was not necessary for the plaintiff to aver his readiness and willingness to convey at every period of the contract. It is enough if he is ready and able to convey at the time when the title is to be made out. I also think that it is no objection that he has not averred that he had a title to the land. According to the terms of the agreement, no time is fixed for the sale; but a time is limited within which the

(1) 3 R. R. 263 (6 T. R. 570).   (3) 1 Saund. 319.
(2) 4 R. R. 700 (8 T. R. 366).

principal money is to be paid, with interest in the mean time. The consideration for the defendant's paying the interest is the plaintiff's undertaking to sell the land, not the actual sale of it. The plaintiff is not bound to do anything before the money is paid. The rule, as laid down in the notes to *Pordage* v. *Cole*, applies strictly to this case. No time, then, being fixed by the agreement for the conveyance of the land, it cannot be a condition precedent ; nor can we imply that a conveyance was intended to be made before the interest was paid, else we should be supposing that the plaintiff intended to part with his estate before the money was paid, and such an intention certainly cannot be implied from the nature of the contract. It may be, that no conveyance need be made till the principal money is paid, that is, at the end of four years. The question here is, whether or not interest is to be paid before the plaintiff has given up possession of the land. I think it is, and that the conveyance is not a condition precedent. The plaintiff is therefore entitled to our judgment.

ALDERSON, B.:

I am of the same opinion. If one act is to be done in consideration of another, the party suing for the non-performance must aver performance on his *part. But if there be two acts, one fixed in [*361] point of time, and the other not, the latter is not a condition precedent. Here the defendant relied not upon the plaintiff's performance, but upon his promise to perform.

ROLFE, B.:

The case of *Luxton* v. *Robinson*, cited by *Mr. Warren*, is distinguishable from this case, because there possession was to be delivered to the defendant on a given day. But here there is no such obligation to deliver possession. No such intention appears on the face of the contract ; and if we were to hold, that possession was to be given by the plaintiff, our decision would be at variance with the meaning of the parties. The vendor was not to convey the estate before he got the purchase-money.

Judgment for the plaintiff.

1842.   **HICKINBOTHAM** *v.* **LEACH.**
June 22.
                    (10 Meeson & Welsby, 361—364; S. C. 11 L. J. Ex. 341; 2 Dowl. N. S. 270.)
Exch. of
Pleas.   To a declaration for words, imputing to the plaintiff, a pawnbroker, that
[361]   he had committed the unfair and dishonourable practice of duffing, that is,
                    of replenishing or doing up goods, being in his hands in a damaged or
                    worn-out condition, and pledging them with other pawnbrokers, the
                    defendant pleaded, that the plaintiff did replenish and do up divers goods,
                    being in his hands in a damaged or worn-out condition, and pledge them
                    with divers other pawnbrokers : Held bad on special demurrer, as not being
                    sufficiently specific.

SLANDER. The declaration stated, that the defendant charged the
plaintiff, a pawnbroker and silversmith, with committing the unfair
and dishonourable practice of "duffing," *i.e.*, of replenishing or
doing up goods being in his hands in a damaged or worn-out
condition, and pledging the same with other pawnbrokers.

Plea, that the plaintiff did replenish and do up divers goods,
then being in his hands in a damaged and worn-out condition, and
did pledge the said goods with divers other good and worthy subjects
of this realm, then being pawnbrokers. Verification.

[362]   Special demurrer, assigning for causes, that it was not stated by
the plea what goods, or what kind of goods, being in a damaged
condition, the plaintiff replenished and did up, nor with what
pawnbroker or pawnbrokers the said goods so replenished and done
up were pledged.

Erle, in support of the demurrer :

This plea is much too general and vague in its statements; the
plaintiff cannot learn from it what he is to come to prove or disprove.
It is in effect only a general plea that the plaintiff carried on his
business in a disreputable manner, which is the libel itself. The
defendant cannot justify by merely repeating the general imputations
of the slanderous words. This plea would not give the plaintiff any
notion what were the goods alleged to be replenished and done up,
or when or with whom they were pledged. If the defendant had
the evidence of his statement, he might have specified the goods
and the persons. The justification must set forth issuable facts :
Jones v. *Stevens* (1), *Newman* v. *Bailey* (2), *J'anson* v. *Stuart* (3),
Holmes v. *Catesby* (4).

(PARKE, B. : It is very difficult to distinguish this case from
Newman v. *Bailey*.)

(1) 25 R. R. 714 (11 Price, 235).   (3) 1 R. R. 392 (1 T. R. 748).
(2) 1 R. R. 393 (2 Chit. R. 665).   (4) 1 Taunt. 543.

The COURT then called on

G. T. White, contra:

The case of *Newman* v. *Bailey* is distinguishable, on the ground that there, for aught that appeared specifically on the plea, the plaintiff might have inflicted penalties for many different kinds of offences, and collected fines from all sorts of people : nothing specific was there alleged.   Here the plea begins by charging the plaintiff with an unfair mode of conducting the business of a pawnbroker and silversmith ; and then the defendant points out, with sufficient precision, with reference to the *rule which prevents him from pleading a multiplicity of matters, the kind and nature of such dishonourable dealings.   What goods the plaintiff did up, or with what pawnbrokers he pledged them, must (assuming the plea to be true) be peculiarly within his own knowledge.

[*363]

(PARKE, B. : Your argument would be equally good, if it were a plea that the plaintiff had committed divers felonies.

ALDERSON, B. : The plea ought to state the charge with the same precision as in an indictment.)

It is clearly not necessary to set forth a multitude of specific instances ; " it being a rule of pleading, that where a subject comprehends multiplicity of matter, there, in order to avoid prolixity, the law allows of general pleading : " 2 Saund. 411, *n.* (4) ; *Cornwallis* v. *Savery* (1), *Shum* v. *Farrington* (2), *Barton* v. *Webb* (3).

(ALDERSON, B. : In those cases the substantial breach was the not accounting for a gross sum, received in parts.   But here every individual act of duffing would be a sufficient answer to the action.)

But the defendant ought not to be tied up to plead and prove one particular act.   He is not to plead matter of evidence, which lies within the plaintiff's knowledge : *Gale* v. *Reed* (4).   The defendant points out a specific class of acts, and that is sufficient.

PARKE, B. :

It is a perfectly well-established rule in cases of libel or slander, that where the charge is general in its nature, the defendant, in a plea of justification, must state some specific instances of the

| (1) 2 Burr. 772. | (3) 8 T. R. 459. |
| (2) 1 Bos. & P. 640. | (4) 9 R. R. 376 (8 East, 80). |

misconduct imputed to the plaintiff. That is settled by the cases of *J'anson* v. *Stuart, Newman* v. *Bailey,* and *Holmes* v. *Catesby.* In some of those cases, perhaps, the statement in the plea was not so specific as it is here, but still this is not specific enough : the plea should have stated the description of the goods, or at least the names of the pawnbrokers with whom they were pledged. As it is,

[*364]

the statement is so general, *that the plaintiff cannot know with what he is intended to be charged. The defendant is bound to give him information of some specific acts with which he intends to charge him. This plea does not do that, and is therefore bad. With respect to the cases which have been referred to, of actions for not accounting for monies, the reason for the exception in those cases is, that there the charge is for not accounting for an aggregate sum received ; and it is held to be sufficient, in order to avoid multiplicity of pleading, to assign a general breach, that the defendant received divers sums of money, which he did not pay over. None of those decisions have any application to cases of libel or slander. The plea is therefore bad, and the judgment must be for the plaintiff.

ALDERSON, B. :

I am of the same opinion. The object of the plea is to give the plaintiff information what it is of which the defendant means to accuse him. *Mr. White* says that must be within the plaintiff's knowledge ; but that is not the case : what the plaintiff has actually done in the course of his business is within his knowledge, but not what the defendant mistakenly or wickedly means to charge him with having done ; that is peculiarly within the defendant's knowledge, and it is because it is so that he is to plead it.

GURNEY, B., and ROLFE, B., concurred.

Judgment for the plaintiff.

1842.
June 22.
July 7.

*Exch. of
Pleas.*
[425]

TURNER AND OTHERS *v.* THE SHEFFIELD AND ROTHERHAM RAILWAY COMPANY.

(10 Meeson & Welsby, 425—435 ; S. C. 3 Ry. Cas. 222.)

By a Railway Act, it was provided, that nothing in the Act contained should authorize the Company to take, injure, or damage, for the purposes of the Act, any house or building which was erected on or before the 30th November, 1835, without the consent in writing of the owner or other person interested therein, other than such as were specified in the schedule to the Act, unless the omission therefrom proceeded from mistake, &c.

A subsequent clause contained provisions for settling all differences which might arise between the Company and the owners or occupiers of any lands which should be taken, used, damaged, or injuriously affected by the execution of any of the powers granted by the Act, and for the payment of satisfaction or compensation, as well for damages already sustained, as for future temporary, or perpetual, or any recurring damages: Held, that the Company were liable, in an action on the case, to the reversioner of a house erected before the 30th November, 1835, and not specified in the schedule, for damage done to it by the obstruction of its lights by a railway station erected by the Company under the Act, and by the dust, &c., drifted from the station and embankment into the house; and that the plaintiff was not bound to come in under the compensation clause.

TURNER
v.
SHEFFIELD
AND
ROTHERHAM
RAILWAY CO.

CASE. The declaration stated, that before and at the time of the committing of the grievances by the defendants as therein-after mentioned, certain messuages, starch-houses, workshops, and buildings, with the appurtenances, did adjoin to certain land in the possession of the defendants, and were in the possession and occupation of certain persons, to wit, James Woodhead and John Woodhead, as tenants thereof to the plaintiffs, the reversion thereof then and still belonging to the plaintiffs, and which said messuages, &c., had been and then were built and fitted up with divers fixtures, implements, and effects of the plaintiffs therein, and had long been and then were used for the purpose of manu-facturing starch therein and therewith, and for divers other purposes, and in which said messuages, &c., during all the time aforesaid there of right had been and were, and still of right ought to be, divers, to wit, 100 ancient windows, through which the light and air, during all the time aforesaid, ought to have entered, and still of right ought to enter into the said messuages, &c., for the convenient and wholesome use, occupation, and enjoyment thereof: yet, the defendants, well knowing the premises, but contriving, &c., to injure, prejudice, and aggrieve the plaintiffs in their reversionary estate and interest of and in the said messuages, &c., while the said messuages, &c., were so in the possession and occupation of the said James Woodhead and John Woodhead as tenants thereof to the plaintiffs, and while the plaintiffs were so interested therein as aforesaid, to wit, on &c., and on divers *other days and times, &c., wrongfully and unjustly, without the leave or license and against the will of the plaintiffs, erected and built a certain railway station, wall, and embankment, in and upon the said land in possession of the defendants as aforesaid, and near to the said messuages, &c., and wrongfully and injuriously kept and continued

[*426]

the said railway station, wall, and embankment for a long time, to wit, &c., by means of which said several premises the light and air, during all the time aforesaid, were and still are hindered and prevented from coming and entering into and through the said windows, or any of them, into the said messuages, &c., and the same have thereby been rendered and are dark, close, uncomfortable, and unwholesome, and less fit and commodious for the purpose of manufacturing starch therein, and for the other purposes for which the same had been heretofore used; and also, by means of the premises, divers large quantities of earth, soil, dust, and dirt were, during all the time aforesaid, and continue to be carried, drifted, blown, scattered, and spread from and off the said railway station, wall, and embankment, so erected by the defendants as aforesaid, against, into, and through the said windows, and into the said messuages, &c., and into and amongst the fixtures, implements, and effects therein; and thereby the said messuages, &c., fixtures, implements, and effects became and were rendered dirty, foul, and clogged up, so that the same became and were less fit and commodious for the said purpose of manufacturing starch therein and therewith, and for the other purposes to which the same had been heretofore used; by means of which said several premises, the said messuages, &c., became and were and are greatly deteriorated in value, and the plaintiffs have been and are greatly damnified, &c., in their reversionary estate, &c.

Pleas, first, not guilty; secondly, as to so much of the declaration
[*427]   as relates to the alleged hindrance and *prevention, by the means therein mentioned, of the light and air from coming and entering into and through the said windows, &c., and as to the supposed causes of action in respect thereof, that they the defendants, before and at the time of the committing of the said alleged grievances were, and still are the body corporate mentioned in a certain Act of Parliament, made and passed in the 7 Will. IV., intituled "An Act for making a Railway from Sheffield to Rotherham," &c., and also in a certain other Act of Parliament, made and passed in the 3 Vict., intituled "An Act to enable the Sheffield and Rotherham Railway Company to raise a further sum of money, and to amend the Act relating to the said railway." And the defendants further say, that the said land so in the possession of the defendants as in the declaration mentioned was, before and at the time of the committing of the said alleged grievances to which this plea is pleaded, and still is, land purchased by the defendants after the

passing of the said first-mentioned Act of Parliament, in pursuance
of the powers and provisions therein contained, for the purpose of
making and providing a certain station, warehouses, and other
buildings and conveniences for receiving, depositing, loading, and
keeping goods, matters, and things conveyed and intended to be
conveyed upon the said railway in the said Act mentioned, and for
other purposes connected with the undertaking thereby authorized.
And the defendants further say, that the said railway station, wall,
and embankment in the declaration mentioned, were so erected,
made, and built in and upon the said land as in the declaration
mentioned, and so kept and continued by the defendants, as therein
mentioned, in the *bonâ fide* execution of the powers by the said
first-mentioned Act granted, and for the purposes and according to
the provisions and restrictions of the same Act, the said railway
station, wall, and embankment having been respectively adjudged
requisite, and having been constructed and made by the *defendants under the powers and provisions of the said Act, for the
purpose of providing a certain station and yard, buildings, and
conveniences for the purposes of the said undertaking, to wit, at
Rotherham aforesaid, at the termination of the said railway there,
they the defendants then doing as little damage as might be in
that behalf.   Verification.

TURNER
v.
SHEFFIELD
AND
ROTHERHAM
RAILWAY CO.

[*428]

  There was also a similar plea to the residue of the declaration.
  Replication to the second and third pleas, that the said
messuages, &c., in the declaration mentioned are houses and
buildings which were erected before the 30th day of November,
1835, to wit, on &c., and that the said several grievances in the
plea mentioned were committed by the defendants, and the said
messuages, &c., were thereby so injured and damaged as in the
declaration alleged, without the consent in writing of the plaintiffs,
so being owners of the said several messuages, &c., as in the
declaration mentioned, and without the consent in writing of any
other person interested in the said messuages, &c.; and that the
said messuages, &c., were not, nor are nor were, nor are any of
them or any part thereof, specified in the schedule annexed to the
said Act of Parliament of the 7 Will. IV., and that the omission of
the said messuages, &c., from the said schedule did not proceed
from mistake.   Verification.
  General demurrers, and joinders in demurrer.
  The following point was marked for argument on the part of the
defendants: That the railway station, wall, and embankment in

42—2

TURNER
v.
SHEFFIELD
AND
ROTHERHAM
RAILWAY CO.

[*429]

the declaration mentioned, having been (as is admitted upon the pleadings) erected in the *bonâ fide* execution of the powers of the defendants' Act of Parliament, the defendants are protected by such Act, and particularly by the 5th section thereof, from being sued at law in respect of such erection; and further, that the 20th section of the said Act does not extend or apply to injury *or damage of the description and character of that alleged in the declaration.

The case was argued on a former day in these sittings (June 22) by

W. H. Watson, in support of the demurrer:

The Company are not liable in this action. The question depends upon the construction to be put on the 20th section of the Act of Parliament, 6 & 7 Will. IV. c. cix., which provides, that nothing in the Act contained shall authorize the Company to take, injure, or damage, for the purposes of this Act, any house or building which was erected on or before the 30th November, 1835, or any land then set apart and used as a garden, &c., without the consent in writing of the owner or other person interested therein, other than such as are specified in the schedule, unless the omission therefrom proceeded from mistake, &c. The words "injure or damage," in this clause, have reference to injury or damage done in the course of taking or using land, &c., for the purpose of constructing the railway. The clause immediately follows those by which the compulsory powers of entering upon and taking land are vested in the Company, and operates as a proviso on and limitation of those powers. The plaintiffs should have claimed compensation under the 35th section, which contains provisions for the settling all differences which may arise between the Company and the owners and occupiers of any lands which shall be taken, used, damaged, or injuriously affected by the execution of any of the powers thereby granted, and for the payment of satisfaction or compensation, as well for damages already sustained as for future temporary or perpetual, or any recurring damages. Different words being used in the two clauses, it must be supposed that they are employed in different senses; and the words "injuriously affected" are larger in their meaning

[*430]

than those of the 20th section, *and comprise injury of every description, whether done in the taking of the land or not. The 5th section gives the general power to enter upon, survey, and take lands, and to do certain acts thereon, and on any lands adjoining thereto, necessary for making, &c., the railway and works, "making satisfaction in manner hereinafter mentioned to all persons interested in any lands which shall be taken, used, or injured, for all damages to be by them sustained in or by reason of the execution of any of the powers thereby granted." Sect. 20 uses the like words—"to take, injure, or damage, for the purposes of this Act." [He cited *Rex* v. *Pease* (1), *Reg.* v. *Eastern Counties Railway Company*, on the prosecution of *Collingridge* (2).] If an action be maintainable, this erection must be abated altogether, although declared by the Act to be a public benefit. All parties have notice, by the depositing of the plan, and the advertisements in the *Gazette*, of the intended line of the railway, and whether their houses are likely to be affected by the use of it; and the compensation clause gives them a permanent and complete remedy. The Legislature has declared this railway to be, when finished, a public highway: can it then be liable to be pulled to pieces for having injuriously affected some land lying in the neighbourhood, where, perhaps, such injury could not by possibility be foreseen,— as, for example, in the case of a well corrupted or dried up by the construction of the line? It is a most *important question to railway companies, since, if the action be maintainable, there is no limit to such actions until the railway be discontinued; nay, the party may himself enter and abate the alleged nuisance, by pulling down the station and embankment, and altogether destroying the railway. With respect to the injury by the drifting of the dust, that cannot, at all events, be actionable, unless it be caused by negligence in the construction of the works; not for the mere drifting or blowing of sand in dry weather, which is necessarily incident to the use of the railway: *Turbervil* v. *Stamp* (3), *Vaughan* v. *Menlove* (4).

[431]

[*432]

Crompton, contrà :

The question arising on both the pleas is precisely the same; the complaint, as to both these matters, is of a construction of the defendants' works, whereby injury is done to the freehold of the house, so as to affect the reversioner. It is altogether a question as to the proper construction of the 20th section, and it clearly cannot be a case within the compensation clause, unless by

(1) 38 R. R. 207 (4 B. & Ad. 30;   (3) 1 Salk. 13.
1 Nev. & M. 690).   (4) 43 R. R. 711 (3 Bing. N. C. 468;
(2) 1 G. & D. 589.   4 Scott, 244).

TURNER
v.
SHEFFIELD
AND
ROTHERHAM
RAILWAY Co.

[*483]

section 20 the Company were authorized to do this act. It is an
established rule, that private Acts of Parliament of this kind are
in the nature of contracts with the public, and are to be construed
most strongly as against the contracting party whose words they
are. And it is submitted that the true construction is, that with
respect to the favoured cases excepted in section 20, the parties
injured are left to their common-law remedy by action. Such is
the grammatical construction of the words, and why are they to be
restrained as against the parties using them? How can it be said
that it is not an injury to the plaintiff's house? It is averred in
the declaration, and that is confessed by the demurrer, to be a
permanent injury, *i.e.*, to the reversion. With respect to the
argument *ab inconvenienti*, that applies equally against the Company. Suppose in *the course of their operations a well were
tapped at a distance of two miles, which was not discovered until
after the lapse of the six months; in that case the remedy is lost
altogether, if it be only within the compensation clause. This,
however, is purely a question of construction, and is not to be tried
by a balance of inconveniences. It is a special exception in favour
of this particular class of houses, for the very object of leaving the
owners to the exercise of their common-law rights. The 20th
section is not merely a restriction on the deviation clauses, but is a
prohibition of any taking, injuring, or damaging the houses, &c.,
therein specified, for any of the purposes of the Act; and if such
injury is prohibited, it is clear that the compensation clauses do
not apply, as they can only be applicable to the cases where the
Act contemplates that such injury is to be committed. The case is
brought by the replication within the precise terms of the 20th
section. Is it an injury to the premises? That is distinctly
admitted, as the gist of the action is such an injury to the premises
as to affect the reversion. Is it an injury to premises excepted?
All buildings erected before the 30th November, 1835, are excepted,
and these were built before that date. And how can the Court
decide against the replication, without repealing that exception?

Watson, in reply:

Compensation clauses, in Acts of this nature, have always been
largely construed: as, for example, in the cases relating to the
Hungerford Market (1). Here the Legislature must have contem-

(1) *Ex parte Farlow*, 36 R. R. 580   *Market Company*, 38 R. R. 253 (4 B.
(2 B. & Ad. 341); *Rex* v. *Hungerford*   & Ad. 592; 1 Nev. & M. 404).

plated that this railway would pass through a town, and would TURNER
necessarily do some injury of this nature, which ought to be SHEFFIELD
compensated.

AND
ROTHERHAM
RAILWAY CO.

Cur. adv. vult.

The judgment of the COURT was now delivered by   [434]

PARKE, B. :

The question raised by the pleadings in this case is, whether the
defendants were authorized by their Act, in constructing their railway station, to erect a station and embankment so near to the
house of the plaintiff as to obstruct its lights, and cause damage
to it by the dust and dirt drifted from it, such house having been
erected before the 30th November, 1835, the house not having been
specified in the schedule, nor omitted therefrom by mistake, and
no consent in writing to the construction of the station or embankment having been obtained from the plaintiff, or any other person
interested in the house. We think the defendants were not
authorized, and that the plaintiff is entitled to our judgment.

The question turns on the 20th section of the 6 & 7 Will. IV.
c. cix. (His Lordship read it.) Adopting the ordinary grammatical
construction of the clause, the Company could neither take the
house in question, nor do any act by which it should be injured or
damaged ; and such construction certainly ought to prevail, unless
it lead to an absurdity, or be manifestly repugnant to the intention
of the Legislature, as collected from the context, in which case the
language may be modified so as to obviate such absurdity, or cure
such repugnance. The argument, which brought before us all the
material clauses of the Act, and pointed out some inconveniences
arising from construing the proviso according to the ordinary sense
of its words, has failed to convince us that this construction is
repugnant to the rest of the Act, or that any absurdity would
follow if it were adopted.

There is no doubt some inconvenience to the Company, in their
being exposed to actions for unforeseen consequential damages
arising from their acts to houses, buildings, gardens, &c., not comprised within the schedule, as by stopping springs communicating
with them, or the *like : and we are not prepared to say that such   [*435]
inconvenience may not afford a ground, in those cases where the
damage could not be foreseen, for limiting the general expression,
and exempting the Company from liability to an action, leaving

to the party injured his right to compensation for the damage sustained. On that point, however, we pronounce no judgment. But in such a case as this, in which the damage could have been foreseen when the station and embankment were made, we see no reason to qualify the words of the clause, and consequently the Company are liable to an action for damaging the house in question, by reason of the obstructing of its lights, and the nuisance to it by dust and dirt from the erecting of the station and embankment so near to it. As this house was erected before 30th November, 1835, the Company ought to have considered, before the Act was passed, whether the construction of any of these works would be injurious to it, and caused it to be inserted in the schedule; and if that had been done, the owner of the house would have been put on his guard, and might have opposed the passing of the Act. It was the fault of the Company to omit it, and they must suffer for the omission; and as they cannot now be permitted to purchase the house directly without the owner's consent, so they cannot be allowed to buy it indirectly, by causing its lights to be obstructed, and then leaving the owner to receive compensation under the Act.

Judgment for the plaintiff.

1842.
May 28.
July 7.

*Exch. of
Pleas.*

[436]

WENTWORTH *v.* OUTHWAITE AND OTHERS (1).

(10 Meeson & Welsby, 436—452; S. C. 12 L. J. Ex. 172.)

H. & Co., of Hull, having sold to W., of Mickley Mills, near Leeds, twenty mats of flax, they were, on the 10th of August, sent by railway to Leeds, and arrived at the defendants' warehouse at Leeds, where it was the custom for the defendants to receive goods sent for W., and to give him notice of their arrival, and for him to send his carts for them. On the 16th of August, W. sent his cart and took away ten of the mats. On the 18th of August, H. & Co. sold to W. twenty other mats of flax, and a quantity of other goods. The flax was sent by railway to Leeds, and arrived duly at the defendants' warehouse; the other goods were sent by sloop to Boroughbridge. On the arrival of this flax at the defendants' warehouse, notice was given to W. by letter, which stated that unless the goods were sent for, they would remain there at warehouse rents. On the 23rd of August, W. sent his cart and took away ten of the latter mats, and left there ten of the mats last sent, and ten of the former. On the 8th of September, W. having become insolvent, the goods which had been shipped for Boroughbridge were stopped *in transitu* at Hull; and on the same day the ten mats of flax of the second parcel were

---

(1) Cited *Coventry* v. *Gladstone* (1868) L. R. 6 Eq. 44, 50, 37 L. J. Ch. 492; *Ex parte Chalmers, Re Edwards* (1873) L. R. 8 Ch. 289, 292, 42 L. J. Bk. 37; *Ex parte Gibbes, Re Whitworth* (1875)   1 Ch. D. 101, 110, 45 L. J. Bk. 10; and dist. *Ex parte Barrow, Re Worsdell* (1877) 6 Ch. D. 783, 788, 46 L. J. Bk. 71.—A. C.

also stopped at Leeds by H. & Co. On the 11th September the sheriff
entered, and seized all the flax in the defendants' warehouse sent by
H. & Co., under an execution against W. On the 15th of September, there
was also a stoppage by H. & Co. of the remaining ten mats of the first parcel.
It was found by the jury at the trial, that the parties contemplated that the
goods were to be used for the purpose of manufacture at Mickley Mills :
Held, under the above circumstances, that the *transitus* was at an end on
the arrival of the goods at the defendants' warehouse.

Held, also, that the stoppage of the goods which had been shipped to go
to Boroughbridge had not the effect of revesting the property in the parcel
of flax which had been sent to the defendants' warehouse at Leeds, although
comprised in one joint contract with the other goods.

Semble, Lord ABINGER, C. B., *dissentiente*, that the effect of a stoppage
in transitu is not to rescind the contract, but only to replace the vendor in
the same position as if he had not parted with the possession of the goods.

Held, that, at all events, the vendor had no right to retake that part which
had arrived at its journey's end.

TROVER by the sheriff of Yorkshire for twenty mats of flax.
Pleas, not guilty and not possessed ; on which issues were joined.

At the trial before Parke, B., at the last Spring Assizes at York,
it appeared that on the 10th of August, 1841, Messrs. Hill & Co.,
of Hull, having sold to a Mr. Weatherall, of Mickley Mills, a place
about thirty miles from Leeds, twenty mats of flax, they were
forwarded by railway to Leeds, and duly arrived at the warehouse
of the defendants (who are carriers) at that town ; and on the
16th of August, Weatherall sent his cart there and took away ten
of the mats. It appeared that the warehouse was a large shed at
or near the railway terminus at Leeds, and that it was the custom
for the defendants to give notice of the arrival of goods at their
warehouse to Weatherall, who sent his waggons or carts for them,
and carried them to Mickley Mills. On the 18th of August, there
was another sale by Hill & Co. to Weatherall of twenty other mats
of flax, and a quantity of other goods. The flax was sent by railway
to Leeds, and duly arrived at the defendants' warehouse, and the
*other goods were sent by sloop to Boroughbridge. On the arrival   [*437]
of the different parcels of flax at the defendants' warehouse, notice
was given to Weatherall by letter, which stated, that unless the
goods were sent for, they would remain there at warehouse rents.
No rent was however charged to or paid by Weatherall. On the
23rd of August, Weatherall sent his waggon and took away ten of
the latter mats, and left there ten of the mats last sent and ten
of the former. Previously to the 8th of September Weatherall
became bankrupt, and on that day, the goods which had been
shipped for Boroughbridge were stopped *in transitu* on board the
sloop at Hull. On the same day the ten mats of the second parcel

WENTWORTH were also stopped at Leeds. On the 11th of September, the sheriff
v.
OUTHWAITE. entered and seized all the flax in the defendants' warehouse sent
by Hill & Co., under an execution against Weatherall at the suit of
Terry & Co., but the officers saw only the ten mats last sent. The
defendants agreed to hold them for the sheriff, on an indemnity
being given. On the 15th of September, there was a stoppage by
Hill & Co. of the remaining ten mats of the first parcel.

The question at the trial was, whether Hill & Co. had a right to
stop the goods, on the ground that the *transitus* was not at an end
upon their arrival at the defendants' warehouse. The plaintiff's
counsel contended that it was at an end, and that the defendants'
warehouse was constructively the warehouse of Weatherall himself.
The jury, in answer to a question put by the learned Judge, found
that the parties contemplated that the flax was to be used for the
purpose of manufacture at Mickley Mills. His Lordship directed
the jury to find a verdict for the plaintiff, reserving the question of
law for the opinion of this Court. The jury having accordingly
found a verdict for the plaintiff, *Baines*, in Easter Term last,
obtained a rule to show cause why a nonsuit should not be entered;
against which rule

[438]   *Dundas* and *Crompton*, in Trinity Term (May 28), showed
cause :

First, the *transitus* was at an end on the arrival of the goods at
the defendants' warehouse at Leeds. That was constructively the
warehouse of Weatherall himself; the goods were kept there for
him, and if he did not send for them upon notice of their arrival,
he was to pay warehouse rent. The cases on this subject are
collected in the note to *Lickbarrow* v. *Mason*, in Smith's Leading
Cases (1), and there the rule derived from all the cases is stated to
be " that the goods are *in transitu* so long as they are in the hands
of the carrier as such, whether he was or was not appointed by the
consignee, and also so long as they remain in any place of deposit
connected with their transmission. But that, if after their arrival
at their place of destination, they be warehoused with the carrier,
whose store the vendee uses as his own, or if they be warehoused with the vendor himself, and rent be paid to him for
them, that puts an end to the right to stop *in transitu*." [They
referred to *Allan* v. *Gripper* (2), *Richardson* v. *Goss* (3), *Foster* v.

(1) Pages 431—435.   2 Tyr. 217).
(2) 37 R. R. 682 (2 Cr. & J. 218;   (3) 6 R. R. 727 (3 Bos. & P. 127).

Frampton (1), *Rowe* v. *Pickford* (2), *James* v. *Griffin* (3), *Scott* v.   WENTWORTH
Pettit (4), and *Dixon* v. *Baldwen* (5).]   *v.*
                                                                                   OUTHWAITE.
Secondly, the consignee had in fact taken away part of the goods   [440]
sold under one entire contract, and there are *many authorities to   [*441]
show that in such case the right to stop *in transitu* is gone.   Thus,
in *Hammond* v. *Anderson* (6), a number of bales of bacon, then
lying at a wharf, having been sold for an entire sum, to be paid for
by a bill at two months, an order was given to the wharfinger to
deliver them to the vendee, who went to the wharf, weighed the
whole, and took away several bales, and then became bankrupt,
whereupon the vendor, within ten days from the time of the sale,
ordered the wharfinger not to deliver the remainder.   By the
custom of the trade, the charges of warehousing were to be paid
by the vendor for fourteen days after the sale.   It was held
that the vendee had taken possession of the whole, and that the
vendor had no right to stop what remained in the hands of the
wharfinger.

(PARKE, B. : In this case there was a clear intention to separate
the part taken as the cart would not hold more.

ALDERSON, B. : The consignee takes away part of the goods,
after he knows that they are lying at his risk, and at a rent in the
defendants' warehouse.)

[They also cited *Slubey* v. *Heyward* (7), *Betts* v. *Gibbons* (8).]
Thirdly, it is said that as another part of the goods, which *were   [*442]
sent by river navigation to Boroughbridge, were stopped in due time,
and the whole was contained in one joint contract, it had the
effect of rescinding the contract, and revesting the property in the
whole in the consignor.   But that cannot be so; the authorities
are strong against the effect of the stoppage being to rescind the
contract; and even if the stoppage had that effect in general, the
point does not arise in the present case, as here the stoppage of
part of the goods could at most only have the effect of rescinding
the contract *pro tanto*, and revesting the property in the last-
mentioned portion of the goods.

(1) 30 R. R. 255 (6 B. & C. 107;   (5) 7 R. R. 681 (5 East, 175).
2 Dowl. & Ry. 108).   (6) 8 R. R. 763 (1 Bos. & P. N. R.
(2) 19 R. R. 466 (8 Taunt. 83; 1   69).
Moore, 526).   (7) 3 R. R. 486 (2 H. Bl. 504).
(3) 46 R. R. 243 (2 M. & W. 633).   (8) 41 R. R. 381 (2 Ad. & El. 57;
(4) 7 R. R. 804 (3 Bos. & P. 469).   4 Nev. & M. 64).

WENTWORTH   *Baines, Martin,* and *Liddell,* in support of the rule:
v.
OUTHWAITE.   The rule is, that an unpaid vendor has always a right to stop the
goods which he has forwarded to the vendee under a contract of
sale, whilst they are on their *transitus,* in the event of the vendee
becoming insolvent. Here the twenty mats which were stopped at
Leeds on the 8th of September, were merely at the warehouse of
the carriers on their way to the consignee at Mickley Mills, the
place of their ultimate destination, and the vendor had therefore a
right to stop them. Lord Tenterden, in his Treatise on Shipping (1),
states the true principle applicable to these cases. He there says,
" Goods are deemed to be *in transitu,* not only while they remain
in the possession of the carrier, whether by water or land, and
although such carrier may have been named and appointed by
the consignee; but also where they are in any place of deposit
connected with the transmission and delivery of them, and until
they arrive at the actual or constructive possession of the consignee,
at the place named by the buyer to the seller as their destination.
But if the consignee, before the goods reach their ultimate destination, does any act which is equivalent to taking actual possession of
[*443]   them, the *transitus* is at an *end." Here the place contemplated
between these parties as the destination of the goods was Mickley
Mills, and the vendee had done no act equivalent to taking
possession of them. According, therefore, to the principle laid
down by Lord Tenterden, nothing less than an actual arrival at
the place of destination would take away the vendor's right to stop
the goods. In *Stokes* v. *La Riviere,* which is quoted in the
argument in *Bohtlingk* v. *Inglis* (2), Lord MANSFIELD is stated to
have said, " No point is more clear, than that if goods are sold and
the price not paid, the seller may stop them *in transitu,* I mean in
every sort of passage to the hands of the buyers." Have these
goods come into the actual possession of the consignee? Clearly
not. But then it is said that they were constructively in his
possession, as he was to send for them, and they were there lying
at a rent until he did so. But there was nothing to show that any
actual rent had been agreed to be paid, or ever was paid. * * *

(PARKE, B.: Would not Weatherall have been liable for
warehouse rent?)

No; it is submitted he would not, as it had not been the course of
dealing between them.

(1) Page 464, 6th edit.   (2) 7 R. R. 490 (3 East, 397).

(PARKE, B.: If from the notice Weatherall might be liable to WENTWORTH
v.
OUTHWAITE. warehouse rent, the defendants' not insisting on it may have *been a forbearance to enforce the right, rather than the absence of the right itself.)   [*444]

But that cannot affect the right to stop *in transitu.* [They referred to *Morley* v. *Hay* (1), *Gibson* v. *Carruthers* (2), and *Hanson* v. *Meyer* (3).]   The true question in these cases is, had the goods arrived at the destination given by the vendee to the vendor? and here they clearly had not, for *Mickley Mills was that place of [*445] destination. Although it had been the practice for Weatherall to send his cart for the goods, the vendors knew nothing of it.

(PARKE, B. : It did not appear that the defendants ever sent the goods to Mickley Mills. The finding of the jury was, that the parties contemplated that the flax was to be used at Mickley Mills, but it is not said that that was mentioned as the place of destination.)

The true ground of the right of stoppage *in transitu* is that on which it is put by Lord ABINGER in *Gibson* v. *Carruthers*, namely, that it is no part of the contract, but that the law gives the right.

·   (LORD ABINGER, C. B.: But is it not open to the party to show the fact as to where the vendee intended the goods to be brought?

PARKE, B.: The ultimate place of destination is that place to which the carrier is to carry the goods, and where the vendee is to receive them.)

In *Whitehead* v. *Anderson* (4), PARKE, B., in delivering the judgment of the Court, lays down the law as clearly settled, " that the unpaid vendor has a right to retake the goods before they have arrived at the destination originally contemplated by the purchaser, unless in the meantime they have come to the actual or constructive possession of the vendee." It is admitted, that if it had been communicated to the vendors that the vendee was to send for the goods to Leeds, that would be the terminus of the transit, and the place of destination ; but it was not so. *   *   *

(1) 3 Man. & Ry. 396.   (3) 8 R. R. 572 (6 East, 614).
(2) 58 R. R. 713 (8 M. & W. 321).   (4) 60 R. R. 819 (9 M. & W. 534).

WENTWORTH
v.
OUTHWAITE.

[447]

Secondly, it is said there has been a part delivery of the goods, and that that amounted to a taking possession of the whole by the consignee, whereby the right of stoppage *in transitu* was gone. But this case is distinguishable from those which have been cited on the other side, and even if it be not, the rule has been of late very much restricted. [They cited *Jones* v. *Jones* (1) and *Dixon* v. *Yates* (2).]

[*448]

But thirdly, even if the *transitus* was at an end on the arrival of the goods at the defendants' warehouse, there was here a stoppage of that part of the goods which had been shipped to go to Borough-bridge, and as they were included in one joint contract with the flax last sent, the stoppage *of that part had the effect of rescinding the contract, and revesting the whole in the vendor. If the effect of a stoppage *in transitu* is to rescind the contract (and it is submitted that it is), the vendors are entitled to the whole of the goods comprised in the contract. There is no authority against its having that effect, but the cases lean rather to the contrary, though the point has never yet been expressly decided. [They referred to *Edwards* v. *Brewer* (3), *Clay* v. *Harrison* (4), *James* v. *Griffin* (5), *Kymer* v. *Suwercropp* (6), and *Litt* v. *Cowley* (7).]

[449]   LORD ABINGER, C. B. :

It seems to me that a great part of the very learned argument which we have heard turns upon a question of fact, whether Leeds was the place of destination to which the goods were to be sent. It may be the place of destination at which the goods are to be at the consignee's risk, and I think that in this case it was the place where they were to be at his risk until he sent for them ; and if so, and they were not to be forwarded by the defendants, that was a place of agency to receive the goods, and consequently the *transitus* was at an end. As to the question whether the stoppage *in transitu* had the effect of rescinding the contract, and revesting the property in the ten mats which had not been delivered, we wish to take time to consider.

PARKE, B. :

I entirely concur in the opinion which has been expressed by my
*450]   LORD CHIEF BARON on the principal *question, that the *transitus*

(1) 58 R. R. 765 (8 M. & W. 431, 442).
(2) 39 R. R. 489 (5 B. & Ad. 313 ;
2 Nev. & M. 177).
(3) 46 R. R. 626 (2 M. & W. 379).
(4) 34 R. R. 334 (10 B. & C. 99).
(5) *Id.* 632.
(6) 10 R. R. 646 (1 Camp 109).
(7) 17 R. R. 482 (7 Taunt. 170).

was at an end. It may be considered as having been at an end,   WENTWORTH
both because the goods had come into the constructive possession   *v.*
of the vendee, and because they had arrived at their place of desti-   OUTHWAITE.
nation. In the judgment in *Whitehead* v. *Anderson* (1), the COURT
say, "A case of constructive possession is, where the carrier enters
expressly, or by implication, into a new agreement, distinct from
the original contract for carriage, to hold the goods for the consignee as his agent, not for the purpose of expediting them to the
place of original destination pursuant to that contract, but in a
new character, for the purpose of custody on his account, and
subject to some new or further order to be given to him." That
is applicable to the present case. When the goods arrived at Leeds,
and notice was sent to Weatherall of their arrival, and that he was
to pay rent, the carriers held them, not as agents for forwarding
them, but for their safe custody, and they were constructively in
the possession of the vendee.

Again, I think the goods had arrived at their place of destination,
for that, as I understand, means the place to which they were to be
conveyed, by the carriers and where they would remain unless fresh
orders should be given for their subsequent disposition. In this
respect the case falls within the principle of *Dixon* v. *Baldwen* (2),
in which Lord ELLENBOROUGH lays down the doctrine, that the
transitus is completely at an end when the goods arrive at an
agent's, who is to keep them until he receives the further orders
of the vendee. After referring to the several cases on this subject,
he says, "In those cases, the goods had so far gotten to the end of
their journey that they waited for new orders from the purchaser
to put them again in motion, to communicate to them another substantive destination, and without such orders they would continue
stationary." That appears to have been the case *in the present   [*451]
instance. The parcels of flax were to remain stationary at the
defendants' warehouse till a further direction should be given by
Weatherall, by an order to deliver to a purchaser, or to forward to
himself, by a new conveyance, and, if no further orders had been
given, they would have continued there. I am of opinion, that on
this ground the *transitus* was at an end, on the arrival of the goods
at Leeds. Whether the effect of the stoppage of that part which
had not arrived at its destination was to rescind the contract, or
only to place the vendor in the same position as if he had not
parted with the goods, I wish to take time to consider.

    (1) 60 R. R. 819 (9 M. & W. 534).   (2) 7 R. R. 681 (5 East, 175, 182).

ALDERSON, B., and ROLFE, B., concurred.

Cur. adv. vult.

The judgment of the COURT was now delivered by

PARKE, B.:

In this case, the Court, consisting of my LORD CHIEF BARON, and my brothers ALDERSON and ROLFE, and myself, have already expressed a unanimous opinion, that the *transitus* of the goods was at an end on their arrival at the warehouse at Leeds, that being the place to which the consignee intended them to be conveyed by the carrier, and where they would stop unless the consignee should direct what further should be done with them. One point only was reserved for consideration, namely, the effect of a stoppage of part of the goods contained in one joint contract, before the seizure by the plaintiff. Several parcels of goods were purchased under one entire contract from Hill & Co., at Hull, by the consignee, living at Mickley, about thirty miles from Leeds. A part—two packages— were forwarded by the railroad to Leeds, and arrived on the 20th of August. One of these packages was taken to Mickley Mills by [*452] the consignee on the 23rd of August. The remaining *package was seized by the sheriff, the plaintiff, on the 11th of September. But in the mean time some remaining parcels, comprised in the same contract, which were forwarded by water-carriage to Borough-bridge, were stopped *in transitu* on the 8th September, and it was contended for the defendants, that this had the effect of revesting in the consignor, at that time, all the parcels contained in that contract, and, amongst others, that seized by the sheriff on the 11th September. We are all of opinion that this objection to the plaintiff's right to recover, in respect of the last-mentioned parcel, cannot prevail.

What the effect of stoppage *in transitu* is, whether entirely to rescind the contract, or only to replace the vendor in the same position as if he had not parted with the possession, and entitle him to hold the goods until the price be paid down, is a point not yet finally decided, and there are difficulties attending each construction. If the latter supposition be adopted (as most of us are strongly inclined to think it ought to be, on the weight of authority), the vendor is entitled to retain the part actually stopped *in transitu* till he is paid the price of the whole, but has no right to retake that which has arrived at its journey's end. His right of lien on

the part stopped is revested, but no more. My LORD CHIEF BARON
has expressed an opinion, to which he still adheres, that the contract is rescinded by a stoppage *in transitu*, but he does not think
that this affects the right of the vendee to retain that portion of
the goods which have been actually delivered to him, or, in other
words, have reached the place of their destination, more especially
when the goods and the price may be apportioned, as in the present
case, and a new contract be implied from the actual delivery and
retention of a part. In either view of the subject, the stoppage of
that portion of the goods conveyed by water affords no defence.

The rule must therefore be discharged.

Rule discharged.

LLOYD, ADMINISTRATOR, &c., *v.* MOSTYN (1).

(10 Meeson & Welsby, 478—484; S. C. 12 L. J. Ex. 1; 6 Jur. 974; 2 Dowl.
N. S. 476.)

An action on a bond of indemnity stood for trial at the Flintshire Assizes:
the commission day was on the 27th July; the cause was tried on the 29th.
At 10 A.M. on the 28th, a notice to produce the bond was served on the
defendant's attorney in the action (who resided in London) in the defendant's presence, in the Assize town. The bond was in the possession of one
W., who held it as the representative of a former attorney of the obligors,
and was himself the defendant's general attorney, and who had undertaken
to produce it at the trial, if the Judge should think he was bound to do so.
Before the Assizes, the bond had been sent by W. to the defendant's attorney
in the action, in London, for the purposes of inspection and admission under
a Judge's order; and the plaintiff's attorney had there taken a correct copy
of it. At the trial, W. had the bond in Court, but objected to produce it on
the ground of privilege, and the objection was allowed:

Held, first, that the notice to produce the deed was sufficient, under the
circumstances, to let in secondary evidence of it; secondly, that the copy
so taken by the plaintiff's attorney was admissible as secondary evidence.

DEBT on a joint and several bond, given by the defendant and
his late father, Mr. Samuel Mostyn, to the plaintiff's intestate,
Edward Lloyd, dated 10th June, 1815. Pleas (after craving *oyer*
of the bond, which was set out), *non est factum* and *solvit post diem*,
on which issues were joined. At the trial before Gurney, B., at
the last Flintshire Assizes, it appeared that the claim of the plaintiff
arose under the following circumstances. A legacy of 200*l.* having
been bequeathed by the will of a Miss Myddelton amongst the
younger children of Mr. Samuel Mostyn, who were then infants,
the intestate, Edward Lloyd, who was Miss Myddelton's executor,
paid the money to Samuel Mostyn in the year 1815, on receiving

(1) Foll. *Calcraft* v. *Guest* [1898] 1 Q. B. 759, 67 L. J. Q. B. 505, C. A.—A. C.

*from him and the defendant (who was the eldest son of Samuel Mostyn, and then of age) the bond in question, which was conditioned to save harmless and indemnify the intestate from all actions, suits, claims, and demands whatever of the legatees or any of them, in respect of their shares of the legacy. In March, 1841, a suit in equity was commenced by Thomas Mostyn, one of the legatees, against the plaintiff, as administrator of Edward Lloyd, to recover his third share of the legacy and interest. Various communications had previously passed between the plaintiff and the defendant on the subject of the claim made by Thomas Mostyn; and on the 19th of May, 1841, the plaintiff gave the defendant a formal notice in writing of the suit having been instituted against him, and requiring the defendant to indemnify him against it, pursuant to the condition of the bond. On the 7th of June, an order was made in the suit by the VICE-CHANCELLOR OF ENGLAND, by consent of the parties, that the bill should be dismissed without costs; and the plaintiff thereupon paid to Thomas Mostyn the sum of 117*l.*, being his share of the legacy of 200*l.*, and interest thereon: and he now sought to recover from the defendant, under his bond of indemnity, the amount so paid, together with the further sum of 26*l.* for the plaintiff's own costs in the equity suit.

It appeared at the trial, that the bond had not been known to be in existence until the year 1839, when it was found amongst a basket-full of old papers, in the house of a Mrs. Jones, the widow and executrix of the late attorney of the defendant and his father. It was now in the possession of a Mr. Williams, Mrs. Jones's son-in-law, who acted for her as executrix, and who was also the general attorney for the defendant, although not the attorney on the record in this action. Mr. Williams had not been served with a *subpœna duces tecum* to produce the bond, but had undertaken to do so if the Judge should think that he was bound to produce it, and he had it in Court at the trial. On being called upon to produce it, he objected

*to do so on the ground that he held it in the same character as Mr. Jones, if alive, would have done, namely, as the attorney of the obligors; and the learned Judge allowed the objection. The plaintiff then tendered in evidence a copy of the bond, which had been furnished to the plaintiff's agent, and examined by him with the original, upon the bond's being sent up by Mr. Williams to the defendant's attorney in London to be inspected, for the purposes of admission under a Judge's order. It was objected that this copy was inadmissible, on two grounds: first, that, the bond having

been in the confidential custody of Mr. Williams, a copy so obtained   LLOYD
could not be used in evidence; for which *Fisher* v. *Heming* (1)   *v.*
was cited as an authority; and secondly, on the ground that at all   MOSTYN.
events it was not admissible without proof of notice to produce the
original: and the learned Judge, being of opinion that notice to
produce was necessary, rejected the evidence. The plaintiff then
proved a notice to produce the bond, which had been served upon
the defendant's attorney in this action, the defendant being present,
in Mold, the Assize town, at ten o'clock in the morning of Thursday,
the 28th of July. The commission day was Wednesday, the 27th;
the cause was tried on Friday, the 29th. The defendant resided
about ten miles from Mold; the attorney, Mr. Leigh, was resident
in London. Mr. Williams, who held the bond, resided at Denbigh,
fourteen miles from Mold, and arrived at the latter place, with the
bond, in the afternoon of Thursday the 28th. It was objected for
the defendant, that this notice was too late; the learned Judge,
however, thought that as the bond was actually in Court, the notice
was sufficient, and that the copy was admissible, and it was
accordingly read.

For the defendant it was contended, that the bond ought,
under the circumstances, to be presumed to have been satisfied.
The learned Judge left that question to the jury, who found a
verdict for the plaintiff for the whole amount *claimed by him,   [*481]
133*l.*, leave being given to the defendant to move to enter a nonsuit, if the Court should be of opinion that the copy of the bond
ought not to have been received in evidence.

Kelly now moved accordingly:

First, inasmuch as Mr. Williams, in whose possession the bond
was, represented the attorney of the obligors, he was not bound
to produce the bond; and if so, neither could a copy obtained
from or furnished by him, contrary to his duty, be received in
evidence. * * *

Secondly, the notice to produce was not sufficient. * * *   [482]

LORD ABINGER, C. B.:   [483]

The only question in this case really is, whether the notice to
produce was served in such proper time as would enable the
party to produce the document if he had it. It appears that the
defendant's attorney was in possession of the original bond, and

(1) 1 Phill. Evid. 182 (8th ed.).

LLOYD
v.
MOSTYN.

that a copy was in town. The attorney who was served with the notice to produce must have known that Mr. Williams, who was the attorney for the defendant in the country, had possession of the bond. It would appear that the notice was merely given from over-caution, lest Mr. Williams, when called to produce it, should plead his client's privilege, and decline to do so. There was time enough for the attorney to consider whether it was for his client's interest to produce it or not, and no doubt he determined it was not. I therefore think the notice was sufficient, taking the fact into consideration, that the party on whom the notice was served knew that the instrument was in the possession of another person, who had been subpœnaed to produce it at the trial, and over whom his client had full authority. It is not like the case of a complicated deed, in which there are many parties, and which the attorney might refuse to produce, because he might think it necessary to take the opinion of his counsel before he produced it. This is the case of a simple bond of indemnity. I think, therefore, that the learned Judge was quite right in admitting the secondary evidence, and that no rule ought to be granted.

PARKE, B.:

[*484]

I am of the same opinion. The question is now reduced to this, whether the notice to produce was sufficient. I agree that the principle to be extracted from the cases is, that notice to produce must be given within *a reasonable time before the trial comes on, the Judge at the trial being the proper person to consider whether that reasonable time has been given or not. I think in this case there was ample evidence to warrant the Judge in deciding that the notice was sufficient, even on the principle contended for by *Mr. Kelly*—which, however, is not the principle laid down in the cases,—that it must depend upon the state of facts at the time the notice was given. Here it was given early on the Thursday morning, the case standing for trial on Friday. It is clear the defendant's attorney on the record, Mr. Leigh, well knew that the bond was in the possession of the former attorney, Mr. Williams, and that he would produce it at the Assizes. At the very time he had the notice, he knew it was in the power of their own client, who had nothing more to do than to direct Mr. Williams to produce it. Even if the bond had not been at the time within the control of the defendant, but had afterwards come into his possession, or that of his attorney, so that it could have been produced on the trial, I by no means say that the notice would not in that case have been sufficient; but it is unnecessary to decide that. The cases referred to are all distinguishable. In the case of *Cook* v. *Hearn*, it was endeavoured to supply a want of previous notice, by giving it at the trial. That is no notice at all. In *Doe* v. *Grey*, the notice was served upon the wife, and not upon the attorney himself, and no proof was given that the attorney had received the notice, though · there was proof that the deed was in his possession at the time. Here there was a notice to produce, given to the right party, and the sole question is, whether that has been given a reasonable time before the trial. I should have been sorry if this objection could have prevailed; and I think there is ample ground for holding that this was a sufficient notice, and therefore that the rule should be refused.

GURNEY, B., and ROLFE, B., concurred.

Rule refused.

LLOYD
v.
MOSTYN.

CHEESE *v.* SCALES.

(10 Meeson & Welsby, 488.)

The defendant published a placard stating of the plaintiff, who was an overseer of the poor, "that when out of office he had advocated low rates, and when in office had advocated high rates, and that he (the defendant) would not trust him with 5*l.* of his property:" Held, that these words were actionable *per se*, without any innuendo.

1842.
Nov. 7.

Exch. of
Pleas.

[488]

LIBEL. The declaration stated that the plaintiff had been and was overseer of the poor of the parish of St. Mary, Stratford-le-Bow; and that the defendant published of and concerning him the libellous matter following: "that the plaintiff, when out of office, had advocated low rates, and when in office had advocated high rates, and that he (the defendant) would not trust the plaintiff with 5*l.* of his private property." Plea, not guilty. At the trial before Lord Abinger, C. B., at the sittings in London after last Trinity Term, the plaintiff obtained a verdict, damages 40*s.*

Crowder now moved in arrest of judgment, and contended that the language imputed to the defendant was ambiguous, and might mean either that the plaintiff was dishonest, or merely that he was negligent of his affairs; and therefore that it was not necessarily libellous, and ought to have been explained by an innuendo.

But per CURIAM :

The publication imputes dishonesty to the plaintiff, or at least tends to disparage him; it was for the jury to say whether it was libellous or not, and they have found that it was. There is no ground for arresting the judgment.

Rule refused.

BRAYTHWAYTE *v.* GEORGE HITCHCOCK.

(10 Meeson & Welsby, 494—498; S. C. 12 L. J. Ex. 38; 6 Jur. 976; 2 Dowl. N. S. 444.)

In debt for rent, stating a demise of a messuage &c. by the plaintiff to W. H., for one year, and so on from year to year if they should respectively please, at the yearly rent of 140*l.*, payable quarterly, and an assignment by W. H. to the defendant, the plaintiff proved an agreement (signed by himself only) for a lease of the premises by him to W. H. for seven years, at 140*l.* a year, that no lease had been actually executed, but that W. H. had entered into possession shortly after the date of the agreement, and had paid two quarters' rent, at the rate of 140*l.* a year : Held, that this was sufficient evidence of a tenancy from year to year, as stated in the declaration, and in which W. H. had an assignable interest.

Where, on the non-production of a deed after notice to produce, the opposite party calls a witness who proves a copy compared by him with the original deed, such copy may be read without being stamped; for it is only used, in point of law, to refresh the witness's memory as to the contents of the deed.

DEBT for rent. The first count of the declaration stated a demise, on the 26th of October, 1840, from the plaintiff to William Hitchcock, of a messuage and premises, to hold for one year from the 25th of December then last, and so on from year to year if the plaintiff and the said William Hitchcock should respectively please, at the annual rent of 140*l.*, payable quarterly on &c. : that, during the said tenancy, to wit, on the 17th July, 1841, all the estate and interest of the said W. Hitchcock in the said messuage and premises came to and vested in the defendant, by assignment from the said W. Hitchcock: and alleged as a breach the non-payment by the defendant of 35*l.*, a quarter's rent due at Christmas, 1841. There was also a count on an account stated.

The defendant pleaded, first, *nunquam indebitatus;* secondly (to the first count) a denial of the demise to W. Hitchcock; and thirdly (to the first count), a denial that the estate and interest of W. Hitchcock vested in him the defendant: on which issues were joined.

At the trial before Lord Abinger, C. B., at the Middlesex sittings after last Term, the plaintiff put in evidence an agreement, dated

the 17th December, 1840, and signed by the plaintiff only, whereby
the plaintiff agreed to execute a lease of a cottage, &c. to W.
Hitchcock, for seven years, at a yearly rent of 140*l.*, payable
quarterly. It was proved that no lease had been executed in
pusuance of the agreement, but that W. Hitchcock had entered
into possession of the cottage shortly after the date of the agreement, and had paid two quarters' rent up to Midsummer, 1841, at
the rate of 140*l.* a year. The plaintiff *then proved a notice to the
defendant to produce a deed of assignment, bearing date the
17th July, 1841, of the cottage, from W. Hitchcock to the defendant:
and on its non-production, called a witness, who produced a paper
which he said was a true copy of the original assignment, which he
had read and compared with it. It was objected that this copy
could not be read in evidence for want of a stamp'; but the LORD
CHIEF BARON overruled the objection, and the copy was read: from
which it appeared, that by the deed of assignment, which was
executed both by W. Hitchcock and the defendant, after reciting
the agreement of the 17th December, 1840, and that no lease had
been executed in pursuance thereof, W. Hitchcock assigned to the
defendant, his executors, &c., all the said agreement, and all
benefit and advantage thereof, and all his estate, title, and interest
therein, to hold to the defendant, his executors, &c., absolutely,
subject nevertheless to a proviso for redemption. It was contended
for the defendant, that there was no sufficient evidence of a demise
whereby a tenancy from year to year was created, as alleged in the
declaration. The LORD CHIEF BARON overruled the objection, and
the plaintiff had a verdict for 35*l.*, leave being reserved to the
defendant to move to enter a nonsuit, if the Court should be of
opinion that there was no sufficient evidence of the assignment.

BRAYTH-
WAYTE
v.
HITCHCOCK.

[*495]

Erle now moved accordingly for a rule to enter a nonsuit, and
also for a new trial, on the ground that there was no sufficient
evidence of a tenancy from year to year between the plaintiff and
W. Hitchcock, or of the assignment of such an interest to the
defendant. First, the copy of the assignment was inadmissible for
want of a stamp. The Stamp Acts, 44 Geo. III. c. 98, sched. A.,
and 48 Geo. III. c. 149, sched. I., part 1 (1), impose a duty upon
"every copy attested to be a true copy, in the form which hath
been commonly used for that purpose, or in any other manner
authenticated or declared to be a true copy, or made for the

(1) See now Stamp Act, 1891 (54 & 55 Vict. c. 39), sch. tit. Copy.

BRAYTH-
WAYTE
v.
HITCHCOCK.

[*496]

purpose of being given in evidence as a true copy, of any *agreement, contract, bond, deed, or other instrument of conveyance, or
any other deed whatsoever: " and there is a proviso, that all copies
which shall at any time be offered in evidence, shall be deemed to
have been made for that purpose. A stamp is therefore required
for every copy of an instrument, before it can be read in evidence
as such copy; the only exception to the rule being where the document is not read or receivable as such, but is used merely as a
memorandum to refresh the memory of a witness.

Secondly, under the agreement recited in the deed, W. Hitchcock
was a mere tenant at will, no lease having been executed, and
there was not sufficient evidence from which to infer a demise from
year to year, as alleged in the declaration. He had therefore no
assignable interest in the premises. * * *

LORD ABINGER, C. B.:

I think the evidence was sufficient to show a tenancy from year
to year, under the agreement, which was duly executed by the
plaintiff; the cases which have been decided on this point go fully
that length. Here there is the additional fact of an admission
under the defendant's hand, in the deed of assignment, that an
agreement for the lease was executed by the plaintiff. But the
plaintiff's case does not rest solely on the agreement to let; there
is the fact of William Hitchcock having been in the possession of
the cottage for more than a year, and having paid two quarters'
rent under the agreement. William Hitchcock had therefore an
assignable interest, which passed to the defendant under the deed
proved at the trial. As to the other point, I think the provisions of
the Stamp Acts relate only to such copies as are evidence *per se*,
and that the word " copy" there means an authenticated copy,
receivable as evidence in the first instance. Here the copy was
evidence, only because the party who produced it had compared it
with the original, and swore to the contents of it, word for word.

[497]   PARKE, B.:

I am of the same opinion. Although the law is clearly settled,
that where there has been an agreement for a lease, and an occupation without payment of rent, the occupier is a mere tenant at will;
yet it has been held that if he subsequently pays rent under that
agreement, he thereby becomes tenant from year to year. Payment
of rent, indeed, must be understood to mean a payment with refer-

ence to a yearly holding; for in *Richardson* v. *Langridge* (1), a party who had paid rent under an agreement of this description, but had not paid it with reference to a year, or any aliquot part of a year, was held nevertheless to be a tenant at will only. In the present case, there was distinct proof of the payment of rent for two quarters of a year. There is the additional fact of an occupation for more than a year; but in the case of *Cox* v. *Bent* (2), where a party, under an agreement for a lease, had occupied for more than a year, the Court held that a tenancy from year to year existed, not on the ground of the occupation, but because the party had during that occupation paid a half-year's rent. I think, therefore, the fact of such a payment was the stronger evidence in this case, and that William Hitchcock may be taken to have been a yearly tenant. Then, as to the question whether there has been a due assignment of such his interest, I think it is clear that there has; because, although the deed in its commencement recites only the agreement, the operative part of it conveys and assigns " all that the herein-before recited agreement of the 17th of December, 1840, and all benefit and advantage thereof, and all that and those the said messuage or tenement and premises at &c., and all the right, title, interest, property, claim, and demand whatsoever, at law or in equity, of him the said William Hitchcock in the said premises," &c. On the other point, I quite agree with my LORD CHIEF BARON that no *stamp was requisite, inasmuch as, though the document [*498] might in form have been read as a copy of the original, it was in truth read only as a memorandum to refresh the memory of the witness, who had compared it with the deed.

GURNEY, B., concurred.

ROLFE, B.:

If we look to the context of the schedule to the Stamp Act, it is evident that the word " copy " is not used in its ordinary sense; for a high rate of duty is first imposed on copies authenticated or attested for the security or use of any person being a party thereto, or taking any benefit or interest immediately under it; and after-wards a lower rate of interest is imposed, where the copy is made for the use of any other person not being a party thereto, or taking such interest or benefit.

Rule refused.

(1) 13 R. R. 570 (4 Taunt. 128).   (2) 30 R. R. 566 (5 Bing. 185; 2 Moo. & P. 281).

1842.
Nov. 8.

*Exoh. of
Pleas.*

[498]

KELL *v.* ANDERSON (1).

(10 Meeson & Welsby, 498—502; S. C. 12 L. J. Ex. 101.)

By the stipulations of a charter-party, the vessel was to take in a cargo of coal at Newcastle, and proceed therewith to London, or as near thereto as she could safely get, and deliver the same to the freighters or their assigns, &c.: to be delivered in five working days, demurrage over and above the said lying days 2*l.* per day. The vessel arrived in the port of London, off Gravesend, on the 9th March, and on the 10th the cargo was sold, and the vessel entered by the freighters for a meter. On the 20th she received an order from the harbour-master to proceed to the Pool; on Monday, the 22nd, she commenced working out her cargo, and was cleared on the 27th. It appeared that in consequence of the factor's certificate that she was a metered vessel, the harbour-master had detained her at Gravesend till the 20th, when her turn arrived for her to proceed to the Pool and discharge her cargo; that if she had not been on the meter's list, this regulation would not have applied, and she might have proceeded to the Pool at once; that it was occasionally the practice for factors not to enter such vessels in the meter's list, but that it was desirable that the cargo should be sold, subject to meterage, by a sworn meter:

Held, that under these circumstances the vessel was not to be considered as having arrived at her place of discharge until the 20th, and therefore that the lying days did not begin to count till then.

ASSUMPSIT on a charter-party, brought by the plaintiff, as owner of the ship *Union*, to recover 22*l.* for the detention of the ship on demurrage for eleven days, at 2*l.* per day. The defendant, as to ten days, denied the detention, and paid 2*l.* into Court.

[499]

At the trial, before Lord Abinger, C. B., at the London sittings after last Term, the charter-party was produced in evidence, and was as follows:

"Newcastle-upon-Tyne, the 25th of February, 1841. It is this day mutually agreed between Mr. Edward Kell, owner of the good ship or vessel *Union*, himself master, of the burden of 141 register tons or thereabouts, now in the Tyne, and William Anderson, jun., agent to the affreighters, that the said ship, being staunch and strong, and every way fitted for the voyage, shall, with all convenient speed, sail and proceed to Jarrow Quay, or as near thereto as she may safely get, and there load two keels of coals, and the remainder coke, not exceeding what she can reasonably stow and carry over and above her tackle, apparel, provisions, and furniture, and being so loaded shall therewith proceed to London, or so near thereto as she may safely get, and deliver the same to the said freighters or their assigns, on being paid freight at and after the

(1) Cited *Tapscott* v. *Balfour* (1872) L. R. 8 C. P. 46, 53, 42 L. J. C. P. 16, 27 L. T. 710; dist. *Norden Steam Co.* v. *Dempsey* (1876) 1 C. P. D. 654, 660, 45 L. J. C. P. 764; explained, *Davies* v. *McVeagh* (1879) 4 Ex. D. 265, 269, 48 L. J. Ex. 686.—A. C.

rate of 7*l*. per keel for the quantity taken on board, and also all charges and expenses on the coals and coke, the ship paying trimming, pilotage, tonnage duty, delivery, (the act of God, the Queen's enemies, fire, and all and every other dangers and accidents of the seas, rivers, and navigation of whatever nature or kind during the said voyage always excepted). The freight to be paid in cash for ship's use, and remainder by the factor's note at sixty days' date, one market day to be allowed the said freighter (if the ship is not sooner dispatched) for sale, the vessel to be delivered in five working days, demurrage over and above the said lying days 2*l*. per day. Penalty for non-performance of this agreement 90*l*.

(Signed) " WILLIAM ANDERSON."

It appeared that the vessel arrived in the port of London, off Gravesend, on the 9th of March, and on the 10th, being then ready to deliver her cargo, she was entered (as sold) for a meter. On the 20th she received an order from the harbour-master to proceed to the Pool, whither she *proceeded accordingly; on Monday the 22nd she commenced working out her cargo, and was clear on the 27th. It was proved that, in consequence of the certificate of the factor that she was a metered vessel, the harbour-master had detained her at Gravesend until the 20th, when her turn arrived for her to proceed to the Pool and discharge her cargo; that if she had not been entered on the meter's list, this regulation would not have applied to her, and she might have proceeded to the Pool at once and that it was occasionally the custom for factors not to enter vessels of small burthen and draught, such as she was, in the meter's list, in order to avoid the chance of delay, and ensure a speedy discharge of their cargoes. On the other hand, it was proved that it was desirable that the cargo should be sold subject to metage by a sworn meter, and that the defendant had notice of her arrival at Gravesend on the 10th of March, and sold the cargo accordingly on that day.

[*500]

The LORD CHIEF BARON was of opinion, on these facts, that the ship had not arrived at the termination of her voyage until the 20th of March, and therefore the defendant was liable for demurrage for one day only, which was covered by the payment into Court; and he accordingly nonsuited the plaintiff, reserving leave to him to move to enter a verdict for 20*l*.

Erle now moved accordingly:

The voyage ended, as far as the control of the master was concerned, on the 10th March, when the ship arrived in the port of

London, at Gravesend. She had then, according to the terms of the charter-party, arrived " at London, or so near thereto as she might safely get." On that day the consignee had the perfect control of the vessel and cargo, and the detention complained of arose altogether from the defendant's having entered her name, for his own benefit, in the meter's list, whereby she had to wait her

[*501] turn for a meter *till the 20th of March. The objection made on the part of the defendant at the trial was, that the ship had not until then arrived at her place of delivery : but the answer is, that as between the owner and the consignee, when she had arrived at a place within the port of London, ready to deliver her cargo, and where her subsequent movements were within the control of the consignee, that was virtually the place of delivery. What is the place of discharge must be construed with reference to the nature of the cargo, and to the usage of trade and the requisitions of the port as to such a class of vessels. In *Leer* v. *Yates* (1), a general ship took brandies on board under bills of lading which allowed twenty lay days after arrival for delivery of the goods in London, and stipulated for the payment of demurrage at 4*l.* a day after the expiration of that time. Some of the consignees choosing to have their goods bonded, the vessel was unable to make her delivery at the London Docks until forty-six days after the expiration of the twenty days ; some of the goods, which were undermost, could not, although demanded, be taken out till the upper tiers were cleared. There it was held that each of those consignees was liable for demurrage for the forty-six days. There, no doubt, the vessel was actually in dock, but she could not come to the actual place of unloading. The general rule is laid down in Abbott on Shipping, p. 266, " that if the merchant covenant to do a particular act which it becomes impracticable for him to do, he must answer for his default, unless the act be or become contrary to the law of his country." That rule goes even further than the present argument requires. Here the ship was at her place of delivery, according to the reasonable meaning of the contract as between these parties, on her arrival at a place where she was under the control of the con-

[*502] signee, the defendant *himself being the cause of the subsequent delay, by choosing unnecessarily to have a meter.

LORD ABINGER, C. B.:

I thought, that as no time was limited by the charter-party from

(1) 12 R. R. 671 (3 Taunt. 387).

which the demurrage was to be reckoned, it must be reckoned from
the time of the ship's arrival at the ordinary place of discharge;
and that if she was prevented from discharging sooner by the
default of the defendant, that should have been the subject of an
action on the case, and not of an action for demurrage. I still
retain the opinion I had at the trial, that the days of demurrage
must be counted from the time of the arrival of the vessel at the
place of discharge, according to the usage of the port.

PARKE, B.:

It appears to me that the question in this case is one of fact,
namely, at what time the vessel arrived at her place of discharge,
according to the usage of the port of London for such vessels. No
doubt the general course of business of the port is to have a meter
employed for such vessels; and the occasional practice of not entering small vessels on the meter's list is merely the exception to the
rule. It is purely a question of fact, as to the proper construction
of the charter-party. *Leer* v. *Yates* turned entirely upon the words
"after arrival," by which the parties had bound themselves.

GURNEY, B.:

I am of the same opinion. I think the time from which the days
are to be calculated is the arrival of the vessel in the usual place
of discharge for colliers; that is, in the Pool. If the parties mean
otherwise, it is very easy for them to employ words to express their
meaning.

ROLFE, B., concurred. ——————————— *Rule refused.*

KELL
v.
ANDERSON.

WILSON AND OTHERS *v.* WHITEHEAD, ACKERMANN, AND CARLETON (1).

(10 Meeson & Welsby, 503—504; S. C. 12 L. J. Ex. 43.)

1842.
Nov. 10.

Exch. of Pleas.

[503]

A., B., and C. verbally agreed that they should bring out and be jointly
interested in a periodical publication. A. was to be the publisher, and to
make and receive general payments, B. to be the editor, and C. the printer;
and after payment of all expenses, they were to share the profits of the
work equally. C. was to furnish the paper, and charge it to the account
at cost prices. No profits were ever made, nor any accounts settled. The
plaintiff furnished paper to A., for the purpose of being used by him in
printing the periodical: Held, that B. and C. were not jointly liable with
A. for the price of it.

ASSUMPSIT for goods sold and delivered, and upon an account
stated. The defendants Ackermann and Carleton pleaded *non*

(1) Quest. in *Kilshaw* v. *Jukes* (1863) 3 B. & S. 847, 32 L. J. Q. B. 217.

Wilson
v.
Whitehead.
assumpserunt, on which issue was joined; the defendant Whitehead pleaded his bankruptcy and certificate, and a *nolle prosequi*
was entered as to him. At the trial before Lord Abinger, C. B., at
the London sittings after last Term, it was admitted that paper of
the value of 298*l.* had been delivered by the plaintiffs, who are
wholesale stationers, to the defendant Whitehead, who carried on
business as a printer under the name of Whitehead & Co., for the
purpose of being used by him in printing the "Sporting Review,"
of which publication he was part proprietor. In order to establish
the joint liability with him of the other defendants, Whitehead's
foreman was called, who stated that there had been a verbal agreement between the three defendants, that they should bring out and
be jointly interested in the "Sporting Review": Ackermann was to
be the publisher, and to make and receive general payments, Carleton
to be the editor, and Whitehead the printer; and after payment of
all expenses, the three were to share the profits of the publication
equally. Whitehead was to furnish the paper for the work, and
charge it to the account at cost-price, and was also to charge the
printing at "master's prices." He furnished accounts accordingly
to Ackermann from time to time, but no settlement of accounts ever
took place, nor were any profits ever realized from the work.

On this evidence, the LORD CHIEF BARON was of opinion that the
other defendants were not jointly liable with Whitehead in this
action, and accordingly directed a nonsuit, giving the plaintiffs
leave to move to enter a verdict for 298*l.*

[504]   *W. H. Watson* now moved accordingly:

The agreement proved at the trial, by which the defendants were
to be jointly interested in the profits of the work, constituted a partnership between them in respect of it, and made them all liable,
when the partnership was discovered, for goods supplied to any of
them for the purposes of the work: *Saville* v. *Robertson* (1), *Gouthwaite*
v. *Duckworth* (2).

· (PARKE, B. : The question is, did the other defendants authorize
Whitehead to purchase the paper on their account, or on his own?
It appears to me, on the true construction of the contract, that the
latter was the case. When the paper was in his possession, he was
at liberty to have appropriated it to any other purpose than to the
"Sporting Review." This is very much like the ordinary case of

(1) 4 T. R. 720.   (2) 12 East, 421.

coach proprietors, where each horses the coach for one or more
stages, and each agrees to bring into the concern the work and
labour of his horses, and none of the others has any interest in
them, though all share in the profits.)

Those cases proceed on the ground that it is notorious to all that
each does so work with his own horses.

(PARKE, B.: Not at all; but on the ground that such is the
authority given. So here, on the true construction of the agreement, the view taken by my Lord at the trial was perfectly correct;
the agreement is that Whitehead shall furnish the paper on his
own account.)

LORD ABINGER, C. B. :

I retain the opinion which I expressed at the trial.

PARKE, B., GURNEY, B., and ROLFE, B., concurred.

Rule refused. ·

WILSON
r.
WHITEHEAD.

PRATT *v.* DELARUE (1).

(10 Meeson & Welsby, 509—514; S. C. 12 L. J. Ex. 25; 7 Jur. 91; 2 Dowl.
N. S. 322.)

A plaintiff suing *in formâ pauperis* is exempted from the payment of
interlocutory equally as of final costs.

1842.
Nov. 17.

*Exch. of
Pleas.*
[509]

IN this case the action was commenced on the 6th of October :
on the 15th, the plaintiff obtained an order to sue *in formâ pauperis.*
An order was afterwards made by Lord ABINGER, C. B., allowing
the defendant a month's time to plead. The plaintiff took out a
summons before Rolfe, B., to rescind that order, and after hearing
the parties, the learned Baron (not being aware that the plaintiff
was suing *in formâ pauperis*) ordered that the summons should be
*refused, " with costs to be taxed by the Master, and paid by the
plaintiff."

[*510]

Horn having obtained a rule to show cause why the order should
not be amended, by striking out the latter words,

Otter now showed cause :

There is no distinction between a pauper plaintiff and any other,
in regard to the power of a Judge at Chambers to impose costs. At

(1) See note to *Casey* v. *Tomlin*, 56 R. R. 686.—A. C.

common law, neither plaintiff nor defendant obtained costs ; but by
the stat. of Gloucester, 6 Edw. I., costs were given to the plaintiff
in all cases where he obtained damages.   Now these costs may be
divided into two portions, the one consisting of Court fees and the
fees to counsel and attorney ; the other of the costs incidental to
the prosecution of a suit.   By stat. 11 Hen. VII. c. 12, a pauper
plaintiff was exempted from the payment of the first portion ; and
after the passing of that statute, if a pauper succeeded, he would
recover both descriptions of costs from the opposite party ; if he
failed, he was exempt from payment of the Court fees and fees to
counsel and attorney, and he paid no costs to the opposite party,
because at that time a defendant, though he succeeded in the suit,
got no costs.   To remedy this the stat. 23 Hen. VIII. c. 15, was
passed ; and by the first section of this statute, a defendant was
entitled to his costs where the plaintiff was nonsuited or a verdict
went against him.   Now the words of this clause being general, a
pauper plaintiff would have been liable to costs, if he were nonsuited or a verdict went against him ; but then the second
section enacts, that provided he were admitted to sue *in formâ
pauperis* at the commencement of the suit, he shall not be liable to
the costs imposed by virtue of that statute ; viz., in the case of his
being nonsuited, or a verdict being obtained against him.   If therefore a pauper plaintiff were admitted before the commencement of
[*511]   the suit, he was exempt from payment *of Court fees, and fees to
counsel and attorney, by stat. 11 Hen. VII., and he came directly
within the exemption of the second section of 23 Hen. VIII. ; if he
were admitted after the commencement of the suit, then he was still
exempt from payment of the fees under stat. 11 Hen. VII., but he
would be liable to pay the costs to the opposite party, if he were
nonsuited or a verdict went against him.   It is admitted that a
pauper may be admitted to sue, and so entitled to all the benefits
of the stat. 11 Hen. VII., either before or after the commencement
of the suit.   Now in this case the action was commenced on the
6th October, and the plaintiff was not admitted a pauper until the
15th.   It is submitted, therefore, that there is no distinction
between a pauper and any other person as to his liability to
costs in such a case, upon a consideration of the statutes.   Then
as to the practice.   It is certainly generally stated in the books of
practice, that a pauper may recover costs though he pays none ;
but it is submitted that the proposition must be limited to that
portion of the costs which consists of Court fees and fees to counsel

and attorney : for the reason of this proposition is given in 1 Eq.
Cas. Abr. 125, and 3 Bla. Com. 400, that the counsel and clerks
are bound to give their labour to him, but not to his antagonist.
The cases also which are usually cited in support of this proposition, do not support it. *Rice* v. *Brown* (1) only shows that a pauper
shall recover his costs if he succeed; and the case of *Blood* v. *Lee* (2)
was adjourned, and even if it were considered as a decision, it does
not appear from the report whether the pauper was admitted before
or after the commencement of the suit; and upon the distinction
above taken, this circumstance would be all important.

    Horn, contrà :

    The uniform practice for several centuries has been for paupers
to be exempted from the payment of *costs, without any distinction   [*512]
between interlocutory and final costs; and the Court will not disturb that practice, merely because they think that the language of
ancient statutes, if subjected to strict verbal criticism, will not
support it to the letter. Long usage, in matters of this nature,
has the effect of a binding decision. Before the rule of H. T.
2 Will. IV., the mode of punishing a pauper for any misconduct
in the course of the cause was by dispaupering him; and the
power thereby given to the Court, of inflicting costs on a pauper
plaintiff in the case there mentioned, shows that, in the opinion of
those who framed the rule, no such power existed before. It must
now be considered as settled, since the case of *Casey* v. *Tomlin* (3),
that the admission to sue *in formâ pauperis* after the commencement of the suit makes no difference as to the right of the pauper
to be exempted from the payment of costs (4).   But even admitting
that he may be subject to interlocutory costs, he ought at all events,
by analogy to the rule of H. T. 2 Will. IV., to be called upon by a
rule to show cause why he should not pay them.

LORD ABINGER, C. B. :

    Undoubtedly, if our decision in this case depended solely upon
the wording of the statute of 23 Hen. VIII., I should think that a
pauper would not be protected thereby from the payment of interlocutory costs, for costs in the cause would, as it seems to me, mean
final costs. But the practice of exempting a pauper from the payment of all costs has now become so inveterate that it cannot be

(1) 1 Bos. & P. 39.   (3) 56 R. R. 686 (7 M. & W. 189).
(2) 3 Wils. 24.   (4) See the next case.

PRATT   disturbed. When a pauper has misconducted himself in the course
  v.   of a cause, the proper mode of subjecting him to the payment of
DELARUE.   costs is by dispaupering him.   That has undoubtedly been the
             established practice, and is recognized by one of the cases which
             has been referred to, decided by the Court of Common Pleas, when
[*513]   *Mr. Justice BULLER had a seat in that Court (1). It is not for us
             to overturn a solemn decision of that kind. The rule will there-
             fore be absolute, but without costs, for setting aside so much of my
             brother ROLFE's order as subjects the plaintiff to the payment of costs.

             PARKE, B. :

                It appears to me that this question does not turn on the con-
             struction of the statute, which applies only to costs payable
             between party and party at the termination of the suit.   This
             is a case of interlocutory costs, which stands upon an entirely
             different footing. It has certainly been a long-established practice,
             that a pauper shall pay no costs whatever; and the principle on
             which it rests was doubtless this, that it would be a great wrong to
             compel a person to pay costs who is totally destitute of money.
             This practice, I think, we cannot now overturn. But then a rule of
             Court has been made, which directs " that where a pauper omits to
             proceed to trial pursuant to a notice or undertaking, he may be
             called upon by a rule to show cause why he should not pay costs,
             though he has not been dispaupered :" and the question arises,
             whether by that rule the practice has been so far altered, as that
             the Court has now a general power of inflicting interlocutory costs,
             the two instances mentioned in the rule being put merely by way of
             examples; or whether the power is to be restricted to those parti-
             cular instances. I think it must be considered as confined to the
             particular instances mentioned in that rule, and that we cannot,
             until some further rule be made on the subject, sanction an order
             which compels a pauper to pay interlocutory costs.

                GURNEY, B., concurred.

             ROLFE, B. :

[*514]   When I made the order, I certainly was *not apprised that the
             plaintiff had been admitted to sue as a pauper, or I should not
             have made it. At the same time, I must regret that there is no
             jurisdiction to inflict interlocutory costs; for although the non-

             (1) *Rice* v. *Brown*, 1 Bos. & P. 39; *ante*, p. 689.

payment of costs by a pauper has a popular sound, and may in some cases be extremely proper, it certainly is often made the means of great oppression.   In the present case, for instance, the plaintiff had misconducted himself by not attending before the Judge, although he was twice summoned.   However, as the established practice has been not to inflict costs, I agree that the rule must be absolute to set aside that part of the order.

Rule absolute accordingly.

DOE D. ELLIS *v.* OWENS (1).

(10 Meeson & Welsby, 514—523 ; 12 L. J. Ex. 53; 2 Dowl. N. S. 426; 7 Jur. 91.)

A person admitted to sue *in formâ pauperis* after the commencement of the suit, is liable, on nonsuit or verdict for the defendant, to the costs antecedent to the date of the order.

THE Court having discharged with costs (2) the rule which had been obtained by the defendant in this case, for setting aside the order of ALDERSON, B., admitting the lessor of the plaintiff to sue *in formâ pauperis* after the commencement of the suit, the latter taxed his costs of opposing that rule, which were allowed at the sum of 10*l.* 1*s.*, and the defendant tendered to the Master his bill of costs in the cause, amounting to 25*l.* 10*s.* 10*d.*   The Master being of opinion that the order to sue *in formâ pauperis* did not exempt the plaintiff from the payment of the costs incurred prior to the date of the order, allowed the defendant the sum of 17*l.* 3*s.* 6*d.* for such costs, and 1*l.* 12*s.* 8*d.* for the costs of taxation, and made out an allocatur for the amount of these two sums, 18*l.* 16*s.* 2*d.*, in favour of the defendant.

Townsend obtained a rule, calling on the defendant to show cause why this allocatur should not be set aside as being irregular, and why the defendant should not pay the costs of this application.

[515]

(1) The decision in this case turned upon 23 Hen. VIII. c. 15, s. 2. That statute, and 11 Hen. VII. c. 12 (referred to in the argument) were repealed in 1883 by s. 3 of the Statute Law Revision and Civil Procedure Act, 1883 (46 & 47 Vict. c. 49), which, however, provides (s. 5) that "the repeal effected by this Act shall not affect" (*inter alia*) "any jurisdiction or principle or rule of law or equity established or confirmed . . . under any enactment repealed by this Act."   The practice as to proceedings *in formâ pauperis* is now regulated by Order XVI. of the R. S. C. rr. 22—31, which first appear in the Rules of 1883 (see Wilson, Judicature Acts, 3rd ed., p. 228).   The present practice appears to be in accordance with the decision here reported (see Ch. Archb. Pr. 14th ed. (1885) ch. 104, p. 1182).— A. C.

(2) 60 R. R. 788 (see 9 M. & W. 455).

44—2

Jervis now showed cause :

The question in this case is, whether an order to sue *in formâ pauperis*, obtained after the commencement of the suit, exempts the plaintiff from antecedent costs. The cases on this subject at common law exhibit some contradiction, the true view of the statutes not having been brought before the Court. The 11 Hen. VII. c. 12, which conferred the right to sue *in formâ pauperis*, enacts, "that every poor person or persons which have and hereafter shall have cause of action or actions against any person or persons within the realm shall have, by the discretion of the Chancellor of this realm for the time being, writ or writs original and writs of *subpœna*, according to the nature of their causes, therefor nothing paying; . . . and after the said writ or writs be returned, &c. the justices shall assign to the same poor person or persons counsel learned &c., and . . . shall appoint attorney and attorneys for the same poor person and persons, &c. &c." At the time of this enactment, a plaintiff paid no costs to the defendant, but he paid the fees of Court, and to counsel and attorney. From this the Act relieves him, if he is a poor person, whether admitted so to sue at the commencement of the suit or afterwards. Then the stat. 23 Hen. VIII. c. 15, first gave a defendant, in case of a verdict for him or a nonsuit, costs against a plaintiff; and the second section, upon which the present question arises, enacts that all poor persons, plaintiffs, "which at the commencement of their suits or actions shall be admitted to have their process of charity," &c., "shall not be compelled to pay any costs by virtue and force of this statute." It is a proviso excepting from the general operation of the statute the persons mentioned therein, and them only, viz., those plaintiffs *who are admitted to sue as paupers at the commencement of their suits. On the equitable construction of this statute (although in the cases of *Foss* v. *Racine* (1) and *Lorewell* v. *Curtis* (2), it was doubted by this Court), it must now certainly be taken as being established, since the cases of *Casey* v. *Tomlin* (3) and *Brunt* v. *Wardle* (4), that even where the party is admitted after the commencement of the suit, he is from that time exempted from the payment of costs. But all the cases leave the present point untouched. There are indeed some old authorities, in which it is laid down that a pauper pays no costs, but in none of them was the point now in question presented to the consideration of the

[*516]

(1) 51 R. R. 665 (4 M. & W. 610).   (3) 56 R. R. 686 (7 M. & W. 189).
(2) 5 M. & W. 158.   (4) 60 R. R. 572 (4 Scott, N. R. 188).

Court ; and the rule of this Court of the year 1717 (Com. Dig. Formâ Pauperis (A.)) is express, that " if admitted after the commencement of the suit, the pauper is to give security to pay the costs before admittance." If the pauper was altogether exempt from the payment of costs, the Court would have had no authority to make such a rule. In *Langley* v. *Blackerby* (1), this point did not arise. In *Blood* v. *Lee* (2), which was merely an application to the discretion of the Court to discharge the plaintiff out of custody, the question was adjourned, and it does not appear to what conclusion the Court came. In *Oats* v. *Holliday*, there cited, the Court certainly are said to have resolved, that a person admitted to sue *in formâ pauperis pendente lite* " shall not pay costs from the beginning of the action." On what ground that case was put does not appear : if the question was when the party could be admitted a pauper, the *dictum* as to the effect upon the costs was merely extrajudicial. But there are some authorities in equity expressly in point for the defendant; and the statute applies equally to courts of equity as of common law. In an *Anonymous* case in Moseley's Reports, 68, it *was expressly decided that a pauper admitted after the commencement of the suit was liable to antecedent costs. The same principle was recognised in the cases of *Wilkinson* v. *Belsher* (3), and *Nash* v. *Yorston* (4). And in *Davenport* v. *Davenport* (5), the present LORD CHANCELLOR says, " The plaintiff then proceeds with the suit, and afterwards obtains the common order to sue *in formâ pauperis*, which does not affect costs incurred previously, and up to the date of that order, and for payment whereof by the plaintiff to the defendants a distinct order was made by the Court."

[*517]

Townsend, in support of the rule :

So long as the order allowing the plaintiffs to sue *in formâ pauperis* remains in force, he is exempt from the payment of all costs. The true construction of the statutes is laid down in the judgment of the Court of Common Pleas, in *Brunt* v. *Wardle*. TINDAL, Ch. J., there says, " The statute 11 Hen. VII. c. 12, is an enabling statute, meant to confer a boon on the poor—its title being ' A mean to help and speed poor persons in their suits ; ' and therefore, unless it in express terms or by necessary implication

(1) Andr. 306.
(2) 3 Wils. 24.
(3) 2 Br. C. C. 272.

(4) 4 L. J. (N. S.) Ch. 86.
(5) 1 Turner & Phillips, 124.

requires that the party shall only be admitted to sue as a pauper before he commences his suit, we have no right to import into it any such condition. I find in the Act no words expressive of any such intention on the part of the Legislature ; and certainly there can be no good reason why a man who has fallen into poverty while the suit is proceeding, should be shut out from the benefit of the statute." His Lordship then refers to the statute of 23 Hen. VIII. c. 15, s. 2, and observes upon it, that " the proper construction of that clause is, that, though it may place parties suing *in formâ pauperis* in a less favourable position where they are admitted so to

[*518]

sue *pendente *lite*, it does not deprive them of the benefit of the former statute." And MAULE, J., referring to the cases of *Foss* v. *Racine* and *Lovewell* v. *Curtis*, says, " The attention of the Court was not in those cases called to the undoubted common-law authority of the Court, to admit parties to sue and defend *in formâ pauperis*."

The words of the statute of Hen. VIII., " at the commencement of the suit," cannot properly be interpreted to mean before the commencement of the suit, nor can they mean, strictly, simultaneously with it. It is a case analogous to those decided upon the statutes relating to costs, 22 & 23 Car. II. c. 9, and 3 & 4 Vict. c. 24, s. 2, the words in which, " immediately afterwards," have been construed to include a reasonable time after the verdict : *Thompson* v. *Gibson* (1). So, when the statute 2 Geo. II. c. 28, s. 8, enables certain persons prosecuted by *capias* to defend *in formâ pauperis*, and directs the Judges " according to their discretion, to admit such person to defend himself against such action or information, in the same manner and with the same privilege as the Judges of such Court are by law directed and authorized to admit poor subjects to commence actions for the recovery of their rights,"—the words " to commence actions " cannot be construed literally, because, for upwards of a century before that Act passed, it had been the constant practice to admit persons to sue *in formâ pauperis* after the commencement of the suit. The admission, indeed, must be after the actual commencement of the suit, because until the writ has been issued the Court has no cognizance of the cause. Therefore, in the form of a petition for an order to sue *in formâ pauperis*, it is stated that " the defendant is jointly indebted unto your petitioner for goods sold, &c. &c., and your petitioner hath commenced an action against him for the same" (2). *Langley*

(1) 8 M. & W. 281.   (2) Tidd, App. 17.

v. *Blackerby* and *Brittain* v. *Greenville* (1) are in *favour of the view contended for by the lessor of the plaintiff.

(ROLFE, B.: If you are right, you mislead a defendant greatly in the conduct of his case : he would resist many things, if he knew the plaintiff was suing *in formâ pauperis*, which he allows to go on, under the expectation that he shall obtain costs. A defendant would never force a pauper plaintiff on.

PARKE, B.: If you can show that the cases have put a uniform construction upon the statutes, we must bow to their authority ; otherwise the reasonable construction certainly is, that the party should not be exempted from all costs, unless he were admitted at the commencement of the suit—that is, as soon as the Judges could admit him.)

Oats v. *Holiday* is an express authority for the plaintiff. *Blood* v. *Lee* is to the same effect, and recognises the principle that a pauper plaintiff is exempt from all costs ; it was not adjourned on this point, but on the question whether the plaintiff was entitled to be discharged out of custody, he being in execution upon a judgment of nonsuit. (He referred also to *Jones* v. *Peers* (2), *Gibson* v. *M'Carty* (3), *Sloman* v. *Aynel* (4), and *Morgan* v. *Eastwick* (5).) Costs in equity stand upon a different footing ; see *Corbett* v. *Corbett* (6), Beames on Costs, 112.

LORD ABINGER, C. B.:

The question is, whether a person admitted to sue *in formâ pauperis*, after the suit has made some progress, is by virtue of that admission to be exempted from paying to the defendant costs incurred antecedently, and due from him at the time of his admission so to sue. If the cases had laid down any fixed rule upon the subject, I should have said that it is now too late to over-rule them by putting a new construction on the statute ; but where *the cases are not sufficiently strong, either from their terms, their number, or their authority, to fetter our judgment, we are at liberty to put the best construction we can upon these Acts of Parliament. If we look at the statute of Hen. VIII., I think there can be no doubt that the intention was to give a successful defendant costs

(1) 2 Str. 1121.
(2) M'Clel. & Y. 282.
(3) Cas. temp. Hardw. 311.

(4) Fortesc. 320.
(5) 7 Dowl. P. C. 543.
(6) 16 Ves. 407.

Doe d.
ELLIS
v.
OWENS.

against the plaintiff, and that the Act makes an exception only in favour of paupers admitted at the commencement of the suit. There is a good reason for that distinction; because, as it is now conceded that a person might be admitted to sue *in formâ pauperis* at any time before, or even after trial, and he would in such case have the full benefit of the statute of Hen. VII., as to Court fees and fees to counsel, it became a question whether the Legislature should exempt the pauper from paying the defendant's costs in all cases, whether admitted before, at, or after the commencement of the suit; and therefore they used these words; which I cannot interpret in any other way than according to their ordinary meaning, nor can I see how the word "at" can be construed "after." A person admitted *before* the commencement of the suit, may, in one sense, be said to be admitted *at* the commencement of the suit; but it is difficult to see how a person admitted *after* the commencement of the suit, can be said to be admitted at its commencement. The ingenious interpretation put upon these statutes by the plaintiff's counsel rests upon a mere fallacy. The word "at" in the statutes relating to costs, which have been referred to, is only used to identify the character of the person who is to certify; that is, he must be the Judge who presides "at the trial." But here the words "at the commencement of the suit" have reference to time, and can only apply to a person admitted before or at the commencement of the suit. By an equitable interpretation of the statute of Hen. VII., when a party is once admitted, he is not thereafter liable to costs under the statute of Hen. VIII.; but he is not therefore

[*521]

exempted from the payment of costs incurred previously *to his admission. The lessor of the plaintiff was therefore liable to those costs, and this rule must be discharged.

PARKE, B. :

I am of the same opinion. The question turns upon the proper interpretation to be put upon the second section of the 23 Hen. VIII. c. 15; the action of ejectment, though not provided for by that statute, being placed on the same footing as other actions by the stat. of 4 Jac. I. c. 3. We are called upon, therefore, to put a construction upon the stat. of Hen. VIII.; and the question is, whether or not the second section applies to a pauper not admitted at the commencement of the suit. It is our duty to construe the statute according to the grammatical meaning of the words, unless some absurdity would ensue from so construing it, or an uniform series of decisions had already established a particular construction. I do not think any of the cases cited of sufficient weight to preclude us from putting our own construction on the words of the statute. The principal authority is that of *Oats* v. *Holiday*, which is cited in *Blood* v. *Lee*. In the latter case the point was not decided, and in the former the decision was only that a party might be admitted after the commencement of the suit. That undoubtedly was the principal point decided, but it is said that " the Court resolved that a person so admitted should not pay costs from the beginning of the action." What is the true meaning of that resolution is left in doubt; probably, that he was not bound to pay the whole costs from the commencement of the action. And such is the construction which we put upon the statute; that if a pauper be admitted after the commencement of the suit, he shall not be bound to pay all the costs, but shall be exempt from those incurred subsequent to his admission. There is now no doubt that a party may be admitted to sue *in formâ pauperis* after the commencement of the suit, and it is clear, from the current of authorities, that we were correct in so deciding; but the question is as to the *effect of such an admission as respects the payment of costs. By the second section of the stat. of Hen. VIII., a pauper is exempt from costs only in the event of his being admitted at the commencement of the suit, that is, as soon as the Court or Judge had jurisdiction to admit him. The statute gives a total exemption from the costs only in case of an admission at the commencement of the suit; if admitted after, then, on the equitable construction of the Act, it seems reasonable that he shall not be liable to the payment of the whole costs, but only to those incurred up to the time of his admission. In this case we must therefore hold, that the lessor of the plaintiff is not altogether exempt from costs, but is liable to pay the costs incurred by the defendant up to the time of his admission to sue *in formâ pauperis ;* and it is reasonable also that he should pay the costs of the taxation.

DOE d.
ELLIS
v.
OWENS.

[*522]

GURNEY, B. :

I think my learned brothers have put the true construction on the Act of Parliament, and it is undoubtedly that which meets the justice of the case.

ROLFE, B. :

I entirely concur. Looking at the language of the second section of the statute of Hen. VIII., the first observation that occurs is, that if you follow the words of that Act, it does not exempt this lessor of the plaintiff from the payment of any costs; because, in terms, it only exempts persons admitted to sue *in formâ pauperis* at the commencement of the suit. But then it is said, that the Court should adopt an equitable construction, and that by such construction a pauper should be wholly exempt. I agree that it is reasonable to adopt an equitable construction; that is, such a construction as shall really do equity, not such as shall favour one party, where the statute itself has not favoured him, at the expense of the other. The statute says that a pauper shall be exempt from the payment of costs, if admitted at the commencement of the suit;

[*523]

but *we are asked to leave out the words "at the commencement of the suit," and to say that he is exempt whenever admitted. It is equitable to say that he shall be exempted from the payment of costs subsequent to his admission: but it might work great injustice to the defendant, if it were held that he might be put to costs, under an expectation that he must eventually recover them, and then, by a retrospective order, be exposed to a charge which he never would have thought of incurring, if he had known the plaintiff to be a pauper.

Rule discharged, without costs.

DAVIES *v.* MANN (1).

(10 Meeson & Welsby, 546—549; S. C. 12 L. J. Ex. 10; 6 Jur. 954.)

The general rule of law respecting negligence is, that although there may have been negligence on the part of the plaintiff, yet unless he might by the exercise of ordinary care have avoided the consequences of the defendant's negligence, he is entitled to recover. Therefore, where the defendant negligently drove his horses and waggon against and killed an ass, which had been left in the highway fettered in the forefeet, and thus unable to get out of the way of the defendant's waggon, which was going at a smartish pace along the road, it was held, that the jury were properly directed, that although it was an illegal act on the part of the plaintiff so to put the animal on the highway, the plaintiff was entitled to recover.

Case for negligence. The declaration stated, that the plaintiff theretofore, and at the time of the committing of the grievance thereinafter mentioned, to wit, on &c., was lawfully possessed of a

(1) Foll. *Tuff* v. *Warman* (1858) 5 C. B. N. S. 573, 585, 27 L. J. C. P. 322; appr. *Radley* v. *L. & N. W. Ry. Co.* (1876) 1 App. Ca. 754, 759, 46 L. J. Ex. 573; *Spaight* v. *Tedcastle* (1881) 6 App. Ca. 217, 226; *The Bernina* (1887) 12 P. D. 36, 89, 56 L. J. Adm. 38; and see the case discussed, Harvard Law Review, iii. 272—276.—A. C.

certain donkey, which said donkey of the plaintiff was then lawfully in a certain highway, and the defendant was then possessed of a certain waggon and certain horses drawing the same, which said waggon and horses of the defendant were then under the care, government, and direction of a certain then servant of the defendant, in and along the said highway; nevertheless the defendant, by his said servant, so carelessly, negligently, unskilfully, and improperly governed and directed his said waggon and horses, that by and through the carelessness, negligence, unskilfulness, and improper conduct of the defendant, by his said servant, the said waggon and horses of the defendant then ran and struck with great violence against the said donkey of the plaintiff, and thereby then wounded, crushed, and killed the same, &c.

The defendant pleaded not guilty.

At the trial, before Erskine, J., at the last Summer Assizes *for the county of Worcester, it appeared that the plaintiff, having fettered the forefeet of an ass belonging to him, turned it into a public highway, and at the time in question the ass was grazing on the off side of a road about eight yards wide, when the defendant's waggon, with a team of three horses, coming down a slight descent, at what the witness termed a smartish pace, ran against the ass, knocked it down, and the wheels passing over it, it died soon after. The ass was fettered at the time, and it was proved that the driver of the waggon was some little distance behind the horses. The learned Judge told the jury, that though the act of the plaintiff, in leaving the donkey on the highway so fettered as to prevent his getting out of the way of carriages travelling along it, might be illegal, still, if the proximate cause of the injury was attributable to the want of proper conduct on the part of the driver of the waggon, the action was maintainable against the defendant; and his Lordship directed them, if they thought that the accident might have been avoided by the exercise of ordinary care on the part of the driver, to find for the plaintiff. The jury found their verdict for the plaintiff, damages 40s.

[*547]

Godson now moved for a new trial, on the ground of misdirection:

The act of the plaintiff in turning the donkey into the public highway was an illegal one, and, as the injury arose principally from that act, the plaintiff was not entitled to compensation for that injury which, but for his own unlawful act, would never have occurred.

DAVIES
v.
MANN.

(PARKE, B.: The declaration states that the ass was lawfully on the highway, and the defendant has not traversed that allegation; therefore it must be taken to be admitted.)

The principle of law, as deducible from the cases, is, that where an accident is the result of faults on both sides, neither party can [*548] maintain an action. Thus, in *Butterfield* v. *Forrester* (1), *it was held that one who is injured by an obstruction on a highway, against which he fell, cannot maintain an action, if it appear that he was riding with great violence and want of ordinary care, without which he might have seen and avoided the obstruction. So, in *Vennall* v. *Garner* (2), in case for running down a ship, it was held, that neither party can recover when both are in ‚the wrong; and BAYLEY, B., there says, "I quite agree that if the mischief be the result of the combined negligence of the two, they must both remain *in statu quo*, and neither party can recover against the other." Here the plaintiff, by fettering the donkey, had prevented him from removing himself out of the way of accident; had his forefeet been free, no accident would probably have happened. *Pluckwell* v. *Wilson* (3), *Luxford* v. *Large* (4), and *Lynch* v. *Nurdin* (5), are to the same effect.

LORD ABINGER, C. B.:

I am of opinion that there ought to be no rule in this case. The defendant has not denied that the ass was lawfully in the highway, and therefore we must assume it to have been lawfully there; but even were it otherwise, it would have made no difference, for as the defendant might, by proper care, have avoided injuring the animal, and did not, he is liable for the consequences of his negligence, though the animal may have been improperly there.

PARKE, B.:

This subject was fully considered by this Court in the case of *Bridge* v. *The Grand Junction Railway Company* (6), where, as appears to me, the correct rule is laid down concerning negligence, namely, that the negligence which is to preclude a plaintiff from recovering in an action of this nature, must be such as that he [*549] could, by *ordinary care, have avoided the consequences of the

(1) 10 R. R. 433 (11 East, 60).   (5) 55 R. R. 191 (1 Ad. & El. (N. S.)
(2) 38 R. R. 578 (1 Cr. & M. 21).   29; 4 P. & D. 672).
(3) 5 Car. & P. 375.   (6) 49 R. R. 590 (3 M. & W. 246).
(4) *Ibid.* 421.

defendant's negligence. I am reported to have said in that case, and I believe quite correctly, that "the rule of law is laid down with perfect correctness in the case of *Butterfield* v. *Forrester*, that, although there may have been negligence on the part of the plaintiff, yet unless he might, by the exercise of ordinary care, have avoided the consequences of the defendant's negligence, he is entitled to recover; if by ordinary care he might have avoided them, he is the author of his own wrong." In that case of *Bridge* v. *Grand Junction Railway Company*, there was a plea imputing negligence on both sides; here it is otherwise; and the Judge simply told the jury, that the mere fact of negligence on the part of the plaintiff in leaving his donkey on the public highway, was no answer to the action, unless the donkey's being there was the immediate cause of the injury; and that, if they were of opinion that it was caused by the fault of the defendant's servant in driving too fast, or, which is the same thing, at a smartish pace, the mere fact of putting the ass upon the road would not bar the plaintiff of his action. All that is perfectly correct; for, although the ass may have been wrongfully there, still the defendant was bound to go along the road at such a pace as would be likely to prevent mischief. Were this not so, a man might justify the driving over goods left on a public highway, or even over a man lying asleep there, or the purposely running against a carriage going on the wrong side of the road.

GURNEY, B., and ROLFE, B., concurred.

Rule refused.

DAVIES
v.
MANN.

———————

BOURKE *v.* LLOYD.

(10 Meeson & Welsby, 550—553; S. C. 12 L. J. Ex. 4; 2 Dowl. N. S. 452.)

> Where a cause, in which there are several issues, is referred to an arbitrator, and the costs of the cause are to abide the event of the award, the arbitrator must award specifically on each issue, and a general award, that the plaintiff had good cause of action against the defendant, and that the defendant should pay to the plaintiff a certain sum, together with the costs of the action and of the reference, is bad.

DEBT for money lent, money paid, interest, and on an account stated. Pleas, *nunquam indebitatus*, and payment, on which issues were joined. The cause was referred, before trial, to an arbitrator, by a Judge's order, which directed that the costs of the cause should abide the event of the award, and that the costs of the reference should be in the discretion of the arbitrator. The arbitrator

1842.
Nov. 22.

*Exch. of
Pleas.*

[550]

BOURKE
v.
LLOYD.

awarded, that the plaintiff had good cause of action against the defendant, and directed that the defendant should pay to the plaintiff 20l., together with the costs of the action and of the reference : but he did not award specifically on each issue.

A rule having been obtained for setting aside this award, on the ground that the arbitrator had not determined the issues in the action, so as to enable the Master to tax the costs,

Cowling, in last Easter Term (May 3), showed cause :

This not being a case in which any verdict had been given, it was not strictly necessary for the arbitrator to find specifically on the issues. But if it was, his directing the defendant to pay the plaintiff 20l., after having stated that the plaintiff had good cause of action, amounts in effect to a finding for the plaintiff on all the issues, and makes the award sufficiently certain. In *Dicas* v. *Jay* (1), where the declaration contained eleven special counts for negligence as an attorney, together with common counts for money paid, &c., and the cause was referred by order of Nisi Prius to an arbitrator, who found that the plaintiff had good cause of action for 23l. 14s. 10d., and directed a verdict to be entered up for that sum, the award was

[*551]

held sufficiently *certain. In *Duckworth* v. *Harrison* (2), where, to a declaration in debt, the general issue and a set-off were pleaded, and the cause was referred by consent to arbitration, " the costs of the reference and award to abide the event ; " and the arbitrators found that the plaintiff was not entitled to recover in the action, and had not any cause of action against the defendant, but said nothing as to the set-off ; it was nevertheless held that the award was final, and that the defendant might maintain an action for the costs of the reference and award. In the present case, there could have been no intention that the arbitrator should find specifically on each issue, and there will be no difficulty in taxing the costs, the nding amounting to a general verdict for the plaintiff.

Ramshay, contrà :

The arbitrator was bound, under this order of reference, to find specifically on all the issues, since otherwise there would be no legal event of the cause, to enable the plaintiff, under the new rules, to obtain his costs. [He cited *Norris* v. *Daniel* (3), *Doe* d. *Madkins*

(1) 5 Bing. 281 ; 2 Moo. & P. 448.   (3) 38 R. R. 530 (10 Bing. 507 ; 4
(2) 51 R. R. 671 (4 M. & W. 432).   Moo. & Sc. 383).

v. *Horner* (1), *Gisborne* v. *Hart* (2), *England* v. *Davison* (3),   BOURKE
Dibben v. *Marquis of Anglesea* (4) and *Hunt* v. *Hunt* (5).]   v.
LLOYD.
Cur. adv. vult.

The judgment of the COURT was now delivered by   [552]

LORD ABINGER, C. B. :

This was a rule obtained and argued in Easter Term, to set aside
an award, and the Court took time to consider, in consequence of
a suggestion at the Bar that a case in this Court was at variance
with, and had thrown a doubt upon, the propriety of several
decisions in which it had been laid down, that where a cause with
several issues was referred, the costs of the cause to abide the event,
the arbitrator must award specifically on each issue. The case
referred to was that of *Duckworth* v. *Harrison;* and from the
observations said to have been made on that case by Mr. Justice
COLERIDGE, in *England* v. *Davison,* it would seem that the learned
Judge supposed that I had pronounced an opinion favourable to
the decision in *Dibben* v. *Marquis of Anglesea,* and indeed sustained
that decision. This, however, is a misapprehension *of what I   [*553]
said. In the case of *Duckworth* v. *Harrison,* the costs of the
reference and award, not of the action, were to abide the event;
and the Court, after some hesitation, held that the meaning of the
parties was, that all the costs of the reference and award should
abide the event of the award; so that, if the plaintiff succeeded, he
should have all those costs, and the defendant, on the other hand,
if he succeeded, should have all; and I stated, or certainly meant
to state, that if the parties had intended that the costs of the
reference and award should be divided, and apportioned to each
issue, they should have provided for it in the submission. It is a
mistake, therefore, to suppose that the Court intended to confirm
the case of *Dibben* v. *Marquis of Anglesea.* We must follow the
current of decisions on this subject, by which it is established that
if the cause is referred, where several issues are joined, and the
costs of the cause are to abide the event, the arbitrator must decide
each issue.
Rule absolute.

(1) 47 R. R. 573 (8 Ad. & El. 235 ; 3   (3) 9 Dowl. P. C. 1052.
N. & P. 344).   (4) 2 Cr. & M. 722.
  (2) 52 R. R. 624 (5 M. & W. 50).   (5) 49 R. R. 717 (5 Dowl. P. C. 442).

1842.
Nov. 9.

*Exch. of
Pleas.*

[562]

DAVID WATSON PURDON AND THOMAS PURDON, v. WILLIAM PURDON.

(10 Meeson & Welsby, 562—563 ; S. C. 12 L. J. Ex. 3.)

Assumpsit by the executors of the payee of a promissory note, against the defendant as maker. The plaintiff produced the note with the following indorsement upon it, signed by the defendant and one of the plaintiffs: " HULL, 1838. Memorandum, that the ¦sum of 1*l*. 7*s*. 6*d*., one quarter's interest, was paid on the within note.—WILLIAM PURDON, THOS. PURDON:"
Held, that this was sufficient evidence of an account stated with the executors, without any proof of the time of the testator's death.

ASSUMPSIT by the plaintiffs, as executors of David Purdon, on a promissory note for 110*l*., made by the defendant in the lifetime of David Purdon. There were also counts for money lent by and on an account stated with the testator, alleging promises to him, and on an account stated with the plaintiffs as executors of D. Purdon, and a promise to them as such executors. Plea, the Statute of Limitations.

At the trial before Lord Denman, Ch. J., at the last Yorkshire Assizes, the only evidence given by the plaintiffs was the promissory note (which was above six years old), with the following indorsement upon it: " HULL, 1838. Memorandum, that the sum of 1*l*. 7*s*. 6*d*., one quarter's interest, was paid on the within note.—WILLIAM PURDON (the defendant), THOMAS PURDON," (the plaintiff). No evidence was given of the time of the death of David Purdon, the testator. It was objected for the defendant, that the plaintiffs ought to be nonsuited, since, as there was no proof of the time of the testator's death, there was no evidence of an account stated with him at the date of the memorandum, as he might not be alive at that time: and even admitting the memorandum to be evidence of an account stated with the testator, still there was no count upon an account stated with him, and a promise to pay the executors. It was also contended, that as the plaintiff Thomas Purdon was not alleged in the memorandum to be executor, there was no evidence of an account stated with him. The learned Judge overruled the objections; and the jury, under his direction, having found a verdict for the plaintiffs, he gave the defendant leave to move to enter a nonsuit.

[563]   *Jervis* now moved accordingly :

The indorsement upon this note was not sufficient to bar the statute. Although payment of interest admits the currency of the note, it has not the same effect as payment of part of the principal.

It is a payment collateral to the principal debt. In *Jones* v. *Ryder* (1) it was held, that a mere parol statement of an antecedent debt without any new contract or consideration, made within six years before action brought, does not constitute a sufficient cause of action to prevent the operation of the Statute of Limitations. Here the plaintiff was not stated to be the executor, and there was no ground for inferring that the interest had been paid to him. To make an act amount to an account stated, the plaintiff ought to show something equivalent to a promise to pay.

PURDON
v.
PURDON.

PARKE, B. :

Surely this was evidence to go to the jury, It was strong evidence of payment of 1*l.* 7*s.* 6*d.* on account of the note. The payment of interest, it is true, does not necessarily prove that the principal money is due, but surely it is evidence of that fact, and but for the objection the jury would have no hesitation in so finding.

The rest of the COURT concurred.

Rule refused.

HEMING AND WIFE *v.* POWER.

(10 Meeson & Welsby, 564—571; S. C. 11 L. J. Ex. 323; 6 Jur. 588.)

1842.

Exch. of
Pleas.
[564]

Slander. The declaration, after reciting that A. and B., the plaintiffs, were lawful husband and wife, and that B. was the lawful sister of one C., alleged that the defendant spoke of and concerning the plaintiff B. and her intermarriage, and of and concerning C., the false, &c. words following : "It has been ascertained beyond doubt that C. and B. are not only not brother and sister, but man and wife : " Held, first, that the plaintiffs were not bound to prove the introductory averment that B. was the lawful sister of C.; secondly, that the words amounted to a charge of bigamy against B.

SLANDER. The declaration, after the usual introductory averments in declarations for slander, alleged that the plaintiffs, Dempster Heming and Rhoda Mary Charde his wife, before the committing of the grievances, &c. thereinafter mentioned, had been and were lawful husband and wife, and also that before the committing of the said grievances, and at the time of the intermarriage of the said plaintiffs, the said Rhoda Mary Charde was the lawful sister of one Henry Leigh Alleyne, he the said Henry Leigh Alleyne then residing within this realm : yet that the defendant, well knowing the premises, and wickedly and maliciously intending to injure the plaintiffs in their good name and reputation, and to

(1) 51 R. R. 452 (4 M. & W. 32).

bring them into public scandal, infamy, and disgrace, and to cause it to be believed by their neighbours, and others, that the said Rhoda Mary Charde had been guilty of the crimes and misconduct thereinafter mentioned to have been charged upon her, and to subject her to the pains and penalties by the laws of this kingdom made and provided against persons guilty thereof, to wit, on the 1st day of June, 1841, in a certain discourse which the defendant then had of and concerning the said plaintiffs, and of and concerning their said intermarriage, and of and concerning the said Henry Leigh Alleyne, in the presence and hearing of divers subjects of our lady the Queen, falsely and maliciously spoke and published of and concerning the plaintiffs, and of and concerning their said intermarriage, and of and concerning the said Henry Leigh Alleyne, the false, scandalous, malicious, and defamatory words following, of and concerning the plaintiffs, and of and concerning their said intermarriage, and of and concerning the said H. L. Alleyne, that is to say, "It has been ascertained beyond

[*565] doubt, that Mr. *Alleyne (meaning the said H. L. Alleyne) and Mrs. Dempster Heming (meaning the said Rhoda Mary Charde) are not only not brother and sister, but man and wife," (meaning that the said R. M. Charde, being lawfully married to and the lawful wife of the said H. L. Alleyne, had afterwards feloniously and unlawfully married and taken to husband the said plaintiff, Dempster Heming, the said H. L. Alleyne being then alive, contrary to the form of the statute in such case made and provided) : And also the false, scandalous, malicious, and defamatory words following, of and concerning the plaintiffs, and of and concerning their said intermarriage, and of and concerning the said H. L. Alleyne, that is to say, "It has been ascertained beyond doubt, that Mr. Alleyne (meaning the said H. L. Alleyne) and Mrs. Dempster Heming (meaning &c.) are not only not brother and sister, but man and wife" (meaning that the said R. M. Charde had been guilty of felony in marrying the said plaintiff Dempster Heming): And also the false, scandalous, malicious, defamatory words following, of and concerning the plaintiffs, and of and concerning their said intermarriage, and of and concerning the said H. L. Alleyne, that is to say, "It has been ascertained beyond doubt, that Mr. Alleyne (meaning the said H. L. Alleyne) and Mrs. Heming (meaning &c.) are not only not brother and sister, but man and wife :" And also the false, scandalous, malicious, and defamatory words following, of and concerning the said plaintiffs, and of and concerning their

said intermarriage, and of and concerning the said H. L. A., that is
to say, " Mr. Alleyne (meaning the said H. L. A.) and Mrs. Heming
(meaning &c.) are man and wife ;" by means whereof &c.

The defendant pleaded not guilty.

The cause was tried before Williams, J., at the last Spring
Assizes for the county of Leicester, when it was objected on behalf
of the defendant that the plaintiffs ought to be nonsuited, inasmuch as there was no proof of the introductory *averment in the   [*566]
declaration that the female plaintiff was the lawful sister of Henry
Leigh Alleyne. The learned Judge overruled the objection, and
the plaintiffs obtained a verdict with one farthing damages, leave
being reserved to the defendant to move to enter a nonsuit. The
learned Judge certified under the recent stat. 3 & 4 Vict. c. 24, s. 2,
that the grievance in respect of which the trial was brought was
wilful and malicious.

In last Easter Term (April 19),

> The *Solicitor-General* moved accordingly on the point reserved,
> and also in arrest of judgment :

First, as to the nonsuit. The declaration alleges that Mrs.
Heming was " the lawful sister of Henry Leigh Alleyne," and that
allegation ought to have been proved, as the essence of the slander
rested on the existence of that relationship. * * *

Then the declaration is bad in arrest of judgment. As there is   [567]
no allegation of special damage, if the words do not impute felony,
they are not actionable. The subject-matter of the charge is
bigamy ; but inasmuch as the declaration itself alleges that Mrs.
Heming and Mr. Alleyne were brother and sister, it is clear that
there could have been no valid marriage between them, and consequently in marrying the plaintiff she could not have been guilty
of the crime of bigamy. It is no slander to charge a person with
a crime of which he could not by any possibility be guilty, because
he is in no jeopardy : Buller's N. P. 5. Thus, in *Snag* v. *Gee* (1),
it was held that no action would lie for slander *in asserting that   [*568]
the plaintiff had murdered J. S. when it appeared that J. S. was
still alive. In *Jackson* v. *Adams* (2), it was held that inasmuch
as the property of the bell ropes of a church is in the churchwardens
of the parish, it was not actionable to say of a churchwarden that
he stole the bell ropes of his parish.

(1) 4 Co. Rep. 16.   (2) 42 R. R. 633 (2 Bing. N. C. 402 ;
                                        2 Scott, 599).

(PARKE, B.: That was clearly only a charge of a breach of trust.)

In *Williams* v. *Stott* (1), the Court appears to have been of opinion that a verbal imputation of fraudulent embezzlement in the office of chamberlain of certain commonable lands belonging to a corporation would not be actionable, on the ground that the party was not in such a situation that he could be guilty of such a felony.

PARKE, B.:

I think that in this case we ought to grant no rule.

As to the first objection, that has already received an answer. In the first place, supposing this averment to be an immaterial one, then it was unnecessary to be proved; on the other hand, if it was a material averment, then the defendant, not having traversed. must be taken to have admitted it: but it seems to me it is clearly an immaterial averment, and upon that ground no rule will be granted.

Then as to the other objection, in arrest of judgment, it is this: that the words which are ascribed to the defendant, taken in connection with what the plaintiff has averred, show that the offence of bigamy could not have been committed, and therefore that Mrs. Heming could not have been in any danger, as the person whom she was charged to have previously married was her brother. If it proceeds upon that ground, it appears to me that there is no foundation for the objection. The complaint against the defendant [*569] is *the making of a false charge against the plaintiff, and if you take the words of the defendant altogether, they clearly amount to a charge of felony, and a false one, against Mrs. Heming. According to the averment in the declaration, it is a charge of felony, for the defendant does not admit she was the sister of Alleyne; on the contrary, his statement is, that Mrs. Heming, who is now married to the plaintiff, instead of being sister to Alleyne, was his wife; if so, she was guilty of the offence of bigamy in intermarrying with the plaintiff. The ground of the matter being actionable is that a charge is made, which, if it were true, would endanger the plaintiff in point of law. Here, if it were true, the plaintiff would be in danger of a prosecution for bigamy, and therefore the matter said to have been uttered is actionable. The averment in the declaration, that she was not the wife of Alleyne, but his sister, appears to

(1) 38 R. R. 724 (1 Cr. & M. 675).

me to make no difference in the case; it is no answer to show that
the charge is false, and that is the whole inference to be drawn
from what is averred in the declaration.   The cases which have been
referred to are all distinguishable.   With respect to that of *Snag* v.
Gee, it appears to me that, according to the true understanding of
that case, it is a very different one from the present.   There the
averment was that the defendant said of the plaintiff, "Thou hast
killed my wife;" and there was an allegation in the declaration
that he was speaking of a person who was then alive.   The allegation must have been such as that the Court could not but imply
that, at the time the words were uttered, they were uttered of a
person known to the parties in whose presence they were spoken,
to be alive; and therefore that they could not infer it was meant to
impute a felony.   The fact being known that she was alive at the
time would show that the word "kill" was not used in the sense of
taking away life.   That was also the meaning of the Court in the
case of *Williams* v. *Stott*.   The reason why the action lies is, that
those persons who heard the slander might *infer that the plaintiff   [*570]
had been guilty of a felony, and might make a charge founded
upon it: but if at the time the words are uttered, there are
circumstances which clearly show the words are not used in the
sense of imputing a felony, then the charge falls to the ground,
and no action will lie.   And it is only on that ground that the case
of *Snag* v. *Gee* can be supported in point of law.

Applying this principle of construction, it seems to me that in
this case there is no ground to arrest the judgment.   The words
import a charge of felony, and must be taken so to have been
understood by those who heard them; and that charge is false.
That is sufficient to render them actionable in point of law.

ALDERSON, B. :

I am of the same opinion upon both points.   As to the first, it
seems to me that the *Solicitor-General* never escaped from the
difficulty which the Court put upon him, from the moment it was
admitted by him that this immaterial allegation need not be proved
by the plaintiff.

Then as to the second point that has been made, in arrest of
judgment, I take the rule to be this: the words, to be actionable,
must impute a criminal offence; that is, the words, if true, must
be such that the plaintiff would be guilty of a criminal offence.
Here the words are, "that it is now ascertained beyond all doubt

that Mrs. Heming and Mr. Alleyne are not brother and sister, but man and wife:" imputing that she was the wife of Alleyne. Surely it is for a jury to say whether the defendant does not mean that she has committed the crime of bigamy. Undoubtedly, if the fact were well known by the persons who heard the words uttered, that Mr. Alleyne was the brother of Mrs. Heming, it would be a very proper question to submit to the jury, that their verdict ought to be that there was no *intention of imputing bigamy, but incest. It might be a question in that case whether the words did not convey an imputation different from that charged in the declaration. But as the case stands, it appears not only that the defendant spoke the words, but that he spoke them with the meaning alleged in the declaration. That question has been submitted to the jury, and very properly found for the plaintiffs.

[*571]

ROLFE, B. concurred.

Rule refused.

FURSDON, EXECUTRIX OF FURSDON, *v.* CLOGG.

(10 Meeson & Welsby, 572—576.)

Quære, whether a verbal statement, made by a deceased collector of rents, at the time of paying over to his employer monies received by him from the tenants, as to the person from whom he received a particular sum entered by him in the rental, is admissible in evidence against that person?

Construction of a document given in evidence as an acknowledgment of title under the stat. 3 & 4 Will. IV. c. 27, s. 17 (1).

ASSUMPSIT for the use and occupation of premises alleged to have been held by the defendant as tenant to the plaintiff's testator, who died in 1837. The first count stated a promise to pay to the testator in his lifetime; the second, a promise to the plaintiff as executrix. Pleas, *non assumpsit*, and the Statute of Limitations.

At the trial before Maule, J., at the Devonshire Summer Assizes, 1841, it appeared that the premises in question consisted of a piece of land called the "Four Lords' Land," of which the defendant had been for many years in the occupation, and the property in the several undivided fourth parts whereof had been for a long time in dispute in the Court of Chancery. In the year 1816, the plaintiff's testator obtained a decree of that Court in favour of his title to one undivided fourth part, and for a partition

(1) Rep. by R. P. L. Act, 1874 (37 & 38 Vict. c. 57), s. 9, and replaced by s. 5 of that Act.—A. C.

of the estate; and it appeared that the defendant had attended
before the Commissioner appointed to carry the partition into
effect, and expressed no dissent. It was proved that the testator's
rents were generally collected by his attorney, a Mr. Law: he,
however, on two occasions, had employed one of the plaintiff's
tenants, a person of the name of Charley, who was since dead, to
collect them for him. Mr. Law was examined as a witness for the
plaintiff, and stated that, in the year 1821, he gave Charley the
rentals of the years 1820 and 1821 to collect by, and that Charley
paid him the aggregate of the sums carried out in those rentals in
the paid columns. Among those entries appeared one (in Charley's
handwriting) of the sum of 6*l*. as having been received for the
premises in question; and Mr. Law swore that Charley stated to
him, at the time of making *the above payment, that he had
received that sum from the defendant. This evidence was objected
to by the defendant's counsel, and the learned Judge inclined to
think it inadmissible, but took a note of it. Two letters from the
defendant to the testator's attorney were also put in, which, it was
contended, amounted to a sufficient acknowledgment of title to
prevent the operation of the Statute of Limitations. The first
was dated December 5, 1833, and, after a long statement of the
expenses incurred by the defendant in the course of the litigation
respecting the property, stated that he wished "an arrangement
to be made on reasonable terms, and due consideration and
compensation to be made." The other letter was dated August 30,
1837, (after the testator's death), and was in answer to an application by the attorney for payment of the arrears of rent; and after
stating that the defendant "was involved in law from 1805 to 1816
concerning the Four Lords' Land, which had given him great
trouble and expense, and that with respect to the expenses, it was
reasonable that the lords of the fee should make him some
recompense accordingly," and after detailing certain particulars as
to the several claims which had been made to the property, that
the plaintiff's testator had been applied to to defend his title as to
one-fourth, but had objected so to do, and that "it appeared reasonable that Mr. Fursdon should vindicate his right to the land,"
rather than that the expenses should fall upon the tenants, the
letter concluded by stating that the writer "begged compassion,
mercy, and pity, and recompense in a satisfactory manner." The
learned Judge thought that these letters amounted to a sufficient
acknowledgment of the title of the testator, and accordingly

FURSDON
v.
CLOGG.

[*573]

FURSDON
c.
CLOGG.

directed a verdict for the plaintiff for the amount claimed, reserving leave to the defendant to move to enter a nonsuit.

In the following Michaelmas Term, *Erle* obtained a rule accordingly, against which, in Michaelmas vacation,

[574]

The *Solicitor-General* showed cause, and contended that the declaration of Charley, as to the payment of rent by the defendant in 1821, was clearly admissible, and was sufficient to charge the defendant in this action. He cited 1 Phill. Evid. pp. 312, 321, 325 (8th edit.), *Barker* v. *Ray* (1), and *Skeffington* v. *Whitehurst* (2) : and the COURT then called upon

Erle and *Taprell*, in support of the rule :

They insisted that the parol declaration of Charley, who was merely a person employed on two occasions only, not a regular steward or agent, was not admissible in evidence; that none of the cases went further than to declare the written entries of such a person, charging himself with the receipt of money, evidence after his death, and that it would be very dangerous to extend the rule to mere verbal declarations of such an agent. They referred to the following authorities: *Higham* v. *Ridgway* (3), *Doe* d. *Human* v. *Pettet* (4), *Ivat* v. *Finch* (5), *Davies* v. *Pierce* (6), *Peaceable* v. *Watson* (7), *Holloway* v. *Rakes* (8), *Doe* d. *Foster* v. *Williams* (9), *Barker* v. *Ray*, *Woolway* v. *Rowe* (10).

[*575]

Crowder and *Montague Smith*, who also appeared for the plaintiff, were then heard upon this point, and contended *that there was no distinction in law as to the admissibility of written and parol declarations made by deceased agents : that it was in all such cases a question for the jury as to the weight and value of the evidence, but that the law of England made no distinction whatever between matter by parol and in writing, except where the writing was by deed.

The COURT took time to consider this point, and in Easter Term, desired that the case should be argued also on the other question, as to the effect of the letters as an acknowledgment of title. It was argued accordingly by

(1) 2 Russ. 67.
(2) 3 Y. & C. 21.
(3) 10 R. R. 235 (10 East, 109).
(4) 5 B. & Ald. 223.
(5) 9 R. R. 716 (1 Taunt. 141).
(6) 1 R. R. 419 (2 T. R. 53).

(7) 13 R. R. 552 (4 Taunt. 16).
(8) 1 R. R. 421 (2 T. R. 55).
(9) Cowp. 621.
(10) 40 R. R. 264 (1 Ad. & El. 114 ; 3 Nev. & M. 849).

The *Solicitor-General, Crowder,* and *Montague Smith,* for the plaintiff:

They contended that the letters read in evidence clearly amounted to a sufficient acknowledgment of title, within the terms of the stat. 2 & 3 Will. IV. c. 71, s. 14; that they were in effect an admission of the testator's right to sue for the rent, and an assertion of a claim by way of set-off, by reason of the cost of the litigation about the property.

Taprell (with whom was *Erle*), in support of the rule, argued, first, that the letter of the 30th August, 1837, did not contain a sufficient acknowledgment to prevent the operation of the statute, because it was not made to the party having title to the land; and that the word "rent," in the 14th section, being coupled with the word "land," meant a rent-charge or other freehold rent issuing out of the land, not a mere conventional rent for the occupation of the land: and secondly, that the letters, taken altogether, did not import any explicit or unambiguous acknowledgment of title in the testator.

The COURT (1), however, were clearly of opinion that at *all events the letter of the 30th August, 1837, which was written in answer to a claim for the rent made on behalf of the testator, was in effect an admission that rent was due, and therefore an acknowledgment of the title of the testator, in whose right the plaintiff, the executrix, claimed the rent. It was unnecessary, therefore, to enter upon the other point, which had been so elaborately argued, since on this ground the rule must be discharged. [*576]

Rule discharged.

————•————

THE PARRETT NAVIGATION COMPANY *v.* ROBINS (2).

(10 Meeson & Welsby, 593—602; S. C. 12 L. J. Ex. 81.)

By an Act of Parliament, 6 & 7 Will. IV. c. ci. (local and personal), certain persons were incorporated for the purpose of improving the navigation of the river Parrett, and they were thereby empowered to take tolls in respect of the transit or conveyance of goods thereon: Held, that in the absence of any express enactment on the subject in the Act. the duties of

(1) Lord Abinger, C. B., Parke, B., Alderson, B., and Rolfe, B.
(2) Cited in *Cracknell* v. *Mayor of*

Thetford (1869) 4 C. P. 629, 634; 38 L. J. C. P. 353.—A. C.

the Company were confined to matters relating to the navigation, and that they were not liable for the sewerage of the river, as to clear away weeds, which, though injurious to the adjoining lands, were no detriment to the navigation.

THIS was an action of trespass, for taking four tables of the plaintiffs. The defendant by his plea justified the taking of one table, on the ground, that the plaintiffs were duly fined 1l., at a court of sewers for the southern division of the county of Somerset,

[*594] for not cutting the weeds growing *in the bottom of the river Isle, between Muchelney Bridge and Muchelney Lock. The defendant also pleaded three other pleas, in which he stated that the plaintiffs were duly fined 2l. for not cutting the weeds growing in the bottom of the river Parrett, between Thorney Bridge and the southern boundary of the borough of Langport Eastover ; 3l. for not cutting the weeds growing in the bottom of the river Parrett, which lies within the borough of Langport Eastmore ; and 4l. for not cutting the weeds growing in the bottom of the river Parrett, between the northern boundary of the borough of Langport Eastover and Hatbe. The plaintiffs, in their several replications to these pleas, denied that they had been duly fined, whereupon issue was joined. The facts were stated, under a Judge's order, for the opinion of the Court, in the following case :

The rivers Isle and Yeo, which have been immemorially navigable, fall into the river Parrett a little above Langport, and this river, which has also been immemorially navigable, runs through Langport and Bridgewater into the Bristol Channel. These rivers drain a considerable tract of country, and are under the control of the Commissioners of Sewers for the southern division of the county of Somerset, who cause them to be viewed frequently by their officers, and who present to the Courts all nuisances, annoyances, and impediments therein. Weeds grow up from the bottom of the rivers in the spring of the year, and die in the fall. During the time they are growing, the water is buoyed back by them, and after much rain such water inundates the low lands adjoining. Some of these weeds have immemorially been cut at different times of the summer, so as to prevent them being an impediment to the passage of the water. The neighbouring lands are greatly benefited in winter by the floods, and also in some degree in dry summers, by the water ponded back by the weeds. The corporation of Langport, who hold lands, and receive the rents and profits of them, have the

[*595] exclusive right of fishery *in the river Parrett, both above and below

the town of Langport, to the extent of the bounds of the borough of Langport, which right of fishery, together with the lands, they have held prescriptively from the Crown, but not as parcel of or as annexed to the manor; and the Bishop of Bath and Wells, as lord of the adjoining manor of Huish Episcopi, through which the river Parrett runs, has the exclusive right of fishery above the borough of Langport, to the extent of his manor. The corporation of Langport have always, out of the rents and profits arising from their lands and otherwise, cut the weeds within their fishery. The weeds have never been cut in the river Parrett above Langport, nor in the river Yeo. In the river Isle, they have been cut by the occupiers of ancient inclosures opposite to and to the length of their frontages, as far as the middle of the river. Opposite to the common moors, the occupiers of tenements, to which right of stackage in the moors belonged, have cut specified portions of the weeds, and which portions were marked by posts put into the ground. Below Langport, the weeds in the Parrett through the parishes of Curry Rivell and Aller, the only parishes where it was necessary to cut them, were from beyond the time of living memory down to the passing of the Poor Law Amendment Act (4 & 5 Will. IV. c. 76), cut by the overseers of the poor of the respective parishes. These overseers had no lands as overseers, and the expenses were charged in their accounts. Since the passing of the Act, these expenses have been disallowed by the auditors of the union, and the weeds have remained uncut. In the year 1836, an Act 6 & 7 Will. IV. c. ci., local and personal, was passed, intituled, "An Act for improving the Navigation of a portion of the River Parrett, and for making a Navigable Canal to Barrington, all in the county of Somerset," under which the Parrett Navigation Company, constituted by that Act, have levied the toll thereby authorized to be taken, and have erected several locks across the river, and *they have purchased strips of land abutting upon the rivers Isle and Parrett on one side thereof, throughout the whole of the navigation, for making a towing path on, and have actually formed and are now using that path. They have also made and completed various improvements in the navigation of the Parrett, and have accelerated and improved the drainage of the neighbouring lands. It would be rather a benefit of that Company, although injurious to the landowners, to leave the weeds uncut.

Fines of 1*l.*, 2*l.*, 3*l.*, and 4*l.* have been imposed upon the Parrett Navigation Company, by the Court of Sewers, for not cutting the

PARRETT
NAVIGATION
COMPANY
v.
ROBINS.

[*596]

weeds in the rivers Isle and Parrett, as follows, viz.: The fine of
1*l.* for not cutting the weeds in the river Isle; the fine of 2*l.* for
not cutting the weeds in that part of the river Parrett which
is above Langport; the fine of 3*l.* for not cutting the weeds in
that part of the river Parrett which comprises the fishery of
the Langport corporation; and the fine of 4*l.* for not cutting the
weeds in that part of the river Parrett below Langport.   The
whole of which portions of the rivers are comprised in the Parrett
Navigation Act.

On the 22nd of September, 1841, at the Sewers Court, held at
Langport, it was agreed that the opinion of this Court should be
taken as to the liability of the Navigation Company to cut these
weeds, and the power of the Commissioners of Sewers to compel
them to do so by fine, or any other and what mode; when all the
necessary proceedings, and the levying of the distresses, were to be
admitted to have been made in due form, so as to bring before the
Court the real questions of the liability of the Company to cut the
weeds, and the jurisdiction of the Commissioners in imposing the
fines, which questions were as follows: As to the fines of 1*l.* and
2*l.*, whether the Parrett Navigation Company, or the land-owners,
or the Commissioners of Sewers, or all or any two and which of

[*597]   them jointly, and to what extent, are liable.   As to *the fine of 3*l.*,
whether the Parrett Navigation Company, or the Langport corpora-
tion, or the land-owners, or the Commissioners of Sewers, or any
and which of them, and to what extent, are liable.   As to the fine of
4*l.*, whether the Parrett Navigation Company alone, or the Parrett
Navigation Company and the land-owners jointly, and to what
extent, or the land-owners alone, or the overseers of the poor, or
the Commissioners of Sewers, are so liable.   And whether, in the
above instances, the Commissioners had power to impose fines on
the Company, or to compel them in any other and what mode to
cut the weeds.   And it was agreed, that, in submitting the points
for the opinion of the Court, it should be left to the Court, if they
should think fit so to do, to mark the liability of the Company (if
they should be found to be liable at all), either solely or jointly, by
dividing the fines; either party to be at liberty to refer to any of
the clauses in the above Act "for improving the navigation of a
portion of the river Parrett, and for making a navigable canal to
Barrington, all in the county of Somerset."

The plaintiffs' points marked for argument were, that they were
not subject to the obligation of cutting the weeds growing in the

river mentioned in this case ; and that, at all events, they were not finable for any omission in cutting them.

The defendant's points were, that the right given to the plaintiffs by 6 Will. IV. c. ci. (local and personal), to demand and receive toll in respect of the conveyance of goods on the rivers Parrett and Isle, was such a beneficial interest in those rivers, as to render the plaintiffs liable to the burthen of cleansing and scouring those parts of the two rivers to which the plaintiffs' right extends.

Cowling, for the plaintiffs :

The Company of Proprietors are not liable. They were incorporated for the particular purpose of making the Parrett a navigable river, and of *constructing a canal.   The preamble of the Act of Parliament shows that ; for it recites those, and those only, as the objects contemplated by the Legislature ; and the 3rd section enacts, " that the said Company shall be, and are thereby authorized and required to make, complete, and maintain certain improvements in the navigation of the said river Parrett, as may be necessary to secure a depth of three feet of water in some part of the stream throughout the whole course of the said river," &c.   There is no express direction in the Act that the Company are to be liable to cut these weeds, nor by implication is any such burthen imposed upon them.   They are merely to do such things as are essential for or tend to the improvement of the navigation ; to defray the expense of which, they are, by the 121st section, empowered to take " tolls, rates, or duties," for tonnage.   The 73rd section, which directs the Company to fence off &c. lands adjoining the towing-path, enacts, that " in case the said Company shall make use of the present embankments of the said river Parrett, or of any river or stream which falls into the same, for such towing-paths or other works, they shall thenceforward be liable to the future repairs of such part of the banks as they may use as aforesaid."   Under that section, the Company would clearly not be liable to repair any part of the banks not used by them, but according to the argument on the other side they must be so now.   The Company have a discretionary power, under certain restrictions, to allow the water to come up the river, and in the event of any damage arising therefrom to the adjoining lands, they are made responsible.   But there is no direction to be found in the Act as to the matter in question, and therefore the charge of clearing away the weeds must remain with those to whom it originally belonged.

[*598]

Manning, Serjt., for the defendant :

A common-law obligation rests upon persons having power to navigate a *river, to cleanse and scour it, inasmuch as they have the benefit of the navigation. In the Book of Assize, 37, pl. 10, there is the following passage : " Commission fuit ag al certeines gents denquī dun river que fuit estopp̄ a le anusans de pais, & per q̄ux & en que def. fuit estopp & per enq̄st fuit trouve q̄ il fuit estopp̄ per cause de non user puis la prim̄ pestilence, & q̄ il naū pas este mondr̄ de tep̄s donc memor̄ ne court, ne q̄ nul devoit ceo mondr̄ de droit, mes ils disont oustr̄ que L'abbe de D. avoit seignioury dun part per le ewe, & le countee de H dauter part, & q̄ ils avoient pischerie en m̄ la river, & q̄ iiij villes & nosme lour nosmes avont lour passage en mesm la riṽ pour lour easemēt ; & ce p̄sentmēt fuit maude en bank le Roy, & hors de ceo record issist br̄e a distr̄ L abbe & le coūtee & aux y les iiij villes, de rūdr̄, per q̄ ils ne duissent monder̄ ceo fosse &c. & L abbe & la countee viendront, & dis q'l3 ne duissent estr̄ charge, depuis q̄ fuit trove per m̄ la pres q̄ nul de droit duist mondr̄ le riṽ & a pluis fort q'l puit estre pris touts les villes q̄ avont cōmon passage & easemēt de m̄ la riṽ duissent ceo monder. Greene donq3 vous ne dedites pas q vos naves pischer̄ illonques et issuit ceo est profit, *et saches de cert q̄ en cas si soit troṽe q̄ les villes nout my lour passage en cel river*, que vous deux serra charge del mondr̄ entierment ; & sic ad judicium, &c." Here the plaintiffs have the benefit of this navigation, and are empowered to take the toll, and therefore they are liable to cleanse the river. It matters not whether they are solely liable, or whether other persons are liable with them, because if they are liable at all, they are finable under the statute of 23 Hen. VIII. c. 5, which gives the Commissioners of Sewers jurisdiction : Year Book, 32 Edw. II., fol. 1, pl. 2. In the case of the *Repairs of Bridges*, &c. (1), it is said, " He who hath the land adjoining ought of common right, without prescription, to scour and cleanse the ditches next to the way to his

land, and *therewith agreeth the book of 8 Hen. VII. 5. But he who hath land adjoining, without prescription, is not bound to repair the way. So, of a common river ; of common right, all who have ease and passage by it, ought to cleanse and scour it ; for a common river is as a common street, as it is said in 22 Ass. and 37 Ass. 10. But he who hath land adjoining to the river is not bound to cleanse the river, unless he hath the benefit of it, *scil.*, a toll or a fishery, or other profit." That is an express authority, as

(1) 13 Co. Rep. 33.

here these places have the benefit of a toll upon the river. In
Warren v. *Dix* (1), a jury impanelled to inquire and present at a
Court of Commissioners of Sewers, presented that A. was benefited
by the sewers; and he received a summons to show cause why he
should not pay; he neglected to traverse the presentment, and
a distress was levied for the amount of the rate; and it was held at
Nisi Prius that these facts were a justification in an action of
trespass for taking the distress, as the presentment, if duly made,
and not traversed, justified the Commissioners in issuing the
warrant of distress. That shows that where the Commissioners
have jurisdiction, they may fine.

Cowling, in reply:

There is no general rule of law which imposes this duty of
cleansing the river upon the Company, as arising out of the right
to take toll, and therefore the liability, if any, must arise out of the
Act of Parliament. In *The Lancaster Canal Company* v. *Parnaby* (2),
TINDAL, Ch. J., in delivering judgment in the Court of Exchequer
Chamber, says, "The principal objection in this case was, that the
clause recited in the declaration, and which is therein stated to
have cast a duty on the Company to remove the obstruction caused
by the sunken boat, was not obligatory, but was an enabling or
permissive clause only. And we are all of that opinion. Neither
the clause recited, *nor anything in the Act of Parliament contained,   [*601]
imposes such a duty on the defendants below: and the allegation
in the declaration, as to the duty of the Company, seems to have
been founded on a mistake as to the true meaning and effect of
that clause." To impose any such liability as that contended for
would be a great hardship upon the Company. It is found here
that the cutting of the weeds would be injurious, and it is not said
that the weeds were any nuisance to any one. Suppose the owners
of the adjoining land were liable *ratione tenuræ* to cut these weeds,
this, being an affirmative Act, would not take away their liability.
There is nothing in the Act which shows an intention to cast this
liability upon the Company, and there is no general rule of law
which applies to it. The Company are therefore not liable.

LORD ABINGER, C. B.:

I am of opinion that the Court of Sewers cannot impose these
fines on the plaintiffs. It appears to me that the Act of 6 & 7 Will. IV.

(1) 3 Car. & P. 71.   (2) 52 R. R. 335 (11 Ad. & El. 242).

PARRETT
NAVIGATION
COMPANY
v.
ROBINS.

c. ci., so far as it relates to the river Parrett, was passed for the purpose of improving the navigation of a portion of that river, and gave toll to the Company of Proprietors for that purpose. The Company have a right to do whatever is essential for carrying out the purposes of the Act; but it does not charge them with any liability in respect of matters not essential for the improvement of the navigation; and the case expressly states that it will be for the benefit of the Company to leave the weeds alone. Even supposing that the parties who take toll on a river are liable at common law to cleanse it, still here the toll is given for the purposes of the navigation, and the omission complained of is beneficial for the Company; and I cannot conceive how they can be liable to a fine for acting as the Legislature has directed.

PARKE, B.:

[*602]

The simple question is, what is to be done under the Act of Parliament for the toll which it authorises *the Company to take? We must, therefore, inquire from whom the Company are to take toll, and for what purposes it is imposed by the Act of Parliament. Now, looking to the 121st section, I think it is clear that the Act authorises them to take toll, not with any view to sewerage, but entirely with a view to render the river navigable. No doubt it is their duty to do all such things as are essential for the proper navigation of the river. That duty they have performed; and it seems to me, on this short ground, that the Commissioners of Sewers have no jurisdiction to impose thes finese. As to the common-law liability, the plaintiffs may be bound at common law to do whatever is requisite for the navigation; but here it is sought to impose a fine in respect of an act of omission, the performance of which would be a detriment to the navigation.

GURNEY, B., concurred.

ROLFE, B.:

The Company have not an exclusive right of navigation, but all persons may navigate the river on payment of reasonable toll.

Judgment for the plaintiffs.

ROUND *v.* HATTON.

(10 Meeson & Welsby, 660—662; S. C. 12 L. J. Ex. 7; 2 Dowl. N. S. 446.)

An action of trespass for an injury to the plaintiff's houses and lands was referred to an arbitrator, who was to settle at what price and on what terms the defendant should purchase the plaintiff's "property." The order of reference gave no power to the arbitrator to determine what the property in question was, nor was there any dispute on the subject. The arbitrator fixed a certain sum as the price at which the defendant should purchase the plaintiff's property, and ordered that the defendant might use the plaintiff's name to enforce certain rights and remedies: Held, that the award was not bad, on the ground of its not specifying what the property was, and that the arbitrator did not exceed his authority in awarding that the defendant should be entitled to use the plaintiff's name.

THIS was an action of trespass for an injury to the plaintiff's messuages, houses, and lands, which by an order of Nisi Prius was referred to an arbitrator, who was to " settle at what price and on what terms the defendant should purchase the plaintiff's property." The order of reference gave no power to the arbitrator, to determine which were the premises in question, and no dispute existed on the subject. The arbitrator awarded, that after deducting certain sums, " the plaintiff is entitled to receive from the said defendant the sum of 153*l.* 11*s.* 6*d.*, which, together with the said sums above directed to be deducted, I settle to be the price at which the said defendant shall purchase the plaintiff's property; " and he directed that the defendant, after conveying the property to him, should be entitled to use the plaintiff's name in enforcing his rights. A rule *nisi* having been obtained for setting aside this award, on the grounds, first, that it was uncertain in not specifying the property in question; and secondly, that the arbitrator had exceeded his authority, in directing that the defendant, after conveyance of the property to him, should be entitled to use the plaintiff's name, in enforcing all rights and remedies against certain parties.

R. V. Richards and *F. V. Lee* showed cause :

First, the arbitrator had no authority under this order of reference to determine what property was in dispute; he was merely to settle the terms and state the price at which the defendant was to purchase the plaintiff's land. It is no objection to the award, that any disputes which should hereafter arise as to the property awarded upon must be determined by extrinsic evidence. It is sufficient if the award can be made certain by that species of proof. Secondly, as to the arbitrator's having exceeded *his

[*661]

authority. In *Burton* v. *Wigley* (1), where an arbitrator, who had authority to decide on what terms a partnership agreement should be cancelled, directed, amongst other things, that the agreement should be cancelled, that one of the partners should have all the debts due to the firm, and should, if necessary, sue for them in the name of his late partner ; it was held, that in authorising one of the parties to sue in the name of the other, the arbitrator had not exceeded his authority. That is a decision directly in point.

W. J. Alexander, in support of the rule :

The award is vague and uncertain. The word "property" is a word of very extensive signification, and if the use of so general a term be allowed, litigation will be promoted rather than checked by arbitration. It was the arbitrator's duty to have described the plaintiff's premises correctly. Secondly, he has exceeded his authority in authorising the defendant to sue in the name of the plaintiff.

LORD ABINGER, C. B. :

I am of opinion that there is no reason for setting aside this award on the ground of uncertainty. The affidavits do not show any dispute as to what was the property to be adjudicated upon. We must therefore assume that the defendant was to buy all the plaintiff's property adjoining the litigated spot. What that property was had been before agreed upon by the parties, and the arbitrator was not called upon to set it out by metes and bounds, but merely to decide on what terms it should be purchased. As to the use of the plaintiff's name, that was a matter within the discretion of the arbitrator, and he might, if he had pleased, have fixed the terms on which the defendant was to indemnify the plaintiff against an action. The rule will be discharged, with costs.

[662]   PARKE, B. :

It is clear that the arbitrator had no power to determine what was the property in dispute. He was simply to fix the price, and the other terms on which it was to be conveyed to the defendant. If there be any difficulty as to the premises awarded upon, that may be an answer to an attachment for not performing the award, but forms no objection to the award itself. As to the use of the plaintiff's name, I think the arbitrator had power to impose that

(1) 1 Bing. N. C. 665; 1 Scott, 610.

condition; or if he had not taken that course, he might have reduced the price that the defendant was to pay for the land.

GURNEY, B., and ROLFE, B., concurred.

Rule discharged, with costs.

DOE D. CARTER AND OTHERS *v.* ROE.

(10 Meeson & Welsby, 670—673; S. C. 12 L. J. Ex. 27; 2 Dowl. N. S. 449.)

> Where a person held premises under an agreement in writing, from quarter to quarter, and the agreement provided that the tenant should quit possession upon receiving six months' notice in writing, and in the event of his losing his license to sell ale, &c., through misconduct at any time during the term, should then forthwith quit possession, on being requested so to do by his landlord: Held, that he had neither a tenancy from year to year, nor a term certain in the premises, within 1 Geo. IV. c. 87, s. 1 (1), so as to entitle the landlord in ejectment to compel him to give security for costs under that Act.

BROS had obtained a rule calling upon one Edward Griffin, the tenant in possession of the premises sought to be recovered by this ejectment, to show cause why, on being admitted defendant, besides entering into the common rule and giving the common undertaking, he should not enter into the recognizance required by the stat. 1 Geo. IV. c. 87, s. 1, to pay the costs and damages which should be recovered by the plaintiff. It appeared that Griffin had been put into possession of the premises in question by one James Collins, who had taken them from a Mr. Spenlove, under a memorandum of agreement dated the 14th of October, 1840, and made between James Collins of the one part and John Francis Spenlove of the other part, signed by both parties, which, after reciting that Spenlove had let to Collins all the messuages and premises in question, to hold them from the 31st December, 1840, as tenant from quarter *to quarter, at the quarterly rent of five guineas, it was witnessed, that Collins, his executors, &c., did thereby agree that he would, during the tenure of the said messuage, obtain a license to sell ale, &c., and that he would quit possession at the end of any three calendar months, upon receiving notice in writing; and that if he should lose his license, he would then forthwith quit possession on being requested by Spenlove, and without any notice for that purpose. The lessors of the plaintiff were the devisees of Spenlove, and had given the tenant a three-months' notice to quit, which expired on the 31st of March, 1842.

[*671]

(1) Rep. See note (1) next page.

DOE d.
CARTER
v.
ROE.

Marsh showed cause :

This application is founded on the stat. 1 Geo. IV. c. 87, s. 1 (1), which enacts "that where the term or interest of any tenant now or hereafter holding under a lease or agreement in writing, any lands, tenements, or hereditaments, for any term or number of years certain, or from year to year, shall have expired or been determined either by the landlord or tenant, by regular notice to quit ; and such tenant, or any one holding or claiming by or under him, shall refuse to deliver up possession accordingly, after lawful demand in writing &c., and the landlord shall thereupon proceed by action of ejectment for the recovery of possession &c.," it shall be lawful for the landlord to move the Court for a rule for such tenant or person to show cause why such tenant or person, on being admitted defendant, besides entering into the common rule and giving the common undertaking &c., "should not enter into a recognizance by himself and two sufficient sureties, in a reasonable sum, conditioned to pay the costs and damages which shall be recovered by the plaintiff in the action &c." Now in this case the agreement does not show either a holding for a term or number of years certain, or a tenancy from year to year. This is an Act conferring an extraordinary remedy on landlords, and therefore the Courts will not extend it, if the case be not strictly within the Act.

[*672]

In *Doe* *d. *Pemberton* v. *Roe* (2), a tenancy for years determinable on lives was decided not to be within the Act. So in *Doe* d. *Bradford* v. *Roe* (3), where a tenant held from year to year, but without a lease or agreement in writing, it was held not to be within the Act. In *Doe* d. *Cardigan* v. *Roe* (4), the statute was held not to extend to a lessee holding over after notice to quit given by himself, where the tenancy had not expired by effluxion of time. And in *Doe* d. *Tindal* v. *Roe* (5), Lord TENTERDEN laid it down generally that the statute "applies only to cases where the tenancy, if by lease, has expired by effluxion of time ; or if by a yearly tenancy, where it has been determined by a regular notice to quit," and he adds, "the words used by it are clear and unambiguous." And PARKE, J., there says, "I own that if it were not for the case of *Doe* d. *Cardigan* v. *Roe*, I should be of opinion that this was a case not only within the mischief, but within the fair meaning of the terms of this

(1) Rep. S. L. R. Act, 1861. See now C. L. P. Act, 1862 (15 & 16 Vict. c. 76), s. 213, &c.

(2) 31 R. R. 135 (7 B. & C. 2).

(3) 5 B. & Ald. 770.

(4) 1 Dowl. & Ry. 540.

(5) 2 B. & Ad. 922 ; 1 Dowl. P. C. 146.

Act. But after the decision in that case, which decision has been acquiesced in for some time, I think it better to observe uniformity in the practice, and not overrule that determination, by going out of the words into that which we may conceive to be the substantial meaning of the Act."

Bros, in support of the rule:

Here the agreement constitutes the tenancy. Although it commences by a recital, it fixes the terms of the tenancy, viz., to hold from the 31st of December, as tenant from quarter to quarter at a quarter's notice; that is a holding for half a year at least, as the lessee is to have the premises for one quarter absolutely, subject to a quarter's notice determining the tenancy. That is enough to constitute an agreement for a term certain, within the meaning of the Act. It is a holding for a term certain, though not from year to year, and the Legislature, *by introducing the words " or from year to year," do not render it less a term certain.

[*673]

LORD ABINGER, C. B. :

The statute itself makes a distinction between a tenancy for a term certain and one from year to year, and I am of opinion that the present holding does not come within either description. The rule must therefore be discharged; but as there was a reasonable doubt whether the case was within the Act, it must be discharged without costs.

PARKE, B. :

The tenancy in this case is not for a term certain, as it depends upon the time when notice to quit is given. As soon as notice is given on the first day of the quarter, then it becomes a term for three months certain; until then, the term is uncertain.

ALDERSON, B. :

I am of the same opinion. The mere insertion in the agreement of a particular time does not render the holding a " term certain."

ROLFE, B., concurred.

Rule discharged, without costs.

1842.
Dec. 3.

*Exch. of
Pleas.*
[694]

COOPER *v.* ROBINSON AND ANOTHER.

(10 Meeson & Welsby, 694—696; S. C. 12 L. J. Ex. 48.)

In replevin, the defendant made cognizance for half a year's rent due at Michaelmas, 1841, for a farm held by the plaintiff under J. H. at a rent of 86*l.*, payable half-yearly at Lady Day and Michaelmas: the plaintiff pleaded in bar, that by an indenture made between J. H. and the plaintiff, purporting to be made on the 1st of Feb., 1841, but which was in fact made after Michaelmas, 1841, and after the rent became due, J. H. released the plaintiff from the rent. The replication set out the indenture, which bore date 1st Feb., 1841, and was a lease from J. H. to the plaintiff of the farm, to hold from 30th July, 1840, for fourteen years, at a rent of 86*l.*, payable half-yearly at Lady Day and Michaelmas, the first payment to be made at Lady Day next: Held, that this was no release of the rent for which the cognizance was made.

REPLEVIN. The defendants made cognizance as the bailiffs of one John Heaton, and alleged that the plaintiff was tenant to Heaton of a farm and lands, at a rent of 86*l.*, payable half-yearly on the 25th of March and the 29th of September, and that the defendants distrained for half a year's rent ending the 29th of September, 1841.

Plea in bar, that after the said rent had become due to the said John Heaton as in the cognizance mentioned, before the said time when &c., by a certain indenture made between the said John Heaton and the plaintiff, to wit, on the 18th of November, 1841, and purporting to be made on the 1st of February, 1841, but which was in fact made after the 29th of September, 1841, and after the said rent had become due and payable (*profert*), the said John Heaton released the plaintiff from the said rent which had so become due, and the payment thereof. Verification.

The replication set out the indenture *in hæc verba*. It bore date the 1st of February, 1841, and was a lease from John Heaton to the plaintiff of a messuage and lands, to hold from the 30th of July, 1840, for the term of fourteen years, at a rent of 86*l.*, payable half-yearly on the 25th of March and 29th of September, the first payment to begin and be made "on the 25th of March next." The replication then averred, that the said rent in the cognizance mentioned was and is rent which became due after the 25th day of [*695] *March next after the said 1st day of February, 1841, that is to say, on the 29th day of September, 1841, as in the cognizance alleged. Verification.

Special demurrer, on the ground (*inter alia*), that the replication has not in any way denied the release stated in the plea in bar; it therefore admits such release, and that the plaintiff is entitled to maintain his action. Joinder in demurrer.

Jervis, in support of the demurrer :.

The replication is informal in several respects; but the defendants will probably contend that the plea in bar is bad. The question is, whether the deed set out in the replication, coupling it with the averments in the plea, operates as a release of the rent. It is submitted that the deed took effect only from the day of its actual execution, which was subsequent to the 29th September, 1841, and therefore the effect was that the plaintiff was released from the payment of rent from July, 1840, until the 25th March next after the execution of the lease, that is, the 25th March, 1842.

(PARKE, B.: But what is there to exempt him from payment, under a former contract antecedent to the deed, of rent due before the 25th March?)

The lease is in operation from the 30th July, 1840.

Hayes, contrà :

The cognizance does not claim the rent under the lease set out in the replication, but under a previous contract of tenancy. A demise to the plaintiff is admitted by the plea in bar. It is agreed that a deed has no operation but from the time of its execution : *Clayton's* case (1), *Oshey* v. *Hicks* (2), *Steele* v. *Mart* (3), Shep. Touch. 108 ; this deed therefore took effect from the time of its actual delivery, which was subsequent to the time at which the rent in question became due. How could it have any operation to confer on the tenant a title to the land rent free for the time past? The statement of a term *of fourteen years from the 30th July, 1840, is merely by way of computation of the subsequent period for which the lease is to run.

[*696]

PARKE, B.:

There is nothing to exempt the plaintiff from the payment, under a previous contract, of rent due before the execution of the indenture. The " term " in the lease only designates the time for which it is to run, by way of calculation, not as conveying any interest. It is but a different way of saying that it is a term for twelve years and eight months to come. It is clear the deed does not operate to release the plaintiff from the liability, under the demise which is

(1) 5 Co. Rep. 1.   (3) 28 R. R. 256 (4 B. & C. 272).
(2) Cro. Jac. 263.

COOPER   admitted by the plea in bar, to pay a rent of 86l. half-yearly.   The
v.
ROBINSON.   judgment must be for the defendants.

    GURNEY, B., and ROLFE, B., concurred.

                          Judgment for the defendants.

1842.   WHITEHEAD AND OTHERS *v.* WALKER.
Dec. 6.
         (10 Meeson & Welsby, 696—699 ; S. C. 12 L. J. Ex. 28 ; 7 Jur. 330.)
Exch. of
Pleas.   The indorsee of an overdue bill or note takes it subject to all the equities
[696]   arising out of the bill or note transaction itself, but not subject to any
           collateral claim existing between the earlier parties to it. Therefore, to an
           action by the indorsee of an overdue note against the payee, a distinct debt
           due to the payee from a former indorsee cannot be set off.

    ASSUMPSIT by the assignees of the indorsee against the indorser
of a bill of exchange.   The declaration stated, that on the 8th of
August, 1834, and before the bankruptcy of Benbow, certain persons
made their bill of exchange in writing, directed to Grayhurst & Co.,
and payable to the defendant ; that the defendant indorsed the bill
to W. Swainson, who indorsed it to Willis and Swainson, who
indorsed it to Benbow before his bankruptcy.   Averment, that
Grayhurst & Co. refused to accept the bill, and that the same
was protested, &c. (1).

[697]   Plea, that after the indorsement of the bill to Willis and Swainson,
and before and at the time when it was indorsed by them to
Benbow, Willis and Swainson were, and still are, indebted to the
defendant in certain large sums of money, amounting in the whole
to 1,000l., in respect of certain bills of exchange, &c., goods sold
and delivered, &c. &c.   Averment, that the said sums so due from
Willis and Swainson to the defendant exceeded the amount of the
said bill of exchange ; of all which premises Benbow, at the time
of the said indorsement thereof to him by Willis and Swainson, had
notice ; and that the said bill was indorsed by them to Benbow,
after it had so been refused acceptance and had been protested
as in the declaration mentioned, and after it had become due.
Verification.

    Replication, *de injuriâ.*

    Special demurrer, and joinder therein.

    Bovill, in support of the demurrer :

    First, the replication is clearly bad, for the plea consists not

(1) See the former case of *Whitehead* v. *Walker*, 60 R. R. 811 (9 M. & W. 506).

of matter of excuse, but of matter which goes in discharge or WHITEHEAD
extinguishment of the defendant's liability upon the bill. It will *v.*
WALKER.
be said, however, that the plea is bad in substance, and affords no
answer to the action, on the authority of *Burrough* v. *Moss* (1).
But a party who takes a bill of exchange after it is due, takes
it with all its equities, both direct and collateral. And it was
expressly held by COLERIDGE, J., in *Goodall* v. *Ray* (2), that a party
who takes a promissory note from the payee, with a knowledge
that the payee is indebted to the maker in a larger amount, cannot
recover upon the note against the maker. That case is strictly in
point for the defendant.

    Crompton, contrà, was stopped by the COURT.

PARKE, B. :

    It is unnecessary to determine whether the *replication is good [*698]
or not, for we think the plea is bad in substance, on the authority
of *Burrough* v. *Moss*. That case decides, that the indorsee of an
overdue promissory note takes it, as against the maker, with all
the equities (3) arising out of the note transaction itself, but not
subject to a set-off in respect of a debt due from the indorser to the
maker of the note, arising out of collateral matters. For example,
if the note be released or discharged, the plaintiff under such
circumstances cannot make a title to it. But a set-off is not an
equity; it is a mere collateral matter; it is a right to set off a cross
demand against the plaintiff's cause of action, which was introduced to prevent a multiplicity of actions. The case of *Burrough*
v. *Moss* is good law, and has been recognised in this Court. Nor
do I think that case is affected by the decision of COLERIDGE, J., in
Goodall v. *Ray*. It seems to me that either there must be some
inaccuracy in the report, or there must have been in that case
that sort of formal notice to the plaintiff which is equivalent to an
agreement to set off the cross demand as against him. On that
ground the case may perhaps be supported; otherwise I cannot
assent to the position, that a mere notice of a set-off between the
payee and the maker can operate to restrict the negotiability of
a promissory note. Besides, the decision of the point was unnecessary in that case, inasmuch as the plaintiff's demand was for

(1) 10 B. & C. 558.
(2) 4 Dowl. P. C. 76.
(3) See now Bills of Exchange Act,
1882 (45 & 46 Vict. c. 61), s. 36 (2),

the effect of which is to substitute the
words " defect of title " for the more
ambiguous expression " equities."—
A. C.

WHITEHEAD
v.
WALKER.

a sum less than the amount of the note. I cannot, therefore, consider that case as an authority that mere notice of the set-off makes any difference. Our judgment must be for the plaintiffs.

ALDERSON, B. :

I am of the same opinion. If the doctrine advanced on the defendant's part were correct, no one would be able to tell whether certain instruments were negotiable or not ; for their negotiability would depend on the will of a third person. No one could tell

[*699]

whether the maker would set off his claim against the prior *party or not : if he will not, the note is negotiable, otherwise it is not. *Burrough* v. *Moss* lays down the true rule, that the indorsee of an overdue bill is subject to those equities, and those only, which affect the bill itself.

GURNEY, B., and ROLFE, B., concurred.

Judgment for the plaintiffs.

1842.
Dec. 3, 9.

*Exch. of
Pleas.*

[711]

STEWARD *v.* GREAVES AND OTHERS.

(10 Meeson & Welsby, 711—723 ; S. C. 12 L. J. Ex. 109 ; 2 Dowl. N. S. 485 ;
6 Jur. 1116.)

The creditor of a banking co-partnership, established and carrying on business under the stat. 7 Geo. IV. c. 46, cannot sue an individual member of the Company for his debt, but must proceed against the public officer, pursuant to the 9th section of that Act : at least, where it appears that there is a public officer, and that he is within the jurisdiction.

Therefore, a plea to an action against an individual member of the Company, which stated that the causes of action accrued against a certain banking co-partnership established under the 7 Geo. IV. c. 46, and not otherwise, of which co-partnership the defendant was a member ; that the causes of action accrued against the defendant as such member and not otherwise ; that S. B. and W. D. had been duly appointed and registered pursuant to the statute, as public officers of the co-partnership, to sue and be sued on behalf of the same, and that the said persons, so being, and being duly nominated and appointed and registered as such public officers, at the time of the commencement of the suit, were living and resident in England, and within the jurisdiction of the Court,—was held a good answer to the action.

ASSUMPSIT for money lent, money paid, money had and received, and upon an account stated.

Second plea, that the said causes of action accrued against a certain co-partnership, called "The Southern District Banking Company," established under the 7 Geo. IV. c. 46, and not otherwise, of which said co-partnership the defendants, at the time

of the accruing of the causes of action, were members ; that the
said causes of action accrued against the defendants as such members, and not otherwise ; that one S. Bovill and one W. Dunn had been duly appointed and registered pursuant to the said statute, as public officers of the said co-partnership, to sue and be sued for and on behalf of the same, according to the statute, and the said persons so being, and being duly nominated and appointed and registered as such public officers at the time of the commencement of this suit, were living and resident in England, and within the jurisdiction of this Court at the commencement of this suit. Verification.

Third plea, that the said causes of action accrued against the said co-partnership called " The Southern District Banking Company," of which, at the accruing of the said causes of action, the said defendants were members jointly *with one J. W. Gilbart and   [*712] J. A. Batho, and who, at &c., were resident in England, and the said causes of action accrued against the said defendants jointly with the said J. W. Gilbart and J. A. Batho, and not against the said defendants alone ; that the said J. W. Gilbart and J. A. Batho, before, and at &c., were and from thence hitherto have been and still are, members and co-partners of and in the said co-partnership in the declaration mentioned, called " The East of England Bank," and that the said plaintiff sues as such public officer of such Bank, and as the nominal plaintiff on behalf of the members of the said East of England Bank, and amongst others, of the said J. W. Gilbart and J. A. Batho. Verification.

Special demurrer to the second and third pleas, assigning for causes : To the second plea,—first, that the Act of Parliament does not preclude the plaintiff from suing the said defendants as he has done, and that it is not obligatory on him to bring his action against one of the public officers.   [Certain formal objections were also taken to the second plea which are omitted.]   The third plea   [713] was also demurred to, on the ground that although Gilbart and Batho were members of the co-partnership mentioned in the plea, yet that plea did not show any grounds for absolving the defendants from liability.

Joinder in demurrer.

The case was argued on a former day of these sittings (Dec. 3), by

   Butt, for the plaintiff :

The main question in this case is, whether the 9th section of the

STEWARD Banking Co-partnership Act, 7 Geo. IV. c. 46, which provides,
v. that all actions and suits, &c. to be commenced or instituted by
GREAVES. any persons against such co-partnership, "shall and lawfully
may " be commenced, instituted, and prosecuted against any one
or more of the public officers for the time being of the co-partnership, as the nominal defendant or defendants for and on behalf
of such co-partnership, takes away the common-law right of a
plaintiff to sue the members of the Company, and compels him
to proceed against the public officer alone. It is submitted that
it does not, but only gives an additional and less difficult remedy.
The words of the clause are affirmative, and therefore, according
to the established rule of construction of statutes, do not abrogate
the common law: Dwarris on Statutes, 637, 638; Com. Dig.
Parliament, (R. 23); 1 Bla. Com. 89. * * *

[715]   The third plea is clearly bad. There is nothing to preclude one
Banking Company, by its public officer, from suing another such
Company, although they may be individuals who are shareholders
in both Companies. The action is not brought against them in
respect of bills or notes, or any thing necessarily connected with
the business of bankers.

    Ogle, contrà :

    The second plea is good both in substance and in form. Under
the 7 Geo. IV. c. 46, s. 9, actions must be brought against the
public officers of the co-partnership, and cannot be maintained
against the individual members. The words " shall and lawfully
may " are here imperative, and the remedy pointed out by the
statute must be pursued. Such words are to be construed as
imperative, wherever that is necessary in order to carry out the
intention of the Legislature. * * *

[717]   He admitted that he could not maintain the third plea.

    Butt, in reply. * * *

                                        Cur. adv. vult.

[718]   The judgment of the COURT was now delivered by

PARKE, B. (His Lordship stated the second plea, and continued :)

    Six objections were made on the argument of the demurrer to
this plea, one of substance, the others of a formal nature.

    The principal objection was, that in the case of a Company
established and carrying on business under the provisions of the

statute 7 Geo. IV. c. 46, the individual members of it are liable to
be sued upon the contracts of the Company, as they would have
been but for that statute, which, it was argued, gave an additional
or cumulative, not an exclusive remedy against the Company, by
an action against the public officer.

This question, on account of its importance, the Court took time   [719]
to consider. We have considered it, and are all of opinion, that the
creditors of a Company so established, and having a public officer,
have no remedy against the individual members, as at common law.
And we are of this opinion upon the words of the ninth section,
giving the remedy against the public officers, and upon the whole
purview of the Act.

The words of the section are, that " all actions against the
co-partnership *shall* and lawfully may be commenced, instituted,
and prosecuted against one or more of the public officers nominated
as before mentioned, as the nominal defendant." These words,
according to their ordinary import, are obligatory, and ought to
have that construction, unless it would lead to some absurd or
inconvenient consequence, or would be at variance with the intent
of the Legislature, to be collected from other parts of the Act. But
this construction is manifestly reasonable and consistent with the
context, and in accordance with the intent of the framers of the Act,
to be collected from every part of it.

It is clear from the recital in the Act, and the scope of most of its
provisions, that the Legislature intended to give to corporations,
and to co-partnerships of more than six, within the limits therein
mentioned, the power of being Banks of issue, the Bank of England
waiving its exclusive privilege in their favour, on the condition that
the individuals should be liable for the bills and notes issued or
money borrowed by such corporations or Companies, in the qualified
mode pointed out by the Act. This liability, by the common law,
would not attach at all to individual members of corporations, and
would attach, in a different mode from that provided for by the
statute, to members of Companies: for, at common law, those
members only would be liable who were such when the contract was
entered into, but by the statute, not only those, but all who became
*members afterwards, and until the bills, notes, or debts were paid   :*720]
are made liable. At common law, all the goods of the contracting
parties and their persons would be liable to immediate execution,—
by the statute, the goods of the Company are liable, and the
members for the time being at the period of the execution, in the

first instance, and afterwards those who were so at the time of
the contracts being entered into or carried into effect, or when the
judgment was obtained thereon. In a proceeding against individuals,
they would be liable to simple-contract debts for six years, to
specialties for twenty: in the statutory mode of proceeding, the
members who have ceased to be such for three years are exempt
from debts of every description. Thus the liability created by the
statute is very different from that which would exist without it;
and it cannot be supposed that the Legislature meant to leave it to
the option of any creditor, whether the members of the Company
should be subject to one species of liability or the other, still less
that a creditor should have the power of depriving them of the
statutory protection which is given to each after having ceased for
three years to be a partner. The framers of the Act had in view
the convenience of the public, and thereby provided a more convenient remedy to creditors than at common law; but they had also
in view the benefit of the members of the Company, by restricting
their personal liability. All the clauses of the statute are consistent
with this view, and there is one, the 10th, which seems to show
that the Legislature did not contemplate that an action would lie
for the same debt against the individual members and against the
nominal defendant; for it provides, that if the merits have been
tried in one action against one public officer, the proceeding may be
pleaded in bar of another against any other public officer, and it
does not make a similar provision if the merits have been decided
in an action against individual members.

[721]   It was objected at the Bar, that a creditor must at all events be
entitled to sue the individual members if there should be no public
officer, or if the officer happened to be out of the jurisdiction, so as
not to be capable of being served with process; and that if he *must*
have the remedy in such cases, it might be presumed he was at
liberty to have recourse to it in all.

If it should be conceded that in those special cases it would be
competent for a creditor to sue the members at common law, from
the necessity of the case, to avoid a failure of justice, it would by
no means follow that he would have the right to do so where the
necessity did not exist, and there was, as there is in the present
case, an officer resident within the jurisdiction. Whether, even in
such cases, an action would lie against individual members, it is
not necessary to decide on the present occasion; but there is
strong ground to contend, that the Legislature meant that there

should always be a public officer capable of being sued, and that the STEWARD
Company are compellable by law to appoint one. GREAVES.

The case of *Blewitt* v. *Gordon* (1) was cited as an authority that
the creditor had an option to sue a Company, constituted as this is,
or its individual members; but the Act under which the Company
mentioned in that case was instituted was very different from the
present, and the words "shall and lawfully may" were held, explained
by the context, not to be obligatory.

We are of opinion, therefore, that this Act of Parliament meant
to give one remedy only, and that against the Company, in the
name of its public officer, and that the common-law remedy is taken
away, at least where such officer exists and is in England; and
consequently that the second plea is good in substance.

It remains for us to consider the other five objections, all of a [722]
formal nature, to that plea (2).   *   *   *

The result is, that the defendants are entitled to our judgment
*on the second plea. The third was properly abandoned by the [*723]
defendants' counsel : on that the plaintiff is entitled to judgment.

Judgment for the defendants.

CASES AT NISI PRIUS.

GREEN *v.* THE LONDON CEMETERY COMPANY. 1839.
Dec. 9.
(9 Car. & P. 6—11.)

[6]

> A., himself a leaseholder of a house, entered into an agreement with B.
> to grant him an under-lease of the house for twenty years and a fraction,
> from Midsummer, 1836. B. entered into possession, and paid rent to A.,
> and underlet a portion of the house to C. from Michaelmas, 1836, and
> received from C. the first quarter's rent, due at Christmas, 1836. On the
> 11th of January, 1837, B., wishing to part with his interest before the
> execution of the lease, wrote to A., requesting him to insert the name of D.
> instead of his. D., a few days after, sent to A. a written consent to become
> his tenant, on the same terms as B. had agreed to; and, in consequence,
> the lease was, on the 15th of March, 1837, granted by A. to D., instead of
> to B. D. brought an action for use and occupation against C., to whom B.
> had underlet a part of the house, and claimed the quarter's rent due at
> Lady Day, 1837: Held, that he was entitled to recover.

THE declaration stated that the defendants were indebted to the
plaintiff for the use and occupation of certain apartments. The
plea was the general issue.

(1) 1 Dowl. P. C. (N. S.) 815.   which deals with these objections is
(2) The portion of the judgment   omitted.—A. C.

The action was brought to recover the sum of 25*l.*, being a quarter's rent due at Lady Day, 1837, from the defendants, for apartments in a house No. 64, in Cornhill, which were occupied for the purposes of the Company.   The case was tried chiefly upon admissions from which it appeared that in the month of June, 1836, a person named Steed entered into a written agreement

[*7] with a person named *Lyon, who was the leaseholder under the Merchant Taylors' Company of the house No. 64, Cornhill, by which agreement Lyon agreed to let the house to Steed for twenty years and three-quarters, wanting six days, from Midsummer, 1836, at 300*l.* a year, and Lyon undertook to execute a lease to Steed according to the terms of the agreement.   Under this agreement Steed entered into possession and paid rent to Lyon, and underlet a part of the house to the London Cemetery Company from Michaelmas, 1836, at the rent of 100*l.* a year, and received the first quarter's rent due at Christmas, 1836.   On the 11th of January, 1837, Steed, being desirous of parting with his interest in the premises before the lease was executed to him, wrote to Lyon, stating that he had succeeded in obtaining a tenant for the premises in his stead.   The letter was to this effect: " The gentleman is Richard Green, Esq., the ship-owner, of Blackwall, whose name you will be pleased to cause to be substituted for mine in the lease."   On the 18th of January Mr. Green wrote to Mr. Lyon and consented to become tenant to him of the house on the same terms as Mr. Steed had agreed to ; and in consequence of this arrangement the lease which was intended to have been granted to Mr. Steed, was granted by Mr. Lyon to Mr. Green.   It was executed on the 15th of March, 1837.

Platt, for the plaintiff, contended in his opening, that the plaintiff was entitled to recover the quarter's rent from the defendants because they took under Steed, and were therefore estopped from disputing his interest in the reversion, and because Green acquired that interest from Steed before the rent became due which was sought to be recovered in the action.

In addition to the facts admitted as above, Steed was called as a witness for the plaintiff, and stated that he gave the Cemetery Company notice that he had agreed to part with his interest to

[*8] Mr. Green.   His evidence on the subject *was as follows : " I gave a written notice some time in January, 1837, I think to the clerk,

Mr. Buxton, in the back room in Cornhill, at their place of business; I cannot say whether I gave the notice before or after I wrote the letter to Lyon about Green; I gave it while the negotiation was going on between Lyon, Green, and myself, and before the transaction was complete; I might have given the notice to the managing director; I know it was received, because it was commented upon to me at the board by the chairman; I think this was in the month of January; it was when I applied for my rent up to Christmas; he said, 'We have a letter of yours; how are we to know whether you are the landlord or not? we have a letter stating that we are to consider Mr. Green as landlord;' they objected to pay the Christmas rent, and did not pay till I threatened to distrain for it."

LORD DENMAN, Ch. J.:

I think you may give evidence of the contents of the notice.

Witness:

I told them in the notice that I had negotiated the letting of the house to Mr. Green. On his cross-examination by *Kelly*, he said: "I think the notice was given while it was matter of negotiation, and before it was completed."

Kelly:

Have you not since given notice to the Company not to pay rent to Mr. Green?

Platt objected:

The witness cannot get out of the written paper.

Kelly:

That is assuming the whole question. The other side rely on a notice; surely I am at liberty to show that it was countermanded.

Platt:

If the written documents before your Lordship *operate as a surrender, then he cannot alter it by anything that he subsequently did or said.

[*9]

LORD DENMAN, Ch. J.:

I think it may possibly be material. It is but a notice. I think the question may be asked.

Witness:

I communicated to them that Mr. Green had not paid me the consideration for the transfer, but I never told them not to pay the rent to Mr. Green, nor not to consider themselves as Mr. Green's tenants.

Kelly, for the defendants:

Several questions of law arise in this case. It is said the defendants are estopped from denying Steed's title. I concur in that observation; but the question is, whether Steed's title has been vested in Green, the present plaintiff? I apprehend it has not. Steed came in under an agreement containing words of present demise. He was therefore the lessee of Lyon, a termor, and was himself a termor under Lyon, and entered into possession, and had a reversion to commence on the determination of the defendant's tenancy. The first question will be, was there any surrender by Steed to Lyon of the term or any part of it? I submit that there was not. If there was, then will come the question whether he could surrender that which he had granted to the defendants? Steed says in his letter that he has obtained a tenant—that may be a good license to Lyon to grant the lease to Green; but the question is, whether it is a surrender of Steed's interest? A surrender must take place *eo instanti* and cannot commence *in futuro*. Now this could only operate when the lease was granted, and therefore was not any surrender at all. At the time when the lease was granted nothing was done by Steed, but all was between Lyon and the present plaintiff. It appears that Steed had made the defendants his tenants, and had the *reversion to commence on the determination of their tenancy—he had no present interest in the premises. He might, by a sufficient instrument, have surrendered what interest he had if it was to operate immediately. There is a further difficulty which is insuperable against this plaintiff's recovering. Supposing Steed did surrender at the time, the only effect would be to put Lyon in the same situation as Steed, and that was only a reversion—and as a reversioner, he would be entitled to the rent, but a lease subsequently granted would not pass the reversion.

[*10]

LORD DENMAN, Ch. J. (to *Kelly*):

I think the question about the notice may be very material to your case; otherwise I should view the matter thus: Lyon grants

a lease to commence from Christmas, and the defendants become
tenants to the plaintiff as the person to whom the lease was granted.
I shall direct the jury to find for the plaintiff, and I will give you
leave to move to enter a nonsuit or to have a special case.

GREEN
v.
THE LONDON
CEMETERY
COMPANY.

Platt :

I do not understand your Lordship to recommend any particular
course?

LORD DENMAN, Ch. J. :

No ; I do not feel much doubt about it. I do not know what the
effect may be.

Platt then called the clerk of the Company, who swore that he
had not received the notice spoken of by Mr. Steed, nor had he
heard anything of it.

LORD DENMAN, Ch. J. :

There really is no question about the notice unless the witness is
perjured. He says he mentioned it to the board, and the chairman commented upon his letter. (His Lordship then said to the
jury :) In my opinion the plaintiff is entitled to recover. I think
the defendants are tenants to him. You will therefore find *your
verdict for him, and *Mr. Kelly* will bring it before the Court.

[*11]

Verdict for the plaintiff. Damages, 25l., subject, &c.

Platt and *James*, for the plaintiff.

Kelly, for the defendants.

A rule *nisi* was granted in the ensuing Term pursuant to the
leave given, which was called on for argument in Trinity Term,
1839, when, not being supported, it was, without argument,

Discharged.

SELWOOD *v.* MOUNT, Esq., AND OTHERS.

(9 Car. & P. 75—77.)

1839.

[75]

Magistrates having convicted a party under the Highway Act, they drew
up a conviction and returned it to the clerk of the peace, and on an action
being brought against them, they put in the conviction returned to the
clerk of the peace, (which was open to some formal objections), and also
another conviction drawn up afterwards in a more formal shape : *Semble,*

47—2

SELWOOD
v.
MOUNT.

that there is no impropriety in this course of proceeding, provided the latter conviction is according to the truth and supported by the facts of the case.

Semble, that, on deciding a case, magistrates ought not to take an indemnity. as it has the effect of enabling them to decide more safely in favour of a party who is able to give an indemnity, than of one who cannot do so.

TRESPASS, for entering the plaintiff's house and close, and taking his goods. Plea, Not guilty.

It was opened by *Whateley*, for the plaintiff, that the plaintiff had applied to two magistrates, under the stat. 5 & 6 Will. IV. c. 50 (the Highway Act), s. 84, to cause a footpath to be stopped up, as useless: and that they having, under sec. 85 of the Act, certified that it was so, Mr. Williams, of East Ilsley, had, under sec. 88 of the Act, appealed against their certificate; and on the trial of that appeal at the Quarter Sessions at Abingdon, on the 3rd of July, 1838, the jury found that the footpath was not useless; and the Quarter Sessions ordered that the costs of the appeal should be paid by the respondent. As the order was originally drawn up,

[*76] no respondent's *name was mentioned, though the plaintiff's name was afterwards inserted (as he submitted) improperly, by the direction of the chairman. However, the Sessions did not ascertain the amount of costs, and therefore their order was, on that point, inoperative. After this Mr. Williams went before Mr. Mount and Mr. Bunny, two of the defendants, who were magistrates, and they granted a warrant of distress to levy 112*l*. 0*s*. 4*d*. as the amount of these costs, on the plaintiff's goods, which warrant was executed by the defendant Law, who was the constable. He submitted, that as the Quarter Sessions had not ascertained the amount of costs, the defendants, Mr. Mount and Mr. Bunny, had no authority to issue any warrant. They, however, were mere nominal defendants, as Mr. Williams had given them an indemnity.

The taking of the goods was proved, and the counsel of the defendant Law, put in the warrant of distress, which the defendant Law, had notice to produce. The order of Sessions for the payment of the costs was also put in, and did not specify any sum. The indemnity given by Mr. Williams to Mr. Mount and Mr. Bunny was also put in.

ALDERSON, B. :

Magistrates ought not, I think, to take an indemnity. It is a bad practice, as it has the effect of enabling them more safely to decide in favour of a party who is able to give an indemnity, than of one who cannot do so.

Ludlow, Serjt., for the defendants, Mount and Bunny :

By the 90th sect. of the stat. 5 & 6 Will. IV. c. 50, the Quarter Sessions are bound to order the costs to the successful party, on an appeal of this kind ; and that being so, I submit that the magistrates, by whom the payment of them is to be enforced under the 103rd section, may ascertain the amount ; and that, at all events, even if this *is not so, the plaintiff should have made this his defence when summoned before Mr. Mount and Mr. Bunny ; instead of which, he never either appeared to their summons, or made any defence or objection before them, till a warrant of distress is granted, and then brings his action. I submit, that as the magistrates had jurisdiction over the subject-matter, their conviction is a bar to the present action ; and his remedy, if any, was by appeal under the 105th section. I ought to mention also, that a conviction was returned by the magistrates to the Quarter Sessions, and that that conviction is open to some objections. Since that the magistrates have drawn up another conviction, which is free from those objections. I submit that they are right in doing so. It has long been the practice for magistrates not to draw up their convictions at the time. If the conviction returned to the Sessions is good, *cadet questio ;* and if it is not, it is a nullity, and nothing at all ; and the magistrates are then in the same situation as if no conviction had ever been returned to the Sessions.

[*77]

ALDERSON, B. :

I do not see any impropriety in the magistrates drawing up another conviction in a more formal shape, provided that the latter is according to the truth, and supported by the facts of the case.

Both the convictions were put in, and the learned Baron being of opinion that they were in point of law no answer to the action (1), there was a

> *Verdict for the plaintiff against the defendants Mount and Bunny, and for the defendant Law.*

(1) See this case reported on motion for a new trial 55 R. R. 401 (1 Q. B 726).—A. C.

SELWOOD
r.
MOUNT.

Whateley, Tyrwhitt, and *J. Jeffreys Williams,* for the plaintiff.

Ludlow and *Talfourd,* Serjts., and *Carrington,* for the defendants Mount and Bunny.

[78] *Walesby,* for the defendant Law.

In the ensuing Term, *Ludlow,* Serjt., applied to the Court of Queen's Bench for a new trial, on the ground that the facts before stated were a good defence for the magistrates. The COURT granted a rule to show cause.

1839.
Nov. 28.

[189]

THE ATTORNEY-GENERAL *v.* BOND.

(9 Car. & P. 189—190.)

On the trial of an information by the *Attorney-General* for penalties, the defendant (who had been held to bail) had subpœnaed the officer from the Queen's Remembrancer's Office to produce the affidavit on which he had been held to bail, with a view of being able to give it in evidence to cross-examine the person who had made the affidavit, if he should be called as a witness on the trial. The person who made the affidavit was called as a witness on the trial, and, for the purpose of cross-examining him the defendant's counsel wished to put in the affidavit: Held, that the officer was bound to produce it, and that the defendant had a right to make use of it in this way; but that if the affidavit was made by another deponent besides the witness, and related to other persons besides the defendant, the latter would be only entitled to use so much of the affidavit as was sworn by the witness, and as related to the defendant himself.

INFORMATION by the *Attorney-General* against the defendant for penalties under the statute 3 & 4 Will. IV. c. 53, s. 44 (1). The information stated, that certain merchants, to the *Attorney-General* unknown, had imported certain goods, to wit, 230 gallons of foreign brandy, of the value of 310*l.* 10*s.,* which goods were liable to the payment of duties of Customs, and were deposited by a certain officer of Customs, to wit, one J. D., for security of such duties in certain places of security in the United Kingdom; that is to say, in the Queen's warehouse; and that the goods were, without payment of the duties, removed by persons unknown from the said place of security; and that the defendant did assist in the removal, whereby he had forfeited treble the value of the goods, which the Commissioners of her Majesty's Customs had elected to be sued for in this behalf. There were also six other counts for knowingly concealing the goods, and for assisting in unshipping them, &c. Plea, Not guilty.

(1) Rep. 8 & 9 Vict. c. 84, s. 2.

On the part of the Crown, a witness named Collins was called ; and, with a view to cross-examine him, it was proposed by *Humfrey*, for the defendant, to put into the witness's hand the affidavit made by the witness, and deposited *in the office of the Queen's Remembrancer, upon which the writ of *capias* had issued, to hold the defendant to bail in this case, and which the proper officer was subpoenaed to produce.

Jervis and *Kaye*, for the Crown, objected to the production of the affidavit, on the ground that the production of such affidavits would lead to great inconvenience. They also stated, that there was no instance of such an affidavit ever having been used in this way on any former occasion.

LORD ABINGER, C. B. :

I am clearly of opinion, that the defendant is entitled to use it in the manner proposed by his counsel.

Jervis :

The affidavit is the joint-affidavit of the witness Collins and another, and it relates to other persons besides the defendant.

LORD ABINGER, C. B. :

The defendant will be only entitled to use so much of the affidavit as is sworn by the witness Collins, and which relates to the defendant himself. Anything which relates to other persons, or which is sworn by any other deponent, cannot be made use of by the present defendant on this trial. Let me see the affidavit.

The affidavit was handed to his Lordship, who observed, that he did not see anything in it which would be of any use to the defendant.

The affidavit was given back to the officer.

> *The jury could not agree, and were discharged by the consent of the counsel for the Crown.*

Jervis and *Kaye*, for the Crown.

Humfrey and *Mellor*, for the defendant,

1839.
Nov. 28.

[197]

CRONK *v.* FRITH.

(9 Car. & P. 197—199; S. C. 2 Moo. & Rob. 262.)

If, since the execution of a deed, the subscribing witness to it has become
blind, a party suing on the deed must, if *non est factum* be pleaded, call
the subscribing witness, and it is not enough to prove the handwriting of
the parties executing the deed and of the subscribing witness.

DEBT on a bond.   Pleas, 1st, *non est factum ;* 2nd, that the
defendant was persuaded to execute the bond while he was drunk,
and that he did so ; 3rd, fraud.

Replication, denying the second and third pleas.

It was opened by *Jervis* for the plaintiff, that, since the execution of the bond, Mr. Crundwell, the subscribing witness to it, had
become blind, and he therefore proposed to prove the execution of
the bond in the same way as if the witness were dead.

Evidence was given that the signature to the bond was of the
defendant's handwriting, and that the signature to the attestation
was of the handwriting of Mr. Crundwell ; and it was also proved
that since the date of the bond Mr. Crundwell had become blind ;
[*198]   but the witness who *proved these facts stated, in answer to a
question put by *Humfrey* for the defendant, that Mr. Crundwell was
in Court.

Humfrey, for the defendant :

I submit that the bond cannot be read without calling the subscribing witness.   It is said that he is blind ; but one great object
in having the subscribing witness called is to hear his evidence as
to the circumstances attendant on the making of the instrument;
and he may remember those circumstances though he cannot see,
and his evidence may be of the greatest importance on a plea like
the second.

Jervis and *Erskine Perry*, for the plaintiff, cited *Wood* v.
Drury (1), *Pedler* v. *Paige* (2).   *   *   *

(1) 1 Ld. Ray. 734.   The report of
that case is as follows: "At the
Summer Assizes of Warwick, 1699, a
deed was produced to which there were
two witnesses, one of whom was blind.
It was ruled by HOLT, Ch. J., that
such deed might be proved by the
other witness and read, or might be
proved without proving that this blind
witness is dead, or without having him

at the trial, proving only his hand ;
and so it was done in this case."

(2) 1 Moo. & Rob. 258.   This was an
action of debt on bond, with pleas of
non est factum, and a release by a lost
deed : for the defendant it was proposed to put in an instrument attested
by a witness, who was proved to be
blind, on proving his handwriting.
The evidence was objected to on the

LORD ABINGER, C. B. :

 I am decidedly of opinion that the bond cannot be read without calling the subscribing witness. He might from his recollection of the transaction give most important evidence respecting it.

 Jerris called the subscribing witness.

Verdict for the plaintiff.

Jerris and *Erskine Perry*, for the plaintiff.

Humfrey, for the defendant.

CRONK
v.
FRITH.

[199]

BINNS *v.* PIGOT.

(9 Car. & P. 208—209.)

1840.

[208]

An innkeeper has no lien on a horse placed in his stable for the amount of its keep unless it be placed there by a guest.

If a person is stopped with a horse under suspicious circumstances, and the horse be placed at an inn by the police, the innkeeper has no lien on the horse for its keep; and if an auctioneer, by the direction of the innkeeper, sell the horse for its keep, he is liable to be sued in trover by the owner of the horse.

TROVER for a horse. Pleas, 1st, not guilty ; 2nd, that the plaintiff was not possessed of the horse as of his own property ; 3rd, that a person named Furze was an innkeeper and livery-stable-keeper, and that the horse was placed with him at livery by a person named Miller, the apparent owner thereof, upon the terms that it was to be sold if the keep was not paid for ; and that the keep not being paid for by Miller, the defendant, as an auctioneer, sold the horse by the direction of Furze, who had no notice that the horse belonged to the plaintiff. Replication to the 3rd plea, *de injuriâ*.

 It was opened by *Platt*, for the plaintiff, that on the 10th of June, 1839, the plaintiff, who lived in London, had given the horse into the charge of a bricklayer in his employ to take to Elvetham, in Hampshire, where the plaintiff also had a house ; but although the bricklayer had started from London at seven o'clock in the evening, he was stopped with the horse by the police at Richmond

ground that the witness might recollect the facts of this transaction ; and in support of its reception the case of *Wood* v. *Drury*, and the works of Mr. Starkie and Mr. Roscoe on the Law of Evidence, were cited. Mr. Justice PARK said, "There is great weight in the reasons urged for calling the witness, but under the authority of the case cited I shall receive the evidence ;" and his Lordship received the evidence.

BINNS
v.
PIGOT.

at almost one o'clock the next morning, he being taken into custody, and the horse placed at Mr. Furze's inn. In the month of July the horse was sold by the defendant for the keep. He submitted that the innkeeper could have no lien for the keep of the horse, as it was placed in his hands against the will of the owner.

It was proved that the horse was stopped by the police, as before stated; and that on the 25th of July, 1839, Mr. Thorn, a friend of the plaintiff, went to the defendant and *Mr. Furze, and told them that he came by the authority of the plaintiff to forbid the sale, and that Mr. Furze asked Mr. Thorn if he would pay for the keep of the horse, which he refused to do; and that Furze then directed the defendant to sell the horse, which he did.

[*209]

PARKE, B.:

The plaintiff is in this case entitled to a verdict, as the innkeeper had no lien upon the horse. How the horse got into the innkeeper's hands does not very distinctly appear. It was probably taken to him by the police. It is proved that the friend of the plaintiff refused to pay for the keep of the horse, but the plaintiff was not bound in point of law to pay for the keep, as the horse was not brought to the inn by a guest; and an innkeeper has no lien upon an animal put into his stable unless it be brought by a guest.

Verdict for the plaintiff.

Platt and *G. T. White*, for the plaintiff.

Thesiger and *Montagu Chambers*, for the defendant.

1840.

[209]

BUCKET *v.* CHURCH.
(9 Car. & P. 209—212.)

The acknowledgment in writing to take a case out of the Statute of Limitations must either amount to a distinct promise to pay, or to a distinct acknowledgment that the sum is due.

Semble, that there is some doubt whether it is a question for the Judge or for the jury to determine, whether a letter written by the defendant be or be not a sufficient acknowledgment for this purpose; and till that point is settled, the learned Judge will, to save the parties expense, express his own opinion with respect to the document, and also leave it to the jury.

DEBT for money lent, for interest, and on an account stated. Pleas, *nunquam indebitatus,* and the Statute of Limitations.

It was opened by *Thesiger*, for the plaintiff, that the plaintiff was a person of advanced age and very penurious habits, who had for many years worked in market gardens, *but had amassed a property, of which she had placed 650*l.* in the Funds, and had lent 120*l.* to the defendant, who had married her niece, the defendant having also prevailed on her to transfer her stock into the joint names of herself, the defendant, and his wife.

It was proved, that, in the year 1832, the plaintiff had placed 100*l.* and afterwards 20*l.* more in the hands of the defendant, who had been very kind to the plaintiff for some years, and had sent her Sunday dinners, cakes, tarts, &c., and that when she asked him for the money, which she repeatedly did, he on some occasions said she should have it, and on others that she should not.

To take the case out of the Statute of Limitations, a letter, written by the plaintiff's attorney to the defendant, and the defendant's answer, were relied on.

The letter of the plaintiff's attorney was as follows:

"23rd November, 1838.

"Sir,—A Mrs. Susannah Bucket has instructed me to take proceedings against you to compel the payment of 120*l.* she has placed in your hands, and a retransfer of 650*l.* 3½ per Cent. stock she has placed in your name and your wife's jointly with her own. As she is a very old lady, I do not like to take any steps in the matter without giving you an opportunity of stating whether the charges she makes against you are correct, especially as she wishes me to prepare a will in which your wife and yourself are to have no interest. Unless, however, I hear from you on the matter, I shall treat her statement that you have forcibly deprived her of this money as true, which I cannot believe to be the case. She says you have not even paid her the interest on the 100*l.*; is this true?

"I am, Sir, yours obediently,

"To Mr. Levi Church.   H. F. Philipps."

The letter of the defendant in answer was as follows:

"Brentford, 25th November, 1838.

"Dr. Sir,—I received your letter, and I can assure you *that every thing was done in an upright and fair manner, and before witnesses; it was Mrs. Bucket's own proposing and particular wish, so that when she died it should be no trouble nor expense. The 650*l.* she has been receiving dividend for. The 100*l.* she has been

BUCKET
v.
CHURCH.
[*210]

[*211]

receiving double and treble for, believe me, Sir, and if you will refer to Mr. Peake, broker, he will tell you the same; the transferring was done by Mr. Peake, and I have a bill and receipt for the same; and I fully expect to be in London in a few days at Mr. Branston's, and I will call on you.

"I am, Sir, your most obedient,

" H. PHILIPPS, Esq.   L. CHURCH."

Crowder, for the defendant :

I submit that the letter of the defendant does not take the case out of the Statute of Limitations. I apprehend that that is a question for the Judge and not for the jury. It was so considered in the case of *Morrell* v. *Frith* (1).

PARKE, B. :

From the case of *Lloyd* v. *Maund* (2), it would appear to be a question for the jury. What I have always done is, to express my own opinion, and also take the opinion of the jury. If the two agree, it is well—if they differ, it will be for the Court to decide.

Crowder addressed the jury for the defendant, and contended that this was a gift and not a loan, and that the letter of the defendant did not take the case out of the Statute of Limitations, as the real meaning of the expression, " The 100*l*. she has been receiving double and treble for " was, that she had received more than an equivalent twice or thrice over, in what the defendant and his wife had done for her.

PARKE, B. (in summing up) :

The first question is, whether this 100*l*. was a loan or a gift. That it was put into the hands of the defendant as one or the other is conceded. *Mr. Philipps, in his letter, says that it was a loan, and the defendant does not, by his answer, deny that it was so. We now come to the Statute of Limitations—and, to take the case out of the operation of the statute, the party must either make a distinct promise to pay or else make a distinct acknowledgment that the sum is due; and I think, on the true construction of the defendant's letter, he admits the loan, and says, that so far from not having paid the interest, he asserts that he has paid double and treble interest. As there is some little difficulty whether it is a

[*212]

(1) 49 M. & W. 659 (3 M. & W. 402).   (2) 2 T. R. 760.

question for the Judge or a question for the jury, I shall leave it to
you to say whether the defendant, by his letter, meant to say that
the plaintiff had received double and treble the 100*l.*, or had received
double and treble the interest only.   The expression is not that she
has "received double and treble," but has "received double and
treble *for.*"   The Sunday dinners and cakes would very likely double
and treble the interest, but would not double and treble the capital.
I think there is no evidence to take the case out of the Statute of
Limitations beyond 100*l.*   You will say also whether you will
allow the defendant to deduct the interest up to the date of his
letter, as he, in effect, asserts that it has been satisfied up to that
time.   Still you may, if you think proper, disbelieve one part of
his statement and believe another, or it may be that he may only
mean that, having had the various articles that have been
mentioned, the plaintiff ought not to charge interest.

> *Verdict for the plaintiff—the foreman of the jury
> saying, " We find for the plaintiff for 100l., and
> interest since the date of the defendant's letter."*

Thesiger and *Montagu Chambers,* for the plaintiff.

Crowder and *Fish,* for the defendant.

WHEELER *v.* WHITING.

(9 Car. & P. 262—267.)

A. telling a policeman to take charge of B., is the same as his telling the
policeman to take B. into custody, and is sufficient to support an action for
false imprisonment by B. against A.

Semble, that in an action for false imprisonment, a plea that the defendant was possessed of a house, and that the plaintiff was there making a
great disturbance, and refused to depart when requested, and was in great
heat and fury, ready and desirous to make an affray, and cause a breach
of the peace, whereupon the defendant gave the plaintiff into custody,
is bad.

ASSAULT and false imprisonment. Pleas, 1st, to the whole
declaration, not guilty ; 2nd, as to the assault and battery, that the
defendant was possessed of a house and that the plaintiff made a
disturbance there, and refused to depart when requested so to do,
wherefore the defendant laid hands on him and put him out ; 3rd,
as to the assault and battery and part of the imprisonment, that the
defendant was possessed of a house, and that the plaintiff was and

continued in it making a great noise and disturbance, and refused
to depart when requested so to do, "and was then in great heat
and fury, ready and desirous to make an affray, and cause and
commit a breach of the peace there, whereupon the defendant, in
order to prevent such affray and preserve the peace, and restore
good order and tranquillity in his said house, gave charge of the
plaintiff to William Evans, then being a policeman and police

[*263] constable of the town of Monmouth, and then requested *the said
W. E. to take the said plaintiff into his custody, to be dealt with
according to law; and the said W. E. then being such policeman and police officer as aforesaid, then having view of such
conduct and behaviour, and heat and fury of the plaintiff as aforesaid, then gently laid his hands on the plaintiff, and did then take
the plaintiff into his custody," &c.

On the part of the plaintiff, William Evans was called : he
said, " I am a policeman at Monmouth ; the defendant keeps the
' Beaufort Arms' Hotel ; on the 3rd of October, between eight and
nine in the evening, Thomas Jones, the Boots at the 'Beaufort Arms,'
came to fetch me; in the hall of the 'Beaufort Arms,' I found
the plaintiff and defendant, and Mr. Lawrence; the defendant said,
'Policeman, take that man in charge,' pointing to the plaintiff; I
said I thought I could not do so, as I had not seen him do anything;
the plaintiff was claiming a debt from Mr. Lawrence, and said he
would expose him; Mr. Lawrence was going upstairs, and the
plaintiff followed him and said he would follow him into every room
in the house ; the defendant said, ' Policeman, do your duty ; ' Mr.
Lawrence and the plaintiff had gone up the stairs about five steps,
when Boots pulled the plaintiff by the skirts of his coat, and got
him down into the hall again ; I said, ' If I take him I must claim
assistance,' and the defendant ordered Boots to assist me; Boots
and I took the plaintiff to the station-house, and I locked him in ;
the defendant afterwards said that the plaintiff had been knocking
up a great row at his house, but if it was guaranteed that he
would not disturb his house, he should be liberated ; I then went
to the station-house and let the plaintiff go ; the plaintiff had been
there thirty or thirty-five minutes."

[*264] *Ludlow*, Serjt., for the defendant, in addressing the jury,
submitted, that, with respect to the turning the plaintiff *out of
the house, the defendant was justified in doing it, as the plaintiff

was making a disturbance, and would not depart when requested to
do so; and, with respect to the imprisonment, he stated that it had
not been ordered by the defendant, and even if it had, the defendant
would be justified, as it would be shown that the plaintiff was
desirous of making an affray in view of the police officer, and was
therefore given in charge.

For the defendant, Mr. Lawrence was called: he said, "I was
dining at the 'Beaufort Arms,' on the 3rd of October; it was the
second race day; I received a note and a message from the
plaintiff; I went down stairs, and said that if he would speak to
me, we had better walk into another room; he said there was no
need of that; we went into a room and he said, 'Do you mean to
pay me for those empty sacks?' I said I did not owe for any, and
referred him to Messrs. Sparkes and Bruffham, to whom I had let
my mill; he said, 'I look to you;' I said, 'If you think you have
a right against me, you can bring an action if you choose;' he said
he would have the money before he left the room; he said this in
a loud tone, and I said, 'Mr. Wheeler, you are conducting yourself
like a blackguard;' 'Blackguard!' he replied in a loud voice, 'damn
your eyes, I'll knock you down;' he held his fist over my head; he
said I should not leave the room till I paid him; however, he let
me pass him, and said, 'Very well, I will go with you, if you go to
hell;' I was proceeding up stairs, and not wishing for a disturbance,
I said to Mrs. Whiting, who was at the bar door, 'I appeal
to you for protection;' the plaintiff then said, 'I will go and
show you up before your grand friends, I don't care a damn for
you nor them either;' I begged the servants who were there to
send for a policeman; the defendant then came in at the front door,
and asked what was the matter? I said, 'Mr. Wheeler is making
a disturbance, and I appeal to you for protection;' the defendant
said to the plaintiff, *'You must not make a disturbance, and you   [*265]
must not go up stairs;' the plaintiff said he would, and that I was
a swindler and a robber, and he held his fist over me; the defendant said, 'You shall not go upstairs, Mr. Wheeler;' and the
plaintiff replied, 'I will go into every room in your house in defiance
of you;' the policeman then came in, and I desired him to take the
plaintiff in charge; a scuffle ensued, and the defendant said, 'If
you don't go out of the house peaceably, I will turn you out,' and
the defendant then ordered the policeman to do his duty; he said,
'Do your duty, I won't have a disturbance in this house;' the

plaintiff was then taken from the house; the high sheriff, Sir
Benjamin Hall, and the principal men of the county were dining
up stairs; the defendant did not order the plaintiff to be taken to
the station-house, and I never knew that he had been taken there
till about a week ago; I do not consider that I owe the plaintiff
anything, but he has brought an action against me."

PATTESON, J. (in summing up):

I think that the third plea is not good, and I certainly never saw
such a plea before. The landlord of an inn or a public-house, or
the occupier of a private house, whenever a person conducts himself as the plaintiff did, (even according to the evidence of his own
witness), is justified in telling him to leave the house, and if he
will not do so, he is justified in putting him out by force, and may
call in his servants to assist him in so doing. He might also
authorise a policeman to do it, but it would be no part of a policeman's duty as such, unless the party had committed some offence
punishable by law. But, although it would be no part of a policeman's duty to do this, it might be better in many cases that a
policeman should assist the owner of the house in a matter of this
kind, as he would probably get the person out of the house with
less disturbance than the owner himself could do. I think that
the defendant was quite justified in having the plaintiff turned out
[*266] of the house; *but to give him in charge to a policeman " to be
dealt with according to law," is a very different thing. Telling a
policeman to take charge of him is the same as telling the policeman to keep him in custody. Now as to the imprisonment, the
defendant pleads that the plaintiff was making a disturbance in
the house, and ready and desirous to commit a breach of the peace,
whereupon he gave him in charge to the policeman, to be dealt
with according to law; the policeman, however, was not justified
in taking him, unless he saw some breach of the peace committed:
on a charge of felony it would be different. There are several
questions in this case: 1st. Did the defendant cause the plaintiff
to be assaulted and turned out of the house? It is plain that he
did; 2nd. Was the plaintiff conducting himself in an improper
manner and disturbing the quiet of the house, and did the defendant
desire him to leave, and on his refusal to do so put him out? On
this question it is proved by the plaintiff's own witness that the
plaintiff was so conducting himself, for even if the plaintiff had
been ill used by Mr. Lawrence, he was not justified in saying he

would follow him into every room in the house, and if he did so say, the landlord had a right to tell him to leave the house and insist on his doing so.   Then, did the defendant request the plaintiff to depart before force was used ?   It is essential to the defence that that should be shown, for although a person be in the house of another and misconducting himself, the owner has no right to turn him out by force, without first requesting him to depart.   With respect to the imprisonment, you will consider whether the defendant ordered the policeman to take the plaintiff.   The policeman says he did, but it is said on the other side that the defendant did not tell the policeman to take the plaintiff to the station-house. That may be; but if you give a person in charge to a policeman, you do not tell the policeman what he is to do with him; and you will also consider whether the plaintiff was intending to commit a breach of the peace, as *stated in the last plea.   I think that that plea is not good in point of law, but as the plaintiff has taken no objection to it in point of law, but has denied it to be true in point of fact, I shall take your opinion upon it in point of fact, leaving the Court of Queen's Bench to deal with it hereafter.

[*267]

> *Verdict for the plaintiff on the general issue, and on the 3rd plea with 5l. damages, and for the defendant on the 2nd plea.*

C. Phillips and *Greaves*, for the plaintiff.

Ludlow, Serjt., and *Whateley*, for the defendant.

MUDDLE *v.* STRIDE AND OTHERS.
(9 Car. & P. 380—383.)

In an action against the proprietors of a steam-vessel, to recover compensation for damage done to goods sent by them as carriers, if, on the whole, it be left in doubt what the cause of the injury was, or, if it may as well be attributable to perils of the seas as to negligence, the plaintiff cannot recover; but if the perils of the seas required that more care should be used in the stowing of the goods on board than was bestowed on them, that will be negligence, for which the owners of the vessel will be answerable.

Whether, in such a case, on the arrival, and detention by foul weather, of the vessel at a place from which the goods could be conveyed by land to their destination, the captain of the vessel is bound to give notice to the consignee of the fact, to enable him, if he think proper, to obtain the goods earlier by sending for them—*Quære!*

THIS was an action against the defendants as representatives of the Margate New Steam Packet Company, to recover compensation

for damage sustained by certain goods which they undertook to
convey by one of their vessels from London to the plaintiff, who
was a silk mercer and draper, carrying on business at Dover, to
which place one of the Company's vessels was in the habit of going.
The first count of the declaration stated, that the defendants did
not use due care; and the second, that they promised to deliver
the goods within a reasonable time, but did not. The defendants
pleaded the general issue—not guilty; and also that they never
received the goods.

The evidence for the plaintiff showed that the goods, which were
articles of silk and linen, were bought at a Custom-House sale.
The person who bought them said that they were in good order,
and that he packed them carefully in a three-inch deal packing-
case, in which they were taken on board the *Royal Adelaide*. The
vessel left London Bridge Wharf the same morning as the goods
were put on board—viz. a few days before the end of August—and
met with very rough weather; and, on her arrival off Dover,
signals were made to inform the captain that it would be dangerous
for the vessel to attempt to enter the harbour at Dover, and, in
consequence, she put back, and went to Margate, where she
remained. There was not any vessel went from Margate to Dover
until the 4th of September, on which day the goods were sent by
the *Royal George*, another vessel belonging to the defendants. On
the packing-case being opened at Dover, the goods were found to
be damaged—part of them were wet, and the packing paper at one
side of the case was also wetted, and a very offensive smell issued
from the box. The damage done to the goods altogether was
estimated at 20*l.*

[381]   At the close of the plaintiff's case, Lord DENMAN, Ch. J., was
inclined to think, that the evidence left it in doubt whether the
damage was occasioned by the negligence of the defendants or not.
But the jury expressing a wish to hear the defence,

Thesiger, for the defendants, contended, that there was not
any negligence on the part of those who had the care of the vessel,
but that any damage which happened must have been occasioned
by perils of the seas.

The captain and some of the crew were examined as witnesses
for the defence, and stated, that the vessel was obliged to return to
Margate in consequence of the weather; and that, on her arrival
there, the goods were removed from the deck, and put into the

cabin, from which they were not removed till they were put on board the *Royal George*, on the 4th of September. The man who had the care of the goods during the voyage, swore that they were all dry when the vessel arrived at Margate, and, although she shipped several heavy seas, yet the goods were not any of them damaged by water.

Crowder, for the plaintiff, in reply,* after referring to Story on Carriers, p. 344, and the case of *Golden* v. *Manning* (1), contended, that peril of the seas was the only defence which the defendants could set up; and also that they ought, when the vessel arrived at Margate, to have given notice to the plaintiff, in order that he might, if he *pleased, have sent for the goods himself, and so   [*382] obtained them earlier.

LORD DENMAN, Ch. J. (in summing up):

The first count of the declaration states, that the defendants did not use due care; and the second, that they did not deliver the goods within a reasonable time. The defendants have pleaded— first, not guilty, which puts the whole question of negligence in issue; and secondly and thirdly, that they did not receive the goods in the manner mentioned, which is a pure untruth; and I cannot tell why these things should be done—it is quite disgraceful. On the part of the plaintiff it is said, that the only defence is the perils of the seas; and that is true, I think. I do not see any other mode which the defendants have of excusing themselves. I thought at first, at the close of the plaintiff's case, that it was left in doubt as to whether the damage was occasioned by the negligence of the defendants. But you wished the case to proceed, and I am glad that I suffered it to go on. For the question is now set at rest; for the man in whose care the goods were, says that they were quite dry when they arrived at Margate, so that the sea water could not have damaged them. However, the injury appears to me to be of a very mysterious kind. The goods appear to have been injured by some liquid of an offensive character. If you think that was the consequence of any ill-care in the packing of the goods on board the vessel, the defendants will be liable; and even if the perils of the seas required more care in the packing than was bestowed upon them, then the perils of the seas will not be an answer. If, on the whole, in your opinion, it is left in doubt what

(1) 3 Wils. 429, and 2 W. Bl. 916.

MUDDLE
&
STRIDE.

[*383]

the cause of the damage was, then the defendants will be entitled to your verdict; because you are to see clearly that they were guilty of negligence before you can find your verdict against them. If it turns out, in the consideration of the case, that the injury may as well be *attributable to the one cause as the other, then also the defendants will not be liable for negligence. With respect to the detention of the goods at Margate, I think, perhaps, it would have been as well if the defendants, when the vessel arrived there, had communicated to the plaintiff that the goods were there, as possibly he might not have been willing that they should remain so long a time. But that seems to me to be a very minute circumstance in the case. However, if you think that any damage was sustained in consequence, you may give it. On the whole, you will say, whether the goods were damaged from the want of due care on the part of the defendants, and whether there was a detention of them for an unreasonable time.

Verdict for the plaintiff. Damages 20l.

Crowder and *E. James*, for the plaintiff.

Thesiger and *Bodkin*, for the defendant.

1840.
June 2.

[383]

LORD CAMOYS *v.* SCURR, CLERK.

(9 Car. & P. 383—386.)

[*384]

A horse being for sale, A. asked the agent of the vendor to let him have the horse for the purpose of trying it, and the agent did so: Held, that A. was entitled to put a competent person on the horse for the purpose of trying it, and was not limited to merely trying it himself.

CASE. The first count of the declaration stated, that plaintiff " heretofore, to wit, &c. on &c., at the request of *the defendant, delivered to the defendant, and the defendant at his request had the care and custody of a certain mare of the plaintiff, of great value, to wit, of the value of 100l., for the purpose of the defendant riding and trying the same ; and thereupon it then became and was the duty of the defendant, whilst he had the said mare for the purpose aforesaid, to take due and proper care of the same : yet the defendant, not regarding his duty in that behalf, whilst he so had the said mare for the purpose aforesaid, to wit, on the day and year aforesaid, took so little and such bad and improper care thereof, that by reason of the defendant's carelessness and improper conduct in that behalf, the said mare was injured and died." The

declaration contained also a count in trover. Pleas—1st, to the
whole declaration, not guilty ; 2nd, to the first count, "that the
plaintiff did not deliver to the defendant, nor had the defendant the
care and custody of the said mare in the said first count mentioned
in manner and form as in the said first count is alleged ;" (concluding to the country). 3rd plea, to the last count, "that the
defendant committed the alleged grievance in the said last count
mentioned, by the leave and license of the plaintiff to him for that
purpose first given and granted ;" (concluding with a verification).
Replication denying the license.

It was opened by *Kelly*, for the plaintiff, that the mare was
placed in the hands of Mr. Shackel for the purpose of being sold,
and that the defendant, who appeared to like the mare, asked
permission to have a trial of her, which was granted, and the
defendant having received possession of the mare, not only tried
her himself, but put another person's servant on the mare, and
whilst the servant was riding her, the mare was injured, and afterwards died of the injuries she received. He submitted that a person
who had a mare on trial, had no right to put any other person *on
her back ; and that if he did, it was such a conversion as would make
him liable to the owner in an action of trover. He cited the case
of *Bringloe* v. *Morrice* (1).

It was proved by Mr. Shackel that he gave the mare into the
possession of the defendant, for him to have her for the purpose
of trying her. It was admitted that the mare received injuries, of
which she died, while she was thus lent to the defendant.

It was opened by *Platt*, for the defendant, that when the
defendant had himself tried the mare for a short time, he desired
Robert Hobart, who was a very excellent horseman, and who was the
groom of General Dyson, to mount the mare and try her in Hyde

CAMOYS
v.
SCURR.

[*385]

(1) 1 Mod. 210. This was an action
of trespass for immoderately riding
the plaintiff's mare. The defendant
pleaded that the plaintiff lent him the
mare, and gave him license to ride her,
and that by virtue of this license the
defendant and his servant had ridden
the mare alternately. The plaintiff
demurred to the plea. " Per CURIAM.
—The license is annexed to the person,
and cannot be communicated to
another, for this riding is matter of
pleasure. North took a difference
where certain time is limited for the
loan of the horse, and where not. In
the first case, the party to whom the
horse is lent hath an interest in the
horse during that time, and in that
case his servant may ride ; but in the
other case not ; a difference was taken
betwixt hiring a horse to go to York,
and borrowing a horse ; in the first
place the party may set his servant up,
in the second not."

Park; and that on Hobart riding her down the drive on the east
side of the Park the mare ran away with him, and struck herself
against an iron post near Hyde Park Corner, by which the mare
received injuries of which she died, the groom Hobart also receiving
very severe injuries. Upon these facts it was submitted, that the
defendant was entitled to a verdict, as he had a right to put a
person of competent skill on the back of the mare for the purpose
of trying her.

Evidence was given which proved the facts opened for the
defendant.

[386]   COLERIDGE, J.:

The defendant had this mare for the purpose of trying her, and
I think that he was entitled to put a competent person on the mare
to try her. I shall leave it to the jury to say, whether the groom
of General Dyson was a competent person, and whether he rode
the mare only for the purpose of trying her. On the part of the
plaintiff it has been argued, that the defendant was guilty of a
conversion; but if no accident at all had happened, could it be
said that putting the groom on the mare to try her was such a
conversion as would make the defendant liable in an action of
trover? The only question of fact is, whether the defendant did
any more than was necessary for the purpose of trying the mare.

Kelly, for the plaintiff, elected to be nonsuited.

                                                 Nonsuit.

Kelly and *Humfrey*, for the plaintiff.

Platt and *Petersdorff*, for the defendant.

On a subsequent day *Kelly* applied to the Court to set aside the
nonsuit, on the ground that the defendant had no right to allow
the groom Hobart to ride the mare for him; but the COURT
refused a rule.

————————

GUY *v.* GREGORY.

(9 Car. & P. 584.)

In an action for a libel which imputed that the plaintiff's house was
opened as a gaming-house, under the leadership of a woman of notorious
character. The plaintiff alleged in his declaration that his house was a
club-house, and that divers persons paid annual subscriptions. The payment of subscriptions was denied by one of the defendant's pleas, and

evidence was given that a book was kept for subscribers' names, and that
two gentlemen wrote their names in this book; but no evidence was given
of the payment of any subscription: Held, that there was evidence to go to
the jury in support of the allegation in the declaration.

    The defendant pleaded several pleas, but none of them at all referring to
the plaintiff's wife: Held, that the plaintiff could not go into evidence to
show that his wife was a respectable person, as on these pleadings she
must be taken to be so: Held, also, that the plaintiff could not go into
evidence to show that his wife had become ill, and died soon after the
publication of the libels.

GUY
v.
GREGORY.

LIBEL.   The declaration stated, that before and at the time of
the committing of the grievances, the plaintiff, together with his
wife and family, was the occupier and possessor of a certain
house known by the name or sign of the "Cocoa Tree," for the
purpose of opening the same as a club-house, and carrying on the
business of a club-house tavern and coffee-house keeper, and had
opened the same as *a club-house, and carried on the said business
there; and that divers persons had paid divers annual sums for
the privilege of using and frequenting the said house; and that
the defendant, in a certain newspaper called the *Satirist*, on the
22nd of March, 1840, published a libel on the plaintiff.   This libel
imputed that the "Cocoa Tree" in St. James's Street "was opened
by a party of play-table sharpers, under the recognised leadership
of a woman of notorious character."   The 2nd count stated another
libel, in the *Satirist* of the 29th of March.   This libel contained
imputations that the house was a gaming-house, at which persons
were defrauded of their money.   The 3rd count stated a third
libel, contained in the *Satirist* of the 5th of April, which, after
making similar imputations, stated that a sporting Earl, who had
been plundered of some money there, went with some friends, and
took away a case of fraudulent dice; and it then went on to state,
that "the keeper of the den, a notorious woman, who formerly
kept a house of ill fame at Pimlico, and subsequently lived in
Panton Square, and recently in Bolton Row, being discovered by
the party, they removed the brick-dust from her cheeks, substituting layers of black lead, in order, as they said, that she
might, in colour at least, be a correct representation of her foster-
father, his satanic majesty."   The declaration also stated special
damage, but of this no evidence was given.   Pleas—1st, not guilty;
2nd, as to so much of the declaration as related to the plaintiff's
opening the house as a club-house, and carrying on the business as
a tavern and coffee-house keeper—a plea, denying that the plaintiff
did so; 3rd, as to the allegation that persons paid annual sums for

[*585]

the privilege of using the house as a club-house—a plea, denying that they had done so: 4th, to a part of the first count—a plea, stating in substance that the plaintiff and a person named Smart, and a woman of notorious character, named Harrison, kept the house called the "Cocoa Tree" as a common gaming-house; *5th, as to part of the libel in the second count, that the plaintiff had knowingly suffered loaded dice to be used in the house, whereby persons were defrauded by the plaintiff; 6th, to the whole of the first count, that the plaintiff kept a common gaming-house; 7th and 8th, the like as to the whole of the second and third counts. These three latter pleas were in the usual form of an indictment for keeping a common gaming-house. Replication as to those pleas which concluded to the country, a *similiter*, and as to the other pleas, *de injuria*.

It was opened by *Thesiger* for the plaintiff, that the plaintiff had taken the house known as the "Cocoa Tree" club-house, in St. James's Street, intending to open it as a club-house, and that several gentlemen had become subscribers to it; and that soon after the publication of these libels the plaintiff's wife had become ill, and died.

The publication of the libels by the defendant was proved; and to prove the introductory allegations of the declaration, two of the plaintiff's servants were called, who proved that the house had been fitted-up as a club-house; and one of them proved that a book was kept for subscribers to insert their names, in which book he had seen Count d'Orsay and Colonel Bentinck put their signatures; but there was no evidence of any subscription having been actually paid.

Thesiger, for the plaintiff, proposed to ask one of the witnesses as to the state of health of the plaintiff's wife just after these libels were published.

Chadwicke Jones, for the defendant:

I submit that any thing that has occurred to Mrs. Guy cannot be evidence in this cause.

COLERIDGE, J.:

How is it relevant to any of these issues? The plaintiff could not in this action recover damages either for the sufferings of his wife, or for the *loss occasioned by her death. It does not seem to me to be relevant to the inquiry.

Thesiger :

I submit that it is evidence, as showing the general nature and character of these libels. They refer in direct terms to the plaintiff's wife; and we may therefore be allowed to give general evidence of the effect the libels had on her.

COLERIDGE, J. :

If you had stated her illness on the record, you could not have gone into evidence of it; and I think you cannot do so the more, as you have not stated it.

Thesiger :

As the libels assail the plaintiff's wife, may I show that she is a respectable person ?

COLERIDGE, J. :

I think that she must be taken to be so.

The evidence was rejected.

Chadwicke Jones objected that there was no evidence on the third issue, that any one had paid any subscription.

COLERIDGE, J. :

I think there is evidence to go to the jury.

Chadwicke Jones, for the defendant, addressed the jury on that point, and also in mitigation of damages.

COLERIDGE, J., left it to the jury to say whether, on the evidence, they were satisfied that subscriptions had been paid, or whether they thought, by putting their names in the book, the gentlemen who had been mentioned merely meant to intimate that they were willing to become subscribers.

> *Verdict for the plaintiff on all but the third issue, with 100l. damages; and on the third issue, for the defendant.*

MACKENZIE v. COX.

(9 Car. & P. 632—634.)

[632]

If A. place a dog with B., and the dog be received by B., to be kept by him, for reward to be paid to him by A., B. is not answerable for the loss of the dog if he took reasonable care of it; but if the dog be lost, the *onus* lies on B. to acquit himself by showing that he was not in fault with respect to the loss.

CASE. The declaration stated, that the plaintiff, at the request of the defendant, delivered to the defendant divers, to wit, three dogs of the plaintiff, " to be by the defendant kept, fed, and taken care of, for reward to the defendant in that behalf; and the defendant then had and received the said dogs for the purpose aforesaid; yet the defendant, not regarding his duty on that behalf whilst he had the dogs for the purpose aforesaid, to wit, on, &c., took so little and such bad and improper care of the said dogs, that by and through the negligence, carelessness, and improper conduct of the defendant in that behalf, one of the said dogs became and was wholly lost to the plaintiff." Pleas—first, not guilty, and, second, that the defendant did not receive the dogs, or either of them, to be taken care of for reward.

On the part of the plaintiff, it appeared that three dogs of the plaintiff were put into the stables of the defendant, who was a livery-stable keeper, and that his ostler was paid money to buy them food, and that one of the dogs was afterwards lost; but no evidence was given on the part of the plaintiff as to how the loss of this dog had occurred.

[633]

On the part of the defendant it was proved, that before the dogs were placed in the defendant's stable the plaintiff said to the defendant that he had a horse and three dogs which he wished to place with him, and that the defendant replied, that he did not take in dogs, but he should have no objection to the dogs being with the horse; and that on the plaintiff asking whether the dogs would be safe, the defendant replied that he had never lost anything, and referred the plaintiff to the ostler. With respect to the loss, it was proved by the defendant's ostler, that on the evening of the night on which the dog was lost, he locked it up in the stable, and that he missed it between twelve and one o'clock on that night, the stable-door having been opened by a false key; and this witness further stated, that he gave immediate information of the loss.

Shee, Serjt., in reply :

If a person has goods left with him without reward, he is only

bound to take such care of them as he would take of his own; but if
they are placed with him for hire, he must prove to your satisfaction
that he took every care of them which a person reasonably could take.

GURNEY, B. (in summing up) :

In this case, the plaintiff must make out to your satisfaction that
this dog was received by the defendant for reward to be paid by the
plaintiff to the defendant; and if that be made out to your satisfaction, the next question is, whether the defendant has been negligent.
With respect to the first question, evidence was given on the part
of the plaintiff, that the dogs were placed at the defendant's stable;
but no evidence was given on the part of the plaintiff, as to the
manner in which the dog was lost, the *onus* being on the defendant
to acquit himself, by showing that he was not in fault with respect
to the loss of it.   The defendant has adduced *evidence on both   [*634]
questions, and has called witnesses to show that the dog was not
received for reward, and that the stable was entered by a false key;
and even if a person does take goods into his possession for reward,
he is not answerable for their loss if he takes reasonable care of
them; and it is for you to say, whether, locking these dogs into a
stable, was not taking reasonable care of them; and if you think that
it was, and that a dog-stealer came in the night and stole this dog,
then the defendant is not answerable for the loss.   You will consider
on the whole of the evidence that has been given; first, whether the
defendant received the dogs for reward to be paid him; and secondly,
whether this dog was lost by the negligence of the defendant.

Verdict for the defendant on both issues.

Shee, Serjt., and *R. Gurney,* for the plaintiff.

Platt, and *F. V. Lee,* for the defendant.

DOE D. PITTMAN *v.* SUTTON AND OTHERS (1).

(9 Car. & P. 706—709.)

1841.
Feb. 13.
——
[706]

A covenant "forthwith" to put premises into complete repair, must
receive a reasonable construction (2), and is not to be limited to any specific
time; and therefore it will be for the jury to say upon the evidence, whether
the defendant has done what he reasonably ought in the performance of it.

A lessee covenanted to insure, and the premises were uninsured for a
week: Held, in an ejectment for a forfeiture for a breach of this covenant,

(1) Dist. in *Doe* v. *Gladwin* (1845) 6   "within a reasonable time": *Roberts*
Q. B. 962, 14 L. J. Q. B. 189.—A. C.   v. *Brett* (1865) 11 H. L. C. 337.—F. P.

(2) "Forthwith" held to mean

that the lessor could not recover if he, by his conduct, had led the lessee to believe that the premises were properly insured by himself.

A lease (among other covenants) contained a covenant by the lessee to insure, with a proviso that if he did not do so the lessor might insure and distrain on the lessee for the premiums. The lease contained the usual proviso as to forfeiture. Whether the lessee's omitting to insure would incur a forfeiture—*Quære ?*

EJECTMENT to recover premises in the parish of St. Martin's-in-the-Fields.

It was opened by *F. Robinson* for the plaintiff, that this ejectment was brought by the lessor of the plaintiff as landlord of the house, No. 69, Strand, and a house in Theobald's Court, against the defendant Sutton, by reason of the forfeiture of the lease by breaches of covenant in not putting the premises into "complete and substantial repair," and in not keeping the premises insured; and that the defendant Sutton had been in possession of the premises since the year 1838, although the lease was not granted till the year 1840.

The lease of the premises, dated the 18th of March, 1840, was put in ; it was between the lessor of the plaintiff of the one part, the defendant Sutton of the other part, and by it the property was demised by the former to the latter for twenty-one years from the 24th of June, 1838. This lease contained a covenant that the lessee would "forthwith" put the premises "into complete and

[*707]   substantial repair," and keep them "in good *and substantial repair ; " and also a covenant that the lessee would insure them and keep them insured in the Westminster Fire Office, or in some other office to be approved by the lessor, for 2,500*l*., in the joint names of the lessor and lessee ; and that if the lessee made default in insuring, the lessor might do so, and charge the lessee with the premiums, and recover them by distress. The lease also contained the usual proviso of re-entry for breach of any covenants contained in the lease.

With respect to the insurance, it was proved, that, in the years 1838 and 1839, the premises had been insured for 2,500*l*. in the Westminster Fire Office, in the name of the lessor of the plaintiff only, and that the policy was allowed to expire on the 7th of October, 1839, and that the premises remained uninsured till the 13th of October following, when they were insured by the lessor of the plaintiff in the joint names of himself and Sutton. But it was also proved, that, in the years 1838 and 1839, the premiums of the insurance were paid after the policy had been allowed to expire, and that the lessor of the plaintiff had paid 10s. 4d. additional for the new policy in 1840, which had been repaid him by the defendant Sutton; and it was also proved, that the notices of the premiums becoming due had been always sent to the solicitors of the lessor of the plaintiff, and there was no evidence that they had ever been transmitted to the defendant.

With respect to the repairs, it was proved by Mr. Mayhew, the surveyor of the Westminster Fire Office, that the premises were not in repair, as one of the chimneys had bulged; a drain was stopped; some iron stays were wanting to support a chimney shaft; the roof of a room at the back of No. 69, Strand, was out of repair; a dormer door was defective; the floor of one of the rooms in No. 69, Strand, was shored up; two ridge tiles were broken, and some weather-boarding required repair; and a window was broken. But this witness could not state what amount of repairs was needed.

Thesiger, for the defendant: [708]

I submit that the non-insurance cannot work a forfeiture of this lease; because it is expressly provided, that, if the lessee makes default in insuring, the lessor is to do it, and distrain for the premium.

LORD DENMAN, Ch. J.:

I shall reserve that point if it shall become necessary.

On the part of the defendant, a letter from the solicitors of the lessor of the plaintiff to the defendant Sutton was put in, dated in the year 1839, in which they stated, that the lease could not be granted till the defendant Sutton had shown by receipts that he had expended 500l. in repair on the premises; and a surveyor was called, who stated that as much as 500l. had been expended by the defendant Sutton on repairs, and that the bulging of the chimney was caused by an under-tenant keeping granite to the extent of several tons weight on the floor, which was shored up, and that this did not arise from want of repair. And this witness also stated, that the roof of the room was sufficient to go through the winter, and that he had advised the defendant Sutton to delay its repair till the spring; and that he saw no fault in the drainage, and believed that the iron stays were not deficient.

LORD DENMAN, Ch. J. (in summing up):

Upon this covenant to repair having a reasonable construction

put upon it, you will have to say whether or not the defendant has
or has not performed it. It is absurd to attempt to construe this
covenant according to the strictest view of it, because it is impossible. The word is "forthwith," which cannot here mean either a
day or a week; and you must say, on such reasonable construction
of the terms of the covenant, whether the defendant Sutton has
really done what he reasonably ought in the performance of it.
[*709] With respect to these premises being uninsured for a *week, it
appears that the insurance had previously been in the name of the
lessor of the plaintiff, and the notices always sent to his solicitors,
and, as far as we know, never transmitted to the defendant, the
policy always remaining in the name of the lessor of the plaintiff
only; you will therefore consider, whether the lessor of the plaintiff
by his conduct led the defendant Sutton to believe that the premises
were insured by him; for, if the lessor by his conduct led the lessee
to believe that the premises were properly insured, he cannot come
on the tenant for a forfeiture by reason of their not being insured.

Verdict for the defendant.

C. Cresswell and *F. Robinson*, for the plaintiff.

Thesiger, N. Clarke, and *Fry*, for the defendant.

———————•———————

1841.   DOE D. THE TRUSTEES OF THE SCHOOLS AND
[734]   ALMSHOUSES OF THE CITY OF WORCESTER r.
ROWLANDS.

(9 Car. & P. 734—740; S. C. 5 Jur. 177.)

In an action of covenant the declaration stated, that the defendant covenanted to occupy demised premises in a proper manner, and to keep them
in repair. Breaches—that the defendant did not occupy in a proper manner,
and did not keep the premises in repair. Plea—that the defendant did
occupy in a proper manner, and did keep the premises in repair: Held.
that on these issues the plaintiff had the right to begin.

In an action of covenant for non-repair of premises, held by the defendant
under a lease which has several years to run, the proper measure of damages
is not the amount that would be required to put the premises into repair:
but the amount to which the reversion is injured by the premises being out
of repair.

A tenant's allowing a footpath to be made across a part of demised premises,
is no breach of a covenant to occupy the premises in a proper manner.

COVENANT. The declaration stated that the plaintiffs had, on the
14th of June, 1808, demised to the defendant certain premises,

consisting of a warehouse, a stable and garden-ground, situate at the Butts, in the city of Worcester, for the term of forty-one years from Lady Day, 1806, at a rent of 12*l.* a year; and that the defendant, in and by the said lease, covenanted to occupy the premises in a proper manner, and well and sufficiently to repair and uphold the buildings demised; and, if necessary, to rebuild the warehouse, and also to keep in repair the pales and fences.   Breach —that the defendant did not well and sufficiently repair and uphold the buildings, and keep in repair the pales and fences, and that he did not occupy the demised premises in a proper manner.   Pleas— that the defendant did well and sufficiently repair and uphold the building, and did keep in repair the pales and fences, and also that he did occupy the demised premises in a proper manner.

Talfourd, Serjt., for the defendant, claimed the right to begin.

Ludlow, Serjt., for the plaintiffs: [735]

I submit that the plaintiffs must begin, by showing in what respect the defendant has broken his covenant.   One of the issues is, whether the defendant has occupied in a proper manner.   If the defendant is to prove good occupation, he must prove all that he has ever done from the beginning of his lease; and when he has proved ninety-nine things done, which the plaintiffs care nothing about, the defendant then comes to the hundredth, which is the real matter in dispute; and on the covenant to repair, the defendant will have to prove all that he has done, and that may be for the most part what we do not complain of.

COLERIDGE, J.:

If there was no evidence offered on either side, which party would have the verdict?

Ludlow, Serjt.:

I apprehend that that is not always the criterion, but that the question is, who is the substantial actor.

Talfourd, Serjt.:

That way of putting it would always give the plaintiff the right to begin, as the plaintiff is always the actor in seeking damages. The decisions are not all of them easily reconciled; but at the last sittings there was an action of covenant against a master for not properly teaching his apprentice, and he pleaded that he did properly teach him; and the Lord Chief Justice TINDAL held that there was no issue on the plaintiff. My brother *Channel* was on the one side, and my brother *Bompas* on the other.

COLERIDGE, J. :

There was a case at Bristol, where the question was, whether a horse was sound (1). The defendant pleaded that he was sound, and I allowed him to begin; but I think I was wrong.

[736]   *Talfourd*, Serjt. :

Unsound is an affirmative.

Ludlow, Serjt. :

It is in your Lordship's discretion; but if your Lordship decides against me I can have no new trial if the Court should think I ought to have begun.

COLERIDGE, J. :

I think you should, if I decided against you, and the Court should think that I was wrong in not letting you begin. It would be a disadvantage to you, and I think that you ought to have an opportunity of having the point reconsidered.

Ludlow, Serjt. :

If a defendant alleges collateral matter in answer to the declaration, I apprehend that the defendant begins; but if the plea is a mere denial of the declaration, whether affirmative or negative, the plaintiff should begin.

COLERIDGE, J. :

The rule of the Judges, referred to in the case of *Carter* v. *Jones* (2), is not a rule of general application, but only applies to particular actions, of which this is not one.

Ludlow, Serjt. :

If, in an action of trespass a right of way is set up, it is a new case; but these pleas are really no more than a denial of the plaintiff's cause of action.

[737]   COLERIDGE, J. :

I think that the plaintiffs should begin.

(1) The case of *Fisher* v. *Joyce*, *Thompson*, 9 Car. & P. p. 337. referred to in the case of *Osborn* v.   (2) 6 Car. & P. p. 64.

Ludlow, Serjt., opened his case, and stated, that since the granting of the lease, several cottages and other buildings had been erected on the demised premises, in addition to those which were there at the time of the granting of the lease, and that the whole of the buildings and fences were out of repair. He also stated that the gardens had been converted into masons' yards, and that the defendant had allowed footpaths to be made over a part of the demised premises.

To prove the want of repair, Mr. Edward Lucy was called. He said: " I am an architect and builder; I know the property at the Butts, in the possession of the defendant; on the 25th of February last I surveyed it; the property consists of a large warehouse, and also rooms over the warehouse which are let out for dwellings; the outer walls of the warehouse are in a shattery state; the arches of the windows are tumbling out, and it is, as I think, in a dangerous state; there are four small tenements; they are in a bad state, and want renovating; the roofs want repairing; the fence in front is in a very bad state; some other tenements are at the other end; they are also out of repair; there is some fence that has been attempted to be repaired; I have known the place for forty years; it was a garden then; it is now pigsties, bowling-alleys, cart-sheds, and stone-masons' yards; that is in my judgment not a proper occupation of garden ground; it is a deterioration of the property; my estimate of the repairs is 157*l.* 12*s.*; but I could not undertake to put the premises into repair for that money."

In his cross-examination he said: " I recollect the place *in 1806 or 1808; part of it was then garden ground. I consider the property worth less now than it was then. Four of the tenements have been built since 1808, and the four others were made out of the stable. I don't think 500*l.* has been laid out on the place by Mr. Rowlands. My estimate includes the repairing of all the buildings that are there now. The tenements built of Broseley brick, which are furthest from the Severn, were built since the lease; the repairing of them would amount to 30*l.* The building opposite Broadfield was also built since the lease; the repair of that would be about 5*l.* The mason's shop we put a sovereign down for. I put down a sum of 69*l.* for buildings and fences. The want of repair arises not from any sudden cause but from gradual decay and neglect."

On the part of the plaintiff it was proposed to show, that the defendant allowed foot-paths to be made over the property.

[*738]

COLERIDGE, J. :

How do you make this a breach of these covenants ?

Ludlow, Serjt. :

I put it as occupying the land in an improper manner. I submit, that if a person rents gardens, it is a breach of a covenant to occupy in a proper manner if he make pigsties and roads there, and allow windows to be opened.

M'Mahon, on the same side :

If a person is to occupy gardens in a proper manner, it must be by occupying them as gardens.

COLERIDGE, J. :

I think that the tenant's allowing foot-paths across the property is not a breach of this covenant, because the only way in which it could be so is, that the landlord would be bound by what the tenant did, which he certainly would not be (1).

[739]   *Talfourd*, Serjt., for the defendant, submitted that the defendant was not liable at all for the non-repair of any building erected since the granting of the lease, and with respect to the original buildings the jury ought to give very small damages; first, because the buildings were very old, and secondly because the lease had several years to run, and whatever damages the jury gave in this action, the plaintiffs would not be bound, and could not be compelled, to lay them out in repairs.

COLERIDGE, J. (in summing up) :

In this case there is, for all that appears, a valid subsisting lease of this property, which contains a covenant to repair, which has been to some extent broken; and for that breach of covenant the plaintiffs are entitled to damages, notwithstanding that the lease is in existence and has some years to run. If a lease were granted containing such a covenant as the present, and that lease had 100 years to run, and the covenant was broken in the first year, the landlord would be entitled to some damages for that breach of covenant, though the lease would not expire for 99 years to come; but in estimating the damages in cases where the lease has a long time to run, it is not fair to take the amount that would be necessary

(1) See the case of *Wood* v. *Veal*, 24 R. R. 454 (5 B. & Ald. 454).

to put the premises into repair as the measure of the damages; for
in such cases, when the damages are awarded to the landlord, he
is not bound to expend them in repairs, neither can he do so without the tenant's permission to enter on the premises. The true
question therefore is—to what extent is the reversion injured by
the non-repair of the premises? If the lease had ninety-nine years
to run, it could not make much difference in the value of the reversion whether the premises were now in repair or not. This lease
however will expire in about six years. It appears also that this
property originally consisted of a warehouse, a stable, and gardens;
and the plaintiffs say that the erection of the present tenements
was wrongful; but they (waiving that for the *present) have sent   [*740]
surveyors who make an estimate amounting to between 150*l.* and
160*l.* The defendant says "I may have done wrong by putting up
these tenements, but on the covenants contained in this lease I am
only bound well and sufficiently to repair and uphold, and, if need
be, to rebuild the warehouse and stable, and to keep the hedges,
pales, and other fences in tenantable repair;" and I think that
under this covenant the defendant is only bound to keep in repair
the buildings which were on the premises at the time of the granting
of the lease, and to rebuild them if necessary, and to keep up the
fences; and that in estimating the damages you ought not to take
into consideration the new cottages that have been built since the
granting of the lease. The surveyors have mentioned a sum of
30*l.* for the repair of the Broseley-brick cottages, and also sums
of 5*l.* and 1*l.*, for repairing some other buildings, all of which must
be deducted if these buildings were not in existence at the time
of the granting of the lease. The learned Serjeant (*Talfourd*) has
said that you must make a further deduction on account of the age
of the building; but I do not go that length; for as the tenant is
not only to repair but to rebuild if necessary, the plaintiffs are
entitled to have such parts of the premises, as this covenant relates
to, kept always in good repair. The question therefore that you
have to determine is—how much the reversion is injured by the
breach of this covenant, the covenant being limited to the original
buildings and to the fences.

Verdict for the plaintiffs. Damages 40*l.*

Ludlow, Serjt., *Curwood* and *M'Mahon*, for the plaintiffs.

Talfourd, Serjt., and *R. V. Richards*, for the defendant.

49—

BANNISTER AND ANOTHER *v.* BANNISTER AND OTHERS.

(9 Car. & P. 743—746.)

> The custom is that when butty colliers leave off working a coal mine.
> without giving notice, they are not entitled to be paid for gate roading. air
> heading, or coals undergone; but if they leave after having given notice.
> they are entitled to be paid for these things by the owner of the mine; and
> if the mine be not worked, they are not bound to wait till the working is
> recommenced. and to be then paid by the succeeding butty collier.

ASSUMPSIT for work and labour.   Plea—*non assumpserunt,* by
all the defendants except George Bannister, and as to him judgment
by default.

It was opened by *Ludlow,* Serjt., for the plaintiff, that this
action was brought by the plaintiffs, who were butty colliers,
against the defendants, as owners of the Tividale Colliery, for the
sum of 149*l.* 17*s.* for 125 yards of gate roading, 132 yards of air
heading, and about 42 tons of coals undergone.   He admitted, that
the plaintiffs had been paid for all the coal raised; but he submitted that the custom was, that, when butty colliers left working
at a mine, after giving fourteen days' notice, they were entitled to
be paid for gate roading, air heading, and coals undergone.

On the part of the plaintiff it was proved that the quantities of
gate roading, air heading, and coals undergone were as before
stated, and that the prices charged, which were according to a
valuation made by Mr. Yardley, a mine surveyor, were fair and
reasonable; and it was proved by Mr. John Jones that he was
present when Mr. Aston, one of the plaintiffs, gave a written notice
to Mr. Charles Bannister, the managing clerk at the mine, that the
plaintiffs intended to discontinue the working there.

Several witnesses were called, who stated that the custom was,
that when butty colliers left without giving notice they were not

[*744]   entitled to be paid for either gate *roading or air heading, or coals
undergone; but that if they left after notice, they were entitled to
be paid for that species of work by the owner of the mine, or by
the succeeding butty collier.   A letter from Mr. Hickman Bond, one
of the defendants, was also given in evidence.   It was as follows:

" SIR,—If you will meet here to-morrow morning at nine o'clock.
and bring or send the tools, &c., you took from here, by that time
you can receive the amount of your valuation.

" I am, Sir, yours, &c.

" Mr. H. BANNISTER, Tividale,   " G. H. BOND."
    Tuesday, Sept. 10, 1839."

It was opened by *Talfourd*, Serjt., for the defendants, that he should call Mr. Charles Bannister to prove that he had never received any notice; and he should also call several witnesses to show, that, by the custom, the owner of the mine was never called on to pay for gate roading and air heading, and that if the butty collier left without notice, he was not entitled to be paid for the work by any one; and that if he left after notice he had no claim on the mine owner, but was entitled to receive the amount due for this work from the succeeding butty collier.

For the defendants, Mr. Charles Bannister was called, and he stated that he had never received any notice from Mr. Aston; and with respect to the custom several witnesses were called, who stated that the custom was, that if the working of the mine was stopped, the butty collier was not paid for work of this kind till the working of the mine was recommenced by another butty collier, no matter at what distance of time, but the witnesses could give only a few instances within the last two or three years; and one of them (Mr. Alton), who was a ground bailiff, and whose father and grandfather had been so before him, was aware of only two instances within his own knowledge *where this had occurred; and he stated that, in one of those, a part of the butty collier's claim had been liquidated by the mine owner.

Ludlow, Serjt., in reply, observed that the custom contended for by the defendants came to this: A butty collier might do this work in the year 1841, and because the mine owner did not choose to have his mine worked till the year 1941, the butty collier's representatives were to wait till that time to be paid.

GURNEY, B. (in summing up):

This is an action brought by the plaintiffs, who were butty colliers, against the defendants, as mine owners, for gate roadings, air headings, and coals undergone. The plaintiffs have rested their claim on a custom that, where butty colliers leave after notice, they shall be paid for these things by the mine owner or the succeeding butty collier. The defendants allege that this is not the custom, and that the custom is, that the mine owner is in no case liable to pay for work of this sort, but that the butty collier's claim is only against the new butty collier; and that if the mine be not worked, the person who has done this work would have to go unpaid for any number of years. To show that this is

BANNISTER
v.
BANNISTER.

[*745]

BANNISTER
v.
BANNISTER.

the custom, you would, I think, require the evidence to be strong and complete; but even the witness (Mr. Alton), whose father and grandfather were ground bailiffs before him, can find only two instances, and those within these three years. The plaintiffs say that nothing is to be paid if the parties leave without notice, and that is a reasonable custom. Then you will have to consider whether there was notice given in this case; and upon this point I am sorry to say that the evidence is completely contradictory, and you must decide between the two witnesses; and it is for you to say whether the note from Mr. Bond, which has been put in,

[*746]

does not show in what way the *matter really stood, as in that note Mr. Bond recognised the valuation.

Verdict for the plaintiffs. Damages 149*l.* 17*s.*

Ludlow, Serjt., and *F. V. Lee*, for the plaintiffs.

Talfourd, Serjt., and *R. V. Richards*, for the defendants.

1837.
March 23.

Lancaster.
[28]

DOE d. BAMFORD *v.* BARTON.

(2 Moody & Robinson, 28—29.)

The declarations of an illegitimate member of a family respecting his illegitimate brothers are not admissible as reputation.

THIS was an ejectment to recover certain lands formerly belonging to one Alexander Kershaw. That person died seised in 1788, leaving several illegitimate sons, but no lawful issue; and by his will he devised the property to his illegitimate sons for life, with remainder in tail to their children, the remainder to his own right heirs. The devisees for life being stated to be now dead, without leaving issue, the lessor of the plaintiff claimed as heir-at-law of the testator.

In order to prove that J. S., one of the illegitimate sons of Alexander Kershaw, was dead without issue, the counsel for the plaintiff called a witness, who stated that he was a son-in-law of (X.), another of A. Kershaw's illegitimate sons, (now dead) and that he had heard his father-in-law (X.) say that his natural brother J. S. had died many years ago without issue.

PATTESON, J. expressed an opinion that this was not admissible evidence under the head of reputation.

Atcherley, Serjt., for the plaintiff, said there was no case excluding the declarations of a person *de facto* member of the family on the ground that he was not legitimate, and the principle on which such *declarations were received in evidence (viz. the intimate knowledge which the declarant must be supposed to have of the state of the family) applied as strongly to an illegitimate as to a legitimate member of it, if it were shown, as here it was shown, that he was adopted into the family, and virtually formed part thereof.

PATTESON, J.:

The Courts have not latterly been disposed to enlarge the exception in favour of declarations of this kind. The person whose declarations are now tendered in evidence was not, in point of law, a member of the family of his reputed father; and it would be opening a new and a wide door to such evidence if it were to be received merely because the party was living in habits of intimacy amongst those who were members of the family. I think therefore I cannot receive the evidence.

The evidence was accordingly rejected.

Verdict for the defendant (1).

Atcherley, Serjt., *Wightman*, and *Martin* for the plaintiff.

Cresswell, J. Addison, Cowling, and *J. Henderson* for the defendant.

THORNTON *v.* STEPHEN.

(2 Moody & Robinson, 45—46.)

In an action for a libel contained in a newspaper, the defendant has a right to have read, as part of the plaintiff's case, another part of the same newspaper referred to in the libel complained of.

THIS was an action for a libel contained in the leading article of a newspaper called the *Christian Advocate*.

One paragraph of the libel, set out in the declaration, referred to a report (contained in another column of the same newspaper) of an inquiry which had been instituted by the leading members of a Society of Methodists into the conduct of a Mr. Bullard, at which inquiry the plaintiff took part against him.

The libel alleged various defamatory matters against the plaintiff,

(1) See *Johnson* v. *Lawson*, 27 R. R. 558 (2 Bing. 86).

THORNTON
v.
STEPHEN.

provoked (as the writer said) by the part which the plaintiff had taken against Mr. Bullard.

[46]

R. V. Richards, for the defendant, insisted that he was entitled to have the report of the inquiry read as part of the plaintiff's case.

Sir F. Pollock admitted that the defendant was entitled to have the report brought under the consideration of the jury, inasmuch as it was referred to in the libel complained of, but he contended that the defendant could only do so by making it part of his own evidence.

LORD DENMAN, Ch. J.:

The same point, I think, arose in *Rex* v. *Lambert* and *Perry* (1). It does not indeed distinctly appear in the report whether the remainder of the publication was there read as the defendant's case or as part of the plaintiff's; but I think the import of it is, that it should be considered part of the plaintiff's case.

The report was accordingly read as part of the plaintiff's case.

Verdict for plaintiff. Damages 40s.

Sir F. Pollock and *Matthews* for plaintiff.

R. V. Richards for defendant.

———————

1837.
June 21.
———
Westminster.
[47]

DOE D. CARTER *v.* JAMES.
(2 Moody & Robinson, 47—49.)

A witness is not bound to produce, in obedience to a *subpœna*, a will which he holds as attorney for a devisee claiming under it; although it be suggested that it is a will of personalty, as well as of realty, and ought therefore to be deposited in the Ecclesiastical Court.

EJECTMENT by the heir-at-law of Daniel Symonds, who was heir-at-law of John Symonds.

The defendant claimed as devisee of John Symonds, but admitted the pedigree of the lessor of the plaintiff, and called a witness to produce the will of Daniel Symonds, for the purpose of showing that (after bequeathing his personal property in manner therein mentioned) he devised all his real estate to a stranger (Thomas Minshull). The witness stated himself to be the attorney of

(1) 11 R. R. 748 (2 Camp. 398).

Minshull; that he held the will in question as the attorney of
Minshull, and that he therefore declined to produce it.

Kelly and *B. Andrews*, for the defendant, submitted that the
witness was bound to produce the will. It is a will of personalty
as well as realty, and *should therefore, in strictness, have been
deposited in the Prerogative Office. The person withholding the
will from that place of deposit, where the public may have access
to it, is a wrong-doer, and cannot take advantage of his own wrong
by thus refusing to produce a document which the law has provided
shall be open to the public. If there be any doubt whether the will
be or be not a will of personalty as well as realty, the learned Judge
may himself inspect it for the purpose of ascertaining that fact: a
course which is often taken in questions arising under the stamp
laws. Besides, at present the will is only known as the will of one
Daniel Symonds: whether Thomas Minshull be the devisee under
it, *non constat* until the document be produced.

[*48]

Sir J. Campbell, A.-G. :

It was admitted in the opening that Minshull claimed as devisee
under Symonds's will, which is therefore one of his muniments of
title, and the attorney acts correctly in withholding it. As to the
supposed obligation on the devisee of lodging the will at Doctors'
Commons, the will is here in question only as a will which need not
be so lodged, viz. as a will of realty.

LORD DENMAN, Ch. J. :

. Mr. Minshull has this will as a devisee under it; and that being
so, I do not think I can call on his attorney to produce it. It is
suggested that it is a will of personalty, and that I may refer to it
to ascertain whether the fact be so: but I do not think that a Judge
has any more *privilege to examine the document than any one
else. I cannot call on the witness to produce it.

[*49]

Verdict for defendant.

Sir John Campbell, A.-G. and *Fry* for the prosecution.

Kelly, B. Andrews and *Roberts*, for the defendant.

1837.
July 17.

Derizes.
[54]

DAY *v.* BREAM.

(2 Moody & Robinson, 54—56.)

A porter who in the course of his business delivers parcels containing
libellous handbills, is not liable in an action for libel, if he be shown to be
ignorant of the contents of the parcels.

CASE for a libel. Plea, Not guilty.

[*55]   The libel complained of was a printed handbill, containing imputations on the plaintiff clearly *libellous. The plaintiff lived at
Marlborough; the defendant was the porter of the coach-office at
that place, and it was his business to carry out and deliver the
parcels that came by the different coaches to the office. For the
plaintiff it was shown that the defendant had delivered on the same
day paper parcels, tied up, and containing a large quantity of the
handbills in question, to two or three inhabitants of the place, to
whom the parcels were directed. No carriage was marked or
charged, nor any thing charged for porterage. Nothing was
shown to prove that the defendant was aware of the contents of
the parcels.

Bere submitted that no case was made out to go to the jury.

PATTESON, J. ruled that there was enough to call upon the
defendant to show how he became possessed of the parcels.

Witnesses were then called for the defendant, who proved that
the parcels in question were some of five, which came by the
London coach, inclosed in a large parcel directed to the defendant,
each of the inclosed parcels being directed to some inhabitant of
the place. The defendant was not charged with any carriage for
the parcel, because it was usual to bring things gratis for the
servants of the coach proprietors; and he was directed by a proprietor who happened to be in the office when the parcel arrived,
to deliver the inclosed parcels to the persons to whom they were
directed.

[56]   PATTESON, J., in summing up, left it to the jury to say whether
the defendant delivered the parcels in the course of his business
without any knowledge of their contents; if so, to find for him,
observing, that *primâ facie* he was answerable, inasmuch as he had
in fact delivered and put into publication the libel complained

of, and was therefore called upon to show his ignorance of the contents.

Verdict for the defendant.

Erle and *Barstow* for the plaintiff.

Bere for the defendant.

DOE D. HARVEY *v.* FRANCIS.

(2 Moody & Robinson, 57—58.)

Where the only evidence of a tenancy is payment of rent, the person paying is in all cases at liberty to explain the payment, and to show on whose behalf it was received.

THIS was an ejectment brought for a stamping mill.

The lessor of the plaintiff proved payment of rent to him by the defendant, and the delivery of a notice to quit signed by the lessor of the plaintiff.

Erle proposed to put in evidence an answer in Chancery of the lessor of the plaintiff, in which he had sworn that he had no legal interest in the mill, but had acted as agent for third parties, namely, of the adventurers in a mine, of which the lessor of the plaintiff was one.

Crowder objected, that the tenant was estopped from disputing the title of a person to whom he had paid rent.

PATTESON, J. overruled the objection, and held, that where a tenancy was attempted to be established by mere evidence of payment of rent, without any proof of an actual demise, or of the tenant's having been let into possession by the person to whom the payment was made, evidence is always admissible on the part of the tenant to explain the payment of rent, and to show on whose behalf such rent was received.

Erle was accordingly allowed to give evidence, to show the real interest of the lessor of the plaintiff; but upon such evidence being given, it appeared to the learned Judge, that in point of fact the defendant had taken the mills of the lessor of the plaintiff as

Doe d.
HARVEY
v.
FRANCIS.

his tenant: and thereupon a verdict was directed for the lessor of the plaintiff, subject to a bill of exceptions upon other points.

Crowder and *M. Smith* for the plaintiff.

Erle and *Jardine* for the defendant.

1837.
Aug. 9.

Bridgwater.
[60]

FITZ *v.* RABBITS.
(2 Moody & Robinson, 60—61.)

In order to let in secondary evidence of a document, it is not necessary that the search for that document should have been recent, or made for the purpose of the cause. A search amongst the proper papers three years before the trial of the cause was held sufficient.

ASSUMPSIT for use and occupation.

Plea, *Non assumpsit.*

The defence to this action was, that the premises had been taken by the defendant's father, and not by the defendant. In fact they had been occupied from 1831 by a gamekeeper, put into them by the defendant, and his servant, as it was alleged on the part of the plaintiff.

In order to prove the terms of the original taking, the defendant called his brother, who stated, that he had seen a paper in the handwriting of the plaintiff directed to his father, containing his proposals for the taking. The father died in 1833, and after his death, and nearly three years before the commencement of the present action, the witness and the defendant, who was one of his father's executors, had searched for the paper amongst the papers

[*61]

of the father in his house, and could not find *it. Subsequently to this, the defendant had removed some of the papers from the house, and no further search had been made. It did not appear for what purpose the search had been made. The witness said he believed the paper had been destroyed.

It was objected for the plaintiff, that secondary evidence was inadmissible; that a search ought to have been made for the purpose of the action, both in the house of the father, where the widow and one of the executors were living, and also amongst the papers removed.

PATTESON, J.:

It would certainly have been more satisfactory if a recent search

had been made; but I must take it that the search amongst the
papers shortly after the father's death was sufficient, and would
have been enough to let in secondary evidence at that time; and
though I do not recollect any instance in which a search made for
other purposes than letting in secondary evidence, and so long
ago as three years, has been considered enough, yet I think
I ought not, under the circumstances, to reject the secondary
evidence.

The witness was allowed to state the contents of the paper,
and a verdict for the plaintiff was afterwards taken upon terms
agreed on.

Crowder and *Moody* for the plaintiff.

Erle and *Butt* for the defendant.

ROBERTSON *v.* WYLDE.

(2 Moody & Robinson, 101—102.)

In an action for libel against the publisher of a magazine, evidence of the
writer's personal malice against the plaintiff is inadmissible.

CASE for a libel. Plea, Not guilty.

The defendant was a bookseller, and the publisher of a periodical
called the "Railway Magazine," in which the libel complained
of was published. It appeared on the back of the magazine that
it was edited by one Herapath, and it was alleged by *the plaintiff   [*102]
that that person was the writer of the article in question.

Wilde, Serjt. for the plaintiff, proposed to give evidence of
personal malice on the part of Herapath against the plaintiff, who
was the Secretary to the Eastern Counties Railway Company.
The libel professed to comment on some transactions of the
Company, in whose service Herapath had formerly been.

Erle objected that the evidence was inadmissible; saying that
the defendant, the bookseller, was only liable for the actual
damages resulting from the libel, and could not be charged with
vindictive damages on account of the malice of the supposed writer.
If the plaintiff had chosen, he might have obtained the name
of the writer, and sued him; in which case he would have been
made answerable for his own malice.

Wilde, Serjt. *contrà* :

The action is in fact the action of Herapath : the defendant himself publishes the libel, stating in the very front of it that Herapath was the author : he has thereby identified himself with Herapath.

TINDAL, Ch. J., ruled that the evidence was inadmissible.

Verdict for the plaintiff.   40s. damages.

Wilde, Serjt., *Sir W. Follett*, and *Channell* for the plaintiff.

Erle and *Ogle* for the defendant.

1838.
March 2.

Winton.
[119]

FOWLER *v.* DOWDNEY.

(2 Moody & Robinson, 119—121.)

An action will lie for saying of the plaintiff "he is a returned convict," though the words import that the punishment has been suffered.

SLANDER, for saying of the plaintiff " He is a returned convict."

The declaration averred, as special damage, the loss of a customer to whom the words were spoken, the plaintiff being a tradesman. The proof of the special damage failed ; and thereupon,

Erle, for the defendant, contended that the words were not actionable in themselves, inasmuch as they imputed no present liability to punishment : for, conceding that an offence, for which transportation was the punishment, was imputed, the words imply that the party had already suffered that punishment.

[120]   LORD DENMAN, Ch. J. :

My opinion is, that these words are actionable, because they impute to the plaintiff that he has been guilty of some offence for which parties are liable to be transported : that is, I think, the plain meaning of the words, as set out in the declaration ; they import, to be sure, that the punishment has been suffered—but still the obloquy remains.

Verdict for the plaintiff.   Damages 1s. (1).

Crowder and *Saunders* for the plaintiff.

Erle for the defendant.

(1) The test here applied to ascertain whether the words were actionable seems to be, whether they impute a species of misconduct which, in general, subjects a person to criminal prosecution in the common law Courts.

MAYOR, &c. OF BEVERLEY v. CRAVEN.

(2 Moody & Robinson, 140—141.)

When an ancient document, purporting to be an exemplification, is produced from the proper place of deposit, but has not, at the time of its production, the Great Seal affixed, it is still to be presumed that it is an exemplification, and may be read in evidence as such.

DEBT for tolls.

In order to show that a part of the river Hull, at which a vessel of the defendant had landed, was within certain limits, within which the corporation had a right to take toll, the plaintiffs tendered in evidence a parchment, purporting to be an exemplification of a commission, issued by the Crown in the reign of Queen Elizabeth, to certain persons therein named, directing them to

(Com. Dig. Action on the Case for Defamation, D. 5.) And the principle of that test is, not that the imputation of such a species of misconduct places the person slandered in a situation of actual danger, but that an aggravated degree of obloquy is supposed to attach to such misconduct as the law visits with punishment. Accordingly, we find that in ancient times an action for slander was holden to be maintainable for words imputing that the plaintiff had committed a criminal offence ; and no objection was raised on the ground that the speaker went on (as in the principal case,) to allege that the plaintiff had already suffered the punishment inflicted by law on such offenders. (See *Gainford* v. *Tuke*, Cro. Jac. 536.) The same point was raised in *Boston* v. *Tatum*, Cro. Jac. 622. The words spoken were that the plaintiff " was a thief, and had stolen the defendant's gold." After Not guilty pleaded, and a verdict for the plaintiff, it was moved for the defendant, in arrest of judgment, that as no time was alleged when the theft was committed, it might be it was in former times, since which divers general pardons had been, so as there cannot any loss happen to him, *(the plaintiff). The Court overruled the objection, saying " it was a great slander to be once a thief, for, although a pardon may discharge him of the punishment, yet the scandal of the offence remains; for

' *Pœna potest redimi, culpa perennis erit.*' "

There is one instance, frequently occurring in the old books, from which, perhaps, a different inference might, at first sight, be drawn. It is laid down that words are actionable which subject a party to punishment by the custom of the place. As, in London, to say of a woman living in that city, that she is a common harlot, is actionable (that is, in the City Court, 1 Doug. 380, *n.* 96) by reason of the custom, supposed to exist there, of carting women of that character (Com. Dig. Action on the Case for Defamation, D. 10). It may be said that the immorality is the same, and justly exposed to the same measure of obloquy, whether the woman be living in London or in Westminster; and that it is the liability to punishment, therefore, in the one case, and not in the other, which makes the difference. But, after all, this instance will not be found repugnant to the principle before pointed out as the true one. In London, where such misconduct is visited with punishment, the imputation of it is supposed to be more odious and degrading than elsewhere : words conveying that imputation are, therefore, if spoken in London, actionable; if spoken elsewhere, not. (*Whealer* v. *Welch*, 1 Lev. 116.) [The custom referred to has, of course, long since become obsolete. See Odgers on Libel, 3rd ed. 91.]

[*121, n.]

MAYOR OF
BEVERLEY
v.
CRAVEN.

enquire into the boundaries of the borough of Beverley, and of the proceedings taken in pursuance of that commission: there was a slip of parchment at the foot, corresponding in size and form with those on which the Great Seal is usually affixed; but the seal was in this instance wanting: and whether there ever had been one affixed, it was impossible, from the present appearance of the parchment, to say. It was shown that the document came from the corporation chest.

For the defendant it was objected, that the seal being wanting, the document tendered could not be treated as an exemplification. but only as a copy; and, therefore, could only be received after the usual evidence of its accuracy as a copy.

[141]

No proof was given that a search had been made after the supposed original.

ALDERSON, B.:

The document purports, by its contents, and on the face of it, to be an exemplification; and as it comes from the proper place of deposit for instruments of that kind, I think it must be presumed that it was a complete exemplification, and that the seal has been accidentally removed.

The document was accordingly read for the plaintiffs.

Verdict for defendant.

Alexander, *Dundas*, and *Hildyard* for the plaintiffs.

Cresswell and *Tomlinson*, for the defendant.

1838.
July 13.
———
Winchester.
[151]

DAY *v.* PORTER AND OTHERS.

(2 Moody & Robinson, 151—152.)

In trespass, a recovery of damages against a co-trespasser not sued is not admissible in mitigation of damages under the plea of Not guilty.

TRESPASS, for breaking and entering a dwelling house, and pulling down a wall.

Plea, Not guilty.

The trespass having been proved against the defendants, *Crowder*, for the defendants, in his address to the jury, proposed to prove, that the plaintiff had already brought an action against the landlord

[*152]

(under whose orders the defendants acted, *and who was not joined in the present action), and recovered damages for the same trespass.

Bompas, Serjt. objected, that the evidence was inadmissible, inasmuch as the matter proposed was a bar to the action, and ought to have been pleaded as such.

DAY
v.
PORTER.

Crowder, contrà :

At all events it is evidence in mitigation of damages : *Knight* v. *Legh* (1), *Morris* v. *Robinson* (2). The case may be likened to a case of payment not pleaded.

PARKE, B. :

That is an exception, and depends on peculiar circumstances. In trespass the rule is general, that what may be pleaded to the whole or any part of the action cannot be given in evidence under the general issue. A recovery against one so trespassing is a satisfaction against all for the same trespass.

The evidence was rejected.

Verdict for plaintiff, 1s.

Bompas, Serjt. and *Butt*, for the plaintiff.

Crowder and *Rawlinson*, for the defendants.

COATES *v.* STEPHENS (3).
(2 Moody & Robinson, 157—159.)

1838.
Aug. 18.
———
Bristol.
[157]

A cough, at the time of the sale of a horse warranted sound, is an unsoundness and breach of the warranty, though it be afterwards cured without any permanent injury to the horse.

ASSUMPSIT on the warranty of a horse.

Pleas, *Non assumpsit ;* and, 2ndly, That the horse was sound at the time of the sale.

The sale and warranty were clearly proved. The sale took place on the 20th July, 1837, and evidence was offered to show, that the horse, immediately on being taken home, was found to have a cough, and was submitted to medical treatment ; the cough got worse, and on the 7th August the horse was examined by a veterinary surgeon, who pronounced him to be unsound, from diseased bronchial tube and chronic inflammation, cough being an incident of the disease ; and also that the horse was lame from an enlargement of hock, amounting to bone spavin.

(1) 29 R. R. 645 (4 Bing. 589).
(2) 27 R. R. 322 (3 B. & C. 196).
(3) *Holyday* v. *Morgan* (1858) 28 L. J. Q. B. 9.

COATES
*.
STEPHENS.

For the defendant evidence was offered, that the horse was not afflicted either with cough or spavin at the time of the sale; that the horse was sound at the time of the trial, and free from both cough and spavin; and it was contended, that the cough either commenced after the sale, or, at all events, was so slight at the time [*158] as not to *amount to unsoundness, and to be capable of being cured, which, in fact, it had been.

PARKE, B., in summing up, said:

I have always considered, that a man who buys a horse warranted sound, must be taken as buying for immediate use, and has a right to expect one capable of that use, and of being immediately put to any fair work the owner chooses. The rule as to unsoundness is, that if at the time of the sale the horse has any disease, which either actually does diminish the natural usefulness of the animal, so as to make him less capable of work of any description; or which, in its ordinary progress, will diminish the natural usefulness of the animal; or if the horse has, either from disease or accident, undergone any alteration of structure, that either actually does at the time, or in its ordinary effects will, diminish the natural usefulness of the horse, such a horse is unsound. If the cough actually existed at the time of the sale, as a disease, so as actually to diminish the natural usefulness of the horse at that time, and to make him then less capable of immediate work, he was then unsound: or if you think the cough, which, in fact, did afterwards diminish the usefulness of the horse, existed at all at the time of the sale, you will find for the plaintiff. I am not now delivering an opinion formed on the moment on a new subject; it is the result of a full previous consideration; but as I find I differ from the law as laid down by a learned Judge in a case which has been handed up to me (1), I will thank you, if you find for the plaintiff, to tell me on which ground you so find.

Verdict for the plaintiff, generally (2).

[159]   *Crowder* and *Butt*, for the plaintiff.

Bompas, Serjt. and *Stone*, for the defendant.

(1) *Bolden* v. *Brogden*, 2 Moo. & Rob. 113; overruled in *Kiddell* v. *Burnard*, 60 R. R. 857 (9 M. & W. 670).—A. C.

(2) There are decisions somewhat conflicting as to whether a cough, existing at the time of a sale, be or be not an unsoundness; or whether that question should depend on the subsequent event of the malady being cured or not. (See *Elton* v. *Brogden*, 4 Camp.

RUSH *v.* PEACOCK AND ANOTHER.

1838

[162]

(2 Moody & Robinson, 162—167.)

A document deposited in a court of equity, by a party to a suit there, and scheduled in his answer, but which remains with an officer of that Court, after an order to deliver it to the party, is sufficiently in the control and power of the party to let in secondary evidence after notice to produce, and non-production thereof by the party.

In an action by a special administrator, under st. 38 Geo. III. c. 87, the declarations of the executor named in the will, made by him whilst he was the acting executor, are not admissible against the plaintiff.

COVENANT on a policy of insurance, bearing date the 20th April, 1830, and entered into between the said Helen Frances Phœbe Abercromby, of the one part, and the two defendants (directors of the *Eagle Insurance Company), of the other part, for the sum of 3,000*l.* payable to the executors, &c. of the said H. F. P. Abercromby, in the event of her dying within the space of two years then next. The declaration averred that the said H. F. P. Abercromby made her will, appointing one Thomas Griffiths Wainewright her executor, and died within the two years; the declaration also averred, that probate was, on the 21st May, 1831, granted to the executor Wainewright, and that he residing out of the jurisdiction of his Majesty's Courts of Law and Equity, special administration was

[*163]

281; *Liddard* v. *Kain*, 27 R. R. 582 (9 Moore, 356); *Shillito* v. *Claridge*, 2 Chitty, 425; *Garment* v. *Barrs*, 2 Esp. 673; *Bolden* v. *Brogden*, 2 Moo. & Rob. 113; *Jones* v. *Cowley*, 4 B. & C. 448.)

A similar definition to that laid down in the principal case is found in a work of great merit, and of extensive circulation in the sporting world, and amongst the class of persons exercising the veterinary art, namely, the Treatise on the Horse, published by the Society for the Diffusion of Useful Knowledge, p. 961. It would seem nearly impossible to attach any idea to the term "cough" not ranging under the term "disease," and equally difficult to make disease consist with soundness in any animal. In regard, however, to unsoundness, resulting from, or consisting in, an alteration in the natural structure of the animal, there is an ambiguity in the terms "natural" and "alteration of structure." If they

mean an alteration of the structure or usefulness given by nature to the particular animal, then a horse born blind, or with an enlargement necessarily producing lameness, must be considered sound. (See, however, *Joliff* v. *Bendell*, 27 R. R. 737 (Ry. & M. 136).) On the other hand, if the structure meant, be that natural to horses in general, then the class of cases open to litigation would be that of horses so badly shaped as to approach deformity. (See *Dickinson* v. *Follett*, 42 R. R. 801 (1 Moo. & Rob. 299).) As it may now be considered as settled law, that the breach of a warranty of soundness, does not entitle the purchaser to return the horse, but only to recover the difference of value of the horse with, or without the particular unsoundness, the question of temporary maladies, producing no permanent deterioration of the animal, would, generally speaking, only involve the right to damages merely nominal.

RUSH
v.
PEACOCK.

granted to the plaintiff on 26th Nov. 1836, according to the form of
the statute 38 Geo. III. c. 87 ; and that the plaintiff, before the commencement of this suit, was, by an order of the Court of Chancery,
made in a suit there between Wheatley and Burdett, appointed to
collect and get in the outstanding personal estate of the deceased.

There were several pleas averring that the policy was obtained
by means of a fraudulent conspiracy, entered into between the
deceased and Wainewright for the purpose of defrauding the defendants and various insurance companies, by pretending that the
insurances were effected by the deceased for her own benefit, and on
[*164] her own account, whereas *they were in truth entered into for the
benefit and on the account of Wainewright ; also, that the policy was
void by reason of the concealment of material facts by the assured ;
also, that it was made by the orders and for the use and benefit of
Wainewright, who had not any interest in the life insured, and that
it was consequently null and void under the statute 14 Geo. III. c. 48.

A notice had been served on the plaintiff's attorney, Mr. Frampton,
to produce a certain other policy of insurance effected on the same
life about the same time, and (as was alleged) under similar circumstances.

The plaintiff not producing the policy, the defendants tendered
secondary evidence of it ; and in order to show that the best evidence
was under the control of the plaintiff, a witness was called, who
said that the policy in question had been produced by Mr. Frampton,
as the attorney of the then plaintiff, in a former action, brought by
Wainewright, the executor named in the will of H. F. P. Abercromby,
against the Imperial Insurance Company (1). On cross-examination, the witness said he had last seen the policy, a fortnight ago,
in the Master's office in the equity side of the Court of Exchequer,
where it had been deposited as one of the documents produced by
the present plaintiff in a suit for discovery brought against him
there by the present defendants, and (as usual) was scheduled in
his answer.

[165]   The defendants then called Mr. Bowyer, the clerk in Court of
Rush in the Equity Court, who said he had the policy with him in
Court, but declined producing it. He admitted that an order had
been made by the LORD CHIEF BARON directing the policy in

(1) See a report of this case, *Waine-*   rule for a new trial, which was refused,
wright v. *Bland*, 1 Moo. & Rob. 481   46 R. R. 262 (1 M. & W. 32 ; 5 L. J.
(at Nisi Prius). The case went to the   (N. S.) Ex. 147).—A. C.
Court of Exchequer on motion for a

question, amongst others, to be delivered up to Mr. Frampton, the attorney for the defendant in the equity suit, at the expiration of a fortnight from the date of the order, which fortnight had elapsed some days before the present trial.

RUSH
v.
PEACOCK.

Erle and *Cresswell* objected that the defendants were not in a condition to give secondary evidence of the contents of the policy. It was clear that the document was in the custody of the law in the equity side of the Court of Exchequer. It was brought there by the present plaintiff, as part of his answer to a bill filed against him, and in obedience to the authority of the Court; and if the defendants now wanted to have the document produced in Court, they could only do so by producing it as part of the answer, and were bound to read the answer too.

Sir F. Pollock, contrà, insisted that, as it was clear, on the evidence of Mr. Bowyer, that the plaintiff might, before the trial, have obtained actual possession of the policy, it must be deemed under his control. If so, and he does not choose to produce it, the defendants are entitled to give secondary evidence.

LORD DENMAN, Ch. J.:

That certainly is my opinion. The equity Court has, for all practical *purposes, restored these documents to the attorney for the plaintiff. He might have produced them if he chose; by declining to do so, he opens the door to secondary evidence. I cannot, indeed, compel the plaintiff's attorney to produce the policy, though it is now brought into Court by Mr. Bowyer, as his agent; but by declining to produce it, he opens the door to secondary evidence of the contents.

[*166]

Secondary evidence was accordingly given.

The defendants tendered evidence of declarations made by Wainewright, whilst he was executor, and before the proceedings had taken place for having the present plaintiff appointed special administrator under the statute. The witness, to prove the declarations, had gone to Calais for the purpose of taking Wainewright's answer to a bill for a discovery filed against him in the suit before adverted to, of *Wainewright* v. *Bland;* and the declarations were said to have been made by Wainewright on the occasion of his swearing to the answer.

Erle objected to the evidence:

The declarations are those of a stranger to the suit; and the present plaintiff claims under a title quite independent of him.

The *Attorney-General, contrà* :

All the acts of the executor, between the death of the testator and the time when he ceased to be executor, are admissible in evidence against the plaintiff: the titles of the two individuals link in together, and they may be treated as one executor. If Waine-
[*167] wright had died, and an administrator *de bonis non* *had been appointed, would not Wainewright's declarations have been evidence against the administrator *de bonis non* ? Again, supposing Wainewright had released a debt, whilst he continued to represent the deceased, would not that release be available as against a party stepping, as the plaintiff here does, into Wainewright's place? It appears that a bill for a discovery has been filed against Waine-
wright, as representing the deceased, and that he has put in an answer to that bill ; would not that answer be evidence against all others who subsequently represent her ? And if the answer would be evidence, why not the declaration ? for the addition of the oath cannot affect the admissibility, though it may affect the weight of the evidence.

Lord Denman, Ch. J. :

The acts of the original executor, done by him in that capacity, may be admissible in evidence against the plaintiff who has succeeded, *durante absentiâ*, to the office of executor. But I do not think the mere declarations of the executor stand on the same footing. I am not aware that the point has ever arisen, but I think I ought not to receive the evidence.

The evidence was accordingly rejected.

Verdict for the defendants on all the pleas.

[168]   *Erle, Cresswell,* and *J. Henderson,* for the plaintiff.

The *Attorney-General, Sir F. Pollock, Thesiger,* and *Robinson,* for the defendants.

BRIGGS v. AYNSWORTH.

(2 Moody & Robinson, 168—170.)

1838.
Dec. 4.

Westminster.
[168]

The plaintiff in an action on the case gave, as confirmatory evidence of the defendant's having committed the tort proved at Layton, proof that he was seen near the spot at the time in question, and the defendant called witnesses, who swore that the defendant was at Richmond at that time. The plaintiff was allowed to give in reply additional evidence of the defendant's being at Layton, such evidence being a direct contradiction of the new fact of the defendant's being at Richmond.

CASE for negligent driving of defendant's carriage against a carriage of the plaintiff.

Plea, Not guilty.

The plaintiff gave evidence that his carriage was run against at Layton, in Essex, by another carriage, which the witnesses described as being driven by the defendant; and he called witnesses to show that, about the time in question, the defendant was seen in the neighbourhood of the spot where the collision occurred.

The defendant called witnesses to prove that, at the time in question, he was not at Layton, but at Richmond, in Surrey; and during the progress of the plaintiff's case, the plaintiff's witnesses were cross-examined as to their being certain of the identity of the defendant with the driver of the carriage.

The defendant having closed his case, *Platt*, for the plaintiff, proposed to call further witnesses to disprove the defence, by showing that the defendant was not at Richmond, but at Layton, at the time in question: whereupon

Butt, for the defendant, objected that it was not competent to the plaintiff to take the course proposed: the plaintiff's attention had, by the form of the cross-examination of his witnesses, been directed to the importance of showing that the defendant was at, or in the neighbourhood of, Layton. He had shaped his case accordingly; and having examined some witnesses to prove that the defendant was at Layton on the day, he should have exhausted that line of evidence, and not have reserved part of it to bring forward in reply.

[169]

LORD DENMAN, Ch. J. said:

It would, perhaps, have been more correct had the plaintiff in the first instance called the witnesses now tendered; but he did not think that he could, even at this period of the cause, exclude evidence from the jury which certainly went to contradict the defendant's *alibi*.

BRIGGS   The witnesses were accordingly called, and swore that the
AYNSWORTH. defendant was not at Richmond, for that they saw him at Layton
at the very time he was said to have been at the former place.

Verdict for the defendant.

[170]   *Platt* and *James*, for the plaintiff.

Kelly and *Butt*, for the defendant.

————◆————

1839.   CROWDER *v.* SELF AND ANOTHER.
Feb. 7.
—————   (2 Moody & Robinson, 190—191.)

Westminster.   In case for an excessive distress, though the warrant of distress be for
[190]   a greater sum than is really due, the plaintiff is not entitled to a verdict,
unless the goods seized are excessive in regard to the sum really due.

CASE for an excessive distress. The only charge in the declaration was, that the defendants had seized more goods than were
sufficient to satisfy the amount of rent due by the plaintiff. It
appeared that the warrant of distress contained a demand for 6*l.*
rent in arrear, and some odd shillings for expenses, the sum really
due being only 4*l.*; and that the landlord had been led into a
mistake as to the amount, by supposing that a sum of 2*l.*, which
had been paid by the plaintiff, had been paid on account of an
accruing demand for rent, and not for rent already due. A receipt
had been given to the plaintiff showing this fact; but the receipt
was not produced until the fifth day after the broker's man had
been in possession. When this receipt was shown to the landlord,
he immediately withdrew the distress, stating that he had been
mistaken in the manner above alluded to.

After the case for the plaintiff had concluded,

Byles for the defendant contended that an action in this form
could not be supported, unless some real damage was shown:
Avenel v. *Croker* (1), *Wilkinson* v. *Serres* (2) ; and in his address to
[*191]   the jury he insisted that there was no evidence to show *that the
goods taken were more than sufficient to satisfy the arrear of rent
(4*l.*) actually due.

Lord ABINGER, C. B., in summing up, told the jury that the only
question for their consideration was, whether, notwithstanding the

————

(1) Moo. & Mal. 172.   (2) 1 Moo. & Rob. 377.

sum of 6*l.* occurring in the warrant, the goods actually seized were more than sufficient to satisfy a distress for 4*l.*   There was no evidence of any annoyance to the plaintiff's family other than the circumstance of the man being in the house; and if the jury thought that the same quantity of goods might have been fairly seized for an arrear of 4*l.*, then he thought they ought to find for the defendant.

CROWDER
v.
SELF.

Verdict for the plaintiff.   Damages one shilling.

His Lordship certified to deprive the plaintiff of costs.

Miller, for the plaintiff.

Byles, for the defendant.

WHITELOCK *v.* HUTCHINSON.

(2 Moody & Robinson, 205—207.)

1839.
March 19.
———
York.
[205]

A right of common for cattle "*levant* and *couchant*," upon enclosed land, extends to such cattle as the winter eatage of the land, together with the produce of it during the summer, is capable of maintaining.

ACTION on the case for depasturing a certain common, upon which the plaintiff had a right of common, by means of which the plaintiff was obstructed in the enjoyment of his said right.

Plea: That defendant was seised of a tenement, and in right thereof was entitled to right of common over the *locus in quo* for all his commonable cattle *levant* and *couchant* on that tenement, as appurtenant thereto.

Replication: That the defendant at the said times when, &c. depastured the common with cattle, which were not *levant* and *couchant* upon the tenement.

It was proved that the cattle belonged to the defendant, and the principal question was, whether he put more of them upon the common than were properly *levant* and *couchant* upon the tenement; upon this point there was conflicting evidence.   The defendant further gave evidence that the plaintiff had himself overstocked the common.   A question as to the import of the term "levancy and couchancy" having been raised and discussed in the course of the trial,

[206]

PARKE, B., in summing up the case to the jury, said:

Amongst the older authorities there appears, certainly, some

difference of opinion as to the meaning of the expression "*levant*
and *couchant*." There is one set of cases in which it is laid down,
and the term "cattle *levant* and *couchant* upon enclosed land"
means such cattle as are actually used for the purpose of manuring
and cultivating the enclosed land (1). The rule now is, that such
cattle only are to be holden *levant* and *couchant* upon the enclosed
land, as that land will keep during the winter (2). It has been
argued, that the rule includes such as the land will keep during the
whole, or any part, of the year; but that is not so. The real
question is, has this defendant turned more cattle upon the
common than the winter eatage of his ancient tenement,

[*207] together with the hay and other produce obtained *from it
during the summer, is capable of maintaining? If you think
he has, your verdict must be for the plaintiff; and whether the
plaintiff has himself also overstocked the common, is wholly
immaterial on this record.

Verdict for the plaintiff.

Cresswell and *Watson*, for the plaintiff.

Wightman, for the defendant.

————•————

SCHOLEFIELD *v.* ROBB.

(2 Moody & Robinson, 210—211.)

Crib-biting, which has not yet produced disease, or alteration of structure,
is not an "unsoundness," but is a "vice," under a warranty that a horse
is "sound" and free from "vice."

ASSUMPSIT on the warranty of a horse, "that it was sound and
free from vice." 1st breach, that it was not sound. 2nd, that it
was not free from vice.

Pleas. 1. *Non assumpsit*. 2. (to 1st breach), that the horse was
sound. 3. (to 2nd breach), that it was free from vice.

The horse was bought to be delivered at a future day, and the
case of the plaintiff was, that the horse was a crib-biter and wind-
sucker. Veterinary surgeons were examined, who said that the
habit of crib-biting was injurious to horses; that the air sucked
into the stomach of the animal distended it, and impaired its

———

(1) *Id est*, where a right of common   *Hardman*, 19 R. R. 432 (1 B. & Ald.
appendant is claimed, that right being   710, 711).
confined to arable land. See the judg-   (2) 1 Saund. 28 b, *n.*
ment of BAYLEY, J., in *Cheesman* v.

powers of digestion, occasionally to such an extent as greatly to diminish the value of the horse, and render it incapable of work. Some of the witnesses gave it as their opinion that crib-biting was an unsoundness; it was not, however, shown, that in the present instance the habit of crib-biting had brought on any disease, or (as yet) interfered with the power or usefulness of the horse. The defendant denied that the horse was shown to be a crib-biter at all at the time of the sale, though there was evidence of his being one at the time of the delivery.

SCHOLE-
FIELD
v.
ROBB.

PARKE, B. told the jury, that if they thought the horse, at the time of its being sold, and of the warranty being given, was not a crib-biter, their *verdict on both the last issues must be for the defendant; but, even if the evidence of the plaintiff satisfied them that the horse was a crib-biter at the time of the warranty, such evidence would not, in his opinion, support the allegation that it was then unsound, so as to entitle the plaintiff to a verdict on the second plea. To constitute unsoundness there must either be some alteration in the structure of the animal, whereby it is rendered less able to perform its work, or else there must be some disease (1). Here neither of those facts had been shown. If, however, the jury thought that at the time of the warranty the horse had contracted the habit of crib-biting, he thought that was a " vice," and that the plaintiff would be entitled to a verdict on the third plea. The habit complained of might not, indeed, like some others (for instance, that of kicking), show vice in the temper of the animal; but it was proved to be a habit decidedly injurious to its health, and tending to impair its usefulness, and came, therefore, in his Lordship's opinion, within the meaning of the term " vice," as used on such occasions as the present.

[*211]

> *Verdict for the plaintiff on the general issue; but for the defendant on the two other issues* (2).

Cresswell and *Knowles*, for the plaintiff.

Alexander and *Hoggins*, for the defendant.

(1) *Coates* v. *Stephens, supra*, p. 785.   (2) *Broennenburgh* v. *Haycock*, 17 R. R. 682 (Holt, N. P. C. 630).

CUDLIFF *v.* WALTERS AND ANOTHER.

(2 Moody & Robinson, 232—235.)

An appointment of an umpire by two arbitrators, under a power to appoint before "entering on the cause of the matters in difference," is good, though the arbitrators have, before such appointment, enlarged the time.

If one of the arbitrators insist upon producing further evidence, and the other refuse to allow it to be done, this is a sufficient "disagreement" between the arbitrators to authorise the interference of the umpire.

THIS was an action of covenant upon a deed of reference dated 28th July, 1828, whereby the plaintiff and the defendants agreed to submit all matters in difference to the award final end and determination of Richard Marrack and Henry Rawlings, "or, in case they could not agree, to the award and umpirage of such person as they should, by writing to be thereon indorsed under their hands, before they entered on the cause of the matters in difference, appoint as umpire;" so that the award, &c. should be ready to be delivered on or before the 10th of October then next, with power to the arbitrators or umpire, by indorsement, from time to time to extend the time. The declaration alleged the appointment of the umpire before the arbitrators entered upon the cause of the matters in difference; that the arbitrators proceeded to hear the parties and their witnesses, and could not agree with each other concerning the premises, but, on the contrary, did *disagree; whereupon the umpire, having taken upon himself the umpirage, made his award, &c.

[*233]

The only pleas on which the verdict turned were, 1st, That the arbitrators did not duly nominate, constitute, or appoint the umpire in manner and form, &c.

2ndly, That the arbitrators did not disagree concerning the said disputes and matters in difference in manner and form, &c.

It appeared in evidence that before the arbitrators met on the reference, a correspondence took place as to the time of proceeding, and an enlargement was indorsed on the deed, and signed by the arbitrators as follows: "We, finding it inconvenient to proceed on this reference before the 22nd day of November, do hereby enlarge the time till the 1st day of January next. Dated the 16th day of August, 1838."

On the 22nd of November the arbitrators met; and, before proceeding on the reference, agreed on the umpire, and duly indorsed his appointment on the deed. The arbitrators then proceeded on the reference, and heard evidence for two days; and the attorneys of the parties addressed them, and concluded their case. On the 26th, the arbitrators again met, and could not agree on their decision ; but one of them proposed that further evidence should be given for the defendants, and produced certain documents, which the other arbitrator refused to look at ; and the umpire was thereupon applied to, by letter, to receive the further evidence. The umpire met the arbitrators, but refused to interfere unless they disagreed ; upon *which they each wrote down their opinions on certain points, which they declared to be unalterable ; but one of arbitrators proposed that the further evidence might be received, as they might, perhaps, then agree. The points in difference being, in the opinion of the umpire, decisive, and essential to the merits of the case, he gave a written notice to the parties, stating the disagreement of the arbitrators, and requiring them to attend him, as umpire, on the 19th of December.

[*234]

On that day the parties and their attorneys attended the umpire, as well as the arbitrators, one of whom proposed to interfere, but the umpire refused to allow him, and heard the parties, and made his award.

Crowder, for the defendant, contended that the appointment of the arbitrators, being made after the enlargement of the time, was invalid ; that the enlargement was an important act in the exercise of the discretion of the arbitrators, and was therefore an entering " on the cause of the matters in difference," within the meaning of the deed ; and that this being a submission by deed, the objection could not be waived by the mere attendance of the parties, which distinguished the present case from *In re Hick* (1), and *Matson* v. *Trower* (2). Then as to the disagreement, the arbitrators had not finally disagreed. The umpire had no right to interfere until the arbitrators had exhausted all chances of agreeing. Here, the additional evidence might *have produced an agreement ; and one of the arbitrators had never expressly assented to the umpire's interfering, but had throughout proposed having recourse to the additional evidence.

[*235]

COLERIDGE, J., in summing up, said that he had no doubt of the appointment of the umpire being valid. That the object of this clause in agreements of reference was to insure the appointment of an umpire before the minds of the arbitrators became embarrassed

(1) 21 R. R. 511 (8 Taunt. 694).   (2) 27 R. R. 725 (Ry. & M. 17).

CUDLIFF
v.
WALTERS.

by the discussion of the matters in difference; and that the enlargement of the time being a mere arrangement for the common convenience of the arbitrators themselves, as well as of the parties concerned, could not be said to be an entering upon the cause of the matters in difference. In fact, the case in 8 Taunton was rather an authority for the plaintiff. With regard to the disagreement, it was matter for the jury to say whether there was such an essential difference between the arbitrators as entitled the umpire to interfere: no doubt it ought to be such a difference, after hearing the case, as rendered the agreement of the arbitrators hopeless. Here both parties were heard and closed the case, and one of the arbitrators chooses to get up further evidence, which the other refuses to hear: this is such an essential difference as justifies the interference of the umpire.

Verdict for the plaintiff.

Erle and *Butt*, for the plaintiff.

Crowder, for the defendant.

1839.
Aug. 19.

Bristol.
[240]

DOE D. WILDGOOSE *v.* PEARCE.

(2 Moody & Robinson, 240—242.)

An unproved will more than thirty years old coming from the possession of one of the family of the testator, may be read without accounting for the subscribing witnesses, though the person producing it be not strictly entitled to the custody.

THE lessor of the plaintiff claimed the premises in dispute in this ejectment under the will of his father, who died in 1795. The will was dated in 1792, and by it the testator devised the premises in fee (after the death of his wife, whom he made executrix) to his six children, as tenants in common, of whom the lessor of the plaintiff, the widow of one John Wildgoose, was one. The widow of the testator lived until about eight years before the trial, and the premises had been occupied since the death of the testator by the widow, or by the eldest son, of the testator, and the principal question in the cause was, whether the son had occupied under the widow, or in his own right as heir-at-law. The will had never been proved; but was shown to have been delivered by the widow of the testator, some years after his death, to the lessor of the plaintiff; and one witness, who knew the testator, swore to his handwriting. On the counsel for the lessor of the plaintiff proceeding to have the will read, it was objected that, though thirty years old, it could not be read, inasmuch as it did not *come from the proper custody. No particular right to the custody was shown in the lessor of the plaintiff; and the proper custody of a will disposing of personal property, as this did, though of small amount, was the Ecclesiastical Court of the diocese.

COLERIDGE, J. :

I think the plaintiff is entitled to have the will read. It is not necessary that the custody from which an ancient document comes should be strictly according to the legal right; it is enough if it be brought from a place of deposit where, in the ordinary course of things, such a document, if genuine, might reasonably be expected to be found. This is an unproved will, and the proper place of custody of such a will is not the Bishop's registry; it is natural to find it in the possession of some of the family of the testator, who derive a benefit from it. I think, therefore, the custody is here sufficiently accounted for.

Verdict for the plaintiff (1).

A new trial was moved for in Michaelmas Term on other points, but no objection was made to the above ruling (2).

[242]

(1) See Accord. *Doe* d. *Neale* v. *Samples*, 47 R. R. 528 (8 Ad. & El. 151). The lessor of the plaintiff in that case claimed under a mortgage in fee by J. S. deceased, executed in 1821; and the defendant's case was, that J. S. was, at the date of the mortgage, only seised for life; he having, on his marriage, in 1785, executed a deed by which, being then seised in fee, he had settled the estate, giving himself only a life estate, remainder to his children, &c., of whom the defendant was one; and, in proof of this case, the defendant's attorney produced the deed of settlement, bearing date the 9th of November, 1785, which he had found amongst the papers of J. S. It was objected, that evidence of its due execution was necessary, inasmuch as it did not come from the proper place of deposit; for that it should, if genuine, have been amongst the papers of the trustees of the marriage settlement, not amongst those of the party against whom its provisions were to operate. The LORD CHIEF JUSTICE overruled the objection, and a motion to enter a verdict for the plaintiff on the objection was refused; PATTESON, J. saying, "I never understood that the custody to be shown, for the purpose of making a document evidence without proof of execution, was necessarily that of a person strictly entitled to the possession; it is enough if the person be so connected with the deed that he may reasonably be supposed to be in possession of it without fraud, no such fraud being proved."

(2) 5 M. & W. 506.

1840.
Aug. 13.
———
Wells.
[305]

REG. *v.* THE TITHING OF WESTMARK.

(2 Moody & Robinson, 305—306.)

An indictment for the non-repair of a highway, describing the way as immemorial, is not supported by proof of a highway extinguished, as such, sixty years before, by an Inclosure Act, but since used by the public, and repaired by the district charged (1).

The 23rd section of 5 & 6 Will. IV. c. 50, is not retrospective in respect of roads completely public by dedication at the time of the Act; it applies to roads then made, and in progress of dedication.

THIS was an indictment for the non-repair of a road, which stated that there was and is, within the said tithing, a certain common King's highway for all the subjects, &c. at all times to pass and repass with horses, carriages, &c.; and that the said highway was out of repair, and that the inhabitants of the said tithing of right ought to repair, and from time immemorial had been used and accustomed to repair the said highway.

It was agreed on as a fact, that the way in question had been set out as a private road and driftway under an Inclosure Act, in the year 1784, for the use of the adjoining owners, who were directed to repair it; and the award, under a power in the Act, extinguished all ways, both public and private, not set out in it. The prosecutor's counsel offered to prove that the way had been publicly used before the inclosure, and since had been repaired occasionally by the tithing, and been used to a great extent by the public, and was of great importance.

Before the case was gone into by calling witnesses, it was submitted by the counsel for the defendants, that at all events the indictment, in its present form, could not be supported, [*306] inasmuch *as, whatever might be the facts as to the user and repair by the tithing before and since the inclosure, the award extinguished the road as a public way for some time at least, and therefore the allegation of immemorial user and liability to repair could not be supported. It was further urged, that being a private way at the time of the inclosure, it could not be considered as since dedicated to the public so as to bind the parish or tithing to repair, the stat. 5 & 6 Will. IV. c. 50, s. 23, having prevented such dedication, without the view of the surveyor and justices, and other forms prescribed. The words of the section "no road or occupation way made or hereafter to be made" have a retrospective operation, and make it impossible that this road could be a highway by dedication.

(1) Cf. *Reg.* v. *Turweston* (1850) 16 Q. B. 109, 20 L. J. M. C. 46.—A. C.

MAULE, J. said, that as to the latter point the statute must have a reasonable construction, and could not be considered to extinguish roads already public by dedication; otherwise, almost all roads not being immemorial, however important and public, would become extinguished; that the term "made," as used in the Act, must apply to a road formed or made, but not completely dedicated by user or otherwise, at the passing of the Act; but that roads dedicated at that time would be out of the operation of the section. That, on the other point, the indictment clearly failed on the facts, and the jury must acquit the defendants.

Verdict, Not guilty.

Erle and *Bere*, for the prosecution.

Bompas, Serjt. and *Prideaux*, for the defendants.

REG.
v.
THE
TITHING OF
WESTMARK.

REG. *v.* THE INHABITANTS OF THE PARISH OF PAUL.

(2 Moody & Robinson, 307—310.)

On an indictment for the non-repair of a highway, in the ordinary form, a parish cannot be convicted for not rebuilding a sea wall washed away by the sea, over the top of which the alleged way used to pass.

Where a parish are acquitted on such an indictment, on the ground of there being no highway, the Court is not bound to award costs under the Highway Act, 1835 (5 & 6 Will. IV. c. 50,) s. 95. A Judge who tries at Nisi Prius an indictment for non-repair, removed by *certiorari*, has no power under that section to award costs.

1840.
Aug. 6.

Bodmin.
[307]

THIS was an indictment for the non-repair of a highway, found at the Quarter Sessions, and removed by *certiorari* into the Queen's Bench at the instance of the defendants. The indictment alleged, that there was and yet is a certain common and ancient highway within the parish of Paul, used by and for all the liege subjects, &c., with their horses, coaches, carts, and other carriages, to go, return, pass, ride, and labour, at their free will and pleasure; and that a certain part of the said common and ancient highway, called Guavas Quay, situate &c., containing in length &c., was and yet is very ruinous, miry, deep, broken, and in great decay for want of due reparation and amendment of the same, so that &c.

The way in question led from Penzance to Paul, crossing, at one part, the sea-shore, over the sand of which people used to go a and about low water, that part of the shore being impassable at and about high water. Guavas Quay was a quay of ancient date, built of considerable height against some houses and fish cellars, which

REG.
v.
THE INHABI-
TANTS OF
THE PARISH
OF PAUL.

[*308]

it supported and protected against the sea. It was considerably above high water, and of breadth scarcely sufficient for a small fish-cart to pass along. It had been built by the *proprietors of the cellars, which were used by them for their trade in storing and drying pilchards, the quay being the access for their carts and casks from the sands to the cellars. The quay was, in fact, a thick wall of solid masonry, and the surface of the quay was composed of large pieces of granite mortared together, and had been used by persons going on foot and horseback, and with the small fish-carts used by the fishermen, at such times of the tide as the sands were impassable; but at and about low water, the way by the sands was more direct, and more frequently used. The surface had never been repaired as a way, and the wall had been several times in living memory washed away, and rebuilt by the owners of the cellars by subscription. Two or three years before the indictment the sea had washed away a considerable portion of the quay, leaving a gap which completely broke off the communication; and the indictment was preferred for not rebuilding that part of the wall, and restoring the communication.

At the close of the case for the prosecution,

Erle, for the defendants, submitted that the defendants were entitled to an acquittal. Even if the passage along the quay had been proved to be both frequent and convenient, this could not be called a highway, which anybody could, by allowing the public to use it as a highway, so dedicate as to make a parish liable to repair and rebuild it. Such a liability is limited to the surface of grounds over which the owner allows the public to pass. The quay is an expensive and artificial erection, made *use of when a passage is otherwise impossible. At all events a parish could not be obliged to rebuild the wall, whatever might be the obligation as to the surface: *R. v. Landulph* (1). And he mentioned a case in which a parish in Lincolnshire had successfully resisted such a liability to repair a viaduct made across a fen, which had been carried away by the floods. If the parish might be made so liable, an insufficient wall or viaduct might at any time be made, and the public would of course use it; but it necessarily would soon be washed away, and the parish be saddled with the expense of constructing a good viaduct, instead of merely repairing the surface of land, according to their common law liability.

[*309]

(1) 1 Moo. & Rob. 393.

Bompas, Serjt., *contrà:*

If this argument is to prevail, any road, however extensively used and necessary to the public, would be lost, any part of which rested on masonry. If a road be raised in its passage across a valley, and supported by masonry, which gives way after any lapse of time, can it be said that the parish are not bound to repair? The true test is, the user by the public. If so used by permission of the owners, it is dedicated to the public, and becomes a highway.

MAULE, J.:

My opinion is, that upon the language of this indictment the defendants are entitled to an acquittal. In ordinary language this cannot be said to have been, at the time of the default, a highway which the public were prevented from *conveniently using, for want of due reparation and amendment. It was at one time, at most, a wall or embankment, on the top of which there was a road; and whatever might be the duty of the parish as to a road so in existence and requiring repair, I do not think they are defaulters on this evidence. The interruption of the passage is not from the want of repair, but from the sea having washed away the wall or embankment, and there is no longer anything for them to repair. I do not think they are liable to rebuild the wall.

[*310]

Verdict, Not guilty.

TALBUTT *v.* CLARK AND ANOTHER.

(2 Moody & Robinson, 312—313.)

In an action against the editors of a newspaper for libel, the fact of the libel being published on the communication of a correspondent is not admissible in mitigation of damages.

CASE for libel contained in a newspaper, of which the defendants were the editors.

The plaintiff held the situation of clerk of the Eastern Counties Railway Company, at Rumford; and the publication complained of was a statement (professing to be inserted in the newspaper on the authority of a correspondent of the defendants), that the clerk at that station (thereby meaning the plaintiff) had overcharged a passenger.

The pleas were, Not guilty, and a justification of the truth of the statement.

[313]

Thesiger, for the defendants, after proving certain facts in support of the plea of justification, offered to put in evidence a letter from the correspondent, with his name subscribed, on the authority of which the defendants had inserted the statement, they having refused to insert it without the name; and he contended that this evidence was admissible in mitigation of damages.

Sir F. Pollock objected to the evidence.

LORD DENMAN, Ch. J. :

The evidence certainly does not go to prove any of the issues; and I do not think it admissible. The justification depends on the facts, not on the statement of them by a third party. I know that in a case in the Common Pleas it has been held that a previous statement in another newspaper is admissible; but even that decision has been very much questioned.

The evidence was rejected.

Verdict for the plaintiff.

Sir F. Pollock and *Martin*, for the plaintiff.

Thesiger and *Godson*, for the defendants.

JONES AND ANOTHER *v.* KEENE.

(2 Moody & Robinson, 348—350.)

A policy of insurance on the life of A. had been assigned to the plaintiff: the defendant having privately ascertained that A. was dangerously ill, treats with the plaintiff for the purchase of the policy for a small sum, representing it as the then value of the policy, the plaintiff not being aware of A.'s illness: Held, that the sale was void, and that the plaintiff might recover the value of the policy in an action of trover.

TROVER for a policy of insurance effected with the Britannia Insurance Company for the sum of 999*l.* on the life of one George Laing, and bearing date the 21st November, 1837.

Pleas. 1. Not guilty.

2. That the plaintiffs were not possessed, &c.

It appeared that the plaintiffs had in their possession, as part of the bankrupt's estate, the policy mentioned in the declaration, which had been assigned by Laing to the bankrupt before the bankruptcy. In the early part of 1840 the assignees had endeavoured, through their attorney, to sell the policy, and the price they had asked for it was (to the knowledge of the defendant, who was an auctioneer) 40l., but no purchaser could be procured. On the 15th August, Laing (who up to that time had enjoyed excellent health) was taken suddenly and alarmingly ill, and on the 20th he died. On the 18th the defendant instructed one Cook (an agent for the Britannia Insurance Company) to purchase the policy for him, if it was still in the market, and authorised him to offer as much as sixty guineas for it. Cook accordingly called several times upon the attorney of the assignees (who had been employed *by [*349] them to effect a sale of the policy), and finding him at last at home, Cook asked whether the policy was still in the market? He was answered that it was; and the attorney asked Cook how much he thought it would be worth. Cook answered, not more, perhaps, than three fourths of a year's premium (which would amount to about sixty guineas). A bargain was made for the purchase at that sum, and in the course of the afternoon Cook again called, with the defendant, whom he introduced as the purchaser for whom he was acting; the defendant then paid down the money, and the policy was handed over to him.

The plaintiffs gave evidence, that when the defendant on the 18th caused Cook to treat for the purchase of the policy, both he and Cook were very well aware of the alarming illness of Laing, and that he was then in imminent danger; that the plaintiffs had no knowledge whatever of that fact, and treated on the supposition that he was still in good health: and they contended that, under these circumstances, the bargain was a fraudulent one on the part of the defendant, and that therefore no right of property had passed to him.

Alexander, for the defendant, first denied the defendant's knowledge of Laing's illness; and, secondly, he insisted, that even if the defendant was aware of that fact, his non-communication of it would not avoid the contract. It was the vendor's own fault, if, for want of due inquiry as to the value of the policy, he sold it for less than it was worth. So it had been held that a person, proposing to *purchase an estate, was not called upon to disclose to the [*350] seller that he had discovered a mine under it (1).

ROLFE, B., in summing up to the jury, said, that if the defendant had privately ascertained the illness of Laing, and then treated with the plaintiffs without communicating the fact to them, and

(1) See *Fox* v. *Macreth*, 2 R. R. 55 (2 Br. C. C. 420).

they supposing that he was still in good health, there could be no doubt such conduct was grossly dishonourable. But he had no difficulty in going further than this, and telling them, that if they believed the facts as stated on the part of the plaintiffs, the defendant's conduct amounted to legal fraud, and he could not set up any title to the policy so acquired. The jury would say whether, at the time when Cook applied to the assignees on the 18th, and when he stated his opinion to be that the policy was only worth 60*l.*, he and the defendant knew the state of extreme danger in which Laing was; if they were of that opinion, he recommended them to find for the plaintiffs.

Verdict for the plaintiffs (1).

REDDELL v. STOWEY, Sheriff of Devonshire.

(2 Moody & Robinson, 358—359.)

Where a bailiff in possession of goods under a landlord's distress receives a *fi. fa.* from the sheriff, and sells the goods under it, the sheriff is liable in an action, for pound-breach, and rescue, at the suit of the landlord.

CASE for a rescue of goods seized as a distress ; and for pound breach; and there was also a count for selling under a *fi. fa.* without paying over to the landlord a year's rent. Pleas, Not guilty, and several other pleas immaterial to the point decided.

The facts were, that on the 16th July the landlord (Reddell) had distrained the goods of one Porter, his tenant, employing Thorne, a sheriff's officer, as bailiff, in the distress. Thorne kept possession under the distress till the 22nd July, when a warrant of the sheriff [*359] to levy under a *fi. fa.* issued *against Porter was put into Thorne's hands, and he, notwithstanding the representations of the plaintiff to the contrary, acted under the warrant, and sold the goods for the execution creditors, under circumstances (as alleged) of collusion with the execution creditors on his part.

Bompas, Serjt. contended that at all events this could not be a rescue or pound breach, which must be intended to be the act of adverse persons—a man could not rescue from himself.

ERSKINE, J. :

For the present purposes, Thorne, though he happened to be a

(1) See acc. *Hill* v. *Gray*, 18 R. R. 802 (1 Stark. 434), and *Turner* v. *Harvey*, 23 R. R. 15 (1 Jac. 169).

sheriff's officer, was in possession under the distress, as a mere
stranger to the sheriff: the sheriff then comes forward, takes the
goods from Thorne, and sells them: it is precisely the same as if he
had taken the goods from a third person.

REDDELL
v.
STOWEY.

Verdict for the plaintiff.

Erle and *Butt*, for the plaintiff.

Bompas, Serjt. and *Barstow*, for the defendant.

HARVEY *v.* MITCHELL.

(2 Moody & Robinson, 366—367.)

1841.
May 28.

Westminster.
[366]

Where a document is called for after notice to produce by the plaintiff,
the defendant may during the plaintiff's case produce evidence to show the
document lawfully out of his possession, and such evidence is solely for the
Judge to determine whether secondary evidence be admissible, and gives the
plaintiff's counsel no reply to the jury.

ACTION on the case for taking excessive distress.

The plaintiff proposed to make use of the distress-warrant as part
of his case, and with a view to enable himself to give secondary
evidence of its contents, he had given the defendant a notice to
produce it, and now gave some evidence to show that it was in the
defendant's possession.

Platt thereupon (the plaintiff's case still proceeding) interposed
for the defendant, and insisted that he was entitled, in the present
stage of the trial, to give evidence to show that the distress-warrant
was *not in the possession, or under the controul, of the defendant,
but that it had been handed over, pursuant to the statute, to the
commissioners of excise.

[*367]

PARKE, B. was of opinion that *Platt* was entitled to do so, and the
evidence was accordingly received. His Lordship also expressed a
clear opinion that it was for the Judge to decide on the sufficiency
of the evidence thus adduced, and not for the jury, whose opinion
on the matter his Lordship declined to ask ; and, being of opinion
that the warrant was by the evidence satisfactorily shown not to be
in the defendant's custody, or under his controul, his Lordship
refused to permit the plaintiff to give secondary evidence of its
contents.

The secondary evidence was accordingly rejected.

HARVEY   The plaintiff's case then proceeded; and at its close the
   v.   defendant's counsel addressed the jury, but called no evidence.
MITCHELL.

   Jervis, for the plaintiff, thereupon claimed the right to reply,
contending that the defendant had given evidence; and for the
purpose of entitling the plaintiff to reply, it could not be material
at what stage of the trial such evidence was given.

   PARKE, B., however, would not permit the plaintiff's counsel to
reply : he said, that the evidence which the defendant had given
was merely collateral to the merits of the case, and had been
[*368]   required for the purpose of informing the Judge, and not the *jury,
on a matter which was exclusively within the cognizance of the
former.

   The plaintiff's counsel accordingly did not reply.

                                        Verdict for plaintiff.

   Jervis and *Humfrey*, for the plaintiff.

   Platt and *R. Gurney*, for the defendant.

1841.   DOWNING *v.* BUTCHER.
June 18.   (2 Moody & Robinson, 374—375.)

[374]   In trespass for false imprisonment on a criminal charge, the defendant
          cannot cross-examine as to the bad character of the plaintiff, nor as to
          previous charges made against him.

   TRESPASS for false imprisonment, on a charge of obtaining money
under false pretences.
   Plea, Not guilty.
   A policeman called for the plaintiff was asked, on cross-examination by the defendant's counsel, whether he had not had the plaintiff
in custody before, and also what was her general character.
   Both questions were objected to on the ground that they related
to matters not put in issue, and it was impossible that the plaintiff
could now be prepared to meet such evidence, and *Jones* v.
Stevens (1) was cited.
   For the defendant it was answered, that with a view to ascertain
the amount of injury sustained by the plaintiff, it was clearly most
important that the jury should have information on the points

              (1) 25 R. R. 714 (11 Price, 235).

proposed to be inquired into ; and as they related to matters which, furnishing no bar to the action, could not have been put on the record, the course proposed was the only one by which the defendant had an opportunity of bringing them before the jury.

DOWNING
v.
BUTCHER.

GURNEY, B. (after communicating with the other Judges of this Court, who were sitting *in banco* in the adjoining room,) said he was of opinion that neither of the questions could properly be put, and they were accordingly disallowed (1).

[375]

Verdict for the plaintiff.

Thesiger and *Chambers*, for the plaintiff.

Jervis and *C. Jones*, for the defendant.

ROBINSON *v.* MARKIS.

(2 Moody & Robinson, 375—376.)

1841.
June 21.

In order to let in the deposition of a witness examined on interrogatories, his absence must be shown by some one who can speak to the fact, of his own knowledge : proof of inquiries made at the residence of the witness, and of answers given, is not enough.

[375]

TRESPASS for assault, battery, and false imprisonment. The declaration contained two counts.

Plea, Not guilty.

Witnesses had been examined on interrogatories before the Master on the usual terms, in support of the cause of action set forth in the second count. On the deposition of one of the witnesses (a sailor) *being offered in evidence, the attorney's clerk proved that he had made inquiries for the deponent at his residence; and that a person, whom he believed to be the deponent's wife, said that he was abroad, having sailed in the *Thetis ;* and the witness added that he had made inquiries, and been told the *Thetis* was now on a voyage.

[*376]

(1) In *Rodriguez v. Tadmire,*† which was an action for a malicious prosecution, Lord KENYON is reported to have allowed the defendant to give evidence that the plaintiff was a man of bad character; but WOOD, B. refused to permit the defendant to put questions of this kind in a similar case (*Newsum v. Carr* ‡), saying, that, although such evidence might be given in mitigation of damages in actions of slander, it could afford no proof of probable cause to justify the defendant. In *Cornwall v. Richardson,* § ABBOTT, Ch. J. was of opinion that evidence of character was not receivable on either side in an action where there were counts both for slander and a malicious prosecution.

† 2 Esp. 721.
‡ 19 R. R. 675 (2 Stark. 69).

§ 27 R. R. 753 (Ry. & M. 305).

ROBINSON
v.
MARKIS.

It was objected for the defendant, that this was not sufficient proof of the deponent's being absent, and Roscoe on Evidence, p. 79, was referred to.

LORD ABINGER, C. B. ruled that the deposition could not be read; that it was indispensable to prove, by proper evidence, to the satisfaction of the Judge, that the witness was out of England. Here, there was nothing but hearsay to rely upon. The person who gave the attorney's clerk the information ought to have been produced, or other persons who knew the fact of the deponent's having sailed might have been called.

There was a similar want of evidence as to the absence of the other deponents, and the depositions were accordingly not allowed to be read; and there being no other evidence to support the second count, the defendant obtained a verdict on that, and the plaintiff on the first count.

Damages, 5l. (1).

Thesiger and *Martin*, for the plaintiff.

Jervis and *Butt*, for the defendant.

REYNOLDS *v.* MONKTON.

(2 Moody & Robinson, 384—385.)

1841.
Aug. 12.

Bridgewater.
[384]

The churchwardens have a discretionary power to appropriate the pews in the church amongst the parishioners, and may remove persons intruding on seats already appropriated.

TRESPASS for an assault and battery.

Plea, Not guilty, by statute.

The plaintiff was the occupier of a house and farm in the parish of Longsutton, and claimed as such a right to sit in a particular pew in the parish church. On the other hand, the exclusive right to occupy that pew was claimed by one Gaylard, another inhabitant, for himself and family.

The defendant was one of the churchwardens of the parish; and on the Sunday on which the assault complained of took place, just before divine service, he was informed by Gaylard that the plaintiff was in the pew and refused to leave it. The churchwardens had on previous occasions been appealed to, and had given the plaintiff notice that the pew belonged to the Gaylard family. The defendant,

(1) See *Falconer* v. *Hanson*, 10 R. R. 663 (1 Camp. 172).

on being applied to by Gaylard, went in company with the other REYNOLDS
churchwarden to the pew, and desired the plaintiff to quit it and go *v.*
to another seat, which he refused to do ; whereupon the defendant MONKTON.
laid his hand on him with a view to force him out, when the plaintiff
rose and walked out. The congregation were assembling, but the
clergyman had not entered the church. There was contradictory
evidence as to the violence used ; and for the defendant it was
attempted to establish a prescriptive *right to the pew, as attached   [*385]
to the house in which Gaylard lived, his family having for a great
number of years sat there ; and it was also contended, that at all
events the churchwardens had a right to appropriate the seat, which
had clearly been done in this case ; and Rogers on Ecclesiastical
Law (p. 171) was cited.

ROLFE, B. in summing up to the jury, after stating that, in his
    opinion, the evidence failed to make out the prescription, said,
    as to the other question :

I think that the churchwardens have a right to exercise a
reasonable discretion in directing where the congregation shall sit;
and if the defendant used no unnecessary force, he had a right
to remove the plaintiff from the pew in question to another seat.
If, in the exercise of a fair discretion, the churchwardens thought
it more convenient that the pew should be occupied by Gaylard's
family, and not by the plaintiff, and if the removal could be effected
without public scandal, or the disturbance of divine service, the
defendant was justified. You are to say whether any unnecessary
violence was used.

Verdict for the plaintiff. Damages 5l.

Crowder and *Bere,* for the plaintiff.

Erle and *Moody,* for the defendant.

———————

DOE D. ROWCLIFFE *v.* EARL OF EGREMONT.

(2 Moody & Robinson, 386—387.)

1841.
Aug. 16.

Bridgewater.
[386]

A witness called on his *subpœna duces tecum,* who objects to the production
of documents, has no right to have the question of his liability to produce
argued by his counsel retained for that purpose.

THIS was an ejectment brought by the lessee of a tenant for
life against the remainder-man under the will of a former Earl
of Egremont.

The question in the cause was, whether the lease, made by the tenant for life under a power of leasing, was void by reason of not being in compliance with the power.

The lessor of the plaintiff had let judgment go by default in an ejectment brought by the defendant, on the ground of the lease being void ; and the present action was brought in order to try that question, and to found an action against the executors of the tenant for life under the covenants of the lease.

Mr. Murray, the attorney for the executors, was called on his *subpœna duces tecum*, to produce certain accounts showing how and when the tenant for life had received the rents of the estate in question, and other documents which he held for the executors. He objected to produce those documents, on the ground that it would be prejudicial to the interests of the executors, they being in the nature of title deeds.

[*387]

Greenwood appeared as counsel for the witness to contend that he was not bound to produce the *documents.   He was proceeding to argue the question, when an objection was made to his right so to appear by the counsel for the plaintiff.

ROLFE, B. said :

The course has always been for the witness himself to state to the Judge the grounds upon which he contends he is not bound to produce the document required, and the Judge is to decide on the validity of those grounds, and to give to the witness the protection claimed, if he finds him to be entitled to it (1).

Greenwood was not allowed to be heard ; and in the result the witness was required to produce the documents, which he accordingly did.

Verdict for the defendant.

Bere and *Kinglake*, for the plaintiff.

Erle, Crowder, and *M. Smith,* for the defendant.

(1) So, it has been held that an objection to questions proposed, on the ground of their tendency to criminate the witness, must come from the witness himself (*Thomas* v. *Newton,* Moo. & Mal. 48); and the counsel who calls the witness will not be allowed to argue in support of the objection. (*R.* v. *Adey,* 1 Moo. & Rob. 94.)

LEAKE *v.* THE MARQUIS OF WESTMEATH.

(2 Moody & Robinson, 394—399.)

A decree of the Court of Arches for alimony is not admissible in evidence without proof of the proceedings in the suit.

Where a suit is removed by appeal from the Consistory Court to the Court of Arches, the judgment of the Court of Arches is not admissible in evidence without showing that Court to be duly in possession of such suit by producing the process of appeal, viz. the transcript of the proceedings sent from the Court below.

ASSUMPSIT on an attorney's bill.

Pleas, 1. *Non assumpsit.*   2. Statute of Limitations.

It was stated by the plaintiff's counsel, in opening his case, that the defendant and Lady Westmeath, his wife, living separate, the defendant, in 1821, instituted a suit against her in the Consistory Court of London for restitution of conjugal rights, which was met by Lady Westmeath's putting in a plea for a divorce, on the ground of cruelty and ill-treatment.   In Easter Term, 1821, Sir C. ROBINSON, the Judge of that Court, decided that Lady Westmeath had not substantiated the allegations in her plea, and made a decree that the defendant was entitled to the restitution of conjugal rights, and that Lady Westmeath should be admonished to return to, and cohabit with, him.   Against this judgment Lady Westmeath appealed to the Arches Court of Canterbury; and in Easter Term, 1827, the Judge of that Court (Sir JOHN NICHOL) pronounced judgment in favour of the appellant, divorcing her *à mensâ et toro,* and condemning Lord Westmeath in all the costs, as well of the original suit as of the appeal.   The defendant thereupon appealed to the High Court of Delegates, by which Court the judgment of the Arches Court was, in April, 1829, *affirmed.   The defendant then presented a petition to the King in Council, praying for a commission of review, which, however, after argument, was refused.   The plaintiff had been employed by Lady Westmeath as her solicitor, since 1827, in carrying on these various proceedings, and also in defending an appeal from the Irish Court of Chancery to the House of Lords, in a suit instituted by the Marquis of Westmeath against the Marchioness and her trustees, for the purpose of setting aside a deed of separation, executed by the Marquis in 1818; and the present action was brought to recover the costs incurred in all these proceedings between 1827 and December, 1832.

[*395]

No application had been made by Lady Westmeath to the Ecclesiastical Courts for alimony *pendente lite;* but upon the termination of the proceedings, when the commission of review was refused, she commenced proceedings in the Court of Arches for permanent alimony, by filing in November, 1832, what is called an " allegation of faculties," in that Court.   This allegation was supported by an affidavit of Lady Westmeath, sworn in May, 1833 ; and the defendant having put in his answer to the allegation, the Judge (Sir J. NICHOL) on the 9th July in that year gave judgment, decreeing permanent alimony at a certain sum per annum ; which judgment, on appeal to the Privy Council, was affirmed, the Court of Appeal merely reducing the amount of alimony awarded.

[*396]

The *Attorney-General*, for the purpose (as he alleged) of showing that Lady Westmeath was living apart from her husband under justifiable circumstances, *proposed to put in the judgment of the Arches Court, decreeing alimony; and an officer of that Court was called, who produced a book containing short minutes of the proceedings in Court ; viz. first, an entry of the receipt of the documents from the Court below ; secondly, appointments of the days for hearing ; thirdly, entries of the different steps taken in the suit ; and, fourthly, the judgment of Sir JOHN NICHOL, which was given at full length, and of which it appeared that there was not any formal entry except that contained in the book produced.   On cross-examination he stated that the process of appeal consisted of a transcript of the proceedings sent up from the Court below, and which, on the determination of the appeal, was remitted to the Court below.   That transcript had not been brought by the officer of the Consistory Court with the other documents which he had now in Court, in obedience to the *subpœna* served upon him.

The *Attorney-General* now proposing to read the judgment of Sir J. NICHOL from the book of minutes,

The *Solicitor-General* objected to the admissibility of the evidence :

At present it does not appear that there was any jurisdiction in the Court of Arches to entertain the suit ; or, indeed, what the nature of the suit was, except by the short and incomplete statements of the different proceedings in the Court of Appeal.   To let in evidence of the judgment of the Court of Appeal, first, the transcript of proceedings from the Consistory Court, *which was the process of appeal, ought to have been produced ; secondly, the several proceedings in the suit, which led to that judgment, ought

[*397]

also to be produced; for an inference is, no doubt, intended to be drawn from the amount of provision decreed to Lady Westmeath as alimony, and if so, the defendant is entitled to have before the Court the proceedings on which that decree was founded.

LEAKE
v.
THE
MARQUIS OF
WESTMEATH.

The *Attorney-General:*

The judgment of the Arches Court is tendered, not for the purpose of enforcing it, but merely for collateral purposes; and for such purposes, at all events, we have done enough to make it evidence. There is no formal entry of the judgment except that which the officer now holds in his hand; and credit must be given to the Judge of that Court, that he did not give judgment in a suit which was not duly before him. It never could be necessary that, for the mere purpose of proving separation, all the proceedings in the suit should be given in evidence.

TINDAL, Ch. J. :

A decree of the Court of Chancery cannot be read in evidence against a party, without also putting in the bill and answer; and, on the same principle, the judgment of the Ecclesiastical Court cannot be made evidence, without evidence of the proceedings in the suit. I do not say the plaintiff is bound to produce the affidavits which may have been filed, but I think he is bound to show what the pleadings were, by producing the libel and answer and the defensive allegations. It appears to me also, that the transcript *from the Court below ought to have been produced, to show that the Arches Court was duly in possession of the suit.

[*398]

The judgment of the Arches Court was accordingly rejected.

The *Attorney-General,* to obviate the objection, now called the keeper of the records of the Consistory Court, who produced the citation, libel, appearance, and allegations filed, and judgment pronounced, in that Court, concluding with an entry, at the foot of the judgment, that Lady Westmeath appealed from the judgment, which (the officer said) was the only entry on record ever made of an appeal from the judgment of that Court. The *Attorney-General* contended that he had now done enough to let in the judgment of the Arches Court, having shown a suit duly instituted and terminated in the Court below, and an appeal from that Court; and he added, that in the event of the evidence being now rejected, he should feel it to be his duty to tender a bill of exceptions to the ruling of the LORD CHIEF JUSTICE.

The *Solicitor-General* renewed his objection on both the grounds before urged; and the LORD CHIEF JUSTICE ruled that the judgment for alimony was still inadmissible.

An officer from the Consistory Court afterwards brought the transcript; but the objection was renewed, that though this met the difficulty as to the want of jurisdiction in the Arches Court, still [*399] the *judgment of that Court decreeing alimony in 1838 could not be received without producing the proceedings in the suit which led to that judgment.

TINDAL, Ch. J. :

I am still of opinion that the judgment cannot be put in evidence, until you show the proceedings on which it rested.

The evidence was accordingly again rejected.

The commission under the Great Seal authorising the High Court of Delegates to hear the appeal from the judgment of divorce pronounced by the Arches Court in 1827, and the judgment of the Court of Delegates on that appeal, were read without opposition; and in the result, a verdict was taken for the plaintiff, subject to a special case.

Sir F. Pollock, Attorney-General, *Ludlow*, Serjt., and *Hoggins*, for the plaintiff.

Sir W. Follett, Solicitor-General, *Sir T. Wilde*, and *Shee*, Serjt., for the defendant.

———•———

THE MAYOR, &c., OF LONDON *v.* THE MASTER, WARDENS, &c., OF THE PEWTERERS' COMPANY.

(2 Moody & Robinson, 409—412.)

An actual enjoyment of lights for 20 years, even under a permission verbally asked for by the occupier of a house, and given by the person having right to obstruct, is sufficient to confer a right under 2 & 3 Will. IV. c. 71, s. 3. The enjoyment under that section need not be as of right, or adverse.

THIS was an action on the case brought by the plaintiffs, as reversioners of a house in Leadenhall Market, for the obstruction of certain windows. The declaration alleged, that before and at

THE
MAYOR, &C.
OF LONDON
r.
THE MASTER,
WARDENS,
&C. OF THE
PEWTERERS'
COMPANY.

the time of the committing of the grievances, a certain messuage, &c. had been demised to one E. Chipper, as tenant to the plaintiffs, the reversion thereof belonging to the plaintiffs; in which messuage there were, and still of right ought to be, divers to wit, twenty-four windows, through which the light and air during all the time aforesaid ought to have entered, and still, &c. for the convenient and wholesome use and enjoyment thereof. Yet, &c.

The defendants pleaded (traversing the allegation in the declaration), that "there were not, nor of right ought there to have been, any such windows through which the light and air ought to have entered, or did enter, into the said messuage, in manner and form, &c."

The house in question was built in 1815, on the site of an old house which was then pulled down. *In the new house, the windows in dispute were put in the back part, looking towards the Pewterers' Hall, there being only a yard or court between the premises; and the plaintiffs' case was that they had been enjoyed in fact, and without interruption, up to the time of the obstruction in 1840. The obstruction was then put purposely to try the right; and *Sir T. Wilde* for the plaintiffs rested his case on the right acquired or confirmed by such user, under the 2 & 3 Will. IV. c. 71, s. 3. It appeared that the new house had been extended a few feet further towards the Pewterers' Hall than the former house, that is to say, as far as a wall, belonging to the defendants, that stood between the old house and the premises of the defendants. There were some windows in the old house partly obstructed by the wall.

[*410]

For the defendants, *Channell*, Serjt., proposed to prove, that when the new house was built in 1815, the Pewterers' Company had made objections to the windows in question as well as to others put out by other parties. The tenant of the plaintiffs' house, and the other parties, were then summoned to attend a Court of the Company; and, in 1818, in consequence of a letter sent by the clerk of the Company, the then tenant of the plaintiffs' house, Mr. Chipper, attended, and asked to be allowed to continue the windows on sufferance, and it was agreed verbally that he should pay a rent of 2*l*. a year; and the clerk was directed to prepare an *agreement to that effect. He did so, and sent the draft to Mr. Chipper, who kept it for some time; but, in 1820, returned it, refusing to abide by the agreement; the agreement could not now be found. In 1819 the defendants had leased the

[*411]

THE
MAYOR, &C.
OF LONDON
r.
THE MASTER,
WARDENS,
&C. OF THE
PEWTERERS'
COMPANY.
premises opposite the back of plaintiffs' house. *Channell*, Serjt.,
contended, that these facts would defeat the operation of the
statute; that the enjoyment intended in sect. 3 must be an enjoyment as of right, and adverse to the persons interested in any
opposition to it. Here it was, in fact, an enjoyment by mere
sufferance; and, as to the enjoyment from 1820, the defendants
could not be prejudiced by the acquiescence of their tenant.

Wilde, Serjt. :

The enjoyment need not be as of right. It is sufficient that the
actual user should be for twenty years. Mr. Baron PARKE decided
that point, and the case afterwards went to the Court of Error, and
Lord Chief Justice TINDAL delivered the judgment of the Court:
Flight v. *Thomas* (1). In that case MAULE, J., p. 695, says: "Section 2
requires that the easements therein mentioned shall have been
enjoyed by persons 'claiming right thereto,' but in sect. 3, which
relates to the access of light, there is no such expression, and I
think the omission is made purposely."

[412]   TINDAL, Ch. J., expressed an opinion that the facts opened by
the defendants' counsel would not amount to a defence in law.

Channell, Serjt., called a witness to show that the wall spoken
of, whilst it stood, obstructed the windows of the old house so as to
prevent their overlooking the premises of the Pewterers' Company.
At the close of his examination,

TINDAL, Ch. J., said :

I think that all you have stated will not amount to a defence.
The statute says, where the access of light " shall have been actually
enjoyed for the full period of twenty years without interruption, the
right thereto shall be deemed absolute and indefeasible any local
usage to the contrary notwithstanding, unless it shall appear that
the same was enjoyed by some consent or agreement in writing."
That is the enactment, even if at the outset the windows were
improperly constructed. Here is nothing but a negotiation; and
putting out of question all that relates to the old house, and taking
this from 1815 only, as a new house then first built, and that then
a negotiation is entered into for an agreement which you are unable
to produce, I think that this, if proved, will not meet the expressions

(1) 52 R. R. 468 (11 Ad. & El. 688).

used in the Act of Parliament, that the enjoyment of the right must be by consent or agreement in writing.

Whereupon *Channell*, Serjt., consented to a verdict for the plaintiffs.

THE MAYOR, &C. OF LONDON
r.
THE MASTER, WARDENS, &C. OF THE PEWTERERS' COMPANY.

CHANDLER *v.* HORNE (1).

(2 Moody & Robinson, 423—424.)

1842.
March 4.
—
Salisbury.
[423]

Where a witness remains in Court, after an order that the witnesses shall leave the Court, his testimony cannot on that ground be excluded: it is only matter for observation on his evidence.

CASE for slander.

The witnesses were all ordered out of Court; but one of the witnesses called for the plaintiff admitted *that he had been in Court during the whole case. Upon which *Hodges*, for the defendant, contended that he ought not to be examined.

[*424]

ERSKINE, J., said:

It used to be formerly supposed that it was in the discretion of the Judge whether the witness should be examined. It is now settled and acted upon by all the Judges that the Judge has no right to exclude the witness; he may commit him for the contempt, but he must be examined; and it is then matter of remark on the value of his testimony that he has wilfully disobeyed the order.

Verdict for the plaintiff.

JEANS *v.* WHEEDON.

(2 Moody & Robinson, 486—487.)

1843.
July 4.
—
Guildhall.
[486]

Where on a preliminary hearing of a case, the magistrate's clerk had taken down what a witness said, but neither witness nor magistrate signed it: Held that what the witness said might be proved by any one who heard him, without producing the clerk's note.

CASE for a malicious prosecution.

The defendant had made a charge against the plaintiff before a magistrate, the hearing of which was, in the first instance, adjourned, and on a subsequent occasion the case was heard, and the depositions were gone through, taken down, and the plaintiff committed for trial. A magistrate's clerk attended on the first occasion and

(1) Compare *Att.-Gen.* v. *Bulpit* (1821) 23 R. R. 637; and *Thomas* v. *David* (1836) 48 R. R. 794.—A. C.

JEANS
v.
WHEEDON.

took down what the defendant said, but the defendant did not sign it, nor did the magistrate.

Bompas, Serjt., objected that parol evidence was inadmissible of what the defendant said on the first occasion, and that the writing must be produced.

CRESSWELL, J.:

I know from the depositions returned to me at the Assizes, that, in practice when a case is adjourned, the depositions are not regularly reduced to writing under the statute; and I think that parol evidence is admissible here of what was said on the first occasion. If two persons are present on the examination of a witness, and one takes a note of what the witness says, and the [*487] other *does not, the latter is as competent as the former to prove what he heard.

Verdict for the plaintiff.

Talfourd, Byles, Serjts., and *Hance*, for the plaintiff.

Bompas, Serjt. and *Doane*, for the defendant.

———•———

1843.
July 3.
———
Guildhall.
[489]

SADLER AND OTHERS *v.* BELCHER AND OTHERS.

(2 Moody & Robinson, 489—494.)

By the custom of a Bank money paid in after banking hours, was put into a separate place of deposit, and entered in a counter-book, but not carried to the customer's account till next day: where a customer paid in a Bank note after the banking hours, and the banker having before resolved not to open his Bank again, placed the note in such separate place of deposit, without carrying it to the account of the customer, and next morning stopped payment, and became bankrupt, the Bank note was held to remain the property of the customer.

TROVER for a 500*l.* Bank of England note.

Plea 1. Not guilty.

2. That the plaintiffs were not possessed, &c.

The defendants were assignees of the estate and effects of Messrs. Whitmore, Wells, & Co. who on the 29th of June, A.D. 1841, and for many years previously, carried on business in Lombard Street in the city of London, as bankers. The plaintiffs on that day were, and for many years previously had been, customers of Messrs. Whitmore, Wells, & Co., and on the said 29th June the plaintiffs had an account with Messrs. Whitmore, Wells, & Co. as their

bankers, the balance of which account then was in favour of the
plaintiffs, independently of the Bank note in question in this action.
The course of business at the Bank of Messrs. Whitmore, Wells,
& Co., was to close the business of the day at five o'clock, and then
to make up their books and accounts of all *monies received or
paid in the course of the day, before that hour. It was also their
custom of business at five o'clock to draw in the counter-book a
line under the last entry of monies received prior to that hour,
during the day, and after that hour not to pay any cheques which
might be presented ; but to receive any money which might be
brought and deposit it in a separate place where it could not
become mixed with the receipts of the day, and to enter the sums
so received after five o'clock, together with the names of the persons
on whose account they were paid in, in the counter-book under the
line so drawn as aforesaid, but not to take into the account of the
receipts of that day any money so received after five o'clock, nor to
enter it in any other book than in the counter-book under the line
as before stated, until the following day, when such money was
entered in the books as taken into account as part of the receipts
of such following day; and when money was so paid in, the
customer was entitled to draw upon it at the opening of the Bank
on the following morning. The counter-book was a book in which
an entry was made of all monies paid in to the bankers as the
same were paid in, and was always resorted to to ascertain whether
money had been paid in by a customer during the day, before a
cheque of such customer was dishonoured. The same course of
business appeared to be pursued in the other London Banks,
varying only in the circumstance that in some London Banks no
entry is made in the counter-book of monies received after five
*o'clock until the following day, but such monies are deposited in
a separate place and marked with the name of the party on whose
account they are paid in.

Before five o'clock on the said 29th June, Messrs. Whitmore,
Wells, & Co. had resolved to close their Bank after five o'clock on
that day, and not to open it again for business, and at five o'clock
on the said 29th June a line was drawn in the counter-book, under
the last entry of monies received during that day.

After five o'clock on the said 29th June the plaintiffs sent their
clerk to Messrs. Whitmore, Wells, & Co.'s Bank with the 500*l.*
Bank note in question, to be paid in to their credit. The Bank note
was received by a clerk of Messrs. Whitmore, Wells, & Co., and at

SADLER
v.
BELCHER.

[*490]

[*491]

the time he so received it he told the plaintiffs' clerk from whom he received it that it would not be taken into account that day.   The Bank note was then deposited by the clerk who received it in a separate place, where it could not become mixed with the monies which had been received before five o'clock on that day, and the amount of the said Bank note, together with the names of the plaintiffs, were entered, in the usual way, in the counter-book, under the line so drawn as aforesaid, but the Bank note was not ever entered in any other book belonging to Messrs. Whitmore, Wells, & Co., nor was it in any way (except in the manner before men-

[*492] tioned) carried to the account of the plaintiffs, *nor was it entered in the plaintiffs' pass book, which was afterwards made up to the 80th of June, 1841. Messrs. Whitmore, Wells, & Co. never opened their Bank for business after the said 29th of June, and on the 80th of June, 1841, they stopped payment, and committed an act of bankruptcy. At ten o'clock on the morning of the said 30th of June, the plaintiffs applied to have the Bank note in question returned to them, and were informed that the bankers would have returned it, but that they thought it had better wait until the official assignee was consulted.   On the 1st of July, 1841, a *fiat* in bankruptcy was issued against Whitmore, Wells, & Co., and the defendants, as their assignees, took possession of the Bank note in question, and converted the same to their own use.

For the plaintiffs it was contended, that as the note had never been carried to their credit with the Bank of Messrs. Whitmore, Wells, & Co., at the time when the act of bankruptcy was com-mitted, Whitmore, Wells, & Co. would have been perfectly justified in returning it, and were bound to return it to the plaintiffs when it was demanded on the morning of the 30th of June : and *Thomp-son* v. *Giles* (1) and *Threlfal* v. *Giles* were cited, the latter of which was said to be almost precisely in point. It was an action for money had and received, brought against the assignees of Warwick

[*493] & Co., who were *bankers in Lancashire ; and the facts were, that the plaintiff had, after banking hours, deposited a large sum of money with the manager of Warwick & Co.'s Bank, at their place of business.   The manager knowing that the Bank was on the eve of stopping, although no resolution to that effect had been formally come to by the bankers, placed the money in a place by itself, separate from the funds of the house, and the Bank never after that day opened for business. The action came on to be tried before the

(1) 26 R. R. 392 (2 B. & C. 422).

Lord Chief Justice Abbott at the Lancaster Assizes, in the summer of 1822, and that learned Judge was of opinion that the plaintiff was entitled to recover. Here the case is stronger against the assignees, for a resolution to close their business had been come to by the bankers before the Bank note was paid in.

Upon its being distinctly proved by the plaintiffs' evidence, that the Bank note was paid in after five o'clock, and that Whitmore, Wells, & Co. had before then determined not to carry on their business after that day,

LORD ABINGER, C. B. expressed a strong opinion that the plaintiffs were entitled to recover:

His Lordship observed that the note had never been mixed with the assets of the house, nor had the amount ever been carried to the credit of the plaintiffs in the bankers' books; and having been placed apart by the bankers, after they had come to a resolution not to open their Bank again, it must be *taken that they dealt with it as property held by them on behalf of the plaintiffs, unless some unlooked-for contingency should occur before the next morning which might enable them to alter their resolution. It was therefore like the case of *Atkins* v. *Barwick* (1). There, a trader had bought goods of a creditor, but finding he was in failing circumstances, and could not pay for the goods, he put them aside in the hands of a third party, giving notice to the creditor that he had done so; and it was held that they did not pass to the assignees of the purchaser. And Lord MANSFIELD, in a subsequent case, remarked, that if the trader had, under such circumstances, kept the goods, it would have been a very dishonest act (2).

Sir F. *Pollock*, A.-G., for the defendants, said he had been of counsel for the plaintiff in the case of *Threlfal* v. *Giles*, cited on the other side, and he did not think that after the intimation of his Lordship's opinion he should be justified in continuing the defence. He therefore submitted to a

Verdict for the plaintiffs.

Erle and *Fitzherbert*, for the plaintiffs.

Sir F. *Pollock*, A.-G., and *Peacock*, for the defendants.

SADLER
v.
BELCHER.

[*494]

(1) 1 Str. 165.

(2) See *Harman* v. *Fisher*, 1 Cowp. 125.

1843.
July 31.

Durham.
[495]

THE APOTHECARIES' COMPANY *v.* LOTINGA.

(2 Moody & Robinson, 495—500.)

A surgeon may administer medicines in the cure of a surgical case without being subject to the penalties of the Apothecaries Act (55 Geo. III. c. 194), but he has no right to do so in the case of internal diseases not requiring surgical treatment, such as fever, or consumption.

THIS was an action of debt to recover penalties incurred by the defendant, under 55 Geo. III. c. 194, s. 20, for practising as an apothecary, without having obtained a certificate as directed by the Act.

The first count alleged that after the 1st day of August, 1815, mentioned in the Act, to wit, on &c., the defendant (not being a person who on or before the said 1st day of August was actually practising as an apothecary) did act and practise as an apothecary in England (that is to say) by then and there, as such apothecary, attending and advising, and furnishing and supplying medicines to and for the use of one Ann Pace, without having obtained such certificate as by the said Act is directed, contrary to the form of the statute, &c., whereby, &c. There was another count in the same form, only *alleging one John Palmerly to have been the party advised and supplied with medicine ; and five other counts in the same form, only varying the name of the parties ; and there was a general count at the end, stating that the defendant acted and practised as an apothecary, by then and there, as such apothecary, attending and advising, and supplying and furnishing medicine to and for the use of divers and very many persons without having obtained such certificate as by the said Act is directed, contrary, &c., whereby, &c.

[*496]

Plea, Not guilty, by statute (21 Jac. I. c. 4).

It appeared that the defendant was a foreigner, who resided with a person represented to be his uncle, in the town of Bishop Wearmouth; and in regard to the first count, the evidence was that Ann Pace had been afflicted with a consumption for some months before November, 1842, when the defendant was called in to attend her ; he attended her till the January following, when she died ; he was accustomed to desire the mother of the deceased to go to his house for the medicine, and upon her doing so the defendant gave some directions to his uncle in a language which the witness could not understand; the uncle then went into another room and brought some medicine in bottles, which the defendant examined, and smelt, and said it was all right, and put labels on the bottles, containing

directions how the contents were to be used; and after the death of
Ann Pace the mother received from the uncle a bill, in the *following
form, which was partly engraved and partly in the defendant's
handwriting:

APOTHE-
CARIES'
COMPANY
v.
LOTINGA.
[*497]

" Mr. PACE to Mr. LOTINGA, Surgeon, &c.

	£	s.	d.
Bill delivered - - - - -			
Medicines, &c., from 1st Nov. 1842, to 2nd			
January, 1843 - - - - - 3	3	18	0
Journeys - - - - -			
Surgery - - - - -			
Fees - - - - -			
Account for Servants - - - -			
	3	18	0

" Attendance
" Particulars if required."

In regard to the second count, it appeared that the defendant, at
the request of a Mr. Robson, attended a boy, John Palmerly, for a
complaint which he, the defendant, said was inflammation of the
chest, and the defendant used to visit him at the house of the boy,
and said he would send some medicines, which were in fact afterwards brought by his servant; amongst other things, he directed
leeches to be applied, and sent some, for which the boy's father
paid him 4s. He afterwards sent in a bill as follows: "Mr. Lotinga's
charge for medicine and attendance, from 5th of March till the 30th
of March, 1843, on Mr. Robson for Mr. Palmerly's son, 1l. 17s."

The plaintiffs' counsel then tendered evidence *(on the last count)
that the defendant in the month of January, 1843, had attended one
Lancelot Appleby for a paralytic affection; that the defendant
supplied ten bottles of medicine, some to be used as embrocations,
some to be taken internally; and that he sent in a bill charging
1l. 7s. for medicines, and 10s. 6d. for attendance.

[*498]

Dundas, for the defendant, objected that this evidence could
not be received; the case of Appleby was not referred to in any of
the seven first counts, and the last count was too general; it would
be a great hardship on the defendant if he were thus, without
notice, suddenly required to explain the circumstances of any transaction which the plaintiffs might bring forward as a case of
practising as an apothecary.

APOTHE-
CARIES'
COMPANY
ᴠ.
LOTINGA.

The learned Judge, however, ruled that the evidence was admissible; it was impossible to say that the evidence tendered did not tend to establish the facts charged in the eighth count; and if that count was open to any objection on the ground of its generality, an objection of that nature could not be urged in this stage of the proceedings.

The evidence was accordingly received.

Dundas then went to the jury upon the facts, and contended that the instances of practice relied upon by the plaintiffs were all
[*499] cases in which the *defendant had practised not as an apothecary, but as a surgeon; he had so described himself in his bills, and the cases themselves were properly of that kind. The first case proved (of consumption) was known to require surgical treatment, by bleeding, &c.; and so was the second, in which, in fact, leeches had been applied; and in the last instance, that of Appleby, the defendant (whether correctly or not) had treated the disease as one to be cured by external, applications. He also contended that there was evidence that the defendant supplied the medicines rather as a chemist, than as an apothecary.

CRESSWELL, J. to the jury:

The sole question is, whether the defendant has practised as an apothecary, for it is not pretended that he had obtained any certificate authorizing him to do so. Now I apprehend that an apothecary is a person who professes to judge of internal disease by its symptoms, and applies himself to cure that disease by medicines; and if you think the defendant has, in either of the cases proved before you, acted in that way, I recommend you to find your verdict for the plaintiffs. The mere fact of the defendant's having supplied medicines, does not necessarily show that he practised as an apothecary; for a surgeon may lawfully do that, if the medicines are administered in the cure of a surgical case. If, for instance, in the case of a broken leg it becomes necessary to administer medicine, no doubt the surgeon may lawfully do so; but on the other hand,
[*500] *if a surgeon takes upon himself to cure a fever, he steps out of his lawful province, and is not authorized to administer medicine in such a case. You then, on the whole, are to say whether, in the instances proved before you, the defendant acted as an apothecary, or as a surgeon. Take the case of Ann Pace, It is said that her

was a surgical case ; but can a consumption fairly be so classed ? how does the medical attendant judge of it ? surely by the symptoms of the patient in regard to the internal functions of the body ; and how does he apply himself to cure it ? not by manual operation externally, but by the administration of medicine internally. Apply the same test to the other instances, and if in any of them you think that the defendant was acting as an apothecary, you must find your verdict accordingly.   But then it is said, if he did not supply the medicines as a surgeon, still he did not supply them as an apothecary, but as a chemist.   But a chemist is one who sells medicines which are asked for, whereas if you believe the evidence, the present defendant himself selected the medicines, and determined on which he ought to give.

Verdict for the plaintiffs on the first count, the plaintiffs not seeking to recover more than one penalty.

Wortley and *Robinson*, for the plaintiffs.

Dundas and *R. Ingham*, for the defendant (1).

SCHOLES *v.* CHADWICK.

(2 Moody & Robinson, 507—508.)

On an issue, whether the plaintiff had an easement in the defendant's land, the declaration of a former occupier of the defendant's land is not admissible against him.

THIS was an action on the case.   The declaration alleged, that the plaintiff was possessed of a close, and by reason thereof was entitled to water his cattle at a pond in a field of the defendant's, which adjoined the plaintiff's also ; that the defendant wrongfully drained off the water from the pond, and that in consequence thereof a mare of the plaintiff, in descending into the pond to drink, fell down a steep bank and was drowned.

Plea 1. Not guilty.

2. Denying the right alleged.

Martin, for the plaintiff, in proof of the right alleged, tendered evidence of a declaration made by a former occupier of the defendant's land.   The wife of the occupier had requested him to fence off the pond, on account of its being dangerous to children ; and

1843.
Aug. 21.

Liverpool.
[507]

APOTHE-
CARIES'
COMPANY
v.
LOTINGA.

(1) See *Allison* v. *Haydon*, 29 R. R. 653 (4 Bing. 619); *Apothecaries' Com-* *pany* v. *Greenhough*, 55 R. R. 429 (1 Q. B. 799).

SCHOLES
v.
CHADWICK.

Martin proposed to give in evidence the answer of the occupier, viz. that he could not fence it off, because the owner of the plaintiff's close had a right to water his cattle at it.

[*508]

Murphy, Serjt. objected to the evidence; the statement of a former occupier could not be admissible *evidence against the reversioner. Before the Prescription Act, 2 & 3 Will. IV. c. 71, even the acts of the occupier, if he had only an estate from year to year, did not bind the reversioner; *à fortiori*, it cannot be maintained that his mere declarations should have that effect.

Martin :

The tenant is placed in possession by the reversioner, and represents the reversioner; and what he says in derogation of his own rights and interest at the time must be admissible evidence, though of course the weight due to it may be more or less.

CRESSWELL, J. rejected the evidence.

Verdict for the defendant.

Martin and *Pickering*, for the plaintiff.

Murphy, Serjt. for the defendant.

———•———

1843.
Nov. 2.

Westminster.
[536]

YOUNG *v.* HONNER (1).

(2 Moody & Robinson, 536—538; S. C. 1 C. & K. 51.)

On an issue as to the genuineness of a signature, if a witness denies the genuineness, and assigns as his reason, a peculiarity in such signature, other documents, exhibiting the same peculiarity, may be put into his hands on cross-examination, and the witness may be questioned upon them, for the purpose of testing the value of his evidence as to the genuineness of the disputed signature. If he denies the documents to be genuine, proof is inadmissible of that fact.

ASSUMPSIT against the acceptor of a bill of exchange.

Plea. That the defendant did not accept the bill, and issue thereon.

The only question in the cause was, whether the words "accepted, Robert Honner," appearing on the bill as an acceptance, were the genuine handwriting of the defendant.

A witness called for the defendant swore he believed the signature not to be the genuine signature of the defendant; and as a reason

(1) See now Criminal Evidence Act, 1865 (28 & 29 Vict. c. 18), ss. 1 and 8 —A. C.

for that belief he added, that the defendant always signed his name thus —" R. W. Honner."

Upon this *Lee*, for the plaintiff, in cross-examining the witness, put into his hands a document purporting to be signed "Robert Honner," and asked him whether he believed it to be the *genuine signature of the defendant: and on his answering in the affirmative, he was asked whether the document was not signed "Robert Honner"? and whether, after seeing that document, he would persevere in saying that the defendant always signed his name "R. W. Honner"? The document was not in any way relevant to the present issue.

[*537]

Thesiger objected that this course of cross-examination was not allowable, and insisted that it was merely instituting a comparison of handwriting; he cited *Doe* v. *Suckermore* (1), and *Griffiths* v. *Ivory* (2).

ALDERSON, B. (after consulting the other Barons, who were sitting *in banco*) said the Court was unanimously of opinion that the cross-examination, as far as it had been pursued, was regular, and that the question objected to might be properly put. His Lordship added, that they could not subscribe to the decision of the Court of Queen's Bench in *Griffiths* v. *Ivory;* but the inconvenience there suggested, viz. that the jury would have to try various collateral issues, did not arise here, for the witness had himself admitted the document now put into his hands to be genuine ; and surely, if the peculiarity existed in it which he relied upon, *as disproving the genuineness of the signature now in dispute, that must be a circumstance by which to test the value of his belief on the subject. But if the witness had denied the genuineness of the signature to the document now put into his hands, he should not have allowed any issue to be raised upon that point.

[*538]

The question was accordingly put.

Verdict for the plaintiff.

Humfrey and *R. V. Lee*, for the plaintiff.

Thesiger, Butt, and *Clarkson,* for the defendant.

(1) 44 R. R. 533 (5 Ad. & El. 703)   (2) 3 P. & D. 17.

1844.
April 4.

RISHTON *v.* NESBITT.

(2 Moody & Robinson, 554—556.)

Liverpool.
[554]

In a question of pedigree, when it is important to show that the family had relatives living at a particular place, evidence may be given of declarations by a deceased member of the family, that "he was going to visit his relatives at that place."

THIS was a writ of right brought to recover certain lands in the county of Lancaster.

The demandant claimed as collateral heir to one Barbara Aytoun. The tenant relied on two fines levied by Barbara Aytoun; the first above sixty years before the commencement of this action, by which, and a deed to declare the uses of it, the seisin of Barbara Aytoun was divested; and the tenant showed a derivative title under the parties in whose favour the fines were levied, and a long possession.

[*555] The tenant also undertook to prove that another *party than the demandant was the heir of Barbara Aytoun. It became important for the tenant, in establishing the descent of this party from an ancestor of the name of Nicholas Nabb (a brother of Barbara Aytoun), to show that a member of his family lived at Blackburn; and in order to show that fact, *Starkie* asked a witness who had married into the Nabb family, whether she had heard her husband's father (who lived at Manchester), make any statement on that subject.

The witness answered that, on occasion of his leaving his house at Manchester, she had heard him say he was going to visit his relatives at Blackburn.

Dundas objected that the declaration deposed to by the witness could not be received as evidence in this case. In cases of pedigree, the declarations of deceased members of the family had been admitted in evidence, where such declarations pointed to particular individuals as being members of the family; but there were two objections to the admissibility of the declaration now tendered: 1st, there was no precedent for receiving declarations so vague as to point to no particular individual; 2ndly, reputation as to a place where a thing occurred, is not evidence; it has been so decided in the case of a declaration as to the place of birth (1).

[556] ROLFE, B. :

The declaration is not evidence of the fact that the father of the witness's husband did go to Blackburn, or that any one of the name

(1) See *Rex* v. *The Inhabitants of Erith*, 8 East, 539.

of Nabb was living there; but it is evidence of there being a tradi-
tion in the family, that they had relations living at Blackburn; and
in the event of its being shown by other evidence that there were
persons of the name of Nabb living at Blackburn, this declaration
may be referred to, to connect those persons with the family now
spoken of. In the *Troutbeck* case (1) evidence was received of a tradi-
tion that a particular individual had died in India, for the purpose
of connecting that individual with the family of the claimant.

The tenant made out his case satisfactorily, and in the result, the
demandant submitted to a
Verdict for the tenant.

Dundas and *Archbold*, for the demandant.

Starkie, *Crompton*, and *Tomlinson*, for the tenant.

RICHARDS *v.* RICHARDS (2).

(2 Moody & Robinson, 557—559.)

In an action for defamation, where the defendant at the time of uttering
the words had referred to certain reports current against the plaintiff, which
he stated he had reason to believe were true: Held, that on plea of Not
guilty, the defendant might prove by cross-examination of the plaintiff's
witnesses, that such reports had in fact prevailed in the plaintiff's neighbourhood, and were the common topic of conversation, before the words
were uttered by the defendant.

CASE for words spoken to one A. B. imputing to the plaintiff
that he had grossly ill-treated a woman. The declaration alleged,
generally, that the plaintiff had, in consequence of the slander, lost
the friendship of his neighbours, &c.

Plea : Not guilty.

The evidence on the part of the plaintiff, showed that the words
were spoken to A. B. on the occasion of his going to the defendant
to enquire whether he had not imputed to the plaintiff the offence
charged upon him, and who was the author of the slander ? The
defendant, in reply, stated that he had heard of the imputation;
that the report was generally correct, and that he had reason to
believe it to be true; but he refused to state from whom he had
heard it, and strongly censured the plaintiff.

On the part of the defendant, it was attempted to be shown by

(1) *Monckton* v. *The Attorney-General*,   (2) *Watkin* v. *Hall* (1868), L. R. 3
34 R. R. 38 (2 Russ. & My. 147—151).   Q. B. 396, 37 L. J. Q. B. 125.

RICHARDS
v.
RICHARDS.
[*558]

cross-examination of the plaintiff's *witnesses, that the supposed misconduct of the plaintiff had been a frequent topic of conversation among those who were employed by the plaintiff in his business, and was commonly rumoured in the town in which the plaintiff resided, before the conversation between the defendant and A. B., which was the subject of the action; and such evidence was insisted upon as admissible, because it showed that the defendant was, at all events, not the inventor of the slander, and that the injury arising from the slander could not be wholly ascribed to the defendant: *Moore* v. *Ostler*, and *Hardy* v. *Alexander*, referred to in Roscoe on Evidence, p. 398 (5th ed.), were cited.

On the other hand, it was contended that there was no reported authority in favour of the admission of mere rumours in mitigation, except where it appeared that the defendant had himself heard the rumours, and had founded his statement upon such reports of others.

CRESSWELL, J. stated from his own recollection, that the case of *Hardy* v. *Alexander* was not a decision in point, for that the evidence was there received without opposition; but that in *Moore* v. *Ostler*, such evidence had been objected to and admitted.

After consulting WIGHTMAN, J., the learned Judge allowed the counsel for the defendant to prove the above facts on cross-examination.

[559]

Greenwood, for the defendant, in his address to the jury, urged them to find for the defendant, on the ground that the supposed slander being contained in a reply to enquiries made by the witness for the purpose of ascertaining the author of it, was *primâ facie* a confidential and privileged communication, and that there was no proof of express malice.

CRESSWELL, J. :

It appears to me that the defendant has failed in showing that he had any lawful excuse for the act complained of; the uttering of defamatory matter of an actionable nature is presumed to be malicious, unless it occurred on a lawful occasion. If the defendant had merely stated to the witness what he had heard, with a view to enable him to trace the slander to its real author, the case might have been different. But here the defendant went further, and he

even refused to point out any one as the reporter to him, of the   RICHARDS
slander.   •   RICHARDS.

Verdict for the plaintiff.

Crowder, Cockburn, and M. Smith, for the plaintiff.

Greenwood and Rawlinson, for the defendant.

<hr>

ALLEN v. MARTIN.

(5 Jurist, 239—240.)

1841.
Feb. 12.

A purchaser under an ordinary power of sale in a mortgage cannot
require the mortgagor's concurrence on the ground that the mortgagor
is in possession, if the mortgagee undertakes to deliver possession on
completion.

Rolls Court.
Lord
LANGDALE,
M.R.
[239]

THIS suit was instituted for the specific performance of a contract
for the purchase of a real estate belonging to one John Stephenson,
and sold by the plaintiff as mortgagee, with a power of sale. By
the mortgage-deed, it was provided, that in case default should be
made in payment of the mortgage-money, of which the production
of the mortgage indentures should be conclusive evidence, it should
be lawful for the plaintiff, his heirs and assigns, without any further
concurrence of said John Stephenson, his heirs or assigns, to enter
into possession of the premises, and whether in or out of possession
of the same, to make any lease or leases thereof as he or they
should think fit; and also of his and their own authority to make
sale and absolutely dispose of the same, or any part or parts
thereof, with the appurtenants, for as much money as could be
reasonably obtained for the same; and to convey and assure the
same, when so sold, unto the purchaser or purchasers thereof, his,
her, or their heirs and assigns; and it was declared that the
receipts of the plaintiff, his heirs and assigns, for the purchase-
money, rents and profits, should be good discharges for the same,
and that the person paying him or them any monies, and taking
such receipts, should not afterwards be required to see to the
application of the monies therein expressed to be received, nor be
answerable for the misapplication of the same. By the contract,
dated 28th March, 1837, the defendant agreed to purchase the
premises for 380l., and the purchase-money was to be paid as
soon as peaceable possession was given; at all events, within one

month from the date thereof; and an abstract of title was to be delivered.

The title was approved of by the purchaser; but [the purchaser insisted] on the necessity of Stephenson joining in the conveyance, because he was in possession of a portion of the premises sold, and had informed the purchaser that the vendor had no power to deliver possession, and that he (the mortgagor) claimed some right in opposition to the vendor; but it did not appear on what ground the mortgagor founded his denial of the vendor's right to deliver possession. In reply to this objection, the vendor expressed himself ready to give possession, and offered to guarantee the defendant against all claims by Stephenson. The defendant proposed a reference to a conveyancer, which was not objected to by the vendor; but, to save the expense of such reference, he offered to give 15l. for the concurrence of Stephenson. The concurrence of Stephenson, however, was not obtained by this means; and after a great deal of delay and correspondence between the parties, the vendor always professing himself ready to give possession, and the purchaser insisting on the necessity of Stephenson's concurrence, the bill was filed. The nature of the points in dispute between the parties, and the facts of the case are more fully stated in his Lordship's judgment.

Pemberton (who was absent) 'and *Wilcock*, for the plaintiff.

Kindersley and *Piggott*, for the defendant.

LORD LANGDALE, M. R.:

The contract was entered into on the 28th March, 1837, for the purchase of a certain real estate by Mr. Martin, the defendant, for the sum of 380l., to be paid as soon as peaceable possession was given, or at all events within one month from the date thereof; and no doubt it was intended between the parties that the contract should be completed within one month from the date of it. Very soon after the contract was made an abstract of title was delivered; and if there were any objections to the title, though it does not clearly appear whether there were any, they were very shortly removed. Before the end of the month at the expiration of which the contract was to be completed, objections were made to the proposed conveyance. It appears that the property was vested in the plaintiff as mortgagee, with a power of sale, and that he had a right to sell without the consent of the mortgagor, and in

exercise of that right he had entered into the contract.   Before the
end of the month the solicitor for the defendant insisted, that, as
the sale was by a mortgagee, it was necessary for the mortgagor
to join in the conveyance; and on the 12th April, 1837, he communicated his opinion as to that necessity to the solicitor for the
vendor, who happened to be better informed by the aid of a very
valuable book (Sugd. V. & P.), and he disputed the necessity of the
mortgagor joining.   And it is now admitted, that in that opinion
he was perfectly right.   That, however, was the objection taken,
and it was disputed, and in that interval the time at the expiration
of which the contract was to be completed, expired.   After that
time a question was raised by the defendant as to the power of
the plaintiff to deliver peaceable possession.   The mortgagor, it
appears, was in possession of part of the property; and it was
intimated, on the 9th May, by the solicitor of the defendant to the
solicitor of the plaintiff, that it might not be easy to get possession,
for he was informed that the mortgagor would not give up possession.   To that a proper answer was returned,—" Until we can give
you possession, we don't ask for the purchase-money."   I collect,
from the subsequent part of the correspondence, that the defendant's solicitor began to doubt as to the point of law on which he
had relied, for he did not afterwards insist on the mortgagor's
being a necessary party to the conveyance as such, but he insisted
on the difficulty of obtaining possession, and that on that account
it was necessary for the person, who disputed the vendor's right,
to join in the conveyance.   That was the turn the correspondence
took towards the end of May, 1837; and in the beginning of June
the solicitor for the plaintiff said he was ready to give possession.
It is necessary to observe the situation of the parties at this time.
The defendant was claiming a right as to the conveyance to which
he was not entitled, and it was the duty of the plaintiff to be
prepared to give possession, and he stated, in a letter to the
defendant's solicitor, that he was ready to give possession.   Now,
possession was to be delivered when the purchase-money was paid,
and the conveyance could not be settled until the question whether
the purchaser *was entitled to have the concurrence of the mort-   [*240]
gagor in the conveyance was determined; and though it was the
duty of the plaintiff to give possession, yet, on account of the
objection made by the purchaser, he was not able to prove that he
could give possession.   It was in this state of things when the
vendor said he was ready to give possession, but could not prove,

through the objection of the purchaser, that he was able to do so,
that the letter of the 5th June was written on behalf of the
purchaser, proposing a reference to some conveyancer, which was
willingly acceded to by the solicitor of the vendor. But he said
that the expense of a reference would be greater than giving a sum
of money to the mortgagor, and he, therefore, authorized the
solicitor of the defendant to give 15*l.* to the mortgagor for his
signature. The consequence of that was, that the purchaser
conceived he had prevailed in his objection. But I think the
plaintiff did not intend to admit the right, but was willing to
concede to the wish of the purchaser at the expense of 15*l.* And
accordingly some attempts were made to procure the signature
of the mortgagor, and an authority was given to pay him 15*l.* for
his concurrence. But the payment of that sum was to be on
condition, not only of the mortgagor joining in the conveyance,
but also of releasing all claims, and consenting to give up possession. It is difficult to suppose that there was not something to be
done by the vendor to procure possession, though he might have
done it by a sum of money, or some other means. The mortgagor
got out of the way, and was not to be found from June to August.
Two circumstances took place in the meantime. On the 21st July,
the solicitor for the vendor wrote to the purchaser's solicitor,
saying, his client was ready to give possession, but not taking any
step to do so. Then, on 29th July, a letter was sent by the solicitor
of the purchaser to the vendor's solicitor, stating the complaint
of the mortgagor, that he was unlawfully turned out of possession,
and that he threatened to commence proceedings at law ; to which,
the answer was, that the vendor would guarantee the purchaser
against all claims of the mortgagor. In August, Stephenson the
mortgagor not being to be found, the solicitor of the vendor
revoked the authority to pay him a sum of money for his concurrence, stating that the vendor would deliver possession, and saying,
for the first time, that he should require interest on the purchase-
money. The case seems then to have been in this way : the
vendor saying he was ready to give possession, and the vendee not
doing those things which were necessary to enable the vendor
to put him in possession, but saying that claims were made by
other parties. This was not a proper thing for the purchaser to
do. A purchaser has no right to seek information from other
persons ; and if he attends to such representations, he does so at
his own risk. And I am of opinion that the purchaser, in not

attending to the plaintiff's representation that he was ready to
deliver possession, and in not doing those things which were
necessary to enable the vendor to prove that he was ready to
deliver possession, did so at his own risk. I think the vendor had
a right in August to revoke the authority. He might not have
a right to revoke the authority, without paying the expense incurred
in consequence of it; but it is clear that he consented to pay the
15*l.* only to avoid expense, and not from any notion of the
purchaser's right. And I think that, being prevented, not indeed
by the conduct of the vendee, but by that of the mortgagor, from
effecting his object, he had a right to revoke the authority, and
stand on his contract. And so he expressed himself in his letter
of the 12th August, 1837. Further correspondence took place
between the parties ; and in August, 1838, we find the vendor not
insisting on his contract, but offering 10*l.* to procure Stephenson's
consent. It is not stated what was done upon that. Then, in
February, 1839, the bill was filed. The defendant, by his answer,
insists that Stephenson is a necessary party to the conveyance,
and that he is entitled to have his concurrence therein, and that,
in consequence of the delay that has taken place in completing the
contract, he is entitled to compensation for dilapidations ; and,
lastly, that the plaintiff never was, and is not now in a condition
to deliver possession of the premises. If that is so, the contract
cannot be performed. The evidence on this point is utterly valueless : the witnesses speaking only to their belief that the plaintiff
could not deliver possession, because the parties in possession said
they would not give up possession. The only evidence of importance as to this is, that it appears the plaintiff has himself been
willing to give money to Stephenson for his concurrence ; and it is
not easy to suppose that he would have offered to give money,
unless there was some obstruction which could be overcome by
that means. But it does not follow from this that the plaintiff
would not have been able to deliver possession. Therefore, I do
not think there ought to be a reference to inquire whether, at any
time, the plaintiff could have delivered possession, but only whether
he can deliver possession now; and if he can do so, he will be
entitled to a specific performance, and to the costs of this suit.
For this reason, that he says he was always able to give possession;
but the other party never put him into a situation to do that which
he said he could do. Refer it to the Master to inquire whether
the plaintiff can now deliver peaceable possession.

TORBOCK v. LAINY and Others.

(5 Jurist, 318.)

1841.

Queen's Bench.

Lord
DENMAN,
Ch. J.

PATTESON, J.
WILLIAMS, J.
WIGHTMAN,
J.

[318]

A jury retired to consider their verdict, and, upon their returning into Court and their names being called over, one of the jurors, whose name was on the panel, did not answer to the name which the officer of the Court had marked as the name of the party called and sworn: Held, upon objection taken before the verdict was recorded, that it was not a mis-trial.

ASSUMPSIT for work and labour. * * At the trial before Rolfe, B., at the Lent Assizes at Durham, the jury retired to consider their verdict, and the learned Judge went to his lodgings; upon their coming into Court to deliver their verdict, which it had been agreed should be taken, in the absence of the learned Judge, by the officer of the Court, and upon their names being called over, no juror answered to the name of William Bloomer, but one of the jury said his name was Thomas Fulmer; and they gave a verdict for the plaintiff, damages 40l. 7s. Before the verdict was recorded, the counsel for the plaintiff objected, that there was a mis-trial, and renewed the objection on the following morning, when it appeared that the name of Thomas Fulmer was on the panel as well as that of William Bloomer. The learned Judge ordered the verdict to be recorded, reserving leave to the plaintiff to make what use he could of the objection thereafter. In this Term

 Dundas moved for a rule *nisi* for a new trial, on the ground of a mis-trial:

 * * The jury has not been constituted in the manner prescribed by 6 Geo. IV. c. 50, s. 26, and the plaintiff has not had an opportunity of challenging Fulmer, which he might have desired to do.

(PATTESON, J.: It does not appear that Fulmer was sworn by a wrong name.

Lord DENMAN, Ch. J., referred to *R. v. Tremearne* (1), in which the Court granted a new trial, a party who served on the jury not being on the panel, and not being of age.)

LORD DENMAN, Ch. J.:

There is no ground for our interference in this case. We cannot hold that there has been a mis-trial, unless we can say that the

(1) 29 R. R. 234 (5 B. & C. 254).

marking of the juror's name by the officer of the Court is a con- TORROOK
dition precedent to a correct trial. The only question here is, LAINY.
whether the circumstance of the officer putting a mark against the
name of one person on the panel instead of against the name of
another, when his name was called over, destroys the effect of the
verdict. If it had been shown that any consequences unfavourable
to the party making this application had arisen from the mistake
of the officer, it would be different.

PATTESON, J.:

It is quite consistent with the circumstance of the officer calling
the wrong name when the jury came into Court to deliver their
verdict, that the party was sworn by his right name, and that the
only mistake was in the officer having, when the name was first
called, marked the wrong name.

WILLIAMS and WIGHTMAN, JJ., concurred.

Rule refused.

REG. v. HETHERINGTON.

(5 Jurist, 529—530 ; S. C. 5 J. P. 496.)

It is an indictable offence at common law to publish a blasphemous libel
of and concerning the Old Testament.

1841.
Queen's
Bench.
Lord
DENMAN,
Ch. J.

INDICTMENT for a blasphemous libel on that part of the Holy Bible
called the Old Testament. The defendant had been tried before LITTLEDALE,
J.
Lord Denman, Ch. J., and a special jury, at the sittings in London PATTESON, J.
after last Michaelmas Term, and found guilty, Lord DENMAN, Ch. J., [529]
having told the jury, that if they thought the publication tended to
question or cast disgrace upon the Old Testament, it was a libel.

   Sir John Campbell (Att.-Gen.), having prayed the judgment of
the Court upon the defendant,

   Thomas moved in arrest of judgment, or for a new trial: [530]

   (LORD DENMAN, Ch. J.: You are too late to move for a new trial:
the practice is to move within the first four days of Term, and
then to postpone the argument until the party is brought up for
judgment.)

Then, in arrest of judgment, the offence laid in the indictment is not
punishable at common law. The indictment sets out a libel only

upon the Old Testament, and there is no case of an indictment for a publication discussing matters contained in the Old Testament.

All the cases of indictment for blasphemy against the Holy Scriptures are for matters directed against Christianity and religion together. The first case which is said to have decided that Christianity is part and parcel of the common law of England is in the Year Book (34 Hen. VI. p. 40 (1)); but that opinion seems to be founded on a mistranslation; and all the cases down to *R.* v. *Woolston* (2), proceed upon that mistranslation: *R.* v. *Tayler* (3), in which HALE, Ch. J., said, "The Christian religion is a part and parcel of the laws of England," is a leading authority; but what reliance can be placed on the opinion of that Judge in this matter, seeing he held witchcraft punishable at common law? (4).

(LORD DENMAN, Ch. J.: HALE, Ch. J., refers to the enactments of the statute law, and expressly to the Act of Parliament (5), " which," he says, " hath provided punishments proportionable to the quality of the offence.")

Besides, at the time of the cases referred to, all witnesses must have been sworn on the Bible or New Testament, but that is now altered; and, therefore, the reason for holding that an attack upon Christianity would dissolve and weaken the bonds of society, viz. by overthrowing or weakening the confidence in testimony given in Courts of justice, no longer exists.   *   *   *

LORD DENMAN, Ch. J.:

There is no ground for granting a rule in this case.   Though in

---

(1) The case was *quare impedit* against the Bishop of Lincoln; and the passage, which is obscure, is as follows: "Prisot. A tielx Leis que ils de Saint Eglise ont en ancien Scripture, covient a nous a donner credence; car ceo Common Ley sur quel touts mannieres Leis sont fondes. Et auxy, Sir, nous sumus obliges de conustre lour Ley de Saint Eglise: et semblablement ils sont obliges de conustre nostre Ley." It may be thus translated: "To such laws as they of holy Church have in ancient Scripture, it is proper for us to give credence; for that is (as it were) common law, on which all sorts (of) laws are founded. And thus, Sir, we are obliged to take cognizance of their law of holy Church; and likewise they are obliged to take the same cognizance of our law." Wingate evidently grounds his third maxim on the above passage: "To such lawes as have warrant in Holy Scripture, our law giveth credence, *et contra*." Maximes, p. 6. [The text of the Year Book seems to be corrupt or defective. An obvious error in the translation has been corrected.—F. P.]

(2) 2 Str. 834; *S. C.* more fully in Fitzg. 64.

(3) 3 Keb. 607; 1 Ventr. 293.

(4) 6 How. St. Tr. 701, 702.

(5) Stat. 1 Jac. I. c. 12, repealed by 9 Geo. II. c. 5.

most of the cases, I believe not in all, the libel has been against **REG.** *v.* **HETHERING-TON.** the New Testament; yet the Old Testament is so connected with the New that it is impossible that such a publication as this could be uttered without reflecting upon Christianity in general: and, therefore, I think an attack upon the Old Testament of the nature described in the indictment is clearly indictable. It is our duty to abide by the law as laid down by our predecessors, and, taking the cases which have been referred to as assigning the limits within which a publication becomes a blasphemous libel, the publication in question is one. As to the argument, that the relaxation of oaths is a reason for departing from the law laid down in the old cases, we could not accede to it without saying that there is no mode by which religion holds society together but the administration of oaths; but that is not so, for religion, without reference to oaths, contains the most powerful sanctions for good conduct: and I may observe, that those who have desired the dispensation from the taking of oaths to be extended, have done so from respect to religion, not from indifference to it.

LITTLEDALE, J.:

The Old Testament, independently of its connection with and of its prospective reference to Christianity, contains the law of Almighty God; and, therefore, I have no doubt that this is a libel in law as it has been found to be in fact by the jury.

PATTESON, J.:

The alleged mistranslation of a passage in the Year Book referred to is not material, because there are other abundant authorities; and it is certain that the Christian religion is part of the law of the land. The argument is reduced to this, that an indictment for libel is to be confined to blasphemy against the New Testament. But such an argument is scarcely worth anything, because it is impossible to say that the Old and the New Testament are not so intimately connected, that if the one is true, the other is true also ; and the evidence of Christianity partly consists of the prophecies in the Old Testament.

Rule refused.

1841.
July 14.

Rolls Court.
Lord
LANGDALE,
M.R.

[645]

MATSON *v.* SWIFT.
MATSON *v.* JAMES.

(5 Jurist, 645—647.)

On the sale of an estate, subject to mortgages by trustees, one of the conditions was, that the purchaser should pay a deposit, and agree to pay the remainder of the purchase-money on or before the 11th October, 1840; and, on payment thereof, the purchaser should be entitled to the rents from that day, up to which time all outgoings, including interest to the mortgagees, were to be borne by the vendors; but if from any circumstance the money should not be paid at the time fixed, the purchaser should pay interest at 5*l.* per cent. until the time of payment. The purchaser was ready with his money on the day appointed to complete his purchase, and also to pay off the mortgagees, to whom he had given the usual notices; but the contract for sale could not be carried into effect on that day, in consequence of an order of the Court made subsequently to the contract, and which was not contemplated at the time the contract was entered into, subjecting all contracts entered into by the trustees to the approbation of the Court: Held, that, under the above condition, the purchaser was bound to pay interest on his purchase-money at 5*l.* per cent. from the 11th October, 1840.

An equitable mortgagee, who had proved his debt before the Master, was ordered to reconvey to the purchaser, upon receiving his money, without the usual notice (1).

By indentures of lease and release, dated 12th and 14th November, 1836, certain real estates were conveyed by John Swift to William James and Robert Hinde, upon trust, as they in their discretion should think fit, and without the necessity of any further consent, concurrence, or notice of or to the said John Swift, to sell the same, with power to enter into special stipulations with any purchaser relative to the title or otherwise, and to stand possessed of the purchase-monies, upon the trusts therein declared. The first above-mentioned cause was instituted for the purpose of carrying the will of the said John Swift into execution, and of administering his estate. The second cause was instituted merely to revive the suit against certain parties. The third cause was a supplemental suit instituted against the trustees of the above-mentioned indenture of 14th November, 1836; and by a decree made at the hearing of the said last-mentioned suit, dated 27th January, 1841, it was, amongst other things ordered, that it should be referred to the Master to inquire and state to the Court whether any and what contracts had been entered into by the defendants William James and Robert Hinde, as the trustees under the above-mentioned indentures of the 12th and 14th days of November, 1836, for the

(1) *Day* v. *Day* (1862) 31 Beav. 270,   [1892] 1 Ch. 385, 61 L. J. Ch. 231, 66
and see *Fitzgerald's Trustee* v. *Mellersh*   L. T. 178.

sale of the estates in the pleadings of the said cause mentioned, or
any and what part thereof; and whether such contracts, or any
and which of them, had been performed or carried into execution,
or were proper to be carried into execution.   Some time subsequently
to the institution of the first and secondly above-mentioned suits,
but a few days previously to the filing of the bill in the third suit,
viz. on the 5th December, 1889, the trustees of the indentures of
12th and 14th November, 1836, entered into a contract with Dr.
Cresswell for the sale to him of a portion of the said estates, which
had been previously put up to sale by auction, and bought in, for
the sum of 10,500*l.*   By such contract, which was indorsed on the
printed particulars and conditions of sale which had been used at
the auction, Dr. Cresswell declared, that he had that day purchased by private contract, Lot 1, of the estates in the said printed
particulars of sale, for the sum of 10,500*l.*, and that he had paid
into the hands of John Hinde, the vendor's agent, the sum of 250*l.*
as a deposit and part payment of the said purchase-money; and
he thereby agreed to pay the remaining sum of 10,250*l.* to the
vendors on or before the 11th October, 1840, and, in all other
respects, to fulfil and perform the conditions of sale therein contained; and it was further agreed, that the vendors should pay or
allow the purchaser 3*l.* per cent. on the deposit-money until the
purchase should be completed or the deposit-money returned.   By
the first condition of sale, the purchaser was to take notice that
the purchase was subject to the mortgage debts and incumbrances
as set out in the particulars of sale, and the rights and remedies
of the respective mortgagees in respect thereof; and the purchaser
was to save harmless the vendors from such charges, unless the
purchaser should think proper to discharge the mortgage debts
before the completion of the purchase, which he would have an
opportunity of doing by giving the requisite notice, as more than
six months would elapse before the completion of the purchase.
By the second condition of sale the purchaser was required to pay
into the hands of the vendor's agent a deposit of 250*l.*, in part
payment of his purchase-money, and to sign an agreement for
completing the purchase, *and for payment of the residue of his   [*646]
purchase-money to the vendors, on or before the 11th day of
October, 1840; and on payment thereof the purchaser should be
entitled to the rents and profits as from the 11th day of October,
up to which time all outgoings, including the interest on the several
mortgages, and the mortgagees' costs, if any, should be cleared, or

allowed to the purchaser by the vendors. But if from any circumstance the money should not be paid on or before the 11th day of
October, 1840, the purchaser should pay interest thereon at the
rate of 5l. per cent. until the time of payment. And the vendors
were to deliver an abstract of title, and objections were to be taken
within a limited time. The Master having, pursuant to the aforesaid decree of the 27th January, 1841, made his report, dated
24th June, 1841, in favour of the contract entered into by the
trustees with Dr. Cresswell, the plaintiff now presented a petition
praying, amongst other things, that the defendants, William James
and Robert Hinde, might be ordered to carry into execution the
said contract for sale entered into by them with Dr. Cresswell, in
the manner and according to the terms and conditions thereof;
and that Dr. Cresswell might be at liberty to pay into the Bank in
the usual way the sum of 10,250l., being the residue of his purchase-money, and interest thereon, at the rate of 5l. per cent. per
annum, from the 11th October, 1840, to the time of such payment;
and that, upon payment thereof, the trustees, William James and
Robert Hinde, might convey the premises, subject to the incumbrances affecting the same; and deliver possession thereof to him,
and pay over to him all the rents and profits since 11th October,
1840, and interest on his deposit of 250l. at the rate of 3l. per cent.
This petition, so far as it asked that Dr. Cresswell might be ordered
to pay 5l. per cent. interest on the residue of his purchase-money,
from 11th Oct., 1840, was opposed by him under the circumstances stated in an affidavit of himself and his solicitor, Mr. Cox.
The following are the facts stated in the affidavit: Mr. Cox,
having received abstracts of title from the trustees, laid them
before his conveyancing counsel, who, in his opinion thereon,
observed, that there was a reference in the particulars of sale to a
suit of *Matson* v. *Swift*, and that inquiry should be made respecting
the object of that suit, and whether it affected in any other manner
the conveyance of November, 1836, or the execution of the trusts
thereof; Mr. Cox sent a copy of this opinion to the solicitors of the
trustees, who, in answer, stated, that the suit of *Matson* v. *Swift*
did not in any way affect the conveyance of November, 1836; and
that, since the sale of the estates, a supplemental bill had been
filed; but neither the bill nor the answers impugned in any way
the trust-deed of November, 1836. The answers to the remaining
observations and requisitions on the title being mainly satisfactory,
and Mr. Cox relying on the correctness of the above answer

respecting the proceedings in Chancery, laid the papers again
before his conveyancing counsel, with instructions, if he were in
the main satisfied with the answers to his observations, to prepare
the necessary conveyance. Accordingly, the conveyance and the
assignment of a term were prepared, and returned with the observation, that, if the suit of *Matson* v. *Swift* did not affect the trusts of
the deeds of November, 1836, which should be ascertained by an
inspection of the proceedings, a good title was shown in the trustees.
Copies of the draft conveyance and assignment were sent to the
solicitors of the trustees; and on the 24th September, 1840, an
abstract of the Chancery proceedings in the above suits was
forwarded to Mr. Cox, who, upon inspection, discovered the decree
of 27th January, 1840, making any contracts entered into by the
trustees subject to the approbation of the Court. He was thereupon advised by his counsel, that Dr. Cresswell could not safely,
under the circumstances, pay his purchase-money to the trustees;
and that the conveyances would require altering to meet the new
features of the case. Mr. Cox, previously to the receipt of the last-
mentioned abstract, had forwarded the drafts of the conveyance
and assignment of the term to the solicitors for the respective
mortgagees and assignees of the term for perusal; Dr. Cresswell
having, in due time previously to the time fixed by the contract for
completion, caused notices to be given to, and an arrangement to
be made with the mortgagees to pay off their respective mortgages.
After the difficulties had arisen respecting the completion of the
purchase, and the delay consequent thereon, the mortgagees
refused to receive payment of their mortgage monies without fresh
notices. The affidavit then stated, that Dr. Cresswell, being led
by the representations of the vendors' solicitors to expect, that the
contract would be completed at the time fixed, and that there was
nothing in the above suits to affect the power of the trustees, of
their own authority, to complete the contract, sold out stock and
called in money from other investments, and was prepared to
complete on 11th October last, and to have paid the balance of his
purchase-money, and also to have paid off the mortgages; and
that he informed the vendors' solicitors of the fact, and offered to
lodge the money in the hands of any responsible banker, in the
joint names of himself and the trustees, so that it might be pro-
ductive of interest, and which could then have been accomplished,
and to have paid off the mortgages, so as to stop the payment of
interest on having possession of the estate; but that the said

MATSON
v.
SWIFT.

solicitors declined to give possession upon any terms except the payment of the balance of the purchase-money to the trustees; that, in consequence of this, Dr. Cresswell had to dispose in the best way that he could of the money which he had by the means aforesaid in his possession, and by the calling in of which he had sustained considerable loss; and that, as the solicitors of the vendors then represented, that the delay in their being in a situation to complete the purchase would not be great, Dr. Cresswell determined not to reinvest the greater portion of his money in the purchase of stock, and accordingly he placed the sum of 10,000l., part thereof, in the London Joint Stock Bank, at the rate of 3l. 10s. per cent. per annum interest, and 4,000l. in the London and Westminster Bank, at the like rate of interest, and reinvested the residue in the purchase of 3l. 10s. per cent. Reduced Annuities, so as to make up, with stock then standing in the like annuities in his name, the full remainder of the said purchase-money. That Dr. Cresswell finding, that, on the 1st March last, the vendors were still not in a situation to complete their contract with him, and thinking it indiscreet to trust any joint stock Bank for a long time with so large a sum of money, he, on the fourth day of that month, withdrew from the London Joint Stock Bank the said sum of 10,000l., and purchased Exchequer Bills, then at a premium of 11s., to the amount of 10,000l., which, with the premium, interest due on them, and brokerage, cost him 10,400l. 7s. 6d., and which bills bore interest at the rate 2¼d. per 100l. per day, or about 3l. 7s. 3d. per cent. per annum; so that, besides the expense and commission, he had not been able to make so much as 3l. 10s. per cent. per annum upon all his said purchase-money, whilst the conditions of his contract stipulated for his paying the vendors interest on his purchase-money, at the rate of 5l. per cent. per annum, from the 11th October, notwithstanding the delay consequent on the proceedings in Chancery, over which he had no control. The mortgages, amounting to 5,500l., bore interest at the rate of 5l. per cent. per annum, which Dr. Cresswell could not pay off until six months at least after the vendors should be in a situation to complete their said contract with him. Dr. Cresswell, therefore, submitted to the Court, that the contract ought to be varied, so

[*647]   that *justice should be done to him, as well with reference to the interest on his said purchase-money as the interest on said mortgages, and also in regard to the extra expense to which he had already been, and would be put to by the said Chancery proceedings

and the delay thereby occasioned; that he had always been and
was still ready and willing to pay the residue of his said purchase-
money, as the Court should direct, together with such interest
thereon as the Court should, under the circumstances of the case,
think reasonable and just; and on being allowed the additional
costs, charges, and expenses which he had already incurred and
might incur in consequence of, or incidental to, such proceedings.
It was contended, therefore, on the part of Dr. Cresswell, that,
under the above-circumstances, he ought only to be called upon
to pay the vendors so much interest on his purchase-money, from
the 11th October, 1840, as he had made upon it during that
period; and that he ought only to be liable to pay so much
towards the interest due to the mortgagees on their mortgage
debts from the 11th October till the time at which he would be
able to compel them to receive their money, by giving them six
months' notice, as he had actually made by the money which he
had ready for that purpose on the 10th October; and that the
remainder of such interest ought to be paid by the vendors, or out of
the trust-estate; and that the expense which he had been put to
in reinvesting his money and reselling the stock, as well as any
extra expense he had or would be put to, either in altering the
conveyance or otherwise, in consequence of the obstacles that had
arisen from the proceedings in Chancery, should be borne by the
trust-estate.

Pemberton and *J. Russell*, for the petition.

G. Turner and *Morley*, for Dr. Cresswell:

As the delay in completing the contract was caused by the
vendors, and not by the purchaser, the latter is not, by the
rules of the Court, bound to pay interest at 5*l.* per cent. The
utmost that he can be called upon to pay, is the amount of
interest he had himself made by the money pending the delay.
In *Monk* v. *Huskisson* (1), the contract of purchase contained a
stipulation, that if, by reason of any unforeseen or unavoidable
obstacles, the conveyance could not be perfected for execution
before the time fixed for the completion of the purchase, the
purchaser should from that day pay interest on his purchase-
money, and be entitled to the rents and profits of the premises;
and the vendor not having shown a good title till long after the

(1) 4 Russ. 121, n.

MATSON
v.
SWIFT.

time specified, Sir JOHN LEACH held, that he was not entitled to
interest, except from the time a good title was first shown. So
here the purchaser ought not to be called upon to pay interest
at 5l. per cent. till the title was completed by the order of the
Court confirming the contract: *Esdaile* v. *Stephenson* (1). The
conditions of sale can only be considered to relate to circumstances within the contemplation of the parties at the time, such
as objections to the title. But the circumstance which caused the
delay here was not in the contemplation of the parties, and could
not, therefore, have been intended to fall within the condition.
This, therefore, must be considered as an ordinary case, in which,
there being no provision for payment of interest, the Court fixes
the rate. This is a stringent condition, and the Court will not, in
the interpretation of it, lean against the party to be prejudiced
by it. It will not permit the vendor to avail himself of his own
wrong. The vendor has a legal demand for interest at 5l. per
cent. against the purchaser. The latter is entitled also to recover
against him at law, damages for breach of contract; and the
question is, whether, under these circumstances, the Court will
not say that the vendors shall do equity, and shall not enforce
their contract against Dr. Cresswell, unless they pay him what he
would be entitled to recover for damages at law. The vendors
ought also to bear the loss arising from the necessity of paying to
the mortgagees interest at 5l. per cent. since 11th October, up to
the time at which, in the regular course, Dr. Cresswell will be able
to pay them off. He ought not to be called upon to pay them
them more than 3l. 10s. per cent., the interest made by him of the
money which he had ready to pay them off on the day fixed for
that purpose. The vendors ought also to bear the expense of
making any alterations in the conveyances, in consequence of
these proceedings.

Lord LANGDALE, M. R., said, he thought there were cases in
which the point involved in this case had been decided. There
was no doubt but that Dr. Cresswell had done what was in his
power to complete the contract at the time fixed. But, with a
view to decide the question as to the rate of interest to be paid by
him, it was necessary to look at the words of the condition of
sale. These words were: "But if from any circumstance the
money should not be paid on or before the 11th day of October,

(1) 24 R. R. 151 (1 Sim. & St. 122).

1840, the purchaser should pay interest thereon at the rate of 5*l.*
per cent. until the time of payment." It was not possible to throw
those words out of consideration. It might be true, that the
circumstance which did prevent the payment of the purchase-
money on the day named was not in the contemplation of the
parties at the time of the contract. But how could he say, that
a circumstance not within the contemplation of the parties at
that time was not comprised within these words, "if from any
circumstance." His Lordship ordered, that the contract should
be completed by Dr. Cresswell, and his purchase-money paid into
Court, with interest at 5*l.* per cent. from the 11th October, 1840.
And he made no order as to the interest payable to the mortgagees
or as to the costs of altering the conveyances, which, he observed,
only required the introduction of a recital of the present proceedings
into the draft.

Lorat, for an equitable mortgagee, who had come in and
proved his debt before the Master, said, that the mortgagee was
anxious that the amount of his mortgage debt should be paid by
Dr. Cresswell into Court, and that it should be paid out of Court
to him. In which case, he contended, it would not be necessary
for the mortgagee to join in the conveyance to Dr. Cresswell.

This was opposed by other parties, who asked for an order that
he might reconvey on receiving his money from Dr. Cresswell.

His Lordship observed, that the mortgagee would be bound to
give Dr. Cresswell a release, whether he received the money from
him or from the Court; and he did not see that it could make any
difference to the mortgagee as long as he received his money. But
he had a difficulty in making the order, as he was not sure that
the mortgagee was under an obligation to receive his money from
Dr. Cresswell without the usual notice.

Russell said, that the mortgagee had come in and proved his
debt; and the Court, therefore, was at liberty to make an order
for him to join in the conveyance to Dr. Cresswell on receiving his
money from him.

His Lordship, after some hesitation, made an order accordingly,
for the mortgagee to join in the conveyance, on receiving the
interest on his debt up to the 11th October out of the estate, and
his principal and the remainder of his interest from Dr. Cresswell.

1841.

Queen's Bench.

Lord
DENMAN,
Ch. J.
LITTLEDALE,
J.
PATTESON, J.
COLERIDGE,
J.

[650]

BURNELL *v.* HUNT (1).

(5 Jurist, 650—652.

In pursuance of an agreement between A. and B., A. took premises in his own name, and purchased silk and materials on his own account, to carry on the business of a silk-lace-maker, and provided all the machinery and implements of trade ; and B. was employed to superintend the manufacture of goods. The agreement also stipulated, that all the silk and materials, and all the manufactured goods, and all the machinery and implements, should be the sole property of A., and that B. should receive for his remuneration half the profits, as soon as any accrued, and until such time should receive 2*l.* per week from A. : Held, that this agreement, when carried into effect, did not constitute a partnership between A. and B. as to the separate creditors of B. ; and that, therefore where a sheriff seized goods, manufactured under the agreement, in execution of a writ sued out by a separate creditor of B., and sold the same, the gross receipts of the sale might be recovered by A. in an action on the case for selling the goods against the sheriff.

CASE. The first count stated, that the plaintiff and one James Unsworth had been and were co-partners in the trade and business of silk-lace-manufacturers, which had been carried on by plaintiff and said James Unsworth in partnership together ; that, on the 25th day of May, 1839, a *non omittas fi. fa.* was issued out of the Court of Exchequer, directed to the Sheriff of Derbyshire, commanding him of the goods and chattels of the said James Unsworth to cause to be made 89*l.* 18*s.*, and interest as therein mentioned, and 1*l.* 7*s.*, together with sheriff's poundage, &c., which writ was delivered to defendant as Sheriff of Derbyshire to be executed, by virtue whereof defendant as such sheriff seized and took in execution divers goods and chattels, to wit, &c., of which plaintiff and said James Unsworth were the owners and proprietors, of the value of 200*l.*, and then being the joint property of plaintiff and Unsworth ; that it was the defendant's duty to have sold the interest, share, and part of Unsworth therein, and no more ; but he intending to injure &c. plaintiff, and deprive him of his share, &c., sold the whole and applied the proceeds to satisfy the execution, whereby plaintiff's share is wholly lost to him, &c. Second count stated, that the plaintiff was lawfully possessed, as of his own property, of the goods and chattels in the first count mentioned, and lost them, and defendant found them and converted them to his own use, whereby and for the want of the use of them, &c., plaintiff was injured in his trade, &c., and had been deprived of all profits, &c., is prevented from carrying on his trade, and greatly injured, &c. Damages, 200*l.* Pleas : first, to the whole declaration, not guilty ;

(1) Partnership Act, 1890, s. 2 (3), (*b*).

second, to first count, that the goods were not the joint property of   BURNELL
plaintiff and Unsworth; third, to the second count, that the goods   v.
were the property of plaintiff and Unsworth, and not of plaintiff   HUNT.
alone, and sets out the issuing of the writ of *fi. fa.*, its delivery to
defendant as sheriff, the seizure of the goods as the property of
plaintiff and Unsworth, and the sale of the share and interest of
Unsworth therein.   Replication to the third plea, that the goods
were plaintiff's alone, and not his and Unsworth's.   At the trial
before Lord Abinger, C. B., at the Derbyshire Summer Assizes,
1839, a verdict was given for the plaintiff, subject to a special case,
which is as follows: The defendant, being the Sheriff of Derbyshire,
under a writ of *fi. fa.* to him directed (being the writ alleged in the
first count and third plea), on the 27th May, 1839, on the premises
in Curzon Street hereinafter mentioned, seized the entirety of the
machinery, implements of trade, manufactured goods, and unmanufactured materials, in the declaration hereinafter mentioned, and
sold the entire property in the whole of the same (one lace machine
excepted) absolutely in lots, by auction, to divers persons, who paid
him the prices at which the same were respectively sold, and the
same were delivered over by the defendant, and were taken away by
the several purchasers thereof respectively, and the defendant now
retains the whole of the produce of the said sale.   The value of the
machinery and implements of trade taken and sold is 25*l.*, of the
manufactured goods and unmanufactured materials, 80*l.*   The
defendant, at the time of the trial, still retained the said lace
machine.   The *fi. fa.* was sued out by one Crump against one
Unsworth, for a separate debt of Unsworth due to Crump, and with
which the plaintiff was wholly unconnected in any manner whatever.
Unsworth, about January last, having expended 3*l.* or 4*l.* in making
the said lace machine, and being unable, for want of money, to
complete it, applied to the plaintiff, and it was agreed between them
that the plaintiff should finish the machine; that it should be his,
the plaintiff's, sole property; that he should repay Unsworth the
3*l.* or 4*l.* he had expended; that Unsworth should have no property
whatever in the machine; and that he, the plaintiff, should take
premises in his own name, and purchase silk and materials on his
own account, to carry on the business of a silk-lace-maker; and
that Unsworth should be employed to superintend the manufacture
of goods; and that the plaintiff should provide all the machinery
and implements of trade necessary; and that all the goods and
materials purchased for the manufacturing, and all the goods

                                                        54—2

BURNELL
v.
HUNT.

manufactured, and all the machinery and implements should be the sole property of the plaintiff; and that Unsworth should receive for his remuneration half the profits as soon as any accrued; and until such time he was to receive 2*l.* per week from plaintiff. In pursuance of this agreement, the plaintiff paid Unsworth the 3*l.* or 4*l.* he had expended on the lace-machine, removed it to the premises in Curzon Street, and completed it at an expense of about 50*l.*; he also hired the premises in Curzon Street, for the purpose of the manufactory, in his own name, and himself paid the rent for the same, and purchased in his own name and paid for with his own money various machines and implements of trade, and materials for manufacturing goods, and manufactured part of the same materials into goods fit for sale at his own expense on the premises in Curzon Street. Unsworth never paid for anything, nor brought any money into the concern. The machines, implements of trade, unmanufactured materials, and manufactured goods so purchased and paid for by the plaintiff as aforesaid, are the same that were seized by the defendant as aforesaid. The learned Judge was of opinion that Unsworth was a partner, and that the unmanufactured materials and manufactured goods belonged jointly to him, and the plaintiff was therefore only entitled to recover half the value thereof, viz. 40*l.*, from the defendant; and that the machines and implements of trade were plaintiff's sole property; and that he was entitled to recover the whole value thereof; and directed a verdict to be entered for the plaintiff on all the issues, with 40*l.* damages on the first count, and 25*l.* on the second, subject to a special case as to for what sum and how the verdict ought to be entered, the defendant undertaking to forthwith deliver back the lace machine, which has been done accordingly. The defendant tendered evidence, that, before the action was brought, his attorney offered to the plaintiff's attorney one-half of the clear net proceeds of the sale of the whole property seized, but that such offer was refused. This evidence was objected to, but received subject to the opinion of the Court whether admissible, if not, to be struck out of the case.

Whitehurst, for the plaintiff:

The first question is, whether there was a partnership between the plaintiff *and Unsworth as to any of the goods; if there was not, the plaintiff has proved the first count except the averment of property, and he has established the second count, for the selling is the gist of the action and amounts to a conversion, and will be

[*651]

entitled to recover the whole sum claimed thereby; but he will not
have a verdict on the issue raised by the second plea. If there was
a partnership between the plaintiff and Unsworth, the plaintiff is
entitled to a verdict on all the issues, and there will be a second
question, what the sheriff ought to have sold in executing the writ
against Unsworth at the suit of a separate creditor. [He cited
Waugh v. *Carver* (1), *Dutton* v. *Morrison* (2), and other cases.]
Secondly, if there was a partnership between the plaintiff and
Unsworth, there would be a distinction between the machinery on
the one hand, and the manufactured goods and raw materials on
the other; the former would be the sole property of the plaintiff,
the latter would be the joint property of the plaintiff and Unsworth,
and the plaintiff would be entitled to a verdict for 40*l.* on the first
count, and for 25*l.*, the value of the machinery, on the second. • •
On the third point, as to the admissibility of the evidence of tender
of half the net proceeds of the sale, it is quite clear the plaintiff is
entitled to more; the sheriff has no right to deduct the expenses of
the sale.

BURNELL
v.
HUNT.

Gale, for the defendant:

As to the second point, it is admitted by the declaration and by
all the cases cited on the other side, that the sheriff must seize all
the goods of the partnership; and as soon as he has taken posses-
sion, he becomes tenant in common with the partner against whom
execution did not go; and it is clear that no action at law will lie
by one tenant in common against another (3).

(PATTESON, J.: In *Fennings* v. *Lord Grenville* (4), it was held,
that where one tenant in common of a whale refused to deliver up
one moiety of it to the other, and cut it up and expressed the oil,
that was no destruction, so as to subject him to an action of trover.)

In *Heath* v. *Hubbard* (5), it was questioned, whether the sale of a
ship by one who was part owner, was a conversion of the ship, so
as to enable his co-tenant to maintain trover against him (6).
Therefore, the sheriff in this case has not done wrong in taking the
goods.   The question is, whether what he has done is equivalent to
a destruction of the goods and chattels?

(1) 14 R. R. 845 (2 H. Bl. 235).
(2) 11 R. R. 56 (17 Ves. 193).
(3) Co. Litt. s. 323, fol. 200 a.
(4) 9 R. R. 760 (1 Taunt. 241).
(5) 4 East, 110.
(6) The Court seemed pretty clear
that it would not, "partly, as it should
appear, because the sale passes only
the interest of the seller. But, *quære,*
as to the sale of any other chattel in
market overt?" (Note (*s*) to *Wilbra-
ham* v. *Snow,* 2 Saund. 47 h).

BURNELL
v.
HUNT.

(LITTLEDALE, J. : If the sheriff is tenant in common, he i⸱ so only for the purpose of making sale.

PATTESON, J. : You cannot say that the property in the goods is divested out of the partner by the seizure. There is no change of property by that act : *Giles* v. *Grover*, in the House of Lords (1).)

The sheriff acts as a minister of the Court, and there is no case in which an action has been brought against him by a partner for selling more than he ought under a writ of a *fi. fa.* : *Parker* v. *Pistor* (2), *Chapman* v. *Koops* (3), *Eddie* v. *Davidson* (4), which was a strong case of interference by this Court in referring it to the Master to take an account of the shares in the partnership effects : *Pope* v. *Haman* (5). The remedy of the plaintiff is in equity : a court of equity can take the accounts between the parties, and see what each party is entitled to. But the sheriff has no machinery for ascertaining what the interest of each party is.

(LORD DENMAN, Ch. J. : That observation would apply in the case of the destruction of the property. The Court must try the question of partnership.

PATTESON, J. : The proper course is, for the sheriff to seize the whole, and to sell the share of the execution partner; and the vendee will have to settle the matter in Chancery. The sheriff has no power to take the property out of the hands of the other partner.)

But he is not liable to an action at law. In *Burton* v. *Green* (6), Lord TENTERDEN expressed great doubt as to what interest the sheriff might sell in executing a writ of *fi. fa.* against one of several partners. As to the other point, whether the plaintiff and Unsworth were partners or not, the distinction taken on the other side, is one on which I rely ; but it is desired to introduce a third distinction : that persons may be partners as against the world, and yet not be partners as against separate creditors. This is a case in which one partner finds property and the other partner skill, as put by ABBOTT, Ch. J., in *Reid* v. *Hollinshead* (7), *Ex parte Rowlandson* (8), and *Hesketh* v. *Blanchard* (9). Unsworth was jointly interested in the whole adventure, though only to be paid weekly.

(1) See 36 R. R. 27 (9 Bing. 128, 142, 177, 280).
(2) 3 Bos. & P. 288.
(3) 6 R. R. 788 (3 Bos. & P. 289).
(4) Doug. 650.

(5) Comb. 217.
(6) 3 Car. & P. 306.
(7) 28 R. R. 488 (4 B. & C. 867,878).
(8) 1 Rose, 89 ; 19 Ves. 461.
(9) 4 East, 141.

(COLERIDGE, J. : There is no partnership, unless there is an agreement that the party shall have immediate participation in the profits. Suppose I employ a person for a certain time, and tell him, that, after the end of that time, if profits are made, then he shall become a partner, he would be interested in the adventure, but he would not be a partner in the meantime.

PATTESON, J. : Your argument falls short of the proposition necessary to be established. Suppose he is interested, that alone will not give him a property in the goods; and here it is found that the goods were purchased with the plaintiff's money. But, even if he was a partner, he is not necessarily interested in the goods.)

That is as between the parties themselves.

(PATTESON, J. : It lies upon you to show that Unsworth has property in the *goods *inter se*. It comes to this: what is the real interest in the goods as between the parties ?)

[*652]

As to the tender, it has been decided that the amount of the net proceeds is not so bad a measure of damages as to warrant the Court in setting aside the verdict.

(LORD DENMAN, Ch. J. : That is where the plaintiff affirms the sale.)

Whitehurst, in reply, was stopped by the COURT.

LORD DENMAN, Ch. J., after stating the pleadings, proceeded :

The declaration is a curious one, containing two inconsistent counts : in the first it affirms, and in the second it denies, that the plaintiff was a partner with Unsworth. I can conceive that the mode of establishing a partnership may be very different, according as the question is, whether there was a partnership *inter se*, or only a partnership as to the rest of the world. It is said that it is not shown by the third plea what was the amount of the interest of the respective parties in the property. There would, however, be some cases in which we should presume that that interest was a moiety. But in this case it is unnecessary to enter into that question, for the defendant has unlawfully seized the goods in question. From the agreement it only appears that there was something in contemplation, which, if carried out, might have given Unsworth an interest as partner.

(side note) BURNELL *v.* HUNT.

BURNELL
v.
HUNT.

LITTLEDALE, J. :

There was no actual partnership; for there was no receipt of or title to the profits of the concern in or by Unsworth. It is not necessary to consider what would have been the rights of the parties if a partnership had been actually formed.

PATTESON, J. :

It is found expressly that all the goods were the sole property of the plaintiff, and that Unsworth received 2l. a week from the plaintiff for his services. In order to make out a partnership, it was necessary to show that some profits had accrued; and it is quite clear that there never were any profits. It is not necessary to determine as to the other points mooted, and there is considerable difficulty in some of them.

COLERIDGE, J., concurred.

Judgment for the plaintiff on so much of the first issue as relates to the second count; for the defendant on the second issue; and for the plaintiff on the third issue.   Damages 109l.

1840.
Nov. 5.

Chancery.

Lord
COTTENHAM,
L.C.

[860]

MAUND v. ALLIES.

(5 Jurist, 860—863.)

Partnership accounts—Opening settled accounts.

In order to entitle a party to open a settled account, it is not sufficient merely to prove the existence in the account of errors, which a court of equity might consider improper charges or omissions, without reference to what may have been the conduct of the party in agreeing to such account; because, in the absence of fraud or pressure, every item in an account, of which, at the time of settlement, the parties are fully cognisant, may be considered as the subject of special agreement between them, which neither party is at liberty to repudiate.

A., B., and C. were interested in equal shares in certain coal mines, as copartners in trade together; and, after the decease of B., D., having purchased B.'s share from his representatives, was, but not till after the death of A., admitted a partner in the concern, and, together with C. and the representatives of A., signed a settlement of the partnership accounts up to a certain period. D. then purchased A.'s share from his representatives. A., during his lifetime, was the sole manager of the concern; and, before his death, several settlements of accounts took place between the partners. D. having filed a bill against C. and the representatives of A. and B., alleging errors in the settled accounts, and that they were fraudulently drawn out by A., and praying an account of all the partnership dealings and transactions, and that D. might be at liberty to

surcharge and falsify the accounts, and that what should be found due
from A. might be paid by his representatives: Held, that if any one of
such errors could be established, the result would be only a right in the
other partners to have the amount of such error deducted from the share of
A. coming to D., as the assignee of that share.

BY indenture of the 1st May, 1819, being articles of partnership
between Robert Farquhar, Andrew Maund, and Edwin Allies, it
was agreed, that they should become copartners in the trade or
business of coal merchants, under the style or firm of "Robert
Farquhar & Co.," for and during the term of twenty-one years,
to be considered as commencing from the 1st January then
last, determinable nevertheless, and subject to the covenants and
provisions in the said indenture contained. Farquhar and Maund,
being entitled to eight-ninth parts or shares of the freehold, copyhold, and leasehold hereditaments and premises and chattels
personal in the partnership deed mentioned, of which they were in
possession, for the purpose of working certain mines and veins of
coal, by indentures, dated the 27th and 28th February, 1820,
conveyed and assigned, and covenanted to surrender, one-third of
such eight-ninth parts or shares to Allies. The three copartners
carried on the business together until January, 1829, when Maund
died, having by his will given all his real and personal estate to his
daughter M. A. Maund, and appointed her his sole executrix. The
partnership from that time was carried on by the surviving partners
and M. A. Maund, until the 31st December, 1831, when the plaintiff
John Maund became the purchaser of Andrew Maund's share from
M. A. Maund, but he was not acknowledged as a partner in the
concern until after Farquhar's death, which took place in
December, 1832. By indentures, dated the 4th and 5th March,
1833, Farquhar's real and personal representatives sold and conveyed to the plaintiff the whole of Farquhar's share and interest
in the partnership property, he having previously, on the 25th
January, 1833, been admitted a partner in the concern. The
plaintiff having thus become entitled to two-thirds of the before-
mentioned eight-ninths of the partnership property, afterwards
*purchased the other one-ninth from the representatives of one   [*861]
Wormington. The affairs of the partnership were managed
wholly by Farquhar in his lifetime. Accountants were, on several
occasions, employed to examine and make a statement of the
partnership accounts, and, on the 10th January, 1821, after such
an examination and statement had been made, the then partners
signed the general account in the ledger, and also the following

memorandum at the foot of a separate balance sheet: "We have
examined, and approve of the foregoing as a fair and just account
and estimate of our partnership stock and property." In 1832, a
similar examination and statement of the accounts, up to the 31st
December, 1831, was made, and, after considerable correspondence
and discussion between the solicitors of M. A. Maund and of
Farquhar, was signed, as examined and approved, by Farquhar,
Allies, and M. A. Maund, the last of whom, as the representative
of Andrew Maund and in her own right, received and signed
receipts for sums of money amounting to 4,000l. and upwards, in
respect of the profits, &c. which had arisen from the concern. The
plaintiff was present on this occasion, and attested M. A. Maund's
signature of the accounts and receipts; and, previous to the accounts
being signed, the partnership books were, at his request, given into
his possession, and were examined by him in company with an
accountant of his own selection. The accounts for the year 1832
were investigated, and a balance sheet agreed upon by two
accountants, one being appointed by the plaintiff, and the other by
the other parties interested; and objections having, nevertheless,
been taken by the plaintiff to certain items in the account, and
by consent referred to an umpire, whose decision was acquiesced
in by all parties, ultimately, on the 4th February, 1834, the plaintiff
signed the balance sheet of the accounts up to the 31st December,
1832, adding the words "errors excepted" after his signature. On
the 5th September, 1835, the plaintiff filed his bill in this suit
against Allies, M. A. Maund, and John Farquhar and John Hair, the
real and personal representatives of Robert Farquhar, alleging he
had discovered, that the balance sheets or accounts made out during
the life of, and by or under the superintendence of, R. Farquhar,
were fraudulent and erroneous, and contained errors, omissions,
and overcharges to the amount of many thousand pounds; and
that such balances, being mere general balances, did not show the
items from which they resulted; and, therefore, the plaintiff had
been unable to ascertain from such balance sheets or accounts the
inaccuracy and impropriety of the results contained in them; that
the plaintiff, after becoming a partner and interested in the concern,
was refused inspection of the partnership books and accounts; and
that Allies and R. Farquhar during the life of Farquhar, and
Allies and Farquhar's representatives, since his decease, had
always colluded together to cheat and defraud the plaintiff, and to
prevent him from ascertaining the errors, falsehoods, and frauds

contained in the balance sheets or accounts, and had refused to
make him any payment on account of his share in the partnership
profits, until he had signed the balance sheet on account of the
current year ; · and that under pressure and to obtain such payment
the plaintiff signed the same ; but that he so signed the same
under protest, and with the express reservation of errors excepted,
and without having ascertained, or had the means of ascertaining
the inaccuracy thereof ; that Andrew Maund and M. A. Maund,
during the periods they were interested in the partnership concern,
signed some of the balance sheets or accounts, but that they
signed the same in ignorance of, and without having had the means ·
of ascertaining, the false, fraudulent, and erroneous nature thereof ;
that upon a full and fair discovery of the particulars of the several
items from which the said balances were drawn, and upon taking a
fair and just account of the said partnership, it would appear that
many thousand pounds had been subtracted from the partnership
by Allies and Robert Farquhar, or one of them, beyond their just
shares thereof : that if the said balance sheets, or other the
accounts of or relating to the said partnership, were to be deemed
settled accounts, but which the plaintiff submitted and insisted they
were not, then that he ought to be let in to surcharge and falsify
the same ; and praying, amongst other things, that the partnership
might be forthwith dissolved and the affairs wound up, and an
account taken of all the partnership dealings and transactions ; and
that the plaintiff might be permitted to surcharge and falsify the
accounts ; and that what, in taking the accounts, should be found
due from the defendant Allies and the other defendants, might be
answered and paid by them respectively ; and that what should be
found due from A. Maund, deceased, and R. Farquhar, deceased,
respectively, might be answered and paid by the defendants, their
representatives, out of the assets of their respective testators.   The
bill contained charges respecting sixteen different errors and frauds
alleged to exist in the accounts, as to four of which only, noticed in
the LORD CHANCELLOR's judgment, the plaintiff entered into evidence.
The answers of the defendants denied the errors and frauds imputed,
and insisted on the accounts settled and signed at different times,
as a defence to the plaintiff's bill.   E. Allies having died, a bill of
revivor and supplement was filed, and the suit revived against A.
Allies, his widow, and sole devisee and executrix, and Harvey Allies,
his heir-at-law.   The defendant, Ann Allies having died on the
12th May, 1839, intestate, the suit was revived against Isaac Cooke,

MAUND
v.
ALLIES.

her administrator, he being also the administrator *de bonis non* with the will annexed of Edwin Allies. Evidence was gone into at great length by the plaintiff and defendants, the effect of which, so far as material, is stated in the judgment of the LORD CHANCELLOR, before whom the cause now came on to be heard.

Knight Bruce, Wakefield, and *Rogers,* for the plaintiff.

Wigram and *Piggott* for the defendant.

Nov. 5.

THE LORD CHANCELLOR :

The object of this suit was to open accounts settled between partners on the ground of error. I have had frequent occasion to observe, that, in cases of this description, the party seeking to open the account seems to think he has done enough, if he alleges and proves the existence of what some accountant points out to him as an error, and which a court of equity would probably consider as an improper charge, or an improper omission, if there had been nothing in the conduct of the parties to sanction it, without sufficiently considering how far his own conduct may have deprived him of the right of complaining; for, in the absence of fraud, or abused confidence, or pressure, every item in an account, of which the parties were fully cognizant at the time they settled it, may be considered as the subject of agreement between them, which they are no more at liberty to repudiate than any other contract or undertaking into which they may deliberately have entered. If, instead of the usual memorandum on the settlement of the account, there had been a memorandum signed by the parties, referring to any particular item, and stating they had agreed such item should form part of such account, no attempt could have been made to open the account on proof that such item ought not to have formed part of the account; and yet the ordinary mode of settling the account containing such items, all parties being aware of the circumstances connected with it, cannot well be distinguished from such special agreement. A plaintiff, therefore, seeking to open an account, on proving errors in it, should be prepared not only to prove the fact of error, but to meet any case set up by the defendant of his having settled the account with a knowledge of the circumstances constituting such alleged error.

[*862]

The *partnership in this case was formed in 1819, and from 1819 to 1829 the partners were Robert Farquhar, Andrew Maund, and Edwin Allies. In 1829, Andrew Maund died, and from 1829 to

December, 1832, the partners were Robert Farquhar, Edwin Allies,
and Mary Ann Maund, the representative of Andrew Maund. In
December, 1832, Robert Farquhar died, and in January, 1833, the
plaintiff was admitted a partner, as assignee of Andrew Maund's
share, assigned to him by his representative, and in March, 1833,
he also became assignee of Robert Farquhar's share, so that
from that time the only parties interested were the plaintiff, as
assignee of the shares of Andrew Maund, and Robert Farquhar,
and the defendant Edwin Allies. The bill alleges, that no
accounts were ever settled, according to the provisions of the
articles; but the plaintiff, under pressure of the defendants, Edwin
Allies and Robert Farquhar, signed a balance sheet under protest,
and that Andrew Maund and his representative had signed the
same in ignorance of the fraud intended. It is contended, that the
balance sheets which the plaintiff signed, as assignee of Andrew
Maund and Robert Farquhar's interest in the partnership, were
fraudulently drawn out under the superintendence of the same
Robert Farquhar, stating, that many thousands pounds had, by
means of such fraud, been improperly received by the defendants,
Edwin Allies and Robert Farquhar, his share of which he charges
ought to be paid to him by Edwin Allies and the representative of
Robert Farquhar. The bill then alleges many imputed errors in
those balance sheets, of which four only were relied on, and upon
that ground seeks to surcharge and falsify the account. The
answer insists upon accounts settled and signed, and particularly
one in January, 1821, by the then partners, and another in
February, 1832, by Robert Farquhar, and Edwin Allies, and Mary
Ann Maund, the representative of Andrew Maund, and payment to
her of the balance found due to his estate and to herself as a
partner since that time, and receipts signed by her, acknowledging
the sum paid to be his share of the ascertained and agreed amount
of profits and capital, down to the 8th February, 1832. It then
states the examination of the accounts by Mr. Greathead, at the
request of the plaintiff, and certain alterations suggested by him,
which were acquiesced in by the partners, and finally the accounts
signed by the plaintiff on the 4th February, 1834—the account up
to the 31st December, 1832; and states, that the plaintiff had
knowledge of all the now alleged errors before he signed such
accounts. Of the errors alleged and attempted to be proved by
the plaintiff to meet the case so put by the defendant, four only
were relied on at the Bar, the first of which is thus alleged in the

bill: "That the firm rented the Goitre Wharf of the Brecon and Abergavenny Canal Company, at 50l. per annum, from 1820 to 1824, and that they are overcharged in the account in respect of the said rent, to the amount of 100l., to December, 1820,—50l., to December, 1821,—50l., to 1822,—75l., to 1823,—and 50l., to 1824, making a total overcharge of 325l., and over and above the actual rent due from, and paid by, the partnership during such period in respect of the said wharf." This allegation not only imports these sums were charged as paid to the Brecon and Abergavenny Canal Company beyond what they were entitled to receive, but it is attempted to be supported by the evidence of William Holborn, who, from an examination of the books, says, in the cash book A. of the partnership, it appears, several sums, amounting to 325l., are charged by Robert Farquhar, as paid to him, for the rent of this wharf, during that period, and that 50l. per annum was, during the same period, paid to the Brecon and Abergavenny Canal Company. The first observation that occurs in this evidence is, that the plaintiff is purchaser for a considerable sum of money of all Robert Farquhar's interest in the concern, including his share of debt, and other property, and if these alleged errors were established, the result would be only a right in the other partners to this sum of 325l., as an over payment to Robert Farquhar, and consequently a right to have it deducted from any share coming to him, or any person claiming through him; but if the plaintiff insists on these payments to Robert Farquhar as errors on the account, the question would be,—are these payments erroneous? The answer insists, that Robert Farquhar, being lessee of this wharf under the Brecon and Abergavenny Canal Company, at 50l. per annum, agreed to assign it to the partnership at a profit rent to himself of 50l. per annum. The articles of partnership are ambiguous on the subject. They only provide, that Robert Farquhar should execute an assignment or underlease to the firm, for the remainder of the term, at the yearly rent of 50l., subject to the usual covenants and conditions; but such ambiguity would be removed by the conduct of the parties; and the accounts prove, that, from that time to the expiration of the lease, the partnership paid 50l. per annum to the Brecon and Abergavenny Canal Company, and also 50l. per annum was allowed to Robert Farquhar; and though Farquhar was the manager, the accounts were examined and settled with these charges in them, and by the plaintiff himself in February, 1834; and J. Moxham proves, that,

in 1832, the plaintiff was acquainted with all the circumstances
connected with this matter, which had been the subject of frequent
discussion with him, and no attempt was made by him to prove the
contrary. I am, therefore, of opinion, the plaintiff has entirely
failed on this point, and yet this is, in my opinion, the most
plausible of all the points he has made, because the next error
alleged is merely, "that the accounts from 1819 to 1833 show a
great deficiency in the quantity of coal sold, as compared with the
coal produced from the mines." There is no allegation as to what
has become of those deficient coals, and no charge that any of the
other partners had in any manner received the value of them.
That there always is a deficiency is not disputed, but much
evidence is gone into to prove, that the deficiency in the working
of this mine exceeds what is usual. Assuming that to be so, how
can that be an error for the purpose of opening those settled
accounts? It may have been a fault in the management of the
affairs of this mine; but, if, in fact, no more was made available
for the purposes of sale than what appears in the accounts, it
cannot constitute an error in the accounts. If an error, how is it to
be rectified? If it arose from the fault of any one, it arose from the
mismanagement of Robert Farquhar, through whom and whose
share the plaintiff claims; besides which, the deficiency was evident
on the face of the accounts, and it must have been known to all
the parties at the time of the respective settlements of the
accounts, and it is proved to have been known to the plaintiff in
1832; with that knowledge he purchased Robert Farquhar's share
in 1833, and settled the accounts in 1834. The evidence of
Morton, I think, is conclusive as to this. The third alleged error
is, that the partnership is charged in 1819 with 28l., for making
two seats in a chapel, at that time built by subscription. This
entry, the bill alleges, has been since altered to "a seat," instead
of "two seats;" and Robert Farquhar caused one of such seats to
be appropriated to himself and family, and his representatives now
occupy it. The complaint is, that the firm paid for a seat, which
Mr. Farquhar took to himself, and not that the 28l., or any part of
it, was an unauthorized payment in 1819; and, in proof of this, it
states, that the original entry was for two seats, and was afterwards fraudulently altered. The evidence, however, of Monkhouse,
is to prove, that Farquhar was, in fact, a subscriber of 20l., and
the firm of 8l., and yet *the whole 28l. was charged to the firm.   [*863]
How this is to be explained does not now appear, but the result, if

there was anything wrong in the transaction, would be to establish, that the pew occupied by Mr. Farquhar was in fact the property of the firm, because the charge of 28*l.* is paid by the firm, and stands as an item of payment in their books for 1819, and, after the death of all the parties who were partners at that time, and after what the repeated investigation of the books, and the settlement of the accounts, show at present, it is impossible to hold such payment was not authorized by the firm. This case also, if proved to be an error, would only be a subject of charge against Robert Farquhar's share, and subject to the observations before made on that point. It is also proved the plaintiff had his attention drawn to this charge by the settlement in 1834. The last error relied on was, that whereas the firm was entitled to eight-ninths only of the reserved farm, they occupied the whole, and, therefore, became liable to payment for the one-ninth to which they were not entitled, from 1819 to 1833. In support of this allegation, the only evidence is the deposition of William Holborn, who says, after an examination of the books, he does not find any rent charged for the one-ninth. If the plaintiff had made out the case, as alleged, it would only prove the firm had had the benefit of the one-ninth of the farm, without paying any rent to the owner of that one-ninth. Under what circumstances, whether the liability, if any, arose under any contract between them, or as tenants in common, there is no proof; and it therefore does not appear whether such owners had, at the time of the settlement, proved any claim to such rents; if they had, the result would only be, that what might have been made a charge against the firm, was never made. There is a total absence of proof, that any such charge could now be enforced; how then can that be made a ground for opening the accounts between the parties? The result of the laborious examination of all the papers in this case is, that I am of opinion the plaintiff has wholly failed in the attempt he has made to establish a case for opening the accounts. The representatives of Robert Farquhar and Andrew Maund, having ceased to have any interest in the partnership account, are not necessary parties to any account to be taken; as against them, therefore, the bill must be dismissed, with costs; and, as against the representatives of Edwin Allies, who continued in partnership with the plaintiff after the settlement of accounts, so much of the bill must be dismissed, with costs, as seeks to charge them with fraud, and as seeks, therefore, to surcharge and falsify the accounts. As

between those parties, there must be the usual accounts as between   MAUND
partners,—the account to be taken on the footing of the accounts   *v.*
proved to have been settled.   ALLIES.

JOHNSON *v.* BLENKENSOPP (1).

(5 Jurist, 870—871.)

By a written memorandum of agreement between the defendant and the
plaintiff, the plaintiff was " to have 6*s.* a week, three bolls of wheat, to set
potatoes for his family's use, to have a cow kept, house and firing, to keep
the gardens and pleasure grounds in clean and good order, to assist in the
stables and when required at hay and corn harvest, and to make himself
generally useful.   To enter 12th May, 1838."   The defendant had dismissed the plaintiff upon a month's warning.   In an action brought by
the plaintiff to recover a quarter's wages as being a yearly servant : Held,
that he was a menial servant, and was, therefore, by the general rule of
law, entitled to a month's notice only ; and that the memorandum of
agreement contained nothing which showed an intention in the parties to
exclude that rule.

1841,

*Queen's
Bench.*

Lord
DENMAN,
Ch. J.

PATTESON, J.
WILLIAMS, J.

[870]

ASSUMPSIT for a quarter's wages, on the ground, that the plaintiff
had not been rightfully dismissed from the defendant's service.
Plea, that the plaintiff became servant to the defendant, upon
certain terms, among which were the following : that either of the
said parties might determine the service by giving a month's notice
to the other ; and that, in case of the defendant's determining the
said service, he should pay to the plaintiff a proportionate part of
his wages up to the expiration of such notice.   At the trial before
Coltman, J., at Durham, at the Summer Assizes, 1840, it appeared,
that the following written agreement had been signed by the
parties : "Memorandum of agreement between G. L. Blenkensopp
and Thomas Johnson ; viz. that he is to have 6*s.* a week, three
bolls of wheat, to set potatoes for his family's use, to have a cow
kept, house and firing, and to keep himself a pig, no poultry to be
kept, his wife to keep the museum clean, he is to keep the gardens
and pleasure-grounds in clean and good order, to assist in the
stables, and when required at hay and corn harvest, and to make
himself generally useful: to enter 12th May, 1838."   On behalf
of the defendant, a nonsuit was applied for, on the ground, that
the plaintiff was a menial servant, and, therefore, the defendant
had rightfully dismissed him after a month's notice ; and that,
if he was not a menial servant, the agreement would require
a stamp.   The learned Judge directed a verdict for the plaintiff,

(1) Cp. *Parker* v. *Ibbetson* (1858) 4 C. B. N. S. 346, 27 L. J. C. P. 236.

JOHNSON
v.
BLENKEN-
SOPP.

and gave the defendant leave to move for a nonsuit. In the following Michaelmas Term, *Wortley* obtained a rule *nisi* accordingly ; against which,

Addison now showed cause :

First, the agreement contained a general hiring, and, therefore, it was a hiring for a year ; and the particular stipulations contained in the agreement show, that it could not have been intended that the service under it should be liable to be put an end to by a month's notice ; such as, the liberty to set potatoes, the providing a house for him, which places him *extra mœnia*. There were not such in *Nowlan* v. *Ablett* (1).

(PATTESON, J. : The Stamp Act mentions "labourer" in the exempting clause ; and, therefore, in no case would the agreement require a stamp.)

Wortley, *contrà :*

This case is within the rule as to notice applicable to a menial servant. In *Nowlan* v. *Ablett*, the ground of action and the plea were the same as here ; and the stipulations in this agreement are not so strong to repel the application of the general rule of law as in that case.   *   *   *

LORD DENMAN, Ch. J. :

In this case, we are desired, on behalf of the defendant, to enter a nonsuit, if we think that the defendant had the right to discharge the plaintiff upon a month's notice. The question therefore, is, as to the nature of the service which was to be rendered by the plaintiff to the defendant. The first thing is, that there is a written agreement ; and it is quite clear, that, wherever the agreement between parties is imperfect, evidence must be admissible to supply the omissions. Suppose the case of a short note of an agreement being taken down in a memorandum book, that would be subject to evidence of the understanding between the parties at the time they entered into the contract. Then, here, the term implied by the law, where there is a general hiring, that either party may determine the relation upon a month's warning or a month's wages, may be introduced into this agreement ; and such must be presumed to have been the intention of the parties.

(1) 2 Cr. M. & R. 54.

If, however, the agreement is inconsistent with such an understanding, no doubt the presumption would be rebutted. But, sitting here to form an opinion such as a jury ought to do, I do not see anything in this instrument inconsistent with the general rule; and, therefore, I think the plaintiff is a menial servant, for the purpose of this notice, within the principle laid down in the recent case of *Nowlan* v. *Ablett.*

JOHNSON
v.
BLENKEN-
SOPP.

PATTESON, J. :

The whole question is, whether the plaintiff was not a menial servant. If he was, then there is no doubt that the general custom of the realm as to the determination of the relation of master and servant would apply. Formerly, indeed, the rule as to the importation of custom into a written contract was stated in too strong terms, viz. that the custom applied unless " expressly excluded " by the terms of the contract ; but that was corrected in *Hutton* v. *Warren* (1), where PARKE, B. stated the proper question to be, " whether, from the terms of the lease," which was the instrument then under consideration, " it can be collected, that the parties intended to exclude the customary obligation to make allowances for seeds and labour." Here there is certainly nothing in the memorandum inconsistent with the general custom, that either party might determine the relation upon a month's notice. The plaintiff was, indeed, more a menial servant than the plaintiff in the case of *Nowlan* v. *Ablett ;* and there is the remarkable clause, that he is to make himself generally useful as a servant.

WILLIAMS, J. :

It is difficult to draw any distinct line which may ascertain how much of house service *makes a menial servant ; but, in this case, I think the plaintiff is such a servant.

[*871]

Rule absolute.

(1) 46 R. R. 368 (1 M. & W. 463, 477).

1841.
Nov. 13.
—
Chancery.
SHADWELL,
V.-C.
[1078]

FRANKLIN v. DRAKE.

(5 Jurist, 1078.)

Annuitant—Discovery—Want of equity.

An annuitant, whose annuity is charged by his testator upon all his freehold and copyhold estates, has no equity, so long as the annuity is regularly paid, to file his bill against the heir-at-law or devisee, to compel a discovery of the estates so charged, or the execution of a deed purporting to charge the estates. Bill for that purpose dismissed, with costs.

W. J. HUNT, by his will, dated the 10th May, 1817, made the following bequest: "In the first place, I give unto my mother, E. Hunt, out of my estates, both copyhold and freehold, during her life, 30l. per year; Carl Hunt, her heirs, executors, administrators, and assigns, out of my estates, both freehold and copyhold, an annuity of 20l. per annum; and at the death of the aforesaid E. Hunt, my mother, 10l. per year more to Carl Hunt, her heirs, executors, administrators, and assigns.   The remainder I give unto my sister, S. E. Drake, making her my executrix; and, at her death, the whole of my property out of my estates to be equally divided by her children, share and share alike, first paying the above annuities."   The testator died in 1818.   Carl Hunt was regularly paid her annuity down to 1835, when she died, having devised her annuity to the present plaintiff: the annuity was also regularly paid to the plaintiff down to the time of filing the present bill, which he did against the heir-at-law of the testator, for the purpose of ascertaining out of what lands the annuity was issuable, and to obtain the defendant's signature to a deed, charging the same with the said annuity.

T. *Parker*, in support of the bill:

The testator has not distinguished any particular portion of his lands, as being liable to the payment of the annuity, but has made a general devise, how then can the annuitant know upon what lands to enter, should the annuity be in arrear? The property out of which the annuity is to come is, therefore, uncertain. Now, as the property is uncertain, equity has as much jurisdiction as law, and the plaintiff is not to conjecture out of what property she is to have the annuity, but has a right to have a discovery from the defendant as to the property; and if a right to discovery, then, also, a right to relief. Distress would not lie at law. Uncertainty is a proper ground to come to equity: *Duke of Bridgwater* v. *Edwards* (1),

(1) 6 Br. P. C. 368

Duke of Leeds v. *Corporation of New Radnor* (1), *Cook* v. *Smee* (2), *Cupit* v. *Jackson* (8).

Bethell and *Chandless*, contrà :

No case can be shown where a bill of this description has been entertained, unless where the annuity was in arrear; but plaintiff admits, that the annuity has been regularly paid. The only object of the bill is, to compel the defendant to execute a deed to secure the annuity : *Attorney-General* v. *Jackson* (4), *Attorney-General* v. *Pickard* (6), *Stow* v. *Davenport* (6).

Girdlestone, Speed, and *J. Parker,* for other parties.

T'. Parker, in reply.

THE VICE-CHANCELLOR :

The testator has, by his will, charged his freehold and copyhold estates with the payment of this annuity; and this Court cannot further or more effectually charge those estates. Nothing can be done upon the bill. It appears to me that, so long as the parties pay the annuity, there is no possible relief which can be administered by this Court. Were the annuity in arrear, and the party wanted a discovery, he could have it in the usual way, by filing his bill, and paying all expenses. My opinion is, that I cannot give plaintiff any relief; and he must pay all the costs.

Bill dismissed, with costs.

SNOOK *v*. DUNCAN.

(5 Jurist, 1078—1079.)

Security for costs.
Plaintiff made to give security for costs, the evidence not being clear that he intended to return from abroad.

1841.
Nor. 19.

Chancery.
SHADWELL,
V.-C.
[1078]
[*1079]

KINGLAKE moved on behalf of the defendant, that *plaintiff should give security for costs, he having left England in 1838, and resided in Upper Canada until 1840, when he returned to this country for a short time, but again went out to Canada; insisting, that, according to the rule laid down by Lord ELDON, where the

(1) 2 Br. C. C. 338.
(2) 2 Br. P. C. 184.
(3) 28 R. R. 735 (13 Price, 721).

(4) 37 R. R. 641 (2 Cr. & J. 101).
(5) 3 M. & W. 552.
(6) 39 R. R. 503 (5 B. & Ad. 359).

SNOOK
v.
DUNCAN.

plaintiff has gone abroad, the *onus* is upon him to show that he does not intend to reside abroad.

Freeling opposed the motion, upon the affidavits of plaintiff's daughter and son-in-law, in which they stated, that when plaintiff last left England he went abroad for the purpose of selling his property in Canada, and that he intended to return to England in two years ; and that he does not intend to reside permanently abroad any where. And contended, that this case came within the rule of *White* v. *Greathead* (1).

THE VICE-CHANCELLOR :

There is nothing in your affidavits that makes it clear that the plaintiff will return ; indeed it seems very doubtful whether he will return or not. He must give security for costs.

(1) 15 Ves. 2.

INDEX.